Benjamin Hary, Sarah Bunin Benor (Eds.)
Languages in Jewish Communities, Past and Present

Contributions to the Sociology of Language

Edited by
Ofelia García
Francis M. Hult

Founding editor
Joshua A. Fishman

Volume 112

Languages in Jewish Communities, Past and Present

Edited by
Benjamin Hary
Sarah Bunin Benor

DE GRUYTER
MOUTON

ISBN 978-1-5015-2132-4
e-ISBN (PDF) 978-1-5015-0463-1
e-ISBN (EPUB) 978-1-5015-0455-6
ISSN 1861-0676

Library of Congress Cataloging-in-Publication Data
Names: Benor, Sarah, 1975- editor. | Hary, Benjamin H., editor.
Title: Languages in Jewish communities : past and present / edited by
　Benjamin Hary, Sarah Bunin Benor.
Description: First edition. | Berlin ; Boston : Walter De Gruyter, [2018] |
　Series: Contributions to the Sociology of Language (CSL) ISSN 1861-0676 ;
　112
Identifiers: LCCN 2018027142| ISBN 9781501512988 (print) | ISBN 9781501504556
　(e-book (epub) | ISBN 9781501504631 (e-book (pdf)
Subjects: LCSH: Jews–Languages–History. | Sociolinguistics. |
　Jews–Identity.
Classification: LCC PJ5061 .L35 2018 | DDC 408.9924–dc23 LC record available at
https://lccn.loc.gov/2018027142

Bibliographic information published by the Deutsche Nationalbibliothek
The Deutsche Nationalbibliothek lists this publication in the Deutsche Nationalbibliografie;
detailed bibliographic data are available on the Internet at http://dnb.dnb.de.

© 2020 Walter de Gruyter Inc., Boston/Berlin
This volume is text- and page-identical with the hardback published in 2018.
Typesetting: Integra Software Services Pvt. Ltd
Printing and binding: CPI books GmbH, Leck
Cover image: sculpies/shutterstock

www.degruyter.com

This book is dedicated to the last generations of those who speak endangered languages and to the new generations of those who speak thriving languages. May this volume spark intergenerational and international conversations and collaborations.

מכל מלמדיי השכלתי ומכל חביריי למדתי
From all my teachers I have benefited and from all my friends I have learned

To Ursula, David and Ofer (from Benjamin Hary)   לאורסולה, לדייויד ולעופר

And to Solomon Birnbaum and Max Weinreich, pioneers of the field (from Sarah Bunin Benor)

Contents

Introduction —— 1

Part I: Jewish Language Varieties in Historical Perspective

Geoffrey Khan
Jewish Neo-Aramaic in Kurdistan and Iran —— 9

Benjamin Hary
Judeo-Arabic in the Arabic-Speaking World —— 35

Joseph Chetrit
Judeo-Berber in Morocco —— 70

Michael Ryzhik
Judeo-Italian in Italy —— 94

George Jochnowitz
Judeo-Provençal in Southern France —— 129

Ora (Rodrigue) Schwarzwald
Judeo-Spanish throughout the Sephardic Diaspora —— 145

David M. Bunis
Judezmo (Ladino/Judeo-Spanish): A Historical and Sociolinguistic Portrait —— 185

Jürg Fleischer
Western Yiddish and Judeo-German —— 239

Alexander Beider
Yiddish in Eastern Europe —— 276

Vitaly Shalem
Judeo-Tat in the Eastern Caucasus —— 313

Ophira Gamliel
Jewish Malayalam in Southern India —— 357

Part II: Jewish Language Varieties in the 20th and 21st Centuries

Evelyn Dean-Olmsted and Susana Skura
Jewish Spanish in Buenos Aires and Mexico City —— 383

Sarah Bunin Benor
Jewish English in the United States —— 414

Patric Joshua Klagsbrun Lebenswerd
Jewish Swedish in Sweden —— 431

Judith Rosenhouse
Jewish Hungarian in Hungary and Israel —— 453

Dalit Assouline
Haredi Yiddish in Israel and the United States —— 472

Anbessa Teferra
Hebraized Amharic in Israel —— 489

Renee Perelmutter
Israeli Russian in Israel —— 520

Miriam Ben-Rafael and Eliezer Ben-Rafael
Jewish French in Israel —— 544

Aharon Geva-Kleinberger
Judeo-Arabic in the Holy Land and Lebanon —— 569

Part III: Theoretical and Comparative Perspectives

Bernard Spolsky
Sociolinguistics of Jewish Language Varieties —— 583

Peter T. Daniels
Uses of Hebrew Script in Jewish Language Varieties —— 602

Anna Verschik
Yiddish, Jewish Russian, and Jewish Lithuanian in the Former Soviet Union —— 627

Yehudit Henshke
The Hebrew and Aramaic Component of Judeo-Arabic —— 644

Sarah Bunin Benor and Benjamin Hary
A Research Agenda for Comparative Jewish Linguistic Studies —— 672

Index —— 695

Introduction

Over the past three millennia, Jewish communities around the world have spoken and written somewhat distinctly from their non-Jewish neighbors. In some cases, these differences were as minor as the addition of some Hebrew or Aramaic words, and, in other cases, Jews wrote and spoke a significantly different language variety, unintelligible to their non-Jewish neighbors. Most Jewish communities were located somewhere in the middle of this "continuum of Jewish distinctiveness" (Benor 2008, 2009; Gold 1981, 1989; Hary 2009; Hary and Wein 2013; Prager 1986). The results of this linguistic distinctiveness have been referred to as "Jewish languages" (Birnbaum 1971; Fishman 1985; Kahn and Rubin 2016; Paper 1978; Rabin et al. 1979; Weinreich 2008[1973]), "Jewish language phenomena" (Wexler 1981), "Jewish language varieties" (Hary 2009; Spolsky 2014), "Jewish-defined languages" (Hary 2009; Hary and Wein 2013), "Jewish lects" (Gold 1981; Prager 1986), "Jewish religiolects" (Hary 2009, 2011; Hary and Wein 2013), and "Jewish linguistic repertoires" (Benor 2008).

Whatever name is used, the diverse ways that Jews have spoken and written are worthy of analysis. Several volumes offer descriptions of, collectively, at least two dozen Jewish language varieties (most recently, Edzard and Tirosh-Becker forthcoming, and most comprehensively, Kahn and Rubin 2016; see Benor 2015 for an annotated bibliography). Given this proliferation of information on individual Jewish language varieties, the time is ripe for systematic comparative analysis. The current volume makes a step in this direction by presenting uniform formal and sociolinguistic descriptions of language varieties in many Jewish communities, plus some comparative and theoretical observations.

The language descriptions in this book mostly follow this format:
1. Brief introduction
    1.1 Names of the language
    1.2 Linguistic affiliation
    1.3 Regions where language is/was spoken
    1.4 Attestations and sources
    1.5 Present-day status
2. Historical background
    2.1 Speaker community: settlement, documentation
    2.2 Attestations and sources: elaboration
    2.3 Phases in historical development
    2.4 Sociolinguistic description, community bilingualism, public functions
3. Structural information
    3.1 Relationship to non-Jewish varieties (isoglosses, related dialects)
    3.2 Particular structural features (unique to the Jewish variety)

3.3 Lexicon: Hebrew and Aramaic elements
   3.4 Language contact influences
4. Written and oral traditions
   4.1 Writing system
   4.2 Literature
   4.3 Performance (theatre, film, etc.)
5. State of research
   5.1 History of documentation
   5.2 Corpora
   5.3 Issues of general theoretical interest
   5.4 Current directions in research

Some chapters focus more on some topics or omit others, depending how much documentation and prior research are available. Each of the three most widespread and most deeply researched Jewish language varieties receive extra attention in this book: Judeo-Arabic, Judeo-Spanish, and Yiddish. Each chapter on Judeo-Arabic and Yiddish focuses on a different stage, community, or phenomenon, and both chapters on Judeo-Spanish present many phases and communities, reminding readers that scholars can approach the same material in different ways.

This book is organized into three sections: historical, contemporary, and theoretical/comparative. The first two sections are organized geographically, offering a tour of Jewish communities around the world. The historical section begins in the Middle East, docks briefly in North Africa, sails through Europe, and ends in India. The contemporary section begins in the Americas, flies to Europe, and lands in Israel. In the final section, we offer a few theoretical and comparative essays dealing with a phenomenon in multiple language varieties and several language varieties in a region. Our final chapter details an agenda for comparative linguistic research on Jewish communities.

In previous theoretical research, a common question has been "What constitutes a Jewish language?" Various answers have been offered, some more restrictive, some more inclusive (see Benor 2008). As we have argued elsewhere, we feel this question is not productive (Benor 2008 and Hary 2009; see also Fishman 1981 and Gold 1981). Determinations of what is a "language" and what is a "dialect" vary depending on ethnic, geographic, historical, political, religious, and sociological factors, as well as linguistic criteria (Hary 2009: 10–12). Some analysts might consider two language varieties to be separate languages, rather than dialects, because they are mutually unintelligible, because their speakers consider them separate languages, or because they are used in different political entities. All of these criteria are problematic (Benor 2008: 1066–1067). Consequently, we opted to use the term "Jewish language variety," specifically because of its vagueness. Rather than "what constitutes a Jewish language," we prefer more empirical and comparative questions: How have various Jews in various Jewish communities spoken and written? In what ways have they differed in speech and writing from their non-Jewish neighbors? What are the similarities and differences among Jewish language varieties in various times and places? How and why do Christians and Muslims use elements of Jewish language varieties, and how do they view language use among Jews? What role does language play in the emergence of collective identity and the creation of community boundaries?

This book enables advances in this kind of comparative analysis by providing information about Jewish varieties of Amharic, Arabic, Aramaic, Berber, English, French, German/Yiddish, Hungarian, Italian, Lithuanian, Malayalam, Provençal, Russian, Spanish/Ladino, Swedish, and Tat. Readers can also find descriptions of most of these, plus other language varieties (Jewish varieties of Georgian, Greek, several Iranian varieties, Karaim, Krymchak, Portuguese, Slavic, Syriac, and Turkish) in Kahn and Rubin 2016. The current volume focuses on fewer language varieties, but it offers more uniform descriptions, including some sociolinguistic analysis. While in Kahn and Rubin, the chapters on Jewish English, Jewish Swedish, and other contemporary language varieties are only cursory, this book provides substantial information about language use in several contemporary Jewish communities in the Americas, Europe, and Israel, including how Jewish varieties of Amharic, French, and Russian change based on their intense contact with Modern Hebrew in Israel. This decision reflects our understanding that Jews in the 21st century are continuing age-old language practices and innovating on them, based on new historical realities. The language of the children of French immigrants to Israel and the great-grandchildren of Syrian immigrants to Mexico, for example, are not only worthy of analysis but also have the potential to illuminate Jewish linguistic practices of the past (see Gold 1981).

A note about naming conventions: Any language name is necessarily a reification, an umbrella term covering the diverse language use in many subgroups within a given community. However, we feel it is necessary to give a name to linguistic entities, whether one thinks of them as languages, dialects, ethnolects, jargons, language varieties, lects, religiolects, sociolects, or simply styles. We also feel it is acceptable to discuss the phenomenon using the term "Jewish language varieties," recognizing that many of the "languages" Jews have spoken are not distinct enough from their non-Jewish correlates for most people to consider them separate languages. Hence the term "language variety." We follow the convention of using names to distinguish between language varieties that began in the distant past ("Judeo-X"), language varieties that emerged in recent centuries ("Jewish X"), and post-coterritorial language varieties (Judezmo/

Ladino and Yiddish). (See Kahn and Rubin 2016: 3 for a slightly different take on this naming practice.) Several of the chapters in this book discuss diverse approaches to naming particular language varieties, which represent diverse ideological stances regarding Jewishness and localness.

The study of Jewish language varieties is important not just to Jewish studies. It has contributed to the growing literature on language and race/ethnicity on the one hand, sometimes called raciolinguistics or ethnolinguistics (Alim, Rickford, and Ball 2016; Fishman and García 2010; Fought 2006; Labov 1966), and language and religion on the other, sometimes called religiolinguistics (Hary and Wein 2013; Omoniyi and Fishman 2006; Versteegh 2017; Wein and Hary 2014; Yaeger-Dror 2014, 2015). Theoretical research on Jewish language varieties, including that developed in this book, offers a framework for the study of Christian, Muslim, Hindu, African American, Asian British, and other language varieties. This is an example of a "minority" field (such as Jewish studies) exporting theory into general disciplines (such as sociolinguistics) or other "minority" fields (Muslims studies, African American studies, etc.).

This volume contributes to a growing body of literature on the diverse ways Jews have spoken and written around the world and throughout history. Past research has mostly been either structural or sociological but not both. In some circles of Jewish studies, scholars have lamented the loss of Jewish language use, citing several reasons for the loss; however, these scholars have often ignored the development of newer Jewish language varieties (see Benor 2008). This book addresses these issues, bringing together sociolinguistic and formal approaches and highlighting the 21st-century manifestation of this age-old phenomenon. We hope the book will be useful for scholars and students and will serve as a springboard for further research on religiolinguistics, ethnolinguistics, and language use in Jewish communities, past and present.

Acknowledgments

Many thanks go to the contributors for their chapters and their patience. Much gratitude goes to the reviewers, including many of the contributors, for their valuable suggestions. We are grateful to Uri Tadmor for encouraging us to publish this volume and arranging for its inclusion in the *Contributions to the Sociology of Language* series. Thank you to the series editors, Ofelia García and Francis Hult, and to Lara Wysong for shepherding the manuscript through the publication process. Thank you to our copy editors, Joyce Klein, Matthew Miller, and Orli Robin. We are grateful to Tom Carew, Anne and Joel Eherenkranz Dean of the Faculty of Arts and Science at New York University, for his encouragement and financial help with the copy editing. Finally, thanks to Yaron Matras for his leadership in the initial stages of this volume.

Benjamin Hary, New York University
Sarah Bunin Benor, Hebrew Union College
New York, Tel Aviv, and Los Angeles, December 2017

References

Alim, H. Samy, John R. Rickford, and Arnetha F. Ball (eds.). 2016. *Raciolinguistics: How language shapes our ideas about race*. Oxford: Oxford University Press.
Benor, Sarah Bunin. 2008. Towards a new understanding of Jewish language in the 21st century. *Religion Compass* 2(6). 1062–1080.
Benor, Sarah Bunin. 2009. Do American Jews speak a 'Jewish language'? A model of Jewish linguistic distinctiveness. *Jewish Quarterly Review* 99(2). 230–269.
Benor, Sarah Bunin. 2015. Jewish languages. In David Biale (ed.), *Oxford bibliographies in Jewish studies*. New York: Oxford University Press (updated version).
Birnbaum, Solomon A. 1971. Jewish languages. *Encyclopaedia Judaica*, vol. 10. 66–69.
Edzard, Lutz, and Ofra Tirosh-Becker, eds. Forthcoming. *Jewish languages: Text specimens, grammatical, lexical, and cultural sketches*. Wiesbaden: Harrassowitz.
Fishman, Joshua A. (ed.). 1985. *Readings in the sociology of Jewish languages*. Leiden: Brill.
Fishman, Joshua A., and Ofelia García (eds.). 2010. *Handbook of language and ethnic identity*. Oxford: Oxford University Press.
Fought, Carmen. 2006. *Language and ethnicity*. Cambridge: Cambridge University Press.
Gold, David. 1981. Jewish intralinguistics as a field of study. *International Journal of the Sociology of Language* 30. 31–46.
Gold, David. 1989. *Jewish linguistic studies*. Haifa: Association for the Study of Jewish Languages.
Hary, Benjamin. 2009. *Translating religion: Linguistic analysis of Judeo-Arabic sacred texts from Egypt*. Leiden: Brill.
Hary, Benjamin. 2011. Religiolect. In *Jewish Languages*, 31. Ann Arbor: Frankel Institute for Advanced Jewish Studies, University of Michigan.
Hary, Benjamin and Martin J. Wein. 2013. Religiolinguistics: On Jewish-, Christian-, and Muslim-defined languages. *International Journal for the Sociology of Language* 220. 85–108.
Kahn, Lily, and Aaron D. Rubin (eds.). 2016. *Handbook of Jewish languages*. Leiden: Brill.
Labov, William. 1966. *The social stratification of English in New York City*. Washington, DC: Center for Applied Linguistics.
Omoniyi, Tope, and Joshua A. Fishman (eds.) 2006. *Explorations in the sociology of language and religion*. Amsterdam and Philadelphia: J. Benjamins.
Paper, Herbert (ed.). 1978. *Jewish languages: Themes and variations*. Cambridge, MA: Association for Jewish Studies.
Prager, Leonard. 1986. A preliminary checklist of English names of Jewish lects. *Jewish Language Review* 6. 225–236.
Rabin, Chaim, et al. 1979. The Jewish languages: Commonalities, differences and problems (in Hebrew). *Pe'amim* 1. 40–66.
Spolsky, Bernard. 2014. *The languages of the Jews: A sociolinguistic history*. Cambridge: Cambridge University Press.

Versteegh, Kees. 2017. Religion as a linguistic variable in Christian Greek, Latin, and Arabic. In Nora Sunniva Eggen and Rana Hisham Issa (eds.), *Philologists in the world: A festschrift in honour of Professor of Arabic language and culture, Gunvor Mejdell*. Oslo: Novus Forlag. 55–85.

Wein, Martin J. and Benjamin Hary. 2014. Peoples of the book: Religion, language, nationalism, and sacred text translation. In Sander L. Gilman (ed.), *Judaism, Christianity and Islam: Collaboration and conflict in the age of diaspora*. Hong Kong: Hong Kong University Press. 1–34.

Weinreich, Max. 2008 [1973]. *History of the Yiddish language*. New Haven: Yale University Press.

Wexler, Paul. 1981. Jewish interlinguistics: Facts and conceptual framework. *Language* 57(1). 99–149.

Yaeger-Dror, Malcah. 2014. Religion as a sociolinguistic variable. *Language and Linguistics Compass* 8(11). 577–589.

Yaeger-Dror, Malcah. 2015. Religious choice, religious commitment, and linguistic variation: Religion as a factor in language variation. *Language and Communication* 42. 69–74.

Part I: **Jewish Language Varieties in Historical Perspective**

Geoffrey Khan
Jewish Neo-Aramaic in Kurdistan and Iran

1 Preliminary remarks

Jewish Neo-Aramaic was spoken until the 20th century in Kurdistan and the adjacent regions of Iran and continues to be spoken today, mainly in Israel, by the older generation of immigrants. It is the vestige of the Aramaic that was spoken more widely by Jews in the Middle East at earlier periods. Distinct Jewish varieties of Aramaic begin to be attested in written sources in the first half of the first millennium CE. These contrast in particular with specifically Christian varieties of the language, which emerge into history at approximately the same period. This communal split between Jewish and Christian dialects has survived in the Neo-Aramaic dialects.

1.1 Names of the language

The Neo-Aramaic that is spoken by Jews is generally referred to by modern scholars as Jewish Neo-Aramaic. The speakers used a variety of native terms to refer to their language, which varied from region to region and reflected internal dialectal differences. Conscious of the historical connection of the language with earlier literary forms of Jewish Aramaic, some members of the communities refer to the language as *lišanət targum* 'the language of the Targum'. Many speakers refer to their language simply as 'our language' in their particular region's dialect, e.g., *lišana deni* (Zakho and surrounding region), *lišanət nošan* (south-west Kurdistan), *lišana noša* (western Iran), *lišana didan* (north-west Iran), *lišān dideni* (Barzan region). Some names reflect the consciousness of it being a specifically Jewish language, e.g., *lišan hozaye* 'the language of the Jews' (Zakho), and *hulaula* (western Iran), which is an abstract noun meaning 'Jewishness/Judaism' (< *hūḏāyūṯā). Some names contain characteristic words of the Jewish dialects, arranged in pairs, e.g., *lišanət ʾaxča-w ʾačxa* 'language of "so much, so much"' (Arbel region). In Georgia, the Georgian-speaking Jews used the term *lax-lŭx* to refer to the Aramaic-speaking Jews, and referred to their language as *laxluxe-bis ena* 'the language of the lax-lŭx'.[1] This term is likely to have its origin in the so-called L-suffixes (consisting of the preposition *l-* and a pronominal suffix), which are a distinctive feature of

---

[1] I am grateful to Reuven Enoch (personal communication) for informing me of this Georgian term.

Neo-Aramaic past verbal forms. Aramaic-speaking Jews in Israel sometimes refer to their language by the term *kurdit* 'Kurdish', which relates to the regional origin of the community rather than its linguistic origin.

1.2 Linguistic affiliation

The Jewish Neo-Aramaic dialects belong to the North-Eastern Neo-Aramaic (NENA) subgroup of Neo-Aramaic dialects.[2] This is a highly diverse group of over 150 dialects, spoken by Jews and Christians originating from towns and villages east of the Tigris in northern Iraq, south-eastern Turkey, and western Iran. The NENA subgroup is distinct from three other subgroups of Neo-Aramaic. These include the western subgroup spoken by Christians and Muslims in the villages of Maʿlula, Baxʿa, and Jubʿadin in the region of Damascus; the Ṭuroyo subgroup, spoken by Christians in the Ṭūr ʿAbdīn region of south-eastern Turkey; and Mandaic, spoken by Mandaeans in the cities of Ahwaz and Kermanshahr in Iran. None of these subgroups is as diverse as NENA. Within NENA itself one may identify a number of subgroups. There is a fundamental split between the dialects spoken by the Jews and those spoken by the Christians. This applies even to cases where Jewish and Christian communities lived in the same town, such as Urmi (northwestern Iran), Sanandaj (western Iran), Koy Sanjak, and Sulemaniyya (both in northeastern Iraq). Within Jewish NENA dialects themselves a number of subgroups are identifiable.

1.3 Regions where language is/was spoken

At the beginning of the 20th century, the Aramaic-speaking Jews lived in thriving communities in villages and towns throughout the original NENA area. During the upheavals of the First World War, the Jews of southeastern Turkey and the adjacent region of northwestern Iran underwent considerable hardship and, like the Aramaic-speaking Christian communities of the region, permanent displacement from their original places of residence. Some Jews, notably those from the region of Salmas (Salamas) in the far northwestern tip of Iran, fled into the Caucasus and settled in Tbilisi (Mutzafi 2014a). They suffered further under the regime of Stalin, who, in 1950, moved virtually the entire community to Almaty in Kazakhstan, where a large proportion of the Jews speaking the Salmas dialect can be found to

---

[2] The term was coined by Hobermann (1988: 557).

Map 1: NENA dialect area

this day. A few elderly Salmas Jews can still be found in Tbilisi. Other dialects of Jewish communities who were displaced during the First World War have become extinct, such as those from the region of Gavar.

Since the 19th century, several Jews of the region emigrated to Palestine through religious motives. This emigration increased after the First World War in the first half of the 20th century, due to the activities of the Zionist movement. In the early 1950s, after the foundation of the State of Israel, this migration turned into a mass exodus. As a result, the vast majority of surviving Aramaic-speaking Jews are now resident in Israel. After this exodus, virtually no Aramaic-speaking Jews remained in Iraq. The few who did remain were mostly women who had converted to Islam.[3] In western Iran, however, some remained during the time of the Shah but left after the Iranian Revolution in 1979. In Sanandaj, for example, only about 1,000 Jews of a total population of approximately 4,000 migrated to Israel in 1952. Over the subsequent two decades, there was a gradual emigration of the Jews from the town either to Tehran or abroad, mostly to Israel. After the

---

3 Cf. the story of the sister of Yona Sabar, narrated by his son, Ariel Sabar (2009).

Iranian Revolution in 1979, most of the remaining Jews left Sanandaj, the majority settling in Los Angeles in the USA and the remainder in Israel or Europe (Ben-Yaʿqov 1980: 149; Khan 2009: 1).

1.4 Attestations and sources

There are some written sources of Jewish Neo-Aramaic, which are datable to the 17th century onwards. These are mainly manuscripts of homilies and Bible translations. Literature of this type was also transmitted orally, and after the migration of Jews to Israel a larger corpus was committed to writing.[4] This written material is an important source for the study of the history of Jewish Neo-Aramaic, since it often contains a more archaic form than is found in the surviving spoken dialects. The literature, however, only reflects a limited range of the dialectal diversity. Serious documentation and study of the spoken NENA dialects began only in the second half of the 19th century. Much of the early work was carried out by missionaries, whose main concern was the dialects of the Christians, e.g., Stoddard (1860) and Maclean (1895). Some data on the dialects of the Jews were, nevertheless, published by scholars during this period, together with material from the Christian dialects, e.g., Socin (1882), on the Jewish dialect of Zakho; Duval (1883), on the Jewish dialect of Salmas; and Maclean (1895: 340–344), on the Jewish dialect of Urmi.

Systematic work on the Jewish dialects did not begin, however, until the second half of the 20th century, after the Jews had left their original places of residence and migrated to Israel. So far, several monograph-length descriptions of dialects have been published, including Garbell (1965a: Jewish Urmi and related dialects), Mutzafi (2004a: Jewish Koy Sanjak), Mutzafi (2008a: Jewish Betanure), Fassberg (2010: Jewish Challa), Greenblatt (2011: Jewish Amedia), Cohen (2012: syntax of Jewish Zakho), Khan (1999: Jewish Arbel), Khan (2004a: Jewish Sulemaniyya and Ḥalabja), Khan (2008a: Jewish Urmi), and Khan (2009: Jewish Sanandaj), in addition to numerous shorter sketches and studies. Several scholars, especially Mutzafi, Hopkins, and Khan, have gathered extensive data on most of the other surviving dialects. Much of this material is gradually being made accessible in an online NENA database at the University of Cambridge.

---

4 A large amount of this literature has been edited and studied by Yona Sabar in his numerous publications, e.g., Sabar (1976, 1985, 1991a, 1983, 1988, 1991b, 1994). See also the work of Rees (2008). Sabar was instrumental in having many of the tradents of the oral traditions commit them to writing. Yosef Rivlin also played a role in this respect; see, for example, Rivlin (1959).

1.5 Present-day status

All of the Jewish Neo-Aramaic dialects are now on an inexorable trajectory of extinction as living vernaculars within the next couple of decades or so. As remarked, some are known to have already become extinct; in some cases, descriptions of these have, fortunately, been published, e.g., the Jewish dialect of Challa (Fassberg 2010), or at least unpublished data have been collected for future study, e.g., Jewish Nerwa (Mutzafi). The communities who spoke the various dialects in their original locations were of varying sizes. Some dialects were spoken only by a handful of Jewish families, and it is these that have now become extinct or are in particular danger of extinction, such as Challa in southeastern Turkey (Fassberg 2010), Aradhin (Mutzafi 2002a), Dobe and Hiza (in Iraq). The dialects that were spoken by larger communities in their original locations are in a healthier state, but every year the number of good speakers dwindles and opportunities for systematic linguistic documentation vanish with them.

2 Historical background

2.1 Speaker community: Settlement

There are only scant sources for the history of the Aramaic-speaking Jewish communities. The main written historical sources have been described by Brauer and Patai (1993) and, in greater detail for each community, by Ben-Yaʿqov (1980). It is assumed by these authors that the communities have very deep historical roots, but the first clear historical reference to an Aramaic-speaking Jewish population is by the medieval traveller Benjamin of Tudela (12th century), who states that the Jews of the region spoke the Targum language (Brauer & Patai 1993: 58). Mann (1931, 2: 16) publishes letters datable to the beginning of the 16th century that mention villages in the highlands of Kurdistan that had Jewish communities. Some of these had been abandoned by their Jewish population by the 20th century or the number of Jewish inhabitants had been considerably reduced, reflecting the fact that the Jewish population of the region declined after the 16th century. One reason for this reduction is likely to have been the forcible conversion of some Jews to Islam, especially in the 19th century in some areas (Soane 1912: 186). After the First World War and the setting of the border between Iraq and Turkey by the League of Nations in 1925, some Jewish communities that fell within Turkish territory moved down into Iraq. Fieldworkers on the Jewish Neo-Aramaic dialects have gathered a number of oral accounts from older speakers about the recent history of their communities. These frequently talk of migrations around the region, especially from villages into towns. This applies, for example, to the Jews of the towns of Sulemaniyya and Sanandaj, which were founded in the Ottoman period (Khan 2004a: 3, 2009: 1).

2.2 Phases in historical development

The history of the Aramaic-speaking Jewish communities is reflected also in the linguistic history of the Jewish NENA dialects. These are not direct descendants of any of the earlier literary forms of Aramaic (except, of course, for the written forms of Jewish NENA extant from the 17th century onwards), although they exhibit close affinities to Syriac and Jewish Babylonian Aramaic. The dialects rather have their roots in a vernacular form of Aramaic that existed in antiquity in the region of northern Mesopotamia, which differed from the vernacular underlying the literary languages of Syriac to the west and Jewish Babylonian Aramaic to the south. This is shown by the fact that, although exhibiting numerous innovations, they are more conservative than Syriac and Jewish Babylonian Aramaic in some features (Khan 2007a; Fox 2008). Some of the dialects, moreover, have preserved lexical items of apparently Akkadian origin that do not appear in dictionaries of the earlier forms of literary Aramaic.[5] Structural differences among the NENA dialects are likely to reflect, to some extent, migrations of communities in the northern Mesopotamian region. The clear structural distinction between the Jewish and Christian dialects has been brought about by different migration patterns, as well as social divisions. Within the Jewish dialects, migration history is reflected by concentrations of structural diversity. The greater degree of diversity within the structure of dialects in Iraq from those in western Iran, for example, suggests that Iraq was the original heartland of the Aramaic-speaking population and the communities on the eastern periphery in western Iran were the result of migration from this heartland. The Jewish NENA dialects of western Iran also reflect a greater degree of innovation in their structure.

2.3 Sociolinguistic description, community bilingualism, public functions

In the first half of the 20th century, the Aramaic-speaking Jews of the region mainly lived in towns. Many of these appear to be very old urban settlements.

---

[5] For Christian dialects, see Krotkoff (1985) and Khan (2002: 515), and for Jewish dialects, Sabar (2002: 12).

The structural differences between the Jewish and Christian dialects of some towns, such as Urmi in northwestern Iran, can be correlated with the fact that Christians were recent arrivals from the villages, whereas the Jewish urban settlement had deeper historical roots (Khan 2008a: 1). Some of the Jewish urban population of other towns is, however, known to have migrated from villages in relatively recent times, as is the case in Sanandaj and Sulemaniyya. Most of the Jewish town dwellers were small traders, goldsmiths, tailors, weavers, and dyers. Some of the traders were shopkeepers, while others were peddlers who hawked their wares around the surrounding countryside. Some of the Jews who remained in villages until the 20th century, such as the communities of the villages of Betanure, Shukho, and Sandu, were agriculturalists (Mutzafi 2008a, 2014b).

All Aramaic-speaking Jews were bilingual, and in many cases trilingual. In addition to their Aramaic community language, they also spoke the language of the majority local population. Throughout most of the NENA area, this was Kurdish. In northwestern Iran, it included also Azeri Turkish. Kurdish and Azeri, therefore, have had a particular impact on Jewish NENA. In addition, many Jews spoke the official languages of the modern nation states. This applied in particular to the Jews of Iran, who spoke Farsi, which was the language of education. The knowledge of Arabic by Aramaic-speaking Jews in Iraq in the 20th century was more limited. It appears, however, that Arabic was more widely spoken in the region at earlier periods, and this has survived in the Arabic vernaculars spoken by some of the Jewish communities, such as Sendor, Arbīl, and Aqra (Jastrow 1990a, 1990b). Some features of Jewish NENA in Iraq can be explained as the result of contact with Arabic at earlier periods. All Aramaic-speaking Jews in the region had some knowledge of Hebrew. This was more extensive among the learned members of the communities, but there was a general "Hebrew component" in the vernacular used by all speakers. After their migration to Israel, all Jews rapidly acquired Israeli Hebrew, and this has an impact on the speech of virtually all surviving Aramaic speakers today. The surviving speakers of the Salmas dialect in Almaty in Kazakhstan also use Russian, even among themselves, and this is rapidly overwhelming their Aramaic dialect.

Researchers have documented sporadic differences between the speech of men and women in Jewish NENA-speaking communities. Garbell (1965a: 33), for example, refers to the fact that the speech of many of the older women among her informants differed from that of men, with regard to the phonological feature of suprasegmental emphasis. The older women tended to extend this feature to all items in the lexicon, whereas men distinguished between emphatic and plain lexical items. Among the surviving Jewish NENA speakers today, some men who have been active in communal activities, including religious leaders, exhibit some aspects of dialect-mixing in their speech, which is rarely found in the speech of women.

In their original homeland, the Aramaic-speaking Jews did not have any clear communal organization across the region, but in Israel they have aligned themselves into three broad social groups. These include: (1) Kurdistani Jews, who include those from Iraqi Kurdistan and Iranian Kurdistan (i.e., western Iran). (2) Nash Didan (*nāš didán* 'our people'), which consist of Aramaic-speaking Jews from northwestern Iran (Iranian Azerbaijan), mainly the town of Urmi. (3) Aramaean Jews, which consist of a few hundred Jews from Iranian Kurdistan who regard themselves as Aramaean and reject the Kurdistani identity that other Jews from the same area adopted after their arrival in Israel (Mutzafi 2014b).

3 Structural information

3.1 Relationship to non-Jewish varieties

The Jewish NENA dialects are divided into two main subgroups: (1) The so-called *lišana deni* subgroup, which was spoken in the northwest of Iraq in locations to the west of the Great Zab river, such as Zakho, Dohok, Amedia, and Betanure, and just to the east of the river around the Turkish border, such as Nerwa in Iraq and Challa in southeastern Turkey. (2) Dialects spoken in locations east of the Great Zab river in the Arbīl and Sulemaniyya provinces of Iraq (e.g., Rustaqa, Ruwanduz, Koy Sanjak, villages of the plain of Arbel,[6] Ḥalabja, and Sulemaniyya; also the village of Dobe, which is on the western bank of the Great Zab), in the West Azerbaijan province of Iran (e.g., Urmi, Salmas, Shino, Naghada [Solduz], Sablagh [Mahabad]), and further south in the Kurdistan and Kermanshah provinces of Iran (e.g., Saqqiz, Sanandaj, Kerend, and on the Iraqi side of the border in Khanaqin). This subgroup is generally referred to as trans-Zab (following Mutzafi 2008b). In addition, there was a small cluster of dialects in the region of Barzan, located in Iraq between these two areas, which exhibit a linguistic profile that is transitional between the two main subgroups (Mutzafi 2002b, 2004b).

As remarked, the Jewish Neo-Aramaic dialects exhibit numerous differences in their structure from the Christian dialects of the region. The Christian dialects spoken east of the Tigris and the Jewish dialects do, however, clearly exhibit shared innovations and belong to the same Neo-Aramaic subgroup, viz., NENA.

---

[6] The Jews in the town of Arbel itself spoke Arabic (Jastrow 1990a).

One of the most conspicuous innovations of the NENA subgroup is the replacement of the finite verbal forms *yiqṭul* (prefix-conjugation) and *qṭal* (suffix-conjugation) of earlier Aramaic with conjugations based on the active and passive participles, respectively. The NENA dialects are distinguished from the adjacently located and closely related Ṭuroyo subgroup by several shared innovations. These include the phonological shift *ġ > ʿ > ʾ > ø. The voiced velar fricative *ġ (the erstwhile fricative allophone of the */g/) has been lost in NENA (with the exception of a few lexical items), and has the reflex /ʾ/ or zero, e.g., Jewish Amedia *peʾla*, Jewish Arbel *pela* 'radish' < *paġlā. The /ʾ/ developed from an early pharyngeal /ʿ/, which is preserved in a few words, e.g., Jewish Amedia *raʿola* 'valley' < *rāġōlā. A shared innovation of NENA in the verbal system that distinguishes it from Ṭuroyo is the loss of the middle voice so-called T-stems, which have survived, albeit in reduced form, in Ṭuroyo. There are also a variety of shared lexical innovations in the Jewish and Christian NENA dialects, the most conspicuous one being *baxta* 'woman' (of uncertain etymology, but see Mutzafi [2005: 99 n.79]), as opposed to the conservative Ṭuroyo *ʾaṭto*. These innovations of NENA are of a considerable historical time-depth. The lexical item *baxta*, for example, appears in an 11th century source (Khan 2007a: 11).

In general, the trans-Zab subgroup of Jewish NENA is more innovative than the *lišana deni* subgroup, due to a greater degree of convergence with the non-Semitic languages of the area. The trans-Zab dialects exhibit a greater degree of difference from the neighboring Christian dialects than is the case with the *lišana deni* subgroup. This is a consequence of the fact that the Christian dialects have, in general, not undergone the degree of convergence with contact languages that is found in trans-Zab dialects. Conservative features found in Jewish *lišana deni* and the neighboring Christian dialects include, for example, the preservation of interdental consonants (in some dialects) and the preservation of a predominant SVO word-order, which are not features of Kurdish, the predominant contact language in the region. Trans-Zab dialects, on the other hand, have converged with Kurdish and Azeri Turkish with regard to these features, in that they have lost the interdentals and have a predominantly SOV word order. Moreover, there is a greater proportion of loanwords in their core lexicon than is the case in *lišana deni* dialects. Nevertheless, there are numerous differences between Jewish *lišana deni* dialects and the local Christian dialects. This can be seen in the chart below, which compares the Christian Barwar dialect (Khan 2008b) with the neighboring Jewish dialect of Betanure (Mutzafi 2008a), together with two other Jewish *lišana deni* dialects, Amedia (Greenblatt 2011) and Nerwa. As can be seen, the Jewish dialects exhibit considerable similarities among themselves, which contrast with the Christian dialect:

Table 1.1: Comparison of the Jewish *lišana deni* dialects with the Christian Barwar dialect

	C. Barwar	J. Betanure	J. Amedia	J. Nerwa
loss/preservation of laryngeal	balota 'throat'	balo'ta	balo'ta	balo'ta
reflex of *ay	lɛša 'dough'	leša	leša	leša
reflex of *aw	tawra 'ox'	tora	tora	tora
2s independent pronoun	'ati	'ahət ms. 'ahat fs.	'ahi	'ahət ms. 'ahat fs.
3pl. pron. suffix	-ay, -ɛy, -ey	-u, -ohun	-u, -ohun	-u, -ohun
genitive particle	diye	dide	dide	dide
reciprocal pronoun	ġðaðe	'əxðe	'əġde	'əxde
deictic copula	hole	wəlle	wəlle	wəlle
indicative prefix	i-	k-	k-	k-
'tomorrow'	tamməl	banhe	qadöme	qadome
'now'	diya, hadiya	'atta	'atta	'atta
'last year'	šetət wirra	šətqel	šətqel	šətqel
'quickly'	jalde	hayya	hayya	hayya
'big'	goṛa	'əṛwa	'uṛwa	'uṛwa
'to descend'	ṣlaya	kwaša	kwaša	kwaša
'to stand'	klaya	ḥmala	ḥmala	ḥmala
'to sleep'	ṭlaya	ṭwa'a	ṭwa'a	ṭwa'a
'to grow up'	mqărone	ṛwaya	ṛwaya	ṛwaya
'to speak'	mṣawoθe	mḥakoye	mḥakoye	mḥakoye
'he wants'	băye	gbe	gbe	gbe
'he knows'	yăðe	ki'e	ki'e	kiye

3.2 Particular structural features unique to the Jewish variety

A feature that is unique to all Jewish NENA dialects and contrasts with Christian dialects is the masculine single form and plural form of the adjective 'big', which are *rurwa/ruwwa* and *rurwe/ruwwe* respectively. This has developed by levelling from the original plural form **rawrḇē* (the original masculine singular form being **rabbā*) (Mutzafi 2014b).

The *lišana deni* dialects exhibit a distinctive feature that stands in contrast to the neighboring Christian dialects and the trans-Zab Jewish dialects in the formation of the independent genitive pronominal form. In most of the *lišana deni* dialects, the singular of this is formed by adding pronominal suffixes to the base *did-*, whereas the plural is formed by adding suffixes to the base *d-*. The singular suffixes are monosyllabic and the plural suffixes are bisyllabic, in some cases lengthened, with the result that the paradigm is bisyllabic in all persons:

	Jewish Betanture	Christian Barwar
3ms	did-e	diy-e
3fs	did-a	diy-a
2ms	did-ox	diy-ux
2fs	did-ax	diy-əx
1s	did-i	diy-i
3pl.	d-ohun	diy-ey
2pl.	d-oxun	diy-εxu
1pl.	d-eni	diy-ən

Most features that are unique to the Jewish dialects are found in the innovative trans-Zab dialects. As remarked above, most of these have arisen through a greater convergence with contact languages. These features can be divided into those that are general to all trans-Zab dialects and those that are found only in particular dialects of trans-Zab.

Innovative features that are general to trans-Zab include the shift of the interdental consonants /θ/ and /ð/ to the lateral /l/, e.g.

Christian Barwar	Jewish Arbel		
béθa	belá	'house'	< *baytā
'éða	'elá	'festival'	< *'ēdā

Similar sound shifts have been identified in Kurdish (Kapeliuk 1997). As can be seen from the indication of stress position in the table above, the trans-Zab dialects have word-final stress. This contrasts with the general penultimate stress that is found in Jewish lišana deni and the Christian dialects, and is likely to be induced by contact with the word-final stress position of Kurdish (Khan 2007b: 200).

Another general innovation, under the influence of Kurdish or Azeri Turkish, is the elimination of the distinction between genders in third person singular pronouns, e.g.:

Christian Barwar	Jewish Arbel		
'aw	'o	'he'	< *hāhū
'ay	'o	'she'	< *hāhī

The trans-Zab dialects in and around the Arbīl province of Iraq are, in general, more diverse in their structure than those in Iran and also are, in many cases, more conservative. As remarked above, it is likely that Iraq is the original heartland of the subgroup. This Iraq subgroup of trans-Zab includes dialects such as Koy Sanjaq, Qalʻa Dǝze, Rwanduz, Rustaqa, Dobe, and the Arbel plain. The trans-Zab dialects in Iran may be divided on the basis of shared innovations into (i) the northwestern Iran subgroup, which includes the dialects in the West Azerbaijan province of Iran (e.g., Urmi, Salmas, Shino, Naghada [Solduz], Sablagh [Mahabad]), together with the now extinct dialects that were spoken over the border in southeastern Turkey (e.g., Bashqala [Başkale] and Gavar [Yüksekova]); and (ii) the western Iran subgroup, which includes dialects of the Kurdistan and Kermanshah provinces of Iran (e.g., Saqqiz, Tikab, Bokan, Sanandaj, Kerend) and adjacent dialects over the border in Iraq (e.g., Sulemaniyya, Ḥalabja, Khanaqin). The dialects of this latter west Iran subgroup are referred to by their speakers as *hulaula*.

In phonology, these two Iranian subgroups exhibit unique innovations in the development of the emphatic consonants. These include the developments associated with the original emphatic consonants *ṭ and *ṣ and also more recently evolved emphatic phonemes, such as the sonorants /ṛ/, /ḷ/ and labials /ṃ/, /ḅ/. Such emphatic consonants involve a coarticulation of pharyngealization. In the Christian dialects of Iraq and also the Jewish *lišana deni* dialects, the emphatic consonants maintained their status of pharyngealized consonantal segments, with the phonetic spread of pharyngealization to adjacent vowels and consonants. In the Iraq subgroup of trans-Zab, the pharyngealization is weakened but can still be identified. In the western Iranian subgroup, however, an innovation has taken place whereby the pharyngealization of the emphatic segments has ceased to be a coarticulatory feature, but rather surfaces as a pharyngeal segment in the word. This may either be a historical pharyngeal, which has lost its pharyngeal articulation in non-emphatic contexts, e.g., Jewish Sanandaj *tamʻa* 'she tastes' < *ṭāmʻā vs. *šamya* 'she hears' < *šāmʻā, or a non-etymological pharyngeal, e.g., *tmaʻni* 'eighty' < *tmani* (Khan 2013). Such a development seems to have been brought about by convergence with the phonological structure of neighboring Kurdish (Kahn 1976: 49–52).

In the Jewish Urmi dialect of the northwestern Iran subgroup, the phonetic spreading of coarticulatory pharyngealization of consonantal segments has been reinterpreted as a suprasegmental phoneme that is a property of an entire word. This has come about under the influence of the vowel harmony of Azeri Turkish, with which the dialect was in contact. The same happened to the Christian dialects of the area, but a unique feature of Jewish Urmi is that the historical emphatic stop *ṭ became identical with the non-emphatic stop /t/ on the segmental level:

	Iraq	Northwestern Iran	
	Jewish Arbel	Christian Urmi	Jewish Urmi
*ṭūrā 'mountain'	ṭura	⁺ṭura	⁺tura

The original emphatic *ṭ was distinguished from non-emphatic *t not only in pharyngealization but also in glottal setting, in that *ṭ was unaspirated and *t was aspirated. As remarked, in the Urmi dialects the pharyngealization has become a suprasegmental feature (represented above by a superscribed ⁺). In the Christian dialect, the glottal setting of *ṭ is retained and the consonant is pronounced unaspirated (represented above by the symbol /ṱ/), which contrasts with aspirated /t/. In the Jewish dialect, however, the glottal setting is not retained and *ṭ has become totally assimilated to *t on a segmental level. This can be interpreted as reflecting a greater degree of convergence with the phonology of Azeri, which does not have an unaspirated phoneme equivalent to the /ṱ/ of Christian Urmi. Furthermore, in Jewish Urmi the back vowels /u/ and /o/ are fronted to [y] and [ø], respectively, in non-emphatic words, corresponding to the fronting that is found in the Azeri vowel harmony system, whereas this is not systematically found in Christian Urmi (Khan 2013).

In the Jewish Salmas dialect in the northwestern Iran subgroup, the suprasegmental pharyngealization has been lost in all words that originally used to contain it, but the phonetic effect of this feature on vowels has been preserved. This is most conspicuous in the development of long *a* vowels that were originally pharyngealized. These were backed and rounded to the quality /o/, e.g., *xosa* 'back' < *xāṣā*. This has occurred only in morphological stems and not in inflectional vowels:

	Lexical stem	Inflectional ending	
xosa 'back'	*xos-*	*a*	(nominal singular) < *xāṣā*
tyolana 'player'	*tyol-*	*ana*	(agentive singular) < *ṭyālānā*

This development in Jewish Salmas has occurred due to contact with various non-Semitic languages, including Russian in the recent history of the dialect.

An example of an innovation in morpho-syntax in the western Iranian subgroup is the loss of the genitive particle *d*. This particle, which combines a head noun with a dependent noun in a genitive construction, continues to be used, mainly in the form of a clitic on the head in the trans-Zab dialects of Iraq and northwestern Iran. In the western Iran subgroup, however, it has disappeared. It is possible to explain this as a convergence with Kurdish (Khan 2007b: 202), e.g.:

Jewish Arbel/Jewish Urmi	Jewish Sanandaj	
beləṭ Šlomo	*bela Šlomo*	'the house of Šlomo'
		< *bayṯā d-Šlomo*

In most dialects of the western Iranian subgroup, it has survived only as a vestige in genitive pronouns, but in the dialect of Jewish Kerend it is often omitted even in this context (Khan 2009: 11):

Jewish Sanandaj   Jewish Kerend
bela do   *bela ʾo*   'his house'

The conservative nature of the Iraq subgroup of trans-Zab, vis-à-vis the other trans-Zab subgroups, is reflected in some areas of morphology, such as the copula and the patterns of verbs. Compare the form of the present copula across the dialects:

	Iraq Jewish Arbel	Northwestern Iran Jewish Urmi	Western Iran Jewish Sanandaj
3ms	-ile	-ile	-ye
2ms	-wet	-ilet	-yet
1s	-wen	-ilen	-yena

In Jewish Arbel, the original heterogeneity of the paradigm is preserved, with the /l/ element in the 3rd person and the /w/ element in the 2nd and 1st persons. In Jewish Urmi the /l/ element has been generalized, and in Jewish Sanandaj the /l/ has been lost in the 3rd person and replaced by the glide /y/ (-ye < -ile), then the /y/ element has been generalized.

The northwestern Iran and western Iran subgroups exhibit a greater degree of leveling across the vocalism of the verbal patterns. This can be seen, for example, in the forms of the infinitive:

	Iraq Jewish Arbel	Northwestern Iran Jewish Urmi	Western Iran Jewish Sanandaj
simplex	CCaCa	CaCoCe	CaCoCe
causative	maCCoCe	maCCoCe	maCCoCe

The Iraq subgroup retains the archaic form of the infinitive of the simplex (historically *peʿal*) form, whereas in the other subgroups this has been levelled with the vocalic pattern of the infinitive of the derived causative form (historically *ʾap̄ʿel*). The Jewish Urmi dialect, in fact, exhibits a complete levelling of vocalic patterns across all conjugations of the simplex and derived forms of the verb (Khan 2008a: 65–67).

Another feature of the Iraq subgroup of trans-Zab that can be regarded as conservative is the occurrence of oblique marking of the subject of past perfective verbs in both transitive and intransitive clauses, e.g.:

Jewish Arbel
griš-li   'I pulled' (transitive)
qim-li   'I rose' (intransitive)

In the transitive clauses, the oblique suffix can be interpreted as an ergative marker. It is a feature of Christian NENA dialects, and the Jewish *lišana deni* and Iraqi trans-Zab dialects, that this ergative suffix is used also as a marker of the subject of intransitive verbs in an alignment profile that may be called "extended ergative" (Doron & Khan 2012). This profile is likely to have existed in the proto-form of the NENA subgroup, as a result of partial convergence with Iranian ergative languages of the region. The use of the oblique marker of intransitive subjects is attested in NENA interferences in classical Syriac texts at an early date (Khan 2004b). This is of considerable theoretical interest for studies in language contact and diachrony, in that it involves incomplete pattern matching (Matras & Sakel 2007) and constructional persistence, i.e., the continuing existence of the formal and semantic framework of a particular construction throughout the history of a language (Haig 2004: 55–57).

The innovative trans-Zab dialects of western Iran, however, exhibit a more canonical alignment profile, whereby the subjects of transitive verbs are marked by the oblique ergative suffix, but unaccusative intransitive verbs are marked by direct nominative suffixes, e.g.:

Jewish Sanandaj
grəš-li   'I pulled' (transitive)
qim-na   'I rose' (intransitive)

Such canonical ergative alignment, which is unique in NENA to the Jewish dialects of western Iran, is best considered to be the result of innovation rather than archaism, which has arisen, like other innovations in this subgroup, through a greater degree of convergence with Kurdish. Apart from the general innovative character of the subgroup compared to the Iraqi NENA dialects, there is some more specific evidence for this proposal. The past copula, for example, in the western Iranian trans-Zab dialects is conjugated with oblique ergative suffixes, e.g., *ye-le* 'he was', as is the case in extended ergative dialects such as the Iraqi trans-Zab dialect Jewish Arbel: *we-le*. In a canonical ergative alignment system, a copula would be expected to have nominative subject suffixes. The presence of ergative suffixes must be a relic from an earlier period in which there was extended ergative marking. The shift to nominative marking of the past copula was blocked by the fact that the resulting form would be identical, or nearly identical, to the present copula. In the northwestern Iran subgroup of trans-Zab, nominative subject marking is found on the present perfect of intransitive verbs, but the extended ergative system is retained on verbs when they have perfective function, e.g.:

Jewish Urmi
qəm-li   'I rose' (perfective)
qim-en   'I have risen' (present perfect)

The development of such present perfects with nominative subject may also be regarded as an innovation. It is, indeed, probably the first stage of the shift to the nominative marking of the perfective, the development present perfect > perfective being a common pathway of diachronic evolution. The existence of present perfect verbs with nominative subject suffixes is not, however, unique to Jewish NENA, since it is found also in some Christian dialects in the northwestern periphery of NENA in south-eastern Turkey, such as Hertevin (Jastrow 1988: 58–59) and Bohtan (Fox 2009: 56).[7]

A general innovation that is unique to the trans-Zab dialects of Jewish Neo-Aramaic is the formation of the perfective stem of the simplex pattern (historical *pe'al*) form on the analogy of that of the causative pattern (historical *'ap'el*):

Christian Barwar	Jewish Sanandaj	
simplex	simplex	causative pattern
griš-le	*graš-le* 'he pulled'	cf. *mərxəš-le* 'he caused to walk'
griša-l e	*gərš-a-le* 'he pulled her'	cf. *mərxš-a-le* 'he caused her to walk'

The more conservative trans-Zab dialects of Iraq still retain the *CCiC-a-le* pattern in middle /w/ verbs, e.g.

    Jewish Arbel   Jewish Sanandaj
    dwiq-a-le   *dəwq-a-le*   'he held her'

The small cluster of Jewish dialects in the region of Barzan (Mutzafi 2002b, 2004b), which are transitional between the *lišana deni* and trans-Zab subgroups, exhibit features of both of the other subgroups and also some unique features. Among the unique features is the use of the preverbal indicative-marking particles *y-* and *k-*. These are found elsewhere in NENA, but not with the distribution that is found in this dialect cluster. In these dialects, for example, they may be combined in the order *y + k*, e.g., *y-k-emər* 'he says'. In other NENA dialects such a combination is found only in the reverse order, e.g., Christian Urmi *c-i-patəx* 'he opens'. In some of the dialects of the cluster, the *y* is used in positive verbs and the *k* in negated ones, e.g., *y-saxe* 'he swims', *la k-saxe* 'he does not swim'.

---

[7] For further details of the development of ergative constructions in NENA, see Doron and Khan (2012), Coghill (2016), and Khan (2017). It has generally been assumed by scholars that the alignment patterns that are found in the western Iranian trans-Zab dialects are more archaic than the majority of dialects with generalized marking of oblique subject suffixes, e.g., Hopkins (1989), Mutzafi (2014b), Coghill (2016), and that the extended ergative profile reflects the decay of the orginal ergative system (Barotto 2014).

3.3 Lexicon: Hebrew elements

A common feature of all Jewish Neo-Aramaic dialects is their Hebrew component, which existed in the dialects before the migration of speakers to Israel (Sabar 1975a, 1975b, 2013a, 2013b). The quantity of Hebrew words varies according to whether the speaker is learned or not in Jewish sources, but there is a core of a Hebrew component in the speech of all speakers. The following description will focus on two subgroups of dialects as case studies, viz., the *lišana deni* subgroup and the northwestern Iran subgroup of trans-Zab.

Certain sound shifts that took place early in the history of NENA have not affected the corresponding sounds in the Hebrew words of the Hebrew component. In the Jewish Neo-Aramaic dialect of Zakho (*lišana deni* subgroup), the pharyngeals *ḥ and *ʻ shifted to /x/ and /ʼ/ respectively, whereas these sounds are retained in Hebrew words, e.g., Neo-Aramaic *xamša* (< *ḥamša) 'five', but Hebrew *ḥámmaš* (חֻמָּשׁ) 'Pentateuch', Neo-Aramaic *ʼawər* (< *ʻābər) 'to pass', but Hebrew *ʻavḗra* (עֲבֵרָה) 'transgression'. As seen in the last example, there is also a lack of parallelism between the shift of *ḇ to [w] in Zakho Neo-Aramaic and its realization as [v] in Hebrew. Hebrew *gimel rafeh* was pronounced as a fricative, e.g., *ʻagā́la* (הַגְעָלָה) 'purification of utensils for Passover', whereas a historical fricative *ḡ has generally been lost in NENA and has shifted to /ʼ/ in the Zakho dialect, e.g., *šrāʼa* 'lamp' (< *šrāḡā). It is important to note that, although there is a mismatch in the general sound shifts, all of the aforementioned sounds in Hebrew, [ḥ], [ʻ] and [v], occur in some words of the lexicon of the Jewish Zakho Neo-Aramaic dialect, due to conditioned retention in certain phonetic contexts, e.g., *nḥāqa* 'to touch', *ʻamōqa* 'deep' (Khan 2013: 112), and elsewhere, e.g., *zavāra* 'wanderer', *ġlāqa* 'to close'.

More recent sound shifts, in particular Jewish NENA dialects, have also affected the Hebrew component. This applies, for example, to the Hebrew fricative *bgdkpt* sounds *ḏ and *ṯ, which shifted to /z/ and /s/ respectively in the Jewish Zakho dialect, both in native Aramaic words and also in Hebrew loanwords, e.g., *bēs* ʼ(letter) beth' (בֵּית), *səʻoza* 'festive meal' (סְעוּדָה). This indicates that the Hebrew component entered the dialects after the formation of the proto-NENA subgroup, but before the occurrence of more recent sound shifts. Hebrew loanwords were sometimes pronounced with emphatic (pharyngealized) consonants, in order to distinguish them from Neo-Aramaic homonyms, e.g., *ṭōṛa* 'Torah' vs. plain *tōra* 'bull'. The vowels of Hebrew words in Jewish Zakho generally exhibit the general features of Sephardi pronunciation traditions, i.e., there was no distinction in pronunciation between *qameṣ* and *pataḥ*, on the one hand, or between *ṣere* and *seghol*, on the other. Also *ḥolem* and *shureq* were, at times, pronounced identically. It is noteworthy that *shewa* was often pronounced *a*, e.g., *našā́ma* 'soul' (נְשָׁמָה).

Hebrew loanwords in the *lišana deni* dialects are stressed on the penultimate syllable, which is the normal position of stress in native Aramaic words in these dialects, e.g., *pásuq* 'verse' (פָּסוּק), *tašúva* 'repentance' (תְּשׁוּבָה). In the reading of Biblical Hebrew in liturgy, by contrast, the stress is according to the biblical accents, i.e., generally on the final syllable. In Hebrew loanwords in the spoken language, the stress may be moved onto the short-vowel of a *shewa* with resultant gemination of the following consonant, e.g., *šáṭṭar* 'document' (שְׁטָר). This may be compared to a simlar process in the native Aramaic lexicon to produce bisyllabicity of a monsyllabic noun, e.g., *šə́mma* 'name' < *šma. Innovative gemination also occasionally occurs after the stress in originally bisyllabic words, e.g., *kúmmar* 'Christian priest' (כֹּמֶר). The consonant *resh* was sometimes pronounced geminate in other contexts, e.g., *maṣurrāʿ* 'leper' (מְצוֹרָע). In Hebrew words, original consonant gemination is generally retained, whereas this has often been lost in the Neo-Aramaic dialect, e.g., Jewish Zakho Neo-Aramaic *qaṭā́la* 'killer' (< *qaṭṭālā), but Hebrew *šammaš* 'synagogue beadle'.

In Jewish Urmi of northwestern Iran, suprasegmental pharyngealization of Hebrew loanwords is conditioned by the historical presence of one of the following elements (Khan 2008a: 37–39): (i) The emphatic consonants *ṭ or *ṣ, e.g., ⁺*ṭappa* 'drop' (טִפָּה), ⁺*saddiq* 'pious man' (צַדִּיק); (ii) The pharyngeals *ḥ or *ʿ, which shift to /h/ and zero respectively, e.g., ⁺*hātān* 'bridegroom' (חָתָן), ⁺*gnedem* 'paradise' (גַּן־עֵדֶן). Some exceptions are *ani* 'poor' (עָנִי) and *hanukke* 'Hanukkah' (חֲנֻכָּה), which are not pharyngealized; (iii) Elsewhere, pharyngealization occurs predominantly in words with long rounded back vowels, especially *qameṣ*, the reflex of which is [ɒ], e.g., ⁺*haggada* 'Passover legend' (הַגָּדָה), ⁺*amen* 'amen' (אָמֵן), although some words with long *qameṣ* are pronounced without pharyngealization, e.g., *kawod* 'honour' (כָּבוֹד), *mazuza* 'mezuzah' (מְזוּזָה). As in the *lišana deni* dialects, Hebrew loanwords were sometimes pronounced with suprasegmental emphasis in order to distinguish them from Neo-Aramaic homonyms, e.g., ⁺*tora* 'Torah' vs. *tora* 'bull'. A *gimel rafeh* in Hebrew words in Jewish Urmi is pronounced as a fricative, e.g., ⁺*aġala* (הַגְעָלָה) 'purification of utensils for Passover', although it has become zero in Aramaic words, e.g., *pela* 'radish' (< *paġlā). Original gemination of consonants is lost in most Aramaic words, but is often maintained in Hebrew words, e.g., *šibbat* 'Sabbath' (שַׁבָּת), although it is weakened in some cases, e.g., *sidur* 'prayer book' (סִדּוּר). High front vowels in Hebrew words are often lowered to /a/, e.g., *tašri* 'Tishri' (תִּשְׁרֵי), ⁺*banadam* 'human being' (בֶּן־אָדָם). Conversely the reflex of original /a/ is occasionally /i/, as in *šibbat* 'Sabbath' (שַׁבָּת). *Shewa* is usually pronounced /a/, e.g., *barit mila* 'circumcision' (בְּרִית מִילָה), and occasionally /i/, e.g., *nišama* 'soul' (נְשָׁמָה). Stress is on the final syllable of Hebrew words, as in words in the Aramaic dialect, this being a feature of the trans-Zab dialects (see above).

With regard to morphology, nouns in the Hebrew component of the dialects may retain their Hebrew plural form and accent or, alternatvely, have a Neo-Aramaic plural suffix, e.g., *məṣwṓṯ / məṣwā́ye* 'precepts', *mal'āxī́m / mal'áxe* 'angels'. The gender of Hebrew nouns sometimes changes, e.g., *'olā́m* 'world' and *'awṓn* 'inequity' are usually feminine, but are masculine in Hebrew.

Several Hebrew words are integrated into verbal expressions by combining Hebrew nouns or adjectives with light verbs, e.g., *p-y-š nifṭar* 'to die' (literally: 'to become deceased'). After the migration of the Jews to Israel, Israeli Hebrew verbs began to be integrated into the spoken Aramaic dialects by combining an Israeli Hebrew infinitive form with a light verb, e.g., *lišmor koliwale* 'they used to preserve it' (literally: 'to preserve [= לִשְׁמוֹר] they used to do it') (Khan 2004a: 14).

The Jewish Neo-Aramaic dialects use Hebrew and Rabbinic Aramaic words as cryptic expressions. These replace regular lexical parallels that would have been understood by non-Jewish neighbors (Mutzafi 2010, 2013).

Relating to religion, one finds *təppól, təppul* 'Muslim prayer', literally 'falls' (תִּפֹּל), derived from Exodus 15:16: תִּפֹּל עֲלֵיהֶם אֵימָתָה וָפַחַד 'awe and fear falls upon them'; *beṯ təppul* 'mosque' (literally: 'house of תִּפֹּל'); *šetí waʿereb, šattu-ʿérev, šatta-ʿéruv* 'crucifix' (literally: 'warp and weft; crosswise' שְׁתִי וָעֵרֶב).

Warnings in dangerous situations are sometimes expressed by cryptic expressions, such as *wayyidom, waydóm* (וַיִּדֹּם), based on Leviticus 10:3 וַיִּדֹּם אַהֲרֹן 'and Aaron was silent'. Words with a similar function may be alluded to by referring to the letters of their Hebrew orthography, e.g., *tre lamedé* 'two letter *lameds*', an allusion to the Neo-Aramaic (ultimately Iranian) word *ḷāḷ* 'dumb, mute'.

Aramaic-speaking merchants used Hebrew words in their secret argot, e.g., *kesāfe* 'money' (< כְּסָפִים, with an Aramaic plural suffix replacing the Hebrew one); *šəlmé* also 'money', derived from the Hebrew verbal root שלם 'to pay' with the nominal pattern of the synonymous cryptic word *falsé* (of Arabic etymology). Cryptic words were often used by merchants to refer to products, e.g., *šexar* 'alcoholic drink' (שֵׁכָר), or *zeʿa* (זֵעָה), literally 'sweat' (a Hebrew translation of the primary meaning of the Arabic parallel *ʿaraq* 'sweat', which also denotes 'arrack' as a secondary meaning). The Jewish merchants' secret argot of the dialect of Urmi disguised Aramaic verbs, which might have been understood by local Aramaic-speaking Christians, by replacing the final vowel of the Aramaic infinitive forms with the Hebrew plural suffix *-ím*. Most of these cryptic forms are employed as imperatives, thus *hivalím* 'give it!' (*hiwālá* 'to give'), *šaqolím* 'buy it!' (*šaqolé* 'to buy'), *zaboním* 'sell it!'.

3.4 Language contact influences

In numerous places in the foregoing discussion of grammatical structure, the point has been made that many of the differences between the *lišana deni* dialects and the trans-Zab dialects have come about by the greater convergence of the latter with contact languages. Here we shall restrict ourselves to some remarks on the lexicon.

As expected, the lexicon of the trans-Zab dialects exhibits a greater influence from contact languages than the *lišana deni* dialects. This is reflected by a greater proportion of loanwords in core areas of the lexicon. The table below shows a series of items in the core lexicon that are of native Aramaic etymology in Jewish Amedia, a *lišana deni* dialect, compared to the corresponding items in the trans-Zab dialects Jewish Urmi and Jewish Sanandaj. In each case, at least one of the trans-Zab dialects has a loanword, from Azeri Turkish (T), Kurdish (K), or Persian (P). In some cases both trans-Zab dialects have loanwords.

Table 1.2: Selected core vocabulary in *lišana deni* and trans-Zab dialects

	Amedia	Urmi	Sanandaj
'eyelash'	tәlpa	kәprәg (T)	peḷa (K)
'eyebrow'	bәgwina	⁺qaša (T)	gwenya
'jaw'	le'ma	čanakta (K/T)	čanaga (K)
'spit'	roqe	roqe	tәf (K/P)
'arm'	'ida	⁺qola (T/K)	qoḷa (K)
'mother'	yәmma	⁺daa (K)	daăka (K)
'hail'	barda	⁺dolu (T)	tarzăka (K)
'shade'	ṭalla	kolga (T)	poxa
'green'	yaruqa	⁺yašәl (T)	yăruqa

Outside of the core vocabulary, the extent of influence of contact-languages is greater, especially in nouns. Garbell (1965b) has calculated that in the Jewish Urmi dialect, 69% of the total lexicon of nouns are loanwords, and similar proportions can be identified in other trans-Zab dialects (Khan 2004a: 7).

Although nouns are particularly susceptible to being loaned, as is generally the case cross-linguistically, the impact of contact-languages can be seen in all areas of the lexicon in the Jewish NENA dialects. Many verbal roots have been extracted from loanwords. This applies also to Hebrew loanwords, e.g., Jewish Zakho *t-p-l* 'to pray (Muslims)' < Hebrew תְּפִלֹּ (see above). Some grammatical particles have been borrowed, including discourse connectives and, in the case of some trans-Zab dialects, the Kurdish definite article (Khan 2007b: 201–202).

4 Written and oral traditions

4.1 Writing system

When Jewish Neo-Aramaic speakers began to commit their language to writing in the 17th century, they used Hebrew script, as is the norm with other Jewish languages. The orthography was *plene*, corresponding to the contemporary practice of spelling Hebrew (Sabar 1976: xxxi–xxxiv, 2002: 15–21). There are, however, some differences. The most conspicuous one is the use of *'aleph* to represent long *ā* in word-medial position, e.g., כמארא *xmāra* 'ass', including in Hebrew loanwords, e.g., נשאמוך *nišāmox* 'your soul' (= נְשָׁמָה), and occasionally also medial short /a/, e.g., כאלוי *kalwe* 'dogs'. In contrast to written Christian Neo-Aramaic, which has incorporated historical elements of Syriac orthography, Jewish Neo-Aramaic orthography is phonetic and not based on that of any early literary form of Jewish Aramaic, e.g., כמשא *xamša* (= חמשא), שואא *šō'a* (= שבעא). Scribes sometimes write prosthetic vowels that break initial consonantal clsuters, e.g., אתרי *'ətre* 'two', אטלהא *'əṭlāha* 'three'. These are generally not pronounced in the surviving spoken language. Spread of emphasis is reflected in spellings with emphatic letters, such as צלוצא *ṣlōṣa* 'prayer' (= *ṣlōsa* < *slōṭā), and loss of emphasis by spellings such as שרתי *šarte* < *šarṭe* 'conditions'. Texts written by Jewish Urmi speakers reflect the weakening of pharyngeal consonants in that dialect, e.g., אלחא *ilha* (*ḥet* represents /h/) (Sabar 2013b: 481).

Texts written in Israel since the 1950s exhibit some influence from Israeli Hebrew pronunciation, e.g., ח may be used for Neo-Aramaic /x/ and ק for Neo-Aramaic /k/, דוּמָיֶק *dūmāyək* 'eventually', or Hebrew orthography, e.g., the use of ע, as in cases such as עֵינָא *'ena* 'eye' (cf. Hebrew עַיִן), or the use of שׂ in cases such as שְׂעָארֵי *saʿāre* 'barley' (cf. Hebrew שְׂעוֹרִים).

Hebrew vocalization signs came to be used frequently in texts written down in the 20th century. These reflect Sephardi Hebrew pronunciation, in that the signs *qameṣ* and *pataḥ*, on the one hand, and *ṣere* and *seghol*, on the other, interchange inconsistently. The *shewa* sign is often used to represent /a/, even in closed syllables, e.g., חְכּוֹמָא *ḥakōma* 'king'. A noteworthy feature of vocalization is the insertion of epenthetic vowels breaking initial consonantal clusters, which are generally not pronounced in the spoken dialects. This is found predominantly in verbal forms in Bible translations, e.g., in the trans-Zab Neo-Aramaic Bible translation studied by Rees (2008: 16) פְּלִיכְלֵה 'he opened' (spoken dialects: *plixle*).

A distinctive feature of the Bible translations is their close imitation of the syntax of the Hebrew source text. This results in the fact that their syntax deviates radically from the syntax of the spoken dialects (for details, see Rees 2008).

4.2 Literature

There is no clear distinction between the written literature and the oral literature of the Neo-Aramaic-speaking Jews, since the majority of their literary heritage originates in oral transmission (Aloni 2014: 22). The many bible translations published by Sabar, for example, were committed to writing only in the 20th century, at the request of scholars in Israel.

Jewish Neo-Aramaic literature may be divided into the following categories (Sabar 1976: 161–178, 1982: xxxii–xxxvi; Aloni 2014: 22–24):

I. Religious literature, most of which exists today in manuscripts, including:
   (i) Homilies on portions of the Pentateuch.
   (ii) Expositions on the *Hafṭarot* and *Megillot* in the form of free translations.
   (iii) Literal translations of the Bible, mostly written down from oral traditions in the 20th century.
   (iv) Liturgical literature, including dirges (*qinot*), especially for the Ninth of Ab, paraliturgical songs (*pizmonim*), and expositions of the 613 commandments (*'azharot*)
   (v) Rhymed aggadic narratives (*tafsirim*), loosely based on biblical and midrashic sources. Many of these were published by Rivlin (1959).
II. Oral folk literature. This played a central role in the culture of Neo-Aramaic-speaking Jews. Some of it has been committed to writing by scholars, as part of their documentation of the dialects, and also by native speakers.

In Israel, new performance genres have developed among the Neo-Aramaic speaking community. Theatrical plays have been produced, notably by the performer and singer Nisan Aviv, in the Jewish Urmi dialect (Khan 2008a: xviii, 417). The *lišana deni* community in Jerusalem currently holds monthly cultural gatherings, at which they have poetry readings and stand-up comedy entertainment. Speakers of some of the western Iranian trans-Zab dialects have held phone-in radio programmes, organized by speakers of Sulemaniyya and Sanandaj, including poetry readings and other cultural activities. Participation in these activities dwindles from year to year, as the number of competent speakers gradually diminishes.

5 State of research

Despite the progress that has been made with the documentation of the Jewish Neo-Aramaic dialects, it is very important to strive for a fuller documentation during the last two decades or so of the life of the dialects. This applies both to the description of the linguistic structure of the dialects and also to the collection and transcription of oral literature. This documentation should consist not only of the publication of data, but also the secure archiving of unpublished audio and visual data.

References

Aloni, Oz. 2014. *The Neo-Aramaic speaking Jewish community of Zakho: A survey of the oral culture*. Saarbrücken: Lap Lambert.
Barotto, Alessandra. 2014. Split ergativity in the NENA dialects. In Geoffrey Khan & Lidia Napiorkowska (eds.), *Neo-Aramaic and its linguistic context*, 232–249. Piscataway: Gorgias Press.
Ben-Yaʿqov, Avraham. 1980. קהילות יהודי כורדסתאן, 2nd edn. Jerusalem: Kiryat Sepher.
Brauer, Erich & Rachel Patai. 1993. *The Jews of Kurdistan* (Jewish Folklore and Anthropology Series). Detroit: Wayne State University Press.
Coghill, Eleanor. 2016. *The rise and fall of ergativity in Aramaic: cycles of alignment change*. Oxford Studies in Diachronic and Historical Linguistics 21. Oxford: Oxford University Press.
Cohen, Eran. 2012. *The syntax of neo-Aramaic: The Jewish dialect of Zakho*. (Neo-Aramaic Studies). Piscataway: Gorgias Press.
Doron, Edit & Geoffrey Khan. 2012. The typology of morphological ergativity in Neo-Aramaic. *Lingua* 122. 225–240.
Duval, Rubens. 1883. *Les dialectes Néo-Araméens de Salamâs: Textes sur l'état actuel de la Perse et contes populaires publiés avec une traduction Française*. Paris: F. Vieweg.
Fassberg, Steven Ellis. 2010. *The Jewish Neo-Aramaic dialect of Challa*. Leiden: Brill.
Fox, Samuel E. 2008. North-Eastern Neo-Aramaic and the Middle Aramaic dialects. In Geoffrey Khan (ed.), *Neo-Aramaic Dialect Studies*, 1–18. Piscataway: Gorgias Press.
Fox, Samuel E. 2009. *The Neo-Aramaic dialect of Bohtan*. Piscataway: Gorgias Press.
Garbell, Irene. 1965a. *The Jewish Neo-Aramaic dialect of Persian Azerbaijan: Linguistic anlysis and folkloristic texts* (Janua Linguarum, Series Practica). The Hague: Mouton.
Garbell, Irene. 1965b. The impact of Kurdish and Turkish on the Jewish Neo-Aramaic dialect of Persian Azerbaijan and the adjoining regions. *Journal of the American Oriental Society* 85(2). 159–177.
Greenblatt, Jared R. 2011. *The Jewish Neo-Aramaic dialect of Amadiya* (Studies in Semitic Languages and Linguistics). Leiden: Brill.
Haig, Geoffrey. 2004. *Alignment in Kurdish: A diachronic perspective*. Kiel: University of Kiel Habilitationsschrift.
Hoberman, Robert. 1988. The history of the modern Aramaic pronouns and pronominal suffixes. *Journal of the American Oriental Society* 108. 557–575.
Hopkins, Simon. 1989. Neo-Aramaic dialects and the formation of the preterite. *Journal of Semitic Studies* 37. 74–90.
Jastrow, Otto. 1988. *Der neuaramäische Dialekt von Hertevin (Provinz Siirt)* (Semitica Viva). Wiesbaden: Harrassowitz Verlag.
Jastrow, Otto. 1990a. *Der arabische dialekt der Juden von 'Aqra und Arbīl* (Semitica Viva). Wiesbaden: Harrassowitz Verlag.

Jastrow, Otto. 1990b. Die arabische dialekte der irakischen Juden. In Werner Diem & A. Falaturi (eds.), *XXIV deutscher Orientalistentag vom 26. bis 30. September 1988 in Köln. Ausgewählte vorträge*, 199–206. Stuttgart: Steiner.

Kahn, Margaret. 1976. *Borrowing and Variation in a Phonological Description of Kurdish*. Michigan: University of Michigan PhD thesis.

Kapeliuk, Olga. 1997. Spirantized d and t in Neo-Aramaic. *Massorot* 9–11. 527–544. [Hebrew].

Khan, Geoffrey. 1999. *A grammar of Neo-Aramaic: The dialect of the Jews of Arbel*. Boston: Brill.

Khan, Geoffrey. 2002. *The Neo-Aramaic dialect of Qaraqosh*. (Studies in Semitic Languages and Linguistics). Boston: Brill.

Khan, Geoffrey. 2004a. *The Jewish Neo-Aramaic dialect of Sulemaniyya and Ḥalabja*. (Studies in Semitic Languages and Linguistics). Leiden: Brill.

Khan, Geoffrey. 2004b. Aramaic and the impact of languages in contact with it through the ages. In Pedro Bádenas de la Peña, Sofía Torallas Tovar, Eugenio R. Luján & María Ángeles Gallego (eds.), *Lenguas en contacto: El testimonio escrito*, 87–108. Madrid: Consejo Superior de Investigaciones Científicas.

Khan, Geoffrey. 2007a. The North-Eastern Neo-Aramaic dialects. *Journal of Semitic Studies* 52(1). 1–20.

Khan, Geoffrey. 2007b. North Eastern Neo-Aramaic. In Yaron Matras & Jeanette Sakel (eds.), *Grammatical borrowing in cross-linguistic perspective*, 197–214. Berlin: Mouton de Gruyter.

Khan, Geoffrey. 2008a. *The Jewish Neo-Aramaic dialect of Urmi*. (Gorgias Neo-Aramaic Studies). Piscataway: Gorgias Press.

Khan, Geoffrey. 2008b. *The Neo-Aramaic dialect of Barwar*. Leiden: Brill.

Khan, Geoffrey. 2009. *The Jewish Neo-Aramaic dialect of Sanandaj*. Piscataway: Gorgias Press.

Khan, Geoffrey. 2013. Phonological emphasis in North-Eastern Neo-Aramaic. In Jean Léo Léonard & Samia Naïm (eds.), *Base articulatoire arrière. Backing and backness*, 111–132. Munich: Lincom Europa.

Khan, Geoffrey. 2017. Ergativity in Neo-Aramaic. In Jessica Coon, Diane Massam & Lisa Travis (eds.), *Oxford handbook of ergativity*, 873–899. Oxford: Oxford University Press.

Krotkoff, Georg. 1985. Studies in Neo-Aramaic lexicology. In Ann Kort & Scott Morschauer (eds.), *Biblical and related studies presented to Samuel Iwry*, 123–134. Winona Lake: Eisenbrauns.

Maclean, Arthur John. 1895. *Grammar of the dialects of vernacular Syriac as spoken by the eastern Syrians of Kurdistan*. Cambridge: Cambridge University Press.

Mann, Jacob. 1931. *Texts and studies in Jewish history and literature*. (The Abraham and Hannah Oppenheim Memorial Publications). Cincinnati: Hebrew Union College Press.

Matras, Yaron & Jeanette Sakel. 2007. Investigating the mechanisms of pattern replication in language convergence. *Studies in Language* 31(4). 829–865.

Mutzafi, Hezy. 2002a. On the Jewish Neo-Aramaic dialect of Aradhin and its dialectal affinities. In Werner Arnold (ed.), *Sprich doch mit deinen Knechten aramäisch, wir verstehen es!" 60 Beiträge zur Semitistik, Festschrift für Otto Jastrow zum 60. Geburtstag*, 479–488. Wiesbaden: Harrassowitz Verlag.

Mutzafi, Hezy. 2002b. Barzani Jewish Neo-Aramaic and its dialects. *Mediterranean Language Review* 14. 41–70.

Mutzafi, Hezy. 2004a. *The Jewish Neo-Aramaic dialect of Koy Sanjaq (Iraqi Kurdistan)*. (Semitica Viva). Wiesbaden: Harrassowitz Verlag.

Mutzafi, Hezy. 2004b. Two texts in Barzani Jewish Neo-Aramaic. *Bulletin of the School of Oriental and African Studies* 67(1). 1–13.

Mutzafi, Hezy. 2005. Etymological notes on North-Eastern Neo-Aramaic. *Aramaic Studies* 3(1). 83–107.
Mutzafi, Hezy. 2008a. *The Jewish Neo-Aramaic dialect of Betanure (province of Dihok)*. (Semitica Viva). Wiesbaden: Harrassowitz Verlag.
Mutzafi, Hezy. 2008b. Trans-Zab Jewish Neo-Aramaic. *Bulletin of the School of Oriental and African Studies* 71(3). 409–431.
Mutzafi, Hezy. 2010. Cryptic expressions in Jewish Neo-Aramaic. *Massorot* 15. 113–137. [Hebrew].
Mutzafi, Hezy. 2013. Secret languages, Hebrew in: Aramaic. In Geoffrey Khan, Shmuel Bolozky, Steven E. Fassberg, Gary A. Rendsburg, Aaron D. Rubin, Ora R. Schwartzwald, and Tamar Zewi (eds.), *Encyclopedia of Hebrew Language and Linguistics*. Leiden-Boston: Brill.
Mutzafi, Hezy. 2014a. Christian Salamas and Jewish Salmas: Two separate types of Neo-Aramaic. In Geoffrey Khan & Lidia Napiorkowska (eds.), *Neo-Aramaic and its linguistic context*, 289–304. Piscataway: Gorgias Press.
Mutzafi, Hezy. 2014b. Jewish Neo-Aramaic. In Norman A. Stillman & Phillip Isaac Ackerman-Lieberman (eds.), *Encyclopedia of the Jews of the Islamic World*. Boston: Brill.
Rees, Margo. 2008. *Lishan didan, Targum didan: Translation language in a Neo-Aramaic Targum tradition*. Piscataway: Gorgias Press.
Rivlin, Joseph Joel. 1959. *Shirat Yehude ha-Targum*. Jerusalem: Bialik Institute.
Sabar, Ariel. 2009. *My Father's paradise: A son's search for his family's past*, 1st edn. Chapel Hill: Algonquin Books.
Sabar, Yona. 1975a. The Hebrew elements in the Aramaic dialect of the Jews of Kurdistan. *Lĕšonénu* 38. 206–219. [Hebrew].
Sabar, Yona. 1975b. The Hebrew elements in the Neo-Aramaic dialect of the Jews of Azerbaijan. *Lĕšonénu* 39. 272–294. [Hebrew].
Sabar, Yona. 1976. *Pašaṭ Wayəhî BaŠallaḥ. A Neo-Aramaic midrash on Beshallaḥ (Exodus). Introduction, phonetic transcription, translation, notes and glossary*. Wiesbaden: Harrassowitz Verlag.
Sabar, Yona. 1982. *The folk literature of the Kurdistani Jews: An anthology*. (Yale Judaica Series). New Haven: Yale University Press.
Sabar, Yona. 1983. *Sefer Breshit ba-'Aramit ḥadashah be-nivam shel Yehude Zakho: We-nosfu 'alav ṭeqsṭim be-nivim 'aḥarim shel 'aramit ḥadashah u-milonim*, vol. 9 ('Edah ve-Lashon). Jerusalem: Magnes Press.
Sabar, Yona. 1985. *Midrashim Ba-'Aramit Yehude Kurdisṭan le-parashiot Wayḥi, Beshallaḥ, Yitro*. Jerusalem: Israel Academy of Science and Humanities.
Sabar, Yona. 1988. *Sefer Shemot ba-'Aramit ḥadashah be-nivam shel Yehude Zakho: Ve-nosfu 'alav ṭeqsṭim be-nivim aḥerim shel 'Aramit ḥadashah u-milon* ('Edah ve-Lashon). Jerusalem: Magnes Press.
Sabar, Yona. 1991a. *Targum de-Targum: an old neo-Aramaic version of the Targum on Song of Songs*. Wiesbaden: Harrassowitz Verlag.
Sabar, Yona. 1991b. *Sefer Wa-yiqra' be-'Aramit ḥadashah be-nivam shel Yehude Zakho: ve-nosfu 'alav ṭeqsṭim be-nivim 'aḥerim shel 'Aramit ḥadashah u-milon*. ('Edah ve-Lashon). Jerusalem: Hebrew University Magnes Press.
Sabar, Yona. 1994. *Sefer Devarim ba-Aramit ḥadashah be-nivam shel Yehude Zakho: ve-nosfu 'alav ṭeqsṭim be-nivim aḥerim shel Aramit ḥadashah u-milon*. ('Edah Ye-Lashon). Jerusalem: Magnes Press.
Sabar, Yona. 2002. *Jewish Neo-Aramaic dictionary*. (Semitica Viva). Wiesbaden: Harrassowitz Verlag.

Sabar, Yona. 2013a. Modern Jewish Aramaic, Hebrew component in. In Geoffrey Khan, Shmuel Bolozky, Steven E. Fassberg, Gary A. Rendsburg, Aaron D. Rubin, Ora R. Schwartzwald, and Tamar Zewi (eds.), *Encyclopedia of Hebrew Language and Linguistics*. Leiden & Boston: Brill.

Sabar, Yona. 2013b. Kurdistan, pronunciation tradition. In Geoffrey Khan, Shmuel Bolozky, Steven E. Fassberg, Gary A. Rendsburg, Aaron D. Rubin, Ora R. Schwartzwald, and Tamar Zewi (eds.), *Encyclopedia of Hebrew Language and Linguistics*. Leiden & Boston: Brill.

Soane, E. B. 1912. *To Mesopotamia and Kurdistan in disguise; with historical notices of the Kurdish tribes and the Chaldeans of Kurdistan*. London: J. Murray.

Socin, A. 1882. *Die Neu-Aramäischen Dialekte von Urmia bis Mosul*. Tübingen: H. Laupp.

Stoddard, David Tappan. 1860. *Grammar of the modern Syriac language, as spoken in Oroomiah, Persia, and in Koordistan*. New Haven: B.L. Hamlen.

Benjamin Hary
Judeo-Arabic in the Arabic-Speaking World

1 Introduction

Judeo-Arabic is a *religiolect* that has been spoken and written in various forms by Jews throughout the Arabic-speaking world. A religiolect is a language variety with its own history which is developed within a specific religious community, although some of its distinctive features may later spread outside of the community (Hary 2009: 12–13). Judeo-Arabic literature deals, for the most part, with Jewish topics and is written by Jews for a Jewish readership. Several important features distinguish it from other varieties of Arabic. These include a mixture of elements of Classical and post-Classical Arabic, dialectal components, pseudocorrections,[1] and pseudocorrections that have become standardized. In other words, it is a typical mixed variety. Judeo-Arabic also possesses a number of specific additional sociolinguistic features that set it apart: the use of Hebrew rather than Arabic characters, various traditions of Judeo-Arabic orthography, elements of Hebrew and Aramaic vocabulary and grammar, and the style of the *šarḥ* (a genre composed of literary translations of Jewish religious and liturgical texts from Hebrew and Aramaic into Judeo-Arabic). Users began to employ the religiolect around the eighth century CE, as a linguistic result of the Arab conquests during the seventh century, and have been using it in various forms until today.

1.1 Names of speakers

Judeo-Arabic speakers have been labeled by several names and have been a topic of discussion academically and politically for quite some time, in Israeli society and elsewhere. Many designations for speakers of Judeo-Arabic exist, including *Mizrahim* (lit. 'Easterners' or עדות המזרח, lit. 'The communities of the East'), *Sephardim* (lit. 'Spaniards'), and "Arab Jews." In fact, the term *Mizrahim* (often translated as 'oriental Jews') may be considered a misnomer, since Moroccan Jews, for example, hardly count as being from the east, if the point of reference is Israel. However, an imaginary line drawn diagonally across the Mediterranean,

---

[1] Pseudororrections, which include both hypercorrections and hypocorrections, are a kind of a linguistic "correction," which often stems from speakers' and writers' desires to speak and write with a more prestigious variety of the language. For a full treatment, see Blau 1970 and Hary 2007.

from the Strait of Gibraltar to the Black Sea, has historically distinguished the Jewish "west" (in fact, north) from the Jewish "east" (in fact, south). This raises a number of questions, such as: Who set this imaginary line? Who used it? For what purposes? The term *Mizrahim*, on the other hand, does not necessarily allude to a specific geographical origin, the east. It can also refer to the geopolitical discourse, in particular to the second and third generations of Jews of Middle Eastern and North African origins who were engaged, beginning from the early 1970s (in the writings of Segev, Shohat, Swirski, etc.), in gaining political awareness and raising public consciousness of the Israeli "ethnic" puzzle, whereby systematic, institutional discrimination against the group was part of the practices of Zionism and the State of Israel.

The term *Sephardim* has its own problems. Strictly speaking, it refers to Jews whose ancestors had been expelled from the Iberian Peninsula, up to and especially in 1492 and 1497, and who then settled in the Ottoman Empire and elsewhere. Although many Jews of the Ottoman Empire, especially in Arabic-speaking communities, adopted the religious ways and liturgical customs of the expellees from the Iberian Peninsula, pre-Sephardi traditions also survived in many areas, including North Africa. In popular usage, the term *Sephardim* often includes *Mizrahim* and is used as a default to non-*Ashkenazim*.

The term "Jews of Arab lands," which has often been used in the past (including by me), in retrospect may not be the most appropriate. The expression associates "lands" with a nationality, since the term "Arab" may be used to refer to a specific (pan-)nationalism. The term "Arab" need not necessarily be identified with nationalism. An Iraqi, for example, may ask herself, "Am I an Iraqi or an Arab?" However, there have been attempts to demonstrate that the term "Arab" in the context of pan-nationalism encompasses all Arabic-speaking nations. Thus, the use of the term "Arab lands" would seem to establish a link, in the Romantic sense, between one population group and a specific territory. Such a link is factually inaccurate, since many minorities – Berbers, Jews, Kurds, and others – who live in "Arab lands" – have their own national movements and aspirations. Control of a given territory by a certain population is thus a historical and not a geographical fact; i.e., there is no "natural link" between human population groups and specific territories.

Finally, the term "Arab Jews," attested historically in various documents but now used only sporadically in the general media and more frequently in academic circles, may be misleading because the word "Arab" could be perceived as an "ethnic" marker. This leads to several unresolved issues, two of which are as follows:

(i) The concept of "ethnicity" itself remains unclear in most contexts, the Israeli case included; it is therefore best avoided in academic discourse, unlike the concepts of language or religion, which can be measured and marked more easily.

(ii) The term "Arab Jews" bears controversial political connotations in Israel. For example, it may suggest a connection between "Arab Jews" and "Arab Israelis," whose identity constructions seem similar on the surface, but in fact differ profoundly on various levels. For example, Arab Israelis in general feel less connected to the State of Israel than "Arab Jews." In addition, many "Arab Jews" object to the term, sometimes strongly, because of the current Arab-Israeli conflict, among other reasons. Although some Israeli intellectuals today refer to themselves as "Arab Jews," they are probably quite aware that their use of the term with its current connotations is rather remote from the way it may have been used by Jews in pre-modern Egypt, for example, where the political context was significantly different.

Nationalism in the Middle East developed mainly in the 20th century. Consequently, the term "Arab Jews" as a historical or cultural designation is best avoided in reference to any time before the end of the 19th century. Afterwards the term becomes ambiguous, unless one specifically stipulates that the word "Arab" is not being employed in the more recent sense of nationality. Today, such "Arab Jews" are in reality almost exclusively multilingual Israeli, French, or North American nationals who, for the most part, do not hold any "Arab" citizenship (except for some Moroccan or Tunisian Jews). In fact, many of them do not even speak Arabic or Judeo-Arabic well; only their parents or grandparents do. Therefore, when referring to the time period from the beginning of the 20th century to the present, the term "Jews of Arabic-speaking backgrounds" is thus more suitable. For pre-modern times, the term "Arabic-speaking Jews" is fitting as well. The two latter terms would probably also be acceptable to more people than the term "Arab Jews."

The multiplicity of terms that refer to Judeo-Arabic speakers reveals that it represents a dynamic field and that various names are subject to rethinking the categories, as they imply different political positions. Furthermore, it exposes the efforts of political activists and scholars to engage in making visible a category, that of Arabic-speaking Jews, that has been concealed by the category *Sephardi Jews*, which was and still is "one term fits all," and thus tells us a lot about the discomfort and anxieties in which marginal groups find themselves. This exposure is a fascinating area of investigating the genealogy and emergence of Arabic-speaking Jews and their various political and ideological positions.

1.2 Present-day status

Judeo-Arabic today is endangered and close to becoming extinct. The extensive emigration of Arabic-speaking Jews from the late 1940s through the 1960s is the main reason for this situation. Most of these Arabic-speaking Jews immigrated to Israel (although some also immigrated to France, North America, and other places), where they were under great pressure to drop Judeo-Arabic and adopt Hebrew. Today, there are still sizeable Jewish communities in Morocco (3,000) and Tunisia (1,100). In Morocco, most of the Jewish community uses French rather than Moroccan Judeo-Arabic. There are still speakers of Contemporary Judeo-Arabic in Israel (and elsewhere) who use its various dialects: Iraqi Judeo-Arabic, Libyan Judeo-Arabic, Moroccan Judeo-Arabic, Tunisian Judeo-Arabic, Yemeni Judeo-Arabic, as well as a handful of Egyptian and Syrian Judeo-Arabic speakers. According to the SIL International Ethnologue project, as of the mid-1990s there were close to 500,000 speakers of Judeo-Arabic, and I assume that the number has declined today to just under 400,000 speakers (see also Spolsky and Shoahamy 1999: 3). This population, however, is aging, so that Judeo-Arabic's use as a native religiolect will likely disappear in the near future. Consequently, there is an urgent need for extensive research on Judeo-Arabic.

On the other hand, there has been a rising consciousness among the younger generation with a high degree of Mizrahi identity, especially around literature and the arts. Many examples are noted in sections 4.2 (literature) and 4.3 (performance). Of special note in music is *The Israeli Andalusian Orchestra*, based in Ashdod, the successor to the previous *The New Andalusian Orchestra* (2009) and the previous *Israeli Andalusian Orchestra* (1994), which was terminated in February 2009 due to the dismissal of all of its musicians and workers. Most of those individuals refused to be dissuaded and therefore continued to hold rehearsals and concerts, in a steadfast struggle for government recognition and public funding. This was done mostly as a strong recognition of Judeo-Arabic culture and heritage. According to the orchestra's website, "Their work has brought to life the music and heritage of a culture that had almost disappeared forever." Indeed, the orchestra focuses on reviving archaic music and lyrics. In recent years, more recognition of such music was given in Israel, and, in 2016, an additional group, *Jerusalem Orchestra – East and West*, started to function. Furthermore, as recently as September 2017, the Israeli Minister of Culture announced that an orchestra specializing in Middle Eastern and North African music would be selected soon and would be recognized as a national orchestra (which involves doubling its financial governmental support). This is certainly a change in priorities in Israeli society.

The politics of Judeo-Arabic in Israel and in the United States, where influential Jewish societies reside, has been discussed at length by Hary (2016a), Shohat (2016), and others. Hary concludes that, although Judeo-Arabic is one of the more significant Jewish religiolects (Hary 1992: 73–75; Stillman 1988: 3–4),

Yiddish and Judeo-Spanish enjoy greater recognition and prestige. There are several reasons for this. First, the dominance of Ashkenazi Jewry throughout the 20th and 21st centuries in two influential Jewish societies, in the United States and in Palestine/Israel, has advanced the prestige of Yiddish over other Jewish religiolects. In the United States, the YIVO Institute for Jewish Research was reestablished to support the teaching and study of Yiddish culture. Yiddish continues to enjoy greater prestige than any other Jewish religiolect (except Hebrew).

The tragedy of the Holocaust, coupled with Stalin's crackdown on Yiddish, led to the loss of a large number of Yiddish and Judeo-Spanish speakers. These losses helped to increase nostalgic interest in Yiddish and Judeo-Spanish during the end of the 20th century and the beginning of the 21st century. For example, in 1996, the Knesset, the Israeli legislature, adopted two laws, the Law of the National Authority for Yiddish Culture (1996) and the Law of the National Authority for Ladino Culture (1996), which established national agencies for the study, research, and teaching of Yiddish and Ladino, respectively. In addition, these authorities also actively encourage production of Yiddish and Ladino cultures in Israel. No such authority was established for Judeo-Arabic. Moreover, the Film Industry Regulations of 2001 specify support for films shot in Yiddish and Ladino, but do not mention Judeo-Arabic (support for films shot in Arabic in general is stated, though). In yet another example, the Israeli Post Office issued stamps recognizing Yiddish and Ladino as part of a short set on Jewish languages; however, no stamp about Judeo-Arabic was issued in that set. Moreover, even when the Israeli Post Office issued a stamp in 2005 that commemorated 800 years since the passing of Moses Maimonides, the existence of Judeo-Arabic was not mentioned, nor was it acknowledged. These examples clearly constitute the greater symbolic importance of Yiddish and Judeo-Spanish in Israeli society, compared to Judeo-Arabic.

In the academic world, the study of Classical Judeo-Arabic has enjoyed much more prestige than Later and Modern Judeo-Arabic. There have been financial and academic resources available for scholarship concerning Geniza materials from the classical period, but the use of the term *Arabic* and the emphasis on Arabic studies in this connection have not been sufficiently acknowledged. The Society for Medieval Judeo-Arabic Studies, headquartered at the Ben-Zvi Institute in Jerusalem, has mostly concentrated on the classical medieval period, but no similar society exists for later and modern periods. This may stem from elitist or classicist approaches or subtle prejudice against contemporary Arabic-speaking Jews.

Consequently, the Israeli public has, at most, a limited acquaintance with the term *Judeo-Arabic*. An average graduate of a high school or a university in

Israel would likely recognize the terms *Yiddish* or *Ladino* but would be puzzled if confronted with the term *Judeo-Arabic*.

Even general scholarship on Jewish Bible translation suffers from the same syndrome. Although recognizing Saadia Gaon's tenth-century Judeo-Arabic translation of the Bible, it often ignores the huge project of Judeo-Arabic biblical translations. For example, Frederick Greenspahn quoted Joseph Hertz, the British chief rabbi of the first half of the 20th century, as saying that "the history of Jewish Bible translations would summarize the history of the Jews" and added that "[i]t is particularly striking to note those languages in which there are several Jewish translations. These include Greek, Aramaic, Yiddish/German, and English, which constitute the major centers of Diaspora Jewish life, further illustrating the intimate connection between the history of Jewish Bible translation and of the Jews" (Greenspahn 2006: 181). It is disappointing to see Greenspahn ignore the plethora of Judeo-Arabic biblical translations as well as the Arabic-speaking Jewish Diaspora, which constituted more than half of the Jewish population in the world for many centuries.

On the other hand, the publication of several volumes of *Textual History of the Bible* by Brill (started in 2016) promises to have a more prominent place for Arabic translations. For example, in volume one (*The Hebrew Bible*, edited by Armin Lange and Emanuel Tov), the editors discuss the primary and secondary translations of the Bible with attention to Arabic. In addition, in 2012 the project of *Biblia Arabica: The Bible in Arabic among Jews, Christians and Muslims*, was established by the German-Israeli Project Cooperation and conceived by scholars from Freie Universität Berlin (Sabine Schmidtke) and Ludwig-Maximilians-Universität Munich (Andreas Kapolny and Ronny Vollandt), in cooperation with Tel Aviv University (Camilla Adang and Meira Polliack). The project enabled, in a short time, impressive progress in the study of the rich and varied traditions of translating the Hebrew Bible and New Testament into Arabic, starting from the eighth century CE onwards. This is also seen in the 2017 publication of *Senses of Scripture, Treasures of Tradition: The Bible in Arabic among Jews, Christians and Muslims* (edited by Miriam L. Hjälm, Ludwig-Maximilians-Universität, München).

Other positive developments in the study of Judeo-Arabic deserve to be mentioned. There have been many efforts geared toward better recognition of the religiolect in many recent major publications in Jewish Studies; for example, both the *Encyclopedia of Jews in the Islamic World* (2010) and the *Encyclopedia of Hebrew Language and Linguistics* (2013), published by Brill, grant Judeo-Arabic a prominent place.

In sum, young scholarship in the field has recently advanced the study of Judeo-Arabic, and there is hope that this is the direction in which we are moving.

2 Historical background

Because the period of Jewish cultural creativity in Muslim-controlled lands predates the rise of the modern nation-state, it offers intriguing alternative examples to modern forms of group identity and self-definition. During the Middle Ages, the vast majority of Jews lived under Muslim rule, approximately 90 percent up until 1200 CE. This means that Arabic-speaking Jews were responsible for forging the crucial links between rabbinic literature in Late Antiquity – the Mishnah and the Talmud – and the ever-expanding and growing communities of the Diaspora, thus setting the stage for Jewish continuity over the course of more than a millennium.

One of the major debates in the field is whether Jews in Muslim-controlled lands enjoyed greater freedom, communal autonomy, and cultural integration than their coreligionists in Christian Europe. The fortunes of the Jews waxed and waned, along with those of the Christians and Muslims under caliphate rule. Wherever the Jews were the smaller of two (or three) minority religions, they were not singled out for harsh treatment. During the High Middle Ages, a period of great cultural efflorescence in the Middle East, the Jews enjoyed forms of communal autonomy that contributed to their economic and demographic growth, as well as their cultural creativity. Under Muslim rule, this communal autonomy was a principle enshrined in religious law, while, under Christian rule, autonomy was a principle to be renegotiated at each juncture of power (Cohen 1994).

The Middle Ages were an immensely fertile time for Jewish religious creativity in fields such as law (*halakhah*), mysticism, theology, philosophy, Hebrew grammar, and biblical studies, including biblical translations (see below, section 4.2, literature).

2.1 Phases in historical development

There is some evidence that the Jews on the Arabian Peninsula during the pre-Islamic period used a type of Jewish Arabic dialect called *al-Yahūdiyya* (Gil 1984: 206; Newby 1971, 1988: 21–23). This dialect was similar to the Arabic dialect used by the general public but included some Hebrew and Aramaic lexemes, especially in the domains of religion and culture. Some of these Hebrew and Aramaic words passed into the speech and writing of the Arabs. This may explain the appearance of words of Hebrew and Aramaic origin in the Quran. There is no evidence, however, that *Pre-Islamic Judeo-Arabic* ever served as the vehicle of a distinct literature (see below in 4.2, as-Samaw'al bnu 'Ādiyā''s case). Yet *al-Yahūdiyya* writings in Hebrew characters may also have existed (Newby 1971: 220). After the conquests of early Islam, the Jews in the newly conquered lands adopted the conquerors' language. They began to incorporate Arabic into their writing and gradually developed their own religiolect.

The second phase of Judeo-Arabic began in the eighth century in Egypt and the ninth century elsewhere. This was the period in which the Judeo-Arabic Phonetic orthography was used, though alongside the Arabicized orthography (see below). The appearance of Saadia ibn Yosef al-Fayyūmī's (882–942 CE) translation of the Pentateuch into Judeo-Arabic at the turn of the tenth century marks the beginning of the third phase, *Classical Judeo-Arabic*. Although the written form of this language contained dialectal features as well as pseudocorrections, according to Blau (1999), it tended to follow the model of Classical Arabic to a large extent. The works written in this period covered the entire spectrum of literary composition: theology, philosophy, biblical exegesis, philology, grammar, lexicography, law, ritual, and literature, in addition to commercial and private correspondence. Much of the material from this period has survived in several *genizot*, most notably the Cairo Geniza. The number of works in this period exceeded the number of Judeo-Arabic works of any other single period.

The fourth phase, *Later Judeo-Arabic*, lasted from the 15th to the 19th centuries. The shift from Classical to Later Judeo-Arabic was accompanied by "the increased social isolation of the Jews of the Arab world at the end of the Middle Ages within restrictive quarters, such as the *məllāḥ* and *ḥart il-yahūd*" (Stillman 1988: 5). During this period, many more dialectal elements penetrated into the written language, and the tradition of the *šarḥ* – the literal translation of Hebrew and Aramaic religious sacred texts into Judeo-Arabic – developed. Historical, halakhic, liturgical, and other texts were written in this period, many of them aimed at the general public rather than the erudite elite. Toward the end of this period, and even more so in the following period, an extensive folk literature also came into being. This period witnessed the development of the Hebraized orthography (Hary 1996), i.e., Judeo-Arabic written with spelling conventions that were heavily influenced by Hebrew and Aramaic. It was also at the beginning of this period that Jewish scholars began to write in Hebrew; by the end of the period, Hebrew had become the preferred written language. Yemen was an exception in this development, because its Jewish community was more isolated. The literary language of the third phase, Classical Judeo-Arabic, continued to be used there well past the 15th century.

The emergence of the fifth phase of the religiolect, *Contemporary Judeo-Arabic* of the 20th century, is characterized by greater production of *šurūḥ*, folktales, and other types of popular literature. In this period, the texts are characterized by more dialectal components than in previous periods and exhibit local elements taken from the spoken varieties. However, North Africans had begun to use their local dialect in writing during earlier periods. As a result, Jewish readers from other Arabic-speaking areas found Maghrebi texts difficult, if not impossible, to understand. Furthermore, beginning in the previous phase and continuing into this phase, several dialectal centers developed and flourished among Arabic-speaking Jews. Thus, there arose Maghrebi Judeo-Arabic, Egyptian Judeo-Arabic, Syrian Judeo-Arabic, Iraqi Judeo-Arabic, and Yemenite Judeo-Arabic, each with its own local flavor.

To summarize, the phases of Judeo-Arabic are Pre-Islamic Judeo-Arabic, Early Judeo-Arabic (eighth/ninth to tenth centuries), Classical Judeo-Arabic (tenth to 15th centuries), Later Judeo-Arabic (15th to 19th centuries), and Contemporary Judeo-Arabic (20th century).

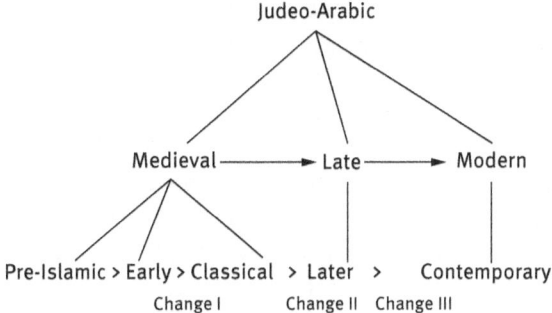

Figure 1: Phases of Judeo-Arabic.

2.2 Sociolinguistic description: The Judeo-Arabic continuum

The description of the various phases in Judeo-Arabic points to a possible linear connection between medieval, late, and modern Judeo-Arabic; however, at three points in its history, the religiolect underwent dramatic changes in its structure and sociolinguistic use. Despite these changes, it can still be divided into successive periods, each of which was influenced by its predecessor.

The first change occurred in the first half of the tenth century CE (see Figure 1 above), after Saadia published his translation of the Bible into Judeo-Arabic, called the *tafsīr*. In the Arab Jewish world, Saadia's *tafsīr* was held in enormous respect and admiration. In fact, Saadia's translation profoundly impacted Judeo-Arabic orthography. Before Saadia, many Judeo-Arabic writers used the Phonetic orthography, where they transferred Arabic sounds into Hebrew characters phonetically (Blau and Hopkins 1987). Saadia's *tafsīr*, modeled after Classical Arabic orthography, indicated the beginning of the Arabicized orthography, marking the first dramatic change in the history of the religiolect. In this orthographic tradition, Arabic characters are transferred mechanically into Hebrew letters, almost without taking into account the phonetic values. Recent studies (by Polliack, Tobi, and more) that have contested the primacy and originality of Saadia's translation do not invalidate the idea of the first major change in Judeo-Arabic. They indicate, though, that some pre-Saadia Bible translations employing the pre-Saadia Phonetic orthography have been identified in the Cairo Geniza. These earlier translations may have supplied Saadia with a lexical reservoir for his translation. It is still unclear whether Saadia's work replaced these earlier phonetic translations or whether the latter continued to be written and used alongside Saadia's version. What remains clear is the major change that occurred in the religiolect in the tenth century.

The second change arose during the 15th century, when Jews in several places reduced their contact with their Muslim counterparts, as well as their language and culture. Although a great number of Jews settled in the Ottoman Empire after their expulsion from Spain in 1492 and experienced even more intense contact with the Muslim world, many Jews felt the need for more separation from their Muslim (and Christian) neighbors. They began to congregate in exclusively Jewish neighborhoods (sometimes with the active encouragement of the authorities, with the result that Jewish isolation became more complete), such as *ḥart il-yahūd* (in Egypt), *məllāḥ* (in North Africa), or *qāʿat il-yahūd* (in Yemen). This change was especially marked in some areas like North Africa but less so in others, like Yemen, where close contacts between Jews and Muslims persisted for some time. This position is well known and well documented (e.g., Blau 1999; Hary 1992; Stillman 1988); however, are there other, internal factors that can explain this change? How did the increased presence of Ottoman Turkish in a large swath of lands with Jewish presence affect this change, if at all? Because of the change in contact between the cultures in the 15th century, not only did the structure of literary written Judeo-Arabic (Hary 1992: 79) come to incorporate more dialectal elements, but more works were written in Hebrew. In fact, Hebrew, Arabic, and Judeo-Arabic were sometimes assigned different usage functions (see Drory 1992, 2000). To conclude, Judeo-Arabic did not develop along the same lines everywhere.

Finally, the religiolect again experienced a dramatic change in the 20th century, with the rise of Arab and Jewish national movements, the outbreak of the Arab-Israeli conflict, and the consequent emigration of Jews from (mostly) Arabic-speaking areas. The religiolect lost ground due to migration, struggle, and nationalism (and the resulting pressure from other languages). This change brought about the near loss of the religiolect.

The aforementioned three changes highlight several different issues. The changes of the 15th and the 20th centuries especially triggered an increased use of dialectal elements in Judeo-Arabic texts. This is important linguistically because we therefore have written evidence for the development of the spoken dialects; such evidence is difficult to find in more standard Arabic texts, where elements of spoken language varieties were not so prevalent. Earlier changes of the tenth and the 15th centuries were unique because they featured the development of the Arabicized orthography and Hebraized orthography, respectively – the latter characterized by, among other things, greater Hebrew/Aramaic influence on Judeo-Arabic spelling. The changes of the 15th and 20th centuries were intimately connected to the decreased contact between Jews and their Arab neighbors.

Furthermore, in the description of the language community of Jews in (mostly) Arabic-speaking areas, we see how continuglossia (Hary 2003, 2009: 37–44) is intimately tied to the use of other languages, Hebrew and Aramaic in the present case. This situation is not unique to Judeo-Arabic. It is compatible with what Ferguson (1959) has said about Tamil and the effect on it of Sanskrit and English, as well as about Arabic in some parts of the Arab world where French, English, Coptic, or Syriac also play or played a role. In fact, continuglossia occurs in many other speech communities; for example, in Faroese (Hary 2016a; Thomsen n.d.).

The continuglossic structure of Judeo-Arabic has been in flux. In fact, the above-mentioned (second and third) dramatic changes in Judeo-Arabic that ensued during the 15th and 20th centuries resulted in a diachronic shift in the nature of the continuglossia, so that more and more dialectal elements penetrated the writings composed in this religiolect. This had the effect of reducing the gap between the left and right poles of the continuum ("linguistic gap"), as is seen in Figure 2 (see below explanations of Varieties B_n and Varieties C):

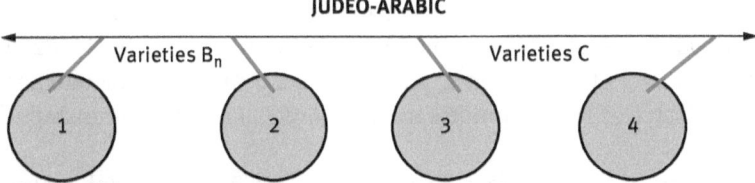

Figure 2: Continuglossia of Judeo-Arabic.
1 = Literary Written Classical Judeo-Arabic
2 = Literary Written Later Judeo-Arabic
3 = Literary Written Contemporary Judeo-Arabic
4 = Spoken Dialectal Judeo-Arabic

In other words, the gap between the more elevated writing (and formal) side of the continuum and the spoken side is narrowed down with the progression of time, as is displayed in Figure 2. Indeed, more dialectal elements penetrated the religiolect in general with the passage of time (see 3.2 below).

There are several possible explanations for why the dialectal components in Judeo-Arabic became more conspicuous with the passage of time. Because of the Jewish separation – or perceived separation – from their Arab Muslim environment, Jews may have taken even less care in preserving Classical Arabic and thus may have allowed more dialectal components to enter their writings. In addition, as time passed, they started to write more in Hebrew. Moreover, in Later Judeo-Arabic, the Hebraized orthography began to develop, heavily influenced by Hebrew/Aramaic spelling conventions. Finally, the increased dialectal components in Later and Contemporary Judeo-Arabic may represent a decline in the level of education in the Muslim world in general and in the Arabic-speaking Jewish world in particular, which started at the end of the Middle Ages, in the 15th century.

The investigation of marginal, minority language varieties such as Judeo-Arabic makes it easier to understand the diachronic development of Arabic in general. In fact, such investigations open a small window onto Arabic continuglossia in general and can explain some of its historical developments, as well as the development of Arabic dialects throughout history, since the periphery (in these cases, Judeo-Arabic) so often points to the center (in this case, Arabic in general).

3 Structural information

3.1 Relationship to non-Jewish varieties

Because it is the meeting point of Classical Arabic, Arabic dialects, Hebrew, and Aramaic, Judeo-Arabic exists in numerous mixed forms. As a result, one feature of literary written Judeo-Arabic (also termed Varieties B_n; Hary 1992: 56, 79–82) is that it contains, among other elements, many colloquial Arabic characteristics. Figure 3 below illustrates the continuum in Judeo-Arabic and its relationship to other languages.

At the right end of the Judeo-Arabic continuum one finds dialectal spoken Judeo-Arabic (also termed Varieties C; Hary 1992: 79). The left side of the Arabic continuum, containing Standard Arabic (the acrolect, also called Variety A, Hary 1992: 55–56, 80), is not found in a fully developed form in literary written Judeo-Arabic; however, it is a source of style shifting that many authors attempted to use, with varying degrees of success. In other words, the language of Judeo-Arabic authors only approached Standard Arabic. Had they written in a language that was too much like Standard Arabic, their writings would have lost their distinctive identity and would not have been considered Judeo-Arabic. Standard Arabic is still the anchor for the left side of the Judeo-Arabic continuum (Variety A). Judeo-Arabic authors

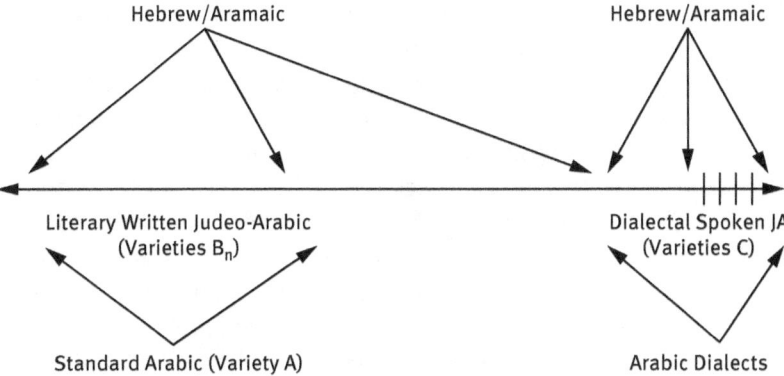

Figure 3: Relationship between Judeo-Arabic and other languages.

quite frequently attempted to follow Standard Arabic, the prestigious Arabic variety, at times without much success, which brought about the creation of pseudocorrections (see Blau 1970; Hary 2007). The motivation for trying to write in Standard Arabic is intimately connected to the desire to use the prestigious variety that was designated as such by the dominant Muslim majority. Thus, it is plausible that the Jews, a minority language community, defined themselves linguistically according to the values of Muslim Arabs, the dominant majority. However, Maimonides, a great philosopher and scholar of the 12th century, was competent in all varieties of Arabic. When he wrote to his coreligionists (e.g., in his *responsa*), he used Judeo-Arabic in Hebrew characters; when he wrote for the general public, as in his medical writings, he employed Standard (Classical) Arabic in Arabic characters.

3.2 Particular structural features (unique to the Jewish variety)

There are several studies that treat the particular structural features of Judeo-Arabic. Among them are Hopkins (2008) for Early Judeo-Arabic; Blau (1995, 1999) for Medieval Judeo-Arabic; Hary (1992), Khan (1991, 1992), and Wagner (2010) for Late Judeo-Arabic; Hary (2017), Mansour (1991), and Stillman (1988) for Modern Judeo-Arabic, and more (see section 5.4 below).

In this section, the distinctive features of Medieval (Classical) Judeo-Arabic and Late/Modern Judeo-Arabic[2] are discussed. Because of the nature of the

---

[2] Whereas the examples for Medieval (Classical) Judeo-Arabic are not regional, as they are taken mostly from Blau (1995), the examples for Late/Modern Judeo-Arabic use Egyptian (and more precisely, Cairene) Judeo-Arabic data (Hary 2009, 2017).

religiolect, the former includes structural features of Varieties B_n and the latter more features of Varieties C as extracted from the written texts, as well as spoken features derived from recordings (Rosenbaum 2008). This is due to the diachronic development of the religiolect (and possibly also due to changing writing conventions, Sarah Benor, personal communication); with the passage of time, more dialectal elements penetrated the religiolect in general (see section 2.2 above).

According to Blau (1995), Classical Judeo-Arabic tends to move more in the direction of the analytic type of language (rather than the synthetic, as is the case in Classical Arabic). In other words, Classical Arabic may express more than one grammatical concept in one word, whereas Classical Judeo-Arabic tends to do so less. This is shown in particular with the disappearance of most case and verbal mood markers in Classical Judeo-Arabic. This is, of course, compared to Standard Arabic in that period (Medieval Classical Arabic).

In phonetics and phonology, final short vowels disappeared, and final long vowels became shorter. Even the phonemic structure of the short vowels changed and became unstable (/miʿnāh/ 'its meaning', instead of /maʿnāh/, Blau 1995: 18); /ā/ > /ē/ (ליכן /lēkən/ 'but', Blau 1995: 19); diphthongs contracted and became monophthongs (אמתא /emta/ 'when', Blau 1995: 20); the glottal stop disappeared, and there was increased use of assimilation processes (for example, *tafxīm* and *tarqīq*).

The most important development that Classical Judeo-Arabic underwent morphosyntactically is, as mentioned above, the disappearance of noun case markers and verbal mood markers. Furthermore, the direct object may be indicated with the preposition /li-/ (וקוא לרוס הדה אלכשב 'and he strengthened the heads of these wooden pieces', Blau 1995: 179); the *iḍāfa* sometime uses analytic possessive pronouns (מתאע or בתאע, Blau 1995: 159); the final /n/ of the dual and the masc. pl. forms may be preserved in the *iḍāfa* construct or with possessive pronouns (אתנינהם 'the two of them', Blau 1995: 104); there is an increase in asyndetic sentences, as in the dialects (לאזם תבון 'you must', Blau 1995: 211); the most common negative marker is מא; the fem. pl. and dual is superseded by the masc. (הדה אלתשובות... וכאן פי אלואחדה מנהם 'one of these responses was …', Blau 1995: 97); and the internal passive is replaced by other verbal patterns.

The collection of several manuscripts in Later Egyptian Judeo-Arabic (LEJA, Hary 2009) is the basis for the description of selected distinctive structural features of that period, especially those features that differ from Classical Judeo-Arabic described above, of which most also made their way into Spoken Later Egyptian Judeo-Arabic (Hary 2017; Rosenbaum 2008).

In phonetics and phonology, there is a clear preference for the vowel /u/. This preference is noticeable in vowel shifts such as /a/ > [u]: תוקעודו /tuʿʿudu/ 'you (pl.) will settle' and אומות /umūt/ 'I die'; /i/ > [u]: חומאר /ḥumār/ 'donkeys' and דול ווקת /dulwàti/ (or /dulwàt/) 'now'; or even from a "zero" vowel to [u]: אהול /ahul/ 'people'. This preference has very little manifestation in standard spoken (non-Jewish) Egyptian dialects; however, sometimes the standard features both the vowels /u/ and /i/ for certain forms. Users of the standard variety, though, prefer the /i/ vowel, while Jews prefer /u/. For example, the standard verbal pattern /fiʻil/ also has the realization of /fuʻul/: standard /xiliṣ/ 'be finished, was saved' and /tiʼil/ 'became heavy' are preferred to their /fuʻul/ variants (in the standard variety). LEJA users clearly prefer the /fuʻul/ variants: כולוץ /xuluṣ/ 'was redeemed' and תוקול /tuʼul/ 'became heavy'. Other vowel shifts in LEJA include the shift /a/ > /ā/ in words originating in Hebrew: בטלאה /baṭalā/ 'in vain'; שולחאן /šulḥān/ 'table'; and the opposite shift /ā/ > /a/ preceding /ʻ/, /ḥ/, or /h/: בתע /bitaʻ/ 'of (masc.), genitive marker'; אלהנא /ilahna/ 'our God'. Finally, another vowel shift in LEJA is the lengthening of /i/ or /e/ (into /ī/ or /ē/ respectively) in words borrowed from Hebrew: גלעיד /galʻēd/ 'Galʼed'; חמיץ /ḥamēṣ/ 'leavened'; עיריב /ʻērēb/ 'evening'. The consonantal inventory of LEJA includes the voiceless bilabial stop /p/: אל פלגשים /il-pilagšīm/ 'the concubines'; פלדש /pildaš/ 'Pildash (name)', as a clear borrowing from the Hebrew. Furthermore, the voiced pharyngeal fricative /ʻ/ sometimes exhibits weakening in LEJA: חדאשר /ḥidaašar/ 'eleven'; אהד /ahd/ 'pact'. In addition, emphatization or velarization (*tafxīm*) occurs quite frequently, usually in the vicinity of other velarized phonemes, as in /t/ > /ṭ/, טוראב /ṭurāb/ 'earth'; /d/ > /ḍ/, מוקצאר /muʼḍāṛ/ 'power'; and /s/ > /ṣ/, פצר /faṣṣaṛ/ 'interpret'. This phonological feature occurs also in Classical Judeo-Arabic (see above). On the other hand, loss of emphatization or de-emphatization (*tarqīq*) may also occur in LEJA: /ṭ/ > /t/, מכטתין /muxattatīn/ 'marked (pl.)'; /ḍ/ > /d/, וידרבו /wi-yidrabo/ 'and they strike it'; and /ṣ/ > /s/, סרכה /sarxa/ 'outcry'. Sometimes the shifts have been more complex, as in /θ/ > /s/ > /ṣ/, צור /ṣōṛ/ 'ox' and /ð/ > /d/ > /ḍ/), אבצורהום /abḍuṛhum/ 'I will scatter them'. In the first example, the interdental /θ/ became a fricative /s/, as is common in urban dialects when an affiliation with Classical Arabic is desired, and then underwent emphatization (/s/ > [ṣ]) in the environment of emphatic [ṛ]. In the second example, interdental /ð/ became a stop /d/, as is common in urban dialects. Then, the latter underwent emphatization (/d/ > [ḍ]) in the environment of emphatic [ṛ].

Morphosyntactically, LEJA features several variant pronominal forms: the third person plural independent pronoun may appear as הומן /humman/ 'they' and the masculine singular demonstrative pronoun has a variant of /dih/ (or /deh/), פטיר דיה /fiṭīr dih/ 'this unleavened bread'. The plural demonstrative pronoun /dōli/ and /hadōli/ appear quite frequently: אל כלאם הדולי /il-kalām hadōli/ 'these words'; אל אראצ'י הדולי /il-ʼarāḍi hadōli/ 'these lands', usually following the noun as modifiers. When the plural demonstrative pronoun appears before the noun as a subject, standard Spoken Egyptian Arabic /dōli/ usually appears: דולי אל צלאטין /dōli l-ṣalaṭīn/ 'these are the rulers', although not always: הדולי אוולאד קטורה /hadōli ʾawlād qiṭūra/ 'all of these are the children of Ketura'. There are also interrogative pronouns that are distinctive in LEJA for the most part (and do not appear in standard Egyptian Arabic): איש /ēš/ 'what'; קד איש /ʾaddēš/ 'how much';ליש /lēš/ 'why'; and כיפ /kēf/ 'how'. These interrogative pronouns are preposed in the sentence (rather than postposed as in the standard Egyptian dialect): איש דה אסתעגלת /ēš da istaʿgalt/ 'what is this that you hurried?' קד איש פעייל טייבין /ʾaddēš faʿāyil ṭaybīn/ 'how many good deeds?' As for the genitive marker pronouns, the singular masculine genitive marker /bitāʿ/ is probably frozen in use in LEJA, כל צרבה וצרבה ... כאנת בתאע כמס צרבאת 'each plague ... was of five plagues'. In other words, while the genitive marker in standard Egyptian is conjugated according to gender and number, in LEJA, it is frozen in its masculine form.

The verbal pattern /fuʿul/ is typical in Later Egyptian Judeo-Arabic (Hary 1992: 280–285). It usually indicates intransitive verbs with "low grade" control and is often equivalent to the /fiʿil/ pattern in standard colloquial Egyptian: שוכת /šuxt/ 'I became old' and כותרו /kutru/ 'they multiplied'. Furthermore, the pattern /fiʿil/, found in the standard dialect, appears in LEJA as well: מיסכת /miskit/ 'she caught' and ביכי /biki/ 'he cried'. Use of the N-dialect imperfect form is quite frequent in LEJA: אנה נערפ /ana niʿraf/ 'I know'; and נישכורוך /niškuruk/ 'we thank you'.

The verb *come* in the texts of Later Egyptian Judeo-Arabic features some forms that are characteristic also of the standard dialect: גית /gēt/ 'I came'; גיה /geh/ and גה /gah/ 'he came'; גינה /gēna/ 'we came' and גיתו/גיתום /gētu(m)/ 'you (pl.) came'. The texts, however, also reveal other forms that are peculiar to LEJA: אגה /ega/ 'he came'; גאתת /gātet/ or /gātit/ 'she came'; גו /gu/ and איגו /egu/ 'they came'. Furthermore, the verb *to go* also features a special form in LEJA: אראח /arāḥ/ 'he went'. In addition, the "long" forms of *eat* and *take* occur frequently in LEJA: אכלתו /akaltu/ 'you (pl.) ate' and אכֿדו /axadu/ 'they took'. As in standard Egyptian dialect, the verbal pattern *itfaʿal* appears very frequently in LEJA: אתבהלו /itbahalu/ 'they were overwhelmed' and אתצלמת /itḍallimt/ 'it became dark'. Finally, in LEJA geminate verbal forms became defective as in גֿשיתני /ġaššētni/ 'you deceived me', which is clearly typical of other modern dialects as well.

In the number system, LEJA employs archaic numerical forms, as is typical of Jewish religiolects in general: אורבוע מאית /urbuʿmiyya/ 'four hundred'. As seen above, this feature is also in line with the characteristic phonological preference in LEJA for the vowel /u/. There are other number forms used in LEJA that correspond to above-mentioned phonological features, for example, the weakening of the voiced pharyngeal fricative /ʿ/ as in אתנאשר /itnaašar/ 'twelve' or the shift of the interdentals to stops (which is also prevalent in Classical Judeo-Arabic, see above) as in אתנין /itnēn/ 'two'; however, the latter is common in standard Cairene and in many sedentary dialects all over the Arab world as well.

LEJA uses an alternative feminine ending morpheme in the first term of an *iḍāfa*, /-it/: ארבעית סאעאת /arbaʿitsaʿāt/ 'four hours' and סרבּיית אל פֿוּקרה /sarxiyyit il-fu'ara/ 'the cry of the poor'. In negation, the particle לם /lam/ is used extensively with perfect verbs: לם כּליתני /lam xallitni/ 'you did not let me' and לם וקפֿ /lam wi'if/ 'he did not withstand'. It is also commonly employed with imperfect verbs: ולם יתגייר /wi-lam yitġayyir/ 'and it will not change' and לם תגי /lam tigi/ 'she will not come'. In addition, it also appears in unexpected contexts, such as with nouns: אנא הוא ולם אבֿור 'I (and) not someone else'; with pronouns: לי ולם לו 'to me and not to him'; with prepositions: ולם עלה יד מוחרק 'and not through a seraph'; and even in isolation: וקאלו אליה לם סידי 'And they told him "No, Sir"'. Finally, LEJA exhibits common colloquial Egyptian adverbial forms, such as הנאךּ /henāk/ 'there'; קווי /'awi/ 'very' or כדה /kəda/ 'so, thus'; however, it uses the unique variant כמאנה /kamāna/ 'also' (in addition to the standard כמאן /kamān/). In short, both Classical Judeo-Arabic and LEJA differ to some degree from their non-Jewish correlates in phonology and morphosyntax. There are many other dialects used in Modern Judeo-Arabic, for example, various North African Judeo-Arabic dialects, Palestinian (see in this volume the chapter on Modern Palestinian Judeo-Arabic by Geva-Kleinberger), Syrian, Iraqi, Yemenite, and more (see 5.4). These modern Judeo-Arabic dialects can be placed on an imaginary continuum stretching from the dialects with the most distinct features (compared to its dominant equivalent among Arab Muslims) to the dialects with the least distinct features. Whereas other North African Judeo-Arabic dialects may approach the most distinct end of the continuum, Egyptian may draw closer to its least distinct end, and yet the latter's distinct features are still plentiful.

3.3 Lexicon: Hebrew and Aramaic elements

In recent years, a plethora of studies on the Hebrew and Aramaic components in Jewish languages in general and in Judeo-Arabic in particular have appeared (to name just a few, Arnold 2013; Avishur 2001; Bar-Asher 1992, 1998a, 1998b, 2013; Blau 2013; Chertrit 1989; Geva-Kleinberger 2013; Goitein 1931; Hary 2009: 144–159, 2016; Henshke 2007, this volume; Maman 2013; Rosenbaum 2002b, 2013; Shachmon 2013; Tedghi 1995; Vollandt 2013; Yoda 2013).

We find many Hebrew lexemes that are employed in Judeo-Arabic mainly in the religious domain, in proper nouns, and in food items, but also in other domains. For example, in Classical Judeo-Arabic: מעשים טובים 'good deeds'; אלמלאכים רעים 'the wicked angels' (Blau 1999: 146). In LEJA, in proper names and place names: יצחק 'Isaac', ירושלים 'Jerusalem'; in liturgical and religious terms: חופה /ḥuppa/ 'marriage', כרפּס /karfaṣ/ 'Karpas, greens for the Passover *Seder*', חול /ḥōl/ (or /ḥol/) 'a week day'; and in other domains: אל פלגשים 'the concubines' (Hary 2009). Moreover, jewelers in Egypt (Jews and non-Jews) use the adjective /yāfet/ 'good' and the verb /yaffet/ 'treat customers nicely', probably derived from Hebrew יפה 'nice' (Rosenbaum 2002b: 125). They also use /šall/ 'at, genitive marker', probably derived from Hebrew של 'genitive marker' (Rosenbaum 2002b: 126). In addition, the verb /'etdardem/ or /'ddardem/ 'fall asleep' is derived from Hebrew נרדם with the same meaning (Rosenbaum 2013). Additionally, the Jews of Tripoli (Libya) use the verb /bdəq/ 'check', probably derived from Hebrew בדק with the same meaning; they also use the verb /xnəb/ 'steal' (from Hebrew גנב; note that in many Jewish religiolects Jews use variants of this verb [Yoda 2013]). In sum, it seems that, as in many other Jewish religiolects, Hebrew loanwords in Judeo-Arabic are used for proper nouns and the religious domain but are also found in other domains.

Hebrew and Aramaic elements tend, for the most part, to be fully incorporated into Judeo-Arabic. In other words, they take the grammatical features of the borrowing (or target) language (I call this Direction A, Hary 2016b). Indeed, Blau (1999: 134) reports that in Classical Judeo-Arabic, we find אצדר /aṣdar/ 'arrange (a prayer)' from Hebrew (תפילה) הסדיר, adapting phonologically to the Arabic structure by the employment of the *tafxīm*. The same is true morphosyntactically, as in, for example, the use of the appropriate feminine singular form, which refers to the non-human plural noun פירות in: אן כאנת תלך אלפירות לא הביאו שליש 'if these fruits have not reached the stage of one-third of maturity' (Blau 1999: 136). Similarly, Hebrew verbs in התפעל are transferred into the equivalent Arabic /tafaʕʕala/: תאבל /taʾabbal/ 'mourn' (from Hebrew התאבל) and תשמד /tašammad/ 'apostatize' (from Hebrew השתמד, Blau 1999: 138), in order to be integrated into the Arabic verbal morphological structure.

At times, though, Hebrew components were not integrated fully into Judeo-Arabic, and kept, for example, some Hebrew structural features (I term this *Direction B*, Hary 2016b). For example, in Classical Judeo-Arabic, the loanword גייר /gayyar/ 'make a proselyte' or אתגייר/תגייר /itgayyar/tagayyar/ 'become a proselyte', although morphologically adapted into the Arabic verbal patterns, phonetically kept the Hebrew /g/ phoneme (Blau 1999: 134–135).

In LEJA, we witness the same types of integration into the Arabic structure (Hary 2009, 2016b, 2017). In phonetics and phonology, most often Hebrew and Aramaic words are incorporated into the Judeo-Arabic phonological system. Thus, the vowels /a/, /i/, and /e/ are lengthened to [ā], [ī], and [ē], as in שמאע /šəmāʕ/ 'the prayer of the *Shema*' and עירב /ʕērēb/ 'evening'. Similarly, the consonantal inventory of words originating in Hebrew adapts itself to the Arabic phonological structure. Thus, Hebrew words with /ṣadi/ (צ) are pronounced in LEJA with the emphatic /ṣ/: חמיץ /ḥameṣ/ 'leavened food'. Additionally, emphatization (*tafxīm*) occurs in Hebrew words borrowed into Judeo-Arabic, thus employing a regular Arabic phonological process: /t/ > /ṭ/: במטי מעט /bi-maṭei mē'aṭ/ 'few in number' (although it alternates with במתי); /z/ > /ẓ/: אליעֿזר /eli'eẓer/ 'Eliezer' (although it may alternate with non-emphatic /z/: אליעזר); and /s/ > /ṣ/: מצובין / maṣubīn/ 'seated' (Hary 2009).

In the same way, we witness morphosyntactic adaptation into the Arabic structure. The following are just a few examples from LEJA: the definite article attached to Hebrew words is the Arabic morpheme /al-/ in a morphophonemic spelling, thus incorporating the Hebrew words into the Judeo-Arabic structure: אל ברכה 'the blessing'; Arabic demonstrative pronouns are employed together with Hebrew words by following their nouns to integrate them into the Arabic text: מורר דה 'this bitter herb'; the Arabic genitive marker /bətā'/ is used with Hebrew components and thus integrated into the Arabic structure: אל מצא בתאע אפיקומן 'the unleavened bread of the *afikoman*'; Hebrew roots take Arabic grammatical patterns, for example, the Hebrew root *s-d-r* of סדרי משנה 'the sections of the Mishna' adopts the Arabic plural form /fa'ā'il/, resulting in Judeo-Arabic סדאדר/sadādir/ 'sections (of the Mishna)'.

As in Classical Judeo-Arabic, Hebrew components in LEJA are not integrated, at times, following *Direction B*. Phonetically, the existence of the phonemes /p/ and /v/ is clearly under the influence of Hebrew. Thus, LEJA possesses the voiceless bilabial stop /p/ (אל פלגשים 'the concubines'), and, more rarely, the voiced labiodental fricative /v/. Also, morphosyntactically, Hebrew nouns used in LEJA do not always receive the Arabic plural, as in עארליין /'arilyyīn/ 'Christian men'. Sometimes these nouns are transferred into Judeo-Arabic "as is" with the Hebrew plural morpheme, as in אל מצריים 'the Egyptians'. There are other cases morphologically where the Hebrew components keep their structure and are not fully adapted into the Arabic structure: the use of /ila/ to imitate the Hebrew definite direct object marker את: אל רב וגד אלה דנב עבידך 'and God found the sin of your servants'; the use of Hebrew pronoun suffixes /-nu/ 'us'; וצוואנו /wa-ṣṣiwānu/ 'and he commanded us'; and the use of the Hebrew directional suffix /-ah/: גראה 'in the direction of Gerar'.

3.4 Language contact influences

As is clear from previous sections, Hebrew, Aramaic, and several Arabic varieties serve as key contact languages for Judeo-Arabic. Especially in the medieval period, Standard Classical Arabic served as the model for Judeo-Arabic writers, and, since they were not always competent in it, they produced many pseudocorrections, both hyper- and hypocorrections.[3] Classical Standard Arabic influenced Judeo-Arabic on all levels of the language, including the grammar and the lexicon. Furthermore, various Arabic dialects have been in regular contact with Judeo-Arabic dialects and have had mutual influence.[4] Finally, as described in the previous section, Hebrew and Aramaic have also been prime contact languages with back-and-forth influence on and by Judeo-Arabic.[5] This influence has not been limited only to the lexicon, but also to the grammar (Hary 2016b). In general, Blau (1999: 133) writes that "however large the ratio of Hebrew elements, they do not alter the basic structure of the text, which still remains Arabic. The fundamental fact concerning the contact of Hebrew with Arabic is that, despite the great prestige of Hebrew as the hallowed language, *it was Arabic, backed by a mother-tongue group, that absorbed Hebrew*, which was no longer a living language." This is what I call *Direction A*, which is indeed the general outcome of all the interactions of several languages in contact with Judeo-Arabic; however, as seen in the previous section, *Direction B* was also employed, as Hebrew elements sometimes maintained their structure in the grammatical and lexical spheres.

4 Written and oral traditions

4.1 Writing systems

The writing system of Judeo-Arabic uses the Hebrew characters with some modifications; however, there are also Judeo-Arabic texts written in Arabic letters, especially among the Karaites (mostly transcriptions of biblical verses into Arabic accompanied by discussions of these verses in Arabic; see Khan 1993; Polliack 1998). There are three spelling traditions used in Judeo-Arabic: the Phonetic, the Arabicized, and the Hebraized traditions (Blau 1995; Blau and Hopkins 1984, 1987; Hary 1992, 1996).

The Phonetic tradition, termed by Blau and Hopkins (1987) "Early Vulgar Judeo-Arabic Spelling," which is based, for the most part, on phonetic principles,

---

[3] See Blau 1970 and Hary 2007 for a detailed explanation of pseudocorrections, including hyper- and hypocorrections.
[4] We have examples of what I term *crossing religious boundaries* (Hary 2009: 16–19), where Judeo-Arabic influences the Arabic of non-Jews, for example, in the professional speech of Christian and Muslim goldsmiths in Cairo and Alexandria (Rosenbaum 2002b).
[5] For the influence of Judeo-Arabic on Hebrew, see Yehudit Henshke's work on the Hebrew spoken by *mizrahim* in the periphery in Israel (2013, 2015).

almost free from the influence of Classical Arabic orthography, was used mostly during the period of Early Judeo-Arabic. Blau and Hopkins (1987: 124) claim, "There is no orthographical feature [in this spelling tradition] that has to be explained as imitation of literary Arabic spelling habits." There are three main characteristics to this tradition: first, marking /ḍ/ and /ẓ/ with Judeo-Arabic ד, representing the closest phoneme in Hebrew to the pronunciation of Arabic ض and ظ; for example, אנדור /unḍur/ 'look', cf. انظر (Blau and Hopkins 1984: 20). Second, use of phonetic *scriptio plena* 'full spelling'; for example, both /u/ and /i/ are frequently denoted with ו and י respectively, unlike Classical Arabic orthography: בידאעתי /biḍā'ati/ 'my goods' (Blau and Hopkins 1984: 20), cf. بضاعتي. At the same time, the tradition also uses *scriptio defectiva*, not marking, for example, the medial *alif* (that denotes /ā/) in ביד /bayāḍ/ 'white', contrary to Classical Arabic بياض (Blau and Hopkins 1984: 20). Finally, spelling the definite article phonetically (and not morphophonetically as in the Arabicized tradition, see below); for example, בילפיום /bi-l-fayyūm/ 'in the Fayyūm', where the *alif* is not written, as it is not heard phonetically (cf. بالفيوم) (Blau and Hopkins 1984: 22); אסלם /as-salām/ 'the peace', where the *lām* is not written, as it is not heard phonetically (cf. السلام) (Blau and Hopkins 1984: 22); and בדנניר /bi-d-danānīr/ 'with the dinars', where both the *alif* and *lām* are not written, as they are not heard phonetically (cf. بالدنانير) (Blau and Hopkins 1984: 23).

The Arabicized spelling tradition, which is based on the imitation of Classical Arabic orthography, replaced the Phonetic spelling tradition with the appearance of Saadia Gaon's translation of the Pentateuch at the turn of the first millennium, especially because of its prestige and widespread distribution all over the Jewish Arab world. Since there are fewer Hebrew characters than Judeo-Arabic phonemes, the Arabicized tradition frequently employs diacritic points that copy those of the Arabic letters.[6] For example, צ̇ for ض /ḍ/; ט̇ for ظ /ẓ/; ד̇ for ذ /ð/; ת̇ for ث /θ/; ה̇ for ة feminine marker; ק̇ for ق /q/; ג̇ for ج /dʒ/; similarly, ג̇ for غ /ɣ/; כ̇ for خ /x/; and פ̇ for ف /f/, although the last three can be interpreted as using a phonetic principle as well. Some of the conventions of Talmudic orthography, influential in many of the Jewish religiolects, are also employed in the Arabicized tradition: occasional rendering of the short /u/ with ו and denoting consonantal /w/ and /j/ with וו and יי (especially geminate). As a general rule, the Arabicized spelling tradition follows the orthography of Classical Arabic closely: The long vowels are marked with long letters (י, ו, and א); the definite article is usually

---

6 It is not unusual to use diacritic points when adopting a specific script for another language; see the adaptation of the Arabic script to Persian and the use of پ, for example, to mark the phoneme /p/, which exists in Persian but not in Standard Arabic.

written morphophonemically אל, regardless of its phonetic value; the distinction between *'alif maqṣūra biṣūrati l-'alif* and *'alif maqṣūra biṣūrati l-yā'* is kept (using א and י, respectively); and even sometimes short vowels, *tašdīd*, and *madda* are written with their Arabic signs over the Hebrew characters. This spelling tradition is typical of Classical Judeo-Arabic but was also used in earlier and later periods.

Finally, the Hebraized spelling tradition developed during Later Judeo-Arabic and was used then alongside the Arabicized. There are three main features to this tradition. First, Hebrew and Aramaic influence: For example, *'alif maqṣūra biṣūrati l-yā'* (which is usually spelled with a *yod* in the Arabicized spelling tradition in imitation of Classical Arabic orthography) is denoted in the Hebraized spelling tradition with a ה, in imitation of Hebrew orthography (ארמה 'throw', cf. ارمى) and מוסה 'Musa', cf. موسى, Hary 1992: 87–88) and not with a י, as is the case in the Arabicized tradition. It can also be spelled with an א, as influenced by the orthography of the Babylonian Talmud (עלא 'on', cf. على and תועטא 'is given', cf. تعطى, Hary 1992: 88). Even *'alif maqṣūra biṣūrati l-'alif* may be spelled with a ה, as is אל דוניה 'this world', cf. الدنيا (Hary 1992: 88). In addition, final *'alif* is frequently spelled with a ה, in imitation of standard Hebrew orthography: הנה 'here', cf. هنا and לחמתנה 'our meat', cf. لحمتنا (Hary 1992: 88). Finally, feminine nouns may be spelled with an א, possibly an influence from the orthography of the Babylonian Talmud, מרא 'time', cf. مرة and עטימא 'big (fem.)', cf. عظيمة (Hary 1992: 88).[7]

The second aspect of the Hebraized spelling tradition is a closer phonetic representation; for example, the use of *scriptio plena* to denote the short vowels /u/, /i/, and /a/ (it is more common to mark it with /u/ than with /i/ or /a/): כותרה /kutra/ 'multitude', כונת /kunt/ 'I was', נאזיז /nāziz/ 'leek', and רתכאת /(i)rtaxət/ 'became loose'; the occasional use of *scriptio defectiva*, possibly reflecting colloquial speech: אטעוה 'they obeyed him' (cf. اطاعوه); marking of final /-a/ even if there is no representation in Classical Arabic orthography or in the Arabicized tradition: תעאלה 'come' (cf. تعال); marking the *'alif mamdūda* according to its phonetic representation with ה or א: נסא 'women' (cf. نساء); not marking *'alf al-fāṣila* (as opposed to occasional marking in the Arabicized tradition, following Classical Arabic orthography): נזלו 'they came down' (cf. نزلوا); *'alif maqṣūra biṣūrati l-yā'* is spelled with a ה, in imitation of Hebrew orthography, as mentioned above, but also according to its phonetic value /-a/: אחכה 'he told' (cf. احكى); writing consonantal /w/ and /y/ with וו and יי, respectively: אבּוואתי /ixwāti/ 'my brothers'; occasional phonetic spelling of the definite article: אנאס /an-nās/ 'the people' (without writing the ל, as it is not heard phonetically, cf. الناس); spelling the first term of *iḍāfa* with a ת, as a reflection of its phonetic value: חארת אל יאוד /ḥart

---

[7] For a more thorough treatment of the subject, see Hary 1992: 82–96 and Hary 1996.

il-yahūd/ 'the Jewish quarter'; occasionally marking the /ḍ/ with a ד for phonetic reasons: דאק 'was annoyed' (cf. ضاق); reduction of *tafxīm* (or *tarqīq*) is seen in the spelling of ص with a ס: רכ'יס 'cheap' (cf. رخيص); frequent spelling of the enclitic conjunction /fə/ or /fe/ 'and' as a separate word, probably for phonetic considerations: פ' (cf. ف); and frequently denoting the frozen accusative *tanwīn* with a ן: כ'וֹפן /xōfan/ 'out of fear' (א in the Arabicized tradition in imitation of Classical Arabic orthography, cf. خوفاً).

Although the Hebraized tradition dominated in the Later Judeo-Arabic period and onward, the Arabicized spelling tradition was also used and continued to exert influence. For example, the spelling of the definite article is more often morphophonemic, אל, as is the case in the Arabicized tradition.

To conclude, the Hebraized tradition differs from the Phonetic in that it has some influence from Classical Arabic orthography (via the Arabicized tradition), whereas the Phonetic tradition has none. Furthermore, the Hebraized tradition differs from the Arabicized in that it shows greater phonetic representation and spelling conventions of Hebrew and Talmudic orthography. In other words, the Hebraized spelling tradition is based neither on the orthography of Classical Arabic (as is the case with the Arabicized tradition), nor on phonetic principles only (as is the case with the Phonetic tradition). The Hebraized tradition is, then, a combination of both the Phonetic and the Arabicized traditions with additional influence from Hebrew and Aramaic spelling.

4.2 Literature

The literature of Judeo-Arabic is varied and vast, stretching from Spain in the west all the way to India in the east and spanning from the seventh century CE until today. As mentioned above, there is not much evidence for literature in Judeo-Arabic from the period before Islam. The writing of the pre-Islamic Jewish poet as-Samaw'al bnu 'Ādiyā' did not differ from that of his Arab contemporaries and, in fact, constitutes part of the canon of Arabic literature, and not of Jewish literature. Were it not for Arab sources reporting that he was Jewish, this fact would probably have remained unknown. In other words, as-Samaw'al bnu 'Ādiyā' was an Arab poet who happened to be Jewish.

As mentioned in 2.1, the period of Classical Judeo-Arabic provides us with a huge production of literature, covering the entire spectrum of literary composition: theology, philosophy, biblical exegesis and translations, philology, grammar and lexicography, law (*halakha*), mysticism, ritual, and literature, in addition to commercial and private correspondence. Some of the classics of medieval rabbinic literature that are widely studied today were composed in Classical

Judeo-Arabic. Of special note are the three giants of Classical Judeo-Arabic. The first is Saadia ibn Yosef al-Fayyūmī (882–942 CE) with his translation of the Pentateuch into Judeo-Arabic (probably at the turn of the tenth century), marking the beginning of the period of Classical Judeo-Arabic, and also his *Book of Beliefs and Opinions* (*kitāb al-'imānāt wa-al-'i'tiqādāt*, Baghdad, 933 CE). The second is Judah Halevi (1075–1141 CE), who composed his 12th-century classic work, *The Kuzari* (*kitāb al-xazari*), in a part of the Iberian Peninsula that had recently been re-conquered by Christians, but he nonetheless wrote it in Judeo-Arabic, the language of the educated Jewish classes. The work was later translated into Hebrew and Yiddish and became one of the most widely read works of Jewish literature in history. The third giant is Moses Maimonides (1138–1204 CE), who wrote his *Guide for the Perplexed* (*dalālat al-ḥā'irīn*) in Cairo in Judeo-Arabic at the close of the 12th century. This work went on to become not just the greatest Jewish philosophical work of the Middle Ages, but one of the greatest philosophical works of all time.

In Later Judeo-Arabic, the tradition of the *šarḥ* – the literal translation of Hebrew and Aramaic religious sacred texts into Judeo-Arabic – developed. Historical, halakhic, liturgical, and other texts were written in this period, many of them aimed at the general public rather than the erudite elite. Toward the end of this period, and even more so in the following period, an extensive folk literature also came into being and grew richer during the period of Modern Judeo-Arabic.

Judeo-Arabic literature continues to be produced. For example, Rabbi David Buskila (born near Ouarzazate in south central Morocco) translated the *Book of Tanya* into Moroccan Judeo-Arabic and published his translation in 1977–1984 (Maman 2011); Asher Cohen (born in Casablanca) wrote the play *Almiseria* in Moroccan Judeo-Arabic (*Miseria* is a Spanish word, borrowed into urban Moroccan Judeo-Arabic, meaning 'miserliness') – he was inspired by Molière's *L'Avare*, which was produced and performed in Israel in 2000. Plays translated into Moroccan Judeo-Arabic and featuring Gad Elmaleh, a famous Canadian Moroccan-born actor, have been produced in Montreal. In addition, over the last 15 years, Rabbi Aharon Farhi, who was born in Aleppo, Syria in 1944 and has been the rabbi of Congregation Beth Yosef in Brooklyn since 1992, has written essays connected to the weekly Torah portions in Hebrew, Arabic (serving the older generation, according to Rabbi Farhi himself), and English (serving the younger generation), posting them in cyberspace. While Farhi writes in Arabic letters, his writing can certainly be classified as Judeo-Arabic, due to its use of Hebrew lexemes, colloquial elements, readership and audience, and more (Matsa 2002).

In sum, even today there is some production of liturgical sermons in Judeo-Arabic, as well as journalism, theater, film, and music (see 1.2 and 4.3).

4.3 Performance (theater, film, etc.)

In recent years, because of increases in Mizrahi identity awareness, and also in connection with nostalgia in Israel and elsewhere, there has been some performance in the religiolect. A program in Moroccan Judeo-Arabic has been broadcast weekly on Israeli radio. Furthermore, in theater, as noted above in 4.2, in the performances of the Canadian actor Gad Elmaleh, and especially in film, there has been some creativity involving Judeo-Arabic. For example, the Israeli films *Sh'chur* (1994, directed by Shmuel Hasfari) and *Turn Left at the End of the World* (2004, directed by Avi Nesher) feature sections in Moroccan Judeo-Arabic, and the 2013/4 film *Farewell Baghdad* (or *The Dove Flyer* [in Hebrew], directed by Nissim Dayan), based largely on the novel by the Israeli writer Eli Amir (born and raised in Iraq), is the first movie to be entirely shot in Judeo-Arabic (Iraqi). The film depicts the volatile political events in Baghdad in the 1940s before the emigration of the Jewish community.

In music, note the performances of the New Andalusian Orchestra in Judeo-Arabic at times, which are described in 1.2 (for the relevance to Mizrahi politics). Likewise, Shimon Bouskila is a well-known Israeli singer who performs in Judeo-Arabic (in addition to Hebrew and Arabic). Recently, we have been witnessing several new developments in the performance of music in Contemporary Judeo-Arabic (especially Moroccan, but also Yemenite and other). For example, Neta Elqayam, born in 1980 in Netivot, Israel, is one of the emerging dedicated young Mizrahi enthusiasts who seek to rediscover their (Moroccan) Judeo-Arabic roots. On her website, although she writes mostly in English (and some in Hebrew and Arabic), she posts some phrases in modern Judeo-Arabic in the Hebraized spelling tradition (מרחבא ביכום 'welcome to all of you!'). She regularly performs in Moroccan Judeo-Arabic and, along with Amit Hai Cohen, appears in Abiadi (https://youtu.be/JoFxzgPTCmY), a tribute to the Jewish Moroccan singer, Zohra Al Fassiya. The latter was born in 1905 in Sefrou, Morocco, and was the first female recording artist in Morocco. She is considered the queen of the Malhun Moroccan music genre, and her songs were mostly secular; however, the melodies were modified to fit the *piyyutim* (Jewish liturgical poems and songs) style.

Additionally, *A Wa* is a band of three sisters who combine Yemenite folk music, some of it in Yemeni Judeo-Arabic, with electronic dance music (https://youtu.be/g3bjZlmsb4A). Furthermore, composer Zafrir Ifrach writes and performs in Moroccan Judeo-Arabic (https://youtu.be/82noV6sPyug). Even more mainstream popular singers such as Miri Masika and *Knesiyat Hasekhel* ('Church of Reason') sometimes sing in Moroccan Judeo-Arabic: Masika sings זהרה 'Zahra' (https://www.youtube.com/watch?v=DHhTAYK2Cg8), and *Knesiyat Hasekhel* sing

כאנת וחדה 'There is a Girl' (https://www.youtube.com/watch?v=nmaEcPDASAk). Finally, the Jerusalem Orchestra – East and West performs at times in Judeo-Arabic.

As these examples from literature, film, and music demonstrate, the Judeo-Arabic cultural heritage is not dying (which is hard to say about the language itself). Much of this cultural activity is postvernacular; the people who produce and consume it are not necessarily frequent and sometimes not even proficient speakers of Judeo-Arabic.

5 State of research

5.1 History of documentation

Most of the Judeo-Arabic texts from the earlier periods, and until Later Judeo-Arabic, come from the Cairo Geniza. The Cairo Geniza is basically an archive; it is a depository of an extensive collection of manuscripts, usually written on vellum and paper, many of which are in Judeo-Arabic; other manuscripts are in Hebrew, Aramaic, and other Jewish religiolects. The Geniza is probably the most important "discovery" or "rediscovery" of a collection in modern Jewish studies, shedding illuminating information on life in the medieval eastern Mediterranean area. The Geniza, consisting of over 200,000 leaves, was found in the attic of the Ben Ezra synagogue in Fustat (Old Cairo) toward the end of the 19th century. Most of the Judeo-Arabic material is from the tenth through the 13th centuries, including documentary and literary sources. Much of the material made its way to various research libraries around the world, most notably to the Geniza Unit at Cambridge University. Furthermore, the Karaite leader and scholar, Abraham Firkovitch, bought many manuscripts in Cairo in the 19th century, and they are located today at the Firkovitch Collection at the Russian National Library in St. Petersburg (Reif 2010).

There are other *genizot* that contain Judeo-Arabic documents. There are probably still *genizot* that are buried in Cairene cemeteries, most probably in al-Basāṭīn. Another type of archive, for Later and Modern (Egyptian) Judeo-Arabic, is the Cairo Collection (Hary 2010). This collection consists of more than one hundred photocopied manuscripts, mostly from Egypt, dating from the 18th through the 20th centuries. In the 1980s this collection was brought from al-Ḥannān synagogue in Cairo to the (today) Department of Manuscripts and the Institute of Microfilmed Hebrew Manuscripts located at the National Library in Jerusalem. The manuscripts contain mainly Jewish liturgical texts written mostly in Judeo-Arabic but also in Hebrew and Aramaic; one manuscript is in

Yiddish. Several manuscripts are written in more than one language: Some are in Hebrew and Aramaic (such as a commentary on Maimonides' *Mishne Torah*, ritual slaughter laws, and *midrashim*); others are in Hebrew and Judeo-Arabic (such as bilingual editions of Passover *Haggadot*); and finally, one manuscript, written in 1906 by the Ashkenazi Rabbi of Cairo, Aharon Mendel Aharon ha-Kohen, comprises testimonies, agreements, and requests for divorce agreements in four languages (Hebrew, Arabic, Yiddish, and French). Some of the literary genres of the Judeo-Arabic manuscripts in the collection are *šurūḥ* (literary translations of sacred and liturgical Hebrew and Aramaic texts into Judeo-Arabic) of Isaiah, Jeremiah (including the *hafṭara* for the ninth of Av), Ezekiel, the twelve Minor Prophets, Psalms, Job, Ecclesiastes, and the Book of Ruth, Passover *Haggadot*, *isrā'ilyyāt*: *qiṣṣat yūsuf* ('The story of Joseph'), *quṣṣat ester* ('The story of the Book of Esther'), *quṣṣat zaxarya* ('The story of Zechariah'), *quṣṣat ḥana* ('The story of Hannah'), *quṣṣat il-xurbān* ('The story of the destruction'), and *quṣṣat ʿašar ḥaxamīm* ('The story of the ten rabbis'). The large number of noteworthy documents in the collection has made it possible to reconstruct many features of Egyptian Judeo-Arabic of the 18th century and later and to give us a good understanding of Jewish life in pre-modern and modern Egypt.

Many Judeo-Arabic newspapers and journals appeared throughout the Arab Jewish world, especially in the 19th and 20th centuries. For example, Yeshurun ('an expression for the people of Israel') published in Baghdad, Iraq, (1920–1921) in Baghdadi Judeo-Arabic (and also in Hebrew); *Misraïm* ('Egypt') published in Cairo, Egypt, (from 1904) in Egyptian Judeo-Arabic; *El-Horria* ('The freedom') published in Tanger, Morocco, (1915–1917 and 1921–1922) in Moroccan Judeo-Arabic, *Maguid Micharim* ('The preacher of righteousness') published in Oran, Algeria, (1895–1896) in Algerian Judeo-Arabic; *Es-Sabah* ('The morning') published in Tunis, Tunisia, (1904–1940) in Tunisian Judeo-Arabic; and *doreš tov le-ʿamo* ('Seeking good for one's people') published in Bombay, India, (1856–1866) in Iraqi Judeo-Arabic. Furthermore, there is extensive folk literature in Modern Judeo-Arabic, produced and published mainly in North Africa and Egypt. Additionally, the Jewish Oral Tradition Research Center at the Hebrew University in Jerusalem, established by Shlomo Morag, encouraged and produced many recordings of Judeo-Arabic speakers from various locations and is a source for the spoken language.

5.2 Corpora

In recent decades and with the development of corpora studies, several attempts have been made at creating corpora for Judeo-Arabic material. Most notable is the Friedberg Jewish Manuscript Society, which houses manuscripts from the Cairo

Geniza, a Judeo-Arabic corpus, and a Judeo-Arabic bibliography. There are other corpora, some of which are housed at leading research universities, e.g., *The Princeton Geniza Project*, which is a searchable database of over 4,300 documentary Geniza texts in Judeo-Arabic, Hebrew, and Aramaic. The project is hosted by the Princeton Geniza Lab, a collaborative space devoted to making the documentary texts of the Cairo Geniza accessible to all. Additionally, the Cairo Geniza Collection of the Bodleian libraries is also found online (http://genizah.bodleian.ox.ac.uk/) and is searchable.

5.3 Issues of general theoretical interest

The field of language contact has focused mainly on spoken language varieties, and less research has been devoted to languages in contact in written texts. Studies of Judeo-Arabic have contributed much in this field, showing mechanisms of interference in written texts. For example, Hary 2016b is devoted to theoretical observations of written texts in Judeo-Arabic constantly in contact with Arabic and Hebrew. Furthermore, Polliack (2018a, 2018b) has recently investigated code switching and mixed-code use of Judeo-Arabic writings (especially medieval) and contributed much to the sociolinguistic contexts of these texts and representation of (minority) identity issues. This is important, as it sheds new light on how we can understand sociolinguistic and identity issues in the Middle Ages in the Mediterranean basin.

Another important issue of theoretical investigation is how written texts can provide us with clues to identify dialectal features of a language variety. Blau laid the foundations to the methodology in the 1960s (Blau 1995, 1999). Through a careful examination of texts, colloquial elements can be extracted in order to reconstruct, at least in part, the dialect spoken by users of the texts in a given time. Hary (2017) shows that the texts of the Judeo-Arabic *šurūḥ* consist of a mixture of several layers: Classical and post-Classical Arabic, pseudocorrections, pseudocorrections that had been standardized in the texts (and therefore synchronically are no longer pseudocorrections), verbatim translations from Hebrew and Aramaic into Judeo-Arabic, traces from earlier translations of sacred texts, especially that of Saadia Gaon, and finally, dialectal components. Consequently, the dialect can be traced by isolating the first five elements mentioned above, thereby allowing elements of the spoken dialect to surface. The findings should then be compared with care to documented standard dialects (modern and pre-modern), in order to confirm the findings. Some complications may arise; for example, sometimes it is not easy to decide whether standardized pseudocorrections had become part of the dialect or had just been standardized in the written texts and became productive only there and not in the spoken dialect.

The methodology of isolating the dialectal elements in the written texts (along with the constraints mentioned above) is exemplified in the following sentence from the Egyptian Judeo-Arabic *šarḥ* to Genesis (Hary 2009: 94), ואל צביה חוסנת אל מנטֹר קווי בכריה וראגל לם ערפהא ונזלת אל עין ומלת גרתהא וטלעת 'and the girl (was) very good looking, a virgin, and no man had known her. She went down to the spring, filled her jar, and came up', which is a translation of והנערה טבת מראה מאֹד בתולה ואיש לא ידעה ותרד העינה ותמלא כדה ותעל (Gen 24:16). In this translation, Classical and post-Classical components stand out clearly, for example, the *iḍāfa ġayr ḥaqīqiyya* in /ḥusnat al-manẓar/ 'good looking'; however, the choice of חוסנת אל מנטֹר 'good looking' by the *šarḥan* may also be connected to the influence of Saadia's work. The verbatim translation elements are also evident: lack of /wa-kānat/ 'and (she) was' at the beginning of the sentence in the *šarḥ*, in order to mirror the Hebrew, lack of *vav* conjunctive before בכריה 'virgin', again, to meticulously copy the Hebrew, the use of the Judeo-Arabic noun עין 'spring' in graphemic and phonetic imitation of Hebrew עין, as other Arabic nouns could have been chosen, and more. It is also possible that the choice of עין 'spring' may have been indirectly influenced by Saadia's translation (another element mentioned above), which was so prevalent among Arabic-speaking Jews. The use of /lam/ before the perfect verb in לם ערפהא '(he) did not know her' may reveal a standardized pseudocorrection in the written texts, which possibly became part of the spoken dialect later (Rosenbaum 2002a). Following the isolation of the above elements, several characteristics that are part of the spoken dialect remain: the adverb /'awi/ 'very', the noun /rāgil/ 'man', the possible use of the negative /lam/ as mentioned above, and more. This is indeed one method to reconstruct the dialect from written materials.

Another useful method for reconstructing various linguistic characteristics of the spoken dialect from written texts is the orthographic tradition. For example, orthography is helpful in detecting the use of the short vowel /u/ in Egyptian Judeo-Arabic dialect. In the Hebraized tradition mentioned above in 4.1, it is virtually obligatory to use *vav* to mark the short vowels /u/ and /o/. The preference for the vowel /u/ is very evident in LEJA texts, and we can assume that such is the case in the spoken variety, as also confirmed by Rosenbaum's recordings and interviews of modern Egyptian Judeo-Arabic (2008). We see this preference in both the phonology and the morphology. For example, the appearance of *vav* clearly indicates the frequent shifts to /u/ among Egyptian Jews in the form of /a/ > [u] and /i/ > [u]. For example, דול ווקת /dul-wåt(i)/ 'now'; תועאלה /tuʿāla/ 'exalt'; שועב /šuʿb/ 'people'; קוצת חנה /'oṣṣet ḥanna/ 'The story of Hanna'. In morphology, the verbal pattern /fuʿul/, typical in LEJA, is common in the spoken dialect as well and can be traced due to the Hebraized tradition, e.g., כותרת /kutrət/ '(it) grew'; כולוץ /xuluṣ/ 'was redeemed' (Hary 2017: 16–17). This all represents the preference for the vowel /u/ among Egyptian Jews. This orthographic tool also should be employed with caution as ambiguous occurrences may occur (Hary 2017: 18–19).

5.4 Current directions in research

Early Judeo-Arabic (Hopkins 2008), Classical Judeo-Arabic (Blau 1995, 1999), and Later Judeo-Arabic (Hary 1992, 2009; Khan 1992, 2013; Wagner 2010) enjoy good detailed grammatical studies. There are also extensive studies on various modern Judeo-Arabic dialects (for example, Bar-Asher 1996 [North Africa]; Blanc 1964 [Egypt]; Chetrit 2014 [North Africa]; Cohen 1981 [North Africa]; Geva-Kleinberger 2009 [Tiberius], this volume [the Holy Land and Lebanon]; Hary 2017 [Cairo, Egypt]; Heath 2002 [Morocco]; Jastrow 1990 [Aqra and Arbil, Iraq]; Mansour 1991 [Baghdad]; Piamenta 2000 [Jerusalem]; Rosenbaum 2008 [Egypt]; Shachmon 2014 [Yemen]; Stillman 1988 [Sefrou, Morocco]; Tirosh-Becker 1989 and 2010 [Constantine, Algeria]; and many more). In recent decades, there has been increased interest in investigating the Hebrew and Aramaic components in Judeo-Arabic (and in Jewish language varieties in general) and much work has been done in the field (see above in 3.3).

Although several dictionaries for Judeo-Arabic have been published (Blau 2006; Diem and Radenberg 1994; Friedman 2016; Piamenta 1990; Ratzabi 1985), there is still a need to develop dialectological atlases, especially for modern Judeo-Arabic dialects, which are still in need of further studies. In addition, the field also needs the composition of dialectological atlases for the various šurūḥ from different places in Later and Modern Judeo-Arabic. There have been recent attempts at sociolinguistic studies of Judeo-Arabic from the medieval period (Polliack 2018a, 2018b, for example), from the later period (Hary 1992 and 2009, for example), and from the modern period (Chetrit 2007, for example). Clearly, more sociolinguistic studies of Judeo-Arabic are a desideratum.

To conclude, Judeo-Arabic is a fascinating mixed religiolect. It is, in fact, the delicate combination of Arabic and Hebrew/Aramaic with significant political and sociolinguistic implications for life in the volatile Middle East. During the 20th century, the Judeo-Arabic tradition waned with the rise of anti-Semitism, Zionism, the Arab-Israeli conflict, and the decline of Jewish communities in Arab-controlled lands. To anyone more accustomed to the current Jewish-Arab conflict, a conflict that began within the global context of colonialism and intensified with the onset of modern nationalism, Judeo-Arabic culture in the medieval, pre-modern, and modern periods is surprisingly cosmopolitan and an especially relevant topic of inquiry for our own increasingly global society, challenging some of us to reflect anew on how we think of ourselves and others.

Acknowledgments

I have benefited from conversations with many scholars while writing this chapter. I wish to thank Sarah Benor, Moti Gigi, Roxani Margariti, Meira Polliack, Marina Rustow, Ella Shohat, Ruth Tsoffar, and Martin J. Wein; however, I bear full responsibility for the contents of this chapter.

References

Arnold, Werner. 2013. Judeo-Arabic, Hebrew component in Syria. In Geoffrey Khan (ed.), *Encyclopedia of Hebrew language and linguistics*, vol. 2, 401–402. Leiden: Brill.

Avishur, Yitzhak. 2001. העברית שבערבית יהודית [Hebrew elements in Judeo-Arabic]. Tel-Aviv-Jaffa: Archaeological Center Publications.

Bahat, Ya'akov. 2002. המרכיב העברי בערבית הכתובה של יהודי מרוקו [The Hebrew component in the written Arabic of the Jews of Morocco]. Jerusalem: Bialik Institute.

Bar-Asher, Moshe. 1991. Hebrew elements in North African Judeo-Arabic: Alterations in meaning and form. In Alan Kaye (ed.), Semitic studies in honor of Wolf Leslau on the occasion of his eighty-fifth birthday, November 14th, 1991, vol. 1, 128–149. Wiesbaden: Harrassowitz.

Bar-Asher, Moshe. 1992. *La composante hebraïque du judéo-arabe algérien (communautés de Tlemcen et Aïn-Temouchent)*. Jerusalem: Magnes Press.

Bar-Asher, Moshe. 1996. La recherche sur les parlers judéo-arabes modernes du Maghreb: État de la question. *Histoire Épistémologie Langage* 18. 167–177.

Bar-Asher, Moshe. 1998a. המילים העבריות בשרח של יהודי מרוקו (מסורות תאפילאלת) [Hebrew words in the *šarḥ* of the Jews of Morocco (traditions of Tafilalet)]. In Moshe Bar-Asher (ed.), מסורות ולשונות של יהודי צפון אפריקה [Linguistic traditions of the Jews of North Africa], 173–197. Jerusalem: Bialik Institute.

Bar-Asher, Moshe. 1998b. על היסודות העבריים בלשון לימודים [About the Hebrew component in *Leshon Limudim*]. In Moshe Bar-Asher (ed.), מסורות ולשונות של יהודי צפון אפריקה [Linguistic traditions of the Jews of North Africa], 198–207. Jerusalem: Bialik Institute.

Bar-Asher, Moshe. 2001. לשון לימודים לרבי רפאל בירדוגו [Rabbi Raphael Berdugo's biblical commentary *Leshon Limmudim*]. Jerusalem: Bialik Institute.

Bar-Asher, Moshe. 2013. Hebrew component in Judeo-Arabic, North Africa. In Geoffrey Khan (ed.), *Encyclopedia of Hebrew language and linguistics*, vol. 2, 397–401. Leiden: Brill.

Blanc, Haim. 1964. *Communal dialects in Baghdad*. Cambridge: Harvard University Press.

Blanc, Haim. 1974. The nekteb-nektebu imperfect in a variety of Cairene Arabic. *Israel Oriental Studies* 4. 206–226.

Blanc, Haim. 1981. Egyptian Arabic in the seventeenth century: Notes on the Judeo-Arabic passages of Darxe No'am (Venice, 1697). In Shlomo Morag, Issachar Ben-Ami & Norman Stillman (eds.), *Studies in Judaism and Islam presented to Shelomo Dov Goitein*, 185–202. Jerusalem: Magnes Press.

Blanc, Haim. 1985. ערבית-יהודית מצרית: עוד לעניין ספר דרכי נועם לר' מרדכי בן יהודה הלוי [Egyptian Judeo-Arabic: More on the subject of R. Mordekhai b. Yehuda Ha-Levi's *Sefer Darxe No'am*]. *Sefunot* 3. 299–314.

Blau, Joshua. 1970. *On pseudo-corrections in some Semitic languages*. Jerusalem: Israel Academy of Sciences and Humanities.

Blau, Joshua. 1995. דקדוק הערבית-היהודית של ימי הביניים [A grammar of Medieval Judeo-Arabic], 2nd edn. Jerusalem: Magnes Press.
Blau, Joshua. 1999. *The emergence and linguistic background of Judaeo-Arabic: A study of the origins of Neo-Arabic and Middle Arabic*, 3rd edn. Jerusalem: Ben-Zvi Institute.
Blau, Joshua. 2006. *A Dictionary of Mediaeval Judaeo-Arabic texts*. Jerusalem: Academy of Hebrew Language, Israel Academy of Science and Humanities.
Blau, Joshua. 2013. Hebrew component in Medieval Judeo-Arabic. In Geoffrey Khan (ed.), *Encyclopedia of Hebrew language and linguistics*, vol. 2, 388–489. Leiden: Brill.
Blau, Joshua & Simon Hopkins. 1984. On early Judaeo-Arabic orthography. *Zeitschrift für Arabische Linguistik* 12. 9–27.
Blau, Joshua & Simon Hopkins. 1987. Judaeo-Arabic papyri: Collected, edited, translated, and analysed. *Jerusalem Studies in Arabic and Islam* 9. 87–160.
Chetrit, Joseph. 1989. יסודות עבריים בערבית של יהודי מרוקו: לשונו של שיר יהודי בלבוש יהודי [The Hebrew-Aramaic component of Moroccan Judeo-Arabic: The language of a Muslim poem in a Jewish presentation]. *Massorot* 3–4. 203–284.
Chetrit, Joseph. 2007. *Diglossie, hybridation, et diversité intra-linguistique: Études socio-pragmatiques sur les langues juives, le judéo-arabe et le judéo-berbère*. Leuven: Peeters Publishers.
Chetrit, Joseph. 2014. Judeo-Arabic dialects in North Africa as communal languages: Lects, polylects, and sociolects. *Journal of Jewish Languages* 2. 202–232.
Cohen, David. 1981. Remarques historiques et sociolinguistiques sur les parlers arabes des Juifs maghrébins. *International Journal of the Sociology of Language* 30. 91–105.
Cohen Mark. 1994. *Under the crescent and cross: The Jews in the Middle Ages*. Princeton: Princeton University Press.
Diem, Werner, Hans-Peter Radenberg & Shelomo Dov. 1994. *A dictionary of the Arabic material of S. D. Goitein's A Mediterranean Society*. Wiesbaden: Harrassowitz Publishing House.
Drory, Rina. 1992. Words beautifully put: Hebrew versus Arabic in tenth-century Jewish literature. In Joshua Blau & Stephan C. Reif (eds.), *Genizah research after ninety years: The case of Judaeo-Arabic*, 53–66. Cambridge: Cambridge University Press.
Drory, Rina. 2000. *Models and contacts: Arabic literature and its impact on medieval Jewish culture*. Leiden: Brill.
Ferguson, Charles. 1959. Diglossia. *Word* 15. 325–340.
Friedman, Mordechai Akiva. 2016. מילון הערבית-היהודית מימי הביניים לתעודות הגניזה של ספר הודו ולטקסטים אחרים [A dictionary of Medieval Judeo-Arabic in the India book letters from the Geniza and in other texts]. Jerusalem: Ben-Zvi Institute.
Gallego, María Ángeles. 2010. Arabic for Jews, Arabic for Muslims: On the Use of Arabic by Jews in the Middle Ages. In Juan Pedro Monferrer & Nader Al Jallad (eds.), *The Arabic language across the ages*, 23–35. Wiesbaden: Reichert Verlag.
Geva-Kleinberger, Aharon. 2009. *Autochthonous texts in the Arabic dialect of the Jews of Tiberias*. Wiesbaden: Harrassowitz Publishing House.
Geva-Kleinberger, Aharon. 2013. Hebrew component in Iraqi Judeo-Arabic. In Geoffrey Khan (ed.), *Encyclopedia of Hebrew language and linguistics*, vol. 2, 391–393. Leiden: Brill.
Gil, Moshe. 1984. The origin of the Jews of Yathrib. *Jerusalem Studies in Arabic and Islam* 4. 203–224.
Goitein, Shelomo Dov. 1931. היסודות העבריים בשפת הדיבור של יהודי תימן [Hebrew elements in the spoken language of the Jews of Yemen]. *Lěšonénu* 3. 356–380.

Gottreich, Emily Benichou. 2008. Historicizing the concept of Arab Jews in the Maghrib. *Jewish Quarterly Review* 98(4). 433–51.
Greenspahn, Frederick E. 2006. Why Jews translate the Bible. In Isaac Kalimi & Peter J. Haas (eds.), *Biblical interpretation in Judaism and Christianity*, 179–195. New York: T&T Clark.
Hary, Benjamin. 1992. *Multiglossia in Judeo-Arabic, with an edition, translation, and grammatical study of the Cairene Purim scroll*. Leiden: Brill.
Hary, Benjamin. 1996. Adaptations of Hebrew Script. In William Bright & Peter T. Daniels (eds.), *The world's writing systems*, 727–34, 741–42. Oxford: Oxford University Press.
Hary, Benjamin. 2003. Judeo-Arabic: A diachronic reexamination. *International Journal for the Sociology of Language* 163. 61–75.
Hary, Benjamin. 2007. Hypercorrection. In Kees Vertseegh (ed.), *Encyclopedia of Arabic language and linguistics*, vol. 2, 275–279. Leiden: Brill.
Hary, Benjamin. 2009. *Translating religion: Linguistic analysis of Judeo-Arabic sacred texts from Egypt*. Leiden: Brill.
Hary, Benjamin. 2016a. *Il-ʿarabi dyālna* (our Arabic): The history and politics of Judeo-Arabic. In Anita Norich & Joshua Miller (eds.), *The languages of Jewish cultures: Comparative perspectives*, 297–320. Ann Arbor: University of Michigan Press.
Hary, Benjamin 2016b. Judeo-Arabic and Hebrew as languages in contact: Some theoretical observations. *Carmillim for the Study of Hebrew and Related Languages* 12. [13]–[30].
Hary, Benjamin 2017. Spoken late Egyptian Judeo-Arabic as reflected in written forms. *Jerusalem Studies in Arabic and Islam* 44. 11–36.
Heath, Jeffrey. 2002. *Jewish and Muslim dialects of Moroccan Arabic*. London: Curzon.
Henshke, Yehudit. 2007. לשון עברי בדיבור ערבי: אוצר המילים העברי בערבית המדוברת של יהודי תוניסיה: מילון ודקדוק [Hebrew elements in daily speech: A grammatical study and lexicon of the Hebrew component of Tunisian Judeo-Arabic]. Jerusalem: Bialik Institute.
Henshke, Yehudit. 2013. On the Mizraḥi sociolect in Israel: A sociolexical consideration of the Hebrew of Israelis of North African origin. *Journal of Jewish Languages* 1. 207–227.
Henshke, Yehudit. 2015. Patterns of dislocation: Judeo-Arabic syntactic influence on modern Hebrew. *Journal of Jewish Languages* 3. 150–164.
Hirschfeld, Hartwig (ed.). 1892. *Arabic chrestomathy in Hebrew characters*. London: Kessinger Publishing.
Hopkins, Simon. 2008. The earliest texts in Judaeo-Middle Arabic. In Jérôme Lentin & Jacques Grand'Henry (eds.), *Moyen arabe et variétés mixtes de l'arabe Aà travers l'histoire: Actes du Premier Colloque International (Louvain-La-Neuve, 10–14 Mai 2004)*, 231–249. Louvain-la-Neuve: Université Catholique de Louvain, Institut orientaliste.
Jastrow, Otto. 1990. *Der arabische Dialekt der Juden von ʾAqra und Arbīl*. Wiesbaden: Harrassowitz Publishing House.
Khan, Geoffrey. 1991. בחינה של הערבית-היהודית בתעודות הגניזה המאוחרות והשוואתה עם הערבית-היהודית הקלאסית [A linguistic analysis of the Judaeo-Arabic of late Genizah documents and its comparison with Classical Judaeo-Arabic]. *Sefunot* 20. 223–234.
Khan, Geoffrey. 1992. Notes on the grammar of a late Judaeo-Arabic text. *Jerusalem Studies in Arabic and Islam* 15. 220–239.
Khan, Geoffrey. 1993. On the question of script in Medieval Karaite manuscripts: New evidence from the Genizah. *Bulletin of the John Rylands University Library of Manchester* 75. 133–141.
Khan, Geoffrey. 2013. A Judaeo-Arabic document from the Ottoman period in the Rylands Genizah Collection. In Renate Smithuis & Philip Alexander (eds.), From Cairo to

Manchester: Studies in the Rylands Genizah fragments, 233–247. Oxford: Oxford University Press.

Khan, Geoffrey. 2016. Judeo-Arabic. In Lily Khan & Aaron Rubin (eds.), *Handbook of Jewish languages*, 22–63. Leiden & Boston: Brill.

Levy, Lital. 2008. Historicizing the concept of Arab Jews in the Mashriq. *Jewish Quarterly Review* 98(4). 452–469.

Maman, Aharon. 2011. המוגרבית היהודית מדוד בוסקילה עד אשר כהן: תחיה או שירת ברבור [Judeo-Magrebian from David Buskila to Asher Cohen: Renaissance or swan song?]. In Yoseph Tobi & Dennis Kurzon (eds.), חקרי מערב ומזרח: לשונות, ספרויות ופרקי תולדה מוגשים ליוסף שטרית [Studies in east and west: Language, literature, and history presented to Joseph Chetrit], 111–134. Jerusalem: Carmel.

Maman, Aharon. 2013. מילון משווה למרכיב העברי בלשונות היהודים, על יסוד האוסף של פרופ׳ שלמה מורג ז״ל [Synoptic dictionary of the Hebrew component in Jewish languages, according to Professor Shlomo Morag's collection]. *Language and Tradition* 31. Jerusalem: Magnes Press.

Mansour, Jacob. 1991. הערבית היהודית של בגדאד [*The Jewish Baghdadi dialect: Studies and texts in the Judaeo-Arabic dialect of Baghdad*]. Or-Yehuda: Babylonian Jewry Heritage Center.

Matsa, Shay. 2002. ערבית-יהודית בארצות הברית: תמורות בלשון הכתיבה של יהודי חלב שבניו יורק [Judeo-Arabic in the United States: Changes in the writings of Aleppo Jews in New York]. בין עבר לערב [Between Hebrew and Arab] 5. 153–164.

Myhill, John. 2004. *Language in Jewish society: Toward a new understanding*. Clevedon: Multilingual Matters.

Neusner, Jacob, Baruch Levine, Bruce Chilton & Vincent Cornell. 2012. *Do Jews, Christians, and Muslims worship the same God?* Nashville: Abingdon Press.

Newby, Gordon Darnell. 1971. Observation about an early Judaeo-Arabic. *Jewish Quarterly Review* 61. 212–221.

Newby, Gordon Darnell. 1988. *A history of the Jews of Arabia from ancient times to their eclipse under Islam*. Columbia: University of South Carolina Press.

Ornan, Uzzi. 1985. Hebrew is not a Jewish language. In Joshua Fishman (ed.), *Readings in the sociology of Jewish languages*, 22–26. Leiden: Brill.

Piamenta, Moshe. 1990. *Dictionary of Post-Classical Yemeni Arabic*. Leiden: Brill.

Piamenta. 2000. *Jewish life in Arabic language and Jerusalem Arabic in communal perspective: A lexico-semantic study*. Leiden: Brill.

Polliack, Meira. 1998. Arabic bible translations in the Cairo Geniza collection. In Ulf Haxen, Hanne Trautner-Kromann & Karen Lisa Goldschmidt Salamon (eds.), *Jewish Studies in a new Europe: Proceedings of the Fifth Congress of Jewish Studies in Copenhagen 1994 under the Auspices of the European Association for Jewish Studies*, 595–620. Copenhagen: C. A. Reitzel.

Polliack, Meria. 2010. Bible translations. In Norman Stillman (ed.), *Encyclopedia of Jews in the Islamic World*, vol. 1, 464–469. Leiden: Brill.

Polliack, Meira. 2018a. Single-script mixed-code literary sources from the Cairo Genizah and their sociolinguistic context. In Lily Kahn (ed.), *Jewish languages in historical perspective* (IJS Studies in Judaica Series 17). Boston & Leiden: Brill.

Polliack, Meira. 2018b. Dual script mixed code sources from the Cairo Genizah. *Journal of the Intellectual History of the Islamicate World* 6.

Ratzaby, Yehudah. 1985. אוצר הלשון הערבית בתפסיר ר׳ סעדיה גאון [A dictionary of Judaeo-Arabic in R. Saadya's Tafsir]. Ramat Gan: Bar-Ilan University Press.

Reif, Stephan. 2010. Cairo Geniza: General survey and history of discovery. In Norman Stillman (ed.), *Encyclopedia of Jews in the Islamic world*, vol. 1, 534–539. Leiden: Brill.
Rosenbaum, Gabriel M. 2002a. The particles *ma* and *lam* and emphatic negation in Egyptian Arabic. In Werner Arnold & Harmut Bobzin (eds.), *Sprich doch mit deinen Knechten aramäisch, wir verstehen es!*, 583–598. Wiesbaden: Harrassowitz Publishing House.
Rosenbaum, Gabriel M. 2002b. מילים עבריות ושפת סתרים של צורפים קראים בפי יהודים ולא-יהודים במצרים המודרנית [Hebrew words and Karaite goldsmiths' secret language used by Jews and non-Jews in modern Egypt]. *Pe'amim* 90. 115–153.
Rosenbaum, Gabriel M. 2008. לשון היהודים במצרים המודרנית [The language of the Jews in modern Egypt]. In Nahem Ilan (ed.), קהילות ישראל במזרח במאות התשע-עשרה והעשרים: מצרים [Jewish communities in the east in the nineteenth and twentieth centuries: Egypt], 245–256. Jerusalem: Ben-Zvi Institute.
Rosenbaum, Gabriel M. 2013. Hebrew component in Egyptian Judeo-Arabic. In Geoffrey Khan (ed.), *Encyclopedia of Hebrew language and linguistics*, vol. 2, 390–391. Leiden: Brill.
Rustow, Marina. 2008. *Heresy and the politics of community: The Jews of the Fatimid caliphate*. Ithaca: Cornell University Press.
Shachmon, Ori. 2013. Hebrew component in Judeo-Arabic, Yemen. In Geoffrey Khan (ed.), *Encyclopedia of Hebrew language and linguistics*, vol. 2, 390–391. Leiden: Brill.
Shachmon, Ori. 2014. Yemenite Judeo-Arabic. In Geoffrey Khan (ed.), *Encyclopedia of Hebrew language and linguistics*. Leiden: Brill.
Shohat, Ella. 2016. The question of Judeo-Arabic(s): Itineraries and belongings. In Anita Norich & Joshua Miller (eds.), *The languages of Jewish cultures: Comparative perspectives*, 94–149. Ann Arbor: University of Michigan Press.
Spolsky, Bernard & Elana Shohamy. 1999. *The languages of Israel: Policy, ideology, and practice*. Clevedon: Multilingual Matters.
Stillman, Norman A. 1979. *The Jews of Arab lands: A history and source book*. Philadelphia: Jewish Publication Society.
Stillman, Norman A. 1988. *The language and culture of the Jews of Sefrou, Morocco: An ethnolinguistic study*. Manchester: University of Manchester.
Tedghi, Joseph. (ed.). 1995. *Les interférences de l'hébreu dans les langues juives*. Paris: Editions de l'INALCO.
Tirosh-Becker, Ofra. 1989. סוגיות לשוניות מן הערבית היהודית של קונסטנטין [A Characterization of the Judeo-Arabic Language of Constantine]. *Massorot* 3–4. 285–312.
Tirosh-Becker, Ofra. 2010. On dialectal roots in Judeo-Arabic texts from Constantine (East Algeria). *Revue des études juives* 169. 497–523.
Thomsen, John. n.d. *Features of Faroese diglossia*. Unpublished manuscript.
Versteegh, Kees. 1997. *The Arabic language*. Edinburgh: Edinburgh University Press.
Vollandt, Ronny. 2013. Hebraisms in Arabic versions of the Hebrew bible. In Geoffrey Khan (ed.), *Encyclopedia of Hebrew language and linguistics*. Leiden: Brill.
Wagner, Esther-Miriam. 2010. *Linguistic variety of Judaeo-Arabic in letters from the Cairo Genizah*. Leiden: Brill.
Yoda, Sumikazu. 2013. Hebrew component in Judeo-Arabic, Libya. In Geoffrey Khan (ed.), *Encyclopedia of Hebrew language and linguistics*, vol. 2, 393–397. Leiden: Brill.

Joseph Chetrit
Judeo-Berber in Morocco

1 Introduction

Berber is the native language of North Africa and is classified as belonging to the Chamito-Semitic or Afro-Asiatic families of world languages. Despite the domination of North Africa by several successive powers, viz., the Carthaginian Empire, the Greco-Roman Empire, the Visigoths of Spain, the Byzantine Empire, and the Arabs (from the end of the seventh century), Berber remained a first language for millions of speakers in Algeria and in Morocco. Before turning to Judeo-Berber, it should be noted that the Jewish presence in North Africa dates back to antiquity, and that remnants of Jewish sites, dated from the third century BCE (in Libya) to the third century CE (in Morocco), were uncovered by archeologists working in Libya, Tunisia, Algeria, and Morocco (Hirschberg 1974: first chapter; Chetrit and Schroeter 2003; Schroeter 1997). However, to the best of our knowledge and despite this long and close association with Berber tribes, Jews did not use Berber as their principal language at any point in their history, apart from in isolated and small communities, as we shall see below. Nonetheless, in rural communities, they usually used it as a second language in Berber-speaking environments, jointly with their Judeo-Arabic as a first language. In Morocco, which stands at the core of our discussion, Berber is still used as a first or second language by some 30% of the population, mostly in rural regions.[1] Until the 1950s, and before the country's independence and the massive departure of its Jews, the number was even greater: Almost 50% of the population had Berber as their first or second language. A large proportion of them even used it as their only language, namely, in the high ranges of the Rif Mountains, the High, Middle and Anti Atlas, and the Sous valley; this language allegiance lasted despite thirteen hundred years of Arabic expansion and domination. As a language spoken by scattered and diverse tribes, Berber is not – and never was – a standardized language. It includes a great diversity of tribal and rural dialects that are brought together in Morocco

---

[1] According to the Moroccan Government Census of 2014 concerning population and settlement, 26.7% of Moroccans speak Berber in its several varieties, and 89.8% speak Spoken Arabic or "Darija," but 70.2% of the Moroccans of the Sous-Massa region speak *Taflhit*, 48.8% in the region of Tafilalt-Draa speak *Tamaziyt*, and 38.4% in eastern regions and 8.2% in the region of Tanger-Tétouan-Al Hoceima speak *Tarifit* (Moroccan Government Source, 2015). I am grateful to my colleague, Professor Mohamed Elmedlaoui of the IRCAM Institute in Rabat, for letting me know the results of this recent census.

in three great sets of closely related dialects: *Taʃlhit* in southwestern Morocco, *Tamaziɣt* in central and southeastern Morocco, and *Tarifit* in eastern-northern Morocco. Berber-speaking Jews were numerous in the *Taʃlhit* regions; it served as the only language for a few of them and as a second language for a large proportion of those who lived in rural and semi-rural communities.

There is no name for the kind of Berber used by Jews, hereafter Judeo-Berber, mostly because of its great proximity to the Berber spoken by Muslims, but also because of its use as the vernacular of small communities and by only a few thousand speakers per generation in total. Even a name like əl-ʕərbija djälnä (=our Arabic), used by Moroccan Jews for distinguishing Judeo-Arabic from Muslim Arabic, was unusual among Judeo-Berber speakers. Since most of the rural communities of speakers resided in the Southern regions of Morocco, where the Berber dialects largely belonged to the *Taʃlhit* set, the name given by the monolingual as well as the bilingual Jewish speakers for their language was *Taʃlhit* or *ʃəlħa*, the same name used by Muslim speakers.

The present study aims to provide a sociolinguistic and linguistic presentation of what we call Judeo-Berber dialects, and to illustrate their discursive production and structural foundations through two unpublished texts, one oral and the other written, from the *Taʃlhit* area.[2] The first is a narrative spontaneous text, while the second is a section from a written translation of the *Haggadah*. The linguistic treatment of the texts presented here may illustrate the directions of research required by the small corpora of yet unpublished oral and written texts.

2 Sociolinguistic and historical background

This study is primarily concerned with the contemporary uses of Berber and Judeo-Berber by Jewish speakers in Morocco, on the basis of oral documentation gathered through ongoing fieldwork among elderly men and women who came from rural communities of the High Atlas, the Anti-Atlas and its valleys, and the large Sous valley in southwestern Morocco. Documentation on the use of these dialects in other North African countries and regions and in ancient times is so scarce that it is extremely difficult to reach any definitive conclusions about it.[3]

---

[2] For more information on the Berber dialects of the *Taʃlhit* regions, see *inter alia* Destaing 1920, 1940; Laoust 1921; El Mountasir 1999.

[3] For Algeria, too, there is some information about Jewish rural communities who lived among Berber tribes and spoke Berber, notably in northeastern Kabylie in the 19th century (Chaker 2004). In Ghardaia in the Algerian Sahara, many Jews used Berber in their trade with Muslim

For Morocco, some scholars[4] expressed doubts about the existence of a linguistic entity that could be named Judeo-Berber, in a manner akin to other Jewish languages such as Yiddish, Judeo-Spanish, and Judeo-Arabic.

After so many theoretical discussions of what constitutes a Jewish language, this opinion concerning the Berber spoken and used by Jews deserves a little more consideration here. Apart from the seminal paper of Haim Rabin (Rabin 1981) about the diglossic constituency of Jewish languages, the endolectalization process that contributed to constituting Jewish languages, suggested by the author in several studies (Chetrit 2007: 18–24, 424–439, 2013, 2014), and the practical and grammatical distinguishing features illustrated in this book, *inter alia*, by the study of Geoffrey Khan on Neo-Aramaic dialects, it is worth emphasizing the importance of semiotic and textual features that also distinguish Jewish languages (Chetrit 2007, 2009). After all, a language – any language – is not only a mental system of phonological and morphological structures that was – and is yet – singled out by linguists and grammarians. It is also – and for the lay speaker this may be the most important feature – a reservoir of fixed and new meanings that permits, through lexical items and their infinite and regular combinations, interaction with other speakers, the conducting of conversations and many kinds of discourse, and the generation of an infinite set of texts within the scope of a given national or communal culture (Chetrit 2007: 3–33). As we will see later, Judeo-Berber dialects had less differentiating phonological and morphological features, in comparison with non-Jewish neighboring dialects, but they developed textual genres and semiotic worlds that refer to specific Jewish referential spaces, such as the texts concerning the Exodus from Egypt and the Passover service, apart from calque translations of para-liturgical Hebrew and Aramaic texts. Therefore, sociolinguistic, semiotic, and cultural features are no less useful for deciding if a language – a dialect or a comprehensive natural language – is to be considered a distinct Jewish language or not (see also Benor 2008; Hary 2009: 5–49).

Despite the lack of walled quarters or distinct streets for the small Jewish populations, varieties of Judeo-Berber clearly developed in some rural and isolated communities of the High Atlas, among Jews who settled in the Ait Bu Ulli tribe near Demnat to the north of Marrakech, and among those who lived in the Tifnout region near the Ait Wawzgit (Ouaouzguite) tribes of the Moroccan Anti-Atlas range, at least during the 19th and the first half of the 20th centuries. For

---

clients, along with their Judeo-Arabic, until their departure in 1962. This information was gathered directly from informants from this community in fieldwork conducted in Strasbourg and Paris, where most of these Jews eventually settled. Cf. Chetrit 2016: 14–15.

4 The doubts were expressed orally during discussions and presentations on the uses of Judeo-Berber in Morocco.

these small communities, Judeo-Berber was the principal and often the only language used by Jews, not merely in their interactions with neighboring Berber Muslims, but also within the Jewish family and in communal institutions. Many testimonies of Moroccan Jews who visited such communities in the 1930s and 1940s, which were recorded in our fieldwork, as well as a Hebrew chronicle from 1899–1902 (Chetrit 2007a: 230–232), attest to these monolingual uses. This linguistic situation lasted until the French Protectorate developed practical roads and paths between 1920–1940, which opened and strengthened the contacts between isolated rural Jews and urban Jews and progressively led monolingual speakers of Judeo-Berber to adopt Judeo-Arabic also and to become bilingual.

While there were relatively few monolingual speakers of Judeo-Berber – only a few thousand per generation, due to the smallness of the isolated Jewish communities in the impenetrable High and Anti-Atlas mountain ranges – bilinguals were very numerous. In fact, almost all of the men and a great number of the women who lived in the hundreds of Jewish rural and semi-rural communities of the High and Anti-Atlas located in the *Taflhit* and *Tamaziyt* areas (Cf. Flamand 1959), and possibly in the Rif Mountains of northern Morocco as well,[5] spoke Berber as a second language along with Judeo-Arabic as their first language, used in family and communal interactions. Rural Jews spoke Berber in Morocco, as well as in Algeria, because of their economic dependence on a primarily Berber-speaking Muslim clientele. Indeed, in order to make their living, almost all the rural Jews, and many Jews in semi-urban communities as well, engaged in small-scale commerce and practiced their trades among Berber populations, traveling in small groups from one village to the next and from one weekly market to the next in order to sell their meager merchandise and offer their services as silversmiths, tinsmiths, makers of mattresses, and so on. Many of them were away from their homes months at a time, usually from after the *Sukkot* [Feast of Tabernacles] autumn festival until the eve of *Pesaħ* [Passover], the spring festival, and from after *Pesaħ* to the eve of *Shavuʕot* [Pentecost]. Moreover, as noted, Jews did not generally live in separated and closed quarters in the rural communities, as they did in urban and semi-urban communities, but lived among their Muslim neighbors, using Berber for their daily interactions with them. Varieties of Judeo-Berber also developed among these perfectly bilingual Jews. These dialects were very similar to the neighboring Muslim Berber dialects. The next section of the

---

5 Information about the existence of a few rural Jewish communities scattered among the Berber tribes of the Rif is scarce. Cf. Moulieras 1895: 76–77, 89, 155. After the establishment of the Spanish Protectorate in northern Morocco in 1912, these communities were progressively extinguished, and their members settled in urban Jewish communities, such as Tetouan and Tangier, where they were considered, with some disdain, *forasteros* [=strangers].

present study will turn towards examining their textual and structural features, through excerpts taken from oral and written texts.

A third kind of Judeo-Berber speaking communities were those that were bilingual at a much earlier point in time, possibly somewhere between the 15th and 18th centuries, and who spoke Judeo-Arabic as well as Judeo-Berber. These communities subsequently became monolingual, in the course of the 19th and 20th centuries, and ended up only speaking Judeo-Arabic. This notwithstanding, they integrated hundreds of Judeo-Berber elements into their Judeo-Arabic as transparent remnants of their second language, including some lexical items which had disappeared from the Muslim dialects. An example is the term *azmumg* and its variants, which continued to indicate the *Ḥinna* ceremony preceding Jewish weddings in numerous communities, but which had totally disappeared from the Muslim Berber dialects. Another example is the term *abəṭṭʊl*, which refers to a *kohen* 'descendant of the tribe of Aharon the priest', whose title of *kohen* was denied by his community on account of his transgression of his religious duties as a *kohen*.

An example of a community that became monolingual and developed a notably hybridized Judeo-Arabic is Taroudant, which was the main Jewish community of the Sous Valley in southwestern Morocco. This community's rich and diversified Judeo-Berber component was extensively presented and commented on (see Chetrit 2007a: 237–267).

After the dispersion of Jewish rural communities and their re-settlement in Israel, monolingual Jews had almost totally disappeared. However, it was still possible, according to numerous testimonies, to find some elderly women in Israel who continued to use their unique mother tongue of Judeo-Berber in their family settings well into the 1960s. But in Morocco, as well as in Israel, many Jews of rural Moroccan origin, both men and women, still speak Berber and some residual Judeo-Berber, principally as an occasional language for dealing with Muslim clients in Morocco or in guided visits of Israeli tourists to rural regions of Morocco. Indeed, in the course of our fieldwork, many of our Israeli informants, 70, 80, and even 90 years old, were able to speak fluently and to give coherent narrations in Judeo-Berber more than 40 years after their departure from Morocco. These informants came from bilingual communities and were recorded in (Judeo-) Berber as well as in Judeo-Arabic.

For the purposes of our discussion, it is therefore important to distinguish between two distinct Jewish groups of Judeo-Berber speakers: the monolinguals, who had used Judeo-Berber exclusively in the past in small and isolated communities, and the bilinguals, who spoke Judeo-Arabic as their first and principal language but used Berber as a second language in their contacts with Berber Muslim clients, as well as with the occasional rural monolingual Jews. The distinction between these two groups is important, because all that we know about the first group, including the texts attributed to rural monolingual speakers, came from members of the second group, who lived in rural as well as urban and semi-urban communities; they spoke Berber and Judeo-Berber, because of their commercial or professional activities, while their family and communal language was Judeo-Arabic. Some Judeo-Berber texts dealing directly with Jewish life in those rural communities are, in fact, parodies mocking the so-called ignorance of isolated rural Jews (Chetrit 2007a: 269–287).

That said, and as stated in the literature (see Chetrit 2007: 7–8, 213–237), Judeo-Berber enjoys a special status among the Jewish languages that have been documented and studied thus far. This stems from the fact that it is a partial Jewish language, meaning that this language was essentially used by Jewish speakers to serve in face-to-face interaction and oral discourse. As such, Judeo-Berber was not used in written texts of any kind, apart from the translations of the *Pesaħ [Passover] Haggadah* and some other rare texts attributable to particular knowledgeable translators; these written texts were not spontaneous or communal texts, as we will see below. Moreover, Judeo-Berber dialects did not generate any original Jewish creations in the traditional Jewish domains of Biblical, *Talmudic,* and *Halakhic* exegeses and essays, in Jewish original poetry or narration, or in any other kind of Jewish intellectual work, apart from some oral homiletic discourse, such as on the occasion of an elderly person's decease. However, Haim Zafrani has argued, in his co-edition of the written Judeo-Berber text of the *Passover Haggadah* from Tinghir (Galand-Pernet and Zafrani 1970: 2), that communal teaching in Judeo-Berber, as is known for other Jewish languages, existed in Morocco. But, as we shall see, his conclusions should be revisited, including his assertion that the traditional communal translation of the *Haggadah* in Tinghir, as well as in other rural communities, was conducted in Judeo-Berber (Galand-Pernet and Zafrani 1970: 3–4).[6]

That said, the author recently uncovered a singular hybridized bilingual poem in a Hebrew manuscript, which was written in Judeo-Arabic and Judeo-Berber (in Hebrew characters) in 1812 in a rural community of the Draa in central-southern Morocco, where the Judeo-Berber component represents some 20% of the text. The poem deals with a romantic affair that made a scandal in the bilingual small community and presents the adventure of a very handsome young man who was found in the company of a married woman, while he was engaged to a young lady. No other romantic text such as this existed in that epoch, either in Judeo-Arabic or in Hebrew, in the Jewish communities of Morocco, rural or urban. But this exception proves the rule: There was no notable literary creation in Judeo-Berber.

Despite the absence of intellectual works, whether oral or written, in Judeo-Berber, Jewish speakers nonetheless had rich repertories of Berber songs and

---

6 See also the text of the *Haggadah* of Tinghir in Zafrani 1980: 321–399.

tales, which they shared with their Muslim neighbors and which they performed separately or jointly with them at their family festivals. Many families of rural origin continued, until recently, to perform their poetic and musical repertory at their family festivals in Israel, particularly on the occasion of weddings, and the songs of some knowledgeable informants, both men and women, were recorded during the fieldwork. According to the information provided by many informants, there were even some Jewish experts, called *rrais* (pl. *rrwais*), who composed original texts to the melodies of rural Moroccan Berber *Aħwaʃ* and *Aħidus* ceremonies, where poetic jousts on love and other lyrical issues were performed in the form of collective dances and individual songs, with male and female dancers arranged in separate rows (Schuyler 1979; Elmedlaoui and Azaryahu 2014). Several sets of such songs were recorded in the course of our fieldwork, and other recordings of Berber songs performed by Jewish informants can be consulted at the Sound Archives of the National Library of Israel in Jerusalem.

3 Judeo-Berber oral and written texts and their distinctive features

3.1 Judeo-Berber discourse and oral texts

As mentioned above, Judeo-Berber dialects were used almost exclusively for oral face-to-face interaction within and outside the family by the Jews who lived in the isolated and small communities of southern Morocco; among bilingual speakers, they were used for oral interactions with Berber-speaking Muslims and the occasional monolingual Jewish speakers. Therefore, oral discourse was the principal outcome of their daily discursive activity; it served in the various social discursive events, with all their associated descriptive, narrative, directive, procedural, and speculative utterances. These discursive activities not only utilized the structural linguistic – phonological, phonetic, syntactic, lexical, and semantic – resources of the dialects, but also the traditional formulaic apparatus which completes them and includes proverbs, blessings, curses, and other empathic formulas that provide oral discourse with its human touch and punctuate its interactional foundations and trends.[7] The present section will illustrate this kind of free and

---

[7] For such a formulaic apparatus in a Moroccan Judeo-Arabic dialect, that of Taroudant in southwestern Morocco, see Chetrit 2009: 529–658.

spontaneous discourse through an unpublished narrative text that we recorded from a bilingual speaker, the late Haron Tedghi, who was born in 1912 and grew up in Oufran/Ifran in southwestern Morocco, moved to Tiznit and then to Inezgan, where he lived for about 50 years; he died in Paris in 2008, when he was 96 years old. His text was recorded in Inezgan in 1998.

Apart from such natural and infinite discursive activities, Judeo-Berber dialects also included, as mentioned above, smaller or larger repertories of traditional oral songs and tales that were performed by the speakers during family ceremonials and were common to both Jews and Berber Muslims (Elmedlaoui and Azaryahu 2014). Apart from these shared modalities and textual repertories, Judeo-Berber dialects also included specific Jewish texts and formulas, such as family, communal, and traditional Jewish tales, Hebrew and mixed formulas, as well as short oral texts referring to Jewish situations and events. The few specific Jewish formulas and texts recorded or documented in the course of our fieldwork were performed by bilingual Jewish speakers, who also provided us with Judeo-Berber texts that supposedly served isolated monolingual communities. These formulaic texts are particularly related to *Passover* ceremonials and to some other liturgical moments forming part of the solemn prayers of Shabbat mornings and Jewish festivals. Nonetheless, extensive inquiries among elderly and knowledgeable Jews, who came from isolated rural communities where Judeo-Berber was used by their parents as their unique language, convinced us that some texts are parodic and satirical texts that were invented or transformed by bilingual Jews whose first language was Judeo-Arabic, in order to mock the so-called ignorance and the ways of life of the poor, isolated Jews. Several parodic texts of this kind were published and commented on in a previous work on the uses of Judeo-Berber in Morocco (cf. Chetrit 2007a: 268–292), including a so-called Talmudic discussion concerning a ridiculous and non-realistic situation. The text reproduces a fictional discussion between two Judeo-Berber-speaking rabbis about the status of an embryo found attached with a string in the stomach of a kosher cow after its slaughter (Chetrit 2007a: 284–287; Chetrit 2015a: 125).

3.2 Written Judeo-Berber texts: The translations of the *Haggadah*

As for written Judeo-Berber texts, were it not for the initiative of some willing individuals in Morocco as well as in Israel during the second half of the 20th century, they would not exist at all. Judeo-Berber culture was entirely oral, but Jewish scholars with writing skills, who lived and served in small monolingual communities, were generally bilingual and even trilingual after obtaining a rabbinical education in a major Judeo-Arabic community. When they needed to write a text, they did so in Judeo-Arabic or even in Hebrew, like their colleagues from other communities. Those who desired Judeo-Berber written texts wanted to leave a written trace of the Jewish Berber culture that developed in Morocco to future generations, and particularly the most popular text representing Jewish culture *par excellence*, the *Pesaḥ Haggadah*. Thus, they directly or indirectly contacted bilingual scholars or well-read individuals who were able to produce such a written document, similar to the numerous translations that had existed in other Jewish communities in a Jewish or general language. The scholars were persuaded to translate the whole text of the *Haggadah* into Judeo-Berber, although the *Haggadah* was not recited in Berber before then (or afterwards) in any Jewish community.[8] Did Judeo-Berber speakers recite the Haggadah or parts of it in calque Judeo-Berber in earlier generations? No trace of such translations has yet been found.

This was the path that led to three different written versions of the *Pesaḥ Haggadah*, two of which contain the complete text, and the third containing selected sections. As the three versions were largely presented and commented on in a previous work (Chetrit 2007a: 220–225, 292–321), there is no need to linger over their specific particularities in the present discussion. Instead, we will just mention the names of the initiators and writers of the three versions and the circumstances in which they were written.

The first known translation of the *Haggadah* was written in 1959 in Tinghir in southern central Morocco by Yossef Malka and published by Haim Zafrani and Paulette Galand-Pernet in 1970. As he personally told us in 1987, Yossef Malka, the translator, prepared it in the early 1950s after being approached by a Jewish notable of his community, Meir Elhaddad, who engaged in some commerce in Casablanca, where he was convinced by the communal leader, Raphael Benazeraf, to provide him with such a text. During our meeting, the writer insisted that the text is a personal translation and not a communal tradition. Other old informants from Tinghir, including Rabbi Mimoun, Yossef's brother, who read the text for Haim Zafrani, categorically told me that in Tinghir, as well as in Asfallu, the

---

[8] Apart from the text of the *Haggadah*, there are only two other short Hebrew texts that were translated as Judeo-Berber calque and known to many of our informants who came from diverse rural communities. The first is a biblical verse (*Genesis* 29:9), and the second is a stanza from the famous poem by Rabbi Yehudah Halevi, - מי כמוך ואין כמוך *Mi Kamoxa ve-en Kamoxa* 'Who can be like You, and none can be like You', that was sung in all Moroccan communities, in Hebrew and in Judeo-Arabic, on the Shabbat before Purim. The stanza begins with the words נערות אסתר *Naʕarot Ester* 'the handmaidens of Esther'. For more information about these texts and their diverse translations, see Chetrit 2007a: 287–292.

neighboring rural community where the Malka brothers were born, Jews recited the *Haggadah* in Judeo-Arabic and not in Judeo-Berber. In the course of our fieldwork, hundreds of informants from rural communities in Berber-speaking environments gave us the same information.

The second translation of the *Haggadah* into Judeo-Berber was written by Rabbi Masʕud Ben Shabbat who was born in the 1880s or 1890s in Aqqa, in far southwestern Morocco. He spent a long period of time sojourning in the rural and Berber speaking communities of the Sous Valley, where he served as *Ḥazzan* 'cantor', *Shoḥet* 'ritual slaughterer', and teacher. After the Second World War, he migrated to Casablanca, where he continued his rabbinical activities and his poetic writing in both Hebrew and Judeo-Arabic. As he was also fluent in Berber, his editors, the brothers Hadida of Casablanca, suggested in the late 1940s that he prepare a translation of the *Haggadah* for publication along with the Hebrew original for the Judeo-Berber-speaking communities of southern Morocco, using the same model they had used to publish a Judeo-Arabic and French *Haggadah*. However, the rapid dispersion of these rural communities in 1954 and their emigration to Israel thwarted their project. Rabbi Masʕud Ben Shabbat passed away in Casablanca in 1959, but the brothers Hadida brought his manuscript of the Judeo-Berber *Haggadah* with them to Israel. They later made the document available to scholar Hanania Dahan, who collected many documents and manuscripts from Moroccan Jews, and sent me a copy of the original.[9] The text covers all of the sections that form the *Haggadah* and is entitled הגדה בלשאן שלוח *həggädä b-lsän ʃ-ʃluḥ*, literally meaning '*Haggadah* in the language of the *ʃluḥ*', without any mention of a Jewish language. However, even if the title is neutral, the text's calque translation is very Jewish, as it imitates and continues the long tradition of calque translations of biblical and liturgical Hebrew texts, which are characterized by their non-natural syntax, their literal word-for-word translation, and their adaptation of meanings in a manner far from the semantic and semiotic worlds of the ordinary Berber or Judeo-Berber texts and discourses (cf. Chetrit 2007a: 292–321). We will present and comment on a new section from the Ben Shabbat manuscript (see Figure 1) in a later part of the present study.

The third version is a partial translation of about ten sections of the *Haggadah*, including the translation of the final text, חד גדיא *Ḥad gadya* 'one kid', which was not translated in the two previous versions. This written translation is

---

[9] The historian Dr. David Cohen from Holon provided me with another copy of the same document, as well as with copies of other texts published by the Hadida Brothers, and I thank him for that.

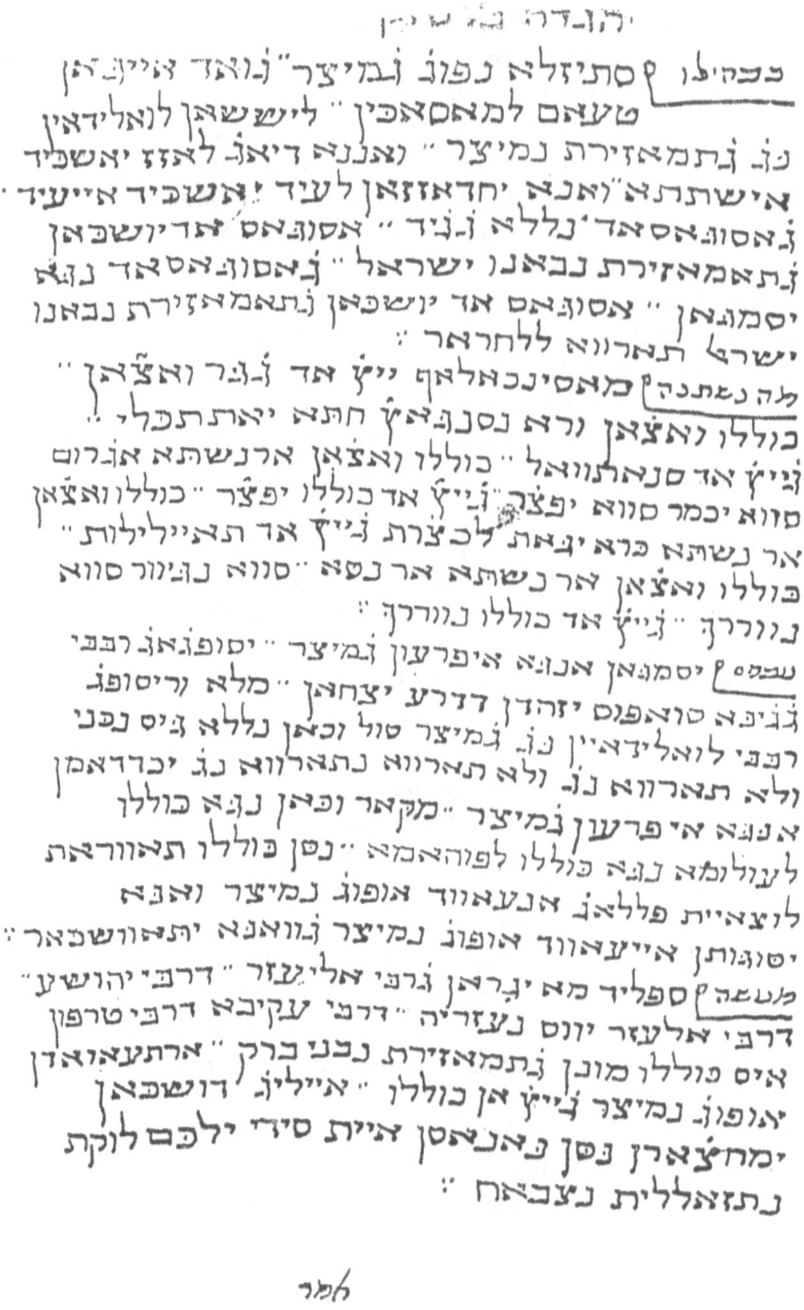

הגדה של פסח

כבהילו פ סתיזלא נפונ נמיצר נואד זיינדן
טעאם למאסאכין ליש שאן לנאלידאין
כז נתמאזירת נמיצר נאננא דיאנ לאזז יאשפיד
אישתרתא ואנא יחדאזזאן לעד יעשביד אייעיד
נאסונאסאד נללא נעיד אסונגאס אד יושבדאן
נתאמאזירת נבאננ ישראל נאסונאסאד ננא
יסמנאן אסונגאס אד יושפאן נתאמאזירת נבאננ
ישראל תאהרונא ללחראר

מה נשתנה פ מאסינכאלאף נייץ אד נ_נר ואצאן
כוללו ואצאן ודא נסנגאץ חתא יארתתכלי
נייץ אד סנאתונאל כוללו ואצאן ארנשתא אנרום
סוא יכמר סוא יפצר נייץ אד כוללו יפצר כוללו ואצאן
אר נשתא כרא יגאת לכצרת נייץ אד תאיילילות
כוללו ואצאן אר נשתא אר נסא סוא נגיור סוא
נוורדן נייץ אד כוללו נוורדן

שבס פ יסמנאן אנונא איפרעון נמיצר יסופגאנ רבני
נגינא סואפס יזהדן דדרע יצחאן מלא וריסופ
רבני לואלידאיין נז נמיצר סול וכאן נללאן ג׳יס נבני
ולא תארווא נז ולא תארונא נתארלווא נז יכדדאמן
אננא אי פרעון נמיצר מקאר וכאן נגא כוללו
לעולומא ננא כוללו לפוהאמדא נסן כוללו תאווראת
לוצאיית פללאנ אנעאוד אופונ נמיצר ונגא
יסוגות אייעאווד אופונ נמיצר נואנא יתאוושבאר

מעשה פ ספליד מא יגראן גרבי אליעזר דרבי יהושע
דרבי אלעזר יונס נעזריה דרבי עקיבא דרבי טרפון
איס כוללו מובן נתמאזירת נבנ ברק ארתעאואדן
אופונ נמיצר נייץ אן כוללו איילין דושבאן
ימחצארן נסן נאנאסן צאית סיד ילכם לוקת
נתזאללית נצבאח

לכוני

Figure 1: Excerpt from the manuscript of Masʕud Ben Shabbat (without pagination). The first page of the manuscript (from Joseph Chetrit's personal archives).

due to Yehuda Derʕi, who was born in the 1920s in Ighil n-Ughu, upstream from the Sous Valley, and who settled in Ashdod, Israel in 1962, where the author met him in 1994 as part of the fieldwork he conducted among Judeo-Berber speakers and asked him to translate the *Haggadah*. At his request, Yehuda wrote another rare text for him in Judeo-Berber. He composed a poem about the young Solika Hatshwel from Tangier, who was beheaded in Fes in June 1834 for her refusal to recant her Jewish faith and convert to Islam, and who became a great saintly figure among the Jews of Morocco. Dozens of poems were written in Hebrew, in Judeo-Arabic, and in Judeo-Spanish after her martyrdom, but none were written in Berber. For his Judeo-Berber poem, Derʕi was inspired by some Judeo-Arabic poems and adapted their contents to Berber poetic structures.

The writing system used by all three authors is almost identical for the three manuscripts, and the system of transcription is similar to that used for Judeo-Arabic texts. The writers used square Hebrew letters with punctuation vowels, except for Rabbi Masʕud Ben Shabbat, who limited himself to marking the voiced fricative velar consonant |ɣ|, the ɣ*imel* (גּ), and the voiced emphatic dental consonant |ḍ| (צּ, קּ) with an upper dot, the voiced post-alveolar |ʒ| (ג̣) with a subscript dot, and the palato-velar stop consonant (|g| - ג , |k| - כ) or the geminate consonants, that are very frequent in Berber, with an internal dot or *dagesh*. The vocalization of the other two texts is meaningful for the distinctive realization of the vowels |i| and |u| by Jewish speakers of Judeo-Berber; these pronounce the two vowels as the centralized vowels [ɨ] and [ʉ], as in their Judeo-Arabic dialects. Therefore, Yehuda Derʕi transcribed them respectively with a *Segol* (ֶ), representing a vowel close to [e], and with a *Ḥolam* (ֹ, וֹ), a vowel close to [œ] in a non-emphatic environment or to [o] in an emphatic one, while Yossef Malka transcribed |i| with a *Ḥiriq* (ִ), but |u| in the same manner as the former, and sometimes also with a *Šuruq* (וּ), as for [u]. For example, Yehuda wrote לְמוֹפְהֵימִין for *lmufhimin* 'clever', and Yossef wrote נוּגְרוֹם אוֹר יְמְתִין for *n uɣrum ur imtin[n]* (literally, 'of bread that was not leavened').

4 Structural components of Judeo-Berber dialects and their distinctive features

4.1 The consonants and vowels of Judeo-Berber

As a rule, the phonological and morphological structures of Moroccan Judeo-Berber dialects were universally very close to those of their neighboring Muslim dialects, because of the intimate proximity between Jews and Muslims in rural settings. The essential reason for that is because Judeo-Berber speakers, monolinguals or bilinguals, generally lived in permanent and daily contact with their Berber Muslim rural neighbors, on the same streets and even in the same buildings as most of them, and not in walled Jewish quarters, as was the case for Judeo-Arabic speakers in Moroccan urban and semi-urban places. However, the Jewish pronunciation of Berber and its Judeo-Berber varieties has several distinctive features, originating in a Judeo-Arabic first language that largely interfered with its phonetic articulations, as we saw above for the vowels |i| and |u|.

Despite the lack of distinct phonological and morphological features, Judeo-Berber should be classified, as stated above, as a Jewish language, at least for its sociolinguistic and cultural features, which determined the Jewish discourse, and its semiotics and meanings, the points of view and attitudes of the speakers in their daily life, as well as in their religious conduct and forms of life. Through its specific texts, Judeo-Berber also has distinctive syntactic and semantic features. On the syntactic level, the artificial wording of translated texts mirroring the syntax of the Hebrew originals is entirely unknown in Muslim Berber texts and discourse. On the semantic level, too, the distinctive Jewish vision of the world filters through the calque translations of biblical and traditional Jewish expressions, as well as through the implicit references to cultural and spiritual proper Jewish entities.[10]

Before engaging in a detailed discussion of these features, let us present the transcription system used for the present oral and written texts:

Consonants	labial	dental-alveaolar	alveolar	post-alveolar
unvoiced stops	[p]	t tt ṭ ṭṭ		
voiced stops	b bb [ḇ ḇḇ]	d dd ḍ ḍḍ		
nasals	m mm [ṃ ṃṃ]	n nn [ṇ ṇṇ]		
unvoiced fricatives	f ff		s ss ṣ ṣṣ	ʃ ʃʃ
voiced fricatives			z zz ẓ ẓẓ	ʒ ʒʒ
coronal		r rr [ṛ ṛṛ]		
lateral			l ll [ḷ ḷḷ]	
semi-consonant	w [ɥ] ww [w̰]			

	palato-velar	uvular	pharyngeal	laryngeal
unvoiced stops	k kk kʷ kkʷ	q qq qʷ qqʷ		
voiced stops	g gg gʷ ggʷ			
unvoiced fricatives	x xx xʷ xxʷ		ḥ ḥḥ	h hh

---

10 For theoretical discussion of the distinctive features of Jewish languages, see Chetrit 2007: 3–38; Benor 2008; Hary 2009: 5–49.

voiced fricatives	ɣ ɣɣ ɣʷ ɣɣʷ		ʕ ʕʕ
semi-vowel	j jj [j]		
Cʷ	labio-velarized consonant		
̣	emphatic consonant		
[C]	particular phonetic element due to an emphatic environment or a foreign loan, like the [p] in *palistin*, *pisäḥ*		
Vowels	front high	back high	mid-low centered	lower central
	i [ɨ ï]	u [ʉ o]	[ə]	a [ä ɒ]
Diphthongs	i̯	u̯		
[V]	Phonetic realization of a phonemic vowel due to an emphatic environment [ï], [o], [ɒ], or to the usual centralized realizations of Jewish speakers in southern Judeo-Arabic dialects: [ɨ], [ʉ]. [ə] is a very short vowel, frequent in Judeo-Arabic dialects; in Judeo-Berber discourse, it serves to avoid clusters containing too many consonants.		

4.2 Some distinctive features of Judeo-Berber

4.2.1 Morphophonemic features

On the morphophonemic level, the most salient distinctive features are:
a. Apart from the tendency to centralize the articulations of |i| and |u|, the low central vowel |a| is performed with a lesser degree of lowness in ordinary phonetic contexts, i.e., without emphatic consonants, under the influence of the *Imala* pronunciation of Judeo-Arabic. This feature is represented in the present study by the complex character [ä]. In direct emphatic contexts, |a| is velarized, particularly directly after or before an emphatic consonant as the root of the tongue moves back and high; it is transcribed here as [ɒ]. In non-direct contact with an emphatic consonant, the *Imala* is cancelled. Examples from the oral text: *täddärt* (the name of a village near Ifran /Oufran), *nənnä i̯äs* 'We told him'; *i̯ät lmyɒṛɒ* 'a cemetery' – loaned from Arabic; *är i̯aqqṛɒ* 'he recited some prayer'. As for the realizations of the |i| and |u| by the speaker of the following oral text, they are not generally centralized, due to his great fluency in the Berber that he spoke on a daily basis with his Muslim clients in Inezgan, southwestern Morocco. Another particularity of Judeo-Berber is the tendency to expand, as in Judeo-Arabic, the pharyngealization of emphatic consonants, not only to neighboring vowels, but also to other syllables of the lexical unit. In such emphatic environments, the realization of the vowel |i| is lowered as for |e|; it is represented here by [ï]. The realization of |u| is also affected, and it is rounded and lowered as for [o].

b. The frequent cancelling of the labio-velarization of palatal and velar consonants: kʷ > k, kkʷ > kk, gʷ > g, ggʷ > gg, xʷ > x, ɣʷ > ɣ, as in our oral text: Muslim Berber *nkkʷni/nukkni* > *nəkkni* 'we'. This tendency also distinguishes Judeo-Arabic dialects from Muslim Arabic dialects in Morocco, where labial, palatal, and velar consonants are also frequently velarized, but not by Judeo-Arabic speakers.
c. The frequent performance of the post-alveolar consonant |ʃ| as a dental-alveolar |s| with a weak stridency, particularly by speakers living in separate Jewish quarters, in big villages, or in urban and semi-urban communities. As in the Judeo-Arabic dialects, the stridency of such an archiphonemic |s| is not the same from one community of Judeo-Berber speakers to the next and can be close to [ʃ], between [s] and [ʃ], or close to [s]. In our oral text, there is a clear distinction between the two phonemes /ʃ/ and /s/ because of the speaker's long life among Muslim Berbers after the Jews of his community departed in the early 1960s.
d. The realization of the unvoiced labial stop |p| of Hebrew and European languages as a borrowed consonant in Judeo-Berber, while Muslim speakers articulate it as [b] or [bb], e.g., *palistin* in the oral text or *pisäħ (Pesaħ)* in daily discourse.
e. The occasional nasalization of the liquid consonant |l|: l > [n] by Jewish speakers from southwestern Moroccan communities, such as Iligh, Tahala, or Oufran/Ifran. Here is an illustrating brief excerpt from a famous Jewish joke told by Jaïs Bensabbat, who was born in Ifran but lived for dozens of years in Marrakech, where he was recorded:

> *innä-k jän ḍ-ḍoṛ juʃkäd jän nħəzzän s jät ṭmäziṛṭ. tämäzirt-än id bäb-nns gän kunnu iɣʷjän, ur ssən wänu* 'It is said that a Rabbi once arrived in a [rural Jewish community]. The locals of the place, all of them were donkeys, they did know nothing' (*nħəzzän* 'a/the Rabbi' renders *lħəzzän*; *kunnu* 'all of them' is used in place of *kullu*; and *wänu* instead of *wälu* 'nothing').

4.2.2 Syntax

a. The use of mixed syntactic schemes in oral translated texts, combining calque schemes, as well as the free or natural syntactic structures of the Berber clause. This hybrid syntax appears particularly in the translations of the first sections of the *Pesaħ Haggadah*, of which there are many communal oral versions, as well as in other liturgical texts (cf. Chetrit 2007a: 272–292). But in the individual written translations of Yossef Malka and Masʕud Ben Shabbat, as well in the other two short oral texts, the calque schemes of the Hebrew – and, in fact, of the Judeo-Arabic – are respected and truly illustrated.

b. The use in ordinary, specific, or professional discourse of Hebrew lexemes, compounds, and formulas that refer to specific Jewish cultural entities from all domains of Jewish life as in other Jewish languages (cf. all the chapters in Chetrit 2009). The loans are perceived as a kind of technical terminology and are mostly borrowed from Judeo-Arabic and not directly from the Hebrew texts. In the oral text, we have, for example: *lhorban* חורבן 'the destruction [of the temple of Jerusalem]', *lqiborʊ* קבורה, here 'tombs', used along with *lqibor* and *lqbor*, and *lmiʕorʊ* מערה 'cemetery' used with its Arabic/Berber equivalent *lmyorʊ*. In the other oral texts, the parodic texts, we have the argumentative expression *illä wəddäj* אלא ודאי 'that is sure', and references to rabbinical works, like *ʃulħan ʕarux* שולחן ערוך, which is the canon of the *Halakhic* precepts and behaviors, or to biblical figures of ill repute such as *Datan* and *Abira[m]* דתן ואבירם (Numbers 16: 1–38) (cf. Chetrit 2015a: 124–125). On the other hand, there are no Hebrew terms in the following translation of the text from the *Haggadah*, but that is a usual and even foundational principle in calque translations of biblical and liturgical texts. As was largely proved in a previous study (Chetrit 2007a: 292–320), the three Judeo-Berber translations of the *Haggadah* presented above are, in fact, a duplication or an adaptation of the traditional Judeo-Arabic translation and not a direct translation of the Hebrew original.

4.2.3 Semantics and lexicon

On the semantic and lexical level, and apart from the Hebrew and Judeo-Arabic elements that distinguish the Judeo-Berber dialects, the entire lexicon is shared with Muslim speakers. However, in the parodic texts, presented as supposedly used in monolingual Jewish communities, there are some lexical forms that indicate cultural Jewish entities in a comical manner. For example, the *ħaroset* חרוסת, which symbolizes the mortar that the Hebrews were constrained to produce during their servitude in Egypt and figures on the *Seder* plate of the *Pesaħ* tradition, is called *ṣṣʊbħon ixṣərn*, literally 'spoiled soap', instead of the simple Judeo-Arabic Hebrew loan *əl-ħarusit* (or *əl-hilk* in southeastern communities). Another example is the compound *ämän wʊḍîl*, literally 'water of grapes' for 'wine', instead of the Arabic loans *ʃʃrʊb* (or *ṣṣrʊḥ* in the usual Jewish pronunciation) or *lxmər* (*lxmər* in Jewish use) (cf. Chetrit 2007a: 270–272).

All of these distinctive features clearly show that modern Judeo-Berber is a hybridized language like all other Jewish languages (Chetrit 2007: 3–38, 407–543,

2013). It combines a Judeo-Arabic substrate, a Berber matrix, and a Hebrew component borrowed through Judeo-Arabic uses. But unlike other Jewish languages, Judeo-Berber is not a complete diglossic language, because of the lack of an intensive manipulation of Hebrew texts or other texts through exegesis, homilies, teaching, and so on, as the long-lasting field research teaches us. Yet, as shown in other studies (Chetrit 2007: 8–14, 2013: 182–184), diglossia consists not only of differential social uses of two languages by the same speakers, but also of the formation of many intertwined and hybridized forms and structures in the two languages, due to their continuous interference. Likewise, we have no evidence that a secret language, based on a combination of Hebrew terms and Berber syntax as in Judeo-Arabic (cf. Chetrit 2007: 545–564, 2009: 241–249), was used in Judeo-Berber communities. All of these characteristics make Judeo-Berber dialects partial Jewish languages.

5 Example texts

5.1 An oral narrative text

The following text was recorded in August 1998 in Inezgan near Agadir.[11] As previously noted, Haron Tedghi, the narrator, was born in 1912 in Ifran (Jews say Oufran),[12] in the Bani mountains of southwestern Morocco, stayed for some time in Tiznit after his adolescence, and came to Inezgan in the 1950s, where he lived until 2008. He lived all of his life in a Berber environment and engaged in small-scale commerce with Muslim Berbers. He was fluent in Berber as well as in Judeo-Arabic and had a good comprehension of his Jewish and Berber environment, though he did not have a formal education. Haron was interviewed about his community and its traditional texts, including the *Pesaḥ Haggadah*, first in Judeo-Arabic and immediately after that in Judeo-Berber, his second language. He gave us some Judeo-Berber excerpts of the first sections of the *Haggadah* and other short texts (see Chetrit 2007a: 276–277) and told us about his community's

---

11 The interview, including the text, was carried out as part of a study of the Jewish presence in a Moroccan-Berber environment; the Binational Science Foundation Israel – U.S.A. (BSF) provided us with an important grant for the study, funding the summers of 1997, 1998, 1999, and 2000. Members of the research team, apart from the author, included Professor Daniel J. Schroeter from the University of Minnesota, Professor Abderrahman Lakhsassi from Mohammed V University of Rabat, and, in 1999 and 2000, the filmmaker Haim Shiran as well.
12 For more information about the community of Ifran/Oufran, see Chetrit 2015b; Monteil 1948.

beliefs concerning the genesis of the Jewish community of Ifran, which, according to the local oral tradition, was the most ancient in Morocco.[13] Jewish Ifran was also known for its holy Jewish cemetery, containing the graves of Kabbalists and martyrs, and into which it was forbidden to enter without serious mystic preparation (cf. Chetrit 2015b). After a narration of the legendary history of his community, Haron told us of an event concerning the holy cemetery to which he was an eye-witness.

As for the language of the Judeo-Berber text,[14] which belongs to the *Taʃlḥit* area, it is important to note that it is a free and spontaneous oral text, performed in the course of an interview that included leading questions expressed from time to time by the interviewers. As such, the text is characterized by:
- The chronological and logical organization of the narrative contents in autonomous fragments, with almost no subordinations between them and within them.
- Various repetitions of contents, e.g., in fragments (4, 5, 16).
- The use of the phatic expressions: *i̯äk?* (1), *yäi̯illi* (8); *yᵘwälli* (12, 13, 16), that also mark the speaker's hesitations.
- The use of particular descriptive and repetitive syntactic structures resembling mimetic theatrical scenes: *iyər gis äi̯illi iyər* (13); *är i̯aqqṛʋ är i̯aqqṛʋ är i̯aqqṛʋ äi̯illiy iyʷli* (14).
- Some slackening in the formulation of intent: *nənnä äsən - äsən* 'them' instead of *äs* 'him' (8). However, the use of the pronoun complement *–[ä]k* 'you' in the repetitive verbal phrase *innä i̯[ä]k* 'he told you' (7, 8, 9, 10, 11), in place of *–äy* 'us, he told us' is a calque translation of the Judeo-Arabic expression *qal-lk* meaning 'he said', where the indirect complement *-lk* serves as a phatic element. Compare the ordinary use of *innä* 'he said' without a complement in fragment (13).
- The appearance of some cases of consonantal assimilation: *äʃkənt-t [=d] s ifrän* (1); *iffuy är imi l [=n] lmyʋṛʋ* (15), and of consonantal omission: *k[r]ä i̯gät* (3, 5), *jaḍni[n]* (6), or of vocalic omission: *timy[a]ṛin* (10).
- The expansion of the pharyngealization of an emphatic consonant to neighboring consonants and vowels: *iḍəṛ, oḍʋṛ* nns, *imṃoḷḷẓ* (15).

---

[13] In our visit to Ifran in August 1998, elderly Muslims spontaneously told us that they knew that Jews had been living in Ifran for eighteen centuries.
[14] The text was transcribed from tape in Rabat in 2013 with the assistance of three Berber-speaking research students from Mohammed V University: Lahcen Oubas, Anir Bala, and Rachid Sadik. I am grateful to them for their precious assistance, as well as to Professor Mina El-Mghari, who recommended them, and Professor Jama'i Baida, the head of the Archives Marocaines in Rabat, for his help.

The first four features described here are due to the narrative nature of the text, but the others are due to idiosyncratic usages of the speaker as a Jewish Berber-speaker.

The narrative structure of the text is also characterized by the passive form of some descriptive verbs, particularly in the first part of the narration, which pertains to a non-personal experience and to a distant report for the speaker: *ttuḥṣʊrn udäi̯n* (4), *ttumḍʊln y i̯ät lmyʊrʊ* (5), *ttumḍʊln gis səbʕä, sät täswin* (5). In the second part there is also a passive form: *ur ittumkin* (8). The speaker also uses conclusive formulas borrowed from Muslim spoken Arabic on two occasions, for marking the end of a narrative episode: *häkkäk hij*ä (5); *kän hä lḥäl* (17).[15]

(1) mən *lḥoṛban* lli i̯zwärn – i̯äk? – ʃəttitn udäi̯n; ffuyən, äʃkənt-t s ifrän. (2) ifrän kullu äs zwärn kullu s lmɣrib; yinn äɣ zdyən. (3) kkän zzäwit, kkän idä u̯ ʃqrʊ, kkän täddärt, kkän tinkərt; llän ɣ k[r]ä i̯gät mäni; är yinnä är lməlläḥ zdyən gis. [...]
(4) mən lliy mmäyən ḥəttä nəttni d imusəlmin, mmäyən disən, ttuḥṣʊṛn udäi̯n, mmtən gisən, gigän ä gisən imutən. (5) ttumḍʊln ɣ i̯ät lmyʊrʊ, är äs ttinin lmyii̯rʊ, ɣ ifrän. k[rä] i̯gät lqiḇoṛ, k[r]äi̯gät *lqiḇoṛʊ*; ttumḍʊln gis səbʕä, sät täswin, sä lqḇoṛ i̯än f i̯än. *häkkäk hij*ä. (6) *lmiʕʊrʊ* jaḍni[n], ɣ tälli lmyʊrʊ lli mqqoṛn, ur ä sərs ikəʃʃəm ḥəttä i̯än. – ʕl-äʃ? – är sərs dḍuwoṛn, udäi̯n. – udäi̯, ur ikʃim? – uhu, ur imkin.
(7) ʕəqqəly äs nəkki, i̯uʃkäd i̯än ɣ *palistin*, innä i̯[ä]k rä i̯zoṛ [...] iffuy yinnä ɣ ifrän. (8) nənnä äsən [! – äs]: *äwäddi*, nəkkni hän ur äd – yäi̯lli – ur ä nəkʃəm s ugʷəns. innä i̯k: *mä-xəʃ-ʃäi̯n* ä nəkʃəm s ugʷəns. nnän äs: uhu, ur ittumkin. (9) inkər innä i̯k nəttän: ml-ät iji yir mäniy ä ttʕumənt, mäniy ä ttʕumǝy. (10) nmun dis äi̯lliy äs nəmlä yilli ɣ ä ttʕumənt timy[a]ṛin; innä i̯k: yid, uhu. (11) nmun dis s i̯ät lḥəfrʊ ɣ uzṛu, är gis äqläi̯n ämän yikäd ɣ izəddär; innä i̯k: yid, äy räd ʕumɣ. (12) näwi äs lḥwäi̯ʒ nns, ndəl t yikäd s - ɣʷwälli - l-izoṛ äi̯lliy iʕum. (13) iqəssəs - ɣʷwälli - äskärn; iyər gis äi̯lli iyər; iyʷli d. innä: yiläd, äy räd yliy didun äd zoṛɣ. (14) nmun dis äi̯lliy nn ikʃəm d ɣʷwälli d ugəns; iyərq, jakʷin d izəddär u wäkäl yärɣi; är i̯aqqṛʊ är i̯aqqṛʊ är i̯aqqṛʊ äi̯lliy iyʷli. (15) iffuy är imi l [=n] lmyʊrʊ; iḍəṛ f oḍʊṛ nns, immoḷḷẓ. (16) näsi t id ɣ uḥäi̯k är tigəmmi n mərdxäi̯ lli i̯gän ädəlli ttäʒər mqqoṛn, igʷun gis. niwi t in s - ɣwälli - tigəmmi n mərdxäi̯ igʷun gis. (17) äʃkin äs ɣ iḍṣ nns, nnän äs: sir, ḥäti nəskər äk äsəggʷäs woḍʊn; är kiy tffuyt ɣ lmayrib är d iy tlkəmt därun, rä tmmətt. *kän hä lḥäl*.

[(1) After the first destruction [of the Temple of Jerusalem], of course, Jews were dispersed. They went out [from Palestine], they arrived at Ifran. (2) Ifran is the very first [Jewish community] in all Morocco; they settled there. (3) They were in the Zaouia, in Ida u Shqra, in Taddart, in Tinkert, and in many other places. They lived there in the Mellah. [...] (4) As they struggled against Muslims, fought them, the Jews were besieged; some of them perished; there were dead men among

---

15 For an extensive analysis of the narrative and poetic texts of the Berber tradition, see Galand-Pernet, 1998.

them. (5) These were buried in a cemetery, which is named Al-Mghiyra, in Ifran, where there are many tombs. They were buried there in seven, in seven levels, one tomb over the other. It was in that way. (6) The other cemetery, which is very large, no one can enter there. – Why? – Jews walk around. – A Jew does not enter there? – No, it is impossible.

(7) I remember that someone came from Palestine, he said that he wanted to go on pilgrimage [to the cemetery]. [...] He came to Ifran. (8) We said to him: Dear fellow, we do not – how to say that – enter there. He said to us: I must enter. It was said to him: No, it is forbidden. (9) But he was determined, he said: Show me just where women immerse [for their purification], where I can immerse. (10) We went with him to the place where women immerse. He said: Here, no. (11) We went with him until arriving at a crevasse in a rock, where water was flowing at the bottom. He said: It's here that I want to immerse. (12) We took his clothes and made with them a kind of curtain until he had immersed. (13) He cut, how to say that, his nails. He read what he read and went up. He said: Now, I want to go up and go with you for pilgrimage. (14) We accompanied him until he entered inside, how to say, he was there. He immersed, he jumped to the bottom of the crevasse. He recited prayer after prayer until he had gone back up. (15) He made his way to the door of the cemetery, then he fell down on his leg and sprained his leg. (16) We carried him on a sheet until arriving at the house of Mordekhai, who was then a very rich man, where he lived. We brought him round, how to say that, to Mordekhai's home, where he slept. (17) During his sleep, they came and said to him: Attention, what happened to you [means] that we had assigned to you a year of misfortune; when you will leave Morocco and return back to your home, you will die. It's what happened.]

5.2 A section from the written translation of the *Haggadah* by MasʕudBen Shabbat

The text is taken from the written translation of the *Haggadah* of *Pesaħ* by Rabbi MasʕudBen Shabbat. It deals with the reason why matzot must be eaten on *Pesaħ*, arguing that it should be done in order to remember that, during their brusque exodus from Egypt, the Hebrews took unleavened dough with them to make their bread. As usual, the biblical source of this habit is also given, through the citation of Exodus 12:39.

As for the Judeo-Berber translation appearing there, it generally reproduces the contents of the Hebrew and Judeo-Arabic text through a word-by-word translation, in calque mode. There are, however, some noteworthy exceptions, all of which concern the divine apparition who saved the Israelites, where literal translation becomes an adaptation and even an exegesis. In the Hebrew source of the Haggadah, the fragment is:

> עד שנגלה עליהם מלך מלכי המלכים הקדוש ברוך הוא ʕad ʃe-niγla: ʕăle:hem melex malxe: ham-mëla:xi:m haq-qa:do:ʃ ba:ru:x hu:, literally meaning: 'until the King of kings of kings, He of blessed holiness, appeared before them', which was transformed by the translator in several ways:

- Instead of the passive verb נגלה עליהם niγla: ʕăle:hem 'appeared before them', the translator preferred to use an active verb representing the Israelites' sight: 'they saw…'. Another passive verb appearing in the Hebrew source, 'they were driven out', is also rendered with an active Berber verb, דחינתן dḥin-tən 'they drove them out'.
- What the Israelites saw was the light representing the Honor of God נור נסידי רבבי nnur n-sidi ṛəḅḅi 'the light of God' – and not God Himself, as that is impossible for human beings. By his exegetic adaptation, the translator continued a long tradition by which rabbinical scholars have avoided the personification of God by mentioning Him indirectly with figurative symbols and metaphors.
- The translator did not translate the name of God, 'He of blessed holiness', literally, and rendered it with the ordinary Moroccan-Jewish appellation סידי רבי sidi ṛəḅḅi, literally meaning 'my Master, my Sovereign'.
- The phrase 'the King of kings of kings' is rendered with a two-term expression, אגלליד ניגלדאן agəllid n-igəldan 'the Kings of kings', rather than the original three-term expression.

Similarly, for the marker of citation in the Hebrew source שנאמר, ʃe-neʔĕmar 'as it was said', the translator adopted and adapted the traditional Judeo-Arabic equivalent expression פחאל מא קאל לפסוק f-ḥal ma qal l-päsuq 'as the biblical verse said', but instead of 'verse', the translator preferred to mention the whole book, and used לכתאב lktab 'the Bible'.

As for the morpho-syntactic level: there are strange uses of the pronoun -ak 'to/for you', either as an addition to the original where it does not exist: וראכיכמר ur-ak-ixmər 'which did not become leavened to you', or instead of –asən 'to/for them' in the verbal phrase ורתאכסכירן ur-t-ak-skirən 'they did not prepare any provisions for themselves either', where the pronoun –ak refers to the Israelites and should be asən. It might be the case that for this translator, this special use of –ak served as a phatic element as we saw in the previous text.

לפציר אדללי אר נשתא אשכו פמית? אשכו ור ידיאל לעגין לואלידאיין נג אייכמר נור נסידי רבי אגלליד ניגלדאן יפוכותן גלחין. גמכלי סינא לכתאב: סנוואן לעגין ללי סופגן גמיצר ירכסאס פצרנין וראכיכמר, אשכו דחינתן גמיצר ורזדיארן אדמאטלן; חתא לעוין ורתאכסכירן.

lfḍiṛ ad-əlli ar nʃətta, aʃku f-mit? aʃku ur idjaɣ lʕʒin [n]-lwalidạin-nnəɣ
a-ịxmər ạilliɣ ẓṛɒn nnur n-sidi ṛəḅḅị agəllid n-igəldan ifukku-tən
ɣ-lḥin. ɣmkəlli sinna lktab: "sənwan lʕʒin-lli suffɣən ɣ-miṣəṛ irxsas fḍəṛnin
ur-ak-ixmər, aʃku dḥin-tən ɣ-miṣəṛ ur-zdarən ad-maṭəln, həṭṭa lʕwin
ur-t-ak-skirən" (Exodus 12:39).

[This matzah that we eat, for what reason? Because the dough of our fathers did not have time to become leavened before they saw the light of God, the King of kings, who saved them then. Such as said the Book: "They baked from the dough that they had brought out from Egypt unleavened cakes, which had not become leavened, because they drove them out from Egypt, and could not tarry; and they did not prepare also any [other] provisions for themselves" (Exodus 12:39).]

6 Conclusion

Linguistic and literary research in the domain of Judeo-Berber is very limited. Likewise, apart from some recordings of songs by men and women from communities in Berber regions that were deposited in the National Sound Archives of Jerusalem, almost all of the existing oral material was gathered in our ongoing fieldwork.

The fieldwork began in 1978, among the rural Jews who settled in Shlomi in northwestern Israel, and then extended to numerous other places in Israel and Morocco. It still continues, but less intensely. In the course of the fieldwork, hundreds of elderly men and women were approached and recorded in Judeo-Arabic about their life in a Berber speaking environment and about their uses of Berber and Judeo-Berber. Some of them sang traditional Berber songs and others recited short Judeo-Berber texts concerning the *Pesaḥ* festival, the *Haggadah*, and other liturgical settings. Some oral texts have been published (Chetrit 2007: 268–292, 2015b: 125), but several other versions of these texts remain unpublished. Likewise, there are other narrative texts recorded from bilingual informants, who told us their anecdotes and personal events in both Judeo-Arabic and Judeo-Berber versions.

Apart from this corpus, which was digitalized in part, it was recently possible to obtain a copy of the recordings made by the late Professor Haim Zafrani or for him.[16] Apart from the reading of the written *Haggadah* from Tinghir by Mimoun Malka, which was published and largely commented on in Galand-Pernet and Zafrani 1970, the digitalized corpus includes:

---

[16] I am grateful to Dr. Mohamed Haddaoui from the Ministry of Culture in Rabat, who sent me these recordings.

a. The translation into Judeo-Arabic and Judeo-Berber by an anonymous informant from Ifran/Oufran of some verses of the Book of Esther, of the three first sections of the *Haggadah*, and of some biblical verses from Genesis (17 minutes). In another recording, the informant reads a part of the manuscript of the *Haggadah* written in Tinghir (9 minutes).
b. A monologue in Judeo-Berber by another informant (10 minutes), who also performs several Berber songs (16 minutes).
c. A conversation between two Judeo-Berber speakers about Jewish life in their community, followed by the performance of some Berber songs (15:52 minutes).

Nonetheless, as a partially living Jewish language, Judeo-Berber is now a dying language. Elderly speakers who have conducted a great part of their life in Judeo-Berber and Berber are becoming increasingly rare. For the near future, the goal is, therefore, to edit and publish the entire text of the *Haggadah* written by Rabbi Masʕud Ben Shabbat and the bilingual poem of 1812 from the Draa region, as well as the oral corpora described above.

References

Benor, Sarah Bunin. 2008. Towards a new understanding of Jewish language in the twenty-first century. *Religion Compass* 2(6). 1062–1080.

Chaker, Salem. 2004. Traces juives en Kabylie: Pour une exploration systématique. In Nicole S. Serfaty & Joseph Tedghi (eds.), *Présence Juive au Maghreb: Hommage à Haïm Zafrani*, 95–102. Paris: Editions Bouchène.

Chetrit, Joseph. 2007. *Diglossie, hybridation et diversité intra-linguistique: Etudes socio-pragmatiques sur les langues juives, le judéo-arabe et le judéo-berbère*. Paris & Louvain: Peeters.

Chetrit, Joseph. 2009. *Trésors et textures d'une langue: Etudes socio-pragmatiques sur le judéo-arabe en Afrique du Nord et son composant hébraïque: Articles, poèmes, récits et proverbes*. Jerusalem: Bialik Institute. [Hebrew].

Chetrit, Joseph. 2013. Formation and diversity of Jewish languages and of Judeo-Arabic in North Africa. I. Middle Judeo-Arabic and its forms of hybridization. *Journal of Jewish Languages* 1(2). 177–206.

Chetrit, Joseph. 2014. Judeo-Arabic dialects in North Africa as communal languages: Lects, polylects, sociolects. *Journal of Jewish Languages* 2(2). 202–232.

Chetrit, Joseph. 2015a. Jewish Berber. In Lily Kahn & Aaron Rubin (eds.), *Handbook of Jewish languages*, 118–129. Leiden: Brill.

Chetrit, Joseph. 2015b. Une communauté au passé légendaire, Oufrane. In M. Mezzine, A. Sasson et A. Gomel (eds.), *Communautés juives au sud de l'Anti-Atlas*, 93–105. Casablanca: La Croisée des Chemins.

Chetrit, Joseph. 2016. Diversity of Judeo-Arabic dialects in North Africa: Eqa:l, Wqal, kʲal and ʔal dilalects. *Journal of Jewish Languages* 4(1). 1–43.
Chetrit, Joseph & Schroeter, Daniel. 2003. Les rapports entre Juifs et Berbères en Afrique du Nord: Aspects historiques et culturels. In Paul Balta, Catherine Dana & Régine Dhoquois-Cohen (eds.), *La Médirerranée des Juifs: Exodes et enracinements*, 75–87. Paris: L'Harmattan.
Destaing, Edmond. 1920. *Etude sur la tachelhit du Sous: Vocabulaire français-berbère*, vol. 1. Paris: Imprimerie Nationale.
Destaing, Edmond. 1940. *Textes berbères en parler des chleuhs du Sous*. Paris: Librairie Orientaliste Paul Geuthner.
El Mounastir, Abdallah. 1999. *Initiation au Tachelhit, langue berbère du sud du Maroc*. Paris: L'Harmattan.
Elmedlaoui, Mohamed & Sigal Azaryahu. 2014. The 'Aḥwash' Berber singing ceremony shift from Morocco to Israel: An ethno-musicological Approach. *Etudes et Documents Berbères* 33. 171–186.
Flamand, Pierre. 1959. *Diaspora juive en terre d'Islam: Les communautés israélites du sud marocain: Essai de description et d'analyse de la vie juive en milieu berbère*. Casablanca: Imprimeries Réunies.
Galand-Pernet, Paulette. 1998. *Littératures berbères: Des voix, des lettres*. Paris: Presses Universitaires de France.
Galand-Pernet, Paulette & Haim Zafrani. 1970. *Une version de la Haggadah de Pesah: Texte de Tinghir du Todrha (Haut-Atlas), Maroc, Paris*. Paris: Librairie Orientaliste Paul Geuthner.
Hary, Benjamin H. 2009. *Translating religion: Linguistic analysis of Judeo-Arabic sacred texts from Egypt*. Leiden & The Netherlands: Brill.
Hirschberg, Haim Z. 1974. *A history of Jews in North Africa*. Vol. 1. Leiden: Brill.
Laoust, Emile. 1921. *Cours de berbère marocain: Dialectes du Sous, du Haut et de l'Anti-Atlas*. Paris: Augustin Challamel.
Monteil, Vincent. 1948. Les Juifs d'Ifrane. *Hespéris* 35. 151–162.
Moroccan Government. 2015. Recensement général de la population et de l'habitat 2014. Présentation des principaux résultats. Rabat: Haut Commissariat du Plan.
Moulieras, Auguste. 1895. *Le Maroc inconnu. I. Exploration du Rif (Maroc septentrional)*. Oran: Private Edition.
Rabin, Chaim. 1981. What constitutes a Jewish language? *International Journal of the Sociology of Language* 30. 19–30.
Schroeter, Daniel J. 1997. La découverte des Juifs berbères. In Michel Abitbol (ed.), *Relations judéo-musulmanes au Maroc: Perceptions et réalités*, 169–187. Paris: Stavit.
Schuyler, Philip D. 1979. *A repertory of ideas: The music of the rwais, Berber professional musicians from southwestern Morocco*. Seattle: University of Washington PhD thesis.
Zafrani, Haim. 1980. *Littératures dialectales et populaires juives en Occident Musulman: l'écrit et l'oral*. Paris: Geuthner.

Michael Ryzhik
Judeo-Italian in Italy

1 Introduction

Some general factors have influenced the development and the history of Judeo-Italian from the beginning in a very decisive manner, so that these factors must be called *ab initio*. The history of Judeo-Italian seems to parallel the history of the Italian language much more than the history of Yiddish or Ladino parallels German and Spanish. The reasons for this similarity seem clear. First, Judeo-Italian followed a homoglottal development: It developed in the Italian *milieu*, while Yiddish and Ladino were spoken and written in a heteroglossic environment, Yiddish mostly in Eastern Europe, and Ladino mostly in the Ottoman Empire and North Africa. The second reason, connected to the first but not identical to it, is the great influence of Italian cultural processes on the culture of Italian Jewry.[1]

Jewish culture in Italy, with regard to the use of language or languages, was always very Italianized, e.g., very influenced by the dominant culture. Sometimes Jewish Italian culture preceded common (Christian) Italian developments. As one well-known example, we can cite the case of the sonnets. The Hebrew Italian poet, Emmanuel Romano, wrote his Hebrew sonnets in octets, using the scheme ABBA ABBA exclusively, while in the Italian sonnets this scheme became prevalent only with Petrarch, who was born after Emmanuel had already written his sonnets (Bregman 1995).

It is clear, but must be underlined, that Emmanuel Romano did not invent this scheme, which was widespread but not used exclusively from the end of the 13th century. The scheme of the CD CD CD sextet remained common before Petrarch, e.g., divided into three parts (and not in two). The scheme CDE CDE was in use in the Sicilian School but was rare. While Emmanuel used the scheme ABBA ABBA exclusively for the octet and CDE CDE almost exclusively for the sextet, he was not its inventor; but he understood before others the inner force of these schemes.

Similarly, the writing of romance dialects in Hebrew characters in the territory of Italy began almost simultaneously with writing them in Latin characters and sometimes preceded it. In Salento, for example, one of the earliest cases of writing in the local dialect is the case of the romance glosses to the *Mishna*. As Cuomo has demonstrated (Cuomo 1977), these glosses, found on the margins of

---

[1] See, for example, the classic study by Bonfil 1994a.

https://doi.org/10.1515/9781501504631-005

Ms Parma 138, were written in the 11th century in the Otranto dialect (or in some dialect very close to it).

We shall return to these facts and processes later. However, it seemed important to emphasize, from the very beginning, the parallelism in the development, history, and social and general attitude to the problems of language, in the land in which the *questione della lingua* [the problem of language] always occupied a central place in cultural and social life.[2]

1.1 Names of the language

Judeo-Italian is the modern English name given to the dialects and sociolects spoken and written in Italy by Jews during the long centuries of their sojourn there. Their mutual affinities and connections is the greatest problem with Judeo-Italian, which may be formulated in the question, "Does Judeo-Italian exist as one internally connected entity?" Italian linguists use the parallel term *giudeo-italiano*,[3] but Italian scholars generally prefer definitions that are more precise: *giudeo-romanesco*, *giudeo-piemontese*, *giudeo-fiorentino*, etc. (Terracini 1937; Mayer-Modena & Massariello-Merzagora 1973; Mancini 1992). Italians also tend to use the term *parlata* instead of *dialetto* (for example, Massariello Merzagora 1980, 1983; Scazzochio Sestieri 1970; Fortis and Zolli 1979; Fortis 2006), seemingly because *parlata* (more or less 'the way of speech') is less precise and very general, and subsequently less binding.

The Hebrew denomination of the Jewish language of the Italian Jews in the Middle Ages and in the Renaissance was very general: לעז *laʕaz* 'foreign language'. We find, in the notes to the Passover Seder, in the famous halachic compilation of the 13th century שיבולי הלקט *Šibbole leqet*, written by R. Sidqiyya ben Avraham Anaw:

> מה שאומרים אותו בלשון ארמית לפי שהוא היה הלעז שלהם שהרי בבבל ניתקן ואומרים אותו בלעז כדי להבין הנשים והתינוקות לקיים מצות והגדת לבנך

[*ma še-ʔomerim ʔoto be-lašon ʔaramit lefi še-hu haya ha-laʕaz šellahem še-hare be-bavel nitqan we-ʔomerim ʔoto be-laʕaz kede le-havin ha-našim we-ha-tinoqot le-qayyem miṣwat we-higgadta le-vinka*]

---

2 See Migliorini 1987, *passim*; Marrazini 1993 and the bibliography. Many other articles in the volume Serianni & Trifone are useful, especially Serianni 1993.
3 About other possible names for Judeo-Italian, see Cuomo 1982.

[... it is said in the Aramaic, because it was their *laʕaz*, as this phrase was established in Babylonia, and it is said in the *laʕaz* to make it understandable to women and children, to fulfill the commandment "tell it to your son"] (Buber 1886: 186)

The commentary on the *Seder* in the book לקט האומר, *Leqet ha-ʔomer*, Venice 1718, is called פרוש בלשון לעז, *Peruš bi-lšon laʕaz* [commentary in the *laʕaz* language], as it is in many other editions of the *Haggada* with Judeo-Italian translations. This word is also used in the manuscript comment on the *Haggada* written by Apulian Jews in Corfu: ונוטל הכרפס הנקרא אצו בלעז[4] *we-noṭel ha-karpas ha-niqra* acciu *be-laʕaz* [and takes the celery, which is called *acciu* in *laʕaz*]. The same Apulian Jews also use the Hebrew term לשוננו, *lešonenu* 'our language', which attests, it seems, to their linguistic self-consciousness: לוקחין מין עשב שנקרא בלשוננו שלינו,[5] *loqeḥin min ʕeśev še-niqra bi-lšonenu selinu* [they take some of the herb, which is called in our language *selinu*.] Another term used is *latino, latini*. The Siddur in its Judeo-Italian translation is called *Tefillot latini* in the printed edition from Bologna, 1538. The relationship between the two terms לעז *laʕaz* and *latino* may be clarified by the translation of the Biblical verse בית יעקב מעם לעז *bet yaʕaqov me-ʕam loʕez* [the House of *Yaʕaqov* from the people that speaks a foreign language] (Psalms 114:1): *casata de ya'kov da popolo* **latino**[6] [the House of *Yaʕaqov* from the Latin people]. Yet another term that was used in the titles of books with Judeo-Italian translations is simply *italiano*. This term is problematic in Italian (in the Italian linguistic tradition, it refers to the written literary language based on the Florentine dialect of Petrarch and Boccaccio, as opposed to other spoken dialects). It is also very late: The first attestation is from 1698 (Battaglia 1961). But, as Cuomo has shown (Cuomo 1982: 17 n. 43), in Judeo-Italian sources it was used more than a century earlier, in the title of the Hebrew-Italian-Latin dictionary *Ṣemaḥ David* by David de' Pomis, Venice 1587: "קֵי קוֹרִיסְפּוֹנְדֵינוֹ אַל יְטָאלִיאָנוֹ וֹולְגָרֵי *ke korrispondeno al italiano volgare*" [which corresponds to the spoken Italian].

In modern times, we have evidence of the Judeo-Italian dialect from Lugo, near Ferrara. It was recorded in the 1920s by R. Giacomelli and published by B. Terracini: "kuando io èro micéna, in lo kascèr de Luk, parlévene tuti **in judio**, e sé konformévene a parlèr in rumagnol e in italiano" [when I was a child, in the ghetto of Luco, each one spoke **in Judio** and understood Romagnolo

---

[4] Ms. Schocken 22, c. 60r; Ms. Parma, Biblioteca Palatina, De Rossi 89, c. 3v. *Acciu* is 'sedan' in the Salentinian dialects, see Rolhfs 1976.
[5] Ms. New York, JTSA 5439, c. 3r. Also *selinu* (שלינו) is the dialect term for 'sedan', see Cortelazzo & Zolli 1999.
[6] F. ex. in the *editio princeps* of the Siddur in Judeo-Italian translation, Fano 1506, c. 83b. This verse is part of the *Hallel*, so it was widespread and very well known.

and Italian] (Terracini 1962: 288). Here the *Judio* stays in contraposition to the *Romagnolo* (non-Jewish local dialect) and to the *Italiano* (official language), in this case also providing evidence of the linguistic self-consciousness of its speakers.

Unique in its name, as in all other features, is the dialect of Livorno Jews, *bagitto* (Bedarida 1956). The Livorno Jews are mostly of Iberian provenance, the descendants of the Sephardic Jews expelled from Spain and Portugal, and the term itself is the diminutive of *bajo* [low]. There are also some other local denominations, such as *pugghisu* [Apulian], for the language of the Apulian Jews transferred to Corfu (Sermoneta 1990), but this is the rare case of a Judeo-Italian dialect existing in a heteroglossic (Greek) environment.

1.2 Linguistic affiliation

All Judeo-Italian dialects belong to the same regional dialect groups as their non-Jewish counterparts,[7] though many of them contain linguistic traits from other dialects, due to the constant dislocations of Jews on the peninsula, mostly from the South to the North. Their great diversity is the result of parallelism between the Jewish and non-Jewish cultural and linguistic processes which was mentioned above. The Italian dialects are very different and belong to two great dialectal groups: the Northern dialects, which are generally closer to the so-called gallo-romance dialects (comprising French and Provencal dialects), and the Central and Southern dialects.[8]

Modern spoken Italian, based on the 14th century Florence dialect, belongs to the Central group of dialects. Italian Jewish dialects developed mostly on the basis of local dialects, with the subsequent dislocations within the Apennine Peninsula. Consequently, the linguistic affiliation of the Jewish dialects in Italy is closely related to the geographical distribution of the Jewish communities and their migrating processes.[9] Jewish settlement in Italy began in the deep South (Salento), which is the region of Italy closest to Palestine and to Rome, the capital of the Empire. The earliest texts in *Judeo-Italiano*, which demonstrate something about the spoken language, were written in one of the dialects of Salento[10] or in a dialect that is closely related to Marchigiano and ancient Romanesco. One

---

7 Except the Judeo-Livornese, *bagitto*, see above.
8 The literature dedicated to Italian dialectology is infinite. For a very general description see Renzi 1994: 176–178. For more detailed studies: Castellani 2000; Cortelazzo et al. 2002.
9 For the general scheme see Milano 1963.
10 Marginal glosses on the Mishnah in Ms Parma de' Rossi 138, see above (Cuomo 1977).

example is the case of the *Elegy for the 9th of the Av*, written in the 13th or 14th century[11] and published by Cassuto (Cassuto 1929).

Somewhat later, the intensive cultural life of Italian Jewry, mostly in Central Italy (Umbria, Marche, Rome and Lazio, Toscana), found its romantic[12] linguistic expression mostly in translations of the known religious and ritual texts, such as the Bible and the Siddur, but also in compilations of rabbinical literature (Cassuto 1930a, 1930b, 1934; Cuomo 1985). This literature was written in a language with salient central-southern features, so that Cuomo and Sermoneta classified it as a "central-southern koiné" (Cuomo 1976; Sermoneta 1976). In reality, the majority of traits are from the Romanesco and Umbro-Marcheggiano dialects (Cuomo 1988, *passim*). There are also many dialectal variations between, for example, different translations of the Siddur (Ryzhik 2013a). However, these "central-southern" dialects, used for Jewish Italian literature, also preserved some lexical and grammatical traits of the deep South, of Calabria and Salento (Ryzhik 2008a, 2014a). With the expulsion of the Jews from Southern Italy, which constituted the Kingdom of Naples, a satellite of Spain, in 1493–1512, the center of Jewish life passed to the Northern cities (Jewish communities in the South remained only in the State of the Pope, particularly in Rome and in Ancona). Translations of the Bible from the 16th century, and especially the translation of the Siddur from the 17th century, feature a language with many more Toscana influences, with a clear Northern bias (Cassuto 1930a; Ryzhik 2012).

The closure of the ghettoes in 1555 confined the Jews to special zones in the Northern cities (and in Rome, Florence, and Ancona), and it led to the formation of the ghetto dialects, almost exclusively based on Northern speech, with some remnants of their Southern origin.[13] These ghetto dialects remained as they were, as did most Italian local dialects, up to the Unity of Italy in 1865.

1.3 Regions where the languages were spoken

From the above it is clear that the geographic distribution of the historical and dialect varieties of Judeo-Italian is closely related to the history of Jewish presence and movement on the peninsula. In antiquity and in the earlier Middle Ages, this meant Rome and the regions that are nearest to Palestine – Apulia and

---

11 For its dating see Contini 1960: 35–36: "the archaic jester stile and its similarity to the *Sant'Alessio* have suggested to Cassuto, not followed by all scientists, to date it in the earlier 13th century or even in the preceding century; but it is not possible to date it earlier than the 13th century."
12 E.g., non-Hebrew.
13 See the pioneering work by Jochnowitz 1974.

Basilicata. In the late Middle Ages and in the Renaissance, there is documentation of a massive presence of Jews in the central regions of Umbria, Marche, and Lazio, and the Judeo-Italian of this period is clearly related closely to the corresponding dialects.

Later, in the ghetto period, the geography of the spoken Judeo-Italian ghetto dialects is much more Northern-based: Venice, Mantova, Modena, Piemonte and Torino, Reggio Emilia, Treviso, Trieste, and Ferrara (Terracini 1937, 1951; Mayer-Modena and Massariello-Merzagora 1973; Massariello Merzagora 1980; Polacco and Fortis 1972; Fortis 1991; Foresti 1986; Fortis & Zolli 1979; Colorni 1970; all these centers belong to the Northern zone, from the linguistic point of view). Ghetto dialects existed also in the Central-Southern zone, primarily in the best-known ghetto, in Rome, and also in Tuscany, e.g., in Pitigliano and in Florence (Terracini 1951; Massariello Merzagora 1983).

Outside Italy, a Judeo-Italian dialect existed on the island of Corfù. It was spoken by the Apulian (Salentinian) Jews, expelled during the general expulsion from the Kingdom of Naples in the beginning of the 16th century. It is called *pugghisu* (= *pugliese* 'Apulian'; Sermoneta 1990). Linguistically, it is very similar to extreme Southern Italian dialects (with traits not only from Salento), but because Corfù was in the zone under strong Venetian influence, there are also some Venetian traits (Ryzhik 2013b). Another case of a Judeo-Italian dialect outside Italy may be the Sicilian dialect of Saloniki Jews. Sermoneta has shown that the older Sicilian tradition of the Hebrew Siddur was preserved by the expelled Jews in Greece before it was replaced by the Jews expelled from Spain (Sermoneta 1988). In the manuscripts of this Hebrew Makhzor, there are several sentences in the dialect that can be called Judeo-Sicilian; it may be that this dialect was spoken at least until the 17th century by the expelled Jews, but we do not know when it was replaced by Judezmo.

1.4 Attestations and sources

The type and amount of documentation and sources available provide strong evidence of the distinction between the Southern / Northern and the medieval / modern periods of Judeo-Italian. The ancient and medieval period is represented by translations of the sacred literature and by some original texts. I have mentioned above the Salentine glosses in the margins of Ms Parma A of the Mishna, which is one of the earliest documentations of Salentine (South-Italian) dialects in general. One of the earliest poetic texts in the central-southern dialects is also written in Hebrew characters. It is the *Elegy for the 9th of the Av*, written in the 13th or 14th century, mentioned above. In the 14th–15th centuries, the

Judeo-Italian texts are represented by Biblical and Siddur translations and by fragmentary translations of collections of Rabbinical literature, such as *Pesiqta Rabbati* (Cuomo 1985).

The 16th century saw the rapid and vast development of preaching in all countries, related to the religious wars between Catholics and Protestants (e.g., in Central and Western Europe); it was a century of religious dissensions. Consequently, we have some manuscript collections of Judeo-Italian sermons from this period (Bonfil 1976; Ryzhik 2008). The 16th century was also a time of great changes in the linguistic landscape of Italy. Two main factors brought about the unification of the written language based on the Tuscan dialect and the rejection of other dialects. One was the revolution started by Pietro Bembo, who sanctified the language of the "three crowns" (Dante, Petrarc, and Boccaccio).[14] The other factor was decisions by the Tridentine council, and subsequent counter-reformation acts, which tended to standardize normative language against the dialect and "corrupted" forms, enforced by the newfound means of print.

As I have said before, processes in the cultural life of Italian Jewry were very closely connected to general Italian processes. So it was in this case; there were drastic changes in the life of Judeo-Italian. As a written language, it gradually ceased to exist during the course of the 16th–17th centuries, drifting from Judeo-Italian to standard Italian, as we will see below, through some examples of texts belonging to the same genres, or translations of the same texts. In the case of the Jewish communities, Judeo-Italian gave up its place not only to literary Italian, but also to Hebrew, always highly cultivated by Italian Jewry. As Bonfil has demonstrated, this switch to the two literary languages occurred in the middle of the 16th century (Bonfil 1994).

On the other hand, the above-mentioned formation of the ghetto dialects changed the field of use of Judeo-Italian: from the literary dialect of the translations of classic texts to a low vernacular.

In this way, the history of Judeo-Italian drastically changed at this time, and correspondingly the means of documentation changed as well. No more translations of classical texts or sermons; the main source became "Judeo" ways of speech in comic plays or other comic genres. Later, in the 19th century, when interest began to grow in the romantic side of life of the "simple people," leading to increased interest in dialects, this interest found its expression in the Jewish world in the collections of "Jewish ways of speech." These collections were created, especially in the beginning, by amateurs. They were frequently written down as

---

14 In reality, Petrarch and Boccaccio (Dante was too rough for Bembo), see Marazzini 1993; Dionisotti 1960, Introduction.

some type of home-made transcription without a precise place of recording noted and mostly concerned with the Hebrew-Aramaic component of Judeo-Italian, as more romantic, more interesting, and usually more comic. Nevertheless, they are highly important for the reconstruction of Judeo-Italian dialects.[15]

Later, these Judeo-Italian dialects were collected by some very precise recorders and sometimes elaborated upon by illustrious scholars; two examples are the case of Pitigliano, Ferrara, and Forenze, collected by R. Giacomelli and published by Terracini (Terracini 1962), and the case of Judeo-Modenese, collected by the same Giacomelli and published by Modena Mayer and Merzagora Massariello (1973).

Another important source from the period of the ghetto is popular (or quasi-popular) songs and rhymes, usually of late registration. For example, the ballad from the ghetto of Moncalvo "La gran battaja dj'abrei d'Moncalv," written at the end of the 18th century and published by Colombo (Colombo 1970), or two little poetic compositions in Judeo-Piemontese, brilliantly exposed by B. Terracini (Terracini 1937). Besides the authentic popular dialect writings, there are some texts in dialect composed by educated (sometimes very educated) people, mostly as an attempt to revive or to recreate the Judeo-Italian literature in the ghetto dialects. In this case, as well, parallel developments exist in the "great" Italian word, e.g., the use of dialect by educated authors, who didn't speak (and didn't write) dialect in everyday life, for literary, ideological, or ethnographic purposes. Benedetto Croce called this kind of literature "*letteratura dialettale riflessa*" [reflected dialect literature] (Croce 1952).

Such are the sonnet collections by Crescenzo Del Monte, written in Judeo-Romanesco (Del Monte 1927, 1932, 1955); they are particularly rich in Hebrew-Aramaic elements, but the romance component is also of great importance. The well-known scholar, David (Umberto) Cassuto, wrote a play with his children in Judeo-Fiorentino, "Gnora Luna" (Bene Kedem 1932; Bene Kedem is a pseudonym of *Bene* [= 'children of' in Hebrew] *Cassuto David Moshe*), which may serve as an important source of this dialect in the first half of the 20th century.

The Second World War and the Holocaust, with the subsequent post-war changes in the style of life, have brought with them a drastic decrease in the living use of Judeo-Italian. In the last decades of the century, some representatives of "reflected dialect literature" appeared who recorded the last (final) phases of Judeo-Italian. For example, "Chiacchere alla giudia" da Mirella Calò (Calò 1990), a collection of short dialogues in Judeo-Romanesco from the 1980s, that try to be realistic and modern (in which they succeed), but they are also extremely nostalgic.

---

[15] For the full list of these collections, see Aprile 2012:297–308.

1.5 Present-day status

The history of Judeo-Italian as a living language will end, or has already ended, in our day. There are still some elderly Italians who speak or understand remnants of the ghetto dialects. I personally met a street actor from Rome who spoke the dialect in his childhood and still remembers some words, such as *sikkinimmə* 'knife'. However, it seems (maybe I am wrong) that real, live use has ended. There is internet activity; for example, the Facebook page of "*Laboratorio teatro giudaico romanesco*," and this may be of some interest. Regarding the possible future, I cannot, and do not want to try to, predict the fate of Judeo-Italian in unpredictable Italy. What is really interesting, from the socio-linguistic point of view, is the question of whether the Italian of modern Italian Jews is different from the Italian of their non-Jewish neighbors and, if so, in what ways? Are there remnants of Judeo-Italian lexemes and expressions; is there a considerable presence of Modern Hebrew in that Italian's presumable Hebrew component?

2 Historical background

2.1 Speaker community: Settlement, documentation

The first Jews settled in Southern Italy and in Rome. We have many historical sources from this earliest period, in epigraphic form and in archives. Much information can be derived from tomb inscriptions, written from the third to the ninth centuries, mostly in the catacombs of Rome and in the cemeteries of Venosa and Naples (Ascoli 1880; Galante 1911; Lacerenza 1999). These inscriptions were in Latin in the earlier period, but slowly Hebrew replaced Latin. Initially, this was only in single key words, such as שלום *šalom* (written also שאלום), then in short Hebrew phrases (e.g., משכבו של ביטה בן פיוסטנה נוחנפש נשמתולחי עולם *miškavo šel-Vita ben Fayustina noaḥ-nefeš nišmato-le-ḥay ʕolam* [The place of rest of Vita son of Faustina let his soul rest for Eternal life]), and finally in long, fully Hebrew inscriptions. Archive sources about this period are very rich and were collected and studied mostly by Cesare Colafemmina (Colafemmina 1990). Jewish literary sources and chronicles are also important for this earlier medieval period; the most important of these is *Megillat Ahima'az*, which describes the types of Jews in various cities of Southern Italy (Oria, Otranto, Capua).[16]

---

[16] See the recent edition with a comment, Bonfil 2009.

Sicily was also densely populated by Jewish communities up to the expulsion of 1493 (for their history see Simonsohn 2011). Later, the center of Jewish life shifted to Central Italy, to Umbria, Marche, and Toscana. After the establishment of the ghettoes, Jewish communities were restricted to cities in which there were ghettoes, such as Rome, Ancona, Mantua, Padua, Ferrara, Venice, and Torino. This period of Jewish history is very rich in archive documentation, collected, elaborated, and studied by generations of historians and philologists from the beginning of the Judenwissenschaft to our days. From our point of view, the creation of isolated ghetto communities is important, as it led to the formation of ghetto dialects.

Finally, the Unity of Italy (1865) led to the opening of the ghettoes. The Jewish communities partially dispersed into other centers, partially remained in the same cities, but were no longer confined to a special zone and isolated from the Christian population. The result, from a linguistic point of view, was the cessation of speaking in ghetto dialects, which were also perceived as the symbol of medieval darkness.

2.2 Attestations and sources: Elaboration

Phases in historical development (the ancient Salentinian Judeo-Italian dialect; earlier medieval Judeo-Italian, mostly Roman and Umbrian; medieval and Renaissance Judeo-Italian on the basis of the Central-Southern dialects; the late Judeo-Italian ghetto dialects, mostly Northern but also Roman and Tuscan):

The earliest sources of the Italian dialects spoken (more accurately, written) by Jews reach us from Southern Italy and Rome. Perhaps the most ancient are the marginal glosses in the Mishna, in Ms Parma 138, mentioned above (Cuomo 1977). These glosses, as Cuomo has shown, were written in the dialect of Central-Southern Salento (Cuomo 1977: 221). These are the phenomena that are concerned with realization of vowels (e.g., latin ē > i; latin ō > u; Cuomo 1977: 208–209), morphology (e.g., 3pl of the indicative with the suffix -ane: *puligane* '(they) clean' *separane* '(they) separate' etc.; Cuomo 1977: 218) and lexicon (e.g., Salentine forms *kòrnula* 'carob', *serrùla* 'little vase', *ânastùle* 'buttons').

From the ancient period and the central-southern zone, we have the elegy for the 9th of Av, mentioned above. This elegy appears in many anthologies of ancient Italian literature (e.g., Contini 1960: 37–42; Sampson 1980: 181–183). The beginning of Judeo-Italian literature may also be important for general Italian literature. The following is a quote from the beginning of the *Elegy* in the transliteration of Contini (Contini 1960: 35–36):

לָאיֶנְטִי דְּצִיוֹן פָּלְנְיֵי אֵילוּטָא / דִּיצֵי טָאוּפִּינָא מָלֵי סוֹ קוֹנְדּוּטָא / אַמָאנוּ דְּלוֹנֵימִיקוּ קֵי מָאוֹשְׁטְרוּטָא / לָא נוֹטִי אֶלָא דִיאֵי שְׁטָא פְּלוֹרַנְדוֹ / לִי סוֹאִי גְרַנְדֶיצִי רֵמֶימְרַאנְדוֹ / אֵימוֹ פִּילוֹמוּנְדוּ בָאוֹ גַאטִיבַאנְדוֹ

> la-ienti de-şiyon planji e-lutta / dice taupina male so condutta / a-manu dello-nemicu ke m-ao-štrutta / la notti e-la die šta plorando / li so-i grandezz-i remembr-ando / e-mo pel-lo-mundu vao gattivando
>
> [The people of Zion cry and mourn / saying: 'Miserable, I am badly led / in the hand of the enemy that has destroyed me' / night and day they are crying / remembering its greatness / and now wander the world in captivity]

Two stories are included in this elegy. One is about young captives who threw themselves in the sea so as not to be sold to brothels, and the other is about Rabbi Yišma'el ben 'Eliša's children, who recognized each other in slavery when their owners wanted to marry them to each other. They are found in tractate *Niddah* (57a-58b) in the Babylonian Talmud and in a parallel text in the *Midrash Ekha Rabbah*. They are among other stories about the destruction of the Second Temple and the successive expulsion and captivity. This text is very typical of Jewish Italianized culture. On one hand, the theme of the elegy, its rhythm, four stressed words in each line,[17] and the rhyme structure, e.g., the monorhyme tercets, are typical traits of the Hebrew elegies. On the other hand, there are multiple similarities to contemporary Marchigian poetry (Marches is the region in central Italian in which Italian literature began), such as *Ritmo di Sant'Alessio* or *Ritmo Laurenziano*. Additionally, the story about the brother and sister is somewhat similar to a medieval Italian novella. The language has many traits of the central-southern dialects, primarily of the ancient *Marchigiano* and ancient *Romanesco*.[18]

The Salentine glosses of the Mishna and the *Marchegiano-Romanesco* elegy are the first examples of written Judeo-Italian that represent the high level of the language (rabbinical glosses and excellent poetry, in the case of the elegy). The full history of the Italian dialects used by Jews may be divided into two main stages; they differ in (almost) all of their general and particular traits, purely linguistic and meta-linguistic. The first stage, called 'classical' or 'medieval' Judeo-Italian, is represented mostly by vulgarizations (translations) of the classical Hebrew

---

[17] One of the stresses may be secondary, in the polysyllabic word, or may fall on the proclitic.
[18] Examples: assimilation of the clusters -nd- (*bennerelli* 'venderli' 'to sell them' in the quoted fragment), but not constant (*venduta* 'sold' in the quoted fragment) and -nv- ('*mmediati* 'invidiati' 'envied, v. 15), but with hypercorrections (*afflambato* 'affiammato' 'burned', v. 30); the change of the sibilant to the affricate in the cluster -ns- (*pinzaro* 'thought' in the quoted fragment); the conservation of the clusters of the labial + l (*plo, planto* in the quoted fragment, but also *pianto* 'cry'); the 1sg.pres. of the verb 'avere' *aju* (in the quoted fragment), the future form *faraio* 'I'll do' (in the quoted fragment), the 3sg. pres. forms *ao* 'I go', *vao* 'I come', *fao* 'I do' (*passim*); the interchangeability of the final *i* and *e*: *porti* 'doors', *donni* 'women', *flambi* 'flame' / m. *figlie* 'sons', *isse* 'these m.' See Contini (1969: 35–42).

texts, such as the Bible and Talmudic and liturgical literature. The language of these texts is generally homogenous. It is central-southern, according to its characteristic traits (as we have seen in the case of the Elegy to the 9th of Av), and it may be defined as 'high' or 'written', which is not surprising, considering the content of these texts. In contrast, the late Judeo-Italian represents various ghetto dialects, heterogeneous and belonging to different zones, almost all Northern (as spoken in the Northern communities),[19] and defined as 'low', functioning as the spoken jargon.[20] This 'lowness' is expressed even in the self-nomination of the Livorno Jewish dialect, 'bagitto' (from *bajo* 'low').

Therefore, the first important question to ask is: What may the upper time limit of the medieval (classic) Judeo-Italian be; when did the use of the medieval Judeo-Italian of the texts end and that of the modern Judeo-Italian of the dialects spoken in the ghetto begin?

The answer differs from the answer to (partially) similar questions concerning two great Indo-European Jewish languages, Yiddish and Ladino. First, in the case of these languages, the great change occurred with the changing of the linguistic *milieu*: These became heteroglossic after the eastward migration, in the case of Yiddish, and with the expulsion from Spain in the case of Ladino, while Judeo-Italian remained in the same homoglottic Italian environment. Second, both Yiddish and Ladino remained written languages for Ashkenazic and Sephardic Jews respectively, while written Judeo-Italian ceased to exist in the modern period.

In the case of Judeo-Italian, the reasons for the changes and their characters must be sought, not in the transfer of the Jews to another country, but in the changes that occurred in Italy. The main factors for this change were of two different types: the establishment of the ghetto, on one hand, and the tuscanization of written Italian on the other.

The spoken ghetto dialects begin their existence with the establishment of the ghettoes in the middle of the 16th century (the first ghetto, in Rome, was created in 1555). This was also the time of the expulsion of Jews from Southern Italy, which began in 1493, almost simultaneously with the expulsion from Spain (Southern Italy was governed by Spanish royal families and was practically under Spanish rule). This is one of the reasons for the great difference between the southern character of medieval Judeo-Italian and the (light)northern character of late Judeo-Italian (in the latter, the northern traits are not very salient, and most of them are also found in common Italian). But the real reason for the cessation

---

19 With the evident exceptions of some communities, such as Rome, Florence, and Pitigliano.
20 Sometimes used expressly as the 'secret language', also by the (half)-criminal population.

of medieval Judeo-Italian being used in the translation of sacred texts seems to be the same one that caused the tuscanization of all written forms of language in Italy in the 16th century – the debates around the *questione della lingua*, which led to the unification and tuscanization of written Italian.

The first person who demonstrated and analyzed the differences between Judeo-Italian translations of the 15th and 16th centuries was Cassuto, with the example of translations of the Book of Amos (Cassuto 1930c: 19–38). Another example of the change is in the language of sermons.

Rabbinical sermons in Italy were printed in Hebrew. However, it is clear that they were delivered from the pulpit in some Italian dialect, and, up to the second half of the 16th century, they were delivered in Judeo-Italian. Some of these sermons are preserved in manuscripts (Ryzhik 2008b). A comparison of the sermons that were written in the first half of the century with the sermons written in the second half reveals clear differences in their language. It became much more tuscanized, according to the general trend in Italy in this epoch.

Let us examine a short fragment from one sermon of Rabbi Samuel ben Rafael Modena, from the year 1535[21]:

> *Per* **plu** *rascioni [...] lareppresenteziona mia in questo maqom qadoš è molto inquetaente e d'onne altre arrecorderemo sola questa una. Che* **essenno** *io minore ein safeq che non è lecito amme [...] avere una simila prosunziona innanzi una* **replubbeca** *[...] lacavesa che mi ha* **indotto** *aquesto è stato* **locomannamento** *de lo mio superiore* **onorandissimo patere**
>
> [For many reasons [...] my appearance in this *holy place*[22] is very exciting and from all other <reasons> let us mention only this one. That being a minor, *without doubt*, it is not permitted to me [...] to have similar presumption before a public [...] the reason that induced to it was the commandment of my superior honorable father]

We do not know precisely where this sermon was written, but it was undoubtedly written in Central or Northern Italy (Modena is the family name of the preacher, not his place of birth). Nevertheless, there are many traits that are characteristic of the old and/or Southern Italian dialects, which are also found in medieval Judeo-Italian. These include assimilation *nd>nn* (with the only exception in the scholarly Latinized form *onorandissimo* 'very honorable'); the form *onne* instead of *ogni* 'each'; the masculine articles *lo* and *li*; the epenthetic vowel in the word

---

[21] Ms. Guenzburg 1317, f. 184b. As in other examples in this article, the original writing is in Hebrew characters, and I use transliterations.
[22] Italicization indicates Hebrew words.

patere (instead of *padre* 'father'); the form *cavesa* (instead of *causa* 'case') and the scripture *plu* (instead of *più* 'more') with the conservation of the nexus *pl*.

There are multiple southern traits. For example, forms similar to *replubbeca* with metathesis, which we see here, are found in different places in the South: *plubbicu* [Calabria], the toponym *Piobbico<publicus* in the Marches (Rohlfs 1966: 323).

But in the sermons of R. Ya'aqov ben Mordecai Pogetto, written in 1579, the language is very different. All of the southern and ancient traits that appear in the sermon of Samuel Modena are eliminated. In addition, the period became much more complex, "baroque," and not simple and medieval. An example from his sermons will serve as an illustration[23]:

> *che se si allegra l'acricultor per i vaghi e belli fiori che li soi alberi e campagni fioriščono nella prima quanto maggiormente si esulta per i maturi frutti che da quelli raccoglia nella state certo che quanto è più degno al frutto delli fiori tanto più contento a per la produzione delle perot che per la germinazione delli peraxim*

> [as a peasant is happy for wonderful and beautiful flowers, that his trees and fields flower in the spingtime, but he exults much more over the mature fruits that he gathers in the summer, surely because, as the fruits are more honorable than the flowers, so is he more satisfied over the production of the *fruits* than for the germination of the *flowers*]

It is clear that there had been decisive changes in Judeo-Italian in the course of the 16th century, parallel to corresponding changes in common Italian.

Another example of changes in Judeo-Italian during the 16th century may be found in a comparison of translations of the Siddur.[24] There are several manuscripts of the 15th century (whose abbreviations below in this article are Q1, Q2, and Q3),[25] three identical printed editions from the 16th century (we will use the *editio princeps*, Fano 1505, whose abbreviation will be F),[26] and one manuscript from the 17th century (called S).[27] The translation in the S manuscript is very different from the others in many ways and at all linguistic levels. The language of the medieval translations (F and 15th century manuscripts) is Southern in many

---

[23] Ms. JTS 1588, f. 42b.
[24] About these translations see Cassuto 1930b; Ryzhik 2007; idem 2013a and the bibliography there.
[25] Ms. Parma de' Rossi ital. 7, written in 1484 (according to the collophone) in Florence or in its nearest neighborhood. Its abbreviation in this article is Q1; Ms. London 625 [Or. 2443], written in 1483 in Montalboddo [Ostra] (according to the collophone), with the abbreviation Q2; Ms. JTS Mic. 4076, written in the 15th century in the same zone (Tuscany-Umbria), there is no collophone. Its abbreviation in this article is Q3.
[26] We will use *editio princeps* Fano 1506, its abbreviation is F. In the scientific literature it is called Rite of Fano (*rito di Fano*).
[27] Ms. London Or. 10517, written in Northern Italy. Its abbreviation in this article is S.

of its phonological features, while in S, modern and Northern, Northern traits (or the absence of Southern ones) are documented, e.g.:

1) absence of gemination;
2) intervocal sonorization (סְטִיפִּידִי = *stipidi* instead of *stipiti* 'doorposts') (Rohlfs 1966, 201);
3) elimination of the final vowel, e.g., רַאיּוֹנַאר קְוֵוילִי [...] סֵידֵיר טוּאוֹ = *rajjonar queli [...] seder tuo* (instead of *sedere* 'to sit', *ragionare* 'to discuss'), נֵיל [...] נֵיל קַאמִינַאר טוּאוֹ יַיאצֵיר טוּאוֹ אֵי נֵיל רִיצַאר טוּאוֹ = *nel caminar tuo [...] nel jacer tuo e nel rizar tuo* (instead of *camminare* 'to walk', *rizzare* 'to come up', *giacere* 'to lie down')[28];
4) absence of assimilation *nd > nn* (Rohlfs 1966: 253), which is obligatory in F and 15th century manuscripts, e.g.: קוֹמַאנְדוֹ = *comando* 'command' in S vs. קוֹמַנּוֹ *comanno* in Q3; פֵּינְדַאלְיִי = *pendalji* (translation of ציצית *ṣiṣit* 'tassel') in S vs. פֵּינַּלְיִי = *pennalji* in Q3.

Distinctions are also clear on other linguistic levels. The use of the *passato remoto* tense stands out among morphosyntactic traits in F and 15th century manuscripts vs. the use of *passato prossimo* in S,[29] e.g., in Numbers 15:41 (in *Shema' Israel*):

The Hebrew text: אני ה' אלהיכם אשר הוצאתי אתכם מארץ מצרים ʔ*ani H' ʔElohekem ʔašer hoṣeti ʔetkem me-ʔEreṣ Miṣrayim* [I am God your Lord that has taken you from the Land of Egypt]
Q1: איאו דומֵדֵת לו דֵית בוֹשְטְרוֹ קֵי טְרָאסִי בּוֹאִי דֵלְטֵירָה דֵי מִצְרַיִם
io Domedet lo Det *vo*štro che **trassi** voi della-terra de *Miṣraim*
Q2: איאו דומֵדִיד דֵיד בּוֹשְטְרֵין קִי טְרָאסֵי בּוֹאִי דַלְטִירָה דְמְצְרָיִם
io Domeded Ded *vo*štro che **trasse** *vo*e dalla-terra de-*Misraim*
Q3: איאו סוֹ דוֹמֵדֵת דֵית וֹשְטְרוֹ קֵיטְרָאסֵי ווֹאי דַלְטִירָה דְמְצְרָיִם
io so Domeded Det uoštro che-trasse uoi dalla-terra de-*Misraim*
S: איאו איל סִינְיוֹר אִידְיאוֹ וֹסְטְרוֹ קְוַואל אוֹ קַאוַואטוֹ ווֹאי דַה לַה טֵירָה דֵי מְצְרָיִם
io il Sinjor Idio uostro qual **o cauato**[30] uoi da la tera de *Misraim*

There is a clear line of development that can be called historic-geographic from medieval Judeo-Italian, rich in ancient (and /or) southern traits, to post-medieval Judeo-Italian, Tuscanized and rich in the northern traits.[31]

---

[28] The language of S is very Tuscanized and normalized. So the dialectal Northern traits are very attenuated, and, for example, the elimination of the final vowel is used almost only after the /r/. But as is seen, in all cited cases this elimination is documented before the consonant, the position that usually protects the final vowel. It also seems to be significant that this elimination is almost obligatory in S.

[29] *Passato prossimo* is characteristic of the northern, *passato remoto* of the southern dialects; see Rohlfs 1966: 672, 673.

[30] In this case the lexemes (*trarre / cavare*) are also different.

[31] Additional examples will appear later, in the discussion of isoglosses and structural features.

It must be underlined that all of these texts, comprising those from the 17th century, Tuscanized and lightly northern, are written in Hebrew characters. But just a little later, from the end of the 18th century onwards, characters became (almost) exclusively Latin, and Judeo-Italian written in Hebrew characters ceased to exist.

The ultimate phase of the development of Judeo-Italian, that of the ghetto dialects, seems to be neatly separated from what preceded it. The ghetto dialects are mostly Northern and more similar to local non-Jewish dialects than to each other. But there are three trends in the late ghetto dialects that must be underlined.

First, like most Jewish languages, these dialects are somewhat archaic in contrast to their gentile counterparts. Second, they are also somewhat more southern. This is not surprising if we consider the general direction of migration of Jewish communities during the centuries of their story in Italy. Third, there are some (mostly lexical) remnants of medieval Judeo-Italian that are preserved in these dialects.

Let us examine some examples of the first two trends. The most archaic of the Jewish dialects appears at the very beginning of the closure of the ghettoes. Mancini (1992) has demonstrated that the language of the Roman ghetto in the Renaissance and Baroque period was based on the Roman dialect of the "first stage," e.g., on the medieval Roman dialect, and not on the Roman dialect of the "second stage," which was formed in the 16th century, mostly under the massive influence of the Florentine traits. C. Del Monte (1935) has shown that the ghetto dialect of the first half of the 20th century also had great affinity with the old Roman dialect. Finally, even in the street scenes written by M. Calò in the 'postwar ghetto dialect of Rome' (Calò 1990), there are clear remnants of the ancient phases, e.g., *ajo* 1sg. ind. pres. of the verb *avere* [to have] (instead of the normative *ho*), the form which belongs to the first stage of the Roman dialect, or *fio* [son] (instead of the normative *figlio*), characteristic of the second stage.

Another example of the presence of archaic and southern traits may be the Judeo-Mantuan described by Vittore Colorni (1970). In the field of phonology, Judeo-Mantuan lacks the vowels *ü* and *ö*, typical for the Lombard dialects[32] and usual in the Mantuan non-Jewish dialect; so *cor* 'heart' and not *cör* (as in the Mantuan non-Jewish dialect), *fiol* 'son' and not *fiöl*, *mur* 'wall' and not *mür*, *du* 'two' and not *dü* (Colorni 1970: 115). The epenthetic vowel is not *a*, as in the non-Jewish Mantuan (*pádar* 'father', *mádar* 'mother', *líbar* 'book', *áltar* 'other'), but *e* (*páder, máder, líber, álter*; Colorni 1970: 115), coinciding, fortuitously or not, with the epenthetic vowel typical for medieval Judeo-Italian (see Cuomo 1988: 41). In the field of morphology, e.g., Judeo-Mantuan lacks the pleonastic repetition of the

---

[32] As a result of the gallic substrate.

atonic pronoun in verb conjugation, which is obligatory in non-Jewish Mantuan, as is usual in the Northern dialects. In Judeo-Mantuan we see *mi son* 'I am' and not *mi a son*, as in non-Jewish Mantuan; *ti sit* 'you are' and not *ti at sè*; *lu è* 'he is' and not *lü l'è* (Colorni 1970: 122). Judeo-Mantuan is more southern in its traits than its Christian counterpart.

There are additional affinities with medieval Judeo-Italian in other Jewish dialects. So, in the prayer that the Jewish children in Pitigliano say (that is, said seventy years ago) at the end of the Sabbath, there were feminine nouns in singular with the suffix *-ezze*: "Bona sera, bona stimana, bon'anno, sanità, pace, bene e berahà, vita lunga e *allegrezze e contentezze* a noi e a tutti ki bbène ce vò" (Terracini 1951) [Good evening, good week, good year, health, peace, well-being, and *berakha* (blessing), long life and *happiness* and *satisfaction* to us and to all that want well-being for us]. The suffix *-ezze* for the singular noun (not plural!), which has its origin in the Latin -ITIES, is found in ancient Italian and in the Southern dialects (Rohlfs 1966: 355). It is also found in the Rite of Fano, e.g., *fortezze mia* 'my force' (c.5r), *lagrannezze toa* 'your greatness' (c.18v). Also the word *allegrezze* 'happiness' itself is documented in the Rite of Fan: *lallegrezze vostra* 'your happiness' (c.114v).[33]

Finally, there is one ghetto dialect, Judeo-Ferrarese, which has preserved multiple traits of medieval Judeo-Italian, so that it can be considered a real remnant of it (or as some sort of a missing link between the medieval and ghetto dialects).[34] This preservation is especially meaningful because Judeo-Ferrarese has preserved ancient and / or southern traits in the northern linguistic *milieu*. The traits in question are found on all levels of linguistic analysis. Here are some examples:

Phonological traits: (1) /j/ instead of /dž/ at the beginning of the word: *jornèta* 'day' (= giornata), buta *jò* la menèstra 'poured out (down) the soup' (= giù), *yènte* 'people' (= gente), un *yudío* 'Jew' (= giudeo); (2) the absence of intervocalic sonorization: *voluto* 'wanted', è *ito* 'has gone', *vinuto* 'came', *marito* 'husband', lo *fóko* 'the fire', *jokèr* 'to play' (= giocare); (3) the assimilation nd > nn [35]: s'è *rakomanèta* 'recommended' (= raccomandata), *grani* 'great pl.' (grandi), *grana* 'great f.' (= granda), *mána* 'sends' (= manda), *véner* 'to sell' (= vender), *kanèla* 'candle' (= candela), *responévo* '(I) answered' (= rispondevo).

Morphological traits: (1) personal pronouns (3rd person) *esso, essa, essi*, instead of the Northern *lo (lu), la, li*, and similar; (2) pres. indic. 2sg of the verb *essere* 'to be' is (sometimes) *si* as in the South, and not *sei* as in the North and in

---

[33] Ryzhik 2007: 11. Other cases of affinity between the Hebrew component of the ghetto dialects and medieval Judeo-Italian will be cited below, in the discussion of the Hebrew elements in Judeo-Italian.
[34] For a detailed description, see Ryzhik 2014b.
[35] Naturally, in the North the double consonant is simplified, so *nn* > *n*.

Standard Italian; (3) the pres. indic. 1sg of the verb *sapere* 'to know' is based on the southern form *saccio*: *sac*, instead of the regular *so*; (4) the pres. indic. 1sg. of the verb *avere* 'to have' is the southern *ay* (*ayo*), instead of *ho*; (5) accordingly (as the two forms are connected to each other), the suffix of the 1sg. fut. is the southern *-ai* (from *-ayo*): *dirai* 'I shall say', *anderai* 'I shall go', *sentirái* 'I shall hear', instead of *-o*.

Lexical: there are some salient southern lexemes in Judeo-Ferrarese, e.g., *paravola* 'word', *cre* 'tomorrow' (Ryzhik 2014b).

A very important word, characteristic of Judeo-Ferrarese, is the verb *nescere / innescere* in the sense of "to teach": "*kuscí favelerem dè quel ke tu sè. Una hamortá ke inèscia a un profesor*" [So I shall tell you who you are. A *hamorta* [she-ass] that teaches a professor]. This verb is not documented in any other ghetto dialect. But it is one of the most characteristic verbs in medieval Judeo-Italiano (Cuomo 1976: 49). For example, in the Rite of Fano: "*e per la lejje toa che nescesti noi*" [and for your *Torah* that you have taught to us] (179v); "*tu cordolji allomo sapere nesce allomo intelletto*" [you give the man knowledge and teach the man intelligence] (78r); or in the 16th century sermons: "*la Tora ennesce a lo ben adam*" (Ryzhik 2008b: 539) [the *Torah* teaches the *man*]. In the non-Jewish sources, this verb is extremely rare and is documented only in 13th century texts written in an ancient Roman dialect (where it is also very rare). For example, in the *Storie de Troia e de Roma*, 1252/1258: "*Et a li cavaleri novilemente nescea cavallaria; De Adriano imperatore. [...] Questo fece granne spesa ad nescere lectera greca*" (Ryzhik 2008a:168) [and he nobly taught the knights the principles of knighthood; about the emperor Hadrian [...] he invested much to teach the Greek letters].

In the latest phase of its development, in the late ghetto period, most ghetto Judeo-Italian dialects were very similar to their local Christian counterparts, but they preserved more southern and more ancient traits, showing the possible (genetic?) connection with older Judeo-Italian. At least one dialect, the Judeo-Ferrarese, had multiple traits demonstrating its genetic relation to medieval Judeo-Italian.

2.3 Sociolinguistic description, community bilingualism, public functions

Judeo-Italian served various social uses during its long history, from the quasi-liturgical purpose of the medieval translations to the secret language and taboo uses in the ghetto period.

It is difficult to decide what the precise purpose of the Bible medieval translations was, apart from evidently being a useful tool with which to understand the text. But the Siddur translations seemed to be intended for women, at least those in which the first page, with the morning benedictions, is preserved (Q3 and S; for the abbreviations see above and see the bibliography at the end of the article), which contain the versions characteristic to women.

For instance, the benediction שעשני לרצונו *še-ʕaśani li-rṣono* [that has made me according to his will] (instead of שלא עשני אשה *še-lo ʕaśani ʔišša* [that has not made me a woman], which is the "male version" of this benediction) is translated in this way in these two manuscripts:

> Q3: **בֶּנֶדֵיטוֹ טוּ דּוֹמֶדַת דֵית נוֹשְׁטְרוֹ רֵי דֵלוֹ** עוֹלָם קֵי פֵיצֵי מֵי קוֹמֵי לַבוֹלֵינְטָה סוֹאָה
> benede*tt*o tu Domedet Det noštro re de*ll*o ʻolam che fece me come la-volonta soa
> [blessed are You our God Almighty, King of the world, that has made me according to his wish]
> S: **לָאוֹדָאטוֹ טוּ סִינְיוֹר אִידְיאוֹ נוֹסְטְרוֹ רֵי דֵיל מוֹנְדוֹ קְוָואל מִי קְרֵיאוֹ קוֹנְפוֹרְמֵי אַלָה וֹלוֹנְטָה סוּאָה**
> laodato tu Sinjor Idio nostro re del mondo qual mi creo con*f*orme ala uolonta sua
> [praised are You, our God Almighty, King of the world, that has created me according to his wish]

Similarly in the benediction "that has not made me a slave":

> Q3: **בֶּנֶדֵיטוֹ טוּ דּוֹמֶדַת דֵית נוֹשְׁטְרוֹ רֵי דֵלוֹ** עוֹלָם קֵי נוֹן פֵיצֵי מִי שְׁפְחָה
> benede*tt*o tu Domedet Det noštro re de*ll*o ʻolam che non fece me *šifha*
> [blessed are You, our God Almighty, King of the world, that has not made me *shifha* (slave fem.)]
> S: **לָאוֹדָאטוֹ טוּ סִינְיוֹר אִידְיאוֹ נוֹסְטְרוֹ רֵי דֵיל מוֹנְדוֹ קֵי נוֹן מִי פֵיצֵי סְקִיאַוּוה**
> laodato tu Sinjor Idio nostro re del mondo che non mi fece schiaua
> [praised are You, our God Almighty, King of the world, that has not made me slave (fem.)]

So also in the benediction "that has not made me a *goy* [= non-Jew]," with the characteristic (sociolinguistic) change of the version in the 17th century manuscript:

> Q3: **בֶּנֶדֵיטוֹ טוּ דּוֹמֶדַת דֵית נוֹשְׁטְרוֹ רֵי דֵלוֹ** עוֹלָם קֵי נוֹן פֵיצֵי מֵי גוּיָה
> benede*tt*o tu Domedet Det noštro re de*ll*o ʻolam che non fece me *guya*
> [blessed are You, our God Almighty, King of the world, that has not made me gentile (fem.)]
> S: **לָאוֹדָאטוֹ טוּ סִינְיוֹר אִידְיאוֹ נוֹסְטְרוֹ רֵי דֵיל מוֹנְדוֹ קְוָואל קְרֵיאוֹ מִי יְהוּדִית**
> laodato tu Sinjor Idio nostro re del mondo qual creo mi *yehudit*
> [praised are You, our God Almighty, King of the world, that has created me *yehudit* (Jew fem.)]

The "female" target audience of the translations explains the absence of Mishnaic texts from the 15th century manuscripts, because it was forbidden for women to study Talmud or its parts. In the 16th century print (the Rite of Fano) and in the 17th century manuscript this rule is no longer valid, at least in its strict form, and there are translations of the ritually read Mishnah chapters (*Shabbat* 2; *Zebahim* 5).

The translations seem meant for use during the synagogue service. The clear proof of that can be seen in the instruction notes. These notes are very precise; for example, in Q3, after the *Shemonaʻ ʻesre*, before the *Tahanun*, p. 13a:

אֵילוֹ לוּנְדִי אֵילוֹ יוֹבֶדִי סֶידִיצֵי וְעַתָּה אֵילַלְטְרִי דִי סֵיקוֹמִינְצָה אַשְׁרֵי אֵי פּוֹאִי סֵידִיצֵי וּבָא לְצִיוֹן
e-lo lundi e-lo jovedi se-dice *we-'atta* e-l-altri di se-comincia *'ašre* e poi se-dice *u-va le-Ṣijon*
[on Monday and Thursday *we-'atta* is said and on other days begin with *'ašre* and then *u-va le-Ṣijon* is said]

Many of the notes describe the full service in the synagogue, not only the "female" part. For example, in F, describing the reading of the Torah on Saturday, p. 71b:

קְוָוה קְיָימָה לוֹ כּוֹהֵן אֵי לֵיִי אַסֶפֶּר אֵי דִיצֵי לָה תְהִילָה אֵי רֵיפּוֹנֵי לוֹ סֶפֶר אֵי דִיצֵי לוֹ מוּסַף
qua chiama lo *kohen* e lejje a-*sefer* e dice la *tehilla* e repone lo *sefer* e dice lo *musaf*
[here he calls the *kohen* and reads in-*sefer* and says *tehilla* and returns the *sefer* and says *musaf*]

Another sign of the synagogue destination of the translation is the presence of passages that can be read only in a *minyan*. So, in S (in which the morning benedictions have only the "female" form), the *Shemona' 'esre* includes *Modim de-rabanan* (pp. 41ab) and *Qeduša* (pp. 35b-36a).

As mentioned above, during the 16th and 17th centuries Judeo-Italian was ousted from the liturgical sphere. Let us see a little example of this process (for the details see Ryzhik 2010).

Each medieval manuscript of the Makhzor (the annual Hebrew prayerbook) of the Italian rite contains three short prayers in Judeo-Italian[36]: *Seder hattarat qelalot* [Order of the annulment of curses], *Mi še-berak* [He that blessed], *Hazkarat nešamot* [Commemoration of the souls (of the passed)]. The three prayers, located after the Passover liturgy, are composed in a mixture of Judeo-Italian and Hebrew. The fixed liturgical formulas common to all rites are written in Hebrew, while expressions that are found only in the Italian rite are in Judeo-Italian. The texts of these prayers are (almost) identical in all manuscripts.

In order to follow the withdrawal of Judeo-Italian, it is important to see what happens in the printed editions in the 16th century. In the first printed editions of the Siddur according to the Italian rite, Soncino 1486 and Fano 1506, these texts are written in Judeo-Italian, as in the medieval manuscripts. But in the Rimini edition of 1521, the Hebrew translation is printed next to the usual Judeo-Italian text. This is also the case in the famous Bologna Makhzor, 1540. While in the next edition of the Siddur, Mantua 1560, only the Hebrew translation is printed, and the same is true in all of the subsequent editions (Venice 1587, 1606, 1626, and so on), up to our days (in the modern Italian translations of the Siddur, this text is simply translated backwards from the Hebrew to the standard Italian, e.g., it is not printed in its original Judeo-Italian form).

---

36 Scazzocchio 1988. Scazzocchio described these prayers in Ms Casatenense 71(2881), but they are found in all medieval manuscripts of the Mahzor.

At least in this case, the development is exactly parallel to the processes in the Christian Italian world, dictated by the grammarians of the beginning of the century and by decisions of the Council of Trent. It must be noted that the period from 1540 to 1560 is the period in which decisive changes occurred in the post-biblical Hebrew tradition, as it is represented in printed editions of the Siddur (the same editions that are quoted above) (Ryzhik 2012). This coincidence may not be accidental.

Judeo-Italian in the synagogue service was replaced by Hebrew.[37] The replacement of Judeo-Italian by Italian during the same 16th century was mentioned above, in the example of written sermons.

This refusal to use Judeo-Italian for literature and liturgical purposes coincided with the closure of the ghettoes and the rise of the ghetto dialects. Of course, these dialects may also have existed before 1555, the official date of the confinement of the Jews to ghettoes. But there are two reasons that compel us to speak about the ghetto period when we discuss these dialects. The first is a technical reason: Medieval documentation is limited to the written texts. The second reason is a socio-linguistic one: After the closure of the ghettoes, the Jews were much more confined to specific geographical places and much more isolated from the surrounding non-Jewish population – two factors that are propitious to forming dialects. Ghetto dialects represented the low level of sociolects. In real life, it was a spoken language, like all other Italian dialects; in literature, reproductions of it were used mostly for comic effect. The Second World War put an end to the living use of these dialects. Nostalgia and the halo of antiquity have gradually changed its status from a low jargon to an elitist symbol of unity among Roman Jews. This does not mean that anybody speaks it or knows it; it means that some expressions are used as a sign of belonging to a group. Nowadays it is more spoken about than used in the above mentioned social networks.

3 Structural information

3.1 Relationship to non-Jewish varieties (isoglosses, related dialects)

Judeo-Italian dialects are not distinguished from other Italian dialects by clear morphologic or syntactic traits that are unique to Judeo-Italian. We have seen

---

[37] With very few exceptions; one example: in the Siddur (entirely in Hebrew) that was printed in Venice in 1710, Tractate Avot appears in Italian written in Hebrew characters.

above that Judeo-Italian is almost always somewhat more southern and somewhat more ancient than its Christian counterparts; but all the traits that are found in Judeo-Italian can be found in some other Italian dialects, albeit sometimes chronologically or geographically remote from the immediate surroundings.

The peculiarity of medieval Judeo-Italian vs. other Italian dialects finds its expression in the common lexicon (of both Hebrew and Romance elements) that is sometimes restricted to the Jewish Italian dialects. For instance, the verb יְפַתֶּה *yifte* 'seduce' in the biblical verse Deuteronomy 11:16 in the *Shema' Israel* is translated with the verb "semonire" (in the appropriate form "semonisca") in all translations, including the late one, S.

In the Christian translations, other words are used in this verse[38]: Vulgata: decipiatur; Bibbia Volgare: ingannato; Diodati: sedotto; Brucioli: disuiato. The verb "semonire" is found only in the Judeo-Italian sources, such as Yudah Romano's glosses, published by Debenedetti Stow, and in *Maqre Dardeqe*, a Hebrew-(Judeo-)Italian-Arabic vocabulary published in Naples, 1488 (Debenedetti Stow 1990: 246; Maqre Dardeqe, Napoli 1488. In both, the root פתה *PTH* [seduce] is translated with the word סימונימנטו = simonimento, and our verse (Deut. 11:16) is cited as a Biblical example.

In spite of its evident Christian origin (from "simonia" 'simony', the trade in sacred tasks, from the name of Simon the Magus from the Acts of Apostols), the verb "semonire," in the general sense of seduction, is completely absent from the Christian sources and present only in the Jewish ones. It may be this total absence from Christian sources that is the reason for keeping this verb, with such clear Christian etymology, in Judeo-Italian. From the example of this verb, we can perceive the existence of a common tradition underlying the Judeo-Italian translations, from ancient to more recent ones.

Sometimes a specific Judeo-Italian word is also found in some Christian source, but in an isolated and rare appearance. That is the case with the word גואל *go?el* 'redeemer', which is traditionally translated as "sconperatore" or a similar term, such as in the first benediction of the *Shemona' 'esre*. That is the word used in all of the Jewish translations, including the 17th century's S.

The verb form of this word, *scomparare* 'to redeem', is very common in Judeo-Italian, and the form סקונפיראו = *sconperao* is also found in the *Maqre Dardeqe* as a translation of the root גאל *G?L* 'redeem' (Cuomo 1985: 111). The word is

---

38 Christian translations used for comparison with the Jewish-Italian ones are the Vulgata Clementina, the Bibbia Volgare, originally published by N. Jenson in Venice, 1471, and the translations of Brucioli [Bruccioli, Antonio,1562. Bibbia (trad.), Ginevra, F. Durone] and Diodati [Diodati, Giovanni, 1607. *La Bibbia, cioè, I libri del Vecchio e del Nuouo Testamento nuouamente traslatati in lingua Italiana da Giovanni Diodati, di nation Lucchese*, Ginevra, Jean de Tournes].

documented at the end of the 16th century in the elegy in Judeo-Italian published by Roth (Roth 1950: 155). But in the Christian sources, this word is found only in one Venetian document written in 1371.[39] In this case, the tradition is established very well in Judeo-Italian and is very rare in the Christian world.

Another important example may be the Judeo-Italian verb *nescere* 'to teach', which was preserved through the centuries by its existence in the ghetto dialect of Ferrara, see above.

3.2 Particular structural features (unique to the Jewish variety)

Generally speaking, there are no specific structural features that are unique to the Jewish variety (varieties) of Italian (Cuomo 1976, 1988; Aprile 2012: 8–9). What is unique is the combination of isoglosses, which seems to be the result of koineization, and which may have had three stages. One, the ancient stage, is more Southern and has its expression in the translation of the *Hosh'anot* (Ryzhik 2014a); the second is in translations into the classic medieval Judeo-Italian of the 15th and early 16th centuries and is Central-Southern (Cuomo 1976; see also Ryzhik 2013a); the third is the Central-Northern *koiné* of the late 16th–17th centuries (Mayer-Modena 1997: 953), which ought to be investigated on the basis of the later translations and texts.

One innovative morphological trait that may be considered is the use of the Hebrew abstract nominal suffix *-ut* (Aprile 2012: 34; see the bibliography there) with a Romance lexical base. This suffix is also vital with the Hebrew component of Judeo-Italian, such as the Judeo-Modenese *mahalut* 'illness' < מחלה *maḥala* 'illness' and the Judeo-Ferrarese *gnofud* 'vanity' < עוֹף *ſof* 'bird'. There are also interesting cases of the addition of this suffix to the Romance base: Judeo-Roman *cancherigiùdde* 'object, mean thing' < Italian *canchero* 'cancer', Judeo-Piemont *scürchnüd* < Piem. *scür* 'dark'.

3.3 Hebrew and Aramaic elements

The Hebrew / Aramaic component is an important part of Judeo-Italian, as it is in other Jewish languages. Most works that deal with Judeo-Italian focus (almost)

---

39 In Johann de Bona, *Lettera "autentica" del rettore di Ragusa Johann de Bona a dei giudici e consiglieri della città, al console dei Veneziani a Salonicco, a Lucha Pençin veneziano* (Monumenta Ragusina. Libri Reformationum, t. IV, ed. by J. Gelcic, MSHSM, XXVIII, 1896, pp. 129–30).

exclusively on this component.⁴⁰ Even the excellent recent (2012) book by Marcello Aprile, "*Grammatica storica delle parlate giudeo-italiane*," in spite of its title [Historical grammar of the Judeo-Italian dialects], concentrates exclusively on the Hebrew (and Aramaic) components⁴¹ of the lexicon.⁴² According to Aprile (Aprile 2012: 37), who has compiled the fullest description of all possible sources, ghetto Judeo-Italian used 189 nouns, 17 adjectives, 35 verbs, and a dozen other words (pronouns, numerals etc.) with Hebrew origins. What follows are some aspects of the Semitic component.⁴³

Generally speaking, there are several principal features that characterize the Hebrew words that enter the Judeo-Italian ghetto dialects. First, as in other Jewish languages, a word that is cited in the synagogue during the service, or in the *Haggada* of Pesah, has more chance to enter the lexicon of Judeo-Italian. Second, these words often (not always) tend to be used in the expressive (mostly comic⁴⁴) or taboo⁴⁵ sense, or as a secret language. A good example of these two tendencies is the word *scefoc* (from the Hebrew שְׁפוֹךְ *šefok* 'pour') from the end of the *Haggada* (שפוך חמתך *šefok ḥamatka* [pour out your anger]), that is used in the sense of "to vomit" (because at this stage of the Passover Seder the participants may be drunk).

Let us examine some examples from the five principal categories: the semantic field of Jewish religious observance, the expressive or comic, the taboo, the secret languages and "general" (common everyday) use (may initially belong to the first four categories). Citations are from an excellent collection of the Judeo-Italian of Rome, compiled by Milano, 1932.⁴⁶

(1) Religious field (usually words that have no non-Jewish parallel in Italian): *farsi aggomèlle* [to recite the prayer of thankfulness for an escape from danger] (< *ha-gomel* 'benefactor'); *Aronne Accodesh* 'the Holy Ark' (< ארון הקדש ʔ*aron ha-qodeš* the same); *cuppa* 'wedding' (< חֻפָּה *ḥuppa* the same).

---

40 Beginning from the pionering studies by Cammeo 1909–1911.
41 And some other words from non-Italian dialects, mostly German and Iberian.
42 The illustrious exceptions are the works of Luisa Cuomo, especially Cuomo 1988, in which she has done a detailed and very important analysis of the grammar of medieval Judeo-Italian.
43 For detailed studies of the Hebrew component, see many of the articles and books cited in this article, especially those by Maria Modena-Mayer and Aprile 2012, as well as my review of Aprile 2012 (Ryzhik 2016).
44 See, for example, Mayer-Modena 1990; idem 2001.
45 See Mayer-Modena 1999 and Aprile 2012. See Mayer-Modena 1978 specifically about the taboo.
46 The guttural ע (ʕ*ayin*) was pronounced in ghetto Judeo-Italian as a nasal sound, which found different expression in the orthography of collectors of the Hebrew component in different dialects.

(2) Comic or expressive use: *faccia di Aggada* 'typical Jewish face' (< 'a face of the Haggada'); *bangkavanodde!* [expressive exclamation as a negative reaction] (< בעוונות *ba-ʕawanot* 'because of sins'); *sciofaroddi* 'horned (betrayed husband)' (< שופרות *šofarot* 'ram's horn, shofar' pl.).

(3) Taboo use and euphemisms: *aveludde* 'mourning' (< אבל *ʔavel* the same); *beridde* 'penis' (< ברית מילה *berit mila* 'circumcision')[47]; *cholaimmi* 'illnesses' (< חלאים *ḥolaʔim* the same + Italian plural suffix); *macomme* 'toilet' (< מקום *maqom* 'place').

(4) Secret language: *bechave bechave* 'secretly' (< בהחבא *be-heḥave* 'secretly'), *Befiorre* 'Pope' (< אפיפיור *ʔepifyor* the same) (also: *peferimmi* 'paoli', the Roman coins); *Carovve* 'Jesus' (< קרוב *qarov* 'close, relative'); *cumarre* 'priest' (< כֹּמֶר *komer* the same); *gallach* 'priest' (< גלח *gallaḥ* 'person with cut hair'); *gannav* 'thief', *gannaviare* 'to steal' (< גנב *gannav* the same); *jorbedimmi* 'policemen' (from the two Hebrew letters *yod* and *bet*, with the numeric value 12, which was the number with the significance "policemen" in some 19th century lottery); *ngkarelle* 'Christian' (< ערל *ʕarel* 'uncircumsized'); *ngkesavve* 'Christians' (< עשו, *ʕEsaw* 'Esau'); *rura* 'cursed f.' (< ארורה *ʔarura* the same).

(5) Common everyday life: *achlare* 'to eat' (< אכל *ʔakal* 'to eat' + Italian verb suffix); *bangkal* 'husband, owner' (< בעל *baʕal* the same) with derivation *bangkalessa* 'wife, female owner' (< Italian feminine suffix *-essa*); *benzachar* 'male' (< בן זכר *ben zakar* 'male'); *dabberrare* 'to speak, to talk' (< דבר *dibber* the same + Italian verb suffix); *iscia* 'women, wife' (< אשה *ʔišša* the same).

There are many cases in which the Hebrew component of Judeo-Italian preserves authentic forms of post-biblical (Mishnaic) words which were "corrected" (in reality corrupted) in the printed editions of the Mishnah, e.g., *chavora* 'society' (Milano 1932: 241), from חֲבוֹרָה *ḥavora*, corrupted to חֲבוּרָה *ḥavura* in the printed editions.

In some cases, different post-biblical traditions of a specific word were fossilized in different Judeo-Italian dialects. In this way the word חנק has two different forms in Judeo-Italian (Aprile 2012: 61, and see the bibliography there). The Judeo-Piemont form is *hanèc*, Judeo-Torinese is *khanèc*, Judeo-Mantovan *chanèk*; in Livorno: *héneq*; in Venice two types coexist: *hénec*, *hanèc*. In discussing these forms we must take into account the fact that the form *ḥèneq* is a late one. In MSS Kaufmann and Paris of the Mishna (which also represent the ancient Italian tradition), the form is חָנֶק *ḥaneq*, as it is in Palestinian and Babylonian vocalization (Eldar 1979: 94), as well as in the medieval *Makhzorim* of the Italian rite (Ryzhik 2008: 352–353). Only much later does the form חֶנֶק *ḥeneq* appear, which seems to be derived from Spain at the time of the expulsion. Perhaps it is here that we see a true example of the Sephardic influence on Judeo-Italian.[48] We expect the Sephardic tradition to influence Livorno and to penetrate into Venice, both historically and geographically.

---

[47] It is also used in the 'normal' use of circumcision.
[48] But in the earlier medieval tradition in Sepharad, it is also חָנֶק *ḥaneq*; see Dodi 2002: 33.

Very important to the study of the history of Judeo-Italian are words and expressions that unite medieval Judeo-Italian and the ghetto dialects. This concerns not only obvious verbs such as *darshare* 'to preach' (< דרש *deraš* 'sermon'), but also rarer constructions such as *ta'anare* 'to quarrel' (from the Hebrew טַעֲנָה *taʕana* 'argument, claim'). In the Rite of Fano, the phrase כתלמיד חולק על רבו *ke-talmid ḥoleq ʕal rabbo* [as a pupil that **disagrees** with his teacher] (c. 137a, part of the *Rosh HaShana* service) is translated קוֹמֵי לוֹ תַלְמִיד קִי טַעֲנָה קוֹלוֹ רוֹבִּי סוּאוֹ (*come lo talmid che ta'ana collo robbi suo*). The Hebrew word קלוח *ḥoleq* 'disagrees' is translated by the Hebrew-based hybrid verb *ta'anare*. If one Hebrew word is translated by another (adapted to the Italian morphology), that means that the second one must be very present in the vernacular of the Jews. And, in fact, we find this verb several centuries later in the dialect of the ghetto of Moncalvo in a comic poem, in the expression "*L'ha tanhanà coul Penacas*" (Colombo 1970: 440) [he quarreled with Pincas], with the same slight change of the meaning ('quarrel, dispute') and the same preposition, *con* as in the Rite of Fano. The change of genre of the literature, in the historic period and in the geographic position, do not prevent the analogous use of the Hebrew component.

There are many other important traits and trends in the use of the Hebrew component, especially those connected to the use of the comic genres, as a secret language, and for *taboo* purposes; but the connection between old and new Judeo-Italian seems very important to stress.

3.4 Language contact influences

The entire history of Judeo-Italian is the history of inter-dialectal influences, as was shown above. An important part of these inter-dialectal contacts is the forming of the *koiné* (Cuomo 1976; Sermoneta 1976). The contacts with other languages were not very strong, because the Italian Jews lived in a homoglossic surrounding (with the exception of the Apulian community in Corfù, in whose language there are some signs of a neo-Greek influence, as, for example, in the absence of the infinitive; see Ryzhik 2013b: 391).

Some examples of foreign influence may be seen in the Hebrew component of Judeo-Italian. The classic example is the word *chamiscioser* [the plate of fruits for the 15th of Shevat] < חמשה עשר *ḥamiša ʕaśar* 'fifteen' (Fortis 2009: 253). This is certain to be a Yiddish loan-word, because of the pronounciation of qamaṣ = /o/ and because of the absence of the nasal ע *ʕayin* (= *ng* or *ngk*) characteristic of Judeo-Italian.

There are also some signs of a Judeo-Spanish (or, in general, Judeo-Iberian) influence on Judeo-Italian. For example, in the *Maqre Dardeqe*, the root תרף TRF 'idol' is translated by the word פסיליש *psiles*, formed from the Hebrew component

פֶּסֶל *pesel* 'idol' and the Iberian plural suffix *-es*. Another example may be the word *negro* 'black' instead of the Italian *nero* (such as in Bene Qedem 1932). Aprile (2012: 123–130) dedicates much space to the probable Spanish (Judezmo) influence on Judeo-Italian, but it seems that, in spite of some fine examples,[49] he exaggerates, as most of the words that Aprile considers loan words are widely known from the liturgy and enter the Jewish languages independently (such as *Adar* 'the month of Adar', *agada* 'the Passover Haggadah', and so on).

4 Written and oral traditions

4.1 Writing system

From the beginning, Judeo-Italian was written in Hebrew characters; this is so in the marginal glosses to the Mishna in Ms Parma 138, in the *Elegy for the 9th of Av*, in all translations of the Siddur and of the Bible up to the latest, those of the 17th century, and in the Renaissance sermons. Even when Judeo-Italian became very similar to general literary Italian, e.g., in the translations of the 17th century, it was written in Hebrew characters, sometimes very close to the Italian orthography in the Latin characters. For example, in Italian the *n* is often written above the next letter in the form of a tilde, as in *secodo,* with the tilde above the *d*. This way of writing was copied in some late manuscripts, such as with נ *nun* above the ד *dalet* in the word סקודו *seco(n)do.*

All of the letters of the Hebrew alphabet are represented in Judeo-Italian script, except those that signify the sounds that do not exist in Italian, e.g., the gutturals ה, ח, ע (א is used to signify the vowel /a/); כ and ת are also not used (only ק and ט), with the exception of the Name of God, which is *Domedet Det* in Judeo-Italian (from *Dominus Deus*) and which is written דומדת דית. The gutturals are used in the Hebrew component of medieval Judeo-Italian, e.g., מחלארי *maḥlare* 'to forgive' (< מחל *maḥal* the same), עסקינו *ʕasqino* 'they were occupied' (< עסק *ʕasaq* 'to be occupied').

Writing in Hebrew characters ceased in the beginning of the 18th century. The collections of ghetto dialects from the 19–20th centuries are registered in Latin characters. Also, the somewhat artificial prose and poetry written in the

---

[49] For example, Judeo-Roman *shevàtte a barba sbatte* [it is cold and there is wind] (< שבט *ševaṭ*, the winter month, "which beats the beard") vs. *ševat ke la barva bate* with the same meaning in Judeo-Spanish.

Judeo-Roman dialect in the 20th century (Del Monte 1927, 1932, 1955; Calò 1990) are written in Latin characters. In these writings, there are some peculiarities connected to the sounds that are absent from standard Italian: ע ʕayin, which is pronunced as a nasal sound, is designated in different ways, mostly ngk; the fricative velar is designated as ch.

4.2 Literature

There is no great literature in Judeo-Italian. Most of the relevant texts are named in Section 2.2 above, because it is difficult to divide discussing Judeo-Italian linguistic properties from the scarce literature that was written in it. So we have the marginal notes on the Mishna as the earliest testimonies. They are followed by the *Elegy for the 9th of Av*, written in the 13th–14th centuries; the Siddur translations of the 15th–17th centuries; the Bible translations of the same period; the *Pesiqta Rabbati* partial translation of the 16th century. After the 16th century, there are some manuscript collections of sermons, the most important being that of R. Mordecai Dato.

Some other compilations must be added: one sabbatical poem of the 16th century (Roth 1925a, 1925b); an elegy for the Ancona martyrs (burned by the Inquisition in 1556; Roth 1950); the "Masseket Hamor," a comic composition of the 16th century (Mayer-Modena 2001). For some late minor compositions, mostly in Judeo-Venetian, see Fortis 2006: 19–37; in Judeo-Piemontese, see Terracini 1937; Colombo 1970.

From the late period, there are collections of sonnets written by C. Del Monte in Judeo-Romano (Del Monte 1927, 1932, 1955).

4.3 Performance (theatre, film, etc.)

In the Renaissance and Baroque Italian theatre, Judeo-Italian was used along with other linguistic minorities of Italy (mostly for comic purposes). So it is in a scene in the loan bank in the 1594 comedy *Amfiparnaso* by Orazio Vecchi (Fortis 2006: 19), in the comedies by Donzellini (1605; Mayer-Modena 2003: 69) and Andreini (1612; Mayer-Modena 1990).

The real theatre pieces written by Jews in Judeo-Italian belong to the later period and represent mostly "reflected dialect literature" (Croce 1952). This includes some compositions in Judeo-Venetian (Fortis 1989) and numerous pieces by Bedarida (1928; 1934; 1935). The most important of these texts is the *Gnora Luna* (Bene Kedem 1932), written by U. Cassuto and based on a 17th century story of the love of two young Jews, rich with examples of *Judeo-Florentino*.

Finally, the second half of the 20th century saw some revival of theatrical writing in Judeo-Romano, such as the texts by M. Calò (1990), and this was true even in the 21st century, as in *Da dove à da venì 'o freddo, vè 'o callo* by Piperno, Calò, and Sermoneta of 2004 (Fortis 2006: 37).

5 State of research

5.1 History of documentation

The sources and their collection are described in the previous sections; in the case of Judeo-Italian, it is somewhat artificial to distinguish between the relatively scarce literature, its collection, and the study of the language. The Italian part of the *Maqre Dardeqe*, the trilingual (Hebrew-Italian-Arab) dictionary printed in Naples in 1488, may be considered the first "collection" of Judeo-Italian. But the real collecting of the Judeo-Italian of the ghetto began only in the late period, with the pioneering work of Cammeo (1909–1911). I have already mentioned most of the great collections created in the 20th century; almost all of them are gathered in the bibliography of Aprile 2012, and the Introduction to Fortis 2006 is very useful. Specifically, I would like to mention the important work by Pavoncello from 1986 to 1988. Medieval and Renaissance sources, mostly translations, were gathered and described primarily by Cassuto, Sermoneta, and Cuomo (see bibliography).

5.2 Corpora

It is almost impossible to speak about corpora in the case of Judeo-Italian; in some sense, only the great translations of the Bible and of the Siddur and the 16th century collections of sermons may be considered as such. The collections of sonnets by C. Del Monte also represent great (or at least long) works.

5.3 Issues of general theoretical interest

In spite of the relative scarcity of documentation, Judeo-Italian may be very useful as a model for the study of some general processes and trends. Generally speaking, these processes and issues may be considered as a number of oppositions: written vs. spoken, ancient vs. modern, the Jewish variety vs. the corresponding common (non-Jewish) variety, different Jewish dialects vs. *koiné*. In the ancient and Renaissance / Baroque periods, the processes of koineization on the different dialect bases are most important: first, the extreme Southern, then the Central-Southern, then the Central-Northern, as well as the transitions between these stages. Theoretically important is the opposition between ancient written (high) Judeo-Italian and late ghetto spoken (low) Judeo-Italian and the study of relations between them. This transition, from the written high language to the spoken low language, is also very interesting from the socio-linguistic point of view; the return to Judeo-Italian in the 20th and 21st centuries by part of the elitist Jewish Roman youth is interesting, as well. But there is also socio-linguistic interest in the study of Judeo-Italian in medieval times, its role in the liturgy, and the fact that it was (at least formally) designated for women.

But perhaps the most theoretically interesting feature of Judeo-Italian is its power, even in its weakness. On one hand, there are no morphological or clear syntactic features that distinguish between the Jewish variety of Italian and the common Italian (non-Jewish) dialects. On the other hand, language consciousness of this Jewish variety has long existed, among both Jews and gentiles. So this distinction must be based on very tenuous traits and intonations, whose analysis may also help us to understand other tenuous Jewish languages, such as Jewish Russian or Jewish American English.

5.4 Current directions in research

In the field of medieval and Renaissance Judeo-Italian, first of all, present-day research must concentrate on preparing scientific (critical or diplomatic) editions of the main texts which remain in manuscripts, such as translations of the Siddur and of the Bible and collections of sermons. Second, a dictionary and a comprehensive grammar of the Romance component of the language must be written; besides general scientific interest, it will help us to understand where the distinctions lay between the Jewish and non-Jewish varieties.

Another prospective (and technically very difficult) direction may be the investigation of another 'weak' Jewish variety – the modern Italian of Jews. The article by Romano in 1967 may be considered the beginning of this direction; Romano studied the Hebrew element in novels written by Italian Jews.

In conclusion, I would like to say that the main problem in studying Judeo-Italian seems to be the very existence (or non-existence) of this Jewish language, in other words, the relationship between different dialects and "types of speech" referred to by this name (Judeo-Italian), the diachronic connections between different epochs and (synchronic) connections between different geographic zones, with the aim of establishing the measure of significant common traits with other Judeo-Italian dialects and with other non-Jewish dialects, and understanding which features make a dialect Judeo-Italian. But these problems are also in great measure common to the general dialectology of Italy.

References

Judeo-Italian translations of the Siddur:
F = *Editio princeps*, Fano 1506
Q1 = Ms. Parma de' Rossi ital. 7 (y. 1484)
Q2 = Ms. London 625 [Or. 2443] (y. 1483)
Q3 = Ms. JTS Mic. 4076 (15th century)
S = Ms. London Or. 10517 (17th century)

Aprile, Marcello. 2012. *Grammatica storica delle parlate giudeo-italiane*. Salento: Congedo Editore.
Ascoli, Graziadio Isaia. 1880. Iscrizioni inedite o mal note, greche, latine, ebraiche, di antichi sepolcri giudaici del Napolitano. In *Atti del IV Congresso Internazionale degli Orientalisti (Firenze 1878)*, vol. I, 239–354. Florence: Le Monnier.
Battaglia, Salvatore. 1961–2002. *Grande dizionario della lingua italiana*. Turin: Unione Tipografico-Editrice Torinese.
Bedarida, Guido. 1928. Un intermezzo di canzioni antiche da cantarsi quando é Purim. *La Rassegna Mensile di Israel* 3. 271–302.
Bedarida, Guido. 1934. Vigilia di Sabato. *Rassegna Mensile di Israel* 9. 183–200, 292–305, 342–361.
Bedarida, Guido. 1935. *Il siclo d'argento*. Città di Castello: Unione Arti Grafiche.
Bedarida, Guido. 1956. *Ebrei a Livorno: Tradizioni e gergo: In 180 sonetti giudaico-livornesi*. Flornece: Le Monnier.
Bené Kedem. 1932. Gnora Luna: Scene di vita ebraica fiorentina. *Rassegna Mensile di Israel* 6. 546–579.
Bonfil, Robert. 1976. ʔAḥat mi-derašot ha-ʔitalqiyyot šel R. Mordekay Dato [One of the Italian sermons by R. Mordecai Dato]. *Italia* 1. 1–32.
Bonfil, Robert. 1994a. *Be-marʔa kesufa (ḥayye ha-yehudim be-ʔItaliya bime ha-Renessans)* [In the enchanted mirror (Jewish life in the Renaissance Italy)]. Jerusalem: Merkaz Zalman Shazar Le-Toldot Israel.
Bonfil, Robert. 1994b. Changing mentalities of Italian Jews between the periods of the Renaissance and the Baroque. *Italia* 11. 61–79.
Bonfil, Robert. 2009. *History and folklore in a Medieval Jewish Chronicle: The family chronicle of Ahima'az ben Paltiel*. Leiden: Brill.
Bregman, Devora. 1995. *Ševil ha-zahav: Ha-soneṭ ha-ʕivri bi-tqufat ha-Renessans we-ha-Baroq* [Il sentiero d'oro: Il sonetto ebraico nel Rinascimento e nel barocco]. Beer-Sheva: Makon Ben-Ṣevi we-Hoṣaʔat ha-sefarim šel ʔUniversiṭat Ben-Gurion ba-Negev.
Buber, Solomon (ed.). 1886. *Šibbole ha-leqet ha-šalem* [The full ears of gleaning]. Vilna: Ha-ʔalmana we-ha-ʔaḥim Romm.
Calò, Mirella. 1990. *Chiacchere alla giudia*. Roma: Carucci.

Cammeo, Giuseppe. 1909. Studj dialettali. *Il Vessillo Israelitico* 57. 169–170, 214–215, 315–316, 359–361, 459–461, 504–505.
Cammeo, Giuseppe. 1910. Studj dialettali. *Il Vessillo Israelitico* 58. 8–9, 148–49, 403–4, 448–450, 506–507, 543–545.
Cammeo, Giuseppe. 1911. Studj dialettali. *Il Vessillo Israelitico* 59. 25–26, 52–53, 102–104, 143–144.
Cassuto, Umberto. 1929. Un'antichissima elegia in dialetto giudeo-italiano. *Archivio Glottologico Italiano* 32–33. 349–408.
Cassuto, Umberto. 1930a. La tradizione giudeo-italiana per la traduzione della Bibbia. In *Atti del I Congresso per le tradizioni popolari*, 114–121. Florence: Rinascimento del Libro.
Cassuto, Umberto. 1930b. Les traductions judeo-italennes du ritual. *Revude des Études Juives* 89. 260–281.
Cassuto, Umberto. 1930c. Il Libro di Amos in traduzione giudeo-italiana. In Elia Samuele Artom, Umberto Cassuto & Eugenio Zolli (eds.), *Miscellanea di studi ebraici in memoria di H.P. Chajes*, 19–38. Florence: Casa Editrice Israel.
Cassuto, Umberto. 1934. Saggi delle antiche traduzioni giudeo-italiane della Bibbia. *Annuario di Studi Ebraici* 1. 101–135.
Castellani, Arrigo. 2000. *Grammatica storica della lingua italiana*. Bologna: il Mulino.
Colafemmina, Cesare. 1990. *Documenti per la storia degli ebrei in Puglia nell'archivio di stato di Napoli*. Bari: Regione Puglia, Assessorato alla Cultura- Istituto Ecumenico S. Nicola.
Colombo, Dino. 1970. Il ghetto di Moncalvo e una sua poesia. *Rassegna Mensile di Israel* 36. 435–441.
Colorni, Vittore. 1970. La parlata degli ebrei mantovani. *Rassegna Mensile di Israel* 36. 109–164.
Contini, Gianfranco (ed.). 1960. *Poeti del duecento*, vol. I. Milan & Naples: Ricciardi.
Cortelazzo, Manlio & Paolo Zolli. 1999. *Il nuovo etimologico: Dizionario etimologico della lingua italiana (=DELI)*. Bologna: Zanichelli.
Cortelazzo, Manlio, Carla Marcato, Nicola De Blasi & Gianrenzo P. Clivio (eds.). 2002. *I dialetti italiani. Storia, struttura, uso*. Turin: Unione Tipografico-Editrice Torinese.
Croce, Benedetto. 1952. La letteratura dialettale riflessa, la sua origine nel Seicento e il suo ufficio storico. In Benedetto Croce (ed.), *Filosofia. Poesia. Storia, pagine tratte da tutte le opere a cura dell'autore*, 355–364. Milan & Naples: Riccardo Ricciardi Editore.
Cuomo, Luisa. 1976. In margine al giudeo-italiano: Note fonetiche, morfologiche e lessicali. *Italia* 1. 30–53.
Cuomo, Luisa. 1977. Antichissime glosse salentine nel codice ebraico di Parma, De Rossi, 138. *Medioevo Romanzo* 4. 185–271.
Cuomo, Luisa. 1982. Italkiano versus giudeo-italiano versus 0 (zero), una questione metodologica. *Italia* 3. 7–32.
Cuomo, Luisa. 1985. Pesicheta Rabbati: Un florilegio midrascico giudeo-italiano al confine fra la Toscana e l'Umbria nel XVI sec. In Isaac Benabu & Joseph Baruch Sermoneta (eds.), *Judeo-Romance Languages*, 69–125. Jerusalem: Misgav Yerushalayim.
Cuomo, Luisa. 1988. *Una traduzione giudeo-romanesca del libro di Giona*. Tübingen: Max Niemeyer Verlag.
Debenedetti Stow, Sandra (ed.). 1990. *Yehuda ben Moshe ben Daniel Romano, 14th cent. La chiarificazione in volgare delle "espressioni difficili" ricorrenti nel Mishneh Torah di Mose Maimonide: Glossario inedito del XIV secolo*. Rome: Carocci.

Del Monte, Crescenzo. 1927. *Sonetti giudaico-romaneschi con note esplicative e un discorso preliminare sul dialetto giudaico-romanesco e sulle sue origini*. Florence: Israel.
Del Monte, Crescenzo. 1932. *Nuovi sonetti giudaico-romaneschi con note esplicative ed alcune osservazioni sulle pecularitàe sulla presumibile derivazione del dialetto romano giudaico*. Rome: Cremonese.
Del Monte, Crescenzo. 1935. Il dialetto di Roma al sec. XVI e le sue sopravvivenze. Alcune battute romano vernacole di una commedia del '500 con versione giudaico-romanesca. *Rassegna Mensile di Israel* 10. 290–296.
Del Monte, Crescenzo. 1955. *Sonetti postumi giudaico-romaneschi e romaneschi*. Rome: Israel.
Dionisotti, Carlo. (ed.). 1966. *Prose e rime di Pietro Bembo*. Turin: Unione Tipografico-Editrice Torinese.
Dodi, Amos. 2002. *ʕIyyunim be-masoret ha-lašon šel yehude Sefarad lifne ha-geruš* [Studies in the linguistic tradition of Spanish Jews before the Expulsion]. Beer Sheva: Hoṣaʔat ha-sefarim šel ʔUniversiṭat Ben-Gurion ba-Negev.
Eldar, Ilan. 1979. *Masoret ha-qeriʔa ha-qedam-ʔAškenazit* [The Hebrew language tradition in Medieval Ashkenaz (ca. 950–1350 C.E.)], vol. 2. Jerusalem: Magnes Press.
Foresti, Fabio. 1986. Il giudeo-reggiano (da testi dei secoli XVII-XIX). *Studi Orientali e Linguistici* 3. 479–506.
Fortis, Umberto. 1989. *Il ghetto in scena. Teatro giudeo-italiano del novecento. Storia e testi*. Rome: Carucci.
Fortis, Umberto. 1991. Il lessico di origine ebraica in alcune composizioni giudeo-triestine. In Giampaolo Borghello, Manlio Cortelazzo & Giorgio Padoan (eds.), *Saggi di linguistica e di letteratura in memoria di Paolo Zolli*, 177–201. Padua: Antenore.
Fortis, Umberto. 2006. *La parlata degli ebrei di Venezia*. Florence: Giuntina.
Fortis, Umberto & Paolo Zolli. 1979. *La parlata giudeo-veneziana*. Assisi & Rome: Carucci.
Galante, Gennaro Aspreno. 1913. Un sepolcreto giudaico recentemente scoperto in Napoli. *Memorie della R. Accademia di Archeologia, Lettere e Belle Arti* 2. 232–248.
Jochnowitz, George. 1974. Parole di origine romanza ed ebraica in giudeo-italiano. *Rassegna Mensile di Israel* 40. 212–219.
Lacerenza, Giancarlo. 1999. L'iscrizione di Claudia Aster Hierosolymitana. In Luigi Cagni (ed.), *Biblica et Semitica: Studi in memoria di Francesco Vattioni*, 303–313. Naples: Istituto Universitario Orientale.
Mancini, Marco. 1992. Sulla formazione dell'identita linguistica giudeo-romanesca fra tardo medioevo e rinascimento. *Roma nel Rinascimento* 8. 53–122.
Marazzini, Claudio. Le teorie. In Luca Serianni & Pietro Trifone (eds.), *Storia della lingua italiana*, vol. I: I Luoghi della codificazione, 231–330. Turin: Einaudi.
Massariello Merzagora, Giovanna. 1980. La parlata giudeo-piemontese. *L'Archivio Glottologico Italiano* 65. 105–136.
Massariello Merzagora, Giovanna. 1983. Elementi lessicali della parlata giudeo-fiorentina. *Quaderni dell'Atlante Lessicale Toscano* 1. 69–101.
Modena-Mayer, Maria-Luisa. 1978. Osservazioni sul tabu' linguistico in giudeo-livornese. in Robert Bonfil, Daniel Carpi, Maria Modena Mayer, Giulio Romano & Giuseppe Baruch Sermoneta (eds.), *Scritti in memoria di Umberto Nahon*, 166–179. Jerusalem: Fondazione S. Mayer e R. Cantoni.
Mayer-Modena, Maria-Luisa. 1990. A proposito di una scena "All'ebraica" nello Schiavetto dell'Andreini. *Annali della Facolta di Lettere e Filosofia dell'Universita degli Studi di Milano* 43. 74–81.

Mayer-Modena, Maria-Luisa. 1997. Le parlate giudeo-italiane. In Corrado Vivanti (ed.), *Storia d'Italia. Annali 11/2. Gli ebrei in italia*, 937–963. Turin: Einaudi.
Mayer-Modena, Maria-Luisa. 1999. La composante hebraique dans le judeo-italien de la Renaissance. In Shlomo Morag, Moshe Bar-Asher & Maria-Luisa Mayer-Modena (eds.), *Vena Hebraica in Judaeorum linguis*, 93–107. Milano: Centro Studi Camito-Semitici.
Mayer-Modena, Maria-Luisa. 2001. La Masseket Hamor di Gedalya ibn Yahia. *Italia* 13–15. 303–342.
Mayer-Modena, Maria-Luisa. 2003. Il giudeo-italiano: Riflessioni sulle fonti. *Materia giudaica* 8. 65–73.
Mayer-Modena, Maria-Luisa & Giovanna Massariello-Merzagora. 1973. Il giudeo-modenese nei testi raccolti da A. Giacomelli. *Rendiconti dell'Istituto Lombardo Accademia di scienze e lettere, classe I lettere* 107. 869–938.
Migliorini, Bruno. 1987. *Storia della lingua italiana*. Flornece: Sansoni.
Milano, Attilio. 1932. *Glossario dei vocaboli e delle espressioni di origine ebraica in uso del dialetto giudaico-romanesco*, In Crescenzo Del Monte, *Nuovi sonetti giudaico-romaneschi*, 236–259. Rome: Cremonese.
Milano, Attilio. 1963. *Storia degli ebrei in italia*. Turin: Einaudi.
Pavoncello, Nello. 1986. *Modi di dire ed espressioni dialettali degli ebrei di Roma*, vol. 1. Rome: Tipografia Veneziana.
Pavoncello, Nello. 1988. *Modi di dire ed espressioni dialettali degli ebrei di Roma*, vol. 2. Rome: Tipografia Veneziana.
Polacco, Bruno & Umberto Fortis. 1972. Quarant'anni fa (tre tempi in giudeo-veneziano). *Rassegna Mensile di Israel* 38. 584–617.
Renzi, Lorenzo. 1994. *Nuova introduzione alla filologia romanza*, Bologna: Il Mulino.
Rohlfs, Gerhard. 1966–1969. *Grammatica storica della lingua italiana e dei suoi dialetti*, 3 vols. Turin: Einaudi.
Rohlfs, Gerhard. 1976 [1961]. *Vocabulario dei dialetti salentini*, 2nd edn. Galatina: Congedo Editore.
Romano, Giulio. 1967. L'elemento ebraico in romanzi di scrittori ebrei italiani. In Daniel Carpi, Attilio Milano & Alexander Rofe (eds.), *Scritti in memoria di Leone Carpi*, 185–207. Jerusalem: Fondazione Sally Mayer.
Roth, Cecil. 1925a. Un hymne sabbatique du XVIe siècle en judéo-italien. *Revue des Études Juives* 80. 60–80, 182–206.
Roth, Cecil. 1925b. Un hymne sabbatique du XVIe siècle en judéo-italien. *Revue des Études Juives* 81. 55–78.
Roth, Cecil. 1950. Un'elegia giudeo-italiana sui martiri di Ancona (1556–57). *Rassegna Mensile di Israele* 16. 147–156.
Ryzhik, Michael. 2007. *Ha-qawwim ha-lešoniyyim be-targum ha-siddur la-ʔiṭalqit ha-yehudit lefi defus Fano 266 [1506]: ʕIyyun rišoni* [The linguistic traits of the Judeo-Italian prayer book translation according to the Fano edition, 1506]. *Italia* 17. 7–17.
Ryzhik, Michael. 2008a. Lessico delle traduzioni dei testi liturgici ebraici in dialetti giudeo italiani. In Emmanuela Cresti (ed.), *Prospettive nello studio del lessico italiano: Atti del ix Congresso della Società Internazionale di Linguistica e Filologia Italiana*, 165–172. Florence: Firenze University Press.
Ryzhik, Michael. 2008b. I cambiamenti nel giudeo-italiano in corso del Cinquecento: Le prediche. In Francesco Aspesi, Vermondo Brugnatelli, Anna Linda Callow & Claudia Rosenzweig (eds.), *Il mio cuore è a Oriente, studi di linguistica storica, filologia e cultura ebraica dedicati a Maria Luisa Mayer Modena*, 527–545. Milano: Cisalpino.

Ryzhik, Michael. 2010. Ha-lašon we-ha-nusaḥ be-targume ha-siddur be-ʔIṭalia [The language and the prayer traditions in the Judeo-Italian prayer book translations]. *Italia* 20. 7–28.

Ryzhik, Michael. 2012. *Mi-kitve ha-yad la-defusim: Hipatteḥuyyot masorot ha-niqqud bi-dfuse ha-siddur ha-ʔiṭalqi be-sof ha-meʔa ha-15 u-ve-maḥaṣit ha-rišona šel ha-meʔa ha-16* [From the manuscripts to the printed editions: Development of the tradition of the vocalization in the Italian Siddur editions at the end of the 15th and in the first half of the 16th centuries]. *Leshonenu* 74. 333–357.

Ryzhik, Michael. 2013a. Preliminaries to the critical edition of the Jewish-Italian translation of the Siddur. *Journal of Jewish Languages* 1. 229–260.

Ryzhik, Michael. 2013b. Le didascalie per la cena pasquale nella tradizione degli ebrei nell'Italia meridionale. In Fabrizio Lelli (ed.), *Gli ebrei nel Salento (secoli IX-XVI)*, [=Università di Salento, Studi Storici 106]. 379–406. Galatina: Congedo Editore.

Ryzhik, Michael. 2014a. La traduzione delle poesie antiche per la festa delle Capanne (*Hoshʻanot*) nei volgarizzamenti del libro di preghiere ebraico in giudeo-italiano. In Ivano Paccagnella, Elisa Gregori (eds.), *Lingue, testi, culture. L'eredità di Folena, vent'anni dopo (Atti del XL Convegno Interuniversitario, Bressanone-Brixen, 12–15 luglio 2012)*, 173–184. Padua: Esedra.

Ryzhik, Michael. 2014b. Il dialetto giudeo-ferrarese ed il giudeo-italiano antico. *Medioevo Romanzo* 38. 152–169.

Ryzhik, Michael. 2016. Review of *Grammatica storica delle parlate giudeo-italiane*, by Marcello Aprile. *Journal of Jewish Languages* 4. 261–266.

Sampson, Rodney (ed.). 1980. *Early Romance texts: An anthology*. Cambridge: Cambridge University Press.

Scazzocchio Sestieri, Leah. 1970. Sulla parlata giudaico-romanesca. In Daniel Carpi, Attilio Milano & Umberto Nahon (eds.), *Scritti in memoria di Enzo Sereni*, 101–129. Milan & Jerusalem: Fondazione Sally Mayer.

Scazzocchio Sestieri, Leah. 1988. Un breve testo in giudeo-italiano. In Haim Beinart (ed.), *Jews in Italy: Studies dedicated to the memory of U. Cassuto on the 100th anniversary of his birth*, 94–102. Jerusalem: Magnes Press.

Serianni, Luca. 1993. La prosa. In Luca Serianni & Pietro Trifone (eds.), *Storia della lingua italiana*, vol. I: *I luoghi della codificazione*, 451–580. Turin: Einaudi

Serianni, Luca & Pietro Trifone (eds.). 1993. *Storia della lingua italiana*, vol. I: *I luoghi della codificazione*. Turin: Einaudi.

Sermoneta, Joseph Baruch. 1976. Considerazioni frammentarie sul giudeo-italiano. *Italia* 1. 1–29.

Sermoneta, Joseph Baruch. 1988. *Nusaḥ ha-tefilla šel yehude Siṣiliya* [Prayer tradition of the Sicilian Jews]. In Haim Beinart (ed.), *Jews in Italy: Studies dedicated to the memory of U. Cassuto on the 100th anniversary of his birth*, 131–217. Jerusalem: Magnes Press.

Sermoneta, Joseph Baruch. 1990. Testimonianze degli ebrei pugliesi a Corfù. *Medioevo Romanzo* 15. 408–437.

Simohnson, Shlomo. 2011. *Ben ha-paṭṭiš we-ha-saddan: Ha-yehudim be-Siṣiliya* [Between Scylla and Charybdis: the Jews in Sicily]. Jerusalem: Magnes Press.

Terracini, Benvenuto. 1937. Due composizioni in versi giudeo-piemontesi del secolo XIX. *Rassegna Mensile di Israel* 12. 164–183.

Terracini, Benvenuto. 1951. Residui di parlate giudeo-italiane raccolti a Pitigliano, Roma, Ferrara. *Rassegna Mensile d'Israel* 17. 3–11, 62–72, 111–121.

Terracini, Benvenuto. 1962. Le parlate giudaico-italiane negli appunti di Raffaelle Giacomelli. *Rassegna Mensile di Israel* 28. 260–295.

George Jochnowitz
Judeo-Provençal in Southern France

1 Brief introduction

Judeo-Provençal is also known as Judeo-Occitan, Judéo-Comtadin, Hébraïco-Comtadin, Hébraïco-Provençal, Shuadit, Chouadit, Chouadite, Chuadit, and Chuadite. It is the Jewish analog of Provençal and is therefore a Romance language. The age of the language is a matter of dispute, as is the case with other Judeo-Romance languages. It was spoken in only four towns in southern France: Avignon, Cavaillon, Caprentras, and l'Isle-sur-Sorgue. A women's prayer book, some poems, and a play are the sources of the medieval language, and transcriptions of Passover songs and theatrical representations are the sources for the modern language. In addition, my own interviews in 1968 with the language's last known speaker, Armand Lunel, provide data (Jochnowitz 1978, 1985). Lunel, who learned the language from his grandparents, not his parents, did not have occasion to converse in it. Judeo-Provençal/Shuadit is now extinct, since Armand Lunel died in 1977.

Sometimes Jewish languages have a name meaning "Jewish," such as Yiddish or Judezmo – from Hebrew *Yehudit* or other forms of *Yehuda*. This is the case with Shuadit, due to a sound change of /y/ to [š]. I use the name Judeo-Provençal for the medieval language and Shuadit for the modern language.

2 Historical background

2.1 Speaker community: Settlement, documentation

Jews had lived in Provence at least as early as the first century CE. They were officially expelled from France in 1306, readmitted in 1315, expelled again in 1322, readmitted in 1359, and expelled in 1394 for a period that lasted until the French Revolution. However, Provence was not yet ruled by the kings of France in 1394. This changed in 1481, and there was pressure to expel the Jews from there as well, which happened in 1498 but was not completely enforced until 1501 (Shapiro 1972).

The city of Avignon in Provence became the residence of the Popes in 1309. Avignon and the neighboring area, the Comtat-Venaissin, belonged to the Holy See and did not become part of France until two years after the French

Revolution, in 1791. The Jews in the Papal States were not affected by the expulsions from France and Provence. Isolated Jewish communities existed in four towns: Avignon, Carpentras, Cavaillon, and l'Isle-sur-Sorgue. After the last Jews had been expelled from France in 1501, the Papal States became an island with a Jewish minority surrounded by a France without Jews. Life was not easy for the Jews in the Papal States – Avignon and the Comtat-Venaissin. Jews were the victims of violence. In the period after it had abated, they were permitted to live only in restricted areas. "Dans la seconde moitié du XVè siècle, après avoir été un peu partout molestés et pillés par la population chrétienne, ils furent réduits à se cantonner dans une seule rue des localités où ils demeurent,--la carrière des juifs: ainsi, en 1453, à Cavaillon, en 1486 à Carpentras, après une première limitation à deux rues, en 1461" ("In the second half of the 15th century, after having been harassed and robbed almost everywhere by the Christian population, they were forced to restrict themselves to a single street in each of the communities where they lived – the Jewish quarter – thus, in 1453 in Cavaillon, in 1486 in Carpentras, after a previous limitation to two streets in 1461") (Chobaut 1937, vol. I, no. 1, p. 6). Under the circumstances, it was natural for their language to differ from that of their neighbors.

Immigration from North Africa became a major factor after Morocco and Tunisia became independent in 1956 and reached a peak when Algeria became independent in 1962. Algerians (unlike Moroccans and Tunisians) were French citizens before independence, and Algerian Jews left for France in great numbers. Today, Jewish rituals and culture in the Comtat-Venaissin are North African.

2.2 Attestations and sources

When is a language born? In the case of both French and German, the Oaths of Strasbourg, written in 842 and signed by King Louis the German and King Charles the Bald, ruler of West Francia, give us an early, official document in both French and German defining the existence of these two languages. On the other hand, it is impossible to decide when French and Provençal (today generally known as Occitan) split off from each other. There is dispute about whether they split into two or three languages, the third being Franco-Provençal, also known as Arpitan (Jochnowitz 1973).

As for Jewish languages, it is hard to determine whether an early text is written in Judeo-French or Judeo-Provençal, or simply in French or Provençal spelled out in Hebrew characters. David S. Blondheim (1925) discusses in detail the lexical items common to various Judeo-Romance languages. He is thus agreeing with the point of view behind Max Weinreich's belief that there was a common origin of Judeo-Romance (Weinreich 1980). Menachem Banitt wrote an article arguing that there had never been such a language as Judeo-French and that medieval texts from France in Hebrew characters were simply in French (Banitt 1963). Kirsten Fudeman, in her book analyzing many of these texts, writes, "In this volume I use the term 'Hebraico-French' to refer to Old and Middle French texts written in Hebrew letters" (Fudeman 2010: 5). Her choice of the term "Hebraico-French" suggests that she agrees with Banitt. However, she adds, "To say that the Jews spoke the same language as their non-Jewish neighbors is not to say that they spoke it in an identical way" (Fudeman 2010: 58), thus recognizing that there may have been a Jewish way of speaking Middle French.

Many Jewish languages are characterized by the presence of words of Hebrew, or perhaps Aramaic, origin. Such words are lacking in the Provençal texts written in the Hebrew alphabet in the Middle Ages. The notable exception is the word *goya* meaning "Gentile woman," which is found in the Judeo-Provençal women's prayerbook that is Roth Manuscript 32 (Jochnowitz 1981). Should we say that the appearance of this Hebrew word, in what otherwise was a word-for-word translation into Provençal of the daily prayers, marks the birth of Judeo-Provençal at some unspecified point in the 14th or 15th century? Whatever answer we choose does not answer the question of when the everyday language of Jews in southern France – or in the Roman Empire – started mixing words of Hebrew origin into their everyday speech. We do not have enough evidence to answer this question, which explains why Blondheim and Banitt differ in their responses.

2.3 Phases in historical development

A small number of texts survive from the medieval period, all written in Hebrew characters. There are glosses, the oldest of which is the *Ittur* of Isaac b. Abba Mari of Marseilles, written between 1170 and 1193 (Guttel 1972: 439), the Esther poem analyzed by Susan Milner Silberstein and discussed below, and the prayerbook preserved as Roth Manuscript 32 (Jochnowitz 1981). From the modern period – the 19th and 20th centuries – we have a number of texts representing liturgical language and spoken language, the latter often portrayed in comical ways. I will use the terms "Provençal" and "Judeo-Provençal" when talking about the older texts in the Hebrew alphabet and the term "Shuadit" when discussing the newer texts in Latin characters.

2.3.1 Judeo-Provençal texts in Hebrew letters

Susan Milner Silberstein wrote a detailed analysis of a poem written in 1327 in Hebrew characters, in a language that may or may not have been Judeo-Provençal (Silberstein 1973). The title of her book simply says it is in Provençal. The text is quite hard to read (see Figure 1) for a number of reasons. It is handwritten, and the style of the characters is unfamiliar to contemporary readers. "The script in this text is of the *Sephardic* Type and, more specifically, of the *Sephardic Mashait* style, an elaborate, semi-cursive book hand sometimes called 'rabbinic'" (Silberstein 1973: 72). The spaces occur in unpredictable locations, and the same Hebrew letter is sometimes used for different sounds.

The poem is an original work and only partly reflects the biblical story of Esther. The name Nebuchadnezzar occurs twice in the opening section of this Esther poem, despite the fact that he is nowhere mentioned in the Biblical Book of Esther (Nebuchadnezzar is mentioned in the Book of Chronicles II and in the Book of Daniel, and a different spelling, Nebuchadrezzar, is found in the Books of Jeremiah and Ezekiel). On the first page of the poem, we find two different spellings. On line 6, we find נבוכ דנצר. The word *de* (of) is written as a prefix. There is a space in the middle of the word, perhaps indicating that the author viewed *de* as a preposition. On line 10, we find אנבוקאדנדור. The word *a* (to) is written as a prefix.

The second spelling is an indication that the Provençal change of intervocalic -*d*- to [z] had reached Judeo-Provençal. The writing of prepositions as prefixes shows that the Hebrew language has influenced the conceptions of what word boundaries are. It also suggests an ignorance of the way in which words are spelled in the Latin alphabet.

The spelling דייב for the word for *God* occurs both in the Esther poem and in the women's prayerbook in the Cecil Roth Collection (Jochnowitz 1981). It was probably pronounced [diew].

The title line of the text, written in Hebrew, is translated by Silberstein as opening with the words: "I will begin to write the vernacular [text] composed by Maestre Crescas" (pp. 71–72). The word for "vernacular" is *la'az*, spelled in Hebrew, לעז – the word meaning "foreign language" used by Rashi for his glosses into French. It is possible that *la'az* was a commonly-used word for the local language, whether French or Provençal.

Crescas wrote Esther poems in both Hebrew and Provençal. Silberstein informs us that, in the Hebrew version, there is an acrostic that reads: "The doctor called Israel son of Joseph Caslari, of the family of Yitzhar, who lives in the town of Avignon..." (pp. 66–67). The name "Crescas" is not mentioned, but it is probably implied by the words "son of Joseph." Crescas, a surname found

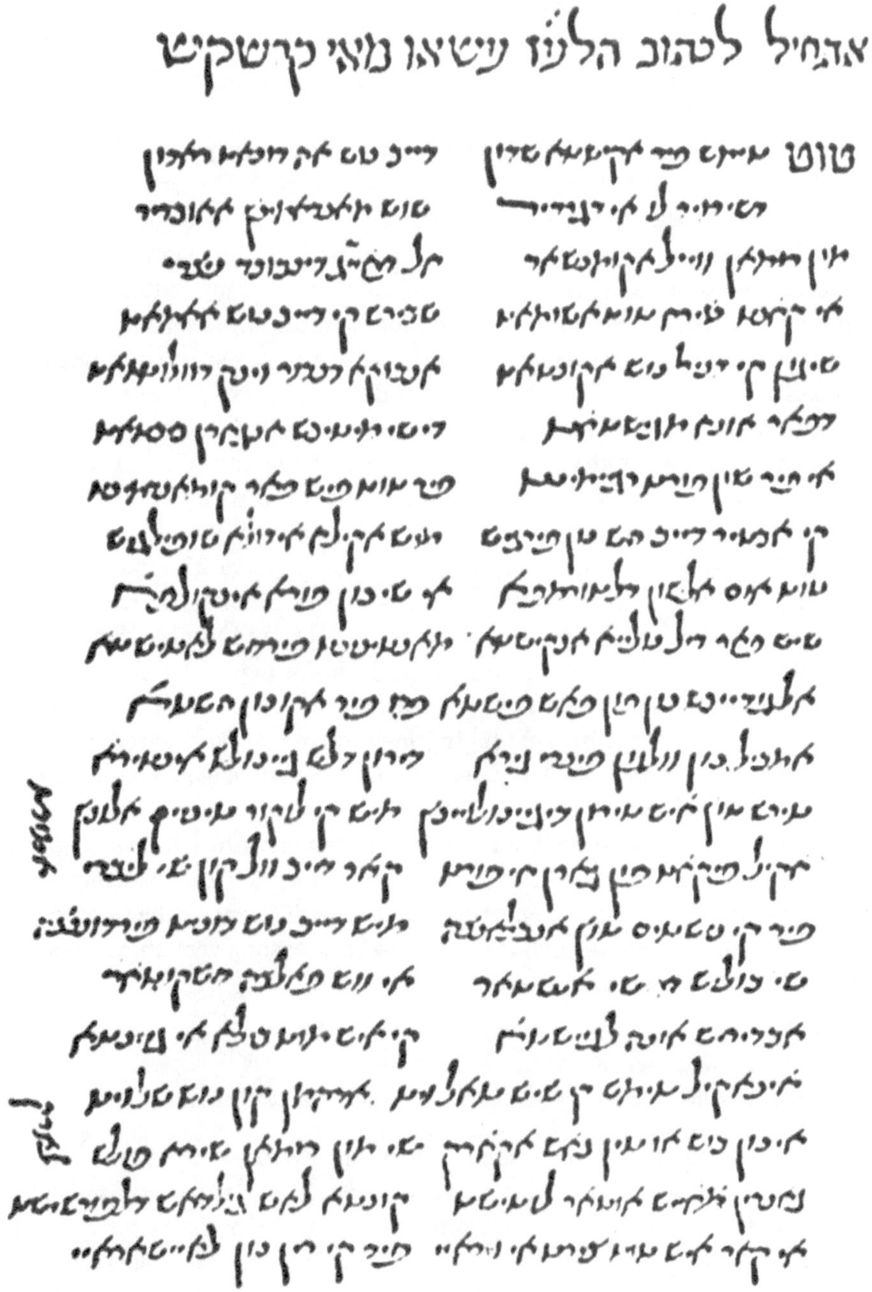
אתחיל לכתוב הלעז עשאו מאי קרשקש

טוט

Figure 1: The first page of the original version of the poem (Silberstein 1973: 260), reproduced with the author's permission.

among the Jews of both Catalonia and southern France, means *increase* (cognate with the second syllable of *increase* as well as with the words *crescent* and *crescendo*) and is no doubt a translation of "Joseph" or "son of Joseph" (Encyclopedia Judaica 1972). Puritan minister Increase Mather (1639 – 1723) was probably given his name, because it is the English translation of "Joseph."

We saw above that the second spelling of "Nebuchadnezzar" shows that the [d] had become a [z] in both Provençal and Judeo-Provençal. Nebuchadnezzar is the name of a king in the Bible, and so it is not a word of Romance origin. If we examine the transcription of the Hebrew letters into Latin letters done by Silberstein, we find the words for "season" and "reason" in verses 1 and 2 are transcribed *sazon* and *razon*, which is not surprising when we think of Provençal. It becomes more surprising when we look at the spelling in the Hebrew alphabet, where the [z] sounds are spelled with a ד. Apparently, in Judeo-Provençal, that was the way to spell the sound [z]. The words for "season" and "reason" were never at any time spelled with a *d* in Provençal. Intervocalic *s*, like intervocalic *d*, had become *z*. This merger was not reflected in texts in Latin letters, but did appear in the Esther poem. The independence of Hebrew-letter spelling traditions in this case reminds us of the fact that the prepositions *de* and *a* were written as prefixes, and not separate words, in Crescas' poem. The use of ב in final position for [w], as we saw above, is further evidence that the author was not bound by Provençal orthographic traditions. Final *-d* also became [z] in Judeo-Provençal. This is reflected in a contemporary version of the Passover song *Had Gadya*, in which the first word is pronounced [haz].

In the version of *Had Gadya* sung by Armand Lunel, we hear both [had gadya] and [hay gadya], rather than [haz gadya] (Jochnowitz 1985). Did the song vary in different parts of the Comtat-Venaissin? Were there different family traditions of how to sing it? Further research is needed. In Lunel's sung version, we hear the lines at the opening of the last verse:

> *Es vengü a kadoš baruš u*
> *K a čaata lu malak amavet*
> ([then] came the Holy One, Blessed be He, Who killed the angel of death)

The words "*kadoš baruš u*" and "*malak amavet*" are of Hebrew origin. This is apparently the only evidence, aside from *goya* in Roth Ms. 32, of Hebrew words in Judeo-Provençal. Of course, we don't know the age of a tradition of singing. Moulinas writes that *Had Gadya* was one of the rituals done in Provençal (Moulinas 1981: 193). Did Moulinas hear a different version without the Hebrew words? Whether he did or not, we have to consider this song an example of Judeo-Provençal, rather than of Provençal. Moulinas does not give us a version of *Had Gadya*, but he expresses doubt that there ever was a Jewish language spoken in the Comtat-Venaissin. He asks, "Comment imaginer qu'ils aient pu pousser le désir de se distinguer au point de s'imposer un bilinguisme bien inutile, en se servant du dialecte vernaculaire pour leurs contacts incessants avec les chrétiens et d'une langue différente pour les relations intérieures de la communauté juive?" (How could anyone imagine that they could have pursued the desire to maintain their identity to the point of imposing a useless bilingual situation upon themselves, using the local vernacular in their everyday contacts with Christians and a different language for internal relationships within the Jewish community?) (Moulinas 1981: 191).

On the one hand, Moulinas seems unaware that Jewish languages are the rule and not the exception. Furthermore, he does not know about the fact that language is always changing and that regional, professional, cultural, and other groups are always developing their own dialects and sub-dialects. On the other hand, even though the last speaker of Judeo-Provençal, Armand Lunel, lived until 1977, he did not speak the language to anybody. He had learned it from his grandparents, not from his parents. Moulinas could not have come across direct evidence of Shuadit when he wrote his book in 1981.

Moulinas ends his book with a chapter about the disappearance of the culture of the Jews of the Comtat-Venaissin, a process which he says began immediately after the French Revolution. He writes that once Jews were free to move out of the area, and once Jews of different backgrounds were free to move into the area, cultural eradication began to take place (Moulinas 1981: 459).

As the culture changed and there were more contacts with Jews from other areas, new religious rituals were adopted, and old ones became incomprehensible. As Moulinas (1981: 475) explains, "The confusion created by different traditions of liturgical singing and of pronouncing Hebrew should have led to cultural gaps with other Jewish communities." Today, the rituals, traditions, and pronunciations heard in the synagogues in the Comtat-Venaissin are those of the Jews of North Africa, who are now the majority in the Jewish communities there.

2.3.2 Texts in Latin letters

The texts written in Hebrew characters have no Hebrew words – or very few. The texts in Latin characters are filled with words of Hebrew or Aramaic origin. They are typical of Jewish languages, in that they have many borrowings and a unique local pronunciation of Hebrew. The use of an alphabet that is not Hebrew makes it clear that the words of Hebrew etymology are pronounced according to the rules of the local Jewish form of speech.

The play *Harcanot et Barcanot* was written in the 18th century, at least in part, to demonstrate the nature of Shuadit. Armand Lunel, in his introduction to the libretto of his opera *Esther de Carpentras*, tells us that the play was written by someone named Bédarride, "qui s'amusa à écrire une bouffonerie judéo-comtadine" (who enjoyed writing a farce in Shuadit) (Lunel 1926: 17). In other words, he wrote it for fun. Pierre Pansier, in his introduction to the play, spells the author's name Bédarrides and says the manuscript can be found in the Bibliothèque de Carpentras, coté No. 1009 (Pansier 1925: 113). The play not only tells us about the phonology and vocabulary of the language, but reflects the fact that it was considered funny. Regional, ethnic, and other non-standard languages are often considered undignified or comical or both, and this has often been the case with Jewish languages.

Here is an English translation of the French translation at the bottom of the page of the original Shuadit:

> The Rector: Gueneruf (theft)! But what does it mean?
> Barcanot: Would you believe that he doesn't know what a gueneruf is?
> Someone who steals an egg can steal a bull.
> It's true that by ganauta (to steal) I mean
> As if Harcanot took the money of another
> Which he believed his...
> Harcanot: A plague on your lung!
> You're telling him...
> The Rector: I begin to understand.
> Gueneruf is...
> Larcanot [sic] (Should be Barcanot): Yes.
> The Rector: It's when one wants to take
> What is not his; a thief in one word.

Not all non-Provençal words in the play are from Hebrew. Pansier tells us the *haoumoun* (rector) is the "gouverneur (hebr. *haegmôn*)" (1925: 113). According to my research, the word *haegmôn* seems to come from the Greek word *hegemon*, meaning "leader," rather than Hebrew.

The play is filled with words of Hebrew origin. For example (Pansier 1925: 127):

> *Réellement, Harcanot, as dedins ta <u>chadayim</u>*
> *Lou <u>sekel</u> dòu <u>holam</u>.*
> ('Really, Harcanot, you have within your hands the wisdom of the world').

The word *chadayim*, meaning "hands," illustrates the change of Hebrew ׳ to [š], the same change that explains the name *Shuadit* from יהודית. We also see the borrowing *sekel*, meaning "wisdom," and *holam*, meaning "world." Another example of a word derived from Hebrew with a negative meaning is *siccor*, meaning "drunkard" (Pansier 1925: 131).

UNE COMÉDIE EN ARGOT HÉBRAÏCO-PROVENÇAL

LOU HAOUMOUN
Le gueneruf! Mais qu'est-ce que ça signifie?

BARCANOT
Lou cresès, lou saup pas de qu'èi un gueneruf!
220 Un que ganauto un uf, pòu ganauta un buf.
Es emef; moussu, pèr ganauta vole dire,
Coume se Harcanot apavo lo maou d'éu
Que lou cresèsse siéu...

HARCANOT
Lou mau caud sus toun léu!
Ié dabères aqui...

LOU HAOUMOUN
Je commence à comprendre;
225 Le gueneruf c'est...

BARCANOT
Oui.

LOM HAOUMOUN
C'est lorsque l'on veut prendre
Ce qui n'est pas à soi: un voleur en un mot.

LE RECTEUR
Le gueneruf (vol)! Mais qu'est-ce que ça signifie?

BARCANOT
Le croyez-vous, il ne sait pas ce que c'est qu'un gueneruf?
220 Un qui vole un œuf, peut voler un buef.
C'est vrai par ganauta (voler) je veux dire
Comme si Harcanot prenait l'argent d'un autre
Qu'il croyait sien...

HARCANOT
La peste sur ton poumon!
Tu lui dis là...

LE RECTEUR
Je commence à comprendre.
225 Le gueneruf c'est...

LARCANOT
Oui.

LE RECTEUR
C'est lorsque l'on veut prendre
Ce qui n'est pas à soi; un voleur en un mot.

Figure 2: Excerpt from Pansier, 1925.

A chain shift took place in Shuadit, reflecting sound changes in Provençal. This can be seen in the transcription of Hebrew letters:

ת,צ,ס, and שׁ all became [θ], which then became [f].[1]
שׁ became [s].
י became [š].

In another chain shift, ד became [z] between vowels and [s] at the end of a word, and ז became [v]. These could have been pull shifts, meaning after a sound change left a gap in the pattern, another sound moved in to fill the gap. Or they could have been push shifts, meaning as one sound began to change, speakers had to alter the sound it was changing to, in order to maintain the distinction.

And so, the Jews of southern France said *emef* rather than *emeθ* ('true') and *Ifrael* rather than *Israel*. They also said *mamver* instead of *mamzer*, meaning "bastard," and *vona* instead of *zona*, meaning "prostitute." Instead of *Talmud*, they said *Talmus*. And, as we have already seen, instead of *Yehudit*, meaning 'Jewish', for the name of their language, they said *Shuadit*.

> *Sémâ Ifrael, Adonaï Elohenu, Adonaï e'had (Baru'h sem kevod mal'hufo l:olam vaed). Véaaouta ef Adonaï Elohe'ha be'houl lebabe'ha uou'houl naphse'ha uou'houl méode'ka, véayu adévarim ahélé asser ano'hi méfave'ha ayom al lebabe'ha, véssinantam lébane'ha, védibarta bam béssioute'ha bébéfe'ha uoule'hte'ha badere'h uoussou'hbe'ha uoukumé'ha ; uksartam léof al iade'ha, véayu létotaphof béén e'ha, u'hfaoutan al mévuvof befe'ha ubishare'ha.*

Figure 3: Shema from *Archives Juives* 1843: 695.

Sound changes in the Hebrew component of the spoken language also affected the language of prayer. The extent of these changes is generally not evident when we look at the prayers in the original Hebrew, since the spelling does not change. It is somewhat more evident when we read texts in the vernacular spelled with Hebrew characters but, as we saw above, the Esther poem in Judeo-Provençal leaves many questions unanswered. On the other hand, the following transcription of the שמע tells us a great deal.

---

[1] We know that [f] and [θ] are acoustically similar. It is not unusual for there to be confusion or merger of these sounds; such a merger has taken place in certain non-standard varieties of English, where people say *mouf* instead of *mouth*.

This segment of the daily prayers is found in a report on a detailed visit to southern and eastern France that appeared in *Archives Juives* in 1843 (also in Szajkowski 1948: iii). The reporter described the language transcribed into Latin letters as *vicieuse* (defective, faulty), but it is a treasure. It provides evidence that, in 1843, צ, שׂ, ס, and ת were pronounced [f]. The spelling *Véaaouta* confirms the interpretation of the ב in דייב as [w] finally and pre-consonantally, but between vowels as [v], since the word ואהבת is transcribed as *Véaauta*, while the word הדברים is transcribed as *adévarim*. It further documents that ו was pronounced [v], as we see in the spelling *mévuvof* for מזוזות. On the other hand, initial י is spelled *i* and likely pronounced [y] in the word *iade'ha*, Hebrew ידך, and is silent in *Ifrael*, perhaps because a [y] frequently vanishes before the acoustically similar [i]. There is no example of י becoming [š], which is the sound change that gave us the word *Shuadit*, among others.

By 1843, speakers of Shuadit had become less isolated from other Jewish communities. The isolation lasted from 1501 through 1791. The pronunciations we encountered in *Harcanot et Barcanot* survived through 1843, in whole Hebrew as well as in the spoken language. They survive in the Passover song *Had Gadya* but are no longer used in synagogues in the Comtat-Venaissin and Avignon, where new immigrants have moved in from North Africa. These immigrants and their descendants have introduced the interdental fricative [θ] into whole Hebrew to represent the letter ת.

3 Structural information

3.1 Relationship to non-Jewish varieties (isoglosses, related dialects)

Shuadit has words ending in final [p], [t], and [k]. These final consonants lasted into the 20th century in southwestern France (see Jochnowitz 1973: 116), but are not found in the area of the Papal States. Most Shuadit examples are words of Hebrew origin, but there are other words, like [kat] ('cat'), of Romance origin. The survival of these final consonants may reflect the expulsion from most of France that was completed in 1501, or it may reflect the role that words of Hebrew origin played in the phonology of Shuadit. It is hard to know when the final consonants disappeared from the varieties of Provençal, since they could have remained in the written language long after they were no longer pronounced, as is the case in contemporary French, in which the word spelled *chat* ('cat') is pronounced [ša].

Final stops are found in the southwestern province of Gascony and the adjacent region of southern Languedoc. When Jews were expelled from southern France, those who fled to the Comtat-Venaissin could have brought their dialects with them.

The word "*juge*" ('judge') was pronounced "*chuche*" (Guttel 1972, vol. 10: 441). The fricative sounds were originally affricates – a change that occurred in most of France. Affricates are unvoiced in a small area in the eastern part of Gascony and in southern Languedoc (Jochnowitz 1973: 111). As was the case with final stops, Jews moving to the Papal States could have brought the unvoiced africates with them. Then the affricates would have become fricatives as part of a major sound change.

We also see in Guttel (1972, vol. 10: 440) that "*plus*" is pronounced "*pius*" in Shuadit. This feature is found in eastern France, in parts of Lorraine and in Champagne (Jochnowitz 1973: 141). Could this pronunciation have been brought south when Jews left northern France in 1394? Perhaps. I did not come across any of these pronunciations in my own explorations.

3.2 Lexicon: Hebrew and Aramaic elements

A few terms refer to language. *Lashon hakodesh* ('language of holiness') is used in many Jewish communities to refer to Hebrew/Aramaic. In Shuadit, it is spelled *lassan akodes* and refers to the Shuadit language, as can be found in the comedy *Harcanot et Barcanot*, the play discussed above, which is a self-conscious attempt at capturing and preserving Shuadit. My informant, Armand Lunel, whom I interviewed in 1968, said his parents used to say "*Daber davar devant lou nar*" ('Say nothing in front of the boy') when they did not want him to understand.[2]

Jewish languages frequently have words referring to negative concepts that are of Hebrew origin. This is part of the tradition of using words of Hebrew origin as euphemisms and dysphemisms (Jochnowitz 2009). In Shuadit, we find [*ganaw*] meaning 'thief' from Hebrew גנב. The final [w] is also found in the Judeo-Italian spoken in Italy's Piedmont province, which is adjacent to France. In all likelihood, this pronunciation was brought by Jews expelled from France. In the play *Harcanot et Barcanot*, the word spelled *gueneruf* is the topic of the comic misunderstanding. The final -*uf* is the Shuadit pronunciation of the Hebrew noun-forming suffix -ות, reflecting the pronunciation [f] for ת. גנבות is one of the Hebrew words for "theft." The letter *r* in the word is a mystery, perhaps reflecting the elongation of *vav* into *resh*, a regional sound change, or perhaps it is simply an illustration of how the Rector misheard the word. Other words derived from גנב occur throughout the play. In *ganaut* (Pansier 1925: 119), the final –*t* is probably silent, and the word was pronounced [*ganaw*] with a final ב pronounced [w], just

---

2 In Judeo-Piedmontese, *dabra davar* means 'don't speak' according to Bachi (1929: 31).

as we saw in the word דייב meaning "God." The plural, however, is *ganavín*, since the ב is not final and retains its [v] pronunciation.

3.3 Language contact influences

Judeo-Provençal shares with Judeo-Italian and Ladino a negative word that is of Romance origin. In Judeo-Italian and Ladino, the word is *negro* and means 'bad, unfortunate' and does not mean "black," which is *prieto* in Ladino and *nero* in Judeo-Italian. In Judeo-Provençal the word is *nècre*, which is different from the Provençal *negre* for "black." It is also different from the Judeo-Provençal *negre*, meaning "foreigner" or "gentile," and which comes from Hebrew *nokhri*, according to Pierre Pansier (1925: 144). I have my doubts about this etymology, since the vowels do not correspond, and I am not aware of another case where Hebrew [o] is realized as [e] in Judeo-Provençal. Be that as it may, we also find a more familiar word for "gentiles," which is *gouïen*, obviously from Hebrew *goyim* (Pansier: 142).

4 Written and oral traditions

4.1 Writing system

Judeo-Provençal was written in Hebrew characters, with final and pre-consonantal ב representing the sound [w] and intervocal ד representing [z]. Shuadit was written in Latin characters following the spelling traditions of Provençal.

4.2 Literature

There were liturgical poems called *piyyutim*, designed to be sung or chanted during religious observances. A number of these poems in Judeo-Provençal were transcribed by Emperor Dom Pedro II of Brazil (Pedro Alacantara 1891).

5 State of research

Zosa Szajkowki's major work on Shuadit (1948) was written in Yiddish, and no doubt there were scholars in France and elsewhere who did not read it. Now that there is a French translation of this book by Michel Alessio (Szajkowski 2010), there may be increased interest in the subject. In the United States, Adam Strich has entered the category of scholars who have written about Judeo-Occitan (Provençal) (see, e.g., Strich with Jochnowitz 2015).

5.1 History of documentation

Non-Jews were aware of the existence of Shuadit and wrote works in which Jewish characters speak in this language. It was the custom in Carpentras to read a comic work called *Lou Sermoun di Jusiou* (The Sermon of the Jew) on Ash Wednesday. The work is attributed to Cardinal Jacques Sadolet and was supposedly composed in 1517. Since it is a comic work, written by non-native speakers, the Shuadit we find may not be accurate. Another such work is *Noué Juzioou* (Jewish Christmas carols), one of which is named *Reviho-te, Nanan* (Wake up, Nanan). It is a song in the form of a dialog between a convert from Judaism to Christianity and Nanan (a nickname for Abraham), who decides that he, too, will convert at the end of the song. It is attributed to N. Saboly, who lived from 1615 to 1675.

5.2 Corpora

There were various sets of glosses dating from the early Middle Ages. In addition to *Ittur* (mentioned above in section 2.3), there are "the glosses found in the anonymous *Sefer ha-Shorashim* appended to the *Farhi Bible* Ms. Sassoon no. 368, p. 42–165" (Guttel 1972: 439).

5.3 Issues of general theoretical interest

It would be of great interest to learn when Judeo-Romance varieties became spoken languages. The disagreement between Blondheim and Banitt continues, since there is no hard data concerning the way Jews spoke to each other as Romance languages were evolving.

References

Archives juives. 1843. Un voyage dans les communautés islaélites [sic] de l'est et du midi de la France. 624–643 and 685–696.

Banitt, Menachem. 1963. Une langue fantôme: Le Judéo-français. *Revue de Linguistique Romane*, 245–294.
Blondheim, David S. 1925. *Les parlers Judéo-romans et la Vetus Latina*. Paris: Librairie Ancienne Edouard Champion.
Chobaut, Hyacinthe. 1937. Les Juifs d'Avignon. *Revue des études Juives* 2 (new series): Janvier 5–52; Juillet-Décembre 3–39.
Colorni, Vittore. 1970. La parlata degli ebrei mantovani. *Rassegna Mensile di Israel* 36 (Scritti in memoria di Atillio Milano), 109–181.
Encyclopedia Judaica. 1972. Crescas. In *Encyclopedia Judaica*, Vol. 5, 1078.
Fudeman, Kirsten. 2010. *Language and identity in medieval French communities*. Philadelphia: University of Pennsylvania Press.
Guttel, Henri. 1972. Judeo-Provençal. In *Encyclopedia Judaica*, vol. 10, 439–441. Jerusalem: Keter.
Jochnowitz, George. 1973. *Dialect boundaries and the question of Franco-Provençal*. Berlin: De Gruyter (Hardcover edition, 2013).
Jochnowitz, George. 1978. Shuadit: La langue juive de Provence. *Archives Juives* 14, 63–67.
Jochnowitz, George. 1981. …Who made me a woman. *Commentary* 71/4, 63–64.
Jochnowitz, George. 1985. Had Gadya in Judeo-Italian and Shuadit (Judeo-Provençal). In Joshua Fishman (ed.), *Readings in the sociology of Jewish languages*, 241–245. Leiden: Brill.
Jochnowitz, George. 2009. Wrestling with God: Fear and fearlessness in Jewish languages. *Midstream* 54/3, 26–28.
Levy, Raphael. 1964. *Trésor de la langue des juifs français au Moyen Age*. Austin: University of Texas Press.
Lunel, Armand. 1926. *Esther de Carpentras ou le carnival hébraïque*. Paris. Editions de la Nouvelle Revue française.
Lunel, Armand. 1964. Quelques aspects du parler judéo-comtadin. *L'arche*. 94, 43–45.
Lunel, Armand. 1967–68. Les conversations chez les judéo-comtadins. *Les nouveaux cahiers* 2, 51–54.
Lunel, Armand. 1975. *Juifs de Languedoc, de la Provence et des Etats français du Pape*. Paris: Albin Michel.
Moulinas, René. 1981. *Les juifs du Pape en France: Les communautés d'Avignon et du Comtat Venaissin aus 17e et 18e siècles*. Paris: Commission française des Archives juives.
Ornan, Uzzi. 1972. Hebrew grammar. In *Encyclopedia Judaica* Vol. 8, cols. 77–175. Jerusalem: Keter.
Pansier, Pierre. 1925. Une comédie en argot hébraïco-provençal de la fin du XVIIIe siècle. *Revue des études juives* 81, 113–145.
Pedro Alcantara (Dom Pedro II). 1891. Poésies hébraico-provençales du rituel comtadin. Avignon: Séguin Frères.
Saboly, Nicholas. [Lived 1615–1675] 1824 [new edition]. *Noué juzioou*. Avignon.
Sadolet, Jacques. 1517. Lou sermoun di Jusiou. Printed version in *Armana Prouvençau* 21 (1875), 27–32.
Shapiro, Alexander. Provençal. In *Encyclopedia Judaica*, vol. 13, cols. 1259–64. Jerusalem: Keter.
Silberstein, Susan Milner. 1973. *The Provençal Esther poem written in Hebrew characters c. 1327*. Dissertation. University of Pennsylvania.
Strich, Adam (with George Jochnowitz). 2015. Judeo-Occitan (Judeo-Provençal). In Lily Kahn and Aaron D. Rubin (eds.), *Handbook of Jewish languages*. Leiden: Brill. 517–551.

Szajkowski, Zosa. 1948. *Dos loshn fun di yidn in di arbe kehiles fun Komta-Venesen* [The language of the Jews in the four communities of Comtat-Venaissin]. New York: YIVO. (Translated into French by Michel Alessio, 2010, as *La langue des Juifs du Pape*. Valence, France: Vent Terral.)

Weinreich, Max. 1980. *History of the Yiddish language*. Chicago: University of Chicago Press. (Translation of *Geshikhte fun der Yidisher shprakh*. 1973. New York: YIVO Institute.)

Wexler, Paul. 1987. Reconstructing the genesis of Yiddish in the light of its non-native components. In Dovid Katz (ed.), *Origins of the Yiddish language*, 135–142. Oxford: Pergamon Press, 135–42.

Ora (Rodrigue) Schwarzwald
Judeo-Spanish throughout the Sephardic Diaspora

1 Brief introduction

Judeo-Spanish (JS) is the language used by the Jews originating from Spain. It flourished in the Ottoman Empire immediately after the Expulsion from the Iberian Peninsula in 1492 and is still spoken in the same geographical areas today. Another branch of the expelled Jews, much smaller than the eastern one, settled in North Africa and continued to speak a JS language variety known as Ḥakitía (Ḥaketía) until the 20th century.[1]

At the beginning of the 21st century, JS seems to be in the process of becoming an endangered language. However, in spite of the decreasing number of speakers, there is an increasing interest in JS, both from an academic and folkloristic perspective.

1.1 Names of the language

Several names refer to the language used by the expelled Jews from Spain, e.g., *Spanyolit* or *Espanyolit* (especially in Israel), *Espanyol, Ladino, Romance, Franco Espanyol, Judeo Espanyol, Jidyo* or *Judyo, Judezmo, Zhargon*, etc., in the Ottoman Empire communities, and either *Ḥakitía* or just *Espanyol* in North Africa (Bunis 1999a: 17–18). Each community used a different name for the language. Three names, however, are commonly used today to denote the language of the Ottoman Empire Jewish communities: *Judezmo* (meaning both Judaism and the language name, parallel to Yiddish), *Ladino,* and *Judeo-Espanyol* (Judeo-Spanish). Many scholars use the name *Ladino* to specifically denote the JS calque type language of liturgical translations from Hebrew, while JS or *Judezmo* refers to the vernacular used for all other purposes.

---

[1] The following books refer to the history and sociolinguistic aspects of JS: Wagner (1990), Marcus (1965), Renard (1967), Díaz-Mas (1992), Bunis (1999a), and Sephiha (1986). See also Hernández González (2001) for an overview of the language. A detailed research bibliography through 1980 is listed in Bunis (1981). The best description of Ḥakitía is given in Benoliel's book (1977).

Note: This is an updated revised version of my article "Judeo-Spanish Studies," published in The *Oxford Handbook of Jewish Studies*, edited by Martin Goodman, Jeremy Cohen and David Sorkin, Oxford University Press 2002, pp. 572–600, by permission of Oxford University Press.

1.2 Linguistic affiliation

Judeo-Spanish is considered a dialect of Spanish (Zamora Vicente 1985: 349–377). Its first affiliation is with Iberian Spanish. The Jews in Spain before 1492 were familiar with Hebrew and Aramaic, Arabic (the language of the Muslim conquerors), and Romance (the language of the Christians). Ibero-Romance was used as the main vernacular language of the Jews from the time of the *Reconquista* in Christian Spain. By the time of the Jewish Expulsion, several Spanish dialects had formed in the Iberian Peninsula. The Jews carried these dialectal varieties to their new countries of settlement, and these dialects continued to serve as the languages of communication until they were gradually unified into a kind of koiné (see 2.1 below). The language then developed autonomously. JS kept some features of medieval Spanish which changed in modern Castilian Spain. Contact with neighboring languages, as well as constant interaction with Hebrew-Aramaic, the language of religion and education, influenced the vocabulary, grammar, and semantics of JS. Hence, although its basic grammatical structure and vocabulary are based on medieval Spanish, there are many differences between Judeo-Spanish and Spanish.

1.3 Regions where the language is/was spoken

Most of the Jews expelled from Spain in 1492 settled throughout the Ottoman Empire, especially in what is known today as Turkey and the Balkans, where they spoke JS (and Ḥakitía in North Africa). Most of the ex-converted Jews (*anusim*) who gradually left Spain and Portugal settled in the Netherlands, in southern France, Italy, Germany, and later on in the United States. The main language spoken by these communities during the 17th–18th centuries was Portuguese, though they used Hebrew, Spanish, Latin, and local languages for writing (den Boer 1996). Spanish was specifically used for liturgical Ladino translations. From the 19th century, they started using the local languages. Some ex-converted Jews immigrated to Sephardic Jewish population centers throughout the Ottoman Empire and were fully assimilated into these communities.

From the end of the 19th century, North African Ḥakitía was gradually replaced by Modern Spanish. The ex-converted communities adopted the languages of the countries in which they lived, and their usage of Ladino texts became quite limited.

Nowadays, JS is still spoken in some communities in Israel, in the United States, in France, in Belgium, and in the Balkans, although the number of native speakers is gradually decreasing.

1.4 Attestations and sources

Yaari (1934) lists the names of books and documents written in JS found in the National Library in Jerusalem, but his list is partial because many books have been added to the library since 1934, and much additional material exists in other libraries and private collections around the world. More sources can be found in the online Bibliography of Hebrew Books from 1460 to 1960 in the National Library Catalogue in Jerusalem. A search for JS books reveals thousands of titles (Cohen 2011). Gaon's (1964) catalogue of Ladino newspapers is also partial. Other catalogues around the world demonstrate the enormous volume of material written in JS (e.g., Refael's 1999 review, as well as catalogues such as Steinschneider 1852–60, Cowley 1971 and others).

In addition to written texts, oral JS sources have been collected and documented since the end of the 19th century (see 4.2 below). Many books have been written on these oral sources; recordings exist in various institutions and private collections (see sections 4 and 5 below).

1.5 Present-day status

Eastern JS is still alive today and is spoken in Israel and around the world by individual native speakers, mostly elderly. The language of ex-converted Sephardic Jewish communities has become totally assimilated into that of the wider host societies. North African descendants of the exiled Jews use standard Spanish today, and remnants of Ḥakitía can only be heard in proverb citations, special words and nicknames, and some songs and folk stories.

2 Historical background

Max Weinreich (1973: 126) distinguished two periods in the development of JS (*Dzhudezmo*): Sepharad I, before the Expulsion from the Iberian Peninsula, and Sepharad II, from the 16th century onwards. The Expulsion caused the expelled Jews (Sephardim) to become almost exclusively a Diaspora community. Only the ex-converted communities from Spain and Portugal kept some ties with Spain and Portugal, long after they left the Iberian Peninsula and returned to Judaism.

Apparently, JS developed in the Iberian Peninsula, although what evidence we have is difficult to assess (Marcus 1962; Várvaro 1987; Revah 1970: 238–240; Weinreich 1973: 126). It is reasonable to assume that the language was already shaped as a Jewish language, based on the following considerations, in addition to the Hebrew script JS speakers used when writing Spanish: 1. The Jews formed a religious ethno-sociological group that was different in customs and beliefs from non-Jewish groups, and such groups form special language varieties (Spolsky 2014: 129–140); 2. There was an extensive Hebrew-Aramaic fused component in the JS language that included not only religious terms but general ones as well (e.g., *dezmazalado* 'unlucky, miserable' from Hebrew *mazal* 'luck'); 3. Some linguistic forms developed in Iberian Spanish were adopted by the Jews and preserved in their speech while abandoned by their neighbors (e.g., *ansina* 'so, this way'; Spanish *así*); 4. The linguistic similarity between the North African and Ottoman Empire Sephardic communities after the Expulsion cannot be explained as accidental. They both ascended from the same medieval Jewish sources (Bunis 1992, 2004a; Schwarzwald 1999, 2002).

On the other hand, Minervini (1992: 131–133) carefully examined a variety of medieval *aljamiado*[2] JS texts and showed that phonological, morphological, and lexical evidence proves that the Jews used the same dialectal variety as their Christian neighbors (Penny 1996: 55). However, because of the Hebrew-Aramaic component in these texts, Hebrew orthography, and special Jewish content, it is reasonable to conclude that some forms of JS already existed in medieval Spain.

2.1 Phases in historical development

The periodization of JS after the Expulsion from Spain varies among scholars. Based on historical, literary, and linguistic processes, one can distinguish between 16th century JS and 17th–20th century JS (Revah 1970: 240–242; Sephiha 1979: 26, 1986). On the other hand, various linguistic considerations support a division of JS between the 16th–18th centuries and the 19th–20th centuries (Bunis 1992: 404–412). In the 16th century, immediately after the Expulsion, written material, either in Rashi script or in square Hebrew letters, followed certain norms that retained the Roman-script spelling of Spanish. Towards the end of the 16th century and during the 17th century, the (Judeo) Spanish and [Judeo-] Portuguese varieties turned slowly into a *koiné*, which served the Sephardic Jews as the JS in their new settlements (Minervini 2002; Quintana 2006, 2012). Because of the distances between the settlements, various dialects were formed.

---

2 *Aljamiado* is a Spanish text written in non-Roman characters.

The distance from Spain and the natural development of JS contributed to the changes in various literary and linguistic features of the language from the 19th century onwards (some say from the second half of the 18th century), and modern JS was formed at this stage. Vernacular forms entered the written language, and many words and expressions from the local languages were fused with JS.

From World War I to the present day, JS underwent another change (see 2.2 below). This period is marked by a gradual shift from Hebrew orthography to Roman script and by an increase of French and Italian influences that replaced Turkish, Greek, and sometimes Hebrew elements by more "Romanized" forms.

2.2 The current state of Judeo-Spanish

In the early years of the 21st century, the number of JS speakers is gradually decreasing, the quantity of creative writing being produced is small, and its target is a Hispanic audience, not necessarily a JS one. Harris (1994: 197–229) lists 24 reasons that have caused the present predicament of JS, many of which relate to one another. Here are a few of the most important ones:

a. With the formation of separate nationalities in the Balkans and Eastern Europe during the 19th century, and with Kemal Ataturk's reforms in Turkey, local languages turned into national ones, thus changing JS into an informal, mundane family language.
b. The secularization of communities where JS was once spoken has also led to its decline. JS was associated with a religious, traditional way of life. Newer generations increasingly wanted modernism and therefore slowly abandoned their roots.
c. Since World War II, JS has not been taught as a primary language and has not been studied as a second language in elementary or high schools (but see section 5.4.2 below). North African Sephardic communities replaced Ḥakitía with Modern Castilian Spanish, while French replaced JS as the language of culture in the eastern Mediterranean.
d. JS did not have the prestigious status of Spanish, French, or Italian. JS speakers did not consider it important and replaced it with the more revered languages.
e. Many members of Sephardic communities immigrated to various countries around the world for commercial and other reasons. In their new settlements they adopted the local languages. Moreover, with the rise of the Zionist ideology from the 19th century onwards, many members of the Sephardic communities immigrated to Israel. The Israeli ideology to speak only Hebrew in Israel caused the gradual loss of JS among the younger generations.

f. Thousands of JS-speaking Sephardic Jews, especially from Greece, were killed during the Holocaust.
g. Many Sephardic JS speakers married Jews from other communities. Communication between married couples and their children was not in JS, but rather in the language of the country in which they resided.
h. The replacement of Hebrew or Rashi orthography by Roman script, although meant for the benefit of the speakers, had a negative effect. It prevented JS speakers from enriching their vocabulary and grammar with written JS literature. A language without literature is a living language but cannot be as rich as a written one (Fishman 1972: 24–28).
i. There were no unifying forces working for the retention of the language because its speakers did not consider it important enough to retain.

3 Structural information

As described in section 2, Spanish Jews became familiar with Arabic during the Islamic invasion of Spain and with Romance languages after the *Reconquista* in the Iberian Peninsula. JS-speaking Jews used Hebrew and Aramaic as their languages of liturgy, education, and correspondence with other Jewish communities, JS to communicate between themselves, and the language of their host society to converse with non-Jews.

JS was influenced by the various medieval Romance dialects that existed, and still exist, in the Iberian Peninsula (Wright 1982; Zamora Vicente 1985). Traces of all these dialects can be found in the JS that developed after the Expulsion.

The archaic JS vocabulary reflecting Iberian Spanish is revealed through words like *abokarse* 'bend' (Spanish *agacharse, imclinarse*; Spanish *abocarse* 'approach, meet with'), *agora* 'now' (Spanish *ahora*), *ambezar* 'teach, learn' (Old Spanish *avisar*), *avagar* 'slowly [adverb]' (Spanish *despacio, lentamente*; Spanish *vagar* 'wander, roam [verb]; leisure, idelness [noun]'), *eskapar* 'finish; save' (Spanish *terminar, acabar; salvar*; Spanish *escapar* 'escape; ride [a horse]'), *kavesal* 'pillow' (Spanish *almohada*, Old Spanish *cabezal*), and many others.

The influence of Iberian dialects can be found in various words, e.g., *alfinete* 'pin' and *preto* 'black' (from Portuguese; Spanish *alfiler; negro*; JS *negro* is 'bad'; Spanish *prieto* 'dark; mean; tight'), *ponte* 'bridge' and *luvia* 'rain' (from Leonese; Spanish *puente, lluvia*), *mangrana* 'pomegranate' (from Aragonese and Catalan; Spanish *granada*), *atorgar* 'consent to, allow' (from Aragonese and used in Salamanca; Spanish *consentir, otorgar*), *alḥað* 'Sunday' (from Arabic; Spanish *domingo*), etc.

3.1 Relationship to non-Jewish varieties

After the Expulsion from Spain, Jewish communities were in constant contact with local languages in the Ottoman Empire to the east (Turkish, Greek, Serbo-Croatian, etc.) and with Arabic and Berber in the west. Later on in the development of JS, the Jews were exposed to French and Italian in the Balkans and Turkey, and French and Spanish in North Africa. Traces of all these languages can be found in JS. This influence is expressed lexically, but at times grammatically as well, e.g.,

    Turkish: *džep* 'pocket' (alternating with *aldikera~faldukwera*; Spanish *bolsillo, faltriquera*), *tendžeré* 'pot' (Spanish *cacharro*), *musafír* 'guest' (Spanish *convidado*), *doláp* 'cupboard' (Spanish *armario*; JS also *almario*) (Varol-Bornes 2008)
    Greek: *piron* 'fork' (Spanish *tenedor*), *fusta* 'skirt' (Spanish *falda*), *abramila~avramila* 'small prune' (Spanish *ciruela*)
    Serbo-Croatioan: *ludo* 'crazy' (Spanish *loco*), *misirke* 'turkey' (Spanish *pavo*), *rizá~riðá* 'handkerchief' (Spanish *pañuelo*)
    French: *elévo* 'student' (alternating with literary *desipulo, estudiante*; Spanish *alumno, estudiante*)
    Italian: *adíyo* 'bye' (Spanish ¡*hasta luego*!), *komerčo* 'commerce' (Spanish *comercio*), *capače* 'capable' (Spanish *capaz, competente*)
    Arabic: *kira* 'rent' (Spanish *alquiler*), *adafina* 'Jewish Shabbat dish, cholent', *šarife* 'noble', *dendná* 'music' (in Ḥakitía; Spanish *música*)

The Turkish suffixes *-lí* and *-dží~-čí* were adopted by JS and added to words of non-Turkish origin, e.g., *xenli* 'graceful person' (Hebrew ḥen + Turkish *-li*), *azlaxadží* 'successful' (Hebrew haṣlaḥa + Turkish *-dži*). Turkish verbs take the Spanish ending *ear* and conjugate like any other JS words, e.g., *adžidear* 'pity' (Turkish *acımak* [adžımak] + *-ear*), *bozear* 'damage, ruin' (Turkish *bozmak* + *ear*).

Dialectal differences are listed in many descriptions of JS. Zamora Vicente (1985: 362) lists many differences between eastern and western dialects within the eastern Ottoman Empire communities, e.g., *agranada – mangrana* 'pomegranate', *bostezar – bostežar* 'yawn', *blando – moye* 'soft', *ruvio – royo* 'reddish'. Quintana (2006) mapped isoglosses of the various eastern JS dialects based on some grammatical and lexical features. Some of these features can be traced back to the Iberian Peninsula, while others are independent developments of the language due to distances between communities. Quintana showed that the most significant dialectal centers focused around Constantinople (Istanbul) in Turkey and Thessaloniki in Greece. Communities that were more detached from these centers show greater variations in JS.

3.2 Particular structural features

There are several common linguistic features in all JS dialects, and these features make them different from other varieties of Spanish (although several features can also be found sporadically in some Spanish dialects around the world). Most of these features existed in Ḥakitía until the 19th century (Benoliel 1977). A few of the features are listed here (Crews 1935; Marcus 1965: 70–95; Wagner 1990[I]: 9–28; Zamora Vicente 1985: 349–377; Bunis 1992: 414–420, 1999a; Penny 2000: 174–193; Quintana 2006: 3–23):

a. The medieval phonemes /š/, /dž/, and /ž/ were retained in JS, but changed in Modern Spanish into /x/ (Spanish <g> or <j>), e.g., *pašaro* 'bird', *džente* 'people', *ižo* 'son' (Spanish *pájaro, gente, hijo* pronounced [páxaro, xénte, íxo]).

b. The phoneme /x/ occurs in words of Hebrew-Aramaic, Arabic, or Turkish origin, e.g., *xanukíya* 'Hanukkah lamp' (from Hebrew *ḥanukka*), *alxáð* 'Sunday' (from Arabic *al+ḥad* 'the one'; Spanish *domingo*), *xanum* 'affectionate address to a woman or a girl' (Turkish *hanım* 'woman, lady, Ms., Mrs.' It also occurs as a variant of *we* in some dialects; see feature f on page 154 below).

c. JS /v/ and /b/ are distinct phonemes, while their status is allophonic in Spanish ([ß] and [b]), e.g., *xavér* 'partner, friend' (from Hebrew *ḥaber*), *xabér* 'news' (from Turkish *haber*), *bivir* 'live', *bever* 'drink', *vazo* 'glass' (Spanish *vivir, beber, vaso*, pronounced [biβir, beβer, baso]).

d. Spanish *u* in historical sequences of *-bC- is often realized in JS as *v*, e.g., *sivdað~sivda* 'city', *kavza* 'cause, reason', *devda* 'debt' (Spanish *ciudad, causa, deuda*).

e. The equivalents to the Spanish letters <c> and <z> ([θ] in Castilian Spanish) are pronounced [s] and [z], e.g., *serar* 'shut' (Spanish *cerrar*), *(f)azer* 'do' (Spanish *hacer*), *(f)izo* 'did (3SG)' (Spanish *hizo*).

f. Residues of the historical affricates *c* or *z* are pronounced as [dž] or [ž] in a few words, e.g., *dodže~dože* 'twelve' (Spanish *doce*).

g. The historical /s/ would often be pronounced [z] between vowels, e.g., *kaza* 'house' (Spanish *casa*).

h. Spanish <s> before *k* is pronounced [š] in JS, e.g., *moška* 'fly [n]', *buškar* 'search' (Spanish *mosca, buscar*).

i. Spanish <ll> is pronounced [y] or lost in some cases in JS, e.g., *yave* 'key' (Spanish *llave*), *estrea* 'star' (Spanish *estrella*).

j. There is no clear distinction between flap *r* and trill *r* in JS. In all the texts, the letter *resh* represents both, e.g., JS <pero> Spanish *pero* 'but', *perro* 'dog'. Trill *r* is common in spoken JS in word initial and medial position, especially after *a*, as in Spanish, e.g., *arreglar* 'arrange'.

k. Vowels are not always as in Spanish, e.g., *kuzir* 'sew' (Spanish *coser*), *džugo* 'game' (Spanish *juego*), *pilago* 'lake' (Spanish *piélago*).
l. There is metathesis in many consonant clusters, especially with *d* or *r*, e.g., *pedrer* 'lose' (Spanish *perder*), *porfeta* 'prophet' (Spanish *profeta*).
m. Clitic pronouns also undergo metathesis in imperative plural forms, e.g., *kitalda* 'take it.F out' (Spanish *quitadla*).
n. The JS diminutive is *-iko/-ika* (M/F) rather than Spanish *-ito/-ita*, e.g., *livriko* 'small book' (Spanish *librito*), *ermanika* 'small sister' (Spanish *hermanita*).
o. Some conjugational suffixes are systematically different from Spanish. The suffixes *-í* '1SG', *-tes* '2SG', and *-imos* '1PL' are used in the preterite instead of *-é*, *-ste*, and *-amos* (in *-ar* verbs). The suffix *-š* '2PL' is used instead of *-eis* and *-ais* in Spanish, e.g., *avlí* 'I spoke' (Spanish *hablé*), *avlates* 'you.SG talked' (Spanish *hablaste*), *avalimos* 'we talked' (Spanish *hablamos*), *avláteš* 'you.PL talked' (Spanish *hablateis*), *avlaráš* 'you.PL shall speak' (Spanish *hablarais*).
p. The verbs *ser* 'to be', *dar* 'give', *estar* 'be', and *ir* 'go' conjugate in the 1st person as *so, do, esto, vo* (Spanish *soy, doy, estoy, voy*; and see feature e on page 154 below).
q. There are fewer tenses in JS than in Spanish.
r. The copulative verb is often *tener* rather than *aver* (Spanish *haber*), e.g., *tengo avlado* 'I have been talking', *tenía iðo~avía iðo* 'I had gone' (Spanish *he hablado, había ido*).
s. The Spanish *ustedes* formal polite addressee form is absent. Polite forms are expressed by 2PL forms, *vos*, or by conjugated forms of the 2PL forms.
t. Although *nos* 'us' (accusative pronoun) and *nuestro* 'our' are known and used in a literary style, the vernacular forms are *mos* and *muestro*, respectively.
u. The initial *mue* instead of the Spanish *nue* also occurs in other words, e.g. *muevo* 'new' (Spanish *nuevo*), *mueve* 'nine' (Spanish *nueve*).
v. The accusative pronoun can occur before the verb or following it, e.g., *alegrar mos emos*, next to *mos alegraremos* 'we shall rejoice' (Spanish *nos alegraremos*; in medieval Spanish also *alegrar nos hemos*).
w. Definite articles before possessive pronouns follow medieval forms, e.g., *la mi (f)iža* 'my daughter' (literally the my daughter; Spanish *mi hija*), and are still used, especially in literary and poetic styles.

Some phonological and morphological features are dialectal and occur in specific areas (Quintana 2006):
a. The initial historical *f* is preserved in some dialects, e.g., *forno* 'oven', *fazer* 'do', *fígado~fégaðo* 'liver' (*orno, azar, igaðo* in other dialects; Spanish *horno, hacer, hígado*). This phenomenon also occurs in the dialects of Asturia, Galicia, and Leon, as well as in Portugal.

b. In some dialects, /g/ is velarized and pronounced as [γ], e.g., in Thessaloniki. In some dialects, /d/ is not spirantized after a vowel, e.g., in Bulgaria.
c. In some dialects, the semivowel *w* is inserted after the velar *g*, e.g., *lečuga>lečugwa* 'lettuce' (Spanish *lechuga*).
d. Unstressed mid-vowels *o* and *e* become high vowels *u* and *i*, respectively, in unstressed position in northeastern communities, e.g., *sigúnda* 'second.F', *tupár* 'find', *dibášu* 'under' (in most dialects *segúnda*, *topar*, *debašo*; Spanish *segunda*, *topar*, *debajo*).
e. Some verbs have special conjugations when compared to standard Spanish, and these fluctuate in various locations, e.g., *se~so*, *sos*, *es*, *semos~somos*, *soš*, *son* 'be.PRES' (Spanish *soy*, *eres*, *es*, *somos*, *sois*, *son*).
f. The Spanish diphthong *we* in *swe* and *fwe* (Spanish spelled <sue, fue>) is realized in JS as [swe, fwe], [sxwe, xwe], or [sfwe] in various dialects, e.g., *swenyo~esxwenyo~esfwenyo* 'sleep' (Spanish *sueño*), *fwego~xwego* 'fire' (Spanish *fuego*).

3.3 Lexicon: Hebrew and Aramaic elements

The Hebrew-Aramaic (HA) component is quite heavy in JS. Most words are stressed as in Hebrew. The letters *dalet* after a vowel and sometimes *tav* at the end of a word are pronounced [ð], the letter *ṣadi* is pronounced [s], and *ḥet* is pronounced [x]. Especially in Thessaloniki, *ayin* at the end of a word or when closing syllables is pronounced [x], and *shin* is pronounced [s]. The letter *he* is not pronounced in JS (Schwarzwald 1981, 1985; Bunis 1993).

Many HA words in JS relate to the Jewish calendar, traditions, and life cycle and carry the same meanings as in Hebrew, e.g., *roš šaná* 'Rosh Hashana, New Year's Day', *kipúr* 'Kippur, Day of Atonement', *pésax* 'Passover' (Hebrew *pesaḥ*), *šavuóð~sevó* 'Pentecost' (Hebrew. *šavuʕot*), *tišá beáv* 'The 9th of Av' (Hebrew *tišˁá beʔáv*); *tefilá* 'prayer; morning prayer', *kadíš* 'Kaddish', *xazán* 'cantor' (Hebrew *ḥazan*), *pasúk* 'biblical verse', *kilá~keilá* 'community' (Hebrew *qehilá*); *berít* 'circumcision', *bar mizvá* 'Bar Mitzvah', *xupá* 'wedding ceremony' (Hebrew *ḥupa*), *arón* 'coffin', etc. Other words are not related to Jewish concepts, e.g., *avel* 'mourner', *afilú* 'even', *gezerá* 'decree', *sadik* 'righteous person' (Hebrew *ṣadiq*), *seuðá* 'meal' (Hebrew *seˁudá*), etc.

Some HA words in JS carry both Hebrew and additional meanings, e.g., *rebí* 'rabbi; teacher', *xavér* 'friend; partner' (Hebrew *ḥaver*), *gemará* 'Talmud; booklet', *megilá* 'the Book of Esther; a long boring document', *sar* 'sadness; suffering' (Hebrew *ṣaˁar*), *misva~mizva* 'alm; dead person' (Hebrew *miṣva*).

Many HA words totally changed their original Hebrew meanings in JS, e.g., *garon* 'voice' (Hebrew 'throat'), *veaðar* 'second month of Adar in a leap year' (Hebrew *veʔadar* 'and Adar'), *mišmara~mismara* 'study night' (rabbinical Hebrew 'third part of a night'), *mabul* 'a lot' (Hebrew 'flood'), *kal* 'synagogue' (Hebrew *qahal* 'congregation, public'). Other words are newly formed as Hebrew words carrying special meanings, e.g., *daatán~daxtán* 'someone who considers himself knowledgeable; pest' (Hebrew *deˤa* 'opinion') *yoðéa lašón~yoðéax lašón* 'warning to point out someone who's not Jewish but understands JS or Spanish' (Hebrew *yodeaˤ* 'knows[SG.PRS]', *lašón* 'language, tongue'), *xaxamút~xaxamúð* 'the rabbi's duty' (Hebrew *ḥaxám* 'wise; in JS also rabbi'), etc.

The morphological fusion of HA words in JS is revealed when Hebrew words take inflectional or derivational suffixes from Hebrew, Turkish, or Spanish, e.g., *balabáy-balabáya* 'good householder.M-F' (Hebrew *baˤal habbayit, baˤalat habbayit* 'the owner of the house'), *axenarse* 'beautify oneself' (Hebrew *ḥen* 'grace'), *(guevo) enxaminado* 'hard boiled [egg]', *enxaminarse* 'get burnt, stay long in the sun' (Hebrew *ḥamin* '(Sabbath) stew'). From the word *aspan* 'insolent' (Hebrew *ˤaz panim*), the abstract form *aspanut* 'insolence' is formed; from *xaver* 'partner', the word *xavransa* 'partnership' is formed (in addition to *xaverut*), and *xaveriko* is a partner or a spouse.

Hebrew influence is revealed in syntactic structures, as well. Many phrases are based on Hebrew expressions, e.g., *el santo bendičo el* 'the Holy blessed (be) He' is based on the Hebrew *haqadoš barux hu*; *el era dizien* 'he used to say, irritant' is based on the common Mishnaic saying *hu haya ʔomer*; *asta aki* 'until here, the end of citation' is coined after Hebrew *ˤad kan*. *Salir de ovligasyon* 'act perfunctorily' is based on the Hebrew *laṣet yede ḥova*, and *tener zexu~zaxuð~zaxu* 'have merit' reflects *yeš (lo) zəxut*.

Many proverbs use Hebrew words, some based on Hebrew sources, others on Hispanic traditions or those of neighboring languages. For example: *ni de tu myel ni de tu fiel* 'neither from your honey, nor from your needle; no trust in you' (cf. Hebrew *lo meˤuqṣex velo miduvšex* 'not from your sting nor from your honey'). *Abaša maðrega~eskalon i toma mužer, suve maðrega~eskalon i toma xaver* 'descend a step and take a wife, climb a step and take a partner' is based on a Talmudic saying (Bavli, Yevamot 63a). The proverb *ben kax uven kax gway de~bolo la iža de iftax* 'in the meantime, alas~was lost the daughter of Jephthah' is based on the biblical story from Judges (chapter 11). Learned JS speakers used to say *axaré eamál veatórax vaikáx kórax* 'after labor and effort Koraḥ took; referring to someone who wants the fruits of the achievements that others worked on'. All the words are Hebrew, but this is a JS proverb that does not exist in Hebrew.

3.4 Language contact influences

In the previous sections, some features were described referring to the dialectal variations caused by language contact. The terms eastern and western are often used in JS research, referring to different communities:
1. Eastern are the expelled Jews; western are the ex-converted communities that originated mainly from western Spain and Portugal and settled in western Europe.
2. Eastern are the Ottoman Empire Sephardic Jews; western are the North African Sephardic Jews.
3. Eastern are the dialects in the Ottoman Empire that reflect features of central Iberian Spanish; western are the dialects in the Ottoman Empire that reflect west and north Iberian Spanish.

The ex-converted communities are considered western dialects only with regard to Ladino liturgical translations, which carry more features of standard Spanish than the eastern ones. They are mostly written in Roman letters though a few Ladino texts are printed in Hebrew letters. They also include less Hebrew words in the translations than the eastern ones.

According to the second classification, the eastern communities include the Ottoman Empire JS speakers, whereas the western communities include Ḥakitía speakers. In addition to its general JS grammatical and lexical features, JS of the western communities is typified by extensive borrowings from Arabic, the neighboring language, and by different lexical choices. The Jews of the western communities retained the pharyngeal /ḥ/ and /ʕ/ in words of Hebrew and Arabic origin like their Judeo-Arabic-speaking neighbors. The oral literary genres are slightly different from the eastern ones. Very little has been published in writing in Ḥakitía, but we know that the oral JS literary tradition was well preserved in this community.

The most comprehensive studies on various JS Ottoman Empire eastern dialects were conducted by Crews (1935) and Wagner (1990[I]: 7–109, 1990[I]: 111–235, and more in 1990), and later by Bunis (1981: 42–50, 1988), and Quintana (2006) in various publications.

Researchers distinguish between groups of dialects in the Ottoman Empire reflecting various areas in the Iberian Peninsula – western versus eastern; however, there are further differences, which have come about due to local influences and natural language development. Quintana shows that this classification into east and west is not clear, because many isoglosses are formed distinctly, depending on the features described (see 3.2 above). Dictionaries show the common vocabulary in various JS languages, but in many cases the dialectal differences are not indicated, e.g., *faldukwera* in Thessaloniki, *aldikera* or *džep* 'pocket' in Turkey, *seðakero* (Hebrew *ṣədaqá*) means philanthropist in Thessaloniki, but a beggar in Turkey and Israel (*seðakadži* in Thessaloniki).

Because of the continued migrations of Jews in various communities, dialectal study is very difficult, especially now that there are hardly any living native JS speakers that carry on the tradition.

4 Written and oral traditions

4.1 Writing system

From its beginnings, Spanish was written by Jews in Hebrew characters, in the form that was later named Rashi script. This way of writing in handwritten texts was named *Solitreo* by the Sephardic Jews (*ganchos* 'hooks' in the vernacular). Printed material in JS was written in either Hebrew Rashi script or square Hebrew letters, sometimes vocalized, especially for liturgical translations.

The only Sephardi Jewish group that mainly used Roman characters in Ladino from the beginning was the ex-converted Jews. For liturgical Ladino translations, they often used the conventional Spanish spellings of their time, with some adaptations for the transliteration of Jewish or Hebrew terms. Most of their creative writing was written in Portuguese and in Spanish, naturally in Roman script (and rarely in Hebrew or in the local languages). Therefore, this group will not be discussed any further in this section, except in reference to Ladino translations.

Throughout its history, JS developed a certain kind of conventional spelling to represent Spanish and JS in Hebrew letters; however, this was not always consistent. Spelling became more regularized during the 19th century (Pascual Recuero 1988; Bunis 2004b; Schwarzwald 2004). Here is a comparison of spelling changes from the 16th to the 19th century (the pronunciation is given in square brackets):

מחז׳יר > מוג׳יר [mužer] 'woman' (Spanish *mujer* [muxer])
איז׳ו > היג׳ו~פ׳יג׳ו [(f)ižo], rarely פ׳יג׳ו, 'son' (Spanish *hijo* [ixo])
ייאמאר > לייאמאר [yamar] 'call' (Spanish *llamar*, dialectal [λamar, yamar])
איסטרייא~איסטריאה > אישטרילייה~אישטרילייא [estreya~estrea] 'star' (Spanish *estrella* [estreλa, estreya])
אוייר > אואיר~אולייר~אואיר 'hear' (Spanish *oír*)
סי > שי~סי [si] 'yes; if' (Spanish *sí*)
סאלוד > שלוד~סלוד~סאלוד [salu(ð)] 'health' (Spanish *salud*)
באשו > באש׳ו~בשו~בש׳ו [bašo] 'low' (Spanish *bajo* [baxo])
ב׳ינו > וינו [vino] 'wine; he came' (Spanish *vino* [bino])
ביב׳יר > ביביר~ביב׳יר~ביויר [bivir] 'live' (Spanish *vivir* [biβir])
ביב׳יר > ביביר ~ ביב׳יר [bever] 'drink' (Spanish *beber* [beβer])

As can be seen from the examples above, spelling conventions became more consistent, more distinctive, and more systematic in the 19th century. *Zayin* with a diacritic replaced the ambiguous *gimel* with a diacritic, to represent the sound /ž/. Initial historical /f/ and /h/ in JS were ignored. The combination of *lamed* and *yod* reflected the Spanish <ll>, pronounced [y] in JS, and was replaced by the Hebrew double *yod*, not always consistently, sometimes causing hypercorrections as in *oír*. *Shin* for the representation of /s/ was substituted by *samech*. *Shin* with a diacritic was replaced by *shin* without a diacritic. *Vav* or *bet* with a diacritic was systematically replaced by *bet* with a diacritic.

Gimel with a diacritic continued being used for the representation of /č/ and /dž/, e.g., ג'יקו [čiko] 'small' (Spanish *chico*), ג'וסטו > ג'וסטו~ג'ושטו [džusto] 'right' (Spanish *justo* [xusto]). *Kof* represented /k/ (e.g., קאמינו 'way', Spanish *camino*; קילו 'kilo'; קואנדו 'when', Spanish *cuando*). The letters *kaf*, *tzadi*, and *tav* were normally used in words of Hebrew origin (e.g., כבוד 'honor', צדקה 'charity', תורה 'Bible'), while *ḥet* could occur in Hebrew words, in words of Arabic or Turkish origin, as well as in dialectal varieties (e.g., חכם 'rabbi' (Hebrew), חאביר [xaber] 'news' (Turkish), חואי [xwe] 'was.3m', *fwe* in other JS dialects; Spanish *fue*). Sometimes *tzadi* would represent the Spanish <c> or <ç>, in early texts immediately after the Expulsion from Spain (e.g., סינציניאה [sencenia] 'matzah'). *Nun* and *yod* represented the Spanish <ñ> (e.g., דאנייו, Spanish *daño* 'damage').

During the 20th century, many JS texts were written in Roman script; however, the orthographic conventions are controversial among scholars (see, for instance, Sephiha 1973: 31–38; Hassán 1978; Varol 1998: 27–28; Lazar 1988: xiii-xvi). The most commonly used orthographic convention today in transcribing JS is the one used in *Aki Yerushalayim* (Shaul 1979–2016; see 5.4.5 below). A few examples are listed here. The last example in each row refers to the *Aki Yerushalayim* convention:

אזיר 'do' – haćer, azer (Spanish *hacer*)
איזו 'did(3SG)' – hiźo, izo (Spanish *hizo*)
ג'יקו 'small' – chico, čico, čiko, tchiko, tchico, chiko (Spanish *chico*)
ג'ודיריאה 'Jewish quarter' – ĵudería, ǵuderia, ǧuderiya, ǰuderia, djuderia (Spanish *judería*)
ג'ינטי 'people' – ĝente, ǧente, djente (Spanish *gente*)
קאזה 'house' – caśa, caza, kaza (Spanish *casa*)
בולאר 'fly(v)' – yolar, bolar (Spanish *volar*)
באשו 'low' – baĵo, bašo, bacho, basho (Spanish *bajo*)
נינייו 'child(M)' – niño, ninio, ninyo (Spanish *niño*)
אאי 'there' – allí, ayí, ayi (Spanish *allí*)
חכם 'rabbi; smart' – ḥajam, jajam, ḥakam, haham (Hebrew)
ג'יפ 'pocket' – ĝep, ǧep, djep (Turkish *cep*)
חבר 'friend, partner' – ḥaber, ḥaver, javer, haver (Hebrew)

חאביר 'news' – ḥaber, jaber, ḥaber, haber (Turkish *haber*)
צדקה 'charity' – šedaca, sedaka (Hebrew)
שאלב'אר 'baggy trousers' – šalvar, chalvar, shalvar (Turkish şalvar)

The examples above reflect different writers' viewpoints on the system. Some claim JS Roman-script spelling ought to reflect Spanish spelling as much as possible; others are in favor of a single equivalent sign for each JS phoneme.

Early Ḥakitía texts were written in Hebrew letters, as in the east, but Spanish and Arabic influence caused them to use *kaf rafa* for [x], while *ḥet* was maintained in words of Hebrew and Arabic origin. Late Hakitía texts from North Africa were written in standard Spanish, with some Spanish adjustments to loan words.

4.2 Written literature

As in any living language, one can distinguish between canonical or genuine written literature and folk (oral) literature. The former are not always known to all the members of the community, but rather to learned individuals, mostly men; the latter are widespread, well-known, fluently used by each and every member of the community, and are widely used by women. Both are part of the cultural heritage of any speech community (Romero 1992b).

While the innovators of folk literature are mostly completely anonymous, the authorship of most printed JS material is known. Printed materials include scientific, historical, geographical, and religious literature, poetry, rabbinic text translations, other translations, prose, plays, books about the Jewish calendar, communal publications, etc. From the late 19th century onwards, written press, newspapers, journals, and periodicals were also published.

Another two points should be raised concerning various JS literary genres. 1. Sources: Some of the genres are Spanish in origin and were later developed independently by Sephardic Jews. Some of the genres are genuine JS innovations, independent of any prior tradition, yet some of these are influenced by local literary genres. 2. Jewishness: Some of the genres are Jewish in nature because of their content, while others are not. The use of JS and its Hebrew-script orthography, sources, and target audience, for whom specific material was written, all contribute to the Jewishness of various genres (Hassán 1982; Romero 1992a).

In the following sections, a distinction will be made between the existent literature in JS before and after the Expulsion from Spain. In the literature after the Expulsion, the following genres will be discussed: Ladino translations; rabbinical literature including *Meam loez*; press; drama; *belles lettres*; and popular literature. Other literary genres listed in catalogues and in Cohen's (2011) work will not be discussed here.

4.2.1 Sepharad I

Very little was created by Jews in JS prior to the Expulsion, e.g., *Coplas de Yosef* by an anonymous writer (Girón-Negrón and Minervini 2006) and *Proverbios morales* by Sem Tob de Carrión (Ardutiel) (Díaz-Mas and Mota 1998; Zemke 1997). The *Kharjas* and The Valladolid Statutes are examples of interactions between languages used by the Jews. The *Kharjas* indicate the concluding Spanish verses of a Hebrew poem (Hitchcock 1977). The combination of languages is systematic where the rhymes and the metric structure fit. The *Kharjas* probably belonged to the oral literary tradition, although they were sometimes written by well-reputed poets.

The Valladolid Statutes (*Taqanot Valladolid*) for the communities in Castile, formulated by the Jewish council in 1432 (April 22–May 2), give additional proof of the contact between Hebrew and Spanish. The text, written in Hebrew characters, is primarily Spanish with the incorporation of Hebrew (Baer 1936: 280–297; Minervini 1992: 181–255), where the use of Hebrew words is not restricted to cultural or religious terms.

The 25 texts Minervini (1992) studied include instructions for conducting the Seder on Passover,[3] some contracts between Jews, written oaths, commercial contracts, declarations, medical recipes, and various agreements, most of which are short and fragmental, and all of which are written in Hebrew characters. The other small documents seem to follow certain JS stylistic formulae, commonly used by JS speakers.

Lazar has published some texts from Sepharad I in the *Sephardic classical library*. His texts are Ladino by definition, because they are mainly translations of Hebrew texts.

Texts written by Jews in Roman script in Spain were mainly composed for the benefit of Christian patrons, and as such are written in the Spanish of their era. *Sefer Tešuva* 'Book for Repentance', although written in Roman script, is very Jewish in its contents. Its main text is based on Maimonides and "The Gates of Repentance" by Jonah Gerundi. This book also includes several short tractates, i.e., *Pirqē ʾābōth* 'Ethics of the Fathers', *Megillat ʾEstēr* 'the Book of Esther', *ʾOraḥ haḥayyim* 'Way of life' (a translation from Jacob ben Asher), and *Midraš ʿaśeret ha-dibrōt* 'Midrash on the Ten Commandments' (Lazar 1993b). The original translator is unknown, and, according to Lazar (1993b: xii-xiii), the work was composed at the end of the 14th or the beginning of the 15th century. The aim of the book was "to present in the familiar vernacular of the Spanish Jews a condensed version of religious and ethical

---

3 The instructions for conducting the Seder after the Expulsion from Spain continue the same pre-exilic tradition.

texts otherwise not accessible to them" (Lazar 1993b: xi). It was probably written in Roman script for the benefit of the converted Jews. Another text that existed in Ladino prior to the Expulsion from Spain was a translation of *Sefer hakuzari* 'Book of the Kuzari' by Yehudah HaLevy (Lazar 1990). Both *Sefer tešuva* and *Sefer hakuzari* were originally published in Roman script, probably by converted Jews. The Jewishness of the texts is apparent through their contents and their linguistic nature, which supports the claim that JS did exist before the Expulsion.

4.2.2 Sepharad II

Ladino translations

Ladino translations are perhaps the most popular literary genre to accompany Sephardic Jews throughout the ages. The seemingly Ladino translations from Spain in Roman script from before the Expulsion are in fact free Spanish translations made for Catholic patrons by either Jews, converted Jews, or others (Schwarzwald 2010, 2012b). The only extant Ladino translations are those published after the Expulsion from Spain in various Sephardic Diaspora locations: Italy, the Ottoman Empire, the Netherlands, and England.

This genre is famous for its inflexibility, on the one hand, and for its archaic nature on the other. The translations reflect Hebrew syntactic structures, and they retain grammatical and lexical features typical of medieval Spanish (Lazar 1964; Revah 1970; Sephiha 1973, 1979; Benabu 1985; Schwarzwald 1989, 2008, 2012a; Bunis 1994, 1996).

Several liturgical texts were translated into Ladino for educational reasons, each to be read on special dates:

a. The Bible: the Pentateuch; Psalms; the *Megillot* (Scrolls) – Song of Songs, Ruth, Lamentation, Ecclesiastes, and Esther; several *Haftarot*, especially those of the Ninth of Av, Rosh Hashanah, Yom Kippur, Passover, etc. The Bible was translated in full in Ferrara in 1553, in Roman characters, whereas, in the Ottoman Empire, it was translated in parts in Constantinople and Thessaloniki, in Hebrew characters (Lazar 1988, 1992a, 1992b, 1993a, 1995c, 2000; Hassán 1994).
b. *Sidur* and *Maḥzor*: The daily prayer book and prayer book for holidays were also published in Ladino translations in full in Ferrara in 1552, in Roman script,[4] whereas, in the Ottoman Empire communities, only certain passages of these books were translated (in Hebrew script), mostly since the 18th century. In the 16th century, two prayer books for women were published,

---

4 The later Amsterdam editions were copies of the Ferrara original.

one in Thessaloniki (Schwarzwald 2012a), the other in Italy, probably in Venice. The former *Siddur* includes many instructions for women, while the latter contains very few instructions, all of which are related to prayers. Lazar considered the latter *Siddur* as pre-exilic, but it has been proven that it was post-exilic (Lazar 1995b; Minervini 1998; Schwarzwald 2011).

c. The Passover (Pesaḥ) Haggadah is read on the first night of Passover; the first two nights outside Israel. It was published as part of the *Maḥzor* in Ferrara and in the Ottoman communities, as well as in separate booklets after 1609 (Schwarzwald 2008).

d. Ethics of the Fathers, known as *Pirke avot*, read every Saturday between Passover and Pentecost. This text also appeared in the Ferrara *Maḥzor* and in *Maḥzors* throughout the Ottoman Empire, as well as in separate booklets after 1601 (Schwarzwald 1989).

The two main types of Ladino translations are those made for the expelled eastern Jewish communities, which spoke JS and used only the Hebrew alphabet, and those made for western ex-converted communities, which spoke Portuguese or Spanish and mainly used the Roman alphabet.

The binary classification of east and west is based mainly on the following linguistic criteria:

1. Conventional JS spelling is used in eastern Hebrew-script translations. The western texts reflect Hispanic spelling of the time.
2. The western Roman-script translations only contain a few Hebrew words, such as God's name ([A.] for *Adonai*), proper names, and a number of Jewish concepts which have no Spanish equivalents. The western Hebrew-script Ladino translations contain some additional Hebrew words. The eastern translations include the largest number of Hebrew words (Schwarzwald 1996: 61).
3. Different words and phrases are used consistently in both east and west (Sephiha 1973: 238 ff; Schwarzwald 1996).

Lazar (1964, 1995a) claims that the Spanish translations of the Middle Ages set the foundations for Ladino translations published after the Expulsion. Wexler (1987) shows that there are clear tendencies in the Roman-script Ladino translations of the 18th century to make the text more Jewish, on the one hand, yet more Hispanic in nature, on the other – which also assumes old pre-exilic versions as the origin for the Ladino translations. Bunis (1996) argues for the oral nature of Ladino translations. In his view, the translations emerged from a Jewish oral tradition that had already existed in Spain. Based on various linguistic features in the Spanish and Ladino Bible translations, Schwarzwald demonstrates that the post-exilic translations are independent of the Spanish pre-exilic translations (Schwarzwald 2003, 2010, 2012b).

Rabbinical literature

Rabbinical literature refers to literature written by Sephardic rabbis on subjects such as Jewish law, morals, education, Jewish customs, commentaries on and interpretations of various canonical texts, judicial matters, Responsa literature, etc.

Most of this rabbinical literature was written in Hebrew (e.g., Bornstein-Makovetsky 2001). Rabbi Moses (ben Barukh) Almosnino was exceptional in writing *Crónica de los reyes otomanos,* known as *Extremos y grandezas de Constantinopla* 'The History of the Ottoman Kings: The Values and Greatness of Constantinople' in Thessaloniki in the 16th century. He wrote this book in (Judeo-) Spanish in Hebrew script, but his work became famous through its transliteration into Roman characters, which was done for the benefit of Christian Spanish speakers (Romeu Ferré 1998). Almosnino also wrote the halakhic book *Sefer hanhagat haḥayyim: El regimiento de la vida* 'The management of life' (Zemke 2004). Almosnino and his contemporaries also wrote other rabbinical, educational, moral, and legal literature in Hebrew.

Other rabbinical literature written in JS includes Meir Benveniste's edited translation of *the Shulḥan arukh,* called *Meza de la alma* (*Shulḥan hapanim* in Hebrew); Zadiq Forman translated *Ḥovat halevavot* by Baḥye Ibn Pakuda and named it *El deber de los corazones* (both published in Thessaloniki circa 1568) (Schwarzwald 2014, 2017). An anonymous writer published *Compendio delas šeḥiṭót* in Constantinople circa 1510 (Cohen & Schwarzwald 2018).

Various changes in the economic, political, and social circumstances of the Jews caused some decrease in the Hebrew education of later generations. The majority of the population spoke JS, but their knowledge of Hebrew kept deteriorating. At the same time, various trends in non-Jewish societies which promoted dialects to the status of languages changed the attitudes towards spoken JS among the Jews. The educated Sephardic leaders grasped the need to elevate the layperson's knowledge of Judaism and started writing in JS as well. In addition to *Meam loez* (see the discussion below), other books were written in JS, e.g., Abraham ben Isaac Asa's translation of *ʾotiyot de Rabbi Akiva* (Constantinople 1729), *Sefer meshivat nefesh* by Shabetay ben Yaacob Vitas (Constantinople 1743–1744), *Tiqqune hanefesh* by Reuben ben Abraham of Shtip (Thessaloniki 1775), *Shelom Yerushalaim* by Yehuda ben Shlomo Hai Alcalay (Belgrade 1840), *Pele yoʿets* by Yehudah Eliezer Papo (Constantinople 1870–1874), *Sefer meshek beti* by Eliezer Papo (Sarayevo 1872–1874; Šmid 2012), and many others.

Rabbinical JS literature, either original or translated, is loaded with Hebrew words, phrases, and citations due to the contents of its treatises and its reliance on common Jewish knowledge of Hebrew words. The number of Turkish and various Balkan terms increases during the 19th and 20th centuries.

Responsa literature and rabbinical homilies were mostly written in Hebrew, although they were mainly addressed to a Sephardic audience. Occasionally, in citation of actual cases or JS wills, expressions or whole conversations would combine JS with Hebrew text, as can been seen in early Responsa from the 16th century (Benaim 2012).

Sermon collections were delivered in JS but were mostly published in Hebrew. *Vehokhiaḥ Avraham* by Abraham Palachi (Izmir 1862), for instance, includes sermons and Bar Mizvah homilies. *Sefer vayyiqra Moshe* by Moshe Shimon Pesah (Volos 1891–1937) includes sermons of a Halakhic nature and lamentations in Hebrew and JS (Yaari 1934; Refael 1999; Cohen 2011).

Meam loez

Meam loez [meꜤam loꜤez] ('from a people of strange language'; Psalms 114:1), one of the most volumnious and important literary works ever compiled in JS, was started by Rabbi Jacob Khuli (1689?–1732). He gathered biblical commentaries from various classical Jewish sources, as well as rabbinical commentaries on the Bible from all periods.

Jacob Khuli completed the commentary on the whole book of Genesis, and this was published in 1730 in Istanbul in Rashi script. Khuli's commentary on Exodus, however, ended at the 27th chapter (*Teruma*) and was published posthumously in 1733. Following his guidelines, the following individuals carried on his work, but even their efforts failed to bring this monumental work to completion: Rabbis Isaac Magriso (end of Exodus, Leviticus, Numbers), Isaac Shemaria Argueti (Deutronomy), Menachem Mitrani (Joshua), Isaac Abba (first Prophets; Isaiah), Rafael Isaac Meir Ben Veniste (Ruth), Hayim Shaki (Song of Songs), Nissim Aboud (Ecclesiastics), and Rafael Hiya Pontrimoli (Esther). This JS classic was eventually published in its unfinished form in Constantinople, Thessaloniki, Leghorn, Smyrna, etc., and ran for several editions.

Because of its educational value, *Meam loez* was translated into Hebrew by Shmuel Yerushalmi with some adjustments. Yerushalmi also added a few volumes in Hebrew, based on the same principles initiated by Khuli (Sh. Yerushalmi 1957–1981). *Meam loez* has been translated in full into English (Kaplan 1977–1997) and partly into French as well.

Although the language of *Meam loez* is JS, the echo of its Hebrew sources is apparent. On the one hand, 12%–15% of the words and phrases in the text are in Hebrew; on the other, the syntax is influenced by Hebrew word order.

Several studies of *Meam loez* have examined its literary aspects (e.g., Landau 1980, 1981; Alexander 1986; Ginio Meyuhas 2001, 2004, 2006–2007, and many others). The sources that served the writers and its lexicon have also been analysed (e.g., Wiesner 1981; Romeu Ferré 2000). The study of various editions of the work by different authors at various times and in different locations sheds light on the language and varieties of Ottoman JS in the 18th–19th centuries (Maeso and Pascual Recuero 1964–1970; García Moreno 2004; Schwarzwald 2006–2007, 2012c; Bunis and Adar-Bunis 2011; Quintana 2004).

Drama

The first Sephardic drama writers were ex-converted Jews from the Netherlands, but their writing cannot be considered JS. JS drama developed around Jewish themes in the early centuries after the Expulsion. The story of Esther and the drama of Joseph and his brothers were repeated themes performed around Purim in various communities, although these are not documented. From the middle of the 19th century, many new plays were written and produced. Some of these exist in print, some in manuscripts; others are mentioned in various newspapers, but their original sources have been lost. Bunis (1995) describes the (apparently) first JS play published in the Ottoman Empire. Other plays are described in catalogues (Yaari 1934). Romero (1979) gives the broadest description of JS plays.

In addition to biblical themes like David and Goliath, Esther, Deborah, and Jephthah, JS plays were also written and translated around other themes, religiously oriented or entirely secular, e.g., *La famía misterioza* 'The mysterious family' by Jakim Behar, *El bet din de los syelos* 'The court of law of heaven' (translated from Polish), *El ḥazino imažinado* 'The imaginary invalid' (translated from Moliere's French *The hypochondriac*), *Los budžukes* 'The twins' (translated from Shakespeare's *Comedy of errors*), etc.

The spectrum of JS plays encompassed all dramatic genres – comedy, tragedy, tragicomedy, etc., and reflected various themes – historical, religious, and secular. The plays were often musicals or semi-musicals and were written in verse form or in plain prose. In most cases, the plays were performed by amateur actors and were frequently produced and performed by members of Zionist youth or national organizations in various cities. One such play was edited by Alexander and Weich-Shahak (1994).

Belles lettres

The second half of the 19th century also marks the turning point for JS secular literature. From this time onwards, novels would be written in JS on historical Jewish matters, but not from a religious perspective. Most of the stories were devoted to human matters, love, tragedies, luck, etc. The names of the authors are given in some of the original texts, e.g., *La džudía salvada del konvento* 'The

Jewess saved from the convent' (Y. de Boton), *Muerta por el amor* 'Dead for Love' (Moiz Ḥabib).

Some of the novels published in JS were adaptations or translations of European and Hebrew literature, e.g., *Les miserables, The count of Monte Cristo, The Karamazov brothers*, as well as Hebrew *Ahavat Zion 'Amor de Zion'* (Abraham Mapu), *Kisme moledet 'Sharmes de patria'* 'The magic of homeland' (Yehuda Burla). The source is specifically mentioned in some cases, but in others it is the duty of the researcher to trace the source used by the writer. This is why Hassán (1982) does not view JS secular literature as genuine, but rather as an adaptation of neighboring cultures. However, it is unjust to claim that all JS literature is adapted. Much JS creative writing is original and deserves to be researched. Also, it should be recalled that Sephardic Jews continued publishing and creating all kinds of literary genres, from science to *belles-lettres* (e.g., Elias Kaneti), in languages other than JS.

Romero (1993) described and analyzed this literature; Barquín Lopez (1995) edited and studied twelve JS novels in depth. This genre is continually being studied by JS researchers.

Press

Although Hassán (1982) considers all kinds of press published in JS as an adapted genre, it should really be considered an independent creative genre. The first JS newspaper, *Shaʿare hamizrah* 'The gates of the east' was published in Izmir in 1845 (Cohen 2011: 63). Since then, hundreds of JS newspapers have been published in many cities (Gaon 1964), notably in Thessaloniki (since 1865) and Constantinople (since 1853), but also in Izmir, Vienna, Jerusalem, Sofia, Filipopoli, Rusjuk, and Tel Aviv. A few editions of other newspapers have also been published in smaller cities throughout the Ottoman Empire (all written in Rashi script).

The first JS newspapers included only translated news; however, the publication of *La epoka* 'The era' in Thessaloniki in 1875 marked the turning point in the development of JS journalism. It included original articles on political matters, as well as local news. Other publications followed suit and reduced the number of translated articles.

JS newspapers were only very rarely published on a daily basis. Most of them appeared just once or twice a week, and they varied a great deal in their ideology. Several of the newspapers were political; others were satirical-humorist, and some were Zionist in nature or were the voice of national-political movements. The language of the newspapers varied accordingly: vernacular JS was freely used in the satirical-humorist newspapers (Bunis 1999b); a literary variety of JS was used in the more politically oriented papers. A Hebrew component was widely utilized in the satirical-humorist papers, while Hebrew and Turkish were avoided and replaced by Hispanized (French-like, Italian-like) forms in other publications.

In addition to news and editorial articles, the JS newspapers included stories (some of which were serialized and later published in books), songs in Hebrew and in JS, and various sections, just as we find in newspapers today.

A number of JS journals in Hebrew Rashi letters still existed at the beginning of the 20th century in the Balkans and in Israel, but their number gradually decreased. Moreover, newspapers began to favor the use of Roman letters over Hebrew letters. Current newspapers written in JS are all written in Roman letters (see 5.4 below).

4.3 Popular literature

4.3.1 Poetic literature

The oral folkloristic poetic tradition of JS is extremely rich and has been recorded and written down since the end of the 19th century. The poetic tradition includes varieties of sung material – *romansas* (or *romances*), *coplas* (or *complas*), and *cantigas* (or *canticas*). The *romansa* is a ballad with six- or eight-syllable lines rhyming on the even-numbered lines. The *copla* is a poem of educational origin, written in assorted narrative or descriptive rather than lyric themes, formed in stanzas, frequently using acrostics, with various types of rhyming. The most famous *coplas* are dedicated to Jewish holidays, e.g., Purim, Passover, Tu Bishvat, etc. The *cantiga* is a lyric song, usually written about love. Men used to sing many of the *coplas* on religious or Jewish oriented themes, whereas the romances and *cantigas* were usually sung by women (Menéndez Pidal 1928; Romero 1988, 1992c, 2008; Díaz-Mas 1992: 105–106, 119; Alexander et al. 1994; Refael 1998, 2004; Weich-Shahak 1997).

These three types of sung poetry are as old as JS itself. The *romansa* is rooted in Spain, and the manuscript *Coplas de Yosef* already existed in Sepharad I, as mentioned above. Only a few of the *romansas* are related to Jewish themes or historical Jewish characters. They became Jewish because of their use in Sephardic communities (see, for instance, Armistead and Silverman 1971, 1979, 1982; Attias 1972). Although their poetic form was rooted in Spain, *coplas* are more Jewish in nature, because they are historical or communal descriptions of events.

Many studies have been dedicated to the *romansa*, most of which are collections of the traditions in some communities (Menéndez Pidal 1906, 1907; Benichou 1944; Attias 1961). Menéndez Pidal, in his numerous works, analyzed the themes of *romansas* and their Hispanic roots. Specific *romansas* have been analyzed too, e.g., by Refael (1998). Analysis of the musical and poetic structures has been conducted by Seroussi (1989, 1995), Havassy (2007), Weich-Shahak (1997, 2007), and others.

A careful analysis of the various JS oral poetry traditions reveals that, although there is no doubt about their Iberian ancestry, many of the *romansas*, *coplas*, and *cantigas* are late innovations. These innovations follow two trends. The first is an adoption of local traditions in the Ottoman Empire – Turkish, Greek, Bulgarian, etc. – and in North Africa. The second is an independent innovation by creative writers on the lines of old traditions, especially of *coplas* and *cantigas*. One finds, for instance, Zionist *coplas* (*Zionidas*) at the beginning of the 20th century, with no former tradition. Many songs were written during the Holocaust (Lévy 1989; Refael 2008). Newspapers and other pamphlets include new poems and ballads, some of which carry instructions stating that they should be sung to the specific tune of another song. Hence, *coplas* and *cantigas* are different from *romansas* because for many of them, especially the modern ones, the identity of the authors is known (e.g., Shlomo Reuven, Moshe Kazes, and Zadik Gershon). Some *coplas* are written, like *cantes* (songs), and not all of them are sung.

The language of these genres varies, depending on their contents and the year in which they were written. *Romansas* that originated from Hispanic sources carry features of Old Spanish with almost no markers of JS. *Romansas*, *coplas*, and *cantigas* with Jewish themes have definite Jewish markers, reflected by either a Hebrew component, reference to Jewish tradition and customs, or phrases from Ladino translations. Late *coplas* and *cantigas* have heavy Turkish and Greek components, as well. Vernacular forms appear in many of these texts.

4.3.2 Proverbs

There are several collections of JS proverbs. Lévy (1969), Alexander-Frizer (2004), and Alexander-Frizer and Bentolila (2008) list these collections and add many proverbs gathered through their field work. Many JS and Ḥakitía proverbs can be traced back to Spain, although others are based either on Hebrew sources or on neighboring cultures, or are completely new innovations.

The studies undertaken on JS proverbs demonstrate that they can be classified according to four criteria – message, theme, form, and lexicon – with respect to Hispanic proverbs. Some proverbs of Hispanic origin seem to be kept intact, although the vocabulary may vary, e.g., Spanish *Cada uno sabe donde le aprieta el zapato* 'Everyone knows where his shoe hurts; everybody is aware of his problems' is retained in eastern JS as *kada uno save onde le ergwele el sapato~el kalsado*.

The proverb *xoxma i bina i kyošk enriva* 'wisdom and knowledge [building] and a tower on top of them, i.e., great stupidity' includes the Hebrew synonyms *ḥokma* and *bina* 'wisdom'. *Bina*, like *kyošk*, is also a Turkish word for building, hence the pun on the Hebrew word, whereas in Turkish the proverb has an entirely different meaning (see discussion above in 3.3). The same principles apply to other folkloristic genres.

4.3.3 Miscellaneous

Other genres exist in JS. Most examples of these genres were transmitted orally, especially by women. They are comprised of folk tales, fables, riddles, satirical tales, jokes, etc., some of which were included in the written JS texts listed above. There are many collections of JS folk tales exisiting today, but the study of this field is still in its infancy (Haboucha 1992; Alexander-Frizer 2000; Alexander and Romero 1990; Romero 2009; Held 2009). Bunis (1999b) studied the satirical correspondence between two typical folk characters, a husband and a wife, as published in the Thessaloniki JS press. His description is important from both a linguistic and literary stand point. These genres and others need to be researched further.

5 State of research

As stated above, in spite of the diminishing numbers of JS native speakers, there is a growing interest in the research and discovery of the cultural heritage of JS by descendents of Sephardic communities and by others who are fascinated by the literature and folklore of Sephardic society.

5.1 History of documentation

Documentation started towards the end of the 19th century and continues extensively today, especially with an effort to preserve the oral traditions as much as possible.

The growth of interest in recent years in Sephardic studies in general, and in the language spoken by the descendents of the expelled Jews from Spain in particular, has led to the publication of numerous textbooks and dictionaries to help both teacher and student. The textbooks are primarily designated for university students, whereas the dictionaries are meant for anyone interested in the language.

Four JS textbooks have been published in Israel. In two of them, JS is spelled in Roman script (Koén-Sarano 1999a, 1999b; Shaul 1999); in the other two, JS is spelled in Hebrew Rashi script (Gattegno and Refael 1995, 1998[5]; Bunis 1999a). Varol's (1998) textbook in France and Markova's (2008) in the United States include Judeo-Spanish conversations and short texts in Roman script, as well. Both books are accompanied by CDs. The choice of scripts marks the different attitudes to the language: JS is taught as a language of communication in Roman script, whereas in Hebrew script it is taught as a language of culture and research.

The only JS dictionary written in Hebrew script is Cherezli (1899), with French translations.[6] All other JS dictionaries are published in Roman script. In the first group, JS words are explained in various languages: Nehama (1977) JS – French; Pascual Recuero (1977) JS – Spanish; Romano (1995 [1933]) JS – multilingual; Bendayan de Bendelac (1995) Ḥakitía – Spanish; Perahya and Perahya (1998) JS – French; Perez and Pimienta (2007) JS – Hebrew.[7] In the second group one can find the translation from and into JS: Perahya et al. (1997) JS – Turkish / Turkish – JS; Passy (1999) and Kohen and Kohen-Gordon (2000) JS – English / English – JS; Bunis (1999a: 463–551) and Koén-Sarano (2009–10) JS – Hebrew / Hebrew – JS. Other dictionaries are planned to be published online in Germany.

Lazar's (1999) *Ladino reader* is a great supplement to the list given above. This reader includes representative texts of the various JS genres from all of its language periods, most of which are written in Roman-script transliteration in order to facilitate the availability of the texts to anyone interested in JS and its wide-ranging literary heritage.

5.2 Corpora

As stated above in sections 1.4 and 4, all written and oral materials are subjects for research in the JS genres.

---

[5] The textbooks have been revised by Nivi Gomel and Shmuel Refael (2018).
[6] I do not include here Lazar's (1976) limited dictionary because it includes only JS entries beginning with the letter *gimel*. Bunis (1981: 24) lists another two dictionaries, which I could not trace: 1. *Milon kis sefaradi-ivri* (A pocket Spanish-Hebrew dictionary), authored by M. Moše (Thessaloniki 5694 [=1933–1934]); 2. *Diksyonaryo žudeo-espanyol—bulgaro* (Judeo-Spanish—Bulgarian dictionary), authored by A.D. Pipano (Sofia 1913).
[7] Perez in *Machon Maale Adumim* has now an online JS – Hebrew / Hebrew – JS dictionary: http://folkmasa.org/milon/yachad2.php?mishtane=br.

5.3 Issues of general theoretical interest

Linguistic, literary, musical, folkloristic, historical, and social aspects of JS are studied today by various researchers around the world, many of whom are based in Israel and Spain. Many of the studies are either collections of data (e.g., recordings, transcriptions of texts in Rashi script into Roman letters) or descriptions of the various corpora. The theoretical issues pertain to the following questions: 1. The linguistic structure of the language; 2. The relationships between Hispanic and JS traditions; 3. The penetration of various components from Hebrew and Aramaic, neighboring languages, and prestigious educational languages and their fusion in JS; 4. The sources of the JS corpus, be they lexical, musical, grammatical, literary, or folkloristic; 5. The sociolinguistic aspects of creativity in JS; 6. The historical development of JS and its relationship to social and political factors; 7. The geographical dispersion of JS and the sources for its dialectal differences; 8. The differences between the various literary genres (e.g., liturgical translations, halakhic translations, halakhic independent writings, Jewish novels, translated novels, etc.); 9. The themes and contents of the works.

5.4 Current enterprises in JS

5.4.1 Academic publications

The following periodicals are devoted solely to JS: *Ladinar* (at Bar-Ilan University); *El presente* (at Ben-Gurion University); *Judenspanisch* (*Neue Romania*) and *Sephardica* (in Germany by Peter Lang Publisher). Other journals, such as *Sefarad, Hispania Judaica Bulletin, Revista de Filología Española*, and *Estudios sefardíes* are focused on Hispanic or Sephardic matters, not all of them related to JS studies.

Tirocinio Publications in Barcelona devotes most of its academic publications to JS studies. Also, CSIC in Madrid and the Ben-Zvi Institute in Jerusalem include many publications on Sephardic and JS issues.

5.4.2 Academic instruction

In spite of the growing interest in JS, not many institutions are involved in formal systematic instruction of the language. Three universities in Israel have special programs for the study of JS: 1. Bar-Ilan University in Ramat Gan, at The

Salti Institute for Ladino Studies (http://www.ladinobiu.co.il/). 2. Ben-Gurion University in Beer Sheva at the David Gaon Ladino Center for the study of language and culture (http://www.ladino.org.il/186467/%D7%9E%D7%95%D7%A1%D7%93%D7%95%D7%AA-%D7%9E%D7%97%D7%A7%D7%A8). 3. The Department of Hebrew and Jewish Languages at the Hebrew University in Jerusalem, where JS is studied intensively.

At the Consejo Superior de Investigaciones Cientificas (CSIC) in Madrid, serious academic work is conducted into the preservation, documentation, and publication of JS materials. Haim Vidal Sephiha taught and Marie Christine Varol still teaches introductory courses in JS in Paris. Michael HaLevy-Studemund teaches JS and its literature in Hamburg and at other locations as a subject in summer schools. Gloria Ascher teaches JS in Boston. There are sporadic university courses in JS at various locations in North America and in Europe in departments of Romance languages, depending on the availability of teachers (and students). The late Moshe Lazar, for example, was a visiting professor at the University of California in Los Angeles (UCLA), David M. Bunis taught Judezmo in 2014 at the University of Washington in Seattle, and I taught an introductory course in JS at Emory University in Atlanta in 1998.

5.4.3 Conferences

Since 1979, bi-annual conferences specifically devoted to Judeo-Spanish have been organized. They were initiated in England, but since 2012 they have taken place in turn at Bar-Ilan University in Ramat Gan, at CSIC in Madrid, and at the University of London. The Center for Jewish Languages and Literatures at the Hebrew University in Jerusalem has organized an international conference on Jewish Languages every two or three years since 2003, at which JS is well represented. Misgav Yerushalayim, the Institute for Research on the Sephardic and Oriental Jewish Heritage, organizes international conferences every four years, in which many papers regarding JS are presented. The UC Ladino Club at UCLA organizes conferences about Ladino. Around 1992, the year that marked 500 years since the Expulsion from Spain and the discovery of the New World, there were several international academic conferences dealing with the linguistic, historical, literary, philosophical, musical, and cultural impact of the Expulsion on the Sephardic Diaspora. JS is also discussed at length at the World Congress on Jewish Studies in Israel and at congresses of the European Association for Jewish Studies.

5.4.4 Special institutions and enterprises

Several important enterprises deserve special remarks:
1. *The National Authority for Ladino and Its Culture*, established in 1997 by the Israeli government, sets its aim to keep and preserve JS and its culture (http://www.ladino-authority.com/). Yitshak Navon (1921–2015), the fifth president of Israel and a native speaker of JS, was the head of the Authority until recently and one of the sources of its inspiration. In addition to supporting many of the enterprises related to JS in Israel mentioned above, the National Authority works at several levels for the development of activities in JS.
2. *Instituto de Estudios Sefardíes* (formerly Arias Montano Institute) of the Consejo Superior de Investigaciones Cientificas (CSIC) in Madrid, Spain, aims to collect, preserve, and study JS language and literature. A large collection of Ramon Menéndez Pidal's (1928) transcripts and catalogues, thousands of manuscripts, printed texts, newspapers, Michael Molho's library, etc., are gathered there, catalogued, and analyzed. The project was initiated by the late Iacob Hassán (1936–2006) and continued by Elena Romero, Aitor García Moreno, colleagues, and students.
3. *Sefarad: Society for Sefardic Studies* (http://www.sefarad-studies.org/). This society incorporates scholars from all over the world whose research and interests are mainly concentrated on the history and culture of the Jews of Sefarad and their descendants in all fields and disciplines, including history, philosophy, mysticism, literature, languages, art, music, folklore, education, archeology, liturgy, halakhah, Biblical and Talmudic studies, etc.
4. *Amutat Sfarad* (Sepharad Association) in Israel, headed by Mordechai Arbel and Moshe Shaul, is a nonprofit organization that aims to preserve the JS language and its culture. Their most important executive branch (in addition to publishing *Aki Yerushalaim*, see above) is *Machon Maale Adumim* (Maale Adumim Institute) *for the Documentation of the Language and its Culture*, founded and directed by Avner Perez (http://web.macam.ac.il/~yon/av.htm).
5. Moshe Lazar's (1928–2012) edition of the *Sephardic classical library*. This collection of JS classical texts is copied from its Hebrew script, edited, and carefully transcribed into Roman characters. This enterprise makes rare books available to the JS researcher.
6. Isaac Jerushalmi's (Yerushalmi) edition of *Ladino books*. Rabbi Jerushalmi of Cincinnato, Ohio, collected several Sephardic texts, edited them, transcribed, and translated them into English, e.g., I. Yerushalmi (1989, 1993), and others.

Researchers do similar work in other places, but for lack of space there is no way to mention them all. All of these efforts are important for the protection and documentation of the JS tradition before it is gone forever.

5.4.5 Non-academic publications

The most prominent and best known recent publication is *Aki Yerushalayim: Revista Kulturala Djudeo-Espanyola*, founded in 1979 by the editor Moshe Shaul as a supplement for the Israeli Radio program in JS. It had the following aims: 1. To improve knowledge of the culture, folklore, history, and current status of Sephardic Jews; 2. To renovate the active literary and folkloristic creation of JS as much as possible. This publication ceased to exist recently, and the National Ladino Authority in Israel is trying to establish a new format with a new name.

There are other activities and publications around the world in which JS and Sephardic culture are the focus. The *Shalom* (Şalom) weekly Jewish newspaper in Istanbul was established in 1947 by Avram Leon as a JS journal, but today includes only one page in JS, while the rest is written in Turkish. *El amaneser* is a monthly newspaper published in Istanbul and is entirely written in JS. *Los Muestros: La Boz de los Sefardim*, published in Brussels and edited by Moshe Rahmani, is a multilingual quarterly. Haim Vidal Sephiha was responsible for the publications of *Vidas Largas* in Paris. *La Lettre Sepharade* has been published since 2000 and originally appeared in print at the same time in the USA in English and in France in French (today, it is published only on the Internet – through Institut Sepharade Europeen, http://sefarad.org/). All of these publications have a few hundred readers, although some of them are distributed by the thousands. All of the publications listed above are written in Roman letters, and, with the exception of *Aki Yerushalayim* and *El amaneser*, only rarely feature articles written in JS.

5.4.6 Online activities

Ladinokomunita is the most popular online discussion group in which JS is actively used (http://www.sephardicstudies.org/komunita.html). Other groups on the internet are either societies or organizations that relate to Sephardic groups as communities which are not Ashkenazi and deliver news and information about this world mainly in English (e.g., http://sefarad-studies.org/, https://groups.yahoo.com/neo/groups/sephardicnewsletter/info, sephardimizrahicaucus@googlegroups.com) and in Spanish (e.g., http://www.proyectos.cchs.csic.es/sefardiweb/, http://www.bibliothecasefarad.com/). Also, the Jewish Languages site includes a small JS section (http://jewish-languages.org/judeo-spanish.html). Weekly information about the Sephardic world, especially regarding JS, is given in Spanish and in English in eSefarad: Noticias del Mundo Sefarad (http://esefarad.com/).

5.4.7 Performances

Yitshak Navon, the fifth president of the State of Israel, wrote a play, *Bustan Sepharadi* 'A Sephardic Orchard', which portrayed Sephardic life in Jerusalem at the beginning of the 20th century. The play has been produced continually through the years at the Israeli National Theater, *Habima*. Although in Hebrew, the songs, proverbs, and translated idioms in the play carry a JS flavor. Other original plays in JS are produced from time to time by amateur groups in Israel and Turkey, and they attract JS lovers. In recent years, *Festiladino*, a contest of newly written JS songs in Israel, has been established, in which performers and writers from around the world present new songs in JS. It is possible to hear singers, bands, and orchestras performing old and new JS songs all over the world.

5.4.8 Poetry

A few poets (e.g., Margalit Matityahu and Avner Perez in Israel, Claris Nikodisky in France, and a few others) write JS poetry. Their poems have been published in bilingual editions, although most of their compositions are in their mother tongues and not in JS. Individuals sometimes publish books in JS printed in Roman letters, e.g., Moshe Ha-Elion, Yehuda Hatsvi. Their target audience is small.

5.4.9 Other non-academic activities

At a non-academic level, the following should be mentioned: Matilda Koén-Sarano started a big enterprise several years ago, in which she recorded JS folktales and songs and published them in Roman script with their Hebrew translations. Several books relating to this work have been published so far, e.g., *Cuentos* 'Stories' (1986), *Djoha ke dize?* 'What does Djoha say?' (1991), *Vini kantaremos* 'Let's sing' (1993), *Konsejas i konsejikas* 'Stories and anecdotes' (1994), *Gizar kon gozo* 'Cooking with (Ladino) Taste' (2010), and more.

Informal meetings relating to JS and Sephardic culture flourish in Israel and abroad. There are meetings which occur either monthly or bi-monthly, where JS speakers join together to study JS texts, chant *romansas* and *complas*, discuss folk tales and proverbs, and practice Sephardic culinary traditions. These meetings are not academically oriented but rather nostalgic in nature.

Many popular events sporadically involve JS and attract JS enthusiasts. For instance, in 2013, a "Ladino International Day" was initiated, and since then it is celebrated each year in December around the world with lectures, music, and performances that reflect the JS cultural heritage. A special evening is dedicated to JS stories and folk tales at the Festival of Storytellers in Israel (during Sukkot). Two study weekends are organized each year, between February and March, in which various issues of JS are discussed. The Salti Center at Bar-Ilan University organizes Ladino study days twice a year (*Maraton Ladino*), which are open to the public and where various issues are studied, etc. In Israel, the National Authority for Ladino and Its Culture organizes various activities. All these gatherings generally involve musical, culinary, and other entertaining folkloristic events, but most of the talks are in Hebrew.

In recent years, new initiatives have been established or are in the works, including the Sephardic Studies Digital Archive in Seattle in the USA (https://jewishstudies.washington.edu/sephardic-studies/sephardic-studies-digital-library-museum/) and the Israeli National Judeo-Spanish (Ladino) Academy, supported by the Royal Spanish Academy in Spain. There are also some private collections of proverbs, songs, and stories. Unless these are either published or brought to institutions whose aim is to gather this kind of text, this material will surely disappear.

Finally, Israeli authors, when writing about Sephardic JS speakers, characterize their speech by inserting JS sentences and phrases into the Hebrew discourse of their novels.

5.5 A look to the future

The most imperative necessity today is to record living JS native speakers in their use of various literary genres and to transcribe their language, as is done in the Maale Adumim Institute and the National Sound Archives at the National Library of Israel in Jerusalem. This basic data can later serve as a corpus for any study of literary, linguistic, musical, and textual analysis. It is really urgent to collect this material as soon as possible, as the number of native JS speakers is gradually diminishing.

The second important task is to gather all extant JS documents, handwritten and printed. In spite of existing detailed catalogues of JS creativity, much material only exists in handwritten form, and much printed material is not held by libraries. These documents exist either in private collections or in the personal belongings of people who do not always appreciate their value, and sometimes they are lost for various reasons. It is important to catalogue them and write a monograph series on the variety of documents. With the developing technologies today, it is also important to present them in an electronically searchable format, for the benefit of researchers. The analysis of these data can be used for the study of vocabulary, grammatical structures, dialects, and other linguistic issues. Although phonology and the JS lexicon have been researched quite intensively, very few studies have been undertaken on JS morphology, syntax, and semantics.

Time plays an important role in the salvation of whatever remains of JS and its rich linguistic heritage. As things stand now, it seems that only academic research will actively survive, long after the last native JS speakers pass away.

References

Alexander, Tamar. 1986. The character of Rabbi Isaac Luria in the Judeo-Spanish story "The converso and the shewbread." *Pe'amim* 26. 87–107. [Hebrew].

Alexander-Frizer, Tamar. 2000. *Maʕase ahuv vaḥetsi* [The beloved friend-and-a-half]. Jerusalem & Beer Sheva: Magnes & Ben-Gurion University Press. [Hebrew].

Alexander-Frizer, Tamar. 2004. *Words are better than bread: A study of the Judeo-Spanish proverb*. Jerusalem & Beer Sheva: Ben-Zvi Institute & Ben-Gurion University Press. [Hebrew].

Alexander-Frizer, Tamar & Yaakov Bentolila. 2008. *La palabra en su hora de oro: El refrán judeo-español del norte de Marruecos*. Jerusalem: Ben Zvi Insitute & The Hebrew University of Jerusalem.

Alexander, Tamar & Elena Romero. 1990. *Erase una vez – Maimonides: Cuentos tradicionales hebreos*. Cordoba: El Almendro.

Alexander, Tamar & Weich-Shahak, Susana. 1994. *En este tiempo: Drama musical para Purim en Salónika*. Tel Aviv: Tag. [Hebrew].

Alexander, Tamar, Isaac Benabu, Yaacov Gelman, Ora Schwarzwald & Susana Weich-Shahak. 1994. Towards a typology of the Judeo-Spanish folksong: Gerineldo and the romance model. *Yuval: Jewish Oral Traditions: An Interdisciplinary Approach* 6. 68–163.

Armistead, Samuel G. & Joseph H. Silverman. 1971. *The Judeo-Spanish ballad chapbooks of Yacob Abraham Yona*. Berkeley: University of California Press.

Armistead, Samuel G. & Joseph H. Silverman. 1979. *Tres calas en el romancero sefardí (Rodas, Jerusalén, Estados Unidos)*. Madrid: Castalia.

Armistead, Samuel G. & Joseph H. Silverman. 1982. *En torno al romancero sefardí-hispánico y balcánico de la tradición judeo-española*. Madrid: Seminario Menéndez Pidal.

Attias, Moshe. 1961. *Romancero Sefaradi*. Jerusalem: Ben Zvi Institute & Kiryat Sefer. [Hebrew].

Attias, Moshe. 1972. *Cancionero Sefaradi*. Jerusalem & Tel Aviv: The Center for the Study of Saloniki. [Hebrew].

Baer, Fritz. 1936. *Die Juden im christlichen Spanien*, vol. 2. Berlin: Akademie Verlag.

Barquín Lopez, Amelia. 1995. *Edición y estudio de doce novelas aljamiadas sefardíes de principios del siglo XX*. Universidad del País Vasco: Servicio Editorial.

Benabu, Isaac. 1985. On the transmission of the Judeo-Spanish translations of the Bible: The eastern and western traditions compared. In Isaac Benabu & Joseph Sermoneta (eds.), *Judeo-Romance languages*, 1–26. Jerusalem: Misgav Yerushalayim.
Benaim, Annette. 2012. *Sixteenth-century Judeo-Spanish testimonies*. Leiden & Boston: Brill.
Benichou, Pierre. 1944. Romances judeo-espanolas de Marruecos. *Revista de Filología Hispánica* 6. 36–76, 105–138, 255–279, 313–381.
Bendayan de Bendelac, Alegria. 1995. *Diccionario del judeoespañol de los Sefardíes del Norte de Marruecos*. Caracas: Centro de Estudios Sefardises de Caracas.
Benoliel, José. 1977. *Dialecto Judeo-hispano-marroquí o hakitía*. Madrid: Varona.
Bibliography of the Hebrew Books 1460–1960. http://www.hebrew-bibliography.com (accessed 29 August 2016).
Bornstein-Makovetsky, Leah. 2001. Halakhic and rabbinic literature in Turkey, Greece and the Balkans, 1750–1900. *Pe'amim* 86–87. 124–174. [Hebrew].
Bunis, David M. 1981. *Sephardics studies: A research bibliography*. New York: Garland Publications.
Bunis, David M. 1988. The dialect of the Old Yišuv Sephardic community in Jerusalem: A preliminary linguistic analysis. In Moshe Bar-Asher (ed.), *Studies in Jewish languages*, *1–*40. Jerusalem: Misgav Yerushalayim.
Bunis, David M. 1992. The language of the Sephardim: A historical overview. In Haim Beinart (ed.), *Moreshet Sepharad: The Sephardi legacy*, 399–422. Jerusalem: Magnes.
Bunis, David M. 1993. *A lexicon of the Hebrew and Aramaic elements in modern Judezmo*. Jerusalem: Magnes & Misgav Yerushalayim.
Bunis, David M. 1994. Tres formas de ladinar la biblia en Italia en los siglos XVI–XVII. In Iacob Hassán (ed.), *Introducción a la biblia de Ferrara*, 315–345. Madrid, Colección Encuentros.
Bunis, David M. 1995. Pyesa di Yaakov Avinu kun sus ijus (Bucharest, 1862): The first Judezmo play? *Revue des Études Juives* 154(3–4). 387–428.
Bunis, David M. 1996. Translating from the head and from the heart: The essentially oral nature of the Ladino Bible-translation tradition. In Winfred Busse & Marie-Christine Varol-Bornes (eds.), *Hommage á Haïm Vidal Sephiha*, 337–357. Berne: Peter Lang.
Bunis, David M. 1999a. *Judezmo: An introduction to the language of the Sephardic Jews of the Ottoman Empire*. Jerusalem: Magnes. [Hebrew].
Bunis, David M. 1999b. *Voices from Jewish Salonika*. Jerusalem & Thessaloniki: Misgav Yerushalayim, The National Authority for Ladino & Ets Ahaim. [Hebrew & English].
Bunis, David M. 2004a. Distinctive characteristics of Jewish Ibero-Romance, circa 1492. In Yom Tov Assis & Raquel Ibáñez-Sperber (eds.), *Hispania Judaica Bulletin*, 105–137. Jerusalem: The Hebrew University of Jerusalem.
Bunis, David M. 2004b. Writing systems as a national-religious symbol – on the development of Judezmo writing. *Pe'amim* 101–102. 111–171.
Bunis, David M. & Mattat Adar-Bunis. 2011. Spoken Judezmo in written Judezmo: Dialogues in Sefer Me-'am Lo'ez on Leviticus and Numbers (Istanbul 1753-64) by Rabbi Yiṣḥaq Magriso. *Pe'amim* 125–127. 409–502. [Hebrew].
Cherezli, Shlomo I. 1899. *Nuevo chiko diksyonario Judeo-Espagnol – Française*. Jerusalem: Abraham Lunz.
Cohen, Dov. 2011. *The Ladino bookshelf: Research and mapping*. Ramat Gan: Bar-Ilan University PhD thesis.
Cohen, Dov & Ora (Rodrigue) Schwarzwald. 2018. *Compendio delas šeḥiṭót (Constantinople ca. 1510): The First Book Printed in Ladino*. Paper presented at the XIth Congress of the European Association for Jewish Studies. Krakow, Poland.

Cowley, Arthur Ernest. 1971. *Concise catalogue of the Hebrew printed books in the Bodleian library*. Oxford: Clarendon Press.
Crews, Cynthia M. 1935. *Recherches sur le judeo-espagnol dans les pays balkaniques*. Paris: DROZ.
Den Boer, Harm. 1996. *La literatura sefardí de Amesterdão*. Alcalá de Henares: Instituto Internacional de Estudios Sefardíes y Andalusíes.
Díaz-Mas, Paloma & George K. Zucker (trans.). 1992. *Sephardim: The Jews from Spain*. Chicago: The University of Chicago Press.
Díaz-Mas, Paloma & Carlos Mota. 1998. *Sem Tob de Carrión proverbios morales*. Madrid: Catedra.
Fishman, Joshua A. 1972. *Sociolinguistics*. Rowley, MA.: Newbury House.
Gaon, Moshe D. 1964. *A bibliography of the Judeo-Spanish (Ladino) press*. Jerusalem: Ben Zvi Institute & The Hebrew National Library. [Hebrew].
García Moreno, Aitor. 2004. *Relatos del pueblo ladinán: Me'am lo'ez de Éxodo*. Madrid: CSIC.
Gattegno, Erella & Shmuel Refael. 1995. *Primeros pasos en judeo-español*. Tel Aviv: The Institute for the Study of Salonika Jewry. [Hebrew].
Gattegno, Erella & Shmuel Refael. 1998. *Kurso avansado i superior en judeo-español (Ladino)*. Tel Aviv: The Institute for the Study of Salonika Jewry. [Hebrew].
Ginio Meyuhas, Aliza. 2001. Everyday life in the Sephardic community of Jerusalem according to the *Meam Loez* of Rabbi Jacob Kuli. *Studia Rosenthaliana* 35(2). 133–142.
Ginio Meyuhas, Aliza. 2004. Ecos de las polémicas cristianas contra los judíos en *Meam Loez*. *Convivencia de culturas y sociedades mediterráneas* [Encuentros Judaicos de Tudela] 5. 143–155.
Ginio Meyuhas, Alisa. 2006–2007. Navegar kreaturas: L'éducation des enfants selon le commentaire de Ya'aqov Khuli des livres de la Genése et de 'Exode dans le Me'am Lo'ez (1730). *Yod* 11–12. 35–52.
Girón-Negrón, Luis M. & Laura Minervini. 2006. *Las coplas de Yosef: Entre la Biblia y el Midrash en la poesía judeoespañola*. Madrid: Gredos.
Gomel, Nivi & Shmuel Refael. 2018. *Ladino language: Reading, writing and speaking*, I, II. Ramat Gan: Salti Institute.
Ha-Elion, Moshe. 2000. *En los kampos de la muerte*. Maale Adumim: Instituto Maale Adumim. [Hebrew].
Haboucha, Reginetta. 1992. *Types and motifs in the Judeo-Spanish folktales*. New York: Garland.
Harris, Tracy K. 1994. *Death of a language: The history of Judeo-Spanish*. Newark: University of Delaware Press.
Hassán, Iacob M. 1978. Transcripción normalizada de textos judeoespañoles. *Estudios Sefardíes* 1. 147–150.
Hassán, Iacob M. 1982. Visión panorámica de la literatura sefardí. *Hispánia Judaica* 2. 25–44.
Hassán, Iacob M. (ed.). 1994. *Introducción a la biblia de Ferrara*. Madrid: Colección Encuentros.
Havassy, Rivka. 2007. The Ladino song in the 20th century: A study of the collections of Emily Sene and Bouena Sarfatty-Garfinkle. Ramat Gan: Bar-Ilan PhD thesis. [Hebrew].
Held, Michal. 2009. *Let me tell you a story / Ven te kontare: The personal narratives of Judeo-Spanishs speaking storytelling women, an interdisciplinary study*. Jerusalem: Ben-Zvi Institute.
Hernández González, Carmen. 2001. Un viaje por SEFARAD: La fortuna del judeoespañol. *El español en el mundo (Anuario del instituto Cervantes)*, 281–332. Barcelona: Plaza & Janés Editores.
Hitchcock, Richard. 1977. *The Kharjas: A critical bibliography*. London: Grand and Cutler.

Kaplan, Aryeh. 1977–1997. *Yalkut Meʿam Loʿez: The Torah anthology*. New York: Moznaim.
Koén-Sarano, Matilda. 1999a. *Kurso de Djudeo-Espanyol (Ladino) para prinsipiantes*. Beer Sheva: Ben-Gurion University Press. [Hebrew].
Koén-Sarano, Matilda. 1999b. *Kurso de Djudeo-Espanyol (Ladino) para adelantados*. Beer Sheva: Ben-Gurion University Press. [Hebrew].
Koén-Sarano, Matilda. 2009–2010. *Diksionario Ladino (Djudeo-Espanyol-Ebreo – Ebreo-Ladino (Djudeo-Espanyol)*. Jerusalem: Zack.
Koén-Sarano, Matilda. 2010. *Gizar kon gozo*. Jerusalem: Zack.
Kohen, Elie & Dahlia Kohen-Gordon. 2000. *Ladino-English / English-Ladino concise encyclopedic dictionary*. New York: Hippocrene Books.
Landau, Luis. 1980. Content and form in the Meʿam Loʿez of Rabbi Jacob Culi. Jerusalem: The Hebrew University of Jerusalem PhD thesis.
Landau, Luis. 1981. The transformation of the talmudic story in *Meʿam Loʿez*. Pe'amim 7. 35–49. [Hebrew].
Lazar, Moshe. 1964. Bible translations in Ladino from after the Expulsion. *Sefunot* 8. 337–375. [Hebrew].
Lazar, Moshe. 1976. *Diccionario Ladino-Hebrew* (Fasciculo de muestra G). Jerusalem: Ben-Zvi Institute.
Lazar, Moshe (ed.). 1988. *Ladino pentateuch: Constantinople 1547*. Culver City: Labyrinthos.
Lazar, Moshe (ed.). 1990. *Yehudah Halevi: Book of the Kuzari [15th c.]*. Culver City: Labyrinthos.
Lazar, Moshe (ed.). 1992a. *The Ladino Bible of Ferrara [1553]*. Culver City: Labyrinthos.
Lazar, Moshe (ed.). 1992b. *The Ladino Five Scrolls (Abraham Asa's versions of 1744)*. Culver City: Labyrinthos.
Lazar, Moshe (ed.). 1993a. *The Ladino Maḥzōr of Ferrara [1553]*. Culver City: Labyrinthos.
Lazar, Moshe (ed.). 1993b. *Sefer Tešuḇāh: A Ladino compedium of Jewish law and ethics*. Culver City: Labyrinthos.
Lazar, Moshe (ed.). 1995a. *Biblia Ladinada: Escorial I.j.3*. Madison: The Hispanic Seminary of Medieval Studies.
Lazar, Moshe (ed.). 1995b. *Siddur Tefillot: A woman's Ladino prayer book*. Culver City: Labyrinthos.
Lazar, Moshe (ed.). 1995c. *Libro de oracyones: Ferrara Ladino Siddur*, Lancaster: Labyrinthos.
Lazar, Moshe (ed.). 1999. *Sefarad in my heart: A Ladino reader*. Lancaster: Labyrinthos.
Lazar, Moshe (ed.). 2000. *The Ladino scriptures: Constantinople – Salonica [1540–1572]*, vol. 1–2. Lancaster: Labyrinthos.
Lévy, Isaac J. 1969. *Prolegomena to the study of the 'Refranero Sefardi'*. New York: Las Americas Publishing House
Lévy, Isaac J. 1989. *And the world stood silent: The Sephardic poetry of the Holocaust*. Urbana: University of Illinois Press.
Maeso, David G. & Pascual Pascual Recuero (eds.). 1964–1970. *Meʿam Loʿez: El gran comentario bíblico sefardí*, vol. 1: *Prolegómenos*, vol. 2: *Genesis* (I-XXV, 18), vol. 3: *Genesis* (XXV, 18–L, 26). Madrid: Gredos.
Marcus, Simon. 1962. A-t-il existé en Espagne un dialecte judéo-espagnol. *Sefarad* 22. 129–149.
Marcus, Simon. 1965. *The Judeo-Spanish language*. Jerusalem: Kiryat Sefer. [Hebrew].
Markova, Alla. 2008. *Beginner's Ladino with 2 audio CDs*. New York: Hipocrene Books.
Menéndez Pidal, Ramon. 1906. Catalogo del romancero judeo español. *Cultura Española* 4. 1045–1077.
Menéndez Pidal, Ramon. 1907. Catalogo del romancero judeo español. *Cultura Española* 5. 161–199.

Menéndez Pidal, Ramon. 1928. *El romancero judeo-español, teorías e investigaciones*. Madrid: Espasa Calpe.
Minervini, Laura. 1992. *Testi giudeospagnoli medievali*, vol. 1–2. Napoli: Liguori Editore.
Minervini, Laura. 1998. Review of Moshe Lazar's edition of Siddur Tefillot: A woman's Ladino prayer book. *Romance Philology* 31. 404–419.
Minervini, Laura. 2002. La formación de la *koiné* judeo-española en el siglo XVI. *Revue de Linguistique Romane* 263–264. 497–512.
Nehama, Joseph. 1977. *Dicctionaire du judéo-espagnol*. Madrid: CSIC.
Pascual Recuero, Pascual. 1977. *Diccionario básico ladino-español*. Barcelona: Ameller Ediciones.
Pascual Recuero, Pascual. 1988. *Ortografía del ladino*. Granada: Universidad de Granada.
Passy, Albert M. 1999. *Sephardic folk dictionary English to Ladino – Ladino to English*. Los Angeles: Author's edition.
Penny, Ralph. 1996. Judeo-Spanish varieties before and after the Expulsion. *Donaire* 6. 54–58.
Penny, Ralph. 2000. *Variation and change in Spanish*. Cambridge: Cambridge University Press.
Perahya, Clara, R. Meranda, S. Danon, R. Sedaka & Ç. Zakuto. 1997. *Diksyonaryo/ Sözlük Judeo-Espanyol – Türkçe/ Türkçe – Judeo-Espanyol*. Istanbul: Gozlem Gazetecilik Basin Yayin.
Perahya, Klara & Elie Perahya. 1998. *Dictionnaire français judéo-espagnol*. Paris: Langues and Mondes.
Perez, Avner & Gladys Pimienta. 2007. *Diksionario amplio djudeo-espanyol – ebreo: Lashon me-Aspamia*. Maale-Adumim: La Autoridad Nasionala del Ladino i su Kultur and Sefarad – El Instituto Maale Adumim.
Quintana, Aldina. 2004. Sobre la transmisión y el formulismo en el ME'AM LO'EZ de Yacob Juli. In Hilary Pomeroy and Michael Alpert (eds.), *IJS Studies in Judaica 3: Proceedings of the Twelfth British Conference on Judeo-Spanish Studies (24–26 June 2001)*, 69–80. Leiden: Brill.
Quintana, Aldina. 2006. *Geografía lingüística del judeoespañol*. Bern: Peter Lang.
Quintana, Aldina. 2012. Judeo-Spanish: From linguistic segregation outside the common framework of Hispanic languages to a *de facto* standard. In Malka Muchnik & Tsvi Sadan (eds.), *Studies in modern Hebrew and Jewish languages*, 697–714. Jerusalem: Carmel.
Refael, Shmuel. 1998. *The knight and the captive lady*. Ramat Gan: Bar-Ilan University Press. [Hebrew].
Refael, Shmuel. 1999. Trends and goals in catalogues and bibliographies of Ladino printed books. *Pe'amim* 81. 120–154. [Hebrew].
Refael, Shmuel. 2004. *I will tell a poem: A study of the Judeo-Spanish (Ladino) coplas*. Jerusalem: Carmel. [Hebrew].
Refael, Shmuel. 2008. *Un grito en el silencio: La poesía sobre el Holocausto en lengua sefaredí*. Barcelona: Tirocinio.
Renard, Raymond. 1967. *Sépharad: Le monde et la langue judéo-espagnole des séphardim*. Mons: Annales Universitaires de Mons.
Revah, Israel S. 1970. Hispanisme et judaïsme des langues parlées et écrites par les Sefardim. In Iacob M. Hassán (ed.), *Actas del primer simposio de estudios sefardíes*, 233–241. Madrid: Instituto Arias Montano.
Romano, Samuel. 1995 [1933]. *Dictionary of spoken Judeo-Spanish/ French/ German*. Jerusalem: Misgav Yerushalayim.
Romero, Elena. 1979. *El teatro de los sefardíes orientales*, vol. 1–3. Madrid: Instituto Arias Montano.
Romero, Elena. 1988. *Coplas sefardíes*. Cordoba: El Almendro.
Romero, Elena. 1992a. *La creación literaria en lengua Sefardí*. Madrid: MAPFRE.

Romero, Elena. 1992b. Literary creation in the Sephardic diaspora. In Haim Beinart (ed.), *Moreshet Sepharad: The Sephardi legacy*, 438–460. Jerusalem: Magnes.
Romero, Elena. 1992c. *Bibliografía analítica de ediciones de coplas sefardíes*. Madrid CSIC.
Romero, Elena. 1993. Nuevos aspectos de la narrativa judeoespañola. In Eufemio Leorenzo Sanz (ed.), *Proyección histórica de España en sus tres culturas: Castilla y León, America y el Mediterrneo III*, 175–194. Valladolid: Junta de Castilla y León.
Romero, Elena. 2008. *Entre dos (o más) fuegos: Fuentes poéticas para la historia de los Balcanes*. Madrid: CSIC.
Romero, Elena. 2009. *Dos colecciones de cuentos sefardíes de carácter mágico: Sipuré Noraot y Sipuré Pelaot*. Madrid: CSIC.
Romeu Ferré, Pilar (ed.). 1998. *Moisés Almosnino Crónica de los Reyes Otomanos*. Barcelona: Tirocinio.
Romeu Ferré, Pilar. 2000. *Las llaves del Meam Loez: Edición crítica, concordada y analítica de los Índices del Meam loez de la Tora*. Barcelona: Tirocinio.
Schwarzwald (Rodrigue), Ora. 1981. The pronunciation of 'ayin in the East-Ladino Speaking Communities. *Lešonenu* 46. 72–75. [Hebrew].
Schwarzwald (Rodrigue), Ora. 1985. The fusion of the Hebrew-Aramaic lexical component in Judeo-Spanish. In Isaac Benabu & Joseph Sermoneta (eds.), *Judeo-Romance languages*, 139–159. Jerusalem: Misgav Yerushalayim.
Schwarzwald (Rodrigue), Ora. 1989. *The Ladino translations of Pirke Aboth (Eda VeLashon* 13). Jerusalem: Magnes. [Hebrew].
Schwarzwald (Rodrigue), Ora. 1996. Linguistic variations among Ladino translations as determined by geographical, temporal and textual factors. *Folia Linguistica Historica* 17. 57–72.
Schwarzwald (Rodrigue), Ora. 1999. Language choice and language varieties before and after the Expulsion. In Yedida K. Stillman & Norman A. Stillman (eds.), *From Iberia to diaspora: Studies in Sephardic history and culture*, 399–415. Leiden: Brill.
Schwarzwald (Rodrigue), Ora. 2002. Judeo-Spanish studies. In Martin Goodman (ed.), *Oxford handbook of Jewish studies*, 572–600. Oxford: Oxford University Press.
Schwarzwald (Rodrigue), Ora. 2003. A new look at the origin and transmission of the Ladino translations. In Daniel Sivan & Pablo-Itshak Kirchuk (eds.), *Bentolila jubilee book*, 359–369. Beer Sheva: Ben-Gurion University Press. [Hebrew].
Schwarzwald (Rodrigue), Ora. 2004. Spelling and orthography in Ladino translations from the 16th Century on. *Pe'amim* 101–102. 173–185. [Hebrew].
Schwarzwald (Rodrigue), Ora. 2006–2007. Le style du Me'am Loez: Une tradition linguistique. *Yod* 11–12. 77–112.
Schwarzwald (Rodrigue), Ora. 2008. *A dictionary of the Ladino Passover Haggadot (Eda Velashon* 27). Jerusalem: Magnes.
Schwarzwald (Rodrigue), Ora. 2010. On the Jewish nature of medieval Spanish biblical translations: Linguistic differences between medieval and post exilic Spanish translations. *Sefarad* 70. 117–140.
Schwarzwald (Rodrigue), Ora. 2011. Lexical variations in two Ladino prayer books for women. In Winfried Busse & Michael Studemund-Halévy (eds.), *Lexicología y lexicografía judeoespañolas*, 53–86. Bern: Peter Lang.
Schwarzwald (Rodrigue), Ora. 2012a. *Sidur para mujeres en ladino, Salónica, siglo xvi*. Jerusalem: Ben-Zvi Institute.

Schwarzwald (Rodrigue), Ora. 2012b. The Relationship between Ladino liturgical texts and Spanish Bibles. In Jonathan Decter & Arturo Prats (eds.), *The Hebrew Bible in Fifteenth-Century Spain: Exegesis, literature, philosophy and the arts*, 223–243. Leiden & Boston: Brill.

Schwarzwald (Rodrigue), Ora. 2012c. Discourse aspects in *Meam Loez*. In Ephraim Hazan & Shmuel Refael (eds.), *Mahbarot liyehudit: Studies presented to Professor Judith Dishon*, 291–309. Ramat Gan: Bar-Ilan University Press. [Hebrew].

Schwarzwald (Rodrigue), Ora. 2014. Linguistic variations in early Ladino translations. *Journal of Jewish Languages* 2. 1–48.

Schwarzwald (Rodrigue), Ora. 2017. Thessaloniki 1568 and Venice 1713: Language differences in two Ladino books. In Elena Romero, Hilary Pomeroy, & Shmuel Refael (eds.), *Actas del xviii congreso de estudios sefardíes*, 289–305. Madrid: CSIC.

Sephiha, Haim V. 1973. *Le Ladino: Deutéronome*. Paris: Centre de Recherches Hispaniques.

Sephiha, Haim V. 1979. *Le Ladino (judéo-espagnol calque)*. Paris: Association Vidas Largas.

Sephiha, Haim V. 1986. *Le judéo-espagnol*. Paris: Éditions Entente.

Seroussi, Edwin. 1989. *Mizimrat qedem: The life and music of R. Isaac Algazi from Turkey*. Jerusalem: Renanot, Institute for Jewish Music. [Hebrew]

Seroussi, Edwin (ed.). 1995. *Alberto Hemsi: Cancionero Sefardí*. Jerusalem: The Jewish Music Research centre, The Hebrew University.

Shaul, Moshe (ed.). 1979–2016. *Aki Yerushalayim: Revista kulturala djudeo-espanyola*. Jerusalem: Emision Djudeo-Espanyola de Kol Israel i Sefarad.

Shaul, Moshe. 1999. *Ladino (Spanyolit) for beginners*. Maale Adumim: The Institute for the Documentation of Judeo-Spanish and Its Culture. [Hebrew].

Šmid, Katja. 2012. *El sefer mešec beti de Eliézer Papo: Ritos y costumbres sabáticas de los sefardíes de Bosnia*. Madrid: CSIC.

Spolsky, Bernard. 2014. *The languages of the Jews: A sociolinguistic history*. Cambridge: University Press.

Steinschneider, Moritz. 1852–1860. *Catalogue librorum Hebraeorum in bibliotheca Bodleiana*. Berlin: Welt-Verlag.

Varole, Marie-Christine 1998. *Manuel de judéoespagnol: Langue et culture*. Paris: Langues et Mondes.

Varol-Bornes, Marie-Christine. 2008. *Le judéo-espagnol vernaculaire d'Istanbul*. Berne: Peter Lang.

Várvaro, Alberto. 1987. Il giudeo-spagnolo prima dell'espulsione del 1492. *Medioevo Romanzo* 12. 154–72.

Wagner, Max L. 1990. *Juden-Spanish I-II*. Stuttgart: Franz Steiner.

Weich-Shahak, Susana. 1997. *Romancero sefardí de Marruecos: Antología de tradición oral*. Madrid: Alpuerto.

Weich-Shahak, Susana. 2007. *Voces sefardíes de Sarajevo*. Madrid: Tecnosaga.

Weinreich, Max & Shlomo Noble (trans.). 1973. *History of the Yiddish language*. Chicago: The University of Chicago Press.

Wexler, Paul. 1987. De-Judaicization and incipient re-Judaicization in 18th century Portuguese Ladino. *Iberoromania* 25. 23–37.

Wiesner, Christa. 1981. *Jüdisch-Spanisches glossar zum ME'AM LO'EZ des Iacob Kuli*. Hamburg: Helmut Buske.

Wright, Roger. 1982. *Late Latin and early Romance*. Liverpool: Francis Cairns.

Yaari, Abraham. 1934. *Catalogue of Judeo-Spanish books*. Jerusalem: The Hebrew University. [Hebrew].

Yerushalmi, Isaac. 1989. *Reuven Eliyahu Yisrael's traduksyon livre de las poezias Ebraikas de Rosh ha-Shana I Kippur 5670 and the six Selihoth of the 5682 edition*. Cincinnati: Ladino Books.

Yerushalmi, Isaac. 1993. *The Song of Songs in the targumic tradition*. Cincinnati: Ladino Books.

Yerushalmi, Shmuel. 1957–1981. *Yalkut Meʿam Loʿez* [Meam Loez collection], 20 vol. Jerusalem: Or Hadash. [Hebrew].

Zamora Vicente, Alonso. 1985. *Dialectología española*. Madrid: Gredos.

Zemke, John. 1997. *Critical approaches to the proverbios morales of Shen Tov de Carrión: An annotated bibliography*. Newark, Delaware: Juan de la Cuesta.

Zemke, John. 2004. *Moshe ben Bariḵ Almosnino's Regimiento de la Vida* and *Tratado de los Sueños*. Tempe: Arizona Center for Medieval and Renaissance Studies.

David M. Bunis
Judezmo (Ladino/Judeo-Spanish): A Historical and Sociolinguistic Portrait

1 Brief introduction

The interaction in medieval Iberia of Jews, Christians, and, from 711, Muslims, led to the rise of Jewish varieties of medieval Ibero-Romance. Since the largest group of Sephardim, or medieval Iberian Jews, was concentrated in Castile, the variety of Jewish Ibero-Romance having the largest number of speakers was Jewish Castilian. In addition to its adaptations of Castilian elements used by local non-Jews, sometimes in unique forms, it incorporated elements of Hebrew-Aramaic, Jewish Greek/Latin, Jewish Ibero-Arabic, and non-Castilian Hispanic origin. With the expulsions of the Jews from Castile and Aragon in 1492, their varieties of Ibero-Romance were transported with them to the places in which they found refuge. The greatest numbers made their way to the Ottoman Empire, at the invitation of Sultan Bayezid II (1447–1512); others settled in North Africa, Italy, and other parts of the Mediterranean basin. The descendants of the medieval Spanish Jews who re-established themselves in the Ottoman Empire, as well as those who remained in the region after the empire gave way to new nation-states, continued to use evolved forms of their distinctive, principally Ibero-Romance Jewish language into the 21st century. The present chapter is devoted to the language of the Jews of the Ottoman Empire and its successor states and the literature created in it, with additional information about pre-expulsion Iberian and post-Ottoman Judezmo.

1.1 Names of the language

In their writings in Hebrew, the Jews of medieval Iberia, as well as their descendants throughout the world, into the modern era, referred to their language by the same name used by Jews throughout the Romance-speaking regions to denote their local varieties of Jewish Romance: *la'az* or *lo'ez*, which in the Bible (Ps. 114:1) denoted the speaking of a 'foreign language' – in that context, specifically Ancient Egyptian. In the Mishnah, *la'az* denoted Greek, and in the Middle Ages, it came to designate Romance or Jewish Romance (perhaps influenced by the phonological proximity to Romance LATINUS or 'Latin', from which the Jews knew that Romance varieties derived). In order to distinguish their variety of Romance

https://doi.org/10.1515/9781501504631-008

from varieties used by Jews in other regions, the Sephardim sometimes called it *la'az sĕfaradi* or 'Sephardic/Spanish La'az'.

In their writings in the language itself, the Jews of the 16th century Ottoman Empire continued to use Romance-origin names, which they presumably had used in Spain and which were also in use among medieval Spanish non-Jews (Bunis 2008a), e.g., *ladino*,[1] from LATINUS, an allusion to its popular Latin origin; *romanse*, from ROMANICE, further demonstrating an awareness of its Romance origins; *espanyol*, from HISPANIOLUS, specifying that this version of Romance was that used in HISPANIA, or Spain.

Although it has been argued that *Ladino* properly denotes only the 'archaizing' calque variety used in the literal translation of sacred texts (e.g., Sephiha 1973), many texts in the language demonstrate that the word in fact has many meanings, among them, 'translation', 'meaning', and especially 'the vernacular of the Sephardim (in its diverse written and spoken varieties), particularly as opposed to Hebrew' (in Hebrew writings this opposition is denoted by *la'az* vs. *lĕšon ha-qodeš* 'Holy Tongue'; and in the vernacular itself by *ladino* vs. *lashón [akódesh]*). Devoid of the negative connotations (e.g., 'sly', 'shrewd') which the word *ladino* has in Spanish, as well as of those acquired after the Spanish conquest of Latin America (e.g., 'mestizo', 'Spanish-speaking Indian'), *ladino* has enjoyed widespread use as a linguanym throughout the history of the language.

That the Ottoman Sephardic masses began to lose cognizance of the Iberian origins of their language is suggested early on by other names they used to denote it. For example, one of the linguanyms used by the first generation of Sephardim born in the empire and used by some speakers into the 20th century, but which evidently had not been used by medieval Spanish non-Jews, was *franko*, meaning 'Western European language'. Perhaps this was a Jewish adaptation of Turkish

---

[1] Except when using I.P.A. transcription symbols enclosed within square brackets [ ], or angular < > brackets enclosing text originally appearing in Latin letters, Judezmo citations are here transcribed from sources originally in the traditional Hebrew-letter Judezmo alphabet, using a modification of the romanized orthography proposed by the Israel National Authority for Ladino Culture (for a summary see *Aki Yerushalayim* 35: 96 [2014]: 2). Note the values of the following special symbols: *ch* = [tʃ]; *d̲* = [ð]; *dj* = [dʒ]; *ġ* = [ɣ]; *ḥ* = [χ]; *i* =[i] or, usually preceding a vowel, [j]; *j* = [ʒ]; *ny* = [ɲ]; *r* = flapped [ɾ] or trilled [r] (depending on the particular word and the regional Judezmo dialect being cited); *rr* = trilled [r]; *s* = [z] before a word-initial voiced phone, otherwise [s]; *sh* =[ʒ] before a word-initial voiced phone, otherwise [ʃ]; *s·h* = [sχ]; *u* = [u] or, usually preceding a vowel, [w]; *v* = [v]; *y* = [j] (usually word-initially or finally or between vowels); *z* = [z]. The stress in words ending in a vowel or *n* or *s* is generally penultimate, and that in words ending in other consonants is ordinarily ultimate; exceptional stress is indicated by an acute accent mark. Unless otherwise noted, the references are to Modern Judezmo.

Frenkçe, a generic name used among the Turks to denote a language spoken by *Frenkler*, or the peoples of *Frengistan* 'Christian Western Europe', seemingly demonstrating a local perception of the Jews' language as originating in the west, from whence they had reached the empire. By the 18th century another distinctive linguanym arose among the Jews, which demonstrated their geographic reorientation and self-perception: *levantino* 'Levantine language' or 'language of the Levant', showing that by then the Ottoman Sephardim saw the Levantine Basin as their home.

By the first half of the 18th century, the Ottoman Sephardim were using the word *djudezmo* – originally meaning 'Judaism' (cf. Sp. *judaísmo* < Lat. IUDAISMUS) – in the sense of 'Jewish language'. It was used to translate Hebrew *yĕhudit* 'language of the Judaeans', 'Jews'/Jewish language' in the vernacular Bible translation published by Avraham Asa in Constantinople in the early 18th century (e.g., II Kings 18:26, 1743); by the early 19th century, it appeared textually in the specific sense of 'vernacular of the Ottoman Sephardim', which its speakers and their non-Jewish neighbors perceived as the local 'Jewish language' (e.g., in Turkish it was called *Yahudice* 'Jewish language').[2] As illustrated in native writings in the language and as documented by scholars belonging to the community, the use of *djudezmo* – along with *djudió/djidió*, also meaning 'Jewish' – to denote the language of the Ottoman Sephardim was widespread into the 20th century (Bunis 2011a). From the late 19th century, with the intensification of Haskalah and later, western academic influence on the speaker community, the names *djudezmo* and *djudió/djidió* lost ground to pseudo-scientific names such as *djudeo-espanyol* 'Judeo-Spanish' and simply *espanyol*, the latter widely used today among popular speakers, who thereby fail to mark any distinction between their own language and the Spanish language. Nevertheless, *djudezmo* still enjoys some popular use among native speakers and is the name preferred by many Jewish-language scholars – as a unique innovation arising within the speaker community; because of its designation of the language as a 'Jewish language', sharing terminological parallels with some other Jewish languages (e.g., Yiddish); and as a memorial to major Judezmo-speaking communities, such as those of Salonika, Bitola (Monastir), and Rhodes, many of whose everyday members called their language *djudezmo* until they were annihilated in the Holocaust.

---

[2] Among Spaniards, Spanish is often called *cristiano* 'Christian' – a reminder of the fact that Christian Spaniards associated Spanish with Iberia's Christian population, in opposition to the Arabic used by Muslims. But it is unclear whether this Spanish Christian practice had any influence on the use of *djudezmo* as a linguanym among the Ottoman Jews.

1.2 Linguistic affiliation

As was already noted, Judezmo first arose in medieval Iberia, and most of its linguistic raw material, including its lexicon, morphology, and syntactic structure, has always derived from Ibero-Romance, particularly popular Jewish Castilian, with additional elements apparently adapted from other varieties of popular Jewish Ibero-Romance, such as Jewish varieties of Leonese, Andalusian, Galician, Portuguese, Aragonese, and Catalan. Thus the language is of great interest to Hispanists and Romanists in general for the light it sheds on medieval Ibero-Romance, and on the distinctive, partially unique patterns of development which evolved over half a millennium in this Jewish variety of Ibero-Romance, as used in its Ottoman and post-Ottoman locales – places in which other varieties of Ibero-Romance never enjoyed prolonged use. Since the incipient varieties of Judezmo used in medieval Iberia also incorporated material from Hebrew-Aramaic and Ibero-Arabic, and post-expulsion varieties of Judezmo developed in contact with Arabic and Jewish Arabic in parts of the Middle East and North Africa (see section 1.3 below), the language is also of interest to Semitists. Its contact over centuries with Turkish and Balkan languages, and consequent extensive borrowing from those languages, also makes Judezmo intriguing for Turkish and Balkan linguists (Stankiewicz 1964; Gabinskij 1996; Friedman and Joseph 2014), and offers a basis for comparative studies with other Balkan languages, as well as with heavily Arabic-influenced Ḥaketía (another Spanish-based Jewish language) in Spanish Morocco (Bunis 2008b, 2011b, 2012.).

1.3 Regions where languages is/was spoken

Jews used varieties of Ibero-Romance in all of the numerous cities and towns of medieval Christian Iberia in which they resided. In each area the Hispanic component of the Jews' language appears to have borne a closer resemblance to the Ibero-Romance used by the local non-Jews than to varieties used by Jews in distant communities. Since Castilian enjoyed special prestige in medieval Spain, and the majority of its Jews resided in Castile, it is likely that cultured Jews in other parts of Iberia also had some knowledge of Castilian as used by Jews. With the expulsions of the Jews from Castile and Aragon in 1492 and from Portugal in 1497, the Jewish exiles to the Ottoman regions brought their diverse varieties of Jewish Ibero-Romance first to the major port cities in which they settled, primarily Constantinople and Salonika and their environs, as well as to parts of the Middle East, such as the cities of the Land of Israel sacred to the Jews (Jerusalem,

Hebron, Safed, Tiberias), Syria, Lebanon, and Egypt. Later, Jews migrated – of their own volition, in search of new markets for their skills and merchandise, or through royal edict, as part of the Ottoman *sürgün* population transfers – to more distant parts of the realm, leading to the establishment of Judezmo speaker communities throughout Anatolia and Rumelia, in regions that, with the dismemberment of the empire, were to become Turkey, Greece, Bulgaria, Yugoslavia, and Romania, as well as daughter communities in parts of the Austro-Hungarian Empire, such as Vienna and Budapest, and in Italy.

From the middle of the 19th century, education in schools established by the governments of the nation-states carved out of parts of the Ottoman Empire led Judezmo-speaking children to start replacing Judezmo with the local language: Turkish, Greek, South Slavic languages, Romanian. From the second half of the 19th century, the network of Jewish and non-Jewish colonialist-oriented educational institutions established in the Ottoman regions by organizations such as the Alliance Israélite Universelle (AIU; founded in Paris, 1860) and Società Dante Alighieri (founded in 1889) drew young Judezmo speakers into the linguistic and cultural spheres of the primary languages of instruction in their schools – primarily French and Italian. Teachers in these institutions encouraged pupils to abandon Judezmo, indoctrinating them to perceive the language as of low prestige and little cultural value or practical utility. Branches of the Zionist movement which were established in various Sephardic communities motivated their students to adopt Hebrew, with the aim of immigrating to the Land of Israel. From the late 19th century, increasingly difficult economic and social conditions, conscription into the local armed services, and a desire for a better life led Judezmo-speaking young men to leave their families' centuries-old places of residence and immigrate to Western Europe, the Americas, European possessions in Africa, such as the Belgian Congo, and far-flung parts of the British Empire, such as Australia. After settling in, husbands sent for their wives and children, and bachelors established families. The immigrant generation continued using Judezmo in the home and synagogue but gradually acquired the local language; the next generation understood Judezmo, and some could also use it actively, but adopted the local language as its primary language; subsequent generations usually had little or no command of the language.

For those who remained *in situ* in Greece and what was to become Yugoslavia, the Holocaust brought a tragic end to the Judezmo speaker communities. The survivors, and most of the Judezmo speakers who remained in Turkey, Bulgaria, and Romania, immigrated to Israel, where they learned Hebrew and their children adopted Hebrew as their primary language.

1.4 Present-day status

Although still enjoying a speaker community of perhaps several thousand individuals, most of them over 60 and living in Israel, Turkey, the Balkans, the United States, and France, Judezmo is today an increasingly endangered language, with no new generations acquiring it as their primary or even secondary language. However, there are some attempts being made to revitalize Judezmo, research and teach it in universities and local community centers, and maintain cultural vitality and foster creativity through the publication of new and re-edited fictional and non-fictional works, reference materials, and recordings, as well as governmental and grassroots encouragement of performances by musical ensembles and theater troupes. In Israel, much of this work is sponsored by the Israel National Authority for Ladino and its Culture, established by the Knesset in 1996. Judezmo also enjoys a virtual homeland on the Internet (see section 4.2).

2 Historical background

Medieval Jewish writings in varieties of Ibero-Romance have survived from various parts of Iberia and constitute representations of some of the diverse regional, social, and stylistic varieties used by medieval Iberian Jewry. Shortly after their arrival in the Ottoman Empire following the expulsions, Jews established printing presses; from around the middle of the 16th century, the presses began to publish works entirely or partly in Judezmo or approximations of it. Numerous works – including books, pamphlets, and, in the 19th century, periodicals – were published in all of the major and several minor Judezmo-speaking population centers of the Ottoman Empire and its successor states and in immigrant centers (for an extensive listing see the *Bibliography of the Hebrew Book* [http://aleph.nli.org.il/F?func=find-b-0&local_base=mbi01]). Original Judezmo works continue to appear, primarily in Israel, Turkey and the Balkans, and the United States. This rich textual corpus provides a glimpse into Judezmo in its regional, social, and stylistic variations from the pre-expulsion period into our own times.

In some of the documents in the 'Sephardic La'az' which first arose in medieval Iberia, one already sees some of the salient features which continue to characterize Judezmo to this day (see section 3 below). With the expatriation of Sephardic La'az and its speakers to the Ottoman Empire, and the virtual detachment of the language from the varieties of non-Jewish Ibero-Romance which subsequently evolved in Iberia and Latin America, Judezmo gained its developmental independence, with free reign granted to its internal tendencies and trends, an increasing incorporation of elements from Hebrew-Aramaic, and a selective openness to elements found in the indigenous contact languages. From the mid-19th century, the profound influence of colonial languages such as Italian, French, and German led to significant structural changes and especially relexification. During all phases, the etymologically diverse and ever-evolving elements together constituting Judezmo formed unique, structurally cohesive linguistic entities. However, especially from the early 20th century onwards, the tendency of the speakers to acquire and then give preference to other languages as their major language led to symptoms of language mixing, loss, and demise, leading to the critical condition in which the language is to be found today.

2.1 Speaker community: settlement, documentation

The documentation of pre-expulsion Sephardic La'az and the extensive corpus exemplifying the use of Judezmo in the Ottoman regions enable us to form an impression of the writers of the texts, their intended audience, and the speaker community at large over the course of the language's development. With few exceptions, the texts surviving from medieval Iberia suggest that they did not reflect the everyday, popular language used by the rank-and-file Jews of the peninsula, but were the creation of an elite sector of educated individuals who were familiar with the evolving variety of literary Spanish becoming normative during that period and who saw that variety as a model for their own writing, at least with respect to its Hispanic component. The popular sectors of Iberian Jewry, who undoubtedly comprised the majority group, must have used linguistic varieties, the Hispanic component of which bore a closer resemblance to the popular varieties used by their non-Jewish neighbors than that found in the 'elitist' writings.

The significant gap which must have existed between the 'elitist' language exemplified in most of the pre-expulsion texts, and the more popular language which many everyday Jews must have used in medieval Iberia, is hinted at by the language used in texts directed at the popular reader which began to be published in the middle of the 16th century in Constantinople and Salonika – the principal immigration centers of the speaker group during the century following the expulsions from Iberia. Comments by the authors of such works suggest the existence of an education-level division of the 16th century speaker community into: (a) *talmidé hahamim* or 'rabbinical scholars', all of whom were proficient in Hebrew, some of whom could use varieties of Judezmo close in their Hispanic component to the emergent non-Jewish Spanish norm, and at least some of whom were familiar with Turkish as well; (b) the *vulgo* or *amón am* 'popular sector', who constituted the majority, and who lacked fluency in Hebrew and, according to authors' comments, could best cope with Judezmo if printed in the vocalized Square (*merubá*) letters ordinarily used in the Hebrew Pentateuch and daily prayer book (although Judezmo-speaking merchants were said to be proficient in so-called Rashí and cursive Judezmo characters); and (c) the women of the group, most of whom were illiterate during this period and would continue to be so into at least the late 19th century. The language used in 16th century texts meant for the popular reader incorporated more elements of Hebrew-Aramaic and perhaps also Ibero-Arabic origin than many of the 'elitist' pre-expulsion texts contained, and their Hispanic components themselves display some unique features (e.g., the inflection *-ásh/-ésh/-ísh*, widely used to denote the second-person plural present indicative in verb conjugations, as opposed to Spanish *-áis/-éis/-ís*).

Already exemplified sporadically from the 16th century, Judezmo rabbinical prose and poetry flourished from the 18th century, perhaps partly in an attempt to provide attractive religious reading material for less educated speakers of the kind who had been attracted to the cult surrounding Sabbatai Zevi (1626–c.1676), the false messiah of Izmir; popular rabbinical Judezmo literature continued to appear into the early 20th century. Reflecting significant changes in the popular language as used by its intended readers, such works offer a glimpse into Judezmo as it developed in the diverse regions of the Ottoman Empire throughout that period.

From the middle of the 19th century, novel varieties of literary Judezmo began to compete with the popular rabbinical variety for literary dominance. One was the Western Europeanized language of the incipient Judezmo periodical press (Sephiha 1976), with its extensive incorporations from Italian and French (and in Vienna, from German), first exemplified in the newspaper *Šaʿare mizraḥ* or *Puertas de Oriente*, edited by Rafaʾel ʿUzziʾel in Izmir, 1845–1846 (Bunis 1993). The variety of language illustrated in such periodicals was actually employed in speech by some members of the community who had been educated in Western European-style schools, such as those of the AIU, and who were imbued with a strong orientation toward Western Europe and secular humanism.

From the late 19th century, linguistically alternative periodicals employing as their base the popular language of the region of publication, rather than Western Europeanized Judezmo, began to appear in the major Judezmo speaker centers; more than any other printed source of the time, such periodicals reflected the highly distinctive features of popular regional speech at their time of publication (Bunis 1982).

In addition, throughout the phases of the language Judezmo speakers cultivated a rich oral literature, including proverbs and sayings (for native terminology see Bunis 2015b), riddles, popular songs, epic ballads, and liturgical poetry, each genre characterized by certain linguistic idiosyncrasies (for an overview of diverse varieties of Judezmo literature see Romero 1992). Some of this corpus of folk literature is documented in the press and in chapbook collections of songs, tales, and proverbs (see for example Armistead and Silverman 1971a, 1971b). Much more was preserved through oral transmission, and some of this corpus has in recent years been committed to writing by members of the community and scholars devoted to documenting their traditions (e.g., Armistead and Silverman 1986; Alexander-Frizer 2008).

2.2 Phases in historical development

The criteria relevant for the division of Judezmo into historical phases include shifts in the names for the language; in orthography; in phonological, morphological, and syntactic structure; and in the lexicon. Comparing the intonation contours of contemporary Judezmo and Spanish, it is clear that Judezmo also underwent changes at this level, probably under local influence, but it seems impossible to assign these changes to specific historical phases.

The earliest stage in the language may be called the **Old Sephardic La'az** – or in retrospect, **Old Judezmo** – phase. Its proto-phase began with the earliest interactions between the Jewish immigrants who first arrived in Romanized Iberia, perhaps with the Roman armies, and the local non-Jewish Romance speakers whose languages developed into early Ibero-Romance in its diverse regional forms. From 711, Jews in Spain under Islam used Jewish varieties of Arabic, and, in some contexts, probably Romance as well. Later, the varieties of Castilian used by the Jews of Castile once again under Christianity exhibited influences from their earlier Jewish Ibero-Arabic. It was during this stage that the fusion of elements was initiated, including distinctive elements from Jewish Castilian (e.g., *el Dio* 'God', cf. Sp. *Dios*) and other Ibero-Romance varieties (e.g., *burako* 'hole', cf. Pt. *buraco*), Hebrew-Aramaic (*haham* 'rabbinical scholar', cf. Heb. *ḥakam*), Jewish Greek/Latin (*meldar* 'to read', cf. Gk. *meletaō*, J.Lat. *meletare*), and Jewish and non-Jewish Ibero-Arabic (e.g., *alḥad* 'Sunday', cf. Ibero-Arab. *al-ḥadd*). This established a model for the synthesis of native and contact elements which was to continue in the Ottoman Empire and other locales to which Judezmo would later be carried.

The **Middle Judezmo** phase (1492–c.1796) began with the arrival of the Jewish exiles from Iberia in the major seaports of the Ottoman Empire and the beginnings of interaction with more veteran Jewish residents, such as the Jewish Greek-speaking Romaniotes, as well as the non-Jewish majority, including Turks, Greeks, South Slavs, Albanians, Armenians, and others, with whom they came to communicate primarily in Turkish, as an Ottoman lingua franca. **Early Middle**

Judezmo (1492–c.1728) was marked by the beginnings of a tendency toward the rejection of certain Ibero-Romance variants characteristic of normative Christian Spanish (perhaps because the variants which came to be preferred in Ottoman Judezmo had already been widely used popularly in Iberia, and possibly also as a rejection of variants used in the Christianized speech of *conversos* arriving from Iberia in order to return to the open practice of Judaism), e.g., Jud. *-amos* as the first-person plural *present* indicative marker of *-ar* verbs vs. *-emos/-imos* as the *preterite* indicative marker, instead of normative Spanish *-amos* used for both tenses. This early stage was also characterized by the elevation to normative status of variant features considered popular, non-standard, substandard, or archaic in normative varieties of Ibero-Romance (especially Castilian) in Iberia and Latin America (e.g., Jud. *adelantre* 'forward' vs. Sp. *adelante*, pop. *adelantre*); the incorporation of certain Ibero-Romance elements of popular non-Castilian origin (e.g., Jud. *kazal* 'village', Pt., Arag. *casal* vs. Sp. *aldea*); the widespread acceptance of certain Ibero-Romance forms unique to Jewish use (*djud̲ezmo* 'Judaism; Jewish language' vs. Sp. *judaísmo* 'Judaism' [only]); the expansion of the Hebrew-Aramaic component (e.g., *kaserar* 'to render fit for Jewish use' < *kaser* [Heb. *kašer*] 'ritually fit for Jewish use'); and the selective borrowing of elements from contact languages such as Jewish and non-Jewish Greek (e.g., *trandafilá* 'rose', Gk. *triandáfyllo*) and especially Turkish (*trushí* 'brine', Tk. *turşu*), thus establishing the foundations of a distinctly Ottoman Judezmo. During this early stage there is already evidence of the beginnings of a bifurcation of Judezmo into distinct regional dialects (see section 3.2 below).

By the **Late Middle Judezmo** phase (1729–1796), the Judezmo speaker communities in the Ottoman Empire had undergone a complete reorientation and shift in self-perception from foreign newcomers to a part and parcel of the Ottoman social structure, constituting what in the early 19th century would be designated by the Ottoman administration as the *Yahudi milleti* 'Jewish national-religious entity'. During Late Middle Judezmo the tendencies observed in the early part of the phase grew more pronounced, and included distinctive normatizations and significant innovations in the grammatical system (e.g., in verbal inflections, such as the establishment as universal in all regional dialects of *-í* as the first-person singular preterite indicative marker in all conjugation groups), and a significant expansion of the Turkish-Balkan component (which by now included representatives of all word classes, including verbs, adjectives, adverbs, and interjections), thus causing the language to diverge still further from non-Jewish Spanish of the Middle Ages, and from the contemporaneous Spanish evolving in Spain and Latin America.

Evidence of the onset of the **Modern Judezmo** phase may be seen at the end of the 18th century. During the **Early Modern Judezmo** phase (c.1797–1844) the internal tendencies toward analogical levelling and simplification of the grammatical system (e.g., -*tes* as the second-person singular preterite indicative marker, from Old and Early Middle Judezmo -*ste* through Late Middle -*stes*; cf. Sp. -*ste*) reached their peak. The **Late Modern Judezmo** phase (1845–present) is characterized by considerable lexical innovation and expansion resulting from novel uses of pre-existing linguistic raw material (e.g., *hazindad* 'illness', *enhazinarse* 'to grow ill' < *hazino* 'ill' + substantivizing -*dad*, verbalizing *en-* -*arse*); and further incorporations from Hebrew-Aramaic (e.g., *purimlik* 'Purim gift' < Heb. *purim* + Tk. substantivizing -*lik*) and local contact languages (e.g., *kolayladear* 'to simplify' < Tk. *kolayladı* [*kolay* + -*la*- -*dı*]+ Jud. -*ear*) and their fusion into a modern linguistic entity distinct at all levels from non-Jewish varieties of Spanish. It is also in this period that the profound influences on Judezmo of colonial languages such as Italian, French, and – in communities under Austro-Hungarian cultural sway – German became increasingly apparent, as a result of direct interaction with merchants, school teachers, and other users of those languages locally, and through the influence of the written literature and journalism in those languages to which Judezmo speakers were exposed in colonial-oriented schools, newly-established community libraries, and periodicals sold at newsstands. From the late 19th century, and especially following World War II, some Judezmo speakers came into contact with Spanish politicians, scholars, and merchants; the scholars demonstrated an interest in Judezmo for the light it could shed on the history of the Spanish language and Spanish oral traditions, but the Spaniards also saw the Judezmo speaker community as a bridge which could assist them in gaining entrée into the Ottoman Empire in order to advance their own commercial and political interests. As a result, some Judezmo-speaking intellectuals advocated bringing their communal language into closer alignment with Spanish or replacing Judezmo with Spanish outright; but such proposals had little echo in the larger speaker community, and the demonstrable impact of Spanish on the language of most Judezmo speakers has remained insignificant.

2.3 Sociolinguistic description, community bilingualism, public functions

From its earliest appearance, Sephardic La'az or Judezmo, like other Jewish languages, has existed in a diglossic relation with Hebrew and Aramaic – the languages of the sacred texts and formal liturgy of its speakers – and with the languages and linguistic varieties used by the neighboring Jewish subculture groups and non-Jewish ethnic groups. At various stages in medieval Iberia, the latter included Arabic speakers, and Christians and Muslims using somewhat different varieties of Ibero-Romance. Following the expulsions, the languages with which Ottoman Judezmo speakers were in contact included Jewish languages such as the Jewish Greek of the Romaniotes, and the Jewish Arabic of Mustaʻarabim ('Judeo-Arabic-speaking Jews of the Middle East') in parts of the Middle East, such as the Land of Israel and Syria; in addition, they had contact, in much smaller numbers, at various points in the development of the language, with speakers of Yiddish, Jewish Italian, and others. They were also in frequent contact with non-Jewish speakers of local languages such as Greek, South Slavic languages (e.g., Bosnian, Serbian, Bulgarian), Romanian, and especially Turkish. Rabbinical responsa demonstrate that Judezmo speakers – both men and women – commanded Turkish to a certain extent from the 16th century on, although, before the proclamation of the Turkish Republic in 1923, their Turkish was perceived by Turks as being spoken with a 'Jewish' (i.e., Judezmo) accent and not necessarily using normative Turkish grammar. In cities in which members of diverse Jewish subculture groups met, such as in Old Yishuv Jerusalem, Judezmo served as a kind of Jewish lingua franca, especially among non-Ashkenazim; but even Yiddish speakers in Jerusalem borrowed lexemes from Judezmo (Kosover 1966). Throughout the Ottoman Empire, Judezmo was considered to be the indigenous Jewish language, and was referred to, in Turkish and other state languages, as 'the Jewish language'. As stipulated in the 1911 regulations concerning the governing body of the Jews of the Ottoman Empire, representatives of the Jewish community in the Ottoman government were required to know how to "*avlar i eskrivir el djudesmo*" 'speak and write Judezmo' (Gran Rabinato de Turkia [1911]: 5), and community documents, such as those regulations, as well as public circulars and communications from the Chief Rabbinate and other Jewish communal institutions, as well as the Ottoman regime, included a Judezmo version. Thus, a postcard in Turkish commemorating the Young Turk Revolution of 1908 included an inscription in Judezmo, as well as the other major non-Jewish languages of the empire. Judezmo was used as the language of instruction in traditional Jewish educational institutions (which mostly taught religion), and as the language of public discourse in synagogues and other Jewish venues, and of literature and periodicals directed toward the popular Jewish reader.

From the Modern Judezmo phase, Judezmo had competition from Hebrew as the language of the incipient Zionist movement; and from French and Italian as the languages of foreign merchants in Ottoman cities and the language of instruction in colonialist-oriented schools attended by children from Judezmo-speaking homes. As the empire gave way to new nation-states, each with its own official language, Judezmo speakers in each state strove to master the local language; among the younger speakers, this generally led to a state of bilingualism, to the mixing of Judezmo with the local non-Jewish language, and, especially after World

War I, to the demise of Judezmo and its replacement by the local state language. Although there are still thousands of Judezmo speakers today, most are over 60, none seem to be monolingual speakers, and, at least as a group, the younger generations of descendants of Judezmo speakers, both in the traditional speech territory and in centers of immigration, are not being taught the language through natural transmission within their families, but only in courses which began to be introduced in universities and community and cultural centers in the 1970s.

Throughout its history, Judezmo was spoken in diverse ways according to various social variables, such as age, gender, religiosity, profession, and so on. For example, individuals – especially males – with a more religious orientation tended to employ more elements of Hebrew-Aramaic origin than their more secular, religiously less-educated counterparts; while males whose professions or trades brought them into close contact with the local non-Jewish population tended to incorporate in their speech more local borrowings than those less in touch with non-Jewish neighbors. Younger speakers who acquired French and Italian through commercial contacts or formal schooling tended to relexify their Judezmo, replacing traditional elements of Hebrew-Aramaic and Turkish-Balkan origin with Gallicisms and Italianisms, leaving those speakers unfamiliar with the European prestige languages baffled by the younger generation's *nuevo linguaje* 'new language' (Bunis 2014). As the speech of westernized/Europeanized/secularized males became enriched through borrowings from French and Italian, and depleted of 'eastern' elements of Hebrew and Turkish origin, the language of females lacking a western education began to seem more old-fashioned and conservative, with greater preservation of 'eastern' elements, and even more traditional, popular forms of Hispanisms than used by males, who now tended to alter the forms of their Hispanisms under French and Italian influence (e.g., *muestro* > *nuestro* 'our', under the influence of French *notre*, Italian *nostro*). In general it may be said that, in the late 19th and 20th centuries, the encounter with diverse new language attitudes, some originating among the local non-Jews, others among local representatives of European Jewish language-related social movements, such as the Haskalah and political Zionism, caused Judezmo speakers of all orientations to introspect about their language and effect changes in it.

3 Structural information

As in other regions in which Jewish languages arose, the need to maintain one's livelihood and ensure physical security necessitated that the earliest Jewish immigrants in Spain have knowledge of their non-Jewish neighbors' everyday language. On the other hand, the religious and ethnic culture which set the Jews apart from their neighbors led to their intracommunal use of elements of language reflecting their distinctiveness; such elements often derived from their oldest ancestral and sacred languages, Hebrew and Aramaic (e.g., popular pronunciations of Hebrew *šabbat*, such as *sabad*, to denote the Sabbath, preferred over *sábado*, used by Christians). Further distinctive linguistic material used by the Jews of Iberia derived from the Jewish Greek and Jewish Latin that the ancestors of the community had used, especially in sacred study, before the migration to Iberia (e.g., *Ayifto* [cf. Gk. *Aígyptos*] 'Egypt'). The Muslim conquest from 711 of parts of Iberia led some Iberian Jewish communities under Islam to adopt Arabic in a Judaized form; centuries later, with the return to Christendom of those regions, Jewish Ibero-Romance again became the primary language of their Jewish residents, but now their Romance included some elements preserved from Jewish Ibero-Arabic (e.g., *[a]dafina* [cf. Ar. *ad-dafina*], one name for the traditional Sabbath lunch stew, kept warm overnight). The Romance component of Jewish Ibero-Romance in Iberia, too, had distinctive features as a result of phonological idiosyncrasies (e.g., the tendency to realize historical word-final vowel + *is* as vowel + *š*, as in *sesh* instead of *seis* for 'six'), and a propensity for fusing morphemes of diverse etymological origins into innovative coinages absent from non-Jewish speech (e.g., *enheremar* 'to excommunicate', from *hérem* [Heb. *ḥerem*] 'excommunication' + Hispanic-origin verbalizing *en--ar*), as well as the selective rejection or alteration of words and forms used by the co-territorial non-Jews (e.g., Jewish *djudezmo* vs. Spanish *judaísmo* 'Judaism').

With the expulsions from Iberia, interaction with new neighbors of diverse ethnicity led to contact with and selective adoption of material from new languages, principally Turkish, Greek, South Slavic, German, and, in parts of the Middle East, Arabic. When Western European languages such as Italian and French began to have an impact on the ethnic groups of the Ottoman Empire, in response to the Ottomans' desire for aid from the Western Europeans and their willingness to grant the Europeans trade capitulations in return for that aid, Judezmo underwent significant modification under the influence of those languages – in the case of French, in good measure through the efforts of the AIU school network established throughout the empire by agents of the Jews of France. With the replacement of the Ottoman Empire by new nation-states, each of which sought to establish the language and ethnicity of the local predominant group at the state level, Jews made strides in acquiring those languages; to the detriment of Judezmo, its speakers eventually adopted the state languages for everyday, intracommunal use, increasingly curtailing the use of Judezmo to occasional intimate interactions within the family and among friends. In each phase of its development, from its medieval antecedents through the varieties still used in the 21st century, the structure of Judezmo reflected linguistically the dynamism of the speaker community within its own communal borders and in interaction with its neighbors.

3.1 Relationship to non-Jewish varieties (isoglosses, related dialects)

The predominance of Castilian in medieval Iberian Jewish communities is illustrated in forms attested in Hebrew-letter Jewish texts from the 15th and 16th centuries and still in use in regional Judezmo, such as מוג'ו/*mucho* '(m.g.) much' and איג'ו/-פ'/*(f)echo* '(m.sg.) done', corresponding to Old Spanish *mucho* and *fecho* (Mod.Sp. *hecho*), as opposed to correspondents such as Aragonese and Portuguese *muito* and *feito*, Galician *moito* and *feito*, and Catalan *molt* and *fet* (cf. Lat. MULTUM, FACTUM).

Throughout the history of Judezmo, its phonological system has shared much with that of Old Castilian, as distinct from that of Modern Spanish. For example, Judezmo has distinct /b/ vs. /v/ phonemes, as opposed to the single Modern Spanish /b/ phoneme, which has the positional allophones [b] and [β]. The Judezmo phoneme corresponding to the phonemes represented graphemically in Old Spanish by <z> and intervocalic <s> is /z/ (e.g., OSp. <dezir> 'to say', <casa> 'house', realized in Old Spanish as [deˈdzir], [ˈkaza] = Mod. Jud. דיזיר [deˈzir], קאזה [ˈkaza]), as opposed to Modern Spanish /θ/ in [deˈθir] (in Castilian) or /s/ [deˈsir] (in Andalusia and Latin America) (<decir>), and /s/ in pan-Spanish [ˈkasa] (<casa>). Also agreeing with Andalusian and Latin American Spanish, the Judezmo correspondents of Old Spanish <ç> [ts] and <s-, -ss-> [s] are both reflected in Judezmo as /s/ [s], e.g., סינקו/*sinko* 'five', פאסאר/*pasar* 'to pass', as opposed to Modern Castilian, which distinguishes them as [θ] (*cinco* [ˈθiŋko]) vs. [s] (*pasar* [paˈsar]). Word final <s> was reflected in Old Spanish as voiced [z] when preceding a voiced sound (e.g., a vowel), and Judezmo preserves this feature, e.g., OSp. <las oras>, Jud. לאס אוראס / / las oras/, realized phonologically as [laz ˈoras] 'the hours'); Modern Spanish instead realizes this as voiceless *s* [las ˈoras]. Old Spanish had a /ʒ/ phoneme, probably having the positional allophones [dʒ] and [ʒ] (or perhaps simply [ʒ]), as well as a /ʃ/ phoneme, realized as [ʃ]; all of these merged in later Spanish in an /χ/ phoneme, realized as [χ] or [h]; but Judezmo still retains the earlier sounds, as the distinct /dj/ [dʒ] vs. /j/ [ʒ] vs. /sh/ [ʃ] phonemes; e.g., OSp. <gente>, Jud. ג'ינטי/*djente* [ˈdʒente] 'people', OSp. <mujer>, Jud. מוז'יר/*mujer* 'wife', OSp.<baxo>, Jud. באשו/*basho* [ˈbaʃo] 'short'.

3.2 Particular structural features (unique to the Jewish variety)

3.2.1 Phonology

Although the phonological systems of all varieties of Modern Judezmo share certain features with Old Castilian, they also diverge from both medieval and modern varieties of Spanish in various ways. For example, the Judezmo correspondent of the Old Spanish sound denoted orthographically as <ll> is neither the palatalized [ʎ] once characteristic of medieval Castilian (and still used in some varieties of Spanish) nor the [dʒ], [ʒ], or [j] phones of contemporary varieties of Spanish, but simply the glide *y* [j], e.g., Sp. <llamar> (Old Spanish [ʎaˈmar], Modern Spanish [ʎ-/dʒ-/ʒ-/jaˈmar] = Jud. ייאמאר/*yamar* 'to call'); the same Judezmo *y* [j] sound also corresponds to Spanish <y>, which is generally realized as [dʒ], [ʒ], or [j] in modern varieties of Spanish, e.g., Sp. <yo> [dʒ-/ʒ-/jo], Jud. יו/*yo* [jo] 'I'). As opposed to the single Old Spanish phoneme /h/ (often reflecting Latin F-, or Arabic *f*, *h*, *x*, or *ḥ*, through earlier Old Spanish *f*-), Old Judezmo evidently had distinct /h/ vs. /χ/ (and perhaps also /ḥ/) phonemes, partly in reflection of lexemes derived from Hebrew-Aramaic and (Jewish) Ibero-Arabic, e.g., OSp. <haragán> [haraˈyan], Mod.Sp. [araˈyan] = Jud. חאראגאן/*haragán* [χaraˈyan] 'lazy'; OSp. <hondo> [from earlier *fondo*] [ˈhondo], OJud. פֿ-/הונדו [ˈf-/ˈhondo] (earlier *fondo*), yielding Mod.J. פֿ-/אונדו [ˈf-/ˈondo]). Also as a result of the incorporation of elements from these Semitic languages, the privilege of occurrence of certain phones differed in the two languages; for example, Judezmo speakers could distinguish *m* from *n* word-finally, while the only nasal permitted in final position in Spanish was *n*, e.g., Jud. ירושלים/*Yerusháláyim* 'Jerusalem', Sp. *Jerusalén*; Jud. אמן/*amén*, Sp. *amén* 'amen'). In certain words, especially those relating to Judaism, Old Judezmo showed popular phonological developments expected in Castilian, whereas Old Spanish showed some more conservative or otherwise divergent forms, e.g., OJud. ג׳ודיגו/*djudego* vs. OSp. *judaico/judiego* 'Jewish, Judaic'. There were also some divergences in stress, e.g., OJud. ג׳ודייו/*djudió* vs. OSp. *judío* 'Jew'.

Judezmo texts produced in the Ottoman Empire revealed further divergences from the sound system known for Old Spanish; some or all of these may already have existed in Old Judezmo, but were perhaps considered by the 'elitist' Jewish writers in medieval Iberia to be of too popular or non-standard a nature for literary use. Three of the most widespread of these divergences are the breaking of a medial *ue* [we] diphthong into two syllables separated by *ǵ*, e.g., ג׳וגיביס/*djuǵeves* 'Thursday' (cf. Sp. *jueves*), and the shifts *nue-* > *mue-*, e.g., מואיס/*mues* 'walnut' (cf. Sp. *nuez*), and *sue* > *(e)s·hue-*, e.g., איסחואיגרו/*(e)s·huegro* 'father-in-law' (cf. Sp. *suegro*). (For some other divergences, see the section on regional dialects below.) At the supra-segmental level, Modern Judezmo correspondents of words having antepenultimate stress in Spanish often have final stress, e.g., Sp. *sábana* = Jud. סאבֿאנה/*savaná* 'sheet'.

3.2.2 Morphology and lexicon

Judezmo morphology shows a propensity for analogical leveling and the simplification of paradigms. For example, in the conjugation of the verb, we find numerous present-tense stems in stressed position lacking the *e > ie* and *o > ue* vowel breaking typical of Modern Spanish, e.g., Jud. אימפיסו/*empeso* vs. Sp. *empiezo* 'I begin' (cf. Jud. infinitive *empesar*, Sp. *empezar*), Jud. *djuġo* vs. Sp. *juego* 'I play' (cf. Jud. infinitive *djuġar*, Sp. *jugar*). On the other hand, in the conjugation of some verbs, Salonika and its environs show vowel breaking throughout the paradigm, e.g., Salonika Jud. *kieremos* vs. Sp. *queremos* 'we want' (cf. Salonika Jud. infinitive *kierer*, Sp. *querer*). All varieties of modern Judezmo show innovative leveling in the inflections marking the preterite indicative, e.g., first-person singular -*í* in *djuġí* 'I played', *komí* 'I ate', *salí* 'I went out', vs. Sp. *jugué, comí, salí*; first-person plural -*imos* in *djuġímos* 'we played', *komimos* 'we ate', *salimos* 'we went out', vs. Sp. *jugamos, comimos, salimos*; (under the influence of the -*s* representing the second-person singular in other tenses:) Jud. second-personal singular -*V̌tes* in *djuġates* 'you played, *komites* 'you ate', *salites* 'you went out', vs. Sp. *jugaste, comiste, saliste*, and second-personal plural -*V̌tesh* in *djuġátesh* 'you played', *komítesh* 'you ate', *salítesh* 'you went out', vs. Sp. *jugasteis, comisteis, salisteis*. Influenced by the *v*- of the imperfect indicative inflection -*ava* (cf. Sp. -*aba*) of the quantitatively predominant -*ar* verb conjugation group (e.g., Jud. *djuġava*, Sp. *jugaba* 's/he was playing'), the historical -*ía* inflection of less frequent -*er* and -*ir* verbs became -*iva* in some verbs in various modern dialects, e.g., Belgrade Jud. *komiva* vs. Sp. *comía* 's/he was eating'. Alternative forms of the gerund and past participle are composed of stems deriving from the preterite rather than the infinitive, e.g., *tuviendo* 'having', *tuvido* 'had' < *tener* 'to have'; cf. Sp. (and alternative Jud.) *teniendo, tenido*. Probably under the influence of the initial [m] in object and reflexive pronouns denoting the first person singular (*me*), the possessive (*mi*), as well as the first person plural inflectional endings with -*mos*, the first-personal plural subject and object pronouns are usually *mozotros* and *mos*, respectively, and, together with the influence of the following bilabial glide [w], the possessive is *muestro* (cf. Sp. *nosotros, nos, nuestro*, but also popular forms with *m*- resembling those in Judezmo).

On the other hand, Judezmo shows some conservatism when compared with Spanish, often opting for alternate forms which existed in Old Spanish but were rejected in the emerging literary standard. For example, substantives ending in

-*or* as well as certain others are feminine in Judezmo, corresponding to variants in Old Spanish (e.g., Mod.Jud. f. *la kolor, la mar* vs. Mod.Sp. m. *el color, el mar* 'the color', 'the sea'). Other forms which became obsolete in Spanish but continue to enjoy use in Judezmo include *aġora* 'now' (OSp. *agora*, Mod.Sp. *ahora*), *bushkar* 'to look for' (OSp. *bus-/buxcar*, Mod.Sp. *buscar*), and many others. Finite verb forms which in Old Spanish existed as variants and were later rejected in Spanish are preserved in Judezmo as the sole, normative forms, e.g., *vo* 'I go', *so* 'I am', *vide* 'I saw'; cf. Mod.Sp. *voy, soy, vi*.

Judezmo lexemes (and their plurals) often resemble analogues in popular, as opposed to normative, Spanish, e.g., Jud. *adelantre* vs. Sp. *adelante* 'forward'; Jud. *veluntá(d)* vs. Sp. *voluntad* 'will'; plural *piezes* (cf. sg. *pie* + pl. *s* + -*es*) vs. normative Sp. *pies* 'feet'. Some Judezmo lexemes are reminiscent of regional, non-Castilian forms of Ibero-Romance, e.g., Jud. *alfinete*, Port., Gal. *alfinete* vs. Sp. *alfiler* 'pin', Jud. *djinoyo*, Cat. *genoll* vs. Sp. *rodilla* 'knee', *indo* 'going', Port., Gal. *indo* vs. Sp. *yendo*. Some forms seem to be internal innovations, e.g., *lap* 'pencil' (cf. Sp. *lápiz*, with final -*iz/-is* reanalyzed by Judezmo speakers as a plural marker).

3.2.3 Regional dialects

From its earliest beginnings, Ottoman Judezmo has shown evidence of subdivision into regional dialects. The principal subdivision is between Northwest Judezmo (=NWJ), spoken essentially in the region which was to fall under the linguistic and cultural sway of the Austro-Hungarian Empire, constituting the former Yugoslavia, Western Bulgaria, Romania, and Austria, and Southeast Judezmo (=SEJ), comprised essentially of the dialects spoken in present-day Turkey and Eastern Bulgaria, with Istanbul as its focal area, and the dialects of Salonika and its environs constituting a transitional or medial zone, showing mostly Southeastern features, but also some typical of the Northwest.

The major phonological isoglosses separating the two major dialect regions are the Northwest *f*- vs. Southeast phonological zero reflection of Old Judezmo (and Old Spanish) word-initial *f*- (< Lat. F-, and Arabic *f*- and sometimes velar consonants), e.g., NWJ *fazer* vs. SEJ *azer* 'to do' (cf. OSp., Port. *fazer*, Mod.Sp. *hacer* < Lat. FACERE); the metathesis of historical -*rð*- as -*ðr*- in the Southeast (including Salonika), but its preservation as -*rd*- in the Northwest, e.g., SEJ *taðrar* vs. NWJ *tardar* 'to delay'; and the raising of nonstressed (especially word-final) historical *e* to *i* and *o* to *u*, respectively, in the Northwest, versus the tendency for the historical vowels to be preserved in the Southeast, e.g. NWJ *dienti, oju* vs. SEJ *diente, ojo* 'tooth', 'eye' (cf. Sp. *diente, ojo*). Note that in these respects, Salonika and its environs resemble the Northwest in preserving old *f-*, but the Southeast in tending to show *-ðr-* metathesis and the preservation of historical nonstressed *e* and *o*. At the syntactic level, the Northwest dialects (as well as Salonika) posit object and reflexive pronouns before verbal infinitives when following prepositions, e.g., *para mos dar* 'in order to give us', while the Southeast dialects prefer to post-posit them after the infinitive, e.g., synonymous *para darmos*. Lexically, the Northwest dialects prefer using *loké?* and *premi* to express 'what?' and 'one must', respectively, while the Southeast (including Salonika) dialects prefer *kualo?* and *kale*.

There is also some subdivision within the two major dialect regions. For example, in Salonika and its environs (e.g., Bitola), the gerund doubles as the second-person plural imperative form, e.g., *viniendo/-u!* 'come!', while most of the Southeast dialects instead use the historical imperative having *-V́ð* (the *ð* may also drop), e.g., *vení(ð)!* 'come!' Within the Northwest, Bitola, and some nearby dialects show the raising of historical nonstressed word-final *a* to *e*, e.g., Bitola *kaze* vs. Salonika *kaza* 'house'; and Sarajevo shows the lowering of stressed *e* to *a* when preceding *r* + consonant or, historically, a trilled *rr*, e.g., Sarajevo *puarta* vs. Salonika *puerta* 'door', *puarus* (< *puarrus*) vs. *puerros* 'leeks'. Influence from the divergent local contact languages also resulted in some additional phonological isoglosses distinguishing Northwest from Southeast Judezmo (see 3.4 below).

3.3 Lexicon: Hebrew and Aramaic elements

As documented in texts in 'Old Sephardic La'az', elements of Hebrew-Aramaic origin have always constituted a significant part of Judezmo, helping to set it apart from its non-Jewish correlates. The phonology of the Hebrew-Aramaic component in Modern Judezmo derives directly from that used among the Jews of medieval Christian Iberia. The distinctive characteristics of the traditional Hebrew-Aramaic phonology of Judezmo speakers in Salonika, as compared with the traditions of Ashkenazim, Jewish Arabic speakers, and other Jewish subcultures, include the following realizations of the letters (as they are known in Judezmo): א/*álef* = phonological zero (e.g., *goel* גואל 'savior'), ב/*ved* = [v] (e.g., *gevir* גביר 'rich man'), pointed ג/*gémal* = [g] (e.g., *gemará* גמרא 'Talmud volume; booklet'), unpointed ג/*yémal* = [y] (e.g., *meǵilá* מגילה 'scroll of Esther'), pointed ד/*dáled* = [d] (e.g., *din* דין 'religious law'), unpointed ד/*dáled* = [ð] (e.g., *adar* אדר 'month of Adar'), ה/*e* = phonological zero (e.g., *aftará* הפטרה 'Haftarah'), ח/*hed* = [χ] (e.g., *hazán* חזן 'cantor'), ט/*ted* = [t] (e.g., *perat* פרט 'detail'), י/*yod* = phonological zero after and often before a front vowel (e.g., *geinam* גיהנם 'hell', *[y]eshivá* ישיבה 'study hall'), otherwise [j] (e.g., *yorésh* יורש 'heir'), ע/*ayn* = phonological zero syllable-initially (e.g., *meará* מערה 'cave'), phonological zero/[χ] syllable-finally (e.g., *rashá[h]* רשע 'evil person'), צ/*sadi* = [s] (*sadik* צדיק 'righteous man'), ק/*kof* = [k] (e.g., *pasuk* פסוק 'Torah verse'), ש/*shin* = [ʃ]/[s] (e.g., *sh-/salom* שלום 'peace'), pointed ת/*tav* = t (e.g., *torá* תורה 'Torah'), unpointed ת/*tav* = [t] syllable-initially, [ð]/[θ] syllable-finally (e.g., *ba<u>d</u>kol* בת קול 'celestial voice; echo'). The vowels ֵ/*seré*, ֶ/*segol* and ְ/ *shevá naá* are generally realized as *e*, e.g., *arel* עָרֵל 'uncircumcised man, Christian', *pésah* פֶּסַח 'Passover', *berahá* בְּרָכָה 'benediction'; ָ/*kamés* and ַ/*patah* are *a*, e.g., *kavo<u>d</u>* כָּבוֹד 'honor', *amsaá* הַמְצָאָה 'ruse'; and חולם/*holem* and קמץ קטן / *kamés katan* are *o*, e.g., *olam* עוֹלָם 'world', *orlá* עָרְלָה 'foreskin'. Consonants with a *dagesh hazak* are generally not geminated (e.g., *maká* מכה 'plague'). The place of stress generally corresponds to that in Hebrew and Aramaic.

Phonological processes characteristic of Judezmo in general apply equally to elements of Hebrew-Aramaic origin, e.g., two adjacent vowels often collapse to one, e.g., *maminím* (< *maamimín*) מאמינים 'believers (esp. in the false messiah, Sabbatai Zevi)'; there is metathesis of -*rð*- > -*ðr*-, e.g., *Mo<u>d</u>roháy* (< *Mor<u>d</u>oháy*) מרדכי 'Mordechai'; word-final -ð/-θ and certain other fricatives are often deleted, e.g., *Daví(<u>d</u>)* דוד 'David'; and word-final voiced consonants are often devoiced, e.g., *raf* (< *rav*) רב 'rabbi'.

Many elements of Hebrew-Aramaic origin used throughout the history of the language denote concepts central to the Jewish religion, culture, and civilization, e.g., *kipur* כיפור 'Yom Kippur', *moe<u>d</u>/mue<u>d</u>* מועד 'Jewish holiday', *kal* קהל 'synagogue', *be<u>d</u>ahé/be<u>d</u>ahaim* בית החיים 'cemetery (literally, 'house of life'); but others are more abstract, or are grammatical elements lacking any direct connection to Judaism, e.g., *zemán* זמן 'time, era', *dor* דור 'generation', *zakén* זקן 'elderly man', *afilú* אפילו 'even', מחמת / *mehamá(<u>d</u>) de* 'on account of'. Words of Hebrew-Aramaic origin supply many of the lexemes used in humoristic, ironic, or cryptic contexts; e.g., emotive words for 'money' or 'cash', such as *perahim* 'coins, money' (cf. Heb. *perahim* פרחים 'flowers', Ital. *fiorini* '[literally flowers] florins'), *gasim* 'coins' (cf. Heb. *gasim* גסים [literally, 'heavy ones']), *hatahás* 'coins, money' (cf. Heb. *hatixa* חתיכה (literally, 'piece [of silver, etc.]'). Elements of Hebrew-Aramaic origin are also the main ingredient in the secret register used in the presence of non-Jews who might understand Judezmo; e.g., *No diburees, ke es yodéah lashón!* 'Don't speak (in Judezmo) because he knows the language!' (cf. *diburear* 'to speak (esp. a foreign language)' < *dibur* דיבור 'speech', *yo<u>d</u>éah lashón* יודע לשון 'knows the language').

The gender of Judezmo nouns of Hebrew-Aramaic origin sometimes diverges from the norm in the source language; for example, nouns ending in a consonant tend to be masculine, e.g., *el lashón* (לשון) 'the language; Hebrew', whereas those ending in *a* are generally feminine, e.g., *la shevá* (שווא) 'the schwa'. Fusions combining stems of Hebrew-Aramaic origin and derivational morphemes of Hispanic origin are known from the Middle Ages on, e.g., pre-expulsion *enheremar* 'to excommunicate' (< *hérem* חרם 'excommunication' + Hispanic-origin verbalizing *en-* *-ar*), post-expulsion *gaviento* 'haughty' (< *ga[a]vá* גאווה 'pride' + Hispanic-origin adjectivizing *-ento*), *mazalozo* 'lucky' (< *mazal* מזל 'luck' + adjectivizing *-ozo*), *kafrador* 'Jewish heretic' (< *kafrar* 'to deny the existence of God' < *k-f-r* כ־פ־ר + actor-denoting *-dor*); *badkamiento* 'search (esp. for leavened food before Passover)' (< *badkar* 'to search < *b-d-q* ב־ד־ק + substantivizing *-miento*).

Before the expulsions, substantives of Hebrew-Aramaic origin sometimes pluralized with the addition of Hispanic-origin plural markers; e.g., *eskavás* 'memorial prayers' (cf. *eskavá* השכבה [Heb. *haškava*] + Hispanic-origin *s*). Following the expulsions, fusion forms also included other inflectional elements of Hispanic origin added to stems of Hebrew origin, e.g., femininizing *-a* in *samasa* 'wife of the synagogue beadle; extra candle used to light the Hanukkah lamp' (cf. Heb.-origin *samás* שמש [*šammaš*] 'beadle'); as well as inflectional endings of Hebrew-Aramaic origin added to stems of other origins, e.g., the Hebrew-origin masculine plural marker *-im* ים- used in forms such as *ladroním* 'thieves' (< Hispanic-origin *ladrón* 'thief'); plural markers of both Hebrew and Hispanic origin appearing in tautological plurals such as *berahodes* 'benedictions' (cf. Hebrew-origin sg. *berahá* ברכה + *-od* [Heb. ־ות] + Hispanic-origin *-es*); and abstract nouns such as *haraġanud* 'laziness' (< Ibero-Arabic-origin *haraġán* 'lazy' + Hebrew-origin abstract substantivizing *-ud* [ות־]). Hypocoristic forms of personal names were often created by suffixing morphemes of Hispanic origin (e.g., *-iko* [Sp. *-ico*]) to Hebrew names, e.g., *Avramiko* (< *Avram* אברהם) and *Sarika* (< *Sará* שרה); probably, such forms had already been used before the expulsions, but most are apparently first documented in Ottoman rabbinical responsa from the 16th century.

Elements of Hebrew-Aramaic origin deriving from passages in the sacred literature also include lexicalized phrases and examples of metonymy displaying semantic shifts, e.g., *([f]azer) oséshalóm* '(to make a) get-away' (cf. *osé shalom* עושה שלום, literally, 'makes peace', an allusion to the three steps backward made at the conclusion of the *amidá* (עמידה) or 'silent devotion' prayer); *mashemeha/-o* 'Ashkenazi Jew' (cf. *ma shemeha* מה שמך 'what is your name?' [Gen. 32:27], used in early interactions between Judezmo speakers and Ashkenazi immigrants in the Ottoman Empire, who often had no common language except a stilted Hebrew based on verses in the sacred sources) – the latter term later yielding the ironic language-name *mashemehesko* 'Yiddish' (cf. Jud. *-esko* [Sp. *-esco*], added to ethnonyms to create linguanyms). Interaction with speakers of local languages in the Ottoman Empire led to further innovations in the use of elements of Hebrew-Aramaic origin.

3.4 Language contact influences

From the Early Middle Judezmo phase, contact with local languages in regions under Ottoman domination had a significant influence on Judezmo at all linguistic levels. In the Northwest region, the influence of the phonological systems of varieties of South Slavic, Italian, and German led to the collapse of the Old Judezmo /d/ versus /ð/, /g/ versus /ɣ/, and /ɾ/ versus /r/ phoneme oppositions, respectively, as occlusive /d/, /g/, and flapped /ɾ/, whereas all six phonemes survived in the Southeast region, with /ð/ and /ɣ/ perhaps reinforced under the influence of neighboring Greek: cf. NWJ [na'dar] vs. SEJ [na'ðar] 'to swim' (Sp. *nadar* [na'ðar]), NWJ [pa'gar] vs. SEJ [pa'ɣar] 'to pay' (Sp. *pagar* [pa'ɣar]), NWJ *para* 'for; grape-leaf' vs. SEJ *para* 'for' vs. *parra* 'grape-leaf' (Sp. *para, parra*). Under the same local influences, in word-final position, the /d/ (< /ð/) phoneme underwent devoicing to /t/ in the Northwest; e.g., NWJ *sivdat* vs. SEJ *sivda̱d* 'city' (cf. OSp. *civdad/-th*). On the other hand, the interaction with the contact languages in the Northwest region led to the introduction in its dialects of the phonemes /ʣ/ (e.g., *podzu* 'well', cf. Sp. *pozo*, It. *pozzo*) and /ts/ (e.g., *natsión* 'nation', cf. It. *nazione*, Ger. *Nation*), which are essentially absent in the Southeast. In contact with Turkish and Balkan languages, Judezmo in various regions acquired palatalized *k´*, e.g., *k´irá* (alternating regionally with *kyirá* and *chirá*) 'rent' < Tk. *kira* (also Bosn. *ćirija*).

The earliest interactions between Jewish immigrants from Iberia and speakers of Balkan languages, such as the Jewish Greek of the Romaniote Jews and especially popular Turkish, led to borrowings reflecting the new realia the Jews encountered in the empire, e.g., terms of Ottoman origin (often borrowed into Turkish from other languages, such as Persian, Arabic and Greek) found in Judezmo texts of the mid-16th century. Such borrowings referred to local culinary traditions, e.g., *sherbet* 'fruit sherbet' (cf. Tk. *şerbet* [< Per. *sherbet* < Ar. *sharbat*],[3] Gk. *sermbéti*) and *hoshap* 'cold fruit compote' (cf. Tk. *hoşap*, Gk. *hosáfi*), costume terms such as *feradjé* and *anterí* 'types of long, loose-fitting Ottoman-style coats or robes' (cf. Tk. *ferace, entari*), institutional and architectural terms such as *han* 'inn' (Tk. *han*) and *taván* 'ceiling' (Tk. *tavan*), and names for local ethnic groups such as *ermenís* 'Armenians' and *arnautes* 'Albanians' (cf. Tk. *ermeni, arnavut*). But prolonged contact with the local languages also led to the replacement of native lexemes by new borrowings, e.g., *elefante* (Sp.) > *fil* (Tk.) 'elephant', *mono* (Sp.) > *maymón(a)* (Tk. *maymun*) 'monkey'.

---

3 Henceforth, only the direct Ottoman etyma of the Judezmo borrowings will be cited.

Especially after the 16th century, the deep-level borrowing of elements from the local contact lexicons belonging to all word classes and semantic spheres is reflected in Judezmo rabbinical and, later on, secular texts. Such borrowings include substantives such as the color term *maví* 'blue' (Tk. *mavi*), adjectives describing physical characteristics such as *shishko* 'fat' and *kyosé* 'beardless' (Tk. *şişko, köse*), verbs such as synthetic *emzalear* 'to sign, authorize in writing' (cf. Tk. *imza-* [< Ar. *imza* 'signature'] + denominal verbalizing *-la-*) and analytic *(f) azer shematá* 'to cause a commotion' (cf. Tk. *şamata et-*), adverbs such as *mahsús* 'intentionally' (Tk. *mahsus*), and interjections such as *ayde!* 'come on!' and *(a) bré!* 'hey!' (Tk. *haydi, b[i]re*). By the Early Modern Judezmo phase, Judezmo contained thousands of such local borrowings. The use of some words and forms tended to be confined to particular dialects or regions; but most were universal, e.g., *parás* 'money' (cf. Tk. *para* 'para coin, money' + Hispanic-origin plural marker *s*), *boyá* 'paint' (Tk. *boya*), *udá* 'room' (Tk. *oda*), *kavé* 'Turkish coffee' (Tk. *kahve*), *bel* 'waist' (Tk. *bel*), *kolay* 'easy' (Tk. *kolay*), *bit(i)rear* 'to finish' (Tk. *bitir*), *konushear* 'to converse' (Tk. *konuş*).

In the 16th century, Turkish lexemes composed of Turkish-origin stems and semantically discrete suffixes were borrowed freely; by the 18th and 19th centuries, the suffixes were also used productively with stems of non-Turkish origin, in fusion constructions such as *pizmondjí* 'singer of Jewish religious hymns' (cf. Heb.-origin *pizmon* פזמון 'hymn' + Tk. agent suffix *-ci*), *hanukalik* 'Hanukkah present' (cf. Heb.-origin *hanuká* חנוכה 'Hanukkah holiday' + Tk. *-lik*, denoting something associated with the object referred to by the stem), *vedrolí* 'greenish' (cf. *vedre* [Sp. *verde*] 'green' + Tk. adjectivizing *-li*), *hahamhaná* 'offices of the chief rabbinate' (cf. Heb.-origin *haham* חכם 'rabbinical scholar' + Tk. *hane* 'building'), and many others. By the 18th century, Judezmo formally distinguished between masculine and feminine forms of nouns and qualifiers of Turkish origin, e.g., m.sg. *estambolí* vs. f.sg. *estambolía* 'resident of Istanbul' (cf. Tk-origin *-li* + Sp.-origin femininizing *-a*). A further sign of the deep-level incorporation of material from contact languages is the occasional attraction to substantives of local origin of inflectional endings such as the Hebrew-origin plural marker (masculine) *-im* (ים-) to lexemes such as *papás* 'priest' (cf. Tk. *papaz*, Gk. *papás*), yielding *papazim* 'priests', and (feminine) *-od* (ות-) to nouns such as *kasabá* 'small town' (Tk. *kasaba*), giving plural *kasabod*. Hypocoristic suffixes of (Jewish) Greek origin were borrowed by Judezmo speakers early on; feminine examples are attested in 16th century rabbinical responsa; e.g., feminine *-oúla* occurs in names such as *Simhula* (< Heb.-origin *Simhá* שמחה), *Rozula* (< Hispanic-origin *Roza* [Sp. *Rosa*]). Examples, mostly masculine, with *-achi* (cf. Gk. *-áki*) are attested from the late 19th century, e.g., *Avramachi* (< *Avram* אברהם).

Turkish also had a significant effect on Judezmo at the level of the idiomatic expression; numerous phrases of Turkish origin are used in full or partial translation, e.g., *De ke?* 'Why?' < Tk. *Neden?*; *Ke haber?* 'What's new?' < Tk. *Ne haber?* And just as idiomatic expressions of Hebrew origin were used as an integral part of Judezmo – e.g., *Haham haham shetiká!* !חכם חכם שתיקה 'A smart man keeps quiet!', so too, numerous Turkish sayings and proverbial expressions were incorporated into everyday Judezmo, either in Judezmo translation, in the original Turkish, or both, e.g., *Son pishmán, faydá etméz – Después ke akontese una dezġrasia, repentirse no aze ningún provecho* ('After a mishap occurs, regretting what might have been does no good'). Repetition of a concept using referents both of Turkish and Hispanic origin is used for emphasis, e.g., *Ich nada!* 'Absolutely nothing!' (cf. Tk. *hiç*, Sp. *nada*, both meaning 'nothing'); elements of Hebrew origin are also employed in such constructions, e.g., *Adonay Dio!* 'My God!' (cf. Heb. *Adonay* י״י, Sp. *Dios*).

Turkish and other local contact languages seem not to have made a profound impact on the syntax of Judezmo until the late 19th and especially 20th and 21st centuries, when speakers of Judezmo and their descendants increasingly adopted Turkish or other state languages as their primary language and restricted their use of Judezmo to the home and synagogue, leading to symptoms of language mixing and language demise. But, especially in certain regions, there appears to have been some syntactic influence. For example, the use of the subjunctive seems to have weakened in areas in which Judezmo speakers were in prolonged contact with speakers of South Slavic languages. In Turkey, Turkish constructions such as *çok para* 'much money', with *para* in the singular because it follows a qualifier denoting plurality, began to be mirrored in Judezmo constructions such as synonymous *muncha pará*, with both the adjective and noun in the singular, whereas in Spanish, analogous constructions (e.g., **mucho ducado*) are impermissible. Since the turn of the 20th century, possessive constructions of the type *el ombre su padre* 'the man's father', reflecting Turkish *adamın babası*, are documented, if rarely (cf. older/usual Judezmo *el padre del ombre*, as in Spanish).

4 Written and oral traditions

4.1 Writing systems

As in the case of other Jewish languages which arose before the modern era, Old Sephardic La'az or Old Judezmo was written primarily in the Hebrew or Jewish alphabet (a practice known as *soletrear* or 'transcribing Judezmo sounds in

Hebrew letters', cf. Bunis 2008a: 431), using the various cursive scripts characteristic of the Jews of Iberia, which came to be called *ḥaṣi qolmos* in Hebrew and, by at least the 16th century, referring both to their cursive and printed forms, *letras provensalas* or *letras de Rashí* in the language itself. The reference to Rashí derived from the fact that the first printed edition of Rashi's commentary, published in Reggio di Calabria in 1475, was printed in a font modeled after the Iberian Jewish cursive; henceforth, the font was popularly known as *Rashí* characters. With the advent of Jewish printing in the Ottoman Empire in the 16th century, the earliest Judezmo texts meant for a popular audience were printed in the vocalized Square (or *merubá*) letters familiar to popular readers from the Hebrew Bible and daily prayer book; but subsequent Judezmo printing most commonly appeared in the *Rashí* font without vocalization, the Square letters being reserved in such prints for titles and as a kind of bold face. From the 19th century, some Judezmo printing was also realized in unvocalized Square letters, especially in immigrant communities (e.g., New York) where *Rashí* type may have been difficult to obtain. Also from the 19th century on, the Judezmo cursive script was commonly denoted as *soletreo*.

The traditional Hebrew-letter writing system underwent modifications during the various historical phases of Judezmo. The representation of the vowels and diphthongs have remained rather similar throughout the historical development of Judezmo: word-initial and -medial *a* = א, word-final -*a* =primarily ה; both *e* and *i* = י, and *o* and *u* = ו, all four vowels being preceded by silent א when in word-initial position; the *y* [j] glide was denoted by single י when preceding *e* or *i*, and by double יי when preceding or following *a*, *o*, or *u*; the *u* [w] glide was denoted by ו. The consonants generally have been represented as follows: /b/ [b] = ב; /ch/ [tʃ] = ג׳; occlusive /d/ [d] = ד; fricative /d/ [ð] = ד, as well as syllable-final ת in Hebrew-Aramaisms, or, especially from the 18th century, ד׳; /dj/ [dʒ] = ג׳; /f/ [f] = פ-/-ף, פ׳; occlusive /g/ [g] and fricative /ġ/ [ɣ] = primarily ג; /j/ [ʒ] = pre-modern ג׳ and, especially from the late 18th century, ז׳, which became the modern norm; /k/ = ק (also כ in some words of Hebrew-Aramaic origin); palatalized /k´/ [k´] (in post-expulsion Judezmo) = קיי or ק׳; /l/ = ל; Old Judezmo /ʎ/ (or at least the Old Judezmo sound corresponding to Old Spanish ʎ) = לי(י), and from the 18th century its reflex, /y/ [j], was often denoted by the variants ליי ~ יי; /m/ [m] = מ-, -ם; /n/ [n] = נ-, -ן; /ny/ [ɲ] = ני(י); /p/ [p] = פ; flapped /r/ [ɾ] = ר; trilled /rr/ [r] = ר, and from the late 19th century, variant רר; /s/ [s], or word-finally, before a voiced phone, [z] = Old Judezmo ש (corresponding to OSp. <s-, -ss-, -s>), ס, and rarer -ץ, צ (corresponding to OSp. <z-, ç, -z>), Middle Judezmo ס/ש, Modern Judezmo ס (the Middle and Modern forms corresponding to both OSp. <s, ss, s> and OSp. <ç, z, z>); /sh/ [ʃ] = ש̃/ש; /t/ [t] = ט (also syllable-initial ת in some Hebrew-Aramaisms); /v/ [v] = Old and Middle Judezmo ב̃-/-ב̃-/-ו-//-ו, Modern Judezmo ב̃; /h/ [χ] = ח (also כ, and syllable final ע, in some Hebrew-Aramaisms); /z/ [z] = Old Judezmo

-ש- (corresponding to OSp. <s->), ז (corresponding to OSp. <z>) and Middle and Modern Judezmo ז (corresponding to both OSp. <s-> and <z>). As noted, the letters א and ה were positional variants for /a/, but in words of Hebrew-Aramaic origin had zero phonological value; ע had zero value in syllable initial position but /h/ [χ] or zero syllable finally. In Northwest Judezmo, the regional phoneme /dz/ [ʣ] was represented by דד (e.g., פודזו *podzu* 'well'); and the /ts/ [ts] phoneme by ץ-/צ (e.g., נאציון *natsión* 'nation').

From the mid-19th century, when some Judezmo-speaking children began to attend foreign-language, colonialist-oriented schools such as those of the AIU, and local state schools such as those in Serbia and Bulgaria, some younger speakers became more proficient in the use of the Roman or Cyrillic alphabet than the traditional Hebrew-letter Judezmo alphabet. From this time, and especially following World War I, there was a gradual shift away from the Hebrew-letter system to Roman orthographies based on French, Serbian, and romanized Turkish, and to the Bulgarian Cyrillic orthography. In 1979, Moshe Shaul, editor of the Jerusalem Judezmo periodical *Aki Yerushalayim*, proposed an early version of the romanization, which has now become the standard system advocated by the Israel National Authority for Ladino and Its Culture; it is used in Judezmo periodicals, *Aki Yerushalayim* and *El Amaneser*, on Internet sites such as Ladinokomunita and the Judezmo section of eSefarad.com, and among everyday native speakers and some scholars. A compromise between Turkish, French, English, and Spanish romanizations, the salient graphemes of this romanization, often called *Aki Yerushalayim* spelling, are: *ch* = [ʧ], *dj* = [ʤ], *h* = [χ], *i* = [i] and [j] (the latter, especially when preceding a vowel), *j* = [ʒ], *k* = [k], *ny* = [ɲ], *r* = [ɾ], *rr* = [r], *s* = [s], *sh* = [ʃ], *u* = [u] and [w], *y* = [j] (in initial, final, and certain medial positions), *z* = [z].

4.2 Literature

The writings in Sephardic La'az surviving from pre-expulsion Spain are somewhat limited; they include Hebrew-letter personal correspondence, business contracts, community records and regulations such as the *taqqanot* or ordinances set down by the rabbis in Valladolid in 1432, prayers in translation with instructions, original poetry (e.g., *Koplas de Yosef Asadik*; *Proverbios morales* of Shem Tov of Carrión), and transliterations of Spanish literature in Hebrew letters, such as the moralistic drama, *Danza general de la muerte*. The registers and styles employed in most of this pre-expulsion material probably diverged considerably from the everyday language used by most Jews of Spain. There are also a few volumes of religious instruction in the Latin alphabet, apparently meant for crypto-Jews posing as Christians who dared not keep Hebrew-letter writings in their homes for fear of discovery by the Inquisition, and who were perhaps no longer familiar with the Hebrew alphabet.

Following the expulsions, Judezmo enjoyed extensive written documentation in the Hebrew alphabet, from the mid-16th into the 20th centuries, and from the late 20th through 21st centuries, in romanization. Publications from the Early Middle Judezmo phase included renditions of rabbinical court testimony incorporated in Ottoman responsa collections; calque translations of sacred Hebrew and Aramaic texts, such as the so-called Constantinople Pentateuch of 1547, Ethics of the fathers, and the women's siddur, *Seder našim*; poetic and dramatic pieces; and rabbinical writings of several types and in several styles, which might collectively be called *djudezmo de hahamim* or 'rabbinical Judezmo' (e.g., *Šulḥan ha-panim ... Meza de el alma*, an adaptation of parts of Yosef Karo's *Šulḥan 'aruḵ*, by Me'ir [Benveniste], Salonika 1568).

From the Late Middle phase, Judezmo rabbinical literature expanded to include original volumes of biblical exegesis such as volumes of *Sefer Me-'am lo'ez* by Ya'aqov Khulí (Constantinople, Genesis, 1730; Exodus, 1733) and his successors, and collections of *ko(m)plas* or rhymed couplets on religious and moralistic themes such as *Koplas de purim* by Avraham de Fes (Constantinople, c.1720) and *Şorḵe şibbur* by Avraham Asa (Constantinople, 1733). There were also translations and adaptations of Hebrew texts and original rabbinical treatises.

In Livorno, 1778, David Atías published a pioneering educational manual for Eastern Sephardim planning to visit Western Europe; entitled *La guerta de oro* (The Golden Garden), it exhibited an innovative fusion of rabbinical, popular, and novel Western Europeanized linguistic features and marked the inception of Judezmo literature of a less specifically religious nature. A further reflection of growing western cultural influences among the Ottoman Sephardi communities from the mid-19th century was the rise of a periodical press. The earliest surviving Judezmo newspaper was *Ša'are Mizraḥ*, published by Rafa'el 'Uzzi'el in Izmir, 1845–1846; its appearance was followed by over 300 Judezmo newspapers, published in Vienna and throughout the Mediterranean Sephardi diaspora, including Jerusalem, Constantinople, Salonika, Izmir, Edirne, and later Sarajevo, Belgrade, Plovdiv, Ruse, Sofia, Rhodes, Paris, New York, and elsewhere. In Salonika, the Hebrew-letter Judezmo press continued to flourish until the Nazis closed the Jewish presses. In the 1930s, the Judezmo press of Istanbul began to appear in Turkish romanization. Especially after the establishment of the State of Israel in 1948, massive immigration from cities such as Salonika and Istanbul led to a revival of the Judezmo press – now in romanization – in Tel Aviv–Yafo. At the same time, diverse material of the kind presented in the periodical press was also published in pamphlets and books in Istanbul and Tel Aviv.

Many of the newspapers and books of the Late Middle phase were written, edited, and published by Sephardi graduates of the AIU and participants in the programs of the Italian Società Dante Alighieri. Although many of the journalists used the highly Europeanized variety of Judezmo first richly documented in 'Uzzi'el's *Ša'are Mizraḥ*, from the late 19th century some writers rejected this highly Gallicized and Italianized *djuḏezmo frankeaḏo* (Western Europeanized Judezmo), preferring instead to imitate the popular, natural *djuḏezmo kabá* or 'common Judezmo' spoken by the masses, which they used in noteworthy periodicals featuring fiction and satire, such as *El Meseret* (ed. Alexandre Benghiatt, Izmir, 1897–1922), *El Djugetón* (ed. Elia R. Karmona, Constantinople, 1909–1933), and *El Kirbach* (ed. Moïse Levy, Salonika,1910–1917).

In more recent years, an appreciation of Judezmo as an independent Jewish language which evolved naturally as a result of the interaction of its speakers – especially those of the less elite echelons – and their neighbors, has led to the growing use in the 21st century of a compromise between the folk and Europeanized varieties in the periodicals *Aki Yerushalayim* of Jerusalem (founded 1979) and *El Amaneser* (founded 2005, continuing *Şalom*, founded 1947) of Istanbul, in messages appearing in the pioneering Ladinokomunita social network site, in Internet sites such as eSefarad.com, which publish news and features in the traditional language (in romanization), and in the brief daily Judezmo (or Djudeo-Espanyol) program of Radio Kol Israel of Jerusalem. Gifted writers such as Moshe Shaul, Matilda Koen-Sarano, Avner Peretz, Moshe Aelion, Eliezer Papo, Roz Koen, Margalit Matitiahu, Klara Perahya, Karen Şarhon, Yehuda Hatsvi, and others continue to employ varieties of the traditional idiom for artistic self-expression, re-creating the vibrant life of Judezmo-speaker communities of the past, erecting monuments to the communities that perished during World War II, and carrying the innovative use of Judezmo into the 21st century.

4.3 Performance (theatre, film, etc.)

Historians of the Turkish shadow theatre (Karagöz) have suggested that Jewish immigrants from Iberia with theatrical experience helped establish that theatrical form in the Ottoman Empire and Judezmo texts from the 16th century create the impression that dramatic presentations were known in the empire from that century. The earliest full performance text we have is the Joseph story, Avraham Toledo's *Koplas de Yosef Asadik* (Constantinople, 1732), in which various figures participate in the re-enactment of the biblical narrative using rhymed verse, enhanced by Ottoman classical music (Perez 2005).

Judezmo dramatic works in the prose format more widely known in Western European theatrical literature began to appear in the Balkans and Ottoman regions in the mid-19th century. One of the earliest pieces was *Piesa de Yaakov Avinu kon sus ijos* (Bucharest, 1862), composed by Moshe Shĕmu'el Kofino for the pupils of the Sephardic religious elementary school in which he taught in Giurgiu (Romania). The dramatic genre proved to be popular among Judezmo speakers in the Ottoman Empire and its successor states. Many of the published plays – often conveying politico-ideological messages such as those of the Haskalah, Zionism, and Jewish nationalism, or meant to enrich the celebration of Jewish festivals and highlight the talents of the pupils in Jewish schools – were performed in schools, community centers, and local theaters by pupils and troupes of amateur actors.

Commercial recordings of Judezmo songs, performed in traditional styles by some of the speaker community's finest singers, had begun to be released early in the 20th century; some, e.g., those by Isaac Algazi and Haim Efendi, have enjoyed re-release in recent years (Seroussi 2002, 2008). Recordings of Judezmo music are still popular – but today the pieces are often performed in styles diverging widely from those traditionally used by native speakers of earlier times, ranging from the medieval and baroque (e.g., recordings of Voice of the Turtle) to heavy rock (e.g., recordings of Sarah Aroeste).

From the founding of the Jewish State, Judezmo theater troupes in Israel, usually organized by immigrants from a particular city or country, have entertained their compatriots with plays and musicals, as part of a broader attempt to maintain and revitalize the Judezmo language and cultural traditions. Similar efforts have been made by Judezmo speakers who remained in the countries of origin, such as Bulgaria, Turkey, and the former Yugoslavia. "Sephardic Romancero" (1968) and "Bustan Sephardi" (Spanish Garden, 1970), two highly popular Hebrew musicals by Yitzhak Navon, Israel's fifth president and himself a native Judezmo speaker, incorporated Judezmo songs and scenes from Sephardic life in the Land of Israel of the 1930s.

Since World War II, Judezmo (or approximations of it) have also been incorporated in films of fiction touching on the lives of Judezmo speakers in Israel, Yugoslavia, Bulgaria, and elsewhere, such as the Moshe Mizrahi films *The House on Chelouche Street* (1973), starring Israeli actors Shaike Ofir and Gila Almagor, and *Every Time We Say Good-bye* (1986), starring Tom Hanks and the Spanish-accented Cristina Marsillach. More recent years have seen documentaries focusing on Judezmo speaker communities of the past and present, such as the historical travelogues of Yehoram Gaon (1988), Yitzhak Navon (2006), and Eliezer Papo (Ángel Nieto 2002), films recounting the Sephardic immigrant experience in the United States, such as "Arvoles Yoran por Luvias" (Trees Cry for Rain), by Bonnie Burt and Rachel Amado Bortnick (1989), treatments of the complex interactions between Jews and non-Jews in the traditional Judezmo homeland, such as "A Turkish-Jewish-Muslim Tale," by Güler Orgun, the autobiographical "The Key From Spain," by Flory Jagoda (c.2000), and slices of Sephardic life, past and present, related by rank-and-file Judezmo speakers and uploaded to YouTube and other websites.

5 State of research

Judezmo language and literature have drawn the attention of scholars since the late 19th century, with the result that there is an extensive research literature on these subjects. Studemund (1975), Sala (1976), and Bunis (1981) provide bibliographical details through their years of publication; subsequent updates have appeared in various sources, such as the MLA International Bibliography and the journal *Sefarad*. Schwarzwald (2002) offers a précis of the development of the field. A valuable bibliography of Sephardic studies, including Judezmo language, linguistics, and literature, is the Bibliografía Sefardí Comentada of CSIC's Sefardiweb (www.proyectos.cchs.csic .es/sefardiweb/bibliografiasefardi/).

5.1 History of documentation

An interest in the Jews of medieval Iberia among the early Haskalah historians, as well as non-Jewish historians of the 19th century, led to a "re-discovery" of the Sephardim of the Ottoman Empire, their history, cultural traditions, and language. The late 19th century saw the publication of pioneering books and articles focusing on topics in Judezmo language and folk literature which were to captivate philologists, linguists, and folklorists into the 21st century. Topics included the distinctive characteristics of the language, especially compared with Spanish; regional dialects; the special language of translations of Hebrew and Aramaic sacred texts; the question of Jewish linguistic distinctiveness in Iberia; the Hebrew-letter writing system; the linguistic components of non-Hispanic origin in the Ottoman regions; Judezmo as a member of the family of Jewish languages; the diverse linguistic varieties used in Ottoman Judezmo literature; and the corpus of proverbs, popular songs, ballads, and other oral folk genres cultivated by Judezmo speakers in the empire and its successor states. The late 19th century also saw the budding of Judezmo lexicography, with early attempts at scientific lexicography appearing after World War I, and a flurry of bilingual, mostly 'practical' dictionaries appearing from the 1970s. Since the 1970s, university-level courses introducing Judezmo as a foreign language and focusing on facets of its structure, history, and literature were introduced in institutions of higher education in Israel, parts of Europe, and the United States; and textbooks enabling this instruction were created.

5.2 Corpora

The advent of the Internet has enabled scholars to advance analysis of written Judezmo with the establishment of fully searchable online corpora and lexical databases, reflecting early literary texts originally in Hebrew letters and now transcribed in romanization, and material of more recent vintage created directly in digitized romanization (e.g., Busse 2001). Online corpora include *El Amaneser* (sephardiccenter.wordpress.com/el-ameneser/), Collections de Corpus Oraux Numériques (cocoon.huma-num.fr/exist/crdo/meta/crdo-COLLECTION_JSFA), Corpus Wiki (http://www.corpuswiki.org/index.php?action=select&id=23), El Corpus MemTet (https://ladino.unibas.ch/proyectos/entre-tradicion-y-modernidad/el-corpus-memtet/), and Perez N.d.

5.3 Issues of general theoretical interest

The considerable discrepancy between the various linguistic registers documented in Iberia before the expulsions and the popular Judezmo published from the mid-16th to 21st centuries in the Ottoman Empire raises the question: Do the pre-expulsion texts actually reflect the contemporaneous linguistic habits of the majority of everyday Jews, or are they essentially the artificial creations of a scholarly elite whose literary model was Spanish as used by Christian literati? Another fundamental question, with broad theoretical implications for the development of minority and enclave languages in general, is: Which internal and external historical, social, and linguistic dynamics were at work in the synthesis of the diverse varieties of incipient Ottoman Judezmo reflected in texts from the 16th and 17th centuries into the unique, relatively cohesive structural whole that constitutes modern Ottoman and post-Ottoman Judezmo? What roles did the shifting ethnic and ideological self-perceptions of members of the speaker community play in the considerable structural and especially lexical reorganization which the language underwent over the course of its historical phases, and how do these shifts tie in with the instability over time of linguistic elements relating to ethnic and linguistic identity, such as names for the language, the alphabet used to write it, its component structure, the relation perceived by members of the speaker community between Judezmo and Spanish, and the speakers' thoughts regarding the future of the language.

5.4 Current directions in research

In recent years, the field of Judezmo language research has drawn a significant number of young researchers to its coterie of veteran scholars. Current researchers diverge considerably in their approaches and interests; some lean toward Hispanic studies, others toward comparative Jewish language research, still others toward general or Romance linguistics, sociolinguistics, or philology. Something of the diversity of interests in current research in the field may be seen in the collective volumes devoted to Judezmo and allied studies – some broad-ranging, others devoted to specific themes – which have seen the light since 2002, including Gatenio 2002; Bürki, Schmid and Schwegler 2006; Guastalla 2007; Molho 2008; Romero, Hassán and Izquierdo Benito 2008; Bunis 2009a; Díaz-Mas and Sánchez Pérez 2010; Molho, Pomeroy and Romero 2011; Romero and García Moreno 2011; Busse and Studemund-Halévy 2011; Bürki, Cimeli and Sánchez 2012; García Moreno 2012e; Bürki and Sinner 2012; Bürki and Romero 2014. The present section will touch on the most prominent topics in Judezmo language research since the beginning of the 21st century.

The history of Judezmo linguistics, and Sephardic Studies in general, were reviewed (e.g., Riaño López 2001; Schwarzwald 2002; Berenguer 2011a), and some of the diverse scholarly approaches to Judezmo were examined (e.g., Hassán 2006). Recent structural introductions to the language include Hetzer 2001; Schmid 2006a; Busse 2011b; Marín Ramos 2014. Broad general overviews of the problematics of the language are provided in Busse 2004; Gabinskij 2011; Minervini 2013; Bunis 2016a. The pedagogical use of Judezmo to teach Hebrew was discussed by Gomel (2006).

Of especially recent vintage in the field of Judezmo are studies devoted to topics in Judezmo syntax (e.g., Berenguer 2002, 2012a, 2012b, 2012c, 2014a, 2014b; Varol 2002a; García Moreno 2003, 2006a, 2012a; Barco 2004; Barme 2004; Montoliu and Van der Auwera 2004; Berenguer, Cerezo and Schmid 2006; Bürki and Schmid 2006; Stulić-Etchevers 2008; Varol 2008, 2009; Schlumpf 2009, 2012a, 2012b, 2014, 2015; Bürki 2012a; Tabares Plasencia, Sinner and Hernández Socas 2012; Von Schmädel 2012; Vuletić 2011; Shafran 2014). Other areas of structure considered include the distinctive features of the language's phonology and morphology (e.g., Bürki 2001; Stulić, Vučina and Zečević 2003; Bunis 2004b, 2006–2007, 2007, 2012a; García Moreno 2006a, 2012a, 2012b; Bradley 2007a, 2007b, 2009; Varol 2008, 2011a; Bradley and Smith 2011; Hualde and

Şaul 2011; Hernández González 2012b); the lexicon (including anthroponyms, and expressions of time and space), lexicography and the use of glosses (e.g., Busse 2001; Varol 2003; Bunis 2006–2007, 2007, 2011e, 2013a, 2015b; García Moreno 2006b, 2010, 2012d, 2013b, 2013c, 2013d, 2013e, 2014; Sanchis i Ferrer and Vuletić 2008; Schwarzwald 2008a, 2011; Stulić-Etchevers 2008; Mancheva 2009; Busse and Studemund-Halévy 2011; Díaz-Mas and Romeu Ferré 2011; Kohring 2011; Platikanova 2011; Quintana 2011a; Studemund-Halévy 2011; Vučina Simović 2011; Bürki and Sinner 2012; Rieder-Zelenko 2012, 2014; Sánchez and Wieland 2012; Von Schmädel 2012; Twardowska 2013; Zečević-Krneta 2013; Hernández Socas, Sinner and Tabares Plasencia 2014); semantics and metaphor use (e.g., Münch 2007; Bürki and Sinner 2012; Hernández González 2012a). Studies of the language's Hispanic and non-Hispanic components (see Busse 2011a; Varol 2011b), continue to draw attention: on Slavisms: Bunis 2001; Grecisms: Symeonidis 2002; Mavrogiannis 2006–2007; Hebrew-Aramaisms and the Whole Hebrew of Judezmo speakers: Münch 2004, 2007; Bunis 2005c, 2006–2007, 2007, 2009b, 2013c, 2013e, 2013f; Rieder-Zelenko 2006; Benaim 2008; Schwarzwald 2013a; Turkisms: Romeu Ferré 2004; Şahin Reis 2005; Bunis 2006–2007, 2008b, 2013b, 2013h; Rieder-Zelenko 2006; Varol 2011a; Vuletić 2011; Gallicisms: Barme 2004; Hispanisms: Papo 2007; Mancheva 2008b; Quintana Rodríguez 2009; Italianisms: Minervini 2008b, 2014; Arabisms: Neuman 2006–2007; Minervini 2011a; Bunis 2017; Germanisms: Papo 2013. Judezmo borrowings in other languages have been noted (e.g., in Greek: Mavrogiannis 2006–2007; in Modern Hebrew: Schwarzwald and Gomel 2001; Schwarzwald 2013b). Judezmo orthographic systems in the Hebrew, Roman, and Cyrillic alphabets have been examined, in their historical development and as identify markers (e.g., Busse 2003, 2005; Salvador Plans 2003; Sephiha 2003; Kohring 2004; Bunis 2005a; Schwarzwald 2005; Neuman 2006–2007; Hassán 2008; García Moreno 2012c; Budor 2013; Studemund-Halévy 2013; Díaz-Mas 2014); and the transcription systems used by scholars to romanize Hebrew-letter Judezmo texts have received attention (Varol 2002b, 2003; Schmid 2006b).

Attempts continue to be made to demarcate the salient phases in the historical development of pre- and post-expulsion Judezmo (e.g., Minervini 2006, 2008a; Quintana Rodríguez 2006b, 2006c, 2007, 2008, 2011b; Bunis 2013h); and to focus attention on particular phases, their characteristic features, and representative texts (e.g., Bunis 2004a; Arnold 2006; Quintana Rodríguez 2006b, 2007, 2008, 2014a; Schmid 2007; Vàrvaro and Minervini 2007; Benaim 2008, 2011; Ayala 2010; Vàrvaro 2012; Berenguer 2014b). The geographic dispersion of Judezmo has also been examined (e.g., Weis 2000; Symeonidis 2002; Gerson Şarhon 2006; Quintana Rodríguez 2006a, 2014b; Schmid 2007; Studemund-Halévy and Collin 2007; Bossong 2008; Bunis 2008c, 2010a, 2012a, 2013d, 2013i; Varol 2008; Soler 2009;

Ayala 2010; Vuletić 2011, 2012; Studemund-Halévy, Liebl and Vučina Simović 2013; Twardowska 2013; Vučina Simović 2013a, 2013b, 2013c).

Various topics relating to Judezmo sociolinguistics and register/style divergence have been addressed. The rise and manifestations of popular Judezmism (or *Djudeoespanyolizmo*, as denoted by journalist Sam Levy of Salonika), as an independent movement and in cognizance of other modern Jewish and non-Jewish language movements such as Modern Hebrew revivalism and Yiddishism, were examined (Bunis 2010b, 2011g, 2012b; Vučina Simović 2013a, 2013b, 2013c), as were the rise of an Ottoman Judezmo culture and its linguistic and literary manifestations (e.g., Bunis 2005b; Borovaya 2012), Judezmo as a homeland (e.g., Díaz-Mas and Romeu Ferré 2013), and issues of language and identity (e.g., Weis 2000; Varol 2011b), and standardization (e.g., Quintana Rodríguez 2012). Scholars have pondered the linguistic outcome of the encounter of Judezmo speakers with modernization and with the languages of Western European colonialism; the effects on Judezmo of the dismemberment of the Ottoman Empire and the rise of local nationalism; the reality of medieval and Ottoman Sephardic multilingualism; and the connection between language, identity, and other societal factors in the Judezmo speaker community, especially as reflected in the Judezmo press and other primary sources (e.g., Altabev 2003; Bunis 2003; Ayala 2006; Ayala and Busse 2006; Ayala and Djaen 2006; Quintana Rodríguez 2006c; Díaz Mas and Sánchez Pérez 2010; Bürki and Sinner 2012; Romero 2012; Bürki 2013; Gutwirth 2013; Sánchez and Bornes-Varol 2013, 2015; Selony and Sarfati 2013; Şaul 2013), as well as in Spanish sources (e.g., Díaz-Mas 2012). Scholars have focused on the names of Judezmo (e.g., Bunis 2008a, 2011a); native and non-native perceptions of and attitudes toward the language (e.g., Altabev 2003; Papo 2009a; Bürki 2010a, 2010b; Schmid 2010; Bunis 2011c, 2011g, 2014, 2016c); and other features distinguishing Judezmo as a Jewish language (e.g., Bunis 2011f, 2013g); as well as contacts between speakers of Judezmo and other (Jewish) languages (e.g., Vučina Simović 2013c). Judezmo within the context of Hispanism has also been discussed (e.g., Hassán 2002, 2006), as has the use of approximations of Spanish by Judezmo speakers (e.g., Varol 2010a). Scholars have also compared distinctive features of Judezmo with those of Ḥaketía and other Jewish languages (e.g., Bunis 2006, 2007, 2008a, 2008c, 2011c, 2012a; Schwarzwald 2008b), as well as of medieval Muslim Ibero-Romance (e.g., Bunis 2015a), of Spanish in its regional and historical variation (e.g., Penny 2000; Quintana Rodríguez 2010), and of Balkan languages (e.g., Friedman and Joseph 2014). The use of Judezmo among victims of the Holocaust was commemorated (e.g., Sephiha 2002; Santa Puche N.d.).

Topics in stylistics and discourse analysis include the language of conversation and literary representations of conversation (e.g., Cerezo 2006; Sánchez 2008b, 2013, 2015; Bunis 2011d), written representations of diverse social and literary registers and genres – including age, gender, and social-level and professional divergence in language use – as well as the registers used in the novel, and autobiographical and dramatic writing (e.g., Varol 2003–2004, 2010b; Barco 2004; Bürki 2006, 2010, 2012b, 2014; Schwarzwald 2006–2007, 2010b; Valladares Ruiz 2007; Sánchez 2008a, 2010, 2011, 2012, 2014; García Moreno 2011a; Bunis 2012c, 2013d, 2013g; Valentín del Barrio 2012); and code-switching (e.g., Held 2009). Calque Judezmo Bible glosses and translations and their distinctiveness vis à vis Christian Spanish Bible-translation traditions, have been treated (e.g., Quintana 2008a; Schwarzwald 2010a, 2011, 2012c; Bunis 2017), as has the calque language of liturgical-text translations for women (Schwarzwald 2012a, 2012b).

Attempts at language maintenance, language planning, and revitalization within the speaker community, in universities, and by the Israeli government, as well as symptoms of Judezmo language death, have been discussed (e.g., Hetzer 2003; Gerson Şarhon 2006, 2011; Harris 2006; Mantcheva 2006, 2008a; Quintana 2006d; Shaul 2006; Vučina Simović 2009, 2011, 2013a); nor has the role of Judezmo in the contemporary print and radio-broadcast media (e.g., Shaul 2004, 2007) and the internet (e.g., Busse 2001; Benveniste 2005; Schmid 2007; Brink-Danan 2011; Bunis 2016b, forthcoming) been neglected.

Numerous scholars, mostly of the Hispanist school, have re-released editions of Judezmo texts originally appearing in the Hebrew alphabet – mostly in romanization, sometimes accompanied by the original Hebrew-letter text and/or Hebrew parallels, and including translations of sacred texts, original rabbinical tracts, correspondence, poetry, periodicals, fictional works, and folk remedies – prefaced by linguistic analysis and complemented by glossaries of words unfamiliar to Spanish speakers (e.g., Lazar 2000a, 2000b; Riaño López 2000; Schmid and Bürki 2000; Collin 2002; Asenjo Orive 2003; Studemund-Halévy Studemund 2003, 2010; García Moreno 2004, 2011a, 2013a; Overbeck de Sumi 2005; Ayala and Busse 2006; Varol and Itzhaki 2006; Von Schmädel 2007, 2011; Albarral 2010a, 2010b; Berenguer 2011b; Minervini 2011b, 2012; Muñoz Molina 2011, 2014; Romeu Ferré 2011; Von Schmädel 2011; Papo 2012; Schwarzwald 2012a, 2012b; Šmid 2012; Bunis 2013d; Platikanova, Busse and Kohring 2014; Sánchez Pérez 2014; Studemund-Halévy with Collin 2014; Studemund-Halévy and Stulić 2015). The challenges of electronic text edition and metadescription were pondered (e.g., Soufiane Roussi and Stulić 2006, 2013).

Considerable efforts have been devoted to the development of tools facilitating the study of Judezmo and its literature. Joseph Nehama's *Dictionnaire du judéo-espagnol*, published posthumously in 1977, provided the foundation for numerous bilingual dictionaries, of varying scope and quality (e.g., Perez and Pimienta 2007; Perahya 2012; Hazan 2013), including internet word-lists and concordances (e.g., "Diksionario de Ladinokomunita" [http://ladinokomunita. tallerdetinoco.org/]; and Trezoro de la Lengua Djudeoespanyola [http://folkmasa. org/milon/pmilonh.php], edited by Avner Perez). Recordings of Judezmo speech have been issued (e.g., Liebl 2009), and large-scale oral documentation projects are underway (e.g., Mavrogiannis 2013).

Acknowledgments
The present article was prepared with the support of a grant from the Israel Science Foundation, no. 41105/11.

References

Albarral, Purificación. 2010a. *Biblia de Abraham Asá: Los doce profetas menores*. Logroño: Cilengua.
Albarral, Purificación (ed.). 2010b. *Quen se cura, dura, el libro de higién de Albert Saúl (Constantinopla, 1922)*. Barcelona: Tirocinio.
Alexander-Frizer, Tamar. 2008. *The heart is a mirror: The Sephardic folktale*. Detroit: Wayne State University Press.
Altabev, Mary. 2003. *Judeo-Spanish in the Turkish social context: Language death, swan song, revival or new arrival?* Istanbul: Isis.
Ángel Nieto, Miguel. 2002. *El último sefardí*. TVE S.A., ARTE G.E.I.E. and Alea TV.
Armistead, Samuel G. & Joseph H. Silverman. 1971a. *The Judeo-Spanish ballad chapbooks of Yacob Abraham Yoná*. Berkeley: University of California Press.
Armistead, Samuel G. & Joseph H. Silverman. 1971b. *Judeo-Spanish ballads from Bosnia*. Philadelphia: University of Pennsylvania Press.
Armistead, Samuel G. & Joseph H. Silverman. 1986. *Judeo-Spanish ballads from oral tradition. I. Epic ballads*. Berkeley: University of California Press.
Arnold, Rafael. 2006. *Spracharkaden: Die Sprache der sephardischen Juden in Italien im 16. und 17. Jahrhundert*. Heidelberg: C. Winter Verlag.
Asa, Avraham ben Yiṣḥaq (tr.). 1743. *Sefer nĕvi'im rišonim ... 'im la'az*. Constantinople.
Asenjo Orive, Rosa. 2003. *El Meam Loez de Cantar de los Cantares: (Šir Haširim de Hayim Y. Šaki, Constantinopla, 1899)*. Barcelona: Tirocinio.
Ayala, Amor. 2006. "Por nu'estra lingu'a" (Sofía 1924): un artículo periodístico sobre la lengua y la identidad entre los sefardíes en la Bulgaria de entreguerras. *Neue Romania* 35 (=*Judenspanisch* X). 83–98.
Ayala, Amor. 2010. El judeoespañol en los textos del periodo moderno (tardío) en Bulgaria. In Paloma Díaz-Mas and María Sánchez Pérez (eds.), *Los sefardíes ante los retos del mundo contemporáneo: Identidad y mentalidades*, 65–74. Madrid: CSIC.
Ayala, Amor & Ricardo Djaen. 2006. El crepúsculo del ladino: reflexiones de S. J. Djaen acerca del djudezmo y su literatura en vísperas de la Segunda Guerra Mundial. *Sefárdica* 16. 37–58.
Ayala, Amor & Winfried Busse. 2006. "Por nu'estra lingu'a": Edición del texto publicado en *El Manadero* (Sofía, 1924). *Neue Romania* 35 (=*Judenspanisch* X). 99–107.
Barco, Francisco Javier del. 2004. Las formas verbales en las biblias de Alba y Ferrara: ¿Fidelidad al texto hebreo? *Sefarad* 64:2. 243–267.

Barme, Stefan. 2004. Syntaktische Gallizismen im modernen südosteuropäischen Judenspanisch. *Neue Romania* 31 (=*Judenspanisch* VIII). 73–91.
Benaim, Annette. 2008. Hebrew lexical borrowing in Judeo-Spanish as represented in some of the Sephardic responsa of the 16th Century. In Hilary Pomeroy, Christopher J. Pountain, and Elena Romero (eds.), *Proceedings of the Fourteenth British Conference on Judeo-Spanish Studies, 26–28 June 2006*, 35–48. London: Department of Hispanic Studies, Queen Mary University of London.
Benaim, Annette. 2011. *Sixteenth-century Judeo-Spanish testimonies*. Leiden: Brill.
Benveniste, Marcelo. 2005. "¿Qué encontramos sobre el judeoespañol en Internet?" *Sefárdica* 15. 117–123.
Berenguer Amador, Ángel. 2002. Rasgos sintácticos y morfológicos del verbo en dos obras de la lengua clásica sefardí. In *Judaísmo Hispano. Estudios en memoria de José Luis Lacave Riaño*, 311–318. Madrid: CSIC.
Berenguer Amador, Ángel. 2011a. Historia de la lingüística judeoespañola. In Elena Romero and Aitor García Moreno (eds.), *Estudios sefardíes dedicados a la memoria de Iacob M. Hassán (z"l)*, 145–155. Madrid: CSIC and Fundación San Millán de la Cogolla.
Berenguer Amador, Ángel. 2011b. Las coplas "El espejo de Amán" y "El retrato de Zereš" de Sa'adí Haleví. In Rena Molho, Hilary Pomeroy, and Elena Romero (eds.), *Judeo Espaniol: Textos satíricos judeoespañoles de Salonicenses o sobre Salonicenses*, 156–176. Thessaloniki: Ets Ahaim Foundation.
Berenguer Amador, Ángel. 2012a. Acerca del gerundio en judeoespañol. In Yvette Bürki, Manuela Cimeli & Rosa Sánchez (eds.), *Lengua, llengua, llingua, lingua, langue: Encuentros filológicos (ibero)románicos: Estudios en homenaje a la profesora Beatrice Schmid*, 33–40. Munich: Peniope.
Berenguer Amador, Ángel. 2012b. Los pretéritos en judeoespañol. In Yvette Bürki & Carsten Sinner (eds.), *Tiempo y espacio y relaciones espacio-temporales en judeoespañol*, 27–34. Munich: Peniope.
Berenguer Amador, Ángel. 2012c. La sintaxis del subjuntivo en judeoespañol. *eHumanista: Journal of Iberian studies* 20. 47–62.
Berenguer Amador, Ángel. 2014a. La preposición *a* como marca del complemento directo de persona en el libro de David M. Atías, *La güerta de oro* (Liorna, 1778). In *La lengua sefardí: Aspectos lingüísticos, literarios y culturales*, ed. Yvette Bürki and Elena Romero. Berlin: Frank and Timme, 21–34.
Berenguer Amador, Ángel. 2014b. Los pretéritos en el judeoespañol del siglo XVIII. *Ladinar* 7–8. 37–48.
Berenguer Amador, Ángel. 2014. The verbal moods in 18th-century Judeo-Spanish. *Massorot* 16. 87–112. (Hebrew.)
Berenguer Amador, Ángel, Manuela Cerezo, and Beatrice Schmid. 2006. "El muerto está vivo": A propósito del infinitivo en judeoespañol. *Acta Romanica Basiliensia* 17. 25–36.
Borovaya, Olga. 2012. *Modern Ladino culture: Press, belles lettres, and theatre in the late Ottoman empire*. Bloomington: Indiana University Press.
Bossong, Georg. 2008. El judeo-español de Salónica, un crisol lingüístico. In Rena Molho (ed.), *Judeo Espagnol: Social and cultural life in Salonika through Judeo-Spanish texts*, 31–49. Thessaloniki: Ets Ahaim Foundation.
Bradley, Travis G. 2007a. Constraints on the metathesis of sonorant consonants in Judeo-Spanish. *Probus* 19. 171–207.

Bradley, Travis G. 2007b. Prosodically-conditioned sibilant voicing in Balkan Judeo-Spanish. In Erin Bainbridge & Brian Agbayani (eds.), *Proceedings of the Thirty-fourth Western Conference on Linguistics, WECOL 2006*, vol. 17, 48–73. Fresno, CA: Department of Linguistics, California State University.

Bradley, Travis G. 2009. On the syllabication of prevocalic /w/ in Judeo-Spanish. In Pascual José Masullo, Erin O'Rourk & Chia-Hui Huang (eds.), *Romance linguistics 2007. Selected papers from the 37th linguistic symposium on Romance languages (LSRL), Pittsburgh, 15–18 March 2007*, 51–87. Philadelphia: John Benjamins.

Bradley, Travis G. & Jason Smith. 2011. The phonology-morphology interface in Judeo-Spanish diminutive formation: A lexical ordering and subcategorization approach. *Studies in Hispanic and Lusophone linguistics* 4. 247–300.

Brink-Danan, Marcy. 2011. The meaning of Ladino: The semiotics of an online speech community. *Language and communication* 31. 107–118.

Budor, Karlo. 2013. Polymorphisme graphique des documents judéo-espagnols des Balkans. In Soufiane Roussi and Ana Stulić-Etchevers (eds.), *Recensement, analyse et traitement numérique des sources écrites pour les études séfarades*, 23–34. Bordeaux: Presses Universitaires de Bordeaux.

Bunis, David M. 1982. Types of non-regional variation in early modern eastern spoken Judezmo. *International journal of the sociology of language* 37. 41–70.

Bunis, David M. 1993. The earliest Judezmo newspapers: Sociolinguistic reflections. *Mediterranean language review* 6–7. 5–66.

Bunis, David M. 2001. On the incorporation of Slavisms in the grammatical system of Yugoslavian Judezmo. *Jews and Slavs* 9. 325–37.

Bunis, David M. 2003. Modernization of Judezmo and Hakitia (Judeo-Spanish). In Reeva S. Simon, Michael M. Laskier, and Sara Reguer (eds.), *The Jews of the Middle East and North Africa in modern times*, 116–128. New York: Columbia University.

Bunis, David M. 2004a. Distinctive characteristics of Jewish Ibero-Romance, circa 1492. *Hispania Judaica Bulletin* 4. 105–37.

Bunis, David M. 2004b. Ottoman Judezmo diminutives and other hypocoristics. In Frank Alvarez-Péreyre and Jean Baumgarten (eds.), *Linguistique des langues juives et linguistique générale*, 193–246. Paris: CNRS.

Bunis, David M. 2005a. Writing as a national-religious symbol: On the development of Judezmo writing. *Pe'amim: Studies in Oriental Jewry* 101–102. 111–171. (Hebrew.)

Bunis, David M. 2005b. Judeo-Spanish culture in medieval and modern times. In Zion Zohar (ed.), *Sephardic and Mizrahi Jewry: From the Golden Age of Spain to modern times*, 55–76. New York: New York University Press.

Bunis, David M. 2005c. A theory of Hebrew-based fusion lexemes in Jewish languages as illustrated by animate nouns in Judezmo and Yiddish. *Mediterranean language review* 16. 1–115.

Bunis, David M. 2006. Les langues juives du moyen-orient et d'Afrique du nord. In Shmuel Trigano (ed.), *Le monde sépharade, vol. 2, Civilisation*, 537–64. Paris: Editions du Seuil.

Bunis, David M. 2006–2007. Judezmo inanimate fusion nouns with non-romance affixes. *Yod. Revue des études hébraïques et juives* 11–12. 359–410.

Bunis, David M. 2007. Judezmo and Haketia inanimate nouns with Hebrew-origin bases and Romance-origin affixes. In A. Maman, S. E. Fassberg & Y. Breuer (eds.), *Sha'are lashon: Studies in Hebrew, Aramaic and Jewish languages presented to Moshe Bar-Asher*, vol. 3, 40–63. Jerusalem: The Bialik Institute.

Bunis, David M. 2008a. The names of Jewish languages: A taxonomy. In Francesco Aspesi, Vermondo Brugnatelli, Anna Linda Callow & Claudia Rosenzweig (eds.), *Il mio cuore è a Oriente. Studi di linguistica storica, filologia e cultura ebraica dedicati a Maria Luisa Mayer Modena*, 415–433. Milan: Cisalpino.

Bunis, David M. 2008b. The differential impact of Arabic on Ḥaketía and Turkish on Judezmo. *El Presente* 2. 177–207.

Bunis, David M. 2008c. Jewish Ibero-Romance in Livorno. *Italia* 18. 7–64.

Bunis, David M. (ed.) 2009a. *Languages and literatures of Sephardic and Oriental Jewry*. Jerusalem: Misgav Yerushalayim and Bialik Institute.

Bunis, David M. 2009b. Judezmo analytic verbs with a Hebrew-origin participle: Evidence of Ottoman influence. In David M. Bunis (ed.), *Languages and literatures of Sephardic and Oriental Jewry*, 94–166. Jerusalem: Misgav Yerushalayim and Bialik Institute.

Bunis, David M. 2010a. The traditional language of the Sephardic Jews (in the Turkish Republic). In Yaron Ben-Naeh (ed.), *Jewish communities in the East in the nineteenth and twentieth centuries: Turkey*, 177–192. Jerusalem: Ben-Zvi Institute (Hebrew).

Bunis, David M. 2010b. Echoes of Yiddishism in Judezmism. *Jews and Slavs* 22. 232–50.

Bunis, David M. 2011a. Native designations of Judezmo as a 'Jewish language'. In Yosef Tobi & Dennis Kurzon (eds.), *Studies in language, literature and history presented to Joseph Chetrit*, *41–81. Haifa–Jerusalem: Haifa University-Karmel.

Bunis, David M. 2011b. The east-west Sephardic *Láʿaź* (Judeo-Spanish) dialect dichotomy as reflected in three editions of *Séfer Dat Yehudit* by Abraham Laredo and Yiŝḥac Haleví. In Elena Romero (ed.), with Aitor García Moreno, *Estudios sefardíes dedicados a la memoria de Iacob M. Hassán (z»l)*, 157–190. Madrid: CSIC and Fundación San Millán de la Cogolla.

Bunis, David M. 2011c. The changing faces of Sephardic identity as reflected in Judezmo sources. *Judenspanisch* 13. 43–71.

Bunis, David M. (with Mattat Adar-Bunis). 2011d. Spoken Judezmo in written Judezmo: Dialogues in *Sefer Me-ʿam Loʿez* on Leviticus and Numbers (Istanbul 1753–64) by Rabbi Yiṣḥaq Magriso. *Peʿamim: Studies in Oriental Jewry* 125–127. 412–505. (Hebrew.)

Bunis, David M. 2011e. Judezmo glossaries and dictionaries by native speakers and the language ideologies behind them. In Winfried Busse & Michael Studemund-Halévy (eds.), *Lexicología y lexicografía judeoespañolas*, 353–446. Bern: Peter Lang.

Bunis, David M. 2011f. Judezmo: The Jewish language of the Ottoman Sephardim. *European Judaism* 44. 22–35.

Bunis, David M. 2011g. A doctrine of popular Judezmism as extrapolated from the Judezmo press, c. 1845–1948. In Rena Molho, Hilary Pomeroy & Elena Romero (eds.), *Satirical texts in Judeo-Spanish by and about the Jews of Thessaloniki*, 244–268. Thessalonica: Ets Ahaim Foundation.

Bunis, David M. 2012a. The Judezmo/Ḥaketía phonological divide as reflected in two editions of *Sefer Dat Yĕhudit* (Livorno 1827/Jerusalem 1878). In Malka Muchnik & Tsvi Sadan (Tsuguya Sasaki) (eds.), *Studies in modern Hebrew and Jewish languages presented to Ora (Rodrigue) Schwarzwald*, 670–696. Jerusalem: Karmel.

Bunis, David M. 2012b. The Anti-Castilianist credo of Judezmo journalist Hizkia M. Franco (1875–1953). In Aitor García Moreno (ed.), *Homenaje a Elena Romero*, 63–97. (www.ehumanista.ucsb.edu/volumes/volume_20).

Bunis, David M. 2012c. 'Recordings' of Judezmo linguistic variation in the early 20th-century Judezmo press. In Yvette Bürki, Manuela Cimeli & Rosa Sánchez (eds.) *Lengua, llengua, llingua, lingua, langue – encuentros filológicos (ibero)románicos: Estudios en homenaje a la profesora Beatrice Schmid*, 92–114. Munich: Peniope.

Bunis, David M. 2013a. The Judezmo press as a forum for modern linguistic discourse. In Rosa Sánchez & Marie-Christine Bornes-Varol (eds.), *La presse judéo-espagnole, support et vecteur de la modernité*, 143–179. Istanbul: Libra.

Bunis, David M. 2013b. Turkish influence on Hebrew in the Ottoman Empire. In Geoffrey Khan (ed.), *Encyclopedia of Hebrew language and linguistics*. Leiden: Brill.

Bunis, David M. 2013c. Judeo-Spanish (Judezmo), Hebrew component in. In Geoffrey Khan et al. (eds.), *Encyclopedia of Hebrew language and linguistics*, vol. 2, 421–427. Leiden: Brill.

Bunis, David M. 2013d. Shem Tov Semo, Yosef Kalwo, and Judezmo fiction in nineteenth-century Vienna. In Michael Studemund-Halévy, Christian Liebl & Ivana Vučina Simović (eds.), *Sefarad an der Donau: Lengua y literatura de los sefardíes en tierras de los Habsburgo*, 39–146. Barcelona: Tirocinio.

Bunis, David M. 2013e. The Whole Hebrew reading tradition of Ottoman Judezmo speakers: The medieval Iberian roots. *Hispania Judaica bulletin* 9. 15–67.

Bunis, David M. 2013f. 'Whole Hebrew': A revised definition. In Yisrael Bartal, Galit Hasan-Rokem, Ada Rapaport-Albert, Claudia Rosenzweig, Vicki Schifriss & Erika Timm (eds.), *A touch of grace: Presented to Chava Turniansky*, vol. 2, *37–68. Jerusalem: Zalman Shazar Center–Center for Research on Polish Jewry.

Bunis, David M. 2013g. Writing more and less 'Jewishly' in Judezmo and Yiddish. *Journal of Jewish languages* 1. 9–75.

Bunis, David M. 2013h. From Early Middle to Late Middle Judezmo: The Ottoman component as a demarcating factor. *El Prezente 7 / Menorah* 3. 115–163.

Bunis, David M. 2013i. Judezmo (Judeo-Spanish; Ladino) as spoken by Greek Jews. In Eyal Ginio (ed.), *Greece*, 311–324. Jerusalem: Ben-Zvi Institute.

Bunis, David M. 2014. Linguistic conservatism versus linguistic pragmatism: Judezmo speakers on 'old' and 'new' language. In Hillel Weiss, Roman Katsman & Dov-Ber Kotlerman (eds.), *Around the point: The literatures of Jews in Jewish and non-Jewish languages*, 135–182. Cambridge: Cambridge Scholars Publishing.

Bunis, David M. 2015a. Jewish and Arab medieval Ibero-Romance: Toward a comparative study. In José Alberto R. S. Tavim, Maria Filomena Lopes de Barro & Lúcia Liba Mucznik (eds.), *In the Iberian Peninsula and beyond*, vol. 2, 64–148. Cambridge: Cambridge Scholars.

Bunis, David M. 2015b. On Judezmo terms for the proverb and saying: A look from within. In Eliezer Papo, Haim Weiss, Yaakov Bentolila & Yuval Harari (eds.), *El Prezente 8–9 / Mikan 15 (=Damta LeTamar)*, vol. 3, 11–53. Beer Sheva: Ben-Gurion University of the Negev.

Bunis, David M. 2016a. Judezmo (Ladino). In Lily Kahn & Aaron D. Rubin (eds.), *Handbook of Jewish languages*, 365–450. Leiden: Brill.

Bunis, David M. 2016b. Twenty-first-century talk about Judezmo on the Ladinokomunita website. In Joshua Miller and Anita Norich (eds.), *Languages of modern Jewish cultures: Comparative perspectives*, 321–360. Ann Arbor: University of Michigan.

Bunis, David M. 2016c. Speakers' 'Jewishness' as a criterion for the classification of languages: The case of the languages of the Sephardim. *Hispania Judaica Bulletin* 12. 1–57.

Bunis, David M. 2017. The Judeo-Arabic roots of the Ladino Bible translation tradition. In Yochanan Breuer, Steven Fassberg & Ofra Tirosh-Becker (eds.), *Jubilee Volume in Honor of*

Aharon Maman (=*Meḥqarim Bĕ-Lashon* 17–18), 65–88. Jerusalem: Department of Hebrew Language. (Hebrew.)

Bunis, David M. Forthcoming. Sephardic customs as a discourse topic in the Ladinokomunita internet correspondence circle. In *Minhagim*, eds. Sara Appel, Hasia Diner, and Jean Baumgarten. Tel Aviv: Goldstein-Goren Diaspora Research Center (Tel Aviv University).

Bürki, Yvette. 2001. Algunos aspectos sobre la formación de palabras en *El hacino imaginado*. In *Actas del I Encuentro Internacional de Filólogos Noveles*, 17–30. Alcalá de Henares: Universidad de Alcalá–Universität Basel.

Bürki, Yvette. 2006. El discurso periodístico en la prensa judeoespañola del siglo xix. *Revista Iberoamericana de Lingüística* 4. 77–97.

Bürki, Yvette. 2010a. «La cuestión de la lingua» y la defensa del judeoespañol en la prensa sefardí de Salónica (1901–1902). *Spanish in context* 7. 78–99.

Bürki, Yvette. 2010b. *La Época* y *El Avenir*: Dos periódicos, dos discursos en contraste. In Paloma Díaz-Mas & María Sánchez Pérez (eds.), *Los sefardíes ante los retos del mundo contemporáneo: Identidad y mentalidades*, 159–170. Madrid: CSIC.

Bürki, Yvette. 2012a. Mecanismos de cohesión gramatical en judeoespañol moderno. In Yvette Burki and Carsten Sinner, *Tiempo y espacio y relaciones espacio-temporales en judeoespañol*, 125–140. Munich: Peniope.

Bürki, Yvette. 2012b. Rasgos de la inmediatez comunicativa en notas de viaje de la época. In G. Cordone, V. Beguelin & M. de la Torre (eds.), *En pos de la palabra viva: Huellas de la oralidad en textos antiguos: Estudios en honor al profesor Rolf Eberenz*, 423–442. Bern: Peter Lang.

Bürki, Yvette. 2013. The status of Judeo-Spanish in the Ottoman Empire. In José del Valle (ed.), *A political history of Spanish*, 335–349. Cambridge: Cambridge University Press,

Bürki, Yvette. 2014. La elaboración textual en la prensa judeoespañola: Las necrologías. In Yvette Bürki and Elena Romero (eds.), *La lengua sefardí: Aspectos lingüísticos, literarios y culturales*, 35–57. Berlin: Frank and Timme.

Bürki, Yvette, Manuela Cimeli & Rosa Sánchez, eds. 2012. *Lengua, llengua, llingua, lingua, langue. Encuentros filológicos (ibero)románicos: Estudios en homenaje a la profesora Beatrice Schmid*. Munich: Peniope.

Bürki, Yvette & Elena Romero (eds.). 2014. *La lengua sefardí: Aspectos lingüísticos, literarios y culturales*. Berlin: Frank and Timme.

Bürki, Yvette & Beatrice Schmid. 2006. El tiempo futuro en judeoespañol: Apuntes para su estudio. In *Proceedings of the Thirteenth British Conference on Judeo-Spanish Studies, 7–9 September 2003*, ed. Hilary Pomeroy. London: Department of Hispanic Studies Queen Mary University of London, 27–41.

Bürki, Yvette, Beatrice Schmid & Armin Schwegler, eds. 2006. *Una lengua en la diáspora: el judeoespañol de Oriente* (=Sección temática de la Revista de lingüística Iberoamericana IV.2 [8]). Frankfurt–Madrid: Vervuert–Iberoamericana.

Bürki, Yvette & Carsten Sinner (eds.). 2012. *Tiempo y espacio y relaciones espacio-temporales en judeoespañol*. Munich: Peniope.

Burt, Bonnie & Rachel Amado Bortnick. 1989. *Trees cry for rain (Arvoles yoran por luvias): A Sephardic journey*. Oakland, CA: Bonnie Burt Productions.

Busse, Winfried. 2001. Lexicographie électronique du judéo-espagnol: Un dictionnaire interactif du judéo-espagnol sur Internet. *Neue Romania* 24 (=*Judenspanisch* V). 63–72.

Busse, Winfried. 2003. Judeo-Spanish writing systems in Roman letters and the normalization of orthography. *Neue Romania* 28 (=*Judenspanisch* VII). 105–128.

Busse, Winfried. 2004. Zur Problematik des Judenspanischen. *Neue Romania* 12 (= *Judenspanisch* I). 37–90.
Busse, Winfried. 2005. Rashí: Transliteración, transcripción y adaptación de textos aljamiados. *Neue Romania* 34 (=*Judenspanisch* IX). 97–108.
Busse, Winfried. 2011a. Contacts linguistiques. In Winfried Busse and Michael Studemund-Halévy (eds.), *Lexicología y lexicografía judeoespañolas*, 11–32. Bern: Peter Lang.
Busse, Winfried. 2011b. Kurzcharakteristik des Judenspanischen. *Neue Romania* 40 (=*Judenspanisch* XIII). 171–196.
Busse, Winfried & Michael Studemund-Halévy (eds.). 2011. *Lexicología y lexicografía judeoespañolas: Actas del simposio internacional organizado por el Instituto de Historia de los Judíos en Alemania (Hamburgo, 7–9 de septiembre de 2008)* [=*Sephardica* 5]. Bern: Peter Lang.
Cerezo, Manuela. 2006. "Ande está el cadavre?" – Apuntes sobre el discurso directo en las novelas policíacas judeoespañolas de Jim Jackson. In *Actas del VI Encuentro Hispano-Suizo de Filólogos Noveles (Oviedo, 9 de mayo de 2006)*. Basel: Romanisches Seminar der Universität Basel (=*ARBA* 17).
Collin, Gaëlle. 2002. *La novya aguna*: Présentation, translittération et édition d'un roman judéo-espagnol de Eliya Karmona. In *Neue Romania* 26 (=*Judenspanisch* VI). 2–132.
Díaz-Mas, Paloma. 2012. El judeoespañol en la prensa española de la Restauración: Informaciones en el diario *El Globo*. In Yvette Bürki, Manuela Cimeli & Rosa Sánchez (eds.), *Lengua, llengua, llingua, lingua, langue. Encuentros filológicos (ibero)románicos. Estudios en homenaje a la profesora Beatrice Schmid*, 190–202. Munich: Peniope.
Díaz-Mas, Paloma. 2014. Writing systems and cultural identities in the Sephardic Diaspora. In Johannes Den Heijer, Andrea Schmidt & Tamara Pataridze (eds.), *Script beyond borders: A survey of allographic traditions in the Euro-Mediterranean world*, 473–510. Louvain: Université Catholique de Louvain-Peeters.
Díaz-Mas, Paloma & Pilar Romeu Ferré. 2011. El léxico de la memoria: Expresiones judeoespañolas en autobiografías sefardíes. In Winfried Busse & Michael Studemund-Halévy (eds.), *Lexicología y lexicografía judeoespañolas*, 123–141. Bern: Peter Lang.
Díaz-Mas, Paloma & Pilar Romeu Ferré. 2013. Being multilingual: Judeo-Spanish as a homeland in the Diaspora as reflected in Jewish Sephardic memoirs. In Andrej Katny, Izabela Olszewska & Aleksandra Twardowska (eds.), *Askenazim and Sephardim: A European perspective*, 227–244. Frankfurt am Main et al.: Peter Lang.
Díaz Mas, Paloma & María Sánchez Pérez (eds.). 2010. *Los sefardíes ante los retos del mundo contemporáneo: Identidad y mentalidades*. Madrid: Consejo Superior de Investigaciones Científicas.
Friedman, Victor A. & Brian D. Joseph. 2014. Lessons from Judezmo about the Balkan Sprachbund and contact linguistics. *International Journal of the Sociology of Language* 226. 3–23.
Gabinskij, Mark A. 2011. *Die sefardische Sprache*. Trans. Heinreich Kohring. Tübingen: Stauffenburg.
Gaon, Yehoram. 1988. *From Toledo to Jerusalem*. Netanya: Globus United. (Judezmo).
García Moreno, Aitor. 2003. La deixis personal en el Me'am Lo'ez de Éxodo (1733–46): Configuración y usos especiales del sistema pronominal judeoespañol. *Res Diachronicae* 2. 127–34.
García Moreno, Aitor. 2004. *Relatos del pueblo ladinán (Me'am Lo'ez de Éxodo)*. Madrid: Consejo Superior de Investigaciones Científicas.

García Moreno, Aitor. 2006a. Innovación y arcaísmo en la morfosintaxis del judeoespañol clásico. *Revista Internacional de Lingüística Iberoamericana* 4. 2:35–51.
García Moreno, Aitor. 2006b. El judeoespañol *ecierdo*. ¿El eslabón perdido en el origen de *izquierdo*?" In José Jesús de Bustos Tovar & José Luis Girón Alconchel (eds.), *Actas del VI Congreso Internacional de Historia de la Lengua Española*, vol. III, 2437–2445. Madrid: Arco/Libros, UCM y AHLE.
García Moreno, Aitor. 2010. Glosas frescas en *La hermosa Hulda de España* (Jerusalén, 1910). In Paloma Díaz-Mas & María Sánchez Pérez (eds.), *Los sefardíes ante los retos del mundo contemporáneo: identidad y mentalidades*, 75–85. Madrid: CSIC.
García Moreno, Aitor. 2011a. Towards a new style in nineteenth century Judeo-Spanish prose: Two Judeo-Spanish versions of the German novel *Der Rabbi und der Minister*. *European Judaism* 44. 9–21.
García Moreno, Aitor. 2011b. Más textos judeoespañoles de Salónica: Avance de la edición de diez cuentos sefardíes tradicionales, recogidos por Cynthia Crews a principios del siglo XX. In Elena Romero and Aitor García Moreno (eds.), *Estudios sefardíes dedicados a la memoria de Iacob M. Hassán (z"l)*, 191–203. Madrid: CSIC and Fundación San Millán de la Cogolla.
García Moreno, Aitor. 2012a. De la pervivencia (o no) de algunas innovaciones morfosintácticas del judeoespañol castizo. *Cuadernos dieciochistas* 13. 229–47.
García Moreno, Aitor. 2012b. Los tiempos pretéritos con cierre vocálico en el judeoespañol de Salónica (1935). In Yvette Bürki & Carsten Sinner (eds.), *Tiempo y espacio y relaciones espacio-temporales en judeoespañol*, 15–26. Munich: Peniope.
García Moreno, Aitor. 2012c. Apuntes sobre la ortografía aljamiada del judeoespañol. In Raquel Suárez García and Ignacio Ceballos Viro (eds.), *Aljamías in memoriam Álvaro Galmés de Fuentes y Iacob M. Hassán*, 217–232. Gijón: Trea.
García Moreno, Aitor. 2012d. Juguetonarios: Diccionarios humorísticos de *El Ĵugueton*. In Yvette Bürki, Manuela Cimeli & Rosa Sánchez (eds.), *Lengua, llengua, llingua, lingua, langue. Encuentros filológicos (ibero)románicos. Estudios en homenaje a la profesora Beatrice Schmid*, 231–248. Munich: Peniope.
García Moreno, Aitor (ed.). 2012e. *Homenaje a Elena Romero* (= Sección monográfica de eHumanista 20). (http://www.ehumanista.ucsb.edu/volumes/20)
García Moreno, Aitor. 2013a. *Der Rabbi und der Minister. Dos versions judeoespañolas de la novela alemana. Edición y estudio filológico*. Barcelona: Tirocinio.
García Moreno, Aitor. 2013b. Glosas de andar por casa en los cuentos sefardíes tradicionales recogidos por Cynthia Crews en Salónica a principios del siglo XX. *Ladinar* 7–8. 95–112.
García Moreno, Aitor. 2013c. Les gloses comme sources pour l'étude du lexique judéo-espagnol: L'example de *Luzero de la Pasensia* (Roumanie). In Soufiane Roussi and Ana Stulic-Etchevers (eds.), *Recensement, analyse et traitement numérique des sources écrites pour les études séfarades*, 249–271. Bordeaux: Presses Universitaires de Bordeaux.
García Moreno, Aitor 2013d. Río abajo, tiempo después: Diferencias léxicas en dos versiones sefardíes danubianas. In Michael Studemund-Halévy, Christian Liebl & Ivana Vučina Simović (eds.), *Sefarad an der Donau: La lengua y literatura de los sefardíes en tierras de los Habsburgo*, 203–219. Barcelona: Tirocinio.
García Moreno, Aitor. 2013e. ¿Ante el primer diccionario monolingüe judeoespañol? *Sefarad* 73. 2, 371–408.
García Moreno, Aitor. 2014. Calcos y préstamos en los sipurim de Yishac Hakohén Perahiá: ¿Variación diafásica o problemas de traducción? In Yvette Bürki & Elena Romero (eds.),

La lengua sefardí: Aspectos lingüísticos, literarios y culturales, 89–108. Berlin: Frank and Timme.

Gatenio, Rafael (ed.). 2002. *Judeo Espaniol: A Jewish language in search of its people: Proceedings of the 2nd Judeo-Espaniol International Conference, Tesalónica, 16–17 de Abril de 2000*. Thessaloniki: Ets Ahaim Foundation.

Gerson Şarhon, Karen. 2006. Las aktividades de la komunita sefardi turka para la konservasion del djudeo-espanyol. *Ladinar* 4. 171–179.

Gerson Şarhon, Karen. 2011. Ladino in Turkey: The situation today as reflected by the Ladino Database Project. *European Judaism* 44(1) (Spring 2011). 62–71.

Gomel, Nivi. 2006. Judeo-Spanish textbooks for teaching Hebrew. In Hilary Pomeroy (ed.), *Proceedings of the Thirteenth British Conference on Judeo-Spanish Studies, 7–9 September 2003*, 53–61. London: Department of Hispanic Studies, Queen Mary and Westfield College.

Guastalla, Silvia (ed.). 2007. *Il giudeo-spagnolo (ladino): Cultura e tradizione sefardita tra presente, passato e futuro*. Livorno: Salomone Belforte.

Gutwirth, Eleazar. 2013. Medieval poliglossia: The Jews in Christian Spain. *Medioevo Romanzo* 37(1). 125–149.

Harris, Tracy K. 2006. Death of a language revisited: Reactions, results and maintenance efforts on behalf of Judeo-Spanish since 1994. In Hilary Pomeroy (ed.), *Proceedings of the Thirteenth British Conference on Judeo-Spanish Studies, 7–9 September 2003*, 63–74. London: Department of Hispanic Studies, Queen Mary University of London.

Hassán, Iacob M. 2002. La lengua y la literatura sefardíes en el marco del hispanismo. *Raíces* 16. 52–53, 20–30.

Hassán, Iacob M. 2006. El estudio del ladino: Entre la tradición española y la tradición israelí. *Ladinar* 4. 43–55.

Hassán, Iacob M. 2008. Sistemas gráficos del español sefardí. In *Sefardíes: Literatura y lengua de una nación dispersa, XV curso de cultura hispanojudía y sefardí de la Universidad de Castilla-La Mancha*, 119–136. Cuenca: Ediciones de la Universidad de Castilla–La Mancha.

Hazan, Isacco. 2013. *Dictionnaire illustré du judéo-espagnol de Turquie*. Paris: Éditions du Divit.

Held, Michal. 2009. 'Ima', 'madre' or 'mama'? Code switching in the personal narratives of Judeo-Spanish-speaking women storytellers. *Ladinar* 5. 67–87. (Hebrew.)

Hernández González, Carmen. 2012a. El componente metafórico en la expresión lingüística del espacio en la lengua sefardí. In Yvette Bürki & Carsten Sinner (eds.), *Tiempo y espacio y relaciones espacio-temporales en judeoespañol*, 103–114. Munich: Peniope.

Hernández González, Carmen. 2012b. Observaciones sobre las formas adverbiales en *-mente* en el español sefardí. *eHumanista: Journal of Iberian Studies* 20. 191–203.

Hernández Socas, Elia, Carsten Sinner & Encarnación Tabares Plasencia. 2014. La función de las glosas en *El trajumán* de Michael Papo (1884). *Zeitschrift für Romanische Philologie* 130(2). 397–429.

Hetzer, Armin. 2001. *Sephardisch. Judeo-español, Djudezmo: Einführung in die Umgangssprache der südoesteuropäischen Juden*. Wiesbaden: Harrassowitz.

Hetzer, Armin. 2003. Problems of language planning and standardization in contemporary Ladino texts. *Neue Romania* 28 (=*Judenspanisch* VII). 129–141.

Hualde, José I. & Mahir Şaul. 2011. Istanbul Judeo-Spanish. *Journal of the International Phonetics Association* 41. 89–110.

Jagoda, Flory. c.2000. *The key from Spain: The songs and stories of Flory Jagoda*. [U.S.A.]: Ankica Petrović.
Koen-Sarano, Matilda. 2009. *Diksionario Ladino – Ebreo / Ebreo – Ladino*. Jerusalem: S. Zack.
Kohring, Heinrich. 2004. Judenspanisch in hebräischer Schrift. *Neue Romania* 12 (= *Judenspanisch* I). 101–179.
Kohring, Heinrich. 2011. Lexicographica Judaeohispanica: Florilegium. In Winfried Busse and Michael Studemund-Halévy (eds.), *Lexicología y lexicografía judeoespañolas*, 287–337. Bern: Peter Lang.
Lazar, Moshe (ed.). 2000a. *The Ladino Scriptures: Constantinople-Salonica [1540–1572]*. 2 vols. Lancaster, CA: Labyrinthos.
Lazar, Moshe (ed.). 2000b. *Sēfer Ben Gurïōn (Yōsipōn): First Ladino translation by Aḇraham Asa [1753]*. Lancaster, CA: Labyrinthos.
Liebl, Christian (ed.). 2009. *Judeo-Spanish from the Balkans: The recordings by Julius Subak (1908) and Max A. Luria (1927)* (= Sound documents from the Phonogrammarchiv of the Austrian Academy of Sciences: The complete historical collections 1899–1950, series 12/ OEAW PHA CD 28). Vienna: Verlag der Österreichischen Akademie der Wissenschaften.
Mancheva, Dora. 2008a. La lengua sefardí en su decadencia. In I. Hassán y R. Izquierdo-Benito (ed.), *Sefardíes: Literatura y lengua de una nación dispersa*, 81–118. Cuenca: Universidad de Castilla–La Mancha.
Mancheva, Dora. 2008b. Los rastros del búlgaro en la parte judeoespañola de un diccionario trilingüe francés-búlgaro-sefardí. *Cuadernos del Instituto Historia de la Lengua* 1. 75–86.
Mancheva, Dora. 2009. *El diccionario judeoespañol-búlgaro de Albert Pipano: edición y estudio*. University of Geneva PhD Dissertation.
Mantcheva, Dora. 2006. La investigación del ladino en las universidades de Europa: ¿Por qué, con qué objetivo y para quién? *Ladinar* 4. 131–143.
Marín Ramos, Ferrán. 2014. *Gramática básica de djudeo-espanyol*. Villaviciosa: Camelot.
Mavrogiannis, Pandelis. 2006–2007. Les emprunts lexicaux du judéo-espagnol au grec dans le dictionnaire de Joseph Néhama. *Yod: Revue des Études Hebraïques et Juives* 11–12. 289–313.
Mavrogiannis, Pandelis. 2013. The Judeo-Spanish Oral Archive (JSA): Data collection, metadata description, results, and perspectives for development. In Michael Studemund-Halévy, Christian Liebl & Ivana Vučina Simović (eds.), *Sefarad an der Donau: La lengua y literatura de los sefardíes en tierras de los Habsburgo*, 385–407. Barcelona: Tirocinio.
Minervini, Laura. 2006. El desarrollo histórico del judeoespañol. *Revista Internacional de Lingüística Iberoamericana* 2. 13–34.
Minervini, Laura. 2008a. Formación de la lengua sefardí. In Iacob M. Hassán, Ricardo Izquierdo Benito & Elena Romero (eds.), *Sefardíes: Literatura y lengua de una nación dispersa. XV curso de cultura hispanojudía y sefardí de la Universidad de Castilla-La Mancha. In memoriam Ana Riaño y Iacob M. Hassán*, 25–49. Cuenca: Ediciones de la Universidad de Castilla-La Mancha.
Minervini, Laura. 2008b. Gli italianismi nel giudeoespagnolo del cinquecento. In Francesco Aspesi, Vermondo Brugnatelli, Anna Linda Callow & Claudia Rosenzweig (eds.), *Il mio cuore è a Oriente. Studi di linguistica storica, filologia e cultura ebraica dedicati a Maria Luisa Mayer Modena*, 511–526. Milano: Cisalpino.
Minervini, Laura. 2011a. El componente léxico árabe en la lengua de los judíos hispánicos. In Winfried Busse & Michael Studemund-Halévy (eds.), *Lexicología y lexicografía judeoespañolas*, 33–52. Bern: Peter Lang.

Minervini, Laura. 2011b. Tres cartas en judeoespañol: Edición crítica y comentario
    lingüístico. In Elena Romero & Aitor García Moreno (eds.), *Estudios sefardíes dedicados a
    la memoria de Iacob M. Hassán (z"l)*, 331–349. Madrid: CSIC and Fundación San Millán de
    la Cogolla.
Minervini, Laura. 2012. Cantiga de Purim a la morisca. In Yvette Bürki, Manuela Cimeli & Rosa
    Sánchez (eds.), *Lengua, llengua, llingua, lingua, langue. Encuentros filológicos (ibero)
    románicos. Estudios en homenaje a la profesora Beatrice Schmid*, 273–287. Munich:
    Peniope.
Minervini, Laura. 2013. Los estudios del español sefardí (judeoespañol, ladino): Aportaciones,
    métodos y problemas actuales. *Studis Romànics* 35(1). 323–334.
Minervini, Laura. 2014. El léxico de origen italiano en el judeoespañol de Oriente. In Winfried
    Busse (ed.), *La lengua de los sefardíes: Tres contribuciones a su historia*, 65–104.
    Tübingen: Stauffenburg.
Molho, Rena (ed.). 2008. *Judeo Espagnol: Social and cultural life in Salonika through
    Judeo-Spanish texts: Proceedings of the 3rd International Conference on Judeo-Spanish,
    Tesalónica, 17–18 de Octubre de 2004*. Thessaloniki: Ets Ahaim Foundation.
Molho, Rena, Hilary Pomeroy & Elena Romero (eds.). 2011. *Judeo Espaniol: Textos satíricos
    judeoespañoles: De Salonicenses o sobre Salonicenses*. Thessaloniki: Ets Ahaim
    Foundation.
Montoliu, César & Johan van der Auwera. 2004. On Judeo-Spanish conditionals. In Olga
    Mišeska Tomić (ed.), *Balkan syntax and semantics*, 461–474. Amsterdam/Philadelphia:
    Benjamins.
Münch, Almuth. 2004. Die hebräisch-aramäische Sprachtradition im Verhältnis zum
    Spanischen der Juden in Sepharad I sowie zum Djudeo-Espanyol in Sepharad II und die
    Rolle des Ladino. *Neue Romania* 12 (= *Judenspanisch* I), 181–252.
Münch, Almuth. 2007. El campo semántico de valoración intelectual representado por los
    préstamos léxicos hebraicos y arameos en el judeoespañol moderno comparado al campo
    castellano correspondiente. *Neue Romania* 37 (= *Judenspanisch* XI), 91–128.
Muñoz Molina, Natalia. 2011. Ediciones aljamiadas del *Séfer Sébet Yehudá*: su problemática.
    In Elena Romero & Aitor García Moreno (eds.), *Estudios sefardíes dedicados a la memoria
    de Iacob M. Hassán (z"l)*, 361–371. Madrid: CSIC and Fundación San Millán de la Cogolla.
Muñoz Molina, Natalia. 2014. Versiones judeoespañolas del *Séfer Sebet Yehudá* y los paralelos
    textuales del *Darjé Haadam*. In Yvette Bürki & Elena Romero (eds.), *La lengua sefardí:
    Aspectos lingüísticos, literarios y culturales*, 125–134. Berlin: Frank and Timme.
Navon, Yitzhak. 2006. *Out of Spain: Jerusalem which was in Sepharad: A journey through
    Spain with the fifth president of Israel* [video recording]. [Jerusalem:] Israel Broadcasting
    Authority.
Neuman, Yishaï. 2006–2007. Un substrat judéo-arabe d'une graphie judéo-espagnole? *Yod:
    Revue des études Hébraïques et Juives* 11–12. 339–357.
Orgun, Güler. N.d. (c.2000). *A Turkish-Jewish-Muslim tale*. [Istanbul]: N.p.
Overbeck de Sumi, Ruth. 2005. Urtext und Übersetzung der hebräischen Bibel im sefardischen
    Judentum: Eine sprachliche Analyse von Ladinoversionen zum Buch Ruth. *Neue Romania*
    34 (=*Judenspanisch* IX). 109–216.
Papo, Eliezer. 2007. Slavic influences on Bosnian Judeo-Spanish as reflected in the literature of
    the 'Sephardic Circle'. In Pedro M. Piñero Ramírez (ed.), *La memoria de Sefarad: Historia
    y cultura de los sefardíes*, 267–286. Sevilla: Fundación Sevilla-Nodo and Fundación
    Machado.

Papo, Eliezer. 2009a. The language policy of Laura Papo ("Bohoreta") in its historical and cultural context. *Pě'amim* 118. 125–175. (Hebrew.)

Papo, Eliezer. 2012. *And thou shalt jest with thy son: Judeo-Spanish parodies on the Passover Haggadah*. 2 vols. Jerusalem: Ben-Zvi Institute. (Hebrew.)

Papo, Eliezer. 2013. From neutral usage to caricature: German influences on Bosnian Judeo-Spanish, as reflected in the writings of the Sephardic Circle. In Michael Studemund-Halévy, Christian Liebl & Ivana Vučina Simović (eds.), *Sefarad an der Donau: La lengua y literatura de los sefardíes en tierras de los Habsburgo*, 295–311. Barcelona: Tirocinio.

Penny, Ralph. 2000. *Variation and change in Spanish*. Cambridge: Cambridge University Press.

Perahya, Klara. 2012. *Diksyonaryo Judeo-Espanyol-Turko Ladino-Türkçe Sözluk*. 2d edn., Karen Gerson Şarhon (ed.). Istanbul: Sefarad Kültürü Araştırma Merkezi–Gözlem.

Perez, Avner (ed.). N.d. *Trezoro de la lengua djudeoespanyola – ladino durante todas las epokas*. Instituto Maale Adumim. http://folkmasa.org/milon/pmilonh.php (retrieved 15 February 2016).

Perez, Avner. 2005. *Las Coplas de Yosef Ha-tsadik*. Jerusalem: Ben-Zvi Institute. (Hebrew.)

Perez, Avner & Gladys Pimienta. 2007. *Diksionario amplio djudeo-espanyol–ebreo: Lashon me-Aspamia*. Jerusalem–Maale Adumim: La Autoridad Nasionala del Ladino i su Kultura–Sefarad: El Instituto Maale-Adumim. (Hebrew.)

Platikanova, Slava. 2011. Notas al léxico en el *Dreyfus* (Sofía, 1903) de Jak Lorya (1860–1948). In Winfried Busse and Michael Studemund-Halévy (eds.), *Lexicologia y lexicografía judeoespañolas*, 181–195. Bern: Peter Lang.

Platikanova, Slava, Winfried Busse & Heinrich Kohring (eds.). 2014. *Jacques Loria: Dreyfus (Sofía 1903)* (=*Sefardische Forschungen* 3). Tübingen: Stauffenberg.

Quintana Rodríguez, Aldina. 2006a. *Geografía lingüística del judeoespañol: Estudio sincrónico y diacrónico*. Bern: Peter Lang.

Quintana Rodríguez, Aldina. 2006b. La evolución del judeoespañol en el siglo XVII. *Judenspanisch* 10 / *Neue Romania* 35. 157–181.

Quintana Rodríguez, Aldina. 2006c. Las lenguas de los judíos de España: Multilingüismo de la sociedad sefardí. In Elisa Cohen de Chervonagura (ed.), *Comunidades lingüísticas: Confines y trayectorias*, 39–59. Tucumán: Facultad de Filosofía y Letras de la Universidad.

Quintana Rodríguez, Aldina. 2006d. Los estudios sefardíes en las universidades y la urgente necesidad de un modelo interdisciplinario autónomo. *Ladinar* 4. 83–94.

Quintana Rodríguez, Aldina. 2006–2007. Formules d'introduction et structure discursive dans le Me'am Lo'ez de Ya'aqov Khuli. *Yod: Revue des études Hebraïques et Juives* 11–12. 113–140.

Quintana Rodríguez, Aldina. 2007. *Responsa* testimonies and letters written in 16th-century Spanish spoken by Sephardim. *Hispania Judaica Bulletin* 5. 283–301.

Quintana Rodríguez, Aldina. 2008a. From the master's voice to the disciple's script: Genizah fragments of a Bible glossary in Ladino. *Hispania Judaica Bulletin* 6. 187–235.

Quintana Rodríguez, Aldina. 2008b. Las lenguas habladas por los judíos de España y su posición social. In Kathleen E. LeMieux (ed.), *Lluís de Santàngel: Primer financier de América*, 307–320. Valencia: Generalitat Valenciana.

Quintana Rodríguez, Aldina. 2009. Aportación lingüística de los romances aragonés y portugués a la *coiné* judeoespañola. In David M. Bunis (ed.), *Languages and literatures of Sephardic and Oriental Jews*, *221–255. Jerusalem: Misgav Yerushalayim and Mosad Bialik.

Quintana Rodríguez, Aldina. 2010. El judeoespañol, una lengua pluricéntrica al margen del español. In Paloma Díaz-Mas and María Sánchez Pérez (eds.), *Los sefardíes ante los retos*

del mundo contemporáneo. Identidad y mentalidades, 31–52. Madrid: Consejo Superior de Investigaciones Científicas.
Quintana Rodríguez, Aldina. 2011a. *Nishkahá, dankavé, marafet grande, pepino muevo, adoneha tu padre!* y otras unidades léxicas del sexolecto masculino del judeoespañol coloquial de Bursa (Turquía). In Winfried Busse and Michael Studemund-Halévy (eds.), *Lexicología y lexicografía judeoespañolas*, 199–220. Bern: Peter Lang.
Quintana Rodríguez, Aldina. 2011b. Geschichte und Soziolinguistik des Judenspanischen. Vom alten Glanz zur virtuellen Sprachgemeinschaft. *Europa Ethnica* 3. 88–96.
Quintana Rodríguez, Aldina. 2012. From linguistic segregation outside the common framework of Hispanic languages to a *de facto* standard. In Malka Muchnik & Tsvi Sadan (eds.), *Studies in Modern Hebrew and Jewish languages presented to Ora (Rodrigue) Schwarzwald*, 697–714. Jerusalem: Carmel.
Quintana Rodríguez, Aldina. 2014a. *Séder našim* (c. 1500) del rabino Meir Benveniste: Variación en la lengua de un miembro de la primera generación de hablantes nativos de Salónica. In Winfried Busse (ed.), *Sefardische Forschungen* 2, 9–63. Tübingen: Stauffenburg Verlag.
Quintana Rodríguez, Aldina. 2014b. Tierra Santa y Egipto: Lugares de encuentro y contacto lingüístico entre los judíos ibéricos y los judíos arabófonos en los siglos XVI-XVII. In Winfried Busse (ed.), *Sefardische Forschungen* 2, 105–143. Tübingen: Stauffenburg Verlag.
Riaño López, Ana Mª. 2000. Los fragmentos en arameo del libro de Daniel (2,4b-7,28), según la versión sefardí de Yisrael Bajar Hayim (Viena, 1815): Edición y estudio comparativo (morfosintáctico y léxico) con la de Abraham Asá (Constantinopla, 1745). *Miscelánea de estudios Árabes y Hebreos* 49. 261–285.
Riaño López, Ana Mª. 2001. Los estudios sefardíes en España (1992–2001). *Miscelánea de Estudios Árabes y Hebraicos. Sección hebreo* 50. 191–220.
Rieder-Zelenko, Elena. 2006. Elementos hebreos y turcos en tres narraciones sefardíes publicadas en *La Buena Esperanza*. In *Actas del VI Encuentro Hispano-Suizo de Filólogos Noveles*, Basilea: Romanischen Seminars der Universität Basel (=*Acta Romanica Basiliensia* 17), 103–116.
Rieder-Zelenko, Elena. 2012. El léxico relacionado con la flora y la fauna en *La Buena Esperanza*. In Yvette Bürki, Manuela Cimeli & Rosa Sánchez (eds.), *Lengua, llengua, llingua, lingua, langue. Encuentros filológicos (ibero)románicos. Estudios en homenaje a la profesora Beatrice Schmid*, 364–373. Munich: Peniope.
Rieder-Zelenko, Elena. 2014. El léxico relacionado con la vida urbana en *La buena esperanza*. In *La lengua sefardí: Aspectos lingüísticos, literarios y culturales*, 135–150. Berlin: Frank and Timme.
Romero, Elena. 1992. *La creación literaria en lengua sefardí*. Madrid: MAPFRE.
Romero, Elena, Iacob M. Hassán & R. Izquierdo Benito (eds.). 2008. *Sefardíes: Literatura y lengua de una nación dispersa*. Cuenca: Ediciones de la Universidad de Castilla-La Mancha.
Romero, Elena & Aitor García Moreno (eds.). 2011. *Estudios sefardíes dedicados a la memoria de Iacob M. Hassán (ź"l)*. Madrid: CSIC and Fundación San Millán de la Cogolla.
Romero, Rey. 2012. *Spanish in the Bosphorus: A sociolinguistic study on the Judeo-Spanish dialect spoken in Istanbul*. Istanbul: Libra.

Romeu Ferré, Pilar. 2004. Turquismos en un manuscrito de medicina o farmacología terapéutica en hebreo y judeoespañol (s. XIX). *Revista de dialectología y tradiciones populares* 59(2). 31–42.
Romeu Ferré, Pilar. 2011. *Yehudá Alcalay y su obra "La paz de Jerusalén" en los orígenes del sionismo*. Barcelona: Tirocinio.
Roussi, Soufiane & Ana Stulić. 2006. Annotation of documents for electronic editing of Judeo-Spanish texts: Problems and solutions. In Isabella Ties (ed.), *LULCL 2005: Proceedings of the Lesser Used Languages and Computer Linguistics Conference (Bolzano, 27th-28th October 2005)*, 265–280. Bolzano: Accademia Europea Bolzano.
Roussi, Soufiane & Ana Stulić. 2013. Métadescription apliquée à l'étude des sources Séfarades de Vienne: Le cas des textes de Yisrael B. Hayim. In Michael Studemund-Halévy, Christian Liebl & Ivana Vučina Simović (eds.), *Sefarad an der Donau: La lengua y literatura de los sefardíes en tierras de los Habsburgo*, 425–436. Barcelona: Tirocinio.
Şahin Reis, Seminur. 2005. Der Einfluss des Türkischen auf das Judenspanische anhand von Analysen judenspanischer Texte. *Neue Romania* 34 (=*Judenspanisch* IX). 261–279.
Salvador Plans, Antonio. 2003. Consideraciones sobre la grafía romanceada judeoespañola. *Neue Romania* 28 (=*Judenspanisch* VII). 31–51.
Sánchez Pérez, María. 2014. *Prensa sefardí de pasatiempo en Salónica*. Barcelona: Tirocinio.
Sánchez, Rosa. 2008a. "¡Tú ya sabes hablar la habla que hablan los 'cilivizados'!" – La lengua como marca de cambio generacional en *El angustiador*. In Hilary Pomeroy, Christopher J. Pountain, and Elena Romero (eds.), *Proceedings of the Fourteenth British Conference on Judeo-Spanish Studies, 26–28 June 2006*, 203–211. London: Department of Hispanic Studies, Queen Mary University of London.
Sánchez, Rosa. 2008b. Marcas de oralidad en *El hacino imaginado*, traducción judeoespañola de *Le malade imaginaire*. In *La oralidad fingida: Descripción y traducción. Teatro, cómic y medios audio visuales*, 135–155. Frankfurt–Madrid: Vervuert–Iberoamericana.
Sánchez, Rosa. 2010. Un personaje prototípico del teatro sefardí oriental: Acerca de la galiparla del franquito. In Paloma Díaz-Mas and María Sánchez Pérez (eds.), *Los sefardíes ante los retos del mundo contemporáneo: Identidad y mentalidades*, 87–97. Madrid: CSIC.
Sánchez, Rosa. 2011. El *belagí* de Alberto Moljo: Una lectura lingüística. In Rena Molho (ed.), *Satirical texts in Judeo-Spanish by and about the Jews of Thessaloniki. Proceedings of the 4th International Conference on Judeo-Spanish Studies*, 269–283. Thessaloniki: Ets Ahaim Foundation.
Sánchez, Rosa. 2012. Consideraciones para la forja de un registro metateatral judeoespañol. In Yvette Bürki, Manuela Cimeli & Rosa Sánchez (eds.), *Lengua, llengua, llingua, lingua, langue. Encuentros filológicos (ibero)románicos. Estudios en homenaje a la profesora Beatrice Schmid*, 390–407. Munich: Peniope.
Sánchez, Rosa. 2013. Reflejos lingüísticos de la sociedad sefardí ante la modernidad: Los diálogos humorísticos publicados en la prensa. In Rosa Sánchez and Marie-Christine Bornes Varol (eds.), *La presse judéo-espagnole, support et vecteur de la modernité*, 181–200. Istanbul: Libra.
Sánchez, Rosa. 2014. ¿Variación lingüística en el teatro de Laura Papo? In Yvette Bürki and Elena Romero (eds.), *La lengua sefardí: Aspectos lingüísticos, literarios y culturales*, 195–208. Berlin: Frank and Timme.
Sánchez, Rosa. 2015. *Los géneros dialogales judeoespañoles: Oralidad fingida y variación lingüística*. Barcelona: Tirocinio.

Sánchez, Rosa & Marie-Christine Bornes-Varol (eds.). 2013. *La presse judéo-espagnole, support et vecteur de la modernité*. Istanbul: Libra.

Sánchez, Rosa & Katharina Wieland. 2012. *Na* y *ec/eg* en un corpus de narrativa y teatro. In Yvette Bürki and Carsten Sinner (eds.), *Tiempo y espacio y relaciones espacio-temporales en judeoespañol*, 115–124. Munich: Peniope.

Sanchis i Ferrer, Pau & Nikola Vuletić. 2008. La construcció *cali que* + subjuntiu de l'espanyol sefardita: De l'aragonés i el català als Balcans. *Alazet* 20. 253–261.

Santa Puche, Salvador. N.d. Una lengua en el infierno: El judeo-español en los campos de exterminio. *Tonos digital* 5, disponible en línea: [https://www.um.es/tonosdigital/znum5/estudios/J-infierno.htm, accessed 20/9/2015]

Şaul, Mahir (ed.). 2013. *Judeo-Spanish in the time of clamoring nationalisms*. Istanbul: Libra.

Schlumpf, Sandra. 2009. 'Si savías portanto cuánto vos amo!' – Acerca de las condicionales irreales en judeoespañol. In *Actas del VIII Encuentro Hispano-Suizo de Filólogos Noveles*. Basilea: Institut für Iberoromanistik der Universität Basel 2009 (=*Acta Romanica Basiliensia* 21). 13–28.

Schlumpf, Sandra. 2012a. Los tiempos verbales en las oraciones condicionales en judeoespañol moderno. In Yvette Bürki and Carsten Sinner (eds.), *Tiempo y espacio y relaciones espacio-temporales en judeoespañol*, 35–50. Munich: Peniope.

Schlumpf, Sandra. 2012b. Notas sobre las oraciones pseudocondicionales en judeoespañol moderno. In Yvette Bürki, Manuela Cimeli & Rosa Sánchez (eds.), *Lengua, llengua, llingua, lingua, langue. Encuentros filológicos (ibero)románicos. Estudios en homenaje a la profesora Beatrice Schmid*, 408–419. Munich: Peniope.

Schlumpf, Sandra. 2014. Las oraciones condicionales concesivas y sus formas de expresión en judeoespañol moderno. In Yvette Bürki and Elena Romero (eds.), *La lengua sefardí: Aspectos lingüísticos, literarios y culturales*, 209–235. Berlin: Frank and Timme.

Schlumpf, Sandra. 2015. Acerca de la expresión de la condicionalidad y de la concesividad en judeoespañol moderno escrito. *Sefarad* 75. 103–161.

Schmid, Beatrice. 2006a. *Ladino (Judenspanisch) – eine Diasporasprache*. Bern: Schweizerische Akademie der Geistes- und Sozialwissenschaften [Akademievorträge, Heft XV].

Schmid, Beatrice. 2006b. La transcripción de datos judeoespañoles de fuentes aljamiadas. In *Trascrivere la lingua: Dalla filologia all'analisi conversazionale / transcribir la lengua: De la filología al análisis conversacional*, 63–83. Bern et al.: Peter Lang.

Schmid, Beatrice. 2007. De Salónica a Ladinokomunita. El judeoespañol desde los umbrales del siglo XX hasta la actualidad. In *Ecologia lingüística i desaparició de llengües*, 9–33. Castelló de la Plana: Universitat Jaume I.

Schmid, Beatrice. 2010. 'Por el adelantamiento de la nación': Las ideas lingüísticas de Abraham A. Cappon. In Paloma Díaz-Mas and María Sánchez Pérez (eds.), *Los sefardíes ante los retos del mundo contemporáneo: identidad y mentalidades*, 99–112. Madrid: CSIC.

Schmid, Beatrice & Ivette Bürki. 2000. *'El hacino imaginado': Comedia de Molière en version judeoespañola. Edición del texto aljamiado, estudio y glosario* (=*Acta Romanica Basiliensia* 11). Basel: Romanischen Seminars der Universität Basel.

Schwarzwald, Ora (Rodrigue). 2002. Judaeo-Spanish Studies. In Martin Goodman (ed.), *The Oxford handbook of Jewish studies*, 572–600. Oxford: Oxford University Press.

Schwarzwald, Ora (Rodrigue). 2005. Spelling and orthography in Ladino translations from the 16th century on. *Pe'amim: Studies in Oriental Jewry* 101–102. 173–185. (Hebrew.)

Schwarzwald, Ora (Rodrigue). 2006–2007. Le style du *Me'am Lo'ez*: Une tradition linguistique. *Yod: Revue des études Hébraïques et Juives* 11–12. 77–112.

Schwarzwald, Ora (Rodrigue). 2008a. *A dictionary of the Ladino Passover haggadot*. Jerusalem: Magnes. (Hebrew.)
Schwarzwald, Ora (Rodrigue). 2008b. Between East and West: Differences between Ottoman and North African Judeo-Spanish haggadoth. *El Presente* 2. 223–241.
Schwarzwald, Ora (Rodrigue). 2010a. On the Jewish nature of medieval Spanish biblical translations: Linguistic differences between medieval and post-exilic Spanish translations of the Bible. *Sefarad* 70. 117–140.
Schwarzwald, Ora (Rodrigue). 2010b. Two sixteenth century Ladino prayer books for women. *European Judaism* 43. 37–51.
Schwarzwald, Ora (Rodrigue). 2011. Lexical variations in two Ladino prayer books for women. In Winfried Busse and Michael Studemund-Halévy (eds.), *Lexicología y lexicografía judeoespañolas*, 53–86. Bern: Peter Lang.
Schwarzwald, Ora (Rodrigue). 2012a. *Seder nashim: A 16th century prayer book for women in Ladino, Saloniki (Sidur para mujeres en Ladino, Salónica, siglo XVI)*. Jerusalem: Ben Zvi Institute.
Schwarzwald, Ora (Rodrigue). 2012b. Linguistic features of a sixteenth century women's Ladino prayer book: The language used for instructions and prayers. In Hilary Pomeroy, Chris J. Pountain & Elena Romero (eds.), *Selected papers from the Fifteenth Conference on Judeo-Spanish Studies*, 247–260. London: Queen Mary University of London.
Schwarzwald, Ora (Rodrigue). 2012c. The relationship between Ladino liturgical texts and Spanish bibles. In Jonathan Decter & Arturo Prats (eds.), *The Hebrew Bible in fifteenth-century Spain. Exegesis, literature, philosophy, and the arts*, 223–244. Leiden-Boston: Brill.
Schwarzwald, Ora (Rodrigue). 2013a. Judeo-Spanish influence on Hebrew. In Geoffrey Khan et al. (eds.), *Encyclopedia of Hebrew language and linguistics*, vol. 2, 427–430. Leiden: Brill.
Schwarzwald, Ora (Rodrigue). 2013b. Judeo-Spanish loanwords. In Geoffrey Khan et al. (eds.), *Encyclopedia of Hebrew language and linguistics*, vol. 2, 430–432. Leiden: Brill.
Schwarzwald, Ora (Rodrigue) & Nivi Gomel. 2001. Judeo-Spanish in Hebrew literature. *Ladinar* 2. 59–94. (Hebrew.)
Selony, Lisya & Yusuf Sarfati. 2013. (Trans)national language ideologies and family language practices: A life history inquiry of Judeo-Spanish in Turkey. *Language Policy* 12(1). 7–26.
Sephiha, Haïm Vidal. 1973. *Le ladino, judéo-espagnol calque: Deutéronome, versions de Constantinople (1547) et de Ferrara (1553)*. Paris: Centre de Recherches Hispaniques.
Sephiha, Haïm Vidal. 1976. Le judéo-fragnol, dernier-né du djudezmo. *Bulletin de la Société Linguistique de Paris* 71. 31–36.
Sephiha, Haïm Vidal. 2002. Le judéo-espagnol à Auschwitz. In Rafael Gatenio (ed.), *Judeo Espaniol: A Jewish language in search of its people*, 153. Thessaloniki: Ets Ahaim Foundation.
Sephiha, Haïm Vidal. 2003. Djudeo-espanyol (espanyolit i ladino): Una grafiya kolay i universal. *Neue Romania* 28 (=*Judenspanisch* VII). 21–25.
Seroussi, Edwin. 2002. *Cantor Isaac Algazi: Sweet singer of Israel: Ottoman Jewish music from the early twentieth century*. Mainz: Wergo.
Seroussi, Edwin & Rivka Havassy. 2008. *An early twentieth-century troubador: The historical recordings of Haim Effendi of Turkey*. Jerusalem: Jewish Music Reseach Centre, The Hebrew University of Jerusalem.
Shafran, Omer. 2014. Topics in the language of Shemuel De Medina's 16th-century rabbinical responsa: *Hoshen mishpat*, responsum 5. *Massorot* 16–17. 239–278. (Hebrew.)
Shaul, Moshe. 2003. Grafía del ladino al uzo de *Aki Yerushalayim*. *Neue Romania* 28 (= *Judenspanisch* VII). 7–11.

Shaul, Moshe. 2004. El djudeo-espanyol en Israel i la aktividad en este kampo de la emision djudeo-espanyola de Kol Israel. *Neue Romania* 12 (= *Judenspanisch* I). 271–280.

Shaul, Moshe. 2006. La Autoridad Nasionala del Ladino. *Ladinar* 4. 185–188.

Shaul, Moshe. 2007. Kontribusion de la revista *Aki Yerushalayim* al renovamiento de la kreasion literaria en ladino. In Pablo Martín Asuero and Karen Gerson Şarhon (eds.), *Ayer y hoy de la prensa en judeoespañol. Cuadernos del Bósforo* VII, 91–96. Istanbul: Isis.

Šmid, Katja. 2012. *El* Séfer Méšec betí, *de Eliézer Papo: Ritos y costumbres sabáticas de los sefardíes de Bosnia*. Madrid: Consejo Superior de Investigaciones Científicas.

Soler, Natividad Peramos. 2009. El judeo-español en Salónica: Influencias lingüísticas. Universidad de La Laguna PhD. dissertation.

Stankiewicz, Edward. 1964. Balkan and Slavic elements in the Judeo-Spanish of Yugoslavia. In Lucy S. Dawidowicz et al (ed.), *For Max Weinreich on his seventieth birthday*, 229–236. New York: De Gruyter.

Studemund(-Halévy), Michael (ed.). 2003. *Ladino kerido mio. Judenspanische Literatur im 20. Jahrhundert*. Munich–Hamburg: Dölling–Galitz Verlag.

Studemund(-Halévy), Michael (ed.). 2010. *Rinyo o el amor salvaje: Una obra teatral en judeoespañol de Abraham Galante publicada en 1906*. Barcelona: Tirocinio.

Studemund(-Halévy), Michael (ed.). 2011. 'Afilu ke es haham se le menea': Placer sexual y juegos de palabras en judeoespañol. In Winfried Busse and Michael Studemund-Halévy eds.), *Lexicología y lexicografía judeoespañola, 221–276*. Bern: Peter Lang.

Studemund(-Halévy), Michael (ed.). 2013. Le judéo-espagnol en caractères cyrilliques. In Soufiane Roussi & Ana Stulić-Etchevers (eds.), *Recensement, analyse et traitement numérique des sources écrites pour les études séfarades*, 35–45. Bordeaux: Presses Universitaires de Bordeaux.

Studemund-Halévy, Michael & Gaelle Collin. 2007. *Entre dos mundos. Catálogo de los impresos búlgaros en lengua sefardí (siglos XIX y XX)*. Barcelona: Tirocinio.

Studemund-Halévy, Michael, with the collaboration of Gaëlle Collin. 2014. *La boz de Bulgaria*, vol. I: *Bukyeto de tekstos en lingua sefardí: Livro de lektura para estudyantes: Teatro*. Barcelona: Tirocinio.

Studemund-Halévy, Michael & Ana Stulić. 2015. *La boz de Bulgaria*, vol 2: *Bukyeto de tekstos en lingua sefardí: Livro de lektura para estudyantes: Novelas*. Barcelona: Tirocinio.

Stulić, Ana, Ivana Vučina & Gorana Zečević. 2003. Quince canciones judeoespañolas provenientes de Sarajevo y Salónica: Análisis fonético y fonológico. *Res Diachronicae* 2. 380–396.

Stulić-Etchevers, Ana. 2008. Analyse diachronique de *siendo (que)* judéo-espagnol: approche litérale. *Bulletin Hispanique* 110. 309–342.

Symeonidis, Haralambos. 2002. *Das Judenspanische von Thessaloniki*. Bern: Peter Lang.

Tabares Plasencia, Encarnación, Carsten Sinner & Elia Hernández Socas. 2012. La expresión del tiempo en *El trujamán* de Michael Papo (Viena 1884). In Yvette Bürki and Carsten Sinner (eds.), *Tiempo y espacio y relaciones espacio-temporales en judeoespañol*, 63–76. Munich: Peniope.

Twardowska, Aleksandra. 2013. The characterization of male names among the Sephardi Jews in Sarajevo. In Andrej Katni, Izabela Olszewska & Aleksandra Twardowska (eds.), *Ashkenazim and Sephardim: A European perspective*, 190–210. Frankfurt am Main: Peter Lang.

Valentín del Barrio & María del Carmen. 2012. Comportamientos lingüísticos de la mujer moderna en el teatro costumbrista sefardí (1900–1930). *eHumanista: Journal of Iberian Studies* 20. 384–401.

Valladares Ruiz, Patricia. 2007. Los dos melicios: traducción literaria y afiliaciones identitarias en la novelística sefardí del Levante. *Hispania* 90(2). 355–366.
Varol(-Bornes), Marie-Christine. 2002a. Les temps du passé en judéo-espagnol (Salonique et Istanbul), une situation linguistique complexe. In Raphael Gatenio (ed.), *Judeo Espaniol: A Jewish language in search of its people*, 139–151. Thessalonica: Ets Ahaim Foundation.
Varol(-Bornes), Marie-Christine. 2002b. Normalisation orthographique du judéo-espagnol. In D. Caubet et al. (ed.), *Codification des langues de France*, 383–398. Paris: L'harmattan.
Varol(-Bornes), Marie-Christine. 2003. Normalización gráfica del judeoespañol: ¿Por qué? y ¿para quién? *Neue Romania* 28 (=*Judenspanisch* VII). 87–104.
Varol(-Bornes), Marie-Christine. 2003–2004. L'autobiographie en judéo-espagnol: La difficile affirmation du sujet entre tradition et modernité. *Yod. Revue des Études Hébraiques et Juives* 9. 231–60.
Varol(-Bornes), Marie-Christine. 2008. *Le judéo-espagnol vernaculaire d'Istanbul*. Bern: Peter Lang.
Varol(-Bornes), Marie-Christine. 2009. Morphosyntactical calques in Judeo-Spanish: Mechanisms and limits. In David M. Bunis (ed.), *Languages and literatures of Sephardic and Oriental Jewry*, *260–273. Jerusalem: Misgav Yerushalayim and Bialik Institute.
Varol(-Bornes), Marie-Christine. 2010a. Un erudito entre dos lenguas: El 'castellano' de Hayim Bejarano en el prólogo a su refranero glosado. In Paloma Díaz-Mas & María Sánchez Pérez (eds.), *Los sefardíes ante los retos del mundo contemporáneo: Identidad y mentalidades*, 113–127. Madrid: CSIC.
Varol(-Bornes), Marie-Christine. 2010b. *Le Proverbier glosé de Mme Flore Gueron Yeschua (Judéo-espagnol – Bulgarie)*. Paris: Geuthner.
Varol(-Bornes), Marie-Christine. 2011a. Les verbes empruntés au turc en judéo-espagnol (Bulgarie). In Winfried Busse and Michael Studemund-Halévy (eds.) *Lexicología y lexicografía judeoespañolas*, 87–105. Bern: Peter Lang.
Varol(-Bornes), Marie-Christine. 2011b. De l'identité dans la langue à l'identification d'équivalences interlinguistiques en situation de contact: Les processus et les limites de l'emprunt en judéo-espagnol (Turquie). In Marie-Christine Varol-Bornes (ed.), *Chocs de langues et de cultures? Un discours de la méthode*, 77–109. Vincennes: University.
Varol(-Bornes), Marie-Christine. 2012. Aznographie judéo-espagnole. In Yvette Bürki, Manuela Cimeli & Rosa Sánchez (eds.), *Lengua, llengua, llingua, lingua, langue. Encuentros filológicos (ibero)románicos. Estudios en homenaje a la profesora Beatrice Schmid*, 60–73. Munich: Peniope.
Varol, Marie-Christine & Masha Itzhaki. 2006. Remèdes miraculeux – étude d'un manuscrit en judéo-espagnol et hébreu du fonds Abraham Danon. *Neue Romania* 35 (=*Judenspanisch* X). 191–215.
Vàrvaro, Alberto. 2012. Il giudeo-spagnuolo prima dell'espulsione del 1492. In Raquel Suárez García & Ignacio Ceballos Viro (eds.), *Aljamías in memoriam Álvaro Galmés de Fuentes y Iacob M. Hassán*, 233–252. Gijón: Trea.
Vàrvaro, Alberto & Laura Minervini. 2007. Orígenes del judeoespañol: Textos. *Revista de historia de la lengua española* 2. 147–172.
Von Schmädel, Stephanie. 2007. *El konde i el djidyo: Istoria muy interesante*, Shem Tov Semo: Textedition. *Judenspanisch* 11. 210–354.
Von Schmädel, Stephanie. 2011. *El Correo Sefaradi de Viena* o el judeoespañol en letras latinas en un periódico sionista sefardí de entreguerras. *Neue Romania* 40 (=*Judenspanisch* XIII). 19–42.

Von Schmädel, Stephanie. 2012. La preposición *sovre* en textos judeoespañoles de Viena (s. XIX). In Yvette Bürki & Carsten Sinner (eds.), *Tiempo y espacio y relaciones espacio-temporales en judeoespañol*, 77–88. Munich: Peniope.

Vučina Simović, Ivana. 2009. El papel de la mujer sefardí en el mantenimiento/desplazamiento del judeoespañol en el territorio de la antigua Yugoslavia. *El Presente* 3. 253–270.

Vučina Simović, Ivana. 2011. El léxico 'lingüícida' vs. 'favorecedor' en el proceso de mantenimiento/desplazamiento del judeoespañol de Oriente. In Winfried Busse and Michael Studemund-Halévy (eds.), *Lexicología y lexicografía judeoespañolas*, 143–164. Bern: Peter Lang.

Vučina Simović, Ivana. 2013a. Los sefardíes ante su lengua: Los esperancistas de Sarajevo. In Michael Studemund-Halévy, Christian Liebl & Ivana Vučina Simović (eds.), *Sefarad an der Donau. La lengua y literatura de los sefardíes en tierras de los Habsburgo*, 341–360. Barcelona: Tirocinio.

Vučina Simović, Ivana. 2013b. Sources écrites séfarades sur le territoire de l'ex-Yougoslavie: Classification dans une perspective sociolinguistique. In Soufiane Roussi & Ana Stulić-Etchevers (eds.), *Recensement, analyse et traitement numérique des sources écrites pour les études séfarades*, 47–68. Bordeaux: Presses Universitaires de Bordeaux.

Vučina Simović, Ivana. 2013c. The Sephardim and Ashkenazim in Sarajevo: From social, cultural and linguistic divergence to convergence. *Transversal* 13(2). 41–64.

Vuletić, Nicola. 2011. Sovre el léksiko turko en el djudeo-espanyol de Bosnia: Muevas propuestas. In Winfried Busse and Michael Studemund-Halévy (eds.), *Lexicología y lexicografía judeoespañolas*, 107–119. Bern: Peter Lang.

Vuletić, Nicola. 2012. El perfecto compuesto en el judeoespañol de Esmirna (Izmir) hoy. In Yvette Bürki and Carsten Sinner (eds.), *Tiempo y espacio y relaciones espacio-temporales en judeoespañol*, 51–62. Munich: Peniope.

Weis, Dorothee. 2000. La agonía del judeoespañol y la identidad sefardita: Un estudio sociolingüístico en Salónica. *Mediterranean Language Review* 12. 144–191.

Zečević-Krneta, Gorana. 2013. Le cas de la forme *fin* en judéo-espagnol balkanique. In Soufiane Roussi and Ana Stulić-Etchevers (eds.), *Recensement, analyse et traitement numérique des sources écrites pour les études séfarades*, 273–286. Bordeaux: Presses Universitaires de Bordeaux.

Jürg Fleischer
Western Yiddish and Judeo-German

1 Introduction

Western Yiddish is the vernacular originally spoken by western Ashkenazic Jews, mostly in German-speaking surroundings. Beginning in the late 18th century and considerably accelerating during the 19th century, it was gradually given up, primarily in favor of German varieties, due to the general process of cultural assimilation into non-Jewish society. It can be differentiated from German, not only by the fact that it contains vocabulary items of Hebrew or Aramaic origin (see Section 3.3), but also by the fact that there are structural differences with respect to (historical) phonology, as well as grammar (see Section 3.2). Some of the original features of Western Yiddish, particularly Semitic-origin vocabulary items (with a western Ashkenazic pronunciation), were retained in the German varieties spoken by Jews that replaced Western Yiddish, as well as in some non-Jewish German varieties with which it was in contact (see Section 2.4).

It is necessary to state that there is no terminological consensus in the academic literature (see Section 1.1.2). Different scholars may understand different linguistic entities when using the terms *West(ern) Yiddish* (or its equivalents, such as Yiddish *mayrev-yidish, mayrevdik yidish*, German *Westjiddisch*, etc.) or *Judeo-German* (or its equivalents, such as *Judaeo-German, Jewish German*, Yiddish *yidish-daytsh*, German *Jüdisch-Deutsch, Judendeutsch*, etc.). In the terminological approach taken here, "Western Yiddish" is used to designate a Jewish variety that differs from coterritorial German, in terms not only of vocabulary but of linguistic structure. In contrast, a variety spoken by Jews containing special vocabulary, but not otherwise differing from (local) German, is designated "Judeo-German." Since Western Yiddish is more distant from German, particular attention is given to its characteristics in this chapter.

The concept of "Western Yiddish" is controversial for several reasons. Although the name "Western Yiddish" was established relatively early in the academic literature (see Section 1.1.2), some scholars would deny altogether the (former) existence of a linguistic entity related to (Eastern) Yiddish, and at the same time different enough from German to justify the designation "(Western) Yiddish" rather than, for example, "Judeo-German." Even if the concept of a separate western Ashkenazic linguistic entity is accepted, however, what exactly belongs to it and which type of source is best when it comes to linguistic description and analysis remains to be discussed. Furthermore, its presumed origin (particularly with respect to the differentiation from German) is a matter of (sometimes fierce) debate. Of course, the intricate question of whether we are dealing with a "language" or a mere "dialect" is linked to these terminological issues. Given that "language" and "dialect" are notoriously difficult to define, the present survey tries to avoid these notions. However, one aim is to describe the characteristic traits of Western Yiddish that set it apart from (coterritorial) German, regardless of whether these traits are viewed as significant enough to speak of a "language."

To some extent, the widely diverging views of Western Yiddish are due to the fact that, as with other Jewish varieties, data are scarce (see Section 1.4). There are many Medieval and Early Modern records written by western Ashkenazic Jews in the Hebrew alphabet, but their relation to the vernacular spoken by this population is difficult to assess. As to the dialects, Western Yiddish disappeared in many regions without having been recorded by any of its speakers, let alone by professional linguists. In the pre-final and final phase of its existence, its social status was usually very low, both inside and outside the Jewish communities. Much of its linguistic and social history has to be inferred, giving way to substantially differing assessments and opinions.

1.1 Names

"Western Yiddish" is a purely academic term that was probably never used by its speakers to refer to their vernacular. Therefore, it makes sense to distinguish between the designations used outside and inside the academic discourse.

1.1.1 Non-academic names

In the 19th and beginning of the 20th century, Western Yiddish, as well as Judeo-German, was most often referred to as "Jewish German" (*Jüdisch-Deutsch*); note, however, that this designation was also used for the rendering of (Standard) German in the Hebrew alphabet (see Section 2.2). Designations such as "Jewish-German/German-Jewish dialect" (*jüdisch-deutscher/deutsch-jüdischer Dialekt*) were also used (see Weinberg 1981: 254–256). In the written sphere, according to Weinreich ([1973] 2008: 315, A302–303), some attestations of the name "Jewish" as a designation for the language appear as early as the 17th century, although in many instances it is difficult to tell whether this designation relates to the language only, to the alphabet, or to the speakers. For a particular type of formulaic language used to translate religious texts, the term *taytsh* (originally meaning 'German') was used (Weinreich [1973] 2008: 316–317, A302–303).

Since the late 18th century, leading figures of German Jewry who promoted assimilation used the French-derived *Jargon* as a derogative designation for Western Yiddish (Weinreich [1973] 2008: 321–322, A309; see Section 2.4 for respective quotes). To some extent, this designation was also used by speakers, its derogative origin notwithstanding.

A particular register used by western Ashkenazic Jews, containing an especially high number of Hebrew-derived lexical items to mask contents in the presence of persons not having access to this lexical stock, was sometimes designated by a name meaning "Hebrew" (see Section 2.4). Although this designation was normally not used for the regular spoken dialect, outsiders having limited insight into the different Jewish varieties might have mistaken this special register for the common Western Yiddish vernacular.

1.1.2 Academic names

The debate on the nature of "Western Yiddish" and "Judeo-German" is reflected in the differing terminologies. Scholars working within what Beider (2013) calls the "Judeo-Centric Approach" use (and sometimes explicitly argue for) names not containing "German," whereas scholars working within the "Germanistic approach" often, though not necessarily, prefer names for which this is the case.

It is appropriate to recall, first, that the language name *Yiddish*, being a transcription of the (Eastern) Yiddish adjective *yidish* 'Jewish', as well as its equivalents in other languages (German *jiddisch/Jiddisch*, French *yid(d)ic/sh*, Russian *idiš*, etc.), is quite young, even when referring to Eastern Yiddish. According to Weinreich ([1973] 2008: 322, A309–310; see also Weinberg 1981: 262–263), in English academic literature *Yiddish*, primarily meaning the language spoken by eastern Ashkenazic Jews, seems to be established by the end of the 19th century, although names of the type *Judeo-German*, which were the usual designation before, continue to be used. In academic literature written in German, as discussed by Weinreich ([1973] 2008: 322) and Weinberg (1981: 263–265), *Jiddisch/jiddisch*, replacing *Jüdisch-Deutsch/jüdisch-deutsch*, *Judendeutsch/judendeutsch*, etc., was established around the time of World War I, with Solomon (Salomo) Birnbaum (1891–1989) playing the most important role in the propagation of this name. Birnbaum, according to himself, was the first to use *jiddisch* for Eastern Yiddish in a 1913 series of articles entitled *Jiddische Dichtung* (Birnbaum [1974] 1997: 27, 165; see also Weinberg 1981: 263), after which he consistently used

Jiddisch/jiddisch, e.g., in his influential *[Praktische] Grammatik der Jiddischen Sprache*, whose preface is dated 1915 (see Birnbaum 1918: 10).

Shortly after the establishment of the new name for Eastern Yiddish, it was extended; first, to designate what still remained of the dialects spoken by western Ashkenazic Jews at that point in time. Mieses (1919) uses *westjiddisch/ Westjiddisch* in an explication of abbreviations ("*westjd. = westjiddisch, die ehemalige Mundart der ethnographisch deutschen Juden*"; Mieses 1919: 4) and in his text ("*im einstigen Westjiddisch*"; Mieses 1919: 17 = Mieses 1924: 18). At about the same time, Prilutski (1920: 85) speaks of *mayrevyidish*. According to Weinreich ([1953] 1958: 158, note 1; see also Weinreich [1923] 1993: 19), Mieses and Prilutski introduced the term. At the same time, Weill (1920a, 1920b, 1920c, 1921) uses *Yiddish* for a very western variety in his collection of vocabulary entitled *Le yidisch alsacien-lorrain*. Second, with some lag in time, *Yiddish* was also used to designate the language of written and printed records of the High Middle Ages and Early Modern period, though usually without the "west(ern)" specification (e.g., in Jakob Meitlis' 1933 monograph *Das Ma'assebuch: Seine Entstehung und Quellengeschichte; zugleich ein Beitrag zur Einführung in die altjiddische Agada*).

West(ern) Yiddish, or simply *Yiddish* (and its equivalents in other languages), referring to western dialects or the language of the older records, quickly spread, even before the Holocaust. For example, Jechiel Fischer/Bin-Nun, whose primary interest is Eastern Yiddish, talks of the "*Spaltung des Jiddischen in zwei Zweige, den ostjiddischen und den westjiddischen*" (Fischer/Bin Nun [1936] 1973: 47). In 1953, Max Weinreich published his seminal article *Roshe-prokim vegn mayrevdikn yidish*, published first in the periodical *Yidishe Shprakh* with the English parallel title *Outlines of Western Yiddish*, an appendixed version of which appeared in 1958. It is with the publication of this article, at the very latest, that the name *West(ern) Yiddish*[1] seems to have been established and was used by many other scholars working in the field (see Weinberg 1981: 274).

After the Holocaust, the Hebraist Werner Weinberg (1915–1997), who was born in the Westphalian town of Rheda and was familiar with the remnants of Western Yiddish still extant in the first decades of the 20th century in this relatively rural surrounding, was the first to take issue with this terminology. He

---

1 To be more precise, Max Weinreich preferred *Western Yiddish* (*mayrevdik yidish*) over *West Yiddish* (*mayrev-yidish*), because the former is "more description than term [*mer bashraybung vi termin*]" (Weinreich [1953] 1958: 163; the same is already stated by Weinreich 1940: 37; see also Weinberg 1981: 273–274). Most authors would only use one of these terms. It seems that in the literature written in English, Yiddish, and French, *Western Yiddish*, *mayrevdik yidish* or *yid(d)is/ch occidental*, respectively, are more widespread, whereas in the German literature *Westjiddisch* (rather than *westliches Jiddisch*) is the established term.

published his important collection of vocabulary under the title *Die Reste des Jüdischdeutschen* (1973 [1969]) and justifies his use of *Jüdischdeutsch* extensively (Weinberg 1973: 13–15). Later on, in an article specifically devoted to the question of the appropriate name, he suggests the re-introduction of *Jüdischdeutsch* instead of *Westjiddisch* because, in addition to the fact that the speakers used the designation *Jüdischdeutsch*, not *Jiddisch* (see Section 1.1.1), he does not see sufficient linguistic differences from German (Weinberg 1981). The same holds for Simon's (1988) account (see also Simon 1991: 178). According to her, two analyzed western texts from the 16th and early 19th century are not distinct enough from German to justify the designation "Western Yiddish." Rather, the language represented by these documents has to be viewed as a sociolect of German; accordingly, it does not make sense to use *Yiddish* as a cover to refer to both Eastern Yiddish and Western Yiddish (Simon 1988: 213). Wexler (e.g., 2002), whose claim that Eastern Yiddish is a relexified Slavic language has met great skepticism, uses similar terminology: Since there is, according to him, no direct link between the western and the eastern linguistic entity spoken by Ashkenazic Jews, he uses "Ashkenazic German" to refer to the western entity.

Despite this criticism, in current research many scholars still use *(West[ern]) Yiddish*, which can be considered established. There is a possible terminological compromise: Since Jewish varieties undoubtedly existed that were different from (coterritorial) German in terms of linguistic structure, on the one hand, and German varieties spoken by Jews that were only different from German in some vocabulary items, on the other, it makes sense to name the former "Western Yiddish," etc., and the latter "Judeo-German," etc. (see, e.g., Matras 1991: 269; Fleischer 2005: 19–20, note 9). This distinction is made in the present chapter, but it must be kept in mind that the literature may differ in this respect.

1.2 Linguistic affiliation

As has partially become clear in the discussion above on the choice of an appropriate name for the vernacular originally spoken by western Ashkenazic Jews, the linguistic affiliation of this vernacular is a matter of debate (see Beider 2013). To begin with, most serious scholars would agree that Western Yiddish belongs to (West) Germanic. That agreed, there are still two more intricate questions where opinions sharply disagree, namely, whether Eastern and Western Yiddish form a genetic entity in the sense of historical linguistics, and to what extent Western Yiddish and German are different (and, if so, at what point in history that occured). Although these two questions are logically independent, one usually observes that scholars, seeing a clear pan-Yiddish entity, would also maintain that Western Yiddish is (and has for quite a long time been) independent from German, whereas scholars seeing no genetic unity between Eastern and Western Yiddish would also maintain that Western Yiddish is a German variety.

According to Max Weinreich's ([1973] 2008) influential *History of the Yiddish language*, Western and Eastern Yiddish form a genetic entity (i.e., they are seen as two branches of a family tree), and Yiddish has been substantially different from German since the beginnings of its existence. Since Eastern Yiddish, according to Weinreich, only came into being in the 13th/14th century, when the migration of Jews from German-speaking lands into the Polish-Lithuanian Commonwealth brought speakers of Yiddish into contact with Slavic languages, all older forms of Yiddish belong to Western Yiddish. In this sense, Weinreich ([1953] 1958: 161) formulated that Western Yiddish is "the older brother" in the Yiddish family tree. Other scholars, who stress the close affiliation to German, would maintain that we are dealing with a sociolect of German, spoken by a particular social group (see Section 1.1.2).

Depending on whether similarities between Western and Eastern Yiddish are viewed as significant indications of pan-Yiddish unity or not, the dating of these similarities can differ. On the one hand, Yiddish scholars of the 20th century, such as Solomon Birnbaum or Max Weinreich, would maintain that (Western) Yiddish was distinct from German from the very beginning, and therefore linguistic similarities between Eastern and Western Yiddish date early. Many philologists of the 19th century, on the other hand, claimed that Western Yiddish became different from German (and more similar to Eastern Yiddish) only as of the 17th century, when a certain re-migration of Eastern European Jews back to Western Europe began (see Weinberg 1981: 267; see Section 2.1).

1.3 Regions where language is/was spoken

The varieties spoken by western Ashkenazic Jews were more or less coterritorial with German, but sometimes reached out beyond the borders of the German-speaking territory. The oldest clearly dated and localized written texts displaying a larger amount of material originate from 14th century western Germany (see Section 1.4), but somewhat later documents can be traced to other regions as well. Written or printed Ashkenazic Hebrew-alphabet documents displaying a Germanic variety are also attested outside of the German-speaking territory: As witnessed by the very rich written culture beginning in the late 15th century, many important texts originate from northern Italy (see the catalogue by Turniansky & Timm 2003), where, however, the spoken language was subsequently given up. Beginning in the 17th century, Amsterdam became an important center of Yiddish printing.

However, the existence of Western Yiddish documents in a certain location does not exclude the possibility that a different spoken variety was used there. In Eastern Europe before the 19th century, there are hardly any texts displaying distinctly Eastern Yiddish forms (see Kerler 1999), although there can be no doubt that Eastern European Jews, at that point in time, spoke a distinctly eastern variety of Yiddish. In that sense, Western Yiddish was also widespread in Eastern European Yiddish printing before (and even into) the 19th century.

For the spoken dialects, given the early disappearance of Western Yiddish, it is difficult to determine its exact areal extension. It was spoken as far west as Switzerland, Alsace (in the south), and the Netherlands (in the north). Its eastern edge is problematic to establish; different suggestions exist as to exactly where the border between Western and Eastern Yiddish should be drawn, as demonstrated, for example, by maps 1–6 of the first volume of the *Language and Culture Atlas of Ashkenazic Jewry* (LCAAJ 1: 50–55). As a matter of fact, on a dialectal level, transitional zones between "Western" and "Eastern Yiddish," as described by Uriel Weinreich (1964) with respect to the Transcarpathians, probably also existed elsewhere. One example might be Burgenland Yiddish (cf. Schäfer 2017b). If a northern transitional area between Western and Eastern Yiddish (*nördliches Übergangsjiddisch* according to Katz 1983: 1023, Map 53.1) is counted as Western Yiddish, then its territory in the east reached beyond Kaliningrad/Königsberg, including the whole north of present-day Poland; further south, Wrocław/ Breslau, Ostrava/Ostrau, and Budapest still belong to the territory of Western Yiddish, whereas Cracow is Eastern Yiddish. Thus, to the east, Western Yiddish was spoken outside the German-speaking lands in the Czech and Slovak language area (where German, however, played a dominating role before the split-up of the Austro-Hungarian Empire) and in Hungary. In Hungary (as well as in some regions belonging to present-day Slovakia), Western Yiddish was superseded by Eastern Yiddish to some extent during the 19th century, due to immigration from the east and, at the same time, losing ground to Hungarian, thus giving rise to a complicated pattern of Western and Eastern Yiddish, both in terms of sociolinguistic distribution and the use of particular forms (see, e.g., Garvin 1965; Hutterer 1994).

1.4 Attestations and sources

Apart from glosses, short individual sentences, and benedictions, the first texts written by Ashkenazic Jews in a Germanic language are attested in the 14th century, the oldest dated example known so far being a text from Cologne (see Timm 2013). These texts are controversial when it comes to their linguistic interpretation. There is a rich Medieval and Early Modern Hebrew-letter literature, continuing into the 18th century, when the situation began to change and western Ashkenazic Hebrew-letter literature documents faded (see Section 2.2). As a spoken language, Western Yiddish continued to exist, at least on some fringes of its original area, especially in the southwest and east, into the 20th century (LCAAJ 1: 10); it also produced a limited body of literature. Southwestern Yiddish was documented by professional efforts, mostly in the second half of the 20th century.

Additional evidence can be found in non-Jewish sources. As of the 16th century and particularly in the 18th century, some linguistic comments, as well as attempts to document the language of German Jews, had been made. Especially in the 19th century, German authors depicted the direct speech of Jewish characters by using forms more or less close to Western Yiddish (see Schäfer 2017a). Although these non-Jewish sources are secondary, they are nevertheless valuable, since we lack other data.

As becomes clear from the discussion, contrary to Eastern Yiddish there exists no standardized Western Yiddish. This has the consequence that, when quoting Western Yiddish linguistic material, no standardized forms can be provided.[2]

1.5 Present-day status

At the beginning of the 21st century, Western Yiddish, designating a variety that differs from German, not only with respect to vocabulary but also in structural aspects, must be considered practically extinct. As discussed in Section 1.4, in most regions this state of affairs was already reached at the beginning of the 20th century, Southwestern Yiddish being an important exception. Most of the Southwestern Yiddish speakers interviewed in the second half of the 20th century were born in the last two decades of the 19th century. They were probably the last generation of speakers acquiring Western Yiddish as a native linguistic system. It seems likely that it was only in Alsace that Western Yiddish was passed on to the next generation on a relatively regular basis even in the 20th century.

Traces of the Jewish vernacular can still be found in Jewish communities not disrupted by the Holocaust (e.g., descendants of Swiss Yiddish speakers may still know vocabulary items going back to Western Yiddish; see Fleischer 2005: 21),

---

[2] For this reason, in the present chapter, examples that are quoted directly from an indicated source are usually provided in the orthography of the respective source (which is often determined by German spelling rules).

or, as already observed by Lowenstein (1969: 17–18), among emigrated speakers (see, e.g., Jochnowitz 2010). Nevertheless, it is clear that these traces are about to disappear.

2 Historical background

2.1 Speaker community: settlement, documentation

The early settlement history of Ashkenazic Jewry is not well documented. This is particularly unfortunate for the study of Yiddish, since various scholars favor different places of origin for Yiddish (see Jacobs 1994: 9–15): According to Max Weinreich ([1973] 2008), Yiddish originated in the west of the German-speaking area (in a territory encompassing the cities of Cologne, Aachen, Bonn, Koblenz, Mainz, Trier, Worms, Speyer, and Metz). Other scholars, however, favor a more eastern place of origin, particularly in the Bavarian area (e.g., Katz 1985; Eggers 1998), often pointing to Regensburg, with one of the most important Jewish communities at the time in question. The presence of many Jewish communities in the German-speaking lands, usually in cities, has been documented as far back as the High Middle Ages. In the 14th century, emigration towards Eastern Europe began, due not only to persecutions and expulsions connected to epidemics and the crusade movement, but also to favorable conditions in Poland, where Casimir III (king from 1333–1370) actively promoted the immigration of Jews to enhance trade and commerce. This development led to the division of Ashkenazic Jewry into a western and an eastern part.

While western Ashkenazic Jewish communities were usually found in the cities during the High Middle Ages, this changed to some extent in the following centuries: Especially in the west and south of the German-speaking area, Jewish settlements were now usually only allowed in rural areas, giving rise to a special form of rural Ashkenazic Jewry (German *Landjudentum*), with Jews usually working as traders of various goods or as craftsmen.

Beginning in the 17th century, a certain Ashkenazic re-emigration from east to west took place, due to a deterioration of conditions in Eastern Europe. One important event was the pogroms during the Cossack uprisings under Bohdan Xmel'nyc'kyj that began in 1648 and lasted for several years. This brought about more intense contact between eastern and western Ashkenazic Jews, with Eastern European religious authorities and erudition in general often held in high esteem. However, as of the 18th and particularly during the 19th century, ties between western and eastern Ashkenazic Jewry became less intense, due to the growing assimilation of western Ashkenazic Jews into German cultural and linguistic norms. From a social point of view, German Jewry was much more deeply affected by modernization and urbanization than the Christian population (see, e.g., Lowenstein 1976, 1980), which is one reason for the rapid disappearance of Western Yiddish.

2.2 Attestations and sources: Elaboration

For the linguistic study of Western Yiddish and Judeo-German, there are various types of (potential) sources, whose linguistic value and interpretation are often assessed quite differently. Hebrew-alphabet glosses written by western Ashkenazic Jews in a Germanic language are attested in the German-speaking lands as early as the High Middle Ages. It is highly likely that some glosses originate from Rashi, who lived mostly during the 11th century. The oldest dated textual witness displaying Rashi's Germanic glosses is dated 1190 (see Timm 1985, especially 55). Apart from some minor other sources, displaying individual sentences and benedictions (see Timm 2013: 426, with note 38), the oldest text known so far originates from 14th century Cologne (see Timm 2013). However, some of the older texts are differentiated from German virtually only by their use of the Hebrew alphabet (this holds especially for some of the earliest sources, including the Cologne text), and the debate as to whether we are dealing with "late Middle High German" (in Hebrew letters) or "Old Western Yiddish" is controversial (see Timm 1987: 357–386, Timm 2013: 433–435). Other, somewhat later documents display some features differing from German, not only in their use of Hebrew-derived vocabulary but also in terms of phonology (as far as it can be reconstructed from the sources) and of grammar.

The tradition of rendering a Germanic variety spoken by western Ashkenazic Jews with the Hebrew alphabet, in writing and later also in print, declined after the late 18th century, but continued until the 19th and even early 20th century. At that point in time, important changes began. As discussed by Lowenstein (1979), in the late 18th century different varieties were written and printed by means of the Hebrew alphabet:
- A supra-regional variety displaying distinctly Western features, called Old Literary Yiddish by Kerler (1999: 21; this corresponds to Weinreich's [(1973) 2008] *written language A*), was also used in Eastern Europe until the first half of the 19th century. It is attested in the west well into the 19th century, but its use declined beginning in the 18th century.
- Western Yiddish dialects were recorded in a few prints and manuscripts, mostly in plays by Maskilic writers who used Western Yiddish dialect

to characterize traditional, uneducated, and unenlightened Jews (see Section 4.2).
– Standard German was printed and written in the Hebrew alphabet, the most prominent example being, arguably, Moses Mendelssohn's translation of the Pentateuch (1783); the practice of rendering Standard German in the Hebrew alphabet was usually called *jüdisch-deutsch* (see Lowenstein 1979: 195–198; Weinberg 1981: 255–256).

However, during the 19th century, western Ashkenazic Jewish communities turned more and more to the Latin alphabet, and the language variety being written or printed in these communities was almost exclusively Standard German. Hebrew-letter documents disappeared gradually. Beginning in the second half of the 19th century, Western Yiddish dialects (and Judeo-German) were occasionally written in Latin script. An important example of this is Tendlau's collection of proverbs, entitled *Sprichwörter und Redensarten deutsch-jüdischer Vorzeit* (Frankfurt 1860), in which an attempt was made to document aspects of the traditions and customs of German Jews, which were already perceived as disappearing at that point in time.

One region in which Western Yiddish was not only retained for a relatively long period as a spoken language, but which also produced a sizable body of dialectal literature, particularly plays, is Alsace, where we find, from the end of the 19th century until the 1930s, more than a dozen Alsatian Yiddish texts (see Section 4.2). There seems to be no direct link from the pre- and early 19th century Hebrew-letter tradition (which is hardly documented for Alsace) to this late-19th century Latin-letter literature, which seems to have closer ties to German dialect literature.

Outside the Jewish communities, we find occasional remarks or longer descriptions in printed Latin-alphabet sources by Christian authors, or by Jewish converts to Christianity, on the language spoken by Jews in German-speaking lands. Especially interesting, from a linguistic point of view, is the publication of several grammars and/or dictionaries in the 18th century (see Katz 1983: 1025–1026; examples are Johann Heinrich Callenberg: *Jüdischteutsches Wörterbüchlein*, Halle 1736; Wilhelm Christian Just Chrysander: *Jüdisch-Teutsche Grammatik*, Leipzig/Wolfenbüttel 1750; Carl Wilhelm Friedrich: *Unterricht in der Judensprache und Schrift*, Prenzlau 1784).

Beginning in the 18th century, Jewish characters in German literature who were mostly (but not exclusively) depicted by Christian authors, who often (though not always) had an anti-Semitic agenda, were characterized by linguistic features deviating from Standard German (cf. Schäfer 2017a). An early example is Karl Borromäus Sessa's comedy *Unser Verkehr* (1813), while the most prominent examples are arguably various texts published under the pseudonym of Itzig Veitel Stern, e.g., *Gedichter Perobeln unn Schnoukes vun dien grausse Lamden der Jüdischkeit mit Nume Itzig Veitel Stern*, 1831 (for more on Itzig Veitel Stern, see Klepsch 2008). Latin-letter sources reached their peak in the 19th century. As already stated by Weinreich ([1953] 1958: 185–186), although these non-Jewish sources are secondary and, in the case of writers with an anti-Semitic motive, repellant, they are nevertheless valuable from a linguistic point of view, since we lack other data.

While Western Yiddish literacy disappeared during the 19th century (the relatively rich Alsatian literature being a remarkable exception), the variety continued to be spoken, especially in the periphery of its original area of extension (and could still be documented, mostly in the 20th century, through both written and audio recordings). During the fieldwork of the *Language and Culture Atlas of Ashkenazic Jewry* (LCAAJ), it soon became evident that most of the western informants for the atlas (with the exception of Alsace, Switzerland, and certain parts of southwestern Germany immediately bordering this area) "did not claim, and cannot objectively be said to have spoken Yiddish in the generation of our informants" (Lowenstein 1969: 17). Similarly, Guggenheim-Grünberg (1973: 9, 29 [map 1]) states that, for the time around 1900, full Yiddish dialect ("jiddische Vollmundart") was spoken only in the southwest. For one of these regions, Alsace, Zuckermann (1969) was able to publish a grammatical sketch, based on his field work for the LCAAJ. Besides the LCAAJ, different sources of Western Yiddish dialect material are extant: For Northwestern Yiddish, Aptroot (1991) provides an overview of the material; Reershemius (2007) provides an extensive linguistic analysis of a Northwestern Yiddish written text. Guggenheim-Grünberg (1961, 1966a) and Fleischer (2005) provide transliterations of Southwestern Yiddish dialect recordings from the Alemannic area.

In his survey, Max Weinreich ([1953] 1958: 162) states that it is best to begin research on Western Yiddish in the modern period, beginning in the late 18th century, since the forms to be found there are easier to interpret. In his view, the modern spoken material is of especially great value when assessing the linguistic position of Western Yiddish.

Given that, at the present point in time, Western Yiddish is practically extinct, secondary sources become all the more important. The Jewish vernacular, or rather the special register used for trade, has left its traces in some German varieties spoken by non-Jews that were in intense local contact with it. Vocabulary items and important sociolinguistic information could be collected in different regions (see Section 2.4). Quite generally, many Hebrew-origin lexemes are attested in local German dialects, as the survey by Stern (2000) shows. For example, *Massel* 'luck', going back to the Hebrew מזל,

is widespread in most German-speaking regions (see Stern 2000: 128–129). As demonstrated in many popular accounts (e.g., Althaus 2003), many lexemes ultimately going back to Hebrew and borrowed into German, due to contact with Western Yiddish and/or the special register, are now widespread in colloquial registers of German, e.g., *Maloche* 'hard work' (Althaus 2003: 124–125), deriving from the Hebrew מלאכה.

2.3 Phases in historical development

For Yiddish in general, Max Weinreich ([1973] 2008) distinguishes between *Early Yiddish* (pre-±1250), *Old Yiddish* (±1250–±1500), *Middle Yiddish* (±1500–±1700), and *New Yiddish* (±1750–present). For the more recent periods, Kerler (1999: 255–256) differentiates between Early New Yiddish (±1650/±1700–±1800) and New Yiddish proper (±1800–present). It is only in the Early New Yiddish and especially in the New Yiddish period that a hiatus between west and east emerges. As discussed by Kerler (1999), up until ca. 1700 no marked differences between documents printed in the west or east can be seen in the records (see Section 1.3); subsequently, however, forms closer to German emerged in the west, whereas, in the east, distinctly Eastern Yiddish forms gradually began to appear in print.

With this development, Ashkenazic Jewry was divided into a western and an eastern part, a development that was paralleled in other cultural spheres. While the New Yiddish period is marked in the east by a thriving written and printed Yiddish, ever more independent from older forms of written language, and intense literary activities, it is a period of decline for Western Yiddish, both on the written and the spoken level, as well as in terms of its social position (see Section 2.4). It is important to keep in mind that many Western Yiddish sources originate from a period in which Western Yiddish was already about to disappear.

2.4 Sociolinguistic description, community bilingualism, public functions

As with most Jewish communities, Hebrew played the central role in western Ashkenazic Jewry, community-internally, with respect to religious matters, as well as in other forms of erudition. This gave rise to diglossic patterns, with Western Yiddish occupying the position of the vernacular, not held in especially high esteem. It is safe to assume that some persons in western Ashkenazic communities had a very good knowledge of Hebrew (sometimes also Aramaic), while, at the same time, others did not have equal access to and mastery of it. Most importantly, while boys attended the traditional *kheyder* school type also known from Eastern Europe, in which learning Hebrew was at the very center, this was not the case for girls (see, e.g., Timm 2005: 11–12).

In the written sphere, authoritative religious texts were almost exclusively written in (Medieval) Hebrew, with Yiddish having hardly any "official" function. There are some systematic exceptions, however, where the vernacular was used. On the one hand, as discussed above, non-religious, Medieval, as well as Early Modern Jewish literature in Yiddish existed, edifying and entertaining. As to the religious sphere, certain texts, for example Bible paraphrases, were written in Yiddish, specifically to serve the needs of those illiterate in Hebrew. Often an archaic, formulaic, supra-regional style, usually called *taytsh*, was used here, which specifically served the need of translating authoritative texts. The so-called *Tsene-rene*, whose title derives from the Ashkenazic Hebrew pronunciation of Song of Songs 3:11 [צְאֶינָה וּרְאֶינָה בְּנוֹת צִיּוֹן] 'Go forth and see [O ye daughters of Zion]', is an important example of a Biblical paraphrase primarily addressed to women, as the title makes clear (see Neuberg 1999: 2). Also, in some instances, community records, e.g., *pinkasim*, were written in Yiddish.

As of the late 18th century, Western Yiddish was held in very low esteem by leading figures of German Jewry. It was viewed as an impediment to emancipation and assimilation, and it was thought that its abolition in favor of ("pure") German as a primary means of communication, both within and outside the Jewish communities, was a precondition to overcoming the deplorable situation of German Jewry. For instance, Anton Rée (1815–1891), reform pedagogue and director of a Jewish school in Hamburg, states (see Lässig 2000: 652–654 for a more thorough contextualization): "If a Jew wants to see the animosity towards him diminished, he has to expulse his dialect entirely, and if we want to reduce animosity against Jewry on the whole, we have to oust the latter from all its classes" (Rée 1844: 39; translation J.F.). Usually, Western Yiddish was referred to by the derogative *Jargon* (see Section 1.1.1). For instance, this designation is found once in the writings of Moses Mendelssohn ("I am afraid that this jargon has contributed not a little to the immorality of the common people [...]"; translation from Altmann 1973: 499). David Fränkel (1779–1865), director of the *Israelitische Haupt- und Freyschule* in Dessau, complains in 1804 that his uneducated co-religionists talk "in a miserable jargon, a mishmash of abject German, Hebrew, and Aramaic" (translation J.F.; quoted from Lässig 2000: 629). Due to the negative attitude towards Western Yiddish, attempts were made to actively prevent the use of the "Jargon"; for instance, there were school rules forbidding the use of Western Yiddish (see Fleischer 2005: 34 for one example). It is difficult to assess how successful such attempts were. In addition, we have to take into account that the receding of Western Yiddish differed from region to region.

With the beginning of the decline of Western Yiddish at the latest, but probably even before that, it seems highly likely that, in addition to Western Yiddish, Jews also spoke German varieties more similar to the language of their Christian neighbors. In the 20th century, examples of bi-dialectal speakers, who code-switch between Western Yiddish and German, are documented (see, e.g., Fleischer 2005: 29–30, 2012). Some Alsatian Jewish writers published both Western Yiddish and Low Alemannic dialect texts, which attest to one person's competence in a Western Yiddish and a German dialect (see Section 4.2).

Apart from the spoken Western Yiddish vernacular (and the Jewish varieties replacing it), there was also a special register, whose name is given as *lošnak-oudeš* by Lowenstein (1969: 17; there are many variants of its name). Literally, this name means 'language of the holy', which usually designates 'Hebrew'. At least in its origins, it was a secret code, with Hebraisms used to disguise certain concepts from those who did not know Hebrew, which must have been particularly useful in matters of trade. It can therefore be characterized as a market code and was used by cattle and horse dealers well into the 20th century (see Guggenheim-Grünberg 1954, 1981). Quite generally, Hebraisms could be used to disguise certain information from non-Jews (the same strategy is also known in Eastern Yiddish; see Max Weinreich [1973] 2008: 657, A688–689). This variety sparked especially vivid interest on the non-Jewish side (and might have been mistaken for the common Western Yiddish vernacular in some instances). Many early accounts devote some attention to this special register, usually with the intention of denouncing it (see, e.g., Chrysander 1750: [28–32] = 1966: 254–258).

On the other hand, Christians who were in contact with Jews using this special register picked up some of its vocabulary items. There are reported cases of Christians using a register whose name is obviously derived from its Jewish original designation (e.g., *Lekoudesch*; Matras 1997) and knowing an impressive number of such market language Hebraisms, even after the Holocaust (see Matras 1991, 1997 with respect to Rexingen, Württemberg, or Shy 1990 and Klepsch 2004: 22–28 with respect to Schopfloch, Franconia). In addition, when the disguise of information was not an essential aim, it is reported that many German Jews would "give their German a 'Jewish flavor' by using specifically Jewish words or proverbs in their German speech" (Lowenstein 1969: 17–18). In this case, the special vocabulary items served the function of an in-group language.

3 Structural information

It has been noted by many scholars that, during the process of the abandonment of Western Yiddish, its Hebrew-origin special vocabulary, which set it apart from German, was most stable. Such vocabulary items were even retained by persons who did not speak Western Yiddish. Therefore, Western Yiddish is in the center of Sections 3.1 and 3.2, which deal with the relationship to non-Jewish varieties and distinct structural features, respectively. In addition to Western Yiddish, Judeo-German is taken into account in Section 3.3, which deals with Hebrew-origin (and Aramaic-origin) vocabulary.

According to the classification of Yiddish dialects by Katz (1983) and many others, Western Yiddish is defined by displaying /aː/ as the continuant phoneme of vowels E_4 (= Middle High German *ei*) and O_4 (= Middle High German *ou*), whereas in Eastern Yiddish these phonemes remain diphthongs. Katz (1983) creates a subclassification of Western Yiddish into a northwestern, a central, and a southwestern area, but in view of the poor data this appears to be more of a practical than linguistic nature.

To illustrate modern Western Yiddish in its different source types, four short text fragments from different regions and times are provided. All of them display examples for the development of vowel O_4 into /aː/ (1: אָהד; 2: *aach*, 3: *glab*, 4: *fraː*) and some also for the respective development of vowel E_4 into /aː/ (2: *waaßt*, 4: *vaːs, flaːfig*). The first excerpt is from an early 19th century play entitled *Die Hochzeit zu Grobsdorf*, originating from Hesse, Central Germany (see Lowenstein 1975, who provides an edition of the first act, and Fleischer & Schäfer 2012: 422). It is given in its original Hebrew-letter form and in a mixed form of transliteration and transcription that eliminates some peculiarities of the spelling and tries to indicate the assumed phonemic distinctions, but does not indicate vowel length (see Lowenstein 1975: 74 for this excerpt).

(1) זען מיינע שמה יונגע אויס דעם
קעלשלאנד קומט און – האנזע
וועללע האן. ז'יס אָבער אָהך אָה
שיא מעדכע, און דוא געטרויא
איך אָה שבועה דרוף צו טהוא,
נאך אָה – בתולה.

*zen majne fume junge
ous dem kelfland kume
un – honze vele hon. z'is
ober ax a fej medxe, un
do getrou ix a fvue druf
tsu tu, nox a – bsule.*

By my soul, boys from the Kelschland (fictive name) came and wanted to have her. But she really is a beautiful girl, and, I would swear on it, still a virgin.

The second fragment from the Latin-letter play *Der abgeblitzte Freier oder Das verfrühte Schulenrufen*, written in the early 20th century, displays the Yiddish variety of Aurich, in northwestern Germany (see Reershemius 2007: 140):

(2) *Sau? No, dodazu is aach noch Zeits genug.*   So? Well, for this there is still enough time.
    Nu sag mol, Seckel, was gibts Chiddusch in   Now tell me, Seckel, what is the news in the
    die Kille? Ich kumm, waaßt du woll, weinig   community? I come, as you know, rarely or
    oder gar nit uf die Gaß.   not at all into town (literally, on the alley).

The third example illustrates folk literature. This excerpt of a formula spoken after the night prayer was collected in Mattersdorf, Burgenland, in southeastern Austria (see Grunwald 1925: 465):

(3) *Baal Cholem, Jezer Hore,*   Master of Dream, Spirit of Temptation,
    geh weg vün mir   go away from me
    Ich glab nix an dir.   I do not believe in you.
    Ich glab nor an allmächtigen Gott, I only believe in almighty God
    Der mich beschaffen hot.   who created me.

The fourth example is a transcription from a 20th century sound recording from Switzerland (see Fleischer 2005: 224):

(4) ja, ets ʋaːs iç ʋidər. ə fraː tsumə rebə kʰumə.   Yes, now I know again. A woman came to
    un nɔx hot si gsagt ghet: "mãĩ flaːʃigə lumpə   a rabbi. And then she had said: "My meaty
    is əm milçigə ʋasər ãĩə gfalə!"   cloth has fallen into the milky water!"

3.1 Relationship to non-Jewish varieties (isoglosses, related dialects)

Western Yiddish displays some (though not all) of the effects of the Old High German consonant shift, which provides the most important isoglosses of German dialects. Thus, Western Yiddish aligns more closely with High German, rather than Low German dialects. Similarly, Western Yiddish displays the effects of the (Early) New High German diphthongization, a development to be found in Central German, as well as Bavarian and East Franconian, and the effects of the (Early) New High German monophthongization, a development typical of Central German. Also, apocope of final *-e* has taken place in Western Yiddish, as in Upper German and many West Central German dialects.

As discussed above, the development of vowel E_4 (= Middle High German *ei*) and vowel O_4 (= Middle High German *ou*) into /aː/ in Western Yiddish is used in many accounts to distinguish Eastern from Western Yiddish. As to German, the monophthongization of Middle High German *ei* to /aː/ can only be found in some Central German dialects, whereas the monophthongization of Middle

High German *ou* to /aː/ is somewhat more widespread, as it can be found in some Central German as well as in certain East Franconian dialects (see Schirmunski 1962: 233–236). Map 1 illustrates the areal distribution of these developments for both Western Yiddish and German, as of the 19th or early 20th century. For the dialects of German, the development of Middle High German *ei* and *ou* (or the corresponding Low German proto-phoneme, respectively) into /aː/ are indicated by shadings in different colors. For Western Yiddish, point symbols, which are proportional to the number of sources attested for the respective locations, indicate written or printed sources from Jewish authors in which there is evidence for the development of both E_4 and O_4 into /aː/ (i.e., for both sound developments). The Western Yiddish data are derived from an analysis of written and printed texts, mostly originating in the 19th century, collected in a research project devoted to identifying and analyzing written and printed (potential) sources of Western Yiddish (see Section 5.2). As can be seen, only a minority of the Jewish sources displaying evidence for both sound developments are located within or close to the German territory in which one or both developments took place.

The diphthongization of vowels E_2 (= Middle High German *ê*) and O_2 (= Middle High German *ô*) is shared by Eastern and Western Yiddish, although the resulting diphthongs vary. In Western Yiddish it yields /ei/ or /ai/ and /ou/ or /au/, respectively (see the forms שײַ and *weinig* from the above examples (1) and (2), respectively). The same development is also found in some West Central German and neighboring Upper German dialects (see Schirmunski 1962: 236–237), but apart from this region it is not widespread among German dialects.

According to the sound developments discussed so far, Western Yiddish appears to be closest to the West Central German and East Franconian dialects. This makes it more difficult to distinguish Western Yiddish from dialectal German in precisely these areas. Note, however, that this similarity might be superficial, as the areal distribution of the various sound developments might have been different in earlier periods.

In the Low German area in the north, and in the Bavarian and Alemannic areas in the south, the difference between Western Yiddish and the local German dialects is usually quite marked. Since Standard German is primarily based on (East) Central German, this may make Western Yiddish look even closer to Standard German than the local German dialects. For example, in example (2), the forms *Zeits* and *was* display the effects of the High German consonant shift, as in Standard German (cf. *Zeit*, *was*), but differ from the coterritorial Low German dialects (which would display *t* instead of <z> = [ts] and *s*). In example (4), the forms *māĩ* and *āĩə* display the effects of the New High German diphthongization,

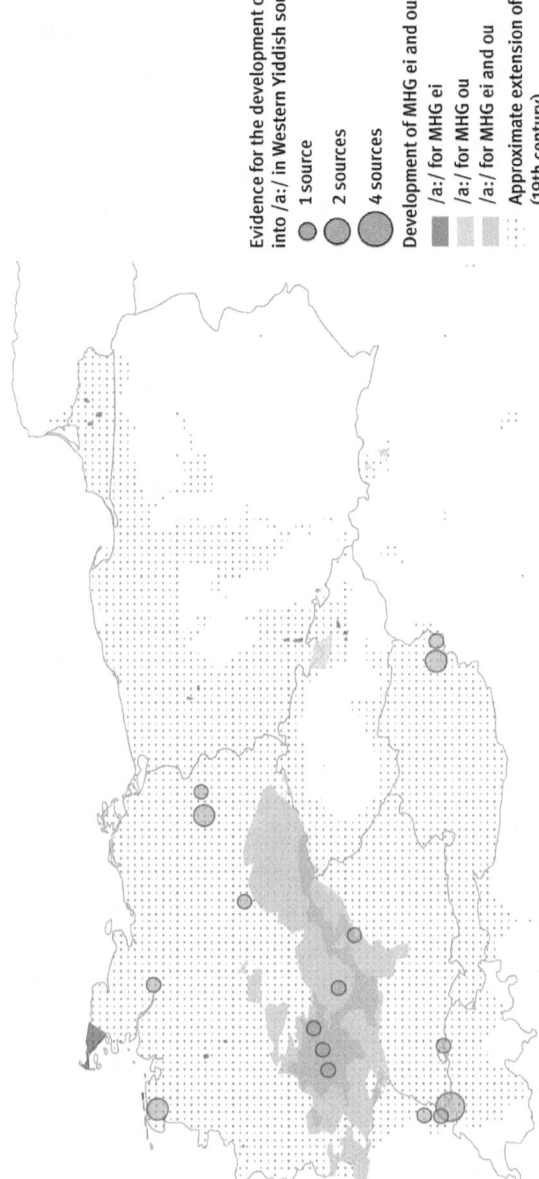

Figure 1: Development of vowels E_4 (= Middle High German *ei*) and O_4 (= Middle High German *ou*) into /aː/ in Western Yiddish written and printed sources, contrasted with the development in coterritorial German dialects (areal extension in German according to WA map 219 and KDSA map 419, indicating the dialectal realizations of Standard German *Fleisch* 'meat', and WA map 125 and KDSA map 425, indicating the dialectal realizations of Standard German *Frau* 'woman', respectively; Yiddish data from written and printed mainly 19th century sources, documentation and attestations accessible electronically: see https://www.online.uni-marburg.de/westjiddisch/.)

as in Standard German (cf. *mein, hinein*), but differ from coterritorial Alemannic dialects (which would display *i(:)* instead of /ai/).

The difference between a local Western Yiddish and coterritorial German dialect is illustrated by the following comparison of Western Yiddish and German (in this case: Bavarian) forms from the town of Frauenkirchen (Burgenland, eastern Austria). In this location, both the local German and Western Yiddish dialect were covered by the same dialect survey for the *Deutscher Sprachatlas*, which, in Austria, took place in the late 1920s. Therefore, we have exactly comparable data that were collected according to the same methodological standards (namely, via a printed questionnaire sent to schoolteachers, including a teacher of the local Jewish school; see Fleischer & Schäfer 2014). Words or phrases from the Yiddish survey forms are contrasted with one German form. The Standard German forms in the first row show the words or phrases as they were provided to the informants[3]:

(5)	Standard German	gloss	Frauenkirchen: Yiddish	Frauenkirchen: German
	heiß	'hot'	*haß*	*hoaß*
	mit rothen Äpfelchen	'with red apples (dim.)'	*mit rajte Eppeloch*	*mit roti kloani Äpfü*
	wieviel	'how much'	*wieviel*	*wiavü*
	für mich	'for me'	*fa mir*	*fia mi*
	Samstag	'Saturday'	*Schabes*	*Soumstoch*

These examples illustrate, on the phonological plan, that the Western Yiddish dialect realizes E_4 = Middle High German *ei* as a monophthong (*haß*), whereas the coterritorial Bavarian variety displays a diphthong (*hoaß*); that the Western Yiddish dialect displays a diphthong for O_2 = Middle High German *ô* (*rajt[e]*), which is realized as a monophthong in the Bavarian variety ([*rot[i]*); that Germanic *-pp- is not affected by the High German consonant shift in Western Yiddish (*Eppeloch*), but is affected in Bavarian, yielding the affricate -pf- (*Äpfü*); that Middle High German *ie* remains a diphthong in the Bavarian dialect (*wiavü*), whereas the corresponding Yiddish form does not differ from Standard German (*wieviel*; note that <ie> most probably stands for a long monophthong here, in accordance with Standard German spelling rules). As to grammar, it becomes

---

3 Both questionnaires can be accessed electronically. The running serial number, which allows unequivocal identification, is 42663 for the Western Yiddish and 42661 for the German questionnaire (note that there are two German questionnaires for this location, with the running numbers 42661 and 42662, respectively; only one of them is included in the above comparison). See http://www.regionalsprache.de/Wenkerbogen/Katalog.aspx.

clear that there is a special diminutive plural ending in the Western Yiddish dialect (*Eppeloch*), whereas in the Bavarian dialect, where no diminutive seems to be common for this lexeme, a circumscription meaning 'small apples' was chosen (*kloani Äpfü*). There is also an instance of the dative case after a preposition, which would be expected to display accusative in High German in the Western Yiddish dialect (*fa mir*), whereas the Bavarian coterritorial dialect displays the accusative (*fia mi*; see Section 3.2 for more on these characteristics). As to vocabulary, the Gentile 'Saturday' was translated by the Hebrew-origin lexeme meaning 'Sabbath' in the Western Yiddish dialect (*Schabes*), but not in the coterritorial (Christian) Bavarian variety (*Soumstoch*; see Section 3.3 for Hebrew-origin vocabulary items).

Of course, on the other hand, there are instances of structural features shared between Western Yiddish and (coterritorial) German, as becomes clear, for example, from Map 1. Note that less widespread Western Yiddish phonological developments might converge with the coterritorial German varieties as well. One possible example is the palatalization of /u/ to /y/ in Alsatian Yiddish in certain phonological contexts (see Zuckermann 1969: 44).[4] Palatalization of /u/ to /y/ is also attested for the German (Low Alemannic) dialects of Alsace (and partially in neighboring Baden; see Beyer 1964). However, the conditions under which this palatalization took place seem not to be identical: In comparison to coterritorial Alsatian Low Alemannic, the development seems to be more restricted in Alsatian Yiddish (Beyer 1964: 355–356).

3.2 Particular structural features (unique to the Jewish variety)

Since Western Yiddish is "coterritorial" (in the sense of Benor 2008) to German, a language notorious for its dialectal diversity, it is difficult to name any Western Yiddish structural feature that is not attested in some German dialect. However, as discussed in Section 3.1, many features typical of Western Yiddish do not show the same areal distribution in Western Yiddish and German. Thus, in terms of historical phonology, the development of vowels E_4, O_4 and E_2, O_2, respectively, are unique to Western Yiddish in much, though not all of its area.

---

[4] The Central Eastern Yiddish palatalization of *u(:)* to *i(:)*, of which *y(:)* is also a likely intermediary stage, seems to be independent from the Alsatian development, given both the areal non-contiguity and the differing phonological contexts. Note that this development is also known from Hungarian and Burgenland Yiddish.

Interestingly, some grammatical features seem to be even more clearly "un-German." For instance, in many Western Yiddish sources, we can find a diminutive formed by a suffix containing -*l* and a diminutive plural suffix, composed of *l* + vowel + fricative, which is clearly a cognate of Eastern Yiddish -*lekh*, e.g., *kʰiɕliɕ* 'cookies (literally small cakes)', *liːdliɕ* 'songs' (Endingen, Switzerland; Fleischer 2005: 74), *maadlox* 'girls', *kinderlox* 'children' (Burgenland, Austria; Cahan 1931: 203, 204; transliteration J.F.; see also the example in the above excerpt [5], which has *Eppeloch* 'apples' in Latin script), *Kneidlich* 'dumplings' (Aurich; Reershemius 2007: 133). This suffix, which is attested in many older sources (see Timm 2005: 109–113), is documented in some modern dialects as well as in older written documents of German. It seems to have spread in Yiddish, whereas it is areally very restricted in modern German dialects (see Fleischer 2014: 112–114), although it might have been somewhat more widespread in earlier periods.

On the syntactic level, there are indications that in Western Yiddish, as in Eastern Yiddish, the case opposition between accusative and dative was neutralized after prepositions, as in the following examples (see also the respective examples in excerpts [4] and [5]):

(6) ix   vil   avail   anous   gei   in   der   kix
    I   want   a_while   out   go   in   ART.DAT.SG.F   kitchen
    'I want to go out for a while into the kitchen'
    (*Die Hochzeit zu Grobsdorf*, transliteration; quoted from Fleischer & Schäfer 2012: 423)

(7) ich   gaih   nit   wieder   in   dem   Gebusch
    I   go   not   again   in   ART.DAT.SG.N   brush
    'I do not go into the brush again'
    (*Der Judenball im Wäldchen*; quoted from Fleischer & Schäfer 2012: 427)

While this neutralization would also appear in Low German, where accusative and dative have been conflated into one single oblique case generally (thus, not only after a preposition), this structural development cannot be found in most High German dialects (see Fleischer & Schäfer 2012; Fleischer 2014: 114–115 for more on this phenomenon).

As far as word order is concerned, occasionally VO structures resembling Eastern Yiddish can be found in western sources, e.g., in the following example from the novel *Die Juden von Zirndorf* by the German-Jewish author Jakob Wassermann (1873–1934). The participle (main clause) and the auxiliary (subordinate clause) are rendered in bold for convenience, to indicate the direct objects occurring post-verbally:

(8) | Hast | de | schon | **gesehn** | en | alten | Mann | über | neunzig,
 | have | you | already | seen | an | old | man | over | ninety
 | wo | **hat** | kein | Haus | un | kein | Hof | un | kein | Bett?
 | REL | has | no | house | and | no | court | and | no | bed

'Have you ever seen an old man over ninety who has no house and no court and no bed?'

However, such examples are relatively rare. It remains to be investigated whether they are authentic, or rather use Eastern Yiddish patterns to characterize the speech of (western rural) Jews.

As discussed in this and the preceding section, it is true that most of the structural characteristics to be found in Western Yiddish are also attested in some German dialect (which, to be sure, would also hold for most Eastern Yiddish features). However, the actual combination of the features to be found in Western Yiddish is not attested for any German dialect in the exact same combination, while these features can be found in many, areally very widespread Western Yiddish sources. Thus, although most of the Western Yiddish features might share their origin with German, the subsequent development in Western Yiddish and German seems to be largely independent.

3.3 Lexicon: Hebrew and Aramaic elements

Many elements of Hebrew (and sometimes Aramaic) origin are attested for both Western Yiddish as well as Judeo-German varieties, as can be seen from the compilations by Weill (1920a, 1920b, 1920c, 1921), Frank (1961), Guggenheim-Grünberg (1976), Weinberg (1973, 1994), and others. It is of little surprise that many lexemes of Hebrew origin are to be found in the sphere of religion, such as *schabbes* 'Sabbath' (e.g., Weinberg 1994: 223–224), *tr̈eife* 'non-kosher' (e.g., Weinberg 1994: 272–273), etc. However, there are also many Hebraisms that are not directly linked to religious items, such as *schicker* 'drunk; drunkard' (e.g., Weinberg 1973: 97), *kinnem* 'lice' (e.g., Weinberg 1973: 72), etc. Much of the Hebrew-derived lexicon parallels Eastern Yiddish (if certain pronunciation differences are disregarded), although there are some lexical isoglosses: For instance, for a '(Jewish) prayer book', Western Yiddish uses *tfile*, whereas Eastern Yiddish uses *sider* (see Katz 1983: 25; cf. Aptroot & Gruschka 2010: 51).

While it is difficult, in many instances, to tell whether a certain Semitic-origin vocabulary item goes back to Hebrew (only) or Aramaic (only), there are some lexemes that can be attributed specifically to Aramaic. This holds, for example, for *nedunje/nedinje* 'bride's dowry', which, according to Weinberg (1994: 197), goes back to the Aramaic נדוניא.

Hebrew-origin nouns usually form their plural according to Hebrew patterns (in Ashkenazic pronunciation). Especially in the masculines, this often entails patterns of vocalic (and accentual) change, which occur together with the distinct plural morpheme deriving from Hebrew ים-, e.g., *chasər – chaséerəm* 'pig(s)' (Guggenheim-Grünberg 1976: 14), *ganəf – ganóufəm* 'thief–thieves' (Guggenheim-Grünberg 1976: 20), *daggəf – daggüfəm* 'fine gentleman/-men' (Guggenheim-Grünberg 1976: 17), *eerəf – əruufəm* 'guarantor(s)' (Guggenheim-Grünberg 1976: 19). In many Hebrew-origin feminines, usually only -s is added to a singular ending in -ə, corresponding to the Hebrew regular feminine plural morpheme ות-, e.g., *chassənə – chassənəs* 'marriage(s)' (Guggenheim-Grünberg 1976: 14). Note, however, that the -ə(s) morpheme can also occur with other, less regular patterns (which are usually not feminine in Hebrew), e.g., *choolm – chalóuməs* 'dream(s), vainness(es)' (Guggenheim-Grünberg 1976: 16).

Hebrew verbal stems are integrated into Western Yiddish and Judeo-German either by adapting them to Germanic morphological patterns, e.g., *ach(e)l(e)n* 'to eat' (e.g., Weinberg 1973: 48), or by creating periphrastic constructions: An invariable form (usually going back to a Hebrew masculine singular participle) is used with the auxiliary 'to be' (see Fleischer 2014: 115–117), e.g., *mauchel sein* 'to excuse' (e.g., Weinberg 1973: 79), *mekaddesch sein* 'to hallow, sanctify' (e.g., Weinberg 1994: 181). Both strategies are also known from Eastern Yiddish (cf. *akhlen, moykhel zayn, mekadesh zayn*), but some lexical items that are morphologically integrated formations in Western Yiddish seem to be lacking in Eastern Yiddish, e.g., *houleche* 'to go' (Guggenheim-Grünberg 1976: 22), *assgene* 'to trade' (Guggenheim-Grünberg 1976: 7).

Some lexemes of Hebrew origin are typical of the special register that allowed Jews to speak secretly in the presence of non-Jews (see Section 2.4). Interestingly, some of the morphologically integrated verbal formations might be especially typical of this register. It is worth mentioning specifically that numerals can be expressed by Hebraisms, usually derived from the names of the respective Hebrew letters; thus, *ollef* '1' (e.g., Weinberg 1973: 88), *beis* '2' (e.g., Weinberg 1973: 51), *gimmel* '3' (e.g., Weinberg 1973: 64), etc. This makes special sense in a trade context. Also, various expressions relating to horse and cattle dealing are attested (reflecting one important profession of rural Jewry), e.g., *beheime* 'cow; piece of cattle' (e.g., Weinberg 1973: 51) and *suss* 'horse' (e.g., Weinberg 1973: 104).

3.4 Language contact influences

If Western Yiddish is viewed as independent from German, then German is surely the most important contact language for Western Yiddish. However, as discussed above, despite the fact that Western Yiddish and German display many identical developments, the areal distribution of these developments differs in many cases. This speaks against the explanation that such parallels are the result of recent contact phenomena (see Sections 3.1 and 3.2). On the other hand, local parallel developments of Western Yiddish and coterritorial German can also be observed, the Alsatian (Low Alemannic and Western Yiddish) palatalization of /u/ to /y/ being one instance in which contact seems to play a role. Also, Swiss Western Yiddish displays cases of interferences from coterritorial Swiss German, but at the same time retains some distinctly Western Yiddish features: While the phonological system is quite far away from coterritorial Alemannic, and while there is evidence for the case merger after preposition, the diminutive plural suffix, and the "periphrastic verbs" (see Fleischer 2004: 129–132), there are Alemannic influences, e.g., in the syntax of the indefinite article or in relative clause formation (see Fleischer 2004: 135–136).

Western Yiddish dialects on the fringes or outside of the German-speaking area might show lexical influences from the neighboring languages. For instance, in Alsatian Yiddish *mɛr* 'mayor', from French *maire*, is attested (see Guggenheim-Grünberg 1966a: 41, 42). In Hungarian Yiddish a few lexemes are borrowed from Hungarian, e.g., *pŭp(əs)* 'hump', from Hungarian *púp* (see Hutterer 1994: 52).

Apart from such areally limited examples, there are indications of earlier contact shared by Western Yiddish as a whole. Of particular interest for historians of Yiddish is the fact that Romance-origin lexemes are attested in older texts, as well as in modern dialects (see Timm 1987: 361–363 for a list of relevant lexemes that are attested before 1500). These lexemes could have come from a language spoken by the Ashkenazic population before Yiddish came into being and/or from contact with Romance-speaking communities in the High Middle Ages. Some Romance-origin lexemes are shared with Eastern Yiddish, e.g., *ben(t)še(n)* 'to bless' (e.g., Timm 2005: 186–187; Weinberg 1994: 67; cf. Eastern Yiddish *bentshn*), deriving from Latin[5] *benedicere*, or *lei(e)ne(n)/lai(e)ne(n)* 'to read' (e.g., Timm 2005: 378–380; Weinberg 1994: 158; cf. Eastern Yiddish *leyenen*), deriving from Latin *legere*. Other Romance-origin lexemes are only attested in Western Yiddish, e.g., *ore(n)* 'to pray' (see, e.g., Timm 2005: 439–442; Weinberg 1994: 204), deriving from Latin *orare* or *praie(n)/braie(n)* 'to ask for; to invite' (see, e.g., Timm 2005: 456–458; cf. Weinberg 1994: 178), deriving from Latin *precari*. The ultimate

---

5 Given that the exact origin of these lexemes is disputed, (Classical) Latin forms are quoted, even though it is impossible that the Yiddish lexemes originate from Latin directly (see Aslanov 2013: 262).

origin of these Romance lexemes is disputed. According to Aslanov (2013), who also discusses older accounts of Romance in Yiddish, both Italian (especially its southern dialects) and French contributed to the Romance lexical stock of (Western) Yiddish.

It is disputed whether Romance influence can be observed beyond the lexicon. One possible instance is the Yiddish *-(e)s* plural, which is attested beyond Hebrew-origin lexemes in older western sources (see Timm 2005: 100–108), as well as in dialectal Western Yiddish, where it is, however, rare. Examples (from an area where coterritorial German does not display *-s* plurals) are *merəs* 'mares' (Guggenheim-Grünberg 1976: 42; cf. German *Mähre – Mähren*), *juŋəs* 'boys' (Fleischer 2005: 112; cf. German *Junge – Jungen*), *kʰuːxəs* 'cakes' (Fleischer 2005: 139; cf. German *Kuchen – Kuchen*). Occasionally, *-s* plurals are even attested with Hebrew-origin lexemes that did not historically build plurals using *-s*, e.g., *bilbúləms* 'pre-texts, false accusations, excuses' (Guggenheim-Grünberg 1976: 10), *mazaˈmatəns* 'businesses' (Fleischer 2005: 122). According to Max Weinreich ([1973] 2008: 408–412, A444–A449; see also Timm 2005: 102), Yiddish *-s* plurals might have a Romance origin, with the realization of the Hebrew-origin feminine plural morpheme ות- as *-əs* also playing a role in this development. In many accounts, however, Romance origin of this morpheme is seen as unlikely (see, e.g., Krogh 2007: 273–275; Aslanov 2013: 270–271; Beider 2014: 85). Krogh (2007: 280–281, note 34) hypothesizes that many of the Old Yiddish instances might turn out to be mere graphic indications of the plural, which might not have had a corresponding spoken form. If this is correct, the Old Yiddish and modern Eastern Yiddish instances of *-(e)s* plurals would turn out to be independent from each other, making the modern Western Yiddish instances of *-(e)s* plurals all the more interesting. Clearly, more research is needed here.

Another interesting structural feature can be found in the grammar of "periphrastic" verbs, which originally formed their present perfect with the auxiliary "to have," not "to be," although the verb "to be" itself, which is part of the periphrastic formations, forms its perfect with "to be," not "to have" (see Fleischer 2014: 115–117). This is illustrated by the following example:

(9) Ich   hab   sie   schon   mekaddesch   gewese (Tendlau 1860: 380)
     I   have   her   already   hallow:INV   been
     'I have already hallowed her (scil. the moon)'

As discussed by Aptroot & Gruschka (2010: 37–38), this distribution is reminscent of French, where the verb "to be" forms its perfect with "to have" as well (*j'ai* *été/*je suis été*), and it therefore seems possible to consider a Romance origin of this construction. As an additional grammatical feature, it is interesting to note that the non-distinction between direction and location after prepositions, observed in Western Yiddish sources (see Section 3.2) but also known from Eastern Yiddish, would also correspond to Romance patterns.

Slavic plays a marginal role for Western Yiddish (see Timm 1987: 360–361), with at best a few lexemes that can be attributed to Slavic (see Beider 2015: 452–453). One Slavic-origin lexeme is the word *kouletsch* (e.g., Guggenheim-Grünberg 1973: 52–53, map 13, Guggenheim-Grünberg 1976: 25), denoting a type of roll (cf. Czech *koláč*, Polish *kołacz*). A Slavic origin is also likely for *nebbich* (e.g., Weinberg 1973: 86, 111), an emotional expression for pity, also known from Eastern Yiddish (*nebekh*): Since Weinreich ([1973] 2008: 542–543), this lexeme is usually attributed to Czech.

4 Written and oral traditions

Given that Western Yiddish was, for most of its time, at the low end of a diglossic relationship (see Section 2.4), it is no surprise that during its history Western Yiddish was written and printed much more rarely than other languages. Many written documents of western Ashkenazic Jews used Hebrew or, later, German, leaving only limited space for Western Yiddish. The oral tradition, on the other hand, is not well documented and therefore difficult to reconstruct.

4.1 Writing system

From the earliest medieval records until the 18th century, documents written or printed by western Ashkenazic Jews almost exclusively used the Hebrew alphabet. Obviously, this alphabet, known primarily from Hebrew texts in the Ashkenazic communities, was the most natural for writing and printing. This state of affairs began to change in the late 18th century, when German made its way into western Ashkenazic Jewry: As discussed by Lowenstein (1979: 199), the use of Hebrew-letter documents among 19th century German Jewry became quite limited (see Section 2.2). For community-internal records, this development might sometimes have been accelerated by the fact that Jewish communities were obliged to keep their records in Latin letters, to make them accessible for inspection by state authorities. As of the second half of the 19th century, if Western Yiddish was recorded in writing or print at all, usually the Latin alphabet was used.

4.2 Literature

While there is quite a rich and interesting Old Yiddish literature (see, e.g., Baumgarten [1993] 2005 and the anthology edited by Frakes 2004), displaying many different genres and text types, Western Yiddish literature became more restricted in the course of the 18th and 19th centuries. Many pre-modern Western Yiddish texts were especially addressed to an audience with limited knowledge of Hebrew (i.e., to women and uneducated men), one important example being the *tsene-rene* (see, e.g., Neuberg 1999; cf. Section 2.4), which was also widespread in Eastern Europe. Western Yiddish seems to have had a fixed place in Purim plays, a late example being Joseph Herz's *Ester oder die belohnte Tugend* (Fürth 1828). Starting in the late 18th century, some Maskilic authors used Western Yiddish dialect in plays to portray traditional, uneducated, and unenlightened Jews, the most famous example arguably being Wolfssohn's *Leichtsinn und Frömmelei* (Breslau 1795/96).

Interestingly, in the 19th century most Western Yiddish sources go back to non-Jewish authors. It is only as of the second half of the century that some texts by Jewish authors, now usually in Latin characters, are attested as manuscripts or prints (presumably with a low number of copies). One example is the comedy *Der abgeblitzte Freier oder Das verfrühte Schulenrufen*, written in 1902 in the Northwestern Yiddish dialect of Aurich (see the edition by Reershemius 2007: 124–151). In Alsace, there is a rich corpus of Western Yiddish literature, consisting mostly of comedies and occasional poems (see the bibliographical entries in Starck 1994: 174–177). The most important writer was Mayer Woog, who published several plays from the 1870s to the 1890s, e.g., *Der Gaasejopper geht auf die Freierei, oder, Die heiratslustige Zipper [...] Vortrag nach dem elsässisch-jüdischen Dialekt* (Hegenheim 1876). Woog also published dialectal texts written in Alsatian German (i.e., in a Low Alemannic dialect), e.g., *Neuigkeite ußem Himmel im Volksdialekt* (Hegenheim 1886). In Alsace, the tradition of Western Yiddish dialect plays continued far into the 20th century, as, for example, attested by comedies by Josy Meyer, such as *Garkisch: Vaudeville en 1 acte* (Mulhouse 1930). The Alsatian plays provide an interesting field for linguistic analysis (see Schäfer 2014). Beside the plays and occasional poems, there are some other texts written in Alsatian Yiddish. The Alsatian Jewish poet Claude Vigée (pen name for Claude Strauss, born 1921 in Bischwiller), who has published mainly French and some Alsatian Low Alemannic texts, is also the author of a few texts in Alsatian Yiddish (two of which can be found in Starck ed. 1994: 167–172).

In addition to the sources outlined so far, a non-written folk literature existed. For instance, many proverbs are known, such as the early collection by Tendlau

(1860), relating to Central Germany. The rich folklore tradition of Austrian Burgenland, including examples of many songs, is documented by, among others, Grunwald (1925: 438–488) and Cahan (1931). The collection of proverbs by Zivy (1966) relates to Alsace; Guggenheim-Grünberg (1966a: 46–47) provides transcriptions of Alsatian proverbs captured in sound recordings. Verses recited by children on Purim are recorded in various variants (see, e.g., Guggenheim-Grünberg 1966a: 50; Fleischer 2005: 211 and references cited there), and a lullaby is documented in a sound recording (see Guggenheim-Grünberg 1966a: 31). This also holds for some occasional poems (see Guggenheim-Grünberg 1966a: 14–19; Fleischer 2005: 73–121).

4.3 Performance

Although plays are one important source of Western Yiddish, little is known about the performance of these texts. While a theatre devoted to performing texts written originally in, or translated into, Eastern Yiddish by professional actors came into being in the 19th century, this was not the case for Western Yiddish. Plays and occasional poems must have been performed in private or semi-private surroundings, on occasions like festivities accompanying Jewish holy days or family celebrations, with the Western Yiddish dialect serving the usually humorous intention.

5 State of research

Western Yiddish and Judeo-German are clearly under-researched. Crucially, for the time being there exist neither a comprehensive dictionary nor grammar of Western Yiddish. In addition to the volume edited by Starck (1994), a periodical, *Cahiers du Centre de Recherche, d'Études et de Documentation du Yidich Occidental/bleter far mayrev-yidish*, of which until today five volumes have appeared, is entirely devoted to research on and documentation of Western Yiddish. At the current point in time, much work, both in finding additional Western Yiddish material and in analyzing it, has yet to be done.

5.1 History of documentation

Western Yiddish was rarely documented systematically. To this day, Max Weinreich's ([1953] 1958) *Outlines of Western Yiddish*, providing a rich survey of sources and numerous bibliographical references, are important. Apart from grammatical analyses of the language of older texts, the *Language and Culture Atlas of Ashkenazic Jewry* (LCAAJ), whose field work was primarily carried out in the 1960s, tried to integrate western data, but could not find Western Yiddish speakers for much of its territory, one important exception being the southwest (see Section 2.2). In Switzerland, beginning in 1949, Florence Guggenheim-Grünberg (1898–1989) conducted interviews and made sound recordings with speakers of Swiss Yiddish, known to her from her husband's family, as well as with speakers of other regions (primarily southern Germany and Alsace), most of whom were then residents of Switzerland. Alongside numerous articles, she published transcriptions of sound recordings (Guggenheim-Grünberg 1961, 1966a), as well as an atlas of Southwestern Yiddish (Guggenheim-Grünberg 1973) and a dictionary of the Swiss variety (Guggenheim-Grünberg 1976). Beranek's (1965) *Westjiddischer Sprachatlas* is methodologically dubious, as discussed by Guggenheim-Grünberg (1966b). The database *Quellen zum Westjiddischen im (langen) 19. Jahrhundert* provides information on (potential) written and printed sources, mainly from the 19th century, and linguistic phenomena typical of Western Yiddish, which were collected in two subsequent research projects. The database can be accessed online. It includes excerpts illustrating phenomena characteristic of Western Yiddish and some maps illustrating their areal extension.[6]

5.2 Corpora

No corpora (in the modern linguistic sense of the word) of Western Yiddish or Judeo-German are publicly available. However, the data base described above provides illustrative text excerpts from (mainly 19th century) written texts. As to dialectal material, there are still sound recordings that await publication in the form of transcriptions, in the collections of the LCAAJ (Columbia University New York, Butler Library), in the collections of the Florence Guggenheim-Archiv, and in various Alsatian locations (see Starck 1994: 177).

5.3 Issues of general theoretical interest

Whereas Eastern Yiddish can be considered "post-coterritorial" (Benor 2008), in the sense that it moved out of the German-speaking area, Western Yiddish, being

---

[6] See: http://www.online.uni-marburg.de/westjiddisch/.

closely related to German, is a "coterritorial" Jewish variety. In that respect, the co-existence of two closely related yet not identical varieties in the same territory is of general interest – and, as stated by Max Weinreich ([1953] 1958: 159), of special interest to students of Yiddish, since the distinctive features of Yiddish in all its variants become most clear if there is immediate contact with German.[7] The framework of bilingual dialectology, sketched by Uriel Weinreich (1952) with respect to Eastern Yiddish (and Slavic), is of particular interest here. As has been pointed out above (see Section 3.1), the same developments can be found in Western Yiddish and German dialects, but often in a different areal distribution, with Western Yiddish usually showing much larger areal spreading and less variation than the German dialects. This suggests a shared origin, but a later split-up, of the respective phenomena in German and Western Yiddish. Given the fact that many phenomena are areally much more widespread in Western Yiddish than in German, it seems that there existed for quite some time a closely-knit network of Jewish communities that were in constant interaction with other, geographically quite distant Jewish communities.

According to the general concepts of Yiddish history by Max Weinreich, it seems very likely that Western Yiddish is closer to the original forms of Yiddish than Eastern Yiddish. Therefore, Western Yiddish data is valuable for the question of the origin of Yiddish, which is of great academic and public interest. Also, structural parallels of Western and Eastern Yiddish are of particular interest, as they might be indicative of a shared origin, antedating the split-up into Western and Eastern Yiddish (and, more generally, into a western and an eastern Ashkenazic cultural sphere).

5.4 Current directions in research

At the present time, the field of Western Yiddish and Judeo-German is still marked by the discovery of new sources, which might change our picture in important ways. This holds true for the Middle Ages (see, e.g., Timm 2013, who edits, describes, and analyzes a text dating from before 1349) as well as for modern times (see, e.g., the editing and subsequent analysis of a play documenting the Western Yiddish variety of Aurich in northwestern Germany, by Reershemius 2007). Current research is characterized by both documentary work (e.g., Fleischer 2005), including analyses of individual (groups of) sources (e.g., Reershemius

---

[7] In Weinreich's ([1953] 1958: 159) original formulation: "[...] *di eynkeyt fun yidish in ale varyantn vayst zikh tsum boyletstn aroys dortn vu es iz faran an umfarmitlter barir mit daytsh.*"

2007; Schäfer 2013, 2014, 2017b), as well as work concerned with the linguistic position of Western Yiddish (e.g., Beider 2010, 2013, 2015; Fleischer 2014). At the present point, much can still be done in identifying additional (potential) sources and analyzing them.

In the future, the Medieval Hebrew responsa literature might emerge as an additional valuable source: Some responsa contain Yiddish witnesses' accounts in what seem to be quite faithful quotations of direct speech. This potential source type, which has not yet been systematically analyzed, might provide especially valuable evidence for older stages of the spoken language. The same might hold for private letters. Also, features of the vernacular might be reconstructed from cases of interference in Medieval Hebrew texts, and thus provide indirect insights into the structure of the Western Yiddish vernacular of earlier periods.

Acknowledgments

The present chapter originated in the context of the research projects "*Westjiddisch im (langen) 19. Jahrhundert: Quellenlage, soziolinguistische Situation und grammatische Phänomene*" and its successor "*Die sprachliche Position des Westjiddischen zwischen Deutsch und Ostjiddisch*," both funded by the *Deutsche Forschungsgemeinschaft* (DFG). Both grants are hereby gratefully acknowledged. I would like to thank Ute Simeon (née Müller) and especially Lea Schäfer for their project work. The chapter profited enormously from discussions with Marion Aptroot, Alexander Beider, Steffen Krogh, and Lea Schäfer, as well as from the feedback by Sarah Benor on behalf of the editors. Thanks are also due to T. Clinton Otte-Ford for checking my English. Needless to state, all remaining errors are mine.

References

Althaus, Hans Peter. 2003. *Kleines Lexikon deutscher Wörter jiddischer Herkunft*. München: Beck.
Altmann, Alexander. 1973. *Moses Mendelssohn: A biographical study*. Tuscaloosa: University of Alabama Press.
Aptroot, Marion. 1991. Northwestern Yiddish: The state of research. In Dov-Ber Kerler (ed.), *History of Yiddish studies: Papers from the Third Annual Oxford Winter Symposium in Yiddish language and literature*, 41–59. Chur: Harwood.
Aptroot, Marion & Roland Gruschka. 2010. *Jiddisch: Geschichte und Kultur einer Weltsprache*. München: Beck.
Aslanov, Cyril. 2013. The Romance component in Yiddish: A reassessment. *Journal of Jewish Languages* 1. 261–273.
Baumgarten, Jean & Jerold C. Frakes (ed.). 2005 [1993]. *Introduction to Old Yiddish literature*. Oxford: Oxford University Press.

Beider, Alexander. 2010. Yiddish Proto-vowels and German dialects. *Journal of Germanic Linguistics* 22. 23–92.
Beider, Alexander. 2013. Reapplying the language tree model to the history of Yiddish. *Journal of Jewish Languages* 1. 77–121.
Beider, Alexander. 2014. Romance elements in Yiddish. *Revue des Études Juives* 173. 41–96.
Beider, Alexander. 2015. *Origins of Yiddish dialects*. Oxford: Oxford University Press.
Benor, Sarah Bunin. 2008. Towards a new understanding of Jewish language in the twenty-first century. *Religion Compass* 2(6). 1062–1080.
Beranek, Franz J. 1965. *Westjiddischer Sprachatlas*. Marburg: Elwert.
Beyer, Ernest. 1964. *La palatalisation vocalique spontanée de l'alsacien et du badois: Sa position dans l'évolution dialectale du germanique continental*. Strasbourg: Section de Dialectologie de la Faculté des Lettres et des Sciences Humaines.
Birnbaum, Salomo. 1918. *Praktische Grammatik der Jiddischen Sprache*. Wien & Leipzig: Hartleben. [No date of publication, preface dated 1915. Later editions, under the title of *Grammatik der Jiddischen Sprache*, indicate 1918 as date of publication of the first edition.]
Birnbaum, Salomo A. 1997 [1974]. *Die jiddische Sprache: Ein kurzer Überblick und Texte aus acht Jahrhunderten*. Mit einem Vorwort zur 3. Auflage von Walter Röll. Hamburg: Buske.
Cahan, Y[eduhda] L[eib]. 1931. Probes fun dem yidishn folklor in Burgnland: Mayselekh un lider [Specimens of the Jewish folklore of Burgenland: Tales and songs]. *YIVO-Bleter* 2. 200–221.
Chrysander, Wilhelm Christian Just. 1750. *Unterricht vom Nutzen des Juden-Teutschen*. Wolfenbüttel: Meißner. Facsimile in Hans Peter Althaus (ed.), Johann Heinrich Callenberg & Wilhelm Christian Just Chrysander: *Schriften zur jiddischen Sprache*. Herausgegeben und mit einem Nachwort versehen von Hans Peter Althaus, 225–280. Marburg 1966: Elwert.
Eggers, Eckhard. 1998. *Sprachwandel und Sprachmischung im Jiddischen*. Frankfurt am Main: Lang.
Fischer/Bin-Nun, Jechiel. 1973 [1936]. *Jiddisch und die deutschen Mundarten. Unter besonderer Berücksichtigung des ostgalizischen Jiddisch*. Tübingen: Niemeyer.
Fleischer, Jürg. 2004. Wie alemannisch ist Surbtaler Jiddisch? Hochalemannische Züge in einem westjiddischen Dialekt. In Elvira Glaser, Peter Ott & Rudolf Schwarzenbach (eds.), *Alemannisch im Sprachvergleich*, 123–140. Stuttgart: Steiner.
Fleischer, Jürg. 2005. *Westjiddisch in der Schweiz und Südwestdeutschland: Tonaufnahmen und Texte zum Surbtaler und Hegauer Jiddisch*. Tübingen: Niemeyer.
Fleischer, Jürg. 2012. Die Minderheit im Spiegel der Mehrheit (und umgekehrt): Zur soziolinguistischen Situation des Westjiddischen im hochalemannischen Sprachgebiet. *Sociolinguistica* 26. 30–40.
Fleischer, Jürg. 2014. The (original) unity of Western and Eastern Yiddish: An assessment based on morphosyntactic phenomena. In Marion Aptroot & Björn Hansen (eds.), *Yiddish language structures*, 107–123. Berlin & Boston: De Gruyter Mouton.
Fleischer, Jürg & Lea Schäfer. 2012. Der Kasus nach Präposition in westjiddischen Quellen des (langen) 19. Jahrhunderts. In Marion Aptroot, Efrat Gal-Ed, Roland Gruschka & Simon Neuberg (eds.), *Leket: Yidishe shtudyes haynt/Jiddistik heute/Yiddish studies today*, 415–436. Düsseldorf: Düsseldorf University Press.
Fleischer, Jürg & Lea Schäfer. 2014. Jiddisch in den Marburger Wenker-Materialien. *Jiddistik-Mitteilungen* 52. 1–34.
Frakes, Jerold C. 2004. *Early Yiddish texts: 1100–1750*. Oxford: Oxford University Press.

Frank, Jehuda Leopold. 1961. *"Loschen Hakodesch": jüdisch-deutsche Ausdrücke, Sprichwörter und Redensarten der Nassauischen Landsjuden*. Tel-Aviv: Private Print.
Garvin, Paul L. 1965. The dialect geography of Hungarian Yiddish. In Uriel Weinreich (ed.), *The field of Yiddish: Second collection*, 92–115. The Hague: Mouton.
Grunwald, Max. 1925. Mattersdorf. *Mitteilungen zur jüdischen Volkskunde* 26/27 [= *Jahrbuch für Jüdische Volkskunde* 1924/1925]. 402–563.
Guggenheim-Grünberg, Florence. 1954. The horse dealers' language of the Swiss Jews in Endingen and Lengnau. In Uriel Weinreich (ed.), *The field of Yiddish: Studies in language, folklore, and literature: First collection*, 48–62. New York: The Linguistic Circle of New York.
Guggenheim-Grünberg, Florence. 1961. *Gailinger Jiddisch*. Göttingen: Vandenhoeck & Ruprecht.
Guggenheim-Grünberg, Florence. 1966a. *Surbtaler Jiddisch: Endingen und Lengnau. Anhang: Jiddische Sprachproben aus Elsaß und Baden*. Frauenfeld: Huber.
Guggenheim-Grünberg, Florence. 1966b. Review of Beranek 1965. *Zeitschrift für Mundartforschung* 33. 353–357.
Guggenheim-Grünberg, Florence. 1973. *Jiddisch auf alemannischem Sprachgebiet*. Zürich: Juris.
Guggenheim-Grünberg, Florence. 1976. *Wörterbuch zu Surbtaler Jiddisch. Die Ausdrücke hebräisch-aramäischen und romanischen Ursprungs. Einige bemerkenswerte Ausdrücke deutschen Ursprungs. Anhang: Häufigkeit und Arten der Wörter hebräisch-aramäischen Ursprungs*. Zürich: Juris.
Guggenheim-Grünberg, Florence. 1981. Die Surbtaler Pferdehändlersprache. *Zeitschrift für deutsche Philologie* 100, *Sonderheft Jiddisch: Beiträge zur Sprach- und Literaturwissenschaft*. 43–55.
Hutterer, Claus Jürgen. 1994. Jiddisch in Ungarn. In Astrid Starck (ed.), *Westjiddisch: Mündlichkeit und Schriftlichkeit*, 43–60. Aarau: Sauerländer.
Jacobs, Neil G. 2005. *Yiddish: A linguistic introduction*. Cambridge: Cambridge University Press.
Jochnowitz, George. 2010. The Western Yiddish of cattle dealers in Orange County. *Cahiers du Centre de Recherche, d'Études et de Documentation du Yidich Occidental/bleter far mayrev-yidish* 5. 5–15.
Katz, Dovid. 1983. Zur Dialektologie des Jiddischen. In Werner Besch, Ulrich Knoop, Wolfgang Putschke & Herbert Ernst Wiegand (eds.), *Dialektologie: Ein Handbuch zur deutschen und allgemeinen Dialektforschung*, 1018–1041. Berlin & New York: De Gruyter.
Katz, Dovid. 1985. Hebrew, Aramaic and the rise of Yiddish. In Joshua A. Fishman (ed.), *Readings in the sociology of Jewish languages*, 85–103. Leiden: Brill.
KDSA: 1984–1999. *Kleiner Deutscher Sprachatlas*. Dialektologisch bearbeitet von Werner H. Veith, computativ bearbeitet von Wolfgang Putschke und Lutz Hummel. Tübingen: Niemeyer.
Kerler, Dov-Ber. 1999. *The origins of modern literary Yiddish*. Oxford: Clarendon.
Klepsch, Alfred. 2004. *Westjiddisches Wörterbuch. Auf der Basis dialektologisher Erhebungen in Mittelfranken*. Tübingen: Niemeyer.
Klepsch, Alfred. 2008. Jüdische Mundartdichtung von Nichtjuden in Franken: Das Rätsel des Itzig Feitel Stern. *Jahrbuch für fränkische Landesforschung* 68. 169–201.
Krogh, Steffen. 2007. Zur Diachronie der nominalen Pluralbildung im Ostjiddischen. In Hans Fix (ed.), *Beiträge zur Morphologie: Germanisch, Baltisch, Ostseefinnisch*, 259–285. Odense: University Press of Southern Denmark.
LCAAJ: Herzog, Marvin, Ulrike Kiefer, Robert Neumann, Wolfgang Putschke, Andrew Sunshine, Vera Baviskar, & Uriel Weinreich (eds.). 1992–2000. *The language and culture atlas of*

Ashkenazic Jewry. Tübingen & New York: Max Niemeyer Verlag & YIVO Institute for Jewish Research.
Lässig, Simone. 2000. Sprachwandel und Verbürgerlichung: Zur Bedeutung der Sprache im innerjüdischen Modernisierungsprozeß des frühen 19. Jahrhunderts. *Historische Zeitschrift* 270. 617–667.
Lowenstein, Steven M. 1969. Results of atlas investigations among Jews of Germany. In Marvin I. Herzog, Wita Ravid & Uriel Weinreich (eds.), *The field of Yiddish: Studies in language, folklore, and literature: Third collection*, 16–35. The Hague: Mouton.
Lowenstein, Steven M. 1975. A mayrev-yidishe pyese fun onheyb 19tn j"h [An early nineteenth-century Western Yiddish drama]. *YIVO-Bleter* 45. 57–83.
Lowenstein, Steven M. 1976. The pace of modernisation of German Jewry in the nineteenth century. *Leo Baeck Institute Year Book* 21. 41–56. [Slightly revised in Lowenstein 1992: 9–28.]
Lowenstein, Steven M. 1979. The Yiddish written word in nineteenth-century Germany. *Leo Baeck Institute Year Book* 24. 179–192. [Slightly revised in Lowenstein 1992: 183–199.]
Lowenstein, Steven M. 1980. The rural community and the urbanisation of German Jewry. *Central European History* 13. 218–236. [Slightly revised in Lowenstein 1992: 133–151.]
Lowenstein, Steven M. 1992. *The mechanics of change: Essays in the social history of German Jewry*. Atlanta: Scholars Press.
Matras, Yaron. 1991. Zur Rekonstruktion des jüdischdeutschen Wortschatzes in den Mundarten ehemaliger „Judendörfer" in Südwestdeutschland. *Zeitschrift für Dialektologie und Linguistik* 58. 267–293.
Matras, Yaron. 1997. Zur stilistischen Funktion der Sondersprache *Lekoudesch* in südwestdeutschen Erzählungen. In Arno Ruoff & Peter Löffelad (eds.), *Syntax und Stilistik der Alltagssprache*, 97–106. Tübingen: Niemeyer.
Meitlis, Jakob. 1933. *Das Ma'assebuch: Seine Entstehung und Quellengeschichte. Zugleich ein Beitrag zur Einführung in die altjiddische Agada*. Berlin: Mass.
Mieses, Matthias. 1919. Die jiddische Sprache: Ein historisch-grammatischer Versuch. *Mitteilungen zur jüdischen Volkskunde* 21(1/2): 1–29.
Mieses, Matthias. 1920. Die jiddische Sprache (Fortsetzung). *Mitteilungen zur jüdischen Volkskunde* 21(3/4): 33–48
Mieses, Matthias. 1924. *Die jiddische Sprache: Eine historische Grammatik der integralen Juden Ost- und Mitteleuropas*. Berlin & Wien: Harz.
Neuberg, Simon. 1999. *Pragmatische Aspekte der jiddischen Sprachgeschichte am Beispiel der 'Zenerene'*. Hamburg: Buske.
Prilutski, Noyekh. 1920. *Tsum yidishn vokalizm: etyuden. Band 1* [On Yiddish vocalism: Studies. Volume 1]. Warsaw: Voytsikevitsh.
Rée, Anton. 1844. *Die Sprachverhältnisse der heutigen Juden im Interesse der Gegenwart und mit besonderer Rücksicht auf Volkserziehung*. Hamburg: Gobert.
Reershemius, Gertrud. 2007. *Die Sprache der Auricher Juden: Zur Rekonstruktion westjiddischer Sprachreste in Ostfriesland*. Wiesbaden: Harrassowitz.
Schäfer, Lea. 2013. Jiddische Varietäten im Berlin des 19. Jahrhunderts: Analyse der "Lebenserinnerungen" Aron Hirsch Heymanns. *Aschkenas* 21. 155–177.
Schäfer, Lea. 2014. Morphosyntaktische Interferenzen im jiddisch-alemannischen Sprachkontakt: Eine Untersuchung anhand westjiddischer Dialektliteratur des Elsass. In Dominique Huck (ed.), *Alemannische Dialektologie: Dialekte im Kontakt*, 247–259. Stuttgart: Steiner.

Schäfer, Lea. 2017a. *Sprachliche Imitation: Jiddisch in der deutschsprachigen Literatur (18–20. Jahrhundert)*. Berlin: Science Press. doi 10.17169/langsci.b116.259.

Schäfer, Lea. 2017b. On the frontier between Eastern and Western Yiddish: The language of the Jews from Burgenland. *European Journal of Jewish Studies* 11. 130–147.

Schirmunski, Viktor M. 1962 [1956]. *Deutsche Mundartkunde: Vergleichende Laut- und Formenlehre der deutschen Mundarten*. Berlin: Akademie.

Shy, Hadassah. 1990. Di reshtlekh fun yidish in Shopflokh [Remnants of Yiddish in the German of Schopfloch.] *Oksforder Yidish* 1. 333–355.

Simon, Bettina. 1988. *Jiddische Sprachgeschichte: Versuch einer neuen Grundlegung*. Leipzig & Frankfurt am Main: Enzyklopädie & Athenäum.

Simon, Bettina. 1991. Zur Situation des Judendeutschen im 19. Jahrhundert. In Rainer Wimmer (ed.), *Das 19. Jahrhundert: Sprachgeschichtliche Wurzeln des heutigen Deutsch*, 178–184. Berlin & New York: De Gruyter.

Starck, Astrid. 1994. Bibliographie du yidish alsacien. In Astrid Starck (ed.), *Westjiddisch/ Le Yiddish occidental. Actes du colloque de Mulhouse*, 173–184. Aarau: Sauerländer.

Starck, Astrid (ed.). 1994. *Westjiddisch/Le Yiddish occidental. Actes du colloque de Mulhouse*. Aarau: Sauerländer.

Stern, Heidi. 2000. *Wörterbuch zum jiddischen Lehnwortschatz in den deutschen Dialekten*. Tübingen: Niemeyer.

Tendlau, Abraham Moses. 1860. *Sprichwörter und Redensarten deutsch-jüdischer Vorzeit. Als Beitrag zur Volks-, Sprach- und Sprichwörter-Kunde. Aufgezeichnet aus dem Munde des Volkes und nach Wort und Sinn erläutert*. Frankfurt am Main: Kauffmann.

Timm, Erika. 1985. Zur Frage der Echtheit von Raschis jiddischen Glossen. *Beiträge zur Geschichte der deutschen Sprache und Literatur* (Tübingen) 107. 45–81.

Timm, Erika. 1987. *Graphische und phonische Struktur des Westjiddischen unter besonderer Berücksichtigung der Zeit um 1600*. Tübingen: Niemeyer.

Timm, Erika. 2005. *Historische jiddische Semantik: Die Bibelübersetzungssprache als Faktor der Auseinanderentwicklung des jiddischen und des deutschen Wortschatzes*. Tübingen: Niemeyer.

Timm, Erika. 2013. Ein neu entdeckter literarischer Text in hebräischen Lettern aus der Zeit vor 1349. *Zeitschrift für deutsches Altertum und deutsche Literatur* 142. 417–443.

Turniansky, Chava & Erika Timm. 2003. *Yiddish in Italia: Yiddish manuscripts and printed books from the 15th to the 17th century*. With the collaboration of Claudia Rosenzweig. Milan: Associazione Italiana Amici dell'Università di Gerusalemme.

WA: Wenker, Georg. 1889–1923: *Sprachatlas des Deutschen Reichs*. Bearbeitet von Alfred Lameli, Alexandra N. Lenz, Jost Nickel, Roland Kehrein, Karl-Heinz Müller und Stefan Rabanus. Marburg 2001–2005: Forschungszentrum Deutscher Sprachatlas. http://www.regionalsprache.de/ (accessed 22 August 2016).

Weill, Emmanuel. 1920a. Le yidisch alsacien-lorrain. Recueil de mots et locutions hébraeo-araméens employés dans le dialecte des Israélites d'Alsace et de Lorraine. *Revue des Études Juives* 70. 180–194.

Weill, Emmanuel. 1920b. Le yidisch alsacien-lorrain. Recueil de mots et locutions hébraeo-araméens employés dans le dialecte des Israélites d'Alsace et de Lorraine. *Revue des Études Juives* 71. 66–88.

Weill, Emmanuel. 1920c. Le yidisch alsacien-lorrain. Recueil de mots et locutions hébraeo-araméens employés dans le dialecte des Israélites d'Alsace et de Lorraine. *Revue des Études Juives* 71. 165–189.

Weill, Emmanuel. 1921. Le yidisch alsacien-lorrain. Recueil de mots et locutions hébraeo-araméens employés dans le dialecte des Israélites d'Alsace et de Lorraine. *Revue des Études Juives* 72. 65–88.
Weinberg, Werner. 1973 [1969]. *Die Reste des Jüdischdeutschen*. 2nd edn. Stuttgart: Kohlhammer.
Weinberg, Werner. 1981. Die Bezeichnung Jüdischdeutsch: Eine Neubewertung. *Zeitschrift für deutsche Philologie* 100, *Sonderheft Jiddisch: Beiträge zur Sprach- und Literaturwissenschaft*. 253–290.
Weinberg, Werner & Walter Röll (ed.). 1994. *Lexikon zum religiösen Wortschatz und Brauchtum der Juden*. Stuttgart-Bad Cannstatt: Frommann-Holzboog.
Weinreich, Max. 1993 [1923]. *Geschichte der jiddischen Sprachforschung*. Atlanta: Scholar Press.
Weinreich, Max. 1940. Shprakhn bay yidn. *Algemeyne Yidishe entsiklopedye, yidn beys*, 24–90. Paris: Dubnov-Fond.
Weinreich, Max. 1958 [1953]. Roshe-prokim vegn mayrevdikn yidish [Outlines of Western Yiddish]. In Yudl Mark (ed.), *Yuda A. Yoffe-bukh*, 158–194. New York: YIVO.
Weinreich, Max. 2008 [1973]. *History of the Yiddish language*. Edited by Paul Glasser, translated by Shlomo Noble with the assistance of Joshua A. Fishman. New Haven & London: YIVO Institute for Jewish Research & Yale University Press.
Weinreich, Uriel. 1952. *Sábesdiker losn* in Yiddish: A problem of linguistic affinity. *Word* 8. 360–377.
Weinreich, Uriel. 1964. Western traits in Transcarpathian Yiddish. In Lucy S. Dawidowicz, Alexander Erlich, Rachel Erlich, Joshua A. Fishman (eds.), *For Max Weinreich on his seventieth birthday: Studies in Jewish languages, literature, and society*, 245–264. London: Mouton.
Wexler, Paul. 2002. *Two-tiered relexification in Yiddish: Jews, Sorbs, Khazars, and the Kiev-Polessian dialect*. Berlin & New York: Mouton De Gruyter.
Zivy, Arthur. 1966. *Elsässer Jiddisch: Jüdisch-deutsche Sprichwörter und Redensarten, gesammelt und glossiert von Arthur Zivy*. Basel: Goldschmidt.
Zuckermann, Richard. 1969. Alsace: An outpost of Western Yiddish. In Marvin I. Herzog, Wita Ravid & Uriel Weinreich (eds.), *The field of Yiddish: Studies in language, folklore, and literature: Third collection*, 36–57. The Hague: Mouton.

Alexander Beider
Yiddish in Eastern Europe

1 Brief introduction

1.1 Linguistic affiliation and main varieties

According to its main system-level characteristics, Yiddish as a whole belongs to the High German branch of West Germanic languages. During its development, it underwent an important influence from Hebrew and, to a lesser extent, Aramaic, the two Semitic languages central to Ashkenazi culture; they were referred to, in Yiddish, by the collective name *loshn-koydesh* 'language of the holy'. In modern times, we can distinguish three main varieties of Yiddish:
1. Western Yiddish (WY), used in western German-speaking territories;
2. Czech Yiddish (CzY), spoken until the 20th century in the Czech lands;
3. Eastern Yiddish (EY), used in Eastern Europe.[1]

The last of these varieties underwent numerous changes in all of its systems, due to the strong influence of co-territorial Slavic languages: Polish, Ukrainian, and Belarusian. It eventually branched into three sub-dialects: Lithuanian Yiddish (LitY), Polish Yiddish (PolY), and Ukrainian Yiddish (UkrY).[2]

The standard modern literary Yiddish language (StY) is an offspring of EY. Its current written norms were formalized during the first half of the 20th century, at the YIVO Institute for Jewish Research (initially in Vilnius, later in New York). Its pronunciation is primarily based on LitY.

1.2 Regions where languages is/was spoken

After their inception during the Late Middle Ages in German-speaking provinces, Yiddish varieties gradually became widespread over a very large area. During the

---

[1] EY and WY are both generally accepted terms, though the exact list of Yiddish varieties belonging to WY is not consensual (see Fleischer, this volume, for more on WY). CzY is a conventional term introduced and discussed in detail in Beider 2015, the book on which the general exposal of the history of Yiddish in this chapter is based.
[2] In Yiddish studies, other terms are also found for these sub-dialects of EY: Northeastern Yiddish for LitY, Central or Mideastern Yiddish for PolY, and Southeastern Yiddish for UkrY.

https://doi.org/10.1515/9781501504631-010

15th–16th centuries, important communities, consisting of migrants from southern Germany and using Yiddish as their first language, were extant in northern Italy. During the 18th century, Yiddish was already spoken by Jews living in (1) various German-speaking areas (corresponding to modern Germany, Austria, Switzerland, and Alsace), (2) the Netherlands, (3) Western Slavic, Hungarian, Eastern Slavic, and Baltic territories that were parts of the Habsburg Empire or the Polish-Lithuanian Commonwealth, and (4) northern Romania. During the 19th–20th centuries, waves of migrations from these areas contributed to the creation of large Yiddish-speaking communities in the Americas (mainly the US, Canada, and Argentina), the Land of Israel, the UK, South Africa, Australia, France, and Belgium. In 1939, Yiddish was the first language for millions of Jews throughout the world.[3]

1.3 Present-day status

In our days, Yiddish is spoken on a daily basis mainly by certain groups of *Haredi* (Ultra-orthodox) Jews in the US, Israel, and a few European cities such as London and Antwerp (see Assouline, this volume). According to various estimations, the total number of such speakers corresponds to several hundreds of thousands. These communities speak and teach Yiddish to their children, and publish manuals and various types of literary works in this tongue. Among them, one counts numerous followers of the Hasidic dynasties, such as Satmar, Belz, Bobov, Vizhnitz, Klausenburg, Skver, Tosh, and Ger (Katz 2004: 379–391). Tens of thousands of elderly persons, born in Eastern Europe before World War II, still speak Yiddish, though they rarely use it as their first language. Moreover, in various geographic areas, such as North America, Europe, and Israel, one can observe a "postvernacular" engagement with Yiddish, with a variety of symbolic uses and innovative mechanisms for cultural preservation. This includes studies and anthologies compiled by scholars with different levels of command of Yiddish, Yiddish lessons organized by associations of various kinds, and arts festivals centered on Yiddish culture (Shandler 2005).

1.4 Names of the language

For centuries, both Jews and non-Jews considered the vernacular language used by Ashkenazi Jews as a kind of German. For this reason, in Yiddish documents,

---

[3] See figures in Birnbaum 1979: 41.

the language was called by a name that was also applied to German; compare *[tøjč] (טײטש) in sources published in 16th-century Western Europe and *[tajč] (טײַטש) in various sources, both western and eastern, of the following centuries. The latter form corresponds to StY *taytsh* and was still present in certain writings compiled in Lithuania during the 19th century. For the same reason, in Hebrew documents the language was mainly designated by the expression pronounced *loshn ashkenaz* in StY, literally, 'language of Ashkenaz / Germany', which is also applicable to German. It appeared as early as in the commentary by Rashi (11th century) and remained in regular use during the following centuries. For example, it was still common in both Hebrew and Yiddish documents during the 17th century. However, various authors, both Christian and Jewish, gradually recognized a specificity of the everyday idiom of Ashkenazi Jews and felt a necessity to distinguish it from the German language spoken by Christians. In works written in German, this gave rise – from the end of the 17th century – to various expressions literally meaning 'Judeo-German' or 'Jewish German', such as *jüdisch-teutsch* (later, *jüdisch-deutsch*), *juden-teutsch*, *hebraisch-teutsch*, and the like.

It was the first of these expressions that became particularly common. In Yiddish works, an equivalent form, *yidish-taytsh*, had existed from the beginning of the 18th century. By the end of the same century, certain Christian authors in Germany had started to omit any references to the "German" language used by Jews, introducing instead the terms *jüdische Sprache* 'Jewish language' and *Judensprache* 'language of the Jews'. The latter compound was, for example, used by Carl Wilhelm Friedrich (1784), who explained that the idiom in question was a specifically Jewish dialect of German. During the same period, the proponents of Jewish Enlightenment in Germany (*maskilim*) started calling this language a *jargon*, derogatorily, and considering it not a "normal" language, but a mixture of various elements. The term *Jargon* was also used by certain Yiddish authors in Eastern Europe, during the 19th and the beginning of the 20th centuries. However, the term was relatively neutral for them, perhaps containing an ironic nuance, but certainly not pejorative. It was also in that area that, during the second half of the 19th century, a number of references to the noun *yidish* appeared.[4]

At the end of the century, several authors living in English-speaking countries, all immigrants from Eastern Europe, started to use the word "Yiddish" as the English designation for their native language. In the 20th century, this word gradually became universal, accepted not only by its speakers in Eastern Europe, but also in various European languages; compare German *Jiddisch* (appearing

---

[4] Examples: An announcement about the publication of the first weekly Yiddish newspaper *Kol mevaser* by its editor Aleksander Zederbaum (1862), the story *Dos meserl* by Sholem Aleichem (1886), and the poem *Monish* by I. L. Peretz (1888).

for the first time at the beginning of the 20th century), Polish *jidysz*, and Russian *идиш*.[5] However, speakers of WY did not necessarily apply it. For example, Swiss Jews interviewed after World War II call their language *yidish-daytsh* (Fleischer 2005: 17).

2 Historical background

2.1 Attestations and sources

The most ancient attestations of the German-based vernacular language used by Jews appeared in glosses of various kinds; the oldest are those in the commentary by Rashi (11th century).[6] Numerous glosses are also known from the following centuries. The earliest sentence in that language is found in the Worms Mahzor (1272–1273). Along with German words, it also included two words of Hebrew origin that were a part of the specifically Jewish repertoire of the vernacular speech of local Jews. The first known literary source in a Jewish vernacular language dates from the period before 1349. It appears on both sides of a slate shingle recently found in Cologne (Timm 2013). Another literary source, the so-called *Cambridge Codex* (1382), represents a collection of eight manuscript documents – mainly poems – from the Cairo *genizah*.[7] Several documents, written in two scripts (Latin and Hebrew, signed by Christians and Jews, respectively) are known from the 14th–15th centuries. They include "Oaths of Peace" (German, *Urfehdebriefe*)[8] and court depositions.

Numerous sources are known to us from the 16th century and the beginning of the 17th century. They come from northern Italy, Germany, or Switzerland, and include paraphrases of several biblical books (such as *Shmuel-bukh*, *Melokhim-bukh*, and *Daniel-bukh*), biblical translations (for example, those of the Torah published in Augsburg [1544] and Cremona [1560], Psalms by Elia Levita), chivalric verse romances *Bovo-bukh* and *Pariz un' Viene*[9] by Elia Levita, other

---
5 See details in Weinreich 1973.1: 321–333; Bin-Nun 1973: 38–46.
6 Timm (1985) suggests strong arguments showing the authenticity of these glosses; they were not introduced by Ashkenazic scribes several centuries after Rashi.
7 The index of all its words and rhymes can be found in Hakkarainen 1973.
8 Regarding the category of medieval "Oaths of Peace," see Frakes 2004: 43–44.
9 It is mostly agreed that Elia Levita was the author of *Pariz un' Viene*. The strongest arguments are due to Timm and Gehlen (appearing in Shmeruk 1996: 317–320). Shmeruk (1996, introduction) advocates, however, a theory about the authorship by one of Elia Levita's pupils.

literary works of various genres (including collections of stories called *Maysebukh*), dictionaries (*Nomenclatura Hebraica* by Elia Levita), descriptions of customs, various ethical, moral, and medical studies. Some of the works in question were written by Jews born in Poland: poems by Gumprecht from Szczebrzeszyn (Venice, 1555), translations of fables by Jacob Kopelmann (Freiburg, 1583),[10] and *Tsenerene*, a very popular paraphrase of the whole Bible, by Jacob ben Isaac Ashkenazi (first available printed version is from Basel, 1622).[11]

In Slavic countries, the earliest known texts are the translations of Psalms and Proverbs by Eliezer ben Israel from Prague (1532) and *Mirkevet ha-mishne* by Rabbi Asher Anshel (Cracow, circa 1534), a printed concordance of words from biblical Hebrew with their Yiddish translation. Both these sources, as well as numerous other documents from the same region from the 16th–18th centuries, show numerous features typical for CzY. Their presence in sources compiled by Polish Jews can be at least partly explained by the normative conventions established for written Yiddish texts followed by their authors. On the other hand, the first known sources revealing peculiarities of spoken EY date only from the turn of the 19th century.

For the hundred years between the mid-19th century and World War II, sources for EY are abundant, including a vast body of modern secular and religious literature. Yet, sources for Yiddish in Western and Central Europe diminish dramatically, beginning with the end of the 18th century, because of the gradual shift among local Jews from Yiddish to German. For CzY, we find only a few small collections of proverbs from Bohemia and Moravia, compiled at the end of the 19th century. Western varieties of Yiddish continued to be living idioms until the mid-20th century in Alsace, two Swiss localities (Endingen and Lengnau), and the city of Amsterdam.[12] For all these areas, a number of detailed glossaries were compiled by their native speakers or field researchers. Yet, the last Yiddish texts available in Germany correspond to literary works from the first two thirds of the 19th century. Those whose authors are Jewish (as is the case for Joseph Herz's comedy *Esther*, published in Fürth in 1854) represent authentic testimonies about WY. Those written by Christians often represent anti-Semitic parodies. For example, that is the case regarding publications during the 1830s by Itzig Feitel

---

10 The whole original text, together with its transcription in Latin characters, an analysis of its numerous aspects (including the linguistic ones), several indices, and a glossary, appears in Schumacher 2006.
11 Numerous linguistic aspects of this work are discussed in Neuberg 1999.
12 See Beider 2015: 66–67; Zivy 1966; Fleischer 2005; Beem 1959.

Stern (pseudonym) and Christian Heinrich Gilardone. Still, these sources also reveal certain real features of Jewish speech in the areas in question.[13]

2.2 Speaker community: Settlement, documentation

An uninterrupted presence of Jews in German territories is attested from the tenth century onwards. The earliest references correspond to the following places: Mainz (circa 950), Magdeburg (965), Merseburg (973), Worms, and Regensburg (both circa 980). During the second half of the 11th century, we also learn about the Jewish presence in Bonn, Cologne, Halle, Speyer, Trier, and Xanten. We do not know what vernacular language was used by these Jews. However, several indirect factors imply that it was German-based in the Rhineland, at least at the end of the 11th century. Some German glosses appear in the commentary by Rashi, while female given names borne by Rhenish Jews often have a pleasant meaning in German, and some of them are unknown among German gentiles. Additionally, more direct factors are known for the 12th, 13th, and the first half of the 14th centuries; numerous German glosses are found in Ashkenazi rabbinic literature and one of these sources (Cologne area, 1290) explicitly says that they are written in "*our language*." Moreover, names having Gallo-Romance / Old French roots did not undergo the vocalic changes that occurred in French (and French Jewish names) during that period. Consequently, Rhenish Jews did not share the same everyday language with their coreligionists from northern France.

During that period, more than 800 new Jewish communities were mentioned in various German-speaking provinces. The massacres at the time of the Black Death (1349) destroyed numerous communities in western Germany. Only 58 communities enjoyed an uninterrupted existence, and all of them are situated in Central Europe (the city of Regensburg, Austria, Czech lands, Saxony, and Silesia). However, in various German provinces, numerous communities were (re-)established during the following 150 years and, by the end of the 15th century, we know of about one thousand localities with Jews. This number (bigger than the number valid before the Black Death) should not be taken as an indicator of a large Jewish population. Indeed, less than five percent of these localities had 20 Jewish families or more, while, in more than half of these places, only one or two families were present. During the 15th and the first half of the 16th centuries,

---

13 Linguistic features of various works mentioned in this section are discussed in Timm 1987, 2005 and/or Beider 2015. Excerpts from these sources, or even their whole texts, are often present in Frakes 2004. See also the exemplary study by Röll (2002) of the glosses for the biblical book of Job, present in a number of early Ashkenazi sources from various regions.

Jews were banned from numerous towns; whole provinces, such as Bavaria and Württemberg, remained without Jews for centuries.[14]

The decline of western Ashkenazi communities displaced the center of cultural gravity to those in Slavic countries. There is knowledge of Jews in the Czech lands and Kievan Rus' from the tenth century, while rabbinical sources mention a regularly functioning religious court in Cracow (Poland) during the first half of the 11th century. During that period, local Jews spoke the Slavic languages of their Gentile neighbors.

In Bohemia-Moravia, Jewish communities gradually shifted to the local colonial Bohemian dialect of German beginning in the 14th century.[15] The gradual abandonment of the Old Czech vernacular language in favor of a German-based idiom, the ancestor of both CzY and EY, was principally related to two factors (Beider 2015: 542–543). The first corresponds to the presence of numerous German Christian colonists in Bohemia and Moravia. Their proportion was especially significant in cities and towns where most Czech Jews dwelled. The second factor is related to the arrival of Jewish immigrants from southeastern Germany and Austria. These settlers were not necessarily more numerous than the indigenous Jews. Due to their cultural importance, and the fact that they were speaking German dialects similar to those used by local German Christian colonists, their linguistic influence could have been disproportional to their population size. CzY continued to be spoken in the Czech lands for many centuries. It was only during the 19th century that Jews gradually shifted to German in the large cities of Bohemia and Moravia.

In Poland, the first documented traces of Jews whose vernacular language was German-based correspond to the 15th century. We can be sure that, beginning with that period, local Jews mainly spoke a language from the same lineage as EY. In the Grand Duchy of Lithuania (covering the territories of modern Belarus, Lithuania, and Ukraine), the Yiddishizing process took place during the 15th–17th centuries. During that period, numerous western migrants came to these territories (mainly from neighboring Poland), and gradually the "autochthonous" Slavic-speaking Jews, of heterogeneous origins (including some early Ashkenazi

---

14 All details concerning the settlement history appearing in this paragraph are taken from Toch 1997.

15 Numerous details concerning the phonology of this medieval dialect – in many aspects intermediary between Bavarian and East Central German – can be found in Moser 1929, 1951. The heterogeneous varieties known during the 19th century and the first half of the 20th century in several German-speaking enclaves within the Czech territories are of little help for its reconstruction; they have been affected by numerous additional influences and innovations. About the shift of the vernacular language spoken by medieval Czech Jews from Old Czech to a German-based idiom, see Jakobson and Halle 1964.

migrants but also descendants of Jews who lived in Rus' during the first centuries of the second millennium CE), also shifted to EY (Beider 2015: 545).

During the 19th century, migrants from what is now eastern Belarus settled in their masses in the Chernigov and Poltava provinces of the Russian Pale of Settlement. Migrants from various areas of the country populated the Kherson, Ekaterinoslav, and Taurida provinces, collectively called New Russia. The largest city of that area, Odessa, also absorbed numerous Galician Jews. The majority of the Yiddish-speaking communities of Hungary and Romania were not created until the 18th–19th centuries, mainly after migrations of Czech and Polish Jews to these territories.

At the turn of the 20th century, numerous Jews migrated from Eastern Europe to other countries. These migrations created the Yiddish-speaking communities in North America (mainly from the Russian Pale of Settlement, the north-eastern part of Congress Poland, and Galicia), Argentina (mainly from Congress Poland, the Grodno area, and Bessarabia), and South Africa (almost exclusively from western Lithuania).

2.3 Phases in historical development

If by the term "Yiddish" we mean an idiom having system-level differences, in comparison to any contemporary dialect of German spoken by Christians, then the birth of Yiddish must be placed in the period encompassing the second half of the 14th century and the 15th century (Beider 2015: 221–226). No data in our possession point to the existence of any difference of this kind before the Black Death. The German language of Jews who lived in western Germany before 1349 definitely possessed a specifically Jewish repertoire: words and given names of Semitic (Hebrew or Aramaic) and Romance (mainly Gallo-Romance / Old French) origin. However, for a spoken language, these are surface-level elements; their presence does not create a new language, and no information is available to assert the existence of the fusion of elements of various origins during this early period. A number of these non-German elements were substratal; they were inherited by Rhenish Jews from their ancestors from northern France. Some other words of French origin were already adstratal; they appeared in the German-based language of Jews of the Rhineland because of their contacts with their French coreligionists.

When Rhenish Jews migrated to other German territories, they adapted their everyday speech to local German dialects, keeping some of their specific Semitic and Romance elements. In the south-eastern, German-speaking territories covering Austria and the easternmost part of Bavaria (Regensburg), Jewish communities, most likely genetically independent of the Rhenish ones, were also using local German dialects. For all these reasons, early Ashkenazi sources dating from the 13th–15th centuries are not homogeneous. They show peculiarities of different German dialects, spoken by co-territorial gentiles.

During the 150 years that followed the massacres during the time of Black Death, the everyday language of Ashkenazi Jews deviated from that used by their Christian neighbors. By the end of the 15th century, we can be sure that we are dealing with a separate idiom, whose usage was limited to Jews. These changes can be observed on several levels.

First, the tradition of biblical translations into the Ashkenazi vernacular gained a particular importance (Timm 2005). This tradition was initially developed in the communities of Western Germany, partly under the influence of principles elaborated in northern France. It gave rise to numerous calques from the original Hebrew text and yielded a special register within the language used by German Jews: StY *Ivre-taytsh*. Because of the education of Jewish boys in elementary schools in which the translations were regularly used, this tradition became widespread, and numerous elements of *Ivre-taytsh* gradually lost their bookish connotation and entered the everyday spoken language. These specifically Jewish elements encompassed numerous semantic idiosyncrasies, some words whose geography was much more restricted for Christians than for Jews, and new words that consisted of German elements brought together by Jews using patterns inspired by the original Hebrew constructions. Here, the system-level innovations were primarily morphological: a widespread use of certain German suffixes, in contexts in which they were not employed by Christians. The vocabulary of German Jews also became enriched by a number of new words coined by Jews, independently of biblical translations (Timm 1987: 375–385). These were words needed for specifically Jewish religious and cultural contexts such as, for example, StY *lernen* 'to study the Talmud', *shulkloper* 'one who knocks on doors calling people to synagogue', *yidishn* 'to circumcise' (compare German *jüdisch* 'Jewish'), and *gut(e)-ort* 'Jewish cemetery' (literally 'good place').

Second, during the 14th–16th centuries, the Semitic elements became fully integrated into the Ashkenazi vernacular, while during the previous period they were at least partly autonomous. For example, such autonomy was valid in the domain of phonology; in the pronunciation of Yiddish words of Hebrew origin, we find no traces of the vocalic and consonantal shifts that took place in the German component of the Ashkenazi vernacular idiom(s).[16] After that period, any phonetic change that operated in the German component was equally applicable

---

[16] The diphthongization of MHG î and û represents an example of such a shift. The long /iː/ and /uː/, present in the phonological chart of Ashkenazi Hebrew of that period, remained unchanged (Beider 2015: 299–300).

to words of Semitic origin. Numerous hybrid German-Hebrew words came into existence individually or, more commonly, following new hybrid morphological patterns. Moreover, a number of Semitic morphological elements were used for words independently of their origin.[17]

Third, and most important, numerous Ashkenazi sources from the 16th century, from western Germany and northern Italy, testify to a linguistic unification process. According to numerous major system-level criteria (primarily phonological and morphological), their language (1) is similar enough, (2) is close to the East Franconian dialect of German, and (3) represents the direct ancestor of modern WY (Beider 2015: 206–220).

In the Czech lands, the vernacular language of local Jews also gradually deviated from the Bohemian dialect of German used by local Christians. It influenced the speech of small Jewish communities in eastern German territories. There is no known historical reference to western mass migrations in Eastern Europe. Local Yiddish-speaking communities were formed gradually, due to a regular influx of Jewish migrants (primarily from Bohemia, Moravia, Silesia, and eastern German territories) during the 15th–16th centuries and the first half of the 17th century. These migrants brought with them their Bohemian-based language (Beider 2015: 559–563). In Poland, precisely during the period of the formation of important Yiddish-speaking communities, new incoming Jewish families met large groups of urban German Christian colonists, who were using an idiom close to their own as their vernacular: the Silesian dialect of German. Close contacts with German-speakers, who lived in Polish towns in great numbers, had an important influence on the development of local dialects of Yiddish without, nevertheless, forcing them to abandon their Bohemian basis. Certain phonological peculiarities of EY, in comparison to CzY, can be explained only by the influence of Silesian. For example, /f/ represents the EY reflex of West Germanic initial *p, contrasting with /pf/ in CzY (StY *fan* 'pan', compare standard German *Pfanne*).[18] On the other hand, contacts with Germans in Poland became a major factor that allowed Ashkenazi immigrants not to shift from their vernacular language to Polish. When the local German-speaking Christian population became Polonized, a large number of important Yiddish-speaking communities had already been firmly established in the area (Beider 2015: 216). During the following centuries, EY was developing in a large area in which the presence of German-speaking Christians

---

17 See details in Section 3.4.
18 This feature is not specific to Silesian, being valid for other East Central German subdialects also. However, according to a set of other major linguistic characteristics, EY is correlated with Silesian only. Among these characteristics: the absence of German neutralization of consonants and the diminutive suffix -*(e)l* (see also Section 3.1).

was rather marginal. As a result of processes internal to Jewish communities, numerous innovations within EY took place. Due to permanent contacts with the Polish Christian population, a large series of adstratal Yiddish elements of Polish origin entered EY. From Poland, EY was brought to the Grand Duchy of Lithuania, most likely during the 15th–16th centuries. In this area (as well as in Red Ruthenia, which, from the mid-14th century, was within Poland), Yiddish-speaking Jews met their coreligionists whose first language was East Slavic, the common ancestor of modern Ukrainian and Belarusian.[19] During the following centuries, local Yiddish sub-dialects acquired numerous Slavic features. This process was due to both the shift to EY of former East Slavic-speaking Jews and to direct everyday contacts with gentile Slavs.

In modern times, the decline of the use of Yiddish as a living language in numerous countries was related to the assimilation of local Jews into the culture of the gentile majority. At the end of the 18th century and during the 19th century, in various German-speaking provinces of Central and Western Europe, local Jews – following the ideology of *Haskalah* – abandoned Yiddish in favor of its cousin language, New High German (NHG). In Hungary, one part of Jewish population became *Magyarized* during the hundred years that followed the revolution of 1848. Similar shifts to the dominant non-Jewish languages took place during the 20th century, in various West European countries (France, Belgium, the UK, and the Netherlands), as well as in South Africa, Latin America, and Australia. In the USSR during the 1920s–1930s, the shift to Russian (or, less commonly, to Ukrainian or Belarusian) was already well advanced in places of traditional Jewish settlement, and especially in the largest cities – such as Moscow, Leningrad, Khar'kov, Dnepropetrovsk, Kiev, Minsk, and Odessa – to which Jews migrated in their masses.[20]

For those who survived the Holocaust, assimilation accelerated during the following decades. In Poland, Lithuania, and, to a lesser extent, Hungary and Romania, Yiddish-speaking communities were decimated by the Holocaust, while the survivors either immigrated to Israel or became linguistically assimilated into dominant cultures. In North America, most immigrant families shifted to English within a generation or two. Yet, because of a permanent influx of masses of native speakers between the 1880s and the 1920s, Yiddish was actively used until the mid-20th century, even in certain secular Jewish groups. However, after the creation of the state of Israel in 1948, the re-orientation to Israeli Hebrew in the education provided by local Jewish communal organizations accelerated

---

19 For the validity of this statement, see arguments (mainly onomastic) in Beider 2015: 433–439.
20 In the last four cities, the Jewish population was already important before the Bolshevik Revolution (1917) that abolished the Jewish Pale of Settlement.

the decline of Yiddish, outside of certain *Haredi* groups (Katz 2004: 344–346). For numerous people who made *aliyah* between 1882 and 1939, Yiddish was their native language. Yet, in the climate of open hostility of local Zionist activists, this language of the Diaspora was gradually abandoned in the Land of Israel, outside of the *Haredi* circles, in favor of the new national language, Hebrew (Katz 2004: 310–323).

2.4 Historical dialectology

The *Language tree* (*Stammbaum*) approach, standard in historical linguistics, is not applicable to Yiddish as a whole; the putative *Proto-Yiddish*, from which all known Yiddish varieties would be derived, has never existed. Moreover, the same approach is not even applicable for WY. The *Language tree* model describes the inception of various dialects, as a result of a series of steps in which every step corresponds to a branching of a proto-dialect into new sub-dialects. Yet, as explained in the previous section, in Western Europe during the 14th–15th centuries, the process was instead the opposite of branching: we observe a gradual unification of various High German Jewish dialects. The result of this partial unification, attained by the start of the 16th century, can be conventionally called *Proto-WY* (Beider 2015: 477–487). For the following centuries, we can already speak about a branching of WY into several sub-dialects, mainly due to the geographic separation of the corresponding communities and the influences of local German dialects. These processes yielded the following varieties:

1. Alsatian, Swiss, and (up to the mid-19th century) Franconian. Because of their close genetic relationship, they can be considered sub-dialects of one entity, conventionally called *Southwestern Yiddish* (SWY).
2. Yiddish in Rhine Palatinate and Hessen. During the 19th century, this idiom disappeared; local Jews mainly shifted to German. However, various traces of it imply that, during the previous two centuries, local Yiddish had major features similar to those observed in SWY.
3. Yiddish in the northern German provinces (including Westphalia and the area of Hamburg) and in Amsterdam. Jewish communities in this region are significantly younger than those mentioned in the two previous points. Moreover, the local Jewish population was fed by migrations from two directions: (a) the south (mainly Rhine Palatinate and Hessen) and (b) the east (mainly East Germany, Bohemia, and Poland-Lithuania; the last region became an important source of migrants only after the Cossack wars of the mid-17th century). As a result, it is not a surprise that during the 20th century remnants of Yiddish still found in northern Germany and the living language in Amsterdam both show not only typical WY features (corresponding to the oldest layer), but also those known in EY and/or CzY. Consequently, at least idioms of Hamburg and Amsterdam can be treated as mixed Yiddish dialects and not just as sub-dialects of WY (Beider 2015: 476–477, 510–514).

In the Slavic countries, the Bohemian-based, specifically Jewish idiom gave rise to both CzY (in the Czech lands) and EY (in the Polish-Lithuanian Commonwealth). Most likely, the corresponding branching took place during the 15th–16th centuries (Beider 2015: 477–479). It was related to migrations eastward by one part of the bearers of this idiom, and the influence of the colonial Silesian dialect of German and local Slavic languages in the new territories. EY, in turn, branched during the 17th century into two sub-dialects: LitY and the dialect representing the ancestor common to PolY and UkrY. The geographic separation between them is related to the Lublin Union (1569). LitY corresponds to the area that remained in the Grand Duchy of Lithuania. Yet, following this treaty, a large part of Ukraine (Podolia, Volhynia, and the Kiev region) that belonged to the Grand Duchy of Lithuania became attached to Poland. Numerous Jewish migrants from ethnically Polish territories came to Ukraine in the decades that followed the Lublin Union, bringing their Yiddish dialect. During the next two hundred years or so, Yiddish in Poland and in Ukraine went through various similar linguistic processes. After the partitions of the Polish-Lithuanian Commonwealth during the last third of the 18th century, and the Napoleonic wars of the beginning of the 19th century, the former Polish area was divided into four parts: (1) the section of Ukraine annexed in 1569 became the southern part of the Russian Pale of Settlement (the area of LitY representing its northern part); (2) Congress Poland became an autonomous part of the Russian Empire; (3) Galicia was annexed by the Austrian Empire; and (4) the western provinces were annexed by Prussia (Posen / Poznań, West Prussia). As a result of this politico-administrative separation, Yiddish in Ukraine during the 19th century gave rise to UkrY, a dialect separate from the PolY used in Congress Poland and Galicia, while the Jewish population in the Prussian section underwent a gradual process of Germanizing.

2.5 Sociolinguistic description, public functions

German dialects, with their specifically Jewish repertoires, and later – after system-level internal changes – Yiddish varieties, represented the vernacular language of traditional Ashkenazi communities. This idiom was not taught publicly itself. However, in the Jewish elementary school (StY *kheyder*), it was used to teach various matters. For example, Yiddish was used to translate and explain biblical and other Hebrew texts. This fact is directly responsible for the verb *taytshn* 'to interpret, translate', derived from the root *taytsh* that designated the Ashkenazi everyday language. However, the social status of that idiom was rather low, in comparison to such prestigious languages of Jewish culture as Hebrew and Aramaic. Books published in the latter two languages were printed in square Hebrew letters. For Yiddish books, considered to have an auxiliary function, the typeface was different. It was popularly called *vaybertaytsh* 'women's Yiddish', which stressed the orientation of these publications to female readers. Moreover, the authors often explicitly stated in the preface that their texts were written in Yiddish so that women and girls could understand them. Actually, this orientation was often ostensible; this literature was also read by men, and some of these books were primarily intended for men.

As explained above, in Western Europe the status of Yiddish became even lower during the 18th century, because of anti-Yiddish propaganda by *maskilim*, and eventually, in many regions, it was abandoned for German. Yet, in Eastern Europe, the situation was totally different: The status of EY increased dramatically. The impetus came from various ideological camps. The first factor is related to the propagation of the Hasidic movement. Certain of its leaders attached a particularly high importance to this language, understandable by all Jews and not only by the learned elite, as was the case with Hebrew and Aramaic. The founder of Hasidism, Israel Baal Shem Tov (circa 1700–1760), preached in Yiddish. His classic texts were published at the beginning of the 19th century, the same period when his great-grandson, Nachman of Bratslav (1772–1810) wrote his famous mystical tales. Generally speaking, Yiddish was extensively used to spread the views of Hasidism and wonder stories of its leaders.

The second impetus came from certain local *maskilim*. The attitude towards Yiddish of Mendel Levin (Lefin) from Satanów (Podolia) (1749–1826) was opposed to that of the western *maskilim*. In 1813, he published his translation of the Book of Proverbs in Tarnopol (Galicia). Instead of the traditional *vaybertaytsh*, here the square Hebrew characters were used. Another revolutionary change was lexical. Before him, numerous Yiddish publications in Eastern Europe followed the written tradition elaborated by Jews of Western and Central Europe that was partly based on the peculiarities of their Yiddish dialects. Levin based his translation on vernacular EY, avoiding words from the German component unknown in EY and actively using Hebrew and Slavic lexemes that were incorporated into the colloquial speech of his time (Fishman 1991: 44–45).

Third, Yiddish acquired importance in Eastern Europe at the turn of the 20th century because of the efforts of a number of authors, whose literary works became well known even outside of Jewish communities because of their high quality. Fourth, a number of Jewish political movements adopted a pro-Yiddish ideological platform, the most important among them being the socialist *Bund* (Jewish labor movement) and the liberal *Folkist* party (whose struggle was focused on Jewish national and cultural autonomy in the Diaspora). Both of them promoted

Yiddish as the Jewish national language in Eastern Europe, published Yiddish periodicals and books, and organized schools.[21] The Yiddish press was of paramount importance for Yiddish cultural life in certain new centers of Ashkenazi emigration. Here, it is worth mentioning the North American socialist-oriented *Jewish Daily Forward* (*Forverts*), whose circulation reached more than 275,000 in the late 1920s / early 1930s.

3 Structural information

3.1 Relationship to non-Jewish varieties

Among various High German dialects, the following are particularly close to Yiddish varieties: (1) East Franconian (the dialect spoken in such cities as Würzburg, Bamberg, and, partially, Nuremberg) to SWY[22]; (2) Bohemian (Prague and other Czech cities) and, to a lesser extent, (3) Silesian to CzY and EY. All aforementioned Yiddish and German dialects share the following major features: (1) the monophthongization of Middle High German (MHG) *ie* and *uo*; (2) the diphthongization of MHG *î* and *û*; (3) the lengthening of short vowels in open syllables and, by analogy, some other contexts; (4) the raising of MHG *â*, and (5) the existence of diphthongal reflexes for MHG *ê* and *ô*, as well as lengthened *e* and *o*. From the point of view of Germanistics, it is appropriate to consider that the inception of Yiddish varieties corresponds to the *Early NHG* (*Frühneuhochdeutsch*); note that the first three of the above five features are often taken as formal criteria for distinguishing between the MHG and NHG periods. Certain other features – specific to certain Yiddish varieties – are listed in the following table:[23]

---

21 Their activity contrasted with that oriented to Hebrew Zionists. However, two eminent Zionists played a crucial role in the development of Yiddish studies. Nathan Birnbaum (1864–1937) became the organizer of the first international Yiddish language conference at Czernowitz, Bukovina (1908). Ber Borokhov (1881–1917), one of the founders of Labor Zionism, wrote the first program for the development of Yiddish studies as a scholarly domain.

22 Section 3 (providing an analysis of Yiddish varieties known to us from sources from the 19th–20th centuries) addresses only one WY sub-dialect, namely, SWY. On one hand, the available information about other sub-dialects from other German-speaking territories is either scanty or ambiguous. On the other hand, as discussed above, Yiddish in Amsterdam represents a mixed dialect.

23 The last column does not provide an exhaustive list of German dialects that include(d) the feature in question. It mentions only the three dialects that are much closer to Yiddish varieties than others. Lists covering all High German dialects appear in Beider 2015: 214–215. In addition

Table 1: Peculiarities: Cross-references between Yiddish and German dialects.

Feature	Jewish varieties concerned	German dialects concerned
Merger of MHG *â* and *ô*	SWY	East Franconian
Raising of lengthened MHG *a*	EY, CzY	Bohemian, Silesian
Diminutive plural suffix –*lekh*	All	East Franconian, Bohemian (older period)
Reflexes of Old West Germanic **p* in the initial position // gemination	*pf // pf* in SWY; *f // p* in EY, CzY	*pf // pf* in East Franconian; *f // p* in Silesian and *pf // p* in Bohemian
German neutralization of consonants	SWY	East Franconian
/št/-reflexes of internal MHG *st*	SWY	East Franconian
/a:/ for MHG *ei* and *ou*	SWY, CzY	East Franconian, Bohemian
Main diminutive singular suffix	-*l* in CzY, EY; -*le* in SWY	-*(e)l* in Bohemian, Silesian; -*le* in East Franconian
Unrounding of front rounded vowels	all	Bohemian, Silesian
Voiced and/or *lenes* reflexes of intervocalic MHG *v*	CzY, EY	Bohemian, Silesian
Apocope of the unstressed vowel	All	East Franconian, Bohemian

Basic SWY vocabulary words *frāle* 'grandmother' and *harle* 'grandfather' are typically East Franconian. On the other hand, several major features of Silesian, unmentioned in the above table, are not found in any Yiddish variety, such as the merging of MHG *uo* and *ô* and the raising of MHG *o* to /u/ in certain contexts.

A few features of SWY are due not to East Franconian but to the influence of more western High German dialects. Among them: /eš/ instead of /aš/ in words cognate to NHG *Tasche* 'bag', *Asche* 'ash', and *waschen* 'to wash'. Moreover, East Franconian is a dialect that combines a number of Upper and Central German features. In the Middle Ages, Jews in western German-speaking provinces lived in areas where both these major subdivisions of High German were used. As a result, in theory, in the set of elements of SWY that seem on the surface typically East Franconian, some may exist in SWY independent of that German dialect.

---

to eleven linguistic elements present in the following table, they cover several dozens of other structural phonological and morphological features.

SWY could have realized its own synthesis of Upper and Central German dialects, whose results could be similar to those observed in East Franconian.

The fact that WY and EY are historically based on different German dialects does not prevent considering them dialects of the same language: Yiddish. Indeed, the notion of language, as opposed to dialect, is sociopolitical. For centuries, Yiddish speakers in different countries were viewed as speakers of varieties of one and the same language. All Yiddish varieties have always been written in Hebrew characters and have a number of specifically Jewish shared elements, unknown in German (Hebrew, Aramaic, Romance, and those inherited from the *Ivre-taytsh* tradition). They were everyday languages in Ashkenazi communities of various countries, in which the origins of numerous members of these communities were often related to migrations from west to east (mainly before the mid-17th century) or vice versa (after that period). For these Jews, changes that were gradually occurring in written German (such as those influenced by the publication of the translation of the Bible by Martin Luther) were irrelevant. Moreover, because of the closeness of East Franconian and Bohemian, numerous elements from the German component, non-specific to Jews, were also pan-Yiddish. It is precisely because of this proximity that, during the 16th–18th centuries, Yiddish printing houses could publish a number of works oriented to the Ashkenazi audience in various countries, avoiding using elements that could only be understood regionally.

3.2 Particular structural features (unique to the Jewish variety)

A large number of features characterizing the German component of Yiddish are unknown in any dialect of German. They are due to linguistic processes internal to Ashkenazi communities. The most striking differences concern vowels: The charts of stressed vowels found in various Yiddish varieties are unique to them. The table below shows reflexes of MHG vowels found in six Yiddish varieties in use during the first half of the 20th century.[24]

The last column presents the corresponding Yiddish "proto-vowels," according to conventional designations introduced by Max Weinreich (1973). As explained above, no *Proto-Yiddish* ever existed (and even *Proto-WY* is a theoretical construction). As a result, for Yiddish as a whole, these "proto-vowels" appear useful only for mnemonic reasons. Yet, for EY, they correspond to historical reality: all three EY sub-dialects have the same Jewish ancestor, *Proto-EY* (Beider 2015: 462–468).

---

24 The information for this table was mainly extracted from Herzog 1992–2000.

Table 2: Realizations of MHG stressed vowels in Yiddish dialects.

MHG	NHG	Swiss Yiddish	Alsatian Yiddish	Dutch Yiddish	PolY	UkrY	LitY	Proto-vowel
â	a [a:]	[ɔu, o:]	[ɔu, o:]	[o:]	[u:]	[u]	[o]	A_2
lengthened a	a [a:]	[a:]	[a:]	[o:]	[u:]	[u]	[o]	A_3
other a	a [a]	[a]	[a]	[a]	[a]	[o]	[a]	A_1
ê, lengthened e	e [e:]	[ɛj]	[ɛj]	[ɛj]	[aj]	[ej]	[ej]	E_2
lengthened ë	e [e:]	[e:]	[e:, ɛj]	[e:]	[ej]	[ej]	[e]	E_5
other e and ë	e [e]	[e]	[e]	[ɛ]	[e]	[e]	[e]	E_1
ei	ei [aj]	[a:]	[a:]	[a:]	[aj]	[ej]	[ej]	E_4
î	ei [aj]	[aj]	[aj]	[ɛj]	[a:]	[a]	[aj]	I_4
ie, lengthened i	ie [i:]	[i:]	[i:]	[i:]	[i:]	[i]	[i]	I_2
other i	i [i]	[i]	[ɪ]	[e]	[i]	[ɪ]	[i]	I_1
ou	au [au]	[a:]	[a:]	[a:]	[oj]	[oj]	[ej]	O_4
ô, lengthened o	o [o:]	[ɔu]	[ɔu]	[ɔu]	[oj]	[oj]	[ej]	O_2
other o	o [o]	[o]	[o]	[ɔ]	[o]	[o]	[o]	O_1
û	au [au]	[ɔu]	[ɔu]	[ɔu]	[ou, o:]	[ou, oj]	[oj]	U_4
uo and lengthened u	u [u:]	[u:]	[y:, y]	[u:]	[i:]	[i]	[u]	U_2
other u	u [u]	[u]	[ʊ]	[o]	[i]	[ɪ]	[u]	U_1

The above table shows several important peculiarities of certain Yiddish varieties unknown in German dialectology:
- The loss of vocalic quantitative contrasts in LitY and UkrY (under the influence of Slavic languages) (U. Weinreich 1958: 260, 1963: 350–351)
- The merger in EY of reflexes of MHG ê and ei, as well as ô and ou
- The pan-Yiddish merger of reflexes of non-lengthened MHG e and ë in closed syllables but different reflexes of their lengthened counterparts (Timm 1987: 121–124, 131–135; Beider 2015: 126–127).[25]

Among EY consonantal innovations, we observe a regular change of the sibilants /s/, /š/, and /z/ into affricates /ts/, /tš/, and /dz/, respectively, in the position after /n/ or /l/; compare StY *fentster* 'window', *gandz* 'goose', *undz* 'us', *haldz* 'neck', *mentsh* 'man', and *faltsh* 'wrong', whose NHG cognates are *Fenster*, *Gans*, *uns*, *Hals*, *Mensch*, and *falsch*, respectively (Beider 2015: 114–115).

EY exhibits numerous grammatical idiosyncrasies that are due to internal innovations. They often correspond to simplifications; for example, the elimination of exceptions in the conjugation of irregular verbs or the diminution of

---

[25] The merger in UkrY and the partial merger in Alsatian Yiddish are relatively recent.

the number of forms of personal and reflexive pronouns. These changes are particularly acute in LitY, in which we also observe such a striking peculiarity as the disappearance of the neuter gender.

3.3 Lexicon: Hebrew and Aramaic elements

In traditional Ashkenazi society, men were expected to read Hebrew, the language taught in elementary schools.[26] Young men who continued their studies in a *yeshiva* also learned Aramaic. Numerous Hebrew and some Aramaic words and expressions were also well known from the sacred texts of Judaism (the Bible and Talmud) and prayers. Knowledge of Semitic lexical elements was prestigious within Ashkenazi communities. Moreover, it could also be particularly attractive from the point of view of the social psychology of separating Jews from non-Jews. This separation was often operational in the religious domain, with Jews avoiding local words associated with the religion of the gentile majority.[27] The separation could also have practical advantages: the possibility of communication between Jews that would not be understood by Christians; compare *Loshne-koudesh*, a secret language devised in the western German-speaking provinces by certain categories of traders (cattle dealers, etc.), primarily on the basis of the Hebrew component of Yiddish (see Matras 1989). All these factors were favorable for the incorporation of new adstratal Semitic elements throughout the history of Yiddish. A number of other elements were inherited from the specifically Jewish repertoires of vernacular Romance and (outside of WY) Slavic languages spoken by the ancestors of Yiddish-speakers.

In the Middle Ages, two groups of Ashkenazi Jews could be distinguished according to their religious customs and their pronunciation of Hebrew, both in the liturgy and (for words of Hebrew origin incorporated into the vernacular language) in everyday speech. The first group, *Bney hes*, lived in the Rhineland, Franconia, Swabia, and a part of Bavaria. The second group, *Bney khes*, dwelled in Austria, the Bavarian city of Regensburg, Eastern Germany, and the Slavic countries. The following phonetic differences between these two groups are known: (1) *heth* was pronounced by *Bney hes* as *he* (sound /h/), while for *Bney khes* its sound /x/ was similar to that of *khaf*; (2) *Bney khes* distinguished between *shin* /š/ and *sin* and *samekh* /s/, while *Bney hes* read all three letters as /s/; (3) for *Bney hes*, certain stressed appearances of *pataḥ*, *ḥatef-pataḥ*, and *qameṣ*,

---

[26] In real life, this knowledge always depended very much on the capabilities of both the boy and the teacher (*melamed*).
[27] In Yiddish studies, this factor, discussed at length in Weinreich 1973, is usually called *L'havdil*.

when adjacent to *heth* or *ayin*, were pronounced as some sort of front mid-vowel; (4) confusion between *ḥolem* and *shureq / qibbuṣ* was observed in different words.[28] Nevertheless, numerous other fundamental features were shared; the Palestinian-like vocalic system with only five qualities (no distinction between *pataḥ* and *qameṣ*, *ṣere* and *segol*), penultimate (and sometimes antepenultimate) stress position, interdental pronunciation of *soft tav* and *soft daleth*, long vowels in open syllables, and short vowels in closed syllables.

During the 13th–16th centuries, the pronunciation of both groups of Jews gradually became standardized, giving rise to norms shared by all Ashkenazi Jews. The *Palestinian*-like vocalic system was replaced with a *Tiberian*-looking system with seven vocalic qualities, in which *pataḥ* and *ṣere* became pronounced differently from *qameṣ* and *segol*, respectively, in open syllables. The fact that the vocalic system of the German component had seven vocalic qualities was determinant for this global normative change in Hebrew pronunciation. The sounds of a number of stressed vowels, whose pronunciation did not originally correspond to their *Tiberian* spelling, changed to fit *Tiberian* norms. Several norms peculiar in the past to *Bney khes* only – such as the velar pronunciation of *heth* and the distinction between sibilants – were adopted by former communities of *Bney hes* as well. Yet, numerous exceptions from the *Tiberian* rules (often already observed in medieval texts by *Bney hes*, and attesting to oral rather than written tradition) survived and became widespread in Central and Eastern Europe also.

During the 14th–16th centuries, a total fusion of the phonetic system of the Ashkenazi vernacular idiom and that of Ashkenazi Hebrew took place. The resulting system included only sounds known in the German component.[29] Beginning with that period, phonetic changes affected Yiddish words independently of their origin. Hebrew and German vowels merged: *qameṣ* with reflexes of MHG *â*, *pataḥ* with MHG *a*, *ṣere* with MHG *ê*, *segol* with MHG *ë*, *shureq* with MHG *ue*, *ḥolem* with MHG *ô*, and *ḥireq* with MHG *ie*.[30]

Throughout Yiddish history, the volume of the Hebrew component was constantly changing: some archaic words disappeared, while numerous new borrowings took place; moreover, numerous new Hebraisms or new meanings were

---

28 Examples of the main phonetic forms of biblical names: Zipporah with /u/ instead of /o/ for *Bney hes*, Samuel with /o/ instead of /u/ for *Bney khes*, Moses with /u/ instead of /o/ for *Bney khes*.
29 The disappearance of interdental consonants with the establishment of /s/ for *soft tav* and /d/ for *soft daleth* represents one of the consequences of this process.
30 M. Weinreich (1958) was the first among Yiddish historical linguists to describe some linguistic details concerning the distinction between *Bney hes* and *Bney khes*. Katz (1985, 1993) emphasized the importance of this distinction for the history of Yiddish. Numerous additional details concerning this topic appear in Beider 2015, with the synthesis on pp. 369–374.

coined within the Ashkenazi culture.[31] The relative volume of this component in Yiddish texts depended on their genres and on authors' choices. Hebraisms were avoided in biblical translations, in the Yiddish sections of various Hebrew-Yiddish dictionaries and glossaries, as well as in literary works following western traditions.[32] On the other hand, their proportion is extremely high in Jewish communal records written in Yiddish; the majority of texts of this type were compiled in Hebrew and, for this reason, the rare Yiddish texts were heavily Hebraicized. Hebraisms comprise about five percent, on average, in EY literature from the turn of the 20th century, reaching nine percent in works by I.L. Peretz and Mendele (Mark 1954).

3.4 Language contact influences

In the history of Yiddish, one can distinguish two kinds of language contact influences: substratal and adstratal. The first corresponds to non-Germanic idioms used by ancestors of Ashkenazi Jews. During the transitional period, corresponding to the shift from these idioms to the German-based Jewish vernacular, the community in question was bilingual. After the end of the period in question, the previously used language was lost, but some of its traces remained in the newly acquired language. In Ashkenazi history, one can distinguish at least three shifts of this kind. The earliest one took place in the Rhineland, at the turn of the second millennium CE. Several Romanisms (mainly with Gallo-Romance / Old French roots) are cases in point, including (among others) StY *bentshn* 'to bless',[33] *leyenen* 'to read', *pen* 'pen', as well as WY *ōren* 'to pray', *dormen* 'to sleep', *bāfen* 'to drink', *prāyen* 'to invite', and *piltsl* 'house maid'.[34]

The second shift took place in Bohemia-Moravia during the 14th century. EY inherited a number of words of Old Czech origin from that shift, such as, for example, StY *zeyde* 'grandfather' (CzY form *deyde* retains the original initial consonant), *bobe* 'grandmother', *treybern* 'to remove forbidden parts from meat

---

31 Weinreich (1973) insisted on the textual origin of numerous Hebraisms in Yiddish. Katz (1985) opposed that view. Following his general idea about Aramaic being the colloquial language of Jews from the Danubian area before they shifted to Yiddish, a language with a German basis created by them, Katz suggests that the Semitic lexical elements in Yiddish are actually mainly inherited from Aramaic (in which, in turn, there was a Hebrew substratum).
32 For example, Hebraisms are almost non-existent in works of this kind before the mid-16th century.
33 The exact etymology of this word is controversial. Contrary to almost all other old Yiddish Romanisms, the Old French origin of it cannot be taken for granted (Beider 2015: 390–402).
34 See details about the Old French lexical substrate in Beider 2015: 392–399.

to make it kosher', and several other butchery and dairy terms. One word of this layer, the interjection *nebekh* 'poor thing!' became pan-Yiddish.[35] The third shift occurred during the 15th–17th centuries in the Grand Duchy of Lithuania and applied to one group of local Jews who abandoned their East Slavic language in favor of EY. Their lexical legacy (if any) cannot be discerned; only a few given names survived, such as the male *Shakhne* and the female *Badane, Sakhne*, and *Vikhne* (Beider 2015: 435). All three of these shifts were of no importance for the structure of Yiddish; their influence was limited to the lexicon.

Adstratal influences correspond to the period when Yiddish varieties were already formed as idioms separate from any contemporary German dialects. For WY, they principally correspond to contacts with co-territorial German dialects. For example, a number of phonetic shifts in Alsatian Yiddish (unknown in Swiss Yiddish) can be explained by the influence of Alsatian (Low Alemannic) German. This is true for the lowering of /i/ and /u/, as well as the fronting-rounding of /u:/ to /y:/ (Zuckerman 1969). Numerous changes due to Dutch occurred in the Yiddish dialect of Amsterdam, in both lexicon and phonology. For example, the original diphthongs [ej] and [aj] (for which no phonemic contrast exists in Dutch) merged to [ɛj], which is peculiar to Dutch phonology (where this diphthong is graphically expressed via 'ij' or 'ei') (Beider 2015: 476).

Massive adstratal changes in EY are due to contacts with Polish, Ukrainian, and Belarusian. They greatly affected all subsystems of EY, even those that are normally relatively closed to external influence. Indeed, Slavic languages are responsible for major grammatical features of EY, including "aspectoid" forms (resembling the Slavic notion of grammatical aspect), calques on Polish models using Germanic verbal prefixes, calques from Belarusian in expressions of LitY, changes of noun genders in comparison to German, borrowings of numerous suffixes (including *-ev, -nik*, and a large collection of diminutive and endearing suffixes), various syntaxic phenomena (for example, the order of words in expressions like *got mayner* 'my God' and *Khayim der kleyner* 'Khayim the small'), a set of phonological traits such as palatal consonantal phonemes, the active use of /tš/ and /ž/, and sibilant confusion in LitY (Weinreich 1973.2: 186–196, 252). No information available to us indicates that the age of these features in Yiddish is old; we do not find them in early Ashkenazi sources. As a result, it is more accurate to consider them adstratal innovations, rather than substratal.[36]

Certain lexical elements of Hebrew or Aramaic origin in Yiddish are clearly substratal; they were inherited from the ancestors of Ashkenazi Jews whose

---

35 See details about the Old Czech lexical substrate in Beider 2015: 429–432.
36 See Beider 2015: 415, 451–452, with the discussion of arguments suggested by Geller (1999, 2009).

vernacular languages were unrelated to German. Among the most plausible candidates for membership in this category are basic religious terms (*malekh* 'angel', *shabes* 'Sabbath', *sotn* 'Satan', *tfile* 'prayer', and *toyre* 'Torah'), directions (*dorem* 'South', *tsofn* 'North', *mizrekh* 'East', *mayrev* 'West'), and a number of abstract words (*mazl* 'star, fortune', *skhus* 'merit', *tsore(s)* 'trouble(s)'). These words are often already found in early Ashkenazi texts, and they are usually present in the Hebrew component of the vernacular languages of non-Ashkenazi Jewish communities as well. Numerous other lexical elements are adstratal; they were incorporated into Yiddish well after its inception. No information available allows us to postulate the existence of substratal system-level influences from Hebrew and Aramaic. All known examples are post-medieval. Among them: (1) the suffix *-te*, of Aramaic origin, used to create feminine forms (*baleboste* 'female owner', *beryete* 'efficient housewife'); (2) the plural suffix *-im* (*poyerim* 'peasants', *doktoyrim* 'physicians', *tayvolim* 'devils'); (3) the plural suffix *-s*, when applied to words with Slavic roots ending in a vowel (*lopetes* 'shovels', *blotes* 'marshes').

During the historical development of Yiddish, there was a fusion of elements taken from various sources. Weinreich (1973.1: 33) illustrates this with the following sentence: *nokhn bentshn hot der zeyde gekoyft a seyfer* 'after the blessing, the grandfather bought a religious book'. In this example, we find words of Romance (root of *bentshn*), Hebrew (*seyfer*), Slavic (*zeyde*), and German (all the other words and the suffix in *bentshn*) origins. However, the importance of this and similar sentences to the question of the fusion character of Yiddish should not be overestimated. Even in this artificially constructed example, the High German basis is evident in all of the grammatical elements: syntax, inflectional endings, and definite and indefinite articles. For this reason, one can effortlessly construct millions of Yiddish sentences in which *all* of the elements are of German origin.

4 Written and oral traditions

4.1 Writing system

Sources compiled by Ashkenazi Jews in their vernacular language traditionally use Hebrew characters.[37] However, throughout Ashkenazi history, the

---

[37] For the period before the 20th century, a manuscript with a Hebrew-Yiddish dictionary kept in Hamburg (Codex 294, compiled around 1500) represents a curious unique exception to this rule: it uses Latin characters (Röll 2013). In the contemporary era, especially with the development of the internet, we find numerous examples of Yiddish transcribed in Latin characters.

correspondence between sounds and the letters used to express these sounds underwent significant changes. The medieval *Bney hes* introduced several rules unknown among non-Ashkenazi Jews: (1) *ayin* for mid-front vowels [e] or [ɛ] and (2) *heth* for [hɛ], [he], [ɛh], or [eh]. The first feature survives in modern Yiddish. The second was abandoned when *heth* ceased to be pronounced as /h/. For *Bney hes*, *shin* was originally used to express both [š] and [s], while *samekh* was not used outside of words of Hebrew origin. However, *samekh* was gradually introduced for [s] in all Ashkenazi communities, while *shin* became limited to [š]. The use of *alef* (with or without a diacritical sign under it) for /o/-colored vowels, typical for modern Yiddish, started in the area of *Bney khes*, while for *Bney hes* the letter *vav* was more commonly used for these sounds. The letter combination (*vav* + *yud*) was used by all Ashkenazi Jews from the Middle Ages onward for both the front rounded vowel [y] or [y:] and various diphthongs whose first element is [a], [ɔ], or [o]. On the other hand, *double yud* originally was used only for diphthongs whose first element was [e] or [ɛ]. Gradually, because of phonetic shifts, this digraph covered not only [ej] and [ɛj], but also [aj].[38] The overall tendency was to avoid phonetic ambiguities. A perfect phonetic match characterizes only StY, in which the pronunciation of any word of non-Semitic origin can be automatically deduced from its spelling. Only lexemes of Hebrew or Aramaic origin are written according to their traditional spelling, which mainly corresponds to that used in the corresponding languages. It was only in the USSR that phonetic spelling became the standard for any word, independent of its origin.

4.2 Modern literature

Numerous literary works are known to us from the 14th–18th centuries. However, even the most popular among them – such as *Tsenerene* and *Bovo-bukh* – remained restricted to internal Jewish use.[39] Modern, internationally acclaimed literature appeared only at the turn of the 20th century, and it is restricted to EY. Its founder was Sholem Yankev Abramovich (1836–1917), who used the pen name Mendele Moykher-Sforim 'Mendele the Bookseller'. His language represents a synthesis of his native LitY and the UkrY spoken by Jews in places where he lived from the age of 19. The publication of his first story, *Dos kleyne mentshele* 'The little man'

---

[38] Details concerning the orthography of Yiddish can be found in Timm 1987; see also the synthesis in Beider 2015: 173–180.
[39] A detailed description of the formation of modern literary Yiddish can be found in Kerler 1999.

(1864), already caused a sensation. His other works (the most popular of which are the novels *Fishke the Lame* and *The Wanderings of Benjamin III*) confirmed his exceptional role in Yiddish literature, because of both their content (often satiric, especially in his early texts, but always with great attention to the sufferings of simple people) and style (an exquisite synthesis of elements from various registers of spoken Yiddish, with extensive use of Hebrew and Slavic lexical elements). His writings had a strong influence on Yiddish writers of the following decades, and it is no surprise that Sholem Aleichem (the pen name of Sholem Rabinovich) called him the "grandfather of Yiddish literature."

Sholem Aleichem (1859–1916) himself became the most popular Yiddish author among Eastern European readers, in his original text and in translation. Many of his short stories are humorous, though the fate of a number of his main characters is tragic. Among his most well-known works are the collections of stories about *Tevye the dairyman* and about *Menakhem-Mendl*, as well as the novels *Mottel the cantor's son*, *Wandering stars*, and *Stempenyu*. I.L. Peretz (1852–1915) is the third classical Yiddish author of short stories who was also a playwright.

During the 20th century, a number of distinguished Yiddish writers and poets worked in various countries (primarily the USSR, Poland, the US, and Lithuania). Among them are David Bergelson, Der Nister, Peretz Markish, Scholem Asch, Joseph Opatoshu, Israel Joshua Singer, Isaac Bashevis Singer (Nobel Prize 1978), Jacob Glatstein, Itzik Manger, Chaim Grade, and Abraham Sutzkever.[40]

4.3 Modern performance (theater, film, etc.)

The first professional Yiddish theater troupe was organized in the 1870s by Abraham Goldfaden (1840–1908) in Romania. Its repertoire was mainly based on texts written by Goldfaden himself and often represented a kind of vaudeville (later more affiliated to operetta) with dancing and songs, in a certain way a continuation of the Ashkenazi tradition of Purim plays. The leading actor and singer of the troupe was Sigmund Mogulesko, who later became famous in the US, the country in which, between 1890 and 1940, Yiddish theater had its Golden Age. The fact that Yiddish theater was banned in the Russian Empire in 1883–1904 played an important indirect role: numerous future leaders of the American Yiddish theater

---

[40] For details concerning Yiddish literature see (among others) Liptzin 1972, Miron 1993, Roskies 1996, Krutikov 2001, and Estraikh 2005.

emigrated from Russia during the period in question. Among the actors whose fame extended well outside of the Yiddish Theater District of New York were Jacob Adler, Boris Thomashefsky, and, during the 1920s, Molly Picon. The original plays were due to Jacob Gordin (who introduced the realistic dramatic direction into Yiddish theater, in contrast to its previous orientation to light genres and pageantry) and David Pinski, as well as classical Yiddish authors Sholem Aleichem and I.L. Peretz. Numerous plays represented translations from various European languages, often executed by Leon Kobrin (who was also an original author). *The Dybbuk* – whose first performance took place in 1919 in Warsaw – became a particularly famous play. Its author, S. Ansky, based it on Hasidic folklore and originally wrote it in Russian before translating it into Yiddish.

During the 1920s in the USSR, Alexis Granowsky organized the Moscow State Jewish Theater (the future GOSET), whose performance acquired great fame. After the emigration of Granowsky (1928), the leading actor of the theater, Solomon Mikhoels, became its artistic director, a position he held for the next 20 years. A Yiddish translation of *King Lear*, the play by Shakespeare, with Mikhoels in the principal role, was the most noteworthy production of the theater during that period. The GOSET was shut down by the Soviet authorities in 1949 after the assassination of Mikhoels and the arrest of another leading actor and director, Benjamin Zuskin (executed in 1952).[41]

During the first half of the 20th century, about one hundred movies were made in Yiddish. Many of them were based directly on theater performances. Among them were a number of Soviet films (often starring Mikhoels or Zuskin; one of them, *Jewish happiness*, was directed by Alexis Granowsky) and several American musical films (including *Yidl mitn fidl*, made in Poland, starring Molly Picon and directed by Joseph Green). *The Dybbuk* (1938), by Polish director Michał Waszyński, became the only Yiddish movie internationally acclaimed for its artistic qualities.[42]

A number of popular Yiddish songs were composed in the territories of the Russian Empire during the 19th century and the first half of the 20th century. Mark Warshavsky, poet and composer, was one of the most appreciated songwriters there (*Oyfn pripetshik*). Some other songs – like *Tumbalalaika* – are anonymous. In the US, a number of Yiddish songs were written for Yiddish theater performances in New York. Perhaps the most popular of them is *Bay mir bistu sheyn*, with lyrics by Jacob Jacobs. During 1940s–1970s, the jazz duo *The Barry Sisters* was particularly popular. Since the 1980s, with the revival of *klezmer* music in the

---

41 For details concerning the history of the Yiddish theater, see Sandrow 1995, Veidlinger 2000, Kanfer 2006, and Berkowitz and Henry 2012.

42 For details concerning the history of the Yiddish cinema, see Hoberman 1995 and Michel 2012.

US, a number of bands have included both instrumental music from this genre and songs with Yiddish lyrics in their performances. Among the best-known examples of the use of Yiddish texts of this kind are those performed by such bands as *The Klezmatics* and *Brave Old World*.

4.4 Naming traditions

The corpus of given names used by Ashkenazi Jews includes numerous biblical names (StY *Avrom* 'Abraham', *Moyshe* 'Moses', *Dvoyre* 'Deborah'), those borrowed from German or Slavic gentiles (*Golde*, *Sonye*), those inherited from Romance-speaking (*Bunem*, *Fayvush*, *Yentl*) or Slavic-speaking (*Beynesh*, *Tsherne*, *Badane*) Jews, and those created in Yiddish (*Alter*) or Hebrew (*Zev*, *Dov*). All personal Yiddish names belong to one of the following classes (Stankiewicz 1969):

– Stylistically neutral full forms (for example, all of the names cited above).
– Hypocoristic forms. These are familiar, intimate, or colloquial. Certain of them carry an expressive nuance; others are completely neutral. In EY and CzY, they are mainly created with the addition of diminutive suffixes: *-l* (*Yankl*, *Berl*, *Velvl*; *Brayndl*, *Gitl*, *Mindl*), *-ke* (*Froymke*, *Moshke*; *Leyke*, *Sorke*), *-ek* and *-ik* (*Moshek*, *Levek*, *Hershlik*, *Pertshik*), *-e* (*Fole*, *Leybe*; *Dobe*, *Tsipe*), *-ush* and *-ish* (*Leybush*, *Berish*), or *-sye* and *-she* (*Dvosye*, *Khisye*, *Khashe*, *Maryashe*). In WY, the main suffixes are *-le* (Alsace, Switzerland, Franconia) and *-khe* / *-khen* (Netherlands, Central and Northern Germany).
– Pet forms that are distinctly expressive and/or emotive. They necessarily include diminutive suffixes in their structure: *-ele* (*Berele*, *Leybele*; *Hindele*, *Rivele*), *-tse* and *-tshe* (*Shlomtse*, *Nyumtshe*; *Khantse*, *Khavtshe*), *-shi* (*Khayemshi*; *Beyleshi*).

Several naming traditions have been valid for Ashkenazi Jews since the Middle Ages. First, all Ashkenazi men have a religious name (*shem ha-qodesh*) and a secular name (*kinnui*). The first category includes full forms of names of Hebrew or Aramaic origin, as well as a few names with Greek roots: Alexander, Kalonymos (StY *Kloynimes*), and Todros (StY *Todres*). All other names are secular. For women, from the religious point of view, all names are equal. Second, names of direct living ancestors cannot be assigned. Third, a series of names may have been assigned to children with precarious health, instead of their previously used names, to protect these children from evil spirits; compare StY *Khayem* and *Khaye* 'life', *Kayem* 'solid', *Kadish* 'the prayer for deceased relatives', *Zeyde* 'grandfather' and *Bobe* 'grandmother', *Alter* / *Zokn* 'old man' and *Alte* / *Skeyne* 'old woman'.⁴³ Numerous given names that first appeared in the medieval Rhineland were gradually introduced by migrants to Eastern Europe.

5 State of research

5.1 History of documentation

The first authors who studied the linguistic peculiarities of Yiddish were Christian scholars. In their publications, E. Schadäus (1592), J. Buxtorf (1609), J.C. Wagenseil (1699), J.H. Callenberg (1733), W.C.J. Chrysander (1750), and F.C.B. Avé-Lallemant (1862) addressed certain aspects of the Hebrew component of Yiddish and formulated the main differences between NHG and Yiddish varieties of Western and Central Europe.⁴⁴ Modern scholarship, in which the comparison is made not to standardized written NHG but to German dialects, was initiated at the end of the 19th century in papers by Lazăr Șăineanu (1889), Alfred Landau (1901, 1911), and Edward Sapir (1916), as well as in the thesis by Jacob Gerzon (1902). These authors founded the scholarly Germanistic approach to the history of Yiddish. The most brilliant representative of that school was Jechiel Fischer / Bin-Nun, whose doctoral research at Heidelberg University (1935–36) concentrated on the phonological comparison between Yiddish and German dialects. His results were published in their totality only in 1973.

A different approach has been elaborated on by Max Weinreich (1894–1969). This scholar insisted on the necessity of analyzing the history of Yiddish not by comparing it to German dialects, but by focusing on factors internal to Jewish linguistic history. Weinreich postulated that Yiddish was born in the Rhine Valley immediately following the creation of the first Jewish communities in German-speaking territories, as a result of a fusion between German elements (due to Christian neighbors) and Hebrew-Aramaic and Romance elements (taken from the languages previously spoken by ancestors of Ashkenazi Jews who, according to Weinreich, migrated to Germany from northern France and northern Italy). This theory is usually called the *Rhine hypothesis* of the origins of Yiddish. Weinreich's posthumous magnum opus, *Geshikhte fun der yidisher shprakh* (1973), represents an encyclopedic-scale history of Yiddish, a unique example of a work covering such a large number of aspects of the inception and development of

---

43 In this list, all names except for the first pair are limited to EY; they already appeared in modern times. See Beider 2001 for details concerning various aspects of Ashkenazi given names.
44 See numerous excerpts from these texts in Frakes 2007 and their analysis in Weinreich 1993.

this language. It provided a general framework for other studies in the domain and introduced numerous fundamental concepts and tools. The publications by Weinreich dramatically changed the domain of Yiddish studies. His influence on all scholars who worked in the same domain after him is enormous. In 1925, he was also a co-founder of what later became the YIVO Institute for Jewish Research and served as its director until 1939.

Among other linguists whose works were particularly important for Yiddish studies, and whose general views roughly corresponded to the *Rhine hypothesis*, were Solomon Birnbaum (who filled the world's first Yiddish chair at Hamburg University, 1922–1933, and was the author of the first scholarly study of the Hebrew component of Yiddish published in 1922), Max Weinreich' son, Uriel (the author of the first modern textbook, *College Yiddish* [1949], and the founder of academic Yiddish studies in the US), and Marvin Herzog (the author of an exemplary study in dialectology, published in 1965, and the chief editor of *Language and Culture Atlas of Ashkenazic Jewry*, a project initiated by Uriel Weinreich).[45]

During the 1980s–1990s, several linguists contributed to the development of the so-called *Danube hypothesis* of the origins of Yiddish. Among them, the most important texts were written by Dovid Katz (1985, 1993), Alice Faber and Robert King (1984), and Eckhard Eggers (1998). They note that modern Yiddish and the German dialects spoken in the Rhineland have virtually no common aspects, while there are a certain number of similarities between Yiddish and the Bavarian dialect of German. Consequently, for scholars who adhere to this school, and especially those who follow Katz, Yiddish originated in Bavaria and the areas bordering it, while the language spoken by Jews in the Rhineland (*Bney hes*) during the first centuries of the second millennium CE had no influence on Yiddish.

The proposed displacement of the area of the inception of Yiddish varieties to areas situated east of the Rhineland is indeed attractive from the point of view of the comparative analysis of Yiddish and German dialects. Numerous positions taken by Katz are also important for a better understanding of the development of the Hebrew component of Yiddish. However, several other major positions of the *Danube hypothesis* are highly controversial. For example, no data corroborate Katz's hypothesis about Aramaic being the spoken language of Jews who migrated in the Middle Ages to the Danube area. In his papers published in 1996–1997, Alexis Manaster Ramer shows that the focus on Bavarian is inappropriate; a large number of pan-Yiddish peculiarities imply that their origins are in west German-speaking territories.

---

45 Previously published atlases (Beranek 1965, Guggenheim-Grünberg 1973) dealt with WY only.

Wexler (1991, 2002) considers Yiddish to be a Slavic language and postulates that it appeared after a relexification of originally Slavic (namely, Upper Sorbian in Central Europe and Polesian in Eastern Europe) words to German. However, the methods he used to corroborate his conclusions contradicted general principles elaborated by historical linguists during the last two centuries. For this reason, his theories have not gained traction with most scholars of Yiddish.

Numerous publications by Erika Timm, including two monumental books (1987, 2005), provide deep insight into the history of the development of the phonetics, orthography, semantics, lexicon, and (to a lesser extent) morphology of Yiddish varieties, especially regarding their German components. They show the inception of a large number of pan-Yiddish features in the West before their propagation in the Ashkenazi communities of Central and Eastern Europe, with a particular emphasis on the *Ivre-taytsh* tradition. The works by Timm and her colleagues from Trier University introduced a new level of rigor in Yiddish studies, thanks to their comparative analysis between Yiddish and German dialects (almost forgotten since the time of Bin-Nun), and their meticulous study of early Ashkenazi sources, which are indispensable for corroborating theories about the history of Yiddish.

The book *Origins of Yiddish dialects* (Beider 2015) addresses numerous aspects of the linguistic history, both horizontal (the unity of all Yiddish varieties known in modern times in Europe) and vertical (the links between vernacular idioms spoken by Ashkenazi Jews during various periods and in different areas).

The aforementioned studies mainly deal with historical linguistics. Numerous sociolinguistic aspects of the history of Yiddish (amply addressed also in Weinreich 1973) are covered by Birnbaum 1979, Shmeruk 1981, Harshav 1990, Fishman 1981 and 1991, Katz 2004, and Jacobs 2005. The synchronic linguistics of modern Yiddish, with a particular emphasis on its grammar, is well covered by Birnbaum 1979 and Jacobs 2005.

5.2 Corpora

The first detailed dictionaries are by Shiye Mordkhe Lifshits: Russian-Yiddish (1869) and Yiddish-Russian (1876). They provide rich, reliable information about his native UkrY. Other excellent quality works are by Alexander Harkavy, who published English-Yiddish and Yiddish-English dictionaries in the 1890s, mainly based on LitY. His Yiddish-English-Hebrew dictionary (1928) remained, for many decades, the most detailed dictionary of EY ever written. Uriel Weinreich's *Modern English-Yiddish and Yiddish-English dictionary* (1968) describes StY, following standards of international lexicography. Works by Yitskhok Niborski (1999 and

2002, co-authored by Bernard Vaisbrot) that also deal with StY reflect important achievements in the domain of Yiddish lexicography. The most comprehensive Yiddish-English dictionary, by Beinfeld and Bochner (2012), with 37,000 entries, is based on Niborski and Vaisbrot 2002. The most comprehensive English-Yiddish dictionary, by Schaechter-Viswanath and Glasser (2016), contains 50,000 entries. A monumental thesaurus was compiled by Stutchkoff (1950).

Today, several major electronic projects concerning Yiddish corpora are underway in Germany. The first one is being conducted by the team of Yiddish scholars at Trier University. It includes materials for a Yiddish-German dictionary and digitalized texts of numerous early sources written by Ashkenazi Jews in their vernacular language; the bulk of the collection corresponds to the 15th–17th centuries. The *Corpus of Modern Yiddish* project of Regensburg University contains texts from 1850 until today. It currently includes about ten million word forms from various published sources (newspapers [primarily the *Forverts*], fiction texts, scientific texts, etc.) and different geographic provenances (Poland, the Americas, the USSR, etc). The *Yiddish Book Center* website (http://www.yiddishbookcenter.org) provides online access to thousands of digitized Yiddish books.[46]

5.3 Issues of general theoretical interest

An analysis of the development of Yiddish touches on a number of questions of interest to linguists that are external to Yiddish studies. The first group of concerned scholars consists of those specializing in Jewish interlinguistics. For them, Yiddish, with its particularly rich documentation and large geographic and chronologic frameworks, represents an ideal object for study. Numerous aspects of the history of the Hebrew component of Yiddish are directly relevant to scholars working on medieval Hebrew. Theoretical issues corresponding to the relationship between Hebrew and Yiddish are of direct interest to scholars who study the influence of sacred (and other high-status) written languages on vernacular tongues, for example, Latin's influence on idioms spoken by Catholics and Protestants, Old Church Slavonic's influence on East and South Slavic languages spoken by Greek Orthodox people, and Arabic's influence on tongues spoken by non-Arabic Muslims. Certain concrete results of the study of early Yiddish can be of benefit to Germanists and Slavists, because they reveal information about the

---

[46] In contrast to the *Corpus of Modern Yiddish*, the digitizations made by the *Yiddish Book Center* are not searchable.

medieval state of the corresponding gentile languages. The gradual separation of Yiddish from German finds parallels in the branching of proto-idioms under certain geographical, political, and/or cultural circumstances. The existence of numerous features shared by all Yiddish varieties is similar to certain linguistic phenomena observed in Afro-American studies. A number of problems in Yiddish studies are applicable to contact linguistics; for example, linguistic changes related to a shift of a population group from one spoken idiom to another, or the development of a minority language in a context in which the majority speaks another tongue (see Rayfield 1970).

5.4 Current directions in research

Despite all of the achievements in Yiddish linguistics during the last hundred years, a number of major aspects of the history of that language are still awaiting adequate linguistic coverage. To this day, no etymological dictionary exists for Yiddish. Such a study would be primarily based on the analysis of references to various words in early Ashkenazi sources. As a result, its compilation depends heavily on the progress of the digitization of documents of this kind. Words from the German component must be compared to their cognate forms in German dialects. The historical aspects of the development of the grammar of Yiddish dialects are almost unexplored.[47] Our knowledge about the history of Yiddish in the Rhine Palatinate-Hessen region (covering Frankfurt, Speyer, Worms, and Mainz) is fragmentary; this dialect was no longer extant in the 19th century. Yet, an analysis of its features during the 17th–18th centuries could provide results of paramount importance for our understanding of the history of the dialects spoken in the 20th century in Alsace, Switzerland, and the Netherlands, as well for the history of WY as a whole.

Another group of open questions concerns specific components. The East Franconian and Bohemian dialects of German seem to be the most important for the inception of WY and EY, respectively. Our knowledge about the history of Yiddish would be greatly enhanced if the information about these two German dialects, and especially their development during the 14th–16th centuries, were less fragmentary. Note that, in contrast to numerous other German dialects, there are no comprehensive dictionaries for these two specific idioms in existence.

---

[47] The studies by Santorini (1989, 1992) are almost the only existing works in the domain of the historical syntax of Yiddish.

The advancement of our knowledge about the Hebrew component of Yiddish could be achieved in several directions. A number of questions concerning the Hebrew pronunciations by medieval *Bney hes* and *Bney khes* remain open. Are their main idiosyncrasies due to internal innovations, or were they inherited from some other traditions? For example, we know that *Bney hes* shared some features with their coreligionists from northern France, while *Bney khes* shared with Old Czech-speaking Jews. However, we are unaware of their precise links to medieval Hebrew pronunciation by Jews in neighboring areas (southern France, Italy, and Byzantium). No comprehensive study of medieval Hebrew exists that would allow estimating the approximate age of numerous Hebrew lexical innovations that were incorporated into Yiddish.

The issues enumerated above all deal with the history of Yiddish. Yet, in our days, hundreds of thousands of *Haredi* Jews still speak it as their everyday language. An adequate linguistic analysis of these contemporary varieties is currently in its initial stage only (see, e.g., Krogh 2012; Assouline, this volume).

References

Beem, Hartog. 1959. *Jerōsche. Jiddische spreekwoorden en zegswijzen uit het Nederlandse taalgebied*. Assen: Van Gorcum–Prakke.
Beider, Alexander. 2001. *A dictionary of Ashkenazic given names: Their origins, structure, pronunciation and migrations*. Bergenfield: Avotaynu.
Beider, Alexander. 2015. *Origins of Yiddish dialects*. Oxford: Oxford University Press.
Beinfeld, Solon & Harry Bochner. 2013. *Comprehensive Yiddish-English dictionary*. Bloomington: Indiana University Press.
Beranek, Franz. 1965. *Westjiddischer Sprachatlas*. Marburg: N.G. Elwert.
Berkowitz, Joel & Barbara Henry (eds.). 2012. *Inventing the modern Yiddish stage: Essays in drama, performance, and show business*. Detroit: Wayne State University Press.
Bin-Nun, Jechiel. 1973. *Jiddisch und die deutschen Mundarten: Unter besonderer Berücksichtigung des ostgalizischen Jiddisch*. Tübingen: Max Niemeyer.
Birnbaum, Salomo. 1922. *Das hebräische und aramäische Element in der jiddischen Sprache*. Kirchhain: Zahn & Baendel.
Birnbaum, Solomon (Salomo). 1979. *Yiddish. A survey and a grammar*. Toronto: University of Toronto Press.
Eggers, Eckhard. 1998. *Sprachwandel und Sprachmischung im Jiddischen*. Frankfurt & New York: Peter Lang.
Estraikh, Gennady. 2005. *In harness: Yiddish writers' romance with communism*. Syracuse: Syracuse University Press.
Faber, Alice & Robert D. King. 1984. Yiddish and the settlement history of Ashkenazic Jews. In David R. Blumenthal (ed.), *Approaches to Judaism in Medieval Times*, vol. 2, 73–108. Chico: Scholars Press.

Fishman, Joshua A. (ed.). 1981. *Never say die! A thousand years of Yiddish in Jewish life and letters*. The Hague: Mouton De Gruyter.
Fishman, Joshua A. 1991. *Yiddish: Turning to life*. Amsterdam & Philadelphia: John Benjamins.
Fleischer, Jürg. 2005. *Westjiddisch in der Schweiz und Südwestdeutschland [Beihefte zum Language and Culture Atlas of Ashkenazic Jewry 4]*. Tübingen: Max Niemeyer.
Frakes, Jerold C. (ed.). 2004. *Early Yiddish texts, 1100–1750*. Oxford: Oxford University Press.
Frakes, Jerold C. 2007. *The cultural study of Yiddish in early modern Europe*. New York: Palgrave Macmillan.
Friedrich, Carl Wilhelm. 1784. *Unterricht in der Judensprache und Schrift*. Prenzlau: Ragoczy.
Geller, Ewa. 1999. Hidden Slavic structure in Modern Yiddish. In Walter Röll & Simon Neuberg (eds.), *Jiddische Philologie. Festschrift für Erika Timm*, 65–89. Tübingen: Max Niemeyer.
Geller, Ewa. 2009. A new portrait of early seventeenth-century Polish Jewry in an unknown Eastern-Yiddish remedy book. *European Judaism* 4(2). 62–67.
Gerzon, Jacob. 1902. *Die jüdischdeutsche Sprache, eine grammatischlexikalische Untersuchung ihres deutschen Grundbestandes*. Cologne: S. Salm.
Guggenheim-Grünberg, Florence. 1973. *Jiddisch auf alemannischem Sprachgebiet*. Zürich: Juris.
Hakkarainen, Heikki J. 1973. *Studien zum Cambridger Codex T-S. 10.K. 22, vol. 3: Lexikon*. Helsinki: Suomalainen Tiedakatemia.
Harkavy, Alexander. 1928. *Yiddish-English-Hebrew Dictionary*, 4th edn. New York: Hebrew Publishing Company.
Harshav (Hrushovski), Benjamin. 1990. *The meaning of Yiddish*. Berkeley, Los Angeles & Oxford: University of California Press.
Herzog, Marvin I. 1965. *The Yiddish language in Northern Poland: Its geography and history*. Bloomington: Indiana University.
Herzog Marvin I. (ed.). 1992–2000. *The language and culture atlas of Ashkenazic Jewry*. Tübingen: Max Niemeyer.
Hoberman, James. 1995. *Bridge of light – Yiddish film between two worlds*. Philadelphia: Temple University Press.
Jacobs, Neil G. 2005. *Yiddish. A linguistic introduction*. Cambridge: Cambridge University Press.
Jakobson, Roman & Morris Halle. 1964. The term *Canaan* in medieval Hebrew. In Lucy S. Dawidowicz, Alexander Erlich, Rachel Erlich & Joshua A. Fishman (eds.), *For Max Weinreich on his seventieth birthday: Studies in Jewish languages, literature and society*, 147–172. The Hague: Mouton.
Kanfer, Stefan. 2006. *Stardust lost: The triumph, tragedy, and mishugas of the Yiddish theater in America*. New York: Knopf.
Katz, Dovid. 1985. Hebrew, Aramaic and the rise of Yiddish. In Joshua A. Fishman (ed.), *Readings in the Sociology of Jewish Languages*, 85–103. Leiden: E.J. Brill.
Katz, Dovid. 1993. East and West, *khes* and *shin* and the origins of Yiddish. In Israel Bartal, Ezra Mendelsohn & Chava Turniansky (eds.), *Studies in Jewish culture in honour of Chone Shmeruk*, 9–37. Jerusalem: The Zalman Shazar Center for Jewish History.
Katz, Dovid. 2004. *Words on fire: The unfinished story of Yiddish*. New York: Basic Books.
Kerler, Dov-Ber. 1999. *The origins of modern literary Yiddish*. Oxford: Clarendon Press.
Krogh, Steffen. 2012. How Satmarish is Haredi Satmar Yiddish. In Marion Aptroot, Efrat Gal-Ed, Roland Gruschka & Simon Neuberg (eds.), *Leket: Jiddistik heute / Yiddish studies today*, 483–506. Düsseldorf: Düsseldorf University Press.
Krutikov, Mikhail. 2001. *Yiddish fiction and the crisis of modernity, 1905–1914*. Stanford: Stanford University Press.

Landau, Alfred. 1901. Der Sprache der Memoiren Glückels von Hameln. *Mitteilungen der Geselschaft für jüdische Volkskunde* 7. 20–67.
Landau, Alfred and Bernhard Wachstein (ed.). 1911. *Jüdische Privatbriefe aus dem Jahre 1619*. Vienna & Leipzig: W. Braumüller.
Lifshits, O. M. 1869. *Russko-novoevrejskij slovar'*. Zhitomir: I.M. Bakst.
Lifshits, O. M. 1876. *Novoevrejsko-russkij slovar'*. Zhitomir: I.M. Bakst.
Liptzin, Sol. 1972. *A history of Yiddish literature*. New York: Jonathan David.
Manaster Ramer, Alexis. 1997. The polygenesis of Western Yiddish – and the monogenesis of Yiddish. In Irén Hegedus, Peter A. Michalove & Alexis Manaster Ramer (eds.), *Indo-European, Nostratic, and beyond: Festschrift for Vitalij V. Shevoroshkin* [*Journal of Indo-European Studies* 22], 206–232. Washington, D.C.: Institute for the Study of Man.
Manaster Ramer, Alexis & Meyer Wolf. 1996. Yiddish origins: The Austro-Bavarian problem. *Folia Linguistica Historica* 17. 193–209.
Mark, Yudel. 1954. A study of the frequency of Hebraisms in Yiddish: Preliminary report. In Uriel Weinreich (ed.), *The field of Yiddish*, 28–47. New York: Linguistic Circle of New York.
Matras, Yaron. 1989. "Lekoudesch": Integration jiddischer Wörter in die Mundart von Rexingen bei Horb. Mit vergleichbarem Material aus Buttenhausen bei Münsingen [*Arbeiten zur Mehrsprachigkeit* 33]. Hamburg: University of Hamburg.
Michel, Chantal Catherine. 2012. *Das Jiddische kino – Aufstiegsinszenierungen zwischen Schtetl und American dream*. Berlin: Metropol.
Miron, Dan. 1973. *A traveler disguised: A study in the rise of modern Yiddish fiction in the nineteenth century*. New York: Schocken.
Moser, Virgil. 1929. *Frühneuhochdeutschen Grammatik. Band 1: Lautlehre. Teil 1: Orthographie, Betonung, Stammsilbevokale*. Heidelberg: Carl Winter.
Moser, Virgil. 1951. *Frühneuhochdeutschen Grammatik. Band 1: Lautlehre. Teil 3: Konsonanten*. Heidelberg: Carl Winter.
Neuberg, Simon. 1999. *Pragmatische Aspekte der jiddischen Sprachgeschichte am Beispiel der Zenerene* [*Jidische Schtudies. Beiträge zur Geschichte der Sprache und Literatur der aschkenasischen Juden* 7]. Hamburg: Helmut Buske.
Niborski, Yitskhok. 1999. *Verterbukh fun loshn-koydesh shtamike verter in yidish*. Paris: Bibliotèque Medem.
Niborski, Yitskhok & Bernard Vajsbrot. 2002. *Dictionnaire yiddish-français*. Paris: Bibliotèque Medem.
Rayfield, Joan R. 1970. *The languages of a bilingual community*. The Hague: Mouton.
Röll, Walter (ed.). 2002. *Die jiddischen Glossen des 14.-16. Jahrhunderts zum Buch Hiob in Handschriftenabdruck und Transkription. Teil 1: Einleitung und Register, Teil 2: Edition*. Tübingen: Max Niemeyer.
Röll, Walter. 2013. A yidish in lataynisher shrift fun arum r"s / 1500. In Israel Bartal, Galit Hasan-Rokem, Ada Rapoport-Albert, Claudia Rosenzweig, Vicky Shifniss & Erika Timm (eds.), *A touch of grace: Studies in Ashkenazi culture, women's history, and the languages of the Jews presented to Chava Turniansky*, 87–117. Jerusalem: The Zalman Shazar Center for Jewish History (Hebrew numbering).
Roskies, David G. 1996. *A bridge of longing: The lost art of Yiddish storytelling*. Cambridge: Harvard University Press.
Șăineanu, Lazăr. 1889. *Studiu dialectologic asupra graiuliu evreo-german*. Bucharest: E. Wiegand.

Sandrow, Nahma. 1995. *Vagabond stars: A world history of Yiddish theater*. Syracuse: Syracuse University Press.
Santorini, Beatrice. 1989. *The generalization of the verb-second constraint in the history of Yiddish*. Philadelphia: University of Pennsylvania PhD thesis.
Santorini, Beatrice. 1992. Variation and change in Yiddish subordinate clause word order. *Natural Language and Linguistic Theory* 10. 595–640.
Sapir, Edward. 1916. Notes on Judeo-German phonology. *Jewish Quarterly Review* 6. 231–266.
Schaechter-Viswanath, Gitl & Paul Glasser (eds.). 2016. *Comprehensive English-Yiddish dictionary*. Bloomington: Indiana University Press.
Schumacher, Jutta (ed.). 2006. *Sefer mišlê šu'olim (Buch der Fuchsfabeln) von Jakob Koppelmann [Jidische Schtudies. Beiträge zur Geschichte der Sprache und Literatur der Aschkenasischen Juden* 12]. Hamburg: Helmut Buske.
Shandler, Jeffrey. 2005. *Adventures in Yiddishland. Postvernacular language and culture*. Berkeley, Los Angeles & Oxford: University of California Press.
Shmeruk, Chone. 1981. *Yiddish literature in Poland. Historical studies and perspectives*. Jerusalem: The Magnes Press. (Hebrew).
Shmeruk, Chone (ed.). 1996. *Paris un' Viena*. Jerusalem: Publications of the Israel Academy of Sciences and Humanities.
Stankiewicz, Edward. 1969. Derivational pattern of Yiddish personal (given) names. In Marvin I. Herzog, Wita Ravid & Uriel Weinreich (eds.), *The field of Yiddish, third collection*, 267–283. The Hague: Mouton.
Stutchkoff, Nahum. 1950. *Der oytser fun der yidisher shprakh*. New York: YIVO Institute for Jewish Research.
Timm, Erika. 1985. Zur Frage der Echtheit von Raschis jiddischen Glossen. *Beiträge zur Geschichte der deutschen Sprache und Literatur* 107. 45–81.
Timm, Erika. 1987. *Graphische und phonische Struktur des Westjiddischen unter besonderer Berücksichtigung der Zeit um 1600*. Tübingen: Max Niemeyer.
Timm, Erika. 2005. *Historische jiddische Semantik: Die Bibelübersetzungssprache als Faktor der Auseinanderentwicklung des jiddischen und des deutschen Wortschatzes*. Tübingen: Max Niemeyer.
Timm, Erika. 2013. Ein neu entdeckter literarischer Text in hebräischen Lettern aus der Zeit vor 1349. *Zeitschrift für Deutsches Altertum und Deutsche Literatur* 142. 417–443.
Toch, Michael. 1977. The Formation of a Diaspora: the settlement of Jews in Medieval German reich. *Aschkenas* 7. 55–78.
Veidlinger, Jeffrey. 2000. *The Moscow State Yiddish theater: Jewish culture on the Soviet stage*. Bloomington: Indiana University Press.
Weinreich, Max. 1958. Bney hes un bney khes in ashkenaz: di problem – un vos zi lozt undz hern. In Shlomo Bickel & Leibush Lehrer (eds.), *Shmuel Niger bukh*, 101–123. New York: YIVO Institute for Jewish Research.
Weinreich, Max. 1973. *Geshikhte fun der yidisher shprakh*. 4 vols. New York: YIVO Institute for Jewish Research (translated as *History of the Yiddish language*. 2 vols. New Haven: Yale University Press, 2008).
Weinreich, Max. 1993. *Geschichte der jiddischen Sprachforschung*. Atlanta: Scholars Press.
Weinreich, Uriel. 1949. *College Yiddish*. New York: YIVO Institute for Jewish Research.

Weinreich, Uriel. 1958. A retrograde sound shift in the guise of a survival: An aspect of Yiddish vowel development. In Diego Catalán (ed.), *Miscelánea homenaje a André Martinet: Estructuralismo e historia* II, 221–267. La Laguna: Biblioteca Filológica.
Weinreich, Uriel. 1963. Four riddles in bilingual dialectology. In *American contributions to the Fifth International Congress of Slavists*, vol. 1, 335–359. The Hague: Mouton.
Weinreich, Uriel. 1968. *Modern English-Yiddish and Yiddish-English dictionary*. New York: YIVO Institute for Jewish Research.
Wexler, Paul. 1991. Yiddish – The fifteenth Slavic language. A study of partial language shift from Judeo-Sorbian to German. *International Journal of the Sociology of Language* 91. 9–150.
Wexler, Paul. 2002. *Two-tiered relexification in Yiddish: Jews, Sorbs, Khazars and the Kiev-Polessian dialect*. Berlin & New York: Mouton de Gruyter.
Zivy, Arthur. 1966. *Jüdisch-deutsche Sprichwörter und Redensarten*. Basel: Victor Goldschmidt.
Zuckerman, Richard. 1969. Alsace: An outpost of Western Yiddish. In Marvin I. Herzog, Wita Ravid, and Uriel Weinreich (eds.), *The field of Yiddish, third collection*, 36–57. The Hague: Mouton.

Vitaly Shalem
Judeo-Tat in the Eastern Caucasus

In loving memory of my grandmother,
Aruvghiz Beniaminova (zichrona le-bracha),
to whom I owe my knowledge of Juhuri...

1 Introduction

Judeo-Tat is a language spoken in the Jewish community of the Eastern Caucasus. This relatively small ethnic group is usually referred to as the *Mountain Jews*. This name is an inaccurate translation of the Russian ethnonym *горские евреи*, which was introduced by the Russian military administration in the 19th century (Semenov 2003: 193, 2007: 181) to distinguish this community from the Ashkenazi Jewish communities in the Russian Empire.[1] The original self-designation of the community is *dʒuhur*, plural forms: *dʒuhur-u(n)* or *dʒuhur-ho*, which is a Judeo-Tat word for 'Jew' and is a cognate of Persian *dʒohud*, Arabic *jæhudi / jæhud*, and Hebrew *jəhudi*.[2]

The name Judeo-Tat indicates the similarity between this Jewish language variety and another one spoken in the same region by a larger, Muslim group of Iranian origin, usually referred to as *Tat*.[3] The ethnonym *Tat*, though to some extent accepted as a self-name by this community, is of unknown origin (Semenov 1992: 4); it was widely used in Azerbaijan to designate people of Iranian origin. Its meaning can vary from the neutral 'settled tribes', as opposed to nomads, to the pejorative 'obedient servants, tribute payers'. Another name used by the community is *pars*, and the language is called *parsi* or *farsi* 'Persian', or by a local village name to distinguish different dialects (Altshuler 1990: 16; Miller 1929: 5, 10, 29, 39, Miller 1892: xvii; Semenov 1992: 4–5). In addition to the Muslim and Jewish ethnolects, scholars have mentioned yet another related language variety that

---

[1] The Russian adjective *горский* was used at that time to describe any ethnic group residing in the Caucasus, regardless of whether they settled in the mountains or not (Semenov 2003: 193). The English translation of *горский* as 'mountain' is not accurate: this adjective is derived from *горец* 'highlander' (as opposed to *горный*, derived from *гора* 'mountain'), and is normally used to describe highlanders, their culture, and their traditions.
[2] Compare with the names for Jews in the languages of the local people in Daghestan: Kumyk *ʒuhut*, Lezgi *tʃuwudar*, Tabasaran *dʒuhud*, Dargwa *ʒuhut'i*, etc. (Nazarova 1996: 123).
[3] The Tat language has nothing to do with a group of Tati languages, which are spoken in Northwestern Iran and belong to the northwestern subgroup of Iranian languages (Grjunberg 1961: 107; Oren and Zand 1982c: 460).

a small Christian community in the same region spoke. These people referred to their vernacular as *farsi* but identified themselves as Armenians (Miller 1929: 16).

The situation in which three different communities speak similar language varieties led to different approaches among the scholars in their historical and linguistic research of this Jewish community, often driven by a non-scientific, political agenda during the Soviet era (Altshuler 1990: 129–132; Nazarova 2002; Semenov 2003: 194–199). Some of the community members adopted those trends, which often caused identity confusion and influenced self-designation and language name(s).

1.1 Names of the language

Russian scholar Vsevolod Miller was the first linguist who studied Judeo-Tat and coined the first language names in professional literature (Miller 1892, 1900, 1901, 1903). Based on previously gathered materials for the Tat language and his study, he concluded that the "Jewish Iranian variety" spoken by the ethnic Jewish population in the Eastern Caucasus was a dialect of the Tat language (1892: xvii, 1903: 160). He systematically referred to it as *еврейско-татский язык / еврейско-татское наречие* 'Judeo-Tat language / dialect', *еврейско-горское наречие* 'Jewish-Highland dialect', *язык горских евреев* 'language of the Highland Jews', or *татское наречие горских евреев* 'Tat dialect of the Highland Jews'. However, during the Soviet period, the terminology underwent significant changes. The three communities were considered one ethnic group of Iranian origin, divided by religion, and the language was referred to as *татский язык* 'Tat language', that was split into two main dialects: *Northern* (Jewish varieties) and *Southern* (Muslim and Christian varieties) (Miller 1929: 37–38; Anisimov 1932; Grjunberg 1963b: 3; Grjunberg and Davydova 1982: 231–232). The traditional distinction between the two varieties, based on linguistic, cultural, and ethnic backgrounds, was restored in the 1990s (Nazarova 1996: 121).

Apparently, the members of the community themselves were not always aware of the distinctiveness of their language and often treated it based on its genealogical relation to other Iranian languages. In the middle of the 19th century, they defined the community vernacular as *Tat*, sometimes even as *the ancient Persian language* (Tsherny 1884, quoted in Altshuler 1990: 359). In the 1860s, Rabbi Yaakov Yitzhaki used the same name in his correspondence with Jewish Russian scholar Avraham Harkavy (Altshuler 1990: 360, 363). In his foreword to the *Jewish Prayer Book* with a Judeo-Tat translation, published in 1909, the translator Asaf Pinkhasov writes about difficulties and complications of translating Jewish prayers into the Tat language: "זוהון תתי" *zuhun tati* (Pinkhasov

1909: vii). In the letters of appreciation written by the Rabbi of Derbent and the leader of the Zionist organization in the Caucasus, published in the same volume, the language is called "זוהון אימו" *zuhun imu* 'our language' as well as "זוהון גלותי זוהון תתי" *zuhun galuti zuhun tati* 'the language of exile, the Tat language' (Pinkhasov 1909: xi, xiii).

Nowadays, the older people and others with a good command of Judeo-Tat refer to this language as *zuhun imu* 'our language', *zuhun ʤuhur* 'language of Jews', or *zuhun ʤuhuri* 'Jewish language'. Some people still use the names that indicate its non-Jewish origin: *zuhun tati* 'Tat language' or *zuhun farsi* 'Persian language', often adding that the true Jewish language is *zuhun ʕivriti* 'Hebrew language'. A similar variety of names is used in Russian: *язык горских евреев* 'language of the Highland Jews', *еврейский язык* 'Jewish language', *горский язык* 'Highlanders' language', *татский язык* 'Tat language', *татский-еврейский* 'Tat-Jewish', *фарси/персидский* 'Farsi/Persian', *диалект персидского* 'dialect of Persian'. However, quite often the Russian words *наш/свой* 'our/one's own' are used, even with the names that do not have a clear indication of the variety being a Jewish language (Shalem 2011). In the English of the Mountain Jewish community of Brooklyn, the word *Gorsky*, a borrowed form of the Russian adjective *горский* 'highland', is used to refer to the language, as well as to distinguish the community from other Jewish communities.

In Israel, Judeo-Tat is called קווקזית *kavkazit* in Hebrew, meaning 'Caucasian'. Although this name is completely wrong and misleading, it is in general use in Israel in colloquial speech. In linguistic literature, טטית-יהודית *tatit-jehudit* 'Judeo-Tat' is used. Recently, the term *Juhuri*, derived from Judeo-Tat *zuhun ʤuhuri* 'Jewish language', is frequently used in all languages, by community members, as well as by some scholars (Bram and Shauli 2001; Podolsky 2002; Nazarova 2002; Agarunov and Agarunov 2010; Authier 2012).[4]

1.2 Linguistic affiliation

The Tat language varieties belong to the southwestern branch of the Iranian languages and are very close to Persian and Tajik (Grjunberg 1961: 107–108; Grjunberg and Davydova 1982: 232; Oren and Zand 1982c: 460; Nazarova 1996: 120). The idea of Judeo-Tat (and Tat) being closely related to Persian was first formulated by Vsevolod Miller (1892: xvi–xvii). However, some scholars claimed that it belongs to the northwestern branch, together with Talysh, Gilaki, and

---

[4] About the preference and specifics of using *Juhuri* vs. *Judeo-Tat*, see Bram (2008: 338).

Mazanderani, the so-called Caspian languages.[5] V. Minorsky (1934) assumes that Tat takes an intermediate position between the Caspian subgroup and the Persian language (quoted in Grjunberg 1961: 106). In his work that discusses the place of Tat among the Iranian languages, Grjunberg quotes some contradictory opinions by Iranian scholars: Some believe that Tat resembles Persian to a great extent, but others assume that Tat, together with Talysh and Semnani, takes an intermediate position between the Caspian languages (Gilaki and Mazanderani) and Central Iranian dialects (1961: 106). Based on his fieldwork with the Muslim varieties of Tat, Grjunberg proves the hypothesis that Tat shows great genetic resemblance to Persian and Tajik, i.e., belongs to the southwestern subgroup of Iranian languages (1961: 107–113). Regarding Judeo-Tat, scholars mention a lesser degree of resemblance to Modern Persian, because the Jewish variety preserves some features that were lost in that language, and it appears more archaic. They are also convinced that it shows greater differences on the lexical level from Modern Persian (Grjunberg and Davydova 1982: 232; Nazarova 1996: 120).

1.3 Regions where language is/was spoken

The historical region of the Judeo-Tat speaking communities in the Eastern Caucasus was limited to Northern Azerbaijan and Daghestan, and most of the population was spread out in numerous small villages. However, starting in the 18th century, many changes took place. For example, many inhabitants abandoned their small villages and moved to towns. By the beginning of the 20th century about 60% of the Mountain Jews already lived in the cities, and some new communities were established in Azerbaijan, Daghestan, and in the Northern Caucasus. The process of urbanization continued after the October revolution, during the Civil War (1917–1922). By the time the Soviet government was established in the region, the urban Mountain Jewish population was concentrated in Quba, Vartashen (now Oghuz), Ganja, Shamakhy, and Baku in Azerbaijan; in Derbent, Petrovsk-Port (Makhachkala), Temir-Khan-Shura (Buynaksk), Khasavyurt, and Kizlyar in Daghestan. Earlier, in the 19th century, new communities were created in the Northern Caucasus in Grozny and Nalchik, which, being Russian army forts, were believed to offer more protection for the Jewish population. The migration of Jews from Vartashen to Tiflis (Tbilisi) created a small Judeo-Tat speaking community in Georgia (Altshuler 1990: 153–235; Anisimov 1888: 10–11, 13; Oren and Zand 1982a: 182; Semenov 1992: 8–10; Nazarova 1996: 123–124; Semenov 2007: 198–215).

---

5 Grjunberg (1961: 106) mentions works by W. Geiger (1898–1901) and A.A. Frejman (1927).

By the end of the 19th century, a small community emerged in Jerusalem. From the beginning of the Zionist movement in the Caucasus and until the establishment of the Soviet government in the region, migration to the Land of Israel continued. As a result, a small community was established in Tel Aviv. During the 1970s, a considerable number of Mountain Jews immigrated to Israel (Altshuler 1990: 477–522). However, drastic changes took place in the 1990s, with the beginning of the post-Soviet *aliyah*. The majority of the Mountain Jews left the former Soviet republics; many of them moved to Israel, but new communities also formed in the United States, Canada, Germany, Austria, Belgium, and Australia. Many of those who stayed in the former Soviet Union left the historical regions as well, creating new large centers in Moscow, Saint Petersburg, and Stavropol Krai (see also Nazarova 196: 124; Semenov 2003: 192).

1.4 Present-day status

The *UNESCO Atlas of the World's Languages in Danger* (2010) classifies Judeo-Tat as an endangered language. The Atlas lists two locations where this language is spoken: the Caucasus and Israel, classifying the degree of endangerment as *definitely endangered* for both. Taking into consideration the current dispersed diaspora of the Mountain Jews, and the fact that members of the newly created communities come from different backgrounds, more groups should be defined and analyzed in a more detailed way. However, one can conclude, that for most of the locations, the degree of endangerment lies between *definitely endangered* and *severely endangered*, depending on the families' origin (Shalem 2013b). The only exception is the community in Qırmızı Qəsəbə (a small municipality next to Quba) in Azerbaijan, where the language is still transmitted from parents to children and is used in everyday life (Clifton et al. 2005). However, almost all of the speakers (except for children of pre-school age) are multilingual; there are no schools where Judeo-Tat is the language of instruction; there is low availability of materials for education and literacy; the language is unable to meet the challenges of modernity and has no official status; and the language is documented in a fragmentary way. All of this makes the status of Judeo-Tat spoken in Qırmızı Qəsəbə *vulnerable* (Shalem 2013b).

2 Historical background

The Jewish settlement in the Caucasus was one of the oldest in the Diaspora (Altshuler 1990: 32). Unfortunately, the Mountain Jews did not preserve any written sources about the community's origin and the creation of the Jewish settlement in the Caucasus. The few fragmental oral traditions do not provide much information, and it is hard to tell if they are original or some later creations, based on the Biblical sources. One of the traditions relates that Jews in the Eastern Caucasus are the descendants of the ten tribes exiled from the Kingdom of Israel and settled in Media in 722 BC by Shalmaneser V, the King of Assyria (Altshuler 1990: 33). Another one claims that the Mountain Jews are the descendants of the Jews exiled from the Kingdom of Judah in the 6th century BC by Nebuchadnezzar II, the King of Babylon (Altshuler 1990: 35).[6] These traditions suggest that the Mountain Jews cannot be descendants of the Second Temple exile. This hypothesis finds support in some ancient Armenian and Georgian chronicles (Altshuler 1990: 35).[7] From the historical, cultural, and linguistic perspectives, this Jewish community most probably originated as a part of Iranian Jewry and was disconnected at some point in its history, because of migration to the Eastern Caucasus.

Regarding the date of the actual arrival of the Mountain Jews in the Eastern Caucasus, there are different approaches among historians, but the general tendency is to link the emerging of this community to the Sasanian Empire (226–651 AD) (Altshuler 1990: 37). The Caucasus, being a strategically important frontier, was very often granted certain liberties and did not always follow the official policies of the emperors, for example, attitudes towards minority religions. During the reign of Bahram I and Bahram II (272–293), the power of the Zoroastrian clergy grew significantly, and the policy of religious tolerance gave way to persecutions against other religions. Later, Yazdegerd II (438–457) and Peroz I (459–483) continued promoting Zoroastrianism and broadened persecutions of the religious minorities. Christians and Jews searched for shelter in the distant and calmer regions of the Empire. This was probably the reason for the establishment and expansion of the Jewish settlement in the Eastern Caucasus (Altshuler 1990: 37–39).[8] Throughout its history, the number of migration waves reinforced the community. The newcomers mainly came from Iran; the latest influx was in the 18th to 19th centuries, from the Gilan Province (Semenov 1992: 20, 2003: 191), and many family oral chronicles still preserve the memory of this relocation.

---

6 See also Miller (1892: xii–xiii) and Semenov (1992: 11–14).
7 Altshuler mentions the Armenian chronicle *History of the Armenians*, written by Movses Khorenatsi, who probably lived in the 5th century AD, and the collection of Georgian chronicles known as *Kartlis Tskhovreba*, probably gathered and edited in the 12th century AD (Altshuler 1990: 36). Semenov (2007: 182–189) lists more medieval sources about the Jewish presence in the region. See also Oren and Zand (1982a: 183).
8 About the establishment of the Jewish community in the Eastern Caucasus see also Semenov (1992: 17–20) and Oren and Zand (1982a: 182–183).

2.1 Speaker community: documentation

Starting in the 17th century, information about the Jewish community of the Eastern Caucasus appeared in European sources. The first attestation is by Adam Olearius, a German scholar, who, while traveling to Iran, visited Derbent in 1637. In his book, *Beschreibung der muscowitischen und persischen Reise* (1647), he wrote that many Jews lived in Tabasaran and that he found both Muslim and Jewish people in Derbent (quoted in Semenov 2007: 190). In 1670, Jan Struys, a Dutch traveler, visited Derbent; like Olearius, he mentioned that the local Jews originated from the tribe of Benjamin (Semenov 2007: 190). In 1690, another Dutch traveler, Nicolaes Witsen, came to Daghestan and reported about the great number of Jews living there (Semenov 2007: 190; Miller 1892: ii). During the Persian Campaign of Peter the Great, by the tsar's order, Captain Johan-Gustaw Gärber made a detailed report about the region. He mentioned Jewish settlements in Derbent, Quba, Rustov, Karakaitag, and Shamakhy (Semenov 2007: 191; Miller 1892: xii–xiii). However, these and similar reports are very fragmentary and do not provide much information about the community.

The first who tried to study this community systematically was the Jewish traveler and ethnographer Yehuda Tsherny. In the 1860s and 1870s, he traveled several times to the Caucasus, published a number of articles in Jewish and Russian periodicals, and planned to publish his study in several volumes. In 1884, Avraham Harkavy posthumously published the parts of his work dedicated to the community of the Mountain Jews (Altshuler 1990: 20–23).

Ilya (Eliyahu) Anisimov was another Jewish ethnographer who contributed to the documentation on this community. In his work, *Кавказские евреи-горцы (Jews-Highlanders from the Caucasus)*, published in 1888, Anisimov criticized Tsherny's work as inaccurate regarding many subjects. He claimed that, being an Ashkenazi Jew, Tsherny could not gain the local Jews' confidence, and they never spoke to him with full trust (1888: 5–6). According to Anisimov, the son of the community Rabbi, he had an advantage in being familiar with the culture and speaking the community language (1888: 9–10).[9]

2.2 Linguistic attestations and sources

In his *Allgemeine historisch-topographische Beschreibung des Caucasus* (1796), Friedrich Enoch Schröder reports that the language spoken by the Jews in the

---

[9] On Anisimov and his work, see also Altshuler (1990: 24–28).

Caucasus is an unknown dialect of Persian (quoted in Altshuler 1990: 359). Another Russian scholar, Eduard Eichwald, who visited the Caucasus in the 1820s, is the first one to mention that Jews in the region speak differently from the Tats (1834, quoted in Altshuler 1990: 359). The Russian orientalist Ilya Berezin wrote the first description of the Tat languages (1851), based on some varieties spoken by the Muslim population (Altshuler 1990: 360). In the late 1850s, another Russian scholar, Bernhard Dorn, collected materials – words and texts – in this language. His fieldwork was also restricted to the varieties spoken by the Muslim population, but, according to his testimony, he also collected some samples of the Jewish variety (1861, quoted in Altshuler 1990: 360). Based on the data collected, he prepared an overview of the grammar and translated some texts, but a large part of the collected materials was never published (Altshuler 1990: 360). Anisimov (1888: 6–7) referred to some words and phrases collected by Yehuda Tsherny (1884) but noted a high inaccuracy in his examples.

Rabbi Yaakov Yitzhaki was the first person who conducted a systematic study of the Jewish variety. In the 1860s, he started to collect words in this language and even tried to deal with the grammar, but most of his work was lost. The remaining manuscript contains about two thousand words with Hebrew translation (Zand 2002: 142–147; Altshuler 1990: 360; Oren and Zand 1982c: 460). Interesting attestations can be found in the correspondence between Rabbi Yaakov and Avraham Harkavy; for example, in one letter he wrote about Judeo-Tat: "This language is growing weaker, and soon the remembrance of it will disappear amongst living [people]" (my translation, quoted in Altshuler 1990: 360; see also Zand 2002: 140–141).

Russian scholar Vsevolod Miller conducted the first significant research of Judeo-Tat. His pioneering work, published in 1892, apart from an introductory chapter on the community's historical background, contains eight texts with Russian translations and a dictionary of about 1500 words. In 1932, his son, Boris Miller, published two additional texts and some proverbs collected in Azerbaijan (276–290).[10]

The first known attestation of Judeo-Tat as a written language, dated 1863, belongs to Yehuda Tsherny: "And they write their letters in the language that they speak" (my translation, quoted in Altshuler 1990: 363). A letter in Hebrew from 1865 "speaks about an already existing tradition of writing in Judeo-Tat, but there are no data revealing when this tradition emerged" (Zand 1991: 388). In this letter,

---

10 Amaldan Kukullu (Amal Kukuliev), a Mountain Jewish writer and folklorist, published a large collection (about three thousand) of Judeo-Tat proverbs, blessings, wishes, and other sayings in 1997.

Rabbi Yitzhak Mizrahi wrote to the police of Derbent (Zand 1991: 433; Altshuler 1990: 363): "We write everything in the sacred language [*lashon ha-kodesh*], but sometimes those, who do not know the sacred language well, write also in the Tat language spoken among us" (my translation, Tsherny 1884: 48, as quoted in Altshuler 1990: 363).

A letter appointing Rabbi Yitzhak ben Yaakov, the father of Rabbi Yaakov Yitzhaki, a rabbinical judge in Derbent (Yitzhaki 1974: 8) illustrates this practice.[11] This document from 1845 consists of two parts: the letter of appointment itself composed in Hebrew (He) and the financial part of this step partially written in Juhuri (Ju).[12] The Juhuri part and its translation can be found in (1). This document is the earliest preserved original using Juhuri as a written language.

1. Early example of Juhuri as written language (P119/3, lines 9–10):

אימו	*imu*	Ju: 'we'
ח'מ'	*ḥātumim maṭāh*	He: abbreviated form of חתומים מטה 'signed below'
ערב קבלן	*ʕāreḇ qabəlān*	He: עָרֵב קַבְלָן 'guarantee' (Jewish legal term)
ארי ר' יצחק	*ɛri rɛbi ishoʁ*	Ju: 'for' + abbreviated form of 'rabbi' + 'Yitzhak'
ארי אני	*ɛri ɛn-i*	Ju: 'for' + 'of' + 'this'
מאה ועשרים	*meʔā vəʕesrim*	He: 'hundred and twenty'
מנת	*monot*	Ju: here 'ruble', used for any currency in Juhuri
נימיו רא	*nimɛ-ju rɛ*	Ju: 'half' + 'it' + accusative marker
ארי פסח	*ɛri pɛseḥ*	Ju: 'for' + He: 'Passover'
דרני	*dorɛni*	Ju: 'to give' PRES.3PER.SING
נימיו רא	*nimɛ-ju rɛ*	Ju: 'half' + 'it' + accusative marker
ארי אאביר סל	*ɛri ɛ-ɛxir sal*	Ju: 'for' + 'to' + 'end' + 'year'
דרני	*dorɛni*	Ju: 'to give' PRES.3PER.SING

The first known text in Judeo-Tat was preserved as a copy made by Yehuda Tsherny in the late 1860s. This is a short list of taxes and services owed by Jews to the prince of Kaitag. Tsherny did not see the original, but a duplicate made

---

[11] This document belongs to Yaakov Yitzhaki Private Collection (P119/3), which is a part of the Central Archives for the History of Jewish People, Jerusalem.
[12] Further examination shows that the Hebrew part of the document is written in Oriental semi-cursive script, whereas the financial part that contains lines in Judeo-Tat is written in letters that are closer to Square Hebrew script (Karina Shalem, personal communication).

by the Rabbi of Tarki from an unknown source. Based on the name of the prince mentioned in the documents, Altshuler assumes that the latest possible time it could have been written is 1820 (1990: 364).

Altshuler concludes that writing in Judeo-Tat was an established tradition in the second half of the 19th century and that Judeo-Tat was mainly used by "simple people" to write letters, business notes, etc. (1990: 363–364).[13] An additional source, revealed recently, supports his assumption: ten letters that were written in 1885–1889 by a Rabbi from the village of Haftaran in Azerbaijan to his son in Quba (Shalem 2013: 153).[14] Some texts in Judeo-Tat can still be found in private collections and family archives. These sources are usually quite recent, from the first half of the 20th century and sometimes even later. Often they are translated copies of religious texts or Bible commentaries, but some are original manuscripts (Shalem 2013: 152).

2.3 Historical development

Unfortunately, written sources or language descriptions dated before the late 19th century are not available. It is hard to trace the historical development of Judeo-Tat prior to that time. Apparently, at some point in its history, the community acquired the language of the neighboring Iranian people. It is hard to judge whether this process took place in the Caucasus or prior to the community's migration to this region. The isolated way of life of the Jewish people led to different paths of development of these two language varieties, creating differences on phonetic, lexical, and grammatical levels. However, the Jewish variety itself is not completely homogeneous and can be divided into several dialects and accents, which show differences mainly in pronunciation and vocabulary.

Judeo-Tat contains four different dialects, based on the geography of settlement and native speakers' attestations. They are: (1) the *Qaitoqi* dialect, named after the historical region of Kaitag in Daghestan, spoken in Northern Daghestan

---

[13] See also Musakhanova (1972: 409) about some attempts to establish written literature in Judeo-Tat in the second half of the 19th century.
[14] This source belongs to the Jerusalem Krupp collection 3257, National Library of Israel f.73617. Documents written in Hebrew often contain notes in Judeo-Tat added by the owners. Sometimes, when an original source had empty pages, they were used to write comments, notes, or even agreements; some of them are in Judeo-Tat. Unfortunately, such additions to the original sources cannot be dated (Shalem 2013: 152). Examples can be found in a collection of various texts from 1882–1958 (Jerusalem Krupp collection 360, National Library of Israel f.75070) that contains Hebrew texts from Quba: letters, community registries, homiletical sermons, and other documents (Karina Shalem, personal communication).

and some regions of the Northern Caucasus; (2) the *Derbendi* dialect, spoken in Derbent and neighboring villages; (3) the *Qubei* dialect, spoken mainly in Quba in Northern Azerbaijan; and (4) the *Shirvoni* dialect, named after the historical region of Shirvan in Azerbaijan, spoken in Vartashen, Ganja, and Shamakhy (Oren and Zand 1982c: 459–460; Nazarova 1996: 124). The Qaitoqi dialect can be further subdivided into three different accents spoken in Northern Daghestan, Grozny, and Nalchik (Nazarova 1996: 124).

Many communities recognized as having distinct dialects or accents emerged quite recently. For example, the Jewish settlement in Quba (modern Qırmızı Qəsəbə) started in the 18th century after the campaign of Nadir Shah, during which many Jewish villages in Northern Azerbaijan and Daghestan were plundered. The local ruler, Hussein-khan, allowed Jews to settle in the town, but on the opposite side of the river. The villages of origin are still remembered in the names of various districts in the settlement. Since then, there have been several influxes of population, including a migration of Jews from the Gilan province in Iran (Semenov 1992: 9; Semenov 2007: 207–208; Oren and Zand 1982a: 183–184; Altshuler 1990: 207–208).

The renewed settlement in Derbent was created in a similar way after the Jewish settlements of *Juhud-Qata* 'Jewish valley' were destroyed in the late 18th century (Oren and Zand 1982a: 184), and their surviving population settled in Derbent and other places in Daghestan. Later, the Derbent community grew continuously, due to migration from the neighboring villages and, during the Civil War, from Quba and other places in Azerbaijan (Semenov 1992: 9, 2007: 205–206). As mentioned above, the communities of Nalchik and Grozny, which are recognized as having separate accents within the Qaitoqi dialect, were created in the 19th century.[15] To conclude, the dialectal division of Judeo-Tat known today emerged in the course of the 18th and 19th centuries and was probably finalized by the beginning of the following century.

The beginning of publishing activities and the formation of a new literary tradition characterize the development of Judeo-Tat in the 20th century. The first two books published in Judeo-Tat were *Mɛtlɛb siyniho* (*The Goal of the Zionists*, 1908), a translation of Yosef Sapir's Russian *Сионизм* (*Zionism*, 1903), and a Jewish prayer book, *Qol tefila* (*Voice of Prayer*, 1909), with a parallel Judeo-Tat translation. Asaf Pinhasov (1884–1920), "an early Mountain Jewish Zionist" (Zand 1985: 6), translated both books. Similar to the written sources mentioned above,

---

15 However, not every new settlement created a new dialect or accent. For example, the Jewish population in Baku (Azerbaijan) mainly comes from Quba and places that are classified as speaking the Shirvoni dialect, but they are still recognized as speakers of either the Qubei or Shirvoni varieties of Judeo-Tat.

Judeo-Tat was written in the Hebrew alphabet in these books. Several issues of the first newspaper in this language were published in 1915–1916 in Baku. This newspaper had a Hebrew title, הד הרים (*The echo of the mountains*). During 1919 in Baku, the local Zionist organization published its own newspaper (Oren and Zand 1982c: 460; Zand 1985: 7). After the establishment of the Soviet government in the Eastern Caucasus, publishing activities continued in Azerbaijan. For a short period in 1922, the first Soviet newspaper in Judeo-Tat, *korsoχ* (*Worker*), was published, as well as the first primer, *taza ſkola* (*New School*, 1921), and the first textbook for Judeo-Tat schools, *gyl doʙi* (*Mountain Flower*, 1927).

Starting in 1927, the center of publishing activity moved to Daghestan (Oren and Zand 1982c: 460–461), where language planning discussions took place starting in 1926 (Musakhanova 1993: 85). As the Derbendi dialect was seen to hold an intermediate position between the Qubei and Qaitoqi varieties, it was selected as the basis for the literary language. The strongest debates were about the sources for lexical enrichment. Three different approaches were discussed: to use Hebrew, Azerbaijani, or Persian as source languages. In practice, Russian, which was generally used by other local languages in Daghestan, became the source language. The use of Hebrew script managed to survive for a while, but, in 1929, the decision to move to Latinized script was accepted (Musakhanova 1993: 85–87; Zand 1991: 412). In 1938, the Cyrillic alphabet replaced the Latinized one (Oren and Zand 1982c: 461; Zand 1991: 416). In the same year, the constitution of Daghestan ASSR declared Tat (de facto Judeo-Tat) one of the ten official languages in the republic (Oren and Zand 1982c: 461).[16]

The weekly newspaper in Judeo-Tat, זחמתכש / *Zaḥmətkəş* / Захьметкеш (*Worker*), was founded in June 1928 in Daghestan, and it played an important role in language development. It was initially published in the Hebrew alphabet, which was gradually replaced by Latinized script in 1930–1931. The newspaper was actively used to propagate the new alphabet. It had a special section called "Xutə boşit!" ("Learn!"), which often published lessons, orthographical norms, and lists of new words in Judeo-Tat. From November 1938 until July 1941, the newspaper was published under the new name *Гъирмизине асдара* (*The Red Star*) (Musakhanova 1993: 87; Zand 1985: 11–12).

After the 1920s, contact of Judeo-Tat with other languages increased drastically. Apart from the communities in the Northern Caucasus, the influence of Russian remained quite low. However, starting in the 1920s, the significance of

---

[16] The speakers of the Muslim variety of Tat in Daghestan were a highly assimilated minority. They were considered speakers of Azerbaijani, which was also one of the ten official languages in the autonomous republic.

the Russian language grew rapidly. It became an important component of community multilingualism and the main source for lexical enrichment of the community language. Starting from that time, new loan words entered the Judeo-Tat language in their original phonetic form, whereas previously words borrowed from Russian underwent phonological adaptations to match the phonetic inventory and phonotactic constraints of the target language (Oren and Zand 1982c: 461–462).

In the 1930s, apart from two schools in Baku and Nalchik, schools with Judeo-Tat as the language of instruction existed mainly in Daghestan, and most of them offered only primary education in the native language. More and more, the Jewish population preferred education in Russian, rather than in local languages. After World War II, all Judeo-Tat schools were converted to Russian schools (Oren and Zand 1982c: 462; Zand 1991: 418, 428). Henceforth, the teaching of Judeo-Tat was offered in some schools, but only for a limited number of hours in elementary schools. A growing number of Judeo-Tat speakers had difficulties reading in their mother tongue, and many "knew it only as a second language, their main language being Russian" (Zand 1991: 418). Publications in Judeo-Tat ceased to appear, as well (Oren and Zand 1982c: 462). The weekly newspaper was renewed in 1947 under yet another name, *Гъирмизине гІэлем* (*The Red Banner*), but closed again in 1952, leaving (Judeo-)Tat the only official language in Daghestan without its own newspaper (Altshuler 1990: 377; Zand 1986: 38, 1991: 417).

It was only at the end of 1953 that books in Judeo-Tat started to appear again, at a very low rate of one or two books per year. In 1959, a volume, *Нуьвуьсдегоргьой мати* (*Tat writers*), was published; this annual collection of literature in Judeo-Tat subsequently appeared almost every year from 1960 to 1980, under a new name, *Ватан Советиму* (*Our Soviet Motherland*) (Zand 1986: 39). It was not until 1975, probably as a reaction to the *aliyah* of the Mountain Jews to Israel, that the weekly newspaper was renewed under its original name, *Захьметкеш*, and broadcasting in Judeo-Tat started on the Daghestanian radio (Oren and Zand 1982c: 462). The newspaper was renamed in 1991 as *Ватан* (*Motherland*), and it is still published in Russian and Judeo-Tat in Derbent. The development of the literature of the Mountain Jews and publishing activities were restricted to Daghestan ASSR, making Judeo-Tat books unavailable outside of Daghestan (Zand 1986: 39).

The limited statistical figures available from the Soviet censuses were based only on those Jews who were officially registered as Tats.[17] They show that,

---

17 This phenomenon, known as *tatization,* was partially a result of confused identity caused by the Soviet approach of one nation split by religion, but was often used by Jews as a convenient escape to avoid persecutions.

already in 1970, only about 70% of the Mountain Jews declared (Judeo-)Tat as their native language; the rest switched to other languages, mainly Russian (about 25%) (Oren and Zand 1982c: 462). The post-Soviet *aliyah* and other migrational processes reinforced the decline of Judeo-Tat among the Jews of the Eastern Caucasus.

2.4 Sociolinguistic description, community bilingualism, public functions

The Judeo-Tat speaking community was usually characterized as multilingual (Zand 1991: 384–385; Altshuler 1990: 357; Musakhanova 1993: 31–32). A description of Russian lands in the Caucasus (1836) mentioned that the Jews of Shirvan, Quba, and Derbent, without any exception, all spoke Azerbaijani (quoted in Altshuler 1990: 357). Yehuda Tsherny (1884) also reported that the local Jews spoke the languages of the neighboring nations, but only a few of them knew some Russian (quoted in Altshuler 1990: 357). The situation was probably slightly different in older times, when the Jewish population led a more isolated way of life, and knowledge of other languages was restricted to people who had contacts with other nations, based on their occupations and traveling habits. The situation changed after the population was forced to leave settlements that were entirely Jewish and moved to mixed villages and towns. However, the community was never exposed to just one language.

2.4.1 Hebrew

Evidence regarding the knowledge of Hebrew among community members was contradictory. Some claimed good knowledge of Hebrew, at least among men, since most of the men took part in religious education. Others reported a high level of illiteracy and a very poor command of Hebrew, often restricted to prayers only. This difference can be explained by the changes that took place in the 19th century: Due to the changes in the socio-economic situation of the community, fewer men were exposed to religious education, and, as a result, knowledge of Hebrew decreased significantly.

Nevertheless, Hebrew and Judeo-Tat were traditionally a diglossic system with a clear division of functions: Hebrew (HIGH) was the language of religion, education, and writing, and Judeo-Tat (LOW), the vernacular language, was used in every day communication and oral traditions (Zand 1991: 386–397). The decreasing knowledge of Hebrew gradually changed this division: Judeo-Tat began to be used in religious education to provide explanations, and the written practice of this language emerged; Hebrew became the language of highly educated religious leaders and the language of the liturgy.

2.4.2 Secret language

The Judeo-Tat speaking community also used a secret language, called *zuhun ʕimroni* or *lybɛlo*,[18] which was used to prevent the gentiles from understanding conversations between Jews (Miller 1929: 19; Shalem 2013a). Similar to other secret jargons created in the Jewish communities in Iran (Yarshater 1977: 1–7), Hebrew (He) and Aramaic were used as sources for lexical materials to create content words. The source words were adapted according to Judeo-Tat (Ju) phonotactical constraints, but some additional techniques were used to disguise the meaning even more: The order of the sounds was often changed (2g); some sounds could be deliberately changed; some words underwent a semantic shift (2a, b), sometimes taking on completely opposite meanings (2g), etc. Regular (2c), as well as periphrastic (2d), verbs were created based on Hebrew roots. Most probably, the numerals were borrowed from Hebrew. In addition, the native vocabulary was used to create encoded expressions with made-up meanings (2l, m). Function words, including pronouns, morphological rules with derivational and inflectional affixes (2f, j), and syntax came from the vernacular language, as well (Shalem 2013a; see also Miller 1929: 18–19).[19]

---

18 In the introduction to his *Материалы для изучения персидских наречий* (*Materials for the study of Persian dialects*, 1888: ix-x), V.A. Zhukovsky mentioned *zebōni imrānī* 'Imranian language', a language used by Jews in Iran for intra-communal communication. Miller (1929: 18–19) mentioned the use of a secret language, called *zuhun ʕymromi*, in the Jewish community of the Eastern Caucasus. The use of this jargon started to disappear a while ago in many Judeo-Tat speaking communities, but it was partially preserved in Quba. The older speakers of other dialects are aware of the phenomenon and still use some words in everyday speech (Shalem 2013a).

The origin of the name *zuhun ʕimroni* is uncertain. Miller was informed that this name comes from the name of a person, *Umrom*, who created this language (1929: 19). The Hebrew name עַמְרָם is indeed pronounced [ʕemrom] in Judeo-Tat. Some scholars assume that it may be derived from the name for the Aramaic language (Mikhail Agarunov, Martin Schwartz, independent personal communication). At the same time, there is a possibility that it was derived from the word *ibrāni* 'Hebrew' used in Arabic (*ʕibrāniy* عِبْرَانِي), Persian (*ibrāni* عبرانی), and Turkish (İbrani) (Shalem 2013a), similar to *qivruli* 'Hebrew', a name of the secret jargon used in the Georgian-speaking Jewish community (Zand 1991: 382).

The name *lybɛlo* comes from Hebrew לֹא 'no' and Aramaic בְּרָא 'outside', suggesting that the secrets should **not** be let **outside** of the community (Shalem 2013a).

19 Miller gives only three words as examples; all were derived from Hebrew and preserved the original meaning: *liham* 'bread' from *leḥem* לֶחֶם, *bosor* 'meat' from *bāsār* בָּשָׂר, *mojɛ* 'water' from

2. Examples of secret language vocabulary (Shalem 2013a):
   a. *posul*   'Muslim, gentile'   He: *pāsul* פָּסוּל 'unacceptable; disqualified'
   b. *ʃoril*   'Armenian, Christian'   He: *ʃārel* עָרֵל '(biblical) uncircumcised'
   c. *mɛtysdɛ*   'to die'   He: *met* מֵת 'dead, deceased' + Ju: -*ysdɛ*
   d. *monuħo birɛ*   'to die'   He: *mənuḥāh* מְנוּחָה 'rest' + Ju: *birɛ* 'to be'
   e. *poʃut*   'simple'   He: *pāšuṭ* פָּשׁוּט 'simple'
   f. *poʃuti*   'simplicity'   He: *pāšuṭ* פָּשׁוּט 'simple' + Ju: -*i* suffix
   g. *ħymχo*   'fool, idiot'   He: *ḥokmāh* חָכְמָה 'wisdom'
   h. *ħoχmo*   'mind, wisdom'   He: *ḥokmāh* חָכְמָה 'wisdom'
   i. *giro*   'money'   He: *gerāh* גֵּרָה '(biblical) 20th part of shekel'
   j. *ħinomi*   'easy money'   He: *ḥinnām* חִנָּם 'free, no charge' + Ju: -*i*
   k. *gɛnov*   'thief'   He: *gannāḇ* גַּנָּב 'thief'
   l. *ʧorduʃi*   'policeman'   Ju: *ʧor* 'four' + *duʃ* 'shoulder' + -*i*
   m. *pysərə kydy*   'very old person'   Ju: *pysərə* 'rotten' + *kydy* 'pumpkin'

2.4.3 Local languages

The knowledge of other local languages varied from region to region. The members of the community in Azerbaijan and Southern Daghestan were Judeo-Tat–Azerbaijani bilinguals. In Northern Daghestan, Kumyk, the main indigenous Turkic language of Daghestan, served as a lingua franca; many Jews spoke it fluently. In the communities of the Northern Caucasus, in Grozny and Nalchik, the Judeo-Tat speakers spoke Chechen and Kabardian (East Circassian), respectively, as a second language (Zand 1991: 384–385; Altshuler 1990: 357; Musakhanova 1993: 31–32). Many knew more than one additional language: The residents of Vartashen (Oghuz) spoke Armenian and possibly Udi (a Lezgic language); in Derbent, Lezgi or Tabasaran might have been spoken as a third language; in Northern Daghestan, Avar or Dargwa often became a component of Judeo-Tat multilingualism (Zand 1991: 385).

---

majim מַיִם (1929: 19). According to Miller, Jews used this secret language to avoid being understood by the neighboring Tat-speaking population. This "artificial language" was based on many Hebrew words, but sometimes not with their usual meaning. The grammar (if it was possible to speak about such) of this secret jargon was the grammar of Judeo-Tat (Tat in Miller). Many of the most frequent verbs ('to speak', 'to eat', 'to give') were replaced by made-up words, which made a conversation less comprehensible. Intelligibility became even more difficult, because one word could have many meanings (1929: 18–19).

2.4.4 Russian bilingualism and language shift

The annexation of the territories by the Russian Empire in the 19th century introduced the Russian language into the region. Gradually it became more important and prestigious, as secular education became more accepted and trade with the Russian speaking areas became more intensive, but knowledge of this language was still restricted to people who were exposed either to education in the Russian language or to contacts with Russian speaking communities. It was only after the October revolution and the Civil War, with the establishment of the Soviet government in the Eastern Caucasus in the 1920s, that Russian became an important part of Judeo-Tat multilingualism (Altshuler 1990: 357–358; Zand 1991: 385–386). Already in the 1950s, many of the Mountain Jews either were fluent Judeo-Tat–Russian bilinguals or knew their community's vernacular only as a second language (Zand 1986: 39, 1991: 418).

The prestige of Russian grew rapidly. It was perceived as the language of educated people and as the key to success in the new environment. Bilingual parents generally used Judeo-Tat as a secret language to hide things from their children, who sometimes acquired some knowledge of the community's language through communication with the older generation. In addition, if the grandparents understood enough Russian, the child did not respond in Judeo-Tat. Often it was not possible to compensate for the lack of communication in the native language inside the family, because there were no schools with Judeo-Tat as the language of instruction. As a result, the next generation produced a great number of semi-speakers: They could understand the language but could barely speak it (Shalem 2009).

The situation was different in the places where the Jewish population was a majority and Judeo-Tat served as a community language. However, the language could not provide up-to-date vocabulary for many subjects and could not compete with Russian or Azerbaijani. When speakers could not find the right words in Judeo-Tat for a conversation, they switched to Russian or Azerbaijani. This often resulted in feelings of inferiority regarding the native language (Shalem 2013b).

The sociolinguistic situation became even more complicated after the majority of the Mountain Jews left the traditional regions of settlement. New languages entered the linguistic scene, and Hebrew, English, or German became additional parts of the multilingualism of the community. Public usage decreased drastically, and Judeo-Tat could be heard only during special family or community gatherings (for example, lamentations for the dead are still performed in the native language). However, there are very strong feelings of nostalgia, especially among the semi-speakers. These feelings often result in some new activities involving the usage of Judeo-Tat, to a certain extent: language lessons, amateur theater performances, and the like. Sporadically, discussions about the future of the language and the necessity of taking action for its preservation emerge, but unfortunately there is no organization focused on these questions and concerns. In spite of the fact that many younger members of the community have a very low command of the language, Judeo-Tat still serves as a very important part of the collective identity of this community (Bram 2008: 347; Shalem 2013b).

3 Structural information

Throughout the history of research, Judeo-Tat has been described as a dialect of Tat (Miller 1892: xvii, 1903: 160), a group of dialects among the dialects of Tat (Oren and Zand 1982c: 460), a Jewish ethnolect (Zand 1991: 379, 429), or a separate language (Nazarova 1994: 120–121, 2002). The question of this language variety being a separate language or a dialect of Tat includes more than structural or lexical aspects (Nazarova 1994: 120–121, 1996: 120–121) and is beyond the scope of this chapter. These two varieties possess common features that distinguish them from immediately genetically related languages, like Modern Persian, and at the same time show significant differences on all levels, which prevent mutual intelligibility between speakers of Muslim and Jewish origin (Nazarova 1996: 120).

3.1 Judeo-Tat vs. Tat in comparison to Persian

Apart from some peculiar differences, the consonant inventory of Tat and Judeo-Tat corresponds to that of Persian. The unique feature of both varieties, not spotted in any other Iranian language, is so-called *rhotacism*, the general substitution of postvocalic /d/ with /r/ (Grjunberg 1961: 107; Grjunberg and Davydova 1982: 246). For example:

3. Rhotacism:
    Tat: *ræsiræn*   Judeo-Tat: *rasirɛ*   Persian: *ræsidæn*   'to reach'
    Tat: *bjar*   Judeo-Tat: *jor*   Persian: *jɒd*   'memory'
    Tat: *dumar*   Judeo-Tat: *dumor*   Persian: *dɒmɒd*   'groom, son-in-law'

Tat varieties mostly preserve word-initial /v/, which in Modern Persian became /b/ (Grjunberg 1961: 107; Grjunberg and Davydova 1982: 246–247). For example:

4. Word-initial /v/:
   Tat: *var*   Judeo-Tat: *vor*   Persian: ***bɒd***   'wind'
   Tat: *værf*   Judeo-Tat: *vɛrf*   Persian: ***bærf***   'snow'
   Tat: *vaʧa*   Judeo-Tat: *vɛʧɛ*   Persian: ***bæʧe***   'child, young [animal]'

Unlike Persian or Tat, the Jewish language variety preserved the two pharyngeal consonants /ħ/ and /ʕ/. These sounds mainly occur in the Semitic vocabulary, borrowings from Arabic and Hebrew (5a), but also appear in some Iranian words (5b) (Grjunberg and Davydova 1982: 241, 247). For example:

5. Pharyngeal consonants:
   a. *sabaħ*   (Arabic)   'morning'
      ʃylħon   (Hebrew)   'small, low table'
      ʕasɛl   (Arabic)   'honey'
      ʕarys   (Arabic)   'bride, daughter-in-law'
      miʕid   (Hebrew)   'holiday'
   b. *ʕasp*   (Iranian)   'horse'
      tɛħl / tɛlħ (Iranian) 'bitter'

According to Miller, the Semitic component in Judeo-Tat is also characterized by the presence of emphatic or pharyngealized alveolar plosives /tˤ/ and /dˤ/, which correspond to Hebrew 'ט' or Arabic 'ط' and Arabic 'ض', respectively (Miller 1900: 18–19, 1903: 163–164). Though Miller indicated these sounds as being of Semitic origin, their appearance was not restricted to the vocabulary borrowed from Arabic or Hebrew. However, later works noticed inconsistent and rare appearances of these sounds (Anisimov 1932: 54), as well as a total absence in some dialects (Miller 1932: 35–36), suggesting that they should not be considered part of the Judeo-Tat consonant inventory (see also Shor 1949: 128, 131–133, 136–137). The status of pharyngealized consonants, which was already unstable at that time, probably continued weakening even more over time, leading to their disappearance. However, their existence might explain the dialectal alternation between /t/ and /d/ in some examples of either Semitic or native origin; the appearance of low /a/ rather than mid-open /ɛ/ next to the dental /t/ and /d/;[20] as well as some cases of post-vocalic /d/

---

[20] Judeo-Tat front mid vowel /ɛ/ is pronounced as more open and sounds like a clear /a/ under the influence of adjacent back – uvular, pharyngeal, and glottal – and possibly once pharyngealized consonants (Miller 1900: 1–2).

that did not undergo *rhotacism*: *dibijo* or *tivijo* from טוּבִיָה 'Tuvia (Hebrew name)', *danusdɛ* or *tanusdɛ* 'to know', *sad* 'hundred', *navad* 'ninety', etc.

The distinction between uvular stop /q~ɢ/ and uvular fricative /ʁ/, which correspond to Hebrew 'ק' or Arabic 'ق' and Arabic 'غ', respectively, weakened as well, resulting in one merged phoneme /ʁ/ (Miller 1900: 15–16, 1903: 164; Shor 1949: 137).

From the 8-vowel system of Middle Persian (MPer), the vowel system of Tat developed in a way similar to Modern Persian (Per): Tat /æ/ corresponds to Per /æ/, developed from MPer /a/; Tat /ɑ/ = Per /ɒ/ < MPer /a:/; Tat /i/ = Per /i/ < MPer /e:/ and /i:/; Tat /u/ = Per /u/ < MPer /o:/ and /u:/. There is one particular difference of short high vowels merged into one high front rounded /y/: Tat /y/ < MPer /i/ and /u/, whereas in Modern Persian these two vowels are still distinguished as front and back mid-closed vowels: Per /e/ < MPer /i/ and Per /o/ < MPer /u/. The emerging of the high front rounded vowel can be seen as a result of the influence of the Turkic languages. However, there is some nonconformity with this strict mapping, due to the secondary phonological processes in the language; for example, the partial vowel harmony that also developed in Tat under Turkic influence (Grjunberg 1961: 108–109; Grjunberg and Davydova 1982: 242–246).

Judeo-Tat (JTat) shows less systematic development of Middle Persian low vowels /a/ and /a:/: MPer /a/ > JTat /ɛ/ and JTat /a/, MPer /a:/ > JTat /o/ and JTat /a/, in this way creating a new phoneme /a/.[21] The raising of MPer /a:/ to /o/ creates very peculiar pronunciation of the Jewish variety (Grjunberg and Davydova 1982: 238–239, 244–245). Similar to Tat, Judeo-Tat vowels are not stable and the pronunciation can vary due to the vowel harmonization, which is stronger in the Qaitoqi dialect than in the rest of the Jewish varieties.

Another characteristic feature of Judeo-Tat historical phonology is the systematic deletion of word-final /n/ (Grjunberg and Davydova 1982: 254). For example:

6. Deletion of word-final /n/:
   Judeo-Tat: *bɛsdɛ*   Tat: *bæstæn*   'to tie'
   Judeo-Tat: *rasirɛ*   Tat: *ræsiræn*   'to reach'
   Judeo-Tat: *χyʃdɛ*   Tat: *χiʃtæn*   reflexive pronoun

The morphology of nouns and adjectives in Tat and Judeo-Tat clearly indicates the closeness of these languages to Persian. Almost all noun suffixes, apart from those that were borrowed from Azerbaijani, either correspond to existent Persian

---

21 The phonemic status of this phone should be checked. Some dialects may have a minimal pair for /a/; for example, the Qaitoqi dialect has two words – *saχd* 'firm, strong' and *suχd* 'burn:PST.3PER.SING', but this is different for the Qubei dialect, where the first word is pronounced as *sɛχd*.

counterparts, or can be understood from the point of view of Persian word formation (Grjunberg 1961: 109). There are very few simple prepositions, but some postpositions are used in combination with prepositions (Grjunberg 1963b: 30–31).

Similar to Persian, both language varieties have a postpositional phrase marker to indicate the accusative case – Tat: *-ræ/-æ* and Judeo-Tat: *-rɛ/-ɛ*, the /r/ consonant is dropped when the word ends in a consonant. This marker sometimes indicates the dative case as well (14b), which can be also marked by a preposition. Tat and Judeo-Tat have developed a similar marker for instrumental/comitative case – Tat: *-raz/-az* and Judeo-Tat: *-rɛvoz/-ɛvoz*,[22] which are used in combination with a preposition 'in, on, to' *bæ* in Tat and *ɛ* in Judeo-Tat (Grjunberg and Davydova 1982: 249).[23] The use of these markers is illustrated below in (7) and (8) by some Tat examples taken from Grjunberg (1963b) and their Judeo-Tat equivalents.[24]

7. Accusative case – Tat (Grjunberg 1963b: 124, 133) vs. Judeo-Tat:
   a. Tat: *bærdæ-gar   biræn bu,   in   χær-æ*
             carrier   be:IRREAL.PST.3PER.SING,   this donkey:ACC.DEF
             bæ   χunæ   mi-fyrsær-ym
             in/on/to   home   send:ITRTV.PST.1PER.SING
      JTat: *bɛrdɛ-gor   mi-bisdo   -gɛ,*
             carrier   be:IMPRF.3PER.SING   CONDPRTCL,
             i   χar-ɛ   ɛ   χunɛ   my-fyrsyr-ym
             this   donkey:ACC.DEF   in/on/to home   send:IMPRF.1PER.SING
      'If there were a carrier [=somebody to take it], I would send this donkey home'.
   b. Tat: *tik baʃ,   baliʃ-æ   byl-ym*
             raise:IMP.SING   pillow:ACC.DEF   put:AORIST.1PER.SING
             bæ   zir   ty
             in/on/to   bottom   you
      JTat: *tik boʃ,   boluʃ-ɛ   dɛn-ym*
             raise:IMP.SING   pillow:ACC.DEF   put:AORIST.1PER.SING
             ɛ   zir   ty
             in/on/to   bottom   you
      'Raise [yourself], I'm going to put the pillow under you'.

---

22 Grjunberg and Davydova (1982: 249) claim that the Judeo-Tat marker of instrumental/comitative case is more archaic.
23 Sometimes this case marker is considered a postposition used in combination with a preposition (Grjunberg 1963a: 30–31).
24 A speaker of the Qaitoqi dialect translated these sentences to Judeo-Tat from Grjunberg's Russian glosses.

8. Instrumental/Comitative case – Tat (Grjunberg 1963b: 30–31) vs. Judeo-Tat:
   a. Tat: insan   bæ   guʃ-aj
            human being   in/on/to   ear:PLUR
            χiʃtæn-**az**   bæ-ʃynøʏræn
            self:**INSTR**   hear:NOTCLEAR
      JTat: odomi   ɛ   guʃ-hoj
            human being   in/on/to   ear:PLUR
            χuʃdɛ-**rovoz**   ʃinovusdɛ
            self:**INSTR**   hear:PRES.3PER.SING
      'A human being hears with his ears'.
   b. Tat: pæni-jæ   bæ   nu-**v-az**
            cheese:ACC.DEF   in/on/to   bread:**COM**
            bu-χardæn-i
            eat:PRES.2PER.SING
      JTat: ty   pɛni-rɛ   ɛ   nu-**rovoz**
            you   cheese:ACC.DEF   in/on/to   bread:**COM**
            χurdɛn-i
            eat:PRES.2PER.SING
      'You eat cheese with bread'.

Genitive case markers are not present in either variety. The possessive case is expressed by the construct state, or by means of the possessive preposition JTat ɛn / Tat æn 'of'. The Persian *ezāfe*, a grammatical particle that links two words together in the construct state, is dropped in both languages. In cases where the first word ends in a vowel, *ezāfe* leaves the linking consonant /j/ in Judeo-Tat and the linking vowels /i/ or /y/ in Tat, which, in combination with the preceding vowel, create a diphthong (Grjunberg and Davydova 1982: 251; Grjunberg 1963b: 25). Here are some examples of the construct state:

9. Construct state – Tat (Grjunberg 1963b: 25) vs. Judeo-Tat:
   a. Tat: duvar   χunæ
      JTat: duvor   χunɛ
             wall   house
      'wall of a house'
   b. Tat: χunɪ   pijær
      JTat: χunɛj   bɛbɛ
             house+*ezāfe* father
      'father's house'

However, unlike Judeo-Tat, the use of the construct state is very limited in Tat and is usually restricted to cases where the two nouns share a very close and organic semantic connection: for example, when the qualified noun is a part of a body or a kinship term: *dym piʃik* 'cat's tail', *duχtæ Masi* 'Masi's daughter', etc. (Grjunberg 1963b: 25). Instead, a different structure was developed under the Azerbaijani influence, and it is used more frequently (Grjunberg and Davydova 1982: 251–252),[25] together with the construction that uses the possessive preposition mentioned above. The examples in (10) illustrate the use of possessive constructions with the preposition 'of' in both languages.

10. Possessive prepositional constructions – Tat (Grjunberg 1963b: 25) vs. Judeo-Tat:
   a. Tat: æn kuʧæ χuvar mæn
           of little sister I
           'of my little sister'
      JTat: i kinig ɛn ʧyklɛ
            this book of little
            χahar-mɛ-n-i
            sister+I[=my sister]+short-copula:3PER.SING[26]
            'This is my little sister's book'.
   b. Tat: æn i ʃæhr
           of this town:SING
           'of this town'
      JTat: zihistɛgor-u ɛn i ʃɛhɛr
            inhabitant:PLUR of this town:SING
            'inhabitants of this town'

Unlike Persian, attributive adjectives precede the qualified noun. Though the linking particle *-ɛ* (*-æ* in Tat) looks similar to Persian *ezāfe*, because it is also used to link noun and adjective (11b), Grjunberg (1961: 114) assumes that this is a special qualifying form, not preserved in Persian, but present in the Caspian

---

[25] In this possessive construction the qualifying noun or pronoun stands before the qualified one and is marked by the accusative marker (Grjunberg 1963b: 26; see example in 16).
[26] The /n/ in *χahar-mɛ-n-i* is an epenthetic consonant that resolves the vowel hiatus created by attaching the short copula. In this case, it can be considered a restoration of the original sound dropped in word final position; compare Tat and Persian *mæn*. But other examples show that /n/ is systematically used as an epenthetic consonant to resolve such cases: *χahar-ty-n-i* 'is your sister', *χahar-imu-n-i* 'is our sister', etc.

languages (Grjunberg and Davydova 1982: 252). If an adjective ends in a vowel, no linking vowel is present (11a).

11. Attributive adjectives – Tat (Grjunberg 1963b: 200, 37) vs. Judeo-Tat:
   a. Tat: æ   zir   sijæ   ɢaʃ-ha   sijæ   ʧum-ha
      JTat: ɛ   zir   sijɛ   ʁoʃ-ho   sijɛ   ʧym-ho
            in/on/to bottom black:ADJ eyebrow:PLUR black:ADJ eye:PLUR
      'under black eyebrows black eyes'
   b. Tat: duraz-æ,   bylynd-æ   χunæ
      JTat: duraz-ɛ,   bylynd-ɛ   χunɛ
            long:ADJ+**particle** high:ADJ+**particle** house
      'long, high house'

In addition, Judeo-Tat has a construction in which an attributive adjective follows the qualified noun. This construction is restricted to certain adjectives, for example, those derived from geographic names and peoples' designations, such as: *zuhun ʤuhuri* 'Jewish language', *zuhun ingilisi* 'English language', etc.

The numerical systems of Judeo-Tat and Tat are very similar to the Persian system, though the system used in Tat shows some interesting differences. Cardinal numbers from 11 to 19 in Tat consist of the word *dæh* 'ten', followed by the words for the numbers from 1 to 9: *dæh-jæk* 'eleven', *dæh-dy* 'twelve', *dæh-sæ* 'thirteen', *dæh-ʧar* 'fourteen', *dæh-panʤ* 'fifteen', *dæh-ʃæʃ* 'sixteen', *dæh-hæft* 'seventeen', *dæh-hæʃt* 'eighteen', *dæh-nyh* 'nineteen'. In contrast, Judeo-Tat uses a formation that is closer to Persian, with the word for 'ten' following the numbers from 1 to 9: *jazdɛh* 'eleven', *dvazdɛh* 'twelve', *sizdɛh* 'thirteen', *ʧordɛh* 'fourteen', *pazdɛh* 'fifteen', *ʃazdɛh* 'sixteen', *hɛvdɛh* 'seventeen', *hɛʒdɛh* 'eighteen', *nazdɛh* 'nineteen'. In addition, most of the Tat dialects use a vigesimal system starting from 60: *sæ-bist* 'sixty', *sæ-bist-dæh* 'seventy', *ʧar-bist* 'eighty', *ʧar-bist-dæh* 'ninety'.[27] Unlike Persian and Tat, Judeo-Tat does not use a linking vowel in the numerals above twenty – Tat: *sad-i bist-i pænʤ*, JTat: *sad bisd pɛnʤ* 'one hundred twenty five'. Ordinal numbers in Judeo-Tat are constructed with a Persian-like suffix *-imi*, whereas Tat uses Azerbaijani ordinal numbers. The Tat variety preserves one measure word *tæ/ta*, whereas the Jewish one does not make use of any (Grjunberg and Davydova 1982: 253–254).

---

[27] Taking into consideration that the vigesimal system is not present in Persian, but widely used in the neighboring Caucasian languages, it makes sense to assume that it is not native to Tat (Grjunberg and Davydova 1982: 253).

The verb morphology of both varieties is similar to Persian, but the formation of tenses, aspects, and moods is different. Similar to Persian, Tat and Judeo-Tat have two verb stems – present and past. The verbs can be either simple or periphrastic, which are constructed with the help of the *light* verbs 'to be' Tat: *biran*, JTat: *birɛ*; 'to strike' Tat: *zæræn*, JTat: *zɛrɛ*; 'to do' Tat: *sæχtæn*, JTat: *soχdɛ*; 'to give' Tat: *dæræn*, JTat: *dorɛ*; and 'to pull' JTat: *kɛʃirɛ*. The content words of the compound verbs can be either native (12a, b) or borrowed lexical materials (12c-g): native or borrowed nouns (12a, b, e), Azerbaijani participles ending with the suffix -*miʃ* (12c, d), or Russian infinitives (12g). Often the first element cannot have an independent meaning (Grjunberg and Davydova 1982: 261). Below are some examples for compound verbs in Judeo-Tat:

12. Compound verbs:
    a. *gof soχdɛ*   'to speak'   < *gof*   'word'
    b. *dʒohob dorɛ*   'to reply'   < *dʒohob*   'voice'
    c. *jonoʃmiʃ birɛ*   'to approach'
    d. *jonoʃmiʃ soχdɛ* 'to move closer'
    e. *ʁɛdiʃ zɛrɛ*   'to read Qadish'   < *ʁɛdiʃ* < קדיש   Hebrew: 'Kaddish'
    f. *fikir soχdɛ*   'to think'
    g. *dumot soχdɛ*   'to think'   < *думать*   Russian: 'to think'

Verb structures comprise a very interesting and complex subject that requires more research, especially those of the Jewish variety. It is not possible to address all points in the scope of this chapter. Below are just some facts that illustrate similarities and differences between these two language varieties. Similar to Persian, both varieties use present and past stems to create different structures, as well as past participles to create complex forms. However, both Tat and Judeo-Tat varieties also use gerundives and infinitives for that purpose. For example, Tat has three different forms created from the infinitive – present tense, irreal past, and past continuous; and Judeo-Tat only one – present tense.[28] Both varieties use gerundives to construct an additional tense that refers to an action that will definitely happen in the future.[29]

---

[28] The Jewish variety has a structure similar to Tat past continuous tense, also created from the infinitive. However, the available literature does not mention it, and it needs more research.
[29] Grjunberg and Davydova mistakenly claim that the "northern dialect," i.e., the Jewish variety, has only one future tense and the "categorical future" is specific to the "southern dialect" (1982: 268–269). In Tat, the formation of this tense varies from dialect to dialect and can be constructed either from a gerundive form used with a short copula, or with the basic forms of aorist

Simple forms are constructed with the help of personal verbal endings, as well as prefixes Tat/JTat *mi-* and Tat *bæ-* or JTat *bi-/bu-* in some of the forms.[30] The use of prefixes is more widespread in the Tat variety; they are used in simple forms and even in complex past progressive, where prefix *mi-* is attached to an infinitive and the past tense of the verb 'to be' is used as an auxiliary. The use of prefixes in Judeo-Tat is much more restricted. Prefix *mi-* is used only in the simple future and imperfect tenses, whereas prefix *bi-* shows no usage in the formation of the verbal structures; it is preserved only in aorist and imperative forms of verbs like *omorɛ* 'to come' and *rafdɛ/raχdɛ* 'to go': *bi-jo* 'come:IMPR.SING' or *bu-ra* 'go:IMPR.SING'. In Judeo-Tat, the verbal prefixes are also omitted if the form is used with the negative particle. Complex verb structures use either past participles or infinitives as the main verb and either short copula (perfect tense[31]) or conjugated forms of the verb 'to be' as an auxiliary.

The passive voice in both varieties is constructed in a similar way: the past participle and an auxiliary verb, conjugated in the desired tense. However, different auxiliaries are used: Tat uses *biræn* 'to be' and Judeo-Tat uses *omorɛ* 'to come', whereas in Modern Persian *ʃodæn* 'to become' is used (Grjunberg and Davydova 1982: 278; Anisimov 1932: 85–119; Grjunberg 1963b: 67–69).

Judeo-Tat, unlike any other genetically related language, has preserved the forms of the optative mood. This structure is used to express a wish or a hope (Grjunberg and Davydova 1982: 267). The optative forms are created with the present stem of a verb and special personal endings.

Similar to Persian, both Tat varieties are subject-object-verb (SOV) languages: The subject group opens the sentence and the verb appears last (Grjunberg 1963b: 106). Compound sentences are rare in oral speech and normally use an asyndetic construction, a practice that results in several simple sentences. Judeo-Tat uses the conjunction 'and' – usually *nɛ(n)* in the Qaitoqi dialect and *vɛ* in other Jewish varieties – to coordinate between phrasal constituents smaller than a clause, like noun or prepositional phrases. In compound sentences, the most frequently used coordinating conjunction is an enclitic *-(i)ʃ* used both as monosyndetic and bisyndetic coordinator (Grjunberg 1963b: 110–111), which is

---

preceded by the invariable particle *bæsæn*, *bistæ*, *bæstæ*, or *sæ*, depending on the region (Grjunberg 1963a: 62–64, 70–71). In Judeo-Tat, categorical future tense is constructed from the gerundive used as a stem with personal verbal endings (Anisimov 1932: 85–119).

30 These prefixes can have a variety of pronunciations, due to the vowel harmony phenomenon.
31 In both varieties, the tendency is to simplify the pronunciation of this complex form with a short copula, and the result looks more like a simple, rather than a periphrastic, structure.

usually attached to the end of a noun or prepositional phrase in a clause. For example:

13. Coordinating conjunction – Tat (Grjunberg 1963b: 110) vs. Judeo-Tat:
    Tat: *duχtær*   *-iʃ*   *ama,*
          daughter   **ANDCLITIC**   come:PST.3PER.SING
          maj   *i-r*   *-iʃ*   *(ama)*
          mother   he/she   **ANDCLITIC**
    JTat: *duχtær*   *-iʃ*   *omo,*
          daughter   **ANDCLITIC**   come:PST.3PER.SING
          dɛdɛ   *ju*   *-ʃ*
          mother   he/she   **ANDCLITIC**
    'The girl/daughter came, and so did her mother.'

Unlike conjunction, disjunction uses only overt coordinators in Judeo-Tat. With phrasal constituents, a bisyndetic coordinator *jɛ ... jɛ* 'either ... or' is used. Monosyndetic coordinators *nɛbugɛ, nɛngɛ, jɛbugɛ* 'if' are complex lexical forms (meaning literally 'if it was not') to express disjunction in complex sentences. An adversative conjunction of Arabic origin *ommo* 'but' is systematically used in written sources; however, it is often omitted in speech, especially by the speakers of the Qaitoqi dialect.

Complex sentences are more frequent: Subordinating conjunctions introduce the dependent clauses, usually followed by the main clause (Grjunberg 1963b: 108–110). Both varieties have a small number of simple subordinating conjunctions, whereas complex conjunctions are more frequent (Grjunberg and Davydova 1982: 282–283; Grjunberg 1963b: 106–111). The peculiar feature of the Tat varieties, well preserved in Judeo-Tat, is the use of clause-final conjunctions, namely enclitics attached to the verb of a subordinate clause (see also Grjunberg and Davydova 1982: 282–283).

In Tat, conditional clauses show some variety in usage: They can be unmarked (14a), marked by the conjunction *ægær* 'if' (14b), or in very rare cases, marked by the particle *-isæ* (14c). However, in Judeo-Tat they show a systematic use of the conditional enclitic *-gɛ* (14). The conjunction *ɛgɛr* 'if' is used in some dialects and in literary language, but the clause-final marker *-gɛ* is never omitted.

14. Conditional clause – Tat (Grjunberg 1963b: 124–125, 108) vs. Judeo-Tat:
    a. Tat: *jæ*   *dærzæn*   *biræn bu,*
             one   needle   be:IRREAL.PST.3PER.SING,
             plaʃ-æ   *mi-duχt-im*
             coat:ACC.DEF   sew:ITRTV.PST.1PER.PLUR

  JTat: dɛrzɛ mi-bisdo   **-gɛ,**
     needle be:ImPrf.3Per.Sing **CondPrtcl,**
     poltoj ty-rɛ   mi-duχd-im
     coat   you:Acc sew:ImPrf.1Per.Plur
  'If there was a needle, we would sew (your) coat'.
 b. Tat: **ægær** mæn-æ paprus biræn bu,
     if   I:Dat   cigarette be:Irreal.Pst.3Per.Sing,
     mæn-æ paprus ty næ-mbajist
     I:Dat   cigarette you Neg-be:NotClear
  JTat: mɛ-rɛ   pɛprus mi-bisdo   **-gɛ,**
     I:Dat   cigarette be:ImPrf.3Per.Sing **CondPrtcl,**
     mɛ-rɛ   pɛprus ty gɛrɛk   nɛ-bisdo
     I:Dat   cigarette you necessary Neg-be:ImPrf.3Per.Sing
  'If I had cigarettes, I would not need yours'.
 c. Tat: bæ   i   tʃyl ruz aftym –
     in/on/to this forty day find:Pst.1Per.Sing
     aftym,[32]   næ-aftym   **-isæ** –
     find:Pst.1Per.Sing, Neg-find:Pst.1Per.Sing **CondPrtcl**
     miam
     come:Ftr.1Per.Sing
  JTat: ɛ   i   tʃyl ruz oχtym   **-gɛ** –
     in/on/to this forty day find:Pst.1Per.Sing **CondPrtcl**
     mi-oχym,   nɛ-oχtym   **-gɛ** –
     come:Ftr.1Per.Sing Neg-find:Pst.1Per.Sing **CondPrtcl**
     ɛ   χunɛ mi-jom
     in/on/to home come:Ftr.1Per.Sing
  'If in these forty days I find – I (will) find, if I don't find – I will come (back home)'.

In Judeo-Tat, the adverbial clauses of time use the infinitive with enclitic -*ki*, whereas Tat varieties use inflected forms of the verb and (usually complex) subordinate conjunctions. For example:

15. Adverbial clause of time – Tat (Grjunberg 1963b: 109) vs. Judeo-Tat:
  Tat: **un** **væχt** **ki**   ty amæræ biri,
    that **time** **that:Conj** you come:Prf.Pst.2Per.Sing

---

[32] The use of the identical verb structure in the main and conditional clauses in this example is probably a stylistic technique used by the storyteller.

	hami	bu,	hyzym	pariz-y,
	summer	be:Pst.3Per.Sing,	now	autumn+short-copula:3Per.Sing
JTat:	ty	omorɛ **-ki,**	hɛmiɛhsal	bu,
	you	come:Inf **WhenPrtcl,**	summer	be:Pst.3Per.Sing,
	honi	porizi-n-i		
	now	autumn+short-copula:3Per.Sing		

'When you came, it was summer; now it is autumn'.

And finally, in Judeo-Tat, clause-final enclitic *-ho* introduces the relative clauses, and Tat uses a subordinate conjunction *ki* 'that'. For example:

16. Relative clause – Tat (Grjunberg 1963b: 109) vs. Judeo-Tat:

    Tat: u   mærd **ki**   bæ   mæn-az gaf bæstæn by,[33]
         that man **that:Conj** in/on/to I:Com   talk:Irreal.Pst.3Per.Sing,
         u   mæn-æ   sigæ   birar-u
         he   I:Acc[=Gen]   sworn:Adj brother+short-copula:3Per.Sing
         'That man who was talking to me, is my sworn brother'.

    JTat: u   odomi   ɛ   mɛ-rɛvoz gof soχdɛ bu   **-ho,**
          that person   in/on/to I:Com   talk:Prf.Pst.3Per.Sing **RltvPrtcl,**
          ku-χolɛ-j   mɛ-n-i
          son+maternal aunt[=maternal cousin]+ ezāfe   I+short-copula:3Per.Sing
          'That person who was talking to me, is my cousin'.

3.2 Lexicon

The basic part of the Judeo-Tat vocabulary is of Iranian origin. A considerable part of the lexicon is of Turkic origin, and the source language is not the same for all dialects of Judeo-Tat: Azerbaijani influenced the vocabulary of the Qubei, Shirvoni, and Derbendi dialects, whereas some Turkic borrowings in the Qaitoqi dialect are from Kumyk. Arabic words in Judeo-Tat are quite numerous and may be borrowed either from the Persian or Turkic languages. Persian could be the source, not only for Arabic words, but also for Iranian words as they were used in Modern Persian.

In spite of the fact that scholars mention a great number of words borrowed from Hebrew and Aramaic (Nazarova 1996: 144), they are not actually very

---

33 The irrelative past structure *gaf bæstæn by* is most probably the result of a typo in the data; the past perfect form *gaf bæstæ by* is more likely in this sentence (similar to 15).

numerous (Miller 1932: 275). The general assumption usually is that, at minimum, words related to religious practice are borrowed from Hebrew. And indeed, some of these words are Hebrew words: ʁediʃ 'Qaddish', mɛlɛ 'brit milah' from Hebrew מִילָה 'circumcision', teflimini 'bar mitzvah' from תְּפִלִּין 'tefillin, phylacteries', syfyr tyro / sifir tiro 'Torah scroll' from סֵפֶר 'book, scroll'. However, many words are actually of Arabic origin, in spite of being related to the Jewish religion, for example: nimaz 'synagogue', hɛloli 'kosher', hɛrimi 'not kosher, forbidden'.[34] Not all Hebrew words in the Judeo-Tat lexicon are related to religious practice, for example: ʃylhon 'small table', hovir 'friend', and others. The low number of borrowings from Hebrew can be explained by the status of the language as a sacred language, but there can be yet another explanation: The Hebrew and Aramaic vocabulary was reserved for use in the secret language mentioned above.

Russian words from earlier stages may have been borrowed via other languages and later directly from the source language. These loans were normally related to the new realities created by the Soviet era: culture, science, technology, etc. Russian words were borrowed as stand-alone words or as stems to be used with native word formation. There are a number of loan translations as well, for example: sɛrnyʃ 'chairman' < sɛr 'head, top, front' + nyʃ 'to sit (present stem)' < Russian председатель, ʤilidbur 'ice-breaker, ice-boat' < ʤilid 'ice' + bur 'to cut (present stem)' < Russian ледокол, ʁonundorɛgor 'legislator' < ʁonun 'law' + dorɛ 'to give' + -gor 'suffix of an agent noun' < Russian законодатель (Shalem 2009).

There were probably some borrowings from the Caucasian languages spoken in the region, but this subject has not been studied.

3.3 Language contact influences

Aside from borrowings, the influence of other languages on Judeo-Tat grammar has not received enough attention in the research. Contact with the Turkic languages is probably the only clear case. On the level of phonetics and phonology, their impact is apparent in the high front rounded vowel /y/ and in the partial

---

[34] In a similar way, some names of the Jewish holidays are different from the familiar Hebrew names: nisonu 'Passover', ʃɛsɛltɛ 'Shavuot, Feast of Weeks', surini 'fast day of the ninth of Av', ʃɛrɛvo '(last day of) Sukkot', homonui / homunu 'Purim'. Some of them may have derived from less familiar names for the same holidays: for example, ʃɛsɛltɛ from the Talmudic name Atzeret, Hebrew עצרת (Mikhail Agarunov, personal communication). For others, the Hebrew names are used: ruʃɛʃune 'Rosh Hashanah', (ruz) kupur / kipur 'Yom Kippur', suko 'Sukkot', and honuko / hɛnukoi 'Hanukkah'.

vowel harmony present in all Judeo-Tat dialects, to some extent. Some Turkic suffixes were borrowed and are productively used in word formation. The special verb structure mentioned above may be a good example of the Turkic influence on Judeo-Tat grammar, though it is not clear if the influence was direct or via contact with speakers of Tat.

4 Written and oral traditions

As mentioned above, Judeo-Tat traditionally served as the community vernacular and was occasionally used in writing, whereas the main written language of the community was Hebrew. Studies of the cultural legacy of the peoples of Daghestan emphasize the importance of the old written literary traditions in Arabic and other oriental languages (Musakhanova 1993: 25). Such studies raise the question of the written literary tradition in Hebrew among Jews in the Eastern Caucasus. This tradition most probably had two parts: the canonical religious literature (Tanakh, Talmud, Biblical commentaries, etc.) and local Hebrew creativity. Unfortunately, the latter could be traced back only in testimonies by the older members of the community (Musakhanova 1993: 28). The earliest sources that reveal some information about the written tradition in Hebrew (similar to the written tradition in Arabic among other peoples in Daghestan) are epigraphic materials: inscriptions on gravestones, synagogues, and some buildings (Sosunov 2007). Other sources were not preserved. The testimonies mention local chronicles written in Hebrew: for example, Hilil from Orogh (Ashaga-Aragh, a village in Daghestan), the author of a history of the Mountain Jews of his village. The other genre was liturgical poetry; two names of poets are mentioned – Elisha' ben Shomoil and Livi ben Mishi Naqdimu, from Abasovo in Juhut-Qata, who lived and created in the 17th and 18th centuries. In the beginning of the 19th century, Matatiyahu Shomoil from Shamakhy wrote poems based on Biblical subjects. Zionist ideas appeared in the liturgical poetry of Rabbi Yusuf (Yosef) Haim from Kurakh in Daghestan and Esef (Asaf) Haim from Quba; both died during the Civil War. Rabbi Ya'anghil Ytskhakovich (Yaakov Yitzhaki, 1846–1917) was a prominent religious writer from Derbent (Musakhanova 1993: 30–31; see also Zand 1985: 5–6). However, apart from the list of Judeo-Tat words with Hebrew explanations by Rabbi Yaakov Yitzhaki, the only remaining written sources in Hebrew are non-literary documents (for example, the documents mentioned above or letters sent from Eretz Yisrael to Quba and written from 1873 to 1881, mentioned by Manoakh [1984: 131–137]) and copies of various religious texts (Shalem 2013: 148–152).

4.1 Writing system

Mountain Jews used Oriental semi-cursive Hebrew script in writing both Hebrew and Judeo-Tat (Altshuler 1990: 364). The written sources occasionally used the square script (Zand 2002: 142), which was later used in print (Pinkhasov 1909). This first known version of the Judeo-Tat alphabet contained some basic adaptations to match the phoneme inventory of the vernacular language: A diacritic *dagesh* was used with the letters ב, כ, and פ, to distinguish plosives [b, k, p] from fricatives [v, χ, f]; the letters ג and צ, when used with *geresh*, corresponded to the affricates [ʤ] and [ʧ]; vowels were indicated by ו [u/y] and some *niqqud* characters: *hiriq* [i], *patach* [a/ɛ], and *kamatz* [o], as well as *schwa* to mark a consonant cluster; a word final vowel marked by a diacritic was followed by an א. The use of this alphabet is illustrated in (17a) by a sentence from Pinkhasov's introduction to the prayer book published in 1909.

17. Alphabets:
    a. ג׳והורון דרבֶּנד ניסא ורסירא אמבּרא גֶּפ הָי אן ג׳והורון גורזנא רא
       גורזנא אן דרבנדא דרבנד אן קובה רא קובה אֲנו הָיְגֶרא.
       (Pinkhasov 1909: viii)[35]
    b. Çuhurun Dərbənd nisə vərəsirə ambarə gofhoj ən çuhurun Guroznərə, Guroznə – ən Dərbəndə, Dərbənd – ən Cubərə, Cubə – ən uhojgərə.
    c. Жугьурун Дербенд нисе вересире амбаре гофгьой эн жугьурун Гурознере, Гурозне – эн Дербенде, Дербенд – эн Гъубере, Гъубе – эн угьойгере.
    d. Чуҳурун Дәрбәнд нисә вәрәсирә амбарә гофhoj эн чуҳурун Курознәрә, Курознә – эн Дәрбәндә, Дәрбәнд – эн Губәрә, Губә – эн уhojкәрә.

ʤuhur-un	dɛrbɛnd	nisɛ	vɛrɛsirɛ	ambar-ɛ	gof-hoj
Jews:PLUR	Derbent	not	understand	many:ADJ+particle	word:PLUR
ɛn	ʤuhur-un	guroznɛ-rɛ,	guroznɛ –	ɛn	dɛrbɛnd-ɛ,
of	Jews:PLUR	Grozny:ACC,	Grozny	of	Derbent:ACC,

---

35 Pinkhasov is inconsistent in his orthography: The spacing differs from one case to another. For example, the accusative particle -rɛ (רא) is written either together with the preceding words or separately, the plural of *gof* 'word' *gof-hoj* is written as two words (גֶּפ הָי), etc. The author's orthography was preserved in the original sentence, written in Hebrew script. When transliterated into the other alphabets, these inconsistencies were corrected; capitalization and punctuation were introduced, in line with actual use in the new alphabets. In the IPA presentation, morpheme boundaries are represented by hyphens.

dɛrbɛnd – ɛn ʁubɛ-rɛ, ʁubɛ – ɛn uhojgɛ-rɛ.
Derbent   of Quba:ACC, Quba   of others:ACC.
'Jews of Derbent do not understand many words of the Jews of Grozny, Grozny – of Derbent, Derbent – of Quba, Quba – of others'.

The late 1920s was the time when many minority peoples in the USSR switched to using the Latinized alphabets. In spite of this general tendency, the Mountain Jewish activists decided to retain an alphabet based on Hebrew, but to "modernize the orthography" by adding vowel graphemes (Musakhanova 1993: 86; Oren and Zand 1982c: 461). However, no standard alphabet was agreed upon. The publications of 1927–1928 used three different alphabets, all based on the Hebrew one: (1) the traditional alphabet described above; (2) another one that used a separate grapheme (constructed with Hebrew *matres lectionis* and vowel points) for every vowel phoneme; and (3) an alphabet that used a combined approach (Oren and Zand 1982c: 461). The chaos in usage of the Hebrew alphabet/s and the inherent difficulty in adapting it led to an inner initiative to replace it, and, in April 1929, the Latinized alphabet was accepted (17b). In 1930, every publication in Judeo-Tat used Latinized script (Zand 1991: 412).

In 1938, written Judeo-Tat changed from using Latinized to Cyrillic script. This new alphabet (17c) used the system of digraphs to indicate the guttural consonants [ʁ, ħ, ʕ, h] and the high front rounded vowel [y]: гъ, хь, гI, гь, and уь, respectively (Oren and Zand 1982c: 461; Zand 1991: 416). The remaining Russian letters, which are not necessary in Judeo-Tat, were widely used in writing Russian loan words and names. This was the last officially accepted alphabet of Judeo-Tat (sometimes called *дербентская кириллица* 'Derbent Cyrillic'). However, for years the communities in Azerbaijan preferred to use a non-official adaptation of Azerbaijani Cyrillic script (17d).

Nowadays, due to the lack of coordination among numerous communities, Judeo-Tat speakers use one of the alphabets mentioned above, depending on people's origin and personal preferences. In Daghestan, where this language is still one of the official languages, works are published in the Derbent Cyrillic alphabet. In Israel several alphabets are used. For example, the *Mirvori* ('Pearl' in Judeo-Tat) publishing house used to accept works in either the Derbent or the Azerbaijani Cyrillic alphabets, but, from time to time, publications in the Latinized alphabet occurred, as well.

4.2 Folklore

A rich oral tradition preceded the written literature of the Mountain Jews (Zand 1985: 4). The work of collecting local folklore started in the 1930s in Daghestan;

interrupted by the war, it never continued in an extensive and systematic way. Two works were published in the 1940s: *Фольклор тати* (*Tat Folklore*), a collection of songs, proverbs, and tales (1940), edited by Khizgil Avshalumov (1913–2001), and *Овосунегьо* (*Fairy Tales*), a collection of tales (1947), edited by Daniil Atnilov (1915–1968). In the 1960s and 1970s, Avshalumov published some proverbs in *Vatan Sovetimu*. Amaldan Kukullu (Amal Kukuliev, 1935–2000), a writer and folklorist, published several collections of Mountain Jewish fairy tales in a Russian translation (Musakhanova 1993: 32–35).

The oral tradition in Judeo-Tat is closely connected to folklore in other local languages, while, at the same time, having a very strong Jewish character (Musakhanova 1993: 35, 48). One of the well-developed genres was *maʕani(ho)* 'song(s)', which could also be subdivided into several categories. Songs that were deeply rooted in the tradition expressed pleas, oaths, and wishes, like, for example, prayers for rain. They were very similar to songs sung by other peoples in the Eastern Caucasus and sometimes had a strong non-Jewish influence (Musakhanova 1993: 36).[36] The love songs could be dramatic, lyrical, or humorous (Musakhanova 1993: 40–41). The lullabies, *nɛnɛm-nɛnuj*, usually expressed maternal love, the mother's readiness to save her child from any possible trouble, and her wishes to see the child growing strong and healthy and having a happy life – but often shifted to a complaint about the hard life of women (Musakhanova 1993: 41–43).

However, the most colorful and diverse genre was traditional wedding poetry. It featured many characters, but its main subject was the bride. Songs praised her beauty and virtues, described her as hard working, and often instructed her how to behave in her new family. Bridesmaids' songs praised the bride and the groom, as well as expressing a sad feeling about the bride leaving her parents' home. Humor played a significant part in wedding poetry; it appeared in debate songs between the two families, as well as in the songs that mocked the groom's mother, the future mother-in-law. The sad motif about the uncertainty of women's happiness also appeared in some songs (Musakhanova 1993: 38–40).

The *maʕani* genre was a part of the oral tradition that created a transition "from anonymous folklore to authored literature" (Zand 1985: 5). First sung by its author, *maʕani-xu*, a song was, at later stages, "repeated from mouth to mouth,

---

[36] For example, Musakhanova (1993: 37) mentions a song sung during the spring holiday *ʃaʕamɛ-vasal* (literally 'candle-spring'), also called *hɛmmɛsali* (constructed from *hɛmmɛ* 'all, whole' and *sal* 'year'), as a Zoroastrian influence. This holiday, which was celebrated to commemorate the beginning of the spring, clearly correlates with *Nowruz*. It might be that the Jewish version was celebrated on the first day of Nissan, which is referred to as the first month of the year in the Bible and is one of four "new year" observances in Jewish tradition.

the author's name being mentioned" (Zand 1985: 5). The best-known songwriters in the late 19th – early 20th centuries were Merdekhey Ovsholum (1850–1925), Shoul Simandu, and Oybolo Turkhuni (Zand 1985: 5).

Another popular genre was *ovosunɛ(ho)* 'folk tale(s)'. The folk tales were usually narrated by "a professional story-teller," the *ovosunɛ-ʧi*, "normally at a special gathering [...], which often lasted late into the night" (Zand 1985: 5). The *ovosunɛ* genre included Oriental heroic, magical, animal, and everyday tales. The tales about everyday life often had strong humorous and satirical aspects (Musakhanova 1993: 46–47); their main hero was Shimmi Derbendi, a "figure resembling the Juha of the Arab Middle East and the Hershele Ostropoler of East European Jewry" (Zand 1991: 5). The tales that originated in the Jewish tradition were a natural part of this genre as well. Their heroes were various Biblical figures: Samson (*ʃymʃun*), Joseph (*isyfɛ sadiʁ*), King Solomon (*ʃɛlmunɛ miliχ*), Moses (*miʃi rabinu*), and others. Unfortunately, these tales stayed undocumented and were forgotten, due to the anti-religious, atheistic attitude during the Soviet era (Musakhanova 1993: 48).

Mɛtɛlɛ(ho) 'proverb(s)' was another folkloristic genre. The life experiences of many centuries were elegantly packed in short and well-formulated sentences (Musakhanova 1993: 49). Similar to *nɛnɛm-nɛnuj*, yet another genre was performed solely by women; the genre of *gɛrɛ(ho), girjɛ(ho), domojos* 'lamentation for the dead' had its specific tune and imagery, but the improvised inclusion of facts and information about the deceased person's life and family made it sound completely different every time (Musakhanova 1993: 40; Zand 1991: 5).

4.3 Literature: Drama, poetry, and prose

Amateur theatrical companies were the first triggers for literary creation in Judeo-Tat in the 20th century. The first known theater was founded in 1904 in Derbent and performed plays based on the Scriptures. However, the content and the authorship of those plays remained unknown (Zand 1985: 6). At the beginning of the Soviet period, there were at least two amateur theaters operating in Baku and in Derbent. The repertoire included plays on Soviet and Biblical themes (Zand 1985: 7–8). Most of the members of such companies, and often the authors of the plays, sympathized with the new government, and this explains attempts to create so-called revolutionary drama, or plays that criticized the traditional structure of the community. The first play that appeared in print (1929) attacked "the custom of paying a dowry for the bride" (Zand 1985: 9). The most prominent playwright of that period was Yuno Semenov (1899–1961), who also wrote poetry and short stories and, beginning in 1922, was in charge of the activities of the theatrical company in Derbent. "Mountain Jewish drama of the 1920s was strongly influenced by the contemporary Azerbaydzhani drama" (Zand 1985: 10).

The establishment of newspapers in Judeo-Tat provided a platform for poets, but also influenced the subjects of their works: Since they were to be published in the newspapers, the poems often dealt with "social and political themes" and practically "reflected [...] current affairs" (Zand 1985: 12). The woman's position in society was one of the popular subjects during that period, as well as the struggle against religion. Prose works were less popular in the beginning but, by the end of the 1920s, short stories started to appear, as well (Zand 1985: 12–13).

The main literary activities were concentrated in Derbent, but, in the 1930s, albeit for a very short period, there were two additional centers, in Moscow and Baku. The most popular genre in the 1930s was poetry. The main subjects were "the struggle against religion," "the solidarity of the workers of the world," "dedication to socialism," and "the friendship of Soviet nations" (Zand 1985: 15) — but the crisis of the traditional society of the Mountain Jews was addressed, as well. The major characteristic of the poetry of this period was its abandonment of "traditional folkloristic prosody and the transition to the syllabo-tonic prosody and rhyming patterns of Russian poetry" (Zand 1985: 16).

The drama of that period concentrated on the establishment of collective farms. The new subject was mixed marriages, a problem previously unknown to the Jewish population. Though the heroes often spoke in slogans, the level of writing was much higher than before; "plots had more turning points, dramatic tension was greater and dialogue was written with greater professional skill" (Zand 1985: 17). Prose developed much more slowly; the first novel appeared, and some short stories were published, but the most interesting development of the period was the beginning of the satirical tradition in Judeo-Tat, started by Khizgil Avshalumov (Zand 1985: 18).

The 1940s through the late 1960s were years of stagnation and decline in cultural activities in Judeo-Tat. Prose became the main genre, having two very strong figures at the forefront: Mishi Bakhshiev and Khizgil Avshalumov. The characteristic feature of that period is the development of documentary writing. Most of the works in this genre by Bakhshiev dealt with general Daghestanian subjects, not necessarily concentrating on the Mountain Jews. In 1963, Mishi Bakhiev published his "greatest achievement in prose," a novel called *Хушегьой онгур* (*The Bunches of Grapes*). The main plot is typical of the genre, known as the "kolkhoz novel": a clash between the innovators and those who prefer the old ways of life in the collective farm; but, at the same time, it addressed several other themes, like war, family stories, and even criticism of life during the time of Stalin (Zand 1985: 41).

Avshalumov was more interested in the present-day life of the Mountain Jews in Daghestan. His short stories, written in the mid-1950s–early 1960s, described everyday life of the Jewish village in Daghestan in a slightly ironic way. He continued developing his satirical skills; his stories often took place in the non-Jewish communities of Daghestan. However, he did not forget the traditional way of life before the Revolution and what happened to it afterwards. His best-known work, *Зен бирор* (*The Sister-in-Law*, 1971), tells the story of upper class Mountain Jews before and after the Revolution. In this and other works, he stays in the ideological category of the "revolutionary epic," but his detailed descriptions of the old way of life reveal some nostalgia (Zand 1985: 42–43). He also took his subjects from Judeo-Tat legends and folklore.

The main figure in Judeo-Tat poetry of the late 1950s was Daniil Atnilov. The subjects he addressed in his works are in the mainstream of the Soviet literature of that period, but his use of language is worth mentioning.

> [...] Atnilov lived permanently in Moscow, where he was isolated from everyday Judeo-Tat speech. This was, evidently, the reason for his acute sensitivity for the language; indeed, his Judeo-Tat is much purer and his loans from Russian fewer than is the case with poets who lived within the Judeo-Tat speaking community. Intent on demonstrating the richness of his mother tongue, Atnilov uses words which are archaic in everyday speech, including Hebrew words displaced by Russian and Azerbaydzhani borrowings. (Zand 1982: 46)

The most remarkable poet of this period was Sergey Izgiyaev. He was an active participant in World War II, and many of his poems dealt with this subject. His poetry was not completely free of the mainstream subjects of the Soviet era, but his works concentrated on human feelings and very touching stories from everyday life. Among his other works, he wrote probably the best love poetry written in Judeo-Tat. He was also well known for experimenting with poetic forms.

Drama in Judeo-Tat never revived after the years of stagnation. The last professional Mountain Jewish theater closed in 1946. Amateur dramatic circles existed in Mountain Jewish collective farms. The two of them that were active in the 1960s in the Derbent area became the base for the "Tat People's Theater," established in 1966. That theater was active, to some extent, until the end of the Soviet period (Zand 1985: 48).

Nowadays, the main publishing activities in Judeo-Tat are concentrated in Israel. However, there are few truly talented writers, poets, and playwrights who are able to produce work of real value. An amateur theater was founded in Hadera (Israel), and it is seen as the continuation of the "Tat People's Theater" mentioned above. Their repertoire is also based on previously published works.

5 State of research

Starting in the late 19th century, research on Judeo-Tat has been fragmentary and sporadic. The pioneering work by Vsevolod Miller mentioned above resulted in several publications. Apart from the collected materials and a small dictionary (1892), he also published overviews of Judeo-Tat phonetics (1900) and morphology (1901), as well as an article about the "Semitic element" in this language (1903). His research concentrated on the Northern (Qaitoqi) variety of Judeo-Tat. His son, the Soviet scholar Boris Miller, continued the study of this language, but he dedicated his work mainly to the Qubei dialect and, in addition to an overview of the Tat speaking communities (1929), published one article on Judeo-Tat (1932) comparing the Qubei dialect to the Northern varieties described by his father. In 1932, Nikolai (Naftali) Anisimov, a Mountain Jewish writer and linguist, published the first grammar of this language written in Judeo-Tat, *Grammatik zuhun tati*. The title refers to the Tat language, but it deals with Judeo-Tat grammar. A short phonetic study by Rozalia Shor (1949) discusses questions of Judeo-Tat consonant inventory, in comparison to the studies by Miller and Anisimov.

The work of the Soviet linguist Aleksandr Grjunberg concentrated on the study of the non-Jewish varieties of the Tat language, and, in 1963, he published a detailed description of the Tat language spoken by Tats in Northern Azerbaijan. However, his discussion of the place of the Tat language among the Iranian languages (1961) is relevant to Judeo-Tat, as well. In the 1970s, Lyudmila Davydova studied the Jewish varieties. She published one article on vowel phonemes (1977). Her work resulted in an unpublished dissertation *Language of the Tats of the Northern Caucasus* (1982).[37] The most prominent work of the Soviet era was a comparative, historical overview of the grammar of the Tat language by Grjunberg and Davydova, published in 1982. It deals mainly with the non-Jewish varieties, the so-called Southern dialect of the Tat language, but throughout the work, it is compared to the "Northern dialect," namely, the Jewish varieties.

Starting in the 1980s, a notable contribution to the study of Judeo-Tat was made by Evgenia Nazarova (Moscow, Russia). She was the first one to confront the approach of Soviet linguistics and raise the question of "language or dialect," advocating the status of the Jewish varieties as an independent language, closely related to Tat (Nazarova 1994, 2002). Chen Bram, an Israeli anthropologist and sociologist, often reveals interest in sociolinguistic questions related to the position and status of Judeo-Tat in Israeli society (Bram 2008; Bram and Shauli 2001).

---

37 Nazarova mentions both works in her overview of Judeo-Tat (1996: 124).

Sociolinguistic studies were also conducted by SIL international (Clifton et al. 2005), but they are mainly focused on the community in Quba (Azerbaijan) as part of the Tat speaking population in Azerbaijan and cannot provide the full picture. The most recent work on this language is the grammar of Juhuri (2012, published in French) by French linguist Gilles Authier.

5.1 History of documentation

The level of documentation of Judeo-Tat is very low. Apart from the small dictionary by Vsevolod Miller (1892), in the course of the 20th century there were several insignificant publications of thematic or specialized dictionaries of this language (for example, Ifraimov 1991; Gavrilov and Izgijaeva 1995). During the last 20 years, some community members have been actively engaged in lexicographic activities, but, unfortunately, most of these works were conducted at a very low and amateur level. Mikhail Agarunov, a Mountain Jewish professor emeritus of chemistry and devoted lexicographer, does the most notable work in this field. His work was initially based on the attempts of his father, Yakov Agarunov, to compile a dictionary of Judeo-Tat, but it went far beyond that, and several editions of his dictionary were published in 1997, 2005, and 2010. The latest edition (Agarunov and Agarunov 2010) contains about 14,000 Judeo-Tat words and phrases with Russian translation. It was published in two versions, using Judeo-Tat Latinized script in one and Cyrillic Azerbaijani script adapted to this language in the other. Unfortunately, the dictionary covers mainly the Qubei dialect, leaving other dialects undocumented. The Derbendi dialect was documented in a dictionary compiled by Edeso (Asja) Izgijaeva (2005), but the level of accuracy and professionalism cannot compete with Agarunov's work.

5.2 Corpora

There are no corpora of Judeo-Tat, but there are two points worth mentioning on this subject. First, Mountain Jewish writer and folklorist Amaldan Kukullu (Amal Kukuliev, 1935–2000) spent about 40 years collecting materials in Judeo-Tat, including tape recordings. His archive is owned by the family, which tries to preserve his legacy within the project called *Золотой сундук Амалдана Кукуллу* (*The Golden Chest of Amaldan Kukullu*), but so far only pieces of Judeo-Tat folklore in Russian have been published. According to the website of the project (gold.amaldanik.ru), run by the family publishing house *Amaldanik* (Moscow), they intend to publish tape recordings in a digital format, but it is unclear when this will occur.

Second, Judeo-Tat is a part of the *Jewish Languages* project started recently by the *Endangered Language Alliance*. The aim of this initiative is to record speakers of Judeo-Tat speaking on various subjects and to make these recordings available to the public. The project is being administered in cooperation with community leaders in Brooklyn, where a considerable number of Mountain Jews have resided since they left the former Soviet republics.

5.3 Issues of general theoretical interest and directions in research

The Judeo-Tat language, as well as Tat, is in need of further study. The fact that, apart from the well-preserved Qubei dialect still spoken in Qırmızı Qəsəbə, its dialects are disappearing (unfortunately, the speech of bilingual speakers often does not represent the full picture) calls for urgent data collection and systematic research on this Jewish language variety. Such study has much to contribute to the field of Iranian linguistics and to the field of Jewish languages.

The basic question of linguistic affiliation was addressed in one work (Grjunberg 1961), and some scholars still think that "although there are many signs that support [the existing] classification, it seems that further study should still examine whether this is the case, or whether it should be considered as a separate Iranian language" (Shaul Shaked, quoted in Bram 2008: 339). The relationship between the Jewish and non-Jewish varieties bears close examination. The influence of other neighboring languages, especially the numerous Caucasian languages spoken in the same region prior to Judeo-Tat–Russian bilingualism, is an interesting subject. The study of the dialectal continuum of Judeo-Tat is quite challenging, due to the decline of the language.

References

Agarunov, Yakov M. & Mikhail Y. Agarunov. 2010. Большой словарь языка горских евреев джуури / Kələ lyqət zuhun çuhuri [Big dictionary of the language of the Mountain Jews, Juhuri]. Pyatigorsk: RIA-KMV.

Altshuler, Mordechai. 1990. יהודי מזרח קאווקאז: תולדות היהודים ההרריים מראשית המאה התשע־עשרה [*The Jews of the Eastern Caucasus: The History of the "Mountain Jews" from the Beginning of the Nineteenth Century*]. Jerusalem: Yad Izhak Ben-Zvi and the Hebrew University of Jerusalem.

Anisimov, Ilya Sh. 1888. *Кавказские евреи-горцы* [Jews-Highlanders from the Caucasus]. Moscow: Dashkov's Ethnographic Museum.
Anisimov, N.A. 1932. *Grammatik zuhun tati* [Grammar of the Tat language]. Moscow: Tsentroizdat.
Authier, Gilles. 2012. *Grammaire juhuri, ou judéo-tat, langue iranienne des Juifs du Caucase de l'est*. Reichert: Wiesbaden.
Bram, Chen & Ran Shauli. 2001. שפה וזהות תרבותית: ג'והורי - שפת יהודי ההר מקווקז ומעמדה בישראל [Language and cultural identity: Juhuri – the language of the Mountain Jews from the Caucasus and its status in Israel]. In: *Наша звезда / Астарайму* [Our star], 180–202. Jerusalem: Ministry of Absorption and the Association of Immigrants from the Caucasus.
Bram, Chen. 2008. The language of Caucasus (sic.) Jews: Language preservation and sociolinguistic dilemmas before and after the migration to Israel. *Irano-Judaica* 6. 337–351.
Clifton, John M., Gabriela Deckinga, Laura Lucht, and Calvin Tiessen. 2005. Sociolinguistic situation of the Tat and Mountain Jews in Azerbaijan. SIL International. http://www.sil.org/resources/publications/entry/9077. (accessed 17 October 2017.)
Gavrilov, B.G. & A.B. Izgijaeva. 1995. *Орфографически гофноме: зугьун тати / Орфографический словарь татского языка* [Orthographical dictionary of the Tat language]. Makhachkala: Daguchpedgiz.
Grjunberg, A.L. 1961. О месте татского среди иранских языков [On the place of Tat among the Iranian languages]. *Вопросы языкознания* [Linguistic issues] 1. 106–114.
Grjunberg, A.L. 1963a. Система глагола в татском языке [Verb system in Tat]. In V.I. Abaev (ed.), *Иранский сборник: К семидесятипятилетию проф. И.И. Зарубина* [Iranian Collection of Studies: To Prof. I.I. Zarubin's 75th anniversary], 121–149. Moscow: Eastern Literature Publishing.
Grjunberg, A.L. 1963b. *Язык североазербайджанских татов* [The language of Tats from Northern Azerbaijan]. Leningrad: USSR Academy of Science Publishing.
Grjunberg, A.L. and L.Kh. Davydova. 1982. Татский язык [Tat language]. In V.S. Rastorgueva (ed.), *Основы иранского языкознания. Новоиранские языки: западная группа, прикаспийские языки* [Introduction to Iranian Linguistics. New Iranian languages: Western Group, Caspian languages], 231–286. Moscow: Nauka.
Ifraimov, I.I. 1991. *Татско-русский иллюстрированный словарь для детей / Гофгьой таты нэ урусинэ э суротгьовоз эри гIэлгьо* [Tat-Russian illustrated dictionary for children]. Nalchik: Nart.
Izgijaeva, Edeso. 2005. *Татско-русский и русско-татский словарь. Татский язык горских евреев Кавказа* [Tat-Russian and Russian-Tat dictionary. Tat language of the Highland Jews of the Caucasus]. Makhachkala: Jupiter.
Kukullu, Amaldan. 1997. *Эхо минувших и зов грядущих эпох* [Echo of the Past and Call of the Epochs to Come]. Moscow: Amaldanik.
Manoakh, B.B. 1984. *Пленники Салманасара (Из истории евреев Восточного Кавказа)* [Prisoners of Shalmaneser (From the history of the Jewish community of the Eastern Caucasus)]. Jerusalem: B. Manoakh.
Miller, Boris. 1929. *Таты, их расселение и говоры (Материалы и вопросы)* [Tats, their settlement and dialects (materials and questions)]. Baku: Scientific Society of Azerbaijan Publishing.
Miller, Boris. 1932. О кубинском говоре татского наречия горских евреев Кавказа [On the Quba subdialect of the Tat language spoken by the Mountain Jews of the Caucasus]. *Записки Института востоковедения Академии Наук СССР* [Proceedings of the Institute of Oriental Studies in Academy of Science of the USSR] 1. 269–290.

Miller, Vsevolod. 1892. *Материалы для изучения еврейско-татского языка. Введение, тексты и словарь* [Materials for study of the Judeo-Tat language. Introduction, texts, and dictionary]. Saint Petersburg: Imperial Academy of Sciences.

Miller, Vsevolod. 1900. *Очерк фонетики еврейско-татского наречия* [An Overview of Judeo-Tat phonetics]. Труды по востоковедению, издаваемые Лазаревским Институтом Восточных Языков [Works in Oriental Studies published by Lazarev's Institute of Oriental Languages] 3. Moscow.

Miller, Vsevolod. 1901. *Очерк морфологии еврейско-татского наречия* [An Overview of Judeo-Tat morphology]. Труды по востоковедению, издаваемые Лазаревским Институтом Восточных Языков [Works in Oriental Studies published by Lazarev's Institute of Oriental Languages] 7. Moscow.

Miller, Vsevolod. 1903. О семитском элементе в татском наречии горских евреев [On Semitic elements in the Tat dialect of the Mountain Jews]. In A.E. Krymsky (ed.), *Древности восточные. Труды Восточной комиссии Императорского Московского археологического общества* [Oriental Antiquities. Works of the Eastern Committee of the Imperial Moscow Archaeological Society] 2(3). 160–168.

Miller, Vsevolod. 1905. *Татские этюды. Часть I. Тексты и татско-русский словарь* [Tat studies. Part I. Texts and Tat-Russian Dictionary]. Труды по востоковедению, издаваемые Лазаревским Институтом Восточных Языков [Works in Oriental Studies published by Lazarev's Institute of Oriental Languages] 24. Moscow.

Miller, Vsevolod. 1907. *Татские этюды. Часть II. Опыт грамматики татского языка* [Tat Studies. Part II. An attempt of a grammar of the Tat language]. Труды по востоковедению, издаваемые Лазаревским Институтом Восточных Языков [Works in Oriental Studies published by Lazarev's Institute of Oriental Languages] 26. Moscow.

Musakhanova, Galina B. 1972. Татская литература [Tat literature]. In A.A. Surkov (ed.), *Краткая литературная энциклопедия* [Short literary encyclopedia], vol. 7, 409–410. Moscow: Soviet Encyclopedia.

Musakhanova, Galina B. 1993. *Татская литература (Очерк истории. 1917–1990)* [Tat Literature (Historical overview. 1917–1990)]. Makhachkala: Dagestanskoje knizhnoje izdatel'stvo.

Nazarova, Evgenia. 1994. К проблеме "язык или диалект" на материале двух разновидностей татского языка [To the problem "language or dialect" based on the materials of two varieties of the Tat language]. In *Тезисы докладов научной сессии, посвященной итогам экспедиционных исследований Института истории, археологии и этнографии, а также Института языка, литературы и искусства в 1992–1993 гг* [Proceedings of the Scientific Session dedicated to the results of field research of the Institute of History, Anthropology, and Ethnography and of the Institute of Language, Literature, and Art in 1992–1993], 120–121. Makhachkala: Scientific Center of Russian Academy of Science in Daghestan.

Nazarova, Evgenia. 1996. Язык горских евреев Дагестана [The language of Daghestan's Mountain Jews]. *Вестник Еврейского университета в Москве* [Bulletin of the Hebrew University in Moscow] 3(13). 120–146.

Nazarova, Evgenia. 2002. Языковые аспекты татского этнического мифа: о терминологической ситуации с названием языка горских евреев [Linguistic aspects of the Tat ethnic myth: On the terminological situation with the name of the language of the Mountain Jews]. Paper presented at the International Conference on The Mountain Jews: From the Caucasus to Israel, Ben-Zvi Institute, Jerusalem, 8–10 October.

Oren, Itzhak and Michael Zand. 1982a. Горские евреи [Mountain Jews]. In Itzhak Oren (Nadel) & Michael Zand (eds.), *Краткая еврейская энциклопедия* [Short Jewish encyclopedia], vol. 2, 182–191. Jerusalem: Society for Research on Jewish Communities.

Oren, Itzhak and Michael Zand. 1982b. Еврейско-татская литература [Judeo-Tat literature]. In Itzhak Oren (Nadel) & Michael Zand (eds.), *Краткая еврейская энциклопедия* [Short Jewish encyclopedia], vol. 2, 455–459. Jerusalem: Society for Research on Jewish Communities.

Oren, Itzhak and Michael Zand. 1982c. Еврейско-татский язык [Judeo-Tat language]. In Itzhak Oren (Nadel) & Michael Zand (eds.), *Краткая еврейская энциклопедия* [Short Jewish encyclopedia], vol. 2, 459–462. Jerusalem: Society for Research on Jewish Communities.

Pinkhasov, Asaf. 1909. סדור קול תפילה עם תרגום להשפה תתית מאת אסף בה״ר פינחסאוו / *Еврейский молитвословъ съ татскимъ переводомъ А. Пинхасова* [Jewish prayer book with Tat translation by A. Pinkhasov]. Vilna: Tipografija Pirozhnikova.

Podolsky, Baruch. 2002. מילים עבריות בלשונם של היהודים ההרריים [Hebrew words in the language of the Mountain Jews]. Paper presented at the International Conference on the Mountain Jews: From the Caucasus to Israel, Ben-Zvi Institute, Jerusalem, 8–10 October.

Semenov, Igor. 1992. *Кавказские таты и горские евреи: Некоторые сведения о них и проблемы происхождения* [The Tats of the Caucasus and the Mountain Jews: Some facts and problems of origin]. Kazan: Tan.

Semenov, Igor. 2003. Горские евреи Кавказа: Некоторые аспекты этнической идентификации [The Mountain Jews of the Caucasus: Some aspects of ethnic identification]. *Центральная Азия и Кавказ* [Central Asia and Caucasus] 3(27). 191–200.

Semenov, Igor. 2007. Очерк истории и географии расселения горских евреев [Historical and geographical overview of the Mountain Jews' settlements]. In Genady Sosunov, *Еврейские памятники восточного Кавказа* [Jewish monuments of the Eastern Caucasus], 180–215. Makhachkala: Epoch.

Shalem, Karina. 2013. Попытка реконструкции еврейской (религиозной) книжной полки горских евреев [An attempt to restore the Jewish (religious) bookshelf of the Mountain Jews]. In L.V. Kalmina, T.A. Karasova, V.Z. Khanin, I.V. Kopchenova, V.V. Mochalova & I.G. Semyonov (eds.), *Материалы XX Международной ежегодной конференции по иудаике* [Proceedings of the twentieth annual International Conference on Jewish Studies], vol. 3, 142–155. Moscow: The Moscow Center for University Teaching of Jewish Civilization "Sefer."

Shalem, Vitaly. 2009. Local culture in global world: A case of Juhuri-Russian bilingualism. Paper presented at the ACLA conference on Global Languages, Local Cultures, Harvard University, 26–29 March.

Shalem, Vitaly. 2011. בין דיאלקט של פרסית ל״שפה שלנו״: עדויות על שפת סתר בקהילת יהודי מזרח קווקז [From dialect of Persian to "our language": Evidence of a secret language in the Jewish community of the Eastern Caucasus]. Paper presented at the third annual Kadmata Conference, Ben-Zvi Institute, Jerusalem, 9 February.

Shalem, Vitaly. 2013a. Secret language in the Jewish community of the Eastern Caucasus. Paper presented at the International Conference on Variation Within and Across Jewish Languages, University of Antwerp, 26–28 June.

Shalem, Vitaly. 2013b. ״בקווקזית אין מילה לאהבה״: איך רוצחים שפה גוססת ["In the language of the Mountain Jews there is no word for *love*": How a dying language is murdered]. Paper presented at the Sixteenth World Congress of Jewish Studies, The Hebrew University in Jerusalem, 28 June – 1 August.

Shor, Rozalia O. 1949. О спорных вопросах в исследовании консонантизма говора татов-евреев [On moot points in the research of consonantism of the dialect of Tat-Jews]. In I.I. Meshchaninov & G.P. Serdjuchenko (eds.), *Языки Северного Кавказа и Дагестана: Сборник лингвистических исследований* [Languages of the Northern Caucasus and Daghestan: A collection of linguistic research] 2, 127–139. Moscow/Leningrad: USSR Academy of Science Publishing.

Sosunov, Genady. 2007. *Еврейские памятники восточного Кавказа* [Jewish monuments of the Eastern Caucasus]. Makhachkala: Epoch.

Tsherny, Yosef Yehuda Ben Ya'akov HaLevy. 1884. ספר המסעות בארץ קוקז ובמדינות אשר מעבר לקוקז וקצת מדינות אחרות בנגב רוסיה, משנת התרכ״ז עד שנת התרל״ה [Book of journeys to the Caucasus, and to the countries over the Caucasus, and some other countries in southern Russia from the year 1867 to the year 1875]. Saint Petersburg.

Yarshater, Ehsan. 1977. The hybrid language of the Jewish communities of Persia. *Journal of the American Oriental Society* 97(1). 1–7.

Yitzhaki, Yaakov. 1974. אגרות ותעודות: מארכיון הרב ר׳ יעקב בהרר״יץ יצחקי ז״ל, רבה הראשי של דגסתן [Letters and documents: From the archive of Rabbi Yaakov Yitzhaki, the chief rabbi of Daghestan]. Jerusalem: The Central Archives for the History of the Jewish People (CAHJP), The Hebrew University Research Center of East European Jewry.

Zand, Michael. 1985. The literature of the Mountain Jews of the Caucasus (Part 1). *Soviet Jewish Affairs* 15(2). 3–22.

Zand, Michael. 1986. The literature of the Mountain Jews of the Caucasus (Part 2). *Soviet Jewish Affairs* 16(1). 35–51.

Zand, Michael. 1991. Notes on the culture of the Non-Ashkenazi Jewish communities under Soviet rule. In Yaacov Ro'i & Avi Beker (eds.), *Jewish culture and identity in the Soviet Union*, 378–444. New York: New York University Press.

Zand, Michael. 2002. Рабби Яаков Ицхаки как лексиограф (sic.) и лексиколог [Rabbi Yaakov Yitzhaki as lexicographer and lexicologist]. In *Материалы международного научного симпозиума "Горские евреи Кавказа", 24–26 апреля 2001 г.* [Proceedings of International Scientific Symposium "The Mountain Jews of the Caucasus," 24–26 April 2001], 140–147. Baku: Elm.

Zhukovsky, Valentin A. 1888. Введение [Introduction]. In V.A. Zhukovsky, *Материалы для изучения персидских наречий, Часть первая* [Materials for the study of Persian dialects, part one], i–xx. Saint Petersburg.

Ophira Gamliel
Jewish Malayalam in Southern India

1 Introduction

Malayalam is the official language of the modern state of Kerala in South India, with approximately 40 million speakers. Jewish Malayalam is a dialect of Malayalam that evolved over centuries of Jewish presence in the region, as attested in records and documents since the mid-ninth century. After the mass migration of Kerala Jews to Israel in 1954, the use of Jewish Malayalam has gradually given way to Modern Hebrew. Currently, there are only a few dozen fluent speakers, mostly in their 60s and older. Their unique dialect of Malayalam was recognized as a Jewish language variety relatively recently (Zacharia 2003a; Gamliel 2009d).

Malayalam, the host language of Jewish Malayalam, is one of the four major literary Dravidian languages, along with Telugu, Kannada, and Tamil. Malayalam is closest in its morphology, syntax, and lexicon to Tamil; both languages branched off from Proto-South Dravidian I (Krishnamurti 2003: 21–22). Though often considered the younger sibling of Tamil, some of the features peculiar to Malayalam suggest that it was a separate language even before the stage of Old Tamil (Govindankutty 1972; Panicker 2006).

Malayalam received its name only as late as the 19th century, notwithstanding its attestation as a distinct language since at least the ninth century. Moreover, it was the German linguist and philologist, Hermann Gundert, who coined the term 'Malayalam' (Zacharia 2014). Until then, the people of Kerala referred to their language by the terms *bhāṣa* 'language', *keraḷa bhāṣa* 'the language of Kerala', or even *tamil̠* 'Tamil', as attested already in the 14th-century treatise on Malayalam literature and grammar, the *Līlātiḷakam* (Freeman 1998: 39). Similarly, Jewish Malayalam is a term coined by contemporary scholars of Kerala Jewry, to represent this religiolect of Malayalam within the spectrum of Jewish language varieties. Speakers use a variety of designations to refer to the language they speak, with the modern term Malayalam being but one of them. The reason for the plurality of terms to denote the spoken language is partly because the mass migration of Kerala Jews occurred in 1954, before the instigation of the Kerala state educational reform (The Kerala Education Act – 1958), which propelled the popularization of the term 'Malayalam' through the school system. Consequently, Kerala Jews retain older terms like Tamil (*tamil̠*) along with the term Malayalam (pronounced *malayāḷǝm*). Additionally, some speakers also use a Hebrew construct to denote their language, namely, Malabarit (pronounced *malbārit*), derived from the old Hebrew and Arabic name for the west coast of South India, *malabār*, and compounded with the Hebrew suffix -*it* for language names. When Kerala Jews take note of their dialect, they either refer to it as *paḻaya bhāṣa* 'old Malayalam' or retort that they speak a broken or 'degraded' (*meʃubeʃet*) Malayalam.

Jewish Malayalam was spoken in Central Kerala, where several Jewish communities existed up to the 1950s – three in Cochin, two in Ernakulam, and one each in Parur, Chennamangalam, and Mala. Documents and records from the pre-modern period provide evidence of Jews settling throughout historical Kerala: Kollam in the south, Kodungallur and Parur in Central Kerala, Koyilandy in the north, and even further north in Mangalore (in South Karnataka). Early modern and modern sources in Hebrew, Dutch, and Portuguese mention Jewish communities in three more places in North Kerala: Madayi, Muttam, and Chaliyam. Currently, the Jews still living in Kerala number less than 50 members, who have adjusted their speech to the Ernakulam and Cochin dialects over the decades following the mass migration to Israel.

In Israel, Kerala Jews clustered in five agrarian settlements – Nevatim, Mesilat Zion, Taʻoz, Aviʻezer, and Kfar Yuval. This enabled them to retain the use of Jewish Malayalam at home and in public gatherings. However, their Jewish Malayalam was influenced by the shift to Modern Hebrew, so that currently Jewish Malayalam is mingled with Israeli Hebrew. This has implications for the syntax, lexicon, and phonology of contemporary Jewish Malayalam, which complicates the analysis and description of speech samples collected during the past decade. For example, it may be difficult to determine whether a lexeme identified as a Hebrew loanword is borrowed from Classical Hebrew or from Modern Hebrew (Gamliel 2013a: 143–144). According to the Expanded Graded Intergenerational Disruption scale (Ethnologue 2015), the status of Jewish Malayalam is currently moribund; the only remaining active users of the language are members of the grandparent generation and older.

Contemporary speakers of Jewish Malayalam in Israel divide between those who emigrated during the 1950s and those who emigrated later on, during the 1970s. The speech of the latter is up-to-date with the dialects of Central Kerala, showing hardly any distinctively Jewish dialectical features. The speech of those who migrated before 1954, while retaining more features of their old religiolect, is heavily influenced by Modern Hebrew, primarily on the lexical level, e.g., loanwords borrowed from Modern Hebrew rather than from Classical Hebrew texts and liturgy. Due to the archaic dialectical retentions in Jewish Malayalam, the late-comers often refer to it as "broken" or "incorrect" Malayalam, while the 1950s migrants often describe their own speech as "old" (*paḻaya*). Generally, this "old" or "incorrect" Malayalam can be, in certain contexts, a source of embarrassment or a target for ridicule. With the exposure to satellite television channels and an increase in heritage tours to Kerala, contemporary Jewish Malayalam is further affected by a renewed contact with contemporary Malayalam. Following the language documentation project in 2008–2009 and the interest of scholars and academicians in Jewish Malayalam, a new phase of efforts to revive the language can be seen in various community functions. The most prominent is a group of women who meet regularly to speak in Malayalam and to study the script in Jerusalem. Prior to this, women in different places formed singing troupes, to rejuvenate Jewish Malayalam wedding songs and perform them at community gatherings.

Some evidence in the manuscripts containing Jewish Malayalam literature suggests that there used to be dialectical variations based on geographical differences. For example, /v/ > /b/ as in: *vāva* > *bāva* 'father' or in *viḷi* > *biḷi* 'call out', with the /b/ variants found mainly (though not exclusively) in manuscripts from the Cochin-Kadavumbhagam community. Similarly, there may have been dialectical variations determined by gender. However, it is difficult to substantiate such claims before conducting a thorough investigation into audio records of casual speech, according to the place of origin and gender of informants.

Among Kerala Jews in Israel, those who migrated in their early childhood are equally fluent in Malayalam and Modern Hebrew; a few have mastered English, as well. All Jewish Malayalam speakers are well versed in the Hebrew script, though their acquaintance with Classical and Biblical Hebrew varies, depending on the level of religious education.

2 Historical background

Kerala is a long strip of land along the Western Ghats, on the west coast of South India. This region has attracted traders from West Asia and the Mediterranean Basin since Hellenistic times, with evidence for imported goods found even in the Hebrew Bible and the Talmud (Rabin 1999: 275–276, 280, 304–305; Weinstein 2000). Although there are references in ancient Jewish texts to products imported from South India, it is reasonable to assume that Jewish traders, travelers, and perhaps also work migrants began to cross the Indian Ocean and settle along the west coast of South India towards the end of the first millennium CE.

Evidence in pre-modern historical records suggests that Jews intermarried with matrilineal Hindu families, like their fellow Christian and Muslim West Asian traders, who were engaged in global trade across the Indian Ocean all through medieval times. It is reasonable to assume that these early traders must have learned Malayalam for conducting their business in the Malayalam-speaking region. In fact, there are quite a few Malayalam loanwords in Judeo-Arabic, found in letters exchanged between Jewish traders traveling along the Indian Ocean trade routes (e.g., דנגלי < *iṭaṅṅali*, a measure of approximately 800 grams; פדיאר < *patiyār*, administrative title; see Gamliel 2018c). Certainly, those who intermarried with Malayali women or temporarily lived in Kerala established extended families of siblings and converts. These family members were native speakers of Malayalam, on the one hand, and observant Jews on the other hand, thus bringing spoken Malayalam and written, liturgical Hebrew into contact with each other. It is reasonable to assume that the early modern Jewish communities in Kerala grew out of such extended families, whose origins can be traced back to Jewish traders hailing from West and Central Asia all through medieval times (Qastro 1783, responsum 99; cf. Segal 1983: 230–232; Gamliel 2018a, 2018b).

The earliest evidence for Jewish presence in the region is the signatures in Judeo-Persian on an Old Malayalam copper plate grant dated 849 CE (Narayanan 1972: 31–37, 2009: 120–122). The place of issue of this grant, often referred to as the Syrian Christian Copper Plates, is the ancient port city of Kollam in South Kerala. This port city was a well-known destination for medieval Jewish traders (Goitein and Friedman 2008: 24). Another ancient port city, Kodungallur, also known as Muziris, was the place of issue of another royal grant associated with Jews and dated 1000 CE. This grant was preserved for generations by Kerala Jews, hence its appellation: The Jewish Copper Plates (Narayanan 1972: 23–30, 2009: 118–120).

The 849 royal grant lists rights and privileges allowing the beneficiaries to develop their business in the region. Additionally, it grants them land and serfs to cultivate it and the right to build a *paḷḷi*, namely, a non-Hindu place of worship. In addition to the signatures in Judeo-Persian, there are signatures in Pahlavi and Kufic Arabic, all belonging to two West Asian trade guilds called, in the grant and in other sources in Old Malayalam, *añcuvaṇṇam* and *maṇigrāmam* (Subbarayalu 2009). The representative of the West Asian traders whose signatures appear on the grant is Maruvān Sapir Īśo, whom scholars presume to be a Nestorian Christian from Persia. Contrarily, the later inscription contains neither signatures nor privileges associated with trade or land grants. The inscription lists class-oriented privileges, suggesting that the beneficiary, Joseph Rabban, was already settled in Kerala at the time of receiving the grant. MGS Narayanan (2009: 122–125) speculates that he might have offered financial and military help to the king, Bhāskara Ravi Varmman, who was engaged in protecting his territory against invaders from the neighboring Cōḻa kingdom in Tamil Nadu.

These two inscriptions are the earliest evidence of Jews in the region. These Malayalam inscriptions are also among the earliest records of the Malayalam language (Sekhar 1953: 11). They are written in the *vaṭṭĕḻuttə* script that was used in Tamil administrative documents during the first millennium CE. Thus, the history of the Malayalam language and the history of Kerala Jewry begin, more or less, in the same period. Moreover, these inscriptions attest the involvement of Jews from West Asia along the long-distance trade routes between the Mediterranean and the West Coast of South India. Jewish history in Kerala is, therefore, closely related to the history of global trade in the Indian Ocean in pre-modern times.

That Jews began to settle on the west coast of South India is further supported by medieval sources in Hebrew and Judeo-Arabic. Benjamin of Tudela mentions Jews settled in and around Kollam in his 12th-century travelogue, transliterating the Malayalam name to Hebrew (קאולם) (Adler 1964: 58). A 12th-century Jewish trader from Tunisia, by the name of Abraham ben Yiju, settled for seventeen years in Mangalore, to the north of Kerala, in what is currently the south of the modern state of Karnataka. He married a woman by the name of Aśu and entered into a business partnership with her brother. This marriage and business alliance must have provided this Jewish trader with the license to construct and manage a workshop for recycling broken metal vessels and utensils shipped from West Asia and back from Mangalore. Furthermore, Ben Yiju employed Jews from Yemen as skilled workers and inspectors (Goitein and Friedman 2008: 52–66). Maimonides also mentions India as a place on the frontier of the Jewish Diaspora in his times. He writes in a letter to the "wise men of Lunel" (Shailat 1995: 559) that rich Jews came from as far as India to acquire copies of his book, Mishna Torah. It is reasonable to assume that Maimonides is refering to the West Coast of South India, as his brother, David, was one of the Jewish traders traveling across the Indian Ocean to the Malabar Coast (Goitein and Friedman 2008: 7–8). There are also references to Jews by non-Jewish travelers from the West; the 14th-century travelogues by Ibn Battuta and Friar Odoric mention Jewish settlements in central and northern Kerala, respectively (Gibb 2005: 238; Yule 1966, 2: 133–134).

2.1 Attestations and sources

Based on these medieval references, we can postulate that Malayalam-speaking Jews lived in Kerala from the beginning of the second millennium CE. These medieval Jewish households must have provided the ground for Jewish Malayalam to sprout and grow. Interestingly, evidence for Jewish literature in Malayalam precedes evidence for the spoken language; Old Malayalam songs on Jewish themes, like biblical stories or Jewish lore, were composed in the style and language of Old Malayalam literature, possibly dating back to the 15th century (Gamliel 2009a, 1: 342–345). This tradition of Jewish Malayalam songs was – and, to some extent, still is – maintained by the female members of the community, with men participating in its textual transmission as scribes or sponsors (Daniel and Johnson 1995: 174–189; Gamliel 2009a, 1: 391–396). However, except for personal names like *yossevə* 'Joseph' and *yākkobə* 'Jacob', these songs contain very few loanwords from Hebrew, and it is difficult to determine whether they represent a fully-fledged Jewish religiolect of the time.

The earliest solid evidence for a distinctive Jewish religiolect of Malayalam is found in a relatively late phase of literary evolution, namely the verbatim translations of Hebrew sacred texts. The language of these translations contains morphemes that were out of use in Malayalam by the 18th century. It also displays distinctive features of Jewish Malayalam, suggesting that, by the time of their composition, Jewish Malayalam had matured into a distinct religiolect of Malayalam. Contrary to the 15th-century songs, these verbatim translations provide the basis for assuming a full-fledged and distinctively Jewish dialect of Malayalam by the 18th century at the latest (Gamliel 2014: 143–148).

Written sources in Jewish Malayalam are, by and large, in the Malayalam script, with the exception of terms or names that appear in Hebrew texts. For example, the term *kāppə* (קאפא) 'vigil', signifying the customary feast that was held on the night after the bridal engagement, appears in Hebrew prayer books for weddings (Qasti'el 1756; Raḥabi 1769; Raḥabi 1916). Place names, too, are occasionally transcribed into Hebrew script in Jewish legal documents like a Ketubah, for example, containing the place name *kovilaṭṭom* (כווילתום) 'Kovilvaṭṭam' (Yosi Oran, personal communication). Otherwise, Jewish Malayalam is attested only in the Malayalam script in handwritten notebooks, containing mainly songs for festive occasions and weddings in particular (Johnson 2002). In the 1980s, Kerala Jews living in Israel began to use Hebrew script for transliterating some Jewish Malayalam songs, to be performed during public celebrations (Isenberg, Daniel, and Dekel-Squires 1984).

The earliest dated manuscript in Jewish Malayalam is a notebook dated 1876 and named after Abigail Madayi, probably its owner. Though manuscripts containing Jewish Malayalam literary texts are rather late, the literary and translation traditions as a whole must be much earlier. Evidence of the tradition of Jewish Malayalam wedding songs dates back to the mid-18th century, in the Hebrew book of prayers mentioned above (Qasti'el 1756: 39a). The editor states that, after certain rites and just before the wedding ceremony, "the women sing according to their custom" (והנשים שרות כמנהגם *ve-ha-našim šarot ke-minhagam*). The phrase "their custom," as opposed to the Hebrew para-liturgical poems that precede and follow it, most probably refers to the tradition of Jewish Malayalam songs mentioned above.

Jewish literature continued to be composed in Malayalam until the mid-20th century, motivated by performative concerns during weddings and, to a much lesser extent, during other life-cycle events. Some of it consisted of folksongs adapted from other communities; some of it is adaptations of Hebrew narrations from the Bible, Talmud, and Hebrew poetry into Malayalam. The history of Jewish

Malayalam literature since the 15th century shows trends of Judaization and, later on, nationalization, but it reveals relatively little about spoken Jewish Malayalam.

Jewish Malayalam speech is attested in audio recordings that were collected by scholars for different purposes. In the 1970s, the anthropologists Shirley Isenberg and Barbara Johnson were the first to record women singing Jewish Malayalam songs in Kerala and in Israel (Seroussi 2004: 4). The recordings are kept in the National Sound Archives of the Jewish National and University Library in Jerusalem. Approximately at the same time, Tapani Harviainen of the University of Helnsinki in Finland, in collaboration with the Jewish Oral Traditions Research Center at Hebrew University, recorded men reciting Hebrew sacred texts (Forsström 2006: 1). Some of these recordings include recitations of verbatim translations in Jewish Malayalam. In 2008, a project of language documentation among the last speakers of Jewish Malayalam in Israel began, under the auspices of the Ben-Zvi Institute in Jerusalem (Gamliel 2009b, 2010, 2013a, 2016b).

2.2 Phases in historical development

The following timeline for the evolution of Jewish Malayalam is based on four types of data sources. First, there is linguistic evidence in spoken Jewish Malayalam, as recorded during the above-mentioned language documentation project. Secondly, the generic classification of Jewish Malayalam literature enables temporal assessment of the period of composition; it is possible to evaluate whether a certain genre preceded or followed another genre. Thirdly, the history of Malayalam literature provides the timeline against which the evolution of genres in Jewish Malayalam is to be estimated (Gamliel 2009a, 1: 53–54; cf. Ayyar 1938: 19–20). Lastly, historical evidence in other languages, such as royal grants and travelogues, provides the timeline of Kerala Jewish history as an anchor for estimating the periods of evolution of Jewish Malayalam.

The 10th–13th centuries constitute the beginning phase, when the ground for a Jewish religiolect to evolve was set. This period begins with the royal grants in Old Malayalam discussed above: the Syrian Christian Copper Plates (849) and the Jewish Copper Plates (1000). External evidence for Jewish settlements in South and North Kerala provides the upper limit of this period, like the mention of Kollam by Benjamin of Tudela (mid-12th century) and the evidence for a Jewish presence in southern and northern Kerala in the Cairo Geniza (11th–13th centuries). This period runs parallel to Early Old Malayalam, which is attested only in royal inscriptions (Sekhar 1953: 1–7).

The 14th–15th centuries constitute the consolidation phase, a period in which the archaic dative morpheme *-ikkə* (after -ṉ), retained in contemporary Jewish

Malayalam, disappeared from Malayalam (Ayyar 1938: 27–28). This period runs parallel to the Early *Maṇiprvāḷam* period and the rare specimens of *pāṭṭə* literature: the *Rāmacaritam* (14th century) and the *Payyannūrpāṭṭə* (15th century). The earliest Jewish compositions in Malayalam must have been composed towards the end of this period, during the 15th century, since they resemble the abovementioned compositions in the Old Malayalam *pāṭṭə* genre in style and language (cf. Freeman 1998: 54–58, 2003: 448–450).

The 16th–17th centuries constitute the phase of Old Jewish Malayalam. It begins with the earliest first-hand accounts in Hebrew of Jewish communities in and around Cochin by an anonymous responsum from ca. 1520 (Qastro 1783: 149, responsum 99) and by the Yemenite traveler, Zacharia Al-Ḍāharī of the mid-16th century (Ratzaby 1965: 130ff.). The genre of Jewish Malayalam *kiḷippāṭṭə* 'parrot song' emerged in this period (Zacharia 2003; Zacharia and Gamliel 2005: 135; Gamliel 2009a 1: 378), which saw the earliest printed indigenous Hebrew poetry (Haʻadani 1688). This phase of Old Jewish Malayalam runs parallel to Early New Malayalam compositions, beginning with Eḻuttacan̠'s *kiḷippāṭṭə* epics, and to the earliest composition in Arabic Malayalam, the *Muḥyiddīn Māla* (1607). This period also possibly marks the onset of verbatim translations of Hebrew sacred texts (Bible and Mishna recitals).

The period between the mid-18th and the mid-20th centuries marks the phase of modern Jewish Malayalam. It begins with the earliest printed Hebrew anthologies of para-liturgy (Qastiʼel 1756; Raḥabi 1769). In this period, with the expansion of European colonialism, the contacts between European Jewry and wealthy Kerala Jewish merchants involved in international trade had a profound effect on Jewish literature composed in Kerala, with a growing trend of Judaization. Thus, a new genre of Jewish songs in Malayalam evolved, in which songs were attributed to wealthy community members. A new trend of wedding songs emerged in this period, based on adaptations of Hebrew para-liturgy to Malayalam. Additionally, scribes in Cochin produced printed and hand-written verbatim translations of Hebrew para-liturgy (HaCohen 1877).

The period from the 1950s to the present day marks the last phase of late Jewish Malayalam, beginning with the mass migration of Kerala Jews to Israel in 1954 and followed by decades of decline in usage.

3 Structural information

Jewish Malayalam is an agglutinative SOV language. Its syntax branches to the left; subordinate clauses and modifiers precede their governing noun phrases;

verbs follow their arguments. Hebrew loanwords are incorporated accordingly, preceding their nominal inflections or governing phrases as in the following examples (1) – (4).[1] Note that all the examples in the present paper are from written sources and transliterated according to Indic transliteration, representing the spelling of words rather than their pronunciation.

(1)   vāst.unn.a   malaāka.ø   van.n.atu   kaṇ.ṭu
    bless.PRS.PRT   angel[H].NOM   come.PST.REL   see.PST
    [She] saw that a blessing angel arrived.
    [Gamliel 2009a, II: 544]

(2)   murddohāyi.ø   ĕḻunner.ṟu   śālom   kŏṭu.tt.atĕ
    Mordechai[H].NOM   rise.NFIN   greeting[H]   give.PST.3SG
    Mordechai got up and greeted him.
    [Zacharia and Gamliel 2005: 88]

(3)   abrām abīṇ.oṭ'   āruḷappāṭ'   ŏṇṭāy.i
    Abraham-our father[H].SOC   divine word   become.PST
    God spoke to Abraham our father.
    [Zacharia and Gamliel 2005: 93]

(4)   kabur.kaḷ.uṭĕ
    tombstone[H].PL.GEN
    of graves
    [HaCohen 1877: 7]

3.1 Relationship to non-Jewish varieties (isoglosses, related dialects)

For Malayalam speakers in Kerala, Jewish Malayalam is one among many dialects and castolects. The degree of intelligibility between Jewish Malayalam and other Malayalam dialects is relatively high. However, it is closest to Māppiḷa Malayalam, the religiolect of Kerala Muslims. For example, Jews and Muslims in Kerala share several kinship terms, distinctively different from those used by

---

[1] The abbreviations used in the glossing for the examples below are as follows: 1=1st person; 3=3rd person; ACC=accusative; ADV=adverb; AUG=augment; CMP=completive; CNJ=conjunctive article; DAT=dative; DSD=desiderative; EXT=existential copula; FUT=future; GEN=genitive; [H]=Hebrew loanword; IMP=imperative; LM=link morph; LOC=locative; LP=link phoneme; M=masculine; NEG=negative; NFIN=nonfinite; NOM=nominative; PL=plural; PRT=participle; PRS=present; PST=past; QUANT=quantifier; QUOT=quotative; REL=relative participle; SG=singular; SOC=sociative; VN=verbal noun; VOC=vocative.

Hindus and Christians (cf. Asher and Kumari 1997: 451–454). See, for example, (5), with the terms for 'father', 'mother', 'elder brother', and 'husband' in Jewish Malayalam, as compared with Māppiḷa Malayalam and with the same terms used by Christians and Hindus. Note that the Christian terms reflect a transition from an older terminology that was closer to that of Muslims and Jews.

(5)		father	mother	elder brother	husband
	Jews	vāva	umma	kākka/ikka	māppiḷa
	Muslims	bāppa	umma	kākka/akka	putiyāppiḷa/ikka
	Christians	appan̠	amma/ammacci	ceṭṭan̠	bharttāvə/māppiḷa
	Hindus	acchan̠	amma	ceṭṭan̠	bharttāvə/ceṭṭan̠

Jewish Malayalam also shares some peculiar morphophonemic features with Māppiḷa Malayalam. For example, the accusative ending /ĕ/ is replaced by /a/, as demonstrated in (6) and (7):

(6) iṅṅu vā ĕnnu makaḷ.a viḷi.ccu
here come.IMP.SG QUOT girl.ACC call.PST
[He] called the daughter, saying: "Come over here!"
[Gamliel 2009a 2: 525]

(7) kan̠.ṭ.a kĕn̠āv.in̠.a cŏll.u.vin̠ niṅṅaḷ
see.PST.PRT. dream.AUG.ACC tell.IMP.PL 2PL
You all tell [me] the dream you saw!
[Gamliel 2009a, 2: 524]

Another example is the replacement of /a/ by /ĕ/ in adjectival participial endings (PRT), as demonstrated in (8) and (9):

(8) kayi.v.il iru.nn.ĕ mutal.um kŏṭu.tt.ūtĕ
hand.LP.LOC sit.PST.PRT wealth.QUANT give.PST.3SG
[Rebecca] gave [Jacob] all the wealth **that** [she] had handy.
[Gamliel 2009a, II: 428]

(9) muṭiy.ā.y.ĕ ñāyĕn̠.ĕ
crown.be.PST.PRT Lord.VOC
Oh, Lord **who** is the top!
[Gamliel 2009a, II: 456]

Such peculiar morphophonemic features can be traced back to an early stage in the evolution of Malayalam, suggesting that Jewish and Māppiḷa Malayalam retain archaic features of Malayalam morphology.

The retention of archaic morphemes is especially evident in the form of the dative after nouns ending in -*an̠*. In most Malayalam dialects, the dative suffix after the singular masculine ending -*an̠* is -*ə*. In Jewish Malayalam, however, the dative ending after -*an̠* is, instead, -*ikkə*, as in example (10). Note that, in manuscripts preceding the mid-20th century, the schwa vowel /ə/ lacks orthographic representation and therefore is represented as /a/.

(10) *avan̠.ikka   pŏkaticcĕ.y.um*
      3sgm.DAT   praise.LM.CNJ
      praise to him
      [Pirke Avot, undated, p. 7]

(11) *nin̠.r̠ĕ   puruśĕn̠.ikku   nūr   vayassə   ŏṇṭa*
      2SG.GEN   man.DAT   hundred   age   EXT
      Your man is a hundred years old.
      [Zacharia and Gamliel 2005: 56]

This feature, occurring also in Muslim dialects of central and north Kerala, is comparable with the dative ending -*ukku* in Tamil, as in *avan̠-ukku* 'for him' (Panicker 2012). Since the dative ending -*ə* is already attested in literary Malayalam in the 14th century, the ending -*ikkə* appears to be an archaism in Jewish (and Māppiḷa) Malayalam.

The link morpheme (LM) -(*i*)*n̠* occurs in Jewish Malayalam after nouns ending in vowels, which is otherwise restricted in Malayalam to nouns ending in a consonant or in the schwa vowel /ə/. For example:

(12) *r̠āel-ummā.n̠.ĕ.y.um   kĕṭṭ.ūt.um-cĕy.t.ūtĕ*
      Rachel-mother.LM.ACC.LP.CNJ   marry.VN.CNJ-do.PST.3SG
      Then, [Jacob] married mother Rachel too.
      [Gamliel 2009a, II: 430]

(13) *ā   vĕlĕ.n̠.a   priyappĕṭa*
      DEM   work.LM.ACC   love.IMP.SG
      Love that work!
      [Anonymous, p. 4]

Some of the dialectical features of Jewish Malayalam reflect affiliations with other dialects of Malayalam. One particularly striking feature is the replacement of the approximant /ḻ/ with /t/, attested also in the northernmost castolects of Nairs and Tiyyas. Compare, for example, the Malayalam words in (14a) and (15a) with their variants in Jewish Malayalam and the Nair dialect in (14b) and (15b), respectively:

(14a) *toḻi*, 'a confidante, bride's maid' [Gundert 1995: 495]
(14b) *tŏti.mār*, 'female companion.PL' [Gamliel 2009a, 2: 420]
(15a) *kiḻaṅṅə*, 'bulb; yam' [Gundert 1995: 251]
(15b) *kĕtaṅṅə*, 'bulb' [Subramoniam 2006: 21]

The alternation /ḻ/ > /t/ is not consistent in the manuscripts. Apparently, Jewish Malayalam underwent a phase of standardization, for scribes began to "correct" the spelling /t/ to /ḻ/. A Malayalam scholar from Ernakulam recalled with amusement that Jewish women of his neighborhood used to pronounce /t/ instead of /ḻ/.[2] Thus, it appears that, gradually, Jewish Malayalam speakers – possibly males first – began to adjust their pronunciation to the speech of their neighbors. Interestingly, this development lead to hypercorrection of /t/ to /ḻ/, attested in manuscripts since the late-19th century, as in (16):

(16) *pĕrima   niṉ.akka*
     glory.SUB   2sg.DAT
     uḻikk.*unn-ā(y)*   *uḷḷa*   *mala-mel*
     shine.PRS.PRT-be.PST.PRT exist.PRS.PRT mountain.ADV
     On a mountain shining with Your glory
     [HaCohen 1877: 42]

The lexeme *uḻikk-*, translating the Hebrew ז.ר.ח 'shine', is derived from the Sanskrit loan verb *udikk-* 'shine' (/d/ is interchangeable with intervocalic /t/ *utikk-*). Since Jewish Malayalam speakers understand it as derived from /ḻ/, they correct it accordingly into *uḻikk-*. Such hypercorrections possibly reflect a transition period, in which speakers began to adjust their religiolect to the central Kerala dialects.

Lastly, the completive aspect (CMP) in Jewish Malayalam is expressed by *kŏṇṭu* instead of *iṭṭa* (< *viṭ-* 'leave'). Note that *kŏṇṭu* is realized as *oṇṭu* in fast speech, as is illustrated in (17):

(17) *vāḻuvu*   *meṭi.cc-***oṇṭu**   *por.unn.a*   *nera.ttu*
     blessing   receive.NFIN-**CMP** come.PRS.PRT   time.LOC
     When [he] was coming **after** receiving the blessing
     [Gamliel 2009a, 2: 427]

All the above-mentioned features are realized in contemporary Jewish Malayalam speech (Gamliel 2013a: 145–147; 2016a). Contrarily, in Jewish Malayalam

---

2 Thuravoor Vishvambharan, personal communication, January 2005.

literature, their realization depends on the scribe and the genre; in some genres, there is a tendency to adhere to literary registers in Modern Malayalam and to standardize the language. On the other hand, archaisms that went out of use in casual speech are realized in literary registers of Jewish Malayalam (Zacharia and Gamliel 2005: 131; Gamliel 2009a, 1: 186–199). For example, the archaic form of periphrastic past in (18):

(18) ummā.ṇ.a   ĕṭu.tt-uṇṭĕ   maṟi.pp.ūt.um-cĕy.t.utĕ
     mother.AUG.ACC   take.NFIN-CMP   bury.FUT.VN.CNJ-do.PST.3SG
     [They] took the mother and buried her.
     [Zacharia and Gamliel 2005: 60]

At the current stage of research of Malayalam dialectology in general, and Jewish Malayalam in particular, it is difficult to determine the boundaries between the Jewish religiolect and other dialects of Malayalam. Certainly, the incorporation of Hebrew loanwords into the lexicon is unique to the Jewish religiolect, whereas Māppiḷa Malayalam, the religiolect closest to Jewish Malayalam, often incorporates Arabic loanwords in a similar way. Compare, for example, the compound verb for 'die' in Māppiḷa Malayalam (19) and in Jewish Malayalam (20):

(19) aruvi.ø   duā.ø   teṭi.kkŏṇṭə   **mautt-ā.yi**
     beauty.NOM   prayer[A].ACC   pray.PRG   **death[A]-be.PST**
     The beautiful woman died while praying.
     [Muhammadali 2007: 51]
(20) mālŏn.ø.um   kiliyŏn.ø.um   **śālŏm-ā.yi.tĕ**
     Mahalon[H].NOM.CNJ Kilayon[H].NOM.CNJ   **peace[H]-be.PST.3SG**
     Malon and Kilayon died.
     [Zacharia and Gamliel 2005: 77]

In both examples, a loanword from the language of sacred texts – Arabic or Hebrew – is embedded in a compound verb to create a lexeme peculiar to the religiolect.

3.2 Lexicon: Hebrew and Aramaic elements

Jewish Malayalam literature freely incorporates Hebrew words into Biblical narrations, devotional songs, or verbatim translations of sacred texts (cf. Zacharia and Gamliel 2005: 205–207; Gamliel 2013b). See for example the fourth verse of the translation of the Zionist/Israeli national anthem, Ha-Tikvah (I24):

(21) yeṛuśalem   paṭṭaṇam   neśar̠.iṉa-pole
    Jerusaelm[H]   town   eagleH.ACC-like
    iṉiyum   putut-ākk.um.eṉ
    again   new-make.FUT.1SG
    We shall renovate once more the town of Jerusalem like an eagle.
    [Gamliel 2009a: 508–9]

This translation-adaptation of a Hebrew song represents a late stage in the history of contact between Hebrew and Malayalam. Hebrew loanwords are attested also in older literary compositions, as in the first lines of the song Feast of the Whale (II42):

(22) tambirāṉ.r̠e   tuṇa-āya   gulatt.innu
    Lord.GEN   help.ADJ   tribe.DAT
    Lord's help for the nation
    olaka   paṭicci-uṇṭākki-vecc.ūte
    world.DO   creat-make-PRF.PST
    He had created the world.
    kālam   ayyayiratti-nannūr̠um-nalpatum-pantiraṇṭum   āyīte
    time   five thousand-four hundred-forty-twelve   be.PST
    Since then, five thousand and four hundred and 52 years went by.
    al̠iññ.a   mīkadāś.iṉr̠e   nāḷ.il
    destroy.ADJ   temple[H].GEN   day.LOC
    per̠unn.a   puruśaṉ.a   peraya-veṇam
    born.ADJ   man.ACC   love-DSD
    Love the man who was born on the day the temple was destroyed.
    [Gamliel 2009a: 437]

In (22), the Hebrew component is expressed also by using the Malayalam numerals to denote the Hebrew year 5452 (1692), besides using the loanword mīkadāś (< מקדש).

It is questionable how many of the Hebrew loanwords in the literature were used in casual daily speech. Preliminary studies on the speech samples collected in 2008–2009 show that Hebrew loanwords were used in casual speech at least to some extent (Gamliel 2009c: 51, 2013a: 142–144, 149–151).

4 Written and oral traditions

The dichotomy between the oral and the written is inapplicable in the case of Jewish Malayalam. For one, in Malayalam literature in general, folksongs (nāṭanpāṭṭu), like the Jewish Malayalam women's songs, are transmitted both orally and textually (Gamliel 2008: 46–49). Secondly, some traditions that are transmitted in writing in other Jewish language varieties (like verbatim translations) are transmitted orally in Jewish Malayalam. Thirdly, a textual tradition like the women's songs displays features characteristic of oral literature, such as variations and repetitions, since it is performative in essence (Zacharia and Gamliel 2005: 131–135). Contrarily, the oral tradition of verbatim translations aims at an accurate rendition of the word-to-word translations for sacred Hebrew texts, with the goal of fulfilling didactic purposes. Lastly, the tradition of verbatim translations, albeit transmitted orally, branched into a written tradition of verbatim translations of Hebrew paraliturgy that appeared in print and in hand-written manuscripts. Interestingly, a parallel tradition of translations for Hebrew paraliturgical texts branched off the performative tradition of women's songs as well (Gamliel 2014: 148–157).

The oral tradition of verbatim translations for reciting Bible and Mishna has its earliest record in manuscripts that were copied down around the late 19th century (Anonymous undated; Hallegua 1898). Bits and pieces of this tradition still exist in the memories of elderly Jewish Malayalam speakers in Israel, who refer to it as *tamsīr*. The *tamsīr* tradition incorporates certain archaisms typical of 18th-century literary Malayalam, which went out of use in Modern Malayalam literature. For example, *kaṇṭān* 'he saw' in (21) incorporates a pronominal suffix, whereas Modern Malayalam would use the bare past form, *kaṇṭu* 'saw', without it:

(23) ŏru   talĕ.n.a   kaṇ.ṭ.āṉ
     one   head.AUG.ACC   see.PST.3SGM
     He saw one skull.
     [Anonymous 9]

The archaic pronominal suffixes in the *tamsīr* tradition suggest that the origin of this tradition cannot be later than the mid-18th century, when the use of the suffixed verbal forms was retained only in formal language registers (Ayyar 1941: 390). Contrarily, the verbatim translations for Hebrew paraliturgy exist only in print, and parallel to a living performative tradition of adaptations of Hebrew poetry to Malayalam (discussed below). This is in stark contrast to the oral tradition of *tamsīr*, which was partially retained in the memory of elderly community members even as late as the 2000s. Therefore, the verbatim translations of Hebrew liturgical poetry must have been compiled close to their publication date, that is, not earlier than the 1870s (Gamliel 2014: 143–148).

The adaptations of Hebrew poetry into Malayalam are contained in the corpus of Jewish Malayalam songs, which was transmitted both in writing and in performance. Such adaptations are called *arttham* 'meaning' in Jewish Malayalam, differentiating them from the pedantic and somewhat artificial verbatim translations called *tamsīr*. These *arttham* translations were performed during weddings and other celebrations; some are still performed in Israel. As opposed to *tamsīr*, these translations are paraphrases adapted to known tunes, and obviously composed with the target language, Malayalam, in mind, whereas the *tamsīr* translation is evidently focused on the source language, Hebrew. Some of these translations must have been composed even before the 18th century. For example, the *arttham* translation for זבד הבת, *zeḇed ha-bat* 'blessing for the daughter' incorporates an Old Malayalam future form marked for the second person singular, which had already fallen out of use as a literary form by the 17th century (Gamliel 2014: 142–57).

Besides the tradition of women's songs and verbatim translations, there must have been a rich tradition of oral literary genres from folk tales to jokes and riddles. This tradition hardly left any records in the recorded heritage of Kerala Jews. A few stories were recorded in Hebrew and archived in the Israel Folktale Archives, where there are about forty stories collected from Kerala Jews in Israel (5327, 8125, 17464–17499, 20403–20405, 20729). These are mostly memorabiles and anecdotes, with only three folktales by definition (8125, 9335, 5327). A few more stories, anecdotes, jokes, riddles, and so forth were recorded in Malayalam, as part of the language documentation project carried out in 2008–2009 (Gamliel 2009b, 2010). This material still awaits thorough transliteration, translation, and analysis.

4.1 Literature

Unlike the major Jewish language varieties that evolved during medieval times, Jewish Malayalam literature is written in the Malayalam script. The corpus of Jewish Malayalam literature is comprised of several genres with a wide spectrum of themes and styles, from retellings of biblical stories to folksongs adapted from Muslim, Christian, and Hindu communities. In previous studies, the generic classification of the corpus has been based on thematic considerations, namely, historical, biblical, devotional, wedding, and miscellaneous songs (Jussay 2005: 105–117; Johnson 2005: 209–210). Arguably, a generic classification of songs based on structural considerations is more useful in constructing the literary history of Jewish Malayalam and juxtaposing its evolution with the history of Malayalam literature (Gamliel 2009a, 1: 171–287). Based on structural features such as rhymes, narration modes, song-titles, linguistic registers, and so forth, Jewish Malayalam songs can be divided into (i) rhyming songs, (ii) formulaic songs, (iii) refrain songs, (iv) composer songs, (v) copperplate songs, and (vi) folksongs. Though this classification is somewhat artificial, it enables the incorporation of indigenous generic classification that may be based on thematic, pragmatic, or structural considerations, depending on the context.

Rhyming Songs have four-line verses, with rhymes in the second syllable of each line (*ĕtuka*) and in the first phoneme of each half-line (*mona*) (Gamliel 2009a, 1: 288–345). These rhymes, combined with Dravidian meters, typify an Old Malayalam literary genre known as *pāṭṭǝ* 'song' (Freeman 1998: 54–58). Since the rhyming songs contain retellings of biblical stories with occasional references to Midrash, they may be called 'biblical *pāṭṭǝ*'. There are very few compositions in Malayalam with structural features comparable to biblical *pāṭṭǝ*. The most similar non-Jewish composition is the Payyannūrpāṭṭǝ ('The Song of *Payyannūr*', ca. 15th century), associated with the *Cĕṭṭi* (merchant) community of north Kerala and with the temple in the town of *Payyannūr* (Freeman 2003: 452, 459). The oldest dated notebook containing biblical *pāṭṭǝ* belonged to Abigail Madayi from Cochin (1876), whose name points to origins in Madayi in north Kerala, not too far from the town of Payyannūr. Interestingly, the Payyannūrpāṭṭǝ mentions the merchant guilds *añcuvaṇṇam* and *maṇigrāmam* (Gundert 2000), suggesting that the structural similarities are not merely coincidental, but rather may be based on historical cross-cultural contacts. Based on both the language register and the style of composition, it is possible to determine that the rhyming songs must be the oldest layer of the Jewish Malayalam songs and, quite likely, predating the *tamsīr* tradition.

Formulaic Songs are stylistically very different from the biblical *pāṭṭǝ* rhyming songs; they contain opening and closing formulas invoking God and do not incorporate the *pāṭṭǝ*-style *ĕtuka* and *mona* rhymes. Many songs of this type are adaptations of biblical stories of the patriarchs, while some are synagogue songs (*paḷḷippāṭṭǝ*), extolling the merits of the different synagogues of Kerala. The biblical formulaic songs resemble in style the *Knānaya* Christian songs from south Kerala (Jussay 2005: 118–28) and were probably composed no earlier than the 16th century and no later than the 17th century.

Refrain Songs are songs with different types of repeated sounds that may consist of meaningless strings of sounds or of lines in fixed intervals. There are several types of refrain songs; they include songs addressing a parrot or a bird, and corresponding to trends in the early Modern Malayalam compositions called parrot songs (*kiḷippāṭṭǝ*), and Malayalam folksongs (Zacharia 2003b). Refrain songs do not necessarily address explicit Jewish themes. Some synagogue songs contain refrains.

Composer Songs are songs attributed to composers, be they actual composers or patrons of anonymous composers. These songs resemble the translation (*arttham*) songs discussed above, in their close affinity with Hebrew liturgy and poetry. Composer songs incorporate more Hebrew loanwords or calque translations, and their style of composition resembles literary registers of Modern Malayalam (Gamliel 2009a: 242–248).

Copperplate Songs are wedding songs obliquely related to the 10th-century copperplate grant (discussed in Section 1); they mention different names and appellations of Muziris/Kodungallur and describe the wedding procession in royal terms. These songs appear solely in notebooks in the possession of the Cochin Paradeśi community, who present the songs as "historically" related to the copperplate grant (Simon 1947). Whether the contents of the 10th-century grant are indeed repeated or alluded to in the songs is dubious.

Folksongs of different types were incorporated into the corpus in different periods and from different communities. There is at least one song which is also a typical Muslim wedding song (Zacharia and Gamliel 2005: 110 [Malayalam]), and several wedding songs that are shared with Christians, though it is difficult to determine who borrowed from whom (Jussay 2006: 118–28). Several songs must have been borrowed from Hindu communities, like the play-song *pŏlika pŏlika* (Narayanan 2005) and the boat-song *kappalilē* (Zacharia and Gamliel 2005: 200 [Malayalam]).

As stated above, Jewish Malayalam songs were performed by women during weddings and, to a lesser extent, during other life-cycle and year-cycle events. Today, with the modernization of life-cycle events and the adjustment to the modern Israeli culture and way of life, the traditional set-up for performances is no more. However, there are women's troupes who present Jewish Malayalam and Malayalam songs for staged performances during communal events and academic conferences (Johnson 2005). The songs they perform are mainly of the translation and composer songs genres, like the translation of the Zionist/Israeli national anthem (see example 21 above) or Malayalam cinema songs that some elderly women still remember from the period prior to their migration to Israel.

5 State of research – past and future

Jewish Malayalam literature has attracted the attention of scholars since the 1970s, prompting them to collect, index, and archive notebooks containing Jewish Malayalam women's songs (Johnson 2002). Rough translations of the songs have appeared in several publications (Daniel and Johnson 1995: 123–191; Jussay 2006: 77–92, 105–128), but it was only in 2002 that the first translations of 28 songs, based on close readings of the Malayalam texts, appeared in publication (Frenz and Zacharia 2002). That publication marked a turning point in the study of the language and the literature of Jewish Malayalam women's songs (Johnson 2007: 135–139). It was followed by a publication of the texts and translations of 52 songs, in a bilingual Malayalam-Hebrew book (Zacharia and Gamliel 2005). Annotated translations of another 62 songs, with transliterated texts based on a critical edition of the manuscripts, are discussed in an unpublished dissertation (Gamliel 2009a, 2). Translations of selected verses of the rhyming songs (Biblical *pāṭṭə*) have appeared in Hebrew (Gamliel 2012), followed by an in-depth study of the translation genres in Jewish Malayalam (Gamliel 2014).

Jewish Malayalam was recognized as a language on the spectrum of Jewish languages in 2003 (Zacharia 2003a), but it was only in 2008 that a project of language documentation was launched, under the auspices of the Ben Zvi Institute in Jerusalem (Gamliel 2009b, 2010). Several articles concerning the initial findings revealed in the audio records have been published since then (Gamliel 2009b-d, 2013a, 2014, 2015, 2016a, 2016b). However, the audio recordings of Jewish Malayalam still await transcriptions for conversations, interviews, and storytelling, which would enable in-depth study of this unique Jewish language variety or Malayalam religiolect.

The study of Jewish Malayalam introduces into the spectrum of Jewish languages a language variety that has evolved for centuries in a region situated on the far margins of the Jewish Diaspora, connected with world Jewry through medieval global trade in the Indian Ocean. Thus, Jewish Malayalam is one of merely two Jewish language varieties affiliated with the Indian linguistic area, the other being Judeo-Marathi (Rubin 2016a; see also Rubin 2016b), which is relatively recent and lacking in literary production and written traditions. It is the only Jewish language variety that evolved through contacts with a Dravidian language, significantly different from the European and West Asian languages with which most Jewish language varieties came into contact. Jewish Malayalam is also unique in its socioreligious setting under Hindu – rather than Muslim or Christian – hegemony.

The study of Jewish Malayalam bears upon several different research concerns beyond the field of Jewish language varieties. First, it is essential for a better and deeper understanding of Kerala Jewish history, culture, and society, whose study has relied too much on second-hand sources, mainly in European languages (Gamliel 2018a). Secondly, it has the potential to contribute comparative perspectives to the fields of Malayalam dialectology and regional literary studies and widen their scope. Thirdly, Jewish Malayalam is the only living contact language directly linking the cultural history of Jews with India from medieval times onwards. The study of Jewish Malayalam, therefore, is also the study of the history and the evolution of cross-cultural contacts in the context of global trade, an emerging field of study (Trivellato 2014).

References

Adler, Nathan Marcus. 1964 [1907]. *The itinerary of Benjamin of Tudela: Critical text, translation and commentary*. New York: Philipp Feldheim. (Hebrew).
Anonymous. פרקי אבות עם תרגום למלבארית [Ethics of the Fathers with translation into Malabarit]. Undated manuscript.
Ayyar, L. V. Ramaswamy. 1993 [1936]. *The evolution of Malayalam morphology*. Thrissur: Kerala Sahitya Akademi.
Ayyar, L. V. Ramaswamy. 1941. Eighteenth-century Malayāḷam Prose by Christians. *New Indian Antiquary* 3(1). 387–397.
Daniel, Ruby & Barbara C. Johnson. 1995. *Ruby of Cochin: An Indian Jewish woman remembers*. Philadelphia: The Jewish Publication Society.
Ethnologue. 2015. Language status. https://www.ethnologue.com/about/language-status (accessed 9 August 2016).
Frenz, Albrecht & Scaria Zacharia. 2002. *In meinem land leben verschiedene völker*. Ostfildern: Schwabenverlag.
Forsström, Jarmo. 2006. מסורת הקריאה המשנאית של יהודי קוצ׳ין במשנה: תורת ההגה [The mishnaic reading tradition of Cochin Jews: Phonology].
Freeman, Rich. 1998. Rubies and corals: The lapidary crafting of language in Kerala. *Journal of Asian Studies* 57(1). 38–65.
Freeman, Rich. 2003. Genre and society: The literary culture of premodern Kerala. In Sheldon Pollock (ed.), *Literary cultures in history: Reconstructions from South Asia*, 437–502. Berkeley: University of California Press.
Gamliel, Ophira. 2008. Malayalam folksongs. In David Shulman & Shalva Weil (eds.), *Karmic passages: Israeli scholarship on India*, 46–82. Delhi: Oxford University Press.
Gamliel, Ophira. 2009a. *Jewish Malayalam women's songs Volumes I and II*. Jerusalem: Hebrew University of Jerusalem PhD thesis.
Gamliel, Ophira. 2009b. Kerala project: On documenting the linguistic heritage of Kerala Jews. Peʾamim 122. 129–153. (Hebrew).
Gamliel, Ophira. 2009c. Oral literary forms in Jewish Malayalam. *Journal of Indo-Judaic Studies* 10. 47–60.
Gamliel, Ophira. 2009d. Jewish Malayalam. *International Journal of Dravidian Linguistics* 38. 147–75.
Gamliel, Ophira. 2010. Documenting Jewish Malayalam in Israel: Fieldwork description and data analysis. *TAPASAM: A Quarterly Journal of Kerala Studies in Malayalam-English* 6. 3–39.
Gamliel, Ophira. 2012. And the women sing their songs: The wedding songs of Kerala Jews. In Haviva Pedaya (ed.), *The piyyut as a cultural prism: New approaches*, 266–315. Jerusalem: Van-Leer Institute (Hebrew).
Gamliel, Ophira. 2013a. Voices yet to be heard: On listening to the last speakers of Jewish Malayalam. *Journal of Jewish Languages* 1. 135–67.
Gamliel, Ophira. 2013b. The Hebrew component in Jewish Malayalam. In Geoffrey Khan (ed.), *Encyclopaedia of Hebrew Language and Linguistics*, vol. 2, 410–13. Leiden: Brill.
Gamliel, Ophira. 2014. סוגות תרגום במליאלם יהודית: בחינה לשונית וסגנונית [Translation genres in Jewish Malayalam: Stylistic and linguistic examination]. *Massorot* 16. 137–72.
Gamliel, Ophira. 2015. Jewish Malayalam. In Norman A. Stillman (ed.), *Encyclopedia of Jews in the Islamic World*. Brill Online. http://www.brillonline.nl/entries/encyclopedia-of-jews-in-the-islamic-world/jewish-malayalam-COM_000710 (accessed 10 August 2016).

Gamliel, Ophira. 2016a. Jewish Malayalam. In Lily Kahn & Aaron Rubin (eds.), *Handbook of Jewish languages*, 503–516. Leiden: Brill.
Gamliel, Ophira. 2016b. Fading Memories and Linguistic Fossils in Jewish Malayalam. In Erich Kasten, Katja Roller, and Joshua Wilburn (eds.), *Oral history meets linguistics*, 83–106. Fürstenberg/Havel: Verlag der Kulturstiftung Sibirien. Available online: http://www.siberian-studies.org/publications/orhili_E.html.
Gamliel, Ophira. 2018a. Back from Shingly: Revisiting the premodern history of Jews in Kerala. *Indian Economic and Social History Review* 55:1. 53–76.
Gamliel, Ophira. 2018b. Aśu the Convert: A slave girl or a Nāyar land owner? *Entangled Religions* 6. 201–246.
Gamliel, Ophira. 2018c. Who was the Fadiyār? Integrating textual evidence in Judeo-Arabic and Old Malayalam. *Ginzei Qedem Genizah Research Annual* 14. 9–40.
Goitein, S. D. & Mordechai Friedman. 2008. *India traders of the Medieval Ages: Documents from the Cairo Geniza "India Book."* Leiden: Brill.
Govindankutty, A. Menon. 1972. From Proto-Tamil-Malayalam to West Coast dialects. *Indo-Iranian Journal* 14. 52–60.
Gundert, Hermann. 2000 [1884]. The legend of *Payyannūr*. In Scaria Zacharia and P. Antony (eds.), *Payyannūrpāṭṭa Pāṭavum Paṭhanaṅṅaḷum*, xli-xliii. Kottayam: D.C. Books.
Ha'adani, Eliyahu. 1688. יד אליהו: סדר אזהרות כמנהג אנשי ארץ הודו ק"ק קוגין [Yad Eliyahu: Liturgical poems for Shavuot according to the rites of the land of India in the holy community of Cochin]. Amsterdam: Sigmund Seligmann.
HaCohen, Daniel Yaʿaqov. 1877. פיוטים עם תרגום מלבארי [Liturgical poems with translation into Malabari]. Cochin: HaCohen Print.
Halegua, Eliya Haim. 1892. Untitled manuscript.
Hary, Benjamin. 2009. *Translating religion: Linguistic analysis of Judeo-Arabic sacred texts from Egypt*. Leiden: Brill.
Isenberg, Shirley, Ruby Daniel & Miriam Dekel-Squires. 1984. *Tišʿa Širey ʿam be-Malayalam* [Nine folksongs in Malayalam]. Jerusalem: Self-Published.
Johnson, Barbara. 2002. הן נושאות את מחברותיהן איתן: שירי נשים יהודיות מקוצ'ין בשפת המקום ["They carry their notebooks with them": Women's vernacular Jewish songs from Cochin, South India]. *Peʿamim: Studies in Oriental Jewry* 82. 64–80.
Johnson, Barbara. 2005. Afterword: The songs and the project. In Scaria Zacharia and Ophira Gamliel (eds.), *יפהפיה: שירת הנשים של יהודי קרלה* [Kārkuḻali – Yefefiah – Gorgeous! Jewish women's songs in Malayalam with Hebrew translations], 208–226. Jerusalem: Ben-Zvi Institute.
Johnson, Barbara. 2007. New research, discoveries and paradigms: A report on the current study of Kerala Jews. In Nathan Katz, Ranabir Chakravarti, Braj M. Sinha & Shalva Weil (eds.), *Indo-Judaic Studies in the Twenty-First Century: A View from the Margins*, 129–146. New York: Palgrave Macmillan.
Jussay, P. M. 2005. *The Jews of Kerala*. Calicut: Calicut University Publication.
Krishnamurti, Bhadriraju. 2003. *The Dravidian languages*. Cambridge: Cambridge University Press.
Shailat, Itzhak. 1995. *The Letters and Essays of Moses Maimonides: A critical edition of the Hebrew and Arabic letters of Maimonides*. Ma'aleh Adumim: Shailat Publishing [Hebrew].
Muhammadali, V. P. 2007. *Māppiḷappāṭṭukaḷ Nūṟṟāṇṭukaḷilūṭĕ* [Mappilla songs over the centuries]. Kottayam: Current Books.

Narayanan, Aju. 2006. Jutarutf Pqlippattum Keralattilf Ma44u Pqlippattukalum [The increase songs of Jews and other increase songs of Kerala]. *TAPASAM: A Quarterly Journal of Kerala Studies in Malayalam-English* 3(2). 653–663.

Narayanan, M. G. S. 1972. *Cultural symbiosis in Kerala*. Trivandrum: Kerala Historical Society.

Narayanan, M. G. S. 2009. The king of Jews in Kodungallur, India. *Pe'amim* 122. 115–128. (Hebrew).

Panicker, T. B. Venugopala. 2006. *Studies on Malayalam language*. Calicut: University of Calicut.

Panicker, T. B. Venugopala. 2012. Jewish Malayalam and the current standard spoken Malayalam. (Unpublished paper).

Qasti'el, David. 1756. סדר תפלות ושירים לימי שמחת תורה וחופת נעורים [Book of prayers and songs for Simḥat Torah and weddings]. Amsterdam: Props.

Qastro, Yaʻqov Ben Abraham. 1783. ספר אהלי יעקב [The tents of Jacob]. Livorno: Avraham Yicḥaq Qastilo and 'Eli'zer Sa'adon.

Rabin, Haim. 1999. *Linguistic studies: Collected papers in Hebrew and Semitic languages*. Jerusalem: The Academy of Hebrew and Bialik Institute. (Hebrew).

Raḥabi, Yeḥezkel. 1769. סדר תפלות כמנהג אנשים שינגלי [Prayerbook according to the rites of Shingli]. Amsterdam: Props.

Raḥabi, Naftali Eliya. 1916. ספר חופת חתנים כמנהג ק״ק קוג׳ין [Prayerbook according to the rites of the holy congregation at Cochin]. Bombay: Lebanon Press.

Ratzaby, Yehuda (ed.). 1965. ספר המוסר: מחברות ר׳ זכריה אלצאהרי [Book of ethics: The notebooks of R. Zacharia Al-Ḍāharī]. Jerusalem: Ben-Zvi Institute.

Rubin, Aaron D. 2016a. "Epilogue: Other Jewish languages, past and present." In Lily Kahn and Aaron D. Rubin (eds.), *Handbook of Jewish languages*, 748–751. Leiden/Boston: Brill.

Rubin, Aaron D. 2016b. *A Unique Hebrew glossary from India: An analysis of Judeo-Urdu*. Piscataway: Gorgias Press.

Segal, J. B. 1983. White and black Jews at Cochin: The story of a controversy. *Journal of the Royal Asiatic Society of Great Britain and Ireland* 2. 228–252.

Sekhar, A. C. 1953. Evolution of Malayalam. *Bulletin of the Deccan College Research Institute* 1951. 1–216.

Seroussi, Edwin (ed.). 2004. *Oh, lovely parrot! Jewish women's songs from Kerala*. Jerusalem: The Jewish Music Research Center, Hebrew University of Jerusalem.

Shailat, Itzhak. 1995. *The letters and essays of Moses Maimonides: A critical edition of the Hebrew and Arabic letters of Maimonides (including response on beliefs and opinions) based on all extant manuscripts, translated and annotated, with introductions and cross-references*. Ma'aleh Adumim: Shailat Publishing [Hebrew].

Simon, A. I. 1947. *The songs of the Jews of Cochin and their historical significance*. Cochin: Pangal Press.

Subbarayalu, Y. 2009. Anjuvannam: A maritime guild in Medieval Times. In Hermann Kulke, K. Kesavapany & Vijay Sakhuja (eds.), *Nagapattinam to Suvarnadwipa: Reflections on Chola Naval expeditions to Southeast Asia*, 158–167. Singapore: Institute of Southeast Asian Studies.

Subramoniam, V. I. (ed.). 2006. *Dialect map of Malayalam: Ezhava-Tiyyar: Dialect map of Malayalam: Nayar*. Trivandrum: International School of Dravidian Linguistics.

Trivellato, Francesca. 2014. Introduction: The historical and comparative study of cross-cultural trade. In Francesca Trivellato, Leor Halevi & Cátia Antunes (eds.), *Religion and trade: Cross-cultural exchanges in world history, 1000–1900*, 1–23. New York: Oxford University Press.

Weinstein, Brian. 2000. Biblical evidence of spice trade between India and the Land of Israel: A historical analysis. *The Indian Historical Review Volume* 27. 12–28.

Zacharia, Scaria. 2003a. Jewish Malayalam. http://www.jewish-languages.org/jewish-malayalam.html (accessed 10 August 2016).

Zacharia, Scaria. 2003b. Possibilities of understanding Jewish Malayalam folksongs. *Journal of Indo-Judaic Studies* 6. 29–47.

Zacharia, Scaria. 2014. Herman Gundert: Ennum prabala matiman. [Herman Gundart: The wisest of all times]. Kottayam: Malayala Manorama. https://drive.google.com/file/d/0ByyN86H3GWkQblgwSXRsV005bnM/edit (accessed 10 August 2016).

Zacharia, Scaria & Ophira Gamliel (eds.). 2005. יפהפיה: שירת הנשים של יהודי קרלה [Kārkuḷali – Yefefiah – Gorgeous! Jewish women's songs in Malayalam with Hebrew translations]. Jerusalem: Ben-Zvi Institute.

Part II: **Jewish Language Varieties in the 20th and 21st Centuries**

Evelyn Dean-Olmsted and Susana Skura
Jewish Spanish in Buenos Aires and Mexico City

1 Brief introduction

The number of Jews living in Central and South America and the Caribbean is estimated at 382,200 (DellaPergola 2015:19), including 286,200 in Spanish-speaking countries (DellaPergola 2015:74).[1,2] The majority of the modern Jewish migrations to the region occurred in the late 19th and early to mid-20th centuries. By and large, Jews born in these countries speak Spanish as their first language. A common perspective, both among linguists and the general public, is that the speech of such individuals is not distinctive enough from that of their non-Jewish neighbors to merit serious investigation. This is true in both traditional Jewish language research, as well as in Spanish sociolinguistics. However, there is a growing body of research in linguistics, anthropology, and related fields, which departs from 'ethnolect' approaches long-dominant in variationist sociolinguistics and instead adopts a more holistic approach to the study of language and ethnic/religious identity (e.g., Reyes and Lo 2009). Along these lines, Benor advocates thinking in terms of a Jewish linguistic repertoire (2009) (or, more broadly, an ethnolinguistic repertoire [2010]), defined as "a fluid set of linguistic resources that members of an ethnic group may use variably as they index their ethnic identities" (Benor 2010: 159). We adopt this perspective in the present exposition of the Spanish spoken among Jewish Latin Americans. We include for consideration an array of communicative practices, ranging from those covered by traditional descriptive linguistics (phonology, morphology, syntax, lexicon, etc.) to discourse practices, speech genres, and language ideologies that are often the focus of ethnographic studies of language and culture.

---

[1] All cited work in Spanish, as well as Skura's original, Spanish-language contributions to this chapter, have been translated by Dean-Olmsted.

[2] The figures presented in this chapter are of estimated "core" Jewish populations, defined by DellaPergola as "all persons who, when asked, identify themselves as Jews, or, if the respondent is a different person in the same household, are identified by him/her as Jews, and do not have another religion" (Della Pergola 2015:19). DellaPergola's estimates of "enlarged" Jewish populations, including those with maternal or paternal Jewish ancestry, are generally greater in each country. While referencing this demographic work, the authors (Dean-Olmsted and Skura) do not necessarily promote these or any specific definition of Jews or Jewishness.

The following entry is largely a comparison of Mexico City, Mexico and Buenos Aires, Argentina, reflecting the co-authors' respective areas of expertise. These two countries represent the largest Jewish populations in Spanish-speaking Latin America, with an estimated 181,000 Jews in Argentina and 40,000 in Mexico (DellaPergola 2015). Furthermore, we argue that key differences in migration histories, residence patterns, and community demographics make for valuable sociolinguistic comparison between the Jewish Spanish spoken in these two locales. In particular, we proffer that Mexico City Jewish Spanish may have more distinctively Jewish features than that in Buenos Aires (and especially, that spoken among Syrian Jewish speakers in Mexico City).

In addition to neglecting the Spanish spoken in other Latin American countries, we do not include for consideration the Portuguese spoken by the 95,200 Jews in Brazil, as the entry is limited to the Spanish language. Moreover, by focusing on 19th through 20th century Jewish migrants and their descendants, we do not consider the language practices of those who identify in some way with Crypto-Jewish or *converso* heritage (that is, Jews forced to convert to Catholicism under the Spanish and Portuguese Inquisitions in the 15th–16th centuries). We suggest that both are important lines of inquiry to include in future comparative research.

The extant research on the Spanish of Jewish Latin Americans is quite limited. Many of the phenomena under discussion come from the authors' own research and observations (some systematic, some anecdotal). Readers may assume the data presented here are previously unpublished unless otherwise indicated. It is our intention that this pioneer effort will stimulate further research on the complex relationships between language, identity, and social life among Jewish Latin Americans.

1.1 Names of the language

In Argentina in the early 20th century, the term *castídish* was used to describe the language of Jewish immigrants from Central and Eastern Europe (that is, a mixture of *castellano* '(Castilian) Spanish' and *ídish* 'Yiddish'). *Castídish* consisted of a principally Yiddish matrix with Spanish loan words (including words from *lunfardo*, the language variety associated with poor Buenos Aires neighborhoods). Many such words were adapted to Yiddish morphology and phonology (e.g., the Spanish *ficha* 'game piece' was pronounced *fiche* [fitšə]) (Fiszman and Skura 2016). *Castídish* was often represented in the Jewish communal press, as well as in literature and music (A. Weinstein and Toker 2004: 17). It was employed as a tool of comic realism in Argentine Jewish theater of the 1930s-1950s (Skura

2007; Fiszman and Skura 2016). We give further examples of *castídish* in theater in Section 4.3.1., below.

Most present-day Latin Americans do not apply a specific label to Jewish speech, aside from vague references such as "*un tonito judío*" 'a Jewish tone/accent'. Nor is there consensus on nomenclature among academics. Linguist David Gold employed terms such as "Contemporary Sephardic Mexican Spanish" and "Eastern Ashkenazi Chilean/Argentine Spanish," emphasizing that

> since each of these (and other) Jewish lects of Spanish is a sublect of the local general Spanish lect (rather than a branch of some originally unified Jewish Spanish [or Ashkenazi Spanish or Sefardic (sic) Spanish, as the case may be], the correct order of the adjectives is Sefardic Argentine Spanish and not 'Argentine Sefardic Spanish,' etc. (Gold 1985: 117).

The phrase "Jewish Latin American Spanish" has recently appeared in academic work (Dean-Olmsted and Skura 2016). There is certainly linguistic and cultural continuity in Jewish populations throughout the region that would support the use of such a term. Several processes facilitate relations across national borders. These include the maintenance of international familial networks; marriages between Jewish Latin Americans of different nationalities; the region-wide circulation of religious functionaries (especially Orthodox rabbis, many of whom are ordained in Israel); the centralized production and distribution of religious texts (both Argentina and Mexico have publishers that export such texts to other Spanish-speaking communities); regional organizations like the *Congreso Judío Latinoamericano*; popular trips to Israel for youth from multiple Latin American countries, hosted by Zionist youth groups *(tnuot)* or international organizations like Aish HaTorah; and activity on digital social media. All of these contribute to a pan-Jewish Latin American identification that can emerge or be invoked in interaction (for example, among Jewish Latin American immigrants in the United States or Israel; see Bokser Liwerant (2013) and Limonic (2014)). Nonetheless, Gold's point remains salient, and we encourage readers to think in terms of local, partially overlapping Jewish Latin American linguistic repertoires, rather than a single, homogeneous code.

1.2 Linguistic affiliation

Contemporary Latin American Spanish is a macrolect with considerable regional and sociolinguistic variation, both between and within countries (as described in Lipski [2012]). In this case, we analyze the Spanish of Mexico City and Buenos Aires, respectively, as used among Jewish speakers.

1.3 Regions where language is/was spoken

Spanish-dominant countries with Jewish populations over 1,000 people include Argentina, Colombia, Costa Rica, Chile, Mexico, Panama, Puerto Rico, Peru, Uruguay, and Venezuela. There are smaller populations in Bolivia, Cuba, Dominican Republic, Ecuador, El Salvador, Guatemala, and Paraguay (DellaPergola 2015). There are also populations of Spanish-speaking Latin American Jews residing in Israel, United States, Canada, and various European cities.

1.4 Attestations and sources

While there is limited academic work dedicated explicitly to linguistic analysis, the Spanish of Jews in Latin America has been captured in numerous institutional and personal documents (letters, memoirs, etc.), in addition to the periodicals, literature, theater, and film that we describe in Section 4. Ethnographic and oral historical research – some communally sponsored – has produced recordings of interviews, oral performances, and other live speech. Much of the above material is housed in Jewish communal archives described in Section 2.2. Finally, the internet provides a rich source of data on contemporary Jewish Latin American Spanish, including news outlets, institutional websites, blogs, and social media sites like Facebook, Twitter, and Instagram. The site *El Léxico Judío Latinoamericano* (Jewish Latin American Lexicon), created and moderated by Evelyn Dean-Olmsted, features a collaborative lexicon in which users contribute words used among Jews in Latin America, along with etymological, sociolinguistic, pragmatic, and other information.

1.5 Present day status

As demographer DellaPergola (2015, 2013) has documented, Jewish populations in Latin America have been slowly decreasing since the 1960s through emigration. Israel is the most common destination, with the United States, Canada, and European countries as options for migrants in higher socio-economic strata. Such migrations are motivated primarily by periods of economic and/or political instability in migrants' respective countries of origin. DellaPergola speculates that such population decline may be offset in the future by growing numbers of converts to Judaism, especially in smaller communities in marginal areas of countries like Peru and Colombia (DellaPergola 2015: 46). Despite overall population loss, the Jewish communities in Mexico City and Buenos Aires (and elsewhere in the region) remain robust and dynamic; so, too, the varieties of Spanish they speak.

2 Historical background

2.1 Speaker community: settlement, documentation

As noted in the introduction, the Jewish presence in Latin America dates to the 15th century, when *conversos* were among the earliest Spanish and Portuguese settlers in the New World colonies (see Gerber 1994; Hordes 2005).[3] Among these individuals, there were varying degrees of Jewish identification and (covert) ritual practice. However, the Inquisition prohibited the open practice of Judaism and, hence, the establishment of any Jewish institution during the colonial period. The situation was different in the Wild Coast (the Guianas) and the Dutch and British Caribbean Islands, where Western Sephardic Jews settled legally in the latter half of the 17th century and maintained an active religious life and regional social networks (see Gerber 2014).

Newly independent Argentina and Mexico abolished the Inquisition in 1813 and 1820, respectively, making legal Jewish migration possible for the first time (Cohen et al. 2007). The majority of early 19th century Jewish migration was from Western Europe, with some Moroccan Jewish migration to Brazil. However, the bulk of modern Jewish migration to Latin America occurred after the 1880s, beginning with waves of Russian Jews from the Pale of Settlement who migrated primarily to Brazil and Argentina. In Argentina, many of these immigrants first lived in rural agricultural settlements established by philanthropist Baron Maurice de Hirsch (see Elkin 2014). By 1920, however, most Argentine Jews lived in urban centers like Buenos Aires, mostly in ethnically diverse neighborhoods that facilitated interactions among Jews of different backgrounds, as well as contact with non-Jews. Although slowing during the First World War, Jewish and other European migration to Argentina continued at a steady pace until the global economic crisis of the late 1920s. Despite restrictive national policies, some 40,000 European Jews settled in Argentina during and after WWII. The last wave of European Jewish migration to the country occurred in the 1950s, primarily from Communist Hungary and Egypt (Lesser and Rein 2008: 8–13).

Mass Jewish migration to Mexico (although in much lower numbers than to Argentina) began in the late 19th and early 20th centuries, including Judeo-Spanish (Judezmo)-speaking Sephardic Jews and Judeo-Arabic-speaking Mizrahi (Middle Eastern) Jews from Ottoman territories. These were part of the migratory waves of religious minorities from the Ottoman Empire that went to various destinations in the Americas. In Mexico (as in Argentina), Sephardi and Mizrahi

---

[3] A version of this section appears in Dean-Olmsted & Skura (2016).

migrations peaked in the 1920s and continued through mid-century. Smaller waves from Syria and Lebanon arrived in Mexico through the 1970s. Substantial Ashkenazi migration to Mexico likewise began in the late 19th-early 20th centuries and swelled in the 1920s, due to official restrictions on migration in the United States and simultaneous efforts on the part of the Mexican government to attract European immigrants (Gleizer Salzman 2011: 56). Ashkenazi immigration essentially halted from 1933–1945, when the Mexican government prohibited Jewish migration via a series of confidential memos (Gleizer Salzman 2014, 2011). It resumed in the postwar years. Most Jewish arrivals to Mexico – Sephardi, Mizrahi, and Ashkenazi – established themselves in port cities like Veracruz and Tampico, as well as in Mexico City, where the majority eventually settled. Mexico's first Jewish communal institution, *La Sociedad de Beneficiencia Alianza Monte Sinaí*, was established in 1912 in Mexico City under the leadership of Salonikan immigrant Isaac Capon. Initially, it represented all ethno-linguistic subgroups until separate Ashkenazi, Sephardic, *Halebi* (Aleppan), and *Shami* (Damascene/Lebanese) institutions formed in later decades.

Today, the majority of Jewish Mexicans (roughly 37,500 out of 40,000) reside in the capital, Mexico City, with smaller communities in Monterrey, Guadalajara, and elsewhere. Communal organization in Mexico City is based on the ethno-geographic origins of their founders. Roughly 42% of the city's Jewish population affiliates with either the Halebi or Shami sectors; another 9% with the Sephardi sector (descendants of Judezmo speakers from Turkey, Greece, and the Balkans); and 20% with the (Orthodox) Ashkenazi community. The remainder – largely Ashkenazi – affiliate with the city's Conservative (Masorti) congregations, other communal institutions, or are unaffiliated (Hamui Halabe 2005: 117). Among diaspora populations, Mexico City Jewry is unusual for its relatively low rates of intermarriage (less than 15% [Della Pergola 2013: 33]), high rates of Jewish day school education for Jewish children (around 93% [Goldstein et al. 2014: 28]), and its "exceptionally strong" concentration of Jewish residence in certain areas of the city (DellaPergola and Lerner 1995: 41). In Mexico City, as in Caracas, Venezuela, the majority of school-aged children are Sephardi or Mizrahi (DellaPergola 2011: 333), evidencing a demographic shift from Ashkenazi to Sephardi/Mizrahi sectors in recent decades. Growing ultra-Orthodox or *Haredi* movements have influenced Jewish Mexican religious and social life since the 1970s, particularly among Halebi Jews (Hamui Halabe 2005, 2012).

Present-day Buenos Aires is home to an estimated 160,000 of Argentina's roughly 181,000 Jews (DellaPergola 2015: 27). The remainder reside primarily in the capital cities of the provinces of Santa Fe, Córdoba, Tucumán, and Entre Ríos. Within the Buenos Aires Jewish population, an estimated 80–90% are Ashkenazim with origins in Eastern and Central Europe. The remainder are mostly

Sephardim descended from Judezmo speakers of the former Ottoman Empire and Morocco, with a smaller subset of Syrian or other Middle Eastern descent (see Bejarano [2005] and Brodsky [2016] for discussions of the size of the Sephardi/Mizrahi population in Buenos Aires). Sephardi and Mizrahi groups have gained greater institutional visibility within the wider Buenos Aires Jewish community in recent decades (DellaPergola 2011: 334). So too have Haredi elements, as evidenced in their political representation in the *Asociación Mutual Israelita Argentina* and in new Haredi religious and educational endeavors. In total, there are thirty Jewish educational institutions serving some 22,000 students. Buenos Aires has a larger secular Jewish population compared to Mexico City, and intermarriage is estimated at 43% (Jmelnitzky and Erdei 2005: 40; Erdei 2014), a rate similar to that documented in the 1980s (Bargman 1997, 1991). Unlike their Mexico City counterparts, most Jews in Buenos Aires have lived for generations in ethnically and religiously mixed neighborhoods.

To summarize, Jews in Mexico City have historically experienced greater social and geographic segregation, as well as political marginalization, than those in Buenos Aires (Hamui de Halabe [2009] and Bokser de Litwerant [2008] describe well the role of Mexican national policy in fostering these exclusions). These differences, we hypothesize, manifest in greater linguistic distinctiveness between Jewish (and especially Syrian Jewish) speakers and non-Jewish speakers in Mexico City than in Buenos Aires – a hypothesis ripe for testing through systematic sociolinguistic investigation.

2.2 Attestations and sources: elaboration

David Gold was one of the first and few linguists to document contemporary Jewish Latin American linguistic phenomena, from the 1960s through the 1980s. These include spoken and written variation in Spanish words for 'Yiddish' (Gold 1980) and analysis of unique phonetic, lexical, and syntactic phenomena, as well as popular songs and sayings, among Ashkenazi Jews in Argentina and Chile (Gold 1982, 1983, 1985). He also remarked on ethnic and religious labeling as well as other lexical practices in Mexico City, identifying variation between the three major ethnic sub-communities (Sephardic, Syrian, and Ashkenazi) (Gold [1985]; Arditti [1986] confirmed or corrected several of these observations). Gurvich Okón (2006) compiled Yiddish words and phrases used in Mexico (some morphologically and/or phonologically adapted to Spanish), in addition to calques from Yiddish to Spanish and vice versa. Of the latter phenomena, Gurvich gives the example of the Yiddish phrase *ich hob kalt* 'I have cold,' which uses Yiddish words but Spanish syntax (a calque of the phrase *tengo frío*, 'I have [am] cold')

(Gurvich Okón 2006: 355). Other studies of the Jewish lexicon in Latin America include Skura's exploration of the use of the word *shikse* in Argentina (Skura 1997a) and Dean-Olmsted's work on ethnic labeling (2011) and Hebrew and Judeo-Arabic loans in Mexico City (2012a), among other elements of the Jewish Mexican linguistic repertoire (2012b). Schaffer (2015) investigated phonological variation in Jewish Mexico City Spanish. We discuss documentation and analysis of Jewish literature and dramatic arts below in Section 4. In addition, there are several Argentine collections of Jewish oral folklore, including stories, sayings, and jokes (Liacho [1945]; Toker, Finzi and Scliar [1991]; Toker and Finzi [1993]; Toker [1996a; 1996b]; Toker and Toker [2001; 2003; 2005; 2007; 2009; 2009]). Academic analyses of discourse, including narrative, joking, and other forms of oral performance, include Macadar (2009) on Uruguay; Fischman (2011; 2008) on Argentina; and Enríquez Andrade (2004) and Dean-Olmsted (2018) on Mexico.

Many Jewish community archives in Latin America house primary documentation of written or recorded oral Jewish Spanish, as described above in Section 1.4. In Mexico City, these include oral history collections at the Mexican branch of the *Asociación de Amigos de la Universidad Hebraica de Jerusalén* and the *Centro de Documentación e Investigación Judío de México* (an expansion of the *Centro de Documentación e Investigación de la Comunidad Ashkenazí*). Argentina maintains dozens of Jewish archives and libraries in the major cities, as well as in the former agricultural colonies. Among the most prominent in Buenos Aires are the *Archivo Histórico de la Fundación IWO*, *Centro de Documentación e Información sobre el Judaísmo Argentino Marc Turkow (AMIA)*, and *Idisher Cultur Farband*.

2.3 Phases in historical development

Yiddish, Judezmo, and Judeo-Arabic were generally replaced by Spanish as the vernacular code among the Latin American-born children of Jewish immigrants. The process of immigrant language shift in Latin America is similar to what has been documented in the United States and elsewhere (Fishman 1966; Veltman 1983). While the children of immigrants usually understood the language of their parents and were perhaps even fully bilingual, subsequent generations lost competence until only using or recognizing isolated words and phrases. A combination of factors contributed to this shift, including education of immigrant children in Spanish-language schools (eventually in Jewish communal as well as public or other private schools), nationalist projects that promoted unified cultural-linguistic citizenries, and stigma from both within and outside the Jewish communities toward immigrants and, by extension, their languages. The shift to

Spanish was preceded in Argentina (and likely in other contexts) by a hybrid form called *castídish*, mentioned above, adopted as Ashkenazi Jews moved from agricultural to urban settings in the first decades of the 20th century.

In both Mexico and Argentina, pre-WWII Ashkenazi intellectual elites engaged in serious reflection and debate on the merits and drawbacks of using Spanish instead of Yiddish in Jewish educational and cultural contexts, both oral and written (Dujovne 2014; Cimet 1996; Cimet 1997). Yiddish thrived for a period in Jewish literature, journalism, and theater in Latin America and was or is taught as a second language in Jewish schools.[4] This was not the case for Judeo-Arabic or Judezmo. Upon the creation of the State of Israel in 1948, most Jewish institutions adopted a Zionist orientation, and Modern Israeli Hebrew became the favored second language to teach in Jewish schools, as is the case today (although Yiddish and Judezmo have enjoyed renewed popularity in an age of pluralist official discourses; see Skura and Fiszman [2005] and Balbuena [2012]). The process of language shift in Mexico is also explored by Hawayek de Ezcurdia et al. (1992); Enríquez Andrade and Revah Donath (1998); Hamui de Halabe (2009); and DellaPergola and Lerner (1995). Language shift among Jews in Argentina is discussed by Virkel de Sandler (1991); Skura (1997b; 2006 (1998)); Skura and Fiszman (2005); and Ansaldo (2016). At the time of writing, a research team lead by Susana Skura is pursuing a project on *"Actores y escenarios del proceso de cambio lingüístico ídish-castellano. Teatro, prensa y escolarización judía en Buenos Aires durante la primera mitad del siglo XX"* [Actors and stages in the process of Yiddish-to-Spanish language shift. Theater, press and Jewish education in Buenos Aires in the first half of the 20th century] (Secretaría de Ciencia y Técnica de la Universidad de Buenos Aires, 2014–2018).

2.4 Sociolinguistic description, community bilingualism, public functions

In addition to regional differences, linguistic variation *within* each Jewish population reflects internal ethnic, religious, generational, ideological, and other diversity. This includes varying degrees of familiarity with and usage of ancestral languages, as well as Modern Israeli Hebrew and (primarily North American) English, corresponding with variables like age, migration/travel experiences,

---

4 Yiddish was taught as a second language in some Jewish day schools in Mexico City until the early 2010s. This was the result of a gradual process, over the previous 25 years, of replacing Yiddish with Hebrew language instruction (Natalia Gurvich Okón, personal communication, April 15, 2016).

and educational background (both Hebrew and English are taught as second languages in most Jewish schools). Another important factor influencing variation is the degree to which speakers align with Haredi Judaism; this constitutes a fascinating area for future comparative research with other Jewish communities around the world. We discuss such variation in greater detail with regards to specific practices below.

3 Structural information

3.1 Relationship to non-Jewish varieties

As discussed in the introduction, the Spanish of Jews in Mexico and Argentina is structurally similar to that of their non-Jewish neighbors. Most differences are the result of influences from textual Hebrew/Aramaic, Modern Israeli Hebrew, and pre-migration languages including Yiddish, Judezmo, and Judeo-Arabic. There are also unique semantic, pragmatic, and other discursive practices that characterize Jewish Latin American linguistic practice.

3.2 Particular structural features

Although lexicon is the most salient area of difference between Jewish and non-Jewish speech in Latin America, there are phonetic and morphosyntactic phenomena that merit further investigation. Generally speaking, the influence of pre-migration languages is most apparent in the Spanish of immigrants; that is, native (L1) Yiddish, Arabic, and Judezmo speakers. L1 Yiddish speakers in Argentina, for example, produce Spanish phrases that conform to Yiddish syntactic structures, such as *nadie no salió*, 'nobody left', a calque of the Yiddish phrase *keyner iz nisht aroysgegangen*. The grammatical version in standard Spanish would be *nadie salió* or *no salió nadie*; the *no* is not preserved in the presence of an antecedent negative pronoun. An example of Yiddish phonological influence is seen in the realization of the Spanish diphthong /ue/ as [oi] among L1 Yiddish speakers. This is exemplified in the typical pronunciation of the word *buenos* ('good [pl.]') as [ʋoiŋos]. This pronunciation also exemplifies the tendency to realize the Spanish voiced bilabial stop as a labiodental approximant [ʋ]. Such speakers also produce a subtle lengthening and dentalization of alveolar fricatives, especially when following a vowel and preceding a plosive consonant. For example, the words *está* (usually [eh'ta] in Rioplatense Spanish) and *cosquilla* (usually [koh'kiʒa] or [koh'kiʃa]) may be realized as [es'ta] and [kos'kiʒa], respectively, with very slight dentalization of the [s]. Likewise, Judezmo influences the lexicon, morphosyntax, and phonology of the Modern Spanish of Sephardi immigrants (for instance, the realization of /x/ as [ʒ] in words like *mujer* [muʒeɾ]). Biondi Assali (1989; 1991a; 1991b; 1992; 1995) has published on the Spanish of non-Jewish Arabic-speaking immigrants in Argentina (for example, the much-stereotyped tendency to pronounce /p/ as [b], due to the lack of phonemic contrast between [p] and [b] in Arabic). To our knowledge, the Spanish spoken by Jewish, Arabic-speaking immigrants in Latin America has not been examined, although it is likely similar to the phenomena documented by Biondi Assali.

Among Jewish L1 Spanish speakers – that is, the descendants of immigrants, born in Latin America – few instances of phonological variation have been observed, although further study may reveal more. Schaffer's (2015) sociophonetic study of Mexico City Jewish Spanish provided an acoustic analysis of two variations first noted by Dean-Olmsted (2012b; Dean-Olmsted and Skura 2016). The first is the production of the voiceless uvular fricative [χ] and, to a lesser degree, the voiceless uvular trill [ʀ̥] as allophones of the voiceless velar fricative /x/ (commonly realized as [x] or [h] in Mexico City Spanish). These variations were present at statistically significant levels in the speech of Syrian Jewish individuals. Research into the social, interactional, and linguistic factors shaping this phenomenon is ongoing; it may reflect the influence of L2 Modern Israeli Hebrew (Lily Schaffer, personal communication). The second phenomenon studied is the realization of the medial /sr/ cluster in the word *Israel*. The most common variant in Mexico City is a single segment fricative rhotic; the product of gestural overlap ([iɾael]). In contrast, the Jewish speakers in her study (both Syrians and Ashkenazim) retained the sibilant and produced an epenthetic, homorganic (alveolar) plosive, as well as an epenthetic vowel; the rhotic was realized as an alveolar tap (for example, as [iz^{də}rael] and [is^{tə}rael]). This phenomenon was observed in Judezmo (Gold and Prager, Leonard 1983: 223), perhaps pointing to the source of this pronunciation. There is at least one instance in Dean-Olmsted's data of a Syrian Jewish Mexican speaker pronouncing the surname *Mizrahi* as [miz^{də}raχi]. Such a pronunciation is reflected in another spelling of that surname in Mexico City: as *Mizdrahi*. Only the /sr/ clusters in these words (*Israel* and *Mizrahi*) have been examined, so we cannot say at this point whether Jewish speakers produce these epethentic sounds within or across other words. To our knowledge, Schaffer's is the first such study of phonological variation in the L1 Spanish of Jewish Latin American speakers. More are surely needed.

Interestingly, there is also a "Jewish pronunciation" of *Israel* in Buenos Aires, although it is not the same as that in Mexico City. The unmarked Buenos Aires version of the word features an alveolar trill [r] following the voiceless alveolar fricative [s]. Jewish speakers, on the other hand, commonly produce a longer [s] followed by an alveolar flap [ɾ] instead of a trill (Scherlis 2014, personal communication). In both Mexico City and Buenos Aires, Jewish and non-Jewish speakers alike (at least those with Jews in their social networks) are conscious of the "Jewish" pronunciation of *Israel* and often cite it when asked about linguistic differences between Jews and non-Jews; it therefore serves as a sort of shibboleth. Such processes of enregisterment – how certain linguistic features become socially recognized and associated with certain groups (Agha 2007) – merit further research in the Latin American context.

Finally, as mentioned in Dean-Olmsted and Skura (2016), there is exciting research to be done on prosodic differences between Jewish and non-Jewish speakers. Both Jews and their non-Jewish acquaintances in Mexico City frequently characterize Jewish speech as *"más cantadito"* 'more sing-song'; a statement that may reflect general awareness of uniquely Jewish prosody. Haredi rabbis in Mexico City – both Ashkenazi and Syrian – often elongate their final syllables and use the rise-fall intonation pattern typical of Ashkenazi Talmudic debate (Dean-Olmsted 2012b), especially during sermons or religious classes. This represents one of many ways in which Haredi Judaism manifests in the Spanish of some Jewish Latin Americans.

3.3 Lexicon: Hebrew and Aramaic elements

Jewish lexical phenomena – including loans from textual Hebrew and Aramaic, Modern Israeli Hebrew, Judeo-Arabic, Judezmo (Judeo-Spanish), and Yiddish – are highly productive in performing identity work in both Mexico City and Buenos Aires. As Skura (2006 (1998)) has emphasized, the inclusion of such words in Spanish discourse can serve as a "password" to discreetly signal Jewishness (or specific kinds of Jewishness) in interaction and thereby include or exclude certain interlocutors. Speakers can also use them to introduce new topics or a shift toward more intimate registers; as such, they function as "triplex signs" (Briggs 1986; Jakobson 1990 [1957]), with heightened pragmatic, social indexical, and poetic functions beyond their referentiality (which Shandler [2006] identifies as characteristic of "post-vernacular" use of Yiddish). Because of their importance in enacting sub-communal identities among Jews in Mexico City, Dean-Olmsted (2012a) refers to these lexical items as "heritage words." Variation in their use reflects and manifests differences in religiosity, ethno-geographic origin, generation, and political orientation among Jewish speakers.

3.3.1 Variation in Hebrew/Aramaic loans

In Mexico City, Syrians, Sephardim, and Ashkenazim each use different Hebrew words, or different pronunciations of the same word, which reflect differences in Hebrew lexicon and phonology in their respective ancestral places of origin (with some overlap between Syrians and Sephardim). For example, Syrians use the word טְבִילָה *tebilá* (Heb. 'ritual immersion') to refer to the ritual bath in which married women immerse before resuming sexual relations with their husbands after menstruation, while Ashkenazim use *mikve* (Heb. 'ritual bath' – Ashkenazi/Modern Israeli Hebrew pronunciation). Syrians also use *tebilá* to refer to the traditional celebration hosted in honor of a bride's first immersion. The spelling of this word also reflects the common Syrian realization of ב as [b] even if it lacks a *dagesh*, while Ashkenazim generally realize this sound in Hebrew loans as [v]. This is one of a number of phonological distinctions in the Hebrew loan words of Syrian vs. Ashkenazi Mexican speakers. Another is the occurrence of a vowel sound between some word-initial stop-rhotic clusters: e.g., Sephardi/Mizrahi *taréf* vs. Ashkenazi *tref* ('not kosher') and Sephardi/Mizrahi *berajá* vs. Ashkenazi *brajá* or *broje* (the latter is likely a more common pronunciation among older Ashkenazi speakers).

Variation in Hebrew loan usage also reflects speaker religiosity, a category that overlaps with ethnic designations in Mexico City (Dean-Olmsted 2011). Overall, use of *both* Hebrew and Arabic loan words (see below) is commonly associated with Shamis and Halebis, more so than with Ashkenazim or Sephardim, as the Syrian groups are reputed to be "more religious" (Dean-Olmsted 2012c). However, within each of these groups, those who are more closely aligned with Haredi Judaism generally use more and different Hebrew phrases than do other speakers. For example, Haredi speakers are more likely to use the phrase *baruj hashem* 'Blessed be the Name (of God)' as a response to the greeting formula *¿Cómo estás?* 'How are you?' Such phrases serve as indexes of speaker religiosity.

Among Ashkenazim in Argentina, the difference between the use of Hebrew versus Yiddish formulas (e.g., *shabat shalom* [Heb.] vs. *gut shabes* [Yid.]; *shaná tová* [Heb.] vs. *a gut yor/ a gityur* [Yid.]) can signal generational differences between native Yiddish speakers and those who learned Hebrew in a Zionist Jewish educational setting.

3.3.2 Gender morphology of loans

All nouns in modern Spanish, including foreign loans, are obligated to take masculine or feminine grammatical gender, as are their corresponding adjectives and determiners.⁵ Processes of gender assignment to Hebrew and other loans among Jewish speakers of Latin American Spanish are an area ripe for research; here we present some preliminary observations. As with Hebrew nouns adopted into Judezmo (analyzed by Romero [2009]), loans denoting female, animate referents are assigned feminine gender (e.g., *la morá* [Heb. 'teacher' feminine]). The gender of other nouns seems to be based primarily on phonological shape, specifically whether the terminal morpheme is -a, usually rendering it feminine in both Hebrew and Spanish. For example, the Hebrew feminine עֲלִיָּה 'migration to Israel' takes the Spanish feminine article (*la aliá*). On the other hand, loans ending in -o, -e, or a consonant may be assigned masculine Spanish gender. For example, speakers in Mexico often use the masculine Spanish article *el* with the Hebrew (feminine) noun זכות zekut 'merit' (*el zejut*; here the grapheme z represents [z], while j represents [x], the latter consistent with Spanish orthographic convention). Variation in gender, as well as plural morphology of loanwords (e.g., whether Hebrew loans take Spanish or Hebrew plural suffixes), likely reflects differences in speaker identities, discourse topics, and social contexts of interaction, as well as the nature and degree of Hebrew language learning.

3.4 Language contact influences

3.4.1 'Heritage words' from ancestral languages, textual Hebrew/Aramaic and Modern Israeli Hebrew

In addition to the phonological and morphosyntactic influences discussed above, pre-migration Jewish languages⁶ provide a rich lexicon for Jewish Latin American Spanish speakers of all ages. The following is a list of the most common semantic/pragmatic areas for heritage words from ancestral languages, along with a few examples from Mexico City and Buenos Aires. Unless otherwise indicated, the Syrian and Sephardic examples have been observed in Mexico City, and Yiddish

---

5 A version of this paragraph appears in Dean-Olmsted and Skura (2016).
6 Of course, in addition to "Jewish languages" (Yiddish, Judezmo, Judeo-Arabic), Jewish migrants also spoke and/or read other co-territorial and colonial languages (including, but not limited to: German, Polish, Russian, and other Slavic languages, in the case of Ashkenazim; Turkish, Greek, and what was formerly called "Serbo-Croatian" (referred to with a variety of labels today, including "Bosnian-Croatian-Montenegrin-Serbian" [BCMS]) among Sephardim. Many Sephardim and Mizrahim read and/or spoke French, largely through the efforts of the French-language schools of the *Alliance Israelite Universelle* (see Rodrigue 1990). The possible influences of such languages on the Spanish of Jewish Latin Americans are not considered in this entry.

examples in both Mexico City and Buenos Aires. More information on Jewish lexicon in Latin America can be found on the website *Léxico Judío Latinoamericano* (http://www.jewish-languages.org/lexico-judio-latinoamericano/). In this section, we use spellings common in Latin America, with phonetic transcription when such standards may cause confusion for English-language readers.

1. Food. These include Ashkenazi *gefilte fish* and *knishes*, Sephardic *burekas* and Syrian *kipes*. Talking about food – in addition to its preparation and consumption – is an important genre for invoking Jewishness, or one's specific Jewish background, in interaction.

2. Religion, rituals, and festivals. These words can serve as sub-ethnic boundary markers in both Mexico City and Buenos Aires; for example, Syrians go to *knis* [kᵊnis] (Ar. 'synagogue') while Ashkenazim go to *shul* or *shil* (Yid. 'synagogue').

3. Institutional life. Many such terms are from Modern Israeli Hebrew (for example, *tnuá* 'youth movement'), reflecting the Zionist orientation of most contemporary Jewish institutions in Latin America, and are used by Jews across ethno-religious boundaries. In Buenos Aires, the word *shule* has been used for decades among Ashkenazim to refer to local Jewish schools (as opposed to *shul/shil* for 'synagogue').

4. Blessings and "verbal-talismans." Matisoff (2000) refers to such phrases as 'psycho-ostensives'. Although there are many such terms in Yiddish, Judezmo, and Judeo-Arabic, there seem to be more items, used more frequently, among contemporary Syrian (and to a lesser degree) Sephardic speakers in both Buenos Aires and Mexico City. Ashkenazi examples include the phrases *zijronó le brajá* (Heb. 'may his/her memory be for a blessing') when mentioning the deceased and *Got tsu danken* (Yid. 'thank God'). Syrian/Sephardic examples include *jamse* [xamse] (Ar. 'five') as protection against the Evil Eye, and *barminán*, originally an Aramaic phrase meaning 'far from us' that was incorporated into both Judeo-Arabic and Judezmo. It is popularly glossed in Mexico as "*Ni Dios lo quiera*" 'Not even God desires it'.

5. Greetings, partings, and courtesy expressions. These include phrases like the Yiddish *a gute nakht* 'good night' among Ashkenazim. Originally a parting phrase only, Gurvich Okón (2006: 357) reports that it is also used as a greeting in Mexico City; that is, speakers impose the pragmatics of the Spanish equivalent *buenas noches* 'good night/evening', which serves to both greet and depart in the evening. The Yiddish phrases *a dank* ('thank you') and *nishtó farvos* (you're welcome) are also common among Ashkenazi speakers. Among Syrians in Mexico, the phrase/word *alamák* (derived from the Arabic *allah ma'ak* 'God [be] with you (masculine)' is used among older people to bless younger relatives upon departing, while younger people often use it

simply to mean 'goodbye'. Ashkenazim may use the Yiddish *tsu gezunt* 'to your health' when someone sneezes; Syrians in Mexico City may use *saja* or *sajtén* (Ar. 'health') for sneezes, burps, or when beginning a meal. During holidays, Ashkenazim often greet with Yiddish formulas while Sephardim/ Mizrahim use Hebrew ones. For example, *a gut yor* (Yiddish) vs. *shaná tová* (Hebrew) 'good year' on the Jewish New Year *Rosh Hashaná*; *gut shabes* (Yiddish) vs. *shabát shalom* (Hebrew) on the Sabbath. As mentioned above, the use of Hebrew rather than Yiddish formulas may also serve to signal generational differences among Ashkenazim in Buenos Aires, with younger people favoring Hebrew.

6. Terms of endearment and affection. These include *jazito/jazit/jazita* [xazito] ('poor little thing' masculine/masculine/feminine) among Syrians and Sephardim in Mexico City; a term that likely derives from the Judezmo [xazin] 'ill'. *Búbele* 'little doll', *mámele* 'little mother (girl)' and *tátele* 'little father (boy)' are Yiddish terms of endearment for children used by Ashkenazim. Asheknazi immigrants in Argentina use the Yiddish *shif shvester/shif bruder* 'ship-sister/ship-brother' to refer to those who immigrated around the same time, although not necessarily on the same boat.

7. Kinship terms. Terms for children include the Judezmo *ishico/ishica* ('little son/daughter') used among Sephardim and the Yiddish *mayn kind* ('my child') among Ashkenazim. Many Syrian Jews use *amí* and *mertamí* to address their fathers- and mothers-in-law, respectively (from the Arabic *'ami* and *merāt 'ami*, literally 'my uncle'/'woman (wife) of my uncle', used as a deferential term of address for older relatives). Ashkenazi grandmothers are often called *bobe/baba* and grandfathers *zayde/zeyde*. Gurvich Okón (2006: 351) reports the hybrid form *bisbobe* for 'great-grandmother', which employs the Yiddish root *bobe* with the Spanish prefix *bis-* (as in the word *bisabuela* 'great-grandmother'). Sephardic grandmothers are called *nona*, while most Syrian grandmothers in Mexico are simply *abuelita* (Sp. 'little grandmother'), likely because the traditional Arabic word for grandmother, *teta*, is a homophone of the Spanish word for 'breast' (and there are local jokes to this effect).

8. Social types: nouns and adjectives for people. These include words for non-Jews, including the Hebrew *goy* (sometimes with the Spanish feminine suffix to refer to female *goya*), the Yiddish *shikse* (non-Jewish woman or female domestic employee) and Judeo-Arabic *ishire* [ɪʒiːre] (female domestic employee). A good Syrian housewife is described as *shatra* (Ar. 'industrious').

9. Taboo language: bad words and insults. These include the Yiddish *pots* (literally 'penis', applied to someone thought to be stupid) and *beheime* ('beast'; i.e., someone without common manners) and the Judeo-Arabic *shajme*

[ʃaxme] (literally 'fat' or 'grease'; glossed as 'clown, idiot' or someone who is wealthy and snobbish).
10. Body parts and bodily functions. Related to the above, such words include the Yiddish *tujes* 'backside' and *beytsim* 'testicles'. The Judezmo *embatacarse* 'to dirty oneself' is used in Mexico to refer, for example, to a baby who has soiled his or her diaper. Also in Mexico City, the verb *pishar* is used ubiquitously among Jews to refer to urination.[7] Although all agree it is a "Jewish" word, there is general disagreement as to its origins, with Ashkenazim claiming it as Yiddish, Sephardim as Judezmo, and Syrians as Arabic. The former two possibilities are more plausible, as some variant of *pish* does indeed exist in Yiddish and Judezmo; Syrian claims that it is 'Arabic' may reflect its association with in-group contexts. In Argentina, *pishar* is not particularly marked for Jewishness, although using *pish* instead of *pis* in the phrase *hacer pis(h)* 'to make piss' (urinate) is more common among Jewish speakers.
11. Other interjections and expressions of emotion. These include the Yiddish *oy* and its variants, the Judezmo *Dio* or *Diosanto*, and the Arabic *jarám* [xaram] (sometimes used as an adjective to describe a forbidden act, and other times as an interjection at tragic or merely regrettable circumstances). In Mexico City, the phrase *Shemá Israel* (Heb. 'Hear Israel') is used to express everything from mild surprise to overwhelming emotion, both positive and negative. It is primarily associated with Syrian Jews, but its use may be spreading to other sectors (Dean-Olmsted even observed it used among non-Jewish classmates of Jewish university students in the late 2000s).
12. Numbers and money. In Mexico City, Arabic numbers and terms for money (for example, the Arabic word *masari*) are sometimes used among Syrians as a "secret language" to discuss financial matters. Ashkenazim in Mexico use the Yiddish phrase *grine lokshn* (literally 'green noodles') to refer to money (Gurvich Okón 2006: 100); those in Argentina use either *grine* or *lokshn* (separately).

Many of these words demonstrate lexical productivity. For example, the nominalizing suffix *-ero* is added to *jaram* to form *jaramero* (one who commits forbidden acts; reported by Gold [1985]); the adjectival suffix *-oso* is added to *shpilkes* (Yid. 'nervous energy') to form *shpilkoso*, used to describe someone who has "ants in his pants." The infinitive verbal suffix *-ear* is frequently added to foreign-origin

---

[7] The verb *pishar* has been documented in general Spanish dictionaries (e.g., in Batchelor [1994: 634]). In Mexico City, at least, it is uniquely associated with Jews.

loans: for example, in Mexico City the Yiddish verb *shlepn* 'to carry' becomes Hispanicized as *shlepear* (Gurvich Okón 2006: 352).

3.4.2 Spanish words and phrases with uniquely Jewish semantics and pragmatics

Jewish Latin American linguistic repertoires also include Spanish words with distinctive semantics and pragmatics, as well as calques from ancestral languages. Perhaps the most well-known example is the word *paisano* (Gold 1985; Dean-Olmsted 2012b). This word is most commonly used to refer to a fellow countryperson in general Latin American Spanish (it may also be used about someone from one's own specific state or region; or, in Argentina, to refer to someone from the countryside, as opposed to the city).[8] Most Jews, however, use it to refer to other Jews (or even more narrowly, to Jews within one's particular ethno-religious community, in Mexico City; the latter may be more common among older speakers). Phrases like *hasta ciento veinte* (Mexico City) or *hasta los ceinto veinte* (Buenos Aires) 'until 120' and *Que nos veamos (siempre) en fiestas* 'May we see each other (always) at holidays/celebrations' are common Hebrew- and Yiddish-to-Spanish calques; the former is posted frequently on the social media site Facebook to congratulate people on their birthdays.

4 Written and oral traditions

4.1 Writing system: Hebrew and other loans in written Spanish

There are various conventions for representing Hebrew and other loans in contemporary written Spanish. Some, mostly academic works employ standardized YIVO conventions for transliterating Yiddish loans. However, most written texts – including literature, prayer books and other sacred texts, institutional newsletters

---

[8] The *Diccionario del Español Usual de México* (1996) lists as one definition of *paisano*, "*persona de orígen semítico*" 'person of Semitic origin'. From the examples provided in the dictionary, it seems that even "non-Semitic" Mexicans use *paisano* to refer to Jews and/or those of Middle Eastern descent in the third person: "*Su patrón es un paisano libanés* 'His boss is a Lebanese *paisano*'; *La playa estaba llena de paisanos, con sus estrellas de David al pecho* 'The beach was full of *paisanos*, with their stars of David on their chests'" (Lara 1996: 666). Dean-Olmsted (2012b: 88) did not observe non-Jews using *paisano* in this way.

and magazines, digital social media, and other websites – feature more popular orthographic norms for transliterating foreign loans. Norms common throughout Latin America include use of *j* to represent the Hebrew letters ח (*chet*) and כ (*chaf*) (for example, חֲנֻכָּה is written *janucá/jánuca* or *januká/jánuka*. The letter *shin* (ש) is represented as *sh* and zayin (ז) as *z*, as they are in English, despite the fact that these sounds are not phonemes in many varieties of Spanish.[9] Words with the Hebrew letter *heh* are sometimes spelled with *h* and sometimes with nothing at all (for example, the word השם (*heh, shin, mem*) is sometimes written *ashem* in Mexico). The latter spelling reflects the common null realization of the sound in Hebrew loans in speech, in both Mexico City and Buenos Aires. Consonants that were geminated via the *dagesh* diacritic in ancient Hebrew pronunciations (as well as in some recent and contemporary varieties of Sephardi and Mizrahi liturgical Hebrew) are often represented with a single letter, e.g., *Shabat* instead of *Shabbat*. Accent markers are often used to indicate stress patterns that deviate from those of general Spanish words. In the example of *janucá* or *jánuca*, the stress marker indicates that final or first syllable is stressed (depending on one's pronunciation; the former seems to be more common in Mexico City, the latter in Buenos Aires). Most non-Jewish Spanish speakers would place stress on the penultimate syllable in this and other three-syllable words that end in a vowel. The word for God in Spanish, *Dios*, is sometimes rendered as *Di-s* or *D-os;* such omission of letters is a common Jewish practice that allows writers to avoid writing the name of God (lest the document eventually become effaced and the name of God desecrated).

In both Buenos Aires and Mexico City, the most common spelling of the word for 'Yiddish' is *ídish*, as we have used throughout this chapter. Gold asserts that in Buenos Aires, given that the grapheme 'y' usually represents a postalveolar fricative [ʒ] or [ʃ], the preference for *ídish* "is definitely so as to avoid suggesting the pronunciation [ʒidiʃ] and not because of any influence from Yiddish dialects with the zero form" (1983: 31). Why most people in Mexico City also seem to prefer this spelling (even though the local pronunciation of /y/ is palatal) is a question for future study.

4.2 Literature

The diversity of Jewish Latin American experience is reflected in a body of literature that spans the 20th and early 21st centuries. Here we mention a few of many

---

9 An exception is Rioplatense Spanish, including that of Buenos Aires, in which the phonemes represented by *y* and *ll* are realized as obstruent fricatives ([ʃ] or [ʒ]).

important authors. For more information, please see the guides and anthologies of Astro (2003); Dolle (2012); Goldberg (2000); Gover de Nasatsky and Weinstein (1994); Heffes (David Viñas) (1999); Lockhart (2013a); Senkman (1983); Sosnowsky (1987); Stavans (2012); Ran and Cahan (2011); and Weinstein and Toker (2004). As Sadow (2013) observes, Jewish Latin American writers "create poetry and narrative that are profoundly Jewish – prayer, home life, mysticism, Biblical exegesis, Talmud, the horrors of the Holocaust, the Spanish and Portuguese Inquisitions, and the State of Israel – and at the same time profoundly Latin American – the immigrant experience, the question of identity, soccer games, and history and politics, the natural beauty of the countryside and the intensity of city life" (2013: 6). Argentine writers Alberto Gerchunoff (author of the classic *Los gauchos judíos* [1910]), Samuel Eichelbaum, Samuel Glusberg, Carlos Grünberg, Enrique Dickman, and Lázaro Liacho are often cited as the pioneers in the field. In addition to those mentioned above, themes common in early Argentine Jewish literature include life in pre-migration Europe, settlement in the agricultural colonies (e.g., Goloboff 1978; Sinay 2013), and sex trafficking of Jewish women in early 20th century Buenos Aires (e.g., Cozarinsky 2002; Schalom 2003). Recent literature (from the mid-1990s on) deals with topics such as the 1994 terrorist attack on the Israeli Embassy and the *Asociación Mutual Israelita Argentina* (AMIA) (see Sadow [2015] for an overview of literary responses to the AMIA bombing), as well as Jewish experiences under the most recent military dictatorship (1976–1983) (e.g., Fingueret 1999; Tarnopolsky 2011). As Lockhart (2013b) signals, the roots of Jewish literary expression in Mexico date to colonization itself, with the writings of Luis de Carbajal *"el Mozo,"* (1567–1596), burned at the stake along with family members for the crime of Judaizing under the Spanish Inquisition. Even in contemporary Jewish Mexican writing, the themes of exile, of secret and discovered Jewishness, and of the Sephardic legacy in general are prominent (e.g., Muñiz-Huberman 1991; 1999). Many novels present recollections of early family life; a majority of these (and, indeed, a majority of all Jewish Mexican literary works) are penned by women. Critiques of patriarchy are prominent in the writing of authors like Rosa Nissan, Sabina Berman, Ethel Krause, and Sara Levi Calderon (Lockhart 2013b: 16–18).

Many Jewish Latin American authors employ lexical, topical, and other markers of Jewishness in their Spanish poetry and prose. Words from Hebrew, Yiddish, Judezmo, and Judeo-Arabic are used for various effects. Many authors employ them as tools of realism, toward creating remembered or fictionalized Jewish social worlds (e.g. Glantz [1981]; Sefamí [2004]; Saed [2003]; and Nissán [1992; 1996] in Mexico; Rozenmacher [1964]; Steimberg [1971, 1992]; Szichman [1971, 1972, 1981]; Kamenszain [1973, 2003, 2010, 2012]; Birmajer [1994]; Plager [1994, 2006]; Fingueret [1995]; Feierstein [1988, 2001]; Rotenberg [2004; 2006]; Sneh [2006]; Krimer [2010, 2013] in Argentina, among many others). Such words also serve as tools of comedy in humorous works (e.g. Shua [1994]; Ulanovsky [2013]). We maintain that linguists stand to contribute a great deal to the current "boom" in Jewish Latin American literary studies (Lockhart 2012) by examining what this canon reveals about the Spanish of Jewish Latin Americans.

4.2.1 Other written texts

Spanish-language Jewish periodicals have thrived in Latin America since the beginning of the 20th century, preceded by Yiddish-language presses established at the end of the 19th century in Argentina and in the 1920s in Mexico (see Bacci 2011; Cimet 1997; Dujovne 2008; Levinsky 2008). Many such publications are online today, including *Mundo Israelita* and *Diario Itón Gadol* in Argentina, and *Enlace Judío* and *Diario Judío de México* in Mexico.

Dujovne (2014) presents an exhaustive sociological examination of the heyday of Jewish Spanish-language book publishing in Argentina from 1919–1974. This began with the translation of Yiddish fiction and non-fiction by an intellectual elite concerned with the younger generations' potential abandonment of their historical and cultural traditions (of which the displacement of Yiddish by Spanish was seen as a major culprit). These early translators and publishers "became cultural pioneers...cementing a new Judeo-Spanish tradition" in 20th century Latin America (Dujovne 2014: 157). Publishers of religious material arose in the mid-20th century, including *Sigal,* which remains active today. In Mexico City, the publisher *Shem Tob* (founded by Halebi [Aleppan] rabbi Shaul Maleh) produces Sephardic liturgical texts with Spanish translations, as well as line-by-line Hebrew transliteration, reflecting the *kiruv* (outreach) dimension of the Syrian Jewish ultra-Orthodox establishment in Mexico (as well as the fact that the target audience is Spanish-language dominant). Both Mexico and Argentina are exporters of Jewish religious texts to communities throughout Latin America.

4.3 Performance

Latin America's tradition of Jewish dramatic arts dates to 1901, the dawn of Yiddish theater in Buenos Aires (Glickman and Waldman 1996). Playwrights began translating works from Yiddish into Spanish in the 1930s, at the same time as Jewish actors and directors began participating in the national scene. Many such artists got their start with the group IDRAMST or *Idishe Dramatishe Studio* (later IFT or *Idisher Folks Teater*). In 1948, the IFT produced "The

Diary of Anne Frank" in Spanish (*"el idioma común de todos los argentinos"* [the common language of all Argentines] (Weltman 1962: 2)). In general, to present in Spanish was understood as a great responsibility. Not only did it bring Jewish culture to a broader public, but it brought Jewish actors and companies into competition with other groups. It also gave Jewish artists greater visibility, which facilitated their participation in national theater. Though not all were in agreement – the famed Max Berliner reportedly left the Jewish youth troupe ARTEA in 1959 when they decided to produce Spanish-language shows of universal themes – the tradition of Jewish theater in the Spanish language continued through the 20th century until the present day. Current Jewish Argentine theater, however, is a smaller-scale endeavor compared to its mid-century peak. Jewish stand-up and other comedic productions in Buenos Aires are a prolific 21st century phenomenon, such as the 2008 production of "Peña Shmeña" and the 2009 production of "NYC 11," both directed by Jorge Schussheim. Their wide popularity, as well as their use of Jewish linguistic markers for comic effect, are yet to be investigated.

While perhaps less prolific (and certainly less studied), theater has also been an important mode of Jewish artistic expression in Mexico City. Glantz (1981) discusses its centrality to social and artistic life among new immigrants. The book *Imágenes de un Encuentro*, the third edition of which was published by the Jewish Mexican communities in 2001, features several posters and photos of Jewish theatrical productions (Bokser de Liwerant 2001, 314–318). Ilan Stavans recounts the experience of his father, Abraham Stavans, "the first openly Jewish actor on Mexico's professional stage; his first exercises were in Yiddish at the CDI (*Centro Deportivo Israelita*)" (Stavans 2001: 103). The CDI remains a center of Jewish Mexican theater, including its annual *Festival de Teatro Habimá*. Some Jewish playwrights – most notably Sabina Berman – are renowned in both the national Mexican and the Jewish literary scenes.

From such roots, an important body of Latin American films with Jewish themes and characters, as well as uniquely Jewish uses of the Spanish language, has emerged (again, little analyzed in the research literature). For more information, please see Dean-Olmsted and Skura (2016); Tall (2011, 2012); the issue of *Jewish Film & New Media* dedicated to Latin America, introduced by Rein and Tal (2014); as well as Gutman (2006); Cherjovsky (2013); and Rud (2016) on Argentine Jewish film. At the time of writing, a new research area on *"Artes del Espectáculo y Judeidad"* (Performing Arts and Jewishness) has recently been created at the Institute of Performing Arts at the Universidad de Buenos Aires. This program, headed by Susana Skura, will bring together scholars of Argentine Jewish theater, film, and music and stimulate further research into the use of linguistic and other semiotic markers of Jewishness in artistic productions.

4.3.1 *Castídish* in Jewish Argentine theater

As Skura (2007) has analyzed, Jewish Argentine plays in Yiddish from the 1920s–1940s provide an excellent repository of the *castídish* (a principally Yiddish matrix with Spanish loans) used among Ashkenazi immigrants.[10] This includes Spanish words and phrases rendered with Yiddish (Hebrew alphabet) orthography, with or without quotation marks to signal their Spanish-language origins. The Yiddish play "Zysie Goy" (Glasserman 1932) is replete with typical phrases of *gauchos (*Argentine cowboys), such as "¡pero qui cosa bárbara!" פּערֶא קי קָאסאַ וואַרוואַראַ (but what a horrible/incredible thing!) (Glasserman 1932: 34). Words such as *sulky* סולקי (a type of horse-drawn carriage) and *galpón* גאַלפּאָן (a primitive storage shed common in rural homesteads) are used repeatedly to invoke life in the Argentine *pampas* 'plains; countryside' (Glasserman 1932: 69). In some such words, the Spanish roots take Yiddish terminal morphemes, as in the example of *zsherbe* זשערבע (Glasserman 1930: 17) for the Spanish word *yerba* (the ingredient in the traditional South American hot drink, *mate*; pronounced [ʒerβa] by most Argentine Spanish-speakers). The hybrid lexical phrase "coseche-arbet" קאָסעטשע אַרבעט 'harvest-work' (Glasserman 1932: 12) includes the Spanish word for harvest, *cosecha* (with the Yiddish terminal morpheme –e), followed by the Yiddish word for work, *arbet*. The phrase employs Yiddish morphosyntax for creating compound lexemes by placing the modifier noun before the head verb, which would be ungrammatical in Spanish.

5 State of research

The study of Jewish Latin American linguistic repertoires is in its infancy. We have suggested many areas for future study throughout this chapter, including systematic inquiry into distinctive lexical, phonological, morphosyntactic, and other practices among Jewish speakers of Latin American Spanish; their possible causes; how they vary according to speaker identities and demographics, discourse topics, and social contexts of interaction; and how they may be used by people who do not identify as Jewish. Comparison with similar phenomena in Judezmo (e.g., the adaptation of foreign loans) will be valuable in many of these endeavors. We also encourage greater attention to contemporary Jewish verbal interactional genres in Latin America, such as humor and narrative, as well as literacy and media practices, taking into account other semiotic modalities in addition to oral and written language. Such research contributes not only to the fields of Jewish languages and Spanish sociolinguistics,

---

[10] See also Skura and Glocer (2016) on Yiddish theater in Argentina from 1930–1950.

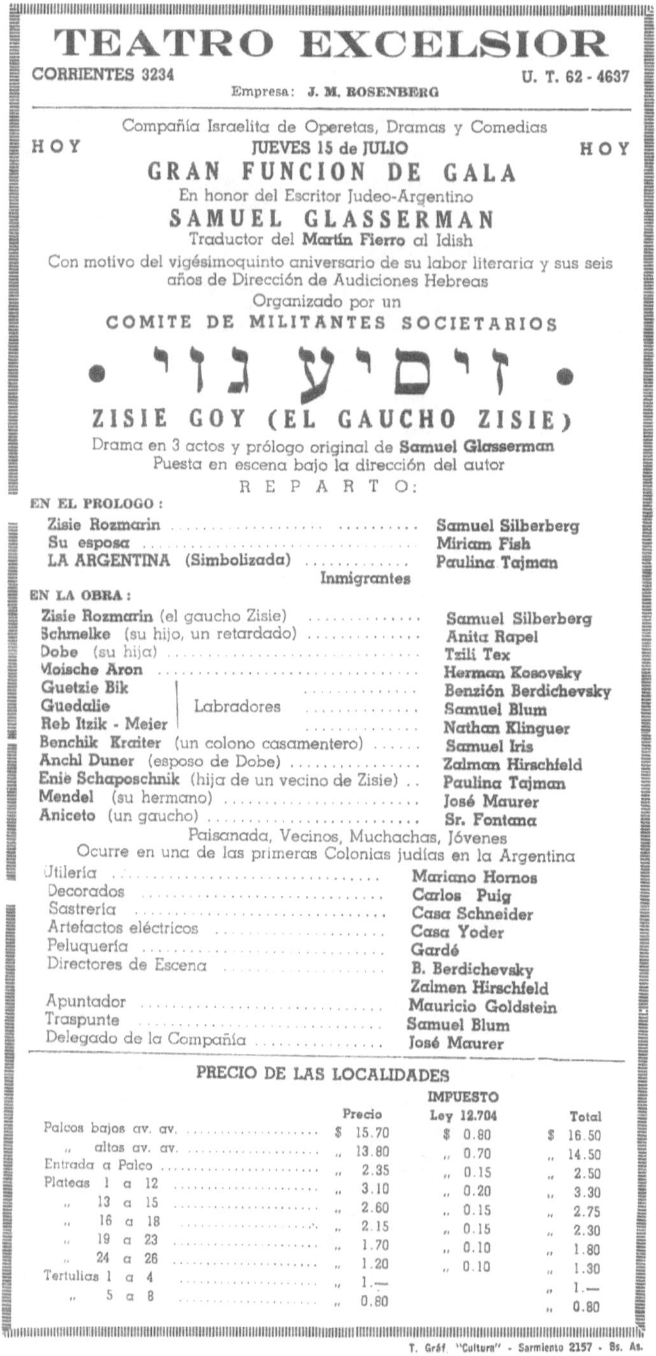

TEATRO EXCELSIOR

CORRIENTES 3234 U. T. 62 - 4637

Empresa: J. M. ROSENBERG

Compañía Israelita de Operetas, Dramas y Comedias

HOY JUEVES 15 de JULIO HOY

GRAN FUNCION DE GALA

En honor del Escritor Judeo-Argentino

SAMUEL GLASSERMAN

Traductor del Martín Fierro al Idish

Con motivo del vigésimoquinto aniversario de su labor literaria y sus seis años de Dirección de Audiciones Hebreas

Organizado por un

COMITE DE MILITANTES SOCIETARIOS

• זיסיע גוי •

ZISIE GOY (EL GAUCHO ZISIE)

Drama en 3 actos y prólogo original de Samuel Glasserman

Puesta en escena bajo la dirección del autor

R E P A R T O:

EN EL PROLOGO:

Zisie Rozmarin .... Samuel Silberberg
Su esposa .... Miriam Fish
LA ARGENTINA (Simbolizada) .... Paulina Tajman

Inmigrantes

EN LA OBRA:

Zisie Rozmarin (el gaucho Zisie) .... Samuel Silberberg
Schmelke (su hijo, un retardado) .... Anita Rapel
Dobe (su hija) .... Tzili Tex
Moische Aron .... Herman Kosovsky
Guetzie Bik (Labradores) .... Benzión Berdichevsky
Guedalie (Labradores) .... Samuel Blum
Reb Itzik - Meier (Labradores) .... Nathan Klinguer
Benchik Kraiter (un colono casamentero) .... Samuel Iris
Anchl Duner (esposo de Dobe) .... Zalman Hirschfeld
Enie Schaposchnik (hija de un vecino de Zisie) .... Paulina Tajman
Mendel (su hermano) .... José Maurer
Aniceto (un gaucho) .... Sr. Fontana

Paisanada, Vecinos, Muchachas, Jóvenes

Ocurre en una de las primeras Colonias judías en la Argentina

Utilería .... Mariano Hornos
Decorados .... Carlos Puig
Sastrería .... Casa Schneider
Artefactos eléctricos .... Casa Yoder
Peluquería .... Gardé
Directores de Escena .... B. Berdichevsky, Zalmen Hirschfeld
Apuntador .... Mauricio Goldstein
Traspunte .... Samuel Blum
Delegado de la Compañía .... José Maurer

PRECIO DE LAS LOCALIDADES

	Precio	IMPUESTO Ley 12.704	Total
Palcos bajos av. av.	$ 15.70	$ 0.80	$ 16.50
„ altos av. av.	„ 13.80	„ 0.70	„ 14.50
Entrada a Palco	„ 2.35	„ 0.15	„ 2.50
Plateas 1 a 12	„ 3.10	„ 0.20	„ 3.30
„ 13 a 15	„ 2.60	„ 0.15	„ 2.75
„ 16 a 18	„ 2.15	„ 0.15	„ 2.30
„ 19 a 23	„ 1.70	„ 0.10	„ 1.80
„ 24 a 26	„ 1.20	„ 0.10	„ 1.30
Tertulias 1 a 4	„ 1.—		„ 1.—
„ 5 a 8	„ 0.80		„ 0.80

T. Gráf. "Cultura" - Sarmiento 2157 - Bs. As.

Figure 1: Poster of the play "Zysie Goy."

but also sheds light on social processes involving Jews and other minority groups in Latin America. For example, how are Jewish and other minority identities changing in an age of multicultural national politics, and how do such changes manifest in language? To what extent are elements of Jewish linguistic repertoires used by non-Jews, whether such practices are marked or not for Jewishness? What does this reveal about relations between Jewish and non-Jewish Latin Americans? How does gender and social class figure into Jewish linguistic practice? How does the growing presence of ultra-Orthodoxy influence language, and how might this be compared to similar phenomena in other non-liberal religious movements (e.g. Evangelical Christianity) in Latin America? What is the nature of the linguistic and general socialization that converts to Judaism experience? By investigating such questions, the study of Jewish language practices in Latin America stands to contribute to areas of general topical and theoretical concerns in the social sciences and humanities, including studies of religion, gender, migration, diaspora, collective memory, citizenship, race and ethnicity, social inequality, hybridity, and alterity.

References

Agha, Asif. 2007. *Language and social relations*. Cambridge: Cambridge University Press.
Arditti, Adolfo. 1986. More on Sefardic Mexican Spanish. *Jewish Language Review* 6. 24–26.
Astro, Alan. 2003. *Yiddish south of the border: An Anthology of Latin American Yiddish writing*. Jewish Latin America. Albuquerque: University of New Mexico Press.
Bacci, Claudia. 2011. Discursos sobre la identidad nacional y la política en el debate entre los semanarios Tribuna y Mundo Israelita (1952–1954). In Emmanuel Kahan, Damián Setton & Alejandro Dujovne (eds.), *Marginados Y consagrados. Nuevos estudios sobre la vida judía en la Argentina*. Buenos Aires: Lumiere.
Balbuena, Monique. 2012. Ladino in Latin America. In Edna Aizenberg & Margalit Bejarano (eds.), *Contemporary Sephardic identity in the Americas: An interdisciplinary approach*, 161–83. Syracuse: Syracuse University Press.
Bargman, Daniel. 1991. *Matrimonios mixtos e identidad judía: Dilemas y desafíos*. Buenos Aires: CEHIS & AMIA.
Bargman, Daniel. 1997. Acerca de la legitimación de la adscripción étnica. Dentro, fuera y sobre los límites del grupo judío en Buenos Aires. Efraim Zadoff & Margalit Bejarano (eds.), *Judaica Latinoamericana*, vol. 3, 93–112. Jerusalem: AMILAT.
Batchelor, R. E. 1994. *Using Spanish synonyms*. Cambridge: Cambridge University Press.
Bejarano, Margalit. 2005. Sephardic communities in Latin America: Past and present. In Efraim Zadoff, Yossi Goldstein & Florinda Goldberg (eds.), *Judaica Latinoamericana V: Estudios históricos, sociales y literarios*, 9–16. Jerusalem: Magnes Press.
Benor, Sarah Bunin. 2009. Do American Jews speak a "Jewish language"? A model of Jewish linguistic distinctiveness. *Jewish Quarterly Review* 99. 230–69.
Benor, Sarah Bunin. 2010. Ethnolinguistic repertoire: Shifting the analytic focus in language and ethnicity. *Journal of Sociolinguistics* 14. 159–83.

Biondi Assali, Estela. 1989. Alternancia de los códigos español-árabe entre los bilingües de Tucumán, Argentina. *Caravelle* 52. 33–55.
Biondi Assali, Estela. 1991a. Lenguas en contacto; el español hablado por los inmigrantes Árabes en la Argentina. In César Hernández Alonso (ed.), *El español de América: Actas Del III Congreso Internacional de El español de América: Valladolid, 3 a 9 de julio de 1989*, vol. 3, 1219–32. Salamanca: Junta de Castilla y León, Consejería de Cultura y Turismo.
Biondi Assali, Estela. 1991b. Mantenimiento de la lengua árabe entre descendientes de sirios y libaneses en Argentina y el concepto de etnicidad. *Anuario de Lingüística Hispánica* 7. 29–44.
Biondi Assali, Estela. 1992. Beine…beineta. El uso de (p) en el habla española de los inmigrantes de origen árabe en la Argentina. *Hispanic Linguistics* 5. 143–168.
Biondi Assali, Estela. 1995. Las formas verbales y su funcionamiento en el español de los inmigrantes árabes en la Argentina: Presente e imperfecto de Indicativo. *Anales de Lingüística Hispánica* 11. 57–80.
Birmajer, Marcelo. 1994. *El alma al diablo*. Bogotá: Grupo Editorial Norma.
Bokser de Liwerant, Judit (ed.). 2001. *Imágenes de un encuentro: La presencia judía en México durante la primera mitad del siglo XX*, 3rd edn. Mexico City: UNAM, Tribuna Israelita, Cómite Central Israelita de México & Multibanco Mercantil Proburs.
Bokser de Liwerant, Judit. 2008. Latin American Jewish identities: Past and present challenges. The Mexican case in a comparative perspective. In Judit Bokser Liwerant (ed.), *Identities in an era of globalization and multiculturalism: Latin America in the Jewish world*, 81–105. Leiden: Brill.
Bokser Liwerant, Judit. 2013. Latin American Jews in the United States: Community and belonging in times of transnationalism. Springer. *Contemporary Jewry* 33(1). 121–143.
Briggs, Charles L. 1986. *Learning how to ask: A sociolinguistic appraisal of the role of the interview in social science research*. Cambridge: Cambridge University Press.
Brodsky, Adriana M. 2016. *Sephardi, Jewish, Argentine: Community and national identity, 1880–1960*. Bloomington: Indiana University Press.
Cherjovsky, Iván. 2013. De la Rusia Zarista a la pampa Argentina. Memoria e identidad en las colonias de la Jewish Colonization Association. Buenos Aires: Universidad de Buenos Aires PhD thesis.
Cimet, Adina. 1996. Nacionalismo y lengua: Los judíos Ashkenazitas en México, 1940–1950. *Revista Mexicana de Sociología* 58(4). 69–96.
Cimet, Adina. 1997. *Ashkenazi Jews in Mexico: Ideologies in the structuring of a community*. Albany: State University of New York Press.
Cohen, Martin A., Margalit Bejarano, Victor A. Mirelman, Haim Avni, Shlom Erel & Efraim Zadoff. 2007. Latin America. In Michael Berenbaum & Fred Skolnik (eds.), *Encyclopaedia Judaica*, 2nd edn., vol. 12, 507–517. Detroit: Macmillan Reference USA. http://go.galegroup.com/ps/i.do?id=GALE%7CCX2587511921&v=2.1&u=imcpl1111&it=r&p=GVRL&sw=w&asid=38e2f97bb2189aa9fb9cc33bd22134f8. (accessed 17 August 2016).
Cozarinsky, Edgardo. 2002. *La novia de Odessa*. Barcelona: Emecé Editores.
Dean-Olmsted, Evelyn. 2011. Shamis, halebis and shajatos: Labels and the dynamics of Syrian Jewishness in Mexico City. *Language & Communication* 31(2). 130–140.
Dean-Olmsted, Evelyn. 2012a. Arabic words in the Spanish of Syrian Jewish Mexicans: A case for "Heritage Words." *Texas Linguistics Forum* 55. 20–32.
Dean-Olmsted, Evelyn. 2012b. *Speaking Shami: Syrian Jewish Mexican language practices as strategies of integration and legitimation*. Bloomington: University of Indiana PhD thesis.

Dean-Olmsted, Evelyn. 2012c. Syrian Jewish Mexicans and the language of everyday Orientalism. *Society for Linguistic Anthropology*. http://linguisticanthropology.org/blog/2012/07/02/syrian-jewish-mexicans-and-the-language-of-everyday-orientalism/ (accessed 17 August 2016).

Dean-Olmsted, Evelyn. 2018. It was (never) relajo: Diasporic chronotope and the social work of Jewish Mexican ethnic joking. *Anthropological Quarterly* 91(2). 669–706.

Dean-Olmsted, Evelyn, & Susana Skura. 2016. Jewish Latin American Spanish. In Lily Kahn & Aaron Rubin (eds.), *The handbook of Jewish languages*, 389–402. Leiden & Boston: Brill.

DellaPergola, Sergio. 2011. ¿Cuantos somos hoy? Investigación y narrativa sobre población judía en America Latina. In Haim Avni (ed.), *Pertenencia y alteridad: judíos en/de América Latina: Cuarenta años de cambios*, 305–330. Madrid, Frankfurt am Main & Mexico City: Iberoamericana, Vervuert & Bonilla Artigas.

DellaPergola, Sergio. 2013a. World Jewish population, 2013. In Arnold Dashefsky & Ira M. Sheskin (eds.), *The American Jewish year book, 2013*, vol. 113, 279–358. Dordecht: Springer. http://www.jewishdatabank.org/Studies/details.cfm?StudyID=737 (accessed 17 August 2016).

DellaPergola, Sergio. 2013. National uniqueness and transnational parallelism: Reflections on the comparative study of Jewish communities in Latin America. Berman Jewish Policy Archive. http://www.bjpa.org/Publications/details.cfm?PublicationID=18558 (accessed 17 August 2016).

DellaPergola, Sergio & Susana Lerner. 1995. *La población judía de México: Perfil demográfico, social y cultural*. Mexico City & Jerusalem: Asociación Mexicana de Amigos de la Universidad Hebrea de Jerusalén.

Dolle, Verena (ed.). 2012. *Múltiples identidades: Literatura judeo-latinoamericana de los siglos XX y XXI*. Madrid, Frankfurt am Main: Iberoamericana & Vervuert.

Dujovne, Alejandro. 2008. Cartografía de las publicaciones periódicas judías de izquierda en Argentina, 1900–1953. Revista del Museo de Antropología 1(1). 121–38.

Dujovne, Alejandro. 2014. *Una historia del libro judío: La cultura judía Argentina a través de sus editores, libreros, traductores, imprentas y bibliotecas*. Buenos Aires: Siglo Veintiuno Editores.

Elkin, Judith Laikin. 2014. *The Jews of Latin America*, 3rd edn. Boulder & London: Lynne Rienner Publishers.

Enríquez Andrade, Héctor Manuel. 2004. *Meollo de Cucuballa: La actuación del narrador y la participación de la audiencia en el relato de vida*. Mexico City: Instituto Nacional de Antropología e Historia.

Enríquez Andrade, Hector Manuel Enríquez, and Renee Karina Revah Donath. 1998. *Estudios sobre el judeo-español en México*. Mexico City: Instituto Nacional de Antropología e Historia.

Fingueret, Manuela. 2006. *Blues de la calle Leiva*. Buenos Aires: Booket.

Fischman, Fernando. 2008. En la conversación fluía. Arte verbal, consideraciones emic y procesos conmemorativos judíos argentinos. *Runa* 29. 123–138.

Fischman, Fernando. 2011. Using Yiddish: Language ideologies, verbal art, and identity among Argentine Jews. *Journal of Folklore Research* 48(1). 37–61.

Fishman, Joshua A. 1966. *Language loyalty in the United States: The maintenance and perpetuation of non-English mother tongues by American ethnic and religious groups*. The Hague: Mouton.

Gerber, Jane S. 1994. *Jews of Spain: A history of the Sephardic experience*. New York: Free Press.

Gerber, Jane S. (ed.). 2014. *The Jews in the Caribbean*. Oxford: The Littman Library of Jewish Civilization.
Gerchunoff, Alberto. 1910. *Los gauchos judíos*. La Plata: Talleres Gráficos Joaquín Sesé.
Glantz, Margo. 1981. *Las genealogías*. Mexico: M. Casillas.
Gleizer Salzman, Daniela. 2011. *El exilio incómodo: México y los refugiados judíos, 1933–1945*. Mexico City: El Colegio de México, Centro de Estudios Históricos: Universidad Autónoma Metropolitana, Cuajimalpa.
Gleizer Salzman, Daniela. 2014. *Unwelcome exiles: Mexico and the Jewish refugees from Nazism, 1933–1945*. Leiden: Brill.
Glickman, Nora & Gloria Waldman. 1996. *Argentine Jewish theatre: A critical anthology*. Lewisburg: Bucknell University Press.
Gold, David L. 1980. The Spanish, Portuguese and Hebrew names for Yiddish and the Yiddish names for Hebrew. *International Journal of the Sociology of Language* 1980(24). 29–42.
Gold, David L. 1982. "La ribeca ista en ventana": A ditty in Buenos Aires Jewish Spanish. *Jewish Language Review* 2. 57–58.
Gold, David L. 1983. More musical and linguistic material from Argentina. *Jewish Language Review* 3. 103–111.
Gold, David L. 1985. More musical and linguistic material from Argentina (Part 2), some Items from contemporary Sefardic Mexican Spanish, and a bit of Eastern Ashkenazic Chilean Spanish and Eastern Ashkenazic Brazilian Portuguese. *Jewish Language Review* 5. 117–122.
Gold, David L. & Leonard Prager. 1983. Reviews and notices. *Jewish Language Review* 3. 183–294.
Goldberg, Florinda. 2000. Literatura judia latinoamericana: Modelos para armar. *Revista Iberoamericana* 66(191): 309–324.
Goldstein, Yossi, Judit Bokser Liwerant, Sergio DellaPergola, Leonardo Senkman, Frida Schwartz, Yael Siman & Maya Shorer Kaplan. 2014. The Latin American Jewish educator in a transnational world: Second year final research report. Jerusalem: The Liwerant Center, The Hebrew University of Jerusalem.
Goloboff, Gerardo Mario. 1978. *Leer Borges*. Buenos Aires: Editorial Huemul.
Gurvich Okón, Natalia. 2006. *En Idish suena mejor: El Idish en la vida cotidiana de los judíos mexicanos: Una colección de palabras, expresiones y refranes*. Mexico City: Universidad Iberoamericana Departamento de Historia Programa de Cultura Judaica.
Gutmann, Luis. 2006. ¿Ídish en el cine de Buenos Aires? ¡Oy Vey! In Perla Sneh (ed.), *Buenos Aires Idish. Temas de patrimonio cultural No 19*, 87–92. Buenos Aires: Comisión para la Preservación del Patrimonio Histórico Cultural de la Ciudad de Buenos Aires.
Hamui de Halabe, Liz. 2009. *El caso de la comunidad judía mexicana: El diseño estructural del estado durante el siglo XX y su interrelación con las minorías*. Mexico City: Consejo Nacional para Prevenir la Discriminación.
Hamui Halabe, Liz. 2005. *Transformaciones en la religiosidad de los judíos en México: Tradición, prtodoxia y fundamentalismo en la modernidad tardía*. Mexico City: Noriega Editores.
Hamui Halabe, Liz. 2012. Religious movements in Mexican Sephardism. In Edna Aizenberg & Margalit Bejarano (eds.), *Contemporary Sephardic identity in the Americas: An interdisciplinary approach*, 105–23. Syracuse University Press.
Hawayek de Ezcurdia, Antoinette, Hugo Yoffe, Enrique Movsovich & Alejandro de la Mora. 1992. Immigrant languages of Mexico. *International Journal of the Sociology of Language* 96. 111–127.

Heffes, Gisela. 1999. *Judios, argentinos, escritores*. Buenos Aires: Ediciones Atril.
Hordes, Stanley M. 2005. *To the end of the Earth: A history of the Crypto-Jews of New Mexico*. New York: Columbia University Press.
Jakobson, Roman. 1990 [1957]. *Shifters, verbal categories and the Russian verb*. In Linda R. Waugh & Monique Monville-Burston (eds.), *On language: Roman Jakobson*, 386–392. Cambridge, MA: Harvard University Russian Language Project.
Jmelnitzky, Adrián & Ezequiel Erdei. 2005. *The Jewish population of Buenos Aires: A sociodemographic survey*. Buenos Aires: AMIA.
Krimer, María Inés. 2010. *Sangre kosher*. Buenos Aires: Aquilina.
Lara, Luis Fernando. 1996. *Diccionario del español usual en México*. Mexico City: El Colegio de México Centro de Estudios Lingüisticos y Literarios.
Lesser, Jeff & Raanan Rein. 2008. *Rethinking Jewish-Latin Americans*. Albuquerque: University of New Mexico Press.
Levinsky, Manuel. 2008. Historia del periodismo judío En México (1a.parte), opinión, diario judío México. *Diario judío: Diario de la vida judía en México y el mundo*. http://diariojudio.com/opinion/historia-del-periodismo-judio-en-mexico-1a-parte/661/. (accessed 18 August 2016).
Liacho, Lázaro. 1945. *Anecdotario judío*. Buenos Aires: Editorial Gleizer.
Limonic, Laura. 2014. The privileged 'in-between' status of Latino Jews in the northeastern United States. New York: City University of New York PhD thesis.
Lipski, John M. 2012. Geographical and social varieties of Spanish: An overview. In José Ignacio Hualde, Antxon Olarrea & Erin O'Rourke (eds.), The *handbook of Hispanic linguistics*, 1–26. Malden: Wiley-Blackwell.
Lockhart, Darrell B. (ed.). 2013a. *Critical approaches to Jewish-Mexican literature [Approximaciones críticas a la literatura judeomexicana]*. [Special Issue]. *Chasqui* 4.
Lockhart, Darrell B. 2013b. Introduction: On the socioliterary dimensions of Jewish-Mexican literature. *Chasqui* 4. 9–26.
Lockhart, Darrell B. 2012. The 'boom' of Latin American-Jewish literary studies. *Chasqui* 41(2). 190–195.
Macadar, Marquesa. 2009. Sephardic diaspora: A case study in Latin America. Bloomington: Indiana University PhD thesis.
Matisoff, James. 2000. *Blessings, curses, hopes, and fears: Psycho-ostensive expressions in Yiddish*. 1st edn. Standford: Stanford University Press.
Muñiz-Huberman, Angelina. 1991. *De cuerpo entero: El juego de escribir*. Mexico: Universidad Nacional Autónoma de México & Corunda.
Muñiz-Huberman, Angelina. 1999. *El canto del peregrino: Hacia una poética del exilio*. Sant Cugat del Valles: GEXEL Universidad Nacional Autónoma de México.
Nissán, Rosa. 1992. *Novia que te vea*. Mexico: Planeta.
Nissán, Rosa. 1996. *Hisho que te nazca*. Mexico City: Plaza y Janés.
Ran, Amalia & Jean Cahan. 2011. *Returning to Babel: Jewish Latin American experiences, representations, and identity*. Leiden & Boston: Brill.
Rein, Raanan & Tzvi Tal. 2014. Becoming part of the moving story: Jews on the Latin American screen. *Jewish Film & New Media* 2(1): 1–8. doi:10.13110/jewifilmnewmedi.2.1.0001 (accessed 18 August 2016).
Reyes, Angela & Adrienne Lo. 2009. *Beyond yellow English: Toward a linguistic anthropology of Asian Pacific America*. New York: Oxford University Press.

Rodrigue, Aron. 1990. *French Jews, Turkish Jews: The Alliance Israélite Universelle and the Politics of Jewish schooling in Turkey, 1860–1925*. Bloomington: Indiana University Press.

Romero, Rey. 2009. Lexical borrowing and gender assignment in Judeo-Spanish. *Ianua: Revista Philologica Romanica* 9. 2–13.

Rotenberg, Abrasha. 2004. *Última carta de Moscú*. Buenos Aires: Editorial Sudamericana.

Rotenberg, Abrasha. 2006. *Raíces y recuerdos: Vivencias judías y otras pasiones*. Madrid: Hebraica Ediciones.

Rozenmacher, Germán. 1964. *Réquiem para un viernes a la noche: Drama en un réquiem y un acto*. Buenos Aires: Talía.

Sadow, Stephen A. (ed.). 2013. *Literatura judía latinoamericana contemporánea: Una antología [Literatura judaica latino-americana contemporânea: Uma antologia*; Contemporary *Jewish Latin American literature: An anthology*). Boston: Northeastern University Libraries.

Sadow, Stephen A. 2015. A kaleidoscope of literary responses to the AMIA bombing. *AZAY Art Magazine*. http://www.azayartmagazine.com/a-kaleidoscope-of-literary-responses-to-the-amia-bombing/ (accessed 18 August 2016).

Saed, Ivonne. 2003. *Triple crónica de un nombre*. Mexico City: Editorial Lectorum.

Schaffer, Lily. 2015. Phonological variation in Mexico City Jewish Spanish. Boulder: University of Colorado MA thesis.

Schalom, Myrtha. 2003. *La polaca: Inmigración, rufianes y esclavas a comienzos del siglo XX*. Buenos Aires: Grupo Editorial Norma.

Sefamí, Jacobo. 2004. *Los Dolientes*. 1st edn. Mexico City: Plaza & Janés.

Senkman, Leonardo. 1983. *La identidad judía en la literatura Argentina*. Buenos Aires: Editorial Pardes.

Shandler, Jeffrey. 2006. *Adventures in Yiddishland: Postvernacular language & culture*. Berkeley: University of California Press.

Sinay, Javier. 2013. *Los crímenes de Moisés Ville: Una historia de gauchos y judíos*. Buenos Aires: Tusquets Editores.

Skura, Susana. 1997a. La Shikse. Signos múltiples en el discurso sobre el "otro." Noticias de Antropología y Arqueología n° 20 http://www.equiponaya.com.ar/congresos/contenido/laplata/LP4/14.htm. (accessed 18 August 2016).

Skura, Susana. 1997b. Usos y representaciones de la lengua de origen en la conformación de procesos identitarios: El idish según sus semi-hablantes Ashkenazíes de la Capital Federal. In Mario Margulis & Marcelo Urresti (eds.), *La cultura en la Argentina de fin de siglo: Ensayos sobre la dimensión cultural*, 109–120. Buenos Aires: Eudeba.

Skura, Susana. 2006 (1998). Usos y representaciones de la lengua de origen en la construcción de la identidad socio-étnica. El ídish en la comunidad ashkenazí de Buenos Aires. En: AAVV *Tesis de Licenciatura del Departamento de Ciencias Antropológicas 1*. Universidad de Buenos Aires. Buenos Aires.

Skura, Susana. 2007. "A por gauchos in chiripá...". Expresiones criollistas en el teatro ídish argentino (1910–1930). *Iberoamericana. América Latina- España-Portugal. Ensayos sobre letras, historia y sociedad* 7(27). 7–23.

Skura, Susana & Lucas Fiszman. 2016. From *shiln* to *shpiln* in Max Perlman's songs: Linguistic and socio-cultural change among Ashkenazi Jews in Argentina. *Journal of Jewish Languages* 4(2). 231–251.

Skura, Susana & Lucas Fiszman. 2005. Ideologías lingüísticas: Silenciamiento y transmisión del ídish en Argentina. In Susana Skura (eds.), *Lenguaje, cultura y sociedad. Perspectivas integradoras*, 63–82. Buenos Aires: Universidad de Buenos Aires.

Skura, Susana & Silvia Glocer (eds.). 2016. *Teatro ídish argentino (1930–1950)*. Buenos Aires: Editorial de la Facultad de Filosofía y Letras de la Universidad de Buenos Aires.
Stavans, Ilan. 2001. *On borrowed words: A memoir of language*. New York: Viking.
Stavans, Ilan. 2012. Latin American Jewish literature. Oxford Bibliographies. http://www.oxford-bibliographies.com/view/document/obo-9780199840731/obo-9780199840731-0009.xml (accessed 18 August 2016).
Steimberg, Alicia. 1992. *Cuando digo Magdalena*. Mexico City: Editorial Planeta Mexicana.
Tarnopolsky, Daniel. 2011. *Betina sin aparecer: Historia íntima del caso Tarnopolsky, una familia diezmada por la dictadura militar*. Buenos Aires: Grupo Editorial Norma.
Toker, Eliahu. 1996a. *Refranerito ídish y las más sabrosas maldiciones judías de Europa Oriental*. Buenos Aires: Arte y Papel.
Toker, Eliahu. 1996b. *Refranerito sefardí y las mejores maldiciones judeo españolas*. Buenos Aires: Arte y Papel.
Toker, Eliahu & Patricia Finzi. 1993. *Las Idishe mames son un pueblo aparte*. Buenos Aires: Grupo Editorial Shalom.
Toker, Eliahu, Patricia Finzi & Moacyr Scliar. 1991. *Del Edén al diván: Humor judío*. Buenos Aires: Shalom.
Toker, Eliahu & Rudy Toker (eds.). 2009. *Si fuese pecado, el rabino no lo haría*. Buenos Aires: Norma.
Toker, Rudy & Eliahu Toker. 2001. *La felicidad no es todo en la vida y otros chistes judíos*. Buenos Aires: Grijalbo.
Toker, Rudy & Eliahu Toker. 2003. *Odiar es pertenecer y otros chistes para sobrevivir al nazismo, racismo, autoritarismo, antisemitismo*. Buenos Aires: Grupo Editorial Norma.
Toker, Rudy & Eliahu Toker. 2005. *No desearás tu mujer al prójimo: Humor sobre los Diez Mandamientos*. Buenos Aires: Grupo Editorial Norma.
Toker, Rudy & Eliahu Toker. 2007. *Reír en Ídish: Humor judío*. Barcelona: Riopiedras.
Toker, Rudy & Eliahu Toker. 2009. *¡Gogl mogl!: El gran libro del humor judío*. Buenos Aires: Sudamericana.
Ulanovsky, Carlos. 2013. *Nunca bailes en dos bodas a la vez*. Barcelona: Grupo Planeta.
Veltman, Calvin. 1983. *Language shift in the United States*. The Hague: Mouton.
Virkel de Sandler, Ana. 1991. El bilingüismo idish-español en dos comunidades bonaerenses. In María Beatriz Fontanella de Weinberg (eds.), *Lengua e Inmigración: Mantenimiento y cambio de lenguas inmigratorias*, 113–132. Bahía Blanca: Departamento de Humanidades, Universidad Nacional del Sur.
Weinstein, Ana E. & Miryam E. Gover de Nasatsky. 1994. *Escritores judeo-argentinos: Bibliografía 1900–1987*. Buenos Aires: Editorial Milá.
Weinstein, Ana E. & Eliahu Toker. 2004. *La letra ídish en tierra Argentina: Bio-bibliografía de sus autores literarios*. Buenos Aires: Editorial Milá.
Weltman, Grisha. 1962. En qué consiste la idea del IFT. In *Teatro IFT: XXX aniversario: Octubre 1962, Buenos Aires*. Buenos Aires: Teatro IFT.

Sarah Bunin Benor
Jewish English in the United States

1 Introduction

Jewish English. Judeo-English. Judaeo-English. Yinglish. Yeshivish. Hebrish. While these terms have different connotations, they all refer to the English used by Jews in English-speaking countries. Jewish English is currently spoken in the United States, Canada, the United Kingdom, Australia, New Zealand, and South Africa, as well as by Anglo-origin immigrants and their children in Israel and elsewhere.

Several scholars have argued that Jewish English should be analyzed as a Jewish language variety (Steinmetz 1981; Fishman 1985; Gold 1985; Weiser 1995; Benor 2009), comparable to language varieties like Judeo-Arabic, Jewish Neo-Aramaic, and Jewish Malayalam, all of which are co-territorial to their non-Jewish base languages (but different from Yiddish and Ladino, which are "post-coterritorial" [Benor 2008]). In contrast to these (mostly) endangered language varieties, Jewish English is currently thriving, as millions of Jews live in English-speaking countries today. Among these Jews, we can talk about a continuum of linguistic distinctness: from the most distinct English of Haredi Orthodox Jews – so heavily influenced by Yiddish that it can sometimes be unintelligible to outsiders – to the English of secular Jews, identical to that of their non-Jewish neighbors, perhaps with the addition of a few Hebrew or Yiddish words. As any attempt to divide this continuum between Jewish English and non-Jewish English would be arbitrary, scholars should include any English-based speech or writing of Jews as appropriate for analysis under the umbrella "Jewish English." Even the most distinctive variety should be seen as a dialect of English, as the structure of English remains mostly intact.

2 Historical background

2.1 Speaker community: Settlement, documentation

In the 11th–13th centuries England had a Jewish community, but we know little about their spoken language, and surviving documents are written in Hebrew or Latin (Spolsky 2014: 127). Expulsions and decrees barred Jews from living in England for many years, but, in the 17th and 18th centuries, former Marranos from Brazil, the Netherlands, and elsewhere in Western Europe settled in England and what would later become the United States. Although there has been little research on the language of Jews in the English-speaking lands of that period, we can assume that the immigrants arrived speaking (Jewish varieties of) the languages of their lands of origin (or ancestral languages) and shifted to (Jewish varieties of) English within a few generations.

In the American colonies, the original Jewish communities were Sephardic, and they assimilated many Ashkenazim over the course of the 18th century. Throughout the 19th century, the United States saw some immigration of Yiddish- and (Jewish-) German-speaking Jews from Central and Eastern Europe; starting in the 1880s, millions of immigrants arrived, many of whom spoke Yiddish. Other languages spoken by Jewish immigrants to the United States included Ladino (Judeo-Spanish, also known as Judezmo) among Jews from Turkey, Greece, and other Balkan countries, (Judeo-) Arabic among Jews from Syria and other parts of the Middle East and North Africa, and (less or more distinctly Jewish versions of) Hungarian, German, and other languages spoken in modernized communities in Europe. After World War II, Holocaust survivors from Central and Eastern Europe immigrated to the United States, including many Haredi Orthodox Jews (especially Hasidim), whose Yiddish would be maintained by their children, grandchildren, and beyond. In the late 20th century, Jews from Israel, Iran, Russia, and other parts of the former Soviet Union arrived in the United States, speaking Hebrew, (Jewish) Farsi, (Jewish) Russian, Juhuri, Bukhari, and other languages. Most members of these communities picked up English within a generation, sometimes maintaining elements of their ancestral languages within their English.

20th-century waves of Jewish immigration to England, Canada, and other English-speaking countries followed similar patterns but with important differences, such as a larger percentage of Jews in Canada and Australia having immigrated after World War II. This chapter focuses primarily on Jews in the United States, the locus of the vast majority of research on Jewish English. For information on Jewish English in the United Kingdom, see Glinert (1993), for Australia see Clyne et al. (2002), and for Canada see Boberg (2004).

2.2 Phases in historical development

Because language use and timelines vary so significantly in different communities (secular, Sephardic, Modern Orthodox, Haredi, Russian, etc.), it is difficult to divide American Jewish history into linguistic phases. For purposes of general analysis, I would suggest the following, somewhat arbitrary, periodization for Jewish American English:

1. 1654–1880: **Early:** Sephardic and then Ashkenazic immigrants create and join small Jewish communities, and their descendants use English with few distinguishing features;
2. 1881–1930: **Immigrant:** Large groups of immigrants, mostly Yiddish speakers, form urban enclaves and use English with system-level influences from Yiddish;
3. 1931–1980: **Integrated:** Descendants of immigrants use English with few distinctive features;
4. 1981–present: **Distinguishing:** While most Jews continue the trends in the Integrated period, many use English with increasing influence from Yiddish, Textual Hebrew/Aramaic, and Modern Hebrew, especially in in-group communication.

Because there was immigration in all periods, this timeline is very much an oversimplification. In all periods, immigrants who learned English spoke with heavy influence from their native languages. In the Early, Immigrant, and Integrated periods, the children of immigrants sometimes learned English with few or no distinctive features, but in immigrant enclaves, especially in the New York area, they often spoke English with some influence from Yiddish. Later generations tended to exhibit diglossia (Ferguson 1959; Fishman 1985): They used nondistinct English for out-group communication and English with some Yiddish and Hebrew words, and sometimes other influences, for in-group communication. In the Distinguishing period, Jews have continued this diglossia, but some have distinguished their in-group language to a greater degree.

As Fishman (1985) theorized, Jewish language varieties tend to arise when a Jewish group migrates to a new language territory. After a period of integration into the surrounding society, in which community members learn and use the local language, the community retracts (because of externally and internally imposed factors) and distinguishes its language more and more. This has been the case with some varieties of Jewish English, as indicated by the suggested timeline above. We can find evidence for the process of distinction from the past few decades in several recent studies. A survey conducted in 2008 found that younger Jews are significantly more likely than older Jews to use certain Hebrew and Yiddish loanwords (like *davka* 'particularly, specifically, even, just to be contrary', *Good Shabbos* [Sabbath greeting], and *leyn* 'chant Torah') and Yiddish grammatical influences (like "staying *by* us" and "enough already"), even as they are less likely than older Jews to use other Yiddish loanwords (like *macher* 'big-shot', *naches* 'pride, often related to offspring', and *heimish* 'homey') (Benor 2012b). In addition, a majority of Jews who responded to the survey report that the number of Yiddish- and Hebrew-derived words they use within English speech has increased over the past 10–15 years (Benor and Cohen 2011).

Quantitative evidence for this distinctiveness can also be found in the Anglo-Jewish press' increasing use of specific Hebrew and Yiddish loanwords, such as *shul* 'synagogue' and *chutzpah* 'nerve', beginning in the 1960s and rising sharply in the 1980s (Benor 2015). We also see increasingly diverse language within specific sectors of the American Jewish community. Documents of the North American Reform movement increased their use of Hebrew loanwords beginning in the 1980s, corresponding to the increasing use of Hebrew as a language of prayer in that movement (Benor 2013a). Among Orthodox Jews, younger survey respondents are much more likely than older ones to report using "staying *by* us," a phenomenon influenced by the increasing insularity within Orthodox communities and the greater acceptance of distinctive language in American society (Benor 2012a).

2.3 Sociolinguistic description, community bilingualism, public functions

The continuum of distinctness mentioned at the beginning of this paper extends beyond Jewish English, as several communities of American Jews speak other languages. In general, this is limited to immigrant populations and sometimes their children, including (Jewish varieties of) Farsi among Jews from Iran, Russian among Jews from the former Soviet Union, Arabic among Jews from Syria, and Hebrew among Jews from Israel. But in some Hasidic communities Yiddish is still a vibrant language, spoken by great-grandchildren of immigrants (Isaacs 1999; Fader 2009; Assouline, this volume). The English used in these bilingual communities is heavily influenced by these other languages, in addition to Hebrew and Yiddish.

Among communities that speak primarily English, the language of each individual can be analyzed comparatively on a continuum of distinctness, from language that is (almost) identical to that of non-Jews to language that incorporates enough other distinctive features that it is sometimes unintelligible to outsiders. The location of any individual along this continuum is influenced by a number of factors, including religiosity, Jewish density of social networks, and time spent in Israel (Benor 2011; Benor and Cohen 2011). For the most part, Jews who observe Shabbat, attend synagogue frequently, have mostly Jewish friends, and/or have spent significant amounts of time in Israel speak English with more Hebrew and Yiddish words and other distinctive features than Jews who are secular, have mostly non-Jewish friends, and have spent little or no time in Israel. This variation stems from several factors, including knowledge of and exposure to biblical, rabbinic, and liturgical Hebrew/Aramaic texts, which have the potential to influence spoken and written English; homogeneity of social networks, which tends to correlate with greater linguistic distinctness in general; and exposure to Israeli Hebrew and to Jews from around the English-speaking world who are spending time in Israel, which tends to correlate with influences from Israeli Hebrew and other distinctive features.

Based on survey data on reported language use, we can speak of this continuum of individuals' linguistic distinctness, correlating with these demographic factors. But given that individuals vary significantly in their use of Jewish features according to topic (what they are speaking or writing about) and audience (who they expect will hear or read their words), a more useful unit of analysis is the utterance. We have data to support the hypothesis that Jews use different variants of certain words (e.g., Passover, PEH-sach, and PAY-sach) when speaking to non-Jews, Jews who are not engaged in religious life, and Jews who are engaged in religious life (Benor 2011). We also know that Orthodox Jews change their language significantly depending on whether their audience is made up of long-time Orthodox Jews, newly Orthodox Jews, non-Orthodox Jews, or non-Jews (Benor 2012a; Stein 2015). And we would expect Jews to use more Hebrew and Yiddish loanwords in Jewish-topic utterances, as many of those loanwords refer to religious and cultural referents, such as *leyn* 'chant Torah', *charoset* 'fruit-nut mixture eaten at the Passover seder [evening ceremony]', and *shiva* 'post-funeral mourning period, gathering'.

3 Structural information

When individuals speak Jewish English, they are speaking English with the incorporation of features from a "distinctive Jewish linguistic repertoire" (Benor 2008; see also Benor 2010 on "ethnolinguistic repertoire"). Most of these features are lexical, but the repertoire also includes system-level distinctive features in phonology, morphosyntax, discourse, and intonation, especially among Orthodox Jews. Because of the wide-ranging diversity among American Jews, some features of the repertoire would only be used by members of a particular community. For example, an Orthodox male yeshiva student might say "The *sugya* we're *learning* is too *lomdish* to *say outside*" ('the [Talmudic] passage we're studying is too complicated to summarize') (Weiser 1995: 92), and a Reform Jewish woman might say "I haven't been to *temple* ['synagogue'] since I was *bat mitzvahed* ['had a coming of age ceremony'], except for *tikkun olam* ['community service/social justice'] events." However, it is extremely unlikely that either individual would utter the other's sentence (Benor 2011). Despite this diversity, there is a good deal of overlap in features used; for example, Jews of many backgrounds would talk about the *maror* 'bitter herbs' and *charoset* on their *seder plate*, even if they pronounce the words differently (and use different fruits, nuts, and bitter herbs for these ritual foods). Given this linguistic overlap and the porous boundaries between communities of Jews, it makes sense to describe one Jewish repertoire from which Jews of all types might use features in their speech.

3.1 Relationship to non-Jewish varieties (isoglosses, related dialects)

The majority of American Jews have ancestry in Ashkenaz (Eastern and Central Europe) and are considered white according to contemporary American racial discourse (this has not always been the case; see Goldstein 2008). These white Jews tend to speak varieties of English that are similar to those of other white Americans, in contrast to African Americans, Latinos, and other non-white groups. African American Jews – a growing group due to adoption, inter-group marriage, and conversion – exhibit diversity: Some use elements of the Jewish repertoire, some use elements of the African American repertoire, and some use elements of both or neither (Benor 2016a). A number of variationist studies have analyzed Jews as a white ethnic group and compared their English speech to that of other white ethnic groups, especially Irish and Italians, finding some phonological differences (Labov 1966; Laferriere 1979; Knack 1991; Boberg 2004). Beyond these city-based studies, we have no systematic research on how Jews around the country compare linguistically to each other or to their non-Jewish neighbors. There is evidence that Jews outside of New York are more likely than local non-Jews to be told they sound like they are from New York and to report using New York regional variants, like [a] for /o/ in "orange" and "Florida" ("ahrange" and "Flahrida") (Knack 1991; Sacknowitz 2007; Benor 2011). The New York influence around the country can be attributed to New York having been and continuing to be a center for Jewish residence, culture, and community.

3.2 Particular structural features (unique to the Jewish variety)

In addition to the above-mentioned vocalic features found among Jews in general, we find some distinct vowels among some Orthodox Jews, including non-raised prenasal /æ/ (e.g., "caandle" – Jochnowitz 1968; Benor 2012a) and back vowels (/o/ and /u/) that are less diphthongized than among most Americans (e.g., "so," "new" – a feature that has not yet received scholarly treatment). We also find distinctive consonants, including devoicing of final voiced consonants (e.g., "beardt") and hyper-aspiration of word-final /t/ (e.g., "right^{h}" – Thomas 1932; Levon 2006; Benor 2012a). Some Jews say they can sometimes identify other Jews (or Orthodox Jews) through their intonation. Distinctive contours include quasi-chanting, rise-fall, and high-falling pitch boundaries (Weinreich 1956; Heilman 1983; Benor 2012a; Burdin 2014).

Morphosyntactically, Jewish English has a number of Yiddish-influenced constructions, especially common among Orthodox Jews. These include present for present perfect progressive tense, sometimes with "already," emulative of Yiddish constructions with *shoyn* (e.g., "I'm living here 10 years *already*"), "should" used to indicate subjunctive after "want," as in "I want that you should come," non-standard prepositions (e.g., "*by* the rehearsal" 'at', "coming *to us*" 'to our house', "her bus gets in *10:15*" 'at 10:15'), and several phrasal verbs (e.g., *say over, answer up, bring down*). Orthodox Jews exhibit some distinctive syntactic placement of adverbial phrases, as in "You'll be stuck studying *all day* Torah" and "You think he's *for sure* Orthodox?" While most of these grammatical features are clearly Yiddish influences, one seems to come from Israeli Hebrew – the use of "so" in a slot that is empty in general American English, emulating Hebrew *az* 'so' ("If I see someone who's using the wrong language, *so* I'll realize that they're just becoming *frum* ['religious']") (Benor 2012a). The Yiddish-influenced topicalization that Feinstein (1980) found in Jewish English a generation ago (e.g., "Some milk you want?") does not seem to be an identifying feature among Orthodox Jews today.

At the discourse level, some studies have pointed to Jews, especially New York Jews, using a highly interactive, overlapping, argumentative speech style, which can be interpreted by some observers as aggressive (Tannen 1981; Schiffrin 1984). Benor and Cohen's survey asked, "Have you ever been told that you interrupt too much or that your speech style is too aggressive?" Jews were more likely than non-Jews to answer "Many times" or "Sometimes" (Benor 2011).

Beyond these phonological, prosodic, morphosyntactic, and discourse differences, which are especially common among Orthodox Jews and others who live in densely Jewish communities, Jews' language tends to be structurally similar or identical to that of their non-Jewish neighbors. The primary area of differentiation is lexicon.

3.3 Lexicon: Hebrew and Aramaic elements

Across a wide variety of Jewish communities in the United States, there are three primary sources of lexical distinction: Yiddish, Textual Hebrew/Aramaic, and Modern Israeli Hebrew. Jewish English includes hundreds – even thousands – of loanwords from these languages. Many loanwords are influenced by some or all of these languages (Yiddish, Textual Hebrew/Aramaic, and Modern Israeli Hebrew), and no single language can be designated as the sole source (Benor 2000). Some Yiddish loanwords have become part of general American English, sometimes with changes in semantics or pragmatics, e.g., *klutz* 'clumsy person', *maven* 'expert, whiz', and *shmooze* 'chat, kiss up, network'. The loanwords discussed below are used primarily by Jews, mostly in in-group speech and writing. Their pronunciation varies: Orthodox Jews, especially those toward the Haredi end of the continuum, tend to use more Yiddish influence, and non-Orthodox

Jews tend to use more Israeli Hebrew influence (e.g., *káshris* vs. *kashrút*). Despite this variation, the examples that follow include just one form for each loanword.

Loanwords are used in reference to prayer and synagogue observance (e.g., *tallis* 'prayer shawl', *minyan* 'prayer quorum/group', *kavana* 'spiritual intention'), holiday-related items (e.g., *lulav* and *esrog* 'palm frond and citron shaken on Sukkot', *haggadah* 'booklet guiding Passover seder', *machzor* 'High Holiday prayer book'), foods (e.g., *matzah* 'unleavened bread for Passover', *homentashen* 'filled cookies for Purim', *gefilte fish* 'fish dumpling'), and lifecycle events (e.g., *brit bat/simchat bat* 'baby girl welcome ceremony, lit. covenant of a daughter/celebration of a daughter', *bar mitzvah* 'boy's coming-of-age ceremony/celebration, boy who has reached adulthood', *chuppah* 'wedding canopy, ceremony').

In addition to specifically Jewish referents, many loanwords refer to general concepts for which there are no simple English equivalents, including *balagan* 'mess, bedlam', *tachlis* 'practical details', *mentsh* 'kind person', and *davka* 'particularly, specifically, even, just to be contrary'. Loanwords not only fill lexical gaps; they are also used for referents for which there are common English equivalents, e.g., *mazel tov* 'congratulations', *polkies* 'thighs', *sheitel* 'wig', *bubbe* 'grandmother', and *chaval* 'a pity'. At many Zionist summer camps, Hebrew loanwords are used for locations, activities, and roles (e.g., *agam* 'lake', *chadar ochel* 'dining hall', *tzrif* 'cabin', *peulat erev* 'evening activity', *nikayon* 'cleaning', *tzevet* 'staff', and *rosh edah* 'unit head') (Benor 2016b).

Especially in Orthodox communities, several psycho-ostensive phrases (Matisoff 2000) are used when speaking about positive, negative, or future events, e.g., *mertsishem / b'ezrat Hashem* 'with God's help', *chas v'sholom* 'God forbid', and *bli neder* 'without a vow'. In Jewish organizational settings, like synagogues and schools, loanwords are often used as communal greetings, e.g., *boker tov* 'good morning', *erev tov* 'good evening', *Shabbat shalom* 'peaceful Sabbath', and *chag sameach / good yontif* 'happy/good holiday'. Hebrew conversational closings are also common, especially in written correspondence among Jews, e.g., *kol tuv* 'all the best', *b'shalom* 'in peace', and *gmar tov* '(may you be) finished well (and inscribed in the Book of Life on Yom Kippur)'.

Several discourse markers are borrowed from Yiddish or Israeli Hebrew, including "oh!" (a short mid-back rounded vowel, cut off by a glottal stop, used to acknowledge an interlocutor's good point in a pedagogical context) and "pshhhhh" (used to indicate being impressed). Many Orthodox Jews, and people of multiple backgrounds who have spent significant time in Israel, use an alveolar tongue click, borrowed from Israeli Hebrew, indicating self-repair and negative response (Benor 2012a).

Loanwords are generally integrated into English sentences phonologically and morpho-syntactically, with a few exceptions. In addition to the phonological system of English, the phoneme [x] is used in words from Hebrew and Yiddish (and occasionally words from non-Jewish languages, like Xavier and Bach). Hebrew- and Yiddish-origin nouns are sometimes pluralized with English morphology (e.g., *menorahs, sukkahs, ba'al teshuvas, shtetls*) and sometimes (especially Hebrew-origin words used by Jewishly educated speakers) with source-language morphology (e.g., *aliyot, talmidei chachamim, siddurim, rugelach*). Hebrew- and Yiddish-origin verbs exhibit heavy influence from Yiddish in how they are integrated morphosyntactically into English: sometimes directly (e.g., "Let's *bentsh*" 'bless, say Grace After Meals' "She *kasher*ed the kitchen" 'rendered kosher', "He learned how to *shecht* chickens" 'ritually slaughter') and – in Orthodox communities – sometimes periphrastically (e.g., "They are *koveya* ['establish'] times to learn" – a calque of the Hebrew *kovea itim latorah*; "We should all be *zoche* ['merit'] the coming of the *Moshiach* ['Messiah']"; "It might be *meorer* ['arouse'] the *tayva* ['lust']"). Also in Orthodox communities, pre-nominal adjectives are sometimes used with the Yiddish suffix *-ə* (e.g., a *choshuve* ['important'] man, *yeshivishe* wedding *shtick* ['entertainment associated with non-Hasidic Haredi Orthodoxy']).

Here are some examples of how Hebrew loanwords are integrated into Jewish English sentences (italics and bracketed translations added):

> [A female visiting scholar] spends one weekend a month at the Orthodox synagogue, where she organizes *y[e]mei iyun* (days of learning), delivers a series of *shiurim* (lectures) and gives 15-minute *drashot* (textual analyses) from the *bima* ['synagogue stage, pulpit'].
> (Snyder, Tamar. "Beyond the rabba-rousing." *New York Jewish Week*, 3/24/2010, http://www.thejewishweek.com/print/7684)

> *L'shem chinuch* ['for the sake of education'], I am leading a "mock" *seder* tomorrow for our Basic Judaism class... I am wondering if anyone out there has already created ... an "essence of" *Haggadah* that is more explanatory than *halachic* ['meeting the requirements of Jewish law']... Thanks in advance for anything you might send my way. I'll teach it all *b'shem omro/omrah* ['in the name of its speaker']!
> (Reform rabbi writing to a pluralistic Jewish professional email list, 2012, reprinted with author's permission)

In the first example, all loanwords are nouns, including a compound noun phrase, and all of those that are pluralized use source-language morphology. The second example includes a few nouns, an adjective, and two phrases.

3.4 Language contact influences

As is clear from the previous sections, Yiddish and Israeli Hebrew serve as key contact languages for distinguishing Jewish English. Other languages continue to exert lexical influence on the speech of specific communities, such as Ladino in the Sephardic community of Seattle (e.g., *kal* 'synagogue', *bragas* 'underwear', *bivas* 'life, bless you') and Judeo-Arabic in the Syrian community of Brooklyn (e.g., *dahak* 'joke', *hadeed* 'awesome'), even among the great-grandchildren of the immigrants who spoke those languages. But due to the numeric and institutional dominance of the descendants of Yiddish speakers among American Jews, some Yiddish loanwords in the religious domain have become so common that even non-Ashkenazi Jews use them, e.g., *shul*, *bentsh*, and *daven* 'pray'.

4 Written and oral traditions

4.1 Writing system

In contrast to most Jewish language varieties whose orthographic practices crystalized in pre-modern times, the English component of Jewish English is generally not represented in Hebrew/Jewish characters; it is written almost identically to non-Jewish English. However, there are exceptions. Many Jews write "God" with a dash ("G-d"), emulating the avoidance of writing the tetragrammaton - God's holy, four-letter Hebrew name. Haredi communities that are bilingual in English and Yiddish sometimes represent English with Hebrew-based Yiddish orthography, as in this sign observed in Williamsburg, New York, in 2012: "מיני מארקעט פלאס [Mini Market Plus] – Fruits, Vegetables and Grocery." Another exception is material items with isolated English words written in Hebrew letters, such as mugs and water bottles with names of American universities (e.g., קולומביה: Columbia), shirts, hats, and *kippot* ('skullcaps') with names of sports teams (e.g., סייאטל סיהוקס: Seattle Seahawks), and pins and bumper stickers with names of political candidates (e.g., ברק אובמה: Barack Obama). These items have the effect of advertising the users' allegiance to the university, team, or candidate while also indicating Jewish pride and the ability to decode Hebrew letters.

When Hebrew, Aramaic, and Yiddish words are inserted into English sentences, they are generally written in English letters, e.g., "bris" 'circumcision ceremony' and "Shabbat shalom." These words are sometimes italicized or otherwise marked as foreign. While the spelling of some non-English words has become fairly standardized (e.g., *bar mitzvah*, *chutzpah* 'nerve', *aron* 'ark'), most have multiple common spellings, even those that have been featured in the U.S. Scripps National Spelling Bee (see Benor 2013b on the 2013 winning word, *knaidel* 'matzah meal and egg dumpling', which is also spelled *knaidle*, *kneidle*, *kneydl*, etc.). Sometimes Hebrew, Aramaic, and Yiddish words inserted into English sentences are rendered in Hebrew letters, as in this quote from a letter sent to campers at a Ramah summer camp: "Come prepared for the קיץ of a lifetime!"

(קיץ 'summer'). This orthographic switching is very common in educational contexts, as well as in Orthodox communities.

4.2 Literature

American Jewish writers have penned tens of thousands of books intended for Jewish audiences – literary and non-literary, poetry and prose; millions of articles in the Jewish press (both in print and online); and thousands of songs sung in Jewish educational and communal settings. Some of these works are in English with few or no distinctive linguistic features, and others, especially those intended for Orthodox audiences, have many Hebrew and Yiddish loanwords and sporadic syntactic influences from Yiddish. However, it is impossible (and futile) to classify the language of some works as Jewish English and others as general English. Instead, we can say that this literature exists on a continuum from least to most distinct, depending primarily on the use of Hebrew and Yiddish words. Within Jewish children's books and songs, there is an emerging metalinguistic genre that teaches Yiddish and Hebrew loanwords, e.g., "Your tati says you are a tayere kint! And your daddy is right. You are a precious child" (Auntie Lili, *My Zeesa Jessica / My Sweet Jessica*, 1997).

4.3 Performance (theater, film, etc.)

Jewish theater troupes in many locations perform English-language plays written by Jews and intended for primarily Jewish audiences, many of which include distinctive language. Films do the same, and some filmmakers have included subtitles for select speakers, especially those using Orthodox Jewish English with many influences from Hebrew and Yiddish (e.g., "Trembling Before G-d," see Horn 2006).

5 State of research

5.1 History of documentation

There is little documentation of pre-modern Jewish English. Jewish-authored English-language documents from the 17th through the 21st centuries can be found in the American Jewish Archives (Cincinnati), the American Jewish Historical Society (New York), and elsewhere.

Description and analysis of American Jews' speech goes back at least to Thomas (1932), who wrote about New York Jews' phonological "errors," including dentalization of alveolar consonants and overaspiration of /t/, and Hurvits (1934), who wrote about Yiddish loanwords in American English. Sporadic studies can be found in the following decades, focusing on Yiddish influence on English among Jews and non-Jews, including Spitzer 1952, Green 1961, Feinsilver 1962, Davis 1967, and Feinstein 1980. Labov's seminal research on language variation in New York (1966) brought about a new tradition: including the analysis of Jews' speech in studies of ethnic variation in urban areas, including Boston (Laferriere 1979), Grand Rapids, Michigan (Knack 1991), and Montreal (Boberg 2004). In the 1980s, researchers began to include Jewish English in comparative research on Jewish language varieties (Steinmetz 1981; Gold 1985). More recent work has focused on sociolinguistic variation and change (see works cited above).

5.2 Corpora

There is no curated corpus of Jewish English texts, sound files, or videos, but the internet is filled with de facto corpora, awaiting systematic variationist research. For example, researchers might compare the use of Hebrew loanwords (including translation and transliteration) on synagogue, school, and summer camp websites of different denominations; the use of Yiddish grammatical influences and intonation in audio recordings of male- and female-led *shiurim* (religious lectures) on the Orthodox site Kol Halashon (http://www.kolhalashon.com); or the songs of contemporary and historical singer-songwriters on Jewish Rock Radio (http://jewishrockradio.com/) and Oy Songs (http://www.oysongs.com/). This type of analysis will give us a better understanding of language variation among American Jews.

5.3 Issues of general theoretical interest

Studies of Jewish English have contributed to theoretical conceptualizations of ethnic language more broadly as the use of a language with the (optional and selective) incorporation of an "ethnolinguistic repertoire," a constellation of distinctive features associated with the ethnic group (Benor 2010). This approach avoids sticky theoretical problems in analysis of ethnic language variation. For example, when African Americans speak English with only a few distinctive features, researchers no longer need to debate whether they are speaking African American English. And, instead of debating whether there is a Korean-American English, we can say that the children of Korean immigrants sometimes make selective use of a repertoire of Korean influences and other distinctive features, especially in in-group speech, even if they generally speak American English in an unmarked way.

Along the same lines, research on Jewish English has contributed to our understanding of Jewish language varieties as existing along a continuum of Jewish linguistic distinctiveness (Benor 2008). Like Jewish English, the language used by Jews in medieval France or Persia might be structurally quite similar to the language used by their non-Jewish neighbors, but it should still be analyzed comparatively, along with Judeo-Arabic, Judeo-Italian, and other Jewish language varieties.

5.4 Current directions and research desiderata

The most widely researched area of Jewish English is lexicon, especially loanwords and loan translations from Hebrew and Yiddish (e.g., Steinmetz 1981; Gold 1985; Benor 2011). This research has resulted in several dictionaries, including a few oriented toward Yiddish influences (Rosten 1968; Steinmetz 1987; Bluestein 1989), one oriented toward Hebrew influences (Glinert 1992), one focused on Yeshivish (Weiser 1995), and a few with a more general focus (Eisenberg and Scolnic 2001; Steinmetz 2005), including the online user-generated dictionary, the *Jewish English Lexicon*. More research is needed on the lexicon of specific domains, such as the many Hebrew words used in Zionist-oriented camps (a research project I am currently conducting with my colleagues Sharon Avni and Jonathan Krasner) and the professional jargon used by leaders of Jewish nonprofit organizations (e.g., *engagement, continuity, peoplehood,* and *linking the silos*).

Several questions remain in the study of Jewish English lexicon. How do American Jews compare to other contemporary and historical Jewish communities in the use of loanwords from ancestral languages and Liturgical, Biblical, and Rabbinic Hebrew? How has the advent of Modern Hebrew changed which words are used and how they are integrated morphosyntactically and phonologically into English? What have been the mechanisms for influence from Israeli Hebrew, e.g., American Jews' network ties with Israelis, Israeli teachers in American Jewish schools, and the policies of Jewish camps, schools, and other organizations regarding Israeli Hebrew influence? Among Yiddish-origin loanwords (including words that are also Hebrew/Aramaic), which dialects (Northeast, Central, Hasidic, etc.) influence their pronunciation (e.g., *kugel*, rather than *kigel* 'quiche-like food', but *punim* rather than *ponim* 'face'), and how did those pronunciations become crystalized within Jewish English? To what extent do the phonotactics of English influence stress patterns and phonological variation within loanwords?

There has been some research on the language of Jewish American English literature (e.g., Loeffler 2002; Wirth-Nesher 2006; Horn 2006), focusing on multilingualism and Yiddish influences in English; see also Levinson 2014 on the use of English in American Yiddish literature. However, there is a need for more linguistic analysis of literature, especially in light of the recent exponential increase in Orthodox publishing (Stolow 2010; Finkelman 2011). Linguistic research on representations of American Jews in cinema and television would be especially welcome, as phonological and prosodic analysis would be possible.

Researchers have begun to study language use in specific groups of American Jews, with several studies on Orthodox Jews (Weiser 1995; Benor 1998, 2000, 2012a; Sacknowitz 2007) and a few on Reform Jews (Levon 2006; Benor 2013a). One study looked at the language of Jews who become Orthodox (Benor 2012a), and another focused on the opposite transition: Orthodox Jews who become secular (Nove 2013). Research is needed on the language of Jewish groups based on ancestry, including the descendants of Bukharan, Persian, Russian, and Syrian Jewish immigrants. Benor (2016a) shows how African American Jews use elements of Jewish English and of African American English as they present themselves to the public as African American Jews. This study is limited to highly performative contexts, and further research is needed to determine how African American, Latino, and other non-white Jews use language in their everyday lives.

A major research desideratum is a large-scale systematic variationist study of Jews around the United States (as well as in other English-speaking countries), analyzing how different groups of Jews compare to each other and to their non-Jewish neighbors. In such a study it would be preferable to use naturalistic recordings (over interview data), controlling for topic, audience, and setting. This type of systematic research would focus primarily on phonology, especially vocalic variables, but could also include acoustic analysis of intonation patterns, an area of research that is becoming more feasible due to technological and analytic advances (see Burdin 2014). Research in these and other areas will increase our understanding, not just of Jewish English, but also of the fascinating phenomenon of Jewish language varieties.

References

Alvarez-Péreyre, Frank. 2003. Vers une typologie des langues juives? In F. Alvarez-Péreyre & J. Baumgarten (eds.), *Linguistique des langues juives et linguistique générale*, 397–421. Paris: Centre National de la Recherche Scientifique.

Benor, Sarah. 1998. Yavnish: A linguistic study of the Orthodox Jewish community at Columbia University. *'Iggrot ha'Ari: Columbia University Student Journal of Jewish Scholarship* 1/2. 8–50.

Benor, Sarah. 2000. Loan words in the English of Modern Orthodox Jews: Yiddish or Hebrew? In Steve S. Chang, Lily Liaw, & Josef Ruppenhofer (eds.), *Proceedings of the Berkeley linguistic society's 25th annual meeting, 1999*, 287–298. Berkeley: Berkeley Linguistic Society.

Benor, Sarah Bunin. 2008. Towards a new understanding of Jewish language in the 21st century. *Religion Compass* 2(6). 1062–1080.

Benor, Sarah Bunin. 2009. Do American Jews speak a Jewish language? A model of Jewish linguistic distinctiveness. *Jewish Quarterly Review* 99(2). 230–269.

Benor, Sarah Bunin. 2010. Ethnolinguistic repertoire: Shifting the analytic focus in language and ethnicity. *Journal of Sociolinguistics* 14(2). 159–183.

Benor, Sarah Bunin. 2011. *Mensch, bentsh,* and *balagan*: Variation in the American Jewish linguistic repertoire. *Language and Communication* 31(2). 141–154.

Benor, Sarah Bunin. 2012a. *Becoming frum: How newcomers learn the language and culture of Orthodox Judaism*. New Brunswick: Rutgers University Press.

Benor, Sarah Bunin. 2012b. Echoes of Yiddish in the speech of twenty-first-century American Jews. In Lara Rabinovitch, Shiri Goren & Hannah Pressman (eds.), *Choosing Yiddish: Studies on Yiddish literature, culture, and history*, 319–337. Detroit: Wayne State Press.

Benor, Sarah Bunin. 2013a. From *Sabbath* to *Shabbat*: Changing language of Reform sisterhood leaders, 1913–2012. In Carole B. Balin, Dana Herman, Jonathan D. Sarna, & Gary P. Zola (eds.), *Sisterhood: A centennial history of Women of Reform Judaism*, 314–337. Cincinnati: American Jewish Archives.

Benor, Sarah Bunin. 2013b. A linguist's take on the *knaidel/kneydl* controversy. *Jewish Journal*, June 10, 2013. http://www.jewishjournal.com/opinion/article/a_linguists_take_on_the_knaidel_kneydl_controversy. (accessed 10 August 2016).

Benor, Sarah Bunin. 2015. How synagogues became *shuls*: The boomerang effect in Yiddish-influenced English, 1895–2010. In Janne Bondi Johannessen & Joseph Salmons (eds.), *Germanic heritage languages in North America*, 217–233. Amsterdam: John Benjamins.

Benor, Sarah Bunin. 2016a. Black and Jewish: Language and multiple strategies for self-presentation. *American Jewish History* 100(1). 51–71.

Benor, Sarah Bunin. 2016b. Hebrew infusion at American Jewish summer camps. Consortium for Applied Studies in Jewish Education. http://www.casje.org/news/hebrew-infusion-american-jewish-summer-camps. (accessed 10 August 2016).

Benor, Sarah Bunin & Steven M. Cohen. 2011. Talking Jewish: The 'ethnic English' of American Jews. In Eli Lederhendler (ed.), *Ethnicity and beyond: Theories and dilemmas of Jewish group demarcation. Studies in contemporary Jewry*, vol. 25, 62–78. Oxford: Oxford University Press.

Birnbaum, Solomon A. 1979. *Yiddish: A survey and a grammar*. Toronto: University of Toronto Press.

Bluestein, Gene. 1989. *Anglish-Yinglish: Yiddish in American life and literature*. Athens: University of Georgia Press.

Boberg, Charles. 2004. Ethnic patterns in the phonetics of Montreal English. *Journal of Sociolinguistics* 8(4). 538–568.

Burdin, Rachel S. 2014. Variation in list intonation in American Jewish English. In Nick Campbell, Dafydd Gibbon, & Daniel Hirst (eds.), *Proceedings of the 7th international conference on speech prosody, Dublin, Ireland*. http://www.ling.ohio-state.edu//~burdin/speechprosody14.pdf. (accessed 10 August 2016).

Clyne, Michael, Edina Eisikovits & Laura Tollfree. 2002. Ethnolects as in-group varieties. In A. Duszak (ed.), *Us and others: Social identities across languages, discourses, and cultures*, 133–157. Amsterdam: John Benjamins.

Davis, Lawrence M. 1967. The stressed vowels of Yiddish-American English. *Publications of the American Dialect Society* 48. 51–59.
Eisenberg, Joyce & Ellen Scolnic. 2001. *The JPS dictionary of Jewish words*. Philadelphia: Jewish Publication Society.
Fader, Ayala. 2009. *Mitzvah girls: Bringing up the next generation of Hasidic Jews in Brooklyn*. Princeton: Princeton University Press.
Feinsilver, Lillian Mermin. 1962. Yiddish idioms in American English. *American Speech* 37(3). 200–206.
Feinstein, Mark H. 1980. Ethnicity and topicalization in New York City English. *International Journal of the Sociology of Language* 26. 15–24.
Ferguson, Charles A. 1959. Diglossia. *Word* 15. 325–340.
Finkelman, Yoel. 2011. *Strictly kosher reading: Popular literature and condition of contemporary Orthodoxy*. Boston: Academic Studies Press.
Fishman, Joshua A. 1985. The sociology of Jewish languages from a general sociolinguistic point of view. In Joshua A. Fishman (ed.), *Readings in the sociology of Jewish languages*, 3–21. Leiden: Brill.
Glinert, Lewis. 1992. *The joys of Hebrew*. New York: Oxford University Press.
Glinert, Lewis. 1993. Language as quasilect: Hebrew in contemporary Anglo-Jewry. In Lewis Glinert (ed.), *Hebrew in Ashkenaz: A language in exile*, 249–264. New York: Oxford University Press.
Gold, David. 1985. Jewish English. In Joshua A. Fishman (ed.), *Readings in the sociology of Jewish languages*, 280–298. Leiden: Brill.
Goldstein, Eric L. 2008. *The price of whiteness: Jews, race, and American identity*. Princeton: Princeton University Press.
Green, Eugene. 1961. *Yiddish and English in Detroit: A survey and analysis of reciprocal influences in bilinguals' pronunciation, grammar, and vocabulary*. Ann Arbor: University of Michigan.
Heilman, Samuel. 1983. *The people of the book: Drama, fellowship, and religion*. Chicago: University of Chicago Press.
Horn, Dara. 2006. The future of Yiddish – in English: Field notes from the New Ashkenaz. *Jewish Quarterly Review* 96(4). 471–480.
Hurvits, M. 1934. Yiddish expressions in American English. *YIVO-Bleter* 6. 187–188 (Yiddish).
Isaacs, Miriam. 1999. Haredi, haymish and frim: Yiddish vitality and language choice in a transnational, multilingual community. *International Journal of the Sociology of Language* 138. 9–30.
Jewish English Lexicon. 2012–present. http://www.jewish-languages.org/jewish-english-lexicon/. Sarah Bunin Benor, creator and editor. (accessed 10 August 2016).
Knack, Rebecca. 1991. Ethnic boundaries in linguistic variation. In Penelope Eckert (ed.), *New Ways of Analyzing Sound Change*, 251–272. San Diego: Academic Press.
Labov, William. 1966. *The social stratification of English in New York City*. Washington, DC: Center for Applied Linguistics.
Laferriere, Martha. 1979. Ethnicity in phonological variation and change. *Language* 55. 603–17.
Levinson, Julian. 2014. *Spatsir durkh* "Lovers' Lane": The uses of English in American Yiddish literature. In Shlomo Berger (ed.), *Margins and centers in Yiddish culture and language* [*Amsterdam Yiddish symposium 9*]. Amsterdam: Menasseh ben Israel Institute.
Levon, Erez. 2006. Mosaic identity and style: Phonological variation among Reform American Jews. *Journal of Sociolinguistics* 10. 185–205.

Loeffler, James. 2002. Neither the King's English nor the rebbetzin's Yiddish: Yinglish literature in America. In Marc Shell (ed.), *American Babel: Literatures of the United States from Abnaki to Zuni*, 133–162. Cambridge: Harvard University Press.

Matisoff, James A. 2000 [1979]. *Blessings, curses, hopes, and fears: Psycho-ostensive expressions in Yiddish*, 2nd edn. Stanford: Stanford University Press.

Nove, Chaya R. 2013. Ambivalence and nostalgia: Stance and identity in the "Off The Derech" community. Paper presented at American Association for Applied Linguistics (AAAL), Dallas.

Paper, Herbert H. 1978. *Jewish languages: Themes and variations; Proceedings of regional conferences sponsored by the Association for Jewish Studies held at the University of Michigan and New York University in March-April 1975*. Cambridge, MA: Association for Jewish Studies.

Rabin, Chaim, Joshua Blau & Haim Blanc. 1979. Haleshonot hayehudiot: Hameshutaf, hameyuhad vehabe'ayati [The Jewish languages: The shared, the unique, and the problematic]. *Pe'amim* 1. 40–66.

Rosten, Leo. 1968. *The Joys of Yiddish*. New York: McGraw-Hill.

Sacknowitz, Aliza. 2007. *Linguistic means of Orthodox Jewish identity construction: Phonological features, lexical features, and the situated discourse*. Washington, D.C.: Georgetown University PhD dissertation.

Schiffrin, Deborah. 1984. Jewish argument as sociability. *Language in Society* 13(3). 311–335.

Spitzer, Leo. 1952. Confusion schmooshun. *Journal of English and Germanic Philology* 51. 226–227.

Stein, Ariel. 2015. Bilingual outreach. *Becoming Frum* Blog, May 13, 2015. http://becomingfrum.weebly.com/discussion-forum/bilingual-outreach. (accessed 11 August 2016).

Steinmetz, Sol. 1981. Jewish English in the United States. *American Speech* 56(1). 3–16.

Steinmetz, Sol. 1987. *Yiddish and English: A century of Yiddish in America*. Tuscaloosa: University of Alabama Press.

Steinmetz, Sol. 2005. *Dictionary of Jewish usage: A guide to the use of Jewish terms*. Lanham: Rowman and Littlefield.

Stolow, Jeremy. 2010. *Orthodox by design: Judaism, print politics, and the ArtScroll revolution*. Berkeley: University of California Press.

Tannen, Deborah. 1981. New York Jewish conversational style. *International Journal of the Sociology of Language* 30. 133–149.

Thomas, C.K. 1932. Jewish dialect and New York dialect. *American Speech* 7(5). 321–326.

Weinreich, Uriel. 1956. Notes on the Yiddish rise-fall intonation contour. In Morris Halle (eds.), *For Roman Jakobson*, 633–643. The Hague: Mouton.

Weinreich, Max. 2008 [1973]. *History of the Yiddish Language*, 2 vols. Edited by Paul Glasser. Translated by Shlomo Noble and Joshua A. Fishman. New Haven: Yale University Press.

Weiser, Chaim. 1995. *Frumspeak: The first dictionary of Yeshivish*. Northvale: Jason Aronson.

Wexler, Paul. 1981. Jewish interlinguistics: Facts and conceptual framework. *Language* 57(1): 99–145.

Wirth-Nesher, Hana. 2006. *Call it English: The languages of Jewish American literature*. Princeton: Princeton University Press.

Patric Joshua Klagsbrun Lebenswerd
Jewish Swedish in Sweden

1 Introduction

This chapter features an introduction to a repertoire of linguistic resources that – when used – distinguish the speech of Swedish Jews vis-à-vis the speech of neighboring non-Jews.[1] Analyzing the speech of Jews from the perspective of a *distinctly Jewish linguistic repertoire* – as opposed to more traditional 'ethnolectal' views – is in line with recent works on Jewish language use (Benor 2008; 2009; Dean-Olmsted 2011; Kiwitt 2014; Klagsbrun Lebenswerd 2015; Verschik 2010), building on the notion of *ethnolinguistic repertoires* (Benor 2010), defined as "a fluid set of linguistic resources that members of an ethnic group may use variably as they index their ethnic identities."

While there are several ways in which Swedish Jews can distinguish themselves linguistically from non-Jews (e.g., by speaking Yiddish, Modern Hebrew, etc.), this chapter will be concerned with *Jewish Swedish*, defined here as the use of linguistic features from the *distinctly Jewish linguistic repertoire* combined with (from a Jewish perspective "unmarked") linguistic features used in the speech of neighboring Swedish non-Jews.

While acknowledging that it is far from unproblematic to treat Swedish as a unified linguistic system, I will, throughout this text, use terms such as '(Standard) Swedish' or 'local varieties of Swedish', etc., when referring to the non-Jewish (mainstream) correlate(s) of Jewish Swedish; these terms are all meant to be understood as the registers of Swedish generally used in the linguistic practices of neighboring groups of Swedish non-Jews, of similar social, economic, and political status as the group of Jews being studied. While this specific issue merits a longer discussion, it is beyond the scope of this chapter.

The distinctive linguistic features in the ethnolinguistic repertoire of Swedish Jews mainly (but not exclusively) derive from Yiddish and (textual and Israeli) Hebrew. These features do not by any means constitute a bounded system, over which all Swedish Jews have identical competence – quite the opposite. There is a great deal of variation regarding which, and how many, repertoire features

---

[1] Data presented in this chapter come from research I am currently conducting for my doctoral dissertation on the linguistic practices of Swedish Jews. My research methods include observations, interviews, online surveys (Lebenswerd 2013), and discourse analysis of community periodicals, inter alia; additionally, a large number of contemporary and historical documents have been collected and analyzed. Results from this research will appear in future publications.

individual Jewish speakers make use of, depending on a whole range of variables, including: interlocutor, context, genre, language ideologies, religious engagement, gender, age (Lebenswerd 2013), etc. Moreover, there is currently no widely used or conventionalized name that Swedish Jews use to refer to their way of speaking; however, for the sake of brevity, as well as for facilitating terminological variation, the ethnolinguistic repertoire of Swedish Jews will henceforth variably be referred to as *Jewish Swedish* or the *repertoire*, etc.

2 Historical background

2.1 Speaker community: Settlement, documentation

Jewish immigration to Sweden can roughly be divided into four historical periods, loosely based on different waves of immigration: 1) the first wave from Central Europe (primarily Northern Germany) between 1775 and the 1860s; 2) the second wave from Eastern Europe between 1860–1917, as well as 3) during and immediately after the Holocaust, and 4) smaller waves of immigration from Hungary (1950s), Poland (1968–1972), and the Soviet Union (late 1980s–early 1990s) (Carlsson 2011).

The origins of the Jewish community of Sweden go back to 1775, the year Aaron Isaac, the first Jew to be granted the right to settle in Sweden without prior conversion to Protestantism, was allowed to establish a *minyan* in Stockholm (Tossavainen 2009). From the beginnings of the Jewish settlement in Sweden in the 1780s until the end of the 1870s, the overwhelming majority of Swedish Jewry was of western Ashkenazi descent, mainly hailing from northern Germany (Mecklenburg in particular), Holland, and Denmark (Carlsson 2011).

During their initial period of settlement (1782–1838), Jews in Sweden were highly restricted socially, economically, and politically, under the so-called *Regulation of the Jews* (*Judereglementet*), according to which Jews were banned from most trades and crafts, only permitted to reside in four cities (Stockholm, Gothenburg, Norrköping, and Karlskrona), and not allowed to marry non-Jews. Moreover, Jews were not only denied access to public schools; they were, additionally, not allowed to establish their own Jewish schools.

In 1838, the *Regulation of the Jews* was abolished, which effectively removed most, but not all, of the discriminating restrictions: Jewish residency was still legally restricted to the four above-mentioned cities (Carlsson 2011). During the following decades, Sweden's tiny Jewish community, numbering approximately 935 individuals in 1855 (Zitomersky 1988), gradually began to experience a true process of emancipation, which was completed by 1870. This process of emancipation occurred concurrently with the establishment of the Reform movement, under which the Jewish community went from being traditionally orthodox to becoming more liberal and assimilated (Carlsson 2011).

Around the same time, in the late 1860s, a second wave of Jewish immigrants started to arrive in Sweden. Up until this point, Jewish immigration to Sweden had been relatively homogenous religiously, culturally, and linguistically. In contrast to the German origins of the first Jewish immigrants, these Jews came overwhelmingly from Eastern Europe, particularly from the Russian Empire. Between the years 1860 and 1920, the Jewish population of Sweden rose from a mere 1,155 to 6,469 (Zitomersky 1988) – a relatively dramatic growth that can be attributed almost entirely to the arrival of Eastern European immigrants. The religious traditionalism and orthodoxy of the new immigrants – who eventually would add a particularly Eastern European character to much of Swedish Jewish identity and culture – stood in stark contrast to the more reformed and liberal orientations of the older, more integrated Jewish community, which had become largely assimilated by then.

By the turn of the century, Swedish Jewry could roughly be divided into two socially, religiously, and ethnically distinct groups: one older group, constituted by more or less assimilated families (mainly) descending from German immigrants who arrived in Sweden between the end of the 18th and the beginning of the 19th century, and the other, newer group, consisting, for the most part, of poor Jews of Eastern European origin, who began to arrive in Sweden in large numbers around the late 1860s. Contact between these two groups was, at most, sporadic; the former group, which had successfully managed to integrate into Swedish society, not only regarded the latter group as foreign, with their backward and pre-modern culture and lifestyle, but they also saw them as a potential threat to their newly acquired acceptance into Swedish society.

During the interbellum period, Jewish immigration to Sweden decreased significantly due to the new stricter immigration policies of 1917. The Nazi party's rise to power in 1933 brought an enormous outbreak of anti-Semitism in Germany, causing German Jews to flee the country. Approximately 3,000 Jewish refugees (the overwhelming majority of which were German) had reached Sweden by July 1939, i.e., two months before WWII broke out (Carlsson 2011: 45). Sweden was never occupied by Nazi Germany, nor were its Jews ever deported during the war. Thousands of Jewish Holocaust survivors, mainly from Poland, Czechoslovakia, Hungary, and Romania (Carlsson 2011: 50), arrived in Sweden during, as well as after, the war. With their arrival, Sweden's Jewish population grew from an estimated 8,000 people in 1940 to approximately 13,000 in 1950 (Zitomersky 1988) – a demographic development quite different from that in the rest of Jewish Europe. Other significant waves of Jewish immigration to Sweden include: 1) 600

Hungarian Jews in 1956, 2) an estimated 2,500 Polish Jews between 1968 and 1972, and 3) approximately 1,000 Soviet Jews in the late 1980s and early 1990s.

The current Jewish population of Sweden is estimated at 15,000–19,000, constituting about 0.2% of Sweden's 9 million people, out of which at least two thirds are said to live in the capital, Stockholm (Dencik 2003: 79; Tossavainen 2009: 1087).

2.2 Phases in historical development

Rather than analyzing historical differences in the speech of Swedish Jews from a linear evolution-like perspective, it makes more sense – given our approach to Jewish Swedish in terms of the relative linguistic distinctiveness of Swedish Jews vis-à-vis the neighboring non-Jews – to instead address how, and to what extent, the linguistic practices of Swedish Jews historically have been distinct from practices among local non-Jews. To complete the picture, I will, additionally, briefly mention a few socio-historical events that may have contributed to some of these changes.

Key to Benor's theoretical construct of distinctively Jewish linguistic repertoires is the concept of speakers "having access" to a set of linguistic features that distinguish Jewish speech (and writing) from that of non-Jews (2008: 1068). Many of the salient historical differences in the speech of Swedish Jews can be attributed to exactly that – i.e., speakers having access to different distinctive features in different historical periods; moreover, shifting ideologies towards linguistic distinctness in different historical periods may also have contributed to historical differences regarding use of distinctive features.

While the vernacular of most Jewish immigrants to Sweden up to the mid-19th century seems to have been varieties of Western Yiddish and/or ("Jewish") German (see Lowenstein's 2002 discussion on shifts from Western Yiddish towards Standard German), it is currently not entirely clear at what point Swedish became an important part of the communicative repertoire of Sweden's Jews. In 1839, a new Jewish ordinance promulgated that the community's accounting had to be kept in Swedish (Valentin 1924: 477). Up until this point, the Jewish communities had kept all community records in Western Yiddish, written in Hebrew orthography (Valentin 1924: 487). Although the requirement to use Swedish only concerned the language used for accounting, the community board decided to use Swedish in all written documents; according to meeting minutes from 1839, the board even decided to avoid using Hebrew expressions whenever possible (Valentin 1924: 487). The shift to Swedish was, more than anything else, a way for Swedish Jews to demonstrate that they, too, were Swedes and not foreigners. It seems, however, that this shift occurred at a time when Swedish was already known and used by most members of the community (Valentin 1924: 487).

Our current knowledge about the linguistic practices in those days is relatively limited. Most external sources mentioning the speech of Jews are not reliable. They mainly belong to an anti-Semitic genre (found in books, pamphlets, cartoons, posters, plays, and other printed works) common in Swedish literature and press from the early 19th century and up until the 1930s (Johannesson 1988; Andersson 2000: 113). In these depictions, Jews were often ridiculed for their speech, characterized as a broken, German-sounding Swedish, which was acquired orthographically by variously substituting: 1) voiced consonants with voiceless consonants (e.g., *jak* for *jag* 'I'); 2) front rounded vowels with unrounded vowels (e.g., *mikke* for *mycket* 'a lot, very'); 3) pre-consonantal ‹s› with ‹sch› (e.g., *schvenska* for *svenska* 'Swedish'). While this mock-register was frequently used to identify characters as Jewish, its ability to do so probably had very little to do with the readers' ability to actually recognize a "real" Jewish accent based on their own encounters with Jews. In fact, at the time when this kind of literature began to emerge, less than 900 Jews lived in the entire country; very few Swedes would actually have had any first-hand experience interacting with Jews.

It is quite unlikely that these depictions of Jewish speech actually tell us anything useful about how Jews spoke in those times. More than anything else, the purpose of using this kind of language was never to accurately reproduce how Jews actually spoke, but to portray Jews as foreigners. Moreover, unlike the genre's German counterparts (cf. Gilman (1986: 138) and Grossman (2000: 137) for similar use of *Mauscheln* in Germany), the Jewish mock-register used in Sweden never included any actual "Jewish" words, most likely because these would have been unknown to most writers as well as readers. Had they done so, they might have been useful.

While there is very little evidence about how Jews in Sweden spoke in the 19th century, lexical analyses of attested documents (including prayer books, letters, community pamphlets, agendas, play scripts, memoirs, etc.), written by community members during the second half of the 19th century, reveal frequent use of features derived from the pre-migration vernacular(s) – Western Yiddish and/or (Jewish) German (Jacobowsky 1955, 1967; Josephson 2006); we find the use of typical "Jewish" German dialectalisms, e.g., *schein*[2] 'beautiful', *bes* 'angry', *jinglinges* 'youngsters', *waibele* 'wife (diminutive)', *schul* 'synagogue', *nos* 'nose' (cf. Standard German *schöne, böse, jüngling, weib(chen?), schule* ('school'), *nase*); Hebraisms: *chein* 'grace, charm', *bocher* 'young man', *jascher kauach* 'well done', *kol* 'Jewish community', *beis hakneses* 'synagogue', *arbekanfes* 'undergarment worn by Orthodox Jews', *mauhl* 'person performing the circumcision', *orel* 'non-Jew', *schammes* 'synagogue usher', *mechulle* 'bankrupt', *naches*

---

2 The spellings used are original.

'pleasure', *schmus* 'chat', *tinef* 'filth', *umchein* 'unpleasantness'. Other items are well known Western Yiddishisms (generally not used in Eastern Yiddish) (Weinreich 2008: 726): *ohrn* 'to pray', *schalet* 'a Sabbath dish', *nebbisch* 'poor thing' (cf. Eastern Yiddish *nebekh* with final [χ]), *schnodern* 'to pledge money when being called to the Torah' (Herzog & Baviskar 2000: 138), *pleite* 'bankruptcy', *zeider* 'Passover dinner' (see Herzog & Baviskar 2000: 100 on initial [s] > [ts] in regional Western Yiddish), and *berches* 'Sabbath loaves'.

Berches happens to be one of a few Yiddish items that have come into the speech of Swedish non-Jews – known as *bergis* in Stockholm and Norrkoping and as *barkis* in Gothenburg (Maler 1979). The differences in pronunciation between *bergis* and *barkis* actually reflect the regional variation of this etymon within the former Western Yiddish speech territory, i.e., the quality of the first vowel, *b[e/a]r-ches*, and the first fricative's place of articulation, *ber[x/ç/š/j]es*. All sources agree that [e] variants dominate in the western parts (west of Elbe), while [a] is predominantly found in the east (Herzog & Baviskar 2000: 356; Beranek 1965: 150; Lowenstein 1969: 19–20). Based on the regional variation of this word in Sweden, it seems reasonable to assume that different varieties of Western Yiddish may have been spoken in these regions, as well.

Attested items of particular interest are those that have been integrated into Swedish verbal morphology; e.g., *schattra* 'to marry off someone' (< *shadkhnen* [same gloss]),[3] *misa sig* 'to make oneself unattractive, ugly' (< *fermiesen zikh* [same gloss]), *krittla* 'to criticize, be difficult' (< *kritlich* 'critical'), and *battla chomez* 'ceremonial search for leavened dough performed the day before Passover' (< *khomets batlen* [same gloss]), in which the latter is also a Western Yiddishism (Herzog & Baviskar 2000: 136; Lowenstein 1969: 21).

Despite the widespread assimilation of the original community of German descent, various findings suggest that the pre-migration vernacular(s) continued to be used, in varying degrees, for several generations – up until the beginning of the 20th century – among community members descended from the initial wave of immigrants (Josephson 2006).

The linguistic practices of the Jewish Eastern European immigrants that started arriving in Sweden during the second half of the 19th century is currently a poorly explored topic. We know that (Eastern) Yiddish was the immigrants' primary vernacular, used both among themselves, as well as with their Swedish-born children (Boyd & Gadelli 1997: 480). Based on the places of origins of most immigrants (overwhelmingly from Suwalki, Kovno, Lomza, Vilna, Grodno, Minsk, Vitebsk etc. [Carlsson 2011: 34]), it is also fairly certain that they spoke various Northeastern

---

[3] The spelling reveals a confusion of /χ/ and /r/, common in many Yiddish dialects.

dialects of Yiddish (Jacobs 2005: 65). It is difficult to say anything about their use of Swedish. However, knowing Swedish seems to have been more common among men and, according to some accounts, many older immigrants never properly learned to speak Swedish (Boyd & Gadelli 1997: 480). Their children, however, all of whom attended Swedish public schools, were Yiddish-Swedish bilinguals; it was common that these children spoke Yiddish at home with their parents and Swedish to each other (Boyd & Gadelli 1997: 480). Several written documents from the first half of the 20th century reveal that Yiddish-derived features constituted a substantial part of their spoken repertoire, which can be exemplified by the text below, featuring an excerpt from a poem, composed in Lund in 1932 by a Swedish-born daughter of Russian immigrants, read at the birthday celebration of one of the city's most revered Jewish teachers (Yiddish-derived features in italics).

> *Swedish original*
> "Jag med dessa rader ville hylla/ "*A lerer*" som i dag de 60 fylla.
> Säkert mången minns den stund/då vår *schåret*[4] kom till Lund.
> Ingen får som han väl jäkta/för att hinna både *davna* och *schäkta*.
> Knappt han hinner vänta *auf a vareme latke*/
> ty tiden är lång, då han bör vara *in jatke*.
> När allting gått *kaseder*/han rusar ner i *cheder*
> för att en stund på dagen/lära barnen den judiska lagen.
> *Schabbes* på den välförtjänta vilodagen/
> då går *Reb schåret* till *schol* med näsduken kring magen"
> (Svenson 1995:93–4).
>
> *Free translation into English*
> With these lines, I wish to celebrate/"*A lerer*" ('a teacher') turning 60 today. Many people probably remember/when our *schåret* ('ritual slaughterer') came to Lund. No one has to rush like he does/ in order to both have time to *davna* ('to pray') and *schäkta* ('to slaughter kosher').
> He barley has time to wait *auf a vareme latke* ('for a hot potato pancake')/ because he is needed *in jatke* ('at the meat shop').
> When everything is *kaseder* ('in order')/he rushes down to *cheder* ('traditional religious school'), for a while every day/to teach children the Jewish law. *Schabbes* ('Sabbath'), the well-deserved day of rest/
> *Reb schåret* ('Mr. slaughterer') goes to *schol* ('synagogue') with a handkerchief around his waist"

In the late 1930s, one specifically conspicuous trend that becomes apparent is the increased use of words and expressions from Modern (Israeli) Hebrew, as well as their pronunciation. Initially, it was primarily a trend among people engaged in

---

4 The spelling of *schåret* (often spelled *shochet* elsewhere) is original and demonstrates a tendency among some Jews in the southern regions of Sweden (Scania) to confuse [χ] and [ʁ] (cf. footnote 3).

Zionistic organizations, evident from words such as: *chalutzim* 'Zionist pioneers', *hachschara* 'preparatory training to become a pioneer in Israel', *galut* 'Jewish diaspora', *chawerim* 'Zionist comrades', *Erez Jisrael* 'the land of Israel'; this trend would eventually spread throughout the entire community.

Most of the approximately 5000 Holocaust survivors that arrived in Sweden during the 1940s were Yiddish speakers (Boyd & Gadelli 1999: 314), and it was, apparently, common that their Swedish born children also grew up speaking Yiddish at home (Boyd & Gadelli 1999: 314). However, unlike both their parents and most of the older Swedish Jews, Jewish children who grew up in Sweden in the 1950s and later were taught Modern (Israeli) Hebrew, which eventually came to replace the traditional Ashkenazi pronunciation that had been used in the liturgy earlier. The influences of Modern (Israeli) Hebrew on the speech of Swedish Jews have, ever since the 1950s, been constantly increasing.

An apt question is: How much did the linguistic practices of 19th century Swedish Jews have in common with the practices of present day Jews? As mentioned above, Swedish Jews have had access to different sets of distinctive linguistic features in different historical periods: In the 19th century, Western Yiddish, varieties of German and western Ashkenazic Hebrew constituted the most important sources of linguistic distinctness; around the turn of the century, Eastern Yiddish and Eastern Ashkenazic Hebrew became the dominant sources for such, which around the 1950s was complemented (and often even replaced) by Modern (Israeli) Hebrew.

Traces of the speech used by previous generations of Swedish Jews can still be found among younger speakers today. Most of the distinctive features attested in the 19th century have not remained, though there are exceptions. For instance, some of the features that currently are still in use (and further discussed in section 3.2) were already used in the 19th century, e.g., *schabbis går in* 'the Sabbath (lit. goes in) begins', *gå i schul* 'go (lit. in) to synagogue', *hålla schabbes* '(lit. hold) keep Sabbath', *gå i mikve* 'to immerse oneself in (lit. go in) ritual bath', *lägga tfillin* 'to put on (lit. lay) phylacteries', as well as the pronunciation of *kosher* (see 3). Although *bergis/barkis* (<*berches*) is still a common kind of bread in Sweden, its Jewish (Yiddish) origins are barely known today, which is also true among Jews: The term was entirely replaced by the Eastern Yiddish term *challe* 'Sabbath loaf'.

While the majority of the Eastern European immigrants that arrived in Sweden at the turn of the century spoke Northeastern dialects of Yiddish, most Yiddish speakers that arrived after the Holocaust came from areas (Poland, Czechoslovakia, Hungary, and Romania [Carlsson 2011: 50]) where Central Yiddish dialects were spoken (Jacobs 2005: 65). These two dialect groups differ significantly in their pronunciations, which is also reflected in the general pronunciations of

Yiddish origin words that are currently used by Swedish Jews; Northeastern Yiddish pronunciation, e.g., *peisachdike* 'fit for Passover', *treif* 'non-kosher', *kneidelach* 'matzo balls', *peyes* 'sidelocks', *leina* 'to read from the Torah', *schul* 'synagogue', *chutzpe* 'audacity', *pupik* 'bellybutton', *chomets* 'leavened food', *beheime* 'moron', etc.; Central Yiddish pronunciations, e.g., *shluffa* 'to sleep', *haymish* 'homey, familiar', *shtippa* 'to have sex', *flayshik* 'meat (food)', *shteytel* 'traditional Jewish village.' The pronunciation of many food terms may differ from family to family, e.g., *bulke/bilke* 'bread roll,' *kugel/kigel* 'a kind of cooked dish', *chrein/chrayn* 'horseradish', *tsholent/tshulent* 'Sabbath dish', etc.

2.3 Sociolinguistic description

According to Lebenswerd (2013), there are several social factors influencing individual speakers' use of distinctive features, among which age, gender, number of Jewish friends, and religious affiliation (particularly Orthodox) were the most important. Some individuals use hundreds of distinctive features in their speech, while others use very few. For instance, speakers regularly attending Modern Orthodox services are significantly more likely to both know and use more distinctive features than speakers who either prefer some other Jewish denomination (Conservative or Reform), or who usually do not attend services.

Furthermore, the use and choice of distinctive features additionally depend on the interlocutor; speakers tend to restrict the use of such features to in-group speech. The sentences below have been constructed (based on how people responded in Lebenswerd's (2013) survey) to illustrate how variation determined by interlocutor can play out in the following three speech contexts[5]: 1) *when talking to Jews you know*, 2) *when talking to Jews you don't know*, and 3) *when talking to non-Jews*.

1) When talking to Jews you know: Det var en *bris i shul* förra *shabbes*, och bland alla *jidden* fanns även några *gojim*.
   Translation: There was a *bris* ('circumcision ceremony') *i shul* ('in the synagogue') last *shabbes* ('Sabbath'), and among all the *jidden* ('Jews') present, there were also a few *gojim* ('gentiles').

---

[5] There are, of course, several other factors that influence word choice. For instance, Orthodox speakers may use more distinctive features when talking to other Orthodox speakers, even if they do not know each other, than they would when talking to close, non-Orthodox friends. In a similar vein, secular Jews, who usually use very few features associated with religion, may increase the use of such items when talking to a rabbi.

2) *When talking to Jews you don't know:* Det var *brit mila* i synagogan förra *shabbat*, och bland alla judar fanns det även några icke-judar.
   Translation: There was a *brit mila* ('circumcision ceremony') in *synagogan* ('the synagogue') last *shabbat* ('Sabbath'), and among all the Jews present, there were also a few gentiles.
3) *When talking to non-Jews:* Det var en omskärelse i synagogan förra *shabbat*, och bland alla judar fanns även en och annan icke-jude.
   Translation: There was a circumcision ceremony in the synagogue last *shabbat* ('Sabbath'), and among all the Jews present, there were also a few gentiles.

These sentences illustrate three things: 1) Yiddish origin features (*bris* 'circumcision ceremony', *shul* 'synagogue', *jidden* 'Jews') are mainly used when speaking to Jews that the speaker is familiar with; 2) Yiddish features are likely to be replaced by Modern Hebrew (*brit mila* 'circumcision ceremony', *shabbat* 'Sabbath') or Swedish counterparts (*judar* 'Jews', *icke-judar* 'gentiles') when speaking to unfamiliar Jews, and 3) in out-group contexts, if distinctive features are used at all, these are from Modern Hebrew (*shabbat* 'Sabbath') (cf. discussion in 3.1 about the social meanings of Yiddish and Modern Hebrew).

3 Structural information

The overwhelming majority of Swedish Jews were born in Sweden and speak local varieties of Swedish that, presumably, are more or less indistinguishable from the speech of neighboring non-Jews – though this has never been systematically studied. As mentioned above and also further elaborated below, Jews may, however, use several distinctive features in their speech (lexical, phonological, morpho-syntactic, semantic, pragmatic, discursive, etc.) that generally are not used in the speech of Swedish non-Jews. Moreover, most Jewish speakers tend to restrict the (intentional) use of such features to in-group communication (see 2.3).

Even when some 'Jewish' features are unintentionally used, speakers perceiving these as 'foreign' would be unlikely to identify them as markers of Jewish speech (cf. Verschik 2010: 295); however, the opposite is also possible, as there are certain features which many Jews identify as shibboleths or markers of non-Jewish (out-group) speech (Lebenswerd 2013). For instance, Jewish speakers tend to pronounce the Standard Swedish words *hebreiska* 'Hebrew (language)' and *kosher* 'kosher' differently than non-Jewish speakers. While most non-Jews pronounce these as [heˈbreːɪska] (four syllables) and [ˈkɔʃːər] (closed, short initial vowel), Jewish speakers tend to prefer [heˈbrɛjska] (three syllables) and [ˈkoːʃər] (open, long initial vowel). The general Jewish pronunciation of *kosher* [ˈkoːʃər] most likely derived from the Western Yiddish pronunciation used by the German-origin founders of Sweden's first Jewish community, as evident from its long initial [oː] vowel, which is not found in any of the Eastern Yiddish dialects nor in Israeli Hebrew (cf. Gold 1985: 283 for a similar discussion about the pronunciation of *kosher* in American Jewish English).

Regarding phonological features: Most varieties of Swedish lack a phonemic /x/; the segment [x] is generally perceived as a variant of /ɧ/ (Riad 2014: 58). Many Jewish speakers, however, maintain a phonemic (and phonetic) distinction between [ɧ] and [x], creating minimal and near-minimal pairs such as *skett* [ɧɛtː] 'happened' and *chet* [xɛtː] 'Hebrew letter ח', and *schack* [ɧakː] 'chess' and *chag* [xagː] '(Jewish) holiday'. Similarly, though [z] is generally not found in most Swedish varieties (often assimilated to [s]), many Jewish speakers, particularly people with (some) proficiency in Yiddish and/or Hebrew, use [z] in words like *mezuza* 'mezuzah', *mazel tov* 'congratulations', and *chazer* 'pork, pig'. It should be mentioned, however, that there are many Jewish speakers who only sporadically make the distinction between [z] and [s], and probably many who never do so.

Phonotactically, Jewish Swedish, additionally, features a number of consonant sequences – frequently occurring in Yiddish and Hebrew – which generally do not occur in most varieties of Swedish. For instance, word initial /ʃ/+consonant sequences are quite unusual in most Swedish varieties; words such as *Schweitz* 'Switzerland' and *schnitzel* often undergo some sort of phonological adjustment, e.g., metathesis: [ʃvɛjːts] → [svɛjːtʃ] and [ʃnitːsɛl] → [snitːʃɛl] (Riad 2014: 285). In Jewish Swedish, these kinds of sequences occur frequently, e.g., *shvitsa* 'to sweat', *shnorrer* 'freeloader', *shluffa* 'to nap, sleep', etc. Other examples of initial consonant sequences in Jewish Swedish that generally do not occur in most varieties of Swedish include: [ts] *tsadik* 'righteous person', [tʃ] *tshulent* 'Sabbath dish', [tx] *tchina* 'sesame paste', [xr] *chrein* 'horseradish', [zm] *zmires* 'Sabbath songs'.

Most Swedish Jews reside in Sweden's three largest cities, Stockholm, Gothenburg and Malmö. Though use of Jewish Swedish has been documented in all of these places (and elsewhere), very little can currently be said regarding regional variation in the use of distinctive features[6]; however, Jews in the Skåne province of southern Sweden (Malmö etc.) generally pronounce *kosher* [ˈkɔʃːəʁ], i.e., as in the Northeastern Yiddish dialects spoken by this community's founders.

---

6 See Muir (2009) regarding the language of Finland's Swedish-speaking Jewish minority.

3.1 Lexicon: Hebrew and Aramaic elements

Features of (ultimately) Hebraic and Aramaic origin are abundant in Jewish Swedish; lexical items such as *shkojach* 'well done, congratulations', *machane* 'camp', *davke* 'just because', *shikker* 'drunk', *kaddish* 'a prayer', *madrich* 'guide, counselor', *ketuba* 'marriage contract', *jontev* 'Jewish holiday', *eretz* 'land (of Israel)', *shuk* 'market', *tuches* 'buttocks', etc., constitute an integral part of the present-day repertoire, most of which derive from Yiddish and/or Israeli Hebrew.

Up until the 1950s, Yiddish was the primary source for Hebraic features. In addition to the many lexical influences from Yiddish, Jewish Swedish exhibits numerous calques of Yiddish strategies for integrating Hebrew-origin items, e.g., *kashra* 'to render kosher' (cf. *kashern*), *göra en bracha* 'to bless (lit. make a blessing)' (cf. *makhn a brokhe*), *gojish* 'non-Jewish' (cf. *goyish*), *lägga tefillin* 'to put on (literally lay) phylacteries' (cf. *leygn tfiln*), etc., (see also section 3.2).

Ever since the founding of the State of Israel in 1948, (Modern) Israeli Hebrew has played an ever-increasing part in the life of Swedish Jews, which, if anything, can be noticed from its influences on their speech. In addition to introducing a new pronunciation norm,[7] Israeli Hebrew has enriched the repertoire with numerous Hebrew 'neologisms', e.g., *hadracha* 'leadership', *tiyul* 'fieldtrip', *shilshul* 'diarrhea', *pigua* 'terrorist attack', *dati* 'religious', *nesia tova* 'bon voyage', etc., as well as providing alternatives to already existing Yiddish counterparts, e.g., *kippa* 'skullcap', *chanukia* 'Chanukah candelabra', *sevivon* 'spinning top', *chag sameach* 'happy holiday', *oznei haman* 'a Purim pastry', *birkat hamazon* 'grace after meals', and *ad mea v'esrim* 'may you live to be 120 (lit. until 120)', respectively corresponding to the Yiddish terms: *jarmulke* (or *kapl*), *menora*, *dreidel*, *gut jontev*, *homentashen*, *benshen*, and *biz hundert un tsvantsik*.

The introduction of Israeli Hebrew has also had sociolinguistic implications. Choices between using features derived from Yiddish or Israeli Hebrew have acquired social meanings; while use of Yiddish items like *shabbes* 'Sabbath', *talles* 'prayer shawl', and *bris* 'circumcision ceremony' tend to be used mainly in informal speech in familiar contexts, use of their Israeli Hebrew counterparts, *shabbat*, *tallit*, and *brit mila*, not only appear to be regarded as more context neutral (Lebenswerd 2013); these forms are also preferred in formal use (written and oral). The sociolinguistic relationship between Yiddish and Israeli Hebrew is currently not fully

---

[7] In the Jewish communities of Sweden, the pronunciation of Hebrew used in the liturgy and the teaching of language was, until the 1950s, based on the Ashkenazi traditions of Central and Eastern Europe. During the second half of the 20th century, the entire community gradually shifted to the pronunciations used in Israel.

understood; however, it probably reflects a history of competing values that people have assigned to them. Future research will, hopefully, round out the picture.

The repertoire, additionally, contains a number of morphological and phonological features (see 3), derived from Yiddish and/or Israeli Hebrew – the use of which involves a great deal of variation. Most Hebraic nouns used in Jewish Swedish can optionally be pluralized by using source language strategies, e.g., *siddur/siddur-im* 'prayer book/s', *kippa/kipp-ot* 'skullcap/s', *shiur/shiur-im* 'seminar/s', as well as Swedish strategies, e.g., *siddur/siddur-er* 'prayer book/s', *kippa/kipp-or* 'skullcap/s', *shiur/shiur-er* 'seminar/s'; the choice of strategy can be stylistic, ideological, as well as reflective of the speakers' general proficiency in these languages. However, for a group of nouns, source language strategies are by far the most common – perhaps even the general norm, e.g., *alija/alij-ot (alij-es)* 'calling to the reading of the Torah', *goj/goj-im* 'gentile/s', *bracha/brach-ot* 'blessing/s', *shaliach/shlichim* 'emissary/ies', *minjan/minjan-im* 'prayer quorum/s'.

In addition to Hebraic items derived from Yiddish and Israeli Hebrew, Jewish Swedish features a number of Hebrew-derived items that can best be classified as local innovations; e.g., *bris(s)a* 'to circumcise', *bris(s)ad* 'circumcised', derived from Yiddish/Ashkenazi Hebrew *bris (mile)* 'circumcision ceremony', and *treifa ned* 'to cause something kosher to become non-kosher', *treifa* 'to eat non-kosher food', derived from Yiddish/Ashkenazi Hebrew *treyf* 'non-kosher'. While the roots of these items are derived from Yiddish, the items per se cannot be derived from Yiddish (or Hebrew), in which these concepts are expressed differently (cf. Yiddish *mal zayn* or *yidshn* 'to circumcise', *gemalet* 'circumcised', *treyf makhn* 'to cause something kosher to become non-kosher'; the last item, *treifa*, lacks a Yiddish counterpart).

3.2 Language contact influences

The repertoire derives most of its features from Yiddish and Israeli Hebrew. In the previous section, we discussed how these two have contributed to the repertoire's Hebraic and Aramaic content; their respective influences on Jewish Swedish, however, are not limited to Hebraisms.

3.2.1 Yiddish

Yiddish – the ancestral language of most Swedish Jews – has been instrumental in the shaping of Jewish Swedish; its influences are noticeable across the board, including a wide variety of lexical categories, ranging from items relating to Jewish religious practices, e.g., *davna* 'to pray', *leina* 'to read from the

Torah', *bensha* 'to recite grace after meals', *shul* 'synagogue', *milchik* 'dairy', *fleishik* 'meat', *parve* 'neither dairy, nor meat', *jahrzeit* 'anniversary of a relative's death', *pushke* 'box for collecting charity (*tzedakah*)', to everyday words and expressions, e.g., *shnorra* 'to beg, mooch', *vajna* 'to complain, whine', *shluffa* 'to nap, sleep', *jid* 'Jew', *heimish* 'homey, familiar', *takke* 'really', *shvitz* 'sweat', *nudnik* 'annoying person', *shpilkes* 'impatience, restlessness', *pupik* 'bellybutton', *pulkes* '(chicken) thighs', *nayes* 'news, gossip', *nebech* 'poor thing', *nasha* 'to snack, nosh'. Yiddish origin verbs are generally integrated (see below for exceptions) into Jewish Swedish by replacing the Yiddish inflectional morphemes with Swedish counterparts:

Yiddish: *shluf-n* 'to sleep' → Jewish Swedish: *shluff-a* 'to sleep, nap'
Yiddish: *daven-en* 'to pray' → Jewish Swedish: *davn-a* 'to pray'
Yiddish: *shvayg-n* 'to keep quiet' → Jewish Swedish: *shvajg-a* 'to keep quiet'

The repertoire, additionally, contains a number of calques, i.e., words and phrases that have been semantically and/or morphosyntactically modeled on Yiddish (and possibly other languages). Examples of Yiddish influenced semantics include literal translations such as *köttig* 'containing meat' and *mjölkig* 'containing dairy products', corresponding to Yiddish *fleyshik* and *milkhik*, e.g., *mjölkiga tallrikar* 'plates used for dairy foods'. A particularly interesting example of semantic calquing is *ljuständning*, which literally means *candle lighting* – a compound of the Swedish nouns *ljus* 'candle' and *tändning* 'lighting' – which is not found in Swedish dictionaries. In Jewish Swedish, *ljuständning* is used with the specific meaning of 'the exact time at which a Jewish holiday begins'; it is noteworthy that use of this particular compound, with this specific meaning, is found in Yiddish *likht-tsindn*, as well as in Jewish American English *candle lighting* (Steinmetz 2005: 23). Other examples of calques include a number of fixed phrases that are word-for-word translations of Yiddish expressions (Table 1 below).

Table 1: Word-for-word calques of Yiddish phrases.

Yiddish	Jewish Swedish	Lit. translation	Translation
geyn in mikve	*gå i mikve*	'go in *mikve*'	'to immerse oneself in the ritual bath'
geyn in shul	*gå i shul*	'go in synagogue'	'to go to synagogue'
hobn yortsayt	*ha jahrzeit*	'have *yortsayt*'	'anniversary of a relative's death'
leygn tfiln	*lägga tefillin*	'lay phylacteries'	'to put on phylacteries'
zitsn shive	*sitta shive*	'sit *shive*'	'to observe the 7 days of mourning'
zogn kadesh	*säga kaddish*	'say *kaddish*'	'to recite the mourner's prayer'

The Swedish verbs *hålla* 'to hold' and *bryta* 'to break' are used in Jewish Swedish with the additional meanings 'to observe' and 'to violate (religious rules)', respectively, e.g., *hålla kosher* 'to keep (lit. hold) kosher', *bryta shabbes* 'to violate the rules of (lit. break) Sabbath', which semantically mirror the alternative meanings used in their Yiddish cognates *haltn* 'to hold (etc.)' and *brekhn* 'to break (etc.)'.

The phrasal verbs *gå in* 'go in, enter' and *gå ut* 'go out, exit' are used in Jewish Swedish to refer to the specific *halachic* time at which the Sabbath or a Jewish holiday begins and ends, respectively, e.g., *Fastan på Jom kippur går in klockan 18.32* 'The Yom Kippur fast (lit. goes in) begins at 6.32 PM'; *Havdalaljuset kan inte tändas innan Shabbat har gått ut* 'The havdalah candle cannot be lit until the Sabbath has (lit. gone out) ended'. This use corresponds to Yiddish *yom kiper geyt arayn* 'Yom Kippur (lit. goes in) begins' and *shabes geyt aroys* 'Sabbath ends'.

While the use of analytic *göra* ('make, do') +noun constructions, as seen in Table 2 below, is fairly common in Jewish Swedish, this kind of verb construction is quite unusual in most varieties of Swedish.

Table 2: Yiddish calqued analytic *göra* +noun constructions.

Yiddish	Jewish Swedish	Lit. translation	Translation
makhn a brokhe	*göra en bracha*	'to make a blessing'	'to bless'
makhn hamotse	*göra hamotsi*	'to make *hamotsi*'	'to recite the blessing of bread'
makhn kidesh	*göra kiddush*	'to make *kiddush*'	'to recite the blessing over wine'
makhn shabes	*göra shabbes*	'to make Sabbath'	'to prepare for the Sabbath'
tshuve ton	*göra tshuva*	'to do repentance'	'to repent'
makhn havdole	*göra havdala*	'to make *havdala*'	'to perform the ceremony concluding the Sabbath'

While most of these constructions have been calqued from Yiddish *makhn* ('to make') +noun or *ton* ('to do') +noun constructions, there are also a few examples where Israeli Hebrew and Jewish English have been the source (see below).

3.2.2 Israeli Hebrew

The major influences of Israeli Hebrew are described in the previous section (3.1). The non-Hebraic influences of Israeli Hebrew on Jewish Swedish – bizarre as this category may be – are perhaps modest, but far from insignificant. As mentioned in the section on Yiddish above, Jewish Swedish features a few examples of the *göra* +noun constructions that have been calqued from Israeli Hebrew.

Table 3: Israeli Hebrew calqued analytic *göra* +noun constructions.

Israeli Hebrew	Jewish Swedish	Lit. translation	Translation
la'asot balagan	*göra balagan*	'to make a mess'	'to create a mess'
la'asot mangal	*göra mangal*	'to make barbecue'	'to barbeque'

These calques are fairly recent and predominantly used by younger speakers. Other examples of influences from Israeli Hebrew include a number of items of originally Arabic origin that are currently used in Israeli Hebrew, e.g., *sababa* 'great!' *tchina* 'sesame paste', *ars* 'a rude and boastful young person', *frecha* 'uncouth female', *yalla* 'come on, let's go'; the use of *yalla* in Sweden is otherwise generally associated with Swedish urban multi-ethnic youth vernacular, primarily used by speakers of immigrant background.

Although the conventionalized Swedish pronunciations of *Hamas* 'Palestinian Islamic organization' and *hummus* 'humus' are [hamːas] and [homːəs], respectively, many Swedish Jews prefer to pronounce these words according to their Israeli pronunciation, i.e., [χamːas] and [χumːus], though many speakers may use the unmarked pronunciation in certain contexts (Lebenswerd 2013).

3.2.3 Jewish American English

Jewish American English (see Benor, this volume) is another source of influence. It is quite difficult to determine if the use of a given Yiddish origin item in Jewish Swedish came directly from Yiddish or from elsewhere. There are, however, a few examples where it is possible to say with certainty that Jewish English is the most probable source. For instance, Gold (1986: 98) describes a change in which the older Jewish English expression *go on Aliyah* 'to emigrate to Israel' became *make Aliyah* around the 1960s; similarly, in Jewish Swedish, the former *gå på alija* 'lit. to go on *aliya*' changed to the current *göra alija* 'lit. to make *aliya*', though somewhat later – perhaps around the 1980s. It is noteworthy that this form is another example of *göra* +noun constructions (see above).

Another example of Jewish English influence is the semantic change that occurred for the Jewish Swedish word *kvetsha*. Among Swedish Jews born before the 1970s, *kvetsha* was apparently used with two meanings: 1) 'to squeeze', as in its original Yiddish meaning (cf. *kvetshn*), and 2) 'to make out (with someone)', which is possibly a local innovation. People born after the 70s, however, overwhelming use *kvetsha* with the meaning 'to complain', which is an American innovation, revealing the influences of Jewish English. This should come as no surprise, as Swedish Jews are frequently exposed to Jewish English through Jewish American popular culture and Jewish educational material, etc. Possibly, the use of many other Yiddishisms in Jewish Swedish such as *shtick* 'typical or signature behavior', *mensch* 'a decent person', *shlepp* 'to carry, lug', *shmus* 'to chat', etc., could very well have come into use through influences by Jewish English, especially among younger speakers, despite existing earlier among local Yiddish speakers.

4 Written and oral traditions

4.1 Writing system

As opposed to written Swedish, repertoire items in Jewish Swedish typically lack standardized spelling. When Swedish Jews started to write in Roman script in the 19th century, the most common practice was to spell Hebraic (and Yiddish/Jüdisch-deutsch) words, as pronounced in their Western Ashkenazi tradition, according to the orthographic principles of German, e.g., ⟨s⟩ for /z/ and /s/, ⟨ch⟩ for /χ/, ⟨sch⟩ for /ʃ/, ⟨w⟩ for /v/, ⟨tz⟩ or ⟨z⟩ for /ts/, ⟨u⟩ for /u/, etc.; however, at times there were a few additions for a couple of Hebrew graphemes: ⟨kk⟩ for כ (*chanukkah* 'Hanukkah'), ⟨ph⟩ for פ (*Schauphor* 'shofar'), ⟨th⟩[8] for ת (*Thphilin* 'phylacteries'), ⟨-h⟩ for final silent ה (*Bar Mitzvoh* 'Bar mitzvah'), ⟨'⟩ for *shva nah* (*Tischo b'Av* 'a Jewish fast day'). The German-based orthography, with some slight modifications (e.g., ⟨v⟩ replaced ⟨w⟩ for /v/), continued to be the most used, at least up until the 1950s, when the spelling underwent another kind of change: a shift from using the traditional Ashkenazi principles of pronunciation to the ones used in Modern (Israeli) Hebrew; *Rausch Haschonoh* 'Jewish new year festival' and *schachris* 'morning service' thus became *Rosch Haschanah* and *schacharit*.

During the 1960s, the Jewish community of Stockholm was working on a new *siddur* (prayer book) that would feature an entirely new transcription system, which, according to its editors, sought to follow the general spelling norms of Swedish (Wilhelm 1970: XIII). This transcription system was markedly

---

8 Cf. ⟨t⟩ for ט *Talis* 'prayer shawl'.

different from previous practices. Not so much in the choice of consonants – which, besides using ‹z› instead of ‹s› for /z/ (*mazkir* 'memorial service'), and ‹ts› instead of ‹tz› for /ts/ (*tsitsit* 'fringes of ritual garment'), remained the same – but in the conspicuous use of vowels: ‹o› for /u/ (*kidosch* 'blessing over wine', *m'zoza* 'mezuzah', *Porim* 'Jewish holiday'), and (the Swedish letter) ‹å› for /o/ (*Sokåt* 'Jewish holiday', *z'miråt* 'Jewish hymns', *m'nåra* 'candelabra'), which, supposedly, was thought to correspond better to Swedish norms.⁹ The new transcription caused many heated debates among Stockholm's Jews; some argued that it was causing confusion, others that it was too Swedish, and that it somehow created a distance between themselves and Jews in the rest of the world. While it never really gained popular acceptance, the system continued, nevertheless, to be used in most official documents issued by the community, such as calendars, magazines, etc., up until 1981, when the community board issued a new official transcription system, which, in addition to reintroducing the older use of ‹u› for /u/ and ‹o› for /o/, also replaced ‹sch› with ‹sh› for /ʃ/, e.g., *shive* 'Jewish mourning reception', *kosher* 'kosher', *chumash* 'five books of Moses', etc., probably due to influences from American and Israeli transcription norms.

While strongly opposed by some, another example of such influences is the increasingly more frequent practice of using ‹y› for /j/, e.g., *yid* 'Jew', *shkoyach* 'good job!', and *halevay* 'if it was only so'. The choice between using a Swedish based transcription or some other system has shown to be guided by language ideologies. While some people claim that they attempt to follow the general norms of Swedish orthography as much as possible, others purposely wish to mark that these words are not 'Swedish' by explicitly adopting a foreign-looking spelling that deviates from established conventions.

Further examples of distinctive orthographic practices include the use of Hebrew abbreviations, such as ז"ל (זכרונו לברכה) 'of blessed memory' – which can appear in the middle of a text – ב"ה (בעזרת השם) 'with God's help', and בס"ד (בסיעתא דשמייא) 'with the help of Heaven', commonly used in the upper right corner of a piece of text. These are sometimes substituted by their corresponding Romanized versions *z"l*, *B"H*, and *BS"D*, respectively. Other examples of distinctive writing include: avoiding writing the word *Gud* 'God', as a sign of respect, by replacing the vowel with a dash, i.e., *G-d;* another example is to purposely use eight letters to spell the holiday of *Hanukkah* (of which there are countless spelling alternatives), as an homage to the miracle that lasted for eight days in the Hanukkah story.

---

9 In Swedish, ‹å› and ‹o› can both be used to indicate /o/; e.g., *gått* [gɔt:] 'went', *gott* [gɔt:] 'good.'

4.2 Literature

Similar to verbal interaction (see 2.3), the use of distinctive features in writing tends to be restricted to texts intended for Jewish audiences, though there are exceptions. Additionally, variables such as topic, type of Jewish audience, type of publication, genre, and degree of formality will, typically, also determine usage. Moreover, ideologies towards using such features in writing have varied historically. Up until the last couple of decades, Jewish publications like prayer books and periodicals would generally feature Swedish-language translations of religious terminology, e.g., *Sabbat* 'Sabbath', *helgdag* 'holiday', *morgonbön* 'morning prayer', and *lövhydda* 'leaf hut' (cf. Gold 1986: 293). In recent decades, however, the general trend is to use Hebrew terms instead, e.g., *Shabbat* 'Sabbath', *Jom tov* 'Jewish holiday', *shacharit* 'morning prayer', and *sukka* 'booth used during Succoth'.

In a similar vein, use of distinctive vocabulary in writing seems to have been markedly less frequent among Jewish authors in the early 20th century than today, though this has never been properly investigated. This general shift is likely related to the "ethnic revival" (Fishman 1999: 301) that occurred among Jews and other minority groups in Sweden in the 1970s (Boyd & Gadelli 1999: 315). Contemporary examples of Jewish writing include novels such as Leif Zern's (2012) *Kaddish på motorcykel*, Stephan Mendel-Enk's (2010) *Tre apor*, and the Swedish translation of *Lachn fun tsores* (Hazdan 2003) – a novel originally published in 1944 in Yiddish, describing Jewish life in Stockholm in the 1940s. (See Rohlén-Wohlgemuth's (1995) review of Swedish Jewish literature between 1775–1994.)

5 State of research

Published research on the speech of Swedish Jews is currently very limited. Lebenswerd's (2013) unpublished study on sociolinguistic variation among Swedish Jews offers an introduction to present-day Jewish Swedish; results from the study can be found in this chapter, as well as in Klagsbrun Lebenswerd (2015). Historical documentation is so far limited to a few sporadic mentions of the use of Yiddish words and phrases in the Swedish spoken by Jews in the late 19th and early 20th century (Jacobowsky 1955, 1967, 1980; Josephson 2006). Additionally, since Yiddish is recognized as one of Sweden's five national minority languages, the use of the language among Swedish Jews has been somewhat studied, though the focus of these studies have centered around the actual use and cultural significance of Yiddish (Boyd & Gadelli 1997, 1999; Sznajderman-Rytz 2007).

5.1 Issues of general theoretical interest

Research on distinctive language practices in relatively small contemporary Jewish communities contributes to a broader understanding of how members of numerically small diaspora communities variously use language to index ethnic (and/or religious) aspects of their identity – especially in cases where the community has undergone a (post-migration) language shift. Furthermore, features from Israeli Hebrew and Jewish English in Jewish Swedish demonstrate how linguistic practices used by members of the same diaspora community in other parts of the world influence each other.

5.2 Corpora

There is no publicly available corpus of Jewish Swedish. However, excerpts can be found online on certain websites, personal blogs, and Facebook groups dedicated to Jewish subjects.

5.3 Current directions in research

Until recently, the linguistic practices of Swedish Jews remained a largely unexplored topic. Forthcoming research will, inter alia, focus on issues such as: the social meanings of using Yiddish and Modern Hebrew words in Jewish Swedish; orthographic practices in Jewish Swedish and how these reflect language ideology; language use among Swedish Jews in the 19th century; the linguistic consequences of the current rise in anti-Semitism in Europe.

References

Andersson, Lars M. 2000. *En jude är en jude är en jude...: Representationer av "juden" i svensks skämtpress omkring 1900–1930* [A Jew is a Jew is a Jew... representations of 'the Jew' in Swedish comic press 1900–1930]. Lund: Nordic Academic Press.
Benor, Sarah Bunin. 2008. Towards a new understanding of Jewish language in the twenty-first century. *Religion Compass* 2(6). 1062–1080.
Benor, Sarah Bunin. 2009. Do American Jews speak a 'Jewish language'? A model of Jewish linguistic distinctiveness. *Jewish Quarterly Review* 99(2). 230–269.
Benor, Sarah Bunin. 2010. Ethnolinguistic repertoire: Shifting the analytic focus in language and ethnicity. *Journal of Sociolinguistics* 14(2). 159–183.

Beranek, Franz J. 1965. *Westjiddischer Sprachatlas [Western Yiddish Language Atlas]*. Marburg: Elwert.
Boyd, Sally & Erland Gadelli. 1997. Jiddisch i Sverige [Yiddish in Sweden]. *SOU 1997: 192. Steg mot en minoritetspolitik. Europarådets konvention om historiska minoritetsspråk*, 467–520.
Boyd, Sally & Erland Gadelli. 1999. Vem tillhör talgemenskapen? Om jiddisch i Sverige [Who belongs to the speech community? About Yiddish in Sweden]. In Kenneth Hyltenstam (ed.), *Sveriges sju inhemska språk – ett minoritetsspråksperspektiv*, 299–328. Lund: Studentlitteratur.
Carlsson, Carl Henrik. 2011. Judisk invandring från Aaron Isaac till idag [Jewish immigration from Aaron Isaac until today]. *Judarna i Sverige: en minoritets historia: fyra föreläsningar*, 17–54. Uppsala: Hugo Valentin-centrum.
Dean-Olmsted, Evelyn. 2011. Shamis, halebis and shajatos: Labels and the dynamics of Syrian Jewishness in Mexico City. *Language & Communication* 31(2). 130–140.
Dencik, Lars. 2003. 'Jewishness' in postmodernity: The case of Sweden. In Z.Y. Gitelman, B.A Kosmin and A. Kovács (eds.), *New Jewish identities: contemporary Europe and beyond*, 75–104. Budapest: Central European University Press.
Fishman, Joshua A. 1999. *Handbook of language & ethnic identity*. New York: Oxford University Press.
Gilman, Sander L. 1986. *Jewish self-hatred: Anti-semitism and the hidden language of the Jews*. Baltimore: Johns Hopkins.
Gold, David L. 1985. Jewish English. In Joshua Fishman (ed.), *Readings in the sociology of Jewish languages*, 280–298. Leiden: Brill.
Gold, David L. 1986. An introduction to Jewish English. *Jewish Language Review*. 6. 94–120.
Grossman, Jeffrey A. 2000. *The discourse on Yiddish in Germany from the Enlightenment to the Second Empire*. Columbia, SC: Camden House.
Hazdan, Israel. 2003. *Lachn fun tsores = Skratta åt eländet* [Laughing at misery]. Bromma: Megilla-förlaget.
Herzog, Marvin & Vera Baviskar. 2000. *The language and culture atlas of Ashkenazic Jewry. Vol. 3, The Eastern Yiddish – Western Yiddish continuum*. Tübingen: Niemeyer.
Holmes, Philip & Ian Hinchliffe. 2008. *Swedish: An essential grammar*. London: Routledge.
Jacobowsky, C. Vilhelm. 1955. *Göteborgs Mosaiska församling 1780–1955 : Minnesskrift till 100-årsdagen av synagogans invigning 12 oktober 1855 [Gothenburg's Mosaic congregation 1780–1955]*. Göteborg: [Mosaiska församlingen].
Jacobowsky, C. Vilhelm. 1967. *Svenskt-judiskt herrgårdsliv [Life on Swedish-Jewish country estates]*. Stockholm: AB Thule.
Jacobowsky, C. Vilhelm. 1980. Mosaiska församlingens historia fram till 1955. *Göteborgs mosaiska församling 1780–1980 [Gothenburg's Mosaic congregation 1780–1980]*. Göteborg: Församl, 13–31.
Jacobs, Neil G. 2005. *Yiddish: A linguistic introduction*. Cambridge and New York: Cambridge University Press.
Johannesson, Lena. 1988. 'Schene rariteten' : Antisemitisk bildagitation i Svensk rabulistpress 1845–1860 ['Schene rariteten' : Anti-Semitic imagery in Swedish fanatic radical press, 1845–1860]. In Gunnar Broberg, Harald Runblom, & Mattias Tydén (eds.), *Judiskt liv i Norden: [Jewish life in Scandinavia]*, 179–208. Studia multiethnica Upsaliensia, 0282-6623; 6. Uppsala: Centre for Multiethnic Research, Uppsala University.

Josephson, Olle. 2006. Moschlade mormorsmor? Bidrag till ett svenskt minoritetsspråks historia [Moschlade great grandmother? A contribution to the history of a Swedish minority language]. In Ann-Marie Ivars (ed.), *Vårt bästa arv. Festskrift till Marika Tandefelt den 21 December 2006*, 141–154. Helsingfors: Svenska handelshögskolan.

Kiwitt, Marc. 2014. The problem of Judeo-French: Between language and cultural dynamics. *International Journal of the Sociology of Language* 226: 25–56.

Klagsbrun Lebenswerd, Patric Joshua. 2016. Jewish Swedish. In Lily Kahn & Aaron D. Rubin (eds.), *Handbook of Jewish languages*, 618–629. Leiden: Brill.

Lebenswerd, Patric Joshua. 2013. *Distinctive features in Jewish Swedish: A description and a survey*. Stockholm: Stockholm University unpublished thesis.

Lowenstein, Steven M. 1969. Results of atlas investigations among Jews in Germany. *The field of Yiddish: Studies in language, folklore, and literature. Third collection*, 16–35. The Hague: Mouton.

Lowenstein, Steven M. 2002. The complicated language situation of German Jewry, 1760–1914. *Studia Rosenthaliana* 36. 3–31.

Maler, Bertil. 1979. Western Yiddish berkhes or barkhes, its origin and offshoots in Scandinavian languages. *Nordisk judaistik – Scandinavian Jewish studies* 2(2). 1–5.

Mendel-Enk, Stephan. 2010. *Tre apor [Three monkeys]*. Stockholm: Atlas.

Muir, Simo. 2009. Jiddišistä ruotsinkautta suomeen: Helsingin juutalaisten kielenvaihdoista ja etnolektistä [From Yiddish via Swedish to Finnish: On the language shifts and ethnolects of the Jewish community in Helsinki]. *Virittäjä* 4. 533–556.

Riad, Tomas. 2014. *The phonology of Swedish*. Oxford: Oxford University Press.

Rohlén-Wohlgemuth, Hilde. 1995. *Svensk-judisk litteratur 1775–1994 : En litteraturhistorisk översikt [Swedish Jewish literature 1775–1994]*. Spånga: Megilla-förl.

Steinmetz, Sol. 2005. *Dictionary of Jewish usage: A guide to the use of Jewish terms*. Lanham, MD: Rowman & Littlefield.

Svenson, Anna. 1995. *Nöden. En shtetl i Lund [Nöden. A shtetl in Lund]*. Lund: Gamla Lund förening för bevarande av stadens minnen.

Sznajderman-Rytz, Susanne. 2007. *Språk utan land med hemvist i Sverige [A Language without a Country Residing in Sweden]*. http://jfst.se/wp-content/uploads/jiddischstudie_0801172.pdf (accessed 15 August, 2016).

Tossavainen, Mikael. 2009. Jews in Sweden. In *Encyclopedia of the Jewish diaspora: Origins, experiences, and culture*, 1087–1092. Santa Barbara, CA: ABC-CLIO.

Valentin, Hugo. 1924. *Judarnas historia i Sverige [The history of the Jews in Sweden]*. Stockholm: Bonnier.

Verschik, Anna. 2010. Ethnolect debate: Evidence from Jewish Lithuanian. *International Journal of Multilingualism* 7(4). 285–305.

Weinreich, Max. 2008. *History of the Yiddish language*, Paul Glasser (ed.). New Haven: Yale University Press.

Wilhelm, Kurt. 1970. *Sidur Šefat Emet: Sidor S'fat Emet*. Basel: Victor Goldschmidt Vlg.

Zern, Leif. 2012. *Kaddish på motorcykel [Kaddish on motorcycle]*. Stockholm: Bonnier.

Zitomersky, Joseph. 1988. The Jewish population in Sweden, 1780–1980: An ethno-demographic study. In Gunnar Broberg, Harald Runblom, & Mattias Tydén (eds.), *Judiskt liv i Norden: [Jewish life in Scandinavia]*, 99–125. Studia multiethnica Upsaliensia, 0282-6623; 6. Uppsala: Centre for Multiethnic Research, Uppsala University.

Judith Rosenhouse
Jewish Hungarian in Hungary and Israel

1 Brief introduction

1.1 Names of the language

The Jewish Hungarian language (*Zsidó-Magyar*, in Hungarian) comprises various elements which reflect the Jewish nature of its users, while being embedded in the general Hungarian language, in Hungary in its current borders and in the earlier, wider areas of the Hungarian Kingdom.[1]

Non-Jews in Hungary have used the derogatory names *biboldó* or, in short, *bibsi* /bibši ~ bipši/, indicating 'Jewish', for various Jewish features (such as behavior or face, Tamas Biró, personal communication, 2016), including the Jewish manner of speech (Márta Fehér, personal communication, 2016). The origin and etymology of the name may be linked to a Roma gypsy word, meaning 'unbaptized' (i.e., Jewish). In Hungarian literature up to the present, the code name for 'Jew' is *urbanus*, following the description of Jewish urban Budapest culture in an anti-Jewish book (as noted in Kőbányai 2010, 2015: 114). However, this does not refer to the language, which is generally not considered to exist.

1.2 Linguistic affiliation

Hungarian is a Finno-Ugric language belonging to the Uralic language family, originating in the region around the Ural Mountains. This group includes Estonian, Finnish, and languages of the Ural region, and is neither Indo-European nor Semitic. However, German is an Indo-European language, and Hebrew and Aramaic are Semitic languages. These languages affected Jewish Hungarian and are integrated into its vocabulary. Thus, the term Jewish Hungarian refers, in my opinion, to the language variety that combines Hungarian, as a Matrix language (Myers-Scotton 2002), with embedded and adapted Hebrew, Aramaic,

---

[1] I extend cordial thanks to Nisan Ararat and Rachel Ararat, Viktoria Bányai, Ruth Bars, Sarah Bunin Benor, Tamás Biró, Márta Fehér, Éva Gábor, and Judith Hidasi for their answers to my various questions about many issues related to this study. It is only due to space limitations that their information is not quoted here in full.

Yiddish, and German elements.[2] As is well known, Yiddish has absorbed Hebrew and Aramaic elements. German elements in Jewish Hungarian follow Standard Hungarian, which absorbed them from German, an official language in Hungary during the Austro-Hungarian (Double-Headed) Monarchy in the 19th and early 20th centuries. We may add to the languages that influenced Jewish Hungarian certain lexical elements of Modern (Israeli) Hebrew. Thus, Jewish Hungarian is a mixed language variety, as is usual in communities whose speakers lead a bilingual or multilingual life, being in constant language contact with dominant local languages.[3]

1.3 Regions where the language is/was spoken

The Hungarian language was spoken in the Hungarian Basin (Pannonia) and Romania (Dacia). It was also spoken in territories that were part of the Austro-Hungarian Monarchy until the Trianon Pact (Paris, 1920), after the end of World War I, and at present belong to the following states: Czech Republic, Slovakia, Austria, Ukraine, Poland, Romania, Serbia, Croatia, and Slovenia (ex-Yugoslavia). When the Nazis overtook Hungary, its borders changed for a few years; when World War II (WWII) ended, the Hungarian borders were again changed in the Paris agreement (1947), which divided the Hungarian territory between Czechoslovakia, Poland, Ukraine, and Yugoslavia. The Hungarian borders have not changed since then.

Before WWII, numerous Jewish communities existed in all the mentioned regions, and their members spoke Jewish Hungarian, usually in addition to a local dialect or language (such as Yiddish, German, or Romanian). Jewish Hungarian also exists in Jewish Hungarian communities around the world, mainly in Canada, the USA, and Israel. Today, only a small proportion of the Jews in Hungary (and elsewhere) are said to use Jewish Hungarian. The main reason is that in Hungary, Jews have "Hungarized" themselves (see below), for fear of recurrent anti-Semitism. Elsewhere, e.g., in Israel, Hungarian-speaking Jewish immigrants have acquired the local dominant languages (Hebrew in Israel),

---

[2] The exact term for the language used by Hungarian-speaking Jews is not yet decided. See a discussion of the definition of Jewish languages in Benor (2008). Simplifying Myers-Scotton's (2002) approach, inter-language code-switching involves the speaker's major language, the matrix language, and a minor language, which provides the code-switched "foreign" elements.

[3] In other cases, such speakers may be immigrants from another country or region and speak dialects or the local dominant language of the country.

and their offspring, from the second generation on, hardly know the parents' mother tongue.[4]

1.4 Attestations and sources

Jewish Hungarian is a rather young language variety, which does not date back earlier than the first quarter of the 19th century. Before that time, Hungarian Jews used Yiddish, and mainly German, outside their community (Komoróczy 2011). Various written (printed) works exist on the history, culture, religion, etc. of Hungarian Jews (e.g., Braham 1966; Katzburg 1992; Patai 1996; Ujvári 1929; Komoróczy 2013), but there are none about their language use. Studied Jewish literature includes humor and jokes (Papp 2016; Patai 2006: 524–534), many Rabbinical works, and various secular "belles-lettres" literature in Hungarian for Orthodox and secular readers, respectively. The few studies that mention their language mainly deal with lexical linguistic elements (Bányai and Komoróczy 2013). Yiddish/ Hebrew/Aramaic elements in existing literature are sometimes written in the traditional Hebrew alphabet in the German or Hungarian text (e.g., *Darkhey Yeshorim*, in Hebrew and Yiddish translation [Komoróczy 2011: 34]; *Hagode shel Peysekh*, written in Hebrew and Aramaic on one page and translated into Hungarian on the opposite page [Komoróczy 2011: 53]). These elements usually reflect traditional objects, actions, customs, etc., used by Jews, including personal names, names of holidays, food types, religious habits, prayers, etc. A different literature type is, e.g., Kishon's (1967) book, written and published in Israel. In that book, Modern Hebrew words appear in the Hebrew alphabet in three humoresques; other words borrowed from Modern Hebrew are transcribed into Hungarian.

1.5 Present-day status

At present, Hungary is an independent country and a member-state of the UN, with Hungarian its official language. The use of Jewish Hungarian is rare, mostly because of the historical, demographic, and political changes that occurred during and after WWII. Some Jews again hide their identities now, trying to assimilate into the Hungarian population. Currently, however, Orthodox and other religious communities in Hungary (e.g., HABAD) and in Israel, and new *olim* (immigrants)

---

[4] In 2015, the Hungarian Embassy in Israel started a once-a-week afternoon kindergarten and a school-age class teaching Hungarian to children whose Hungarian (embassy non-Israeli) or Israeli (Jewish) families enhance its acquisition.

in Israel keep their Hungarian language, including Jewish elements updated with new elements from Modern (Israeli) Hebrew (e.g. *kippának* 'for the *kippa*, the skullcap', in Goldman 2015; cf. *kapeli* in Kishon 1967 and *kapedli* in Szalai 2011, for the same item).

2 Historical background

2.1 Speaker community: Settlement, documentation

Evidence of Jewish existence in Hungary dates back to the second-third centuries CE, when the Romans ruled Dacia and Pannonia (i.e., Hungary and Romania). With the Hungarian tribes that invaded this region in the ninth-tenth centuries, there were presumably also Khazar Jews. From the tenth century, there are Jewish relics, e.g., tombstones with Hebrew engravings. Hungarian Jews are apparently first mentioned in Hebrew documents by Hasday Ibn Shaprut (tenth century CE), where Hungary is called *Hagar* הגר.[5]

During most of the following centuries, Jews continued to live in Hungary. Starting in the Medieval Ages, Jews immigrated to Hungary from Poland, Ukraine, Moldova, and Romania; still later, they also arrived from Austria. Sometimes they earned privileges and lived relatively safely, and at other periods they suffered persecution. An example of persecution was their expulsion from Hungary to the Ottoman Empire territories, following the Muslim Ottoman conquest and occupation of Hungary in the 17th century, ending in 1718.

In the 18th century, Hungary became officially part of the Austro-Hungarian Empire. The Emperor Franz-Joseph granted civil rights to the Jews and other, non-Jewish minorities in 1867.[6] Many Jews, including Orthodox ones, "Hungarized" following this status change. They mingled with the general population, changed their names, and, within two generations, most of them replaced Yiddish with the Hungarian language. The Empire survived until World War I; when the war ended, its territory was divided between adjacent countries, reducing the areas of both Hungary and Austria.

Despite their civil rights, persecution of Hungarian Jews continued between the two World Wars by anti-Semitic, Fascist, and Nazi Hungarians. Even before World War II (in the 1930s), many Jewish Hungarian men were taken to work camps,

---

[5] His emissary to the Khazar King Joseph passed through Hungary and Russia and was aided by local Jews on his way.
[6] The Emperor issued some rights to the Jews in 1840, but they materialized only later.

where most of them perished. The Jewish majority was deported to death camps in Auschwitz-Birkenau in the short period of April-May 1944, from which few survived. At the same time, the Hungarian Arrow-Cross militia murdered thousands of other Jews in Budapest itself. However, a small proportion of Jews managed to leave Hungary in the 1930s and even during the war. Through various European countries, they immigrated to the USA, Palestine (now Israel), and other countries.

Only about a quarter of the Jewish population (according to the 1939 census) returned to Hungary in 1945 after the Holocaust (cf. Benoschofsky 1966). After World War II, a Communist government with USSR support ruled Hungary, and the Jews did not enjoy better conditions than before the War (Patai 1996). In the revolutions of 1956 and 1967, many Hungarian Jews (and non-Jews) left Hungary and immigrated to other countries, including Israel. In the post-communist era (i.e., after 1990), anti-Semitism and xenophobia are expanding again in Hungary, and the Jews there have become anxious about their future.

Before the Holocaust, there were about a million Jews in the large area of Hungary. At present, the estimate is between 48,000 and 100,000 Jews (cf. Della Pergola 2013; Kőbányai 2010) and around 60,000–70,000 in Israel.

Hungarian Jews immigrated to *Eretz Yisrael* (now Israel) even earlier, in the 17th–18th centuries (Neumann 1982; Bányai 2008). The Zionist movement spread in Hungary, and in 1920, 60 members of the Budapest-based Zionist Association *Ha-Mehandes* 'The Engineer' immigrated to the country (Palestine at the time, under British mandate rule). They were influential in establishing modern life in the country, in new settlements and sports groups, culture, and education as teachers, writers, poets, and painters; in national defense and religious activity (rabbinical tasks and religious leadership); medicine (pioneering doctors); science (as Hebrew University and Technion professors), etc. Other waves of (Zionist) newcomers came in the 1930s-1940s. After WWII and the establishment of Israel in 1948, and until about 1951, more new olim came from Hungary (with Jews from all over Europe and Asia). The last two (small) waves of Hungarian immigrants came to Israel in 1956 and in 1991 (Gilady 1991), but since then there has only been a trickle of immigration from Hungary.

2.2 Phases in historical development

Jewish history in Hungary can be divided into six major phases.[7] The first two phases are the longest but least researched, and the last four involve the

---

[7] Patai (1996) gives a more detailed historical classification.

development of Jewish Hungarian. (1) Jews' arrival and settlement in Pannonia (Hungary) since the second-third century, during the Roman Empire. (2) Their continued life in Hungary from about the tenth century to the 19th century. (3) Jews' "Hungarization" after the Monarch's civil rights bill of 1867. (4) World War II and the Holocaust, which nearly caused the Hungarian Jews' total annihilation. (5) Life after the Holocaust until the fall of the Communist regime in 1991. (6) Life under the new Hungarian state from 1991 to the present.

The best period for Hungarian Jews, in my opinion, was phase 3, from the beginning of the 20th century until WWI, in which Jewish culture flourished in Hungary. Those years yielded many Jewish lawyers, doctors, and scientists in all fields of science, as well as talented musicians, painters, writers, journalists, playwrights, actors, and film directors (Balla 1969). In addition, rabbinical institutes and liturgical literature prospered at that time. When persecution increased in the 1930s, many intellectuals and artists abandoned Hungary, along with many others. A major relevant field of culture in the first decades of the 20th century involved Jewish humor and jokes, which spread in the many cabarets of Budapest (particularly noteworthy was the humorous pair called Hacsek és Sajó (Hachek and Shayo).[8] "Jewish-speak" was mainly expressed in its mixed Yiddish lexical items (often originating in Hebrew or Aramaic), e.g., *haverkodik* ('friend' + the verbal suffix of becoming, 3rd person, present tense 'being friendly' < Hebrew *xaver* 'friend'), *valakinek a samesz* (someone-for the servant 'being the servant for someone' < Hebrew *šammaš* 'serving man, synagogue beadle').[9] Such expressions integrated into the informal speech of the Hungarian non-Jewish public, as well as of the Jews.

2.3 Sociolinguistic description, community bilingualism, public functions

Jews lived mostly in Budapest, but there were Jewish communities in smaller towns (e.g., Szeged, Debrecen, Győr, and Sopron), as well as Jewish farmers' villages. The Hungarian language began to spread out from the capital to other locations through the Jewish "Hungarization" movement in the 19th century. Jews used the Hungarian language, mixing it with elements from their original mother tongue, Yiddish (or German). The "Hungarization" process was very quick, and, already

---

8 The original writer of the humoristic skits was László Vadnay (1904–1967). Many writers added skits with these characters to the Budapest cabarets. After WWII they were forgotten, but are now revived on CDs and recent YouTube videos (e.g., Szombat 2015).
9 I thank J. Hidasi for these examples.

by the beginning of the 20th century, most of the Jews used Hungarian at home, as well as in communication with non-Jews. That period yielded the blooming of Jewish education and culture, because children attended general schools, not only Jewish *heider* classes. The "older" generation kept Yiddish for home use for some time, but, outside of Hasidic communities, its use began decreasing rapidly. This process included the religious (Orthodox, Reform, and "Neolog") communities and secularized individuals, but the latter tried to integrate completely into non-Jewish Hungarian society in their intellectual work and daily life, including, for some, conversion to Christianity (Patai 1996: 371–374; László 1969).

The Jewish Hungarian language must have differed in the first generation of "Hungarization" from the non-Jewish population's language in its phonetic system and other structural patterns, as residue of their Yiddish mother tongue. However, from the second generation of this process, Jewish Hungarian was nearly the same as the locally spoken Standard Hungarian (and/or its slang). The rate of Jewish elements (e.g., lexical items) decreased to a minimum or zero in the works of famous *belles lettres* writers; however, in discourse relating to Jewish topics, such lexical items reappeared later, i.e., after WWII (cf. Kaczér 1953; Abádi 1962; Rosenhouse 2015a, 2015b; Sanders 2006; Papp 2016).[10]

A large percentage of Hungarian-speaking Jews in Israel (and elsewhere) are experiencing some attrition in their Hungarian mother tongue. In Israel, this may be due to its disuse for ideological reasons (due to their memories of the Holocaust period), acquisition of Modern Hebrew in classes for adults, or spontaneously acquired Hebrew (cf. Rosenhouse 2012a, b; Rosenhouse 2015a, b; Goldman 2015). Many examples of Hebrew lexical items and expressions occur in books of variegated nature published in Israel by, e.g., Kishon (1956, 1967), Kaczér (1953), and Abádi (1962).

3 Structural information

3.1 Relationship to non-Jewish varieties (isoglosses, related dialects)

Hungary (within its present borders) has six large dialect regions, but Hungarian is spoken also in "language islands" in Romania, Slovakia, Moldavia, and in other neighboring countries that belonged to the Austro-Hungarian Monarchy. As most of the Hungarian Jews lived in a few quarters of Budapest, they spoke

---

[10] This includes anti-Semitic writings (cf. Sanders 2006).

the Hungarian dialect of the capital. Jews who lived elsewhere apparently used those local dialects rather than that of Budapest, but most of them perished in the Holocaust. One testimony of dialect differences is by Mrs. S., who told me that, though her Budapest-born mother-in-law loved her, she could not help mentioning sometimes that Mrs. S. was "provincial" (*vidéki*, in Hungarian), for she was born in Szeged. The typical dialect feature she referred to was using /ö/ instead of the Budapest (Standard Hungarian) /e/.

3.2 Particular structural features (unique to the Jewish variety)

So far, I have not found sufficient material to identify specific structural linguistic features of Jewish Hungarian (e.g., phonology, morphology, syntax, or discourse structure) except vocabulary. The other fields require further research.

3.3 Lexicon: Hebrew and Aramaic elements

Yiddish contains many Hebrew and Aramaic lexical elements, referring to Jewish traditional objects, rituals, or activities. Such lexical items abound in Jewish Hungarian. Jewish Hungarian is, thus, at least a different variety of Hungarian, if not an entirely different language (see a few examples in 3.4). Such Jewish expressions were used in the inter-World Wars period in performed cabaret shows and written humoresques, for example, and apparently most of the non-Jewish audience understood them. Moreover, about 300 of these lexical items penetrated colloquial and Standard Hungarian, where they are used like any other loanword in the language.[11] Some (unknown) part of them are no longer associated with Jewish speech (e.g., /hɔver/ 'friend, guy').

3.4 Language contact influences

The Hungarian language system has translated or adapted various lexical items, including words derived from Yiddish, the earlier Jewish mother tongue of Hungarian Jews. Thus, Jews and non-Jews normally understand, and often actively use (or at least used), these words. Word lists of this vocabulary exist in several publications, but do not exceed about 300 words. The examples below

---

[11] Hungarian has borrowed many lexical items from German, French, Russian, and English, among others. Usually, these elements are adapted to the Hungarian morpho-phonetic structures.

present words derived from Yiddish (which mostly had been previously derived from Hebrew), including words that are also understood by non-Jewish Hungarians, though we do not have written evidence of that for all of them. Basic examples of this common Jewish Hungarian vocabulary are *tréfa* (which in Standard Hungarian now means a 'joke' or 'jovial' and developed from "not legally allowed for Jewish ritual or food"), *hɔver* (in Standard Hungarian 'friend, guy'), *macesz* (the

Table 1: Examples of Jewish Hungarian words and their Yiddish and Hebrew origins.

Jewish Hungarian spelling (<Yiddish)	Meaning	Pronunciation (IPA)	Pronunciation in Modern Hebrew (< Classical Hebrew)	Foreign origin
barchesz	'challah, a special bread used on Shabbat and holidays'	/bɔrxes/ or /bɔrhes/	/braxót/ 'blessings', Yiddish /broxes/	---
cicesz	'prayer fringe (on the prayer shawl)'	/tsitses/	/tsitsít/ 'fringe, tuft'	---
coresz	'problems, troubles'	/tsores/	Biblical Hebrew /tsɔrót/ (Mod. H /tsarót/)	---
Káddis	'prayer commemorating the dead'	/kádiš/	/kadíš/	/qaddíš/ < Aramaic
macesz	'*unleavened bread* for Pesach'	/mɔtsez/	/matsót/	---
maire	'fear, anxiety'	/mɔire/	/morá/	---
minján	'minimal number of men needed for holding a public prayer'	/minjan/	/minján/	---
Rabbi	Jewish priest	/rɔbi/	/rábi, rav/	
sul, zsinagoga	Jewish synagogue	/šu:l, žinɔgoga/	Not from Hebrew	<German; < Greek
sabesz, szombat	Sabbath, Saturday	/šɔbes, sombɔt/	/šabát/	---
talit	'prayer shawl'	/tɔlesz/	Biblical /ṭalít/ Modern /talít/	---
tóra, tójre	The Bible	/tórɔ, tójre/	/torá/	---
tréfa	Originally: 'unholy, illegal thing' Now: 'joke, hilarious'	/tréfɔ/	/trefá/ 'unholy, prohibited for eating'	---

unleavened bread for Passover, also used in Standard Hungarian), and *unberufn* (< Yiddish, 'uncalled for [the devil], protect from the devil'; Bíró 2004, fn. 9, says the latter is used also by non-Jews). Table 1 above presents more examples.

Thus, we find in Jewish Hungarian (1) words that originate in Yiddish (<Hebrew or Aramaic) and (2) words that have changed their meaning in Standard Hungarian and are used by Jews with both meanings, dependent on the context. The words that originate in Yiddish may be partly known to non-Jews. Sometimes they were (and probably still are) used to hide a meaning from non-Jewish listeners.

Hebrew names penetrated Hungarian from translations of the Hebrew Bible long before the Jewish Hungarization process, and both Jews and non-Jews use them in their Hungarian. A few examples of Biblical Hebrew anthroponyms and toponyms in Hungarian are in Table 2.[12]

Table 2: A few biblical personal and place names in Modern Hebrew phonetic pronunciation, Hungarian spelling, and Hungarian phonetic transcription.

	Anthroponyms Male	Female	Toponyms
Modern Hebrew phonetic	*moše*	*xava*	*yerušalaim*
Hungarian spelling	Mózes	Éva	Jeruzsálem
Phonetic Hungarian	mo:zeš	ɛ:vɔ	jeruža:lem
Modern Hebrew phonetic	*josef*	*dvora*	*jerixo*
Hungarian spelling	József	Debora	Jérikhó
Phonetic Hungarian	jo:žef	deborɔ	jeriko
Modern Hebrew phonetic	*šmu'el*	*bat-ševa*	*jarden*
Hungarian spelling	Sámuel	Bethsabé	Jordán
Phonetic Hungarian	šɔmu, ša:muel	betšabe	jorda:n
Modern Hebrew phonetic	*ja'akov/jakov*	*rivká*	*bet-'el*
Hungarian spelling	Jákób	Rebeka	Béthel
Phonetic Hungarian	ja:kob	rebekɔ	bɛ:tel

Many Hebrew and Yiddish words occur, for instance, in Kaczér (1953), Abádi (1962), and Schön (1964). These are novels relating to Jews and their fate, but each in a different historical period. Thus, in Kaczér (1953), which is a saga of three generations of a Jewish family in Hungary since the 19th century (in four volumes),

---

[12] Hebrew Bible versions in Hungarian have existed in the Christian communities since the 16th century, and the names reflect Greek and Latin origins. However, translations of the Bible into Hungarian by Jews appeared only in the 19th century. A 1994 version of the Hebrew Bible in Hebrew and Hungarian apparently reflects the wish to teach the language in addition to the texts.

we find *talmid hacham* 'scholar', *am haaretsz* 'uneducated person, common folk', *mazeltov* 'congratulations', and translated adaptations of biblical and Talmudic passages. Abádi (1962) uses Modern Hebrew words, including *"aszara learba"* 'ten to four' (time of the day), *"hem baim"* 'they are coming', *"šalom, erev tov, adon Boroš"* 'hello, good evening, Mr. Borosh', *"gáfrurim, gáfrurim, átá mevin?"* '... matches, matches (for lighting a cigarette), do you understand?', etc., because his story is about the lives of Jewish Hungarian immigrants who have survived the Holocaust and live in Israel in the 1960s. Schön's book (1964) is a novel about the development of the Hasidic movement at the end of the 19th century, and his vocabulary includes more Yiddish than Hebrew items, e.g., *Smelke* (<Shmuel) 'Samuel', *Reb Mendele* (<Yiddish nickname of Menahem) 'Rabbi Mendele', *a cadik* (<Hebrew) 'the saint (rabbi)', *a Sechina* (/šexina/ <Hebrew) 'the Holy spirit'. As in other literary publications, sometimes these words are translated into Hungarian in the text; in many other cases, the context provides ample elucidation of their meaning, and, on some other occasions, such words remain without explanation or translation. In all these cases, the text reveals code switched Modern Hebrew.

4 Written and oral traditions

Balla (1969: 87–88) writes the following about Jewish development at the end of the 19th century: "The repeal of the oppressive regulations and the developing respect for human freedom brought about an upsurge in the creative spirit that was reflected in the phenomenal development of the press, literature and the arts." Below is a short summary of some of the Jews' intellectual activities in that period.

4.1 Writing system

Jewish written documents have existed in Hungary for many centuries. In the medieval and renaissance periods, they were written in Hebrew, as well as Aramaic, and later in Yiddish or Jewish-High-German (German written in Hebrew letters) (Komoróczy 2011: 12). In the middle of the 19th century, Hungarian became the national language of the country, and the Jews' Hungarization began about then. Since then, Jewish documents have been written mainly in Hungarian (not in Hebrew letters), following the Jews' oral communication. The *haskala* (enlightenment) period in Hungary occurred about half a century after that of Germany (cf. Bíro 2004). However, due to certain goals of a religious or liturgical nature, Hebrew was and is still used (as well as Yiddish and Aramaic elements). Patai

Jozsef's (1903) book, for one, includes interesting Hebrew poetry by him, and some poems that he translated from Hungarian to Hebrew. Prose texts in Modern (Israeli) Hebrew are also available, dating approximately to the inter-World Wars period (e.g., Hameiri's books; see Holzman 1986).

4.2 Literature

From about 1840, and mainly due to the effects of the Hungarian independence war of 1848, the number of Jewish secular (Hungarized) writers increased, until before WWII. Many of them wrote in Hungarian about Hungarian nationality at that time, hardly mentioning their Jewish origins. Jewish poets composed poems about love of the Hungarian homeland, and the wish to become free of the bonds of slavery; they were influenced by Western poetry and ideology. Among the first famous poets were Mihály Helprin (1828–1888), Mór Szegfy (1825–1896), Ignác Reich (1821–1887), Bertalan Ormodi (1836–1869), József Kiss (1843–1921), and others. These and numerous later poets are mentioned in, e.g., Carmilly-Weinberger (1966) and Patai (1996).

Jewish Hungarian secular writing includes prose novels, short stories, essays, travelogues, biographies, autobiographies, humoresques, and literary criticism. These appeared in books, as well as in literary magazines (e.g., *Nyugat* 'West', *A Hét* 'the Week', *Mult és Jövő* 'Past and Future') and literary sections of newspapers, because many of the writers worked as journalists for Budapest newspapers (see, e.g., Patai, 1996: 387–419). We should mention that a proportion of the Jewish-born writers in Hungary converted to Christianity, and their works lacked a Jewish nature. Molnár, Lengyel, Biró, Révész, Balász, and Patai (cf. Patai 1996: 387–419) are among the most famous Jewish writers in the pre-War period who wrote about Jewish themes, explicitly and/or implicitly.

Simultaneously, religious circles continued studying and writing liturgical and Jewish/Judaica studies. Judaic studies flourished in Hungary in the Rabbinical Seminary of Budapest, which began operating in 1877 and was revived after the Holocaust (it is now the Budapest University of Jewish Studies). In addition, other humanities and sciences fields were active.[13] From the end of the 19th century to the beginning of WWI, Hungarian Jewish institutes (mainly, but not only, in Budapest) trained many famous scholars and rabbis; they later occupied important positions in universities and Jewish institutes in such countries as England, Germany, Austria, and the USA.

---

[13] Cf. Patai, 1996: 324–327, about the establishment of the Budapest Rabbinical Seminary and its first professors. Those professors wrote some of their studies in Hebrew, which they knew, among other languages.

After WWII, Jewish survivors returned to Hungary (mainly Budapest), and Jewish writers worked under the limitations of the Communist regime, with participation in cultural life in the 1960s–1970s as intense as before the war (Patai 1996: 640, 659–674). Jewish writers wrote about Jewish issues and the Holocaust, but not immediately after the war. Some cultural Jewish-language elements are assumed to appear in this literature, but their works are still awaiting linguistic research of their use of Hebrew, Aramaic, or Yiddish elements.

4.3 Performance (theater, film, etc.)

Patai (1996: 521–524) describes the Jewish contribution to the performing arts (theater and film) in Hungary before WWII as having a "seminal role in making Budapest a great center of theatrical life" in Europe (Patai 1996: 521; Balla, 1966).[14] Many of the Hungarian playwrights, actors, film directors, and producers of that period were Jews. Many of them (e.g., Endre Nagy, Ferenc Molnár, Menyhért Lengyel, Béla Szenes[15]) also authored novels and short stories (dealing with Jewish topics, among others), as well as essays and satirical and political skits and sketches, published in magazines and newspapers and presented at cabarets and theaters.

Humor was a main feature of Jewish Hungarian cabaret life, which has spread in the written and spoken media since the beginning of the 20th century. Several Jews and non-Jews, native speakers of Hungarian whom I interviewed, indicated the importance of jokes and humor in general in describing Jewish Hungarian speech. Although other aspects of Jewish Hungarian do not appear in literature studies, various viewpoints of Jewish humor do. For example, Papp (2016) describes periods of Jewish-Christian symbiosis and depicts the humor that grew in Hungarian Jewish communities until the Post-Communist years. In many of Papp's quoted jokes, the protagonists are a Jewish rabbi, or two Jews named Kohn and Grün, representing stereotypes of Jewish thinking and worldview (with Christian clergymen representing the non-Jewish society). A typical word in the quoted jokes is /nu/ 'well, then' (< Yiddish), implying the conclusion of the given situation. Linguistically, the jokes in Papp (2016) are in Standard Hungarian, except for some expressions that produce a humorous effect. Jokes,

---

14 In addition to written literature, Jews contributed to other art forms, such as music, painting, and sculpture.
15 Béla Szenes was Hannah (Anikó) Szenes's father.

however, can also reflect linguistic homonyms or puns, and these, too, occur in Jewish joke material.[16]

Jewish topics appeared in Hungarian theaters and films before and after the Holocaust, but without using the special features of the Jewish Hungarian language. However, as noted, before WWII, Jewish expressions were abundant in skits in the Budapest cabarets (Patai 1996). Jewish humor was well known, and there were numerous Jewish actors – "celebrities." Frigyes Karinthy, who was a journalist, novelist, translator, dramatist, poet, critic, and humorist, was the premier and most influential practitioner of the famous Hungarian humor (Kőbányai 2010).[17] In particular, the duo of "Hacsek és Sajo" were the best-known comic characters of the pre-war period. Various writers wrote their skits, and several actor pairs played their roles.[18]

After WWII, like other Hungarian Jews, most of these artists and intellectuals had emigrated, perished, or survived and returned to Hungary. The Communist era silenced Jewish culture and literature (like that of other minorities), but, in the post-Communist era, Jewish writers' activity in Hungary has been on the increase once more (Sanders 2006). Imre Kertész (1929–2015), a Jewish Hungarian writer who survived the Holocaust, won the Nobel Prize for Literature in 2002 for his books which deal with the Holocaust. (His book, "Fatelessness," about a 15-year-old boy during the Holocaust period, in a concentration camp and afterwards, was the basis for a well-known film. This book partly reflects his own biography.)

5 State of research

5.1 History of documentation

Jewish Hungarian has not been considered a separate variety of the Hungarian language or a Jewish language. Even now, not all researchers agree to refer to it as such. Therefore, there is hardly any literature that describes it as a Jewish language. There are, however, isolated studies of Jewish Hungarian writers or speakers in Hungary or Israel (these studies do not specifically deal with their

---

[16] This feature has nothing to do with the biblical heritage, in which there is hardly any joking material, but see Ararat (1997).
[17] His works influenced, among others, the world-famous Ephraim Kishon and George Mikes.
[18] Some of their skits are now on CDs and the internet (YouTube), and their names are also used for political-satirical skits. See, e.g., Hacsek és Sajó (2016a, 2016b).

Jewish Hungarian language), e.g., Györgyey (1980), Patai (1987), Várkonyi (1992), Haraszti (1993), Holzman (1986), and Révész (1942). Ujvári (1929) documented many of the Jewish writers and poets in the pre-WWII era, along with the other topics of his encyclopedic dictionary.[19] Vágo (1991) and Rosenhouse (2012a, 2012b, 2015a, 2015b) studied the speech of Hungarian Jews in Israel. Clearly, much more needs to be done in this field.

5.2 Corpora

There is no corpus of Jewish Hungarian language per se, probably because its existence was not acknowledged. The following few books can serve as corpora for the study of the nature of Jewish Hungarian texts, though at present they have not been used for linguistic studies of the language: Braham (1962), Handler (1935), Haraszti (1935), Komoróczy, G. (2013), Kőbányai (2015), Levy and Levy (2003), and Ujvári (1929).

5.3 Current directions in research

The subject of the Jewish Hungarian language is practically "terra incognita" for research. Many questions come to mind in light of the findings of this study. First, one has to divide the subject into (at least) two parts: Jews in Hungary and Hungarian-speaking Jews outside of Hungary, which, for the present research, are Hungarian-speaking Jews in Israel. These two groups developed in different political and cultural environments and, accordingly, acquired different linguistic features.

The first question raised, therefore, could be, in what linguistic ways do they differ? Considering, for example, lexical aspects, we noted that Biblical Hebrew names were adapted to the Hungarian language. An interesting study, then, would examine the rate of the use of such biblical names in the Jewish and non-Jewish communities in Hungary. A related question concerns the Jewish use of Hungarian personal names (after the Hungarization period) and their use or disuse in Israel, where many people "Hebraize" their names, or did so in the past.

---

19 This encyclopedia is also a first-hand source about the Jews in Hungary until the beginning of the 20th century.

Another possible question could ask how the Jewish Hungarian language is retained in Hungarian-speaking immigrants' homes. Do they or don't they pass it on to their offspring and let it remain (sometimes) an oral heritage language? Is this process similar to, or different from, cases of other Jewish language varieties in Israel or Hungary, and how is it attested?[20]

Furthermore, we can investigate the effect of Modern Hebrew on Jewish Hungarian speech in Israel – in which elements does it differ from Jewish Hungarian in Hungary? Jews in modern Hungary are aware of Israel, and, thus, how and at what rate does Modern Hebrew lexicon infiltrate their speech?

As mentioned, since the beginning of the 20th century, Jewish humor has been an important feature of Jewish Hungarian production, spreading in the written and spoken media. This topic requires a specific study of the discourse structure in jokes and humoristic works, compared to the non-Jewish parallels.

The subject of Jewish Hungarian requires more evidence-based research, because existing research describes neither Jewish Hungarian isoglosses, nor dialect features. Since oral languages develop and/or die with their speakers, these questions, at least, should be studied in Israel as soon as possible.

Our research began with collecting data about Hungarian Jews' speech features in Israel. This aspect of research is important and should continue in both Hungary and Israel. Currently, our focus is on written works of Jewish Hungarian writers from the 20th century before and after the Holocaust. Since a considerable number of Jewish writers write in Hungarian, in Israel and in Hungary, the question arises as to which Jewish elements appear in these works. Rosenhouse (2015b) has studied two of Kishon's humorous books compared with two of Monlár's books, but that study is only the tip of the iceberg. Many works by pre- and post-WWII Jewish writers were lost during WWI, WWII, the Holocaust, and later, but many are still waiting for such studies. I hope not to remain alone in this field.

References

Abádi, Ervin. 1962. *Hárfa Utca [Harp Street]*. Tel-Aviv: Lapid Kiadás.
Ararat, Nisan. 1997. *Drama in the Bible*. Jerusalem: The World Biblical Center. (Hebrew).
Balla, Erzsébet. 1969. The Jews of Hungary: A cultural overview. In Randolph L. Braham (ed.), *Hungarian Jewish Studies*, vol. II, 85–136. New York: World Federation of Hungarian Jews.
Bányai, Viktoria. 2008. Magyar ajku Zsidó közösség a világban [The Hungarian speaking Jewish community in the world]. In N. Bárdi, C. Fedinec & L. Szarka (eds.), *Kisebbségi magyar*

---

[20] On this question cf. the discussion about Former Soviet or Russian Immigrants in Israel (Mendelson-Maoz 2015).

közösségek a 20. században [Hungarian Minority Communities in the 20th Century], 412–417. Budapest: MTA Kisebbségkutató Intézet, http://adatbank.transindex.ro/regio/ kisebbsegkutatas/pdf/VI_fej_16_Banyai.pdf (accessed 2 January, 2016).
Bányai, Viktoria & Komoróczy, Szonja R. 2013. Hungarian, Hebrew loans in. In G. Khan (ed.), *Encyclopedia of Hebrew Language and Linguistic*s, 217–218. Leiden: Brill.
Benkő, Loránd, Bárczi Géza & Jolán Berrár. 1967. *A Magyar Nyelv Története. Etimológiai Szotára* [The history of the Hungarian language. Its etymological dictionary]. Budapest: Akademiai Kiadó.
Benor, Sarah Bunin. 2008. Towards a new understanding of Jewish language in the twenty-first century. *Religion Compass* 2(6). 1062–1080.
Benoschofsky, Ilona. 1966. The position of Hungarian Jewry after the liberation. In Randolph L. Braham (ed.), *Hungarian Jewish Studies*, vol. 3, 237–260. New York: World Federation of Hungarian Jews.
Bíró, Tamás. 2004. Weak interactions: Yiddish influence in Hungarian, Esperanto and Modern Hebrew. In Dicky Gilbers, Maartje Schreuder, & Nienke Knevel (eds.), *On the boundaries of phonology and phonetics: A festschrift presented to Tjeerd de Graaf*, 123–145. Groningen: University of Groningen.
Braham, Randolph L. (ed.). 1962. *The Hungarian Jewish catastrophe: A selected and annotated bibliography*. New York: YIVO-Institute for Jewish Research.
Braham, Randolph L. (ed.). 1966. *Hungarian-Jewish studies*. New York: World Federation of Hungarian Jews.
Carmilly-Weinberger, Moshe. 1966. Hebrew poetry in Hungary. In Randolph L. Braham (ed.), *Jewish-Hungarian Studies*, vol. 1, 295–342. New York: World Federation of Hungarian Jews.
Gilady, David. 1992. *Pesti mérnökök, Izrael országépitői* [Budapest engineers: Builders of Israel]. Budapest: Mult es Jövő.
Goldman, Tamás. 2015. Jewish Hungarian. (unpublished paper).
Györgyey, Clara. 1980. *Ferenc Molnár*. Boston: Twayne.
Handler, Andrew (ed.). 1935. *Ararat: A collection of Hungarian-Jewish short stories*. Rutherford, NJ: Fairleigh Dickinson University Press.
Hacsek és Sajo. 2016a. Nevessünk! [Let us laugh!]. Hacsek és sajó (1.Rész). https://www.youtube.com/watch?v=wKm5ANikJ8I (accessed 28 July, 2016).
Hacsek és Sajo. 2016b. Sajóné sportol [Mrs. Shajo is doing sports]. Hacsek és sajó. https://www.youtube.com/watch?v=LEivXzJDJBc (accessed 28 July, 2016).
Haraszti, György. 1993a. *Magyar Zsidó Levéltári Repertorium (B)* [Directory of archival holdings relating to the history of Jews in Hungary: Hungarian archives]. Budapest: MTA Judaistica Research Team. (Hungarian & English).
Holzman, Avner. 1986. *Avigdor Hameiri and war literature*. Tel-Aviv: Ma'arakhot. (Hebrew).
Kaczér, Illés. 1953. *Ne Félj, Szolgám Jákob* [Fear not my servant Jacob]. Tel-Aviv: Alexander Könyvkiadó R.T.
Katzburg, Nathaniel. 1981. Assimilation in Hungary during the nineteenth century: Orthodox positions. In Béla Vágo (ed.), *Jewish assimilation in modern times*, 49–56. Boulder: Westview Press.
Katzburg, Nathaniel. 1992. Before the Holocaust. In Randolph L. Braham (ed.), *History of the Holocaust: Hungary,* 1–141. Jerusalem: Yad Vashem.
Kishont, Ferenc (Efráim Kishon). 1956. *Hinta Palinta – Humoreszkek* [See-saw humoresques]. Tel-Aviv: Forum.
Kishont, Ferenc (Efráim Kishon). 1967. *Humoreszk* [Humoresque]. Tel-Aviv: Tversky.

Kőbányai, János. 2010. Hungarian literature. In Gershon Hundert (ed.), *The YIVO encyclopedia of Jews in Eastern Europe*. New Haven: Yale University Press. http://www.yivoencyclopedia.org/article.aspx/Hungarian_Literature.

Kőbányai, János. 2015. *Két évszázad magyar-zsidó költészete I. – Kivirágzás 1840–1919* [Two centuries of Hungarian-Jewish poetry I. Flowering 1840–1919]. Budapest: Múlt és Jövő Alapítvány.

Komoróczy, Géza. 2013. *"Nekem itt zsidónak kell lenni": Források és dokumentok (965–2012): A Zsidók története Magyarországon.* ["Here I have to be Jewish": Publications and Documents (965–2012): The Jewish History in Hungary.] Pozsony: Kalligram.

Komoróczy, Szonja R. 2011. *Yiddish printing in Hungary: An annotated bibliography*. Budapest: Center for Jewish Studies at the Hungarian Academy of Sciences.

Lászlo, Ernő. 1969. Hungary's Jewry: A demographic overview, 1918–1945. In Randolph L. Braham (ed.), *Hungarian Jewish studies*, 137–182. New Yok: World Federation of Hungarian Jews.

Levy Simha & Levy, Arie. 2003. *Books written in Hungary for teaching the Jewish religion from the end of the 18th century until 1950*. Tel-Aviv: Tel-Aviv University. (Hebrew).

Mendelson-Maoz, Adia. 2015. *Multiculturalism in Israel: Literary perspectives*. West Lafayette: Purdue University Press.

Myers-Scotton, Carol. 2002. *Contact linguistics: Bilingual encounters and grammatical outcomes*. Oxford: Oxford University Press.

Papp, Richard. 2016. "De hol van a Kohn?" A magyarországi zsidóság modernkori történelme egy budapesti zsidó közösség humorának tükrében. ["But where is Kohn?" Hungarian Jewry history in the mirror of a Budapest Jewish community.] In Peter Barta (ed.), *A humor nagyítón keresztül, IV: Magyar Interdiszciplináris Humorkonferencia*, [Humor in the magnifying glass IV: Hungarian Interdisciplinary Humor Conference] 80–95. Tinta Könyv Kiadó: Budapest.

Patai Jozsef (Ha-Patai Yosef). 1903. Sha'ashu'ey 'Alumim [Youth Entertainment]. Budapest: Schlesinger.

Patai Raphael. 1987. *Ignaz Goldziher and his Oriental diary: A translation and psychological portrait*. Detroit: Wayne State University Press.

Patai, Raphael. 1996. *The Jews of Hungary: History, culture, psychology*. Detroit: Wayne State University Press.

Portuges, Catherine. 2006. Imre Kertész's *Fateless* on film: A Hungarian Holocaust saga. In Randolph L. Braham & Brewer S. Chamberlin (eds.), *The Holocaust in Hungary: Sixty years later*, 349–363. New York: The Rosenthal Institute for Holocaust Studies, Graduate Center of the City University of New York, Social Science Monographs, Boulder, CO, United States Holocaust Memorial Museum & Columbia University Press.

Rosenhouse, Judith. 2012a. Two generations of Hungarian and Hebrew in Israel: A sociolinguistic study. *Helqat Lashon* 45. 159–183. (Hebrew).

Rosenhouse, Judith. 2012b. Israeli Hebrew and Hungarian interaction: Phonetic/phonological issues. In Dafydd Gibbon, Daniel Hirst, & Nick Campbell (eds.), *Rhythm, melody and harmony in speech: Studies in honour of Wiktor Jassem. Special Issue* of *Speech and Language Technology* 14/15, 211–224. Poznan: Polskie Towarzystwo Fonetyczne.

Rosenhouse, Judith. 2015a. Molnár and Kishon: Hungarian and Hebrew in Israel and Hungary. Paper read at IAAL (ILASH) Conference. Jerusalem: Levinsky College.

Rosenhouse Judith. 2015b. Hebrew in Hungarian texts: A lexical comparison. Paper read at LACUS Conference. New York: Rockville Center.

Sanders, Ivan. 2006. Jewish literary renaissance in post-Communist Hungary. In Randolph L. Braham & Brewer S. Chamberlin (eds.), *The Holocaust in Hungary: Sixty Years Later*, 365–376. New York: The Rosenthal Institute for Holocaust Studies, Graduate Center of the City University of New York, Social Science Monographs, Boulder, CO, United States Holocaust Memorial Museum & Columbia University Press.

Scheiber, Sándor, Livia Sheiberné Bernáth & Györgyi Barabás. 1993. *Magyar Zsidó Hírlapok és folyóiratok bibliografiaja* [Bibliography of Hungarian Jewish journals and magazines]. Budapest: MTA Judaisztikai Kutatócsoport.

Szalai, Anna. 2011. *Magyar-Héber, Héber-Magyar szótár* [Hungarian-Hebrew, Hebrew-Hungarian Dictionary]. Jerusalem: S. Zack Könyvkiadó.

Ujvári, Peter. 1929. *Magyar Zsidó lexicon* [Hungarian Jewish Lexicon]. Budapest: Magyar Zsidó Lexicon Kiadása.

Vágo, Robert. 1991. Paradigmatic regularity in first language attrition. In Herbert W. Seliger and Robert M. Vágo (eds.), *First language attrition*, 241–251. Cambridge: Cambridge University Press.

Várkonyi, István. 1992. *Ferenc Molnár and the Austro-Hungarian "fin de Siècle."* New York: Peter Lang.

Dalit Assouline
Haredi Yiddish in Israel and the United States

1 Introduction

As of the beginning of the 21st century, Yiddish is a diminishing language. Prior to the Holocaust it was the language of millions, spoken daily by both secular and traditional Jews in Eastern Europe and in various localities of Jewish immigration throughout the world. Today it exists as a daily means of communication primarily in some *Haredi* (ultra-Orthodox) communities, mainly in urban neighborhoods such as *Mea She'arim* in Jerusalem or "the Jewish quarter" of Antwerp. Yiddish is used inside these communities, while the majority language serves for communication with the outside world: English in the USA, Canada, and the UK; Hebrew in Israel; and Flemish or French in Belgium. In these bilingual settings, the majority language may also assume additional functions (such as being a major medium for written language use), thus causing a reduction in function in addition to the demographic and geographic decline of Yiddish. Serving in a few restricted insider domains, primarily within the home, Haredi Yiddish is facing increased lexical, structural, and stylistic attrition, with some varieties gradually converging (mainly lexically) towards the majority language. Nonetheless, even in its current reduced state, Yiddish enjoys great prestige in Haredi, mostly Hasidic, communities, where it functions as a powerful symbol of a distinct ethnic and religious identity, so that Hasidim continue to speak Yiddish and to pass it on to their children. Yiddish is also spoken outside the Haredi world, by elderly Jews born in Eastern Europe before World War II and by some of their descendants, serving, in addition, as a cultural language among Yiddish-lovers, most of whom have acquired the language in academic institutions (Section 4). Yet Yiddish-speaking communities with Yiddish-speaking children can be found almost exclusively among the ultra-Orthodox.

1.1 Demographics

The number of contemporary Yiddish speakers is hard to calculate. A generous estimate of 1.5 million includes both Haredi speakers who use Yiddish daily, as well as partial speakers and semi-speakers, who have only limited, largely passive familiarity with Yiddish (Fishman 2007, see also Ethnologue, Yiddish: www.ethnologue.com/language/ydd; see also Fishman's estimations of 600,000 speakers in 2001, Shandler 2006: 203, note 1, and 500,000 speakers in Shaechter 1999), while the highest estimate of Haredi Yiddish speakers comes to about half a million (Katz 2004: 387–388; Glinert 1999a: 3). Most Haredi speakers are located in the US and Israel. Examples include: in the United States, in the Brooklyn neighborhoods of Williamsburg and Borough Park, in Kiryas Joel (Orange County, NY), Monsey and the village of New Square (Rockland County, NY), and in Lakewood, New Jersey; and in Israel, in Jerusalem, Bet-Shemesh, Bnei Brak, Betar Illit, and Ashdod (Mintz 1992; Rubin 1997; Isaacs 1999a, Isaacs 1999b; Katz 2004: 385–386; Assouline 2012: 104). Significant Yiddish-speaking Hasidic communities can also be found in Antwerp, London, Manchester, and Montreal, and the language is used in smaller communities as well, such as those located in Melbourne and Sao Paolo. The level of command and use of Yiddish varies within these communities, ranging from fluent speakers who also read and write in Yiddish (such as American Satmar Hasidim) to less proficient speakers with minimal Yiddish literacy, as in some Israeli Hasidic sects (see Isaacs 1999b; Assouline 2012). Some of these less proficient communities are gradually shifting towards the majority language, yet Yiddish is still stubbornly maintained in more extreme, segregated sects. Consequently, even though it is never possible to predict the fate of a minority language, Haredi Yiddish seems to stand a reasonable chance of survival in the coming generations.

1.2 Historical background

Most speakers of Haredi Yiddish are descendants of Eastern European Jews who settled in the US, Israel, and Western Europe after World War II, joining Hasidic sects that were reestablished after their near destruction in the Holocaust (see, for example, Mintz 1992; Rubin 1997). These Hasidic sects are closely knit groups, united around a spiritual leader (the *Rebbe*), and maintaining a close affinity to their idealized Eastern European past. This affinity is manifested by the names of the various Hasidic sects, typically deriving from the Eastern European towns or villages from which they originated (such as the *Belz* and *Vizhnitz* Hasidic sects, named after Belz and Vyzhnytsia, both in present day Ukraine), as well as by the deliberate efforts of Hasidim to replicate their ancestral way of life, maintaining as many of its traditions and customs as possible, including the preservation of their ancestors' language, Yiddish (Isaacs 1999a; Heilman 1995: xiii; Belcove-Shalin 1995). The reestablished postwar sects attracted both Holocaust survivors and Jews who had left Eastern Europe before the war, many of whom joined sects with a geographic provenance different from their own (Fader 2009: 8–9). Nevertheless, the mixed makeup of the new sects has generally not resulted in dialect leveling, since distinct Yiddish dialects function as communal markers, denoting specific group membership within the Hasidic world (see below, Section 1.3). Only a few contemporary Yiddish-speaking communities have enjoyed continuous existence over the last century – one example being the Israeli "Jerusalemites," the descendants of an ascetic group that left Lithuania at the beginning of the 19th century to settle in the holy cities of Jerusalem and Safed (Assouline 2010b) – and so the revived Hasidic sects constitute the majority of speakers.

1.3 Yiddish dialects

Originally, Eastern European Yiddish dialects were divided into three major regional varieties: northeastern, central, and southeastern Yiddish (Weinreich 1980: 16–21). Today, these dialects have acquired a new function, so that they are no longer geographical but rather serve as communal dialects, marking sect affiliation as well as ethnic background (Isaacs 1999b: 114–117). The most widespread Hasidic dialect today derives from central Yiddish, in the shape of the so-called "Hungarian" Yiddish, and is spoken in several sects, primarily in the dominant Satmar Hasidic sect (Krogh 2012a, 2014, 2018. See also Poll 1965). So-called "Polish" Yiddish is also maintained in several sects (Sadock & Masor 2018). Dialects of southeastern origin are less common, preserved, for example, in the language of the Vizhnitz Hasidic sect, and northeastern Yiddish is relatively rare, spoken primarily by some "Jerusalemites" as well as by several groups of Chabad-Lubavitch Hasidim. Since the dialects signal sect affiliation, they are deliberately maintained by their speakers: Children are sent to sect-specific educational institutions where, in those cases in which the parents speak differently, they acquire the dialect of the group, and Hasidim may change their dialect when joining a different sect (Isaacs 1999b: 114–115). Although many original dialectal features are lost, speakers maintain the salient dialectal vowel distinctions, which are readily identified by them as intra-communal markers (Assouline 2015), as well as certain other phonological features such as the apical *r* of "Hungarian" Yiddish (Krogh 2012a: 485). Besides such phonological distinctions, some speakers are also aware of certain lexical dialectal differences, mainly regarding loanwords from former contact languages, such as the Hungarian word *tsúmi* 'pacifier' in "Hungarian" Hasidic Yiddish or the Judeo-Spanish *meníye* 'bracelet' in "Jerusalemite" Yiddish (see also Kosover 1966: 357).

1.4 Sociolinguistic background

Haredi Yiddish is maintained today in a multilingual setting: All adult speakers are bilingual, speaking Yiddish as well as the majority language, while also using the Hebrew-Aramaic variety known as *loshn-kóydesh* (literally, Holy Tongue) in specific domains such as prayer and study. Significantly, the level of command and use of Haredi Yiddish is often gender-differentiated, with men using Yiddish more than women (Fader 2007; Bogoch 1999: 131; Baumel 2003; Ben Rafael 1994: 154). Yet in the Hasidic communities where Yiddish is best preserved, gender differences are minimal, with Yiddish being acquired as a native tongue, serving as the main language spoken with family and friends and employed in communal educational institutions. Yiddish is also the dominant language in the *yeshiva*, where it serves the oral study of sacred Hebrew and Aramaic texts (Isaacs 1999a: 18; 1999b: 108; cf. Heilman 1981). This "scholarly" or "learned" Yiddish, full of Hebrew and Aramaic code-switches, is a highly prestigious variety, which also serves as the language of public address for the Haredi spiritual and scholarly elite. In fact, even in Haredi sects and branches where Yiddish has almost disappeared as a spoken language, it may still be used in certain prestigious scholarly or spiritual contexts – such as advanced yeshiva lessons in Yiddish in some Litvish branches that have otherwise shifted to English or Hebrew (Fishman 1989: 4; Katz 2004: 384). Through this use of the prestigious insider language, primarily English- or Hebrew-speaking Haredim are able to gain access to all parts of Ashkenazi Haredi society (Baumel 2003: 105).

Haredi Yiddish is primarily a spoken language, yet it is also used as a written medium, together with *loshn-kóydesh* (in specific contexts) and the majority language. Yiddish literacy varies greatly from one Haredi community to the next and is commonly gender-determined. For example, Israeli speakers maintain the traditional Ashkenazi diglossia, with Yiddish as a spoken language and Hebrew as the main written medium (Assouline 2010b: 2), with only women from extreme, segregated sects reading in Yiddish, while other women, as well as almost all men, read predominantly in Hebrew. By contrast, the American Hasidic women studied by Fader read mostly in English (Fader 2009: 168–169). In general, Yiddish literacy is higher in American and European communities than in Israel, as demonstrated by the fact that there is not a single Haredi Yiddish newspaper published in Israel (cf. Section 3.2).

The maintenance of Haredi Yiddish is supported by its prestigious status: Yiddish is identified with idealized generations from the past and is therefore deemed vital in the pursuit of an authentic Hasidic way of life (Isaacs 1998b: 167; Isaacs 1999a: 18–20; cf. Fishman 1981: 11–12). Furthermore, Yiddish is considered a holy language in certain Haredi circles, sanctified by its use by generations of righteous Jews (Glinert and Shilhav 1991: 78–81; Fishman 2002: 131–136; Bogoch 1999: 133; Granot 2007: 377–384). The prestige of Yiddish is the driving force behind Haredi efforts to preserve the language. In Israel, these efforts include the translation of books for toddlers and children into Yiddish, the establishment of new Yiddish schools, and the addition of Yiddish lessons in Hebrew-speaking schools (Biglayzn 2007; R.N. 2007). The prestige of the language may even lead

Hebrew-speaking parents, who wish to improve their children's chances of marrying into a "good" family, to send them to Yiddish-speaking schools (R.N. 2007; Bogoch 1999: 140–141; Isaacs 1999b: 110, 112). Command of Yiddish may thus function as an effective vehicle of social mobility.

The efforts to maintain Yiddish, and the wide acknowledgment of its significance for the preservation of what is perceived as the ideal Haredi way of life, are not accompanied by a corresponding ambition to speak "good" Yiddish. Haredi speakers do not attribute any socio-cultural value to "correct" language and believe that Yiddish "has no grammar" (Glinert and Shilhav 1991: 64; Isaacs 1998b: 181–185; Spitzer 2008: 12). There is no standard variety, no structured study of Yiddish in Haredi schools, and Haredi Yiddish publications reveal broad orthographic, dialectal, lexical, and structural variation (Fader 2007: 6–7; Bogoch 1999: 136–137; Krogh 2014: 65; Katz 2004: 389–390). Significantly, the absence of normative pressures in a bilingual setting makes Haredi Yiddish highly susceptible to external influences from the majority languages. At the same time, speakers' tolerant attitude towards external interference supports the survival of Yiddish, mainly because it facilitates compensation for the growing lexical gaps in the Haredi vernacular: "Linguistically, openness permits Haredim to hold onto the traditional while incorporating the necessities of the contemporary world" (Isaacs 1999a: 26. See also Fader 2009: 93; Assouline 2012: 114–115).

2 Past and present Yiddish: Linguistic differences

Comparison between the structure of contemporary and former varieties of Yiddish is no easy task, since the most widespread contemporary "Hungarian" variety derives from the least documented Eastern European Yiddish dialect (Weinreich 1964: 264; Krogh 2012a, 2014). Nonetheless several salient distinctive features of Haredi Yiddish can be identified, mainly with respect to its relative structural simplification. Most conspicuously, the nominal declension manifests considerable simplification and variation, with a gradual shift, for example, to a single definite article (*de/di*), devoid of gender and case distinctions (Jacobs 2005: 292; Mitchell 2006: 121; Assouline 2014: 41–43; Szendrői, Belk, & Kahn 2018; cf. Peltz 1990: 70. See also Nove, forthcoming, on pronominal case syncretism). Another example of structural simplification concerns the marking of the indirect object and some direct objects with the preposition *far* 'for', replacing morphological case marking as well as other prepositions (Assouline 2009, 2014). The most noticeable differences between Eastern European and contemporary Yiddish, however, are attributable to the effect of language contact.

2.1 Language contact influences

The majority languages, mainly American English and Israeli Hebrew, exert a profound impact on Haredi Yiddish. Code-switching and lexical borrowing are common phenomena, varying in extent depending on levels of bilingualism and the attitudes of the community towards the majority language (Isaacs 1999a: 25–27; Jacobs 2005: 293; Vaisman 2008; Assouline 2018). Consider, for example, the English lexical interference in (a), from a lecture delivered by an American Hasidic woman in 2008. All examples in this chapter are taken from a spoken corpus of American and Israeli public speakers, recorded in 2000–2010 (see Section 3.4).

a. | de | tenshen level | iz hoyekh, | yetst, siz | zayer zayer |
|---|---|---|---|---|
| the | tension level | is high | now it is | very very |
| kamen | in aza | tsat | az | me | vert |
| common | in such_a | time | that | IMPERSONAL | becomes |
| nerveyz, | in | me | shrayt, | in | me |
| nervous | and | IMPERSONAL | shouts | and | IMPERSONAL |
| ken | hurtn | aynems | filings. | | |
| can | hurt | one's | feelings | | |

'The tension level is high, now, it's very very common in such a time that we become nervous, and we shout, and we can hurt someone's feelings.' (Note the calque of the English 'to hurt someone's feelings', with the English verb morphologically integrated into Yiddish, and the two English loans 'tension level' and 'common').

English loanwords are frequently employed in American Hasidic Yiddish, while Israeli Hebrew loanwords may be considered problematic in some extreme Israeli Haredi sects, who ideologically oppose Israeli Hebrew (Assouline 2017: 45–47). Nevertheless, most Israeli speakers use many Hebrew loanwords, to much the same extent as their American counterparts use borrowings from English (Assouline 2012: 110, 2013, 2017: 125). English and Hebrew loanwords may be differently integrated morphologically into Yiddish, particularly where verbs and adjectives are concerned. Consider the synthetic morphological integration of the English verb *change* in (b), versus the compound construction used for the integration of the colloquial Hebrew verb *mefasfés* 'miss' in (c) (with the Germanic light verb *zayn* 'to be' and the Hebrew participial form known as *beynoni* as the lexical core of the periphrasis. Both integration patterns are documented in Yiddish, see Sasaki 1993: 137–140; Sadan 2013: 1038; Assouline 2010a):

b. *er hot getsheyndzht zayn maynd*
   he has change.PTCP his mind
   'He changed his mind'

c. *er ot mefasfés geven de yaád.*
   he has miss be.PTCP the purpose(Israeli Hebrew)
   'He missed the purpose'

Adjectives also tend to be integrated differently, with English adjectives often directly inserted, as in (d), while Hebrew adjectives usually undergo morphological integration, as in (e), here with the Germanic derivational suffix *–dik*:

d. *a deyndzheres zakh*
   a dangerous thing
   'a dangerous thing'

e. *meshúkhlel-dik-e oto-s*
   improved-derivative suffix-PL car-PL
   'latest-model cars' (from Israeli Hebrew *meshukhlál* 'improved, topnotch')

Among some speakers, lexical borrowing is so extensive that their Yiddish can almost be viewed as a mixed variety, with a Yiddish grammatical matrix and a largely Hebrew/English lexicon. Note that among most native speakers the Yiddish grammatical structure as such has not been significantly affected by the contact languages.

Another common contact-induced change is semantic convergence of similar sounding elements. This is especially common in American Yiddish, where Germanic Yiddish elements may be influenced by their English cognates (see an example in Nove 2018: 122). Consider the unusual use of the Yiddish preposition *far* 'for' in (f), influenced by the English 'for' (in Eastern European Yiddish *oyf dray voxn* 'for three weeks', see also Estraikh 2007):

f. *man mame iz gezesn neybn mayn babe*
   my mother is sit.PTCP beside my grandmother
   oleo ashulem far dray vokhn in shpitul
   may_she_rest_in_peace for three weeks in hospital
   'My mother sat beside my grandmother, may she rest in peace, for three weeks in the hospital'

Phonological influence is also attested among some Haredi Yiddish speakers, as in the case, for example, of American speakers with an alveolar approximant [ɹ], or Israeli speakers who avoid Yiddish consonant clusters by epenthesis (e.g. *dorten* instead of *dortn* 'there'). There is to date, however, no comprehensive research available on the phonology of Haredi Yiddish.

2.2 Lexicon: Hebrew and Aramaic elements

The Hebrew-Aramaic component in American and European Haredi varieties is lexically and morphologically similar to that in Eastern European Yiddish. Additionally, since Haredim constantly use *loshn-kóydesh* in prayer and study, *loshn-kóydesh* excerpts may be integrated into their Yiddish, mainly by men and particularly in scholastic settings (Assouline 2010c, 2014b). These excerpts or code-switches, articulated in the Ashkenazi pronunciation, were termed "Whole Hebrew" by Max Weinreich, as opposed to the Hebrew-Aramaic component consisting of Hebrew and Aramaic loanwords, which he termed "Merged Hebrew" (Weinreich 1980: 351–353).

In the Israeli varieties, however, the merged component differs from that in Eastern European Yiddish. This is because "Merged Hebrew" reflects a diglossic setting, while the bilingual setting in Israel provides speakers with an unprecedented familiarity with and hence knowledge of Hebrew – as compared to the limited command of Hebrew in the past, which was formerly restricted mainly to a small, learned male elite (Weinreich 1980: 225; Stampfer 1993). As a result, the Hebrew component in Israeli Haredi Yiddish is very extensive, including both documented elements as well as new loanwords from Israeli Hebrew, phonologically and sometimes also morphologically integrated into Yiddish. In addition, the speakers' command of Israeli Hebrew affects the meaning as well as the integration patterns of the Hebrew loanwords. Semantically, the meaning of Hebrew elements usually coincides with the one common in Israeli Hebrew, as in (g), where the documented element *nisóyen* 'temptation' (Weinreich 1990: 527) is semantically modified under the impact of Israeli Hebrew *nisayón* 'experience' (cf. Kantor 1997: 137):

g. ikh ob   nisóyen
   I   have experience
   'I am experienced'

The integration patterns of Hebrew elements may also change in the Israeli bilingual setting, in cases where they reassume some of their original grammatical traits (Assouline 2010a, 2010c: 18–21). For example, the nominal plural inflection of Hebrew-derived Yiddish nouns usually conforms to the regular Hebrew pluralization, as in *sho* 'hour' – *shóes* 'hours' (cf. Israeli Hebrew *shaá* – *shaót*), and not as in Eastern European Yiddish (*sho* – *shóen*, with a Germanic pluralization, Weinreich 1990: 382).

3 Written and oral traditions

3.1 Writing system

Haredi Yiddish orthography differs from Standard Yiddish orthography and is not always consistent. In children's books, which constitute the bulk of Haredi Yiddish literature, additional Hebrew diacritics (*niqqud*) are commonly used (Isaacs 2004). In newspapers and other publications for adults, features of traditional orthography are common, such as "Germanized" (*daytshmerish*) spelling, grammatical apostrophes separating stems from affixes, and omission of diacritics (Mitchell 2006: 76–97; Isaacs 2004; Katz 2004: 382; Krogh 2014; Berman 2013; Kahn 2016: 669. And see, too, Haredi claims in favor of this orthography as opposed to YIVO standard orthography in the section *mame-loshn* in the Haredi monthly Yiddish magazine *Mayles* [*Mallos*], 2005–2006).

3.2 Literature

Haredi Yiddish literature is printed mainly in the US, and includes books (mostly children's books, Katz 2004: 389; and schoolbooks, Kutzik 2018), newspapers, and magazines (such as *der Yid, der Blat, di Tsaytung, Mayles, der Blik, Balaykhtungen, der Shtern* and others, see Mitchell 1999, Krogh 2014, Isaacs 1998b: 177–178, Katz 2003; for additional Haredi periodicals, see the Yiddish Wikipedia under the categories *frume tsaytungen* and *frume magazinen*). Yiddish is also a common written medium on Haredi (mostly American) websites, such as *idishe velt* (www.ivelt.com) and *kave shtibl* (www.kaveshtiebel.com), blogs, and the Yiddish Wikipedia, written almost exclusively by American Hasidim (see also Schaechter 2011).

3.3 Performance

In addition to its primary function as an insider spoken variety, Haredi Yiddish also serves in performative contexts, often on festive occasions such as holidays and weddings. Yiddish plays are usually performed on the carnivalesque Jewish holiday of Purim, as well as in the intermediate days of Passover and Sukkot (Heb. *khol hamoed*). These include the traditional Purim play known as the *purim-shpil* (see, for example, Epstein's study of the "*Daniel–shpil*" in the American Bobov Hasidic sect, Epstein 1998; see also Isaacs 1998b: 175–177), as well as more modern plays, usually based on historical events such as the expulsion from Spain. Recorded plays are distributed in Haredi stores, as is the single Haredi movie in Yiddish produced to date (*a gesheft*, 2005). Hasidic communities also maintain the tradition of the *badkhn* (lit. jester), who performs at weddings as well as at the festive meals during the week following the wedding (Heb. *sheva brakhot*). The *badkhn* recites rhymed verses (*gramen*, see, for example, Mazor and Taube 1994), while some *badkhonim* also perform Yiddish stand-up routines (mainly at the *sheva brakhot* meals). Another form of entertainment common at weddings is the performance of a Hasidic singer, singing in Yiddish, *loshn-kóydesh*, or often in a mixture of both. Popular Hasidic singers also perform at concerts, and their songs are widely distributed throughout the Haredi world (Isaacs 1998b: 171–174). Significantly, all of the genres mentioned above involve only men: players, *badkhonim*, and singers. A woman's voice is perceived to be sexually stimulating, and hence must be silenced in public settings (Berman 1980). Therefore, women's performances are restricted to women-only audiences, such as some amateur plays performed by women to all-female audiences. See also the documentation of a poem recited to a bride at a Satmar wedding (Kahan-Newman 1999) and a study of religiously didactic Hasidic women's songs (Vaisman 2013; see also Isaacs 1998b: 172).

3.4 Haredi Yiddish in the electronic media

Yiddish is used in Haredi radio stations called "hotlines," which are broadcast by telephone (Assouline & Dori-Hacohen 2017). Most American "hotlines" are in Yiddish, featuring Haredi news reports and interviews with Yiddish-speaking Haredim from around the world. Recorded (audio and sometimes also video) Yiddish lectures, lessons, and sermons are also available on hundreds of Haredi websites, such as www.kolhalashon.com, as are recorded plays, shows, *purim-shpiln*, and video clips of Yiddish songs.

4 Yiddish outside the Haredi world

Outside the Haredi world, most contemporary Yiddish speakers are elderly Jews, born in Eastern Europe. Postwar immigrant Yiddish is discussed in several studies conducted in the USA, such as Rayfield (1970), Peltz (1990, 1998a), and Levine (2000) (See additional references in Peltz 1998b). Today, with the number of native Eastern European Yiddish speakers constantly decreasing, current research tends to focus on the cultural role of Yiddish among the descendants of these immigrants as a "postvernacular language" (Shandler 2006; see also Benor 2013. Cf. Avineri's (2012, 2015) "metalinguistic community") serving largely nostalgic and ethno-symbolic functions. Since Yiddish is acquired as a native tongue by children almost exclusively in Haredi communities, non-Haredi contemporary Yiddish is largely dependent on academic and cultural centers, such as the YIVO Institute for Jewish Research in New York, the National Yiddish Book Center (Amherst, Massachusetts), Beth Sholem Aleykhem (Tel Aviv), the *Medem* Paris Yiddish center, and universities offering Yiddish classes, advanced studies and intensive summer courses (Katz 2004: 355–360; see also Burko 2008 on young Yiddishists in New York).

5 State of research

The earliest studies of Haredi Yiddish focused on sociolinguistic issues, such as language ideologies (Poll 1965, 1980; Glinert and Shilhav 1991; Fishman 1981: 11, 53) and the multilingual settings of Yiddish speakers (Jochnowitz 1968; Heilman 1981). Since the late 1990s, sociolinguistic research has expanded to include general studies of Haredi Yiddish (Isaacs 1999a; Katz 2004: 379–391), Haredi Yiddish in Israel (Isaacs 1998a, 1999b; Bogoch 1999; Assouline 2012) and in the UK (Glinert 1999; Baumel 2003; Mitchell 2006), and studies of language and gender in Haredi communities (Fader 2001, 2006, 2007, 2008, 2009: 87–144; Assouline 2014b).

Contemporary linguistic research on Yiddish is based on both written and spoken sources. Written Haredi Yiddish is discussed in Mitchell 2006: 73–117 (written Haredi British Yiddish), Isaacs 2004 (American children's books), Krogh 2012a, 2012b, 2014, 2015, 2018 (written Satmar Yiddish), Bleaman 2017 (syntactic variation), Kantor 1997 (lexical interference), Kahan-Newman 2008 (Hebrew component), and Berman 2013 (Israeli-Hebrew component). Spoken varieties have been studied in the UK (Mitchell 2006: 117–134; Szendrői, Belk, & Kahn 2018), in Israel (Berman-Assouline 2007; Berman 2007; Assouline 2010a, 2010b, 2010c, 2014a, 2014b, 2017), and in the US (Kahan-Newman 2015; Assouline (ed.) 2018; Nove forthcoming). Another new direction of research concerns children's acquisition of Yiddish as a native language, conducted in several Haredi, Yiddish-speaking communities, for example, by Barriere (2010) in Brooklyn, Abugov and Ravid (2013, 2014a, b) in Israel, and Abugov and Gillis (2016) in Antwerp.

References

Abugov, Netta & Steven Gillis. 2016. Nominal plurals in Antwerp Hasidic Yiddish: An empirical study. *Linguistics* 54(6). 1397–1415.

Abugov, Netta & Dorit Ravid. 2013. Assessing Yiddish plurals in acquisition: Impacts of bilingualism. In Virginia C. Mueller Gathercole (ed.), *Bilinguals and assessment: Issues*, 90–110. Bristol: Multilingual Matters.

Abugov, Netta & Dorit Ravid. 2014a. Noun plurals in Israeli Ultra-Orthodox Yiddish: A psycholinguistic perspective. In Marion Aptroot & Björen Hansen (eds.), *Yiddish language structures*, 9–39. Berlin: Mouton De Gruyter.

Abugov, Netta & Dorit Ravid. 2014b. Home language usage and the impact of modern Hebrew on Israeli Hasidic Yiddish nouns and noun plurals. *International Journal of the Sociology of Language* 226. 189–211.

Assouline, Dalit. 2009. Grammatical change and language contact: The case of *far* in Israeli and American Haredi Yiddish. Paper presented at the *Yiddish Language Structures* conference. Regensburg, Germany.

Assouline, Dalit. 2010a. Pe'alim mimotsa ivri baidish hakharedit beisrael [Verbs of Hebrew origin in Israeli Haredi Yiddish]. In Rina Ben Shahar, Gideon Toury & Nitsa Ben-Ari (eds.), *Ha'ivrit safa haya* [Hebrew: A living language], vol. 5, 27–45. Tel Aviv: Hakibutz Hameukhad and the Porter Institute for Poetics and Semiotics, Tel Aviv University.

Assouline, Dalit. 2010b. The emergence of two first person plural pronouns in Haredi Jerusalemite Yiddish. *Journal of Germanic Linguistics* 22(1). 1–22.

Assouline, Dalit. 2010c. Ma'avarim ben idish ve'ivrit bilshon darshanim kharediim beisrael [Codeswitching in Israeli Haredi Yiddish sermons]. *Massorot* 15. 1–24.

Assouline, Dalit. 2012. "Shelo shinu et leshonam": Idish kharedit beisrael ["They had not changed their language": Haredi Yiddish in Israel]. In Kimmy Caplan & Nurit Stadler (eds.), *Mehisardut lehitbasesut: Tmurot bakhevra hakharedit uvekhikra* [From survival to consolidation: Changes in Israeli Haredi society and its scholarly study], 101–115. Jerusalem: Van Leer.

Assouline, Dalit. 2013. Ben tahor letame: Hahavkhana hakharedit ben leshon-kodesh leivrit [The Haredi distinction between *Ivrit* and *Loshn-Koydesh*]. In Yotam Benziman (ed.), *Leshon rabim: Ha'ivrit kisfat tarbut* [Language as culture: New perspectives on Hebrew], 145–163. Jerusalem: Van Leer.

Assouline, Dalit. 2014a. Language change in a bilingual community: The preposition *far* in Israeli Haredi Yiddish. In Marion Aptroot & Björen Hansen (eds.), *Yiddish language structures* (Empirical approaches to language typology), 39–61. Berlin: Mouton de Gruyter.

Assouline, Dalit. 2014b. Veiling knowledge: Hebrew sources in the Yiddish sermons of ultra-Orthodox women. *International Journal of the Sociology of Language* 226. 163–188.

Assouline, Dalit. 2015. Linguistic outcomes of a Hasidic renewal: The case of Skver. *Language & Communication* 42. 141–146.

Assouline, Dalit & Gonen Dori-Hacohen. 2017. Yiddish across borders: Interviews in the Yiddish ultra-Orthodox Jewish audio mass medium. *Language & Communication* 56. 69–81.

Assouline, Dalit. 2017. *Contact and ideology in a multilingual community: Yiddish and Hebrew among the ultra-Orthodox*. Berlin: de Gruyter.

Assouline, Dalit (ed.). 2018. American Hasidic Yiddish. *Journal of Jewish Languages* 6(1) (thematic issue).

Assouline, Dalit. 2018. English can be Jewish but Hebrew cannot: Code-switching patterns among Yiddish-speaking Hasidic women. *Journal of Jewish Languages* 6(1). 43–59.

Avineri, Netta Rose. 2012. *Heritage language socialization practices in secular Yiddish educational contexts: The creation of a metalinguistic community.* Los Angeles: UCLA PhD thesis.

Avineri, Netta Rose. 2015. Yiddish language socialization across communities: Religion, ideologies and variation. *Language and Communication* 42. 135–140.

Barrière, Isabelle. 2010. The vitality of Yiddish among Hasidic infants and toddlers in a low SES preschool in Brooklyn. In W. Moskovich, (ed.), *Yiddish – a Jewish national language at 100. Proceedings of Czernowitz Yiddish language 2008 international centenary conference, (Jews and Slavs 22)*, 170–196. Jerusalem: Hebrew University.

Baumel, Simeon D. 2003. Black hats and holy tongues: Language and culture among British Haredim. *European Judaism* 36(2). 91–109.

Baumel, Simeon D. 2006. *Sacred speakers: Language and culture among the Haredim in Israel.* New York: Berghahn Books.

Belcove-Shalin, Janet S. 1995. Introduction: New world Hasidim. In Janet S. Belcove-Shalin (ed.), *New world Hasidim: Ethnographic studies of Hasidic Jews in America*, 1–30. Albany: State University of New York Press.

Ben-Rafael, Eliezer. 1994. *Language, identity, and social division – the case of Israel.* Oxford & New York: Clarendon Press & Oxford University Press.

Benor, Sarah Bunin. 2013. Echoes of Yiddish in the speech of twenty-first-century American Jews. In Lara Rabinovitch, Shiri Goren & Hannah S. Pressman (eds.), *Choosing Yiddish: New frontiers of language and culture*, 319–337. Detroit: Wayne State University Press.

Berman, Dalit. 2007. Ivrit isre'elit begaluy uvemasve baidish hakharedit [Israeli Hebrew in Haredi Yiddish, visible and camouflaged]. In Rina Ben Shahar & Gideon Toury (eds.), *Ha'ivrit safa haya* [Hebrew: A living language], vol. 4, 107–126. Tel Aviv: Hakibutz Hameukhad and the Porter Institute for Poetics and Semiotics.

Berman, Dalit. 2013. Ivrit ve'ivrit':Ktivan shel milim ivriyot bashavu'on hakharedi 'dos idishe likht' [Hebrew and 'Hebrew': Hebrew words in the Haredi weekly 'Dos Idishe Likht']. In Israel Bartal, Claudia Rosenzweig, Ada Rapoport-Albert, Viki Shifris, Galit Hasan-Rokem & Erika Timm (eds.), *Khut shel khen: Shay lekhava turniansky* [Studies in Ashkenazi culture, women's history, and the languages of the Jews, presented to Chava Turniansky], 539–549. Jerusalem: Shazar.

Berman, Saul J. 1980. Kol 'isha [Woman's voice]. In Leo Landman (ed.), *Rabbi Joseph H. Lookstein memorial volume*, 45–66. New York: Ktav Publishing House.

Berman-Assouline, Dalit. 2007. *Shimur utmura baidish hakharedit beisrael* [Linguistic maintenance and change in Israeli Haredi Yiddish]. Jerusalem: The Hebrew University of Jerusalem dissertation.

Biglayzn, Hersh. 2007. Tate-mame, higanu leveit shemesh! [Father and mother, we have arrived at Beit-Shemesh!]. *Davka* 3. 28–31.

Bleaman, Isaac L. 2017. Variation in Hasidic Yiddish syntax: A corpus study of language change on the internet. Paper presented at the 49th AJS annual conference, Washington DC.

Bogoch, Bryna. 1999. Gender, literacy and religiosity: Dimensions of Yiddish education in Israeli government-supported schools. *International Journal of the Sociology of Language* 138. 123–160.

Burko, Leyzer. 2008. Leshana haba'a bebruklin habnuya [Next year in a rebuilt Brooklyn]. *Davka* 5. 10–11.

Epstein, Shifra. 1998. *'Daniel shpil' bekhasidut bobov* [The Daniel-shpil in the Bobover Hasidic community]. Jerusalem: Magnes Press.
Estraikh, Gennady. 2007. Di shprakh fun khsidisher beletristik [The Language of Hasidic belles-lettres]. *Forverts*, 26 January, 2007.
Fader, Ayala. 2001. Literacy, bilingualism and gender in a Hasidic community. *Linguistics and Education* 12(3). 261–283.
Fader, Ayala. 2006. Learning faith: Language socialization in a Hasidic community. *Language in Society* 35(2). 207–229.
Fader, Ayala. 2007. Reclaiming sacred sparks: Linguistic syncretism and gendered language shift among Hasidic Jews in New York. *Journal of Linguistic Anthropology* 17(1). 1–22.
Fader, Ayala. 2008. Reading Jewish signs: The socialization of multilingual literacies among Hasidic women and girls in Brooklyn, New York. *Text & Talk* 28(5). 621–641.
Fader, Ayala. 2009. *Mitzvah girls: Bringing up the next generation of Hasidic women in Brooklyn*. Princeton: Princeton University Press.
Fishman, Joshua A. 1981. The sociology of Yiddish: A foreword. In Joshua A. Fishman (ed.), *Never say die! A thousand years of Yiddish in Jewish life and letters*, 1–97. The Hague: Mouton.
Fishman, Joshua A. 1989. Yidish ba di khareydim: Frishe koykhes un naye tsores [Yiddish among the Haredim: Fresh forces and new problems]. *Oyfn Shvel* 276. 1–5.
Fishman, Joshua A. 2002. The holiness of Yiddish: Who says Yiddish is holy and why? *Language Policy* 1. 123–141.
Fishman, Shikl [Joshua A.]. 2007. Vifl reders muz a loshn farmogn, kedey tsu blaybn tsvishn di lebedike? [How many speakers must a language have, in order to remain a living language?]. *Forverts*, 3 August, 2007.
Glinert, Lewis & Yosseph Shilhav. 1991. Holy land, holy language: A study of an Ultraorthodox Jewish ideology. *Language in Society* 20. 59–86.
Glinert, Lewis. 1999a. Foreword. In Lewis Glinert & Miriam Isaacs (eds.), Pious voices: Languages among Ultra-Orthodox Jews [*International Journal of the Sociology of Language* 138]. 1–4. Berlin & New York: Mouton de Gruyter.
Glinert, Lewis. 1999b. We never changed our language: Attitudes to Yiddish acquisition among Hasidic educators in Britain. *International Journal of the Sociology of Language* 138. 31–52.
Granot, Tamir. 2007. 'Galut Israel be'erets Israel': Hayidish vehamivta haashkenazi bapsika uvahagut hakharedit bizmanenu [Yiddish and Ashkenazi pronunciation in contemporary Haredi (halakhic) ruling and thought]. *Maim Midalyav* 18. 371–402.
Heilman, Samuel C. 1981. Sounds of Modern Orthodoxy: The language of Talmud study. In Joshua A. Fishman (ed.), *Never say die! A thousand years of Yiddish in Jewish life and letters*, 232–243. The Hague: Mouton.
Heilman, Samuel C. 1995. Foreword. In Janet S. Belcove-Shalin (ed.), *New world Hasidim: Ethnographic studies of Hasidic Jews in America*, xi-xv. Albany: State University of New York Press.
Isaacs, Miriam. 1998a. Yiddish in the Orthodox communities of Jerusalem. In Dov-Ber Kerler (ed.), *The politics of Yiddish: Studies in language, literature and society*, 85–96. Walnut Creek: AltaMira Press.
Isaacs, Miriam. 1998b. Yiddish "then and now": Creativity in contemporary Hasidic communities. In Leonard Jay Greenspoon (ed.), *Yiddish language and culture then and now* [Studies in Jewish Civilization Series 9], 165–188. Omaha: Creighton University Press.

Isaacs, Miriam. 1999a. Haredi, *haymish* and *frim*: Yiddish vitality and language choice in a transnational, multilingual community. *International Journal of the Sociology of Language* 138. 9–30.
Isaacs, Miriam. 1999b. Contentious partners: Yiddish and Hebrew in Haredi Israel. *International Journal of the Sociology of Language* 138. 101–121.
Isaacs, Miriam. 2004. Languages sometimes in contact: Components in Yiddish Hasidic children's literature. In Joseph Shreman (ed.), *Yiddish after the Holocaust*, 131–149. Oxford: Boulevard Books.
Jacobs, Neil. 2005. *Yiddish: A linguistic introduction*. Cambridge: Cambridge University Press.
Jochnowitz, George. 1968. Bilingualism and dialect mixture among Lubavitcher Hasidic children. *American Speech* 43. 188–200.
Kahn, Lily. 2016. Yiddish. In Lily Kahn & Aaron D. Rubin (eds.), *Handbook of Jewish languages*, 641–747. Leiden / Boston: Brill.
Kahan-Newman, Zelda. 1999. Women's badkhones: The Satmar poem sung to a bride. *International Journal of the Sociology of Language* 138. 81–99.
Kahan-Newman, Zelda. 2008. Layered, zippered and buttoned: The importation of Hebrew into '*Dos Yidishe Vort*'. *Journal of Language Contact* 1(2). 1–16.
Kahan-Newman, Zelda. 2015. Discourse markers in the narratives of New York Hassidim: More V2 attrition. In Janne Bondi Johannessen & Joseph Salmons (eds.), *Germanic heritage languages in North America: Acquisition, attrition and change*, 178–198. Amsterdam: John Benjamins.
Kantor, Hadassah. 1997. Triglossia baitonut hakharedit be'artsot habrit [Triglossia in the American Haredi press]. *Balshanut Ivrit* 41–42. 131–139.
Katz, Dovid. 2003. Men baraykhert dos yidish – ba khsidishe kinderlakh [Enriching Yiddish among Hasidic children]. *Yerusholaimer Almanakh* 27. 290–293.
Katz, Dovid. 2004. *Words on fire: The unfinished story of Yiddish*. New York: Basic Books.
Kosover, Mordecai. 1966. *Arabic elements in Palestinian Yiddish*. Jerusalem: Achva Press.
Krogh, Steffen. 2012a. How Satmarish is Haredi Satmar Yiddish? In Marion Aptroot, Efrat Gal-Ed, Roland Gruschka & Simeon Neuberg (eds.), *Leket: Yidishe shtudyes haynt* [Yiddish studies today] 1, 483–506. Düsseldorf: Düsseldorf University Press.
Krogh, Steffen. 2012b. Tsvey alt-naye yidishe romanen fun der khareydisher svive – batrakhtungen fun a lingvistishn shtandpunkt. [Two old novels in new garments from the Haredi environment. Observations from a linguistic perspective.] *Yerusholaimer Almanakh* 29. 308–335.
Krogh, Steffen. 2014. The foundations of written Yiddish among Haredi Satmar Jews. In Marion Aptroot & Björen Hansen (eds.), *Yiddish language structures* (Empirical approaches to language typology), 63–103. Berlin: Mouton de Gruyter.
Krogh, Steffen. 2015. Some remarks on the morphology and syntax of written Yiddish among Haredi Satmar Jews. In Michael Elmentaler, Markus Hundt & Jürgen Erich Schmidt (eds.), *Deutsche Dialekte. Konzepte, Probleme, Handlungsfelder*, 379–413. Stuttgart: Franz Steiner.
Krogh, Steffen. 2018. How Yiddish is Haredi Satmar Yiddish? *Journal of Jewish Languages* 6(1). 5–42.
Kutzik, Jordan. 2018. American Hasidic Yiddish pedagogical materials: A sociological and sociolinguistic survey of 50 years of post-war publishing. *Journal of Jewish Languages* 6(1). 60–88.

Levine, Glenn S. 2000. *Incomplete L1 acquisition in the immigrant situation: Yiddish in the United States*. Tübingen: Max Niemeyer.

Mazor, Yaakov & Moshe Taube. 1994. A Hassidic ritual dance: The mitsve-tants in Jerusalemite weddings. In Israel Adler, Frank Alvarez-Pereyre, Edwin Serrousi & Lea Shalem (eds.), *Masorot yehudiyot shebeal pe: Gisha ben tkhumit* [Jewish oral traditions: An interdisciplinary approach], *Yuval* 6, 164–224. Jerusalem: Magnes Press.

Mintz, Jerome R. 1992. *Hasidic people: A place in the new world*. Cambridge, MA: Harvard University Press.

Mitchell, Bruce. 1999. London's *Haredi* periodicals in Yiddish: Language, literature and Ultra-Orthodox ideology. *European Judaism* 32. 51–66.

Mitchell, Bruce. 2006. *Language politics and language survival: Yiddish among the Haredim in post-war Britain*. Paris & Louvain: Peeters Publishers.

Nove, Chaya R. 2018. The erasure of Hasidic Yiddish from twentieth century Yiddish linguistics. *Journal of Jewish Languages* 6(1). 109–141.

Nove, Chaya R. Forthcoming. Nisht mir, nisht dir: Social and linguistic predictors of case syncretism in contemporary Hasidic Yiddish. In Rebecca Margolis (ed.), *Yiddish in the New Millennium*. Detroit, Michigan: Wayne State University Press.

Peltz, Rakhmiel. 1990. Spoken Yiddish in America: Variation in dialect and grammar. In Paul Wexler (ed.), *Studies in Yiddish linguistics*, 55–73. Tübingen: Max Niemeyer Verlag.

Peltz, Rakhmiel. 1998a. *From immigrant to ethnic culture: American Yiddish in south Philadelphia*. Stanford: Stanford University Press.

Peltz, Rakhmiel. 1998b. The politics of research on spoken Yiddish. In Dov-Ber Kerler (ed.), *Politics of Yiddish: Studies in language, literature and society*, 63–73. Walnut Creek: AltaMira Press.

Poll, Solomon. 1965. The role of Yiddish in American ultra-Orthodox and Hassidic communities. *Yivo Annual of Jewish Social Science* 13. 125–152.

Poll, Solomon. 1980. The sacred-secular conflict in the use of Hebrew and Yiddish among the ultra-Orthodox Jews of Jerusalem. *International Journal of the Sociology of Language* 24. 109–125.

Rayfield, J.R. 1970. *The languages of a bilingual community*. The Hague: Mouton.

R.N. 2007. Harakhaman hu yakim lanu et sukat david hanofelet [May the Merciful One raise up the tabernacle of David that is fallen]. *Davka* 2: 43–44.

Rubin, Israel. 1997. *Satmar: Two generations of an urban island*. New York: Peter Lang.

Sadan, Tsvi. 2013. Hebrew component in Yiddish. In Geoffrey Khan (ed.), *Encyclopedia of Hebrew language and linguistics*, 1034–1038. Leiden & Boston: Brill.

Sadock, Benjamin & Alyssa Masor. 2018. Bobover Yiddish: "Polish" or "Hungarian"? *Journal of Jewish Languages* 6(1). 89–110.

Sasaki, Tsuguya. 1993. Hamarkiv ha'ivri-arami bayidish: Torat hatsurot vetorat hamashmaut [The Hebrew-Aramaic component in Yiddish: Morphology and semantics]. *Massorot* [Studies in Language Traditions and Jewish Languages] 7. 129–144.

Schaechter, Binyumen. 1999. Vifl yidn redn yidish? [How many Jews speak Yiddish?]. *Oyfn Shvel* 316. 22.

Schaechter, Sure-Rokhl. 2011. Khsidish Yidish [Hasidic Yiddish]. *Forverts*, 23 December, 2011.

Shandler, Jeffrey. 2006. *Adventures in Yiddishland: Postvernacular language and culture*. Berkley & Los Angeles: University of California Press.

Spitzer, Zvi. 2008. Veromamtanu mikol halshonot [And Thou hast raised our language above all languages], *Davka* 5. 12–14.

Stampfer, Shaul. 1993. What did "knowing Hebrew" mean in Eastern Europe? In Lewis Glinert (ed.), *Hebrew in Ashkenaz: A language in exile*, 129–140. New York: Oxford University Press.

Szendrői, Kriszta Eszter, Zoë Belk & Lily Kahn. 2018. No case for case (or gender) in Stamford Hill Hasidic Yiddish. Paper presented at the Language, Logic and Cognition Center, The Hebrew University, Jerusalem.

Vaisman, Asya. 2008. English in the Yiddish speech of Hasidic women. *Yiddish* 15(3). 17–28.

Vaisman, Ester-Basya (Asya). 2013. "Hold on tightly to tradition": Generational differences in Yiddish song repertoires among contemporary Hasidic women. In Lara Rabinovitch, Shiri Goren & Hannah S. Pressman (eds.), *Choosing Yiddish: New frontiers of language and culture*, 339–356. Detroit: Wayne State University Press.

Weinreich, Max. 1980. *History of the Yiddish language*. Chicago: The University of Chicago Press.

Weinreich, Uriel. 1964. Western traits in Transcarpathian Yiddish. In *For Max Weinreich on his seventieth birthday: Studies in Jewish languages, literature, and society*, 245–264. London, The Hague & Paris: Mouton.

Weinreich, Uriel. 1990. *Modern English-Yiddish Yiddish-English dictionary*. New York: Yivo Institute for Jewish Research.

Anbessa Teferra
Hebraized Amharic in Israel

1 Introduction

Most of the Ethiopian Jews immigrated to Israel during the 1980s and 1990s. In former publications, they were known as *Falasha*, whose meaning is "stranger" or "exile."[1] However, members of the community consider this appellation to be a derogatory one and call themselves *Betä Israel* 'House of Israel' (this was sometimes shortened to *Israel* [pl. *Israeloch*] while they resided in Ethiopia). In Israel, the name *Betä Israel* is not widely known, except among Ethiopian Jews themselves and scholars who research them. Hence, they are simply labeled as "Ethiopian Jews" or "the Ethiopian community" by the Israeli public. Within the Ethiopian Jewish community, one also finds a large group known as *"Falashmura."* Their ancestors were Ethiopian Jews who were converted to Christianity in the 18th and 19th centuries by European missionaries. Several thousand of them started to move to Israel a few years after "Operation Solomon," which took place in 1991. Most of the *Falashmura* entered Israel, not by virtue of "Law of Return," but by a provision known as "family reunification."

The aim of this chapter is to investigate the linguistic features of "Hebraized Amharic" (henceforth HA). The term HA refers to the variety of Amharic spoken in Israel, mostly by Ethiopian Jews, but also by non-Jewish Ethiopians, such as temporary residents and refugees. The two features which distinguish the HA-speaking group are their age and educational level. Most of the speakers are aged 20 or older, including senior citizens, although some youngsters may speak HA. Various governmental and non-governmental bodies that deal with the integration of Ethiopian Jews have labelled this age group *dor hamidbar* 'the desert generation'. This is an allusion to the Hebrews/Israelites who wandered for 40 years in the Sinai desert and did not make it to the Promised Land. Similarly, the group designated *dor hamidbar* among Ethiopian Jews are viewed as those who cannot be integrated into mainstream Israeli society. With regard to education, the people in this group are either pre-literate (have no formal education) or semi-literate (with a very minimal amount of education).

This chapter contains four sections. The first section is a brief introduction. The second presents various theories regarding the origin of Ethiopian Jews, historical background, immigration to Israel, and integration challenges. The third

---

[1] The term *Falasha* is derived from Geʻez *falasa* (to emigrate, go into exile, be removed).

https://doi.org/10.1515/9781501504631-018

section deals with the languages spoken by Ethiopian Jews (earlier and current) and with the status of current languages, i.e., Amharic and Tigrinya (heritage languages of Ethiopian Jews) in Israel. Finally, linguistic features of HA are discussed in detail in the fourth and main section of the chapter.

2 Origins of Ethiopian Jews

2.1 Introduction

The traditional territory of Ethiopian Jews is the northern part of Ethiopia. Most of them lived in the Gondar region, while a small percentage lived in Tigray. In these two regions, they inhabited hundreds of small villages, among populations that were predominantly Christian. Several groups of Ethiopian Jews also dwelled in other parts of Ethiopia, such as Gojjam, Wello, Addis Ababa, etc. There are several publications that present a general picture about Ethiopian Jews. Quirin (1992) and Kaplan (1992) are general introductions to the Beta Israel community. An annotated bibliography on Ethiopian Jews up to 1997 is provided by Kaplan and Salamon (1998). Leslau (1951) is a collection of texts in English translation, while Shelemay (1989) discusses various cultural aspects of Betä Israel. While the above authors deal with the historical aspects of Ethiopian Jews, Schwarz (2001) focuses on their current life in Israel and their arduous struggle for integration.

2.2 The origins of Ethiopian Jews

There are no written sources about Betä Israel prior to the 14th century. Given this lack of historical data, their origin remained shrouded in mystery and, consequently, different theories arose. The earliest ascribed the origin of Ethiopian Jews to the travels of the Queen of Sheba to Jerusalem and her meeting with King Solomon, as stated in Kings I (10:1–10). This brief biblical tale was elaborated in a book known as Kəbrä Nägäst 'The Glory of the Kings'. According to Kəbrä Nägäst, Menelik I was the offspring of this legendary meeting. He returned to Ethiopia, accompanied by a large contingent of first-born Hebrew sons and, upon arriving in Ethiopia, established the first "Solomonic Dynasty" in the ancient city of Aksum. Until recently, the Kəbrä Nägäst was a national ethos of Ethiopia and, according to Marrassini (2003, 3: 364–368), "it was primarily intended to glorify the Solomonic dynasty of Ethiopia." Hence, according to the proponents of this theory, Judaism was introduced to Ethiopia by the ancient Israelites who accompanied Menelik I. However, the legend as expounded in the Kəbrä Nägäst is rejected by Ethiopian Jews, because its main aim was legitimizing Christian Aksumite kings.[2]

The second theory postulates that ancient Israelites migrated to Egypt after the destruction of the First Temple by the Babylonians in 586 BCE. First, they settled on Elephantine (Yebu) Island. After the destruction of Elephantine, they travelled to Sudan along the route of the River Nile and then continued to Ethiopia. Most Betä Israel accept this theory, and they believe that they are descendants of the ancient Israelites. The argument put forward supporting this theory is that Ethiopian Jews have the Torah ("Written Law") but not the Talmud ("Oral Law"). Moreover, their religious leaders are *qesoch* 'priests' (*kohanim*) and not rabbis. In addition, they do not have post-biblical Jewish holidays, such as *Chanukah* or *Purim*.

According to the third theory, Jews from the South Arabian Peninsula of Yemen arrived in Ethiopia, either as merchants or as captives, taken when King Kaleb crossed from Axum to Yemen and defeated the ruler Dhū Nuwās, ca. 523 CE.

A number of scholars have proposed internal Ethiopian factors, rather than external, as the reason for the emergence of Ethiopian Jews. According to them, the Betä Israel are descendants of the indigenous inhabitants of Ethiopia who converted to Judaism at a certain point in time. The proponents of this theory are Shelemay (1989), Quirin (1992), and Kaplan (1992).

2.3 Immigration to Israel and historical background

The immigration of Ethiopian Jews to Israel was fraught with untold hardships. It included an arduous and long journey over a hostile desert, robbery by armed bandits, infectious diseases, hunger, etc. Ethiopian Jews claim that there is no other Jewish group that suffered more while trying to fulfill its long dream of returning to the Promised Land. In this section, a history of the immigration of Ethiopian Jews to Israel will be discussed briefly.
A. Between 1965 and 1975, a relatively small group of Ethiopian Jews immigrated to Israel. The group consisted of a few men who came to Israel on tourist visas and then remained in the country illegally.

---

[2] Before Ethiopian Jews began immigrating to Israel, this was the preponderant theory that was accepted by them regarding their origin.

B. From late 1979 until the beginning of 1984, thousands of Ethiopian Jews travelled to Sudan on foot, facing untold hardships, and settled in refugee camps. From there, small groups were brought to Israel in a clandestine operation. During this time, the community suffered from malnutrition and various infectious diseases and, consequently, more than 1500 perished.
C. Between late 1984 and early 1985, more than 7,000 Betä Israel arrived in Israel in an operation which was dubbed "Operation Moses." The process continued until an Israeli newspaper exposed the operation and brought it to a halt, stranding hundreds of Ethiopian Jews in the Sudanese camps. Later on, the remaining group was airlifted to Israel by the US Air Force.
D. When allies in the socialist bloc began to crumble, the then Marxist regime of Ethiopia started to lose military support from the former Soviet Union. Hence, diplomatic relations with Israel, which had been severed during the 1973 Yom Kippur War, were reinstated in 1989.[3] The regime began to strengthen its relations with Israel, and it also allowed the legal migration of Ethiopian Jews, in small groups. This was carried out in hopes of getting military support from Israel and in order to establish ties with the US, through Israeli mediation. It is believed that several thousand Ethiopian Jews arrived in Israel between 1989 and May 1991.
E. In May 1991, conditions in Ethiopia started to deteriorate quickly. The rebels from north Ethiopia and their allies surrounded Addis Ababa, and it was clear that the city would fall into their hands within a day or two. Israel was worried about the safety of the thousands of Ethiopian Jews who had temporarily settled in the capital. Thanks to the intervention of the US, the rebels halted their advance to the capital for a few days. Consequently, in a daring campaign named "Operation Solomon," more than 14,500 Ethiopian Jews were airlifted to Israel in the course of 36 hours.
F. In 1999, around 3,500 Ethiopian Jews from the Quara area arrived in Israel.
G. The largest group, which started to arrive in 1992, is known as *Falash Mura*. As was mentioned earlier, they are descendants of Betä Israel whose ancestors converted to Christianity in the 18th and 19th centuries. They are now returning to Judaism and are admitted to Israel on the basis of Orthodox conversion and "family reunification" rules. The *Falash Mura* languished

---

[3] Ethiopia severed its diplomatic relations with Israel in 1973, during the Yom Kippur War. It was claimed that this was one of the reasons why Emperor Haile Sellasie I was toppled in 1974. This is because a year earlier, his Israeli advisors were expelled and, hence, there was no one to warn the senile emperor of the imminent danger to his long rule (Haggai Erlich, personal communication).

in transit camps in Addis Ababa and Gondar before immigrating to Israel. Around 9,000 of them are still waiting in these two camps. The heart-wrenching part is that most family members are in Israel, while only one member is stranded in Ethiopia. Hundreds of them perished because of disease and malnutrition. Their brethren in Israel have staged numerous demonstrations, requesting their immediate immigration to Israel. Ethiopian Jews attribute this situation to blatant racism on the part of the government.

2.4 Integration and various hardships

Ethiopian Jews are gradually becoming part of mainstream Israeli society in many fields. Nevertheless, there are numerous integration problems affecting this group. Some of the general problems are listed below, with particular emphasis on those related to language.

2.4.1 General problems

Contact between Betä Israel, who mostly hail from remote Ethiopian rural villages, and modern and advanced Israeli society initially led to a cultural shock. This is because most of them had never lived in modern apartments or used electrical appliances and were not familiar with Israeli foods, etc. In addition, the Ethiopian Jewish family was an extended one, in which close relatives usually lived in proximity to each other. The breakup of such a close-knit group by placing its members in various absorption centers was very traumatic for many of the new immigrants.

The biggest challenge to Ethiopian Jews probably lies in their very low level of formal education. When they first arrived in Israel, most of them had no useful training for a developed economy like that of Israel. Compared to middle-aged and older immigrants from Ethiopia, the younger generation born in Israel is more successful in being absorbed into the economy, due to the modern education it has received. However, compared to other immigrant groups, even the young Betä Israel college graduates often experience trouble finding a suitable job. Hence, many of them either work as guards or are engaged in low-paying menial jobs, and only a few have found work in their professions.

The Ethiopian Jews have also suffered various manifestations of racism because of their skin color. These have included the refusal of schools to admit Betä Israel children, refusal to sell apartments to them, not allowing Betä Israel youngsters into nightclubs, etc.

2.4.2 Language-related challenges

2.4.2.1 Naming

According to Baye (2006) and Zelalem (2003), in most Ethiopian cultures, names are given to children either by parents or close relatives, based on various factors. These include the status of the family, the general condition prevailing in the country, the physical traits of the child, the aspirations of the family, and others. When Ethiopian Jews started to arrive in Israel in the early 1980s, the authorities at various levels (absorption workers, social workers, school principals, etc.) pressured the group to adopt Hebrew names. Sometimes the reason given for the name change was the difficulty of pronouncing Ethiopian names.

However, although a few of the Hebrew names were phonetically similar to Ethiopian names, they did not match them semantically. For instance, a name such as *šaräw* 'cancel it' was replaced by the Hebrew *Sharon*, while *ayyäləññ* 'he saw it for me' was substituted by the Hebrew name *Ilan*. Neither of the Hebrew names is related semantically to the Amharic ones. In other cases, Hebrew names were selected arbitrarily, at the whim of the officials, without even a slight effort for some sort of phonetic matching. Some members of the community joked that Hebrew names such as Avraham, Yitzhaq, Moshe, etc., which were on the verge of extinction, were suddenly revived thanks to the influx of Ethiopian Jews. The automatic bestowing of Hebrew names was discontinued by the government in the mid-90s. Because a name represents one's identity, arbitrary name changing caused a symbolic break with the new immigrant's past. In rare instances, educated Ethiopian Jews chose Hebrew names that somehow matched the meaning of their original names. For example, the author of this chapter knows an Ethiopian named *Mähari*, meaning 'one who pardons' in Amharic, who replaced his name with the semantically identical Hebrew *Rachamim* 'pardon/mercy'.

The most profound change regarding names was requiring Ethiopian Jews to have family names. In the Ethiopian naming system, there are no family names. One's full name consists of first name followed by the name of the father. For instance, my name is *Anbessa*, and that of my father is *Teferra*. Hence, my full name is *Anbessa Teferra*. One of my sons is named *Yarin*. Had we been in Ethiopia, his full name would have been *Yarin Anbessa*. Regarding Ethiopian Jews, the Israeli authorities decided that a grandfather's name should serve as the family name.

The other related change enacted regarding names was the requirement of married women to take their husband's family name, a practice that was alien to Ethiopian culture. In Ethiopia, women, even after getting married, retain their father's name and do not take their husband's father's name. For instance, in Ethiopia, a woman named *Rachel*, whose father's name is *Solomon*, would remain *Rachel Solomon* all of her life, even if she were married. Compelling

Ethiopian Jewish women to take their husband's family name has sometimes caused friction. Some of the women argued against taking their husbands' family name, claiming that it was their biological father who raised them and not their father-in-law.

2.4.2.2 Learning the Hebrew language
Hebrew was difficult for the new immigrants, and the majority of them (in particular "the desert generation") did not manage to master the language, even after living many years in Israel, resulting in a strong social marginalization. Many elders symbolically referred to themselves as *denqoro* (Amharic 'deaf' or 'ignorant') or *af yälläññəmm* 'I don't have a language' (lit. 'I don't have a mouth'), because of their inability to communicate, since their command of Hebrew was very poor.

2.4.2.3 Abandoning one's native language
Ethiopian Jews who arrived in the 1980s complain that they were encouraged to abandon their native language and adopt Hebrew. This could explain the fact that Ethiopians are quickly losing their languages (Amharic and Tigrinya) and are adopting Hebrew. On the other hand, immigrants from the former Soviet Union often speak Russian with their children (see Perelmutter, this volume). However, since the mid-1990s, the government has adopted a multi-cultural approach and allowed the teaching of various immigrant languages, Amharic being one of them.

3 Languages of Ethiopian Jews

The next portion of this chapter will relate to the original languages of Ethiopian Jews, while the following section will focus on languages spoken by them at the present time, Amharic in particular.

3.1 The earlier languages of Ethiopian Jews

Ethiopia is a multilingual nation, in which more than 70 languages and numerous dialects are spoken.[4] Most of the languages spoken in Ethiopia belong to an

---

[4] The number of languages spoken varies. According to Hudson (2003), there are officially 73 languages, while others claim there are more than 80.

Afro-Asiatic phylum, while a few belong to the Nilo-Saharan. The Afro-Asiatic phylum comprises six sub-families; these are: Ancient Egyptian, Berber, Chadic, Semitic, Cushitic, and Omotic.[5] The last three sub-families, i.e., Semitic, Cushitic, and Omotic, are spoken in Ethiopia. Since Ethiopian Jews used to speak a Cushitic language, due attention will be given to this sub-family. Cushitic comprises five groups: North, Central, East, West, and South Cushitic. Of the five groups, three of them, i.e., Central, East, and West Cushitic, are spoken in Ethiopia.

The earliest reference to Ethiopian Jews' language is in James Bruce's *Travels to discover the source of the Nile* (1790). Although this book is mainly a narrative of Bruce's journey and exploits, it also contains a brief linguistic section entitled "Vocabulary of the Amharic, Falashan (emphasis mine), Gafat, Agow (*sic*.), and Theretch (??) Agow (*sic*.) languages." Among other things, Bruce (1790: 275) writes the following about the language of the Kemant: "…their language is the same as that of the Falasha with some small differences of idiom." The Kəmant (also known as Qəmant) are the neighbors of Betä Israel.[6] Traditionally, they practiced a pagan Hebraic religion, but most of them converted and joined the Ethiopian Orthodox church (Gamst 1969). The Kəmants speak a dialect which belongs to the Agäw group (Central Cushitic) and which is very close to that of Betä Israel.

The English missionary, Flad (1866: 18), also mentions the languages of Ethiopian Jews and writes the following: "There is a striking resemblance between the Falashas and the Kamants (*sic*.), except that the latter are in still greater ignorance and darkness than the former. There are but some slight dialectal variations in their language, so that they can understand each other perfectly well." Flad presents a 12-page grammatical sketch, which is followed by a 57-page lexicon. Flad's assertion sits well with Zelalem's claim that both Kemants and Ethiopian Jews spoke the Kemant language, but with slightly varying dialects.

Leslau (1951: xx-xxi) writes the following, regarding the languages of Ethiopian Jews:

> The Falasha literature is Geez or Old Ethiopic but the spoken language varies. Those Falashas who live in the regions of central Ethiopia speak Amharic, the national language of Ethiopia; in the northern part of Ethiopia, they speak Tigrinya, another important Semitic language of Ethiopia. From all historical evidence, it would seem that the Falashas never have been a Hebrew-speaking people but they once had a language different from the one spoken now. It was of Cushitic origin, as are the languages still spoken by the Bogos, Kemants, and other Agau population. In the mountainous region of Semyen, the northern

---

[5] The source of the name Cush can be traced to the Bible. Noah was the father of Shem, Ham, and Japheth. Ham begat several children, and one of them was Cush (Gen 10:6).
[6] In Israel, the term Kemant/Qemant is used by Ethiopian Jews to refer to Arabs in the public sphere, since the Arabs will not know that they are being talked about.

part of Begemder, the Falashas still seem to speak some of the Agau dialects such as Quarenya and Khamir. In Uzaba, southeast of Gondar, I came across an old priest from Semyen who still spoke Agau.

In continuing to discuss the language use of Ethiopian Jews, Leslau adds the following: "...The former language of Agau is still used in many prayers and benedictions, though in general the priests utter these words without understanding them" (Leslau 1951: xxi).

Appleyard extensively researched the Agäw languages and presents the following family tree of proto Agäw, based on phonological, morphological, and lexical similarities (Appleyard 1996: 1):

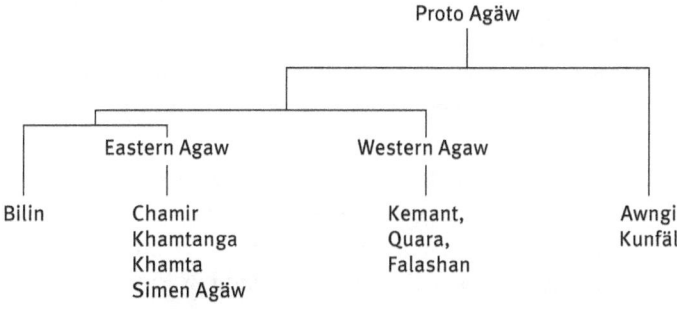

Figure 1: Family tree of Proto-Agaw.

According to Appleyard (2003, 1: 139), the language of the Ethiopian Jews appears to be a dialect of Qemant. He states, "the Qəmant (Kəmant)[7] of Kärkär and Č'əlga north of Lake Tana, together with the Betä əsra'el, who preserve their dialect in some of their liturgy, and most of whom now live in Israel having emigrated in recent years from Ethiopia..." Elaborating on this claim, Appleyard (2003, 1: 140) writes, "The A. [Agäw] speech of the Betä əsra'el also belongs to the same dialect cluster [i.e., Qəmant] and differs from Kəmantnäy only in a small percentage of vocabulary and some morphology. This dialect, called variously "Falaašan," or "Qʷarənya" in the literature (...), is moribund today, spoken by a mere handful of elderly people now living in Israel, though it is still used in Betä Israel liturgy" (Appleyard 1994, 1998).[8]

---

7 As can be seen above, the Kemant language has various labels: Kemant, Qemant, and Kəmantnäy. The term Kəmantnäy was introduced by Zelalem, who wrote his doctoral research on the language and claims that it is the self-name of Kemant as used by the language speakers; nevertheless, I use the more conventional Kemant unless I am quoting Zelalem.
8 This statement may not be accurate. It has been speculated that that there could be very few Qʷarənya speakers among the Ethiopian Jews. The writers of this paper, Prof. Hezy Mutzafi, and

The Agäw dialects spoken by Ethiopian Jews were variously known as Qʷaräñña and Falashan. However, according to Zelalem (2003: 43–44), these were dialects of Kemant. Corroborating his claim, he writes, "This can be proven by comparing the Qʷaräñña texts (Appleyard 1994; Reinisch 1887) with the Kemantney texts." Earlier on, Appleyard (1984: 34) assumed Qʷaräñña to be a dialect of Kemant, and therefore wrote: "Indeed, there is evidence to suggest that what has been called Quara, for instance, can be included within the language here called Kemant." Regarding the languages of Ethiopian Jews, Zelalem (2003: 43–44) adds the following: "Kemantney is a language spoken by the Kemant people. In fact, the Falasha who lived near the Kemant people spoke proper Kemantney, whereas the Falasha who lived around Quara spoke the dialect Quarenya or Quaräsa." The language of Ethiopian Jews was not restricted to Kemantney. It varied in accordance with their area of settlement. Concerning this, Zelalem (2003: 43–44) adds: "in very many other places where the Falasha lived with the Amhara, they were native speakers of Amharic. ...the Falasha who settled among Tigrinya speakers spoke Tigrinya."

The various points raised regarding the earlier languages of Ethiopian Jews can be summarized as follows: According to Appleyard (2003), Ethiopian Jews spoke an Agäw language that belonged to the Kəmantnäy (Kemant) dialect cluster. This dialect was also known as *Fälašan* or *Qʷaräñña*. It is believed that Ethiopian Jews spoke Qʷaräñña, perhaps until the 19th century (see Berry 2010). In the Gondar administrative region, it was completely replaced by Amharic, while in the Tigrai region it was replaced by Tigrinya. By contrast, all religious texts of the Ethiopian Jews are written in Geʿez (also known as 'Ethiopic' or 'Classical Ethiopic'), with a sprinkling of *Qʷaräñña* words here and there. Geʿez is an ancient attested Ethiopian Semitic language and remained the primary written language of Ethiopia into the beginning of the 20th century. Geʿez is not a spoken language and survives mostly as the liturgical language of the Ethiopian and Eritrean Orthodox Tewahedo Church, plus among the traditional religious leaders of Ethiopian Jews.[9]

Dr. Baruch Podolsky of Tel Aviv University tried to find Kemant or Qʷara speakers in 1992 at one of the absorption centers in Central Israel in the immediate aftermath of "Operation Solomon." To our dismay, not a single speaker could be located, there or elsewhere.

9 In addition to various liturgical uses, Geʿez also serves as the source language in the creation of neologisms from various foreign languages, in particular from English, which make their way into Amharic.

3.2 The present-day languages of Ethiopian Jews

It appears that Ethiopian Jews who spoke the various languages of Agäw gradually adopted Amharic. According to Zelalem, almost the same fate awaited Kemant speakers; today, 99% speak Amharic and only 1% of them speak Kemant. Regarding this fact, Appleyard (2003, 1: 140) writes: "...Almost all speakers of Kəmantnäy are bilingual in Amharic, and the majority of people who identify themselves as Qəmant no longer speak the language."

At present, approximately 137,000 Ethiopian Jews live in Israel. Of these, roughly 40% were born in Israel and speak Hebrew.[10] The majority of the rest speak Amharic, while a small percentage speaks Tigrinya. Most Tigrinya speakers are bilingual in Amharic.[11] The degree of fluency in Amharic correlates with the age of the speakers. It appears that those who were aged 30 and beyond continued to use Amharic, with a spattering of Hebrew. This is particularly true with middle aged and older people and is more pronounced among those who were illiterate when they immigrated to Israel. Those between the ages of 10 and 30 became bilinguals, fluent in both languages. The younger ones, however, adopted Hebrew and speak a heavily accented Amharic (if they speak it at all). Ge'ez (Classical Ethiopic) has a special place for Ethiopian Jews. Traditional religious leaders, known as *qesočč* 'priests' (*qes* 'priest' is its singular form), pray in Ge'ez, and all religious texts are written in it (Gamst 1995), interspersed with some Agäw words.[12]

3.3 The place of Amharic in Israel

This section is devoted to the usage of Amharic in Israel. In the introductory section, the usage of Amharic in Israel amongst different age groups and

---

[10] The cited figure of the Ethiopian Jewish population and the various percentages are according to information I received from various bodies that deal with Ethiopian Jews, such as the Ministry of Absorption, the Jewish Agency for Israel, etc.

[11] This is the percentage usually presented in various forums; I do not know if there has been systematic research regarding the number of native Amharic and Tigrigna speakers and bilinguals. In addition to Amharic and Tigrinya, several speakers of other Ethiopian languages also immigrated to Israel, usually because of family ties. Some of the languages brought by these new immigrants are Oromo, Soddo (Kəstane), Wolayta, Sidaama, etc. However, their number is quite insignificant.

[12] The word *qes* 'priest' has an interesting morphology. Although its plural is marked by -*očč* in Amharic, in Israel it has acquired the Hebrew plural -*im* (the only Amharic word to do so), and hence the blend form *qesim* 'priests' is the prevalent one.

contributing factors will be analyzed. In addition, the place of Amharic in the educational system and mass media will be discussed in some detail.

3.3.1 Introduction

The exact number of Amharic speakers in Israel is not known, and I have not come across research that deals with the topic. That being the case, some Israeli sociolinguists have proposed a general figure. For instance, according to Shohamy and Spolsky (1999: 244), "The language spoken by the majority of Beta Israeli is Amharic ... However, at least 10,000 of the Ethiopian Jews in Israel speak Tigrinya as their first language."

The figures of Shohamy and Spolsky were based on immigrants who arrived in Israel before1997. However, since 1992 (and until today), there has been a continuous flow of Ethiopian Jews who are known as "*Falashmura*." Several thousand of them began moving to Israel after "Operation Solomon" in 1992. Most of the "*Falashmura*" come from the Gondar Zone, where Amharic is the dominant language; hence, most of them are native Amharic speakers. Consequently, if those born in Israel are excluded, the majority of those who emigrated from Ethiopia speak Amharic, while a small minority speak Tigrinya. This briefly illustrates the importance of Amharic within the Ethiopian Jewish community in Israel.

Use of the Amharic language in Israel varies according to age group. Almost all of the children born in Israel and those who arrived when they were below the age of 10 speak Hebrew exclusively. This can be explained from a practical point of view. New immigrants from Ethiopia quickly realized that, in Israel, the rapid learning of Hebrew is the key to integration and the concomitant educational and economic advancement. Prodding children to learn Hebrew quickly also has a practical benefit. Most Ethiopian Jewish parents did not speak or read Hebrew when they immigrated to Israel. Hence, if the child is fluent in Hebrew, he can take his parents to various offices and bodies, such as the clinic, bank, post office, the National Insurance Institute, etc., and assist in translating for them.

It has also been observed that the shift from Amharic to Hebrew is more pronounced among Ethiopian Jewish children and youngsters, as opposed, for instance, to new immigrants from the former Soviet Union. The reasons are varied. Some Ethiopian youngsters have low esteem regarding their language and consequently do not want to speak it. In addition, most of the Ethiopian Jewish parents do not pressure their children to speak Amharic. In contrast, most immigrants from the former Soviet Union are educated and very proud of their language and culture.

The other factor that can be cited is the attitude of Ethiopian Jewish youngsters. Most of them think that dropping Amharic and shifting to Hebrew will strengthen their Israeli identity and will raise their acceptance by the mainstream.[13] Moreover, uneducated parents are delighted when they hear their children speaking Hebrew. They are heard saying "*ləj-e yä-färänj qʷanqʷa yəčəlall*," which can be translated as "my child speaks the language of the whites."[14] This probably emanates from the fact that enormous hegemonic pressures were applied to the community members who immigrated to Israel in the eighties to adopt the Hebrew language.

3.3.2 Amharic in the Israeli school system

Amharic is one of several immigrant languages taught at Israeli high schools and colleges, either as 3-unit or 5-unit mother tongue classes. It is taught in more than 40 schools and is primarily intended to allow Ethiopian Jewish youngsters to receive a matriculation (*bagrut*) certificate. According to the guidelines of the Israeli Ministry of Education, a student must matriculate in at least one subject of 5 units. It is very difficult for an Ethiopian new immigrant to study and matriculate in a 5-unit subject, such as Geography or Civics. Amharic fills this crucial gap and has enabled many students to complete their matriculation. Amharic is taught not only for immediate practical significance, but also to enable the student to preserve their native tongue and culture. It may also enhance communication between children and their parents, who usually speak two different languages. The teaching of Amharic has an added advantage, in that it is not only a job source and means of livelihood for several Ethiopian immigrant teachers, but it also creates positive role models for the Ethiopian youngsters, since almost all of their teachers are non-Ethiopians.

The teaching of Amharic began in 1988, at the Yemin Orde Religious Boarding School. However, it became widespread around 1994, i.e., three years after "Operation Solomon." The main reason was the influx of youngsters arriving from Ethiopia with at least a primary education. This can be contrasted with immigrants of "Operation Moses," who were less educated. After "Operation Solomon" the trend was strengthened, because the new immigrants had resided for several years in either Addis or Gondar and were, therefore, educated in the community

---

13 Some of the youngsters may eventually realize that it is a mistake to despise one's own language and culture. This happens, in particular, when they suffer from various manifestations of racism, despite their native fluency in Hebrew.
14 Ethiopians call a white Westerner *färänj*, a term borrowed from Arabic *al-ifranj* (Kane 1990: 2283). An alternative term used instead of *färänj* is *näčč* 'white'.

schools that were opened in both cities in Ethiopia. The other factor which contributed for the sudden expansion of Amharic in schools was "The Blood Affair" of 1996.[15] The youngsters were incensed by this act and decided to return to their roots by studying their language and by trying to preserve their culture.

Some actions have been taken to strengthen the status of Amharic in Israeli high schools. For instance, before 2001, three examiners traveled around Israel and gave written or oral examinations on different days. However, since 2001, a written *bagrut* examination of Amharic is prepared by the Henrietta Szold Institute, and all students sit for the exam on the same day.[16] Each year since 2001, between 550 and 600 students have taken Amharic *bagrut* exams. Additional improvements were the appointment of a Chief Supervisor for Amharic instruction in 2002, as well as the establishment of a steering committee for Amharic education.[17]

The teaching of Amharic is not restricted to the formal educational system. For instance, since 2011, a non-profit organization known as *ənnəmmar* 'let us learn' has started to teach Amharic to children and adult second-generation immigrants.[18] Currently, the program operates in several cities. Moreover, some "absorption centers" ("*mokdey qlita*" in Hebrew) have also started to teach Amharic to parents who want to return to their roots.[19]

3.3.3 Amharic in Israeli mass media

In addition to school use, Amharic also has a limited place in the Israeli mass media. Every day there is an Amharic radio broadcast for two hours on REQA (*Rashut Qlitat Aliyah* 'The Aliyah Absorption Network') and a television broadcast in Amharic and other Ethiopian languages 24 hours a day on Israel Ethiopian Television (IETV). Most of the TV programming originates in Ethiopia; the local content is not more

---

[15] This was the incident in which blood donations were accepted from Ethiopians and surreptitiously thrown out, because of the fear that the blood was contaminated with the virus that causes AIDS. The plot was uncovered by an investigative journalist. When the news of the dumping of the blood leaked, enraged community members, numbering around 10,000, staged a violent protest on January 28, 1996, in front of the office of the then prime minister (Shimon Peres) and clashed with riot police. In order to investigate the matter and present recommendations, the Navon Commission (headed by former President Yitzhak Navon) was established. The incident became known as "*Parashat ha-Dam*" (The Blood Affair). See Seeman 2010.
[16] The Hebrew word "*bagrut*" can be translated roughly as a matriculation exam or as the national Israeli examination after graduation from high school.
[17] The author of this chapter is currently Chief Supervisor for Amharic Instruction in Israeli schools.
[18] Avi Ayeh (director of the [ənnəmar] 'let us learn' project), personal communication.
[19] For instance, I was instrumental in the opening of such a program in the city of Hadera.

than 10%. Some Ethiopian Jews with external dish antennas receive Amharic TV programs from Ethiopia. Others tune in to internet-based Amharic broadcasts of VOA (Voice of America), *Deutsche Welle* (German Voice) and, most recently, various TV and radio channels of the Ethiopian Broadcasting Corporation (EBC).

Regarding print media, one Amharic-Hebrew newspaper, *Yedi'ot Nəgat*, was published until 2016.[20] It was a bi-monthly newspaper which contained various articles, in both Amharic and Hebrew, and the ratio of the content was 70% Hebrew and 30% Amharic. The newspaper contained articles on educational, social, political, economic, and health issues related to Ethiopian Jews. In addition, it sometimes included articles on practical daily matters. Several Ethiopian shopkeepers sell Amharic music CDs, drama VCDs or DVDs, and a limited selection of books. However, unlike for immigrants from the former Soviet Union, there is not a single dedicated bookshop. This stems from the fact that many of the elderly Ethiopian immigrants are uneducated, while those born in Israel do not speak Amharic. Consequently, the number of Amharic readers is very low, and this explains the dearth of Amharic book shops in Israel.

4 Linguistic features of Hebraized Amharic

This section forms the main body of the chapter and contains four sub-sections. The first part is an introduction, in which differences between standard Amharic and the variety spoken by Ethiopian Jews are discussed. The second part briefly treats phonological differences between HA and Hebrew. The third and main part deals with the lexicon, while the morphological section treats the morphological integration of loanwords.

4.1 Introduction

The Amharic spoken by Ethiopian Jews in Ethiopia was not different phonologically, morphologically, or syntactically from that of their Christian neighbors. This means that both Jews and Christians from a certain region of Gondar usually spoke a dialect that was particular to that region.[21] The differences lie

---

[20] The author of this chapter was the Amharic editor of the newspaper and translated various articles which appeared in the newspaper from Hebrew to Amharic.
[21] Regarding dialectal differences between the Amharic of Addis Ababa (the "standard" dialect) and that of Gondar, see Anbessa 1999.

solely in the area of the lexicon, and even these are quite minute. Such lexical differences usually emanate from religious differences between Ethiopian Jews and their Christian neighbors. Ethiopian Jews refrained from words, phrases, and expressions that were related to Christianity and contained the names of Jesus, Mary, names of the Disciples, etc. For instance, when startled, Ethiopian Orthodox Christians use the phrase *bä-səmä ab* 'for Heaven's sake' (lit. 'by the name of the Father'). The way to say "rainbow" is *qästä dämmäna* (lit. 'arrow of a cloud'); its rare synonym, usually used by Christians, is *yämaryam mäqännät* 'Mary's girdle'. However, Ethiopian Jews will avoid this type of phrase, because of its Christian associations. Orthodox Christian Amharic speakers say to a woman in childbirth, *Maryam təqräbəš* 'May Mary approach you' or *Maryam tədabsəš* 'May Mary touch you' (i.e., heal you). These expressions are based on a widespread tradition among Orthodox Christian Ethiopians that Mary, being the mother of Jesus, intervenes during critical times, such as during the labor of child birth. In such instances, Ethiopian Jews may use the expression *'Egzi'abher yərdaš* 'May G-d help you'.

Although the Amharic variety spoken by Ethiopian Jews was identical to that spoken by their Christian neighbors, their liturgical heritage differed. For instance, the holiest book of Ethiopian Jews is known as *Orit* (Aramaic *Oraita* 'Torah'). It consists of the Octateuch: the Five Books of Moses plus Joshua, Judges, and Ruth. The Betä Israel also possessed several important non-biblical writings, such as *Motä Muse* 'Death of Moses', *Motä Aaron* 'Death of Aaron', *Nägärä Muse* 'The Conversation of Moses', *Tə'əzazä Sänbät* 'Precepts of the Sabbath', etc.

The variety of Amharic currently spoken by Ethiopian Jews in Israel contains some phonological and many lexical features that distinguish it from the Amharic spoken in Ethiopia. This newly evolving Hebrew-Amharic contact language can be called "Hebraized Amharic." Ethiopian Jews are not the only speakers of Hebraized Amharic. It is also spoken by some non-Jewish Ethiopian refugees and temporary residents living in Israel. (See Benor 2008: 1067–1068 and Hary 2009: 16–19 for a discussion of Jewish languages spoken by non-Jews.) When Ethiopian Jews go back to visit Ethiopia, they often use common Hebrew words like שלום 'hello', כן *ken* 'yes', and בסדר *bə-seder* 'okay', and are easily identified as Israelis of Ethiopian origin.

In the following sections, some phonological, morphological, and lexical features of Hebraized Amharic will be presented. The spoken data for the research on HA was gathered from different sources; most of it was collected from the daily speech of Ethiopian Jews, with some obtained from the Amharic programs on Israeli radio and television. The sources for written HA are the newspaper entitled የዲዖት ነገት *Yedi'ot Nəgat* and compositions of some native Amharic-speaking students who were taught by this author.

4.2 Phonology

Amharic and Hebrew have different phonemic inventories. In order to demonstrate the phonemic differences between the two languages, the consonantal chart of both languages is presented below. A vowel chart is not included, because it is beyond the scope of this chapter. Amharic has 30 consonant phonemes, displayed according to their place and manner of articulation in Table 1. The Amharic chart was adapted from Baye (2007: 7) and Leslau (2000: 1).

Table 1: Amharic consonant phonemes.

		Labials	Alveolars	Palatals	Velars	Glottals
Stops						
	VL	p	t	č	k kʷ	ʔ
	VD	b	d	ǧ	g gʷ	
	EJ	p'	t'	č'	k' k'ʷ	
Fricatives	VL	f	s	š		h
	VD		z	ž		
	EJ		s'			
Nasals		m	n	ñ		
Liquids			l r			
Glides		w		j		

Hebrew has 30 consonant phonemes, displayed according to their place and manner of articulation in Table 2.

Some comments are in order regarding Hebrew consonant phonemes.

(1) The approximant /w/, the fricative /ž/, and the affricates /č/ and /ǧ/ occur in loanwords only, as in: žaket 'jacket', ǧuk 'cockroach', wat 'watt' (of electricity, also pronounced vat by most speakers). The phoneme /č/ is found in Modern Hebrew mostly in Slavic and Yiddish loanwords, such as čikčak 'in a hasty way' and everyday words such as ček 'check'.

(2) The consonant /r/ has a number of variants. It may occur as a uvular fricative, a uvular approximant, or simply as a flap.

Table 2: Modern Hebrew consonant phonemes (adapted from Schwarzwald 2001).

		Labial	Alveolar	Palato-alveolar	Palatal	Velar	Uvular	Pharyngeal	Glottal
Plosives									
	VL	p	t			k		ʕ	ʔ
	VD	b	d			g			
Fricatives	VL	f	s	š		x	R	ħ	h
	VD	v	z	ž					
Affricates			c	č					
				ğ					
Nasals		m	n						
Laterals			l						
			r[b]						
Approximants		w			j		R		

(3) The pharyngeals /ʕ/ and /ħ/ occur in the speech of speakers who came from Arabic speaking countries.

If the consonant phonemes of Amharic and Hebrew are compared, the following generalizations can be made:
(i) Amharic has a set of five palatal consonants, while Hebrew has only one, /j/. All the other palatals occur in Hebrew only in loan words, as was shown above.
(ii) In addition, Amharic has five ejectives, while Hebrew has none. On the other hand, some varieties of Hebrew are rich in laryngeal sounds, while Amharic has only /ʔ/, /ʕ/, and /h/. Even among these three sounds, the only Amharic laryngeal which occurs in everyday speech is /h/. The letters /ʔ/ and /ʕ/ occur in written forms, such as in አንድ /and/ 'one', አባት /abbat/ 'father', ዓለም /aläm/ 'world', ዓርብ /arb/ 'Friday', and ዐይን /ayn/ 'eye'. However, at the phonemic or phonetic level, neither the letter /ʔ/ nor /ʕ/ are written in synchronic Amharic. The orthographic symbols of these consonants simply serve as vowels and no longer as consonants. These can be seen clearly in the above examples written in IPA, plus in the dictionaries of Leslau (1976) and Kane (1990), where neither /ʔ/ nor /ʕ/ are written at the phonetic level, although they appear as consonant letters in the same examples.

Amharic and Hebrew have different phonemic inventories. First, Amharic has a set of five palatal phonemes (č, č', j, ñ, and ž), which are not found in Hebrew. Secondly, Amharic has five ejective consonants (č', k', p', s', and t'), while Hebrew has none. Thirdly, Amharic lacks the Hebrew gutturals ʻ, ḥ, and x.[22] See Leslau (1995) for further details of Amharic consonant phonology.

As a consequence of these differences, speakers of HA replace certain Hebrew phonemes with Amharic equivalents when incorporating Hebrew loanwords into their speech, as illustrated in Table 3.

Table 3: Phonemic replacement in Hebrew loanwords.

Hebrew phoneme	Amharic replacement	Hebrew word		Hebraized Amharic equivalent	Gloss
פ p	f ~ bb ~ p	פנימיה	pnimiya	finima	'boarding school'
		טיפה	tipa	tibba	'a little bit'
		פרה	para	para	'cow'
ח ḥ or x	h ~ k	חולה	xole	hole	'patient'
		חדר	xeder	heder	'room'
		לחם	lexem	lehem	'bread'
		שחור	šaxor	šakor	'black'
ט t	t' ~ t	משטרה	mišt'ara	mišt'ara	'police'
		טעם	taʻam	t'aʻam	'taste'
		טחן	taxan	t'ahan	'grind'
		טמא	tame	t'ame	'unclean, impure'
ק k	k' ~ k	קטן	katan	k'at'an	'small'
		קצר	katsar	k'as'ar	'short'
		קשה	kaše	k'aše	'difficult'
		דקה	daka	dak'a	'minute'
		רחוק	raxok	rahok'	'far'
		קרה	kara	k'ara	'happen'
צ ṣ	s' ~ t'	צום	ṣom	t'om	'fast'
		ציפור	ṣipor	s'ipor	'bird'
		צר	ṣar	s'ar	'narrow'
		צריך	ṣarix	s'arix	'must, need'

Note that the substitution of p by f appears to be optional when p is word-initial; however, in word-medial position, there is usually no substitution, but occasionally bb.

---

[22] The gutturals ʻ and x are preserved in the Ethiopic script which Amharic uses. Nevertheless, these gutturals are not pronounced in Amharic, and all of them are invariably replaced by h.

The substitution of Hebrew צ ṣ [c] by either the phonemes s' or t' reveals an interesting aspect of Amharic phonology. In Ethiopia, the phoneme s' is a marker of social status; it is found in the speech of educated speakers, while the non-educated use t' in its place (Takkele 1992). In Israel, however, the picture appears to be different, in that HA speakers appear to be acquiring s' in order to replace (the much closer sounding) Hebrew ṣ, as the examples above illustrate.

4.3 Lexicon

Following their immigration to Israel and their exposure to Hebrew, Ethiopian Jews have adopted and are adopting many Hebrew words that are becoming part of the HA lexicon. There are various reasons for the adoption and integration of Hebrew vocabulary into HA, and these are discussed below.

4.3.1 Lack of an Amharic equivalent

In some instances, a Hebrew word is adopted by HA speakers, because the Hebrew terms do not have equivalents, even in standard Amharic.[23] Because there are hundreds of such lexical items from various domains, only a sample list from various domains is presented here. Some of the domains are health, food items, education, banking, etc. As noted above, some of the Hebrew words undergo phonological adjustment when adopted by HA speakers.

(i) Health

Hebrew word	Transcription	HA equivalent	Gloss
טיפול	tipul	t'ipul	'treatment'
קופת חולים	kupat xolim	kubbat holim	'health fund'
אחות	axot	ahot	'nurse'
דלקת	daleket	dalek'et	'inflammation'
ניתוח	nituax	nituah	'surgery'
חובש	xoveš	hobeš	'paramedic'
קלקול קיבה	kilkul keva	k'ilk'ul k'eba	'upset stomach'
חום	xom	hom	'fever'
מצונן	metsunan	mes'unan	'has a cold'

---

[23] Note that some of these words (in particular words for fruits and vegetables) do have Amharic equivalents listed in dictionaries, but many Amharic speakers do not use or understand these terms, some of which seem to be loans from Arabic.

(ii) Food items

Hebrew word	Transcription	HA equivalent	Gloss
מלפפון	melafefon	melafefon	'cucumber'
תפוח	tapuax	tapuwa ~ tabbuwa	'apple'
חציל	xatsil	ħas'il	'eggplant'
פיתה	pita	bit'a	'flat bread'
ביצה	beitsa	bes'a	'egg'
טחינה	texina	t'ihina	'sesame paste'
קמח	kemax	k'ema	'flour'
קציצה	kətsitsa	k'əs'is'a	'ground beef patty'
לחמנייה	laxmania	laħmanya	'roll'
סלט	salat	salat'	'salad'
שקדים	škedim	šək'edim	'almonds'

(iii) Education

Hebrew word	Transcription	HA equivalent	Gloss
חינוך	xinux	hinuh	'education'
תיכון	tixon	tihon	'high school'
מדריך	madrix	madrih	'educator, instructor'

(iv) Banking, insurance, and shopping

Hebrew word	Transcription	HA equivalent	Gloss
משכנתא	maškanta	maškanta	'mortgage'
ביטוח	bituax	bit'uah	'insurance'
חשבון	xešbon	hešbon	'account'
צמוד למדד	tsamud lemadad	s'amud lemadad	'inflation adjusted'
הנחה	hanaxa	hanaha	'discount'
מציאה	metsi'a	mes'ia	'bargain'
יקר	yakar	yak'ar	'expensive'
קבלה	kabala	k'abala	'receipt'
שטר	štar	əšt'ar	'banknote'

(v) Transportation

Hebrew word	Transcription	HA equivalent	Gloss
תחבורה	taxbura	tahbura	'transport'
מכונית	mexonit	mehonit	'car'
רכב	rexev	rekev	'vehicle'

(continued)

(continued)

Hebrew word	Transcription	HA equivalent	Gloss
תחנה	taxana	tahana	'station'
אור צהוב	or tsahov	or s'ahob	'yellow light'
מקום חנייה	makom xanaya	mak'om hanaya	'parking space'

(vi) Home

Hebrew word	Transcription	HA equivalent	Gloss
מקלחת	miklaxat	miklahat	'shower'
מסרק	masrek	masrek'	'comb'
מצעים	matsa'im	mas'aim	'bedding'
רצפה	ritspa	ris'pa	'floor'
מטלית אבק	matlit avak	mat'lit avak'	'duster'

(vii) Miscellaneous terms

Hebrew word	Transcription	HA equivalent	Gloss
מלצר	meltsar	mels'ar	'waiter'
טיול	tiyul	t'iyul	'tour'
משקל	miškal	mišk'al	'balance'
מקרר	mekarer	mek'arer	'fridge'
קפוא	kafu	k'afu	'frozen'
טרי	tari	t'ari	'raw, fresh'
צמא	tsama	s'ama	'thirst'
קומקום	kumkum	k'umk'um	'kettle'

4.3.2 Words with Amharic equivalents

In the above section, examples from various domains were presented, and it was demonstrated that the adoption of Hebrew lexicon involved various phonological adjustments. Sometimes, although the Hebrew word has an Amharic equivalent, the percentage of those who know it and use it was very small. This is because most Ethiopian Jewish immigrants hail from rural Ethiopia and are not aware of the learned Amharic equivalents. In addition, less exposure to mass media may also play its part.

What is striking is that even educated Amharic speakers are heard using Hebrew words, instead of their Amharic equivalents. This could be related to the speakers' desire to demonstrate their mastery of Hebrew; indirectly, it may hint at a linguistic hegemony felt by the new immigrants. The same phenomenon is observed in Ethiopia among educated speakers, who intersperse their speech with English lexical items (Zelalem 1998; Anbessa 2008), In addition, since the percentage of Ethiopian Jews who use Hebrew words is quite large, and also since even educated Ethiopians are bombarded daily with Hebrew lexemes, it appears that they want to conform to the majority and adopt the Hebrew words. Below are some examples of Hebrew words used in HA, despite having Amharic equivalents. Some Amharic equivalents themselves are loans from various languages, as indicated below.

Hebrew word	Transcription	Amharic equivalent	Gloss
מזלג	mazleg	šuka (<Ar. šauka)	'fork'
נהג	nahag	aškärkari/šofär (<Fr. chauffeur)	'driver'
גשר	gešer	dəldəy	'bridge'
קבלה	kabala	därräsäññ	'receipt'
צלם	tsalam	fotograf anši	'photographer'
משטרה	mištara	polis (<Fr. police)	'police'
מונית	monit	taksi	'taxi'
עירייה	'iriya	mazzägaja bet	'municipality'
מסעדה	mis'ada	məgb bet	'restaurant'
אנדרטה	andarta	hawəlt	'monument'
טיול	tiyul	gubəññət	'tour'

4.3.3 Substitution of Hebrew place names with Amharic ones

Speakers of Amharic sometimes substitute Hebrew place names and words with Amharic words and phrases that sound similar. In many cases, the Amharic replacements carry semantic content that is unrelated to the Hebrew word or phrase.

Hebrew word/phrase	HA substitute	Amharic meaning
מבשרת ציון mevaseret tsiyon 'Mevaseret Zion' (suburb of Jerusalem)	mäsärätä s'əyon (mäsärät 'foundation' -ä' compounding suffix')	'foundation of Zion'
מזכרת בתיה mazkeret batya 'Mazkeret Batya' (town in central Israel)	mäskäräm batya	'Meskerem Batia' (personal name)

(continued)

(continued)

Hebrew word/phrase	HA substitute	Amharic meaning
מכמורת mixmoret 'Mikhmoret' (moshav in central Israel)	muk' märet (muk' 'hot' märet 'earth')	'hot ground'
איילת השחר 'ayelet ha-šaḥar 'Ayelet HaShachar' (kibbutz in northern Israel)	ayyäle täšalä	'Ayyele Teshale' (personal name)
קריית נורדאו (kiryat nordau) 'Kiryat Nordau' (neighborhood in the city of Netanya)	kəryat märdo	'Kəryat Merdo'

4.3.4 Substitution of Hebrew phrases with Amharic ones

Speakers of HA sometimes substitute Hebrew phrases with Amharic ones that sound similar. The examples for such type of substitution are very few. In many cases, the Amharic replacements carry a meaning that is unrelated to the Hebrew word or phrase.

Hebrew word/phrase	HA substitute	Amharic gloss
עובדת סוציאלית 'ovedet sotsi'alit 'social worker'	wofe t'olt'walit	'my meddlesome bird'
סופרמרקט supermarket 'supermarket'	sukkar mankiya	'sugar spoon'

The substitution of Hebrew place names, words, and phrases with similar sounding Amharic ones is not restricted to Ethiopian Jews only. It is also practiced by other, non-Jewish Ethiopians (such as temporary residents and refugees) residing in Israel. Although most non-Jewish Ethiopians are educated, their command of Hebrew is poor. Therefore, their pattern of substitution can be compared to that of the non-educated Ethiopian Jews. However, the rate of substitution among non-Jewish Ethiopians is quite limited, because they form a tight-knit group that has little interaction with the Israeli mainstream. Below are some illustrative examples used by this group.

Hebrew word/phrase	HA substitute	Amharic gloss
גן שמואל gan šəmu'el 'Gan Shmuel' (kibbutz east of Hadera)	gašš šəmu'el	'Mr. Samuel'
ראשון לציון rišon letsion, 'Rishon Lezion' (city in central Israel)	əršo läs'əyon	'yeast for Zion'
אסף הרופא asaf harofe 'Asaf Harofe' (hospital in central Israel)	asäffa rofe (Aseffa is a common Amharic name)	'Aseffa, the doctor'
דמי הבראה dmey havra'a 'recuperation payment'	bet abraham (bet is 'house' in Amharic)	'Abraham's house'

4.3.5 Creative innovations

At their initial stage of integration into the Israeli environment, the new immigrants (in particular those with little or no formal education) did not know the Hebrew equivalents for certain lexical items. Hence, they created their own descriptive Hebrew words and phrases. However, these substitutions were temporary in nature. After the new immigrants adapted to Hebrew, they replaced them with the correct equivalents. Below, some illustrative examples are provided.

Hebrew word	Transcription	Gloss	Creative equivalent	Translation
שווארמה	šwarma	'shwarma'	basar mistovev	'revolving meat'
מברשת	mivrešet	'(tooth)brush'	matate kit'ana	'small broom'
נער	na'ar	'lad, youth'	baxur va-hes'i	'a boy and half'
קולה	kola	'cola'	mayim kofs'im	'leaping water'
תחתונים	taxtonim	'underpants'	ben šel miknasayim	'son of trousers'

The HA speakers' use of the feminine form *kitana* 'small (f.)' with the Hebrew masculine noun *matate* 'broom' seems to be an influence from Amharic gender usage. In Amharic, unlike Hebrew, the default gender is masculine, save for a few biologically feminine nouns. Nevertheless, an inanimate noun can be either masculine or feminine, depending on the relative size of the object, with larger objects treated as masculine and smaller ones as feminine. Thus, the feminine adjective *kitana* is used in *matate kitana*, because a toothbrush is relatively small in size.

The creative equivalent of תחתונים *taxtonim* 'underpants', *ben šel miknasayim* 'son of trousers', seems to be another influence of Amharic, an import from the Gondar dialect of Amharic. The word for 'underpants' is *mutanta* in standard Amharic (a loan from Italian *mutande*), while in the northern Amharic dialects, i.e., Gojjam and Gondar, it is *gəlgäl surri* 'small trousers', from the words *gəlgäl* 'lamb' and *surri* 'trousers'.

4.4 Morphological integration of borrowings

In the data collected for this study, no morphological innovations were observed in HA. Nevertheless, HA is replete with instances of the incorporation of Hebrew words and verbal roots into the Amharic system of nominal and verbal morphology.

4.4.1 Borrowing of nouns

The main feature which characterizes HA is the sheer number of nouns borrowed into speech. The noun can appear either as a single item or as part of a phrase. Consider the examples below, where Hebrew words are marked in bold letters.

(i) Examples of "bare" nouns
(1) *ləj-očč-u*   **hofeš**   *yə-fälləg-allu*
    Child-PL-DEF   recesses   3IMPERF-want-3PL:AUX
    'The children want recesses'

(2) *lä-nägä*   *särg*   *əne*   **s'alami**   *näññ*
    For-tomorrow   wedding   I   photographer   1SG:COP
    'I am a photographer for tomorrow's wedding'

(3) *nägä*   **k'abala**   *a-mt'a*
    tomorrow   recipt   CAUS-bring2SG:IMP
    'Tomorrow, bring the receipt'

(4) *särg- očč*   *hulätäñña*   **maškanta**   *hon-u-bbə-n*
    Wedding-PL   second   mortgage   become-3PL:PERF-DETR-1PL:OBJ
    'The weddings became for us a second mortgage' (i.e., became unbearable/a burden)

(5) *lä-ənat-e*   **hafta'a**   *əyyä-wäsäd-ku-ll-at*   *näw*
    For-mother-1SG:POSS   surprise   CONT-take-1SG:PERF-for-her   COP-3M.SG
    'I am taking a surprise to my mother'

(6) *hamus*   *yä-däm*[24]   **bədika**   *allä-bbə-ññ*
    Thursday   of-blood   test   exist-must-1SG:OBJ
    'I have a blood test on Thursday'

(ii) Examples of borrowed lexical items with Amharic affixes
Another feature of HA is the appearance of borrowed lexical items with Amharic grammatical affixes and adpositions.[25]

---

24 When one sees the Amharic word *däm* 'blood', one may mistakenly think that it is the Hebrew word *dam* or a borrowing from Hebrew into Amharic. However, this is not the case. The Amharic *däm* and Hebrew *dam* 'blood' are simply examples of Proto-Semitic cognates.
25 Adposition is a cover term both for prepositions and postpositions.

(7) **nahag**-*očč-u*   *zare*   *ay-sär-u-mm*
driver-PL-DEF   today   NEG-work-3PL:IMPERF-FNLZR
'The drivers will not work today'

(8) *kä*-**gešer**-*u*   *at'ägäb*   *wəräd*
from-bridge-DEF   near   get.off.IMPV.M.SG
'Get off near the bridge'

(9) **kenes**-*u-n*   *y-azägajjä-w*   *man*   *näw*
conference-DEF-OBJ   REL:PERF-prepare-3SG:M:OBJ   WHO   COP-3M.SG
'Who organized the conference?'

(10) *suq-u*   *kä*-**tahana**   **merkazit**-*u*   *at'ägäb*   *näw*
shop-DEF   from-station   central-DEF   near   COP-3M.SG
'The shop is near the central bus station'

(iii) Examples of Hebrew verbal roots with Amharic nominal patterns
Borrowed Hebrew verbal roots can sometimes appear in derived Amharic nominal patterns. Although Amharic is rich in different ypes of nominal patterns, the one found in this type of borrowing is the Amharic agentive pattern *CäCaCi*.

(11) *sälomon*   *t'əru*   **s'älami**   *näw*
Solomon   good   photographer   COP-3M.SG
'Solomon is a good photographer'

The second pattern is an abstract noun, which is regularly formed in Amharic by suffixing /–*nät*/ to adjectives or nouns. However, in the case of HA, an abstract noun is formed by suffixing /–*nät*/ to an agentive noun. Such abstract nouns are very rare.

(12) *yä*-**s'älam**-*i-nät*   *muya*   *qällal*   *aydälläm*
GEN-photographer-AG-ABS   profession   easy   NEG COP
'The profession of photography is not easy'

(iv) Examples of borrowed phrases
HA is also characterized by borrowed phrases, as illustrated below.

(13) *yä*-**mišt'ara**-*w*   **modi'in**   *yä-täsasat-ä*   *näbbär*
GEN-police-DEF   information   GEN-err-3M.SG.PERF   WAS
'The information of the police was erroneous'

(14) ləj-očč-e   lä- **hufšat**   **pesah**   yə-mät'-allu
    child-PL-1:GEN for-vacation Passover 3IMPERF-come-3PL:AUX
    'My children will come for Passover vacation'

4.4.2 Borrowing of verbs

The number of borrowed verbs from Hebrew into Amharic is quite insignificant compared to the large number of borrowed nouns. It appears that virtually all borrowed Hebrew verbs are adapted to the Type B basic stem, which is characterized by gemination in the imperfect. This is true even when the Hebrew verb appears in the *pa'al* stem (for instance, *yəbäddəkal* 'he will examine' from the Hebrew *badak* 'examine').[26] Some Hebrew verbs borrowed into HA are presented below.

(15)

Hebrew stem	Hebrew verb	Transcription	HA verb	Gloss
pa'al	בדק	badak	bäddäkä	'he examined'
pi'el	סידר	sider	säddärä	'he arranged'
pi'el	טיפל	tipel	täppälä	'he treated'
pi'el	צילם	tsilem	s'ällämä	'he took a picture'
pi'el	צייר	tsiyer	s'äyyärä	'he drew a picture'

The following example illustrates the use of such verbs within an Amharic sentence.

(16) ləj-e-n   **ahot**-wa   zare   tə-**täpl**-at-alläčč
    child-1:GEN-OBJ nurse-DEF today 3F:IMPERF-treat-3F:OBJ-3F:AUX
    'The nurse will treat my child today'

In one case, a verb in the *hif'il* stem was borrowed using the equivalent Amharic causative pattern, which is marked by the prefix /-a/. For instance, the Hebrew verb הזמין *hizmin* 'invite', which is in the *hif'il* stem, has the Amharic equivalent *a-zämmänä* 'he invited'. Consider the sentence in (17), which contains the above-mentioned verb.

(17) **monit**   a-**zmən**-äw   wädä-särg-u   hed-u
    taxi   CAUS-invite-3:PL:CNV to-wedding-DEF go-3PL:PERF
    'They went to the wedding by calling a taxi'

---

[26] See Leslau 1995 or Baye 2007 for details of the Amharic verbal system.

5 Summary and conclusion

In this chapter, an attempt was made to investigate the structure of HA. Unlike several other Jewish communities, Ethiopian Jews did not have their own language, which was completely different from the surrounding communities. Until the beginning of the 19th century, Ethiopian Jews spoke a dialect known as Qʷäräñña, which belongs to the Agaw language cluster (Central Cushitic). Later on, Ethiopian Jews slowly abandoned Qʷäräñña and started to adopt Amharic. The process appears to have been completed by the mid-19th century. Nevertheless, the Amharic spoken by Ethiopian Jews and the Amharic spoken by their neighbors were not different, aside from some Christian religious terms, names, and expressions that Ethiopian Jews avoided. Hebraized Amharic differs from standard Hebrew in phonology, morphology, and lexicon. The main difference is in the area of lexicon, followed by phonology. Morphology shows only a slight variation. Syntax is not affected, at least at the synchronic stage. Regarding phonology, the differences are phoneme substitution, in particular of those Hebrew sounds which are unfamiliar to HA speakers. With regard to the lexicon, Hebrew words are used where there is lack of equivalent forms in Amharic, or where the HA speakers are not aware of such equivalents in Amharic, because they are uneducated. In addition, HA speakers substitute Hebrew place names with Amharic ones, which sound similar but may not necessarily carry the same meaning. The other interesting area of lexicon is the use of Hebrew-Amharic interlanguage forms, also known as "sandwich expressions." Although some of the lexical items come from Hebrew, all of the grammatical affixes originate in Amharic. Creative innovations are also another feature of the lexicon, although there are very few such lexical items. Regarding morphology, Hebraized Amharic is characterized by pattern substitution in certain verbs.

As can be seen from the above discussions, and taking into account various factors, it is possible to conclude that Hebraized Amharic is heavily used by the immigrant generation, but not by their children. This implies that, as long as there is immigration (*aliya*) of Ethiopian Jews to Israel, the process will continue. Conversely, if the immigration ceases at some point, then Hebraized Amharic will definitely recede and may finally die out. Only time will tell if this hypothesis proves to be true.

The research discussed in this chapter is only a starting point; not all features may have been covered. The collection of a larger amount of data over an extensive period, and from various areas and sources, may create a clearer picture of Hebraized Amharic.

References

Anbessa Teferra. 1999. Differences between the Amharic dialects of Gondär and Addis Abäba. In Tudor Parfitt and Emanuela Trevisan Semi (eds.), *The Beta Israel in Ethiopia and Israel: Studies on the Ethiopian Jews*, 257–263. London: Curzon Press.

Anbessa Teferra & Grover Hudson. 2007. *Essentials of Amharic*. Cologne: Rüdiger Köppe.

Anbessa Teferra. 2008. Amharic: Political and social effects on English loanwords. In Judith Rosenhouse & Rotem Kowner (eds.), *Globally speaking: Motives for adopting English vocabulary in other languages*, 164–186. Clevedon, Buffalo & Toronto: Multilingual Matters.

Appleyard, David. 1994. A Falasha prayer text in Agaw. In Gideon Goldenberg & Shlomo Raz (eds.), *Semitic and Cushitic Studies*, 206–251. Wiesbaden: Harrassowitz.

Appleyard, David. 1996. Kaïliña – A "new" dialect and its implications for dialectology. In R. J. Hayward & I. M. Lewis (eds.), *Voice and power: The culture of language in North-East Africa: Essays in honour of B.W. Andrzejewski*, 1–19. London: School of Oriental and African Studies.

Appleyard, David. 1998. Language death: The case of Qwarenya (Ethiopia). In Matthias Brenzinger (ed.), *Endangered languages in Africa*, 143–161. Cologne: Rüdiger Koppe.

Appleyard, David. 2003. Agäw. In Siegbert Uhlig (ed.), *Encyclopaedia Aethiopica*, vol. 1, 139–142. Wiesbaden: Harrassowitz.

Baye Yimam. 1997. The pragmatics of greeting, felicitation and condolence expressions in four Ethiopian languages. *African Languages and Cultures* 10. 103–28.

Baye Yimam. 2006. Personal names and identity formation: A cross-cultural perspective. In Ivo Strecker & Jean Lydal (eds.), *The perils of face, 37–70*. Berlin: Lit Verlag.

Baye Yimam. 2007 *Amharic grammar*. Addis Ababa: Eleni. (Amharic).

Benor, Sarah Bunin. 2008. Towards a new understanding of Jewish language in the twenty-first century. *Religion Compass* 2. 1062–1080.

Berry, LaVerle. 2010. Qwara. In Siegbart Uhlig (ed.), *Encyclopaedia Aethiopica*, vol. 4, 312–314. Wiesbaden: Otto Harrassowitz.

Bruce, James. 1790. *Travels to discover the source of the Nile: In the years 1768, 1769, 1770, 1771, 1772, 1773*, 5 vols. Edinburgh: G. J. and J. Robinson.

Corbeil, Jean-Claude. 1991. *Amharic-English visual dictionary*. Addis Ababa: Educational Materials Production and Distribution Agency Artistic Printers.

Flad, Martin. 1866. *A short description of the Falasha and Kamants in Abyssinia*. Chrishona: Mission Press.

Gamst, Frederick C. 1969. *The Qemant: A Pagan-Hebraic peasantry of Ethiopia*. New York: Hold, Rinehart and Winston.

Hary, Benjamin. 2009. *Translating religion: Linguistic analysis of Judeo-Arabic sacred texts from Egypt*. Leiden: Brill.

Hetzron, Robert. 1976. The Agaw languages. *Afroasiatic Linguistics* 3. 31–71.

Hudson, Grover. 2003. Linguistic analysis of the 1994 Ethiopian census. *Northeast African Studies* 6(3). 89–107.

Kane, Thomas L. 1990. *Amharic-English dictionary*. Wiesbaden: Harrassowitz.

Kaplan, Steven. 1992. *The Beta Israel (Falasha) in Ethiopia: From earliest times to the twentieth century*. New York: New York University Press.

Kaplan, Steven & Hagar Salamon. 1998. יהודי אתיופיה: ביבליוגרפיה מוערת [Ethiopian Jewry: An annotated bibliography]. Jerusalem: Ben-Zvi Institute.
Leslau, Wolf. 1951. *Falasha anthology*. New Haven: Yale University Press.
Leslau, Wolf. 1976. *Concise Amharic dictionary*. Wiesbaden: Harrassowitz.
Leslau, Wolf. 1995. *Reference grammar of Amharic*. Wiesbaden: Harrassowitz.
Leslau, Wolf. 2000. *Introductory grammar of Amharic*. Wiesbaden: Harrassowitz.
Marrassini, Paolo. 2007. Kebrä Nägäst. In Siegbart Uhlig (ed.), *Encyclopaedia Aethiopica*, vol. 3, 364–368. Wiesbaden: Harrassowitz.
Quirin, James. 1992. *The evolution of the Ethiopian Jews: A history of the Beta Israel (Falasha) to 1920*. Philadelphia: University of Pennsylvania Press.
Schwarz, Tanya. 2001. Ethiopian Jewish immigrants in Israel: The homeland postponed. Richmond: Curzon Press.
Seeman, Don. 2010. *One people one blood: Ethiopian-Israelis and the return to Judaism*. Piscataway, NJ: Rutgers University Press.
Shelemay, Kay Kaufman. 1989. *Music, ritual, and Falasha history*, 2nd edn. East Lansing: Michigan State University Press.
Shohamy, Elana & Bernard Spolsky. 1999. *The languages of Israel: Policy, ideology and practice*. Clevedon: Multilingual Matters.
Takkele Taddese. 1992. Are s' [θ] and t' [ጥ] variants of an Amharic variable? A sociolinguistic analysis. *Journal of Ethiopian Languages and Literature* 2. 107–121.
Zelalem Leyew. 1998. Code switching: Amharic-English. *Journal of African Cultural Studies* 11(2). 192–216.
Zelalem Leyew. 2003. Amharic personal nomenclature: A grammar and sociolinguistic insight. *Journal of African Cultural Studies* 16(2). 181–211.

Renee Perelmutter
Israeli Russian in Israel

1 Introduction

Israeli Russian (IR) is spoken in Israel by ex-Soviet immigrants, predominantly those who arrived with the so-called Great Wave or the Great Aliya. Almost a million people arrived in Israel from the former Soviet Union (FSU) between 1989 and 2000, making the Great Aliya the biggest immigration wave in Israeli history. This is also the largest immigrant group in present-day Israel, constituting about 20% of the Israeli Jewish population (Donitsa-Schmidt 1999; Fialkova and Yelenevskaya 2007; Kopeliovich 2011; Remennick 2003a, 2003b, 2004). This wave of immigration, like many others, brought extended families rather than individuals to Israel – thus the Great Aliya is a "family resettlement movement" (Remennick 2003b).

Members of this immigration exhibit linguistic and cultural attitudes which are often positioned in contrast to the attitudes of the members of other *aliyot* (Ben Rafael, Olshtain, and Geijst 1997; Leshem and Lissak 1999; Olshtain and Kotik 2000). Some scholars even question to what extent the term *aliya* is applicable to the immigrants of the Great Wave, whose immigration was largely unmotivated by Zionism (e.g., Leshem and Lissak 1999).

Immigrants from the former FSU are, as a rule, proud of their Russian-language culture and tend to regard Russian as an integral identity component. While Zionist language policy in Israel has pressured speakers of diasporic Jewish languages to switch to Hebrew (Olshtain and Kotik 2000; Shohamy 1994; Spolsky and Shohamy 1999), the immigrants of the Great Aliya have sustained an interest in maintaining Russian, and have advocated for and established numerous Russian-language institutions, such as newspapers, periodicals, theatres, and schools (Ben-Rafael, Olshtain, and Geijst 1997; Donitsa-Schmidt 1999; Leshem and Lissak 1999; Schwartz et al. 2009).

While much of the research literature treats the language of the immigrants as simply "Russian" (with a focus on maintenance or attrition), Israeli Russian (IR) is quite different from Modern Standard Russian (MSR). IR is a spoken and sometimes written vernacular which formed under the influence of Hebrew. It exhibits such phenomena as lexical code-mixing, code-switching, phonological and morphological adaptation of Hebrew lexical elements into the Russian matrix, adoption of Hebrew intonation contours, etc. (cf. Naiditch 2004, 2008). The development of IR in Israel showcases similarities and important differences in comparison to diasporic Jewish languages.

Generational differences abound among IR-speaking immigrants of the Great Wave, both in terms of sociolinguistic usage and in terms of the lexical, morphological, and syntactic phenomena attested. As the immigrants of the Great Aliya age and new generations acquire linguistic competency, the IR situation continues to develop and change. Language attrition and shift have been described for the younger speakers of IR (Donitsa-Schmidt 1999; Niznik 2005); on the other hand, a resistance to language shift and a strong bicultural and bilingual identity have been reported even for younger generations (cf. discussion in Golan-Cook and Olshtain 2011).

1.1 Names of the language

Names for the language spoken by the ex-Soviets in Israel tend to vary. Speakers usually identify their language as Russian, often glossing over the fact that they do not speak Modern Standard Russian (MSR), but rather a contact variant of Russian (IR) with a range of linguistic phenomena characteristic of such immigrant variants. Speakers who do discuss their Russian as different from MSR often do so in negative terms, calling their variant *surzhyk* and *smes' russkogo i ivrita* 'a mix of Russian and Hebrew'.[1]

Surzhyk is a term originally used for certain Ukrainian language variants with a strong Russian component. Often understood by speakers as a mixture of Russian and Ukrainian, the concept of *surzhyk* carries with it multiple negative connotations, including lack of education, cultural inferiority, lack of prestige, parochialism, and lack of concern for language purity – as it is neither standard Russian nor standard Ukrainian (cf. Bilaniuk 2004; Kent 2010). For many Russian speakers, the meaning of the word *surzhyk* has extended to encompass any language variants perceived as an "impure" mix of two or more languages in which language contact phenomena such as lexical borrowing, code switching, etc., are present.

Both insiders (speakers of IR) and outsiders, such as journalists, reporters, and bloggers, may describe IR as a *surzhyk* or a linguistic mix, often with the addition of adjectives denoting negativity, like the speaker below:

> I have repeatedly heard the appalling mix [*smes'*] of Russian and Hebrew: "I have just been to the *shuk* 'market', there the socks are – *shalosh be-eser* 'three pairs for ten shekels'" (*translation mine-RP*).[2]

---

1 Russian in this article has been transliterated using the Library of Congress system.
2 http://www.about-russian-language.com/obzor.html

This situation is similarly described in an online BBC article by Semyon Dovzhik, an ex-Soviet who immigrated to Israel in 1991 with the Great Wave but relocated to London in 2008. The two issues he outlines are spoken IR as "immigrant *surzhyk*" and its strong associations as a diglossic Low, a language spoken by those who do not belong to the undefined "Russian-Israeli intelligentsia."[3]

> Many "Russians" in Israel speak Israeli *surzhyk* – an immigrant mix (*smes'*) of Russian and Hebrew, which ruthlessly aggravates anyone who speaks either of these languages well. If, somewhere in Haifa or Ashdod, you approach a passer-by on the street and ask directions in Russian, they'll explain it to you, but you would need to repeatedly ask for clarifications.[4] Obviously, the above does not relate to the Russian-Israeli intelligentsia, among whom the inclusion of Hebrew loanwords '*ivritizmy*' into the spoken language is unacceptable. God forbid you accidentally say "*mazgan*" instead of air conditioner (the first word which every repatriant learns) – you will receive such a side-eye that no air conditioner will help you (*translation mine-RP*).

The last excerpt showcases many of the common stereotypical attitudes that both IR speakers and certain observers adopt towards IR – it is a *surzhyk, smes'* 'mix', i.e., a non-prestigious variant or a diglossic Low; it is spoken by people who do not have a good command of either MSR or Hebrew; speakers of IR are people of lower status who are contrasted to an undefined "intelligentsia," and who live, perhaps, in Russian-language enclaves rather than in neighborhoods where Russian-speaking immigrants of the Great Wave routinely socialize with Hebrew speakers.

These stereotypical attitudes do not necessarily reflect reality. IR is spoken among people of various social classes and educational levels, with the exclusion, perhaps, of Russian-language professionals (e.g., teachers, professors, editors), for whom a strict adherence to MSR and exclusion of IR carries both symbolic and identity capital (however, it can be argued that even among such speakers IR is still in use, but the attitude towards the contexts in which IR can be spoken is much more guarded). Even among the speakers who adhere to MSR, certain contact phenomena, such as intonation contours, are present (cf. Naiditch 2004, 2008).

---

[3] "Intelligentsia" is a problematic concept here, as over 60% of FSU immigrants have academic degrees, and had professional/white-collar careers, which links them to intelligentsia (Naiditch 2004; Remennick 2003a: 433). The writer likely refers to those Russian-language professionals (e.g., journalists, writers, teachers, and academics) for whom speaking MSR in Israel is an identity need.

[4] http://www.bbc.co.uk/russian/blogs/2014/11/141112_blog_dovzhik_hebrew

An additional emerging designation for IR among its speakers is *ivrusit* (from Heb. words *ivrit* 'Hebrew' and *rusit* 'Russian').[5] From a blog comment: "Unfortunately, in Israel the majority of the so-called Russian speakers speak [a] horrific '*surzhyk*'... Here it is called '*ivrusit*'" (*translation mine-RP*).[6]

Scholars and social scientists writing about the language of the immigrants of the Great Wave tend to focus on the immigrants' desire for Russian language maintenance (cf. Abu Rabia 1999; Donitsa-Schmidt 1999; Kopeliovich 2011; Leshem and Lissak 1999). The differences between Israeli Russian and MSR are rarely discussed. Scholars who do discuss IR refer to "Russian in Israel," (Naiditch 2004, 2008; Orel 1994), HebRush (Remennick 2003a, 2003b), which is described by her as a "mixed lingo" (Remennick 2003b: 62), or a kind of "lingo that is used in both public and private realms" (Remennick 2003a: 432), and "Israeli Russian" (Perelmutter, current article; under review).

1.2 Linguistic affiliation

IR is an immigrant variant of Russian, which incorporates a significant Hebrew component (mostly, though not exclusively, lexical) into the Russian-language morphological and syntactic matrix. Depending on the generation, occupation, location, and sociolinguistic context of speech, IR may also be influenced by Hebrew morphosyntax.

Orel (1994, 1999) argues that IR is of complicated origin, with the grammar and vocabulary of the Russian matrix related, not to MSR, but rather to a Jewish Russian vernacular spoken in the Pale of Settlement. According to Orel (1994), given that the majority of Russian-speaking Jews lived in – and many immigrated from – the Pale of Settlement, Ukrainian features inform IR, especially in the domain of pronunciation and syntax. At the same time, many Russian Jews in the USSR viewed their Jewish Russian as undesirable and strove to adhere to the literary Russian standard. These influences and tensions inform IR. According to Orel's analysis, IR has three components: "literary Russian, Slavonic languages of the Pale, mainly Ukrainian, Belarusian, and Polish, and, finally, Yiddish in various dialectal variations," in addition to Hebrew interference (Orel 1994, 1999: 378). Yiddish influences in Jewish Russian (and IR) are notable, especially in the domain of pronunciation and intonation contours, as well as some lexicon (Verschik, this volume). Niznik

---

[5] This designation seems newer and not in use by all IR speakers; not all informants I surveyed knew about the term.
[6] http://www.exler.ru/blog/item/7356/50/

(2005) also notes South Russian features in IR. The IR matrix is primarily East Slavic (Russian), making IR a part of the Indo-European language family.

1.3 Regions where the language is spoken

IR is spoken primarily in Israel, though immigrant Israeli Russians may continue to use it after immigrating to other countries. IR may be especially frequently used in the so-called Russian enclaves in Israel. While Russian-speaking immigrants settled in a variety of geographic regions in Israel, Russian speakers notably concentrate in some towns (e.g., Ashdod, Beer-Sheva, Haifa, and others) where their share in the population may be as high as 30%-40% (Naiditch 2008; Remennick 2003a). The immigrants' attitudes towards these enclaves is variable: In Donitsa-Schmidt's extensive study (1999), some immigrants blamed the state for creating the enclaves by offering FSU immigrants of the Great Wave attractive loan assistance packages to purchase real estate in these towns, previously mostly low-income neighborhoods; other informants stressed that Russian speakers themselves prefer such neighborhoods and the sense of an ethnolinguistic community these neighborhoods support (Donitsa-Schmidt 1999: 192). The enclaves provide not only a milieu for IR, but also opportunities for socialization and Russian-language institutions such as shops, educational and entertainment opportunities, and more (Ben-Rafael, Olshtain, and Geijst, 1997; Schwartz et al. 2009).

1.4 Attestations and sources

Two major sources of IR material are spoken language and informal online writing, such as forum discourse. A corpus of spoken IR has not yet been created, though individual researchers have collected speech data in various formats (e.g., Naiditch 2004, 2008; Niznik 2005; Remennick 2003a, 2003b) and online (Perelmutter 2018).

1.5 Present-day status

In the wake of the Great Aliya, about 20% of the Jews in Israel are Russian speakers (Naiditch 2004, 2008; Remennick 2003a, 2003b). Russian-speaking Israelis of the Great Wave, especially those who immigrated as adults, are oriented towards maintenance of Russian, and work hard to transmit this language to younger generations (Ben-Rafael, Olshtain, and Geijst 1997; Donitsa-Schmidt 1999; Leshem and Lissak 1999; Schwartz et al. 2009; Remennick 2003a, 2003b). The Russian-speaking immigrants have created extensive informal and formal structures to support the maintenance of Russian in their community, including schools, newspapers, magazines, theatre, intellectual games, a dedicated Israeli Russian TV channel, book/music/video stores, food stores, music festivals, political representation in the Knesset, and social networks in private and public spheres (Ben-Rafael, Olshtain, and Geijst 1997; Kopeliovich 2011; Leshem and Lissak 1999; Remennick 2003a, 2003b, 2004, 2005; Zilberg and Leshem 1996).

However, while Russian is currently successful in both the public and private domains, intergenerational transmission is often noted by scholars as a vulnerability for language maintenance (Donitsa-Schmidt 1999; Kopeliovich 2011), with notable tensions and differences in attitudes between those who immigrated as adults, those who immigrated as adolescents (the 1.5 generation), and those who immigrated as children or were born in Israel to immigrant parents.

While adults are oriented towards language maintenance and have displayed positive attitudes to Russian throughout, attitudes of the members of the 1.5 generation have been shifting throughout the years. In Kraemer's study, adolescents who immigrated between 1990–1992 reported not wanting to maintain Russian in any context, preferring to integrate by learning and switching to Hebrew (Kraemer 1995); a decade later, Niznik's (2005) study reports the opposite, with most adolescents reporting positive attitudes towards Russian and a desire to improve their Russian proficiency (88.8% of respondents). Niznik attributes the fluctuating results of such studies (e.g., Ben-Rafael, Olshtain, and Geijst 1997; Donitsa-Schmidt 1999; Kraemer 1995) to a "hesitant identity of the newcomers" (Niznik 2005: 1703). Naiditch (2004) explains these discrepancies by differences in such factors as place of residence, the family's social status, age at immigration, and others. It is also possible that the discrepancy between the attitudes reported reflects the changes that occurred in the intervening decade; in the early days of the Great Aliya, adolescents asserted themselves by wanting to distance themselves from their families' culture by linguistically integrating into their Hebrew-speaking milieu (something their parents likely struggled with), while by 2005, given the Great Aliya's increased social standing, maintaining Russian became desirable for adolescents of Russian-Jewish extraction.

Remennick reports that adolescents of the 1.5 generation tend to form social ties with other Russian-speaking 1.5 generation immigrants, including in institutions such as schools, the army, and higher education (Remennick 2003c: 44); while the social repertoire of the 1.5 generation Russian-speaking immigrants gradually expanded to include Israelis, most reported having predominantly Russian-speaking friends and spouses (Remennick 2003c: 52). In Olshtain and

Kotik (2000), immigrant adolescents reported a range of attitudes from more assimilationist to more stand-offish (all Russian friends); Naiditch likewise reports a range of attitudes among this group, ranging from Russian-oriented, Hebrew-oriented, and bicultural. Regardless of their social ties and attitudes, all respondents of the 1.5 generation seem to have extremely positive feelings towards Russian (Niznik 2005; Olshtain and Kotik 2000) reports that 100% of the 1.5 generation immigrants surveyed want their children to learn at least some Russian.

Generational shifts also include a decreased level of proficiency in children of immigrants and those who immigrated in childhood. Younger generations may have Russian language attrition, transitioning to Hebrew as their L1 (Kopeliovich 2011; Niznik 2005, 2011). Russian-speaking children may have different levels of proficiency in various tasks, e.g., they could be fluent in reading but not in writing (Naiditch 2004).

In a study testing vocabulary knowledge among 70 children of Russian speaking immigrants of the Great Wave, Schwartz et al. (2009) found more breadth (defined as the number of words acquired) than depth (defined as understanding and familiarity with the words) in the children's lexical knowledge of Russian.

Despite coming from Russian-speaking enclaves, these children seemed to regard Hebrew as their L1, pointing towards a language shift occurring within two generations (Schwartz et al. 2009). In a recent study of language development of the preschool children of FSU immigrants, Altman et al. (2014) show that the Russian knowledge of the children depends on family language policies (strict-Russian, mild-Russian, and pro-bilingual). Preschool children from strict-Russian families demonstrated significantly better results in the Russian-language lexical task than those from pro-bilingual homes; however, children from all types of families performed the syntactic task better in Hebrew than in Russian. Altman's study shows resistance to language shift through family language policy; however, children whose L1 is Russian preferred to communicate in Hebrew with their siblings, while communicating in Russian with their parents, grandparents, and other older family members.

Niznik (2005, 2011), like Donitsa-Schmidt (1999), predicts that Russian-speaking immigrants of the Great Wave will follow the patterns of other immigration waves and gradually shift from their home language to Hebrew. A lot of emotion accompanies such language shift, creating intergenerational tensions (Donitsa-Schmidt 1999; Kopeliovich 2011).

Though the Israeli de-facto language policy has shifted towards a greater acceptance of multilingualism and multiculturalism, many immigrants of the Great Wave feel that Russian is not sufficiently supported at the state level. Some support exists, as Russian is offered in several schools (Naiditch 2004), and there are TV and radio broadcasts in this language. However, Russian – along with most other diasporic languages – is not widely available as an educational option in high schools and universities. Despite the obvious demand, only 200–250 students were enrolled nationally in Russian classes in 2000 (Olshtain and Kotik 2000; Remennick 2003a). The future prospects of Israeli Russian remain uncertain.

2 Historical background

The two main immigration waves of Russian speakers to Israel were the Russian Aliya of the 1970s and the Great Wave, or the Great Aliya, of 1989–2000. The two immigration waves are different demographically, linguistically, and ideologically.

The first immigration wave, beginning in 1966, peaking in 1971, and ending roughly by the end of that decade, brought about 200,000 immigrants from the Soviet republics to Israel. Members of this aliya are typically described as motivated by Zionism and characterized by a strong Jewish identity, especially as opposed to those who opted to immigrate to the USA and Western Europe during the same period (Olshtain and Kotik 2000; Remennick 2003a). The Russian-speaking immigrants of the 1970s did not, as a rule, maintain ties with families and cultural institutions in their original homeland, due to Soviet policies that discouraged visits and placed all correspondence under surveillance (Kheimets and Epstein 2001). The integration of these educated, professional immigrants into Israeli society was "largely smooth and excellent" (Remennick 2003a: 433–434). The majority chose to switch to Hebrew in both the private and public spheres, following the Zionist policy of Hebrew monolingual ideology, which puts emphasis on Hebrew in all contexts and encourages subtractive bilingualism/abandoning of diasporic Jewish languages (Shohamy 1994; Spolsky and Shohamy 1999).

In contrast, the Great Aliya differed from most preceding immigration waves in attitudes towards nationalism, knowledge of Hebrew, as well as in cultural and linguistic attitudes. In Donitsa-Schmidt's questionnaires, the motivation for immigration was often stated as economic (44.5%) or political, i.e., motivated by anti-Semitism or the disintegration of the Soviet regime (33.1%), while only 3.5% of respondents mentioned ideology or nationalism (Donitsa-Schmidt 1999: 96).

After immigration, these members of the Great Aliya appeared reluctant to relinquish the language and culture of the former Soviet Union, often maintaining a feeling of cultural superiority over Israelis; Israeli culture was described in denigrating terms, such as Levantine, Oriental, non-European, parochial – in short, contrasting with the immigrants' own perception of their Russian-language culture as high culture – i.e., educated, European, sophisticated, desirable, and central (cf. Fialkova and Yelenevskaya 2007; Trier 1996; Kheimets and Epstein 2001). It is not, therefore, a surprise that the immigrants of the Great Aliya are focused on language maintenance. IR, in particular, is a phenomenon associated with the Great Wave; the immigrants of the 1970s as a rule chose not to maintain their Russian, even at home, and only regained interest in the language under the influence of the immigrants of the Great Wave (Olshtain and Kotik 2000; Remennick 2003a). The timing of the Great Aliya made it easier for immigrants to maintain ties with Russian cultural production and with Russian speakers abroad through the internet, availability of Russian TV programming and books, greater ease of travel, visits from Russian-speaking artists and singers, etc. Immigrant Russian Israelis of the Great Wave were often denigrated by veteran Israelis for their linguistic and cultural separatism and lack of Zionist values (Remennick 2005); a common insult dubs this immigration wave the Sausage Aliya, implying that these immigrants valued personal prosperity over ideology (Fialkova and Yelenevskaya 2007). Despite these often negative attitudes, the Great Aliya is a Jewish immigration wave, a tightly-knit community with its own sense of ethnic and cultural identity which was strongly Jewish, though much less prominently Israeli-oriented (Caspi et al. 2002; Golan-Cook and Olshtain 2011).

One of the crucial differences between the immigrants of the Great Aliya and other waves is the Israeli ex-Soviets' attitude towards Hebrew. Jewish communities around the world coexist with Hebrew in a diglossic situation. Though both Aramaic and Hebrew are associated with traditional Jewish learning, Hebrew holds a special place within Jewish multilingualisms: it is a symbolic component of Jewish identity even for Jews who do not know it. It has the status of a holy, highly prestigious language that connects Jews to their traditions. Since the 20th century, Hebrew has also connected Jews to the State of Israel, an important identity component for many diasporic Jews. Most Jewish immigrants to Israel have some connection to Hebrew through Jewish education, prayer, and other sources.

In Israel, Hebrew is positioned as the ultimate Jewish language, a symbol of Jewish independence and national unity. While Israeli society is de-facto multicultural and multilingual, subtractive bilingualism is practiced by new Jewish immigrants: they are encouraged and often pressured to learn and adopt Hebrew as a means of acculturation, not just to life in Israel, but to Zionist values. At the same time, they are also encouraged to abandon their diasporic languages. Even in the absence of a legally codified language policy, Hebrew had been positioned as the unifying language of the Jews in pre-State Palestine, and a common denominator necessary for the survival of the Jewish State. Diasporic Jewish languages, such as Russian, Ladino, and Yiddish, were not supported; moreover, they were often perceived as an active threat to the survival of Hebrew. Therefore, diasporic home languages have been discouraged in Israel as providing ties to ways of life perceived as non-Zionist. The monolingual policy has weakened the status of diasporic JLs in Israel, and such languages are often in danger of attrition (Ben-Rafael, Olshtain, and Geijst 1997; Kheimets and Epstein 2001; Naiditch 2004; Shohamy 1994).

Hebrew thus emerges as a hegemonic language positioned and maintained by the state not only as a High, but as a language necessary for the survival of the state. It is a language which is positioned as fragile and which is endangered by Jewish multilingualisms (Abu-Rabia 1999; Donitsa-Schmidt 1999; Kheimets and Epstein 2001; Shohamy 1994; Spolsky and Shohamy 1999). However, some scholars speak about a greater openness to multilingualism and a "decline in Hebrew monolingual nation-building ideology" (Kopeliovich 2011: 108) in a post-Zionist society. This greater acceptance of multilingualism might be emerging as a result of the linguistic attitudes of the Great Aliya, as well as a result of competition with English as a global High (Kopeliovich 2011; Naiditch 2004; Spolsky and Shohamy 1999).

In contrast to most other diasporic Jews, Soviet Jews did not have access to religious education and were denied opportunities to learn Hebrew. Interestingly, both Soviet and Zionist language policies emphasized subtractive bilingualism as essential to the successful building of a state. Just like Zionist ideology pressured Jewish immigrants to shift to Hebrew while abandoning diasporic JLs, Soviet language policy actively encouraged a shift to Russian, and positioned certain languages as lesser. In particular, this applied to Jewish languages. Hebrew, a language associated with religion, had been prohibited by the Soviet authorities; any education or cultural activity in Hebrew was forbidden and, until the late 1980s, even Hebrew instruction was considered a crime punishable by a 5-year imprisonment (Kheimets and Epstein 2001; cf. Leshem and Lissak 1999). The result was a "Soviet Jewish intelligentsia [which] identifies itself with a unique combination of Jewish (mostly Yiddish) ethnic and cultural, but not religious, elements and the heritage of Russian culture" (Kheimets and Epstein 2001: 130).

Thus, Hebrew played, at best, a minor role in these Jews' identity. Lacking opportunities to learn Hebrew, Russian Jews refocused on Yiddish. While the opportunities for speaking and writing Yiddish gradually dwindled during the Soviet regime, many Soviet Jews considered it the Jewish language that symbolically connected them to Jewishness (cf. Kheimets and Epshtein 2011; Shternshis 2006; Verschik, this volume) Yet, even though Yiddish held a position of cultural and emotional importance for Soviet Jews, Russian was their primary language of communication, both at home and in the cultural and professional spheres. 90% of FSU Jews cited Russian as their native language in the last Soviet census of 1989 (Remennick 2003a: 433).

In the late 1980s and early 1990s, Hebrew language instruction became permissible in the FSU. As a result, many Russian Jews took Hebrew lessons before immigrating to Israel; however, many recorded feelings of trepidation towards the process of learning Hebrew. Unlike many other diasporic Jews, who have at least some familiarity with Hebrew, many Russian Jews felt intimidated by the unfamiliar script, the right-to-left writing orientation, and the fact that Hebrew is written in an abjad rather than an alphabet (cf. Fialkova and Elenevskaya 2007).

Upon arrival, newly minted Russian Israelis found themselves in an immersion situation with Hebrew just as they faced challenges in all areas of life, such as finding appropriate housing and jobs, integrating into an unfamiliar culture in the community and in the workplace, and dealing with sometimes unfriendly or even hostile attitudes from veteran Israelis. Many immigrants reported negative attitudes towards Hebrew; for those immigrants, cultural and linguistic separatism, informal networks, and strong in-group solidarity helped them survive in an unfamiliar and disorienting environment (cf. Donitsa-Schmidt 1999; Fialkova and Yelenevskaya 2007; Naiditch 2004).

Employment opportunities for immigrants of the Great Wave is an issue often discussed in the literature, as it has influenced and continues to influence both socioeconomic integration and language maintenance. Immigrants of the Great Wave are often stigmatized in Israel as "professors who sweep the streets," i.e., highly-educated professionals who cannot find employment on the level they held in the FSU (Dubson 2007; Remennick 2003a, 2003b); according to Remennick, "Only about one-third of former Soviet professionals and specialists managed to find work suited to their qualifications, while the rest made their living by unskilled manual work" (Remennick 2003b: 42).

Russian is often discouraged in the workplace, as well as in the army (Kopeliovich 2011; Remennick 2004, 2005). Native Israelis often feel uncomfortable about the use of Russian by Russian speakers in the workplace; Russian may be seen as an obstacle to acculturation, or a way for Russian-speaking immigrants to signal their cultural superiority or to exclude native Israelis (Remennick 2004, 2005). Russian speakers may thus opt to speak Hebrew to each other in work situations, and Russian in casual environments.

Language choice and usage thus varies according to social context – at home, with parents and grandparents, with Russian-speaking peers, with colleagues, with veteran Israelis (Remennick 2003a). According to Remennick's 2003 study, phenomena such as lexical borrowings, code-switching, etc., and the "relative shares of Russian and Hebrew in the speech" (Remennick 2003a: 438), i.e., the usage of IR, are conditioned by the speakers' age, social standing, employment status, and contact opportunities with Hebrew speakers. Russian may be used in the domestic sphere, especially when joking, gossiping, and scolding; certain types of code-switching may signal in-group solidarity (Donitsa-Schmidt 1999; Naiditch 2004, 2008). In home situations, most people would use IR rather than MSR: Remennick reported that only 2 families out of 10 surveyed "stuck to pure Russian with almost no Hebrew inclusions throughout many hours of a family gathering" (Remennick 2003a: 438–439).

Naiditch describes two situations of Russian-language usage, positioning them as two extremes of a usage continuum: one reflects younger speakers who use Russian at home to communicate with parents and grandparents. They use Hebrew in school, in the army, at the university, and in the workplace, for cultural consumption and production, as well as with friends. The second situation reflects speakers who use Russian at home and with friends, for media consumption, as well as partially in the workplace; Hebrew is used in work, army, and educational contexts, as well as in reading official material, such as textbooks and official letters (Naiditch 2004: 294).

In more recent studies surveying linguistic attitudes of the immigrants, Hebrew is no longer regarded with negativity or trepidation, even though difficulty with reading Hebrew remains for some, especially older, FSU immigrants. The Israeli identity of the immigrants has also strengthened over the years, while retaining a strong Jewish and Russian component (Golan-Cook and Olshtain 2011). In surveys of immigrants' attitudes, the Hebrew languages ranked positively in some respects, such as in relation to Jewishness and aesthetics; however, in a number of studies involving informant questionnaires, Russian consistently outscored Hebrew, including in such areas as usefulness as an international language, beauty, and Jewish connection. In short, while FSU Jews surveyed do appreciate Hebrew, Russian linguistic identity emerges as having higher emotional value (Ben-Rafael et al. 1997; Kheimets and Epstein 2001; Olshtain and Kotik 2000). Young immigrants also share positive attitudes towards Russian (Kheimets and Epstein 2001; Olshtain and Kotik 2000).

The linguistic situation of FSU immigrants in Israel may be regarded as that of multiglossia (cf. Schiffman 1997), with various languages (Russian, Hebrew, sometimes English) vying for the status of a High. In the beginning, FSU immigrants clearly preferred Russian (specifically, MSR) as a High in which they were highly proficient, and which they often regarded – perhaps under the influence of Soviet imperialism – as a culturally prestigious language possessing a richer vocabulary than Hebrew, as well as a tradition of excellence in sciences and the arts. These immigrants also perceived Russian as more international than Hebrew. Though initially the Great Wave immigrants had a fair amount of resistance to accepting Hebrew as a High, over the years this language of government, education, and job opportunities has increased in prestige for FSU immigrants, whose command of Hebrew has also increased in that same period. Russian has continued to be emotionally and socially significant for FSU immigrants; however, an anxiety over Russian language maintenance has emerged, as younger generations may be undergoing a language shift.

In the situation of multiglossia, both Russian and Hebrew may act interchangeably as a High, depending on the speakers' proficiency, attitudes, genre, subject of communication, etc. (cf. discussion in Naiditch 2004: 295). Between the co-ethnic/in-group High (Modern Standard Russian), and the general Israeli hegemonic High of Hebrew, IR's position is that of an almost-unmentionable Low, a contact vernacular all too often regarded as "impure" and which may be perceived as detrimental to the immigrants' efforts to preserve Standard Russian as the language of culture and prestige. Thus, some speakers may attempt to distance themselves epistemologically from their own spoken vernacular, especially when talking to high-prestige individuals such as researchers and/or Russian-language professionals, or when writing for an audience. At the same time, usage of IR may signal affiliation, solidarity, and in-grouping (Perelmutter 2018).

3 Structural information

The most prominent feature of IR is influence from Hebrew, which is evident across domains but is especially notable in the lexicon. IR incorporates significant amounts of Hebrew lexical elements, often adapted to the Russian phonological and morphological matrix. The amount of code-mixing and code-switching is often situational, varying between individuals, as well as between particular situations (work, home, with friends), genres, and contexts. The lexical incorporation of Hebrew words into the Russian matrix has received the most attention from scholars so far, most notably from Larissa Naiditch, who has conducted extensive fieldwork and has written a series of detailed and insightful articles on IR (2000, 2002, 2004, 2008), as well as Niznik (2005, 2011) and Remennick (2003a, 2003b, 2004, 2005), though the latter has mostly focused on the sociolinguistic aspects of Russian usage and maintenance. The fieldwork done by these scholars focuses on immigrants, rather than on native-born Israelis with Russian-speaking parents.

3.1 Phonetics and phonology; intonation contours

Orel (1994:31) notes in passing that Russian-style consonantal phonemes are often replaced by Hebrew ones in IR.

According to Orel (1994), intonation contours are one of the distinguishing features of Jewish Russian in the former Soviet Union, being heavily influenced by Yiddish. Even when Russian-speaking immigrants adhere to MSR intonation contours, they recognize Hebrew intonation contours as being much closer to Yiddish (and hence, to Jewish Russian) than MSR, and readily adapt Hebrew-style intonation contours in IR (Orel 1994: 37).

3.2 Lexicon

3.2.1 Shifts in Russian word usage

Russian lexemes may change or expand their semantic meanings under the influence of Hebrew. For example, MSR distinguishes between *lekciia* 'lecture' and *doklad* 'a scholarly talk, conference paper or report'; however, since the Hebrew word for both is *hartsaa*, IR expands the domain of *lekciia*: IR *professor iz Ameriki chital lekciiu na seminare* 'A professor from America gave a talk at a seminar' vs MSR *professor iz Ameriki chital doklad na seminare* (Naiditch 2004: 297). The word *salon*, which in IR means 'living room' (under the influence of Hebrew), in MSR largely denotes an Enlightenment-era salon; the word for living room is *gostinnaia* (Niznik 2005: 1710).

IR also uses such loan translations of Hebrew idioms as *brat'/vziat'* 'to take. IMPF/PF' and *delat'/sdelat'* 'to do.IMPF/PF': *vziat' kurs* 'to take a course' (Hebrew *lakakhat kurs*) as opposed to MSR *proslushat' kurs* 'to hear a course' or *zapisat'sia na kurs* 'to register for a course'; *sdelat' pervuiu stepen'* 'to do a BA degree' (Hebrew *laasot toar rishon*) as opposed to MSR *poluchit' stepen' bakalavra* 'to receive a BA degree' (Naiditch 2004: 296; cf. Niznik 2005: 1710). Extending the usage of verbs such as *brat'/vziat'* 'to take' and *delat'/sdelat'* 'to do' to an almost auxiliary-like status is also a feature of other immigrant Russian variants (Naiditch 2004).

3.2.2 Lexical elements of Hebrew origin in IR

Naiditch (2008, 2004) discusses the difficulty in distinguishing between borrowings/loanwords, mixes, and code-switching when describing Hebrew lexical elements incorporated into IR. She suggests that borrowings and code-switching represent two ends of a continuum; whether something may be classified as a borrowing or a switch may depend on the frequency and regularity of a certain word's usage; the speaker's degree of competence in both embedded and matrix languages, in this case Hebrew and Russian; how well a word is integrated (phonetically, morphologically, etc.) into the Russian matrix; the stylistic markedness of a word; and whether the Hebrew word can be relatively easily replaced by Russian.

Nouns are the most frequently encountered Hebrew elements in IR. Most Russian speakers in Israel, regardless of their level of Hebrew proficiency, incorporate nouns that denote concepts particular to life in Israel (Niznik 2005; Naiditch 2004). Examples include *misrad* 'office', *pkida* 'female clerk', *mazkira* 'secretary', *mishtara* 'police', *mazgan* 'air conditioner', *bagrut* 'matriculation exam', and others (Naiditch 2004, 2008). Such words feel unmarked and appropriate to the speakers of IR, where a MSR word would feel unnatural (Naiditch 2004: 299).

Even speakers who may profess negativity towards IR admit that they adopt certain Hebrew words that denote new, formerly unfamiliar phenomena. For example, writer Lidiya Yoffe articulates a range of these common sentiments:

> I do not like when people speak "*surzhyk*": a word in Russian followed by a word in Hebrew. It sounds horrible. At the same time, some Hebrew words I use always or often. Usually these words denote concepts we have initially encountered in Israel. One could translate them into Russian, but in a way that is lengthy and clumsy. And one simply feels that it is not quite the same thing. "*Bitakhon*" and "*bezopastnost'*" ['security'], "*misrad*" and "*uchrezhdenie*" ['office'], "*bituakh leumi*" and "*social'noe obespechenie*" ['social security']. Different connotations. Compare "*sobes*" [short for "*social'noe obespechenie*" 'social security' – RP] and "*bituakh leumi*."[7] (*translation mine-RP*)

In addition, IR may include Hebrew nouns classified as transitional loans or nonce loans, i.e., occasionally incorporated Hebrew words which, according to Naiditch (2004: 299), are stylistically marked and are borderline between mixes and switches: *Ia etu sugiiu uzhe reshil* 'I have already solved this problem' (Hebrew *sugia* 'problem'); *u nee net gvulia* 'she has no limit' (Hebrew *gvul* 'limit, border'). Incorporaton of such nonce loans may mark emotive speech and in-group affiliation. Professional and educational terms may also be frequently incorporated into IR, and the usage of such mixes may also signal in-grouping (Naiditch 2004).

IR readily incorporates a range of discourse markers, such as *yofi* 'great', *beseder* 'all right', *baemet* 'really' (cf. Niznik 2005: 1710). Adjectives and verbs of Hebrew origin appear less frequently in IR (though see 3.3.4 for further discussion).

Yiddish influences in IR lexicon are often hard to discuss in the context of Hebrew lexical influences, as much of the Yiddish lexicon in Jewish Russian was of Hebrew lexical origin, and it is exactly this lexicon that becomes (re)activated in

---

[7] http://varana.livejournal.com/78011.html

Israel under the influence of Hebrew; immigrants recognize and (re)incorporate into IR certain Yiddish words of Hebrew origin, in their Hebrew pronunciation, for example Yiddish *bekitser* > Hebrew *bekitsur*, Yiddish *balabus* > Hebrew *balabait*, Yiddish *bris* > Hebrew *brit*, arguably a case of reborrowing (see discussion in Orel 1994: 30–31).

Hebrew lexical elements in IR are, generally speaking, adapted to Russian phonology. For example, the Russian soft alveolar approximant /l'/ may replace the Hebrew approximant /l/, depending on position, e.g., word-finally: /gvul'/ 'border', /tijul'/ 'excursion'; word-final consonant devoicing is present: Hebrew *makhshev* 'computer' – IR /maxshef/, Heb. *misrad* – IR /misrat/; and Russian rules of vowel neutralization in unstressed syllables apply to Hebrew mixes, e.g., Hebrew *tokhna* 'program' – IR /takhna/ (Naiditch 2004: 300).

3.2.3 Morphological adaptation of Hebrew lexical elements

Hebrew mixes in IR, as a rule, are adapted to Russian morphology, e.g., grammatical gender, case, number for nouns (grammatical gender, case, number, and animacy for masculine nouns). There is a fair bit of surface similarity in form between Russian and Hebrew nouns, e.g., Hebrew nouns ending in *–a* tend to be grammatically feminine, while those ending in a consonant (with the exception of those ending in *–t*) tend to be masculine. Hebrew nouns are thus incorporated into the corresponding Russian lexical classes, depending on ending and stress: e.g., feminine Hebrew nouns like *mishtara* 'police', *sifriia* 'library' will decline like Russian *lisa* 'fox' and *koleia* 'rail'; masculine *ul'pan* 'Hebrew language course/school' like Russian *tuman* 'fog'. Nouns ending in *–e*, such as *khoze* 'contract', do not decline, similar to established Russian loanwords such as *esse* 'essay', etc. (Naiditch 2004: 300–301).

Since the grammatical gender of Russian nominals depends on their word-final consonant or vowel, some Hebrew inanimate nouns change grammatical gender when incorporated into IR, e.g., *khanut* 'store', *pirsomet* 'advertisement' (feminine in Hebrew, masculine in IR).

The formation of plural nouns is an area of variation in IR. There are three main ways of forming plural nouns from Hebrew lexical mixes: 1) adding a regular Russian plural ending: *mivkhany* 'tests', Hebrew *mivkhan* 'test'); 2) using a Hebrew plural ending in *–im* and *–ot* (*khadashot* 'news'); 3) using a hybrid plural ending which would involve both the Hebrew plural suffix and the Russian plural suffix (*khadashoty* 'news', *olimy* 'repatriants').

One of the Hebrew phenomena that migrate to IR is a Hebrew compound binomial with the first noun in status constructus. Only the second part of such binomials declines in IR: *gde vashi teudat zeuty* 'where are your identity cards?' (cf. Hebrew singular *teudat zeut*, plural *teudot zeut*). (Naiditch 2004: 305).

Adjectives of Hebrew origin are rarer in IR than nouns. Adjectives may be formed through Russian suffixation, with some stable adjectives such as *galutnyi* 'diasporic', *datishnyi* 'religious', *shabatnyi* 'pertaining to Shabbat' and more occasional ones such as *khamudnyi* 'cute'. Adjectives without suffixation may be postposed to nouns: e.g., *datishnyi dedushka* vs. *dedushka dati*, both meaning 'a religious grandfather' (Naiditch 2008: 51–53).

Hebrew verbs appear in IR with lesser frequency than nouns; however, some are used regularly, usually with denominal formation: *(ot)ciliumit'* 'to make a copy' (Hebrew *tsilum* 'photograph, photocopy'), *shvitovat'* 'to strike' (Hebrew *shvita* 'strike'), *metapelit'/prometapelit'* 'to care, nurse' (Hebrew *metapel/metapelet* 'nurse'), *shomerit'*, *shomrit'*, *shmirit'* 'to work as a watchman' (Hebrew *shomer* 'watchman', *shmira* 'work of a watchman') (Naiditch 2004; Niznik 2005). Grammatical aspects may be marked by Russian prefixes, thus *ciliumit'* 'to make a copy.IMPF' versus *otciljumit'* 'to make a copy.PF'. Switching of a whole Hebrew verb is also attested, usually with the infinitive: *ty mozhesh, nakonec, lehiraga?* 'can you finally calm down?' Verbs can also be incorporated via a construction *delat'/sdelat'* 'to do.IMPF/PF' + Hebrew noun': *sdelat' khipus* 'to search', *delat' khisakhon* 'to save'. Naiditch notes that noun mixes often feel stylistically unmarked to speakers, while verb switching tends to be more marked (Naiditch 2004: 308–9).

3.3 Grammar

Naiditch (2004) argues that shifts in grammar are minimal, with two exceptions where Hebrew syntax has influenced the syntax of IR: 1) the usage of the Russian conjunction *esli* 'if' in indirect questions: *ia ne znaiu, esli on pridet* 'I do not know if he will come', under the influence of Hebrew *im* 'if' in *ani lo yodea/yodaat im hu yavo* as opposed to MSR *ia ne znaiu, pridet li on* 'I do not know whether he will come'; 2) replacement of relative pronoun *kotoryi* 'which' by the conjunction *chto* 'that': IR *knigi, chto my chitali* 'books that we have read' under the influence of Hebrew *she-* 'that' in *sfarim shekaranu*, as opposed to MSR *knigi, kotorye my chitali* 'books which we have read' (Naiditch 2004: 295). Orel (1994) also emphasizes the influence of Hebrew on the structure of complex clauses in IR, with calques such as *v minutu chto on prishel* 'the minute he came' (Hebrew *berega shehu ba*) instead of MSR *kogda on prishel* 'when he came'; as well as replacing the relative pronoun *kotoryi* 'which' with *chto* 'that', a calque of Hebrew *she-* (similar to Naiditch 2004, above).

4 Cultural institutions

Newspapers play an important role in the FSU immigrant community. The number of Russian-language publications reported in scholarship varies throughout the years, presumably as the number of newspapers has fluctuated, e.g., "20 newspapers and magazines" are reported by Zilberg and Leshem (1996), fifty "dailies, weeklies, and monthlies" by Leshem and Lissak (1999); over 120 Russian-language publications are reported in a detailed study of Russian-language media by Caspi et al. (2002), including "four dailies, nearly 60 weeklies and local papers, 43 monthlies and bimonthlies, and 10 other periodicals" (Caspi et al. 2002: 543). *Vesti* is cited as the most popular newspaper among Russian-speakers in Israel (Kopeliovich 2011). Though the scholars do not indicate whether newspapers use MSR or IR, my ongoing research indicates that newspaper publications adhere to Standard Russian, as it is a variant associated with prestige and literacy, as opposed to IR. However, IR is attested in advertisements (especially in regional/less prominent newspapers), as well as in some humor writing. I am planning to conduct research on IR in Israeli Russian newspapers and periodicals, which will hopefully reveal additional patterns of language usage.

Literary periodicals play an important role in a developing emigré literature, with journals such as *Zven'ia, Zerkalo, Solnechnoe Spleteniie, Dvoetochie, Ierusalimskii zhurnal*, and others, publishing important immigrant literary writers as Evgeny Steiner, Dina Rubina, Igor Guberman, Alexander Goldstein, and many others (Krutikov 2016).

Kol Yisrael, the state radio network of Israel, operates an immigrant channel, Radio REKA, which launched in 1991. While the initial goal was to consolidate radio broadcasts in various immigrant languages, the majority of broadcasts are in Russian (12 daily hours) (Caspi et al. 2002; Kopeliovich 2011). An additional radio station, Channel 7, was established in 1988 as a "pirate station by the Israeli extreme political right" (Caspi 2002: 542); a Russian channel, Channel 8, was established in 1991. There is also a commercial station, Pervoe Radio 'First Radio' (Kopeliovich 2011).

Additional media include a dedicated Russian TV channel in Israel, and several original TV channels from Russia are available as well (with the most popular being NTV, ORT, and RTR (Caspi et al. 2002).

Another famous cultural institution established by Russian-speaking FSU immigrants is the Gesher ('Bridge') Theater; performances are staged in both Russian and Hebrew (Kopeliovich 2011). Musical culture includes such figures as Arkady Duchin, performance artists Vulkan (rap) and Sadyle (hip-hop), and an international fusion band, Los Caparos, which includes both Russian- and Hebrew-speaking musicians (Niznik 2011: 102). In addition, numerous classically trained musicians immigrated to Israel with the Great Wave, finding employment in Israeli orchestras, teaching music, etc.

Of particular interest is the Mofet school project, "a national system of complementary classes (followed by several full-time schools) run by immigrant teachers mainly for immigrant students in order to transfer high standards of teaching of math, physics and humanities from Russian to Israeli schools" (Remennick 2003b: 87). Interestingly, Mofet instruction is in Hebrew. Russian-speaking parents and grandparents support this effort, as well as Russian-language daycare centers and kindergartens, evening and extra-curricular schools, and organizations such as Mapat, IGUM, Shiton, Impulse, Radost, Kidma, and others that supplement the existing educational opportunities (Kopeliovich 2011).

IR speakers also congregate online; this is an underresearched area of linguistic activity for Israeli Russians. Elias and Lemish's survey (2009) shows that younger immigrants use Russian-language websites and social networks, not just for media consumption but for communication with Russian-speaking peers in Israel and abroad, as well as for learning about the host country and establishing social connections to local peers. Online communication provides a "safe ground" for these young immigrants anxious about integration in Israel.

FSU immigrants of all ages may participate in media consumption, production, and social networking online. Prominent Israeli Russian public figures, as well as private individuals, might have Livejournal blogs (Livejournal, in Russian Zhivoi Zhurnal or ZhZh, is an important platform for Russian-language bloggers in a variety of countries, cf. Perelmutter 2013). In addition, IR speakers congregate in especially designated forums, such as souz.co.il (Perelmutter 2018).

5 State of research

5.1 Issues of general theoretical interest

IR is a specific and unusual case in the context of Jewish multilingualisms. Fishman's (1981) concept of a fusion language may or may not be applicable to IR. According to Fishman, each fusion JL draws on resources from a non-Jewish vernacular, and incorporates Hebrew lexicon into this matrix, and, in some cases, morphology and syntax. Spolsky and Benor (2006) point out that diasporic Jewish languages tend to share a number of features – most importantly, a vernacular non-Jewish language as a matrix, with a significant number of borrowings from Hebrew and/or Aramaic; JLs can also incorporate elements from other contact languages.

IR incorporates Hebrew lexicon into the matrix of a non-Jewish vernacular (Russian). However, IR differs from other fusion languages in several important respects. Fishman describes the process of fusion as occurring specifically in Jewish traditional communities. A fusion language involves an oral medium (usually a non-Jewish vernacular), and a Hebrew/Aramaic literacy tradition which is of high emotional value to the community. IR speakers do not fit this model, having been barred from religious observance in the Soviet regime. They had no access to Hebrew literacy through traditional Jewish education; under the Soviet regime, Hebrew literacy was forbidden.

While Soviet Jews had their own specific secular-cultural Jewish identity (cf. Shternshis 2006), they did not congregate in traditional communities, and had mostly switched to Russian not only in speech, but also in writing for daily tasks as well as for cultural production. Russian is, therefore, the language of high prestige with which they feel an emotional connection. These immigrants' encounter with Hebrew occurred either shortly before immigration to Israel or shortly after arrival.

Like other JLs, IR may incorporate a fair amount of religion-specific Hebrew vocabulary, but the process of its incorporation is different from that of other JLs – since many FSU immigrants encountered religious concepts only after arrival to Israel, such words as *shabat, koshernyj, mezuza, matsa,* and others became incorporated into IR.

An additional consideration is that of orthography: while most JLs adapt the Hebrew script to the vernacular, IR uses Cyrillic (IR writing often occurs informally, in online contexts such as blogs and forums, as well as in some newspapers). Using Cyrillic further ties IR to the Russian literacy tradition rather than to the Hebrew literacy tradition, to which Russian-speaking Jews had no access before their arrival in Israel.

While IR may or may not fit into the fusion paradigm, it is nevertheless the vernacular of a specific Jewish community with its own highly idiosyncratic history, which influenced the development of this vernacular. The speech community possesses both a strong connection to Jewishness (although in different ways than most traditional Jewish communities) and a strong sense of group cohesion. IR also presents an interesting case of an immigrant Russian, with similarities and differences to other immigrant Russians around the world. Like many other immigrant vernaculars, IR faces an uncertain future, due to generational shifts and processes of language attrition.

5.2 Directions in current and future research

Studies of Russian in Israel tend to focus on questions of language maintenance and shift. The patterns of language shift observed by recent studies are somewhat unusual for the IR situation, due to this ethnolinguistic group's cohesion and tendency towards additive bilingualism and language maintenance; processes of maintenance and shift remain important to study as new speakers are born and acquire linguistic proficiency.

Unfortunately, IR itself is rarely the focus of such studies. At times, concepts of linguistic purity are raised in discussions of IR by both informants and scholars; MSR is positioned as clean, or pure, Russian and IR as a kind of undesirable variant which might hinder the acquisition of either Russian or Hebrew. Some studies mention IR only as "codeswitching to Hebrew" (Kopeliovich 2011: 119) or "code-switching and bilingualism" (Niznik 2005: 1709). Further studies of intergenerational patterns of IR usage would be very useful, as well as studies of IR across contexts (in the workplace, in the army, etc.).

A corpus of spoken IR is yet to be developed, though individual scholars have collected various linguistic data for their own projects. Fialkova and Yelenevskaya (2007) collected multiple narratives of personal experience from FSU immigrants and conducted anthropological and folkloric analysis using these narratives; these and other IR narratives would benefit from linguistic analysis. Online, vernacular writing presents especially interesting material for the study of IR (cf. Perelmutter 2018).

Other fruitful directions for possible research include Jewish language formation; multiglossic tensions between Hebrew, MSR, and IR; detailed studies of differences in gesture patterns and intonation contours between speakers of MSR and IR; and more.

Acknowledgments

I am grateful to Larissa Naiditsch (Hebrew University) for her groundbreaking work and mentoring over the years and to my spouse Bogi Perelmutter (University of Iowa), for support, encouragement, and many excellent suggestions. This article is dedicated to Irina Paperno (UC Berkeley); this paper could not have been written without her generosity, kindness, and friendship.

References

Altman, Carmit, Zhanna Burstein-Feldman, Dafna Yitzhaki, Sharon Armon Lotem & Joel Walters. 2014. Family language policies, reported language use and proficiency in Russian-Hebrew bilingual children in Israel. *Journal of Multilingual and Multicultural Development* 35(3). 216–234.

Abu-Rabia, Salim. 1999. Attitudes and psycholinguistic aspects of first language maintenance among Russian-Jewish immigrants in Israel. *Educational Psychology* 19. 133–148.

Ben-Rafael, Eliezer, Elite Olshtain & Idit Geijst. 1997. Identity and language: The social insertion of Soviet Jews in Israel. In Lewin-Epstein, Noah, Paul Ritterband & Yaacov Ro'i (eds.), *Russian Jews on three continents: Migration and resettlement*, 364–388. London & New York: Frank Cass & Co.

Bilaniuk, Laada. 2004. A typology of Surzhyk: Mixed Ukrainian-Russian language. *International Journal of Bilingualism* 8(4). 409–425.

Caspi, Dan, Hanna Adoni, Akiba A. Cohen & Nelly Elias. 2002. The Red, the white and the blue: The Russian media in Israel. *International Communication Gazette* 64. 537–556.

Donitsa-Schmidt, Smadar. 1999. *Language maintenance or shift – Determinants of language choice among Soviet immigrants in Israel.* Toronto: University of Toronto PhD thesis.

Dubson, Boris I. 2007. Sotsial'no-professional'nyi' status russkoiazychnykh immigrantov v Izraile. *Sotsiologicheskie Issledovaniia* 4. 96–102.

Elias, Nelly & Dafna Lemish. 2009. Spinning the web of identity: The roles of the internet in the lives of immigrant adolescents. *New Media and Society* 11(4). 1–19.

Fialkova, Larisa & Maria N. Yelenevskaya. 2007. *Ex-Soviets in Israel, from personal narratives to a group portrait.* Detroit: Wayne State University Press.

Fishman, Joshua A. 1981. The sociology of Jewish languages from the perspective of the general sociology of language: A preliminary formulation. *International Journal of the Sociology of Language* 30. 5–16.

Golan-Cook, Pnina & Elite Olshtain. 2011. The impact of identity on patterns of national and ethnic language attitudes and use: The case of immigrant students from the former Soviet Union in Israel. *Israel Studies in Language and Society* 4(1). 10–38.

Kent, Kateryna. 2010. Language contact: Morphosyntactic analysis of Surzhyk spoken in central Ukraine. *LSO Working Papers in Linguistics* 8. 33–53.

Kheimets, Nina G. & Alek D. Epstein. 2001. Confronting the languages of statehood: Theoretical and historical frameworks for the analysis of the multilingual identity of the Russian Jewish intelligentsia in Israel. *Language Problems and Language Planning* 25. 217–230.

Kopeliovich, Shulamit. 2011. How long is 'the Russian street' in Israel? Prospects of maintaining the Russian language. *Israel Affairs* 17(1). 108–124.

Kraemer, Roberta, David Zisenwine, Michal Levy Keren & David Schers. 1995. A study of Jewish adolescent Russian immigrants to Israel: Language and identity. *International Journal of the Sociology of Language* 116(1). 153–159.

Krutikov, Mikhail. 2016. Four voices from the last Soviet generation: Evgeny Steiner, Alexander Goldshtein, Oleg Yuryev, and Alexander Ilichevsky. In Zvi Gitelman (ed.), *The new Jewish Diaspora: Russian-speaking immigrants in the United States, Israel, and Germany*, 251–265. New Brunswick, New Jersey: Rutgers University Press.

Leshem, Elazar and Moshe Lissak. 1999. Development and consolidation of the Russian Community in Israel. In Shalva Weil (ed.), *Roots and routes: Ethnicity and migration in global perspective*, 135–171. Jerusalem: Magnes Press.

Naiditch, Larissa. 2000. Code-switching and -mixing in Russian-Hebrew bilinguals. In Dicky Gilbers, John A. Nerbonne and J. Schaeken (eds.), *Languages in contact: Studies in Slavic and general linguistics*, 277–282. Amsterdam: Rodopi.

Naiditch, Larissa. 2002. Russkii iazyk v Izraile. *Slavianovedenie* 4. 35–43.

Naiditch, Larissa. 2004. Russian immigrants of the last wave in Israel. Patterns and characteristics of language usage. *Wiener Slawistischer Almanach* 53. 291–314.

Naiditch, Larissa. 2008. Tendentsii razvitiia russkogo iazyka za rubezhom: Russkii iazyk v Izraile. *Russian Linguistics* 32. 43–57.

Niznik, Marina. 2005. Searching for a new identity: The acculturation of Russian-born adolescents in Israel. In James Cohen, Kara T. McAlister, Kellie Rolstad & Jeff MacSwan (eds.), *Proceedings of the 4th International Symposium on bilingualism*, 1703–1721. Somerville: Cascadilla Press.

Niznik, Marina. 2011. Cultural practices and preferences of 'Russian' youth in Israel. Israel Affairs 17(1). 89–107.

Olshtain, Elite & Bella Kotik. 2000. The development of bilingualism in an immigrant community. In Elite Olshtain & Gabriel Horenczyk (eds.), *Language, identity and immigration*, 201–208. Jerusalem: Magnes Press.

Orel, Vladimir. 1994. Russkii uazyk v Izraile. *Slavianovedenie* 4. 35–43.

Orel, Vladimir. 1999. Russian émigré literature in Israel: In search of a new language. *Canadian-American Slavic Studies* 33(2–4). 375–382.

Perelmutter, Renee. 2013. Klassika zhanra: The flamewar as a genre in the Russian blogosphere. *Journal of Pragmatics* 45(1). 74–89.

Perelmutter, Renee. 2018. Globalization, conflict discourse, and Jewish identity in an Israeli Russian-speaking online community. *Journal of Pragmatics* 134. 134–148.

Remennick, Larissa. 2003a. From Russian to Hebrew via HebRush: Integrational patterns of language use among former Soviet immigrants in Israel. *Journal of Multilingual and Multicultural Development* 24. 431–453.

Remennick, Larissa. 2003b. Language acquisition as the main vehicle of social integration: Russian immigrants in the 1990s in Israel. *International Journal of the Sociology of Language* 164. 83–105.

Remennick, Larissa. 2003c. The 1.5 generation of Russian immigrants in Israel: Between integration and sociocultural retention. *Diaspora: A Journal of Transnational Studies* 12(1). 39–66.

Remennick, Larissa. 2004. Work relations between immigrants and old-timers in an Israeli organization: Social interactions and inter-group attitudes. *International Journal of Comparative Sociology* 45(1–2). 45–71.

Remennick, Larissa. 2005. Resetting the rules of the game: Language preferences and social relations of work between Russian immigrants and veteran professionals in an Israeli organization. *Journal of International Migration and Integration* 6(1). 1–28.

Schiffman, Harold F. 1997. Diglossia as a sociolinguistic situation. In Florian Coulmas (ed.), *The handbook of sociolinguistics*, 205–216. Malden: Blackwell Publishing.

Schwartz, Milar, Ely Kozminsky & Mark Leikin. 2009. Toward a better understanding of first language vocabulary knowledge: The case of second-generation Russian- Jewish immigrants in Israel. *Diaspora, Indigenous, and Minority Education: Studies of Migration, Integration, Equity, and Cultural Survival* 3(4). 226–244.

Shohamy, Elana. 1994. Issues in language planning in Israel: Language and ideology. In Richard D. Lambert (ed.), *Language planning around the world: Contexts and systematic change*, 131–142. Washington, D.C: National Foreign Language Center.

Spolsky, Bernard & Sarah Benor. 2006. Jewish languages. In Keith Brown (ed.), *Encyclopedia of language and linguistics*, 120–124. Oxford: Elsevier.

Spolsky, Bernard & Elana Shohamy. 1999. Language practice and policy in Israel. In Bernard Spolsky & Elana Shohamy (eds.), *The languages of Israel: Policy, ideology and practice*, 1–29. Clevedon: Multilingual Matters.

Shternshis, Anna. 2006. *Soviet and kosher: Jewish popular culture in the Soviet Union, 1923–1939*. Bloomington: Indiana University Press.
Trier, Tom. 1996. Reversed diaspora, Russian Jewry, the transition in Russia and the migration to Israel. *Anthropology of East Europe Review* 14(1). 34–42.
Zilberg, Narspy & Elazar Leshem. 1996. Russian-language press and immigrant community in Israel. *Revue Européenne de Migrations Internationals* 12(3). 173–189.

Miriam Ben-Rafael and Eliezer Ben-Rafael
Jewish French in Israel

1 Introduction

This chapter focuses on Franbreu, an Israeli Jewish French. It starts with the assessment (French Ambassador 1995) that over 20% of Israeli adults have some knowledge of French. Of this population, 250,000 to 350,000 people could be considered French speakers. However, there is great diversity among the many original Francophones. One model is the French vernacular (see Boudras-Chapon 2008) of North African immigrants drawn from poor socioeconomic background. The second model is illustrated by immigrants of the same origin as well as from other countries where French was considered, at the time of their emigration, the cultural language of the period (especially the Balkans, Turkey, and Egypt). A third, and more recent, model is exemplified by the wave of emigration from France to Israel that began in the 1990s, in the context of the Jewish population's unease as regards surging Judeophobia on the European continent.

All of these models consist of the contact of French with Israel's majority language – Hebrew. Under that influence, they display changes that crystallize, in a quite convergent manner, into a hybrid form that Miriam Ben-Rafael (2001b) called "Franbreu." Even if the recent wave of Francophone immigration appears more determined than any previous cohort to maintain "its" French, the immigrants will inevitably be submitted to the influence of Hebrew, which everyone in Israel is exposed to and acquires – at one level or another. This is the context in which the work presented here focuses on the sociological background, the sociolinguistic evolution of Franbreu, and eventual lines of further developments in this society.

As mentioned, during the 1950s and 1960s a large number of people from North Africa immigrated to Israel (E. Ben-Rafael and Sharot 2007). For those immigrants who had secondary or higher education, and had enjoyed an average social status in an urban environment, French was the daily language and the major vehicle of culture, notwithstanding its impregnation by characteristic accents stemming from the influences of Judeo-Arabic and Arabic. People who arrived with primary education only and joined the underprivileged spoke mostly Judeo-Arabic as their primary vernacular, and an additional French parlance influenced by this Judeo-Arabic. Like other groups – Yemenite, Kurdish, and Libyan Jews – who had similar experiences, these North Africans tended to adhere to their traditional spirit, and to reproduce longstanding models of life, ethnic synagogue attendance, pilgrimages to the tombs of sages, wedding and bar-mitzvah festivals, and rituals. Despite that attachment to the past, the Israeli environment irremediably altered behaviors through the combined influence of the school system, military service, new livelihoods, and the constraints of a consumer society.

At the level of linguistic activity, the main factor of change was the acquisition and practice of Hebrew. The very transition to Modern Hebrew was legitimized by the fact that it was the language common to all Jewish heritages and grounded in the Bible. Within a few years, all of the new populations gained a command of the language, which did not necessarily involve the immediate and total abandonment of Judeo-Arabic or popular French. Many members of the second generation inherited these codes from their parents, at least partially (Hofman and Fisherman 1972). Accordingly, that French barely survived among the descendants of North Africans in disadvantaged social strata. It remained alive mainly among those immigrants of the same origin who arrived with cultural and material resources, joined the middle class, and who had grown up in French culture for decades before their immigration (Chouraqui 1998). In Israel, they learned Hebrew and easily integrated into society, while French remained, in their view, a marker of distinction that they endeavored to preserve. In this, they illustrated the same syndrome as other middle-class immigrants who arrived from non-Francophone countries, where French was a highly praised resource acquired by the bourgeoisie as a "must" – such as Romania, Bulgaria, Turkey, Egypt, and Lebanon. However, in Israel of the 1950s-1970s, the dominant ideology adamantly required new citizens to acquire and speak Hebrew (M. Ben-Rafael 2001b; M. Ben-Rafael and Schmid 2007). These pressures, it is true, did not prevent Francophones, like speakers of other languages, from using their original codes, whether with spouses, among friends, or in cultural activities.

The situation changed completely with the wave of French immigration that began in the late 1980s, with 2,000–5,000 immigrants arriving per year.[1] In 2014, estimates show that about 60,000–70,000 people – not including those who were born in Israel – now living in this country arrived with that immigration. These newcomers (NVs in this chapter,[2] from the French *nouveaux venus* meaning 'newcomers') are a type of hitherto unknown population of Francophones in Israel. Their singular path is first expressed in the linguistic landscape of the localities where they tend to settle (E. Ben-Rafael & M. Ben-Rafael 2008). In the city of Netanya, for example, where NVs are relatively numerous, French is predominant

---

[1] In 2015, the number was especially high at 7,500 (according to official briefing by the Ministry of Absorption).
[2] NV is a term forged by the authors in relation to this research, for the sake of abbreviation.

on signs and panels – from real estate agents, cafés, and shops, to synagogues. French is omnipresent, sometimes exclusively, sometimes alongside Hebrew, English, and Russian. The multiculturalism that has characterized Israeli society since the 1980s, with the emergence of local political ethno-religious forces, explains the ease with which new immigrants can assert their identity in public. This change in the social climate also reflects our present-day era of globalization, typified by the multiplicity of transnational diasporas (see Glick, Schiller, and Fouron 2003). Like many other current cohorts of immigrants of the same type, these NVs aspire to fit into their new environment while still maintaining strong solidarity and institutional ties with their original communities and society.

1.1 Hebrew in the French of Jews in France

Hebrew was not totally foreign to NVs, as can be said of many other groups of Jewish immigrants in Israel. In fact, as elaborated on by Michel Masson (2013), in the case of these NVs, one may point out several sources of Hebrew loanwords in the French language that they spoke on arrival. French itself counts only a number of words originating from Hebrew which have been integrated into the French language – Sabbath (from the Hebrew word *Shabat*), Amen, eden, or messie (from the Hebrew *messaiah*). French has also integrated some words from Hebrew referring to the Jewish religion, like *kippa* (skullcap) or *cacher* (for kosher food, i.e., responding to the exigencies of Jewish dietary laws). Another category of Hebrew loanwords stems from common knowledge about Israel, due to the large exposure of Israeli reality in international media and their sustained interest in the events of the Middle East. Here one counts examples like *kibbutz* (collective settlement), *Tsahal* (the Israeli Defense Army), or the *Mossad* (lit: Agency, designating the Israeli intelligence agency).[3]

---

[3] It is important to remark here that French-speaking Jews of the relatively recent waves of immigration are themselves children or grandchildren of immigrants to France and, as such, are not completely detached from languages originating elsewhere. Many still convey some sparse markers of the linguistic past of their families. As documented by Aslanov (2016), North African Judeo-Arabic or Arabic tokens can be heard, in some circumstances, in the speech of offspring of Algerian, Moroccan, or Tunisian families (the majority of the recent French immigration to Israel). Moreover, as reported by Ertel (see Baumgarten, Astro, and Ertel 1996), the same is quite true of Yiddish expressions among the daughters and sons of families originating from Eastern Europe who make up a non-negligible minority of Israel's French newcomers. Though, in either group, the research reported in the following shows a high level of education, which, as a rule, correlates with detachment from past ethnic parlance.

Religious rituals and synagogue attendance are designated by Hebrew terms, starting with the names and texts of prayers, as well as the songs of ceremonies and the titles of officials. Many youngsters have been members of Jewish youth movements, where they learned a whole lexicon of Hebrew terms – from *madrikh* for educator and *haver* for member to *mesiba* for party. Many French Jews have visited Israel, where they have relatives and friends, and these visits are the occasion for catching up on some practical words – from *malon* for hotel to *shoter(et)* for policeman or policewoman. Above all, there is the influence of the curriculum of Jewish schools attended today, in France, by about 40% of all Jewish youngsters. In most of these schools, Hebrew is taught as a second language recognized as the first Jewish language in the world. This teaching, whatever its success, inculcates some knowledge of the language.

One might still add, among other sources, the educational impact of the linguistic landscape in Jewish neighborhoods. In the quarter called *pletzel* (square in Yiddish), in the heart of Paris, or the Jewish quarter of Sarcelles in the outskirts of France's capital, Hebrew terms are frequent on the billboards of businesses, restaurants, and agencies. One finds, for instance, a supermarket in Sarcelles called *Mazone Cacher* (kosher food). Last but not least, Israeli songs in Hebrew are a "must" at a bar mitzvah or Jewish wedding party.

Whether or not all of this amounts to what could be called "France's Jewish French" is still to be validated by thorough research, and the answer to this question will require more than an enumeration of lexical elements. It is with this kind of questioning in mind that the following delves into what is called in these pages Franbreu, that is, the French spoken by French Jews in Israel.

1.2 Investigating NVs

This research on French citizens of Israel confirms that NVs, in general, often belong to the better educated and professional sectors. Many of them are ambitious young couples with small children. Moreover, the majority of these immigrants were born in North Africa or are offspring of parents originating there. Most of them define themselves as religious or traditional, and their cultural practices and activities are marked by a strong allegiance to the French language and culture. They retain French as the language of the family and social life. French naturally gives way to Hebrew, as the language most used by children among themselves, but it is not an exclusive trend. NVs' ongoing ties with relatives, friends, and institutions in the country of origin shape their character as a transnational diaspora – i.e., they are willing to learn the local majority language and culture, but without sacrificing allegiance to their original singularity.

These NVs constitute a unique group in the human landscape of present-day Israel. Due to their education and professions, they contrast with the major bulk of the Francophone population, which settled in Israel several decades ago, who still define themselves as "North African" and often belong to socially disadvantaged layers. On the other hand, NVs also contrast with their immediate middle-class environment in several ways. They tend to be religious, unlike most middle-class Israelis; French is their first language and, even when they become fluent in Hebrew, they are still "different" from bourgeois Israelis, whose second language is English. Hence, their cultural orientation outside Israel turns them toward France, while most Israelis' external horizon is turned towards the United States. In all these attributes, NVs are a "special" social element in Israel, as well as a singular type of Francophone population.

From their very first steps in the country, these newcomers speak a French that reflects the influence of their contact with Hebrew; in this, they converge toward the "Franbreu" that old-timers of the same linguistic origin as theirs "invented" decades ago. This newer population, it is true, produces frames of socialization and foci of activities where standard French predominates, and that reflect its transnational character: associations for humanitarian purposes, help centers for new immigrants, cultural fora, professional clubs, and newsletters, as well as the French-Israeli websites that have recently mushroomed.

Thus, from the very beginning, NVs speak in French of their *aliya*, not of 'immigration', of the *Sokhnut* and not of the 'Agence juive', of *kupat kholim* and not of 'dispensaire', or of the *iriya* but not of the 'municipalité'. Hebrew elements filter into French and tend to promote the development of the special kind of "speaking French" exemplified by Francophone immigrants who settled in Israel at any time and from anywhere and who, in one way or another, were reluctant to completely abandon their original language. This is the kind of speech that we call "Franbreu" – a kind of French that can be seen as "Israeli Jewish French."

2 Franbreu

Over the years, French could not avoid being marked by contact with Hebrew. No few Francophones share a sense of language loss, reflected by the difficulty of finding, in the presence of other Francophones, the appropriate words to express ideas and feelings. While they still believe it is imperative to speak Hebrew, in terms of their Israeli identity, often they attach no less importance to reconciling their desire to become full Hebrew speakers with preserving their French.

Willy-nilly, this French is changing, engendering Franbreu through the constant contact with Hebrew. It consists primarily of an oral variety that, as such, does not necessarily affect the quality of expression of speakers when they wish to adhere to standard French in normative situations or during cultural events. As oral practice, Franbreu – which as a rule is generated during casual speech – is expressed in lexicon, syntax, and morphology. As such, it may figure among the new codes emerging from language contact in a variety of fields.

Research in language contact indeed shows that a multiplicity of linguistic varieties are generated in most language contact situations (Grosjean 1982; Romaine 1989; Gardner-Chloros 2009). The literature speaks of interference, lexical borrowing, codeswitching, simplification, attrition, and grammatical and lexical innovations. These models characterize the language of groups moving into new environments (Jacobson 1998, 2001; Bentahila 1983; Myers-Scotton 1993). From the same perspective, Miriam Ben-Rafael (2001a, 2001b) studied French-speaking immigrants and found that Franbreu is a good illustration of such processes, both in the context of language contact in general, and regarding the peculiarities, which characterize the French language.

Franbreu is also just one example of linguistic hybridization among many others observed in Israel. Research has shown Hebrew's influence on English (Olshtain and Blum-Kulka 1989), Spanish (Berk-Seligson 1986), Arabic (Koplewitz 1990), and German (Fishman and Kressel 1974). At the same time, it also concerns the influence of diverse dominant languages on French in contact situations – English in Quebec (Pergnier ed. 1989) and in Welland (Mougeon and Beniak 1989), Flemish in Belgium (Witte and Beatens Beardsmore eds. 1987), and Arabic in Morocco (Bentahila 1983).

2.1 Methodology

The basic study that established Franbreu's major traits draws from investigations conducted in the 1990s and is further elaborated in a variety of works (M. Ben-Rafael 2001a, 2001b, 2002, 2003; M. Ben-Rafael and Schmid 2007), culminating in a 2013 book updating the current knowledge available on Israel's Francophones (E. Ben-Rafael and M. Ben-Rafael 2013).

The main group of subjects in the original Franbreu research in the 1990s consisted of 150 Francophones who emigrated to Israel at the ages of 18–30, during the 1950s-1970s, and were aged between 45 and 60 at the time of data collection. Their educational and social condition was relatively homogeneous: secondary education or higher and middle socioeconomic class. Subjects were investigated according to diverse methods: recorded discussions among friends; recorded discussions among colleagues which took place at professional meetings of teachers of French; as well as face-to-face interviews of Franbreophones. Moreover, a set of 15 interviews was conducted individually by Miriam Ben-Rafael in 2007 (M. Ben-Rafael and Schmid 2007) among Franbreophones who reported on their linguistic endeavors at the time of their immigration. This range of speech settings is widely representative of linguistic activity in general and makes it possible to sketch the general profile of Israel's Jewish French. In addition, background data about linguistic knowledge – including French – were collected by quantitative methods of large representative surveys led by E. Ben-Rafael (E. Ben-Rafael and Sternberg 2009; E. Ben-Rafael and A. Goroszeiskaya 1999).

The data obtained presented an opportunity to assess the impact of contact with Hebrew, to draw the contours of attrition, and to judge the pertinence of alternate hypotheses of linguistic change. Focusing on selected aspects of codeswitching, lexicon, and syntax, this research confirms the contention that speakers in different speech situations diverge from standard L1 in different ways, revealing thereby that L1 attrition is not a sufficient explanation for occurrences that are characteristic in L1-L2 contact.

2.2 Language mixing: Codeswitching (CS) and borrowing

CS and borrowing manifestations are the most salient linguistic traits generated by language contact. They are interpreted in various ways (Poplack 1980, 1988, 2004; Poplack, Willer, and Westwood 1989; Clyne 1987; Jacobson 1998, 2001; Myers-Scotton 2002). For some (Dorian 2010; Hamers and Blanc 1983), they reflect attrition or a certain loss of L1; for others, they make up for a deficiency in L1 and provide lexical and semantic enrichment. Some researchers (Auer 1984, 1995, 1996; Lüdi 1990; Myers-Scotton 1993) consider codeswitching and borrowings as new discursive tools at the speaker's disposal that may convey self-identity. For still others, CS and borrowings essentially fulfil pragmatic, ludic, or mystic functions (Pergnier ed. 1989), emphasizing that one should differentiate between L2 influence on L1 and L1 attrition. This issue, as Köpke and Schmid (2004) report, contradicts the widely accepted assumption that all cases of interference are due to attrition. One major trend in the literature does not differentiate conceptually between borrowing and CS. It sees in borrowing the insertion of a single term – e.g., a unitarian CS – and understands CS more generally as a continuum of alternations from the borrowing of one unit up to larger segments – e.g., segmental CS (Romaine 1989; Meyers Scotton 1993; Gardner-Chloros 1995; Grosjean 1995). It is in this comprehensive perspective that we will tackle the question of: What, in this respect, has happened in the case of Franbreu?

French-Hebrew CS is the most remarkable feature in Franbreu. CS may vary from the insertion of a single Hebrew element to the insertion of entire Hebrew sequences. The large majority of single-element CS, or borrowings, are nouns; they may be collective borrowings as well as personal ones. Many of them replace French equivalents; others compensate for the absence of appropriate French terms (*garin* = 'core group', from the language of youth movements) or for terms that exist in French but carry special connotations in their Hebrew versions (*aliya* = 'immigration of Jews to Israel'). Some borrowings may alternate with their French equivalents, but others are fixed and are never switched with French terms, lest they lose their inherent meaning. Thus, there is a clear distinction between what is said in French and in Hebrew. Both French *marriage* (wedding) and Hebrew *khatuna* occur, for example, but a *khupa* (the Jewish nuptial ceremony) is referred to only in Hebrew. Similarly, both the terms *gouvernement* (government) and *memshala* occur, but no French equivalent of the *knesset* (the Israeli parliament) is used. Most borrowed nouns relate to the Israeli public sphere and given areas of activity – such as immigration, education, work, economy, health, religion, or army (see examples in Table 1).

Table 1: Examples of unitarian and segmental CS referring to different contexts.

H terms referring to kibbutz life		H terms that refer to (public) institutions	
khaverim	kibbutz members	khaver knesset	parliament member
asefot	assemblies	kupat kholim	health center
vaadot	commissions	bituakh mashlim	health insurance
makolet	grocery	mashkanta	loan for housing
shkhuna	quarter	arnona	municipal tax
arvut adadit	community help	bituakh leumi	national security
tnua	youth movement	pardes	citrus groves
Expressions of emotion		falkha	agricultural field
		mifalim	factories
tsarot	worries	pkida	secretary
mesubakh	complicated	roe kheshbon	accountant
jafe meod	very nice	ganenet	kindergarten teacher
shalem im atsmi	I feel good about it	ozeret bajit	house helper
gush zar	outsider	tafkid	role
le-mazalenu	by good luck	akhraj	in charge
ma she jesh	it's what it is	atsmaj	self-employed
al tagidi jije be-seder, af paam lo be-seder	don't say it will be ok, it's never ok		

In the field of immigration, there is substantial use of words like *alija*/ immigration, *garin*/ core group, *khanikhim*/ trainees or youth-movement members, *olim khadashim*/ new immigrants, *shaliakh*/ emissary, *ajarat pituakh*/ development town.

Similarly, in the field of education, one has *hinukh/* education, *morim/* teachers, *ganenet/* kindergarten teacher, *bet sefer/* school, *sifrija/* library, *joets/* adviser, *miktsoot bekhira/* elective subjects (at school), *bagrut/* high-school matriculation, *mefakeakh/* school inspector.

In the field of work: *avoda/* work, *parnasa/* livelihood, *kalkala/* economy, *kablan/* building contractor, *shutaf/* associate, *musakh/* garage, *misim/* taxes.

Most often, Franbreophone speakers prefer these Hebrew terms even when French equivalents are available, since the Hebrew element better reflects Israeli cultural values taken for granted. CS, in fact, fulfills several functions in Franbreophone discourse, especially in spontaneous conversation (M. Ben-Rafael 2001b). It may indicate the development of a discursive sequence or a rhetorical juxtaposition:

> H: il adore le chocolat *u mamash makhur le-ze*
> ---he loves chocolate, he is really addicted to it

CS also occurs in the forms of ready-made expressions, idioms of religious nature, greetings, and congratulations: *toda la-el* 'thank God', *zikhrono livrakha* 'may his memory be blessed', *barukh hashem* 'bless God', *halevaj* 'may it only be', *mazal tov* 'good luck', *kol ha-kavod* 'congratulations'.

CS also defines the relationship among different speakers and provides a way of structuring the constellation of the conversation. In the following example, S speaks in French with her two interlocutors, switches to Hebrew when she turns specifically to E, and reverts to French when she addresses M:

> -S addressing E and M: J'ai appelé Avi pour analyser avec lui la situation... (to E) *u khakham non?* ... (to M.) tu sais qui c'est Avi?
> ---I called Avi to analyze the situation with him ...(To E) he's clever isn't he? (To M) you know who Avi is?

CS is also often used for subjective and expressive support. Segmental CS and borrowings become means of judgmental and personal expression. In the following example, the speaker becomes agitated when speaking about a friend who has just lost her husband:

> -oh bien elle est vaillante ... c'est lui qui faisait tout et ... elle est *beseder at jodaat* ... *i mamash beseder* ... *ze haja nora ve-ajom* ... on lui dit ton mari est mort ... *at jodaat ma ze efshar lehishtolel*
> ---oh yeah she is courageous ... he's the one who did everything and ... she's OK you know ... she's really OK ... it was awful and terrible ...you're told that your husband is dead ... you know what it is you can go crazy

Another speaker uses a similar strategy in reference to the present situation in Israel:

> -oh j'en ai assez j'en ai marre *mamash nimas li*
> ---oh I have had enough I'm sick of it I've really had enough

In these cases, the switch from one language to the other takes place in a very fluid way. Unitarian CS (borrowings) and segmental CS are generally unflagged and are inserted in a Franbreu discourse that remains fluid and uninterrupted, both in spontaneous and professional conversations, as well as in interviews. In all these settings, casual CS can be evaluated according to discursive efficiency and evoke no special reaction from interlocutors.

On the other hand, there are also cases where speakers encounter difficulties in retrieving specific French terms. Aware of their problems, they themselves may speak of oblivion and loss of memory, and express embarrassment:

> -y a certains mots que je retrouve pas ... je commence une phrase et je m'arrête parce que ce mot j'arrive pas à le retrouver
> ---there are words I can't find .... I begin a sentence and I stop because I can't manage to find this word

In such cases, CS appears as a stratagem of last resort for overcoming lexical inaccessibility:

> -mon père est venu avec plein de ...un tas de livres ... avec des choses comment on appelle ça ... une *krikha* ...une *krikha* en cuir
> ---my father came with a lot of ...plenty of books ...with things ... how do you say it ... binding ... a leather binding

One strategy for dealing with an inaccessible French term is to switch to Hebrew and then repeat the term in French

> -dans la *khevra* des français ...dans la société française

Another strategy is to attempt to express oneself in French before switching to Hebrew and eventually finding the appropriate French word:

> -c'est mon pays ... *moledet* ... patrie
> ---it's my country... homeland... homeland

But sometimes the reconstruction remains unsuccessful. In the following, the speaker feels that the word "dettes" (debts) is not appropriate [indicated in the example by *], but since she cannot remember "emprunt" (loans), she switches to the Hebrew equivalent *halvaot*:

-nous avons fait des *dettes ...*halvaot*
---we have taken *debts ...loans

Briefly stated, lexical attrition appears, especially when speakers need precise terms.

2.3 Lexicon

In the lexicon, too, wide deviations appear from standard French. One encounters a large number of lexical interferences, and some of them are almost literal translations:

-hier j'ai fermé vingt-huit kgs /cf. *etmol sagarti esrim veshmone kilo* – instead of: hier j'ai perdu mon vingt-huitième kg.
---yesterday I lost my 28th kilo

Confusion, groping for words, and self-questioning about the accuracy of given terms are evident. Whether under the influence of Hebrew or because of a certain French attrition, speakers may also stumble over certain words and distort ready-made expressions:

-je suis née *le 1937 – instead of: je suis née le (date and month) 1937 or:...en 1937
---I was born in 1937
-j'ai mis des prunes *à table – instead of: j'ai mis des prunes sur la table
---I put prunes on the table

All-purpose words like "truc," "machin," and "chose" (stuff, thing) are substitutes for problematic terms, the verb "faire" (to do) is used frequently, and lexical repetitions are abundant as the locutor does not easily provide different wordings:

-c'est vrai que chacun a ses raisons pour lesquelles il décide d'aller vivre au kibuts ... des raisons ... des raisons ... chacun a ses raisons ... des raisons qui sont liées avec des raisons économiques peut-être quelquefois des raisons ....
---it's true that everybody has his reasons for deciding to go and live on a kibbutz ...reasons ...reasons ...each one has his reasons ... reasons that are connected with economic reasons, perhaps sometimes reasons ...

Lexical confusion, calques, and attrition mingle and intersect, while another typical Franbreu feature in the lexical domain is the tendency to simplify, i.e., to bend French items to a semantic reduction that reflects the semantic scope of Hebrew equivalents:

-*chanson ('song') instead of: poème ('poem') / cf. *shir* (= song, poem);
-*métier ('profession') instead of: matière scolaire / cf. *miktsoa* (= school topic, profession);
-*apporter ('to bring something') instead of: amener ('to bring somebody') / cf. *lehavi* (=to bring somebody or something);
-il me *donne pas à travailler, instead of: il me laisse pas travailler / cf. *u lo noten li la-avod* ...(= 'he doesn't let me work').

The same in the following:

-le docteur *invite tous les gens à la même heure, instead of: le docteur convoque ... / cf. *a-rofe mazmin et kol a-anashim be-ota a-shaa*
---the doctor summons all the people [to come for their appointments] at the same time

In addition to such cases, there is also a tendency to lexical innovation in this context of oblivion and confusion, a pattern that applies primarily to verbs: *profaniser ('to profane') instead of: profaner; *légitimiser ('to legitimize') instead of: légitimer; *activiser ('to activate') instead of: activer.

Generally speaking, new Franbreu verbs are often combinations of Hebrew nominal forms and French verbal suffixes, with priority given to the French first verbal group and its "er" suffixe: *tsilum*er (*tsilum* + er) ('to make a photo'); *sidur*er (*sidur* + er) ('to organize'); *tikhnun*er (*tikhnun*+er) ('to plan').

Hence, one may hear:

-peut-être qu'on a *fisfus*é le concert
---maybe we missed the concert

It should be mentioned that these Franbreu neologisms are not necessarily indications of attrition; they may simply be considered as new lexical Franbreu variants that are semantically convenient for Franbreophone discourse.

2.4 Syntax

As for the syntax, the language-in-contact literature also mentions changes and phenomena of attrition (Appel and Muysken 1987; Schmid 2002). Hence, Acadian and Ontario Canadian French, for instance, evince a tendency to omit some verbal forms and alter word order (Mougeon and Beniak 1989, 1991). American Spanish tends to simplify the verbal system and favor morphological innovations (Silva Corvalan 2008). Québécois French speakers underuse the subjunctive form (Chantefort 1976) and often omit "que" in relative and circumstantial phrases (Martineau 1985). Some scholars, however, focus primarily on lexical changes, claiming that grammatical ones are relatively infrequent.

For them, syntax belongs to the hard core of the language and is more resistant to the influence of other languages and new social or cultural circumstances (Hagège 1987, 2000). Grammatical changes in general, and particularly in language-contact situations, progress very slowly in any case (Leeman-Bouix 1994; Walter 1988).

In Franbreu, however, grammatical deviations from standard French are quite frequent. Most of these deviations result from the contact between Hebrew and French. One example among many is the tendency to simplify the verbal system. Hence, the sequence of tenses is rarely respected. The distinction between past tenses – passé composé and imparfait, which does not exist in Hebrew– is not always retained, while the conditional form is often expressed by the future tense – again, like in Hebrew:

>-on va voir si la cassette *marchera, instead of: marche
>---we will see if the cassette *will work

The subjunctive mode is also often disregarded – under the influence of Hebrew, which lacks this verbal form:

>-je veux que vous *saviez, instead of: sachiez
>---I want you to know

Verbal valences differ from standard French and are often calques of Hebrew equivalents:

>-elle aide *à sa mère, cf. *I ozeret le-ima*, instead of: elle aide sa mère
>---she helps her mother

Speakers also experience difficulties with relative pronouns. "Que," for instance, may be used instead of "qui," "que," "dont," and "où":

>-tu me donnes ce *que j'ai besoin, cf. *ata noten li ma she-ani tsarikh*, instead of: ce dont j'ai besoin
>---you give me what I need

This corresponds to the Hebrew grammatical system, in which only one element, "she," expresses the French relative pronouns. Speakers also omit adverbial pronouns, such as "y" and "en," that have no Hebrew equivalents. Where this occurs, French adverbs such as "là" and "là-bas" ("there") are used as "y" substitutes:

>-je vais souvent là, instead of: j'y vais souvent, cf.: *ani holekhet leitim krovot lesham*
>---I often go there

Finally, indefinite determinants are sometimes omitted, again, like in Hebrew, which does not have such articles:

-le français est *[] jolie langue, cf. *tsarfatit i* []*safa yafa*, instead of: le français est une jolie langue
---French is *[] nice language

These grammatical changes may be construed as Hebrew grammatical interferences. Yet one must also point out that some Franbreu grammatical variants – especially those that concern the conditional and subjunctive modes and relative pronouns – are also recurrent in some discursive registers of native spoken French. They have been identified as typical syntax variation tendencies, even outside any contact situation (Ager 1990: 138; Blanche-Benveniste 1997: 53–54; Gadet 1989: 148). These features are slips, confusions, and variants, which belong to the reality of a spoken language (Leeman-Bouix 1994: 101–104) and depend, among other factors, on the variety of discursive situations. Blanche-Benveniste (1990, 1997) and Gadet (1989) note that, according to circumstances, one may witness a simplification of the verbal system and a tendency to misuse or omit the subjunctive mode. In a similar vein, Frei (1971: 200) speaks of the problematics of the conditional, while Leeman-Bouix (1994: 101, 102) reports confusions between the preterite and the compound past (il *disa vs. dit) and regularized forms of the present tense (vous *disez vs. dites). Numerous researchers (Blanche-Benveniste 1997: 42; Gadet 1989: 147–159; Leeman-Bouix 1994; Walter 1988: 296–297) show that the relative pronoun "que" tends to replace "qui" and that the compound relatives ("lequel," "laquelle" etc.) tend to disappear. There is also a tendency to extend and generalize the use of "que" as a link word (Ager 1990: 138; Gadet 1989: 161–168). These tendencies are endemic to spoken French and characterize specific discursive situations, and they converge with what was found in the present research. The hypothesis that may be suggested here refers to the convergence of features of spoken French and Hebrew grammar. More precisely, it is when typical features of spoken French converge with equivalent grammatical features in Hebrew that their emergence in Franbreu is accelerated, through the contact of French with Hebrew. On the other hand, when French grammatical features have no equivalent in Hebrew, they probably tend to resist its influence.

This assertion is well illustrated and validated when it comes to the negative, the gender of nouns, and the prepositional system.

2.5 Negative forms

The French negative can take on two forms in spoken language – the simple form – "pas" – following the verb, and the compound form – "ne...pas" – on both sides of the verb or the auxiliairy – je (ne) parle pas, je (n') ai pas parlé. "Pas" is frequent in informal spoken French, while "ne...pas" appears in more formal contexts (Gadet 1989; Moreau 1986; Posner 1985; Sanders 1993).

The Hebrew negative system, on the other hand, consists of only the preverbal negator "lo" (except for the "al" form in the imperative mode). Hence, the difference between the French and the Hebrew negative systems concerns both word order and the number of eventual negators. Franbreu, it appears, is not influenced by Hebrew. In spontaneous Franbreu conversations, like in spoken French, "pas" often overcomes the bipartite negation "ne...pas," and in the interviews, which are more formal, the two models are used interchangeably. The resistance of the French negative system is such that, even when the negator itself is borrowed, the French word order remains intact:

- le *jajin* était *lo tov*; cf. le vin était pas bon vs. *hajajin lo haja tov*
---the wine was not good

2.6 The syntax of genders

Both French and Hebrew have two genders – masculine and feminine; however, the gender of nouns does not necessarily correspond in the two languages. Findings show that, where differences exist between French and Hebrew words, the Hebrew gender often influences the French article of borrowed words, which are adopted en bloc with their gender. Thus, the Hebrew borrowings *gvina* (cheese in Hebrew) and *miflaga* (political party), which are masculine in French, become feminine in Franbreu, like in Hebrew: le fromage becomes la *gvina* and le party politique la *miflaga*.

The same goes for French adjectives that are paired with borrowed nouns, and which also often take the gender of those borrowed Hebrew terms:

- il y a toujours des choses que tu peux acheter à des *tnajim* (m.) spéciaux (m.) vs. il y a toujours des chose que tu peux acheter à des conditions (f.) spéciales (f)
---there are always things you can buy on special terms

2.7 Prepositions

The prepositional system is another area where French shows resistance to Hebrew influence, in the context of a lack of equivalence. Some French forms, however, do not appear in Franbreu, causing confusion and Hebrew interference:

-*à la fin de compte il fait tomber le nid, instead of: en fin de compte...
---at the end he drops the nest
- on voit bien là *dans cette photo, cf. ...*ba-tmuna hazot*, instead of: sur cette photo
---it is quite clear here in the picture

Most prepositional changes in Franbreu concern the verbal valences which are Hebrew calques. However, despite these variations, French prepositions remain relatively stable and even Hebrew borrowings do not lead to incorrect usages of French prepositions (see also M. Ben-Rafael, 2002a):

- je vais essayer de faire *mimun*er, cf. je vais essayer de faire financer
---I will try to get some financial help

In conclusion, two essential factors stand behind changes in Franbreu syntax: the effect of Hebrew and the acceleration of natural tendencies in French grammar through language contact. The Hebrew syntax influences French mainly when it concurs with syntactic variation tendencies in spoken French. French shows a stronger capacity to resist the influence of Hebrew when a discrepancy exists between the two systems.

3 Extensions of Franbreu: A new agenda

Before concluding this short description of Israel's Jewish-French, or Franbreu, it is also noteworthy that, in the context of the current revolution in communication, Franbreu — which has always been an essentially oral language — is also increasingly characterized by written applications. If today's oral communication has taken on new importance with contemporary electronic means of interaction, this very same development has also amplified written linguistic production. Computers, smart phones, internet connectivity, tablets, and other devices are indeed awarding writing an unprecedented boom. People now spend more and more time writing for themselves (notes, lists, reflections), while for others they use text-messages, emails, or different kinds of messages. New and unique forms of writing that are flourishing are referred to in a broad sense as "SMS language." These are genuine sociolects, possessing new forms of spelling, lexical, and grammatical rules; grosso modo, they are characterized by concise exchanges and phonetic transcripts.[4]

---

4 See: "Language texto: Les formules courantes," on *Notrefamille.com* (retrieved 6.3.14); "Dico SMS" http://www.dictionnaire-sms.com/ (retrieved 6.3.2014); "Le language texto" *Français*

Franbreu also fits into this new profusion of written products. Typical forms of oral Franbreu become natural components of texting and email language. In particular, a profusion of loans written in Hebrew words, using Hebrew or Latin characters, now abound in the electronic exchanges of Franbreophones: French-dominant messages start with *shalom*, ask if *hakol beseder*? (is everything fine?), and end up with *neshikot* (kisses). These are but a few examples of expressions found in this kind of written material. Alternating codes bring up new Franbreu texts, which may be more or less complex productions.

In the memo section of mobile phones, for example, one may find grocery lists that include French and Hebrew items as well as combinations of the two languages, while Hebrew words may appear in Latin characters and French words in Hebrew ones. One can find, in the same list, one after the other, items such as:

French words in Latin characters	French words in Hebrew characters	Hebrew words in Latin characters	Hebrew words in Hebrew characters	
Carottes (carrots)	Petit beurre*	פטיבר	Ariel nozli (Ariel liquid soap)	Klementinot (clementines)	קלמנטינות
Fraises (strawberries)	Vache qui rit*	וואשקירי	Bananot (bananas) Pilpelim (peppers)	Lekhem parus (sliced bread)	לחם פרוס

*Petit beurre (*Tiny butter*) is a French cookie popular in Israel; Vache qui rit (*Laughing cow*) is the name of a French spread cheese.

This written Franbreu is often used in exchanges between Franbreophones, as well as between them and Hebrew-speaking relatives who share some familiarity with the French language. This kind of linguistic activity, it is also worth noting, is affected by the present-day multicultural atmosphere prevailing in Israel, which has become far more tolerant of linguistic diversity than in the past. It is, moreover, an opportunity for Franbreophone parents or grandparents, who long avoided speaking French with their children out of ideological identification, or pressures of the atmosphere in the country, to pass on some basic French to

---

(29.5.13); Candice Satara-Bartko (13.9.11); "Comprendre le language SMS des ados" *Terrafemina.com*; for a crtitical approach, "Les handicappés du clavier," *Tizel Web Blog* (15.11.05). See also the first French novel in SMS language by Phil Marso (1999), *Tueur de portable sans mobile apparent* Paris: Megacom-ik.

their children and grandchildren, thanks to these electronic exchanges. Thus, in current text-messages, one often finds written conversations where Franbreu expressions stemming from Franbreophones alternate with written Hebrew of Hebrew speakers:

Example 1
M, a Franbreophone who has returned to Israel after a long journey, sends an email to her Franbreophone friend:
    Lajla tov (good night) Rivkele! Nous sommes de retour (We're back) [---] et avons trouvé toutes sortes de problèmes d'*instalatsia* (and found all kinds of plumbing problems). *Tov* (well) tu dois être en pleine activité *khevra*tique avec ta famille de *khutz laarets* (you must be in full social activity with your family from abroad)

Example 2
E. (a Franbreophone parent) and her daughter L. (Hebrew-speaking) text each other:
    E. ton fils va mieux? (Does your son feel better?) Il va au *gan hayom*? (Is he going to kindergarten today?) Et toi comment ça va? (and you how are you?)
    L. *karega samti oto ba gan* (I just brought him to the kindergarten)

In these Franbreophones' messages addressed to Hebrew speakers familiar with French, codeswitches (especially long CS sequences) – are common. One often finds repetitions or passages written in French, with translation into Hebrew for easing understanding. In addition, Franbreophone locutors who feel special emotions which they want to convey to their Hebrew-speaking interlocutors tend often to express these emotions in Hebrew. Hence, in the following example, S. (Hebrew-speaking) and her mother, M. (Franbreophone), communicate via text messages, while the latter expresses her worry about her granddaughter, i.e., S's daughter. After a first sequence in French, she continues in Hebrew until the end of the exchange:

Example 3
M. j'espère que L. se sent mieux. Bonne nuit (I hope L. feels better. Good night).
    S. לא הולך טוב לצערי. ל'. ממש לא בסדר...מקווה שמחר יהיה אחרת
lo holekh tov letsaari. L. mamash lo beseder... mekava she makhar jije akheret
(unfortunately it's not going well. L. feels really bad ... hope that tomorrow it will be different)
    M. מה אמר הרופא בדיוק? מה הוא נתן לה?

ma amar harofe bedijuk? ma hu natan la? (what did the doctor say exactly? what has he given her?)

S. מוקסיפן...חושב זה וירוס.

moksipen... khoshev ze virus (moxypen ... thinks it is a virus)

M. לא הבנתי... חושב או לא חושב שזה וירוס?

lo hevanti... khoshev o lo khoshev sheze virus? (I didn't understand ... thinks or doesn't think that it is a virus?)

This kind of exchange may also characterize written contacts between Israeli Franbreophones and Francophones living outside Israel, who are familiar with Hebrew. Franbreu provides them with a transnational means of exchange:

Example 4
Francophone friends from France send an e-mail to a Franbreophone couple residing in Israel, on the occasion of the new year, writing Hebrew terms in Latin characters, seemingly like in France's Jewish French discourse:

-Nous vous souhaitons *chana tova ve metuka ve bria ve chalom* (We wish you a good and sweet and healthy year and peace)

The Israeli Franbreophone couple replies in French, with a Hebrew expression in Latin characters:

Bonne année à vous et vos proches et espérons qu'un jour *jije ktsat joter tov* (Happy new year to you and your family and hope that one day it'll be a little better) ...

Example 5
Two friends, B, a Franbreophone, and W, a Francophone, e-mail each other using Hebrew terms written in Latin characters in their French:

W. pour information on a visité grâce à vous le magnifique, l'extraordinaire musée Louvre/Lens!!! *Mazal tov*! (for your information we visited thanks to you the beautiful, the extraordinary Louvre / Lens museum! Good Luck!)

B. Bravo les explorateurs! *Kol hakavod*! La prochaine fois visitez le musée "la Piscine" à Roubaix c'est aussi *nekhmad*! *Shabbat shalom* et *kol tuv*! (Bravo the explorers! Well done! Next time visit the museum "La Piscine" in Roubaix it is also nice! Have a good Shabbat and all the best!)

These examples show that Franbreu, originally an exclusively oral code, has taken on significant written dimensions in the current reality of the communications revolution. This aspect deserves further study, that would address the development of systematic aspects of written Franbreu.

4 Conclusion

Franbreu, we have shown, is dynamic regarding major aspects of lexicon, syntax, and morphology. One example of language hybridization in Israel, it exemplifies phenomena well-known from other languages, generated by contact with Hebrew. One major feature of Franbreu is the high frequency of codeswitching – whether unitarian or segmental. Nouns represent the largest number of borrowings, but one also finds in this category phatics, adverbs, adjectives, conjunctions, and verbs.

Borrowings often replace French equivalents but, in more than a few cases, fill in the absence of missing terms in French. Some of them are used when French equivalents would be unable to express the exact feeling or significance intended by locutors. Hence, even where equivalents are available, borrowing may seem preferable.

As we have also shown here, codeswitching may express personal, even intimate, feelings stemming from personal identity or the self. They may support discursive developments or provide rhetorical effects. They signal the turn to new topics and narratives or report indirect discourse. An important category of codeswitching consists of Hebrew idioms, forms of congratulations, and well-wishing. In a general manner, this alternation of languages does not cause difficulties among participants in a conversation; on the contrary, it flows along as the interaction unfolds.

Franbreu numbers many significant deviations from standard French, through lexical interferences and calques. Speakers tend to reduce the semantic contents of French terms and associate them with meanings shared by their equivalents in Hebrew. Occurrences are often calques from Hebrew, and lexical confusions are numerous. In many cases, all-purpose words are used to designate topics, objects, or acts, instead of their accurate designations; there is also a tendency for lexical innovations, especially regarding verbs.

As for Franbreu grammar, syntactic deviations from normative French are found. The conditional mode is often expressed in Franbreu by the future, as is done in Hebrew, while the subjunctive mode, which does not exist in Hebrew, is often ignored. Moreover, verbal valences which differ from standard French are duplicates of Hebrew. Confusions may, similarly, refer to relative pronouns, as the Hebrew *she-* stands for all forms of Hebrew relatives.

In brief, language shifts, lexical interference, confusion, tendencies to simplify the lexicon and the grammar, and innovations are all means that attest to attrition, as well as the productive dynamics of the French-Hebrew contact. They reflect the locutors' life experience in their present-day society. Codeswitching, more especially, is not simply the consequence of forgetting French; it is a new means at the disposal of locutors to build up new forms of discourse in language contact.

While all these refer to Franbreu as an oral code, we emphasize that, in the context of the current revolution in communications, Franbreu is also increasingly characterized by written uses. If today's oral communication has taken on a new importance with contemporary electronic means of verbal interaction, this same development has even more amplified written linguistic production. It is a development that has caused an unprecedented boom in opportunities for writing. People now spend more time than ever writing, for themselves as well as to others. Written sociolects emerge with new spelling rules, at the margins of normative lexicons or grammars. These codes are marked by concision and rapid exchanges. Franbreu fits into this profusion of written production. Typical forms of oral Franbreu become natural components of text messages and email language. Hebrew borrowings, written in Hebrew or Latin characters, are customary, and alternating codes in these written Franbreu texts run from simple to more complex. Franbreu — which until recently was exclusively oral — is now assuming a significant written dimension, which deserves research to address the systematic aspects of this written Franbreu.

A question of acute significance, which still arises at this point regarding the status of Franbreu, concerns the chances of its conservation with the turnover of generations. In other words, will children of Francophone immigrants born in Israel, and whose first language is Hebrew, perpetuate Franbreu? Only future research will answer this question. However, some elements can already be presented here, on the basis of what is known. The research has found that NVs tend to continue to speak French with their children – which was not done by many other groups in previous eras. Hence, offspring born in Israel do learn, and probably use, the language in their family – alongside the fact that Hebrew is now their first language. One may suppose that the French which they practice conveys some forms of speech they have inherited from their parents' parlance. The traits of Franbreu have certainly weakened among them, and this will be still more pronounced among the third generation. In this respect, Franbreu is not warranted a promising future within the families of Francophone immigrants. Yet, it is also important to keep in mind that, starting in the early 1990s and up to the present, French-speaking immigrants have continued to arrive in Israel – 7,500 during 2015 alone – and go through the same experience as the first NVs had. Consequently, while Franbreu may decline in vitality within the immigrants' individual families, its presence in the country's public life may be guaranteed by the continuation of French-speaking immigration. As long as this immigration continues, Franbreu has a good chance of continuing to be a facet of Israel's multilingualism.

Whatever the future of this Israeli-Jewish-French language – another term for Franbreu – it may be said that, at the present time, this language is indeed "alive and kicking" among the tens of thousands of native French-speakers who are inserting themselves into Israeli society. They are acquiring the prevailing language and becoming accustomed to its culture, but without abandoning their original linguistic and cultural resources. Their experience in life in their new condition expresses itself in the use of Franbreu.

References

Ager, Dennis. 1990. *Sociolinguistics and contemporary French*. Cambridge: Cambridge University Press.
Appel, René & Pieter Muysken. 1987. *Language contact and bilingualism*. London: Edward Arnold.
Aslanov, Cyril. 2016. Remnants of Maghrabi Judeo-Arabic among French-born Jews of North African descent. *Journal of Jewish Languages* 4. 69–84.
Auer, Peter. 1984. *Bilingual conversation*. Amsterdam: John Benjamins.
Auer, Peter. 1995. The pragmatics of code-switching: A sequential approach. In Leslie Milroy & Pieter Muysken (eds.), *One speaker, two languages*, 115–135. Cambridge: Cambridge University Press.
Auer, Peter. 1996. Bilingual conversation, dix ans après [Bilingual conversation, ten years later]. *Acquisition et Interaction en Langue Étrangère* 7. 9–34.
Baumgarten, Jean, Alan Astro & Rachel Ertel. 1996. Yiddish in France: A conversation with Rachel Ertel. *Shofar* 14(3). 125–137
Ben-Rafael, Eliezer. 1993. *Le public I.F.T.A.: Une enquête sociologique* [The public I.F.T.A: A sociological study]. Tel-Aviv: Ambassade de France.
Ben-Rafael, Eliezer. 1994. *Language, identity and social division: The case of Israel*. Oxford & New York: Clarendon Press/Oxford University Press.
Ben-Rafael, Eliezer & Miriam Ben-Rafael. 2008. Linguistic landscape and transnationalism: Sarcelles-Natanya. *Israel Studies in Language and Society Electronic Interdisciplinary Journal* 1(1).
Ben-Rafael, Eliezer & Miriam Ben-Rafael. 2013. *Sociologie et sociolinguistique des Francophonies Israéliennes* [Sociology and sociolinguistics of Israeli Francophones]. Frankfurt am Main: Peter Lang.
Ben-Rafael, Eliezer, Léon Gani, Rivka Herzlich & Jean-Pierre Van Deth. 1985. *Enquête sur les motivations des élèves apprenant le Français dans le cadre du système scolaire Israélien* [Investigation of the motivations of students learning French in the Israeli school system]. Tel-Aviv: Recherche conjointe Franco-Israélienne, Ambassade de France.
Ben-Rafael, Eliezer, Léon Gani & Rivka Herzlich. 1989. *Enquête auprès des parents d'élèves, des professeurs de français et des directeurs d'écoles en Israel* [Survey of the parents of students, French teachers and school principals in Israel]. Tel-Aviv: Recherche conjointe Franco-israélienne, Ambassade de France.
Ben-Rafael, Eliezer & Anastazia Goroszeiskaya. 1999. *Les langues d'Israel et le statut du Français* [The languages of Israel and the status of French]. Tel-Aviv: Services culturels, Ambassade de France.

Ben-Rafael, Eliezer, Rivka Herzlich & Mira Freund. 1990. Symbole d'identité ou capital symbolique: le parcours social du français en Israel [Symbol of identity and symbolic capital: The social background of French in Israel]. *Revue Française de Sociologie* 31. 315–329.
Ben-Rafael, Eliezer, Francine Lévy. 1991. *Les études françaises dans l'enseignement supérieur en Israel: Motivations et utilisations* [French studies in higher education in Israel: Motivations and uses]. Tel-Aviv: Ambassade de France.
Ben-Rafael, Eliezer & Stephen Sharot. 2007. *Ethnicity, religion and class in Israel*, 2nd edn. Cambridge & New York. Cambridge University Press.
Ben-Rafael, Eliezer & Yitzhak Sternberg. 2009. *La communauté franco-israélienne: Composition, dispositions et structuration* [The Franco-Israeli community: Composition, arrangements and structuring]. Tel-Aviv: Les Services culturels, Ambassade de France, Mars.
Ben-Rafael, Eliezer & Yitzhak Sternberg (eds.). 2010. *World religions and multiculturalism: A dialectic relation*. Leiden & Boston: Brill.
Ben-Rafael, Miriam. 2001a. *Contact de langues: Le Français parlé des francophones Israéliens* [Language contact: French spoken by Israeli Francophones]. Tel-Aviv: University of Tel Aviv doctoral dissertation.
Ben-Rafael, Miriam. 2001b. Codeswitching in the immigrants' language: The case of Franbreu. In Jacobson, Rodolfo (ed.), *Codeswitching worldwide II*, 251–307. Berlin: Mouton de Gruyter.
Ben-Rafael, Miriam. 2002. The French preposition in contact with Hebrew. In Susanne Feigenbaum & Dennis Kurzon (eds.), *Prepositions in their syntactic, semantic and pragmatic context*, 209–229. Amsterdam: John Benjamins.
Ben-Rafael, Miriam. 2003. Pratique discursive et mise en place grammaticale [Discursive practice and grammatical implementation]. *Marges Linguistiques* 4(2). 168–180.
Ben-Rafael, Miriam & Monika S. Schmid. 2007. Language attrition and ideology: Two groups of immigrants in Israel. In Barbara Köpke, Monika S. Schmid, Merel Keijzer & Susan Dostert (eds.), *Language attrition: theoretical perspectives*, 205–226. Amsterdam: John Benjamins.
Bentahila, Abdelali. 1983. *Language attitudes among Arabic-French bilinguals in Morocco*. Clevedon: Multilingual Matters.
Berk-Seligson, Susan. 1986. Linguistic constraints on intra-sequential code-switching: Study of Spanish/Hebrew bilingualism. *Language in Society* 15. 313–348.
Blanche-Benveniste, Claire. 1997. *Approches de la langue parlée en français* [Approaches to spoken French]. Paris: Ophrys Editions.
Blanche-Benveniste, Claire, Mireille Bilger, Christine Rouget & Karel van den Eynde. 1990. *Le Français parlé: Études grammaticales* [Spoken French: Grammatical studies]. Paris: CNRS Editions.
Boudras-Chapon, Valentin. 2008. Langue nationale, langue officielle, langue vernaculaire, langue véhiculaire, langue maternelle [National language, official language, vernacular language, common language, mother tongue]. *Riposte laïque,* http://ripostelaique.com/Langue-nationale-langue-officielle.html (accessed 11 August 2016).
Chantefort, Pierre. 1976. Diglossie au Québec, limites et tendances actuelles [Diglossa in Quebec, current limits and trends]. *Langue Française* 3(1). 91–104.
Chouraqui, André. 1998. *Histoire des juifs en Afrique du Nord* [History of the Jews of North Africa]. Paris: Du Rocher.

Clyne, Michael. 1987. Constraints on code-switching: How universal are they? *Linguistics* 25. 739–764.
Dorian, Nancy C. 2010. *Investigating variation: The effects of social organization and social setting*. Oxford: Oxford University Press.
Fishman, Joshua A. & R.H. Kressel. 1974. The uses of Hebrew loan-words in spoken German in two bilingual communities. *Linguistics* 139. 69–78.
Frei, Henri. 1971 [1929]. *La Grammaire des fautes* [Grammatical errors], 2nd edn. Geneva: Slatkine.
French Embassy. 1995. *Rapport de recherche* [Research report]. Tel-Aviv: Services Culturels.
Gadet, Françoise. 1989. *Le Français ordinaire* [Ordinary French]. Paris: Armand Colin.
Gardner-Chloros, Penelope. 2009. *Code-switching*. Cambridge: Cambridge University Press.
Glick-Schiller, Nina & Georges Fouron. 2003. *Georges woke up laughing Long-distance nationalism and the apparent state*. Durham: Duke University.
Grosjean, François. 1982. *Life with two languages: An introduction to bilingualism*. Cambridge, Mass: Harvard University Press.
Hagège, Claude. 1987. *Le Français et les siècles* [French through the centuries]. Paris: Odile Jacob.
Hagège, Claude. 2000. *Halte à la mort des langues* [Stop the death of languages]. Paris: Odile Jacob.
Hamers, Josiane F. & Michel Blanc. 1983. *Bilingualité et bilinguisme* [Bilinguality and bilingualism]. Bruxelles: Pierre Mardaga.
Hofman, John E. & Haya Fisherman. 1972. Language shift and language maintenance in Israel, in Joshua A. Fishman (ed.), *Advances in the sociology of language*, Vol. 2, 342–364. The Hague: Mouton de Gruyter.
Jacobson, Rodolfo (ed.). 1998. *Codeswitching worldwide, vol. I*. New York: Mouton de Gruyter.
Jacobson, Rodolfo (ed.). 2001. *Codeswitching worldwide, vol. II*. New York: Mouton de Gruyter.
Koplewitz, Immanuel. 1990. The use and integration of Hebrew lexemes in Israeli spoken Arabic. In Durk Gorter, Jarich F. Hoekstra, Lammert G. Jansma & Jehannes Ytsma (eds.), *Fourth International Conference on Minority Languages*, Vol. 2, 181–195. Clevedon: Multilingual Matters.
Köpke, Barbara & Monika S. Schmid. 2004. Language attrition: the next phase. In Monika S. Schmid, Barbara Köpke, Merel Keijzer & Lina Weilemar (eds.), *First language attrition: interdisciplinary perspectives on methodological issues*, 1–43. Amsterdam: John Benjamins.
Leeman-Bouix, Danielle. 1994. *Les fautes de français existent-elles?* [Are there errors in French?]. Paris: Editions du Seuil.
Lüdi, Georges. 1990. Les migrants comme minorité linguistique en Europe [Migrants as a linguistic minority in Europe]. *Sociolinguistica* 4(1). 113–135.
Masson, Michel. 2013. French, Hebrew loanwords. In Geoffrey Khan (ed.), *Encyclopedia of Hebrew language and linguistics*. Boston & Leiden: Brill.
Martineau, France. 1985. L'élision variable de 'que' dans le parler d'Ottawa-Hull [The variable elision of 'that' of speakers from Ottawa-Hull]. *Cahiers Linguistiques d'Ottawa* 14. 53–70.'
Mougeon, Raymond & Edouard Beniak. 1989. Language contraction and linguistic change: The case of Welland French. In Nancy C. Dorian (ed.), *Investigating obsolescence: Studies in language contraction and death*, 287–312. Cambridge: Cambridge University Press.
Mougeon, Raymond & Edouard Beniak. 1991. *Linguistic consequences of language contact and restriction: The case of French in Ontario, Canada*. Oxford: Oxford University Press.

Moreau, Marie-Louise. 1986. Les séquences préformées: Entre les combinaisons libres et les idiomatismes: le cas de la négation avec ou sans ne [Preformed sequences: Between free combination and idioms: The case of negation with or without 'ne']. *Le Français Moderne* 54. 137–160.

Myers-Scotton, Carol. 1993. *Social motivations for code-switching: Evidence from Africa*. Oxford: Clarendon Press.

Myers-Scotton, Carol. 2002. *Contact linguistics: Bilingual encounters and grammatical outcomes*. Oxford: Oxford University Press.

Olshtain, Elite & Shoshana Blum-Kulka. 1989. Happy Hebrish: Mixing and switching in American-Israeli family interactions. In Suzan Gass, Carolyn Madden, Dennis Preston & Larry Selinker (eds.), *Variation in second language acquisition: Discourse and pragmatics*, Vol. 1, 59–83. Clevedon: Multilingual Matters.

Pergnier, Maurice (ed.). 1988. *Le Français en contact avec l'Anglais* [French in contact with English]. Paris: Didier Erudition.

Poplack, Shana. 1980. Sometimes I'll start a sentence in Spanish y termino en español: Toward a typology of code-switching. *Linguistics* 18(7/8). 581–618.

Poplack, Shana. 1988. Conséquences linguistiques du contact des langues: Un modèle d'analyse variationniste [Linguistic consequences of language contact: A variationist model of analysis]. *Langage et Société* 43(1). 23–48.

Poplack, Shana. 2004. Code-switching. In Ulrich Ammon, Norbert Dittmar, Klaus J. Mattheier & Peter Trudgill, *Sociolinguistics: An international handbook of the science of language and society* (2nd edn.), 589–596. Berlin: Walter de Gruyter.

Poplack, Shana, Susan Willer & Anneli Westwood. 1989. Distinguishing language contact phenomena: Evidence from Finnish-English bilingualism. In Kenneth Hyltenstan & Loraine Obler (eds.), *Bilingualism across the life-span: aspects of acquisition, maturity and loss*, 132–154. Cambridge: Cambridge University Press.

Posner, Rebecca. 1985. Post-verbal negation in non-standard French: A historical and comparative view. *Romance Philology* 39. 170–197.

Romaine, Suzan. 1989. *Bilingualism*. Oxford: Basil Blackwell.

Sanders, Carol. 1993. Sociosituational variation. In Carol Sanders (ed.), *French today: Language in its social context*, 27–53. Cambridge: Cambridge University Press.

Schmid, Monika S. 2002. *First language attrition, use and maintenance: The case of German Jews in Anglophone countries*. Amsterdam & Philadelphia: John Benjamin.

Schmid, Monika S. 2009. On L1 attrition and the linguistic system. In Leah Roberts, Daniel Véronique, Anna-Carin Nilsson & Marion Tellier (eds.), *EUROSLA Yearbook 9*, 212–244. Amsterdam & Philadelphia: John Benjamins.

Silva-Corvalan, Carmen. 2008. The limits of convergence in language contact. *Journal of Language Contact* 2(1). pp. 213–224.

Walter, Henriette. 1988. *Le français dans tous les sens* [French in every sense]. Paris: Éditions Robert Laffont.

Witte, Els & Hugo Beatens Beardsmore (eds.). 1987. *The interdisciplinary study of urban bilingualism in Brussels*. Clevedon & Philadelphia: Multilingual Matters.

Aharon Geva-Kleinberger
Judeo-Arabic in the Holy Land and Lebanon

1 Brief introduction

When we speak of Palestinian Arabic we generally imagine Muslim- and Christian-Arab speakers. This article concentrates on Modern Palestinian Judeo-Arabic (hereinafter MPJA), its roots, creation, and death. MPJA was the mother tongue of thousands of Jewish speakers in the Holy Land. Roughly speaking, it formed out of a conglomerate of Maghrebi Jewish dialects and Palestinian non-Jewish dialects. Over time, MPJA came to resemble the non-Jewish Palestinian dialects more and more, yet it retained its own characteristics.

1.1 Names of the language

The dialects of the Maghrebi Jews in the Holy Land communities can be called Modern Palestinian Judeo-Arabic (MPJA). They introduced Maghrebi dialectal features as an infrastructure; but in time, because of the close geographical and cultural relations with their Arab neighbors, who spoke macro Palestinian dialects, these Jewish dialects became linguistically more Palestinian than Maghrebi. On the other hand, there is a close historical and cultural affinity to the Jewish communities northward, in Lebanon; hence, there is also a strong linguistic proximity between the two groups, as they share the dialectal substrate of the Maghrebi North Moroccan type. Not surprisingly, therefore, the language of the Jewish communities in Lebanon resembles those of the Jewish communities in the Holy Land dialectally and differs in various linguistic aspects from the Lebanese dialects. In Lebanon not all the Jews spoke the Maghrebi-influenced type, since the influence of the Damascus and Aleppo Jews was also significant, especially in Beirut. So linguistically, but not politically, the dialects of Lebanese Jews belonged to MPJA even though they were located outside the borders of Mandatory Palestine, and some of them, especially those of Beirut, were influenced by Syrian Jewry in religious observance and culture. Thus, these Lebanese Jewish dialects, although heavily influenced by Syrian dialectal features and components, display a vivid Maghrebi Jewish linguistic substrate even today. Furthermore, the Jewish community of Beirut, and even of Damascus – both of them today mostly residing outside Lebanon – still use the term *Maghrebi* for Jews originating in North Africa and thus differing also in their language.

In his first studies (2000, 2009), Geva-Kleinberger calls the northern dialects of MPJA "Galilean Judaeo-Arabic." As for the Jewish dialect of Jerusalem, which belongs to MPJA, Moshe Piamenta calls it "JJ" (=Judaeo-Jerusalem [Arabic vernacular]), in contrast to what he calls "J," meaning the "intercommunal Jerusalem Arabic dialect," which is spoken by Christian and Muslim residents.

1.2 Linguistic affiliation

In the 16th century, the Palestinian Jewish dialects belonged to the Jewish North African Arabic macro-group of dialects. But the Maghrebi dialectal features gradually diminished, disappearing almost completely by the 20th century. At the same time, these dialects were increasingly influenced by the Palestinian dialects in the Holy Land and by Lebanese dialects in Lebanon. Still, the North African Arabic macro-group features persisted in both groups: within the Holy Land borders and on its threshold. Fieldwork in the late 20th and early 21st centuries attests that these dialects moved closer to the Syro-Palestinian macro type, with MPJA tending more to Palestinian dialects and the Lebanon Jewish dialects more towards Lebanese micro dialects.

1.3 Regions where the language is/was spoken

Within the Holy Land, MPJA can be divided into two main groups. The locations of group 1 are in the Galilee region, first in Safed (Upper Galilee; Arabic: *Ṣafad*) and Tiberias (Lower Galilee: Arabic: *Ṭabariyya*) from the late 15th and early 16th century, and then in Pqiʿīn (Arabic: *il-Bʔēʿa*) in western Upper Galilee and Shfarʿām (Arabic: *Šāfaʿamr*) and Kufr Yāsîf in Lower Galilee. Later still, from the second half of the 20th century, this group is joined by the gradually expanding town of Haifa (Arabic: *Ḥēfa*) on the Mediterranean coastline and, at about the same time, also Rosh-Pina (East Galilee; Arabic: *Žaʿūni*), on a very small scale. Group 2 was mainly in Jerusalem and to a moderate extent in Hebron, where MPJA gradually developed somewhat differently linguistically. Note that MPJA was not the only daily language spoken by Jews in the same communities in the Holy Land: Yiddish flourished there, too. Not surprisingly, some MPJA speakers could converse in Yiddish as well, while some native Yiddish speakers could speak basic Palestinian Arabic.

In Lebanon, several Jewish communities were influenced by the Maghrebi component of the population, hence by the dialectal variant. There were Maghrebi communities in Beirut, Dayr il-Qamar, and also north of Beirut in Tripoli (Arabic:

Ṭarāblus). In South Lebanon, the Jewish communities were more of the Maghrebi type, especially in the cities of Sidon (Arabic: Ṣēda) and Tyre (Arabic: Ṣūr) on the Mediterranean coast. There was also a Maghrebi community in the south Lebanese village of Ḥāṣbayya. South Lebanon also had some very small and ephemeral Jewish communities in Rmēš and perhaps in other villages on the border with the Holy Land. The Sidon Jewish community was mainly of Maghrebi origin, hence influenced by the Maghrebi dialect, and they lived in a quarter of their own. In Beirut, too, there was a Jewish quarter (*Wādi Bu-Žmīl*), but there the Jewish community was a conglomerate of several types, of which Maghrebi was only one.

1.4 Present-day status

In 2016, MPJA can be regarded cautiously as "nearly extinct." The number of speakers of Galilean MPJA does not exceed five, like the number of speakers of the Jerusalem MPJA-type. So, not surprisingly, we can find articles about MPJA with titles containing phrases such as "The last informants..." (e.g., Geva-Kleinberger 2005). By comparison, the number of MPJA speakers at the end of the 20th century was still more than one hundred in its Galilean and Jerusalem branches. Presumably, the numbers of MPJA speakers in the first third of the 20th century reached several thousand and possibly more than ten thousand at its peak. However, today the number of speakers of Jewish Lebanese dialects originating from Maghrebi speakers may still be several hundred, although most of them reside outside of Lebanon.

2 Historical background

Jews have been living in the holy cities of Judaism, especially Jerusalem and Tiberias, for the last two millennia, with only occasional brief interruptions. They spoke Arabic as their mother tongue, many of them first in a Maghrebi Jewish dialect. In Safed, some Sephardi Jews spoke Yiddish in addition to Judeo-Arabic. According to local tradition, the Jews of Pqiʕīn never left the Holy Land, but found shelter in caves in the high mountains of the Upper Galilee. Arabic-speaking Jews were also found in Shfarʕam until the 1920s, when they had to migrate to Haifa. Other Arabic-speaking Jews had settled in Haifa from the beginning of the 19th century, especially between 1831 and 1840, during the Egyptian occupation of the region. Gradually, those Arabic-speaking Jews of Galilee and some Jerusalem Jews speaking MPJA came to identify themselves by the all-inclusive term "Arab Jews (*ilYahūd ilʕarab*)," an expression that had disappeared by the time of the establishment of the State of Israel. The core group of Jews who spoke Arabic as a first language was urban, yet there were also some villages where Jews spoke Arabic for briefer periods, such as Rosh-Pina (Arabic: *Žaʕūni*), a Jewish settlement some thirty kilometers north of Tiberias, on the eastern slopes of Mount Canaan.

As for Jerusalem, Piamenta (2000) maintains that, in the 19th and 20th centuries, JJ ("Judaeo-Jerusalem") was spoken by an indigenous Jewish community, whose mother tongue was the local Arabic dialect of its day-to-day contact by trade with its Arab neighbors, especially in the Old City. According to Piamenta, JJ and the communal Jerusalem dialect diverged because of differences in Jewish customs, traditions, and calendar. But he does not refer to the creation of this dialect.

We hold that JJ is undoubtedly a sub-southern branch of MPJA, but Piamenta did not treat it as such. JJ differs from the dialects of the city's other religious communities, as it does also from MPJA's northern branch in Tiberias, Safed, Pqiʕīn, and especially Haifa in the first half of the 20th century.

2.1 Speaker community: Settlement, documentation

Substantial documentation of the MPJA speakers exists, including their names and sometimes details of their age and lifestyle in several settlements in the Galilee and northern Israel. All the interviews were conducted by Geva-Kleinberger between 1995 and 2005. The recordings cover MPJA speakers from Haifa, Pqiʕīn, Tiberias, and Safed. There is no documentation of informants from Shfarʕām and Kufr Yāsīf, as they had to leave their settlements in 1927; the last of them died elsewhere in the late 1980s. In his research on JJ, Moshe Piamenta gives no details about his informants, but simply mentions "JJ" versus "J."

2.2 Phases in historical development

When the Jews were expelled from Spain in 1492, some of them went to the Holy Land, mostly after spending years in Morocco. In the first stages, they settled mainly in the holy cities in the ancient Land of Israel, such as Jerusalem, Safed, and Tiberias, but in time they also settled in other villages and small towns, such as Shfarʕām, Pqiʕīn, and Haifa. Concurrently, another movement of Jews, mostly traders, established some communities in the Levant, especially in the area that later became Lebanon. Jewish communities in Beirut, Dayr il-Qamar (Arabic:

Dēr il-ʔamar), Sidon, and Tyre can be regarded as lying on the threshold of the Holy Land, very close to places that have served as magnets for the Jewish people throughout history. Over time, some other Jewish communities formed in places in present-day South Lebanon. The tiny Jewish community of Tyre (Arabic: Ṣūr) is a very good example of a Jewish community in Lebanon, just a stone's throw from the Holy Land, that celebrated the three Jewish pilgrimage festivals according to the rite of the Land of Israel and not of the Diaspora: thus, they celebrated the Passover Seder only on one night, not two, as elsewhere in the Lebanese or Syrian Diasporas. Because these Jews of Andalusian origin had fled to the northern parts of the country now called Morocco before moving to the Levant, they became recognized, and even identified themselves, as *Maghrebi Jews*. In sum, we can identify two main macro Maghrebi Jewish communities: one in the Holy Land and the other on its threshold. Most of the communities established by the two groups were new, in contrast to the Damascene Jewish community, which was older, and only later absorbed these Maghrebi Jews.

As mentioned, after being driven out of Spain in 1492 the Jews presumably stopped in northern Morocco. Many MPJA informants refer to Tétouan or Tangier as their city of origin. Accordingly, the dialects of the Jews moving toward the eastern Mediterranean basin, determined to reach the Holy Land after years of yearning, were more Maghrebi in their speech type. Once there, after years of interactions with their Muslim, Christian, and Druze neighbors, their dialect had become more of the Syro-Palestinian type, or, more precisely, bearing more Palestinian features in the Holy Land and more Lebanese features in Lebanon. However, in my opinion, the dialects of the Jews of Lebanon show more Palestinian than Lebanese features, perhaps because of a halt made by these Lebanese Jews in the Galilee region before continuing northward to Lebanon. Over the years, MPJA became more and more Palestinian on many levels of its linguistic data.

2.3 Sociolinguistic description, community bilingualism, public functions

As noted, many MPJA speakers identified themselves as "Arab Jews." As in many other places in the Muslim world, they preferred to live near their Muslim neighbors rather than near the Christians, due to the common language and similar religious practices such as *Kashrut* and *Ḥalāl* food rules, circumcision, and the absence of graven images in the synagogues and mosques. Relations between Muslims and Jews before the riots in the late 1920s and mid-1930s, and the establishment of the State of Israel in 1948, were generally brotherly. This was the case with the Jews of Tiberias as well as Haifa, Safed, and elsewhere; in Tiberias, for example, for centuries there were relations of "brothers through breast-feeding" [Arabic: ʔixwān bi-rriḍāʕa], as Jewish women would have their infants wet-nursed by Muslim women if they did not have enough milk themselves, and vice-versa. Due to this custom, when they grew up, Jewish and Muslim children were obliged to protect each other as if they were natural siblings. Sometimes a linguistic consultant showed an unexpected attitude to the Muslims, expressed in the phrase "There is nothing better than the rule of the Ishmaelites," or, in a more nostalgic version, "[Better] is the rule of Ishmael and not the rule of Israel" [ḥukum Yišmaʕél w lā ḥukum Yisraʔél] (Geva-Kleinberger 2009).

The difference between the Jews of the Galilean cities of Tiberias and Safed is not limited to dialect but arises from wide anthropological dissimilarity and antagonism. This difference undoubtedly had a topographical cause. Tiberias is located some two hundred meters below sea level on the shores of the Sea of Galilee, while Safed lies on the slopes of Upper Galilee, some eight hundred meters above sea level. The two settlements, therefore, have significantly different climates. Safed is characterized by its cold weather, with snow and heavy rains in winter; these, unfortunately, do not tend to remain long in the city but stream down to the Sea of Galilee. Tiberias is located on the lake and enjoys hot and humid weather with less rain but lots of water, some originating in the region of Safed and the rest drawn from the Sea of Galilee itself. The scarcity in Safed of available water, which descends to Tiberias, the less rainy city, caused differences between the cities. The inhabitants of Safed were said to be stingy, because they had to go to a communal well in the city, whereas the Tiberians had water and vegetables all year round in their gardens that were watered directly, and without any significant effort, from the lake itself. So the people of Safed claimed that the Tiberians were exploitative, too lazy, and too happy. In comparison, the Safedis were considered gloomy, besides being mean and tightfisted. The Tiberians could wash their clothes right in the Sea of Galilee, but the Safedis could wash theirs on Fridays alone, for the Sabbath. The Safedis had to be sparing in washing themselves, while the inhabitants of Tiberias could easily go to the Sea of Galilee to bathe. This also led to antagonistic sayings: The Safedis said about Tiberias: "Ṭabariyya ḥžārha sūd w sukkānha ʔrūd" 'Tiberias has black stones, and its dwellers are monkeys', whereas the people of Tiberias used to say: "Ṣáfaḍi - ráfaḍi!" 'One has always to say *no* to a Safadi!'. No wonder then that there were also dialectal differences between the Jewish dwellers of the two cities. These dissimilarities are easily located, especially in the lexicon. Since Tiberias is located on the Sea of Galilee, and therefore nourished by it, we find in Tiberias names of various fish and lake-life, while these terms are not used and are even unknown in Safed.

As for Haifa, in the mid-19th century a little fishing village on the Mediterranean coast some 25 kilometers south of Acre (Palestinian Arabic: ʕakka), it gradually developed a Jewish community of Arabic-speaking Jews of Maghrebi origin. In the first third of the 20th century most of these Jews dwelt in two Jewish quarters that were not far apart: Ḥārt il-Yahūd 'The Jewish Neighborhood' and ʔarḍ il-Yahūd 'The Jewish Land'.

3 Structural information on MPJA

3.1 Particular structural features (unique to the Jewish variety)

In MPJA speech, one finds what we can call *Maghrebisms*, namely, substrates of North-African Arabic macro dialects, especially Moroccan. These structures are not found in Palestinian dialects (Geva-Kleinberger 2004b):

a. The use of the article in Jewish MPJA deviates from Classical Arabic structures, e.g., *ruḥna bi-lḥódeš ʔelúl* 'We went in the month of *Elul*' <*ruḥna bi-ḥódeš ʔelúl*; *lwlād zġār* instead of *wlād zġār* 'little children'.
b. MPJA has a structure typical of Maghrebi Arabic dialects that is not found in other Palestinian dialects: *il-* follows the numbers from 11 to 99, e.g., *xamasṭāš ilwalad* 'fifteen children' or *kān ʕumri xamasṭāš sittāš issini* 'I was [at that time] fifteen or sixteen years old'.
c. Maghrebisms in MPJA also appear in the verb system. The root √s-k-n has a different inflection from that in Palestinian dialects: *skinna* 'we were living in...' and not *sakanna* as in Palestinian dialects. Hence *skint* [sg.1.c.and 2.m]-*skinti* [sg.2.f.]-*skinna* [pl.1.c]-*skintu* [pl.2.c.]-*siknu* [pl.3.c]; for sg.3.m and sg.3.f two variants: *sikin* together with *sakan* (rare) and *síknat* together with *sáknat*.

Parallel to the Maghrebi substrate, there are some other typical morphological structures in MPJA that are decidedly not Palestinian:

a. Certain male Jewish informants use the elative form *ʔáfʕala*, while the normal prevailing form is *ʔáfʕal*; e.g., *ʔáḥsana* [better]; *ʔákbara* [bigger] and not *ʔáḥsan* and *ʔákbar* as in Palestinian dialects.
b. MPJA informants use a frozen *ʔallek*, which is not inflected and variously has the sense of "I mean," "namely," "that is to say": e.g., *yinzalu ʔallek ʕala lbahara* '[It was said that] they went down to the sea [of Galilee], near the sea'; in other cases, *ʔallek* is a frozen form that is not conjugated, e.g., *ʔultillo baʕdēn la-ʔeliyáhu, ʔallek: xuft minna w xāf mi-libint!* 'I said to *Eliyahu* afterwards, as follows: "I was afraid of the girl!" Yet he was afraid of this girl'.

c. Another verb that acts differently but has the same patterns in MPJA is the verb "to say." There is an assimilation of *l* which exists side by side with the regular form in other Palestinian dialects, whereas the assimilated form is not found there, e.g., sg.1. ʔutt vs. ʔult compared with ʔult vs. ʔilt 'I said' in Palestinian dialects (and also in the rest of the paradigm 2.m. ʔutt vs. ʔult compared with ʔult vs. ʔilt 'you said' and so on).

d. Lexically, in MPJA, especially in Galilean dialects, the word *knīse* is often used to denote "synagogue," while in Palestinian dialects *knīse* 'church' is differentiated from *knīs* 'synagogue'. Piamenta notes a vast spectrum of vocabulary used in JJ and not used by Palestinians in Jerusalem in the field of the house and its contents (e.g., JJ *derredōr* 'circumference' versus J *dāyer*), foods and refreshments (e.g., JJ ʕ*ug(g)ā* 'cake' versus J *gatō*), dress and footwear e.g., *swēder* (English via Hebrew *svēder* versus J *žērse*), occupations (e.g., JJ *smāne* 'groceries' versus J *bʔāle*), entertainment (e.g., J *tiyātro* [Spanish-Italian 'teatro'] versus J/JJ *masraḥ*], arts and crafts (e.g., JJ *ġaniyye* 'song' versus J *ġunawiyye*), communication (e.g., JJ *telegrāf* [<French] versus J *talliġāf* 'telegram, telegraphic message'], and even flora and fauna (e.g., JJ *mayyorāna* [Ladino < Spanish '*mejorána*'] versus J *burdʔoš* [~*burdʔōš*] 'sweet marjoram'). JJ has a broad spectrum of Ladino words, e.g., *kūkla* (pl. *kūklas*), literally 'dolls' in Ladino. This JJ versus J list evinces widespread use of Ladino/Spanish loanwords, which reminds us of the origin of the Jerusalem Jews in Andalusia.

The Maghrebi Jews in Galilee and Jerusalem had a special dish for each day of the week, e.g., pasta on Sundays; one was a special Sephardi-Maghrebi dish called *Kalsōnes* in MPJA (Geva-Kleinberger 2009: 72, n. 183).

3.2 Lexicon: Hebrew and Aramaic elements

3.2.1 Hebrew

Piamenta notes that JJ uses what he calls a "Hebrew religious" (H.r.) lexicon. He adds that religion was "essential to their entity and the main factor for establishing their residence in Jerusalem" (Piamenta 2000: 258). Thus we find a very detailed Hebrew lexicon intermingled with JJ Arabic for ritual items, e.g., *təffillīn* 'phylacteries' with its interesting plural *təffillĭmōt*, and also for the liturgy, Jewish law, the Sabbath (e.g., *habdălā* [H.r. 'separation' between the sacred and the secular], the Jewish calendar and holidays (e.g., *Sukkot* 'the feast of Tabernacles'), and the Jewish life cycle (e.g., *gēṭ* 'divorce'). JJ contains remnants of Ladino besides

Hebrew, e.g., *šabbāt di nōvyo* (Piamenta 2000: 27–32, 60). Although Piamenta does not point out the historical link of JJ forms to their Sephardic roots in Andalusia, JJ undoubtedly has shared origins with Galilean MPJA, whose speakers were exiled from Spain and arrived in the Holy Land after a stay in North Africa. Piamenta also writes:

> At the turn of the 20th century, Modern Hebrew as a spoken language and the language of formal education presented itself in schools and outdoors, mainly among youngsters including speakers of JJ, as a domestic language when contacting their Jewish peers whose domestic language was different. After Ladino in the Sephardic community, Hebrew took the lead as the *lingua franca* of both Ashkenazi and Sephardic communities despite their different accents at the beginning. (Piamenta 2000: 6)

In the Galilee region, through recordings of MPJA informants, we can distinguish three phases of the use of Hebrew words (Geva-Kleinberger 2004a: 67–69):

– In the first stage, we find Hebrew words used in the Jewish liturgy and Jewish life, e.g., *sēfer* [normally in the sense of a holy book or the Bible]; *tsadīq* 'righteous'. At this stage, there are long and short vowels in Hebrew and gemination is still preserved, e.g., *mazzāl* 'luck'.
– In the second phase, beginning in 1936 during the massive penetration of Modern Hebrew into daily life, the long vowels are still preserved, yet gemination disappears, e.g., *mazāl* 'luck'. There is a shift of several consonants into their modern variety of Hebrew speech, as well as a shift toward de-emphasis, e.g., *tṣadīq* 'righteous'> *tsadīk*.
– In the third phase, since the establishment of the State of Israel in 1948, long vowels are lost. There is also no gemination and the consonant and vowel system are identical to the Modern Hebrew pronunciation. Thus, *mazāl* becomes *mazál* and *tsadīk* becomes *tsadík*. With time and the consolidation of Modern Hebrew as the state's official language, more Modern Hebrew lexicon enters the informants' speech and full Hebrew sentences appear more frequently.

3.2.2 Aramaic

At the traditional ritual of the *Sēder* or *Lelt is-Sēder* on Passover (*Pēsaḥ*) eve, JJ speakers read the *Haggǎdā*. The Aramaic introduction to the *Haggǎdā*, reading *hā laḥmā ʿanyā dī axǎlū abhǎtāna...* 'This poor bread which our forefathers ate ...' (Piamenta 2000: 42)], is chanted.

All MPJA dialects, including JJ, use the word *ḥammīn* for Shabbat food kept warm from Friday evening – literally 'hot', with the Aramaic plural ending.

Some Aramaic proverbs are used by the informants of MPJA, such as *kol de-'alím gvár* 'might is right!' (Geva-Kleinberg 2009: 150–151).

4 State of research

Two primary scholars have published research studies on MPJA, although neither applied the term to this dialect, used to denote the Arabic speech of the Maghrebi Jews in the Holy Land. This research is also among the earliest to posit MPJA as connected to the dialect of the Maghrebi Jews in historic Lebanon.

The first researcher in the field was Moshe Piamenta, who treated the communal Arabic dialect of Jerusalem, spoken by Muslims, Christians, and Jews. He himself was a native MPJA speaker (Piamenta 1981: 203). In 1958, Piamenta wrote his doctoral dissertation, titled *The use of tenses, aspects, and moods in the Arabic dialects of Jerusalem*, which concentrates on the verb system of the city's Jews.

The other researcher of Galilean Judeo-Arabic, which is a parallel name for MPJA, is Aharon Geva-Kleinberger, who began his interest in the urban dialects of Haifa, encountering for the first time Jewish informants of that city who were native Arabic speakers. Through his research, Geva-Kleinberger came to realize that this dialect was not the only Galilean Judeo-Arabic. His informants told him about the Arabic dialect of the Safed Jews and later about that of the Tiberias Jews. Working on the dialect of the latter, he heard about the last Jewish speaker of this Arabic, a woman from Pqiʕin village in western Upper Galilee. It is a common belief among some MPJA linguistic consultants that the family of this woman had not left the Holy Land after the expulsion of the Jews by the Romans.

4.1 History of documentation

Following his 1958 dissertation and his 1973 and 1979 articles, Piamenta published his best contribution to JJ research in 2000, a book titled *Jewish life in Arabic language and Jerusalem Arabic in communal perspective*. It details the vocabulary of the Jerusalem Jews' dialect, as compared with the communal dialects of the city's Muslims and Christians.

Aryeh Levin (1994) also based his book on the Jewish dialect of Jerusalem, beside the dialect of the city's Arabs. He tends to generalize his descriptions by communalizing the dialects of the city under one roof, without referring to specific linguistic phenomena among the Jews (see, e.g., Levin 1994: 13, note 1).

Geva-Kleinberger's book, *Die arabischen Stadtdialekte von Haifa in der ersten Hälfte des 20. Jahrhunderts*, was published in 2004, although it originated as a doctoral dissertation in 2000 based on fieldwork recordings made between 1995 and 2000. The same year, Geva-Kleinberger (2000) published an article about the Galilean dialect of the Jews of Safed. In 2005, he wrote another paper about the aforementioned last Jewish informant of Pqiˁin, after having finally persuaded this woman to be recorded following three years of effort (Geva-Kleinberger 2005). In 2009, Geva-Kleinberger published a book on the dialect of the Jews of Tiberias, a research endeavor that began when he was gathering material on the Jews of Haifa (Geva-Kleinberger 2009).

4.2 Corpora

Future scholars can use texts in Galilean MPJA recorded by Geva-Kleinberger from Haifa, Safed, and Tiberias, some of which appear on the Heidelberger Internet site of *Semarch*. These texts should stimulate further research, applying Oral History methodology.

4.3 Issues of general theoretical interest

In their studies, apart from linguistic data and analysis, both Piamenta and Geva-Kleinberger introduced anthropological investigations as well. Geva-Kleinberger also presents the historical background to his research. Theoretically, the texts that appear in their works can serve scholars of various academic interests: sociologists, historians, and anthropologists. In addition, MPJA's historical roots and its relation with Maghrebi dialects must be further investigated.

Something else that needs to be further explored is the link between MPJA and Jewish dialects in Lebanon and Syria. Since MPJA has North African and Andalusian roots but developed over time into a dialect more Palestinian in nature, there is a great need to investigate the mechanisms of dialects that change their geographical, hence dialectological, environment through shifting to another region. To date, no written texts have been discovered in these dialects. If some are found in the future, they might cause a revision of some ideas about the dialects' formation and history.

Moshe Piamenta has passed away. There are still recordings made by Geva-Kleinberger that can be transcribed and analyzed. MPJA may already be regarded as an almost obsolete set of dialects even though some linguistic consultants were still alive at the end of the 20th century. Without the studies conducted to date, there is every likelihood that no one would have known anything about the existence of these dialects, as if they had never been.

References

Geva-Kleinberger, Aharon. 2000. Living amongst the spirits: Death and superstition as reflected in the Arabic and Hebrew vocabulary of the Jews of Safed. *Mediterranean Language Review* 12. 18–40.

Geva-Kleinberger, Aharon. 2004a. *Die arabischen Stadtdialecte von Haifa in der ersten Hälfte des 20. Jahrhunderts.* Wiesbaden: Harrassowitz Verlag.

Geva-Kleinberger, Aharon. 2004b. Memories of the Sea of Galilee: A text in the Arabic dialect of the Jews of Tiberias, with a short sketch of the dialect. *Jerusalem Studies in Arabic and Islam* 29. 145–165.

Geva-Kleinberger, Aharon. 2005. Last informants of the Jewish-Arabic dialect of the ancient community of Peqi'in. *Wiener Zeitschrift für die Kunde des Morgenlandes* 95. 45–16.

Geva-Kleinberger, Aharon. 2009. *Autochthonous texts in the Arabic dialect of the Jews of Tiberias.* Wiesbaden: Harrassowitz Verlag.

Levin, Aryeh. 1994. *A Grammar of the Arabic dialect of Jerusalem.* Jerusalem: Magnes Press.

Piamenta, Moshe. 1958. *The use of tenses, aspects, and moods in the Arabic dialects of Jerusalem.* Jerusalem: Hebrew University of Jerusalem PhD thesis. [Hebrew].

Piamenta, Moshe. 1981. Selected syntactic phenomena of Jerusalem Arabic narrative style in 1900. In Shelomo Morag, Issachar Ben-Ami & Norman A. Stillman (eds.), *Studies in Judaism and Islam, presented to Shelomo Dov Goitein on the occasion of his eightieth birthday by his students, colleagues and friends.* Jerusalem: Magnes Press.

Piamenta, Moshe. 1992. Note on the decay of Jerusalem Judaeo-Arabic under the impact of sociopolitical transformation. *Asian and African Studies* 26. 81–88.

Piamenta, Moshe. 2000. *Jewish life in Arabic language and Jerusalem Arabic in communal perspective: A lexico-semantic study.* Leiden, Boston & Cologne: Brill.

Part III: **Theoretical and Comparative Perspectives**

Bernard Spolsky
Sociolinguistics of Jewish Language Varieties

1 Introduction

The close connection between sociolinguistics and Jewish language varieties[1] has been shown again in three recent books: Benor (2012) provides an account of the development of a variety of Jewish English by newly observant young Jews, Spolsky (2014) presents a sociolinguistic history of the languages of the Jews, and Kahn & Rubin (2016) is the first handbook of Jewish languages. Academic study of Jewish language varieties originally focused on them as dialects of the non-Jewish languages from which they were derived, so that the study of Yiddish was considered part of German dialectology and Judeo-Spanish[2] part of Romance dialects study. One of the earliest scholarly treatments of Yiddish (Mieses 1915) appeared in the journal *Dialekte* and refers in its title to Jewish dialects. Dialectology is, of course, a sub-field or predecessor of sociolinguistics, although it changed direction when Labov (1962, 1966) added socially-defined variation to the geographically-defined variations studied by traditional dialectology.[3]

Yiddish dialectology (independent of Germanics) became newly important when Uriel Weinreich started work on the Yiddish dialect atlas (Herzog et al. 1992–2000), production of which included the matching of isoglosses with food preferences (Herzog 1965).[4] Herzog was a student of Uriel Weinreich; another student of his was William Labov, considered the founder of variationist sociolinguistics. A close friend and associate of Weinreich, with whom he nearly wrote a pioneering work on sociolinguistic theory, was Joshua Fishman (Spolsky 2011), the founder of the branch of sociolinguistics known as the sociology of language (Fishman 1968) and one of the pioneers of the study of Jewish languages (Fishman 1985b).

The close ties between the study of Jewish varieties and sociolinguistics are exhibited by the emphasis on ties between language and society in the work of Uriel Weinreich's father, Max Weinreich, whose classic history of Yiddish

---

[1] I used the term "variety" to leave open the sociolinguistically relevant question as to whether they are languages, dialects, creoles, or religiolects, to mention a few of the possible classifications.
[2] Judeo-Spanish includes Ladino, Judezmo, and Hakétia, to mention three recognizable varieties.
[3] Fishman is unhappy that Labov only added social class as a factor, leaving out, for example, the religious factor he finds so important (Fishman 2006a).
[4] For example, northern phonetic features were associated with adding salt to gefilte fish, while southern coincided with the use of sugar.

stressed the sociolinguistic environment and included a pioneering chapter on other Jewish varieties (M. Weinreich 1980, 2008).[5] Fishman's personal goal, at the "supra-rational level," was to find out if any languages were in a stronger state of preservation than Yiddish; he admitted that his work was "Yiddish-centric," with a conscious effort to preserve a scientific perspective by studying other cases and languages (Fishman 2006c). Fishman's early study of language loyalty (Fishman 1966), as well as launching a major trend of studying language shift, provided him with a way of comparing the fate of Yiddish in America with that of other US immigrant languages. In these ways, the study of Jewish varieties was closely tied to the growth of the field of sociolinguistics.

2 What is a Jewish variety?

Jewish varieties are community languages, first and foremost, and their study is a key to exploring the relation between language and society. Of course one can describe a Jewish variety without reference to its use and to the sociolinguistic repertoire in which it exists, but fundamentally these are what define it. Rabin (1981) stressed that a Jewish language was to be recognized, because it was spoken and written by a Jewish community in conjunction with Hebrew (or Hebrew-Aramaic, to be precise) and a non-Jewish co-territorial vernacular (or standard) language. In this triglossic relationship, Hebrew-Aramaic was the high-status language used for literary and religious purposes, the non-Jewish language was used for communication outside the community, and the Jewish variety was used for all vernacular functions (home, school, business) within the Jewish community.

Fishman too included the social in his definition:

> I define as "Jewish" any language that is phonologically, morpho-syntactically, lexico-semantically or orthographically different from that of non-Jewish sociocultural networks and that has some demonstrably unique function in the role-repertoire of a Jewish sociocultural network, which function is not normatively present in the role-repertoire of non-Jews and/or is not normally discharged via varieties identical with those utilized by non-Jews. (Fishman 1981, 1985a)

In this, he was echoing Weinreich's social emphasis when he said: "Without communal separateness there is no separate language" (M. Weinreich 2008: 175).

---

[5] Originally published in Yiddish (1973), the first translation into English (1980) excluded the footnotes, which are translated in the 2008 two-volume edition.

Weinreich opens his major work by describing the nature of Jewish "exclusion" before considering its linguistic results. Thus, for him, the definition of Jewish language varieties is more sociolinguistic than linguistic. While there is still a need for the strictly linguistic analysis that shows how a Jewish variety is different from others, as in the classic study of sectarian Baghdadi dialects (Blanc 1964), the sociolinguistic question of what constitutes a Jewish variety remains critical.

3 Recognizing Jewish varieties

One of the central issues concerning Jewish varieties is their recognition. A first question is recognition by whom? One answer is by a government, acknowledging a language as official or assigning it some other defined legal status. Many languages are listed in the national constitution of the country where they are spoken; others (like Māori and Sign in New Zealand, Welsh in Wales, or French in Quebec) have laws recognizing their status.[6] But Jewish varieties have never had governments, or their own armies and navies,[7] so that apart from Hebrew, which is excluded from the listing of Jewish varieties by scholars such as Ornan (1985), there are only occasional cases of government recognition. The Israeli government has finally established and funded "authorities" for Yiddish and Ladino, but these are intended to support post-vernacular heritage activities (Shandler 2006) and do not provide official functional recognition. In the 1920s and 1930s in the Soviet Union, Yiddish was treated as a minority language and recognized for the Jewish Autonomous Oblast of Birobidzan; this status has not been maintained by the Russian Federation. It was an official language of the Ukrainian People's Republic from 1917 to 1921, and briefly in other nations created by the Treaty of Versailles. It is included in the minority languages of some countries which ratified the 1992 European Charter for Regional or Minority languages: the

---

[6] This regularly recognizes them as "official," but the status needs further definition. Arabic was, until July 2018, the second "official" language of Israel, but it maintained the limitation of official status established by the British Mandatory government to some defined situations, like the publication of government regulations and the provision of interpreters in law courts (in the new Israeli Nationality Bill of 18 July 2018, Arabic was granted "special status"). The New Zealand Māori language act of 1987 gave Māori the right to speak, but not be addressed in, the language in legal proceedings. Some constitutions require that candidates for public office know the official language.
[7] M. Weinreich (1945) explains that the definition of a language as a dialect with an army and navy was suggested by an auditor in one of his classes.

Netherlands, Sweden,[8] Poland, Romania, Bosnia and Herzegovina, and a modified mention in Ukraine.

A second answer is recognition by linguists, who set out to describe and classify what they see as their central objects of study, and by information technology experts who need to know how to translate a text. There can be purely linguistic classification, such as language taxonomies that trace family relationships (this automatically attaches Jewish varieties to the non-Jewish language from which they are derived), or based on morphological or syntactic patterns (agglutinative versus polysynthetic languages, subject-verb-object versus verb-subject-object, or other order languages), but it was sociolinguistics that provided the relevant classification of language status. Stewart (1968) proposed definitions for standard language, vernacular, dialect, creole, pidgin, and classical language. In the case of Jewish varieties, generally lacking standardization, all but Yiddish and perhaps Judeo-Arabic and Ladino can be no more than vernaculars, and most are seen as dialects, or, if considered for their admixture of Hebrew-Aramaic and earlier Jewish varieties, as creoles.[9]

There is an alternative view suggested by studies of multilingual cities, which, following Blommaert (2001, 2007, 2010) and Estraikh (1999), moves the emphasis from named language varieties to the polycentric repertoires developed by migrants in super diverse language environments. This approach has been applied to Jewish speech varieties by Benor (2009, 2011, 2012), who sees the speech of Orthodox Jews, as well as other co-territorial Jewish languages, as varieties of the local language with the addition of distinctive features, such as Yiddish and Hebrew-Aramaic lexicon and syntactic features. Dealing with repertoires rather than named varieties seems a better way of accounting for the large amount of variation between and within individual speakers, and recognizes the plurilingualism and pluridialectism of many speakers; it also makes clear the usefulness of adding the discourse features revealed by Tannen (1981) in her study of New York conversational style.

But sociolinguists continue to look for theoretical or empirical definitions. Fishman (1981, 1985a: 4) provides the definition cited earlier that is quite widely used. His definition has both linguistic and social components, but requires establishing what is "different" (e.g., Ladino has a smaller Hebrew-Aramaic component than Yiddish) and what a "normative" function constitutes. Rabin (1981) concentrates on the sociolinguistic aspect, specifically the diglossic relation of

---

8 In Sweden, the government has issued two documents in Yiddish and permits its use in internet domain names.
9 J. A. Fishman (1987) discusses this issue and concludes, like most scholars, that Jewish varieties are not creoles.

a Jewish variety as an L variety, in relation to Hebrew-Aramaic as the H variety. It was Ferguson (1959) who proposed diglossia to account for the situations in which there is a high-status standard language (H) used in a community that also has a lower status vernacular (L): in his definition, the languages need to be related, such as, for example, Classical Arabic and the regional spoken varieties, High German and Swiss German, or French and Haitian Creole. Fishman (1967) expanded the definition to cases where the languages are not related, such as English and Spanish in the Jersey City Barrio, or Hebrew and Yiddish in the *shtetl*. For Jewish varieties, one needs to add a third variety, the non-Jewish co-territorial variety, used for communication outside the Jewish community.

There is another sociolinguistic criterion used by linguists to distinguish language varieties, as followed (with many exceptions) by ISO, the International Organization for Standardization, an independent, non-governmental organization made up of members from the national standards bodies of 162 member nations around the world. They are responsible for many published standards; for language, the relevant one is ISO 639-3: 2007, which provides a three-letter identifier for all "living, extinct, ancient and constructed languages, whether major or minor, written or unwritten." Languages recognized in this way are listed in Lewis et al. (2013), a recent edition of *Ethnologue*, produced annually by International SIL since Pittman (1969). According to ISO policy, recognizing a distinct language requires it to be mutually unintelligible with all others, although an exception is regularly made for national languages like the Scandinavian languages, which each have their flag and ISO identifier. Intelligibility might work for Jewish varieties, but there are some questionable decisions. In *Ethnologue*, for instance, Hakétia is not recognized as distinct from Ladino, there is a mistaken identification of a Yiddish Sign Language,[10] and only some varieties are ISO recognized.

4 Popular perceptions

Governments and linguists, then, have their criteria for recognizing Jewish varieties; but what about non-experts, whether speakers or not? The popular (as opposed to scientific) recognition of differences in language varieties has been labeled perceptual dialectology by Preston (1999), who illustrates its application

---

10 The editors of *Ethnologue* took it from a single mention in the preface to Sacks (2009), but Sign Language scholars have found no evidence for such a variety, noting that Sign Languages are named for country (British, American) and not language. Such a variety may have existed in schools for the Jewish deaf in Poland before the wars, but there is no firm evidence.

to surveys in various parts of the US; there have also been studies of differences recognized in European American and African American English (Thomas and Reaser 2004). In the case of Jewish varieties, most reports are anecdotal, but one study, by an International SIL team of a sample of speakers in a large number of Tat speaking villages, reported that in every village, residents reported that the Jewish varieties were noticeably different in pronunciation and lexicon, but in some cases these differences were not enough to make the variety unintelligible (Clifton et al. 2005).

There is, Jacobs (2005: 60) says, much anecdotal evidence for Jewish recognition of Yiddish dialect differences, but popular perceptions of these differences do not necessarily coincide with linguistic descriptions. M. Weinreich (2008) says that an 18th century claim that Yiddish was unintelligible to a speaker of German was certainly exaggerated: "The basic difference between Yiddish and German has no direct bearing on the question of whether a German and a Jew, say in the year 1000 in Cologne, could communicate. Communication was possible even 900 years later, when Yiddish and German were most certainly independent linguistic systems" (2008: 350). Trudgill (1992) notes that Ladino would be considered a variety of Spanish if it were spoken in Spain.[11]

What are the common cues for recognizing that Jewish varieties are different? Recent work in linguistic anthropology has used the concept of enregisterment, derived by Agha (2005) from the word "register," a term developed by Ferguson (1964) to refer to varieties of speech like baby talk, foreigner talk, and sports announcer talk. For Agha, register (he takes his examples from Ferguson) overlaps in some way with voice, which marks individual and social dimensions like gender and age. An enregistered dialect, then, is one that contains forms that are associated with a place (a city or district) or a group of people. Johnstone, Andrus, and Danielson (2006) show how this applies to Pittsburgh English.

Jewish varieties are also likely to be marked in this way. The speech of Orthodox Jews that Benor (2011, 2012) has studied is marked by Yiddish and Hebrew words and grammatical influences; the New York Jewish conversational study that Tannen (1981) described was marked by discourse features, such as interruption. The college student speech that C. K. Thomas (1932) tried to correct had phonological features that marked speakers as New York Jews. Jacobs (1996) investigated the varieties of German spoken by Viennese Jews in the 1920s. These are just a few of many examples of outsiders noticing marked features in modern Jewish varieties.

---

[11] When we asked some New Mexico speakers of Spanish how they reacted to the Ladino of a visiting Israeli, they replied it sounded just like their grandparents.

What about recognition by the speakers of the varieties themselves? This might be expected to show up in answers to the question, "What language do you speak?" The answers to a recent US survey conducted by the US Census Bureau found 212,747 adults claiming to speak Hebrew, 155,582 who claimed Yiddish, and only 130 who claimed Ladino (United States Census Bureau 2015). One may assume that many Ladino speakers answered that they spoke Spanish. I was informed by one person that the members of a Sephardi synagogue in New York, 60% of whom knew Ladino, confirmed this hypothesis, and there was a similar report from Los Angeles.

Summing up, then, it seems that many Jewish varieties are mutually intelligible with the non-Jewish variety from which they are derived, with the possibility of added elements to decrease comprehension by outsiders, such as the Hebrew words for a number of characteristics of horses used in their Yiddish by Swiss horse dealers (Bartal and Naor 2006). But they are recognized by speakers as different (they are often called "Jewish" or a translation of the word, or "our language"), and they are recognized by local non-Jews as Jewish.

5 Multilingualism

Fishman (1991b: 308) writes that any sociolinguistic consideration of Yiddish must be in the context of multilingualism: "Multilingualism appears to have been the natural state of Yiddish-using communities for the entire millennium in which the language has existed." But this is likely to be true of every Jewish variety, with the regular pattern of associated use of Hebrew-Aramaic and the non-Jewish variety. As religious and ethnic minorities, Jews have been bound to live with individual plurilingualism and social multilingualism. Multilingualism, Weiser (2011: 8) notes "was thus the norm in Jewish society." Berger et al. (2003) present a number of studies of the various patterns that occurred in Jewish communities in Western Europe. There have also been studies of multilingualism in Spain before the expulsion (Miller 2000). Spolsky (1985) describes the multilingual pattern in Judah before the Roman expulsion; Spolsky and Shohamy (1999) look at the current situation in Israel; and Spolsky (2010) investigates the effect of religion on language maintenance. Shandler (2002) says that the appearance of signs in Yiddish revealed the arrival of Jewish immigrants in New York. Spolsky (2008: 32) notes that the Yiddish public signage that helped represent the linguistic landscape of the Lower East Side of New York has given way to signs in Chinese and Spanish. However, in a Yiddish-speaking Hasidic neighborhood like Meah Shearim in Jerusalem, most signs are written in Hebrew (or in English if intended for tourists).

6 Standardization and modernization of Yiddish

A central concern of applied sociolinguistics is the developing of a standardized version of a variety, with the selection or creation of a writing system, a consensus on orthography, the writing of a standard grammar determining "pure" speech, and the publication of a dictionary that determines acceptance of the standard lexicon. While in some languages like English, this is ultimately left to the individual efforts of scholars or publishers, in many others it is the task of a governmentally empowered institution, an academy, or a collection of committees. As far as writing systems are concerned, most Jewish varieties were written in Hebrew letters, though occasionally with modification (see Daniels, this volume), and with more recent Latinization.

In the case of Yiddish, the Czernowitz conference in 1908 (Fishman 1980, 1993) had on its agenda the standardization of Yiddish, though it spent most of its time on the question of status. Formal efforts at standardization followed later, in two competing schemes, one proposed in Moscow by the Soviet Yiddish committees and the other in Vilna with the foundation of YIVO.

In 1918, with the establishment of the *Evkom* (Jewish commissariat) and the Soviet granting to national minorities of the right to offer education in languages other than Russian, the Yiddish-Hebrew struggle began in earnest in the Soviet Union ('Ôdēd 1979). The Commissariat aimed to set up a network of Jewish schools, but among the many questions it faced was Hebrew language and Jewish religious instruction. The Education Commissariat opposed both and successfully petitioned the Commissariat on Nationalities to ban teaching in a national school in a non-native language. The Hebraists appealed to the authorities, but it was the secular Yiddishists who dominated Jewish education. In 1919, the Jewish Subdivision of the Commissariat on Enlightenment ruled that Hebrew was not the vernacular of the Jewish masses; it could only be treated as a foreign language, and its use as language of instruction was to cease. Petitions for use of Hebrew continued, but were firmly blocked. Privately supported adult education in Hebrew was tolerated but discouraged as nationalistic. In 1925, some Zionist youth groups submitted new petitions arguing for acceptance of Hebrew, but they too were denied and, in the late 1920s, an attack began on Hebrew printed material of all kinds. In 1920, there was a major campaign against the Hebrew calendar, and the Jewish Division imposed a ban on any Hebrew language publishing. There were later attempts at legalizing Hebrew, but the Yiddishists finally succeeded in driving it underground ('Ôdēd 1979: 52). Thus Yiddish became the only Jewish variety recognized under Soviet rule.

This produced a problem for non-Ashkenazi Jews, in particular for the Judeo-Tat speaking Jews of Dagestan. The Jewish section *Evseksiia* claimed authority and denied petitions to use Hebrew in Jewish schools in Dagestan, but it did produce textbooks in Judeo-Tat. In Uzbekistan, material was published in Judeo-Tadzhik, including three translations of Shalom Aleichem ('Ôdēd 1979: 52–55).

Less successful than the war against Hebrew were the efforts of the Yiddishists to oppose the increasing use of Russian by Jews and their related desire to send their children to Russian schools. Slowly but inevitably, Soviet Jews were seeing the value of complete assimilation, so that the Yiddish intelligentsia that controlled the various Soviet Jewish organs was fighting a losing battle ('Ôdēd 1979: 59–60).

As part of this struggle to establish Yiddish as the Jewish national language, the Soviet Yiddishist intelligentsia saw modernization as a critical task, a step being undertaken for other minority languages in Leninist Soviet Russia. They had some advantages: Yiddish already existed as a spoken and written variety, though it had been stigmatized as *zhargon* during the Czarist period by rabbis and "Jewish cultural elites." They argued that it was the language of the people, in contrast to Hebrew, which they associated with the bourgeoisie. One goal of modernization was to distance Yiddish from Hebrew, but the basic goal was to develop it as the national language of the Jewish people.

Soviet Yiddish modernization was a continuation of earlier unorganized modernization, but directed by Soviet Yiddishists without external control: They controlled their own institutions. Although the spelling reform was formally implemented by the State Commissariat of Education and Culture in 1928, it was enacting the decisions of a conference of Yiddishists in 1927 ('Ôdēd 1979: 62).

A first Yiddish-German dictionary had been published in 1867. Debate about modernization followed; one trend was to Germanize, another proposal was to write Hebrew phonetically, or even to Romanize it. A Yiddish philological journal, *Der Pinkas*, appeared in 1913; it was edited by Shmuel Niger, with an opening essay by Ber Borochov arguing that language standardization, which was needed for mass literacy, was the path to nationhood. There had been calls for modernization from Yiddish teachers before World War I and several competing proposals; as mentioned above, the Czernowitz conference was supposed to deal with orthography and other aspects of standardization.

One suggestion accepted by the socialists was a proposal to spell Hebrew words phonetically and not traditionally, as they were in Hebrew. Thus, the word for the Sabbath would be spelled שאבעס, as it was pronounced in some regions,[12]

---

[12] Yiddish dialect differences made it necessary to standardize phonetic spelling. YIVO selected northeastern (Litvak) versions rather than southern (Galicianer). While there are probably now more speakers of Hasidic dialects, there has been no move to change this by YIVO.

and not שבת as in Hebrew. The new Communist Yiddish newspaper, *Emes*, established in 1918, began by dropping German based spelling (the 'h' added in *zer*, from German *sehr*) and a year later started spelling Hebrew words phonetically (*torah* became *toyre*). The arguments were both pedagogical (it was easier to read for someone who did not know Hebrew) and anti-Zionist.

In 1919, the Jewish subdivision of the Enlightenment Commissariat set up a Yiddish Philological Commission whose proposals were approved by the First All-Russian Jewish Conference in 1920. One of the leading reformers was Itschik Zaretsky, who later founded a Philological Commission in Kharkov but returned to Moscow. Another important center was Minsk in Belorussia, where Mordechai Veynger published a collection of articles. In 1926, an Institute for Jewish Research was founded in Kiev, and it published a journal, *Di Yidishe Sprakh*, which became a means of disseminating reform. Many people and institutions were involved, and all met at the Second All-Union Cultural Congress in Kharkov in 1928. There were two major factions, some favoring moderate reform and others proposing radical changes even at the cost of losing support from Jews elsewhere. One major change that was approved was the elimination of five final letters. Implementation was to take place by 1932. There were arguments put forward for Latinization (echoing those with other languages in the Soviet Union), but they were not powerful with the Yiddishists.

In the 1930s, Shneer (2004) says, activity continued but the Yiddish intelligentsia felt its power fading, as communist ideology strengthened its grip. Many of the Leninist policies encouraging ethnic and national cultures were ended and Yiddish schools, newspapers, and institutions were closed down. In the purges under Stalin, many Yiddish leaders were imprisoned or killed. During the war and the Holocaust, masses of speakers of Yiddish died, so that the work of status building for Yiddish ended.

The second major program of standardization and modernization was the work of YIVO, *Yidisher Visnshaftlekher Institut* 'the Institute for Jewish Research', founded in 1925 in Vilna (then part of Poland) by Max Weinreich and the historian Elias Tcherikover, with branches in Berlin and Warsaw, and relocated to New York in 1940. Its goal was to collect evidence of the language and culture of East European Jewry and to work to preserve it; the tasks of Yiddish standardization and modernization were central in its activities. But secular Yiddish continued for a while in the US in the first half of 20th century (Freidenreich 2010; David Fishman 2005).

Neusner (2008) points out that most language management efforts in the case of Yiddish, with the exception of the Soviet Union, have been non-governmental activities and restricted to the form rather than the status of the language. Most have been concerned with lexicon (new terminology) rather than grammar. From the beginning of the 19th century, Yiddish publishing and Yiddish language activity were concentrated in Eastern Europe, although nowadays the YIVO Institute for Jewish Research and the League for Yiddish (founded in 1979 by Mordkhe Schaechter), both based in New York, are the recognized authorities.

Fishman (2006b) has written on the topic of language standardization and suggests that the dimensions relevant to Yiddish and other reviving languages are purity versus vernacularity, *ausbau* versus *einbau*, uniqueness versus regionalization, and internationalisms versus classicism. *Purity* is important for Yiddish in order to maintain distance from neighboring languages, and is marked by a tendency to avoid borrowings. This remains the YIVO approach; but Katz (2004) notes that modern Hasidic Yiddish does not respect the standardization of the secular Yiddishists, and is marked by "diverse experiments in language, grammar, and spelling" (Katz 2004: 390), as well as using a markedly different pronunciation.

Ausbau, a term proposed by Kloss (1967) to describe efforts to distance one variety from another (as opposed to *abstand*, languages which are naturally different), refers, Fishman suggests, to "building away" one variety from another, as Yiddish was desired to be different from German.[13] The call for differentiation ("*Avek fun daytsh!*" 'away from German') had already been made in the 19th century and was a key motto of the Czernowitz conference; it was applied to spelling, grammar, and lexicon. Soviet standardization, Fishman points out, was not as strict about lexicon, but even more anti-German (and as noted, anti-Hebrew) in orthography than YIVO. But since 1961, Russian Yiddish has moved closer to YIVO, with the restoration of final letters and discontinuing the phonetization of Hebrew words. The opposite tendency, *einbau*, refers to the attempt to fuse varieties, such as the endeavors of some leaders of the Jewish Enlightenment and of the Tsarist government to move Yiddish closer to German. Yiddish was (and in orthodox circles still is) influenced by German.

Uniqueness, Fishman says, is for those who find both purity and *ausbau* too mild, and involves incorporating archaic forms of Yiddish gathered from old texts or folklore. *Regionalization*, on the other hand, suggests selecting

---

13 The same process occurred when Nathaniel Webster produced a dictionary to distinguish American from British English, when the various Scandinavian national languages set out to move away from Danish, when India and Pakistan each developed their own variety of Hindustani, and when the various Yugoslav successor states established their own national languages.

lexicon from the same area or language family, such as favoring Arabic for coining new words for Hebrew. For example, Soviet Yiddishists preferred borrowings from Russian. *Internationalisms* refer to borrowing or coinage of terms used in Western languages, especially in the physical, natural, and social sciences. Associated with this was the move for Latinization of script, which never succeeded with Yiddish.[14] *Classicism* seems to refer, rather, to the stress (common in the Yiddish of observant Jews) on including an unlimited number of Hebrew/Aramaic words and expressions and the use of traditional "classic" punctuation and spelling. This puts an extra burden on those men and women without traditional Hebrew religious education. In the Soviet Union, "naturalization" (phonetic spelling) of Hebrew was the approach. Since the break up of the Soviet Union, "classicism" (restoration of the final letters and use of Hebrew spelling) and internationalism in lexicon have both become accepted.

7 Standardization of Judeo-Spanish

There has not, until recently, been the same history of standardization with regard to Judeo-Spanish. Because Jews in the middle ages were exceptionally literate in Hebrew, they could use it as a method of writing other languages. Kenrick (2007) notes a tendency towards standardization in Jewish medieval Spanish written in Hebrew letters, but there was never any institutionally imposed normativism. Fishman (1965) says that, in modern times, some writers and leaders tried to persuade Sephardim to take on their local language, and this occurred especially after the Young Turk Revolution in 1908, when many Jews left Turkey to avoid military service. Most of these migrants switched within a generation, so the few Ladino publications did not last. Some, however, encouraged the maintenance of the language, proposing various models for standardization; there was a movement for castilization, but others sought to maintain folk models.

In the late 19th century, an ideological struggle developed over the status of Judeo-Spanish in the Ottoman Empire. The opening of Westernized schools, especially those of Alliance Israélite Universelle (Laskier 2012), the new recognition of "real Spanish," the renewed call for Hebrew, and the growing status of Turkish all added up to threats to Judeo-Spanish, denigrated as a jargon. Bürki (2010) summarized the defense of Judeo-Spanish as presented in the

---

14 It has, however, been generally accepted for Ladino.

Salonika newspaper *La Época* by Sam Lévy, son of the editor-in-chief, in a series of lectures and articles in 1901 and 1902. Basing his attack on those who called it jargon on linguistic science, Lévy argued that Ladino had developed in the way languages normally do. It was, he said, not only widely spoken but increasingly being written in literature that was widely read. He agreed that Turkish Jews should learn Turkish, but believed that they should maintain and cultivate Judeo-Spanish as the language of Ottoman Jewry. Sadly, though, Ladino could not overcome the pressure of Turkish and other national languages; it was soon restricted to domestic use and has since been left with few and elderly speakers.

But there are sparks of life. Bortnick (2004) reports on a Judeo-Spanish online discussion group, *Ladinokomunita*, which has been operating since 2000 and permits postings only in Ladino; its goal is the maintenance, revitalization, and standardization of the language. One of the central debates has been whether the language is still a vernacular; it is recognized that most speakers have other languages for communication, so that it might better be called post-vernacular. Another debate concerns the name: Ladino was referred to as "Judezmo" (Jewish) within the community.[15] The list does not only insist on the use of Ladino but on standard orthography, following the lead of the magazine *Aki Yerushalayim*, published two or three times a year under the auspices of the Israeli National Authority of Ladino Culture. While every page of the site urges standard spelling (avoiding "c" and "w"), Brink-Danan (2012) notes that even the moderators are not consistent. She cites Stein (2006: 506):

> No language academy or central organization that would oversee the standardization or promotion of Ladino was ever created. Thus when Turkish was Romanized in the 1920s, nearly all writers of Ladino followed suit, abandoning Rashi script in favor of the Roman alphabet. In the absence of a linguistic authority to oversee this process, speakers and writers of Ladino were now more than ever inclined towards linguistic borrowing.

The online list has also debated the issue of script, with some proposing the use of Hebrew or the traditional Solitreo, a cursive Rashi script once common but now rare. A web-based program offers LadinoType, a method of producing Solitreo on a normal keyboard, but it has not been taken up. There are regular arguments for purity, especially in opposition to the use of English borrowings, but borrowings from other languages are generally not noticed (the name of the list includes a borrowing from Italian).

---

15 An online survey of Ladinokomunita followers in 2001 found half preferred Ladino, 20% accepted Djudeo-Espanyol, and none Judezmo.

8 The fragility of Jewish varieties

Arising as they do in contact situations (U. Weinreich 1953), Jewish varieties pass through a number of identifiable sociolinguistic stages. They start not unlike pidgins, as spoken varieties that show a high level of code shifting and mixture; but, as children grow up speaking them, they undergo a process similar to creolization (Bickerton 1977; Hymes, 1971), in which they develop merged grammatical and lexical systems. Most remain at the level of spoken vernaculars, though some are written (usually with Hebrew letters) and a few standardized. However, with rare exceptions, they turn out to last for a limited time, soon to be replaced, after a move to a new environment, by another Jewish variety. In this sense, Jewish varieties, always in minority status and created in stigmatized and closed communities, are currently endangered or threatened languages, a central topic in sociolinguistics for the last two decades (Fishman 2002; Grenoble and Whaley 1998; Hale 1991; Krauss 1991; Moseley 2001; Spolsky 2009). This represents the development of an earlier sociolinguistic concern for studying language shift (Fishman 1964; Gal 1979; Tabouret-Keller 1968) and has been only lately challenged by a call to focus attention on speakers rather than languages (Labov 2008).

One of the results has been a growing interest in the activities of linguists and enthusiasts who attempt to counteract language loss, or to revive dying varieties, labeled by Fishman (1990, 1991a) as "reversing language shift." Many studies have focused on the exceptional revival of Hebrew (Fellman 1973; Ó Laoire 1999; Pilowsky 1985; Shohamy 2007; Spolsky 2007), some of which refer to its unfortunate effect in encouraging the loss of Jewish varieties (Shohamy 2007; Spolsky and Shohamy 1999), but there is also the post-vernacular activism that some Jewish varieties are now showing.

9 Jewish varieties and sociolinguistics

As contact languages, Jewish varieties are an obvious field for sociolinguistic study. As this review has shown, the scholars who have worked on the study of Jewish varieties have also been exploring the topics covered by the growing field of sociolinguistics. Without sociolinguistics, the work on Jewish varieties would be highly constrained, missing its most important dimensions. The Jewish varieties have provided excellent opportunities for the study of socially determined languages, for all have arisen in multilingual situations, in diasporas and cities that have grown with increasing migration. They are enabling the study of complex and dynamic patterns of language repertoires and setting methodological challenges that lead to advances in the field.

References

Agha, Asif. 2005. Voice, footing, enregisterment. *Journal of Linguistic Anthropology* 15(1). 38–59.
Bartal, Israel & Chaya Naor (trans.). 2006. *The Jews of Eastern Europe, 1772–1881*. Philadelphia: University of Pennsylvania Press.
Benor, Sarah Bunin. 2009. Do American Jews speak a "Jewish language"? A model of Jewish linguistic distinctiveness. *Jewish Quarterly Review* 99(2). 230–269.
Benor, Sarah Bunin. 2011. *Mensch, bentsh,* and *balagan*: Variation in the American Jewish linguistic repertoire. *Language and Communication* 31(2). 141–154.
Benor, Sarah Bunin. 2012. *Becoming frum: How newcomers learn the language and culture of Orthodox Judaism*. New Brunswick: Rutgers University Press.
Berger, Shlomo, Aubrey Pomeranz, Andrea Schatz, & Emile Schrijver (eds.). 2003. *Speaking Jewish: Jewish speak: Multilingualism in western Ashkenazic culture*. Leuven: Peeters.
Bickerton, Derek. 1977. Pidginization and creolization: Language acquisition and language universals. In Albert Valdman (ed.), *Pidgin and creole linguistics*, 49–69. Bloomington: Indiana University Press.
Blanc, Haim. 1964. *Communal dialects in Baghdad*. Cambridge, MA.: Harvard University Press.
Blommaert, Jan. 2001. The Asmara Declaration as a sociolinguistic problem: Reflections on scholarship and linguistic rights. *Journal of Sociolinguistics* 5(1). 131–142.
Blommaert, Jan. 2007. Sociolinguistics and discourse analysis: Orders of indexicality and polycentricity. *Journal of multicultural discourses* 2(2). 115–130.
Blommaert, Jan. 2010. *The sociolinguistics of globalization*. Cambridge: Cambridge University Press.
Bortnick, Rachel Amado. 2004. The internet and Judeo-Spanish: Impact and implications of a virtual community. Paper presented at the Proceedings of the Twelfth British Conference on Judeo-Spanish Studies.
Brink-Danan, Marcy. 2012. *Jewish life in 21st-century Turkey: The other side of tolerance*. Bloomington: Indiana University Press.
Bürki, Yvette. 2010. The Ottoman press at the dawn of the twentieth century through the Salonica Newspapers La Época and El Avenir. *European Judaism* 43(2). 102–116.
Clifton, John M., Gabriela Deckinga, Laura Lucht & Calvin Tiessen. 2005. Sociolinguistic situation of the Tat and Mountain Jews in Azerbaijan. SIL International.
Estraikh, Gennady. 1999. *Soviet Yiddish: Language planning and linguistic development*. Oxford: Oxford University Press.
Fellman, Jack. 1973. Concerning the "revival" of the Hebrew language. *Anthropological Linguistics* 15. 250–257.
Ferguson, Charles A. 1959. Diglossia. *Word* 15. 325–340.
Ferguson, Charles A. 1964. Baby talk in six languages. *American Anthropologist* 66(6). 103–114.
Fishman, David E. 2005. *The rise of modern Yiddish culture*. Pittsburgh: University of Pittsburgh Press.

Fishman, Joshua A. 1964. Language maintenance and language shift as fields of enquiry. *Linguistics* 9. 32–70.
Fishman, Joshua A. 1965. Yiddish in America. *International Journal of American Linguistics* 31(2). Part 2.
Fishman, Joshua A. 1967. Bilingualism with and without diglossia; diglossia with and without bilingualism. *Journal of Social Issues* 23(2). 29–38.
Fishman, Joshua A. 1980. Attracting a following to high-culture functions for a language of everyday life: The role of the Tshernovits conference in the 'rise of Yiddish'. *International Journal of the Sociology of Language* 24. 43–73.
Fishman, Joshua A. 1981. The sociology of Jewish languages from the perspective of the general sociology of language: A preliminary formulation. *International Journal of the Sociology of Language* 30. 5–16.
Fishman, Joshua A. 1985a. The sociology of Jewish languages from a general sociolinguistic point of view. In Joshua A. Fishman (ed.), *Readings in the sociology of Jewish languages*, 3–21. Leiden: Brill.
Fishman, Joshua A. (ed.). 1985b. *Readings in the sociology of Jewish languages*. Leiden: Brill.
Fishman, Joshua A. 1987. Post-exilic Jewish languages and pidgins/creoles: Two mutually clarifying perspectives. *Multilingua- Journal of Cross-Cultural and Interlanguage Communication* 6(1). 7–24.
Fishman, Joshua A. 1990. What is reversing language shift (RLS) and how can it succeed? *Journal of Multilingual and Multicultural Development* 11(1/2). 5–36.
Fishman, Joshua A. 1991a. *Reversing language shift: Theoretical and empirical foundations of assistance to threatened languages*. Clevedon: Multilingual Matters.
Fishman, Joshua A. 1991b. *Yiddish: Turning to life*. Amsterdam & Philadelphia: John Benjamins Publishing Company.
Fishman, Joshua A. 1993. The Tschernovits Congress revisited: The First World Congress for Yiddish revisited, 85 years later. In Joshua A. Fishman (ed.), *The earliest stage of language planning: The "first congress" phenomenon*, 321–332. Berlin: Mouton de Gruyter.
Fishman, Joshua A. 2002. Endangered minority languages: Prospects for sociolinguistic research. *MOST Journal of Multicultural Studies* 4(2). 270–275.
Fishman, Joshua A. 2006a. A decalogue of basic theoretical perspectives for a sociology of language and religion. In Tope Omoniyi & Joshua A. Fishman (eds.), *The sociology of language and religion: Change, conflict and accommodation*, 13–25. Basingstoke: Palgrave Macmillan.
Fishman, Joshua A. 2006b. *Do not leave your language alone: The hidden status agendas within corpus planning in language policy*. Mahwah: Lawrence Erlbaum Associates.
Fishman, Joshua A. 2006c. A week in the life of a man from the moon. In Ofelia García, Rakhmiel Peltz, Harold Schiffman & Gella Schweid Fishman (eds.), *Language loyalty, continuity and change: Joshua A. Fishman's contributions to international sociolinguistics*, 111–121. Clevedon: Multilingual Matters.
Fishman, Joshua A. (ed.). 1966. *Language loyalty in the United States: The maintenance and perpetuation of non-English mother tongues by American ethnic and religious groups*. The Hague: Mouton.
Fishman, Joshua A. (ed.). 1968. *Readings in the sociology of language*. The Hague: Mouton.
Freidenreich, Fradle Pomerantz. 2010. *Passionate Pioneers: The story of Yiddish secular education in North America, 1910–1960*. Teaneck, NJ: Holmes and Meier Publishers.

Gal, Susan. 1979. *Language shift: Social determinants of linguistic change*. New York: Academic Press.
Grenoble, Lenore A. & Lindsay J. Whaley (eds.). 1998. *Endangered languages: Current issues and future prospects*. Cambridge: Cambridge University Press.
Hale, Ken. 1991. On endangered languages and the safeguarding of diversity. *Language* 68(1). 1–3.
Herzog, Marvin. 1965. The Yiddish language in Northern Poland: Its geography and history. *International Journal of American Linguistics* 31(2).
Herzog, Marvin, Ulrike Kiefer, Robert Neumann, Wolfgang Putschke, Andrew Sunshine, Vera Baviskar, & Uriel Weinreich (eds.). 1992–2000. *The language and culture atlas of Ashkenazic Jewry*. Tübingen & New York: Max Niemeyer Verlag & YIVO Institute for Jewish Research.
Hymes, Dell (ed.). 1971. *Pidginisation and creolization of languages: Proceedings of a conference held at the University of the West Indies, April 1968*. New York: Cambridge University press.
Jacobs, Neil G. 1996. On the investigation of 1920s Vienna Jewish speech: Ideology and linguistics. *Journal of Germanic Linguistics* 8(2). 177–217.
Jacobs, Neil G. 2005. *Yiddish: A linguistic introduction*. Cambridge: Cambridge University Press.
Johnstone, Barbara, Jennifer Andrus, & Andrew E. Danielson. 2006. Mobility, indexicality, and the enregisterment of "Pittsburghese". *Journal of English Linguistics* 34(2). 77–104.
Kahn, Lily & Aaron D. Rubin (eds.). 2016. *Handbook of Jewish languages*. Leiden: Brill.
Katz, Dovid. 2004. *Words on fire: The unfinished story of Yiddish*. New York: Basic Books.
Kenrick, Donald. 2007. *Historical dictionary of the Gypsies (Romanies)*. Lanham: Scarecrow Press.
Kloss, Heinz. 1967. Abstand-languages and Ausbau-languages. *Anthropological Linguistics* 9. 29–41.
Krauss, Michael. 1991. *Endangered languages*. Paper presented at the Linguistic Society of America annual meeting.
Labov, William. 1962. The social motivation of a sound change. *Word* 19. 273–309.
Labov, William. 1966. *The social stratification of English in New York City*. Washington, DC: Center for Applied Linguistics.
Labov, William. 2008. Unendangered dialects, endangered people. In Kendall A. King, Natalie Schilling-Estes, Lyn Fogle, Jia Jackie Lou & Barbara Soukup (eds.), *Sustaining linguistic diversity: Endangered and minority languages and language varieties (Georgetown University round table on languages and linguistics)*, 219–238. Washington, DC: Georgetown University Press.
Laskier, Michael M. 2012. *The Alliance Israélite Universelle and the Jewish communities of Morocco, 1862–1962*, vol. 45. New York: SUNY Press.
Lewis, M. Paul, Gary F. Simons, and Charles D. Fennig (eds.). 2013. *Ethnologue*, 17th edn. Dallas: SIL International.
Matras, Yaron. 2002. *Romani: A linguistic introduction*. Cambridge: Cambridge University Press.
May, S. 2009. *Pasifika languages strategy: Key issues*. Wellington: Pasifika Languages Strategy, Ministry of Pacific Island Affairs.
Mieses, Matthias. 1915. *Die Entstehungsursache der jüdeschen Dialekte*. Vienna: R. Lőwit.
Miller, Elaine Rebecca. 2000. *Jewish multiglossia: Hebrew, Arabic, & Castilian in Medieval Spain*. Newark: Linguatext.
Moseley, Christopher (ed.). 2001. *Encyclopedia of the world's endangered languages*. Richmond, Surrey: Curzon Press.

Neusner, Jacob. 2008. *A history of the Jews in Babylonia, Part V: Later Sasanian times*, vol. 5. Eugene: Wipf and Stock Publishers.

Ó Laoire, Muiris. 1999. *Athbheochan na heabhraise: Ceacht don Ghaeilge?* [Revival of Hebrew: Example for Irish]. Baile Atha Cliath: An Clochohar Tta.

Ornan, Uzzi. 1985. Hebrew is not a Jewish language. In Joshua A. Fishman (ed.), *Readings in the sociology of Jewish languages*, 22–26. Leiden: Brill.

Pilowsky, Arye L. 1985. Yiddish alongside the revival of Hebrew: Public polemics on the status of Yiddish in Eretz Israel, 1907–1929. In Joshua A. Fishman (ed.), *Readings in the sociology of Jewish languages*, 104–124. Leiden: Brill.

Pittman, Richard S. (ed.). 1969. *Ethnologue: Languages of the world*. Dallas: Summer Institute of Linguistics.

Preston, Dennis R. (ed.). 1999. *Handbook of perceptual dialectology*. Amsterdam & Philadelphia: John Benjamins.

Rabin, Chaim. 1981. What constitutes a Jewish language? *International Journal of the Sociology of Language 30*. 19–28.

Sacks, Oliver. 2009. *Seeing voices: A journey into the world of the deaf*. London: Pan Macmillan.

Shandler, Jeffrey. 2002. Shopping for Yiddish in Boro Park. *Pakn Treger* 40. 21–27.

Shandler, Jeffey. 2006. *Adventures in Yiddishland: Postvernacular language and culture*. Berkeley: University of California Press.

Shneer, David. 2004. *Yiddish and the creation of Soviet Jewish culture: 1918–1930*. Cambridge: Cambridge University Press.

Shohamy, Elana. 2007. At what cost? Methods of language revival and protection: Examples from Hebrew. In Kendall A. King, Natalie Schilling-Estes, Jia Jackie Lou, Lyn Fogle & Barbara Soukup (eds.), *Endangered and minority languages and language varieties: Defining, documenting and developing*. Washington, DC: Georgetown University.

Spolsky, Bernard. 1985. Jewish multilingualism in the first century: An essay in historical sociolinguistics. In Joshua A. Fishman (ed.), *Readings in the sociology of Jewish languages*, 35–50. Leiden: Brill.

Spolsky, Bernard. 1997. Multilingualism in Israel. In William Grabe (ed.), *Annual review of applied linguistics*, vol. 17, 138–150. Cambridge: Cambridge University Press.

Spolsky, Bernard. 2007. The dynamics of the revival of Hebrew. Paper presented at the Symposium Framework on the social history of Basque at the Royal Academy of the Basque Language, Donastia/San Sebastian.

Spolsky, Bernard. 2008. Prolegomena to a sociolinguistic theory of public signage. In Elana Shohamy & Durk Gorter (eds.), *The linguistic landscape: Expanding the scenery*. London: Routledge.

Spolsky, Bernard. 2009. Language beliefs and the management of endangered languages. Paper presented at the Endangered language project workshop on beliefs and ideology in endangered languages, Department of Linguistics SOAS.

Spolsky, Bernard. 2010. Jewish religious multilingualism. In Tope Omoniyi (ed.), *The sociology of language and religion: Change, conflict and accommodation*, 14–28. Basingstoke: Palgrave Macmillan.

Spolsky, Bernard. 2011. Ferguson and Fishman: Sociolinguistics and the sociology of language. In Ruth Wodak, Barbara Johnstone & Paul Kerswill (eds.), *The Sage handbook of sociolinguistics*, 11–23. London: Sage Publications.

Spolsky, Bernard. 2014. *The languages of the Jews: A sociolinguistic history*. Cambridge: Cambridge University Press.
Spolsky, Bernard, Ofra Inbar-Lourie, & Michal Tannenbaum (eds.). 2014. *Challenges for language education and policy: Making space for people*. London: Routledge.
Spolsky, Bernard, & Elana Shohamy. 1999. *The languages of Israel: Policy, ideology and practice*. Clevedon: Multilingual Matters.
Stein, Sarah Abrevaya. 2006. Asymmetric fates: Secular Yiddish and Ladino culture in comparison. *Jewish Quarterly Review* 96(4). 498–509.
Stewart, William. 1968. A sociolinguistic typology for describing national multilingualism. In Joshua A. Fishman (ed.), *Readings in the sociology of language*, 531–545. The Hague: Mouton.
Tabouret-Keller, Andrée. 1968. Sociological factors of language maintenance and language shift: A methodological approach based on European and African examples. In Joshua A. Fishman, Charles Albert Ferguson & Jyotirindra Das Gupta (eds.), *Language problems of developing nations*, 107–127. New York: John Wiley and Sons.
Tannen, Deborah. 1981. New York Jewish conversational style. *International Journal of the Sociology of Language* 30. 133–149.
Thomas, Charles K. 1932. Jewish dialect and New York dialect. *American Speech* 17. 321–326.
Thomas, Erik R. & Jeffrey Reaser. 2004. Delimiting perceptual cues used for the ethnic labeling of African American and European American voices. *Journal Sociolinguistics* 8(1). 54–87.
Trudgill, Peter. 1992. Ausbau sociolinguistics and the perception of language status in contemporary Europe. *International Journal of Applied Linguistics* 2(2). 167–177.
United States Census Bureau. 2015. "Detailed Languages Spoken at Home and Ability to Speak English for the Population 5 Years and Over: 2009–2013." American Community Survey. U.S. Census Bureau. https://www.census.gov/data/tables/2013/demo/2009-2013-lang-tables.html (accessed 6 October, 2016).
Weinreich, Max. 1945. Der YIVO un di problemen fun undzer tsayt [YIVO and the problems of our time]. *YIVO-Bleter* 25(1). 3–18.
Weinreich, Max, Joshua A. Fishman, Shlomo Noble (trans.). 1980. *History of the Yiddish language*. Chicago: University of Chicago Press.
Weinreich, Max, Shlomo Noble, Joshua A. Fishman, Paul Glasser (trans.). 2008. *History of the Yiddish language*. New Haven & London: Yale University Press.
Weinreich, Uriel. 1953. *Languages in contact: Findings and problems*. New York: Linguistic Circle of New York.
Weiser, Keith Ian. 2011. *Jewish people, Yiddish nation: Noah Prylucki and the folkists in Poland*: University of Toronto Press.
ʽÔdēd, Bûstenây. 1979. *Mass deportations and deportees in the Neo-Assyrian Empire*. Wiesbaden: Reichert.

Peter T. Daniels
Uses of Hebrew Script in Jewish Language Varieties

Kahn and Rubin's (2015) *Handbook of Jewish Languages*[1] is an impressive accomplishment, bringing together descriptions, in comparable formats, of nearly every distinctive language form that has been used by Jewish communities around the world, including some that have not usually been recognized in this context. The social situations of those communities are described, as well as the (usually written) sources of data that are available. The editors have helpfully introduced a terminological distinction between "Judeo-X" and "Jewish X" (where X is the name of a language), with the former identifying languages written with Hebrew script and the latter reserved for those written in the language's standard orthography (or in a few cases, with no written form). There is no overall treatment of the adaptation of Hebrew script to the wide variety of languages discussed, but sufficient data are presented on each language for the question to be asked whether general principles, or at least trends, or commonalities, can be observed in those adaptations, and that is the purpose of this chapter.

1 Semitic languages

1.1 Before Hebrew

In the absence of a chapter on the original "Jewish language," Hebrew, to serve as a baseline for later developments, the essentials are presented here (cf. Daniels 2013a). The earliest West Semitic signary comprised 27 or 28 letters, one for each consonant of Proto-Semitic, inspired by Egyptian hieroglyphic writing. It is attested in a handful of brief inscriptions whose letters retain some of the pictographic nature of their models (Naveh 1987; Sass 1988; Hamilton 2006), but the earliest sizable corpus

---

[1] This chapter originated as a review article of L. Kahn and A. D. Rubin, eds., *Handbook of Jewish Languages* (2015); it will have appeared in somewhat different form in *Written Language and Literacy*. Citations to authors without explicit references refer to their contributions in that volume; the author has not had access to any of the contributions to the present volume. This chapter has benefited greatly from the comments of the editors and of several other friends and colleagues mentioned at appropriate places in the text.

https://doi.org/10.1515/9781501504631-023

in a West Semitic script is the Ugaritic texts (Bordreuil and Pardee 2009), whose letters (relatable in shape to the contemporary "linear" forms) are impressed with the corner of a stylus onto a damp clay surface, imitating the technique but not the forms of Mesopotamian cuneiform characters. The majority of Ugaritic clay tablets survive because they were caught in the conflagration that destroyed the city, probably in 1185 BCE. A few that were deemed worthy of preservation by their scribes were found in kilns where they were to be baked like pottery for permanency.

Extensive literary texts were among the first to be discovered, in 1929 at Ras Shamra near the Syrian coast north of Lebanon, and by 1931 the decipherment of the script was essentially complete (Daniels in press b). Scholars discovered that Ugaritic religious poetry was astonishingly like the poetic forms found in the Hebrew Scriptures, involving "parallel structures" and familiar word pairs – but unlike them in an unfamiliar orthographic technique: like the Phoenician texts first attested from about two centuries later, the Ugaritic texts provide no indication of the vowels used in the language.[2] Stanley Gevirtz (1961) noticed that a reasonable emendation (from 𐎗 ḫ to 𐎊 y) in a passage in the Kirta epic (KTU 1.16 i 26–28)[3] yielded a striking parallel to the verse Jeremiah 8:23 (9:1 in English versions) (Table 1): the four central, cognate, words appear in the two texts in opposite orders, making this passage especially apposite for illustrating the unfamiliar (Ugaritic) and familiar (Hebrew) orthographic feature, namely, the use of *matres lectionis* 'mothers of reading' (Latin, a calque of the Hebrew expression אֵם קְרִיאָה *ēm qərîʔâ*). Compare Ug. *qr* with Heb. *mqwr* (*m-* is a nominal preformative), Ug. *ûdmʕt* (*ŭ-* indicates a "broken plural" inflection) with Heb. *dmʕh* (the case marker **i* and the *t-* "consonantal glide" [according to Gelb 1969] were lost, leaving *ā*). Most revealing is the difference between Ug. *rîšk* 'thy head' and Heb. *rʔšy* 'my head', with the first person possessive pronoun spelled י- *y*. As is shown by Ug. *bn*, where the context permits no other reading than 'my son', i.e., **binî*, the *ī* has no expression whatsoever in the text but must be supplied by the reader.

The Ugaritic script may have been in use for as little as a century or less (Bordreuil and Pardee 2009: 19), and there are minimal, if any, indications of incipient use of *matres* (Tropper 2000: 50–56 §§ 21.341–342 greeted with considerable skepticism by Pardee 2003–2004: 28–29, 33–35). Phoenician, however, continued for nearly a millennium and a half and did not employ any

---

[2] With the unique exception that /ʔ/ has three letters according as it is followed by /a/, /i/ or no vowel, or /u/, transliterated *ă ĭ ŭ* respectively.

[3] Known to earlier generations of researchers by the number assigned in Cyrus Gordon's series (beginning in 1940) of *Ugaritic Grammar/Handbook/Manual/Textbook* (1965) as 125:26–28. I thank Mark S. Smith for assistance with this topic.

Table 1: Parallel passages in Ugaritic and Hebrew.

	Ugaritic text	Transliteration	Transliteration	Conjectural vocalization	Translation
KTU 1.16 i 26–28	[cuneiform]	אל תכל : בן קר : ענך מי : ראשך אדמעת	⟨ảl tkl.bn qr.ʕnk. myʰ.rišk ủdmʕt⟩	(ʔal tukalli binî) qōra ʕēnika mēya raʔšika udmaʕāti	'(Do not empty, my son,) the fount of thine eye, the water¹ of thy head with tears.'¹
	Hebrew text	**Masoretic text**	**Transliteration**	**Masoretic vocalization**	**Translation**
Jeremiah 8:23	מי יתן ראשי מים ועני מקור דמעה	מִי־יִתֵּן רֹאשִׁי מַיִם וְעֵינִי מְקוֹר דִּמְעָה	⟨my ytn rʔšy mym wʕny mqwr dmʕh⟩	(mî-yittēn) rôšî máyim wəʕēnî maqôr dimʕâ	'(Who can make) my head waters and my eyes a fount of tears?'²

Notes:
¹ Gevirtz's translation. Compare 'Do not empty out, my son, the fountain of your eyes, the water from your head, your tears' (Pardee 1997: 339b).
² Translation after Lundbom 1999: 535; Lundbom explains (537) that *mî-yittēn* "expresses a wish contrary to fact" in a number of biblical passages, accounting for the traditional rendering 'O that my head were waters …'.

indication of vowels before the Late Punic period, when, presumably in imitation of Latin and/or Greek, some were notated in an alphabetic fashion. Thus either the strength of tradition prevailed, or scribes never felt a deficiency in vowelless writing.

1.2 Hebrew

The earliest known inscription that some have claimed to be Archaic Hebrew, the Qeiyafa Ostracon, exhibits no *matres*.[4] It is epigraphically dated to shortly before the turn of the first millennium BCE, or around 1100 BCE, earlier than any known Phoenician inscription. *Matres* are not found in the earliest Hebrew texts, such as the Gezer Calendar (late 10th century?). The interpretation set forth in Cross and Freedman 1952: 58–60, based on the analysis of their teacher Albright (1943:

---

[4] Rollston 2011 includes various transliterations and interpretations that had been proposed since the text's discovery in 2008.

24), has (with modifications from Kutscher 1970: 349–50 on the basis of new epigraphic discoveries) stood the test of time. The Gezer calendar enumerates months by twos and ones. ירחו must mean 'his two months' and ירח 'his month' (with no expression of the possessive, as seen in Ug. בן), respectively *yarḥēw and *yarḥō; ו- could not represent ō in part because when, subsequently, ō received a *mater*, it was ה-.

> The general development of *matres lectionis* seems to have been along these lines. In the case of י and ו, they first were used in the final position to represent ī and ū respectively. After a considerable period, their use was extended to the medial position, with the same values. During the same period, the diphthongs *aw* and *ay* also were represented by ו and י. When these diphthongs were contracted, the ו and י were retained in the spelling, and they became signs for ô and ê. (The preservation of these signs medially after the contraction of the diphthong, would only take place after the introduction of medial *matres lectionis* generally; in earlier times, the ו or י dropped out when the diphthong was contracted.) The next stage in the use of these *matres lectionis* was the extension of the ו for ô to the final position, where the ô formerly was represented by ה. This unquestionably was a post-monarchic development, since 1) the diphthongs *ay* and *aw* were not yet contracted in Judahite, 2) there is not a single instance of ו = ô in any pre-exilic Hebrew inscription. (Cross and Freedman 1952: 52 n. 37 [letter names replaced with Hebrew letters])

Similarly, after quiescence of final /ʔ/, א- displaced ה- as the *mater* for *ā*, especially in Aramaic.

Matres are found in the earliest Aramaic inscriptions, both those that were available to Cross and Freedman, on which their historical analysis was based, and in earlier ones that were discovered subsequently, notably the earliest known, the bilingual Fekheriye inscription dating to the middle of the ninth c. BCE, where *matres* already occur both word-finally and word-medially (Abou-Assaf, Bordreuil, and Millard 1982: 39–42). It seems not unlikely that Hebrew scribes learned to appreciate and use *matres* from the cosmopolitan Aramaic scribes they presumably came into diplomatic contact with. Hebrew final *matres* begin to appear in the early eighth c. (Samaria ostraca), medial in the early sixth c. (a couple of possible examples in the Lachish letters, dated to the eve of the Exile; Cross and Freedman 1952: 49, 54–56 ## 60, 76, 96).

Texts belonging to the three known scribal traditions regarding the Hebrew Scriptures have been identified among the Dead Sea Scrolls (DSS), which began to come to light in 1947: (a) that underlying the Greek translation known as the Septuagint ("LXX") that dates to the mid third c. BCE; (b) the consonantal basis of the Masoretic Text ("MT") that was provided with vowel indications by several schools of Masoretes, textual scholars, in the mid first millennium CE (the school that prevailed was that of Tiberias, in the Galilee, hence the name "Tiberian Hebrew" for the standard language); and (c) the tradition preserved in the

Samaritan Pentateuch.[5] A surprise appeared with the first Scroll to be examined, the "Isaiah Scroll" from Cave I at Qumran (1 Q Isaᵃ). The text is largely the same in content as the MT, but uses appreciably more *matres*. An intriguing suggestion regarding the reason for the increased use of *matres* is found in Kutscher 1974: 20–23, "Spelling – an Aid to Hebrew–Aramaic Differentiation": not because it was difficult to read a minimally voweled Hebrew text, but because Aramaic and Hebrew words spelled the same could be vocalized differently. This, he says, is

> why we constantly find לא = לוא lest the word be read as לָא, יאמר = יואמר lest it be pronounced יֵאמַר (Aramaic); יוכל to obviate the Aramaistic reading יֵאכַל and רואש for ראוש because of the similar Aramaic word רֵאשׁ.[6] (20)

1.3 Aramaic

It is with the variety of Aramaic used by a Jewish community in southern Egypt – at the island of Elephantine – a few centuries before the DSS, in the later fifth c. BCE, that the study of Jewish language varieties begins. As authors have so often been asked to do in surveys of Semitic languages, Steven Fassberg compresses some 2500 years of attested Judeo-Aramaic into a single chapter.[7] Within the usual five-period subdivision of the Aramaic languages,[8] Fassberg (disregarding the pre-Jewish Old Aramaic that provided much of the data for Cross and Freedman) treats no less than

---

5 Tov (1982) cautions that this pre-DSS partition of the recensions is inadequate in view of the variety of manuscripts found at Qumran: in addition to texts that can be assigned to one or another of the traditions, there are texts intermediate among the traditions.

6 The Hebrew words are pronounced respectively *lô, yômer, yûḵal, rôš*; in Aramaic: *lâ, yêmar, yêḵal, rêš*. A vowel written with a *mater* is conventionally transliterated with a circumflex accent.

7 Inasmuch as the modern or "Square Hebrew" script is an Aramaic variety that replaced the Phoenician-like Old Hebrew script at the time of or in the wake of the Babylonian Exile, when the (by that time) Jewish intelligentsia lived and studied for some two generations in the Aramaic-speaking and -writing milieu of the East, Aramaic would seem to be the Judeo-language *ab initio* and *par excellence*. Recently discovered Akkadian-language evidence for such interaction is discussed in Finkel 2014, esp. ch. 11; this approach has not yet received technical treatment (M. J. Geller, personal communication, 9 June 2016).

The regional and temporal variations in Hebrew handwriting are not considered here. A wide variety of quality reproductions can be consulted in Birnbaum 1971; 1954–57. The selected articles in Birnbaum 2011a, vol. 2, deal primarily with ancient Hebrew, with a few short ones on Yiddish paleography, but Birnbaum 2011b is a previously unpublished tabulation of Jewish language varieties and the variety of scripts used to write them.

8 Gzella 2015: 48 cautions that the standard periodization, due to Fitzmyer 1966: 22–23 n. 60, expanded in Fitzmyer 1979, is based on external historical circumstances and proposes the use of subdivisions based on linguistic phenomena instead; cf. already Daniels 1980: 218–19.

ten separate corpora (though criteria for distinguishing them are not always explicit). Nothing distinctive can be observed about Elephantine orthography – but, I would note, it is in the Elephantine papyri that the "final forms" of Hebrew letters – incipient versions of ץ ף ן ם ך – can first be observed: they are likely the result of a momentary pause of the pen before leaving a space before the next word. When writing without word breaks or with word-dividers, such a pause would not be needed.

A word of caution is required regarding Biblical Aramaic, the second corpus (actually two groups, the transcripts of genuine fifth-c. official Achaemenid documents in Ezra, and second-c. Hellenistic Daniel).[9] Fassberg appears to accept the Masoretic vocalization, created some thousand years after the text was composed, as an accurate reproduction of the sounds of the language, calling the anomalies "influence of Hebrew phonology," examples including pausal lengthening (not otherwise known

---

9 The first Biblical Aramaic grammar representing the modern linguistic, or at least philological, tradition, Kautzsch 1884: 3 assigns the final redaction of Ezra to the end of the fourth c. BCE (and does not offer an opinion on the genuineness of the Aramaic documents quoted) and Daniel to 167 BCE, observing (22) that the two text-groups differ more in lexical than in grammatical details. This opinion is found also in the first pedagogical grammar, which considers the language of Ezra somewhat corrupt and bases the grammar on the Daniel text (Marti 1896: vi–vii). Strack (1905) says nothing at all about the dating of the passages and appears not to recognize differences between the two corpora (though Kautzsch 1884: 4 notes that elsewhere Strack put the book of Daniel back at least to the time of Alexander); the importance of this work is its use of manuscript sources, including some with Babylonian (i.e., non-Tiberian) Masoretic vocalization. Brockelmann (1908–13, 1: 15 § 15) matter-of-factly reports the date of Daniel as 168 or 167 BCE. Historical on top of linguistic arguments for the late dating of Daniel are found in Driver 1926. Bauer and Leander (1927: 9 § 1r) offer some differentiating morphological characteristics that developed over the three centuries or so separating the subdialects, but they are less careful about distinguishing the strata within the body of their grammar. Kutscher (1970: 400–403) reviews the arguments following Driver's publication and, adducing recently discovered inscriptions, denies that they prove a late date for Daniel. Rosenthal (1961: 5) acknowledges the different times and probably places of origin but asserts that "the language they use appears to all intents and purposes uniform, with only minor divergences." Folmer (e.g. 2012: 130) largely concurs: "Notwithstanding that the final redaction of Daniel took place in the middle of the second century BCE, considerably later than Ezra (fourth c.), Daniel Aramaic has preserved linguistic features that ultimately go back to the Achaemenid period." Kaufman (1997: 115–16), on the other hand, avers that "The Aramaic 'official' letters in the book of Ezra are almost certainly to be viewed as composed in Imperial Aramaic, for both their language and their style are appropriate to the period. ... The Aramaic portion of [Daniel] (in contrast to the material in Ezra) clearly belongs to [Middle Aramaic] rather than to Imperial Aramaic." Gzella (2015: 205–8 § 4.4.2), using a plethora of specific orthographic and linguistic details, indicates that the Aramaic portions of both Ezra and Daniel reflect both an earlier bureaucratic style and influence of contemporary language, postulating the existence of a "local literary style" to account for similarities between Aramaic Daniel and contemporary literary compositions, including sectarian DSS and Targums Onqelos and Jonathan, an approach taken with more nuance by Greenfield 1974. Creason 2004 does not consider Biblical Aramaic.

in Aramaic) and segolization (but segolization itself – e.g., מֶלֶךְ *mélek̲* for **malk* 'king', so called from the name *segol* of the symbol for the vowel /ɛ/ – is widely understood as the Masoretes' record of their inability to articulate a word-final consonant cluster). Instead, Biblical Aramaic vocalization should be reconstructed on the basis of the meager evidence from contemporary transcriptions in scripts that specify vowels, and plausible historical retrojection. Compare the Masoretic vocalization[10] of Daniel 7:9//14 with the probable contemporary vocalization as reconstructed by Beyer (2013: 21).[11]

⁹ חָזֵה הֲוֵית עַד דִּי כָרְסָוָן רְמִיו וְעַתִּיק יוֹמִין יְתִב לְבוּשֵׁהּ כִּתְלַג חִוָּר וּשְׂעַר רֵאשֵׁהּ כַּעֲמַר נְקֵא כָּרְסְיֵהּ שְׁבִיבִין דִּי־נוּר גַּלְגִּלּוֹהִי נוּר דָּלִק: ¹⁰ נְהַר דִּי־נוּר נָגֵד וְנָפֵק מִן־קֳדָמוֹהִי אֶלֶף אַלְפִין (כתיב אַלְפִים) יְשַׁמְּשׁוּנֵּהּ וְרִבּוֹ רִבְבָן קָדָמוֹהִי יְקוּמוּן דִּינָא יְתִב וְסִפְרִין פְּתִיחוּ: ... ¹³ חָזֵה הֲוֵית בְּחֶזְוֵי לֵילְיָא וַאֲרוּ עִם־עֲנָנֵי שְׁמַיָּא כְּבַר אֱנָשׁ אָתֵה הֲוָה וְעַד־עַתִּיק יוֹמַיָּא מְטָה וּקְדָמוֹהִי הַקְרְבוּהִי: ¹⁴ וְלֵהּ יְהִב שָׁלְטָן וִיקָר וּמַלְכוּ וְכֹל עַמְמַיָּא אֻמַּיָּא וְלִשָּׁנַיָּא לֵהּ יִפְלְחוּן שָׁלְטָנֵהּ שָׁלְטָן עָלַם דִּי־לָא יֶעְדֵּה וּמַלְכוּתֵהּ דִּי־לָא תִתְחַבַּל:

⁹ ḥəzē hăwêt̲ ʿad dî k̲ɔrsɔwɔ̄n rəmîw wə-ʿattîq yômîn yət̲ib̲ lə-b̲ûšeh kit̲lɔḡ ḥiwwɔr uśaʿar rêšeh kaʿamar nəqē k̲ɔrsəyeh šəb̲îb̲în dî-nûr galgillôhî nûr dɔliq. ¹⁰ nəhar dî-nûr nɔḡēd̲ wən-ɔp̲ēq min-qɔd̲môhî ʾɛlep̲ ʾaləp̲în[12] yəšamməšŭnneh wəribbô rib̲wɔn qɔd̲môhî yəqûmûn dînɔ yət̲ib̲ wəsip̲rîn pət̲îḥû. ... ¹³ ḥəzē hăwêt̲ bəḥezwê lêləyɔ waʾărû ʾim-ʿănɔnê šəmayyɔ kəb̲ar ʾɛnɔš ʾɔt̲ê hăwɔ wə-ʿad̲-ʿattîq yômayyɔ̄ maṭɔ ûqəd̲ɔmôhî haqrəb̲ûhî. ¹⁴ wəleh yəhib̲ šolṭɔn wîqɔr ûmələk̲û wək̲ol ʿaməmayyɔ̄ ʿummayyɔ̄ wəliššɔnayyɔ̄ leh yip̲ləḥûn šɔlṭɔneh šɔlṭɔn ʿɔlam dî-lɔ yeʿdê ûmalk̲ût̲eh[13] dî-lɔ tit̲ḥabbal. (MT)

⁹ ḥăzē hawḗt̲ʰ ʿàd dī kʰorsawān ramīw wa-ʿattʰīq yōmīn yatʰáb̲ lab̲ūšéh kʰa-tʰáleg ḥewwār wa-śàʿar rēšéh kʰa-ʿàmar neqḗ kʰorsiyéh šab̲ībīn dī nūr galgalôhī nūr dāleq ¹⁰ nahār dī nūr nagád̲ wa-nap̲ʰáq mèn qodāmôhī ʾáləpʰ ʾaləpʰín yešammešunnéh wa-rebbó̲ rebbawán qodāmôhī yaqūmūn dīnā yatʰáb̲ wa-sep̲ʰarīn pʰatʰīhū ... ¹³ ḥăzē hawḗtʰ ba-ḥezawḕ lēliyā wa-ʾárū ʾèm ʿanānḕ šammayyā kʰa-b̲ar ʾenāś́ ʾā́tʰḗ hawā́ wa-ʿàd̲ ʿattʰīq yōmayyā maṭā́ wa-qodāmôhī ʾaqrəb̲ū́hī ¹⁴ wa-leh yahī́b̲ šolṭā́n wa-yaqā́r wa-malkʰū́ wa-kʰòl ʿamamayyā́ ʾommayyā́ wa-leššānayyā́ leh yepʰloḥū́n šolṭānéh šolṭān ʿālám dī lā yeʿdḗ wa-malkʰūtʰéh <malkʰū́> dī lā tʰetʰabbā́l. (Beyer)

'⁹ As I watched, thrones were set in place, and an Ancient of Days took his throne, his clothing was white as snow, and the hair of his head like pure wool; his throne was fiery flames, and its wheels were burning fire. ¹⁰ A stream of fire issued and flowed out from his presence. A thousand thousands served him, and ten thousand times ten thousand stood attending him, the court sat in judgment, and the books were opened. ... ¹³ As I watched in the night visions, I saw one like a son of man coming with the clouds of heaven. And he came to the Ancient of Days and was presented before him. ¹⁴ To him was given dominion and glory and kingship, that all

---

10 My transliterations are based on those of Meyer 1966–1972: any of the Masoretic vowels can be long in an open syllable, short in a closed syllable; the circumflex accent indicates presence of a *mater lectionis*; the acute accent marks a stressed syllable that is non-final; under- or over-bars note the spirantized (fricative) pronunciation of the stops.
11 I am grateful to Holger Gzella for assistance with this topic.
12 Corrected in the margin from the consonantal text's *ʾaləp̲îm*.
13 *malk̲û* is a conjectural emendation.

peoples, nations, and languages should serve him. His dominion is an everlasting dominion that shall not pass away, and his kingship is one that shall never be destroyed.' (NRSV)

Among the many Hebraisms introduced (not into the language, but) into the pointing are: postvocalic spirantization of all stops, vs. aspiration of only voiceless stops (Beyer applies spirantization in the Bar Kokba letters dated some 300 years later); leveling of various /ā/s, /o/s, and /u/s to /ɔ/ (the vowel indicated by *qameṣ*); allomorphy *û-* ~ *wə-* for *wa-* 'and'; and a number of stress-conditioned vowel reductions.

A few pages on, Fassberg describes the same situation with regard to manuscripts of Targums Onqelos and Jonathan somewhat differently and more satisfactorily:[14]

> Hebrew pointing rules appear to varying degrees in different manuscripts: the rules of Hebrew pretonic and tonic lengthening as well as shortening of long vowels in closed syllables sometimes apply in Tiberian manuscripts: .... There are also Hebraisms that are not scribal mistakes ....

Fassberg's large assortment of examples from those many Judeo-Aramaic corpora show that the use of *matres* barely changed over the centuries. In his example of a "magic bowl" from Mesopotamia, from the second half of the first millennium CE, some final -*â*'s are written with ה-, others still with א-. This might reflect colloquial use (innovation seems more likely than conservatism) in contrast to the literary texts that are more familiar to modern scholars.[15]

---

14 Goshen-Gottstein (1973: viii) suggests that because Christian Palestinian Aramaic emerged in the same dialect milieu as Jewish Palestinian Aramaic, we might look to this targumic language for parallels and distinctive components. As regards orthography, though, this (West Aramaic) language of the Melkite offshoot of Syriac Christianity (written with a form of Syriac script) exhibits features more like those of the (East Aramaic) Syriac of the church, described in great detail in Müller-Kessler 1991: 29–47 §§ 2.2–2.10. Goshen-Gottstein 1973 presents his text in Hebrew transliteration, Müller-Kessler and Sokoloff 1997 (etc.) in the distinctive script (cf. n. 17).

15 The very common magic bowls or "incantation bowls" that warded off demons in many parts of Mesopotamia were inscribed, in ink on the inside, spiraling outward, in Jewish Babylonian Aramaic, Mandaic, or (Iranian) Pahlavi; some are inscribed with writing-like scrawls, showing that their efficacy lay not in their message but in the act of inscription, presumably along with the recital of the incantations contained or supposedly contained. Mandaic is of special interest because its orthography is nearly fully alphabetic (Daniels 1996; Burtea 2011). The vowel letters are not *matres* because they no longer have any consonantal reading; Häberl (2006: 60–61) attributes their use not to an inherited Aramaic tradition, but to the orthography of the Parthian writing system (which developed out of *matres*-using Aramaic; Henning 1958: 61–63 § 22) from which he derives the Mandaic lettershapes. It is noteworthy that the three letters for vowels, historically *alep̄*, *waw*, and *yod̲*, are smaller than any of the consonant letters, a feature obscured when Mandaic is presented in Hebrew-script transliteration as in the magisterial grammar Nöldeke 1875 and often since. I thank Charles G. Häberl for discussion of this topic, who observes moreover that many of the names in the Mandaic bowls are Iranian.

Nearly a thousand years later, we have a few precious texts written in Modern Aramaic in the mid 17th century, in a Jewish community in western Iraqi Kurdistan. The orthography is unusual in that nearly every medial *u* (long or short) is written with -ו- and even a few medial *ā*'s are written with -א-. The influence of Arabic orthography might be suspected – except that there, *all* (and only) long vowels are notated with *matres*. Is it inconceivable to suggest that literate Jews might have had some exposure to the literature of their fellow-Aramaic-speaking Christians, which was written in Syriac, their East Aramaic literary language, which shows kinship with Babylonian Jewish Aramaic, in its own distinctive script with the same 22 letters as Hebrew/Jewish Aramaic? A distinctive feature of Syriac orthography is that every *ŭ* (except in the two common particles *kul* 'all' and *metul* 'because') is written with the equivalent of -ו-.[16]

A curious pendant to Judeo-Aramaic is the brief treatment of Judeo-Syriac by Siam Bhayro. A single Cairo Geniza leaf from a medical treatise is said to represent this language on the sole basis of the use of י- instead of א- for word-final -*ê* (if there are any other criteria, they are not stated). A few quotations from the Syriac Bible, the Peshiṭta, were cited/translated into Judeo-Aramaic by Jewish sages, and they show the same alteration. The existence, however marginal, of this phenomenon lends credence to my parallel suggestion as to the influence of Syriac on 17th-century orthography.

1.4 Arabic

What, then, of the third great Jewish Semitic language, Judeo-Arabic? The Arabic script developed from that of Nabataean Aramaic (Gruendler 1993),[17] taking over

---

16 The Modern Aramaic written language, developed as a pan-dialectal koine by American Protestant missionaries, beginning in 1836 and culminating in the Bible translation published at Urmia in 1852, uses the Eastern (mistakenly called "Nestorian") form of the Syriac script and etymologizing orthography. It is fairly generous with *matres* but, unlike in Classical Syriac, Hebrew, and Arabic, the vowel pointing is obligatory. The output of the missionary press provided the basis for the description of the language, first by Stoddard 1856, then definitively by Nöldeke 1868, though Nöldeke transliterates the Modern Syriac into the more familiar western *Serṭo* script. The first comprehensive grammar and dictionary of Vernacular Syriac, by an English Anglican missionary, improve a bit on the American missionary orthography and include instructions on interpreting it for various of the dialects covered (Maclean 1895; 1901). Generally, the plethora of linguistic grammars of individual dialects that have appeared over the decades since use phonological transcriptions only; the few primers for small children use orthography only or orthography with Roman transcription.
17 Earlier arguments that Arabic script derived from Syriac script can no longer be sustained (Daniels 2013b: 422, with references).

matres for long (only) *ī* and *ū*. Long (only) *ā* now received a *mater*, the letter that originally represented *ʔ, but not by inheritance from Aramaic; it reflects the loss within Arabic of *ʔ and compensatory lengthening of an adjacent *ă* (Diem 1976; 1979–1983).

For the first time we encounter a Jewish language variety for which the consonant inventory of Hebrew script is inadequate: beside the 22 Phoenician letters that had to suffice for Aramaic and Hebrew,[18] Arabic had had to innovate 6 additional letters (compare Ugaritic) for consonants that remained stubbornly distinct. The earliest scribes – the system was already in place in the first decades of Islam, ca. 640 CE – worked out a system for *etymologically*, rather than phonetically, deriving new letters by adding dots to appropriate letters: ت *t* → ث *ṯ*, د *d* → ذ *ḏ*, ص *ṣ* → ض *ḍ*, ط *ṭ* → ظ *ẓ*, ح *ḥ* → خ *ḫ*, ع *ʕ* → غ *ġ* (Daniels 2013c: 64, 2000: 81–82). These were above and beyond the cases where letterforms had become uncomfortably similar within Nabataean/Proto-Arabic, and in nine cases dots were added to differentiate them: ب *b* ت *t* ن *n* ي *y*, ح *ḥ* ج *ǧ*, ر *r* ز *z*, س *s* ش *š*,[19] ف *f* ق *q*. Judeo-Arabic has no problem with the second group, since no Square Hebrew letters had converged sufficiently for confusion. The first, etymological, group, however, presented a dilemma.

Geoffrey Khan divides the use of the language into three periods: Early, before the early 10th c.; Classical, 10th–15th c.; and Late, after the 15th c. Early Judeo-Arabic orthography is phonetic, following the principles of Rabbinic Hebrew and Aramaic, including omission of א for *ā* and use of י and ו for both short and long *i u*, and sometimes וו for *w*; for the additional consonants Khan notes that the letter for the phonetically closest consonant is used, adducing עדה = عظة *ʕiẓah* 'admonition' but a few lines later citing עידת אלחיאה = عظة الحياة *ʕiẓat al-ḥayāh* 'the admonition of life' (with dotted *daleṯ*). Early Judeo-Arabic texts occasionally received Tiberian pointing.[20]

Classical Judeo-Arabic adopts Classical Arabic orthography: compare EJA סלם, CIJA סלאם = سلام *salām* 'greeting', EJA אלחיכמה, CIJA אלחכמה = الحكمة *al-ḥikma*

---

[18] At least into the third c. BCE when the LXX was written, Hebrew still distinguished *ḥ* and *ḫ*, *ʕ* and *ġ*, for though the members of each pair are written with ח and ע respectively, those consonants are spelled differently in Greek transcriptions containing them (Meyer 1966–1972: §§4.3a, 22.3c–d).

[19] Various reasons have been suggested for the non-importation of the Nabataean letter for *s*.

[20] Regarding one of the first examples to come to light, Blau (1981: 225 ad 34–35) suggested that "the writer was well aware that his spelling was uncustomary [i.e., deviating from Classical Arabic]. For this reason, it seems, he vocalized his letter completely; he realized that otherwise it would be unintelligible." Blau and Hopkins (1984) describe the differences between Early and Classical Judeo-Arabic orthography, but largely in terms of *deviation* of Early from Classical.

'wisdom'; -ā spelled with *alif maqṣūra* (a dotless form of *yā'*) now appears as ײַ: אלי = الى *ilā* 'to'. The additional consonants are now spelled etymologically for the most part, with dots over the respective Hebrew letters, so that *'iẓah* is now עטה – but so is *'iẓat*, for the *tā' marbūṭa*, a morphophonological device placing the two dots of *t* on the *h* shape, is written only with ה- – but *ḥ* and *ġ* are not spelled ח̇ and ע̇ in imitation of Arabic, but כ̇ and ג̇ because *k* and *g* have postvocalic allophones [x] and [ɣ], which, however, in carefully pointed Masoretic Hebrew are written כ and ג.

Finally, Late Judeo-Arabic reverts to the Rabbinic model in preference to the Arabic model, for instance in spelling *-ā* with ה-: אלה *ilā* 'to'; short vowels with *matres*: איבני for ابنى *ibni* 'my son', קולת for قلت *qult* 'I said'; and semivowels with digraphs: בוואליץ 'money orders', бייאנהום 'their specification', cf. Modern Cairene *bawalīṣ*, *bayanhum* respectively.[21]

These languages, then, provide the three sources that we may assume were the models as Hebrew script came to be adopted to vernaculars in Europe and Asia. We now turn to Indo-European.

2 Indo-European languages

2.1 Greek

Literary Jewish Greek is represented by sizable corpora such as the LXX and the writings of Philo of Alexandria and Josephus. The Cairo Geniza yielded a few scraps of Judeo-Greek, and the Ottoman era saw a trickle of Judeo-Greek through the 19th c. Julia G. Krivoruchko offers one sample from each of those groups; both are vocalized. The first words of the Geniza passage (Qoh 2:18), וּגֵי כָּאמִישְׁשָׂא אֶגוֹ = καὶ ἐμίσησα ἐγὼ 'and I hated', show that *šin* not *samek* is used for the voiceless sibilant, that lenition of Gk. /g/ was noteworthy, and that the point for *i* was not needed when the *mater* י was present but that for *o* ו was; unpointed ו corresponds to ου *u*. The "early modern" hymn text begins טְרֵימִי אָיִיס אַפּוֹמְפְּרוֹסְטָסוּ = Τρέμει ἡ γῆς ἀπὸ μπροστά σου 'The land shakes in front of You'. ו *u* is now pointed, /g/ or [ɣ] is swallowed up between two *i*'s, the Modern Greek device of indicating a voiced stop with nasal+voiceless stop is imitated in *brosta* 'shake violently', and the collapse of the high vowels is not quite complete, as signaled by the רֵי *re*

---

21 Hary 1996: 732 refers to this stage as "Hebraized orthography."

corresponding to pε and the מִי *mi* to μει. Of significance for many other Judeo-languages, *t* appears as ט, not ת.

2.2 Iranian

As with Judeo-Aramaic, the "Judeo-Iranian" chapter must cover a broad range, some half a dozen languages – only one of which deserves the prefix, namely Judeo-Persian; virtually all literary production in the others was in Soviet-era Roman or Cyrillic print. Habib Borjian mentions a few orthographic features of Early Judeo-Persian. Only from Classical Judeo-Persian do we find text and transcription of one passage, and several texts with translation only – and, frustratingly, the longest sample in transcription but without text.

Parallel with the ט-not-ת for *t* just seen, in the oldest paleographic Judeo-Persian text yet known (eighth c. CE), which is also the earliest evidence for Modern Persian overall, ק is used for *k*;[22] but subsequently כ is used for both *k* and *x* (which is occasionally כּ, but not ח), and at the latest stage, כ/ב. The earliest Modern Persian (i.e., Arabic-script) manuscript is dated 1056 CE (Moritz 1918; Afshar 2009). We do not know when or by whom Perso-Arabic writing was devised; it took advantage of the dotting-differentiating device described above to allow for four Persian consonants not found in Arabic (پ *p* چ *č* ژ *ž* گ *g*).[23] However, when the prime Arab grammarian, Sībawayh (late eighth c.), a native speaker of Persian, needed to discuss the sound [tʃ] (i.e., *č*), he used not the Persian letter چ but circumlocution (Daniels 2014: 29). It is then possible that Early Judeo-Persian orthography applies Hebrew script to Middle Persian orthography (cf. n. 17 above and Perry 2009) – transliterating it, one might say, though not letter for letter, since the shapes of many letters had merged in the Parthian, Sassanian, and Pahlavi scripts (Skjærvø 1996) – rather than Perso-Arabic orthography. This impression is enhanced by the Early Judeo-Persian renditions of sounds not

---

[22] Note that in Ivrit (to adopt Meyer's [1966–1972] compact term for Modern Hebrew), BH *k and *q have merged as *k*, but the letters continue as morphophonemic symbols of the *k*-that-alternates-with-*x* כ versus the *k*-that-doesn't ק, and similarly for *t and *ṭ in the Ashkenazi pronunciation where ת is *s*, so that borrowed words contain ק and ט with no suggestion of "emphatic" phonetics (כּ and תּ would introduce an undesirable element of the pointing system into ordinary text). Another feature of the orthography of Ivrit that can also be found in Judeo-languages is the use of the apostrophe to mark affricates in recently borrowed words, such as ג'ורג' 'George' and מאצ'ו 'macho'.

[23] This device was then used throughout the Islamic world when scripts were devised for unwritten languages that included consonants not found in Arabic (Daniels 1997, also 2014 with tables mangled).

found in Hebrew: *č* and *ǰ* are both written with a variety of letters with or without diacritics, so that *panǰ* 'five' is spelled פנג׳, פנג׳, פנג, or [24]פנצ׳ (the last of these is consistent with Middle Persian but not with Perso-Arabic spelling); as in Hebrew, [ð], post-vocalic allophone of *d*, is sometimes written ד׳.

Information on Classical Judeo-Persian orthography is shockingly unavailable; the following summary is from an encyclopedia article.

> The main linguistic importance of classical J[udeo-]P[ersian] poetry lies in its orthography, which reveals pronunciations very similar to today's colloquial Persian. The poets take great freedom in spelling: e.g., on the one and the same page of Bābā'i ben Farhād's chronicle (18th century), one may find און *'wn* as well as אן *'n* "that" (N[ew]P[ersian]) *ān* or *un*, spelled ان *'n*), פרמון *prmwn* alongside פרמאן *frm'n* "command" (NP *fermān, fermun*, spelled فرمان *frm'n*), and בירון *byr'n* (a hypercorrection) besides בירון *byrwn* "out" (NP برن *birun*). קרבן *Qrbn* "sacrifice," rhymes with מלאון *ml'wn* "cursed." The loss of *v* from the *kv-* cluster reflects in JP spelling: e.g., כאהד *k'hd* "he/she wants" (NP *kāhad*, spelled خواهد *kv'hd*), כאב *k'b* "dream" (NP *kāb*, spelled خواب *kv'b*). In NP, the Arabic phonemes ز *z* (*zai*), ż (*żā*), ض *z̤* (*z̤āz̤*) and ذ *d* (*dāl*), all pronounced *z*, still keep their original spellings [i.e., in Arabic loanwords]. EJP usually distinguishes between them, but classical JP uses four renditions – ד *d*, ז *z*, צ *ṣ* and ט *ṭ* (mostly ז *z*) – for each of these letters, e.g., ראזי *r'zy* "satisfied" (NP راضى *r'zy*) and לחזה *lḥzh* "moment" (NP لحظه *lḥżh*). Other phonemes the copyists tend to confuse are ', *h*, *ḥ*, and ', all probably pronounced as ' (NP: ' and ' pronounced as ', *h* and *ḥ* as *h*). (Gindin 2009 [all Hebrew (*dageš* and *rape* conjectural), Arabic, and Persian characters added])

It thus appears that Judeo-Persian orthography was not influenced by Perso-Arabic orthography in the way Judeo-Arabic orthography was influenced by Arabic orthography.

2.3 Romance

Among the Romance languages, Judeo-French writings are known from the 11th to the 14th century, but with connected texts (as opposed to glosses) only from the second half of the 13th; Judeo-Occitan (better known as Judeo-Provençal) from the 12th to the 14th; Judeo-Portuguese, from the 15th century "and earlier"; Judeo-Italian, from the 15th to the 17th; and Judezmo or Ladino (Judeo-Spanish) from after the Expulsion from Spain in 1492 to the present. Thus they include the first texts in European languages to be written with Hebrew script.

Marc Kiwitt and Stephen Dürr provide an elaborate table of Judeo-French "graphemic values" (*recte* phonet/mic values) of Old French from which certain

---

24 *Sic* not using the final form ץ – perhaps a typographical error?

properties can immediately be seen. (a) *Rap̄e* is used for fricatives and not *dageš* for stops (ב *b* בֿ *v*, ג *g* גֿ *ǰ* or *ž*, ד *d* דֿ *z*, פ *p* פֿ *f*, ק *k* קֿ *č*[25] or *š*); a hachek-like diacritic is offered as an alternate for *rap̄e* in most cases but is given as the only possibility in ז *z* ז̌ *ž*[26] and נ *n* נ̌ *ñ* – but is not the sole alternative for palatals, in view of the option ל *ʎ*. (b) As elsewhere, ט and שׁ have ousted ת and ס in native words, but כ too has fallen to ק. Unsurprisingly, the French vocabulary has no need of ח or ע. (c) Full complements both of vowel letters (א, ו, and י with points) – א precedes word-initial vowel letter ו and י – and of Masoretic points are given, without indication of whether their distribution is complementary (vowel length is not phonemic). Both *qameṣ* and *pataḥ* are transcribed as *a*, but the only *qameṣ* in all the pointed examples is in the word מָרְטְרִינְשׁ (OFr *marterines*) 'wildcats' (gloss to Isa 34:14), suggesting that the *qameṣ* may have been used to indicate an [ɔ]-coloring of /a/ before /r/ – but cf. אִיקַרדוּנְשׁ *e charduns* 'and briars' (Isa 34:13, same manuscript).[27] (d) The front rounded vowels are not distinguished in writing: *y* is spelled like *u*; but the mid vowels ø œ are spelled like *o* or *u*; and ɔ is spelled like *o*. However, because no phonemic transcriptions are provided – only Judeo-French and Old French orthography – no occurrences can be identified in the examples. (e) Though צ is given as *ts* or *s*, glosses (from three different manuscripts) provide additional data: אֵישְׁטוֹפֵּיץ *estopez* 'hemorrhoids' (1Sam 5:9), אִיקַץ *e chaz* 'hyenas' (Isa 34:14, adjacent to the שׁ *s* above), פּוּרצָא *force* (i.e., [ts]) (Hos 9:4).

Additional observations by the authors are that Judeo-French orthography was to some extent both conservative and reflective of Old French orthography; and that the spelling of Old French vocabulary ultimately derives from the spelling of Greek and Latin loanwords in "Talmudic" orthography (though without specifying Mishnaic Hebrew or Palestinian or Babylonian Aramaic).[28]

The politically correct term "Judeo-Occitan"[29] is preferred by Adam Strich with George Jochnowitz, even though the latter, conforming to tradition, has

---

25 This is the Old French ⟨ch⟩ that by the time of Modern French had become *š*.
26 The table also gives *z* for ז̌; could this be dittography of "voiced alveolar fricative /z/" from the previous line?
27 *Segol* is also very sparse – the only example given is in אֵיפִּינֵשׁ *epines* 'nettles' (Isa 34:13), arguably epenthetic (cf. Lat. *spina*), but compare both אֵישְׁטוֹפֵּיץ (also epenthetic) and אִיקַרדוּנְשׁ, אִיקַץ with "real" *e* 'and' with *ṣere*.
28 Bar-Asher Siegal 2013: 37–43's presentation of Jewish Babylonian Aramaic orthography says nothing about the treatment of loanwords. I thank Eleanor Yadi, librarian of the Dorot Jewish Division, New York Public Library, for providing the relevant chapter.
29 The authors suggest that three unpointed wedding songs (Lazar 1971) may be Judeo-Catalan (and hence outside their purview – but Catalan is the other main member of Occitan), noting that a crucial bit of evidence was mistranscribed by their editor.

used "Judeo-Provençal" in his publications for decades.³⁰ While two full folios in the language are reproduced in clear photographs, there is no information at all on orthography, and only a single sentence is given with text and Old Provençal spelling: בְּנדִיג׳ טוּ שַׁנט בְּנְֶדִּיט נוֹשְׁטְרִי דֵּייב רְיי דַלשֶׁגְּלִי קִי פִּיש מִי פִּינָה *bendich tu sant benezet nost(e)re dieu rei dal seg(e)le que fis mi fen(n)a* 'blessed art thou, holy blessed one, our god, king of the epoch, who made me a woman'. From this brief passage we see that both *dageš* and *rap̄e* are used; the *shwa* seems to represent more than one color of vowel, some supported by a *mater* that differentiates them; and ש, ט, and ק have taken over for ס, ת, and כ. Most interesting is דֵּייב for *dieu*. Given that וו could represent *v* in rabbinic texts, and ב presumably does in this language, could it be a hypercorrection for a spelling דייוו or even דייו?

Devon Strolovitch provides a detailed though somewhat old-fashioned, occasionally confusing description of Judeo-Portuguese orthography (e.g., writing "the glottal fricative ה" instead of "the letter ה"), more in terms of deviations from a standard or a model than on its own terms – but this has the advantage of isolating Hebrew-, Roman-, and Arabic-script components, or subsystems, of the orthography. The familiar abandonment of כ, ת, ח, and ע is found, but ש does not replace ס; rather ש is used for "etymological" *s* (actually, where ⟨s⟩ is used in Roman orthography) and ס for *s* from other sources (actually, where ⟨c/ç⟩ are used). For *v*, there are elaborate, sometimes conflicting principles for choosing between ב (often ב׳), ו, and וו, now etymological, now phonotactic, now graphotactic. Nearly all vowels are notated with *matres*, even *a*; but there is at least some free variation: פרנטש *pr^{a}net^{a}s* ~ פראניטאש *pranetas* 'planets'.³¹ Vowel letters "in hiatus" (*recte* syllable-initial) are preceded by א, leading to odd-looking forms like ויראאוש *veraos* 'summers' and אאוטונוש *autonos* 'winters'.

From the few examples of Judeo-Italian provided by Aaron D. Rubin, we can glean that ט, ס, and ק perform as expected, and even *a* is regularly written with א; interesting are ברֵיבי *breve* '(papal) brief', יוסטי *giusti* 'just', and יוקארי *giocare* 'to play'. Where Judeo-Italian is pointed, *qameṣ* appears not to be used.

---

30 E.g., Jochnowitz 1978, in a volume that was a pioneering attempt at a linguistic approach (cf. Daniels 1982).
31 The absence of י in the first spelling may be a typographical error. Understanding of the materials is hampered by the absence of Roman-orthography Old Portuguese correspondences: alongside transliterations, only (sometimes reconstructed) Vulgar Romance forms are offered, in the conventional small capitals.

Without explanation in this article, David M. Bunis chooses "Judezmo" as the name for the language[32] long known as Ladino, i.e., Judeo-Spanish. The extensive corpus enables him to distinguish several stages of the written language and trace historical developments, relating them to both sound changes within the language and influence of neighboring alphabetic orthographies. The basics are as we have seen for the other Judeo-Romance languages, including א for nearly every initial and medial *a* (אמאר *amar* 'to love') and again "in hiatus" (דיאה *día* 'day', where the *a* is spelled with the ה, not the א). Interesting things are found among the labials: בואינו *bueno* ['bweno] 'good', ביזו *bezo* 'kiss', early ביויר or ביביר *bever* 'to drink',ויר *ver* 'to see', later ביביר, ביר. [dʒ/ʒ] was early ג֗, then [ʒ] was ї, and most recently [dʒ] was ד֗ז. Striking is ש֗ – and not ש – for *š* and some other uses.

2.4 Slavic

Brad Sabin Hill describes glosses and commentaries in West Judeo-Slavic (perhaps akin to Czech; 10th–13th centuries) and glosses in East Judeo-Slavic (perhaps akin to Belarusian/Ukrainian; 10th–17th centuries, with one group in Judeo-Russian) but gives not a single example nor any discussion of orthography. Modern Slavic languages were occasionally written in Hebrew characters under extraordinary circumstances into the mid 20th century.

2.5 Germanic

Grammars of Yiddish generally present a coherent, strictly alphabetic writing system for the language, but Lily Kahn shows that this was a recent regularization, dating only from 1936 and far from universally employed in the thriving Yiddish-speaking community today. In the earliest period of written attestation (14th–16th c.), Yiddish shares some features that have been seen in other Judeo-languages of Europe, including ב֗ for *v*, ש for *s*, ו for *o* and *u*, and א for *a*; but also, unfamiliarly, ע for *e*. א precedes morpheme-initial vowel letters; י is *i*, יי is *ay*.

19th-century Yiddish tended to imitate Standard German orthography, with "epenthetic" ע before syllabic sonorants (געבען *gebn* 'to give' = Ger. *geben*), double consonants pronounced singly (ראססע *rase* 'race' = *Rasse*), ה after vowels

---

32 As he did in his earliest publications more than forty years ago.

that are long in German (שטוהל *štul* 'chair' = *Stuhl*), and *for-*, the equivalent of Ger. *ver-*, spelled פֿער־. Semitic loans are, as usual, spelled as in the source language, but Germanic affixes are marked off with an apostrophe: גע׳גאנב׳עט *ge'ganv'et* 'stolen'. There was also a 19th-century style that used (essentially redundant) pointing of Yiddish alongside that of the Hebrew lexical components of texts.[33]

By the time of the novels and stories of Sholem Aleichem (around the turn of the 20th century), the orthography has become quasi-alphabetic – the only points used are found in אַ *a* and אָ *o* – but it is still Germanizing: שטאָדט *štot* 'city' (cf. *Stadt*), בעקאַנטע *bakante* 'acquaintances' (*Bekannte*): in Weinreich 1968 these are שטאָט, באַקאַנט(ע). The 1936 YIVO (Institute for Jewish Research) orthography systematizes and de-Germanizes. Always referring to non-Semitic vocabulary, each vowel and diphthong has its own letter, and the vowel points are integral parts of those letters: אַ *a* and אָ *o* (with א occurring only word-initially before a vowel letter ו or י), but also יי *ey*, ײַ *ay*, וי *oy*; *v* can only be וו. י almost

---

33 Missing from the volume is any mention of Judeo-German, i.e., Standard German written in Hebrew script. Some ten years ago, I somehow came across a Hebrew-script printing of Moses Mendelssohn's German translation of the Torah, in the library of the Leo Baeck Institute at the Center for Jewish History, possibly a unique copy (Mendelssohn 1834); it had been miscatalogued as Yiddish, which seemed unlikely for a book by Mendelssohn, and indeed when it was brought from the stacks the YIVO librarian at the adjacent desk peered at it and announced, "This is not Yiddish. I do not know what it is, but it is not Yiddish." Unfortunately I was refused permission to photograph a few pages so that I could analyze the orthography at leisure: The head librarian insisted that I did not need it because Mendelssohn's rendition was available in his Collected Works – in Roman orthography (and, I noticed, not without typographical errors in the first page or so). The photocopy of Genesis 1–11 I received a few days later was not really usable. WorldCat reveals that both the New York Public Library and Yeshiva University hold copies (properly catalogued as German) of an 1826 printing of presumably the same edition.

Sarah Benor makes me aware of a different edition of this work, incorporated into a Rabbinic *Chumash* "עם תרגום אשכנזי ובאור" [Hebrew] *'im targûm aškənazî ûbi'ûr* 'with German translation and commentary' (Mendelssohn 1795); the audience for the volume is unclear, since the text is preceded by a סובשקריבענטען פּערצייכניס [German] *Subskribenten Verzeichnis* 'subscribers index' but there is a lengthy introduction in Hebrew (in the Rabbinic typeface), and the parallel columns of a few lines of Torah text and German translation above extensive Hebrew commentary begin on the 68th image of the pdf (pages/folios unnumbered). Mendelssohn's text begins אים אנפֿאנגע ערשוף גאט דיא הימּעל אונד דיא ערדע *Im Anfange erschuf Gott die Himmel und die Erde* (confirmed in Mendelssohn 1845: 3, in Fraktur; cf. Martin Luther's *Am anfang ſchuff Gott himmel vnd erden*: Luther 1534) 'In the beginning God created the Heauen, and the Earth' [1611 orthography]. Note the alphabetic use of א for /a/ (not necessarily for the letter ⟨a⟩), cf. גאט ⟨g?t⟩ *Gott* and not, for instance, גוטט, but the double מּ reflecting *Himmel*; on the other hand, אונד *und* is spelled with the letter for the phoneme /d/ rather than the word-final allophone [t]. דיא *die* seems to indicate disfavor for two-letter words, cf. Yid. די.

does double duty, as in ייִדיש *yidiš* 'Yiddish'.³⁴, ³⁵ There is one other consonantal digraph, זש for *ž*. This development of a Yiddish *alphabet* (in the technical sense),³⁶ apparently with roots in the imitation of German orthography, has gone largely unremarked, in particular by earlier writing-systems theorists for whom this might be tenuous evidence supporting their insistence that "the alphabet" is the *ne plus ultra* of writing system types. Ultra-Orthodox Yiddish orthography retains the earlier Germanisms, and Soviet – atheistic? – Yiddish spelled Semitic vocabulary phonetically (so the letters בּ כ ח שׂ תּ ת were not used at all) and abandoned the word-final forms ן ם ך ף ץ of צ פ נ מ כ (but brought them back later on; Aronson 1996: 737).

3 Turkic languages

Henryk Jankowski describes the two Judeo-Kipchak languages (known from the 16th to the 20th centuries), the moribund Karaim of Karaite communities from Crimea to Lithuania, and the extinct Krymchak of Rabbinic Jews. The most distinctive spelling-relevant aspects of these languages are palatalization of consonants, indicated with י (in imitation of Polish practice, it is suggested), and vowel harmony; the transcriptions include a single occurrence of *ö* and several of *i*, with no differentiation from the writings of *o* and *i*, regarding either *matres* or vowel pointing.³⁷ It is noted that after the historic change *č ğ š ž > ts dz s z* in

---

34 It also marks palatals in Slavic words.
35 The term "Jiddisch" seems to have been controversial in Germany about a century ago. An anthology of excerpts from Bible translations into the language excoriates Birnbaum 1918:

> Diese aus dem Englischen herübergenommene Bezeichnung (Yiddish) sollte vermieden werden, ebenso wie das nichtssagende Jargon. Wissenschaftliche Bezeichnung der von Juden gesprochenen deutschen Dialekte ist Jüdisch-Deutsch (Judeo-German). Auf Befragen haben viele Ostjuden dem Vf. gegenüber ihre heimische Sprache immer nur als judisch oder mameloschen (= Muttersprache) bezeichnet. (Stärk and Leitzmann 1923: xix n. 1)

That did not stop them, however, from recommending the book as a "wissenschaftlich Musterhafte Grammatik" of the contemporary language (xxx). Perhaps Birnbaum had not yet clearly articulated his position that the Jewish language varieties are not dialects deviant from a standard, but independent languages each deserving of a distinctive name (emphasized by the editors of Birnbaum 2011a, 1: 1 n. 1).
36 As opposed to the Hebrew/Aramaic *abjad* (consonantary; Daniels 1990).
37 Compare Osmanli (Ottoman Turkish) Arabic script, where the surplus of consonant letters was put to good use indicating the feature-class of the vowels within a word or morpheme, e.g., صوص ⟨şwş⟩ *suş* 'be quiet', سوس ⟨sws⟩ *süs* 'ornamental'; طارلا ⟨ṭārlā⟩ *tarlá* 'field', ترله ⟨trlh⟩ *terlé* 'sweat' (Jehlitschka 1895: 16, cf. Daniels 1997: 379–80).

Halich Karaim, the sounds were spelled etymologically. ǧ š were ג׳ ש, but how were č ž spelled?

Judeo-Turkish, described by Laurent Mignon, was found, with some puzzling antecedents from earlier centuries, in a few late-19th-century periodicals. It attempted to notate front-rounded ö and ü, both of them as יו but both with other alternatives; א often represents a when it was ā in Arabic, as in זמאן for زمان zamān 'time' – and also when it was not, as in the alternative זאמאן, as well as plain זמן and surprising זמאאן; the curious placing of the *pataḥ* is parallelled in the spelling of قاضى ⟨qāḍy⟩ 'judge' as קאזי or קאזא. א could also appear in Turkish words, where vowel length does not apply: טאש taš 'stone'. Disregard for the Osmanli spelling in numerous particulars is noteworthy; Roman-orthography Turkish was decades in the future. Lending a curious aspect to Judeo-Turkish texts is the use of the final form ך for h as in דולאנדך Holanda 'Holland' and ג׳אדארשאנבא (Pers. چهار شنبه čehār šenbe) Çarşamba [1928 reformed orthography, i.e., *J̌aršamba*] 'Wednesday'.

4 Preliminary conclusions

Are there, then, principles, trends, or commonalities to be found in the adaptation of Hebrew script to the array of Judeo-languages?

Chronologically, the first obvious point is that all the non-Semitic Judeo-languages began to be written after Masoretic pointing of the biblical text was well established. Scribes in each case, then, had the option of pointing their texts or not. For the most part, it appears, the pointing was dispensed with, though it was sometimes called upon but not always with full consistency or coherence. A contrast between secular and religious texts (non-pointed and pointed) can sometimes be noted.

There is often a mismatch between the consonant inventory of Hebrew script and that of the language to be represented. For languages with more consonants, several possibilities have been used: diacritics (*rap̄e*, upper dot, apostrophe, occasionally *dageš*); a letter used as a somewhat consistent diacritic, as י for palatal consonants; and a few digraphs, notably וו for v. The Hebrew affricate צ ts (see Steiner 1982 for values of this letter over the centuries) could be pressed into service to denote other affricates, such as ƭ (č). For languages with fewer consonants than Hebrew has letters, discards are frequent: again and again the ordinary כ ת yield to ט ק – but the opposite is occasionally found; languages with but one voiceless sibilant seem torn between whether to use ס or ש (but not, it seems, שׂ); ח and ע are rarely used.

There are several cases where the standard language's orthography has influenced the application of Hebrew letters. A sociological question to be answered for every example is the extent to which a Jewish population would have been familiar with the writing of their non-Jewish neighbors. In a number of these languages we see Hebrew letters deployed in undeniable imitation of alphabetical spellings in the standard language, but only once did the Hebrew script become strictly alphabetical.

It is worth pausing to consider Kiwitt and Dürr's suggestion (see § 2.3 above) that the orthography of non-Semitic words in Judeo-French (and presumably other Judeo-languages) rests ultimately on the techniques used for assimilating Greek and Latin words into Rabbinic Hebrew and Aramaic texts.[38] This would presuppose that Medieval scribes were able to identify foreign vocabulary in the texts before them, but there is little about a Greek or Latin or Persian word included in a Hebrew text to mark it as foreign; indeed, the dictionary of Jastrow 1903 is notorious for its imagined Semitic etymologies of non-native words. Presumably Krauss 1898–99 is more reliable, but must suffer from the reduced knowledge of manuscript materials in the 19th century.[39] Many data for investigating this question are now available in Sokoloff 1990, 2002 (but there is nothing similar for Rabbinic Hebrew), so this is one of a number of questions that now may find an answer. Sometimes, though, a simple answer is best. In the Hebrew and Aramaic models, ט and ק had constant readings; ת and כ did not (cf. n. 24 above).

Finally, we may wonder what sort of interaction there might have been between Judeo-languages. Occasionally, it is clear: Judeo-Turkish was at least stimulated by the local Judezmo. *Responsa*, written in Rabbinic Hebrew influenced by local vernaculars (as Ecclesiastical Latin varied according to the native languages of its writers), circulated throughout Europe: but would Jews in distant lands have written to each other in their native languages at the same time?[40] Many of the texts in Judeo-languages emerged from the Cairo Geniza, and it is difficult to guess what treasures may still come to light.

---

38 Moreover the spelling of Iranian words in Imperial and Biblical Aramaic should also be considered; cf. Daniels in press a, between nn. 14 and 18.

39 Krauss's discussion of the orthography (1898–99, 1: 1–28) shows that there was sufficient inconsistency in the writing of Greek and Latin sounds that even if such loanwords could be identified by later scribes, they would provide little guidance for the writing of other non-Semitic languages. I am grateful to Stewart Felker for this reference.

40 Sarah Benor adds the observation that occasionally local loanwords made their way into wider use, presumably by such means, as for example Yid. יארצייט *yo/artsayt* < Ger. *Jahrzeit* 'anniversary of a death', which appeared in a medieval Hebrew text and made its way into several Jewish language varieties.

References

Abou-Assaf, Ali, Pierre Bordreuil & Alan R. Millard. 1982. *La Statue de Tell Fekheriye et son inscription bilingue assyro-araméenne* (Cahiers 7). Paris: Editions Recherche sur les Civilisations.
Afshar, I. 2009. Manuscripts in the domains of the Persian language. In Ehsan Yarshater & J.T.P de Bruijn (eds.), *A history of Persian literature*, vol. 1: *General introduction to Persian literature*, 408–429. London: I. B. Taurus.
Albright, William Foxwell. 1943. The Gezer Calendar. *Bulletin of the American Schools of Oriental Research* 92. 16–26.
Aronson, Howard I. 1996. Adaptations of Hebrew script: Yiddish. In Peter T. Daniels & William Bright (eds.), *The world's writing systems*, 735–741. New York: Oxford University Press.
Bar-Asher Siegal, Elitzur. 2013. *Introduction to the grammar of Jewish Babylonian Aramaic*. Münster: Ugaritica-Verlag.
Bauer, Hans & Pontus Leander. 1927. *Grammatik des Biblisch-Aramäischen*. Tübingen: Niemeyer. (Repr. Hildesheim: Olms, 1969.)
Beyer, Klaus. 2013. Der Wandel des Aramäischen veranschaulicht durch Transkriptionen alter aramäischer Texte. In Alejandro F. Botta (ed.), *In the shadow of Bezalel: Aramaic, biblical, and ancient Near Eastern studies in honor of Bezalel Porten*, 13–28. Leiden: Brill.
Birnbaum, Solomon A. 1918. *Praktische Grammatik der jiddischen Sprache für den Selbstunterricht* (Die Kunst der Polyglottie 128). Vienna: A. Hartleben.
Birnbaum, Solomon A. 1954–1957. *The Hebrew scripts*, vol. 2: *Plates*. London: Palaeographica.
Birnbaum, Solomon A. 1971. *The Hebrew scripts*, vol. 1: *Text*. Leiden: Brill.
Birnbaum, Solomon A. 2011a. *Solomon A. Birnbaum, A lifetime of achievement: Six decades of scholarly articles*, vol. 1: *Linguistics*; vol. 2: *Palaeography*, edited by Erika Timm, Eleazar Birnbaum, and David Birnbaum. Berlin: de Gruyter.
Birnbaum, Solomon A. 2011b. Table of Jewish languages and scripts. In Erika Timm, Eleazar Birnbaum & David Birnbaum (eds.), *Solomon A. Birnbaum, A lifetime of achievement: Six decades of scholarly articles*, vol. 1: *Linguistics*, 7–18. Berlin: de Gruyter.
Blau, Joshua. 1981. *The emergence and linguistic background of Judaeo-Arabic: A study of the origins of Middle Arabic*, 2nd edn. Jerusalem: Ben-Zvi Institute for the Study of Jewish Communities in the East.
Blau, Joshua & Simon Hopkins. 1984. On early Judaeo-Arabic orthography. *Zeitschrift für Arabische Linguistik* 12. 9–27.
Bordreuil, Pierre & Dennis Pardee. 2009. *A manual of Ugaritic* (Linguistic Studies in Ancient West Semitic 3). Winona Lake: Eisenbrauns.
Brockelmann, Carl. 1908–1913. *Vergleichende Grammatik der semitischen Sprachen*, 2 vol. Berlin: Reuther & Reichard.
Burtea, Bogdan. 2011. Mandaic. In Stefan Weninger, Geoffrey Khan, Michael P. Streck & Janet C. E. Watson (eds.), *The Semitic languages: An international handbook* (Handbücher zur Sprach- und Kommunikationswissenschaft 36), 670–685. Berlin: De Gruyter Mouton.
Creason, Stuart. 2004. Aramaic. In Roger D. Woodard (ed.), *The Cambridge encyclopedia of the world's ancient languages*, 391–426. Cambridge: Cambridge University Press.
Cross, Frank Moore & David Noel Freedman. 1952. *Early Hebrew orthography: A study of the epigraphic evidence* (American Oriental Series 36). New Haven: American Oriental Society.

Daniels, Peter T. 1980. Review of *A wandering Aramean: Collected Aramaic essays*, by Joseph A. Fitzmyer. *Journal of Near Eastern Studies* 39(3). 217–219.
Daniels, Peter T. 1982. Review of *Jewish languages, theme and variations*, edited by Herbert H. Paper. *Journal of Near Eastern Studies* 41(1): 70–72.
Daniels, Peter T. 1990. Fundamentals of grammatology. *Journal of the American Oriental Society* 110. 727–731.
Daniels, Peter T. 1996. Mandaic. In Peter T. Daniels & William Bright (eds.), *The world's writing systems*, 511–514. New York: Oxford University Press.
Daniels, Peter T. 1997. The protean Arabic abjad. In Asma Afsaruddin & A. H. Mathias Zahniser (eds.), *Humanism, culture, and language in the Near East: Studies in honor of Georg Krotkoff*, 83–110. Winona Lake: Eisenbrauns.
Daniels, Peter T. 2000. On writing syllables: Three episodes of script transfer. *Studies in the Linguistic Sciences* 30. 73–86.
Daniels, Peter T. 2013a. Alphabet, origin of. In Geoffrey L. Khan (ed.), *Encyclopedia of Hebrew language and linguistics*, vol. 1, 87–95. Leiden: Brill.
Daniels, Peter T. 2013b. The Arabic writing system. In Jonathan Owens (ed.), *Oxford handbook of Arabic linguistics*, 412–432. Oxford: Oxford University Press.
Daniels, Peter T. 2013c. The history of writing as a history of linguistics. In Keith Allan (ed.), *Oxford handbook of the history of linguistics*, 53–69. Oxford: Oxford University Press.
Daniels, Peter T. 2014. The type and spread of Arabic script. In Meikal Mumin & Kees Versteegh (eds.), *The Arabic Script in Africa* (Studies in Semitic languages and linguistics 71), 17–31. Leiden: Brill.
Daniels, Peter T. in press a. Aramaic documents from Achaemenid Bactria: Connections to the West – and the East – and the future. In Andreas Kaplony & Daniel Potthast (eds.), *From Barcelona to Qom: Documents from the Medieval Muslim World*. (Islamic History and Civilization). Leiden: Brill.
Daniels, Peter T. in press b. The further quest for Ugaritic. In H. H. Hardy II, Joseph Lam, & Eric D. Reymond (eds.), *"Like 'Ilu Are You Wise": Studies in Northwest Semitic Languages and Literature in Honor of Dennis G. Pardee*. Chicago: Oriental Institute Press.
Diem, Werner. 1976. Some glimpses of the rise and early development of the Arabic orthography. *Orientalia* N.S. 45. 251–261.
Diem, Werner. 1979. Untersuchungen zur frühen Geschichte der arabischen Orthographie: Die Schreibung der Vokale. *Orientalia* N.S. 48(2). 207–257.
Diem, Werner. 1980. Untersuchungen zur frühen Geschichte der arabischen Orthographie: Die Schreibung der Konsonanten. *Orientalia* N.S. 49(2). 67–106.
Diem, Werner. 1981. Untersuchungen zur frühen Geschichte der arabischen Orthographie: Endungen und Endschreibung. *Orientalia* N.S. 50(4). 332–383.
Diem, Werner. 1983. Untersuchungen zur frühen Geschichte der arabischen Orthographie: Die Schreibung der zusammenhängenden Rede. *Orientalia* N.S. 52(3). 357–404.
Driver, G. R. 1926. The Aramaic of the book of Daniel. *Journal of Biblical Literature* 45. 110–119.
Finkel, Irving. 2014. *The Ark before Noah: Decoding the story of the Flood*. London: Hodder & Stoughton.
Fitzmyer, Joseph A. 1966. *The Genesis Apocryphon of Qumran Cave I: A commentary* (Biblica et Orientalia 18). Rome: Pontifical Biblical Institute.
Fitzmyer, Joseph A. 1979. The phases of the Aramaic language. In *A Wandering Aramean: Collected Aramaic Essays*, by Joseph A. Fitzmyer, 57–84. Society of Biblical Literature Monograph Series 25. Missoula: Scholars Press.

Folmer, Margaretha. 2012. Old and Imperial Aramaic. In Holger Gzella (ed.), *Languages from the world of the Bible*, 128–159. Boston: De Gruyter.
Gelb, I. J. 1969. *Sequential reconstruction of Proto-Akkadian* (Assyriological Studies 18). Chicago: University of Chicago Press.
Gevirtz, Stanley. 1961. The Ugaritic parallel to Jeremiah 8:23. *Journal of Near Eastern Studies* 20. 41–46.
Gindin, Thamar E. 2009. Judeo-Persian communities of Iran: viii. Judeo-Persian language. In Ehsan Yarshater (ed.), *Encyclopædia Iranica*, vol. 15, 132–139. New York: Encyclopædia Iranica Foundation. http://www.iranicaonline.org/articles/judeo-persian-viii-judeo-persian-language (Accessed 8 November 2016).
Gordon, Cyrus H. 1965. *Ugaritic textbook* (Analecta Orientalia 38). Rome: Pontifical Biblical Institute.
Goshen-Gottstein, Moshe. 1973. *The Bible in the Syropalestinian version*, part 1: *Pentateuch and Prophets* (Publications of the Hebrew University Bible Project Monograph Series 4.1). Jerusalem: Magnes Press.
Greenfield, Jonas C. 1974. Standard Literary Aramaic. In André Caquot & David Cohen (eds.), *Actes du Premier Congrès International de Linguistique Sémitique et Chamito-Sémitique, Paris 16–19 juillet 1969* (Janua Linguarum Series Practica 159), 280–289. The Hague: Mouton.
Gruendler, Beatrice. 1993. *The development of the Arabic scripts: From the Nabataean era to the first Islamic century according to dated texts* (Harvard Semitic Studies 43). Atlanta: Scholars Press.
Gzella, Holger. 2015. *A cultural history of Aramaic: From the beginnings to the advent of Islam.* (Handbuch der Orientalistik 1:111). Leiden: Brill.
Häberl, Charles G. 2006. Iranian scripts for Aramaic languages: The origin of the Mandaic script. *Bulletin of the American Schools of Oriental Research* 341. 53–62.
Hamilton, Gordon J. 2006. *The origins of the West Semitic alphabet in Egyptian scripts* (Catholic Biblical Quarterly Monograph Series 40). Washington, D.C.: Catholic Biblical Association of America.
Hary, Benjamin. 1996. Adaptations of Hebrew script: Judeo-Arabic. In Peter T. Daniels & William Bright (eds.), *The world's writing systems*, 728–734. New York: Oxford University Press.
Henning, W. B. 1958. Mitteliranisch. In Bertold Spuler (ed.), *Iranistik* (Handbuch der Orientalistik I/4.1), 20–130. Leiden: Brill.
Jastrow, Marcus. 1903. *A dictionary of the Targumim, the Talmud Babli and Yerushalmi, and the midrashic Literature*, 2 vol. London & New York: Luzac & Putnam's.
Jehlitschka, Henry. 1895. *Türkische Konversations-Grammatik*. Heidelberg: Groos.
Jochnowitz, George. 1978. Judeo-Romance languages. In Herbert H. Paper (ed.), *Jewish languages, theme and variations: Proceedings of Regional Conferences of the Association for Jewish Studies held at the University of Michigan and New York University in March– April 1975*, 65–74. Cambridge, MA: Association for Jewish Studies.
Kahn, Lily & Aaron D. Rubin (eds.). 2015. *Handbook of Jewish languages* (Brill's Handbooks in Linguistics 2). Leiden: Brill.
Kaufman, Stephen A. 1997. Aramaic. In Robert Hetzron (ed.), *The Semitic languages* (Routledge Language Family Descriptions), 114–130. London: Routledge.
Kautzsch, Emil. 1884. *Grammatik des Biblisch-Aramäischen: Mit einer kritischen Erörterung der aramäischen Wörter im Neuen Testament*. Leipzig: Vogel.

Krauss, Samuel. 1898–1899. *Griechische und Lateinische Lehnwörter im Talmud, Midrasch und Targum*, 2 vol. Berlin: Calvary.
Kutscher, E. Y. 1970. Aramaic. In Thomas A. Sebeok (ed.), *Current trends in linguistics*, vol. 6: *Linguistics in South West Asia and North Africa*, 347–412. The Hague: Mouton.
Kutscher, E. Y. 1974. *The language and linguistic background of the Isaiah Scroll (1 Q Isa^a)* (Studies on the Texts of the Desert of Judah 6). Leiden: Brill.
Lazar, Moshe. 1971. Epithalames bilingues hébraïco-romanes dans deux manuscrits du XVe siècle. In Irénée Marcel Cluzel & François Pirot (eds.), *Mélanges de philologie romane dédiés à la mémoire de Jean Boutière (1899–1967)*, vol. 1: 339–346. Liège: Soledi.
Lundbom, Jack R. 1999. *Jeremiah 1–20* (Anchor Bible Series 21A). New York: Doubleday.
Luther, Martin, trans. 1534. *Biblia/ das ist/ die gantze Heilige Schrifft Deudsch*. Wittenberg. (Facsimile Cologne: Taschen, 2016.)
Maclean, Arthur John. 1895. *Grammar of the dialects of Vernacular Syriac as spoken by the Eastern Syrians of Kurdistan, North-West Persia, and the Plain of Mosul with notices of the vernacular of the Jews of Azerbaijan and of Zakhu near Mosul*. Cambridge: Cambridge University Press.
Maclean, Arthur John. 1901. *A dictionary of the dialects of Vernacular Syriac as spoken by the Eastern Syrians of Kurdistan North-West Persia, and the Plain of Moṣul with illustrations from the dialects of the Jews of Zakhu and Azerbaijan, and of the Western Syrians of Ṭur'Abdin and Ma'lula*. Oxford: Clarendon.
Marti, Karl. 1896. *Kurzgefasste Grammatik der biblisch-aramäischen Sprache: Litteratur, Paradigmen, kritisch berichtigte Texte und Glossar* (Porta Linguarum Orientalium 18). Berlin: Reuther & Reichard.
Mendelssohn, Moses. 1795. נתיבות השלום [The paths of peace (translation and commentary on the Torah)], vol. 1. Vienna: Anton Schmidt. https://books.google.com/books?id=EUE-AAAAYAAJ&pg=PT4#v=onepage&q&f=false (Accessed 8 November 2016).
Mendelssohn, Moses. 1834. ספר עץ חיים, אדער, דייטשע איבערזעטצונג דער חמשה חומשי תורה: עם חומש מגילות, והפטרות [Book of the tree of life, or, German translation of the Pentateuch, along with the Five Scrolls and the Haftaroth]. Sulzbach: S. Arnstein.
Mendelssohn, Moses. 1845. *Gesammelte Schriften, nach den Originaldrucken und Handschriften*, vol. 7: [*Die fünf Bücher Mose, übersetzt*], edited by G. B. Mendelssohn. Leipzig: Brockhaus.
Meyer, Rudolf. 1966–1972. *Hebräische Grammatik*, 3rd edn., 3+1 vols. Sammlung Göschen 763, 764, 5765, 4765. Berlin: de Gruyter.
Moritz, Bernhard. 1918. Arabia. d. Arabic writing. In *The Encyclopaedia of Islam*, vol. 1, 381–393. Leiden: Brill.
Müller-Kessler, Christa. 1991. *Grammatik des Christlich-Palästinisch-Aramäischen* (Texte und Studien zur Orientalistik 6). Hildesheim: Olms.
Müller-Kessler, Christa & Michael Sokoloff. 1997. *The Christian Palestinian Aramaic Old Testament and Apocrypha version from the Early Period* (A Corpus of Christian Palestinian Aramaic 1). Groningen: Styx.
Naveh, Joseph. 1987. *Early history of the alphabet*, 2nd edn. Jerusalem: Magnes Press.
Nöldeke, Theodor. 1868. *Grammatik der neusyrischen Sprache am Urmia-See und in Kurdistan*. Leipzig: Weigel.
Nöldeke, Theodor. 1875. *Mandäische Grammatik*. Halle: Waisenhaus.

Pardee, Dennis G. 1997. West Semitic canonical compositions, B: Royal Focus, 1: Epic, [a:] The Kirta Epic. In William W. Hallo & K. Lawson Younger (eds.), *The context of scripture*, vol. 1: *Canonical compositions from the biblical world*, 333–343. Leiden: Brill.

Pardee, Dennis G. 2003–2004. Review of *Ugaritische Grammatik*, by Josef Tropper. *Archiv für Orientforschung* online version 50. 1–404. http://orientalistik.univie.ac.at/fileadmin/documents/Rezension_Tropper_AOAT273.pdf (Accessed October 29, 2012).

Perry, John. 2009. The origin and development of Literary Persian. In Ehsan Yarshater & J.T.P de Bruyn (eds.), *A history of Persian literature*, vol. 1: *General introduction to Persian literature*, 43–70. London: I. B. Taurus.

Rollston, Christopher. 2011. The Khirbet Qeiyafa ostracon: Methodological musings and caveats. *Tel Aviv* 38. 67–82.

Rosenthal, Franz. 1961. *A grammar of Biblical Aramaic* (Porta Linguarum Orientalium NS 5). Wiesbaden: Harrassowitz.

Sass, Benjamin. 1988. *The genesis of the alphabet and its development in the second millennium B.C.* (Ägypten und Altes Testament 13). Wiesbaden: Harrassowitz.

Skjærvø, P. Oktor. 1996. Aramaic scripts for Iranian languages. In Peter T. Daniels & William Bright (eds.), *The world's writing systems*, 515–535. New York: Oxford University Press.

Sokoloff, Michael. 1990. *A dictionary of Jewish Palestinian Aramaic of the Byzantine Period* (Dictionaries of Talmud, Midrash and Targum 2). Ramat Gan: Bar Ilan University Press.

Sokoloff, Michael. 2002. *A dictionary of Jewish Babylonian Aramaic of the Talmudic and Geonic Periods* (Dictionaries of Talmud, Midrash and Targum 3). Ramat Gan & Baltimore: Bar Ilan University Press & The Johns Hopkins University Press.

Stärk, Willy & Albert Leitzmann. 1923. *Die jüdisch-deutschen Bibelübersetzungen von den Anfangen bis zum Ausgang des 18. Jahrhunderts*. Frankfurt: J. Kauffmann.

Steiner, Richard C. 1982. *Affricated ṣade in the Semitic languages* (American Academy for Jewish Research Monograph Series 3). New York: American Academy for Jewish Research.

Stoddard, D. T. 1856. Grammar of the modern Syriac language, as spoken in Oroomiah, Persia, and in Koordistan. *Proceedings of the American Oriental Society* 5. i–180, 180a–h.

Strack, Hermann L. 1905. *Grammatik des Biblisch-Aramäischen*, 4th edn. Leipzig: Hinrichs. (1st ed., 1895.)

Tov, Emanuel. 1982. A modern textual outlook based on the Qumran Scrolls. *Hebrew Union College Annual* 53. 11–27.

Tropper, Josef. 2000. *Ugaritische Grammatik* (Alter Orient und Altes Testament 273). Munich: Ugarit-Verlag.

Weinreich, Uriel. 1968. *Modern English–Yiddish Yiddish–English Dictionary*. New York: YIVO.

Anna Verschik
Yiddish, Jewish Russian, and Jewish Lithuanian in the Former Soviet Union

1 Introduction

This chapter focuses on situations where a large majority of speakers have migrated away from the language area and/or undergone a language shift. The Former Soviet Union (FSU) provides a useful test case for such situations. It is probably an impossible task to give equal attention to all Jewish languages that have been or are being used in FSU because of the vast size and ethnolinguistic diversity of the territory. In what follows I will consider Yiddish and its regional varieties and two post-Yiddish ethnolects, Jewish Russian and Jewish Lithuanian.

The languages to be discussed belong to different types of Jewish languages. Yiddish belongs to Type 1 in Wexler's (1987: 6–7) classification: Such languages are links in the chain of language shifts from Hebrew. The remaining varieties, Jewish Russian and Jewish Lithuanian, belong to Type 4: languages that are the result of a language shift to a non-Jewish language. The classification has been justly criticized in the literature (Beider 2013) because different types are determined on the basis of different criteria; nevertheless, it seems rather reasonable to consider languages that are the result of a shift to a "non-Jewish language" under the same heading, because they have many common features (so-called substratum features), caused by the language shift. It is true that the notion "non-Jewish" appears problematic, because it is not clear what a "non-Jewish language" is, especially in view of the fact that many varieties that initially were not spoken by Jews/perceived by laypeople as "non-Jewish" have gradually become a part of Jewish linguistic repertoire. (To give just one example: Jewish folksongs in varieties of Slavic languages are a well-known fact, see Wexler 1987: 188–191 on bilingual Slavic-Yiddish and monolingual Slavic folklore.) In this sense, the label "non-Jewish" appears essentialist (some languages are viewed as essentially inherent to certain ethnolinguistic/ethno-confessional groups and others as foreign; see Hary 2009: 6, footnote 2). In order to avoid essentialist characteristics, one can say that, at least in the case of the shift from Yiddish, the languages in question were not a part of traditional Ashkenazic triglossia (Aramaic-Hebrew-Yiddish); they became gradually internalized and supplanted Yiddish among some segments of the Jewish population. In order to avoid possible misinterpretations, I have adopted the term "post-Yiddish ethnolects," following Neil Jacobs' notion of post-Yiddish Ashkenazic speech (Jacobs 2005: 303–306) and post-Yiddish lects (Jacobs 2005: 303–304).

The term "ethnolect" appears acceptable to some scholars (Clyne 2000) and problematic to others (see discussion in Nortier 2008 and contributions therein, especially Jaspers 2008). Those who suggest discarding the term altogether argue that it equates ethnicity with the way one speaks. However, ethnicity is often understood differently in Western Europe and in Eastern Europe (Verschik 2010: 286); besides, the authors in question mostly refer to new immigrants and their descendents in the West-European situation and do not consider Jewish varieties that have emerged under rather different sociolinguistic circumstances. The label "multiethnolect" that is gaining currency among researchers does not seem to be a "remedy," because it may be descriptively accurate for postmodern, urban immigrant varieties in Western Europe only where people from multiple ethnolinguistic groups contribute to the formation of a new variety (and of general "immigrant" identity as opposed to the local majority). This is not applicable to the Jewish case, where (at least in the synchronic perspective) there is no such diversity to be found.

It is clear that ethnic (or ethno-confessional) background does not automatically turn all speakers of Jewish origin into ethnolect speakers of Russian, English, Polish, and so on; however, a certain ethnolinguistic background (i.e., previous generations of Yiddish-speakers and a shift from Yiddish as L1) can give rise to distinct varieties of L2. Note that these new varieties of mainstream/majority languages do not necessarily arise because of the wish to render Jewish speech and writing different from those of non-Jewish neighbors (the so-called *lehavdil*-factor). Also, the use of Jewish ethnolects may be, but are not always, a sign of a specific style or a distinct identity.

Sometimes it is argued that the speech of the first generation in a language shift situation should not be considered under the heading of an ethnolect, and it is only if L1 features appear in the speech of the next generation that a given variety can be viewed as an ethnolect (Clyne 2000: 86). This view, however, appears counter-intuitive because the situation is often more complex. It is probably impossible to make meaningful distinctions between what is often called "imperfect SLA" in the language shift and speech of subsequent generations; rather, it is the use of a given variety for in-group purposes (i.e., internalization) that matters (Verschik 2010).

Another brand of critique comes from the point of view that "ethnolect" implies a fixed and discrete linguistic entity. Benor (2010) prefers "ethnolinguistic repertoire" instead, showing that speakers do not form a monolithic community, and the circumstances and the degree to which they use ethnolectal features do vary. I use the term "ethnolect" with an understanding that it is not a fixed entity but rather a continuum, and there are immense possibilities for inter- and intraspeaker variation. In fact, ethnolects should be conceptualized like other varieties in multilingual use, for instance, and it is headings like "Turkish in the Netherlands" or "Netherlands Turkish" that are generalizations.

Some researchers assume that the term "religiolect" (Hary 2009: 12–13; Hary and Wein 2013) would be more suitable than ethnolect. Indeed, in an early paper, Gold (1985) noted that there may be a considerable difference between the English of, say, Modern Orthodox and Reform Jews in the USA. No doubt such distinctions are relevant, at least in the USA (Benor 2009; Gold 1985), and the term "religiolect" would be more descriptively accurate than "ethnolect." At the same time, the term is not universally applicable, because Jewish identity may be completely or predominantly considered in ethnolinguistic terms for some people. In certain societies, for instance, in Baltic countries, Jews are usually viewed (both by in- and outsiders) as an ethnic (or ethno-confessional) group and not as an exclusively religious group; also, the wide spectrum of different versions of Judaism, as is the case in the USA and in some West-European countries, is not necessarily present everywhere. It is important to note that, for many Jews shifting to Russian, language shift was a way out of traditional society and a means of distancing oneself from any kind of religion. Thus, Jewish Russian and Jewish Lithuanian would be better described as ethnolects than religiolects. The view that Jews are no longer creating Jewish languages, advocated by Myhill (2004: 151), appears too radical; in his book, he does not mention Jewish Russian, varieties of Jewish English, and the like, although such varieties emerge (see Benor 2009 on the range of contemporary Jewish English lects and the linguistic repertoire of US Jews).

2 Yiddish

The Russian Empire acquired Yiddish-speakers together with the acquisition of its western territories, i.e., the lands gained as the result of the partitions of Poland (the final partition in 1795) and of the Northern War (1700–1721). The territories gained after the partitions of Poland correspond to today's Ukraine, Belarus, Lithuania, and Latgalia (a South-East region of Latvia that, prior to the partitions of Poland in the 18th century, had belonged to the Polish-Lithuanian Commonwealth), and those gained after the Northern War correspond to today's Latvia (excluding Latgalia) and Estonia. Of all these territories, the lands of what is contemporary Estonia had had no Jewish population in the pre-imperial period (the first community emerged in 1829; see more in Verschik 1999). During the Tsarist rule, the governments of Estland, Livland, and Courland (today's Estonia and Northern and Western Latvia) remained outside the Pale of Settlement.

As a result of WWI and the Russian revolution of 1917, Poland and the Baltic states became independent. Poland also included western parts of Ukraine and Belarus. In 1939–1940, the Soviet Union occupied and annexed these territories. Later, the Yiddish-speaking population was almost completely wiped out during the Holocaust. Thus, the sociolinguistic profile of Jewry after WWII dramatically changed: It had a higher share of younger people with Russian as their first language (Altshuler 1998: 190; Estraikh 2008: 66).

The varieties of Yiddish spoken in the Soviet Union belonged to the North-Eastern (Belarus, Northern Ukraine, Lithuania, Latvia, Estonia), South-Eastern (Eastern Ukraine, Moldova), and Central (Western Ukraine) dialects (on regional dialect classification, see Katz 1983; Jacobs 2005: 65), possibly also including transitional and mixed varieties. In Estonia and Latvia, some Jews were speakers of Baltic German, a local variety of the German language. However, it is impossible to draw clear borders between closely related varieties; many Low German lexical items (also part of the Baltic German lexicon) have become conventionalized in Courland Yiddish and Estonian Yiddish, and there are also phonological similarities between the phonology of Baltic German and of Courland and Estonian Yiddish, such as diphthongs [äj], [öü]/[öj]: *väjnen* 'to weep' (cf. North-Eastern *vejnen*), *köjfn* 'to buy' (cf. North-Eastern *kejfn*), etc.

Apparently, it would be accurate to describe the situation as a continuum between Baltic German and Yiddish, especially in view of the fact that some Jews were multilingual, including in Baltic German and their local variety of North-Eastern Yiddish. For speakers of mainstream North-Eastern Yiddish (especially the Vilnius variety) or to proponents of Standard Yiddish, the Yiddish speech of Courland and Estonian Jews sounds "daytshmerish" (a pejorative term labelling German-like features); however, this view would be counter-productive, because it closes the door to contact linguistics and results in a strictly purist approach (see Peltz 1997 on the critique of anti-daytshmerish attitudes).

2.1 The sociolinguistics of Yiddish in the SU and FSU

To a certain degree, language shift among East-European Jews had already started before the collapse of the Russian Empire and the emergence of the Soviet Union (Estraikh 1996 on the shift to Russian). After the revolution of 1917, restrictions concerning professions, access to higher education, place of residence, etc., were lifted, and many Jews moved to the greater urban centers of Ukraine, Belarus, Russia, and other Soviet republics (and after 1934 to Birobidzhan, the Jewish Autonomous District), bringing their varieties of Yiddish with them (this does not concern the Baltic states that became independent in 1918). This coincided in time with a steady decline of *shtetl* economic structures and the Soviet policy of imposed secularization.

The Soviet language policy was anything but straightforward, changing a lot in time and in space (different approaches in different regions). Within the spirit of the early Soviet policy of indigenization (*коренизация*), the languages and cultures of non-Russian ethnic groups were promoted in the 1920s, whereas the discourse of Soviet internationalism was opposed to that of the Russian Empire as "the prison of peoples." It was a way to create local elites loyal to the Soviet cause and to win popularity among non-Russian populations. Yiddish language and cultural institutions, press, and a network of schools were built and cultivated: for example, the Jewish section of the Institute for Belarusian Culture; the Department of Jewish Culture within the Ukrainian Academy of Sciences in Kiev; Moscow State University's Jewish Division; and Leningrad's Institute for Jewish Knowledge and Institute for Jewish History and Literature (Greenbaum 1978, quoted from Le Foll 2012: 256).

By the late 1920s, Soviet Yiddish language planning sought to formulate a new standard that would separate Soviet Yiddish and Yiddish language research from both the previous tradition and from research institutions outside the USSR (especially YIVO) (Le Foll 2012: 272 and references therein). The years 1917–1930 were the formative phase for Soviet Yiddish, whereas the period 1930–1937 witnessed a fierce power struggle among different schools of thought in language planning (Estraikh 1993). Views on de-hebraization (not to be confused with the rendition of Hebrew-origin words in phonetic spelling) differed among scholars (Estraikh 1993); while some language planners saw Hebrew as a source for neologisms, necessary in the new socialist reality, for others Hebrew symbolized "bourgeois" ideologies like Zionism and "reactionary" traditional religious authority.

In the 1930s, Yiddish in the USSR gravitated towards Russian, especially in the creation of neologisms (Soviet-speak, so-to-say), which was a "consequence of the legacy of assimilation" and "demolition of the ecology of Yiddish in the post-revolutionary years" (Estraikh 1993: 36).

Starting from the early 1930s, the policy of indigenization was abandoned, national elites suffered in the course of repressions, and Yiddish research institutions in Ukraine and Belarus were closed or seriously reduced. The traditional area where Yiddish-speakers resided was the one to suffer the most in the course of WWII. After the war, increasing Soviet isolationism and the so-called struggle against cosmopolitanism and bourgeois nationalism destroyed the Yiddish cultural elite and infrastructure (theaters, newspapers, the Jewish section of the Writers Union, etc.), and possibilities for a Soviet Jewish identity via Yiddish (as there had been in the early Soviet years) were excluded. During the so-called Thaw, publishing in Yiddish returned, as the Soviet authorities believed that such a symbolic gesture would help to gain sympathies among left-wing circles (on the magazine *Sovyetish Heymland* and its role, see Estraikh 1995). Still, language shift (mostly to Russian but also to other languages in the Baltic republics), mixed marriages, and emigration continuously contributed to the decrease in the number of Yiddish-speakers.

The situation with Yiddish was different in the Baltic region. During the first period of its independence, Lithuania, even without the Vilnius district, had a substantial Jewish population of 154,000 that was the largest minority in Lithuania and comprised slightly over 7% of the population, as of the census of 1923 (Vaskela 2006: 141). The Jews were predominantly Yiddish-speakers, although Zionist ideology was quite successful. Some drift towards Lithuanian became noticeable in the 1930s (Verschik 2010).

Latvia had about 100,000 Jews, whose sociolinguistic and socioeconomic profile was more diverse than in Lithuania (Mendelsohn 1983: 17–18, 215). There were several competing cultural orientations (Yiddishist, Hebraist, German, Russian, secular, traditional, left- and right-wing, etc.), especially in the capital, Riga (Šteimanis 1995: 38). Jews spoke regional varieties of Yiddish, as well as Russian and (Baltic) German. The use of Russian or German per se should not be automatically equated with assimilation; while for some it was certainly a goal, others created a separate Jewish cultural space functioning in Russian or in German, although this tendency was weakening in the beginning of the 1930s. According to the 1936 census, more than half of the Jewish population in Latvia was proficient in three or four languages. The number of Jews proficient in Latvian as of 1930 was the highest in Courland (for instance, 90.52% in Jelgava) and lowest in Latgalia (18.6% in Daugavpils), where the majority of the population was not Latvian (Dribins 1996: 22).

Estonian Jewry was the smallest (less than 4,500 Jews in 1935), middle-class, urbanized, secularized, and multilingual, yet preserving Jewish ethnic identity (Mendelsohn 1983: 253–254), i.e., having certain characteristics of both West-European and East-European Jewries.

The Hebrew-Yiddish controversy was present, to a smaller or greater measure, in all three Baltic countries, resulting in two different school systems and bitter debates between the adherents of each language. Secondary education in Yiddish was available in all three Baltic countries. School statistics demonstrate different language choice trends: In Estonia and Latvia, Jews opted either for Jewish (Yiddish- or Hebrew-medium) education or for Estonian/Latvian-language schools (especially gymnasiums), at the expense of the languages of former culturally dominant groups, German and Russian. In Lithuania, the number of students in Jewish schools was declining in the middle of the 1930s and growing in Lithuanian-medium schools (there was even a Jewish school with Lithuanian as a language of instruction) (see Mark 1973: 267 for Latvia and Lipets 1965: 308 for Lithuania).

Cultural autonomy, allowing a separate space for the cultivation of national language, press, theater, and cultural institutions, was provided, either de facto or de jure, by the governments in the Baltic countries, and the maintenance of Jewish identity (with Yiddish or Hebrew as its symbol, secular or traditional) was secured for those who wished it. Prior to the Soviet occupation of the Baltic States and WWII, therefore, the sociolinguistic situation of Baltic Jewries differed from that in the USSR. Even after the Holocaust and subsequent Soviet anti-Jewish policies, the remaining Jews and their descendants have upheld the distinctions (and in some cases even emphasized them), maintaining a separate identity from Jews who were Soviet-time newcomers. The older generation of Baltic Jews still has Yiddish, to a certain extent, and is multilingual, while the older generation of those who settled during the Soviet period are Russian monolinguals, as a rule (it is not known whether there are speakers of Jewish Russian among them). Interestingly, in Estonia speakers of Yiddish characterize their variety as "Baltic Yiddish," as opposed to the rest of North-Eastern Yiddish (popularly called "Lithuanian Yiddish"). Some express the opinion that "Lithuanian Yiddish has a lot of Russian words and ours does not"; although there are differences in prosody, phonetics, and lexicon, the claim is not true, because what may appear as Russian is probably of Slavic (but not necessarily Russian) origin. This probably has to do with the internalization of a popular Estonian stereotype about Lithuanian: To an Estonian ear, Lithuanian sounds "Russian-like," because of palatalization and some common words (Lithuanian *knyga* 'book' and Russian *книга*).

As a consequence of the ongoing language shift, population loss during the Holocaust, Soviet anti-Jewish policies, and emigration, the number of Yiddish-speakers has dramatically declined. Let us consider figures for Russia and Ukraine. In Russia, according to the recent census of 2010, the number of Jews was 156,800 (0.1143% of the population, see http://demoscope.ru/weekly/ssp/rus_nac_10.php), as compared to almost 230,000 Jews in 2001. Proficiency in the language of one's ethnicity (a problematic notion in this case) was 5.1%, as opposed to 8.9% in the last Soviet census of 1989 (figures and a more detailed analysis at http://demoscope.ru/weekly/knigi/ns_r10_11/akrobat/glava3.pdf, p. 141; the table refers to Ashkenazic Jews in Russia; the last Soviet census distinguished between Ashkenazic and other groups of Jews, see http://demoscope.ru/weekly/ssp/sng_nac_lan_89_1_1.php).

In Ukraine, according the most recent census of 2001, Jews constituted 0.22% of the population (or 103,500), as opposed to 0.95% (486,300) in 1989 (http://demoscope.ru/weekly/2004/0173/analit05.php). Of the entire Jewish population in Ukraine, 83% listed Russian, and 14.3% Ukrainian, as their mother tongue, while 3% declared it to be Yiddish (http://2001.ukrcensus.gov.ua/rus/results/general/language/).

As is generally true with censuses, there are difficulties associated with such types of statistics. Censuses seldom allow several mother tongues; some censuses do not count languages with a small number of speakers separately; sometimes there is a suggestion to indicate one's mother tongue by choosing from a closed list, containing only the most frequently used languages. Oftentimes, Yiddish is not on the list and falls into the category "language of your ethnicity" or "other languages."

All of the censuses mentioned demonstrate a decline in Jewish population and a language shift away from Yiddish; what censuses do not demonstrate in full is Jewish multilingualism and its complexity: ethnolects and in-between varieties.

There are still some very rare cases of the acquisition of Yiddish as L1 (often together with another language). Individual cases of early Yiddish-Lithuanian bilingualism are described by Verschik (2014). Yiddish as spoken by the informants in this study has both regional North-Eastern features (loss of neuter, syncretism of dative and accusative, realization of certain diphthongs) and Lithuanian impact as well (prosody, Lithuanian-like palatalization, departure from V2 word order, omission of copula in the present tense, omission of past tense auxiliary, and so on). In such instances, Yiddish is a language of the family and closest relatives and not even a community language.

2.2 Yiddish as L2 and L3: Yiddish-X multilingualism

It is common knowledge that, in the past, many Ukrainians, Belarusians, and Lithuanians who resided in localities with substantial Jewish population were able to speak Yiddish with a variable degree of proficiency, depending on their needs and occupations (for instance, some worked with or for Jews; see also Hary 2009: 16–19 on crossing religious boundaries). In the early 2000s, the current author heard from several Yiddish-speakers in Lithuania that their parents had had Lithuanian employees before WWII, and after the war these people were still around and used to visit. Unfortunately, the generation of such speakers of Yiddish as L2 or L3 is already gone and the phenomenon has not been studied, because at that time the field of multilingualism research, as we know it today, did not exist. In more general terms, Yiddish-X multilingualism (that is, including Yiddish and any other language) should be investigated.

At the same time, there is interest about things Yiddish among young people of Jewish and non-Jewish origin alike. Yiddish courses are available at the major universities of Belarus, Lithuania, Russia, and Ukraine. There are diverse reasons for learning Yiddish: It is either heritage language learning (Polinsky and Kagan

2007), i.e., an act of identity (Le Page and Tabouret-Keller 1985), when people want to relate to the language of their grandparents, or dictated by professional needs (klezmer musicians, historians, scholars in folklore, history, literary theory, etc.). It is argued about Yiddish learners in the USA that their commitment to the study of the language is often symbolic; the goal is not as much to achieve serious proficiency, but to demonstrate a stand towards Yiddish. In Avineri's (2012) terms, such learners are joining, not a linguistic but rather a metalinguistic community (see also Shandler 2006: 4 on privileging the secondary level of the signification of Yiddish). A similar research project on Yiddish learners in FSU would be most welcome. There are a growing number of international Yiddish summer programs in Yiddish; the programs are also popular among people of various backgrounds from the FSU. In Eastern Europe, one such program has been regularly functioning in Vilnius since 1998.

3 Jewish Russian

Jewish varieties of Slavic languages (including early varieties before contact with Russian proper) are described to some extent by Wexler (1987). In the 1920s, about 40% of the European Jews resided in Slavic speaking areas and about 10% of those had a Slavic language as L1 (Wexler 1987: 1 and references therein). Many probably spoke at least one Slavic language as L2 or L3. Jewish Russian is a cluster of post-Yiddish varieties, used by Ashkenazi Russian-speaking Jews (Verschik 2007). Apparently, languages of this type are not codified; Jewish Russian is not viewed or perceived by laypeople as a "proper" language; neither does it have a name of its own, but is sometimes referred to in a more indirect way, like "our Russian" (similar to Moroccan Judeo-Arabic that is referred to as "our Arabic," Hary, personal communication). Jewish Russian is a label given by linguists. It does not employ Hebrew script (interestingly, some other post-Yiddish varieties of USA Jewish English have a limited use of Hebrew characters).

Not all Russian-speaking Jews are by default speakers of Jewish Russian. The users of Jewish Russian do not always have it as a single variety but often as a style/register/identity marker. Yet some use one or another version of Jewish Russian as their main variety, as a matter of conscious choice. Note, however, that sociopsychological mechanisms of shift from Yiddish to Russian were different for different segments of the Jewish population: For some, embracing the Russian language was a step into the world existing beyond the realms of shtetl and Jewish environment and a path to what they perceived as world culture; for others, it was a purely practical matter of mastering the language of the majority (especially after leaving the shtetls for greater urban centers). This difference is also emphasized by Estraikh (2008: 63).

Currently, there are varieties of Jewish Russian outside post-Soviet countries, for instance, in Israel. Such instances will not be considered here (but see Perelmutter, this volume). The situation of Russian (including Jewish Russian) in Israel is multilayered: Varieties in the range from the mainstream Russian to rather marked Jewish varieties exist side by side, with a smaller or greater impact of Hebrew, whereas modern Hebrew itself has been influenced by Yiddish and Russian (Zuckermann 2009). The same can be said regarding Jewish Russian in Germany (Berlin) and the US (Coney Island, Brighton Beach).

The main, but not the only, linguistic mechanism is what Thomason and Kaufman (1991) call "interference through shift," that is, various Yiddish features in Russian. Some features, such as a lack of reduction of unstressed vowels or the rendition of the Russian central closed vowel [ɨ] as [i], have almost become obsolete. Realization of [r] as uvular [R] has developed into a marker of Jewish speech, both for in- and outsiders. To an extent, a so-called rise-fall intonation (Weinreich 1956) may be present. Yiddish-origin words (Beider 2013: 93–94; Verschik 2007) are not necessarily limited to cultural vocabulary (customs, religion, food, etc.). Often there are descriptive and emotionally loaded words like *xalojmes ~ xalejmes* 'pointless, unrealistic dreams, castles on sand' (< Yiddish *xalojmes* 'dreams'), *šlimazl* 'ne'er do well', *mešugener* 'crazy'; discourse words and idiomatic expressions: *az ox un vej* 'it is really bad', *bekitser* 'in short, immediately', *vej iz mir* 'woe is me', *taki* < *take* 'really, indeed' (itself of Ukrainian origin). Several word-for-word renditions of Yiddish idioms have even lost their Jewish connotation and become marked as colloquial or funny in mainstream speech: *ja znaju (očen)* 'how should I know' < *ix vejs (zejer)* (literally: 'I know [very much])'.

As other post-Yiddish ethnolects, Jewish Russian has preserved what is sometimes labelled as "Jewish rhetoric," a special conversational strategy of story-telling and arguing. It includes interruptions and overlapping (Safran 2016; Tannen 1981), appellation to hearers by the means of (over)use of rhetorical questions, formulaic expressions such as *čtoby ty znal* 'for your knowledge, pay attention please' (literally, 'you should know'), modelled on Yiddish *zolst visn* with the same meaning and structure, and the like (Verschik 2007: 221–222). For many Russian Jews, this kind of discourse is probably the only remaining Yiddish-derived feature.

But it is not only about the copying of Yiddish items or patterns. Another mechanism, less acknowledged in the ethnolect literature, is the rearrangement of Russian lexical and derivational resources in a new way. This also includes a change in the semantics of originally Russian items. The word *otkaznik* 'refusenik' is probably one of the best known examples of this strategy (Russian *otkaz* 'refusal' + agentive suffix *–nik*), but also *semisvečnik* 'menorah' ('seven' + 'light' + suffix), *zakon* 'Jewish law/religion/customs' (< Russian *zakon* 'law'). Several examples of this kind are listed in Beider (2013: 94).

Fiction and popular culture have contributed considerably to the spread of Jewish Russian features into the mainstream (see Androutsopoulos 2001 on the process in contemporary immigrant ethnolects in Western Europe). Jewish Russian authors (i.e., authors who wrote in Russian, but for a Jewish audience and about Jews) at the turn of the 19th–20th century introduced ethnolectal features for stylization of Jewish direct speech (for instance, Semen Yushkevich; see Cukierman 1980: 37).

For the general public, the so-called Odessa language or Odessa parlance has become the quintessence of Jewish or Jewish-colored speech and humor (perceived as "juicy," expressive, and funny). In fact, Odessa Russian is possibly a multiethnolect with a Yiddish and Ukrainian substratum (that is implied in Cukierman 1980 but not expressed in so many words). Due to the strong impact of Slavic on Yiddish morphosyntax, it is sometimes impossible to say exactly which one is a prototype for a certain construction, because often Yiddish and Ukrainian share argument structure, while Russian is different; for instance, the use of certain prepositions: 'because of' is expressed both in Yiddish and Ukrainian literally as 'over' (*iber* and *čerez* respectively), while Russian has *iz-za* 'because of'. Writers such as Isaac Babel, with his *Odessa stories*, consciously employed word-for-word renditions from Yiddish. For a majority of contemporary readers, the phrase *ja imeju vam skazat' paru slov* 'I have to tell you something' (literally, 'I have to tell you a couple of words') sounds funny, because the construction *imet'* 'to have' + infinitive is not normally used in Russian in such a context and is possibly perceived as having a Jewish sound about it; however, most of Babel's readers do not know Yiddish and would not notice that this is exactly how it sounds in Yiddish: *ix hob ajx tsu zogn a por verter*.

In 2007, the TV series Liquidation, set in post-WWII Odessa, proved to be a great success in Russia, and Yiddishisms, like *bekitser* 'quickly', *šlimazl* 'unlucky person, ne'er-do-well', and others, added flavor, although they remained unintelligible to most of the audience (Estraikh 2008: 68). Those who have access to Jewish Russian would probably recognize and understand them (Beider 2013: 93–94 mentions several such words in a list of Jewish Russian lexical items).

Many widely known and beloved actors and comedians of the Soviet era, e.g., Leonid Utessov, Arkadii Raikin, and Mikhail Zhvanetsky, are of Jewish origin, and whatever their self-identification was/is, they were/are largely perceived as such by the public (Estraikh 2008: 67). Mikhail Zhvanetsky has several humorous sketches that are based on the use of "Jewish rhetoric," but not overt Yiddishisms in the lexicon.

Interestingly, as a counter-reaction to "badly Jewish accented Russian" as spoken by some Jews at early stages of language shift, some highly aware Russian-speaking Jews became over-precise in their use of Russian and avoided any sub-standard and colloquial features. This is not only about avoidance of features perceived as Jewish, but of non-standard usage in general. As Estraikh (2008: 67–68) observes, it is not a coincidence that Ditmar Rozental, born in a Jewish family in Poland, became an ultimate authority on Russian orthography and standard. Interestingly, the same tendency for hypercorrectness is reported by Jacobs (1996) in his paper on Jewish Austrian German. He mentions that, unlike non-Jewish Austrians, who would vary between standard and local dialects depending on the situation, some Austrian Jews would use the supra-regional standard variety in all circumstances.

4 Jewish Lithuanian

Jewish Lithuanian is a cover name for varieties of Lithuanian that are a result of a shift from Yiddish (Verschik 2010; to date, this is the only paper that deals with the subject). Unlike Jewish Russian, Jewish Lithuanian had very little time to develop, because before the establishment of the Republic of Lithuania in 1918 Lithuanian was just a means of communication with neighbors and not an attractive candidate for language shift (unlike "old" and acknowledged languages such as Russian, German, and, to a certain extent, Polish). Mastery of Standard Lithuanian among Jews started through formal schooling; as mentioned in Section 2.1, Lithuanian-medium schools became increasingly popular. In fact, Lithuanian became internalized, that is, used for in-group communication (both alongside Yiddish and other languages and also as a preferred means of expression in a tiny group). The ethnolect remained somewhat ephemeral, because the time was too short for it to develop; there are very few speakers nowadays.

Jewish Lithuanian is characterized by phonetic and prosodic features, such as uvular [R], a lesser degree of palatalization, rendition of the diphthong *ie* [iä] as [ä], occasional rendition of *uo* as *o*, prominence of the first component in all diphthongs as opposed to falling and rising diphthongs in Lithuanian, and occasional rise-fall intonation. As the Jewish population in Lithuania is very tiny, and nowadays Lithuanians have no first-hand contact with the "Jewish accent," it is not clear whether [R] and other Yiddish-origin features are recognized as such and are socially marked. Some younger users have [R] as the only remaining feature and otherwise speak mainstream Lithuanian. Possibly there are certain Yiddish discourse models, as in other post-Yiddish ethnolects.

Based on the features, one can ask whether there are only 12 speakers of Jewish Lithuanian. The question was discussed by Clyne (2000) in a more general way. He argued that one can only speak of ethnolects starting from the second generation and that first-generation phenomena are to be considered SLA. As mentioned earlier in this paper, formal criteria are probably not helpful here. Recall that SLA and a language shift accompanied by imperfect learning produce similar results (Thomason and Kaufman 1991), although SLA is a different case, where speakers do not give up their first language. For a sociolinguist and a contact linguist, it is irrelevant whether a variety or varieties of Lithuanian were "perfect," "target-like" or not; what is relevant is the internalization of any variety of Lithuanian as a part of in-group repertoire (Verschik 2010: 300).

The situation with Lithuanian-speaking Jews was more nuanced than "assimilation." It was not about becoming indistinguishable from Lithuanians; rather, it was often about acquiring a Jewish voice in Lithuanian (Verschik 2010; see Shmeruk 1989 on a similar standing among Polish-speaking Jews). Like in the case with Jewish Russian, religious distinctions are not relevant here.

It is instructive to see how some Lithuanian Jews conceptualize their Lithuanian speech. Such speakers of Lithuanian as L1 presume that, by default, Jews speak Lithuanian differently from non-Jewish Lithuanians, although this is not always the case. This circumstance sheds light on complex relations between markers (i.e., socially relevant features), indicators (i.e., distinct features that have no social meaning but are visible to linguists), and identity (Verschik 2010: 296–297).

5 Yiddish, Russian, Jewish Russian: Putting it all together

It may not be obvious to a layperson that the boundaries between varieties may be porous. For a linguist, it is obvious that there is a lack of clear and needed categories: more or less ethnolectal features depending on speaker/situation/identity conceptualization; typological similarities between East-Slavic languages and Yiddish; similarities in lexicon and structure that have emerged through contact. Many Jews would know that Yiddish has a considerable Slavic component in its lexicon (replication of morphosyntactic models is less obvious to non-specialists), and, for this reason, the language is viewed as a "hybrid": not a "proper language," but a mixture of components from various sources. This mixture may be expressive at times, but still considered inferior (for a non-linguist, foreign patterns and elements in their native Russian are not obvious, and hybridity is perceived as a peculiar characteristic of Yiddish only).

Slavic-origin lexical items in Yiddish are easily detectable by speakers of Russian and are viewed as funny and non-serious (something akin to a comic effect of macaronic rhymes and songs). It is not hard to see the connection between, say, Yiddish *tšajnik* 'teapot' and Russian чайник. The Slavic impact on Yiddish is tremendous in all linguistic subsystems, and Yiddish has conventionalized mechanisms for the morphosyntactic integration of Slavic stems. Consider verbs like *spraven zix* 'to manage to do something', cf. Russian справиться (*sprav-it'sja*); *praven* 'to hold a celebration', cf. Russian править (*pravit'*); descriptive and onomatopoetic words like *xropen* 'to snore', cf. Russian храпеть (*xrapet'*) or *grižen* 'to gnaw', cf. Russian грызть (*gryzt'*); derivative suffixes like -*ovat*- in *kil-ovate* 'somewhat cold', -*ink*- as in *grin-ink-e* '(nice little) green (one)' etc. It is indeed impossible, based on formal criteria, to distinguish between conventionalized Slavicisms and occasional ad hoc use of Russian stems within the Yiddish matrix. Because of some internalized anti-Yiddish attitudes and beliefs about the inferiority of Yiddish due to its "mixed" character, Slavicisms in Yiddish are often perceived as "raw borrowings" and Yiddish speech as impure, half-Russian, half-Yiddish. It is oftentimes believed that there should be a proper Yiddish word, simply forgotten by Yiddish-speakers who are bilingual and Russian-dominant.

However, when Russian-speakers with such attitudes come to study Yiddish, they are surprised to learn that, for instance, the mentioned verbs are an integral part of the "proper" Yiddish lexicon and that familiar Slavicisms in Yiddish they've heard do not prove attrition of Yiddish or its "non-serious" character. At a more advanced stage, they learn to notice dialectal variation, because some varieties of Yiddish have more Slavicisms than others, and Slavic-origin lexical items can vary in shape (consider *nudjen/ nudžen* 'to bore'), depending on a particular Slavic variety that has influenced a given variety of Yiddish. Thus, students of Yiddish begin to reconsider the connections they've made between Yiddish and Russian.

Jewish Russian may also become a relevant point of comparison, as drawing attention to some Jewish Russian constructions contributes to a better understanding of Yiddish morphosyntax, argument structure, idioms, etc., among Russian speakers who learn Yiddish. Figuratively speaking, recall how your grandmother would say it in Russian and then translate back to Yiddish. For instance, while analyzing the Yiddish expression *ix vejs zejer* 'how should I know?' (literally, 'I know very much') it is helpful to mention its Jewish Russian word-for-word rendition *ja znaju očen'* with the same meaning and the same structure, known to many Russian-speaking Jews. Thus, learners of Yiddish come to appreciate fluid borders between linguistic varieties and connections among various components of Yiddish, Jewish Russian, and the Slavic languages.

Although Yiddish is not spoken in FSU on the scale it used to be before the Holocaust, it is not gone without a trace (see also Shandler 2006; Rabinovitch, Goren, and Pressman 2012 about the post-vernacular life of Yiddish). Yiddish elements are re-arranged, re-considered, and included into new linguistic repertoires (Blommaert and Backus 2011). Those who become more familiar with Yiddish and have some access, either to Yiddish or to Jewish Russian, come to appreciate connections among all three. This openness and the complex links between the varieties may remind one of the concept of the polysystem, developed in the 1970s by Israeli literary scholar Itamar Even-Zohar (1990). Cultures and languages are not homogenous and their elements have different statuses at different moments of time in different cultural systems. Drawing on the concept, Shmeruk (1989) refers to the culture of Polish Jews as a Hebrew-Yiddish-Polish trilingual culture and implies that it would be a gross simplification to discuss three separate cultures as closed and isolated systems that are opposed to each other. Appreciation of these connections by laypeople and language learners is much needed, because it contributes to the improvement of meta-linguistic awareness and the development of a more nuanced view on language as such. Using the terms of Benor (2010), all of the components would add up to a certain Jewish ethnolinguistic repertoire.

References

Altshuler, Mordechai. 1998. *Soviet Jewry on the eve of the Holocaust: A social and demographic profile*. Jerusalem: Hebrew University & Yad Vashem.

Avineri, Netta Rose. 2012. *Heritage language socialization practices in secular Yiddish educational context: The creation of a metalinguistic community*. Los Angeles: University of California Los Angeles PhD thesis.

Beider, Alexander. 2013. Reapplying the language tree model to the history of Yiddish. *Journal of Jewish Languages* 1. 77–121.

Benor, Sarah Bunin. 2009. Do American Jews speak a 'Jewish language'? A model of Jewish linguistic distinctiveness. *Jewish Quarterly Review* 99(2). 230–269.

Benor, Sarah Bunin. 2010. Ethnolinguistic repertoire: Shifting the analytic focus in language and ethnicity. *Journal of Sociolinguistics* 14(2). 159–183.

Blommaert, Jan & Ad Backus. 2011. Repertoires revisited: 'Knowing language' in superdiversity. *Working Papers in Urban Language and Literacy* 67. http://www.kcl.ac.uk/innovation/groups/ldc/publications/workingpapers/download.aspx (Accessed 8 November 2016).

Clyne, Michael. 2000. Lingua franca and ethnolects in Europe and beyond. *Sociolinguistica* 14. 83–89.

Cukierman, Walenty. 1980. The Odessan myth and idiom in some early works of Odessa writers. *Canadian-American Slavic Studies* 14(1). 36–51.

Ddribins, Leo. 1996. *Ebreji Latvijā* [Jews in Latvia]. Riga: Latvijas Zinātņu Akadēmijas Filozofijas un Socioloģijas Institūta Etnisko Pētījumu Centrs.

Estraikh, Gennady. 1993. Pyrrhic victories of Soviet Yiddish language planners. *East European Jewish Affairs* 23(2). 25–37.
Estraikh, Gennady. 1995. The era of Sovetish Heymland: Readership of the Yiddish press in the Former Soviet Union. *East European Jewish Affairs* 25(1). 17–22.
Estraikh, Gennady. 1996. On the acculturation of Jews in late Imperial Russia. *Rassegna Mensile di Israel* 62. 217–228.
Estraikh, Gennady. 2008. From Yiddish to Russian: A story of linguistic and cultural appropriation. *Studia Hebraica* 8. 62–71.
Even-Zohar, Itamar (ed.). 1990. Polysystem Studies. [Special issue]. *Poetics Today* 11(1).
Gold, David. 1985. Jewish English. In Joshua A. Fishman (ed.), *Readings in the sociology of Jewish languages*, 280–298. Leiden: Brill.
Greenbaum, Abraham Alfred. 1978. *Jewish scholarship and scholarly institutions in Soviet Russia, 1918–1953*. Jerusalem: Centre for Research and Documentation of East European Jewry.
Hary, Benjamin. 2009. *Translating religion: Linguistic analysis of Judeo-Arabic sacred texts from Egypt*, (Études sur le judaïsme medieval). Leiden & Boston: Brill.
Hary, Benjamin & Martin J. Wein. 2013. Religiolinguistics: on Jewish-, Christian- and Muslim-defined languages. *International Journal of the Sociology of Language* 220. 85–108.
Jacobs, Neil. 1996. On the investigation of 1920s Vienna Jewish speech. *American Journal of Germanic Languages and Literatures* 8. 177–215.
Jacobs, Neil. 2001. Yiddish in the Baltic region. In Östen Dahl & Maria Koptjevskaja-Tamm (eds.), *The circum-Baltic languages*, 285–311. Amsterdam: John Benjamins.
Jacobs, Neil. 2005. *Yiddish. A linguistic introduction*. Cambridge: Cambridge University Press.
Jaspers, Jürgen. 2008. Problematizing ethnolects: Naming linguistic practices in an Antwerp secondary school. *International Journal of Bilingualism* 12(1–2). 85–103.
Katz, Dovid. 1983. Zur Dialektologie des Jiddischen [On Yiddish dialectology]. In Werner Besch, Anne Betten, Oskar Reichmann & Stefan Sonderegger (eds.), *Dialektologie. Ein Handbuch zur deutschen und allgemeinen Dialektforschung*, 2 vol, 1018–1041. Berlin & New York: Walter de Gruyter.
Le Foll, Claire. 2012. The Institute for Belarusian Culture: The constitution of Belarusian and Jewish studies in the BSSR between Soviet and non-Soviet science (1922–1928). *Ab Imperio* 4. 245–274.
Le Page, Robert & André Tabouret-Keller. 1985. *Acts of identity: Creole-based approaches to language and ethnicity*. Cambridge: Cambridge University Press.
Lipets, Dov. 1965. Hebreish shul-vezn un kultur-bavegung in Lite (1919–1939) [Hebrew schools and cultural movement in Lithuania (1919–1939)]. In Haim Laykovich (ed.), *Lite* [Lithuania], vol. 2, 293–323. Tel Aviv: Farlag Y.L. Peretz.
Mark, Mendl. 1973. *Di yidish-veltlekhe shul in Letland* [The secular Yiddish school in Latvia]. New York & Tel-Aviv: Ha-Menora.
Mendelsohn, Ezra. 1983. *The Jews of East Central Europe between the world wars*. Bloomington: Indiana University Press.
Myhill, James. 2004. *Language in Jewish society: Towards a new understanding*. Clevedon: Multilingual Matters.
Nortier, Jacomine. 2008. Introduction. Ethnolects? The emergence of new varieties among adolescents. *International Journal of Bilingualism* 12(1–2). 1–5.

Peltz, Rakhmiel. 1985. The de-hebraization controversy in Soviet Yiddish language planning: standard or symbol. In Joshua A. Fishman (ed.), *Readings in the sociology of Jewish languages,* 125–150. Leiden: Brill.

Peltz, Rakhmiel. 1997. The undoing of language planning from the vantage of cultural history: Two twentieth century examples. In Michael Clyne (ed.), *Undoing and redoing corpus planning,* 327–356. Berlin & New York: Mouton de Gruyter.

Polinsky, Maria & Olga Kagan. 2007. Heritage languages in the "wild" and in the classroom. *Language and Linguistic Compass* 1(5). 368–395.

Rabinovitch, Lara, Shiri Goren & Hannah S. Pressman (eds.). 2012. *Choosing Yiddish: New frontiers of language and culture.* Detroit: Wayne State University Press.

Safran, Gabriella. 2016. Jewish argument style among Russian revolutionaries. *Journal of Jewish Languages* 4(1). 44–68.

Shandler, Jeffrey. 2005. *Adventures in Yiddishland: Postvernacular language and culture.* Berkeley & Los Angeles: University of California Press.

Shmeruk, Chone. 1989. Hebrew-Yiddish-Polish: A trilingual Jewish culture. In Yisrael Gutman, Ezra Mendelsohn, Jehuda Reinharz & Chone Shmeruk (eds.), *The Jews of Poland between two World Wars,* 285–311. Waltham: University Press of New England.

Šteimanis, Josifs. 1995. *Latvijas ebreju vēsture* [History of Latvian Jews]. Daugavpils: Daugavpils Pedagoģiska Universitāte.

Thomason, Sarah Grey & Terence Kaufman. 1991. *Language contact, creolization, and genetic linguistics.* Berkeley & Los Angeles: University of California.

Vaskela, Gediminas. 2006. Lietuvių ir žydų santykiai visuomenės modernėjimo ir socialinės sferos politinio reguliavimo aspektais (XX a. pirmoji pusė). In Vladas Sirutavičius & Darius Staliūnas (eds.), *Žydai Lietuvos ekonominėje-socialinėje stuktūroje: tarp tarpininko ir konkurento* [Jews in the economical and social structure of Lithuania: Between mediator and competitor], 133–176. Vilnius: Lietuvos Istorijos Institutas.

Veynger, Mordkhe. 1929. *Yidishe dialektologye* [Yiddish dialectology]. Minsk: Vaysrusisher Melukhe-Farlag.

Verschik, Anna (ed.). 1999. The Yiddish dialect in Estonia (a description). *Fenno-Ugristica* 22. 265–291.

Verschik, Anna. 2007. Jewish Russian and the field of ethnolect study. *Language in Society* 36(2). 213–232.

Verschik, Anna. 2010. Ethnolect debate: Evidence from Jewish Lithuanian. *International Journal of Multilingualism* 7(4). 285–305.

Verschik, Anna. 2014. Bare participle forms in the speech of Lithuanian Yiddish heritage speakers: Multiple causation. *International Journal of the Sociology of Languge* 226. 213–235.

Weinreich, Uriel. 1956. Note on the Yiddish rise-fall intonation contour. In Morris Halle (ed.), *For Roman Jakobson: Essays on the occasion of his sixtieth birthday,* 633–643. The Hague: Mouton.

Wexler, Paul. 1987. *Explorations in Judeo-Slavic linguistics.* Leiden: Brill.

Zuckermann, Ghil´ad. 2009. Hybridity versus revivability: Multiple causation, forms and patterns. *Journal of Language Contact* 2. 40–67.

Yehudit Henshke
The Hebrew and Aramaic Component of Judeo-Arabic

1 Introduction

This chapter seeks to explore the multilayered and multifaceted development of the Hebrew language in the Middle Ages in the lands of the Muslim east and west, and its interaction with Arabic, the dominant tongue in these countries. It will describe the contact between the high Hebrew of the *beit midrash* and the local Arabic vernaculars.

1.1 The strata of written Hebrew and Aramaic

The body of Hebrew textual sources is both broad and varied. Beginning with the 24 books of the Bible (the latest of which were written during the early Second Temple period, in the last centuries BCE), it continues with post-biblical texts, including the Oral Torah (*tora she-be-'al pe*): the Mishnah, Tosefta and Midreshe Halakha, whose writing continued until the second century CE.

In the second century, Hebrew began declining as a spoken language and gradually became confined to the realms of religious worship and study. It remained in this status for centuries, until its revival as a living language at the close of the 19th century.

In the last centuries BCE and first centuries CE, a state of Hebrew-Aramaic diglossia existed in the Land of Israel. Aramaic gradually replaced Hebrew as the dominant vernacular, while Hebrew, as well as Aramaic mixed with Hebrew, continued to serve as the language of writing and literature. This era saw the composition of great and diverse texts: on the one hand, the Jerusalem Talmud and the *Midreshei Haggadah*, written in Galilean Aramaic mixed with Hebrew, as well as the Babylonian Talmud, written in Babylonian Aramaic mixed with Hebrew; on the other hand, a rich body of liturgical poetry (*piyyut*), which was written in the Land of Israel and was mostly in Hebrew. With the Arabic conquest, Aramaic began to decline as well and over several centuries was gradually replaced by Arabic; the works of the Babylonian *Ge'onim*, composed during this period, were written in both these languages. This brings us to the close of the first millennium CE.

For centuries, Hebrew served as a spoken and written language alongside other tongues from different families, but the most significant contact was with a northwestern Semitic language closely related to it: Aramaic. Due to the kinship and ongoing contact between the two languages, the later biblical literature, as well as a sizable portion of rabbinic literature and the works of the *Ge'onim*, were written in Aramaic, and in many cases Aramaic was itself considered a holy tongue. It comes as no surprise, then, that classical Hebrew and Aramaic continued to coexist as a blended component, and from now on we shall speak of a Hebrew component (integrated into Arabic) that contains within it an Aramaic element.[1]

1.2 Hebrew as a language of prestige

After its decline as a spoken language (in the second century) and until its revival as such (in the late 19th century), Hebrew existed as a living literary tongue, mainly religious in character. It served as the liturgical language of Judaism: for reading the Bible; studying the Mishna; reciting prayers, blessings and liturgical poems; studying the Torah (Responsa, Halakha, commentary and Midrash); delivering sermons; writing poetry, and even composing personal and community documents. In other words, Hebrew, the language of the vast Hebrew (and Aramaic) literature surveyed above, served the Jewish communities as a prestigious language of culture and developed along with the local Jewish communities according to their needs.

1.3 Reading traditions

The first millennium CE saw the development of three traditions in the reading and vocalization of Hebrew – the Tiberian, Palestinian and Babylonian traditions (Eldar 1989). These traditions, and traditions that evolved from them, were used by the Jewish communities well into the 20th century. The tradition practiced in each community was handed down from generation to generation, orally or in writing, and determined the form of various words and the rules of pronunciation, both general and specific. The most widely accepted tradition was the Tiberian, which became established as the authoritative (Masoretic) form of the Bible, imposing a uniform and fixed form of spelling, vocalization, and cantillation of biblical texts. However, this tradition did not necessarily apply to post-biblical texts (Mishna,

---

[1] This brief overview has surveyed the Jewish literature written until 1000 CE, which influenced the languages and cultures of the Jews in the later Middle Ages. The overview did not include the rich literature of Qumeran, which was discovered only in the 20th century, nor ancient Hebrew inscriptions, letters, etc., that were also discovered late and therefore did not directly influence the language of the medieval Jewish communities.

Talmud, *Piyyut* and prayer). As a result, the pronunciation of these texts often preserved remnants of other, independent traditions (Morag 1985; Henshke 2013).

The reading traditions of post-biblical literature fall into two categories: Yemenite and Sephardic. The latter category includes the traditions practiced in Spain, the Muslim east, and the Maghreb (as well as the pre-Ashkenazic tradition). A comparison of the two categories reveals that the Jews of Yemen espoused the Babylonian reading tradition, and those of Sepharad the Palestinian reading tradition (Morag 1963: 11–13 [Introduction]).

1.4 Diglossia

Until the 20th century, Jewish communities were bi/multilingual, and experienced a tension between the language and religious culture of prestige – the many-layered Hebrew traditions – and the local vernaculars. This created an interesting state of diglossia between the local spoken language, which was used in everyday life but whose status in the eyes of the speakers was low, and Hebrew, which was revered and used by the intellectual rabbinic elite, but which was largely confined to religious and spiritual life. This diglossia gave rise to a unique and fascinating type of language-contact that is the most prominent characteristic of the Jewish language varieties.

The diglossia examined in this chapter is one of Hebrew and Arabic. Unlike Jewish communities whose vernacular was non-Semitic, Arabic-speaking communities displayed diglossia between Semitic languages similar in their basic structure (or even triglossia or more, if Aramaic, Standard Arabic, and other Semitic dialects are taken into account).

1.5 Sociolinguistic stratification

Familiarity with the Hebrew tradition had a significant impact on the scope and realization of the language contact. Community members differed in their levels of knowledge; hence, the interaction between the Hebrew tradition and the local vernacular is complex and convoluted in character. Speaking very broadly, most Jewish communities in the Muslim world divided into the following groups in terms of familiarity with the Hebrew tradition:[2] Most conversant in Hebrew culture and tradition were the members (nearly all of them men) of the intellectual

---

[2] This is, of course, a very general characterization; individual communities differed in their precise structure and makeup.

elite – *dayyanim*, rabbis, and Torah scholars, who dealt with Torah on a daily basis. A second group consisted of men who studied Torah in their youth and went on to pursue a profession but maintained ongoing contact with the world of prayer and Torah study. The third group included the women, who in these communities were not taught to read and write Hebrew and were therefore not exposed to this language directly. Rather, their exposure to Hebrew was indirect, through the oral Jewish traditions passed down from mother to daughter, or through the mediation of men from the first and second groups. The third group also included illiterate and uneducated men (Bar-Asher 1999: 150–153). Interestingly, this group is revealed to be a conservative sector that preserved ancient Hebrew forms unchanged, whereas the learned men were more likely to transform and develop the Hebrew traditions, in accordance with new norms or external influences (Henshke 2007: 4–5).

1.6 Judeo-Arabic

For centuries, the Jewish communities in the Muslim world lived apart from the general (non-Jewish) population and were markedly different from their surroundings in their religion, culture, education, and community life. Their language of religion and learning was usually Hebrew, and therefore one of the most prominent characteristics – if not the most prominent characteristic – of their spoken Arabic dialect, namely Judeo-Arabic, is the Hebrew-Aramaic component that was melded into it. This component did not transform the Arabic dramatically but adapted itself to the Arabic grammatical structure (Blau 1999: 123–166); nevertheless, its presence rendered Judeo-Arabic clearly distinct from the language of the environment. Naturally, once incorporated, the Hebrew component took on a life of its own within the Arabic dialect and over the centuries generated fascinating innovations and novel forms that became part of the Jews' distinct language.

1.6.1 Written Judeo-Arabic

The communities of the Muslim world produced a rich and varied literature in Judeo-Arabic, including texts of philosophy, grammar, Halakha, biblical and Mishnaic commentary, etc. The subjects confirm that Judeo-Arabic was a religiolect (Hary 2009). At the same time, writing in Hebrew also continued. Poetry, both religious and secular, was written almost exclusively in this language, and great works in other genres were written in it as well (Drory 1988; Blau 1999: 229–239). The state of diglossia also gave rise to a great enterprise of translation from Arabic to Hebrew for the sake of communities that did not understand Arabic.

Written Judeo-Arabic is divided into two main periods: the classical period, ending in the 15th century, and the later period, from the 16th century onward (see also Hary 2016: 301–307 for a more nuanced periodization). Despite the considerable differences between them, texts from both periods are alike in two ways: they are written in Hebrew characters, and they contain a noticeable Hebrew-Aramaic component, the fruit of the contact between Hebrew, with all its strata, and Arabic. This contact is reflected in every aspect of the language: its morphology, syntax, semantics, and, of course, its lexicon and phraseology. Thus, for example, one finds Hebrew words prefixed with the Arabic definite article: *al-isha* 'the woman', *al-baʕal* 'the husband', *al-bet din* 'the Beit Din'; Hebrew words with Arabic plural forms: *šṭarat* (plural of Hebrew *šṭar* 'deed'), *mazamir* (plural of Hebrew *mizmor* 'song'), *arwaḥ* (plural of Hebrew *rewaḥ* 'profit'); Hebrew words with Arabic pronominal suffixes: *nixbad-na* 'our dignitary', and Hebrew words in Arabic verbal forms: *qaddas* (equivalent of Hebrew *qiddeš* 'sanctified'), *asdar* (equivalent of Hebrew *hisdir* 'arranged, regulated'), and *tašammad* (equivalent of Hebrew *hištamed* 'converted to a different faith') (Blau 1999: 123–166).

1.6.2 Spoken Judeo-Arabic

Though knowledge of written Hebrew was the province of literate men, the Hebrew component percolated into the speech of Jewish society as a whole, and, to some extent, even into the speech of non-Jews. Lacking examples of the medieval Judeo-Arabic vernacular, we shall focus on the vernacular of the 19th and 20th centuries, examples of which do exist.[3]

2 The Hebrew-Aramaic component of spoken Judeo-Arabic

2.1 Languages of origin

Thanks to the contact between the Hebrew texts, written and oral, and the spoken Arabic vernacular, most of the non-Arabic elements that became part of Judeo-Arabic originate in Hebrew. However, there is also a small but prominent

---

[3] The transcription here and throughout the chapter reflects the pronunciation of speakers in various Arabic-speaking communities.

pool of words and expressions that originate in Aramaic. The size of this Aramaic lexicon differed among social strata. Naturally, the language of the scholars was relatively rich in learned Aramaic expressions, such as *deʕabad* 'after the fact' and *en haxe name* 'indeed it is so, all the more so'. Other expressions, sometimes altered in pronunciation, also gained currency in the speech of social strata that did not come into contact with Hebrew on a daily basis, expressions such as *bar minnan* (literally 'except for us', a way of referring to the dead), *sitra ʔaḥra* (literally 'the other side', a way of referring to the devil), *ʕina biša* 'the evil eye', and *raḥmana ləṣlan* 'God forbid' (Bar-Asher 1999: 166–167). Judeo-Arabic also absorbed Aramaic words that were not part of the scholars' jargon, such as *ʕrəbbaʔ* 'the eve of the Sabbath or a holiday', *maʕl* 'the eve of Yom Kippur', *ḥeleq, ḥelq/ ʕleq* 'harosset', *raḥmin* (a personal name meaning 'mercy'), etc. (Bar-Asher 1999: 317–320; Avishur 2001: 133–142, 248–256; Henshke 2009: 190–191).

Another aspect worthy of notice is the special status of Aramaic words among Babylonian Jews, i.e., the Jews of Iraq. In that region, Aramaic served as the Jews' spoken language before it was superseded by Arabic. Hence, the vernacular spoken there was richer in Aramaic expressions, including expressions that were not used elsewhere, e.g., *dara/daġa* 'row', referring to pupils sitting in a row in the *melamed*'s classroom, *damax* 'sleep', *gandar/kandar* 'rolled' (Avishur 2001: 235–287).

Words from other languages, too, found their way into the Jews' speech, through Rabbinic literature and Hebrew-Aramaic halakhic literature, such as the Greek words *esṭanis* 'fastidious person', *boṭrobos* 'patron', which entered via scholarly parlance, and the Yiddish *yarsiyat* (<*yahrzeit* 'anniversary of death'), which was known from the late Responsa literature (Bar-Asher 1999: 154; Henshke 2009: 188–189).

2.2 Lexical categories

As is usually the case in language contact, the majority of the elements comprising the Hebrew component were nouns, especially abstract nouns, but adjectives and adverbs also abounded. Another large category is proper names, some of which were used as given names, while others, associated with hated historical or biblical figures, served as epithets. Verbs also formed a substantial category; most were adapted verbs (Hebrew roots inserted into Arabic patterns), while a small minority were incorporated verbs, maintaining their original Hebrew form.

Also common were constructs, e.g., *bet l-məqdaš* 'the Temple', *braxt kohanim* 'priestly blessing', *qbalt əš-šəbbat* 'reception of the Sabbath', as well as noun+ modifier combinations, e.g., *ṭalet qaṭan* 'small tallit', *siman tob* 'good omen', *qlala nəmrəṣat* 'strong curse'. Lastly, another distinct category was that of proverbs, discussed below (Henshke 1991: 98–100; Bar-Asher 1999: 164–166).

2.3 Domains of use

The most prominent – but by no means the exclusive – domain in which Hebrew expressions were used was the religious domain. The Jewish lifestyle of these communities was immersed in the Hebrew-Aramaic texts of the Holy Scriptures and halakhic literature. We therefore find hundreds of words, phrases, terms, and idioms representing every aspect of Jewish life (Kara 1988: 135–141; Henshke 1991: 100–103; Bar-Asher 1999: 158–163; Rosenbaum 2002: 134–137).

Jewish concepts: *imuna* 'faith', *galut* 'exile', *ṭahara* 'purity', *ṭomʔa* 'impurity', *haš-šem yitbarax* 'God, blessed be He', *yeṣer ha-raʕ* 'evil inclination', *kəbbara* 'atonement', *məbbul* 'flood', *mašiyaḥ* 'messiah', *nbouʔa* 'prophecy', *nes* 'miracle', *qabbala* 'Kabbalah'.

Matters of religious law and custom: *etrog* 'citrus fruit', *braxa* 'blessing', *habdala* 'Havdalah', *həggada* 'Haggadah', *ḥameṣ* 'chametz', *mila* 'circumcision', *məqwe* 'Mikveh'.

Jewish months: *tišre* 'the month of Tishre', *ḥəšwan* 'the month of Heshvan', *raḥamin* (name for the month of Elul).

Holidays and fasts: *sru-ḥag* "Isru Hag', *hošaʕna rabba*, *ḥol moʕed* 'weekday of festival (Sukkot or Passover)', *kəbbor* 'Yom Kippur', *lag la-ʕomer*, *sukkot*. It should be noted that the names of the months and holidays also featured in hybrid Arabic-Hebrew proverbs, such as *tebeṭ l-makala o-qʕad l-bet* 'Tevet (a cold month) is for eating and sitting at home', or *en qəmṣan ila bišaḥ* (literally 'No miser except during Pesach', i.e., "Pesach calls for thrift").

The synagogue and beit midrash: *aron qodeš* 'holy ark', *gniza* 'genizah', *draš* 'rabbi's sermon', *hallel* '(the prayer of) praise', *mənḥa* 'afternoon prayer', *ʕrbit* 'prayer of evening or night', *šaḥrit* 'prayer of morning', *mənyan* 'a quorum of ten men required for public worship', *šifər* 'Torah scroll', *paraša* 'a section of a biblical book', *rəbbi*, *tora*.

Community life: *ʔureyaḥ* 'visitor', specifically from the Land of Israel, *baṭlan* 'Jew who devotes his time to studying in the *beit midrash*', *gizbar* 'treasurer', *ḥəlloq* 'distribution', specifically of funds to the poor, *qahal* 'men of the congregation'.

Terms of praise and blessing: *išət ḥayl* 'woman of valor', *baqi ʕaṣom* 'great scholar', *bin porat yušif* blessing to ward off the evil eye, *ḥaxam* 'wise man, rabbi', *ri šamaym* 'pious person', *kašir* 'kosher', *muʕid ṭob* 'happy holiday', *bəqqeyaḥ* 'sharp-minded, clever person', *ʕalaw əš-šalum* literally 'peace be upon him' (said of the deceased).

Curses and insults: *šmiday* 'devil', *ber šaḥət* literally 'well of dryness' (an expression for a miser), *gaʔawa* 'arrogance', *ḥaṣof* 'insolent person', *dəbbesa* 'fool' in the feminine form, *šəm mawt* literally 'death potion', poison, *ʕaqqeš* 'stubborn person', *šoṭe* 'fool', *šune* 'hater, enemy', *raʕ maʕalalem* 'evildoer', *rasaʕ* 'evil person'.

Other terms: *ʔafəllu* 'even', *bəžžyon* 'shame, fiasco', *gəbbor* 'hero', *dor* 'generation', *hebəl wa-req* 'vanity and emptiness', *zəkkaron* 'memory', *wdday* 'certain, certainly', *ḥatan* 'groom', *ṭaʕot* 'error, mistake', *yayn* 'wine', *kabud* 'honor', *məmmaš* 'really, actually', *li-hefəx* 'on the contrary', *maʕaši* 'story', *naḥt ruwaḥ* 'pleasure', *səddur* 'book' (not necessarily of prayers), *ʕašir* 'rich', *parnasa* 'livelihood', *ṣbeʕot* 'hypocrisy', *qimaḥ* 'flour', *remeəz* 'sign, hint', *təbšil* 'cooked dish'.

2.4 Expressions combining Hebrew and Arabic

The ongoing contact between the languages, and the incorporation of Hebrew elements into Arabic speech, naturally led to the formation of expressions combining Hebrew and Arabic elements. It should be noted that the majority of speakers were not aware of the hybrid nature of these expressions and thought them to be Arabic. Examples are *šid moṭlaq* – Hebrew *šed* 'demon' + Arabic *muṭlaq* 'terrible', an epithet for a naughty boy; *laylat (a)l-fasaḥ* – Arabic *layla* 'night' + Arabic *al-* 'the' + Hebrew *pasaḥ* 'Passover', an expression attested in Yemen meaning the night of the Seder; *ʕanyuṭ midxanzireh* – Hebrew 'poverty' + Arabic 'piggish', meaning abasing poverty (Kara 1988: 134–135); *xu kəbbor* – Arabic 'brother of' + Hebrew 'atonement', namely 'the brother of Yom Kippur', referring to the Fast of Gedalia; *nar u-gəfret* – Arabic 'fire' + Hebrew 'sulphur' (Henshke 2007: 151–153).

3 The secret jargon

An interesting sub-language that forms part of the Hebrew-Aramaic component is the secret jargon, which took advantage of the Hebrew component to form a language opaque to outsiders: children, clients, gentiles (Ratzaby 1978: 22–24 [Introduction]; Chetrit 1989: 262–266; Bar-Asher 1999: 160–162; Avishur 2001: 93–131; Rosenbaum 2002: 138–139; Henshke 2007: 155–156).

This sub-language had many names: *lasun* or *lasuniya* 'language', *lusun qodeš* 'holy tongue', *lasun rakka* 'soft language', *ʕəbri* 'Hebrew', *luġa ʕbriya* 'Hebrew language', *luġat al-yahud* 'the language of the Jews', *taqullit* 'speech', from the Arabic verb *qal*, 'to speak', *slaġot* 'jokes',[4] *slumiyya* 'the language of our own people', *l-iṣoraniya* 'the language of the Jews', etc.

---

[4] This shows that the jargon utilized humorous language to create discourse opaque to outsiders. Professor Joseph Chetrit, p.c.

Unlike the Hebrew component as a whole, the secret jargon tends to avoid Arabic morphology and syntax, and thus features a relatively large number of Hebrew verbs that are not adapted to Arabic patterns, but rather incorporated as they are, e.g., the imperative verbs *dabber* 'speak', *ʕase* 'do', *harḥiq* 'keep away', *lix* 'go', as well as Hebrew sentences featuring Hebrew syntax, e.g., *lo tidabber* 'don't speak' and *al tətten lo* 'don't give him'. The jargon was used in three domains: in the religious domain, to form a barrier between Judaism and Islam, in the domain of trade and business, and to conceal information from children. In the religious domain, there were words for Jew: *yešuroni* (from Deuteronomy 32:15), *ben ʕammenu* 'one of our people'; for a gentile: *goy*, *ummot ha-ʕolam* 'world nations', *yišmaʕel* Ishmael, *qedar* (name of a biblical tribe), *l-qaton* 'young person', *ḥaver* 'friend', and *berex* 'joint, knee', which is a loan translation of the word Ka'ba; for Christian: *ʕarel* or *ʕarir* 'uncircumcised'; and for the Cross: *šti wa-ʕerəb* 'warp and weft'. Dark-skinned gentiles were called *šifaḥ*, a back-formation from the word *šifḥa* 'female slave', to avoid the offensive Arabic word *ʕabd* 'slave' used in spoken Arabic.

Words used in the domain of trade included many verbs, such as *lix* 'go'; *šatta?/štoq/šoteq* 'shut up', used in Iraq, *daber-lo* 'tell him', *ʕaše* 'do', *harḥiq* 'keep away'. Terms referring to the quality of goods included *yafet/yafe* 'beautiful' and *ṭob* 'good'. From the word *yafet*, the Jews also derived the Hebrew-Arabic verb *yaffet* 'to give a good price', which had a *masdar* form (*tayfit*), as well as a passive form (*ʔetyaffet*) and a participle form (*metyaffet*). Other terms referring to prices and money were *baḥim* 'tin', *mammon* 'money', *minyan* 'ten', *ḥeṣi* 'half price', and *šanayen-šanayen* 'two-two', meaning four. Some words denoting sums of money were based on the gematria value of Hebrew letters, such as *daltin* '40', derived from the letter dalet, whose value in gematria is 4, plus the Arabic plural suffix *–in*, *qof* '100', from the letter qof, whose value in gematria is 100. Egyptian Jews coined the word *ša??al*, based on the Aramaic root š-q-l, for 'steal'; North African Jews used the root x-n-b (a variant of the Hebrew root g-n-b) in a similar way. Another word used in commercial contexts was *ʕinayim* 'eyes', meaning 'look out'.

The third domain, concealing information from children, was the most limited. A child was called *qaton/qtiyn* 'small one' or *ḥaber* 'friend'.

4 Preservation of ancient forms

An examination of the Hebrew component reveals a fascinating twofold reality: On the one hand, this component was alive and active and was subject to innovation and development; at the same time, it remained firmly anchored in the ancient Hebrew heritage in which it originated. This section focuses on the latter aspect: the preservation of ancient elements, known from Rabbinic Hebrew and from the non-Tiberian reading traditions – elements that were absorbed into Judeo-Arabic speech, yet faithfully mirror the Hebrew of ancient rabbinic manuscripts. This component of Judeo-Arabic thus provides a fascinating window onto early stages of Classical Hebrew and also sheds light on the ancient Hebrew traditions maintained by the Arabic-speaking communities over the generations (Bar-Asher 1999: 171, 317–320; Henshke 2009).

The ancient Hebrew forms preserved in Judeo-Arabic belong to the phonological, morphological, and syntactic domains; below is a review.

5 Phonology

5.1 Penultimate stress

The question of stress is a central one in Hebrew linguistics, both biblical and post-biblical (Ben-Hayyim 1963; Qimron 1992; Florentin 2002). The dominant tradition is the Tiberian one, which stresses the ultimate syllable in most words (*mileraʕ*), and indeed, most Hebrew words embedded in Judeo-Arabic conform to the Tiberian rule in this regard. However, the speech of some communities incorporates words with penultimate stress (*mileʕel*), reflecting ancient Hebrew traditions that are evidenced in the Dead Sea scrolls, in Samaritan Hebrew, and in rabbinic manuscripts, and which were marginalized when the Tiberian tradition gained dominance. Penultimate stress exists in the Hebrew component of Yemen, Aleppo, Baghdad, Morocco, and Tunisia (as well as in non-Arabic speaking communities such as Zakho and Ashkenaz (Henshke 2007a: 325–331). Thus, in Yemen we find *'ósor* 'forbidden'; in Damascus, *ʕid əlmáṣṣa* (the Festival of Matza, Passover), *'éxa* (Eikhah, the Book of Lamentations), and *ʔafíllu* 'even'; and in Tunisia *habdála* 'Havdalah', *l-haggáda* 'the Haggadah', *mġə́lla* 'the Scroll of Esther', *mášna* 'Mishna', and *nʕíla* 'the prayer of Ne'ila' (Henshke 2007a: 321–325).

5.2 Geminated [r]

Tiberian Hebrew does not geminate the consonant [r], except in rare exceptional cases, but the Eastern tradition of Rabbinic Hebrew does geminate it, e.g., *garraʕ* 'barber', *sir-regan* 'he wove them', *še-rraʔa* 'who saw'. Geminated [r] also appears in some Hebrew words embedded into Judeo-Arabic, such as *ḥarrif* 'keen minded' (Bar-Asher 1999: 324–326), *qarraʔem* 'Karaites', *barroxət* 'parochet'. Again we see the Hebrew component preserving an ancient non-Tiberian tradition (Henshke 2009: 187).

5.3 Pronunciation of the qameṣ

The Palestinian traditions differed from the Babylonian and Tiberian in the realization of the qameṣ. While the first realized it like the *pataḥ* (as an [a] vowel), the other two apparently realized it as a type of [o] vowel. In this case, too, the Sephardic communities adopted a non-Tiberian tradition – the Palestinian – both in their scriptural reading tradition and in the Hebrew component of their speech. However, in some cases they did realize the qameṣ as [o], preserving ancient Babylonian or Tiberian pronunciations. For example, in the speech of some communities, the Aramaic honorific for a father, Mar, was pronounced *mor* and Tish'a be-Av 'the Ninth of Av' was *tšaʕbob*; in Aleppo and Damascus, *šamash* 'synagogue caretaker' was pronounced *šammoš* (which is also the origin of the surname), and the matza was called *maṣṣo* (Bar-Asher 1999: 222–223; Henshke 2007: 63).

6 Morphology

6.1 Plural suffix –iyyot

The Hebrew plural suffix *–iyyot*, which is not biblical but rather an innovation of Rabbinic Hebrew, is prominently preserved in the reading traditions of the Arabic-speaking communities, e.g., *galiyyot* (plural of *galut*, 'diaspora'), *malxiyyot* (plural of *malxut*, 'monarchy, kingship'). The Hebrew component exhibits an even wider distribution of this suffix, applying it to words that do not exist in the Mishnaic reading tradition (Henshke 2009: 192–193), e.g., *hafṭoriyyot* (plural of *hafṭara*), *baqqošiyyot* (plural of *baqqoša* 'request'), *šabboṭiyyot* (plural of *šabbot* 'Sabbath') (Ratzaby 1978: 37, 70; Kara 1992: 138–139),[5] *braxeyot* (plural of *braxa* 'blessing'), *gmariyyot*, (plural of *gmara*), and *l-išibiyut* (plural of *yeshiva*) (Henshke 2007: 92).

6.2 Pausal forms

In biblical Hebrew, pausal forms (characterized by penultimate stress and an alteration of the stressed vowel) occur before a pause and at the end of a verse. In ancient rabbinic manuscripts the phenomenon expanded, with pausal forms

---

[5] These three words are attested in Yemenite Hebrew, which preserves the Babylonian tradition, hence the realization of the *qames* as [o].

appearing in non-pausal contexts. These forms also found their way into the speech of Arabic-speaking Jews, e.g., *ṣaddáket* 'righteous woman' (Ben-Yaacob 1985: 168), *məfsákət* 'last meal before a fast' (Henshke 2009: 192), *boréxu* 'bless', *yagadéšu* 'will make kiddush', *yitgóʕu* 'will blow [the shofar]', *yišléṭu* 'will rule' (Kara 1992: 137; Morag 1995: 187). It should be mentioned that in Yemen, these forms were preserved both in the speech of women and in the speech of men (Kara 1988: 132).

6.3 Nominal and verbal patterns

Gehennam 'Hell' is an ancient form preserved in rabbinic manuscripts, an alternate of the form *gehenom* found in most texts. The former pronunciation was also preserved in most Sephardic communities, e.g., in Tunisia, Morocco, Algeria, Yemen, and Iraq (as well as in Zakho and Persia, and in Judeo-Spanish). Here too, the Hebrew component reflects an ancient Mishnaic tradition (Henshke 2009: 189–190).

The Hebrew component of Judeo-Arabic also preserved rare nominal patterns, such as the *qtala* pattern, e.g., *praṣa* (alongside *paraṣa*, 'parashah', the weekly Torah portion), *tʕana* (alongside *taʕana*, 'claim'), *thara* (alongside *tahara*, 'purity'), *ḥlaṣa* (alongside *ḥliṣa*, the ceremony of *halizah*), *ʕamada* (alongside *ʕamida*, 'standing') (Bar-Asher 1999). Yemenite Judeo-Arabic also incorporated words into the rare pattern of *qtal*, which originated in the Rabbinic Hebrew tradition of that community, e.g., *nagof* 'disease, flaw', *ṭanof* 'filth, contamination' (Morag 1995: 186). In the speech of Iraqi Jews, we find *šbaḥ-šbaḥot* (literally 'praise', referring to a *piyyut*) (Avishur 2001: 161–162).

Also found in Yemen and Iraq is the pattern *qatel* instead of *qatal*, e.g., *goṣer* 'short' (Ratzaby 1978: 251; Ben-Yaacob 1985: 179), as well as other ancient nominal patterns exemplified by *thayat-* instead of *thiyat-* 'resurrection', *homəš* instead of *ḥumaš* 'Pentateuch', and *kummar* rather than *komer* 'Christian priest', which are found in ancient rabbinic manuscripts and in the Babylonian tradition (Henshke 2009: 188–192).

The rabbinic verbal pattern *nitpaʕal*, e.g., *niṣṭaʕar* 'was sad, sorry', was preserved in these communities as well (Kara 1992: 138).

7 Syntax

7.1 Absolute forms in construct-state environments

Another common phenomenon in the Hebrew component is the use of absolute noun forms within a construct (instead of nouns in the construct state). In the communities of Morocco, Tunisia, Algeria, and Iraq we find *šaliyaḥ ṣabbor* (literally 'emissary of the public', 'prayer leader'), rather than the expected *šliyaḥ ṣəbbor; yayn nisx* ('libation wine'), rather than *yen nisx; lašon a-qodəš* (literally, 'the language of sanctity', the Holy Tongue), instead of *lešon a-qodəš*, and *mlaxem ḥabbala* 'angels of destruction' rather than *mlaxe ḥabbala*. Manuscripts and oral traditions indicate that similar forms existed in Rabbinic Hebrew (Henshke 2007: 105–106).

7.2 Absence of definiteness agreement: Indefinite noun with definite modifier

A few examples of this phenomenon are found in the Bible, e.g., *yom haš-šiši* 'the sixth day' (literally 'day the-sixth', Genesis 1:31), but manuscripts indicate that in Rabbinic Hebrew it became much more common and even became an identifying characteristic of this language. The Hebrew component of Judeo-Arabic preserves such forms, e.g., *sʕoda ham-mafsaqet* (literally 'meal the-final', referring to the final meal before a fast) (Reshef 1996: 512–513), *qəddus a-harox* (literally 'kiddush the-long', 'the long kiddush'), *šim a-mfuraš* (literally 'name the-explicit', referring to the Name of God) (Henshke 2007: 108).

ʕeser had-dibberot
The Jews of Tunisia, Morocco, and Algeria called the Ten Commandments and the *piyyutim* associated with them *ʕeser d-dəbbrot* (rather than *ʕaseret-*); even more common was the abbreviated term *l-ʕesər* 'the Ten'. Evidence shows that this seemingly incorrect form is not a late corruption, but an early form found in Rabbinic Hebrew (Bar-Asher 1999: 171).

ḥuṣa la-areṣ
Another ancient form preserved in the speech of the Arabic-speaking communities is *ḥuṣa la-areṣ*, a Rabbinic form that preserves the biblical directional case suffix [-a] (Reshef 1996: 515–516).

In sum, the Hebrew component of Judeo-Arabic preserved many ancient forms, only a small portion of which are presented here. This makes it an invaluable source of information about the history and development of the Hebrew language.

8 Evolution and innovation

The Hebrew component in the Jews' Arabic speech did not just preserve ancient forms. Being part of a living language and a flourishing culture, and due to the ongoing contact with Arabic, it also underwent change and development and generated innovative forms. This section presents morphological, syntactic, and semantic innovations, as well as the special Hebrew sub-dialect used for secret communication.

8.1 Morphology

8.1.1 The Hebrew verb

Since Hebrew and Arabic are sister Semitic tongues, very similar in their morphological structure, Hebrew verbs incorporated into Arabic can be absorbed in two main ways: through a process of adaptation and melding, in which a Hebrew root is inserted into an Arabic verbal pattern, or through straightforward incorporation (without adaptation), whereby a Hebrew verb is embedded as it is, leaving both its Hebrew root and its Hebrew pattern intact.

Adapted verbs
Quite a few Hebrew roots were adapted, i.e., inserted into Arabic patterns; e.g., in Egypt: ʔetdardem 'fell asleep', šaḥwar 'became black' (Rosenbaum 2002: 132–133); in Yemen: fawwar 'celebrated Purim', ʔaysayyeʕ 'will help', and yitraššaʕ (literally 'became evil', i.e., neglected his studies) (Ratzabi 1978: 221, 265; Kara 1992: 137–138); in Iraq: hammaṣ 'recited Hamotzi', the blessing over the bread, šattax 'conducted the Seder', from the Aramaic expression ha-šatta haxa, which appears in the Haggadah, and yfazmen 'sang a piyyut' (Avishur 2001: 163, 201–234); in Aleppo: ʔiyyex 'cried, lamented', from exa, the book of Eikhah, and šaʕbob (from tšaʕbob, Tishʻa be-Av) (Bar-Asher 1999: 213); and in North Africa: miyəl 'performed a ceremony of milah, circumcision', ḥalleṣ 'performed halizah', drəš =daraš, i.e., 'delivered a sermon' and qša =hiqsha, 'asked a Gemara question' (Bar-Asher 1999: 165–166).

In a comprehensive survey of Tunisian Judeo-Arabic (Henshke 2008), 78 Hebrew roots were found to be inserted into various Arabic patterns, forming 94 new forms: verbs, verbal nouns and verbal adjectives. The following is a list of the roots and the Arabic patterns in which they appear:

Faʕala (19): bdl, bdq, gzr, drš, hlx, ḥtm, ṭbl, nṭl, ṭl[6], mṭl[7], ṭmʔ, xnb[8], mṣy[9], fdy, fqd, qšy, ršm, šmr, trm

---

[6] Derived from the root nṭl by omission of the first lateral.
[7] Also a variant of nṭl.
[8] Variant of the root gnb 'to steal', used in the secret jargon.
[9] Derived from 'Hamotzi', the blessing over the bread.

FaʕʕaIa (35): gyr, gml, zmn, ḥyb, ḥll, ḥlṣ, ḥmṣ, ṭbl, ṭmʔ, ṭrf, kwn, xnb, ksy, kšf, kšr, lyx[10], myl, mkl[11], ndy, sdr, ʕyn, ʕqš, pyṭ, ṣdq, qdš, qṭn, rṣy, šbš, šbt, šmd[12], šmš, šqr, tqn, trṣ, trš
Faʕʕala quadrilateral (7): hbdl[13], bṣbṣ, glwd[14], dqdq, mlšn[15], ngzr[16], šbwš[17]
Faʕala (3): ṭhr, mṣy, ṣʕr
Tafaʕʕala (18): ʕbd, bzy, gzr, gyr, wdy, ḥyb, ksy, kšr, nbʔ, ndb, sdr, ʕqš, qnʔ, rṣy, šbš, šmd, snʔ, šfʕ
Tafaʕʕala quadrilateral (3): glwd, mlšn, trdm[18]
Faʕala quadrilateral (4): mwṣy, mwṣn[19], swʕd[20], šwḥd[21]
Tafaʕala quadrilateral (4): ḥwnf, nwḥš, ṣwbʕ, ṣwrr
Quadrilateral with internal vowel (1): nfṭr

The list shows that most of the roots are strong (i.e., comprised of unchanging consonants), whether they are trilateral or quadrilateral. This preference for strong roots is also reflected in the realization of hollow roots. Thus, the Hebrew hollow root m-u-l becomes m-y-l (realized with a consonantal y), and the imperative Hebrew verb *lex* becomes *liyyəx*.

The adapted roots appear in three main verbal patterns, with an apparent preference for the geminated patterns. The most common is *faʕʕala* (accounting for 37% of the roots); next come *tafaʕʕala* and *faʕala* (each accounting for about 20% of the roots). The quadrilateral pattern is also common (accounting for another 20%). The preference for geminated patterns follows from the way these roots were melded into the language: Most were borrowed as nominal, rather than verbal, forms. In other words, in most cases, it is not the roots themselves that were borrowed, but rather nouns, from which the verbs were then derived. In Hebrew, denominal derivation tends to utilize the geminated verbal forms. The semantic aspect also corroborates this assumption, for the meaning of these verbs is generally derived from the meaning of a Hebrew noun. The Judeo-Arabic

---

10 Derived from the imperative form *lex* 'go'.
11 Derived from the noun *maʔaxal* 'dish, food, consumption'.
12 Derived from the noun *šmad* (literally 'annihilation', conversion to a non-Jewish faith).
13 Derived from *habdala* 'Havdalah'.
14 Derived from *galut* 'diaspora'.
15 Derived from *malšin* 'informer'.
16 Derived from the verb *nigzar*, 'in the sense of issuing an oppressive decree'.
17 Derived from *šibbuš* 'distortion, mistake, obsession'.
18 Derived from the noun *tardema* 'sleep'.
19 The last two roots also derived from Hamotzi.
20 Derived from the noun *seʕuda* 'meal'.
21 Derived from the noun *šoḥad* 'bribe'.

verb *ḥallǝl*, for example, comes from the Hebrew noun *ḥillul* 'violation, specifically of the Sabbath', *gǝmmǝl* means 'to say Hagomel', etc.

The ongoing linguistic contact gave rise to an opposite phenomenon as well, namely Arabic roots conjugated in a Hebrew pattern. An example from Tunisia is the verb *mitlaḥafim* 'they wrap themselves', employing the Arabic root l-ḥ-f and the Hebrew *hitpael* pattern.

Embedded verbs
These are verbs that are not inserted into Arabic patterns, but maintain their original Hebrew form, which is alien to the morphological structure of Arabic. The survival of such foreign forms requires extra-linguistic motivation that prevents them from being assimilated into the structure of the host language. Indeed, these verbs occur only in two types of language: the secret jargon and the language of learned Jewish scholars. This clarifies the nature of the extra-linguistic motivation. The secret jargon was used to conceal information from foreign ears. To this end, speakers employed Hebrew words in a way that would provide no clue as to their meaning. Examples of words used in this manner are: *lex* 'go', *dabber* 'speak', *ʕase* 'do', *tiškaḥ* 'forget'.[22] The language of the scholars was rich in scholarly and halakhic Hebrew terms, such as *meʕayen* 'studies in depth', *mitʕanim* 'they fast', *hitnadev* 'gave charity', *yaziq* 'will harm', *mitqadešet* 'marries', *and yiqra* 'will read'.

8.1.2 Nominal forms

Like the verbs, incorporated Hebrew nouns sometimes maintained their Hebrew morphology and sometimes adapted to Arabic morphology.

Plural forms
Some examples incorporated nouns that preserved their Hebrew plural form, while others assumed Arabic plural morphology. Nouns in the former category generally displayed the biblical Hebrew suffixes *-im* and *-ot*, e.g., *mizmor-im* 'songs', *ḥaxam-im* 'scholars', *berax-ot* 'blessings', *dimyon-ot* 'imaginings'. However, as mentioned above, the rabbinic suffix *-iyyot* is also attested, e.g., *parašiyyot* (weekly Torah portions), *maʕasiyyot* (plural of *maʔase* 'story'). Nouns in the latter category exhibited both the "sound plural" forms, e.g., *siddur-siddurat* 'book', *emuna-emunat* 'belief', and the "broken plural" forms, e.g., *siddur-sdadǝr* 'book',

---

[22] These words were usually not incorporated in a sentence but formed single-word utterances, used to convey a covert message to the hearer.

lulab-lwaləb 'palm frond', *šəbbat-šbabət* 'Shabbat', *siman-siyamin* 'sidelock' (Henshke 2007: 91–94; Kara 1985: 134).

Dual forms

Some Hebrew nouns also appeared with the Arabic dual suffix (which, unlike its Hebrew counterpart, remains productive), e.g., *bisqen* 'two verses' (from *pasuq*), *milxin* 'two kings' (from *melex*) (Henshke 2007: 91).

Diminuitive forms

In addition, Hebrew nouns appeared in Arabic diminutive forms, e.g., *sdidər* (diminuitive form of *siddur*); *lwiləb* (diminuitive form of *lulab*, 'palm frond'), *qṭeyən* (derogatory term meaning 'very small, puny'). Even Titus, the name of the reviled Roman emperor, received a diminuitive form – *ṭwiṭaṣ* – meaning 'evil person' (Bar-Asher 1999: 162).

Possessive pronouns

Hebrew nouns with Arabic possessive pronouns are commonly attested, e.g., *šabbat-um* 'their Shabbat', *məzzal-ək* 'your luck'. Conversely, the use of Hebrew possessive pronouns is limited and confined to specific domains. They appear in frozen Hebrew expressions like *zəxrono lə-braxa* 'may his memory be a blessing', said of the deceased, and *yimaḥ šemo* 'may his name be obliterated'; in the secret jargon (e.g., *ḥaver-xa*, 'your friend') and in the language of scholars (e.g., *aboṭe-nu* 'our fathers', *maʕase-hem* 'their deeds') (Henshke 2007: 94–95; Kara 1985: 133).

"Erroneous" derivations

Since the Hebrew component generally conforms to the grammatical rules of Arabic, we find "misderived" Hebrew words, that is, words created after the fashion of Hebrew, while disregarding certain rules of Hebrew morpho-phonology. An example is the word *kašera* (feminine form of the adjective *kašer* 'kosher'), attested in Tunisia and Algeria, formed by combining the Hebrew adjective with the feminine suffix *-a*, while maintaining the [a] vowel after the first lateral, in violation of the Hebrew rule. In Morocco, we also find the singular word *miḡbaʕa* (rather than *miḡbaʕat* 'hat'), a backformation from the plural *miḡbaʕot* (Bar-Asher 1999: 236–237), as well as *mašalot* (plural of *mašal* 'proverb, metaphor') and *basoqem* (plural of *pasuq* 'verse'), which likewise preserve the vowel after the first lateral. The reverse occurs in the word *ṭref*, back-formed from the halakhic term *ṭrefa*, which is in the feminine (Henshke 2007: 99–101).

Masdar patterns

In Tunisia, Morocco, and Algeria, we find the Hebrew root b-d-q inserted into the Arabic *masdar* (verbal noun) patterns *fʕil* and *fʕul*, creating the forms *bdeq* and *bdoq*, used in the expression *bdeq/bdoq al-ḥmeṣ* (=*bdikat ḥamets* 'search for *chametz*'). In Morocco, this root was also realized in another *masdar* pattern, forming *budqan*, used in the expression *lilt l-budqan* 'night of searching for chametz'. The Hebrew word *ḥameṣ* itself underwent a similar process, producing *lilt t-təḥmiṣ*, denoting the same religious ritual (Bar-Asher 1999: 214).

The qitala pattern
In the Arabic of Iraqi Jews, the *qitala* pattern is common, and many Hebrew roots were melded into it, e.g., *simmaxa* 'ordination', *hittara* 'annulment of vows', *šittaxa* 'Seder' (Morag 1995: 186).

The comparative form
In the Arabic of Yemenite Jews, Hebrew roots frequently appear in the Arabic comparative form, e.g., *amʔas* 'more repellent' (from Hebrew *maʔus*), *aršaʕ* 'more evil' (from Hebrew *rašaʕ*), *aʕšar* 'richer' {from Hebrew *ʕašir*), *akšar* 'more kosher' (from Hebrew *kašer*) (Kara 1988: 133).

Feminine forms
Other Hebrew-based innovations include feminine nouns that do not exist in Hebrew, e.g., the form *piyyuta*, found in Tunisian Judeo-Arabic. In this dialect, the singular Hebrew word *piyyut* became a collective noun for religious poems and was used alongside the plural Hebrew word *piyyutim*. Since *piyyut* had acquired a plural meaning, a separate word for the singular was needed. To this end the feminine form word *piyyuta* was coined, after the fashion of Arabic, which uses the singular-feminine to form a singular term from a collective one (Henshke 2007: 97). The Hebrew noun *almana* 'widow', current in many Jewish communities, was sometimes combined with the Arabic definite article: *al-almana*. However, women in Yemen and Tunisia perceived the noun itself as including a definite prefix and thus back-formed the noun *mana*, which took the place of *almana* (Goitein 1983: 174; Henshke 2007: 100–101). Among the Jews of Aleppo, the feminine forms *furiyya* and *šiʕbubiya* were used. These Arabicized forms, based on the Hebrew words Purim and Tish'a be-Av, denoted the gifts given to children on those holidays (Bar-Asher 1999:214).

Nisba *adjectives*
New adjectives were formed by combining Hebrew words with the Arabic *nisba* suffix-*i* (a suffix deriving an adjective from a noun), for example, *ḥəbr-i* ('friend' + *nisba*), to denote a member of the burial society Hevra Qadissha; *baḥuṣ-i* ('outside' + *nisba*), to denote a wandering Jew; *tunf-i* ('filth' + *nisba*), meaning 'dirty, contaminated'; *ʕumruṣ-i* (Hebrew *ʕam ha-ʔretṣ* 'ignoramus' + *nisba),* to denote an ignorant person; *šurṣ-i* (Hebrew *šerets* 'vermin' + *nisba*) (Morag 1995: 186), used as an insult, and *yešurun-i* (Hebrew *yešurun* 'Jew' + *nisba*), used in the secret jargon to refer to a Jew (Henshke 2007: 97).

Arabic roots in Hebrew nominal patterns
While the Hebrew-Arabic contact usually involved Hebrew elements assimilating to Arabic structures, the reverse is attested as well. There are cases of Arabic roots appearing in Hebrew nominal patterns, creating interesting innovations. One example from Morocco is the word *biyutim*, meaning 'water left to stand overnight', formed by combining the Arabic verb *bat* 'spent the night' with the Hebrew plural suffix. Another is the word *glalim* ('poor people'), consisting of the Arabic word *gəllil* and the Hebrew plural suffix (Bar-Asher 1999: 215). Egyptian Jews coined the word *marsim* for 'fragrant herbs' by melding Arabic *marsin* ('myrtle') with Hebrew plural morphology. Tunisian had the word *ṭabbaʕt*, denoting the silver pointer used while reading the Torah, formed by inserting the Arabic root ṭ-b-ʕ ('to follow') into the Hebrew nominal pattern *qaṭṭelet*. The secret Jewish jargon also featured words of this kind, such as *məkseret* ('breakage'), formed by inserting the Arabic root k-s-r ('to break') into the Hebrew nominal pattern of *miqtelet* (Henshke 2007: 97–98).

8.2 Unique Hebrew coinages

Over the centuries, speakers of Judeo-Arabic also coined many "pure" Hebrew words and expressions, devoid of any Arabic element. Most of these coinages, used mainly in speech, were undocumented in Hebrew dictionaries.

8.2.1 Abstract nouns ending in –ut

Judeo-Arabic made robust use of the Hebrew nominal pattern *qatlut*. Many of the nouns appearing in this pattern were unique to the Jewish Arabic dialects, e.g., *əblut* (the seven days of mourning), *ṭərfot* 'impurity, immorality', *kəfrot* 'blasphemy', *merarut* 'sorrow, great difficulty', *ʕnyut* 'poverty', *ʕšrut* 'wealth', *ṣurerut* 'trouble, evil', *ṣaʕarut* 'sorrow', *šaqrut* 'deception', and many others (Ratzaby 1978: 20 [introduction]; Morag 1995: 186; Bar-Asher 1999: 164–165; Avishur 2001: 189–195).

8.2.2 Verbal nouns

The Hebrew verbal nouns *ḥaluqa* and *ḥannuka* appeared in a different pattern, namely *qiṭṭul*, producing *ḥəlloq* and *ḥannox*. The former denoted the distribution of funds to the poor, and the latter appeared in the expression *ḥənnox bayt*, denoting the inauguration of a house (Henshke 2007: 115, 144).

8.2.3 Other nouns

Additional Hebrew nouns coined in Judeo-Arabic are ṣḥeqa 'laughter' (Bar-Asher 1999: 156), baʕya 'problem', daruš or dirša 'sermon', ḥešqa 'enthusiasm' (Ratzabi 1978: 105; Morag 1995: 195), gmila Hagomel recited by women, dəbbora (piyyutim recited before the reading of the Ten Commandments), ṭaruf 'prey', gniž 'place of genizah', ṣleb 'idol', məsmix and məggid (both denoting a person who guides the reader of the Torah in applying the correct cantillation), reṣʕa or reṣʕit (feminine forms of raša, 'evil') (Henshke 2007: 143–146), ḥašuqa 'female lover' (Bar-Asher 1999: 250), among many other examples.

8.2.4 New expressions

In addition to single words, speakers of Judeo-Arabic also coined Hebrew expressions unique to their vernacular. For example, the expression simḥat kuhin 'festival of the kohanim', denoted the 11th of Tishrei, the day after Yom Kippur. This day was dedicated to the kohanim, in memory of the feast held by the Kohen Gadol after emerging, unscathed, from the Holy of Holies, as mentioned in the Mishna (Yoma 7:4) (Henshke 1991: 106–107; Bar-Asher 1999: 304). Adar w-adar and adar mhuddar were names for Second Adar (Henshke 1991: 106; Bar-Asher 1999: 303), and the expression ḥuṣ men-noxri (Bar-Asher 1999: 303) or ḥoṣ mə-k-kabod were uttered before saying words of Torah in the presence of gentiles, or in an inappropriate place. Other expressions included eš balahot (epithet for a hot-tempered woman) and raše məllem 'acronyms', among others (Henshke 2007: 148–150).

8.3 Syntax

Hebrew melded into Arabic is usually confined to the lexical and semantic domains, while the syntax of the host language remains unaffected. Hebrew lexemes and phrases, however numerous they may be, generally remain isolated, embedded within the structures of the incorporating tongue. It would be surprising to find Hebrew syntactic categories within Judeo-Arabic; however, this language does provide some surprises of this kind.

8.3.1 Intensifying constructions

One example is a variety of novel constructions and expressions that produce an intensifying effect. The first of these involves the reduplication of a Hebrew noun or adjective, with a connecting word (in either Hebrew or Arabic) between the two instances of the repeated word: *kašer we-kašer* (literally 'kosher and kosher', meaning 'strictly kosher') and *šeqər fi šeqər* (literally 'a lie within a lie', meaning 'a complete lie'). Speakers also took advantage of the diglossic situation to create such pairs, comprising a Hebrew word and its Arabic equivalent (or near-equivalent): *ḥošəx u-dlam* 'darkness (Heb) and darkness (Ar)'; *bə-səmḥa w-l-fərḥa* 'in happiness (Heb) and happiness (Ar)'; *jirdam wa-ṣaraʕat* 'disease (Ar) and leprosy (Heb)'; *n-nəfxa w-l-gaʔawa* 'in smugness (Ar) and conceit (Heb)'; *bə-l-həmma u-l-giʔut* 'in pride (Ar) and arrogance (Heb)'.

In some cases, the repetition does not involve the same word (or a Hebrew word and its Arabic equivalent), but rather two words that are close, yet not identical, in meaning, i.e., a kind of *hendiadys*. For example: *kšera ṭhora* ('kosher and pure'), *kašer muttar* ('kosher permissible'), and *saṭan o-məsṭen* ('Satan and devil'). Sometimes the two nouns form a construct, in which the first is a singular noun and its dependent is the same noun in the plural, e.g., *ʕereb ʕarabem* ('evening of evenings', meaning late dusk), *ḥerem ḥaramot* ('excommunication of excommunications', meaning 'total excommunication'). Another interesting construction pairs a noun with its cognate in the *mefuʕal* form, e.g., *kašer mkkušar* ('strictly kosher'), after the example of the Mishnaic expression *kaful u-mexuppal*.

Yet another means of creating superlatives involves modifying a noun with a Hebrew word that serves as an intensifier. I found four such intensifiers. Three of them appear in constructs: The first is *elohim* 'God', in the expression *man iluhim* (literally 'manna of God'). The word *man* in this expression means 'delicious food', and the addition of *iluhim/elohim* produces 'extremely delicious food'. Two other words used in a similar manner are *melaxim* 'kings', e.g., *dar mlaxem* (literally 'a house of kings', i.e., a magnificent house), and *šamaym* 'heavens', e.g., *šərba taʕ š-šamaym* (literally 'drink of heaven', an excellent drink). A fourth word, *ʕolam* 'world, eternity', is used as an adverbial: *kənna ʕayšin ʕulam* 'we lived very well' (Henshke 2007: 103–105).

We see then that, despite the limitations, Judeo-Arabic had independent Hebrew syntactic categories that sometimes even preserved unique Hebrew characteristics.

8.3.2 The definite article

The incorporation of Hebrew elements into Arabic structures led to Hebrew nouns appearing with the Arabic definite article, e.g., *al-ḥazzan* 'the cantor'. At the same time, some Hebrew constructs preserved the Hebrew definite article, e.g., *bet ha-miqdaš* 'the temple'. But since this Hebrew definite article eroded over time and became opaque to speakers, some of these expressions acquired a second, Arabic, article, as in *al-malax a-mawet* 'the angel of death' (literally 'the-angel the-death') and *l-abi ab-ben* 'the son's father' (Kara 1988: 133; Bar-Asher 1999: 157; Blau 1999: 146–147; Henshke 2007: 106–110).

8.4 Semantics

The semantics of the Hebrew component were influenced by both Hebrew and Arabic. At the same time, the incorporated Hebrew elements also took on a life of their own and exhibited semantic processes that characterize living languages, thus evolving their own meaning and connotations. In some cases the evolution of their particular sense is transparent, and in other cases it is quite obscure.

8.4.1 Metonymy

The most common type of semantic shift was one of metonymy. The word *adama* 'soil', for example, did not preserve its original Hebrew meaning, but denoted various vegetables, the blessing for which is "*bore peri ha-ʔadama.*" Similarly, the Hebrew word *ʕeṣ* 'tree' denoted fruits the blessing for which is "*bore peri ha-ʕeṣ,*" and *gafan* (Hebrew 'vine') meant 'wine'. The term *zohar* did not refer to the book by that name, but to the celebration held on the night of an infant's circumcision, during which texts from the *Zohar* were read. *Mətta* (Hebrew 'bed') meant 'funeral'; *məzzeq* (Hebrew 'pest') meant 'demon'; *ʕbbor* (a Hebrew term referring to the conception of a baby or to the addition of a thirteenth month to the calendar every four years) meant 'calendar'; *fṭera* (Hebrew 'death') and *fqeda* (Hebrew term for visiting or remembering) referred to the memorial ceremony on the anniversary of a death; *šimut* (Hebrew 'names') was an amulet; *tərgum* (Hebrew 'translation') came to refer to the Aramaic language; *ṭbela* (Hebrew 'immersion') meant 'mikveh'; and *kos* (Hebrew 'cup') meant 'arak' (Morag 1995: 199–100; Bar-Asher 1999: 167–169; Henshke 2007: 114–119).

8.4.2 Textual metonymy

In some cases, the metonymy was based on a reference to the Hebrew sources. For example, *al-tippol* meant 'fear, dread', based on Exodus 15:16: *tippol ʕalehem ʔema wa-faḥad* ('Fear and dread shall fall upon them'). The word *exa* (Eikhah), the Hebrew name of the Book of Lamentations, recited on Tishʻa be-Av, came to denote Tish'a be-Av itself. It also acquired connotations of devastation and tragedy and thus came to describe negative things in general, e.g., ʕurst ixa (literally 'Eikhah bride'), meaning 'widow'; wešš-e ʔ-exa (literally 'Eikhah face'), meaning 'a sour face', etc. (Morag 1995: 200–202; Henshke 2008; Reshef 2009).

8.4.3 Semantic narrowing

Semantic narrowing was common as well. The Hebrew word ʔoreyaḥ 'visitor, guest' was used exclusively for a visitor coming from the Land of Israel, whereas other visitors were referred to as def (the Arabic word for 'guest'). Safeq (Hebrew 'doubt') referred exclusively to doubt in halakhic matters; sʕoda (Hebrew 'meal') meant a feast, especially a religious one; sofer (Hebrew 'writer') meant one who writes contracts and ketubbot; šaliyaḥ (Hebrew 'envoy') was a rabbi's envoy; bdeqa (Hebrew 'examination') referred only to the ritual search for ḥameṣ; səkkin (Hebrew 'knife') meant a slaughterer's knife; baḥur (Hebrew 'young man') referred to a bachelor of any age; stiyya (Hebrew 'drink') referred to arak, and barzel (Hebrew 'iron') meant 'knife' (Bar-Asher 1999: 167–168; Henshke 2007: 119–120).

8.4.4 Omission

Another phenomenon commonly exhibited by the Hebrew component is omission, specifically the omission of parts of Hebrew expressions, e.g., oheb 'lover' for oheb yisrael 'lover of Israel' (Morag 1995: 203); al-meborax 'blessed' for yom kippur al-meborax 'the blessed Yom Kippur' (Avishur 2001: 158–161); ḥəbra for the burial society ḥabra qaddiša, ʕeser 'ten' for ʕeser a-ddibberot 'the Ten Commandments'; sifer 'scroll' for sifer tora 'Torah scroll'; ḥoq for the book ḥoq le-yisrael, which was popular among North African Jews; šmura 'guarded' for maṣa šmura 'guarded matza'; əl-lbana 'the moon' for bərkat əl-lbana 'blessing over the moon', and hafsaqa 'suspension' for hafsaqat ʔaxila (literally 'suspension of eating', denoting a one-week fast) (Henshke 2007: 118–120).

8.4.5 Imagery and metaphor

The Hebrew component of Judeo-Arabic was rich in imagery and metaphor. For example, speakers used the word dbaš 'honey' for anything sweet (literally or metaphorically); ḥošex afela 'darkness murk' for a bad man; miləx 'king' for the first day of the Hebrew month; šorəš 'root' for family lineage; srefa 'conflagration' for a naughty child or a greedy woman; ʕaraba 'willow' for a person devoid of religious knowledge or observance; makka 'blow' for trouble; galut 'exile' for hardship and difficulty, and miṣoraʕim 'lepers' for isolated people or pariahs (Morag 1995: 198–199; Henshke 2007: 121).

8.4.6 Semantic loans and loan translations

The contact between Hebrew and Arabic also gave rise to semantic loans and loan translations. Some of these are easily spotted, but, owing to the similarity of the languages, others are more difficult to discern. The Hebrew word ʕamaleq did not denote only the biblical tribe, but also a tall person, under the influence of Arabic ʕamlaq. The Hebrew word peruš 'interpretation' came to mean an Arabic translation of the Bible, under the influence of the Arabic word šarḥ 'interpretation, explanation', which was used by the Jews to denote the same thing (Henshke 2007: 123–125). In Morocco, we find the word šəllaḥun, literally 'sending'(?), denoting 'selling on credit', a calque of the Arabic word ṭulq (Bar-Asher 1999: 256–257). In Yemen, the Hebrew word gil 'age' came to mean 'generation' under the influence of Arabic jil (Ratzaby 1978: 48).

8.4.7 Names of historical figures

As mentioned, the classical Jewish sources greatly influenced the Jews and were part of their everyday lives. Hence, figures from Jewish history were living emblems whose names took on various metaphorical meanings, with righteous figures representing good and beauty and evil ones representing corruption and ugliness. Thus, in most communities, liyahu n-nbi (Elijah the Prophet) and rəbbi meir (the Mishnaic sage Rabbi Meir Baal Han-nes) were guardian angels evoked in times of trouble; yster l-məlka (Queen Esther) was a symbol of beauty and purity; iyob (Job) was a symbol of suffering and hardship, and barʕo (Pharaoh), gulyat (Golaiath), ṭiṭos (Titus), aman (Haman), ziraš (Zeresh), and izibel (Jezebel) were symbols of evil (Bar-Asher 1999: 162–163; Henshke 2007: 125–127).

8.4.8 Euphemisms and distancing devices

The Hebrew component, perceived to some extent as foreign, also served as a source of euphemisms and devices of psychological distancing. This is evident in three domains. First, the domain of religion, in which Hebrew code-words were used to refer obliquely to non-Jewish figures and symbols, e.g., ʔoto (ha-ʔiš) 'that (man)' for the Prophet Muhammad, šti wa-ʕerəb 'warp and weft' for the Cross, ḥaber 'friend' for a non-Jew. The second domain was that of taboo and embarrassing issues, e.g., bit-kabud 'house of honor' for a toilet and maym qṭənnim 'small water' for urine. The third domain was that of death, e.g., bet a-ḥayyim 'house of life' or bet l-ʕalmin 'eternal home' for a cemetery and nəfṭar 'passed away' for 'died', instead of the explicit Arabic word mat (Ratzaby 1978: 23–24 [Introduction]; Henshke 2007: 122–123).

8.5 Idioms and proverbs

Hebrew sayings and proverbs played an important role in the creation and preservation of the living Hebrew component. Most of these proverbs derived from the Bible or from later classical sources, but some of them took on new forms and meanings as part of the speakers' living language. These sayings thus formed a sort of nexus between the past – their textual origin – and the present and reflected the vitality and complexity of the multi-layered Hebrew component.

8.5.1 Idioms derived from the Jewish sources

Sayings taken from the Bible, or from later classical sources, fall into two categories. First, those that are used exactly as they appear in these sources. The vast majority of these are biblical, e.g., abel wa-ḥafuy roš 'head covered in mourning' (Esther 6:12), bə-nʕare-no u-bəzqene-no 'young and old' (Exodus 10:9). The second category includes expressions and proverbs, which have been altered from the original. In some cases the alteration is very minor and produces no change in the meaning of the expression. For example, yayn isammaḥ libab inuš 'Wine cheers the heart of man' (Psalms 104:15) becomes ha-yayn isammaḥ libab inuš 'The wine cheers...' The small change here – the addition of a definite article – does not change the meaning of the proverb. However, in most cases, the changes, which occurred as unbound phrases, were transformed into bound ones (idioms) and were more significant. The changes could be on the morphological plane or the syntactic.

In the expression ken yirbu (a blessing of fertility meaning 'thus may they multiply'), which originates in the verse 'the more it [the people of Israel] was oppressed the more it increased and spread' (Exodus 1:12), we find a morphological

---

Note: This section is based on Henshke 2008 and references therein.

change, namely a change of number. In the original passage, the verb *yirbe* ('multiply') is singular, whereas in the idiom it is plural.

A syntactic change can occur when two or more words are extracted from a longer expression and joined to form a new one. For example, the phrase of welcome *barux ha-bba* (literally 'blessed is he who comes') derives from Psalms 118:26: "Blessed is he who comes in the name of the Lord." In the verse, the words *barux ha-bba* belong to two separate parts of the sentence and do not express a unified concept. The new phrase was formed by reanalyzing *ha-bba* as part of the main clause, thus producing a single phrase.

The pungent curse, *yimmaḥ šm-o w-zəxr-o* 'may his name and memory be obliterated', is derived from a combination of sources. The expression *yimmaḥ šema-m* 'may their name be obliterated', exhibiting an optative future verb-form common in the Bible, appears in Psalms 109:13. The pairing of *shem* ('name') and *zexer* ('memory') as parallels also appears in the Bible (e.g., Proverbs 10:7). The curse was produced by combining the two.

The meaning of the sayings is generally derived, to a greater or lesser extent, from the original context in which they appear in the sources, reflecting the vitality and depth of the speakers' connection to these ancient Jewish texts. In some cases, the meaning of the original phrase is transparent and is preserved unchanged, as in the abovementioned "Wine cheers the heart of man," and also in *hebel wa-req* 'vanity and emptiness'. In other cases, the meaning is somewhat changed, as in the abovementioned example of *barux ha-bba*. In yet other cases, the meaning of the idiom does not reflect its literal meaning in the original. Instead, it is derived from the general spirit of the original and from other ancient texts associated with it. An example of this kind is the phrase *ben porat yosef*, taken from Jacob's blessing to his sons (Genesis 49:22), which was used by speakers of Judeo-Arabic as a blessing to ward off the evil eye. The literal sense of this blessing does not derive from the meaning of the individual words of which it is composed. Instead, its use is based on the commentary of our sages, who associated it with the concept of the evil eye.

Especially interesting are "metalinguistic" examples, whose meaning refers to some physical feature of the original text in which they appear, for example, *šalom ʕal yisrael* 'peace be upon Israel', which signifies the conclusion or resolution of some problem or affair, because it is the concluding verse of two psalms (125 and 128). An even more striking example of this type is *kaftor taḥat* (literally 'a calyx under'). This expression is repeated three times in Exodus 37:21: "**A calyx under** two branches of the same, **a calyx under** two branches of the same, **a calyx under** two branches of the same, according to the six branches going out of it." Therefore, it is used to refer to a person who repeats himself.

There were also idioms whose meaning was very different from, or even opposed to, their meaning in the original, such as *ḥamor garəm* ('strong-boned donkey') to describe a fool. This idiom, too, is taken from Jacob's blessing (specifically from Genesis 49:14), but in the original text it is a compliment.

8.5.2 New proverbs

The speakers of Judeo-Arabic also coined some proverbs and sayings not based on Jewish sources, such as *mar ḥəšwan ho ʕṣlan* 'The month of Heshvan is lazy', referring to the fact that there are no holidays during the month of Heshvan.

9 Conclusion

This chapter reviewed in detail the Hebrew (and Aramaic) component that was incorporated into the Arabic speech of Jewish communities in the Muslim world, and which developed over centuries of interlingual contact. This Hebrew component has two apparently conflicting characteristics. On the one hand, it preserves ancient Hebrew forms and thus sheds light on the foundations of the Hebrew traditions that were maintained by these age-old communities. Hence, it provides a rare and surprising window onto the development of Classical Hebrew. On the other hand, the Hebrew component maintained an ongoing dialogue with the local Arabic language and became a living part of it. This interlingual contact yielded many important innovations of mixed Hebrew-Arabic character, reflecting the longstanding and fascinating contact between the two tongues.

References

Avishur, Yitzahak. 2001. *Hebrew elements in Judeo-Arabic*. Tel Aviv-Jaffa: Archaeological Center Publications. [Hebrew].

Bar-Asher, Moshe. 1999. *Traditions linguistiques des Juifs d'Afrique du Nord*. Jerusalem: Hebrew University, Bialik Institute & Regional University Institute Ashkelon. [Hebrew].

Ben-Hayyim, Ze'ev. 1963. *Bidvar meqoriyutah shel at'amat mile'el be'ivrit*. In Saul Lieberman, Sheraga Abramson, Yehezkel Kutcher & Saul Ash (eds.), *Sefer Henoch Yalon*, 150–160. Jerusalem: Kiryat Sefer.

Ben-Yaacob, Abraham. 1985. *Hebrew and Aramaic in the language of the Jews of Iraq*. Jerusalem: Ben-Zvi Institute. [Hebrew].

Blau, Joshua. 1999. *The emergence and linguistic background of Judeo-Arabic*. Jerusalem: Ben-Zvi Institute.

Chetrit, Joseph. 1989. The Hebrew-Aramaic component of the Moroccan Judeo-Arabic: The language of a Muslim poem written as Jewish. *Massorot* 3–4. 203–284. [Hebrew].

Drory, Rina. 1988. *The emergence of Jewish-Arabic literary contacts at the beginning of the tenth century*. Tel Aviv: The Porter Institute for Poetics & Semiotics, Tel Aviv University.
Eldar, Ilan. 1989. Pronunciation traditions of Hebrew. *Massorot* 3–4. 3–36. [Hebrew].
Florentin, Moshe. 2002. The stress system of Mishnaic Hebrew. *Lěšonénu* 62. 221–230. [Hebrew].
Goitein, Shelomo Dov & Menahem Ben-Sasson (ed.). 1983. *The Yemenites: History, communal organization, spiritual life*. Jerusalem: Ben-Zvi Institute. [Hebrew].
Hary, Benjamin H. 2009. *Translating religion: Linguistic analysis of Judeo-Arabic sacred texts from Egypt*. Leiden & Boston: Brill.
Hary, Benjamin. 2016. Il-'arabi dyālna (our Arabic): The history and politics of Judeo-Arabic. In A. Norich & J. Miller (eds.), *The languages of Jewish cultures: Comparative perspectives*, 297–320. Ann Arbor: University of Michigan Press.
Henshke, Yehudit. 1991. Hebrew elements in the spoken Arabic of Djerba. *Massorot* 5. 77–118. [Hebrew].
Henshke, Yehudit. 2007. *Hebrew elements in daily speech: A grammatical study and lexicon of the Hebrew component of Tunisian Judeo-Arabic*. Jerusalem: Bialik Institute. [Hebrew].
Henshke, Yehudit. 2007a. Penultimate accentuation: The evidence from Tunisian Jews. In A. Maman, S.E. Fassberg & Y. Breuer (eds.), *Sha'arei Lashon: Studies in Hebrew, Aramaic and Jewish languages presented to Moshe Bar-Asher*, vol. 3, 320–333. Jerusalem: Bialik Institute. [Hebrew].
Henshke, Yehudit. 2008. Hebrew verbs in Tunisian Judeo-Arabic. *Lěšonénu* 70. 679–695. [Hebrew].
Henshke, Yehudit. 2009. Oral language traditions and classical Hebrew: Phonological and morphological phenomena. *Revue des Études Juives* 168. 181–194.
Henshke, Yehudit. 2013. Sepharadi pronunciation traditions of Hebrew. In Geoffrey Khan (ed.), *Encyclopedia of Hebrew Language and Linguistics*, Vol 3, 536–42. Leiden & Boston: Brill.
Kara, Yehiel. 1988. Hebrew and Aramaic elements in the women's language of Yemen. In Moshe Bar-Asher (ed.), *Studies in Jewish Languages: Bible translations and spoken dialects*, 113–145. Jerusalem: Misgav Yerushalayim. [Hebrew].
Kara, Yehiel. 1992. The Hebrew elements and the Hebrew typology of the Hebrew spoken by Jewish Yemenites. *Miqqedem Umiyyam* 5. 131–149.
Morag, Shelomo. 1963. *The Hebrew language tradition of Yemenite Jews*. Jerusalem: The Academy of Hebrew Language. [Hebrew].
Morag, Shelomo. 1985. Hebrew as a language of an elite culture. *Pe'amim* 23. 9–21. [Hebrew].
Morag, Shelomo. 1995. The amalgamated crystallization of Hebrew: Examinations of form and meaning. *Te'uda* 9. 183–208. [Hebrew].
Qimron, Elisha. 1992. Studies in the Hebrew of the Dead Sea Scrolls. *Hebrew Linguistics* 33–35. 79–92.
Ratzaby, Yehuda. 1978. *Osar seshon haqqodesh shellivne Teman* [Dictionary of the Hebrew language used by Yemenite Jews]. Tel-Aviv: The Author (in Hebrew).
Reshef, Yael. 2009. Semantic shifts of textual origin in Jewish languages. In David Bunis (ed.), *Language and literatures of Sepharadic and Oriental Jews*, 21–41. Jerusalem: Bialik Institute [Hebrew].
Reshef, Yael. 1996. Traces of linguistic traditions in the spoken language of Baghdadi Jews. In Moshe Bar-Asher (ed.), *Studies in Hebrew and Jewish languages,* 503–521 [Hebrew].
Rosenbaum, Gabriel M. 2002. Spoken Jewish Arabic in modern Egypt: Hebrew and Non-standard components. *Massorot* 12. 117–148. [Hebrew].

Sarah Bunin Benor and Benjamin Hary
A Research Agenda for Comparative Jewish Linguistic Studies

1 Introduction

Over the past 80 years, several scholars have called for comparative research on Jewish language varieties.[1] In a 1937 Yiddish article about Judezmo (Judeo-Spanish), Solomon Birnbaum dreamt of creating "a new field of linguistics, a Jewish sociology of language based on comparison of all Jewish languages" (1937: 195). In 1973, Max Weinreich suggested a "systematic research program" (2008[1973]: 54) on language use in various Jewish communities and presented such research in his magnum opus about Yiddish. And in 1981, David Gold (1981) proposed Jewish intralinguistics as a field of study and, along with Leonard Prager, offered some of this analysis in the short-lived journal *Jewish Language Review* (1981–1987) and other publications. In this chapter, we present a research agenda for the comparative linguistic study of Jewish communities, building on Birnbaum's, Weinreich's, Gold's, and others' suggestions, on the relatively small amount of comparative research that has been done, and on the language descriptions in this book. We survey past scholarship, discuss preliminaries for comparative study, propose some research questions, and offer reasons why this type of analysis is important.

2 Previous scholarship

The phenomenon of Jewish language varieties came to scholarly attention in the early 20th century as Jewish communal leaders debated the comparative merits of Hebrew and Yiddish as group languages (Loewe 1911; Mieses 1915).[2] In the mid-20th century, Yiddishists spearheaded comparative research on Jewish language varieties (Birnbaum 1937, 1971, 1979; Efroykin 1951; Weinreich 1954, 2008[1973]) and set much of the agenda for the field. The late 1970s and the 1980s saw a slew of edited volumes that dealt with multiple Jewish language varieties (Fishman 1981, 1985, 1987; Gold 1989; Paper 1978; Rabin et al. 1979), two journals (Bar-Asher 1984ff and Gold and Prager 1981–1987), and progress toward a

---
[1] We thank David Bunis for his helpful suggestions on an earlier draft of this chapter.
[2] For a more detailed treatment of the points in this section, see Benor 2015. See Sunshine 1995 for a description of the early history of the field.

theoretical understanding of Jewish language varieties based on comparative analysis (Fishman 1981; Gold 1981; Rabin 1981; and, especially, Wexler 1981a). In more recent decades, the tradition of edited volumes and journals about multiple Jewish language varieties has continued (e.g., Alvarez-Péreyre and Baumgarten 2003; Baumgarten and Kessler-Mesguich 1996; Benor and Sadan 2011; Kahn and Rubin 2016; Tirosh-Becker and Benor 2013ff; Wexler 2006).

In addition, several articles and books have dealt with Jewish language varieties as a phenomenon. Themes discussed in this comparative and theoretical literature include sociology of language (Benor and Sadan 2011; Fishman 1981, 1985, 1987; Myhill 2004; Spolsky 2014), common features (Bar-Asher 2002; Bunis 2009; Weinreich 1954, 2008[1973]), and typology (Alvarez-Péreyre and Baumgarten 2003; Benor 2008; Chetrit 2007; Gold and Prager 1981–1987; Hary 2009; Hary and Wein 2013; Sephiha 1972; Weinreich 1954, 2008[1973]; Wexler 1981a). Several articles and volumes have treated the Hebrew-Aramaic component comparatively (Aslanov 2010; Bunis 1981, 2005a, 2013; Mayer Modena 1986; Morag 1992; Morag, Bar-Asher, and Mayer-Modena 1999; Szulmajster-Celnikier and Varol 1994; Tedghi 1995). A few works have begun to analyze similarities and differences between the language varieties of Jews and other religious and ethnic groups (Fishman 1987; Hary and Wein 2013; Myhill 2009; Stillman 1991; Wein and Hary 2014; Wexler 1974, 1980, 1986).

3 Research questions

Based on this scholarship and our own research interests, we offer a number of research questions for the field of comparative Jewish linguistic studies. When we discuss a "Jewish community," we generally refer to large-scale groupings based on location and language use, like (Judeo-) Georgian-speaking Jews in Georgia, (Jewish) Spanish-speaking Jews in Latin America, and (Judeo-) Arabic-speaking Jews in Yemen. Similar analysis could be done on a smaller scale, such as on Maghrebi-origin Jews versus mustaʻaribīn speaking Egyptian Judeo-Arabic in Cairo (Hary 2017), Syrian-origin versus Eastern European-origin Jews speaking Jewish Latin-American Spanish in Mexico City (Dean-Olmsted and Skura, this volume), or Reform versus Orthodox Jews speaking Jewish English in the United States (Benor, this volume). An even more fine-grained analysis can compare individual speakers, texts, or utterances.

According to our understanding of Jewish linguistic distinctiveness (Benor 2008; Hary 2009), analysis generally focuses on a comparison of a Jewish language variety with its non-Jewish correlate. In the case of coterritorial Jewish language varieties (Benor 2008), like Judeo-Arabic, Judeo-Persian, and Jewish Swedish, the non-Jewish correlate is a language variety spoken by non-Jewish neighbors of the Jewish community under analysis (e.g., 13th-century Judeo-French compared to 13th-century French). In the case of post-coterritorial language varieties like Judezmo and Yiddish, the non-Jewish correlate is the language variety spoken by non-Jewish neighbors of the Jewish community when the Jewish language variety initially developed (medieval varieties of Spanish and German), and there is potentially an additional adstratum of influence from their new coterritorial language varieties (primarily Balkan and Slavic languages, but also Arabic in North Africa), beyond the distinctive features discussed below.

3.1 Sociolinguistic correlations

Our first research question involves a comparison of linguistic distinctiveness in Jewish language varieties, in line with the sociology of language, common features, and typology discussions cited above. As Benor (2008) explains, distinctiveness has multiple aspects. Each Jewish community (or speaker, text, or utterance), might be characterized with regard to each of the following:
1. Hebrew/Aramaic influence:
   To what extent does each community use loanwords and other influences from Hebrew/Aramaic, including those encountered in traditional texts and those transmitted through spoken language?
2. Hebrew script:
   To what extent are non-Hebrew texts in the community written in Hebrew characters and with orthographic conventions influenced by Hebrew-Aramaic texts?
3. Substratal influence:
   To what extent is the language variety influenced by a different language variety spoken by ancestors of (some of) the current community members (including immigrants to the current land)?
4. Archaisms:
   To what extent do Jews maintain more conservative forms of the language? In other words, to what extent have Jews not participated in language changes of local non-Jews?
5. Migrated dialectalism (Hary 2009: 22–23):
   To what extent do disparate Jewish communities within the language territory speak more like each other than their non-Jewish neighbors? To what extent are features from one region used in a different region?

6. Israeli Hebrew influence:
   For communities in the 20th century or later, to what extent do they use loanwords and other influences from Israeli Hebrew?
7. Other features and structural difference:
   Aside from these features, to what extent do Jews differ from their non-Jewish neighbors in phonology, morphosyntax, prosody, and/or discourse? To what extent do these differences exist on a structural versus superficial level?
8. Crossing religious/communal boundaries (Hary 2009: 16–19):
   To what extent does the local non-Jewish population (or a subgroup thereof) acquire features that began as distinctive Jewish characteristics?
9. Overall distinctiveness:
   Based on this list, we can characterize overall distinctness: Where is each Jewish community located on a continuum of Jewish linguistic distinctiveness in comparison to the language of local non-Jews (Benor 2008), also known as the "Jewish linguistic spectrum" (Hary 2009: 5–27, 2011)?

Once we answer these questions for multiple Jewish communities, we can then conduct variationist sociolinguistic analysis, asking how these linguistic variables correlate with several social variables:
1. Openness of society
2. Demographic integration of Jews
3. Textual authority and religiosity
4. Literacy levels in the local standardized language
5. Political Zionism (20th century and later)
6. Time from immigration or language shift
7. Internal migration

We have some hypotheses about how these correlations might play out. We expect that several of the linguistic features listed above – archaisms, other features and structural difference, Hebrew script, and overall distinctness – will correlate inversely with two of the social dimensions: openness of society and demographic integration. Communities in more open societies that are more integrated with their non-Jewish neighbors will likely have fewer distinctive features and structural differences in comparison to the writings and speech of non-Jews. Such a correlation could also be extended to broader hypotheses regarding historical era. For example, compared to the Middle Ages, 21st-century Jewish communities tend to live in more open societies and to be more integrated, and therefore their language varieties tend to be more similar to those of their non-Jewish neighbors. Of course, there are exceptions to this, such as 21st-century Hasidic Jews in the U.S., Belgium, and elsewhere who maintain Yiddish, and medieval French Jews, whose writing suggests that their language did not differ structurally from that of their non-Jewish neighbors.

We expect that communities that are more religiously oriented and those with greater textual authority – that is, ones that revere biblical and rabbinic literature and use it in their everyday lives – will have more influence from textual Hebrew and Aramaic. We also expect that, within a given community, speakers and writers who are more oriented toward biblical and rabbinic literature will use more Hebrew/Aramaic influences. They will also vary according to audience, topic, and setting. We see an instance of variation within a given community and according to topic in Bunis' (2013) analysis of 16th-century Yiddish. Anshl Leyvi's Commentary on *Pirkei Avot* (a section of the Mishna) includes many Hebrew loanwords, while Elijah Levita's epic chivalric romance *Bovo Bukh* includes few. Here are two of the sample quotes Bunis analyzes (transliterated):

> Anshl Leyvi's Commentary on *Pirkei Avot*:
> Un' nit man zol mern fil tsu reydn mit den vayber, afile mit zaynem éyginen vayb habn unzer khakhomim gizágt. Mikolsheken un' toyznt mol véniger mit andern vayber. Un' azó habn gizágt khakhomim zi[khroynem] li[vrokhe] 'Al tsayt das der mensh mert fil tsu reydn mit vayber, er iz goyrem roe tsu zikh zelbert, un' far shtert di toyre, un' zayn sof iz das er nidert in das gehenem.'
>
> [One should not speak much with women, even with one's own wife, our sages said. *A fortiori*, and a thousand times less so, with other women. And so the sages, of blessed memory, said: 'Whenever a man speaks much with women, he brings harm to himself and spoils the Torah, and his end is that he will descend to Hell.'] (Bunis 2013: 33)
>
> Elijah Levita's *Bovo Bukh*:
> Un do er nun keyn feyl mit hit / do tsukh er zeyn shvert ous der sheydn / do lofn zi mit anander in di vit / un shlog of anander mit fröudn / ei einer fun dem andern zeyn lebn rit/ der not shveys ran fun im beydn / Pelukan shtreyt mit groysm shturem / un Bovo vant zikh az eyn lint vurem.
>
> [And when he had no more arrows / he drew his sword from its sheath. / They hurled themselves at one another in battle / and hit one another with glee / until one of the two saved his life. / The sweat from the effort ran from both of them. / Pelukan did combat with great fury / and Bovo fought on like a dragon.] (Bunis 2013: 34)

We see evidence of religiosity correlating with textual Hebrew/Aramaic influence in contemporary Jewish English-speaking communities. As Figure 1 demonstrates, those who identify as Orthodox (including Modern Orthodox and Black Hat) are more likely to report using words like *davka* ('particularly, specifically, even, just to be contrary') than those who identify as Conservative, Reconstructionist, Reform, or no denomination (data in Figures 1 and 2 is from a survey of over 20,000 American Jews who speak English natively; see details in Benor 2011 and Benor and Cohen 2011). This word is common in rabbinic literature, as well as in Yiddish and Israeli Hebrew. Influences from all three of these source languages tend to be more common among Orthodox Jews in the United States.

Another hypothesis is that Jews' literacy levels in the local standardized language will correlate inversely with Hebrew orthography. Jewish communities that

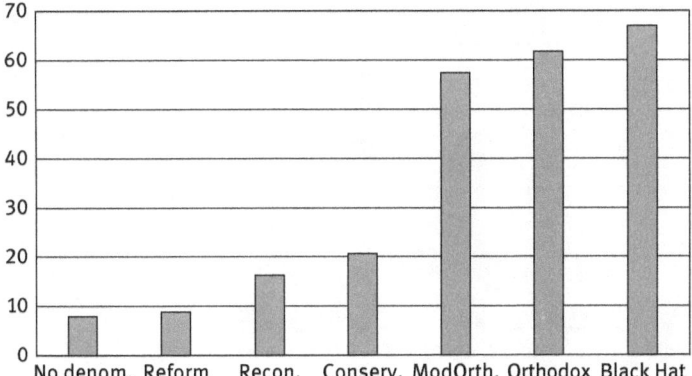

Figure 1: Survey data on % reported use of *davka* among American Jews according to denomination.

live in societies with high literacy levels in the local language will be more likely to write their language varieties in local alphabets. For example, in medieval and late medieval Cairo, Rabbinic Jews' local literacy levels seem to have been lower than those of Karaite Jews there. Consequently, we see that Karaite Jews used Arabic characters in their Judeo-Arabic literature much more frequently than Rabbinic Jews (Hary and Wein 2013: 90, n. 13, 91 and the references there).[3] Contemporary Jewish communities are mostly located in societies where literacy is widespread. Therefore, most (but not all) contemporary Jewish language varieties are written in local alphabets, and Hebrew words are sometimes inserted in Hebrew letters. Judezmo in interwar Saloniki and Yiddish in the United States today are striking counterexamples.

When comparing contemporary communities, we expect that political Zionism will correlate with Israeli Hebrew influence. In communities where many people visit and study in Israel and even make *aliyah* (move to Israel), we expect to see more loanwords and other features from Israeli Hebrew. This is the case among Swedish Jews, who started incorporating Israeli Hebrew loanwords in the 1930s and continue to use them – in evolving ways – today (Klagsbrun Lebenswerd, this volume). In American Orthodox communities, an Israeli click hesitation marker and then-clause "so" (on analogy with Israeli Hebrew *az*, e.g., "If you want to hear it, so you'll have to listen carefully") are common, especially among people who have spent time in Israel and people who spend time with them (Benor, this volume, 2012). Many loanwords in Jewish English are borrowed

---

[3] There are other reasons for the Karaites's choice of script. For example, scholars have argued that the choice of Arabic script was a subtle protest against the Rabbinic authority which was clearly associated with the Hebrew script (ibid.).

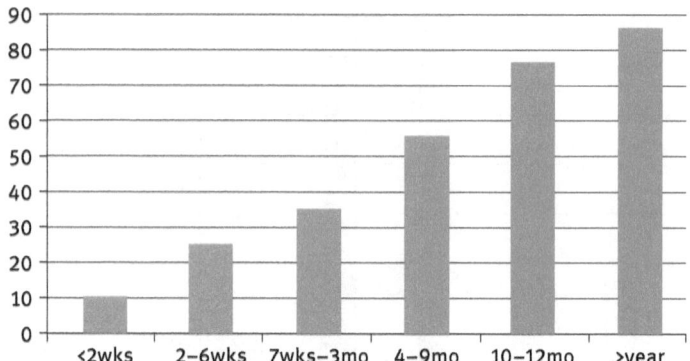

Figure 2: Survey data on the reported use of *balagan* among American Jews according to how much time respondent had spent in Israel.

from Israeli Hebrew, such as *boker tov* (good morning), *bəvakasha* (please), and *bəteavon* (bon appetit). Among American Jews, the word *balagan* (mess, disorder) correlates with time spent in Israel. For example, those who have spent more time in Israel are more likely to report using *balagan* (Figure 2).

Another social variable is time from immigration or language shift: how long the community has been using the language variety it currently uses. In a community that recently immigrated to the current land and/or recently acquired the current language, we expect to see more substratal influence than in a community that has been in its location and using its language for many generations. Substratal influence is what Weinreich (2008[1973]) and Bunis (1981) refer to as "previous Jewish language." For example, in Ottoman Judezmo, centuries removed from substratal contact, we see only a few influences from the substrata of Judeo-Greek (e.g., *meldar* 'to study/read Torah') and Judeo-Arabic (e.g., *al-had* 'Sunday'). But in early 21st-century Jewish English, which is only a few generations removed from the mass wave of Yiddish-speaking immigration, there are hundreds of loanwords and many grammatical features from Yiddish (e.g., *goyish* 'non-Jewish-like', *grager* 'Purim noisemaker', *gornisht* 'nothing', and *give over* 'convey', on analogy with Yiddish *ibergebn*). In general, younger Jews are less likely than older Jews to use Yiddish influences, but in the religious domain, we also see the opposite trend: Younger people are more likely than older people to use words like *shul* and *bentsh* and grammatical influences like *by* (Benor, this volume).

Another hypothesis is that archaisms will correlate with time from immigration or language shift. The more time that has elapsed since the community shifted to its current language or migrated to a location far from its original coterritorial language variety, the more we will find archaic features in relation to the non-Jewish correlate. Archaic features may also correlate inversely with openness of society and demographic integration. In other words, Jewish communities in less open societies that are not integrated well with their non-Jewish surroundings would likely have more archaic features. This is the case in the chapters in the current volume, as those describing contemporary language varieties, like Jewish Latin American Spanish and Jewish Swedish, are less likely to report archaisms. These communities have more recently immigrated to new language territories and acquired new languages, and they are more integrated into their surrounding societies.

We expect post-coterritorial Jewish language varieties to exhibit the most archaic features. Following the expulsion of Jews from Spain in 1492, they maintained their Judeo-Spanish language in various locations, especially in the Ottoman Empire. Since they were distant from their original territory and had limited contact with it, their language variety developed relatively independently from peninsular Spanish and preserved archaic features. An example is the word-initial Latin /f/, which was maintained in some varieties of Judezmo, including in Bosnia, e.g., *fazer* 'to do/make' and *fondo* 'deep (masc. sg.)' in the writings of Bosnian-born Clarisse Nicoïdski (Balbuena 2009: 288–289), but dropped in other varieties of Judezmo and in Spanish, e.g,. *azer* and *ondo*. Furthermore, Judezmo has preserved the Old Spanish phonemes /š/ and /dž/, now both realized as /x/ in modern Spanish (see Bunis, this volume, and Schwarzwald, this volume).

Coterritorial Jewish language varieties also exhibit archaisms. Sermoneta (1976) noted that Judeo-Italian was 100 or 150 years behind Italian in its linguistic characteristics. This may stem from Jewish communities being segregated from their Christian neighbors and therefore not being exposed to their linguistic changes (see Ryzhik, this volume). In Egyptian Judeo-Arabic (Cairene) the verbal pattern /fuʿul/ survived, as opposed to /fiʿil/, which replaced it in the modern Egyptian dialect. Thus, we encounter in Egyptian Judeo-Arabic /xuluṣ/ 'was redeemed' and /kutru/ 'they multiplied' as opposed to the standard Egyptian dialect /xiliṣ/ and /kitru/, respectively. In addition, the interrogative pronouns /ēš/ 'what', /lēš/ 'why', and /kēf/ 'how' of Cairene Judeo-Arabic have survived in sentence-initial position, in contrast to the situation in the standard dialect, where other pronouns, /ēh/ 'what', /lēh/ 'why', and /ezzāy/ 'how' appear at the end of the sentence. Note also that Cairene Judeo-Arabic interrogative pronouns appear in Levant Arabic and may represent migrated dialectalism as well (see below). Furthermore, the demonstrative pronoun /de/ 'this (masc.)', an older Cairene form, survived among Jews through the 20th century (see Hary on Judeo-Arabic, this volume).

Jewish Malayalam also possesses archaic forms, the most striking of which is the dative ending /-ikkŭ/, instead of /-ŭ/, for nouns and pronouns ending in /-an/, e.g., /jīvanikkŭ/ 'for life' (instead of /jīvanŭ/) and /avanikkŭ/ 'for him (third person singular with dative ending)' (instead of /avanŭ/) (Gamliel 2009, this volume). See also archaic features discussed in Jewish Neo-Aramaic (Khan, this volume), Judeo-Tat (Shalem, this volume), and Yiddish (Beider, this volume, and Fleischer, this volume).

The final social variable is internal migration. The more members of a community have migrated within the current language territory, the more we would expect *migrated dialectalism*: regional dialectal characteristics from one region found in another (Hary 2009: 22–23; see also Birnbaum 1979: 12; Blondheim 1925: lxxxvi–vii; Shachmon 2017; Weinreich 2008: A38, A121–22, A533, A584, 708, and many other places; Wexler 1981a: 103–104, 106, especially n. 12). Migrated dialectalism can be found in many languages in various historical periods. It is especially common in Jewish language varieties due to many historical migrations, as well as past and present connections among far-flung Jewish communities. This phenomenon can "move" between the written and spoken forms of language varieties. Some examples include verb forms or a typical vowel shift from Morocco found in Cairene Judeo-Arabic, Baghdadi plural demonstrative pronoun forms found in Cairene Judeo-Arabic, a plural article from Southern Italy used by Jews all over Italy in Judeo-Italian, New York phonological variants used by Jews around the United States in Jewish English, and phonemic alternation between /l/ and /t/ associated with North Malabar used by Jews in Kochin, India, hundreds of kilometers to the south, in Jewish Malayalam (Gamliel, this volume). Another instance of this phenomenon is Jewish varieties of Neo-Aramaic in towns around Kurdistan resembling each other more than the language of their non-Jewish neighbors (Khan, this volume).

We have hypothesized several correlations between social and linguistic variables in Jewish language varieties, based in a tradition of variationist sociolinguistics. By applying these analytic methods to large-scale comparative analysis of Jewish communities in different times and places, we will gain a better understanding of Jewish linguistic distinctiveness, Jewish history, and religious and ethnic language variation.

3.2 Hebrew/Aramaic influences

Now we turn to more in-depth analysis of particular aspects of Jewish language varieties. There are several comparative questions that can be asked about their Hebrew and Aramaic influences. Collectively, these influences are often referred to as a "component," but we prefer to think of them in a less unified way. The most common type of Hebrew/Aramaic influence is loanwords; other types include orthographic practices, morphological blends, and the transfer of syntactic structures from calque translation traditions into the vernacular.

One question we might ask: Which concepts are referred to with Hebrew and Aramaic words? Not surprisingly, most Jewish communities use Hebrew and Aramaic words to refer to Jewish religious concepts, such as holidays, ritual foods, lifecycle events, prohibitions, and halachic (Jewish legal) concepts. A surprising exception is 'synagogue', which is referred to with non-Hebrew/Aramaic words in several Jewish language varieties (see analysis in Wexler 1981b). Similarly, in many verbatim or literal translations of sacred Hebrew/Aramaic texts, translators/interpreters/editors avoided even common Hebrew/Aramaic loanwords; for example, in many of these translations, the Judeo-Arabic *šarḥan* translates Hebrew תורה 'Hebrew Bible, Jewish law' into שריעה /šarī'a/, which means 'Muslim law' in standard Arabic (however, Judeo-Arabic תורה /tōra/ and טורה /tora/, /ṭōra/ also exist).

Non-Jews and their holidays and religious figures are often referred to with Hebrew and Aramaic words, in part as a way of maintaining secrecy. As Table 1 demonstrates, sometimes Jewish religious and non-Jewish concepts are referred to with one Hebrew-origin word in multiple Jewish language varieties (adapted to local pronunciation traditions), as in שבת, and sometimes each language variety uses a different Hebrew-origin word for the same concept, as for evening prayers and Jewish holiday.

Table 1: Hebrew and Aramaic words for concepts related to Jewish religion and to non-Jews in five Jewish language varieties.

	Jewish religion			Non-Jews		
	'Sabbath'	'evening prayers'	'Jewish holiday'	'non-Jewish holiday'	'non-Jew'	'Jesus'
Egyptian Judeo-Arabic	שבת/שבאת/סבת shabbát/sabt	מעריב maariv/f	מועד mo'ēd	---	ערל 'arel, 'Christian'	---
Judeo-Italian	שבת shabáth	השכיבנו ashkivenu	מועד monged	חגא xagá	ערל ngarel	אותו il udó
Judezmo	שבת shabát	ערבית arvit	מועד mwed	חגא hagá	ערל arel	אותו האיש oto aísh
Yiddish	שבת shábes	מעריב mayriv	יום־טוב yontev	חגא khóge	ערל, גוי orl, goy	אותו האיש, תלוי oyse (ho) ísh, tole
Jewish English	שבת shábes, shabát	מעריב, ערבית maariv, mayriv, arvit	יום־טוב, חג yontif, chag	---	גוי goy	---

Another semantic domain of Hebrew and Aramaic influence is euphemism, especially referring to body parts, death, elimination, and sex. Examples include Judeo-Arabic *bit-kabud* 'house of honor, toilet', *maym qṭənnim* 'small water, urine', and *bet a-ḥayyim* 'house of life, cemetery' (Henshke, this volume); Judeo-Greek *rouchoth* 'airs, farts', *rimoním* 'pomegranates, breasts', and *tachath* 'under, rear end' (Krivoruchko 2001); and Judeo-Italian *beridde* 'circumcision, penis' and *macomme* 'place, toilet' (Ryzhik, this volume). In languages in general, people often discuss unpleasant or taboo topics in more pleasant – or euphemistic – ways, including using a positive word but implying the opposite meaning or using a word from a foreign language. This tradition is found in the Bible, when 'curse' is referred to as 'blessing', and continues in rabbinic literature, with the concept of *leshon sagi nahor*, 'euphemism, lit. language of great light', a phrase used ironically to refer to a blind person. Many of the euphemistic Hebrew-origin words used in Jewish language varieties stem from rabbinic literature and are found in multiple Jewish communities. When analyzing euphemism comparatively in Jewish language varieties, we might ask to what extent each variety uses Hebrew/Aramaic words for taboo referents, and we might determine the common sources for such words, perhaps including specific rabbinic texts that deal with taboo concepts or mutual influence among Jewish language varieties.

A slightly different way of conducting comparative analysis of Jewish language varieties' Hebrew and Aramaic influences is by determining which Hebrew words are used in many Jewish language varieties. That leads to the question of origin: How do Hebrew and Aramaic words come to be used in Jewish language varieties, through speakers' contact with texts or through their contact with other language varieties, including a substratum? Any analysis of a Hebrew or Aramaic word should determine whether it has a biblical or rabbinic source, and one might analyze the phonology, morphology, and semantics of the word to determine the likelihood of influence from other language varieties. For example, based on pronunciation norms and plural markers, we know that many of the Hebrew and Aramaic loanwords in Jewish English are heavily influenced by Yiddish and/or Israeli Hebrew (Benor, this volume). However, even if we suspect the influence of a non-textual source, we might ultimately find influence from the texts themselves. For example, variants of the Yiddish-origin word *yortsayt* 'anniversary of a death' are found in many language varieties, including several varieties of Judeo-Arabic, Jewish Dutch, Judezmo, Judeo-Italian, Judeo-Tadjik, and Judeo-Tat. One might assume that Yiddish speakers spread this word to so many locales around the world, but it is more likely that it traveled through Hebrew rabbinic literature. The word apparently first appeared in *Sefer Minhagim* in Amsterdam in 1635, written as יארצייט. If it was borrowed from speakers, one might expect similar pronunciations (with local variants). But the diverse pronunciations, including *yarsyat, yar sayat,* and, in Judeo-Arabic-speaking communities, *yarṣayt* (with the emphatic ṣ reflecting the grapheme צ), suggest that speakers were determining the pronunciation based on the writing in the rabbinic Hebrew text.

This type of analysis leads us to a related question: Which texts are the most common sources for Hebrew and Aramaic loanwords? Prayers and blessings most frequently recited in Jewish religious life? Biblical passages chanted annually in synagogues? Rabbinic literature studied by elite scholars? Such quantitative analysis may give us insight into the process of borrowing and the importance of various texts in various Jewish communities.

Next, we turn to the integration of Hebrew and Aramaic words. How are they incorporated phonologically? Do they use the local inventory of phonemes and local phonological processes? How do they render Hebrew phonemes and phonological processes that are not available in the non-Jewish language variety? Do they use any phonemes that their non-Jewish neighbors do not? If so, are these phonemes also used in words that are not from Hebrew/Aramaic? Users of Egyptian Judeo-Arabic employ the phoneme /p/ and alternate it with /b/, whereas the phonemic inventory of the non-Jews around them does not include the phoneme /p/. The use of /p/ among Egyptian Judeo-Arabic speakers and writers is usually in words borrowed from Hebrew: /purīm/ (also /burīm/ 'Purim'), /il-pilaġšīm/ 'the concubines', and more (Hary 2017: 22).

There are also several questions regarding morphosyntactic integration. Do nouns' plural morphemes come from Hebrew, from the target language, both on different occasions, or both sequentially in the same word? For example, when Egyptian Judeo-Arabic adds the plural morpheme to the noun ערל /'arel/ 'Christian man', it can use either a Hebrew morpheme as in ערלים /'arelim/ or an Arabic morpheme, as in עארליין /'ariliyīn/ (Hary 2016b). A particularly rich research question is how Hebrew-origin verbs are integrated into the local language: directly or periphrastically. Another aspect to this line of inquiry is whether the source of the verbal borrowing is a verb or another part of speech, such as an agentive noun. If the source is a Hebrew verb, what form is borrowed, masculine singular present-tense or a different form?

In Semitic languages, Hebrew-origin verbs tend to be integrated directly through incorporation of the verbal root, as the morphological system of the target language (Judeo-Arabic, Jewish Neo-Aramaic) is similar to that of the origin language (Hebrew). For example, in Egyptian Judeo-Arabic we find אתבהלו /itbahalu/ 'they were overwhelmed' (Hebrew root בהל) and אתזכה /itzaka/ '(he) gained' (Hebrew root זכה, although see Hary 2017: 29–30, especially n. 66); in Palestinian Judeo-Arabic (Peki'in), the Hebrew root אתת 'signal' is used in an Arabic verbal pattern, /bi'áttit/ '(he) sends signals'. Direct integration also happens in some non-Semitic languages, such as Judeo-Italian /gannavi/ 'she steals', from the Hebrew root גנב 'steal'. In some cases, Hebrew-origin nouns are used as the basis for verb formation, e.g., Judezmo שוחאדאר /shohadear/ 'to bribe', from the Hebrew-origin noun שחד 'bribe', and Jewish English /to be bar mitzvahed/ 'have a coming of age ceremony', from בר מצוה. Another strategy is periphrastic integration, such as Jewish Malayalam /śālomāyi/ 'died', from /śālom/ שלום 'peace' + /āyi/ 'to be' (past of /āk-/); Judeo-Tat /monuħo birɛ/ 'to die', from /mənuḥāh/ מנוחה 'rest' + /birɛ/ 'to be'; and Yiddish /maskim zayn/ 'agree', from /maskim/ מסכים 'agree' and /zayn/ 'to be'.

A phenomenon that exists in several Jewish language varieties is doublets, also known as etymologically multilingual tautological compounds (Zuckermann 2003; see also Mayer Modena 1986 and Tedghi 1995). Here are some examples:

> Eastern Yiddish: *mayim akhroynim vaser* 'hand washing after meal'
> Jewish English: *cholov yisroel milk* 'milk prepared by Jews'
> Jewish Neo-Aramaic: *gintid gan-'eden* 'Garden of Eden'
> Judeo-Arabic (Morocco): *bisimha-wilfirha* 'with much delight'
> Judeo-Arabic (Sefrou): *helluf-hazir* 'pig'
> Judeo-Italian: *boni ma'asim tovim* 'good deeds'
> Judezmo: *prove ani* 'very poor'
> Southwestern Yiddish: *e güte simetouve* 'good sign'

When speakers use doublets like these, they might be intending to emphasize the words, or they might not realize they are using Hebrew and non-Hebrew words with the same meaning. When analyzing doublets, we might ask which types of words/phrases tend to be doubled, whether such doublets are more common among speakers with limited knowledge of Hebrew/Aramaic, and whether there is a metalinguistic discourse about doublets as incorrect or unusual.

Another phenomenon found in several Jewish language varieties is coined Hebraisms, words that use Hebrew lexical material but do not exist in the textual tradition. Examples include Jewish English *bat mitzvah* ('girls' coming of age ceremony'), Judezmo *ba'al aftacha* ('optimist'), and Yiddish *khaleshn* ('to faint'). Such words demonstrate the productive relationship between Hebrew and the spoken language. We might analyze how such coinages are formed and which communities are more likely to create them.

So far, we have discussed only lexical influences from Hebrew and Aramaic. Now we turn to semantic and syntactic influence. Many Jewish communities have a tradition of calque (word-for-word, literal) translation of Hebrew and Aramaic texts using lexical material from the local language. Here is an example from Ladino (the Judeo-Spanish translation tradition) with a comparison to the Spanish equivalent:

Hebrew original from *Pirkei Avot* (Ethics of the Fathers):
Kol	Yisrael	yesh	la-hem	heleq	le'olam	ha-ba
All	Israel	there-is	to-them	part	to-the-world	the-coming

Ladino:
Todo	Yisrael	ay	a eyos	parte	a el mundo	el vinyén
All	Israel	there-is	to them	part	to the world	the coming

Spanish:
Todo	Israel	tiene	parte	en el	mundo	venidero
All	Israel	has	part	in the	world	coming

(Source: Bunis 2009)

Based on the English glosses, readers can see that the Ladino translation emulates the words and word order of the Hebrew original, rendering a sentence that is ungrammatical in Spanish but acceptable calque language in Ladino.

The tradition of calque translations leads to another research question: To what extent are such calque phrases found in the spoken language variety? Some examples from Jewish English include "the world to come"– עולם הבא; and "may her memory be for a blessing" – זכרונה לברכה. In Egyptian Judeo-Arabic, it is almost obligatory to mark the definite direct object with /ilā/ in written texts on analogy with Hebrew את. For example, כולנו עארפין אלה אל שריעה 'all of us are learned in the Torah', translating כולנו יודעים את התורה from the Passover *Haggadah* (Hary 2017: 30). This feature may have also penetrated spoken Egyptian Judeo-Arabic, but this question is still debated.

Another aspect of Hebrew/Aramaic influence is script. Beyond the question of whether Hebrew script is used (see above), we can also analyze various script-related practices (see Daniels, this volume). A language variety might have developed different orthographic traditions, sometimes in different periods but sometimes even simultaneously. See, for example, the various orthographic traditions in Judeo-Arabic (Hary 2016a: 301–310, this volume); historical variation in Hebrew-letter Judezmo orthography (Bunis 2005b); and orthographic competition in Yiddish (Estraikh 1999; Hary 1992: 112–113). Analysis of such orthographic variation can shed light on political, literary, cultural, and religious trends (Hary and Wein 2013: 90–91). For example, we can analyze how Jews marked vowel sounds using available (consonantal) letters and/or other signs and whether they adopted various rabbinic writing conventions, such as word-final letter forms. We might expect communities with higher levels of textual authority to use orthography that aligns more closely with biblical and rabbinic literature. In short, Hebrew/Aramaic influence is potentially a very fruitful area for comparative analysis.

3.3 Ideologies, perceptions, and status

Another area for investigation is how speakers and non-speakers perceive Jewish language varieties. To what extent are they seen as separate languages in popular and academic discourse? Are their glottonyms based on their non-Jewish correlate (e.g., Ladino), their Jewishness (e.g., Judezmo), or a combination (e.g., Judeo-Spanish)? Who tends to use which glottonyms? To what extent are the language varieties stigmatized and/or referred to as deficient versions of their non-Jewish correlates (e.g., *zhargon*)? In what ways do attempts at corpus planning engage in *ausbau* and *einbau* – attempts to make Jewish language varieties less or more like various non-Jewish language varieties?

There has been much work on these issues with regard to specific language varieties, especially Yiddish (e.g., Assouline 2017; Fishman 1999; Gilman 1986; Glinert 1999) and Ladino (e.g., Brink-Danan 2011; Bunis 2005b, 2011, 2016). Comparative work on these issues has begun (e.g., Bunis 2008; Fishman 1985; Myhill 2004, 2009; Spolsky 2014), including the influence of ideologies about Yiddish on ideologies about other Jewish language varieties (e.g., Benor 2008; Bunis 2010; Fudeman 2010). But a systematic comparative analysis of multiple questions regarding ideologies, perceptions, and status remains a desideratum. Of course, ideology is implicit in all research, especially in theoretical arguments about what constitutes a Jewish language (variety), including this chapter. We have already seen some meta-analysis of ideology in academic research on Jewish language varieties (e.g., Frakes 1989; Fudeman 2010), reminding us that scholarship is influenced by the author's conceptions of language, identity, and community. We welcome further research on this issue, as well as on how scholarship affects public discourse on Jewish language use.

3.4 Crossing religious/communal boundaries

In various times and places, the language of a Jewish community has influenced the language of local non-Jews; Hary has called this "crossing religious boundaries," and we prefer to fine tune it to "crossing religious/communal boundaries" (Hary 2009: 16–19; also Hary and Wein 2013: 93–96). In the most minimal sense, this can happen through lexical influx in a professional subgroup: Sometimes Christian and Muslim craftsmen borrowed professional terminology from their Jewish colleagues in their respective trade jargons/argots (see, e.g., Fleischer, this volume). For example, Primo Levi has reported the adoption of Judeo-Italian elements in Northern Italy among Christian furriers (Levi 1984, Chapter 1). In Egypt, Christian and Muslim goldsmiths still use an argot they think of as

"Hebrew" or "Jewish," including the word /šaʔʔāl/ 'a thief', which seems to derive from Aramaic /šqal/ 'take' (Rosenbaum 2002). There are also reports from early modern Saloniki, where non-Jews, especially those who worked in the city's harbor, employed Judezmo as their professional language variety, because Jews were such a large percentage of the population and heavily involved in trade surrounding the port.

At times, the lexical influx from Jewish language varieties reached the entire non-Jewish language community, or a large percentage of it. This is the case in contemporary American English, which includes many Yiddish-origin lexemes, such as *shmooze* 'chat, network' (< Yiddish *shmuesn*) and *klutz* 'clumsy person' (< Yiddish *klots*) (Benor, this volume). These transferred loan words, used more by people who live in cities with large Jewish populations, are likely due to Jewish integration into American society and the preponderance of Jews in popular culture and media. However, this is not only a modern phenomenon. There are examples of Hebrew and Aramaic loanwords that entered Christian German language varieties in the Rhine valley via Yiddish, many of which date back to the Middle Ages and are still used today, e.g., *Schmiere stehen* 'to keep a lookout', from Hebrew [šmira] 'guard'; *Ganove* 'thief', from Hebrew [ganav] 'thief' (Reershemius 2006). Similarly, Llanito (or Yanito), a mixture of Andalusian Spanish and British English varieties, spoken by the majority of Gibraltarians, includes many Hebrew lexemes as well as other influences from Haketia, a Judeo-Spanish variety spoken in Northern Morocco and the Spanish exclaves of Ceuta and Melilla (on Llanito, see https://www.ethnologue.com/country/gi/languages and Haller 2000).

More rarely, there was actual bilingualism cutting across religious lines. Muslims in some villages in Iran, such as Sede, used the Judeo-Persian variety employed by Jews in Isfahan and distinguished from the Persian used by Muslims there (Rabin 1979: 53, 56). In Ruthenia (today Western Ukraine), Christian nannies sometimes learned Yiddish and used it to communicate with the Jewish families they worked for. In some cases, they also taught Jewish children the Hebrew prayers. In addition, Hebrew blessings were widespread among the general Greek-Catholic (or Russian-Orthodox) population of the region (Hary 2009: 18, n. 27 and the references there).

As these examples demonstrate, crossing religious/communal boundaries correlates with openness of society and demographic integration of Jews into the local society. When Jews and non-Jews interact intensively in professional or domestic spheres, not only are Jewish language varieties influenced by non-Jewish language varieties, but the influence also goes in the opposite direction. By analyzing this phenomenon comparatively, we may increase our understanding of Jewish language varieties and the historical and contemporary relationships between Jews and their neighbors.

4 Why study Jewish language varieties comparatively?

The research questions discussed above are some of the many areas ripe for analysis in Jewish language varieties around the world and throughout history. Several of these aspects have been discussed in one, two, or multiple Jewish language varieties, but there has not yet been comprehensive and systematic comparative analysis. Taking such a global approach will help to answer old questions and pose new questions in Jewish studies, linguistics, and other fields. It will allow us to compare different locations and eras of Jewish history, exploring various patterns of engagement and insularity with respect to the broader society. It will also allow us to develop theories about language contact, including the influence of texts on spoken language (see Neuman's impressive 2009 treatment of this topic, including his notion of *schriftbund*). Finally, it will allow us to formulate theories about diaspora, ethnicity, migration, and religion that we can then test with other religious, ethnic, and minority groups, such as African Americans, Asian British, Iraqi Christians, the Deaf community, Canadian Hindus, Roma, and others.

How can the analysis of Jewish language varieties help us understand and analyze other religious and ethnic language varieties? Several scholars have already started to write about the linguistic similarities and differences between Jews and other religious and ethnic groups (e.g., Fishman 1987; Hary and Wein 2013; Myhill 2009; Stillman 1991; Wein and Hary 2014; Wexler 1980, 1986). On a broader scale, such research has been formalized in two fields: language and religion, sometimes called *religiolinguistics* (Hary and Wein 2013) (see, for example, Hary and Wein 2013; Omoniyi and Fishman 2006; Versteegh 2017; Wein and Hary 2014; Yaeger-Dror 2014, 2015) and language and ethnicity/race, sometimes called *ethnolinguistics* or *raciolinguistics* (see, for example, Alim, Rickford and Ball 2016; Fishman and García 2010; Fought 2006; Labov 1966).

One area for comparative analysis is script. Communities around the world use orthographic choices to represent their religious and literary affiliations. For example, predominantly Muslim communities use Arabic script for writing Aljamiado, (Muslim) Chinese, Jawi (Malay), Māppiḷa-Malayalam, Persian, Ottoman Turkish, Urdu, and more. Similarly, the Cyrillic script of Serbian symbolizes the importance of the Eastern Orthodox Church in that community, whereas Croatian, although quite similar to Serbian, at least until the breakup of Yugoslavia (1989–1992), is written with Latin script, in line with the Roman Catholic background of most of its users (Hary 2009: 19–20 and the references there). Our comparative Jewish linguistic analysis leads us to several questions about script. In what situations do religious minorities use their own script? What happens to existing orthographic traditions when a new religion spreads in a given territory or when a group migrates to a territory dominated by a different religion or orthographic tradition? Do communities adopt the new dominant script, keep their old script, or create hybrid forms? Answering such questions can shed light on language, religion, and ethnicity, as well as their intersections – religiolinguistics and ethnolinguistics. This is an important academic exercise that heads in an interesting direction: from minority fields (such as Jewish studies) to other minority fields (such as African American studies or Muslim studies), as well as to broader fields, such as sociolinguistics, language contact, and migration studies.

5 Practical considerations and next steps

A practical issue in conducting comparative analysis of Jewish language varieties is the requisite language skills. If one skims the bibliography below, it becomes clear that previous comparative Jewish linguistic scholarship has been written in five languages: English, French, German, Hebrew, and Yiddish. In addition, for each Jewish language variety there is a substantial body of literature in relevant languages, e.g., Spanish for Judezmo, Italian for Judeo-Italian, Russian for Judeo-Tat. (It is also interesting to find lacunae; for example, there are almost no studies of Judeo-Arabic in Arabic.) Of course, to conduct analysis on Jewish Neo-Aramaic, Judeo-Persian, Jewish Swedish, etc., requires knowledge of the language variety and its non-Jewish correlate. Because functional ability in a dozen or more languages is quite rare, comparative Jewish linguistic scholarship requires collaboration. Fortunately, our field has systems in place to facilitate this. Scholars can use the Jewish languages list (jewish-languages.org/ml/), to inquire about a phenomenon in multiple Jewish language varieties (e.g., doublets, how they refer to euphemism or non-Jewish holidays, and whether specific Hebrew words are used). The email list and the Jewish Language Research Website (jewish-languages.org) also enable scholars to easily find others who might be interested in collaborating.

In addition to the opportunities for collaboration, a number of published and online resources facilitate comparative research. If one wanted to conduct a comparative analysis of Hebrew/Aramaic words in multiple Jewish language varieties, one could use the many relevant dictionaries (Aprile 2012 for Judeo-Italian; Bunis 1993 for Judezmo; Glinert 1992 for Jewish English; Henshke 2007 for Tunisian Judeo-Arabic; Niborski 2012 for Yiddish; and Maman 2013 for several Jewish language varieties). In addition, other such dictionaries are in preparation, and there are online collaborative lexicons for Jewish English, Jewish French, Jewish Latin American Spanish, Jewish Russian, and Jewish Swedish (jewish-languages.org). Ideally there would be one comprehensive database for Hebrew/Aramaic word use in all Jewish language varieties, searchable by Hebrew word, referent, and language variety, with information about phonological and morphosyntactic integration, phrases in which the word appears, sociolinguistic variation, and documentation. Another desideratum is a database of language use in all Jewish communities, emphasizing distinctive features and answering some of the questions discussed above. Furthermore, we can collaborate with scholars of other ethnic and religious communities to expand these comparative analyses. To make these ideas a reality, funding is needed, and scholars must be willing to share data and participate in virtual and in-person gatherings devoted to such research. We hope this book will inspire such collaboration and further the field of comparative Jewish linguistic studies on the one hand and comparative religiolinguistics and ethnolinguistics in general.

References

Alvarez-Péreyre, Frank, and Jean Baumgarten (eds.). 2003. *Linguistique des langues juives et linguistique générale*. Paris: CNRS Éditions.

Aprile, Marcello. 2012. *Grammatica storica delle parlate giudeo-italiane*. Galatina: Congedo Editore.

Aslanov, Cyril. 2010. Mekhelek diber lezulato: Milim ivriyot shema'amadan hishtana agav hishtak'utan bileshonot hayehudim [From one part of speech to the other: Hebrew words that changed status once integrated in Jewish languages]. *Massorot* 15. 25–38.

Assouline, Dalit. 2017. *Contact and ideology in a multilingual community: Yiddish and Hebrew among the Ultra-Orthodox*. Boston: De Gruyter.

Balbuena, Monique. 2009. *Dibaxu*: A comparative analysis of Clarisse Nicoïdski's and Juan Gelman's bilingual poetry. *Romance Studies* 27(4). 283–297.

Bar-Asher, Moshe. 1998. Bekhinot bekheker hamarkiv ha'ivri ba'aravit hayehudit hakhadasha bamizrakh uvama'arav [Some aspects in the study of the Hebrew component in Eastern and Western Neo-Judeo-Arabic]. *Massorot* 3–4. 147–169.

Bar-Asher, Moshe. 2002. Behinot be-heker leshonot hayehudim ve-sifruyotehem [Research on the languages and literatures of the Jews]. *Pe'amim* 93. 77–89.

Bar-Asher, Moshe (and others), ed. 1984ff. *Massorot*. Jerusalem: Magnes Press and the Center for the Study of Jewish Languages and Literatures at the Hebrew University of Jerusalem.

Baumgarten, Jean, and Sophie Kessler-Mesguich, eds. 1996. *Special Issue: La linguistique de l'hébreu et des langues juives*. Histoire Epistémologie Langage 18(1).

Benabu, Isaac, and Joseph Sermoneta, eds. 1985. *Judeo-Romance languages*. Jerusalem: Misgav Yerushalayim.

Benor, Sarah Bunin. 2008. Towards a new understanding of Jewish language in the 21st century. *Religion Compass* 2(6). 1062–1080.

Benor, Sarah Bunin. 2009. Do American Jews speak a "Jewish language"? A model of Jewish linguistic distinctiveness. *Jewish Quarterly Review* 99(2). 230–269.

Benor, Sarah Bunin. 2011. *Mensch, bentsh*, and *balagan*: Variation in the American Jewish linguistic repertoire. *Language and Communication* 31(2). 141–154.

Benor, Sarah Bunin. 2012. *Becoming frum: How newcomers learn the language and culture of Orthodox Judaism*. New Brunswick: Rutgers University Press.

Benor, Sarah Bunin. 2015. Jewish languages. In David Biale (ed.), *Oxford bibliographies in Jewish studies*. New York: Oxford University Press (updated version).

Benor, Sarah Bunin and Steven M. Cohen. 2011. Talking Jewish: The 'ethnic English' of American Jews. In Eli Lederhendler (ed.), *Ethnicity and beyond: Theories and dilemmas of Jewish group demarcation. Studies in contemporary Jewry*, vol. 25, 62–7. Oxford: Oxford University Press.

Benor, Sarah Bunin, and Tsvi Sadan, eds. 2011. Special issue: Jewish languages in the age of the internet. *Language and Communication* 31(2).

Birnbaum, Solomon A. 1937. Judezmo. *YIVO Bleter* 11. 192–98. [In Yiddish]

Birnbaum, Solomon A. 1971. Jewish languages. *Encyclopaedia Judaica*, vol. 10. 66–69.

Birnbaum, Solomon A. 1979. *Yiddish: A survey and a grammar*. Toronto: University of Toronto Press.

Blondheim, David S. 1925. *Les parlers judéo-romans et la Vetus Latina*. Paris: Champion.

Brink-Danan, Marcy. 2011. The meaning of Ladino: The semiotics of an online community. *Language & Communication* 31(2). 107–118.

Bunis, David M. 1981. A comparative linguistic analysis of Judezmo and Yiddish. *International Journal of the Sociology of Language* 30. 49–70.

Bunis, David M. 1993. Ha-yesodot ha-'ivriyim ve-ha-aramiyim ba-sefaradit ha-yehudit ha-ḥadashah [*A lexicon of Hebrew and Aramaic elements in modern Judezmo*]. Jerusalem: Magnes.

Bunis, David M. 2005a. A theory of Hebrew-based fusion lexemes in Jewish languages as illustrated by morphologically derived animate nouns in Judezmo and Yiddish. *Mediterranean Language Review* 16. 1–115.

Bunis, David M. 2005b. Writing as a symbol of religio-national identity: On the historical development of Judezmo spelling. *Pe'amim* 101–102. 111–171. [in Hebrew]

Bunis, David M. 2008. The names of Jewish languages: A taxonomy. In *Il mio cuore è a Oriente. Studi di linguistica storica, filologia e cultura ebraica dedicati a Maria Luisa Mayer Modena*, ed. Francesco Aspesi, Vermondo Brugnatelli, Anna Linda Callow, & Claudia Rosenzweig, 415–433. Milan: Cisalpino.

Bunis, David M. 2009. Characteristics of Jewish languages. In M. Avrum Ehrlich (ed.), *Encyclopedia of the Jewish diaspora: origins, experiences, and culture*. Vol. 1, *Themes and phenomena of the Jewish diaspora*, 167–171. Santa Barbara, CA: ABC CLIO.

Bunis, David M. 2010. Echoes of yiddishism in judezmism. In Wolf Moskovich (ed.), *Jews and Slavs* 22, 232–250. Jerusalem: The Hebrew University of Jerusalem.

Bunis, David M. 2011. Native designations of Judezmo as a 'Jewish language'. In Yosef Tobi & Dennis Kurzon (eds.), *Studies in language, literature and history presented to Joseph Chetrit*, *41–81. Haifa: Haifa University & Jerusalem: Carmel.

Bunis, David M. 2013. Writing more and less 'Jewishly' in Judezmo and Yiddish. *Journal of Jewish Languages* 1. 9–75.

Bunis, David M. 2016. Speakers' 'Jewishness' as a criterion for the classification of languages: The case of the languages of the Sephardim. *Hispania Judaica Bulletin* 12. 1–57.

Chetrit, Joseph. 2007. *Diglossie, hybridation et diversité intra-linguistique: Études socio-pragmatiques sur les langues juives, le judéo-arabe et le judéo-berbère*. Paris: Editions Peeters.

Efroykin, Israel. 1951. *Oyfkum un umkum fun yidishe goles-shprakhn un dialektn* (Rise and fall of Jewish diaspora languages and dialects). Paris: Farlag Kiyem.

Estraikh, Gennady. 1999. *Soviet Yiddish: Language planning and linguistic development*. Oxford: Oxford University Press.

Fader, Ayala. 2009. *Mitzvah girls: Bringing up the next generation of Hasidic Jews in Brooklyn*. Princeton: Princeton University Press.

Fishman, Joshua A. 1981. The sociology of Jewish languages from the perspective of the general sociology of language: a preliminary formulation. *International Journal of the Sociology of Language* 30. 5–16.

Fishman, Joshua A. 1987. Post-exilic Jewish languages and pidgins/creoles: Two mutually clarifying perspectives. *Multilingua* 6(1). 7–24.

Fishman, Joshua A. 1991. *Yiddish: Turning to life*. Amsterdam: John Benjamins.

Fishman, Joshua A., ed. 1981. Special issue: The sociology of Jewish languages. *International Journal of the Sociology of Language* 30.

Fishman, Joshua A., ed. 1985. *Readings in the sociology of Jewish languages*. Leiden: Brill.

Fishman, Joshua A., ed. 1987. Special issue: The sociology of Jewish languages. *International Journal of the Sociology of Language* 67.

Frakes, Jerold C. 1989. *The politics of interpretation: Alterity and ideology in old Yiddish studies*. Albany: State University of New York Press.

Fudeman, Kirsten A. 2010. *Vernacular voices: Language and identity in medieval French Jewish communities*. Philadelphia: University of Pennsylvania Press.

Gamliel, Ophira. 2009. Jewish Malayalam. *International Journal of Dravidian Languages* 38(1). 147–175.

Gilman, Sander L. 1986. *Jewish self-hatred: Anti-semitism and the hidden language of the Jews*. Baltimore: Johns Hopkins University Press.

Glinert, Lewis. 1992. *The joys of Hebrew*. New York: Oxford University Press.

Glinert, Lewis H. 1999. We never changed our language: Attitudes to Yiddish acquisition among Hasidic educators in Britain. *International Journal of the Sociology of Language* 138. 31–52.

Gold, David. 1981. Jewish intralinguistics as a field of study. *International Journal of the Sociology of Language* 30. 31–46.

Gold, David. 1989. *Jewish linguistic studies*. Haifa: Association for the Study of Jewish Languages.

Gold, David & Leonard Prager. 1981–1987. *Jewish Language Review*. Haifa: Association for the Study of Jewish Languages.

Haller, Dieter. 2000. Transcending locality, creating identity – a diasporic perspective on the Mediterranean: The Jews of Gibraltar. *Anthropological Journal on European Cultures* 9(2). 3–30.

Hary, Benjamin. 1992. *Multiglossia in Judeo-Arabic: With an edition, translation, and grammatical study of the Cairene Purim scroll*. Leiden, New York and Köln: E. J. Brill.

Hary, Benjamin. 2009. *Translating religion: Linguistic analysis of Judeo-Arabic sacred texts from Egypt*. Leiden: Brill.

Hary, Benjamin. 2011. Religiolect. In *Jewish languages*, 43–46. Ann Arbor: Frankel Institute for Advanced Jewish Studies, The University of Michigan.

Hary, Benjamin. 2016a. *Il-ʿarabi dyālna* (Our Arabic): The history and politics of Judeo-Arabic. In Anita Norich and Joshua Miller (eds.), *The languages of Jewish cultures: comparative perspectives*, 297–320. Ann Arbor: University of Michigan Press.

Hary, Benjamin. 2016b. Judeo-Arabic and Hebrew as languages in contact: Some theoretical observations. *Carmillim for the Study of Hebrew and Related Languages* 12. [13]–[30].

Hary, Benjamin. 2017. Spoken late Egyptian Judeo-Arabic as reflected in written forms. *Jerusalem Studies in Arabic and Islam* 44. 11–36.
Hary, Benjamin & Martin J. Wein. 2013. Religiolinguistics: On Jewish-, Christian-, and Muslim-defined languages. *International Journal for the Sociology of Language* 220. 85–108.
Henshke, Yehudit. 2007. *Lashon 'ivri be-dibur 'aravi: Otsar ha-milim ha-'ivri ba-'aravit ha-meduberet shel yehude tunisyah* [Hebrew elements in daily speech: A grammatical study and lexicon of the Hebrew component of Tunisian Judeo-Arabic]. Jerusalem: Mosad Bialik.
Kahn, Lily & Aaron D. Rubin. 2016. *Handbook of Jewish languages*. Leiden: Brill.
Krivoruchko, Julia. 2001. The Hebrew/Aramaic component in Romaniote [Judeo-Greek] dialects. *Lekket: World Congress of Jewish Studies* 13. 1–8.
Levi, Primo. 1984. *The periodic table*. New York: Schocken Books.
Loewe, Heinrich. 1911. *Die Sprachen der Juden*. Cologne: Jüdischer Verlag.
Maman, Aharon, ed. 2013. *Milon mashveh la-markiv ha-'ivri bilshonot ha-yehudim: 'al yesod ha-osef shel Prof. Shelomo Morag z"l* [Synoptic dictionary of the Hebrew component in Jewish languages]. Edah Ve-lashon 31. Jerusalem: Magnes.
Mayer Modena, Maria Luisa. 1986. Le choix 'hébraique' dans le lexique des langues juives. In David Assaf (ed.), *Divre ha-kongres ha-'olami ha-teshi'i le-mada'e ha-yahadut*, vol. 1, 85–94. Jerusalem: Ha-igud ha-'olami le-mada'e ha-yahadut.
Mieses, Matthias. 1915. *Die Entstehungsursache der jüdischen Dialekte*. Vienna: R. Löwit Verlag.
Morag, Shelomo. 1992. Ha-milim ha-'ivriyot bi-lshonot ha-yehudim: Mispar hebetim klaiyim [Hebrew words in Jewish languages: Several general observations]. *Mi-kedem u-mi-yam* 5. 101–114.
Morag, Shelomo, Moshe Bar-Asher & Maria Mayer-Modena (eds.). 1999. *Vena hebraica in judaeorum linguis: Proceedings of the 2nd international conference on the Hebrew and Aramaic elements in Jewish languages (Milan, October 23–26, 1995)*. Milan: Università degli Studi di Milano, Dipartimento di Scienze dell'Antichità.
Myhill, John. 2004. *Language in Jewish society: Towards a new understanding*. Clevedon: Multilingual Matters.
Myhill, John. 2009. Varieties of Diaspora languages. In M. Avrum Ehrlich (ed.), *Encyclopedia of the Jewish Diaspora: Origins, experiences, and culture. Vol. 1, Themes and phenomena of the Jewish Diaspora*, 172–180. Santa Barbara, CA: ABC CLIO.
Neuman, Yishai. 2009. L'influence de l'écriture sur la langue. Sorbonne Nouvelle Ph.D. dissertation.
Niborski, Isidoro. 2012. *Verterbukh fun loshn-koydesh-shtamike verter in yidish* (Dictionary of holy-tongue-origin words in Yiddish). Paris: Medem Bibliotek.
Paper, Herbert (ed.). 1978. *Jewish languages: Themes and variations*. Cambridge, MA: Association for Jewish Studies.
Rabin, Chaim. 1981. What constitutes a Jewish language? *International Journal of the Sociology of Language* 30. 19–28.
Rabin, Chaim, et al. 1979. The Jewish languages: Commonalities, differences and problems. *Pe'amim* 1. 40–66. [in Hebrew]
Reershemius, Gertrud. 2006. Yiddish words in German. Goethe-Institut. http://www.goethe.de/lhr/prj/mac/msp/en1414420.htm (accessed 17 January, 2018).
Rosenbaum, Gabriel. 2002. Hebrew words and Karaite goldsmiths' secret language used by Jews and non-Jews in modern Egypt. *Pe'amim* 90. 115–153. [in Hebrew]
Sephiha, H. Vidal. 1972. Langues juives, langues calques et langues vivantes. *Linguistique* 8(2). 59–68.

Sermoneta, Giuseppe. 1976. Considerazione frammentarie sul giudeo-italiano. *Italia* 1. 1–29.
Shachmon, Ori. 2017. The Jewish varieties of Yemenite Arabic: Linguistic preservation, innovation and generalization. Paper delivered at Association for Jewish Studies conference, Washington, DC.
Spolsky, Bernard. 2014. *The languages of the Jews: A sociolinguistic history*. Cambridge: Cambridge University Press.
Spolsky, Bernard & Sarah Bunin Benor. 2006. Jewish languages. In Keith Brown (ed.), *Encyclopedia of language and linguistics*, 2nd ed., vol. 6, 120–124. Amsterdam: Elsevier.
Stillman, Norman A. 1991. Language patterns in Islamic and Judaic societies. In Steven M. Wasserstrom (ed.), *Islam and Judaism: 1400 years of shared values*, 41–55. Portland, OR: Institute for Judaic Studies in the Pacific Northwest.
Sunshine, Andrew. 1995. History of Jewish interlinguistics: A preliminary outline. In Kurt R. Jankowsky (ed.), *History of linguistics 1993*, 75–82. Amsterdam: John Benjamins.
Szulmajster-Celnikier, Anne & Marie-Christine Varol. 1994. Yidich et judéo-espagnol: Dynamique comparée de deux langues de Diaspora. *Plurilinguismes* 7. 93–132.
Tedghi, Joseph (ed.). 1995. *Les interférences de l'hébreu dans les langues juives*. Paris: Institut National des Langues et Civilisations Orientales.
Tirosh-Becker, Ofra & Sarah Bunin Benor (eds.). 2013ff. *Journal of Jewish Languages*. Leiden: Brill.
Wein, Martin J. & Benjamin Hary. 2014. Peoples of the book: Religion, language, nationalism, and sacred text translation. In Sander L. Gilman (ed.), *Judaism, Christianity and Islam: Collaboration and conflict in the age of diaspora*, 1–34. Hong Kong: Hong Kong University Press.
Weinreich, Max. 1954. Prehistory and early history of Yiddish: Facts and conceptual framework. In Uriel Weinreich (ed.), *The field of Yiddish: Studies in Yiddish language, folklore, and literature*, 73–101. New York: Linguistic Circle of New York.
Weinreich, Max. 2008 [1973]. *History of the Yiddish language*. New Haven: Yale University Press.
Wexler, Paul. 1974. The cartography of unspoken languages of culture and liturgy: Reflections on the diffusion of Arabic and Hebrew. *Orbis* 23(1). 30–51.
Wexler, Paul. 1980. Periphrastic integration of Semitic verbal material in Slavicized Yiddish and Turkish. In Marvin I. Herzog, Barbara Kirshenblatt-Gimblett, Dan Miron & Ruth Wisse (eds.), *The field of Yiddish: studies in language, folklore, and literature, Fourth Collection*, 431–473. Philadelphia: Institute for the Study of Human Issues.
Wexler, Paul. 1981a. Jewish interlinguistics: Facts and conceptual framework. *Language* 57(1). 99–149.
Wexler, Paul. 1981b. Terms for 'synagogue' in Hebrew and Jewish languages: Explorations in historical Jewish interlinguistics. *Revue des Etudes Juives Paris*, 140(1–2). 101–138.
Wexler, Paul. 1986. Exploring the distinctive features of Wandersprachen: The case of European Romani and Jewish languages. *Mediterranean Language Review* 2. 7–45.
Wexler, Paul. 2006. *Jewish and non-Jewish creators of "Jewish" languages: With special attention to Judaized Arabic, Chinese, German, Greek, Persian, Portuguese, Slavic (Modern Hebrew/Yiddish), Spanish, and Karaite and Semitic Hebrew/Ladino; A collection of reprinted articles from across four decades with a reassessment*. Wiesbaden: Harrassowitz.
Zuckermann, Ghil'ad. 2003. *Language contact and lexical enrichment in Israeli Hebrew*. New York: Palgrave.

Index

Amharic 3, 489
Archaisms 23, 367, 369, 371, 674, 675, 678, 679

Buenos Aires 383

Comparative Jewish linguistic studies 672
Corpora 61, 71, 122, 142, 170, 171, 215, 268, 305, 351, 425, 450, 467, 579, 607, 609, 612
Crossing religious boundaries 634, 686

Demographic integration of Jews 687
Distinctiveness 1, 198, 214, 219, 314, 389, 417, 426, 434, 674, 675, 680

Ethnolinguistics 4, 418, 425, 431, 432, 524, 540, 627, 628, 629, 688, 689

Former Soviet Union 317, 415, 417, 492, 495, 500, 503, 527, 533, 627
France 38, 129, 130, 131, 134, 138, 139, 140, 141, 146, 170, 174, 175, 190, 198, 277, 281, 283, 284, 286, 303, 308, 426, 544, 546, 547, 548, 562

Haredi Yiddish 472
Hebraized Amharic 489
Hebrew and Aramaic component / Hebrew/ Aramaic influence 45, 51, 64, 670, 674, 676, 680, 685
Hebrew script 29, 148, 159, 162, 163, 170, 173, 324, 344, 359, 362, 539, 621, 635, 674, 675, 685
Historical background 13, 41, 71, 102, 129, 147, 190, 247, 279, 317, 320, 359, 387, 414, 432, 459, 473, 489, 493, 532, 575, 579
History of documentation 61, 122, 142, 169, 214, 267, 305, 351, 424, 466, 578
Hungary 245, 283, 286, 387, 432, 433, 438, 453, 454, 455, 456, 457, 458, 459, 462, 463, 464, 465, 466, 467, 468

India 2, 57, 61, 375, 680
Internal migration 680

Israel 2, 3, 9, 10, 11, 12, 15, 16, 25, 27, 29, 30, 35, 36, 37, 38, 39, 40, 58, 59, 61, 74, 76, 77, 79, 81, 91, 108, 115, 132, 138, 146, 147, 149, 157, 162, 167, 170, 171, 172, 173, 175, 176, 188, 189, 190, 196, 210, 211, 212, 213, 215, 277, 280, 286, 287, 289, 300, 315, 317, 318, 325, 345, 349, 357, 358, 359, 362, 363, 364, 371, 372, 374, 385, 386, 391, 393, 394, 396, 399, 414, 415, 417, 418, 421, 438, 442, 446, 468, 482, 517, 540, 565, 572, 573, 574, 589, 636, 644, 666, 669, 677, 678
Israeli Hebrew influence 421, 426, 675, 677
Israeli Russian 540
Italy 124, 140, 146, 161, 162, 185, 189, 244, 277, 279, 285, 303, 308, 680, 686

Jewish
– English 3, 414, 441, 445, 446, 447, 450, 583, 629, 635, 676, 677, 678, 680, 682, 684, 685, 689
– French 565, 689
– Hungarian 453
– linguistic spectrum 675
– Lithuanian 641
– Malayalam 375, 414, 679, 680, 684
– Neo-Aramaic 31, 414, 680, 683, 689
– Russian 123, 314, 523, 533, 534, 627, 629, 633, 638, 639, 640, 641, 689
– Spanish 191, 194, 407
– Swedish 3, 450, 679, 689
Judeo
– Arabic 2, 35, 70, 71, 72, 73, 74, 75, 77, 78, 79, 81, 82, 83, 84, 85, 86, 87, 89, 90, 91, 92, 156, 359, 361, 387, 390, 391, 392, 394, 397, 398, 402, 414, 423, 426, 544, 545, 579, 610, 611, 612, 614, 670, 677, 678, 679, 680, 681, 682, 683, 685, 689
– Berber 92
– German 270, 278, 618
– Italian 124, 140, 141, 426, 614, 616, 679, 680, 682, 684, 686, 689
– Provençal 142, 614, 616

Judeo (*continued*)
– Spanish 2, 39, 72, 81, 119, 177, 220, 387, 394, 403, 415, 474, 583, 595, 614, 617, 655, 672, 679, 685, 686
– Tat 352, 590, 591, 680, 682, 684, 689

Kurdistan 9, 610, 680

Ladino 39, 94, 105, 141, 146, 147, 156, 157, 159, 160, 161, 162, 168, 170, 172, 173, 176, 220, 414, 415, 422, 528, 576, 577, 585, 586, 587, 588, 589, 594, 595, 614, 617, 685, 686
Latin America 186, 190, 194, 199, 286, 383, 384, 385, 386, 387, 389, 390, 391, 392, 393, 394, 396, 397, 400, 401, 402, 403, 404, 405, 407, 679, 689
Literacy levels in the local standardized language 676
Literature 4, 12, 30, 31, 35, 38, 41, 42, 58, 60, 61, 75, 98, 99, 100, 101, 103, 105, 114, 119, 121, 122, 142, 150, 162, 163, 164, 168, 169, 172, 173, 185, 192, 195, 196, 205, 210, 211, 213, 214, 215, 219, 241, 243, 246, 249, 250, 252, 255, 266, 270, 280, 281, 289, 296, 299, 300, 314, 315, 325, 345, 346, 349, 357, 359, 361, 362, 363, 364, 369, 370, 371, 372, 374, 375, 384, 386, 390, 391, 400, 401, 402, 424, 427, 435, 449, 453, 455, 458, 463, 465, 466, 480, 497, 520, 530, 549, 550, 555, 595, 610, 627, 631, 636, 644, 645, 646, 647, 649, 676, 677, 682, 683, 685, 689

Mexico City 407
Migrated dialectalism 674, 679, 680
Modern Palestinian Judeo-Arabic 51, 579
Morocco 38, 58, 59, 61, 64, 92, 130, 188, 389, 549, 572, 573, 653, 655, 656, 660, 661, 662, 667, 680, 687

Openness of society 675, 678, 687

Political Zionism 197, 677

Religiolect 1, 3, 35, 38, 39, 40, 42, 43, 44, 45, 48, 50, 52, 55, 59, 60, 64, 629, 647
Religiolinguistics 4, 688, 689, 690

Repertoire 1, 279, 283, 288, 294, 300, 347, 349, 383, 385, 390, 400, 405, 407, 418, 419, 425, 431, 432, 434, 437, 439, 442, 443, 444, 447, 525, 584, 586, 597, 627, 628, 629, 639, 641
Russian 3, 15, 21, 60, 283, 288, 300, 301, 305, 313, 315, 316, 319, 320, 324, 325, 326, 329, 342, 345, 346, 348, 351, 417, 433, 437, 495, 540, 546, 585, 590, 591, 592, 593, 628, 629, 630, 631, 632, 633, 636, 638, 639, 640, 689

Script 120, 132, 148, 149, 157, 158, 159, 160, 161, 162, 164, 170, 171, 175, 324, 344, 345, 351, 359, 360, 362, 372, 447, 530, 594, 595, 602, 688, 689
Sephardic 97, 105, 118, 132, 177, 186, 189, 190, 191, 193, 195, 203, 208, 210, 213, 214, 216, 218, 385, 387, 388, 389, 396, 397, 398, 402, 403, 415, 416, 422, 577, 646, 654, 655
Sociolinguistics 4, 216, 218, 383, 405, 597, 634, 680, 689
Substratal influence 674, 678
Sweden 431, 586

Textual authority and religiosity 676
Time from immigration or language shift 678

United States 38, 39, 142, 146, 170, 190, 213, 215, 317, 385, 386, 388, 390, 427, 482, 548, 589, 676, 677, 680

Western Yiddish 270, 434, 435, 436, 438, 441

Yiddish 2, 39, 58, 61, 72, 94, 105, 119, 129, 141, 196, 270, 276, 384, 389, 390, 391, 392, 395, 396, 397, 398, 399, 400, 401, 402, 403, 404, 405, 414, 415, 416, 417, 418, 419, 420, 421, 422, 423, 424, 425, 426, 427, 431, 438, 439, 440, 441, 442, 443, 445, 446, 447, 449, 450, 454, 455, 456, 458, 459, 460, 461, 462, 463, 482, 523, 528, 529, 533, 534, 570, 571, 583, 584, 585, 586, 587, 588, 589, 594, 617, 618, 619, 641, 672, 675, 676, 677, 678, 680, 682, 685, 686, 687, 689

www.ingramcontent.com/pod-product-compliance
Lightning Source LLC
Chambersburg PA
CBHW021217300426
44111CB00007B/345